Cybersecurity Best Practices

Michael Bartsch · Stefanie Frey
Hrsg.

Cybersecurity Best Practices

Lösungen zur Erhöhung der Cyberresilienz
für Unternehmen und Behörden

Herausgeber
Michael Bartsch
Bern, Schweiz

Stefanie Frey
Bern, Schweiz

ISBN 978-3-658-21654-2   ISBN 978-3-658-21655-9 (eBook)
https://doi.org/10.1007/978-3-658-21655-9

Die Deutsche Nationalbibliothek verzeichnet diese Publikation in der Deutschen Nationalbibliografie; detaillierte bibliografische Daten sind im Internet über http://dnb.d-nb.de abrufbar.

Springer Vieweg
© Springer Fachmedien Wiesbaden GmbH, ein Teil von Springer Nature 2018

Gedruckt auf säurefreiem und chlorfrei gebleichtem Papier

Springer Vieweg ist ein Imprint der eingetragenen Gesellschaft Springer Fachmedien Wiesbaden GmbH und ist ein Teil von Springer Nature.
Die Anschrift der Gesellschaft ist: Abraham-Lincoln-Str. 46, 65189 Wiesbaden, Germany

Cyber: Risks and Economic Opportunities for Geneva

"Security is not declared, once and for all. It has to be built and maintained. It must also be adapted to the changing risks and needs of the population. It must also take into consideration the changing level of expectations and demands. For all of these reasons, security cannot be taken for granted. It must be upheld every day and regularly requires new reflexions, choices, courage and investment."

Challenges

Today's economic, political and social landscape is marked by international competition, the increasing worldwide inter-linking of numeric data and networks, the multiplication and development of new risks, higher expectations in terms of reactivity or mobility, a relative dematerialisation of borders, but simultaneously an increasing superposition of legal responsibilities and jurisdictions. Norms and regulations also evolve at an increasing pace. And so does the globalisation of information and the media: an incident taking place here can rapidly make worldwide news. In turn, a security incident taking place at a supplier's storehouse may rapidly require action on the behalf of a global firm's international management.

Technology has allowed us to fight crime more efficiently, through forensic sciences, through the development of closed-circuit camera (CCTV) networks our through increasingly sophisticated detectors, for example. These technologies may allow us to curb street violence and theft. A clear trend in the past decade, therefore, has been the reduction of physical violence and, arguable, the transfer of at least some of this criminality toward the information and cyber sphere.

This in itself is not a sufficient cause for celebration. Indeed, new risks do not take the place of more traditional ones. We witness rather an accumulation of risks and forms of criminalities. And for Government officials, law enforcement agencies, local security forces or business teams charged with security matters, the same budgets and numbers are pressed to handle an increasing number of risks and threats. These threats, in turn, have also become generally more complex in nature. As an example, Geneva – as an International business and Humanitarian hub – is faced with almost every single risk or threat outlined in the Swiss Ministry of Defence's Security Policy Report (SiPol Ber 2016), from terrorism to natural or technological challenges.

Security Through Cooperation

Cyber criminality is an example of complex issues. In many cases, a successful attack is not even noticed by the victim. The tracking of the attacks' origin and the prosecution of such criminal activities is in itself a challenge – both technical and legal. They most often require international cooperation, information exchange and conventions. They are therefore by definition time-consuming and costly.

In Geneva, a Common Criminal Policy (PCC) has been established in 2012, and is adapted every 2 years, to align and coordinate the efforts of our Justice system and our law enforcement agencies. We believe the burden of cyber crimes needs to be shared between the Federal and State/regional levels. The first is needed to address the severe or nationwide challenges and attacks, to facilitate international cooperation in situations of emergency. The second can best handle the burden of the immediate response and daily cyber issues, monitoring and end-user reporting.

Geneva at the Heart of the Security Debate

Cyber challenges can also entail technological and economic opportunities. Many of the highly trained and qualified professionals, multilingual and technology savvy, are available on the Swiss labour market.

Businesses in Geneva have, at hand, over 170 permanent diplomatic representations, over 270 international organisations and NGOs. The World Intellectual Propriety Organisation (WIPO), The International Labour Organisation (ILO), the World Trade Organisation (WTO), the UN Training and Research agency (UNITAR) or the International Telecommunications Union (ITU) all have their headquarters here. In other words, many of the decision-makers, essential regulators and actors in the area of new technologies are present here.

Many of the internet-based research and development also takes place in the Geneva area, where it originated some three decades ago. The biotech campus is a true ambition and opportunity for Geneva. Universities, research centres and the CERN are also major international players. Investors and banks are here as well, allowing us to establish a unique economic and technological cluster.

Responses

Geneva's Security Strategy: Horizon 2030, released in 2017, addresses cyber security in several ways. The development of our IT-criminality brigade (BCI) is a direct response to the demands of the population. Similar demands explain the successful vote, earlier in 2016, of a new Law set to reform our national intelligence agencies.

In our *Geneva Economic Strategy*, released in 2015, we have already announced the development of business and strategic intelligence competences, practices and tools, aimed at improving cooperation in our ecosystem and the competitiveness of our companies. The establishment in 2017 of the General Directorate for Economic Development, Research and Innovation (DG DERI) allows us to step up and support more projects in these areas – in particular in the realm of artificial intelligence, blockchain and cyber security.

Security cannot be established solely by decisions or law. Training and the development of a proper information and security culture are needed. For this, conferences and regular meetings have been organised, under the name Geneva Digital Talks.

Innovation

Technology is cumulative and there is no way to turn back in time. We must therefore develop the skills, the structures and the regulations, which will allow us to anticipate the threats and the evolutions of both technologies and markets better and more quickly. This will allow us to pilot and enhance change, applying new technologies to our present and future needs, in an ethical and responsible way.

I am pleased that all of these reflections are taking place in Geneva and in Switzerland. Conferences, forums, research and publications such as this one, associations exchanging experiences and best practices all contribute to the development of networks. They are instrumental in building our societies' resilience levels. And altogether, they give us a decisive comparative advantage: a real and sustainable security.

Pierre Maudet
State Counsellor of Geneva, Switzerland

Politische Strategien zur Bekämpfung der Cyber-Kriminalität – Eine Zukunftsaufgabe

Goethe sagte 1771 in seiner Rede „Zum Schäkespears Tag": „Das, was wir ‚bös' nennen, ist nur die andere Seite vom Guten." Was Digitalisierung und Digitale Wirtschaft betrifft, sind diese Worte hochaktuell. Statista GmbH zufolge nutzten im Jahr 2017 gut sechzig Prozent der Deutschen das Internet. Der Online-Handel boomt und die Wirtschaft verlagert ihre Geschäftsprozesse verstärkt in den Cyber-Raum. Doch die zunehmende Digitalisierung erhöht die Anfälligkeit für Kriminalität im Cyber-Raum im gleichen Maße, wie sie voranschreitet. Wer nicht versteht, dass wir die dunklen Seiten nicht ignorieren können, wenn wir die Vorteile weiter nutzen wollen, der riskiert den Vertrauensverlust von Millionen von Internetnutzern. Daher hat die unionsgeführte Koalition in der 18. Wahlperiode in nahezu historischen Dimensionen gesetzgeberisch gehandelt, was die Verbesserung von Rechtsgrundlagen sowie die personelle und materielle Ausstattung der Sicherheitsbehörden angeht. Mit dem Haushaltspaket 2017 zur Stärkung der Sicherheitsbehörden wurde zusätzlich rund eine Milliarde Euro an Personal- und Sachmitteln zur Verfügung gestellt.

Aus einem Anfang Februar 2017 vorgestellten Bericht des Bundesamts für Sicherheit in der Informationstechnik (BSI) ergibt sich zur Cyber-Bedrohungslage ein beunruhigendes Bild. Sowohl bei der IT-Wirtschaft als auch bei den Anwendern wird noch immer digitale Sorglosigkeit diagnostiziert. Während die Hersteller von Hard- und Software weiterhin zu wenig in die Sicherheit ihrer Produkte investieren, sind die Sicherheitsvorkehrungen der Anwender gegen Cyber-Angriffe weiterhin häufig unterdimensioniert. Die globalen Dimensionen der Gefährdungslage zeigen schon Beispiele wie die Schadsoftware „WannaCry", von der weltweit knapp 100.000 Systeme betroffen waren, oder der Datendiebstahl bei US-Finanzdienstleister Equifax, dem bis zu 143 Millionen Kunden in den USA, Kanada und Großbritannien zum Opfer fielen. Auch die Polizeiliche

Kriminalstatistik des Bundeskriminalamts (BKA) verzeichnet für 2016 einen Anstieg um fast 40 Prozent auf über 100.000 Fälle von Computerkriminalität. Dabei handelt es sich um die Fälschung beweiserheblicher Daten und Täuschung im Rechtsverkehr ebenso, wie um Computersabotage, Datenveränderung und das Ausspähen und Abfangen von Daten. Mit Blick auf die Gesamtstatistik für das „Tatmittel Internet", die auch die Verbreitung pornografischer Schriften, Waren- oder Kreditbetrug einbezöge, fielen die Zahlen noch weit erschreckender aus.

Die Angreifer, Ziele und Absichten für Cyber-Crime sind höchst unterschiedlich. Sie erstrecken sich von Cyber-Spionage ausländischer Nachrichtendienste in Behörden, Militär, Unternehmen und Forschung über Organisierte Kriminalität durch Identitätsdiebstahl, Erpressung, Geldwäsche und Cyber- Bankraub bis hin zu politischen Motiven. Der Verfassungsschutzbericht 2016 nennt erneut Russland und China als Ursprungsländer. Vieles weist auf strategische Informationsbeschaffung aus Politik und Bundesverwaltung durch diese Angriffe hin.

Angesichts dieser Gefährdungslage hat die unionsgeführte Koalition in der 18. Wahlperiode eine Reihe von Initiativen ergriffen, um die IT-Sicherheit in Deutschland substanziell zu verbessern. Mit dem 2015 verabschiedeten IT-Sicherheitsgesetz ist Deutschland, auch im europäischen Vergleich, seiner Vorreiterrolle in Sachen Cyber-Sicherheit gerecht geworden. Es zielt in erster Linie auf die Betreiber kritischer Infrastrukturen (KRITIS), also auf systemrelevante Einrichtungen, Behörden, Organisationen und Unternehmen. Neben der Einführung einer gesetzlichen KRITIS-Definition wurde für die Betreiber eine Meldepflicht für IT-Sicherheitsvorfälle verankert, um künftig realistische Lagebilder erstellen zu können. Zudem wurden Telekommunikationsanbieter verpflichtet, Kunden über Sicherheitsvorfälle zu informieren und Vorschläge zu machen, wie Schäden an Computern, Tablets oder Smartphones behoben werden können. Das BSI wurde gestärkt und die Ermittlungszuständigkeit des BKA im Bereich Cyber-Crime ausgeweitet.

Darüber hinaus hat die Bundesregierung mit der Cyber-Sicherheitsstrategie 2016 mehr als 30 strategische Ziele und Maßnahmen formuliert, um den Schutz vor Cyber-Angriffen durch Prävention, Detektion und Reaktion zu verbessern. Die neuen „Mobile Incident Response Teams" beim BSI etwa sollen auf Anfrage den Verfassungsorganen, Bundesbehörden und KRITIS-Betreibern bei der technischen Bewältigung von Sicherheitsvorfällen helfen. Die „Quick Reaction Force" beim BKA, eine 24/7 Rufbereitschaft aus vier Cyber-Crime-Experten, soll in Zusammenarbeit mit den Ländern notwendige polizeiliche Sofortmaßnahmen außerhalb der Regelarbeitszeit starten können.

Laut der Bitkom-Studie: *Wirtschaftsschutz in der digitalen Welt* vom 21. Juli 2017 waren in den letzten zwei Jahren rund die Hälfte der deutschen Unternehmen Opfer von Cyber-Angriffen. Jedoch haben nur 31 Prozent, nicht einmal ein Drittel, die Vorfälle den Behörden gemeldet. Dabei kann insbesondere die Verwundbarkeit kleiner und mittlerer Unternehmen (KMU) der Volkswirtschaft gefährlich werden, denn viel Know-How liegt heute nicht mehr bei großen Unternehmen, sondern bei den kleinen und mittelständischen Zulieferern. Für die KRITIS-Betreiber und Telekommunikationsanbieter konnten gesetzliche Meldepflichten verankert werden, aber für die Sicherheitsbehörden sind auch darüber hinaus jegliche Informationen über Cyber-Angriffe von immenser Bedeutung. Nur wenn sie davon erfahren, können sie auf Grundlage eines realistischen Lagebildes entsprechende Abwehrstrategien entwickeln. Die Wirtschaft ist auch in Selbstverpflichtung gefordert, solche Vorfälle nicht aus Angst vor Reputationsverlust und Gewinneinbußen zu verschweigen.

Prävention und Schutz von IT-Systemen und schnelle Reaktion auf Vorfälle sind richtig. Sie bleiben essenzielle Säulen der IT-Sicherheit. Sie helfen aber nicht umfassend und sind nicht für jede Lage geeignet. Angesichts der heiklen Cyber-Bedrohungslage wird immer deutlicher, dass auch über aktives Vorgehen gegen solche Gefahren diskutiert werden muss.

Beim Schusswaffenangriff auf das Country Festival in Las Vegas im Oktober 2017 beispielsweise stürmte die Polizei das Hotel, in dem sich der Täter befand, und hätte ihn entwaffnet, festgenommen oder ausgeschaltet, hätte sie rechtzeitig die Chance dazu gehabt. Niemand hätte dieses Vorgehen in der realen Welt in Frage gestellt. Im Cyber-Raum sollen in einer vergleichbaren Angriffssituation besonders hohe Mauern schützen – die Firewalls.

Nicht einmal, wenn angreifende Server identifiziert werden können, dürfen die Sicherheitsbehörden in diese IT-Systeme eindringen oder sie gar unschädlich machen. Für aktive Intervention in fremden IT-Systemen existiert für Bundessicherheitsbehörden – die Bundeswehr einmal ausgenommen – derzeit keine Rechtsgrundlage. Dabei können solche Angriffe bundesweit Krankenhäuser oder Energieversorger, Kernkraftwerke oder die DB-Leitzentrale lahmlegen.

Eines ist sicher: der Staat muss Gefahren auch aktiv begegnen können. Er muss in der Lage sein, seine Bürger, seine Unternehmen, die Zivilgesellschaft und politische Institutionen auch im Cyber-Raum zu schützen. Im Kern müssen Rechtsdurchsetzung und Gefahrenabwehr im Cyber-Raum den Abwehr- und Verfolgungsmöglichkeiten der Sicherheitsbehörden in der realen Welt gleichgestellt werden. Ermittlungsbehörden müssen die Befugnis erhalten Daten und Server zu sichern, in IT-Systeme einzudringen und als Ultima Ratio auch Server abzuschalten. Aufgrund der Eingriffstiefe muss es für eine aktive Cyber-Abwehr rechtlich hohe Hürden geben. Wahrscheinlich wäre auch eine Grundgesetzänderung nötig. Die Vorratsdatenspeicherung ist ein gutes Beispiel für eine ausgewogene Regelung durch die Beschränkung auf schwerwiegende Straftaten und durch den Richtervorbehalt.

Eine künftige Regierungskoalition hat die Aufgabe politisch zu entscheiden, welche Arten aktiver Cyber-Abwehr ermöglicht werden sollten. Dabei sind Eskalationsstufen denkbar, die von der Löschung abgeflossener Daten von einem fremden Server über das Zurückholen von Daten bis hin zur Serverübernahme und -steuerung reichen, ohne dass ein Angreifer dies bemerkt. Von Datendiebstahl betroffene Bürger wären vermutlich höchst einverstanden, wenn ihre persönlichen Daten von einem Server gelöscht und damit die Weiterverbreitung gestoppt werden könnte.

Auch in den Bundesländern wachsen zunehmend die Erwartungen an eine stärkere Rolle des Bundes im Bereich der IT-Sicherheit. Einige Bundesländer haben derzeit und wohl auch künftig nicht die Ressourcen für die komplexen technischen Operationen zur Cyber-Abwehr. Es ist eben wenig sinnvoll, globale Bedrohungen regional bekämpfen zu wollen. Ziel in der 19. Wahlperiode muss deshalb ein deutlich potenteres, zu einem Krisenreaktionszentrum ausgebautes Cyber-Abwehrzentrum sein. Es muss die Aktivitäten von BSI, Bundesamt für Verfassungsschutz, Bundesnachrichtendienst, BKA, der Zentralen Stelle für Informationstechnik im Sicherheitsbereich (ZITiS), der Bundespolizei, der Bundeswehr und der entsprechenden Landesbehörden bündeln und bei komplexen Schadenslagen die Federführung an sich ziehen können. Cyber-Gefahrenabwehr kann nicht länger auf sechzehn Bundesländer verteilt bleiben. Ebenso sollten in Anlehnung an das englische Vorbild der Government Communications Headquarters (GCHQ) die unterschiedlichen technischen Kompetenzen in einer Spezialeinheit zusammengefasst werden.

In der laufenden Wahlperiode müssen darüber hinaus dringend weitere gesetzgeberische Maßnahmen in Angriff genommen werden, um die Kriminalitätsbekämpfung im Internet weiter zu verbessern. Oberste Prämisse muss dabei sein: Opferschutz vor Datenschutz! Öffentlich – oder vom politischen Mitbewerber FDP – wird bei jedem Gesetzesvorhaben schnell der Orwellsche Überwachungsstaat beschworen. Bei den gescheiterten Sondierungen hat die FDP sämtliche Unionsvorschläge in dieser Richtung blockiert und will gar die Regelung zur Vorratsdatenspeicherung wieder aufheben. Dabei wird die Verbindung zu schwerster Kriminalität wie Kinderpornografie oder Terrorgefahr öffentlich kaum gezogen, für deren Bekämpfung die Vorratsdatenspeicherung ein ungemein wichtiges Ermittlungsinstrument ist.

Die CDU/CSU-Fraktion hingegen setzt sich für ein den Gefahren angepasstes, modernes Datengesetz ein, das den Zugang der Sicherheitsbehörden zu vorhandenen Datenbeständen vereinfacht und die Möglichkeiten der Polizei zur Beweissicherung verbessert. Dazu gehört eine klare Rechtsgrundlage zur Überwachung verschlüsselter Internet-Kommunikation für Telemediendienste wie WhatsApp, Skype und E-Mails. Auch eine klare Rechtsgrundlage für die Online-Durchsuchung, eine Ausweitung der Rechtsgrundlage für die DNA-Analyse, ein besserer Zugang zu Mautdaten bei schwerster Kriminalität und Terrorismus und eine verlängerte Speicherfrist für Verkehrsdaten gehört dazu, die derzeit auf nur zehn Wochen beschränkt ist.

Besonders hervorzuheben sind abschließend folgende Punkte: Cyber-Kriminalität ist kein rein deutsches Phänomen. Für alle wichtigen Industrienationen bestehen vergleichbare Risiken. Insofern muss auch in der Bekämpfung eng mit internationalen Partnern auf EU-Ebene, in der NATO oder bei den Vereinten Nationen zusammengearbeitet werden.

Zum anderen hat die unionsgeführte Koalition in der 18. Wahlperiode gesetzgeberisch vieles getan, vieles bleibt zu tun. Zu einer erfolgreichen Strategie gegen Terrorismus, Organisierte Kriminalität und Cyber-Crime gehören in erster Linie personell wie materiell gut ausgestattete Sicherheitsbehörden. IT-Systemtechnik auf dem neuesten Stand, gut ausgebildete IT-Fachkräfte und Spezialisten, gut ausgestattete Spezialeinheiten bei den Bundesbehörden gegen Cyber-Crime, Cyber-Terrorismus und Cyber-Spionage sind Voraussetzung für eine erfolgreiche Kriminalitätsbekämpfung.

Mit den vergangenen Bundeshaushalten konnten entscheidende Schritte auf diesem Weg vorangekommen werden. Erklärtes Ziel der Politik muss aber bleiben jetzt nicht nachzulassen. Die Herausforderungen in den vergangenen Jahren sind nicht kleiner geworden. Auch in den kommenden Jahren müssen die Haushalte der Sicherheitsbehörden weiter gestärkt und für die wachsenden Herausforderungen – auch insbesondere durch Cyber-Kriminalität – ertüchtigt werden.

Armin Schuster
Mitglied des Deutschen Bundestages, CDU/CSU-Fraktion, Deutschland

Vorwort der Herausgeber

Der Global Risks Report 2017 des World Economic Forum bewertet Cyberrisiken nach Terrorismus als die dominierende gesellschaftliche Bedrohung des 21. Jahrhunderts. Wir haben uns daher entschieden, dieses Thema aktiv anzugehen und haben 2017 unser erstes Buch Cyberstrategien für Unternehmen und Behörden: Maßnahmen zur Erhöhung der Resilienz bei Springer Vieweg publiziert.

Wir konnten auch Beiträge von einem weltführenden Unternehmen der IT-Industrie, der deutschen Polizei, der Staatsanwaltschaft Zürich und führenden IT-Unternehmen gewinnen. Es wird aufgezeigt, dass Staaten die Cybersicherheit ernst nehmen und mehr als 80 Staaten bereits eine Cyberstrategie entwickelt haben. Leider konnten weder Best Practice Beispiele noch ein Unternehmen gefunden werden, welches bereit gewesen wäre, über seine Cyberstrategie zu berichten.

So wurde die Idee entwickelt, im Nachgang zum ersten Buch ein zweites Buch über „Best Practice" Beispiele in der Cybersicherheit in Zusammenarbeit mit unseren Co-Autoren aus den Bereichen Staaten und Behörden Cyber Defence, Forschung und Lehre sowie IT-Anwender und Dienstleister herauszugeben. Die IT-Sicherheitsunternehmen, ob groß oder klein, ob Inland oder Ausland, die wir angefragt haben, haben alle zugesagt einen Artikel zu schreiben und zum Schluss mussten wir leider, gebunden durch die vereinbarte Seitenzahl, auch einige Absagen mit schwerem Herzen erteilen. Da wir mit dem Thema lediglich an der Oberfläche kratzen konnten, sind wir zuversichtlich, dass alle noch die Möglichkeit bekommen werden, ihre wertvollen Beiträge zu liefern. Wir werden dazu ein Best Practice Forum einrichten. Bei den IT-Dienstleistern konnten wir leider nur wenige Beiträge finden, da am Ende die Unternehmen entweder anonym bleiben wollten oder weil sie an einer Geheimhaltung gebunden sind, oder weil sie schlichtweg (noch) keine Best Practice Lösungen hatten.

Es sind nun insgesamt mehr als 50 Beiträge und über 600 Seiten zustande gekommen und ein Beitrag ist interessanter als der andere. Es wird dem Leser nicht schwer fallen die vielen Seiten mit großem Interesse zu lesen. Jeder Autor konnte sich entscheiden, ob er auf Deutsch oder auf Englisch schreiben möchte. Daher kam ein gemischtsprachiges Buch zu Stande.

Was liefert dieses Buch?

Cybersicherheit, wie es Prof. Dr. Helmbrecht von der Europäischen Netzwerkagentur ENISA und Herr Generalleutnant Warnecke aus dem Bundesministerium der Verteidigung in Deutschland in ihren Beiträgen erwähnt haben, geht uns ALLE an und ist eine „shared responsibility". Armin Schuster als Mitglied des Deutschen Bundestags nennt es zudem eine „Zukunftsaufgabe" und Pierre Maudet schreibt that „security cannot be taken for granted". Darum soll dieses Cyber Security Best Practice Buch, das gemeinsame Verständnis für Cybersicherheit und die Notwendigkeit der Zusammenarbeit zwischen allen Akteuren und Stakeholdern nachhaltig stärken. Somit soll das Buch auch dazu beitragen, dass die Cybersicherheit anhand der Best Practice Beispiele aus den Bereichen Staaten, Behörden sowie IT-Industrie Dienstleister und Anwender insgesamt nachhaltig erhöht wird.

Aufbau des Buches

Das Fachbuch zu Cybersecurity Best Practices ist in vier Teile gegliedert: Staaten und Behörden, Cyber Defence, Forschung und Lehre und Industrie (Anwender, Hersteller und Dienstleister). Auch haben wir zwei interessante Beispiele aus der Praxis gefunden, bei denen Opfer von Cyberangriffen berichten. Der erste Beitrag beschreibt den Cyberangriff auf das Lukaskrankenhaus in Neuss aus dem Jahre 2016. Der zweite Beitrag beschreibt einen erheblichen E-Commerce PHISHING Angriff dessen Opfer die Familie Gfeller aus Lausanne war und der bereits 2008 stattfand.

Das Geleitwort des Buches wurde vom Staatsrat von Genf Pierre Maudet und Armin Schuster, Mitglied des deutschen Bundestages geliefert. Jedem der vier Teile geht ein Vorwort voraus. In der Einleitung des Buches diskutieren wir, warum eine allgemeine Ignoranz und Selbstgefälligkeit in Bezug auf Cybersicherheit herrscht und wie mögliche Lösungsansätze aussehen könnten.

Folgende Organisationen haben für die vier Teile Beiträge geliefert:

- **Teil I Staaten und Behörden**: Das Vorwort zu Teil I wurde von Arne Schönbohm, Präsident des Bundesamtes für Sicherheit in der Informationstechnik (BSI) und Prof. Dr. Udo Helmbrecht, Executive Director der Europäischen Agentur für Netz- und Informationssicherheit (ENISA) beigesteuert. Mit Beiträgen haben sich Finnland und Serbien, das BSI und die ENISA, die Swiss Cyber Experts, der Sicherheitsverbund Schweiz (SVS) und fünf Landeskriminalämter aus Deutschland, vertreten durch die Sicherheitskooperation Cybercrime, beteiligt.
- **Teil II Cyber Defence**: Das Vorwort wurde von Generalleutnant Dieter Warnecke, Abteilungsleiter Strategie und Einsatz im Bundesministerium der Verteidigung geschrieben. Weitere Beiträge wurden von Ambassador Sorin Ducaru, Senior Fellow the Hudson Institute in Washington DC and a Special Advisor to the Global Commission

on the Stability of Cyberspace (bis Ende 2017 Assistant Secretary General for Emerging Security Challenges to NATO), dem Österreichischen Bundesministerium für Landesverteidigung und Sport (BMLVS) und dem eidgenössischen Departement für Verteidigung, Bevölkerungsschutz und Sport der Schweiz (VBS) geliefert.

- **Teil III IT-Industrie**: Das Vorwort zur IT-Industrie und den Anwendern wurden von Heinz Karrer, Präsident des Schweizer Industrieverbands economisuisse und Dr. Holger Mühlbauer, Geschäftsführer des TeleTrust e.V. erstellt. Des Weiteren haben sich führende Anbieter der IT-Industrie (siehe Inhaltsverzeichnis und Danksagung) bereit erklärt, ihre respektiven Best Practices beizusteuern. Aus der Anwender-Industrie konnten wir die Deutsche Bahn AG, die Schweizer Post und das Lukaskrankenhaus in Neuss gewinnen.

- **Teil IV Forschung und Lehre:** Hier sind Beiträge von der ICT4Peace Foundation, Leiden University, von der Universität Lausanne, vom Institut für Internet-Sicherheit an der Westfälischen Hochschule in Gelsenkirchen, der Technische Universität Delft, der Technischen Universität Berlin, der University of Amsterdam und der Internet Initiative Japan eingeflossen.

An wen richtet sich das Buch?

Das Buch richtet sich an interessierte Leser, die in irgendeiner Weise mit Cybersicherheit zu tun haben oder mehr darüber erfahren wollen. Die Hauptakteure sind:

- Staaten und Behörden;
- Strafverfolgung;
- Verteidigung;
- Forschung und Universitäten;
- Vorstände und Geschäftsleitungen;
- Chief Information Security Officers (CISO);
- IT-Sicherheitsbeauftragte;
- Strategieverantwortliche;
- IT-Verantwortliche;
- Risikomanager;
- Krisenmanager;
- Studierende.

Bern, Schweiz, 2018   Stefanie Frey
                                                                          Michael Bartsch

Preface by the Publishers

The Global Risks Report 2017 of the World Economic Forum rates cyber risks after terrorism as the dominant social threat of the twenty-first century. The editors have decided to tackle this topic and published in 2017 their book Cyberstrategien für Unternehmen und Behörden: Maßnahmen zur Erhöhung der Resilienz with Springer Vieweg. The book has been divided into 2 parts: Part I identifies cyber threats, perpetrators, their motivation and organizational structures, means and methods to address cyber crime, and analyses the potential harm and costs of these attacks. Part II deals with possible solutions and illustrates the importance of taking an all-encompassing and risk-based approach to cyber security, addresses how states approach cyber security, deals with requirements and regulation and offers generic means to develop and cyber strategy and security measures.

We got valuable contributions from a leading global IT company, the German police, the Swiss pubic office of prosecutors and other important IT companies. We illustrated that states take cyber security seriously and today more than 80 states have developed a cyber strategy. Unfortunately, companies are not that advanced in that respect and we did not manage to find a company that was willing to share a best practice with us or report on their cyber strategy.

Against this background, the idea was developed to publish a second book on "best practice" examples in cybersecurity in cooperation with our co-authors from the areas of states, authorities and international organizations, cyber defence, research and education as well as IT users and service providers. IT security companies, whether large or small, whether domestic or foreign, which we approached for a contribution all agreed to be part of this book. In the end we unfortunately, bound by the agreed page numbers, had to reject some contributions. This was not easily done and with a heavy heart. However, since we have only just scratched the surface on cyber security, we are confident that everyone will have the opportunity to deliver their valuable contributions in the next round. The picture on the side of the IT users looks very different. We were only able to find very few contributions from the IT user side that were willing to feature in this book. At the end the companies either wanted to remain anonymous or were bound by secrecy.

We managed to get over 50 contributors and over 600 pages and each contribution is more interesting than the next. The reader will find it easy to plough through what seems at first a huge book and will read its pages with great interest.

What This Book Provides

As Prof. Dr. Helmbrecht and Lieutenant General Warnecke have pointed out in their respective contributions, cyber security concerns ALL of us and is a shared responsibility. Armin Schuster further stated that it is a major task and challenge of the future and Pierre Maudet stated that security cannot be taken for granted. This Cyber Security best practice book should deepen the common understanding for cybersecurity and the need for cooperation between all actors and stakeholders. Thereby contributing to greater cyber security and more resilient states, governments and IT industry.

Structure of the Book

This cybersecurity best practice textbook is divided into 4 parts: states and authorities, cyber defense, research and education and IT industry (users and service providers). It also includes a part with two chapters with interesting examples from real life. One contribution is the cyber attack on the Lukas hospital in Neuss in 2016 and the other an e-commerce PHISHING attack on a private person in 2008.

The preface to the book was delivered by State Councillor of Geneva Pierre Maudet and Armin Schuster member of the German Parliament. Each of the 4 parts is preceded by a preface. The introduction to the book is a contribution by Deutor discussing why there is general ignorance and complacency about cybersecurity and offers possible solutions to eliminate this problem.

The following organizations have contributed to the four respective parts:

- **Part I States and Authorities**: the preface to Part I was written by Arne Schönbohm, President of the Federal Office for Information Security (BSI) and Prof. Dr. Udo Helmbrecht, Executive Director of the European Network and Information Security Agency (ENISA). In addition, there were contributions by Finland and Serbia, the BSI and ENISA, the Swiss Cyber Experts, the Swiss Security Network (SVS) and the State Office of criminal investigation of Germany, represented by the cybercrime security cooperation.
- **Part II Cyber defense**: the foreword was written by Lieutenant General Dieter Warnecke Head of Strategy and Operations in the Federal Ministry of Defense. Other contributions include Ambassador Sorin Ducaru, Senior Fellow the Hudson Institute in Washington DC and a Special Advisor to the Global Commission on the Stability of Cyberspace (until end of 2017 Assistant Secretary General for Emerging Security Challenges to NATO),

who provided a conribution on NATO, based on his experence as Assistant Secretary General for Emerging Security Challenges to NATO. Further contributions include the Austrian Federal Ministry of Defense and Sport (BMLVS) and the Swiss Federal Department of Defense, Civil Protection and Sport (DDPS).

- **Part III IT Industry (service providers and users)**: Heinz Karrer, President of economisuisse and Dr. Ing. Holger Mühlbauer, Managing Director of TeleTrust e.V. contributed the preface to this part. In addition, leading IT companies (see table of contents and acknowledgments) have agreed to contribute their respective best practices. From the user industry we were able to win the Deutsche Bahn AG, the Swiss Post and the Lukaskrankenhaus in Neuss.
- **Part IV Research and Teaching**: Contributions have been made by the ICT4Peace foundation, Leiden University, the University of Lausanne, the Institute for Internet Security at the Westphalian University of Gelsenkirchen, the Technical University of Delft, the Technical University of Berlin, the University of Amsterdam and the Internet Initiative Japan.

Target Groups

The book is aimed at anyone who works or is in any way involved in cyber security or wants to learn more about it. The main target groups are:

- States and authorities;
- Prosecution;
- Defense;
- Research and Universities;
- Management;
- Chief Information Security Officers (CISO);
- IT security officer;
- Strategy managers;
- IT person responsible;
- Risk Manager;
- Crisis manager;
- Students.

Bern, Switzerland, 2018

Stefanie Frey
Michael Bartsch

Danksagung

Wir wollen uns ganz herzlich bei unserem Netzwerk von Geschäftspartnern, Kunden und Freunden bedanken – ohne die dieses Buch niemals möglich gewesen wäre.

Unser Dank gilt den Cybersicherheitsexperten und Fachleuten aus Staaten, Behörden, internationalen Organisationen, Cyber Defence, Forschung und Lehre sowie IT-Anwendern, Herstellern und Dienstleistern für ihre praxisorientierten und wertvollen „Best Practice" Beispiele zur Cybersicherheit in ihren jeweiligen Organisationen.

Unser spezieller Dank geht an die folgenden Personen und Organisationen:

Pierre Maudet, Staatsrat von Genf, Armin Schuster, Mitglied des Deutschen Bundestages, CDU/CSU Fraktion, Generalleutnant Dieter Warnecke Abteilungsleiter Strategie und Einsatz im Bundesministerium der Verteidigung, Ambassador Sorin Ducaru, Senior Fellow the Hudson Institute in Washington DC and a Special Advisor to the Global Commission on the Stability of Cyberspace (bis Ende 2017, Assistant Secretary General for Emerging Security Challenges to NATO), Präsident der economisuisse Heinz Karrer, Geschäftsführer der TeleTrust Dr. Holger Mühlbauer, Präsident des Bundesamtes für Sicherheit in der Informationstechnik (BSI) Arne Schönbohm, Prof. Dr. Udo Helmbrecht, Executive Director der Europäischen Agentur für Netz- und Informationssicherheit (ENISA), dem Geschäftsführer der Städtischen Kliniken Neuss (Lukaskrankenhaus) Dr. Nicolas Krämer, der Pressesprecherin der Städtischen Kliniken Neuss (Lukaskrankenhaus) Ulla Dahmen und der Familie Gfeller für ihre ausführliche Darstellung eines Angriffs auf ihr Online-Konto bei der Ricardo Online Plattform.

Dem Sicherheitsverbund Schweiz (SVS), Andre Duvillard und Melanie Friedli, den Swiss Cyber Expert, Mark Saxer, den 5 Deutschen Landeskriminalämtern vertreten durch die Sicherheitskooperation Cybercrime (SiKo), Dirk Kunze, Aapo Cederberg für seinen Beitrag aus Finnland, Irina Rizmal und der Diplo Foundation für ihren Beitrag aus Serbien, der Allianz für Cybersicherheit des BSI, Stefan Wunderlich, der ENISA, Dimitra Liveri, Anna Sarri und Eleni Darra, dem Abwehramt des Österreichischen Bundesministerium für Landesverteidigung und Sport (BMLVS), Walter Unger, dem Eidgenössischen Departement für Verteidigung, Bevölkerungsschutz und Sport (VBS) Gérald Vernez und Adolf Dörig.

Der ICT4Peace Foundation, Dr. Eneken Tikk, der Universität Lausanne Laura Crespo, Prof. Solange Ghernaouti und Bastien Wanner, dem Institut für Internet-Sicherheit an der Westfälischen Hochschule in Gelsenkirchen Prof. Dr. Norbert Pohlmann, der Technischen Universität Delft Tobias Fiebig und Dr. Jan van den Berg dem Team von der Technischen Universität Berlin, der University of Amsterdam, der Internet Initiative Japan, bestehend aus Prof. Anja Feldmann, Franziska Lichtblau, Florian Streibelt, Thorben Krüger, Pieter Lexis, Randy Bush.

Dem Deutschen Digitalverband Bitkom, Teresa Ritter und Marc Bachmann, SoCoA, Chris Aghroum, Richard Hill von Hill Associates, der Deutschen Bahn, Dr. Matthias Drodt, Ludger Pagel und Thomas Biedorf, der Schweizer Post, Christian Folini und Denis Morel, der genua GmbH, Dr. Magnus Harlander und Dirk Loss, der itWatch GmbH, Ramon Mörl, der Atos Technologies, Jörg Eschweiler, der IBM Schweiz, Dr. Alain Gut und Dr. Andreas Wespi, der Kudelski Security, Martin Dion, der Microsoft Deutschland, Michael Kranawetter, der Secunet AG, Jörg Kebbedies, der A1 Telekom Austria AG, Dr. Wolfgang Schwabl, der Secuvera GmbH, Tobias Glemser, der NSIDE ATTACK LOGIC GmbH, Sascha Herzog, dem Program Manager and InfoSec/GDPR Experten, Lars Minth, dem Senior Manager IT Security and Operations, Claudio Di Salvo, der Comexposium Group, Michael Weatherseed und der Axel Allerkamp, Experte für IT/Cyber-Sicherheit und Krisenmanagement.

Auch danken wir ganz herzlich meiner Mutter Brix Frey für ihre Hilfe bei dem englischen Leseverständnis und insbesondere für die mentale Unterstützung bei der Erstellung des Gesamtwerks. David Philpott und Martin Smith danken wir für ihre Unterstützung bei der Qualitätssicherung bei einigen ausgesuchten Beiträgen.

Auch vielen Dank an Frau Sybille Thelen und Frau Heike Jung vom Springer Vieweg Verlag, die uns auch in diesem Buch mit viel Vertrauen und Geduld begleitet haben.

Dr. Stefanie Frey und Michael Bartsch Deutschland und Schweiz, 2018

Das Best Practice Forum im Internet erreichen Sie unter: www.cybersecurity-best-practice.net

Sie erreichen uns unter: info@deutor.de

Informationen zum Buch Cyberstrategien für Unternehmen und Behörden: www.cyberstrategien-fuer-unternehmen.de

Acknowledgments

We would like to thank our network of business partners, customers and friends without whom the writing of this book would not have been possible. Our gratitude is extended to the cyber security experts from states, authorities and agencies, international organizations, cyber defense, research and education, as well as IT service providers and users for their practice-oriented and valuable "best practice" examples on cybersecurity in their respective organizations.

Our special thanks goes out to the following people and organizations:

State Councillor of Geneva, Pierre Maudet, Armin Schuster, member of the German Parliament, CDU/CSU fraction, Lieutenant General Dieter Warnecke Head of Strategy and Operations in the German Federal Ministry of Defense, Ambassador Sorin Ducaru, Senior Fellow the Hudson Institute in Washington DC and a Special Advisor to the Global Commission on the Stability of Cyberspace (until end of 2017, Assistant Secretary General for Emerging Security Challenges to NATO), president of economisuisse Heinz Karrer, Dr. Ing. Holger Mühlbauer, Managing Director of TeleTrust Association, Arne Schönbohm, President of the Federal Office for Information Security (BSI), Prof. Dr. Udo Helmbrecht, Executive Director of the European Network and Information Security Agency (ENISA), Managing Director of the „Städtischen Kliniken Neuss" (Lukaskrankenhaus), Dr. Nicolas Krämer, spokeswoman Ulla Dahmen from the „Städtische Kliniken Neuss" (Lukaskrankenhaus) and the family Gfeller for their detailed account about the cyber attack on their Ricardo Online account.

The Swiss Security Network (SVS) André Duvillard und Melanie Friedli, the Swiss Cyber Experts Mark Saxer, 5 State Offices of criminal investigation of Germany, represented by the security cooperation on cybercrime (SiKo) Dirk Kunze, Aapo Cederberg for his contribution on Finnland, Irina Rizmal and Diplo Foundation for their contribution on Serbia, Stefan Wunderlich from the Cybersecurity Alliance BSI, Dimitra Liveri, Anna Sarri und Eleni Darra from ENISA, Walter Unger from the Austrian Federal Ministry of Defense and Sport (BMLVS) and Gérald Vernez and Adolf Dörig from the Swiss Federal Department of Defense, Civil Protection and Sport (DDPS)

Dr. Eneken Tikk from the ICT4Peace Foundation, Laura Crespo, Prof. Solange Ghernaouti and Bastien Wanner from the University of Lausanne, Prof. Norbert Pohlmann from the Institute for Internet-Sicherheit from the Westfälische Hochschule in Gelsenkirchen, Tobias Fiebig and Dr. Jan van den Berg from the Technische Universität Delft, the team from the Technische Universität Berlin, University of Amsterdam, the Internet Initiative Japan, Prof. Anja Feldmann, Franziska Lichtblau, Florian Streibelt, Thorben Krüger, Pieter Lexis and Randy Bush.

Teresa Richter und Marc Bachmann from Germany's Digital Association (Bitkom), Chris Aghroum from SoCoA, Richard Hill from Hill Associates, Dr. Matthias Drodt, Ludger Pagel und Thomas Biedorf from Deutsche Bahn, Christian Folini and Denis Morel from Swiss Post AG, Dr. Magnus Harlander und Dirk Loss from genua GmbH, Ramon Mörl from itWatch GmbH, Jörg Eschweiler from Atos Technologies, Dr. Alain Gut and Dr. Andreas Wespi from IBM Switzerland, Martin Dion from Kudelski Security, Michael Kranawetter from Microsoft Deutschland, Jörg Kebbedies from Secunet AG, Dr. Wolfgang Schwabl from A1 Telekom Austria AG, Tobias Glemser from Secuvera GmbH, Sascha Herzog from NSIDE ATTACK LOGIC GmbH, Program Manager and InfoSec/GDPR expert Lars Minth, Senior Manager IT Security and Operations Claudio Di Salvo, Michael Weatherseed from Comexposium Group and Axel Allerkamp, Expert for IT/Cyber-Security and Crisis Management.

An enormous thanks also to my mother Brix Frey, who supported us with her English comprehension skills and mental support. A big thank you to David Philpott and Martin Smith for their quality assurance and proof reading skills in a few selected articles.

A big thank you also to Sybille Thelen and Heike Jung from Springer Vieweg Verlag, who supported us in this second round with patience and trust.

Dr. Stefanie Frey und Michael Bartsch Deutschland und Schweiz, 2018

You can reach us under: info@deutor.de

The Best Practice Forum is available under: www.cybersecurity-bestpractice.net

For more information on our book Cyberstrategien für Unternehmen und Behörden see: www.cyberstrategien-fuer-unternehmen.de

Inhaltsverzeichnis

20 Best Practices in Cybersecurity from Intergovernmental Discussions and a Private Sector Proposal 253

Richard Hill

21 Woher nehmen, wenn nicht stehlen – oder wo haben Sie Ihren CISO her? 261

Michael Bartsch

Über die Autoren

Christian Aghroum is an expert at the Council of Europe and consultant for governments, private and public companies in security, cybersecurity and crisis management. He is founder and Vice-President of a think-tank, CyAN and also founder and CEO of a consulting company, SoCoA. Former chief superintendent of the French national police, he spent 30 years working on organized crime and terrorism. He is a former head of the French national cybercrime unit just before joining an international swiss company as Chief Security Officer. Christian holds two masters in law and informatics, has been auditor of Inhesj Paris. He is lecturer for various universities but also for management schools, ESSEC (Paris) and IMSG (Geneva). He wrote several books alone or in collaboration.

Axel Allerkamp Dipl.-Ing. Axel Allerkamp beschäftigt sich mehr als 20 Jahre mit den Aspekten der IT/Cyber-Sicherheit und Krisenmanagement. Neben seiner beruflichen Tätigkeit in diesem Umfeld, ist er Co-Autor des Wirtschaftsgrundschutzes und Dozent an Hochschulen für diese Themen.

Marc Bachmann M.A., M.Sc., Bereichsleiter Luftfahrt und Verteidigung. Marc Bachmann betreut in der Bitkom Geschäftsstelle die Arbeitskreise Verteidigung und Luftfahrt. Vor seiner Tätigkeit beim Bitkom war Herr Bachmann 13 Jahre bei der Bundeswehr in verschiedenen Bereichen tätig. Unter anderem war er Marineflieger beim Marinefliegergeschwader in Kiel. Zuletzt war er in der regionalen Öffentlichkeitsarbeit des Presse-/Informationsstabes des Bundesministeriums der Verteidigung eingesetzt. Im Freistaat Sachsen war er verantwortlich für die Schnittstellenkommunikation zwischen Bundeswehr, Politik, Wirtschaft, Bildung und Gesellschaft zu bundeswehrspezifischen und sicherheitspolitisch relevanten Themen. Herr Bachmann studierte an der Helmut-Schmidt-Universität der Bundeswehr in Hamburg Geschichte und Sozialwissenschaften sowie Corporate Communication an der Rotterdam School of Management/Erasmus Universität in Rotterdam.

Michael Bartsch Managing Director at Deutor Cyber Security Solutions GmbH is specialized in IT and IT-Security Solutions for Law Enforcement, Enterprises and SMEs. Michael worked for Europe's biggest Telecommunications Provider and oversaw the design and development of secure IT-Systems for public authorities, police, military customers and intelligence services. Michael has also been active for many years as a crisis manager for cyber attacks. He advises companies and governments during the whole process of a cyber attack: before, during and after. As the founder of two public private partnerships in Germany, aimed at fighting cyber crime, he has a deep insight and knowledge of the „modus operandi" of cyber criminals. Michael assists governments and companies in the entire process from prevention to reaction to continuity after a cyber attack and helps in the development and implementation of cyber strategies and cyber blueprints. He is a well known key note speaker and political advisor and has several publications on cyber security.

Jan van den Berg starting in 1970 he studied mathematics and physics at Delft University of Technology. In 1977, he received the diploma of Mathematical Engineer. From 1977–1989, he lectured courses in mathematics, physics and computer science on institutes of higher education in The Netherlands, and mathematics and physics at the secondary school of Nampula (Mozambique). From 1989–2006, he worked at the Econometric Institute of Erasmus University Rotterdam lecturing courses in computer science and economics, and did research in computational intelligence, with applications in combinatorial optimization, finance, agriculture, philosophy, bibliometrics, among others. He finalized his Ph.D.-thesis entitled "Neural Relaxation Dynamics" in 1996. From 2006 up till now, he has been working at Delft University of Technology, mostly on topics related to (Big) Data Analytics and Cyber Security. On 9 July 2013, he was appointed as full professor Cyber Security at this University. He also acts as Scientific Director of the Cyber Security Academy in The Hague. On 26 May 2015, Van den Berg was also appointed as full profess of Cyber Security within the Institute for Security & Global Affairs (ISGA) of Leiden University. More details about his background can be found on his personal webpage at Delft University of Technology.

Thomas Biedorf arbeitet seit 2014 im Konzerndatenschutz der Deutschen Bahn in der Abteilung Audit und technischer Datenschutz. In seiner Rolle berät er die verantwortlichen Stellen im Konzern bei der Einführung konzernrelevanter Verfahren im Hinblick auf die datenschutzkonforme Implementierung und Umsetzung von Technik. Er ist Leiter der internen Arbeitsgruppe „Soziale Netzwerke und neue Technologien", die u. a. laufend datenschutzrechtliche Leitfäden zu aktuellen Themen wie Big Data, Künstliche Intelligenz oder Internet der Dinge für die Konzernunternehmen erstellt. Vorher war er 14 Jahre als Berater und Programmierer tätig und betreut als externer Datenschutzbeauftragter kleine und mittelständische Unternehmen.

Randy Bush is a Research Fellow and Network Operator at Internet Initiative Japan, Japan's first commercial ISP. He specializes in network measurement especially routing, network security, routing protocols, and IPv6 deployment. He is also a lead designer of the BGP security effort. Randy has been in computing for over 50 years, and has a few decades of Internet operations experience. He was the engineering founder of Verio, which is now NTT/Verio. He has been heavily involved in transferring Internet technologies to developing economies for over 25 years. He was a chair of the IETF WG on the DNS for a decade and served as a member of the IESG, as co-chair of the IETF Operations and Management Area. Randy was the first Chair of the NANOG Steering Committee, a co-founder of AfNOG, on the founding Board of Directors of ARIN, helped start AfriNIC, and has participated in APNIC, RIPE, et alia since each was founded.

Aapo Cederberg is currently Executive Adviser to the Finnish Information Security Cluster (FISC). He is also an Associate Fellow of the Global Fellowship Initiative at the Geneva Centre of Security Policy (GCSP). His main area of responsibility is Cyber security and other comprehensive security matters such as Hybrid warfare and to organize training courses and security dialogue on this topic. Aapo Cederberg is also CEO and Co-founder of Cyberwatch Finland. Cyberwatch is providing strategic analysis and better situational awareness of the cyber world for the management of companies and organizations in Finland. The analysis process is utilizing AI and a network of high level cyber experts. Mr. Cederberg has served as a Secretary General for the Security Committee of Finland for 6 years. The Security Committee provides support, advice and expertise for the government in comprehensive security matters and serves as a collaborative platform for the on-going national efforts related to the national crisis preparedness. The security committee also works on various initiatives and issues statements and guidelines, such as Security Strategy for the Society and National Cyber Security Strategy, to assist the national Government. Mr. Cederberg's earlier assignments include working as the head of Strategic Planning and foresight at the Ministry of Defense (2005–2007). Before this he has a long career in the service of Finnish Defense Forces, where his latest assignments include holding the Commander position at the Häme GBAD Battalion (2003–2005) and serving as a Senior Military Adviser at the Permanent Mission of Finland to the OSCE (1999–2003).

Laura Crespo is a researcher at the University of Lausanne, where she is currently writing her dissertation on cyber diplomacy and Switzerland's role regarding the international normative debate in the cyber realm. Furthermore, Ms. Crespo works at the Swiss Federal Department of Foreign Affairs. She has been involved in the implementation of the national Swiss cyber strategy and she has been engaged in different international processes regarding cyber-security, such as United Nations Group of Governmental Experts on Developments in the Field of Information and Telecommunications in the Context of International Security (UN GGE) and the process within the OSCE on confidence building measures. Prior to that she worked at the Project Cyber Defence within the Federal Department of Defence, Civil Protection and Sport.

Ulla Dahmen ist Pressesprecherin der Städtische Kliniken Neuss – Lukaskrankenhaus – GmbH. Nach der Cyberattacke auf das Lukaskrankenhaus war sie Mitglied des Krisenstabs. Die Journalistin arbeitete zuvor als Tageszeitungsredakteurin in verantwortlicher Position, zuletzt als Redaktionsleiterin der WZ in Wuppertal und dem Rhein-Kreis Neuss.

Eleni Darra   The topic of NCSS is covered in ENISA by the NCSS team, namely Anna Sarri, Eleni Darra and Dimitra Liveri, from the Secure Infrastructures and Services Unit. ENISA has been dealing with the topic since 2012 and the team was formed in 2014. The NCSS team in ENISA is running related projects, handles the NCSS online map, facilitates discussion in the NCSS experts group and finally organizes annually the ENISA NCSS workshop.

Claudio Di Salvo   Senior Manager with 18 years of experience in development, implementation and management of complex Enterprise Cyber Security-Information Systems Programs, Information Assurance Risk Management Programs and Digital Transformation Programs.

Recognized as a seasoned IT professional, entrepreneurial minded who provides a practical approach to the security of data, information systems and risk management that meets both the needs and constraints of the organization. Proven track record of achievements, regardless of the technical, non-technical, and political challenges within an organization. Demonstrated team player, with the ability to successfully initiate, lead and manage individuals and multiple projects, from inception to completion. Ensure various divisions, departments and stakeholders are connected and communicating to provide a holistic enterprise risk management approach, eliminating silos. He has professional experience in more than 10 countries in different organizations like the International Air Transport Association (IATA), Swisscom, T-Systems, PWC and TechEdge.

Martin Dion is originally from Montreal, Martin has been navigating the tormented water of cyber security for over 20 years. He was the founder and CTO at Above Security Canada where he worked locally and in the Caribbean's. Twelve years ago, he moved to Switzerland to launch SecureIT, serving EU and MEA fortune 500 clients. When both organizations where acquired by Hitachi Security, he moved to MIG Bank as Chief Security Officer. He is now the VP of EMEA Service Delivery at Kudelski Security, which he joined 5 years ago. Martin originally studied Information System Management at HEC (CA), followed by Operational Risk Management at Kaplan (US) and Criminology at Leicester (UK) which was complemented by executive education at Harvard Business School and at the Center for Creative Leadership. He holds CISSP, CISM, ISO 27001 and OCEG certifications. He focusses on enterprise security strategy definition, cyber intelligence and on top of certification classes, he teaches innovation and business modelling in various Swiss universities.

Adolf J. Dörig ist Berater und Geschäftsführer der Doerig + Partner AG sowie Präsident des Beirates Cyber-Defence VBS. Nach seinem Studium zum Maschineningenieur, seinem Nachdiplom in Systemengineering sowie zwei betriebswirtschaftlichen Studiengängen eignete er sich in 30 Berufsjahren sehr viel Führungs-, Projekt-, Analyse-, Design- und Implementierungserfahrung von komplexen Anwendungen mittels modernsten Technologien an. Erfolgreiche Umsetzungen von grossen, internationalen Strategieentwicklungs-, Risikomanagement- und Sicherheitsprojekten in verschiedenen Industrien runden sein breites und fundiertes Erfahrungswissen ab.

Dr. Matthias Drodt ist aktuell Leiter IT-Security Prozesse und Engineering bei der DB Netz AG. Er ist zuständig für das Management der IT-Security im Bereich der digitalen Leit- und Sicherungstechnik für sicherheitskritische Bahnsysteme. Zuvor begleitete er mehr als 9 Jahre die Funktion des CISO für den Deutsche Bahn Konzern und war verantwortlich für die konzernweiten Richtlinien, Prozesse, Strategie und Governance hinsichtlich IT-Sicherheit. Er hat hierbei maßgeblich den Ausbau der Cyber Resilience innerhalb der Deutschen Bahn umgesetzt sowie die Einführung von sicheren Cloud-Lösungen maßgeblich gesteuert und vorangetrieben. Zuvor bekleidete er mehrere Jahre die Rolle des Chefarchitekten für Security & Continuity Management beim internen IT-Dienstleister DB Systel.

 **Ambassador Sorin Ducaru** is currently a Senior Fellow the Hudson Institute in Washington DC and a Special Advisor to the Global Commission on the Stability of Cyberspace. He is a Romanian career diplomat with a longstanding experience in trans-Atlantic and International Relations and a particular expertise in the field of emerging security challenges and the impact of new technologies upon security. Ambassador Ducaru's professional background reflects a quite rare blend of technical and political studies. Holding degrees both in computer-studies and political science, he has been intensely engaged intellectually and professionally in translating "digital language" into the language of policy and strategy.

Ambassador Ducaru held the post of NATO Assistant Secretary General for Emerging Security Challenges from September 2013 to November 2017. In this capacity he was the head of the Emerging Security Challenges Division at NATO-HQ, Chair of the Cyber Defence Committee and also coordinator and manager NATO's Science for Peace and Security Programme. He has been leading the work on NATO cyber policy development and implementation in a period of most dynamic developments for the Alliance in this field. He has provided expert input and chaired Allied negotiations on NATO's Enhanced Policy on Cyber Defence (adopted at the Wales Summit in 2014), on NATO's Cyber Defence Pledge and the Alliance's Recognition of Cyberspace as Operational Domain (both adopted at the Warsaw Summit in 2016). As Chair of NATO's Cyber Defence Management Board, he has been in charge of supervision NATO Cyber Action Plan implementation. Ambassador Ducaru has championed the cyber multi-stakeholder approach and the development of NATO's cyber partnerships with partner countries, international organizations, industry and academia, displaying at the same time a strong support for the development of international norms of responsible behavior and confidence building measures in cyberspace as important instruments to strengthen stability in cyberspace.

Prior to his appointment as ASG, Ambassador Ducaru served as Romania's Permanent Representative to the North Atlantic Council, from September 2006 to September 2013. From November 2011, Ambassador Ducaru was the Dean of the North Atlantic Council.

Ambassador Ducaru was born on 22 June 1964, in Baia-Mare, Romania. He graduated from the Polytechnic Institute of Bucharest in 1988 with a BA Degree in Applied Electronics and Computer-Studies and from the Romanian National School of Political Studies and Public Administration in 1992, with a Post-Graduate Degree in Political Studies. He holds a MPhil Degree in International Relations from the University of Amsterdam (1993) and a Ph.D. degree in International Economics from the Academy of Economic Studies in Bucharest (2005).

He joined the Romanian Ministry of Foreign Affairs in 1993, assuming various posts such: counsellor to the Minister, spokesman of the MFA, Director of the Minister's Office and Director for NATO and Strategic Issues. From 2001 to 2006, he served as Romania's Ambassador to the United States of America. In 2000–2001, Ambassador Ducaru served as Permanent Representative of Romania to the United Nations, in New York.

In the year 2008 Ambassador Ducaru was awarded the rank of Knight of the National Order "The Star of Romania." He received the title of "Ambassador of the Year" in 2003 and 2012, from the Minister of Foreign Affairs of Romania.

He is married to Carmen Ducaru, Director of the Romanian Cultural Institute in Brussels and has two children. Ambassador Ducaru speaks German, English and French, and enjoys playing the guitar, key-board, skiing, tennis and photography.

Andre Duvillard wurde vom Bund und den Kantonen zum gemeinsamen Delegierten gewählt. Er moderiert den Dialog zwischen dem Bund und den Kantonen im Sicherheitsverbund Schweiz, bearbeitet und führt die Geschäfte der Politischen Plattform, der Operativen Plattform und der Arbeitsgruppen. Er leitet die Operative Plattform, vertritt die Anliegen in der Politischen Plattform und setzt deren Aufträge um. Der Delegierte wird von einer Geschäftsstelle unterstützt. André Duvillard schloss das Studium der Rechtswissenschaften 1987 an der Universität Neuenburg ab. Anschliessend war er als Delegierter des Internationalen Komitees vom Roten Kreuz (IKRK) im Irak, in Israel und im Libanon tätig. Von 1991–1997 arbeitete er bei den Parlamentsdiensten als Sekretär der Sicherheitspolitischen Kommissionen (SiK). Zwischen 1997–2012 war er bei der Kantonspolizei Neuenburg als Stv. Kommandant und ab 2005 als Polizeikommandant tätig.

Jörg Eschweiler has a background in military information security & operations, during his commercial career he served with IBM and Airbus in leadership positions starting their CySec business in DACH region and in international roles. Being known as lateral thinker and promoter of innovations and outside-box-thinking he has a track record in inter-connecting between silos as well as research, technology development and business including close relations with GO/NGO/commercial hubs in the USA, Israel, Singapore, France and the United Kingdom of Great Britain. He pioneered establishing CySec competence centers for gov and private entities incl. exchange and mission accomplishment across silos which includes exploring, advocating and leveraging new ways and innovative approaches. This included founding modern forms of cooperation in the Cyber arena (e.g. Community-ISACs like CSSA e.V. in Germany, PPPs) and supporting innovative tech vendors to focus on right capabilities, to meet demand and enter markets. He went „back" on the gov side 2016 to support German MoD as they build out their new Cyber Command and strategic approach towards innovating & incubating sustainable CySec capabilities. After finishing the assignment he moved on to commercial side joining Atos as major European player to fuel progress in Cyber Security and Intelligence, with scope on civil and national security for German market. Within national standardization he is active as Vice Chair of Council at IT Security Coordination Office (KITS) at the German Institute for Standardization (DIN e.V.). He plays an active role in European strategy and standardization on Cyber Security as co-founder, contributor and deputy chair of the CEN CENELEC Cyber Security Focus Group. On international level he chairs the Cyber Security Standards User Council of the Organization for the Advancement of Structured Information Standards (OASIS), the leading open technology and interoperability standards organization. Within NATO Federated Mission Network capability development community he's supporting next generation mission oriented cloud security as evolution of data centric security on German behalf.

Prof. Anja Feldmann Ph.D. is since 2006 a full professor at the Technische Universität Berlin, Germany. From 2000 to 2006 she headed the network architectures group first at Saarland University and then at TU München. Before that (1995–1999) she was a member of the Networking and Distributed Systems Center at AT&T Labs – Research in Florham Park, New Jersey. Her current research interests include Internet measurement, traffic engineering and traffic characterization, network performance debugging, intrusion detection, network architecture. She has been Co-Chair of ACM SIGCOMM and IMC and Co-PC-Chair of ACM SIGCOMM, ACM IMC, and ACM HotNets. She is a member of the German Academy of Sciences Leopoldina, the BBAW, the supervisory board of SAP SE. She received a M.S. degree in Computer Science from the University of Paderborn in 1990 and M.S. and Ph.D. degrees in CS from CMU in 1991 and 1995, respectively.

Tobias Fiebig is an assistant professor in the Engineering Systems and Services section at TU Delft. He has a M.Sc. degree in System and Network Engineering (SNE) from University of Amsterdam, and obtained a Dr.-Ing. in computer science from TU Berlin. His overall research interest is on how system and network engineering can become more secure by design. For this purpose, he combines the development of technical research tools with qualitative and quantitative methods.

Dr. Christian Folini ist Partner bei der netnea AG in Bern. Er arbeitet als Sicherheitsingenieur für verschiedene nationale und internationale Kunden. Er ist spezialisiert auf Webserver Sicherheit, Bedrohungsanalysen und DDoS Verteidigung. Dank über zehn Jahren praktischer Erfahrung mit der Open Source Web Application Firewall ModSecurity ist er ein gefragter Referent und Kursleiter zu diesem Thema. Christian Folini ist der Autor des ModSecurity Handbuchs und Co-Lead des OWASP ModSecurity Core Rule Projekts. Er fungiert als Vize-Präsident des Public Private Partnerships „Swiss Cyber Experts" und er ist als Program Chair an der Organisation der jährlich stattfindenden Swiss Cyber Storm Konferenz beteiligt.

Dr. Stefanie Frey Ph.D. (Department of War Studies, King's College London, UK) is Managing Director at Deutor Cyber Security Solutions Switzerland GmbH. Stefanie is specialized in developing strategies and solutions against criminal acts in the digital space for states, international organizations and companies in close cooperation with law enforcement and other relevant bodies. She worked several years for the Swiss government as coordinator for the implementation of the National Cyber Strategy of Switzerland. She made contributions to ENISA's Cyber Security Working Group and the OECD Working Party on Security and Privacy in the Digital Economy (SPDE) and has influenced the outcome of the OECD Digital Security Risk Recommendation. Since 2017 she is a member of the Permanent Stakeholder Group of ENISA and is actively engaged in shaping the regional and global cyber security agenda with international and regional organizations. Stefanie also has an MBA from the International School of Management (ISM) in Dortmund and has several publications on cyber security, the Cold War and World War II.

Melanie Friedli ist in Basel aufgewachsen. Sie hat in Genf Politologie und Internationale Beziehungen studiert und mit dem Lizenziat abgeschlossen. Danach absolvierte sie ein LL.M. in Kriminologie an der Rechtswissenschaftlichen Fakultät der Universität Bern. Zurzeit absolviert sie berufsbegleitend an der Universität Freiburg ein CAS+ in Mediation in Wirtschaft, Organisationen und öffentlichem Bereich. Sie hat vier Jahre beim Bundesamt für Polizei gearbeitet, unter anderem bei der Meldestelle für Geldwäscherei, bevor sie zum Sicherheitsverbund Schweiz wechselte, wo sie hauptsächlich für die Koordination der Umsetzung der Nationalen Cyber-Strategie der Schweiz mit den Kantonen zuständig war. Aktuell arbeitet sie beim Staatssekretariat für Internationale Finanzfragen im Bereich Geldwäscherei und Terrorismusfinanzierung. Leichtathletik und Basketball haben schon in sehr jungen Jahren einen wichtigen Teil in ihrem Leben eingenommen. Ersteres übt sie immer noch aktiv und intensiv aus. Sehr früh hat Melanie Friedli Interesse an Kriminalfällen gefunden, deren Verhinderung und Aufdeckung immer anspruchsvoller werden. Diesem Gebiet ist sie bis heute treu geblieben.

Prof. Solange Ghernaouti is director of the Swiss Cybersecurity Advisory and Research Group – University of Lausanne. She holds a Ph.D. in Computer Science (Paris University), is former auditor of the French Institute of Advanced Studies in National Defence, Associate Fellow at the Geneva Center for Security Policy, member of the UNESCO Swiss Commission and of the Swiss Academy of Technical Sciences. She has authored more than 300 publications and thirty books including "Cyberpower: Crime, Conflict and Security in Cyberspace" (EPFL press 2013). She is Chevalier de la *Légion d'Honneur* and has been recognised by the Swiss press as one of the outstanding women in professional and academic circles.

Tobias Glemser ist Geschäftsführer der secuvera GmbH und BSI-zertifizierter Penetrationstester. Er beschäftigt sich seit dem Jahr 2000 intensiv mit technischen und organisatorischen Fragen rund um die Informationssicherheit.

Dr. Alain Gut is Director Public Sector at IBM Switzerland after having been Director of Software Group Switzerland and Austria and Member of the Executive Board Switzerland. Before that he held various management positions at Tata Consultancy Services, Microsoft, A&A Actienbank, UBS AG and DEC Digital Equipment Corporation. Alain Gut holds a M.A. and a Ph.D. in business administration and computer science from the University of Zurich and attended the Program for Executive Development (PED) at IMD Lausanne. Alain Gut is engaged in many associations and organizations on the topics of informatics in education, mobility and cyber security. He is President of the Board of Directors of Swiss Cyber Experts, a Public Private Partnership with the Swiss Government.

Dr. Magnus Harlander hat an der TU-München und am Lawrence-Berkeley-Lab in theoretischer Physik promoviert. 1992 – noch während der Promotion – hat er mit zwei Kollegen die genua GmbH gegründet und in 25 Jahren in diesem Team als Geschäftsführer zu einem führenden Anbieter von IT-Sicherheitsprodukten für anspruchsvolle Märkte entwickelt. Die unter seiner Verantwortung entwickelten Produkte sichern hochsensible Netze von Regierungen und weltweit agierenden Organisationen ab. Dafür wurden in dieser Zeit viele bahnbrechende Neuerungen vorgestellt, wie z. B. die erste BSI-zertifizierte Firewall oder das erste Mikro-Kernel-basierte End-User-System. Magnus Harlander ist von vielen Vorträgen und Panel-Beiträgen zum Thema IT-Sicherheit bekannt, hat eine Reihe von Publikationen veröffentlicht und wirkt in mehreren Organisationen als aktives Mitglied oder, wie beim Münchner Kreis, auch im Vorstand. Anfang 2018 hat er sich aus der Geschäftsleitung der genua GmbH zurückgezogen und agiert nun noch als Gesellschafter, Berater, Investor, IT-Sicherheits-Aktivist und als Vorstand der Harlander-Stiftung.

Prof. Dr. Udo Helmbrecht has more than 40 years of professional management experience in the IT sector. Udo Helmbrecht was born in 1955, in Castrop-Rauxel, North Rhine-Westphalia, Germany. He studied Physics, Mathematics and Computer Science at Ruhr-University, Bochum, and in 1984 he was awarded a Ph.D. in Theoretical Physics. In 2010 Udo Helmbrecht was appointed honorary professor at the Universität der Bundeswehr Munich, Germany. His experience in the field of security has been acquired through work in a variety of areas, including the energy industry, insurance, engineering, aviation, defence, and the space industry. He became the president of the German Federal Office for Information Security (BSI) in 2003. Udo Helmbrecht took office as Executive Director of the European Union Agency for Network and Information Security (ENISA) in October 2009.

Sascha Herzog ist technischer Geschäftsführer der NSIDE ATTACK LOGIC GmbH in München und arbeitet seit 2003 als Penetration Tester und Ethical Hacker. Er führte Penetration Tests und simulierte Angriffe bei zahlreichen internationalen Unternehmen durch. Herr Herzog leitete viele Projekte bei internationalen Konzernen, Finanzinstitutionen, Versicherungen, Medien- und High-Tech Unternehmen, Regierungseinrichtungen, Pharma- und Energieunternehmen, sowie zahlreichen Kunden aus dem deutschen Mittelstand und der Industrie.

Dr. Richard Hill was formerly a senior official at the International Telecommunication Union (ITU); he was involved with operational aspects of service provision, networks and performance, including numbering issues (for example, assignment of international country codes) and charging and accounting matters. He has been involved in internet governance issues since the inception of the Internet and is now an activist in that area, speaking, publishing, and contributing to discussions in various forums. He writes frequently about internet governance issues. Prior to joining ITU, Richard was Department Head, IT Infrastructure Delivery and Support, at Orange Communications (a GSM operator). He previously was the IT Manager at the University of Geneva; held various IT and telecommunications positions in Hewlett-Packard Europe; worked as a Research Statistician for A.C. Nielsen; as a systems designer and manager for software for econometric modeling and the management of financial portfolios at M.I.T. and spinoffs. Richard holds a Ph.D. in Statistics from Harvard University and a B.S. in Mathematics from M.I.T. Prior to his studies in the U.S.A., he obtained the Maturita' from the Liceo Scientifico A. Righi in Rome, Italy.

Heinz Karrer ist seit September 2013 Präsident des Schweizer Wirtschaftsdachverbandes economiesuisse. Bekannt wurde er als ehemaliger CEO der AXPO, die er während 11 Jahren erfolgreich leitete und als früherer Nationalspieler des Handballteams der Schweiz. Er ist dipl. Kaufmann, machte anschliessend die Matura auf dem 2. Bildungsweg und studierte Nationalökonomie an der HSG. Während seiner Berufskarriere war er u. a. für Intersport, Ringier und Swisscom in leitender Funktion tätig. Er hat verschiedene Mandate als Verwaltungsrat und ist Mitglied des Bankrats der SNB.

Dr.-Ing. Jörg Kebbedies (*1958) ist Principal bei der secunet Security Networks AG am Standort Dresden, für die er seit dem Jahr 2000 tätig ist. Aktuell berät er dort im Bereich der Gestaltung sicherheitsrelevanter Prozesse und der Entwicklung von Sicherheitsarchitekturen für Unternehmen und Behörden mit hohen Vertraulichkeitsanforderungen. Er begann seine berufliche Karriere nach dem Abitur 1975 als Facharbeiter für Betriebs-, Mess- und Steuerungstechnik bei der EKO Stahl GmbH. Im Anschluss studierte er 1978–1983 Technische Kybernetik und Automatisierungstechnik an der TU Dresden, wo er 2013–2017 zum Thema „Beschreibung, Verarbeitung und Überprüfung clientseitiger Policies für vertrauenswürdige Cloud-Anwendungen" promovierte. Zwischenzeitlich führte ihn sein beruflicher Werdegang von der EKO Stahl GmbH, wo er 1985–1991 als Ingenieur beschäftigt war, und einer Beratertätigkeit 1991–2000 bei der Systemhaus Scheuschner GmbH zu der secunet Security Networks AG: 2000–2006 zunächst als Sicherheitsberater im Umfeld Web- und Portalsicherheit und Identity-Management und 2006–2010 im Bereich Prozessberatung im Geheimschutz sowie 2010–2015 als Teamleiter im Bereich Informationssicherheitsmanagement. Jörg Kebbedies ist daneben im Besitz mehrerer Zertifizierungen im Bereich IT-Sicherheit.

Dr. Nikolas Krämer ist seit 2014 kaufmännischer Geschäftsführer der Städtischen Kliniken Neuss – Lukaskrankenhaus – GmbH. Davor war er als Kaufmännischer Direktor im Katholischen Hospitalverbund Hellweg, als Bereichsleiter Finanz- und Rechnungswesen in der Kaiserswerther Diakonie in Düsseldorf sowie bei KPMG/BearingPoint als Unternehmensberater tätig. Er promovierte über strategisches Kostenmanagement im Krankenhaus und hält verschiedene Lehraufträge, u. a. an der Dresden International University. Nicolas Krämer hat über 50 Publikationen verfasst. U. a. ist er Autor sowie Herausgeber des Buches „Krankenhausmanagement 2.0". Als Referent gibt er sein Wissen und seine Erfahrungen aus dem Cyberangriff an andere Unternehmen weiter.

Michael Kranawetter arbeitet seit 2007 als National Security Officer, Head of Information Security bei Microsoft Deutschland. In dieser Funktion ist er für die IT-Governance, IT-Compliance und Risikoeinschätzung sowie die gesamte Informations-Sicherheits-Strategie des Unternehmens verantwortlich. Michael Kranawetter hat umfassende und langjährige Erfahrungen in der IT-Sicherheits-Branche. Als Projektmanager und Berater implementierte er eine Reihe bedeutender Infrastruktur-Projekte, bevor er bei der Münchener Rück AG als Senior Service Manager und IT-Architekt unter anderem in Bereichen der Sicherheitsarchitektur, im Service Management und in der IT-Governance tätig war. Zuletzt war er dort für das interne, international aktive Sicherheits-Audit-Team sowie für das Risikomanagement von Informationssicherheit, IT-Compliance und IT-Governance verantwortlich.

Thorben Krüger is a computer scientist and bibliophile. His professional interests include systems engineering, Internet measurement and obscure programming languages. In his free time, he is enthusiastic about innovations in space exploration and sarcastic about politics.

Dirk Kunze trat 1992 in den Polizeidienst ein und versah zunächst Dienst als Streifenpolizist in Köln. Nach dem Bachelor-Studium an der FhöV Köln wechselte er in die kriminalpolizeiliche Sachbearbeitung, zuerst bei der Kriminalwache und anschließend im Kommissariat für Raubdelikte. Ab 2006 entwickelte Dirk Kunze am Landesamt für Ausbildung, Fortbildung und Personalangelegenheiten der Polizei NRW die Fortbildung im Bereich Mobilfunkforensik. Daneben unterrichtete er digitale Beweissicherung und polizeiliche Datenverarbeitung. Außerdem wirkte er an der Einführung landeseinheitlicher Fallbearbeitungssysteme mit. Nach dem Abschluss des Masterstudienganges an der Deutschen Hochschule der Polizei übernahm Dirk Kunze 2015 die Leitung des Dezernats 42 (Ermittlungskommissionen, Zentrale Internetrecherche) im Cybercrime-Kompetenzzentrums des LKA NRW. 2017 bildete er das Cyber-Recherche- und Fahndungszentrum der Polizei Nordrhein-Westfalen beim LKA NRW und übernahm dessen Leitung. Daneben baute er für den operativen Einsatz die Critical Incident Response Group (CIRG) des LKA NRW zur Reaktion auf Angriffe gegen kritische Infrastrukturen auf.

Pieter Lexis received his M.Sc. in Systems and Network Engineering from the University of Amsterdam. After wandering around several companies as a DevOps Engineer focusing on automation, he joined PowerDNS B.V. where he works on the Open-Source nameserver of the same name, automates customer deployments and works with the IETF and other parties to deploy and improve new (security) standards.

Franziska Lichtblau works as a Ph.D. student in the field of Internet Measurement at TU Berlin. Her main focus is on inter-domain traffic measurements, IXPs, security and Internet infrastructure. She has a background as system administrator and is active in the free software community.

Dimitra Liveri The topic of NCSS is covered in ENISA by the NCSS team, namely Anna Sarri, Eleni Darra and Dimitra Liveri, from the Secure Infrastructures and Services Unit. ENISA has been dealing with the topic since 2012 and the team was formed in 2014. The NCSS team in ENISA is running related projects, handles the NCSS online map, facilitates discussion in the NCSS experts group and finally organizes annually the ENISA NCSS workshop.

Dipl. Wirt.-Inf. Dirk Loss unterstützte nach dem Studium zunächst als IT-Sicherheitsberater, IT-Grundschutz-Auditor und Penetration Tester Unternehmen und Behörden bei der Konzeption und Prüfung von IT-Sicherheitsmaßnahmen. Von 2005 bis 2012 war er als Projektleiter und Systemarchitekt verantwortlich für die Entwicklung von Hochsicherheitsfirewalls zur vorschriftenkonformen Kopplung von Netzen mit unterschiedlichem Schutzbedarf. Bei der genua GmbH begleitet er seit 2012 in verschiedenen Funktionen die Entwicklung Microkernel-basierter Separationslösungen für den Geheimschutz – unter anderem als Software Entwickler, Product Owner und Autor von Herstellerdokumentation für Common Criteria Evaluierungen.

Pierre Maudet was elected in the Geneva Government on 17 June 2012. He was previously a member of the Administrative Council (2007–2012) and Mayor of the City of Geneva (2011–2012). As a State Counsellor, he chairs the Department of Security and the Economy (DSE).

Lars Minth is CEO and founder of quantusec. He is a voracious listener, active speaker, author, host and advisor for InfoSec and Cyber topics with a history of working for governments and cities, intelligence and commercial organizations. His current research topics are threat intelligence, cyber governance, IAM, national security management systems and making smart cities resilient and secure.

Dr. Denis Morel arbeitet seit mehr als fünf Jahren bei der Schweizerischen Post und ist dort als Leiter E-Voting verantwortlich für dieses Geschäft für die Post. Denis Morel ist ausgebildeter Mathematiker und arbeitete nach seiner Promotion an der Universität Freiburg mehrere Jahre lang für verschiedene Unternehmen in der IT-Beratung. Dabei bearbeitete er unter anderem Themen wie Geldwäschereibekämpfung, E-Health und E-Government. Denis Morel ist Vorstandsmitglieder des Vereines eGov-Schweiz.

Ramon Mörl since accomplishing his degree in Computer Science in 1987 at the technical University in Munich, Mr. Mörl consulted Companies regarding IT-Security. For well-known Companies such as HP, IBM, Siemens, ICL and Bull he had a leading role steering projects in BELGIUM; Germany; France, Italy, Austria, Switzerland and the USA. He acted as an independent evaluator and consultant for the European Union especially in regards to ECMA, IETF and ISO standards for IT Security. Since 2000 Mr. Mörl holds a patent for costefficient use of secure processes. Since 2002 Mr. Mörl uses his experience as Managing Director of itWatch GmbH.

Prof. Dr. Holger Mühlbauer hat nach seinem Jura-Studium als Wissenschaftlicher Mitarbeiter an der TU Berlin am Fachbereich Informatik im Bereich Datenschutzrecht und Informationsrecht gelehrt. Er promovierte 1994 zum Thema „Einwohnermeldewesen" und arbeitete anschließend bei der Kassenärztlichen Vereinigung Berlin. Ab 1996 war er einer der Normenausschuss-Geschäftsführer im DIN Deutsches Institut für Normung e.V. in Berlin. Dr. Mühlbauer bekleidete die Funktion des ‚Secretary' in mehreren Gremien des Europäischen Komitees für Normung (CEN) und der Internationalen Normungsorganisation (ISO), insbesondere auf dem Gebiet „Dienstleistungsnormung" bzw. „Service standardization".
2008 wechselte er für ein Jahr zu Austrian Standards nach Wien. Seit 2009 ist Dr. Mühlbauer Geschäftsführer des TeleTrusT – Bundesverband IT-Sicherheit e.V. Dr. Mühlbauer ist Autor zahlreicher Publikationen zu standardisierungs- oder IT-sicherheitsrelevanten Themen.

Prof. Dr. Norbert Pohlmann ist Informatikprofessor für Informationssicherheit im Fachbereich Informatik und geschäftsführender Direktor des Instituts für Internet-Sicherheit an der Westfälischen Hochschule Gelsenkirchen. Vorher war er von 1988 bis 1999 geschäftsführender Gesellschafter der Firma KryptoKom, Gesellschaft für kryptographische Informationssicherheit und Kommunikationstechnologie mbH. Nach der Fusion der KryptoKom mit der Utimaco Safeware war er von 1999 bis 2003 Mitglied des Vorstandes der Utimaco Safeware AG. Seit April 1997 ist Prof. Pohlmann Vorstandsvorsitzender des Bundesverbands für IT-Sicherheit TeleTrusT und seit Mai 2015 Mitglied des Vorstandes des eco (Verband der Internetwirtschaft e.V.). Außerdem ist Prof. Pohlmann Mitglied des wissenschaftlichen Beirates der GDD (Gesellschaft für Datenschutz und Datensicherung e.V.) und Mitglied im Lenkungskreis der Initiative „IT-Sicherheit in der Wirtschaft" (Bundesministeriums für Wirtschaft und Technologie). Er war fünf Jahre Mitglied der „Permanent

Stakeholders' Group" der ENISA (European Network and Information Security Agency), die Sicherheitsagentur der europäischen Gemeinschaft. Zahlreiche Fachartikel und mehrere Bücher, Vorträge und Seminare auf dem Gebiet der Informationssicherheit dokumentieren seine Fachkompetenz und sein Engagement auf dem Gebiet IT-Sicherheit.

Ludger Pagel ist seit 2013 bei der DB Systel im Geschäftsbereich Workplace und Infrastructure tätig. Zu seinen Aufgabenfeldern gehören die Konzeption und Umsetzung von Prozessen des Security Managements, die Vertretung des Geschäftsbereiches in IT-Security-bezogenen Gremien sowie die Beratung bei IT-Security Themen. Im Rahmen seiner Tätigkeiten war er verantwortlich für die Evaluierung des Aufbaues eines CSIRT mit zugehörigem SIEM in der DB Systel und später verantwortlich für die Abstimmung und Umsetzung bezüglich prozessualer, normativer und datenschutzrechtlicher Aspekte. Hierzu gehörte und gehört auch die enge Abstimmung mit dem CISO der Deutschen Bahn zwecks Integration in die Cyber Defense des Konzerns. Heute berät er im Rahmen des technischen Security Beratungsteam der DB Systel konzerninterne Kunden bezüglich CSIRT/SIEM-betreffender Aspekte.

Teresa Ritter M.Sc., Bereichsleiterin für Sicherheitspolitik und Verteidigung beim Bitkom. Teresa Ritter betreut als Referentin für Sicherheitspolitik die Themen Wirtschaftsschutz, IT-Sicherheit und Verteidigung beim Bitkom, dem größten Digitalverband Deutschlands. Vor ihrer Tätigkeit beim Bitkom war Teresa Ritter wissenschaftliche Mitarbeiterin bei Nina Warken MdB, Mitglied des Innenausschusses. Im Rahmen ihrer dortigen Arbeit verantwortete sie die Themen Bevölkerungsschutz und innere Sicherheit. Bereits während ihres VWL-Studiums an der Freien Universität Berlin, arbeitete sie als studentische Mitarbeiterin beim Bundestagsabgeordneten Roderich Kiesewetter, Mitglied des Auswärtigen Ausschusses. Dort betreute sie die Themen Außen- und Verteidigungspolitik.

Irina Rizmal is currently working as a Consultant at the Diplo Foundation. She was in charge of setting up the first national cybersecurity drill at policy level in the Republic of Serbia. She was also the lead author of the Guide through Information Security in the Republic of Serbia, published by the OSCE Mission to Serbia and reprinted by the Saga International Frontier Group. Prior to focusing solely on cybersecurity, she worked on other security-related topics including security sector reform, private security, classified information protection, EU and NATO integration and cooperation of the Republic of Serbia. She holds a Master's degree in Security Studies from the University College London (UCL). She is a member of the "Petnica Group."

Anna Sarri The topic of NCSS is covered in ENISA by the NCSS team, namely Anna Sarri, Eleni Darra and Dimitra Liveri, from the Secure Infrastructures and Services Unit. ENISA has been dealing with the topic since 2012 and the team was formed in 2014. The NCSS team in ENISA is running related projects, handles the NCSS online map, facilitates discussion in the NCSS experts group and finally organizes annually the ENISA NCSS workshop.

Mark A. Saxer studierte Politikwissenschaft, Staatsrecht und allgemeine Geschichte an der Universität Zürich und schloß mit einem Lizentiat ab (lic. phil. I). Während des Studiums beschäftigte er sich intensiv mit politischer Philosophie und Ökonomie. Seine berufliche Laufbahn begann er als Sekretär der FDP-Fraktion des Parlaments des Kantons Zürich. Nach einer Station als Redakteur bei einer Tageszeitung wechselte er in die Unternehmenskommunikation großer amerikanischer IT-Anbieter, bis er zur Public Affairs Agentur furrerhugi. AG wechselte, wo er heute Partner ist. Er gehörte zu den maßgeblichen Initianten des Schweizer Polizei Informatik Kongress', dessen Geschäftsführer er heute noch ist, und der Swiss Cyber Experts.

Arne Schönbohm hat am 18. Februar 2016 sein Amt als Präsident des Bundesamtes für Sicherheit in der Informationstechnik (BSI) angetreten.

Der gebürtige Hamburger Arne Schönbohm (Jahrgang 1969) studierte Internationales Management in Dortmund, London und Taipeh und ist seit mehr als zehn Jahren in führenden Positionen im Bereich der IT-Sicherheit tätig. Bevor er 2008 Vorstandsvorsitzender der BSS BuCET Shared Services AG (BSS AG) wurde, einem Unternehmen, das sich unter anderem der Beratung auf dem Feld der Cyber-Sicherheit verschrieben hat, war Schönbohm in verschiedenen Positionen für EADS tätig. Zuletzt war er dort Vizepräsident für Commercial und Defence Solutions. Seine 13-jährige Industriekarriere begann der Diplom-Betriebswirt als Trainee in der zentralen Nachwuchsgruppe bei DaimlerChrysler Aerospace in München. Darüber hinaus arbeitete Schönbohm als Sicherheitsexperte und

Berater verschiedener politischer Entscheidungsträger auf Bundes- und Landesebene, so war er unter anderem Mitglied der Cyber Security Coordination Group der EU.

Vor seiner Ernennung zum BSI-Präsidenten war Arne Schönbohm mehr als drei Jahre als Präsident des 2012 gegründeten Cyber-Sicherheitsrats Deutschland e.V. tätig. Er ist Autor diverser Bücher, darunter auch „Deutschlands Sicherheit – Cybercrime und Cyberwar (2011)".

Armin Schuster Polizeidirektor a.D.; 79576 Weil am Rhein – * 20.05.1961 Andernach/Rhein; kath.; verh., 1 erw. Tochter – 1980/83 Studium FH des Bundes für öffentliche Verwaltung Köln/Lübeck, 1986/92 Fernuniversität Hagen (Wirtschaftswissenschaften), 1993/95 Deutsche Hochschule der Polizei Münster, European Quality System Manager und Auditor, Senior Quality Manager. Seit 1983 versch. Verwendungen im gehobenen und höheren Dienst der Bundespolizei (BP), zuletzt bis 2009 Leiter BP-Amtes/-Inspektion Weil am Rhein, 1985 bis 1989 Bundesinnenministerium Bonn. Ehrenamtl. Mitgl. im Vorstand der Deutschen Gesellschaft für Qualität. Ehrenamtl. Mitgl. Jury-Mitgl. der Initiative Ludwig-Erhard-Preis (Deutscher Qualitätspreis), Dozent und Prüfer Deutsche Gesellschaft für Qualität e.V., Mitgl. International Police Association, Mitgl. Bundespolizeigewerkschaft, Verbund für Innere Sicherheit (BGV), Vors. Stiftungsrat der Sportstiftung Südbaden. Seit 1987 Mitgl. der CDU, seit 2007 im CDU-Stadtverband Weil am Rhein, seit 2012 Kreisvors. des CDU-Kreisverb. Lörrach, Mitgl. im CDU-Bundesfachausschuss Innenpolitik. MdB seit Okt. 2009.

Dr. Wolfgang Schwabl Dipl.-Ing. Dr. techn. studierte an der TU Wien Technische Physik und Informatik. Er promovierte 1989 mit Auszeichnung und erhielt für seine Dissertation den Heinz-Zemanek-Preis der Österreichischen Computer Gesellschaft (OCG). Nach der TU arbeitete er bei Digital Equipment Österreich (DEC) und ging 1996 zu mobilkom Austria, wo er zunächst den Ausbau der IT leitete und später für Datensicherheit verantwortlich war. Er wechselte 2010 zur Telekom Austria als Group Director für „Information Security & Emergency". Seit 2015 ist Wolfgang Schwabl als Cyber Security Officer für A1 tätig. Zu seinen ehrenamtlichen Tätigkeiten zählen: Vortragender beim Strategischen Führungslehrgang der Bundesregierung, Förderbeirat der netidee.at, Mitglied des Beirats der stopline.at und stv. Leiter der Cyber Security Plattform (CSP) des Bundeskanzleramtes.

Florian Streibelt is a Ph.D. student at TU Berlin. Coming from system administration he has a strong interest in understanding the challenges of building reliable and secure distributed systems.

Dr. Eneken Tikk (dr.iur) is Head of Power and Strategy Analysis at the Cyber Policy Institute (CPI) in Jyväskylä, Finland. Her work at CPI focuses on questions of strategic stability, normative leadership and state behavior. Dr. Tikk also serves as senior adviser to the board of the ICT for Peace Foundation in Geneva, Switzerland advising governments, policy makers and parliaments on international peace and security issues in the context of ICTs. In her previous assignment, as Senior Fellow for Cyber Security at the International Institute for Strategic Studies (IISS), Eneken launched and coordinated a network of experts in support of the UK foreign cyber policy. She led the international law thread of the UK-China track 1.5 cyber security dialogue (2014–2017). At the invitation of the Estonian MFA, Eneken has been advising the Estonian expert in the UN First Committee Group of Governmental Experts on International Information Security (UN GGE) (2012–2013; 2014–2015; 2016–2017). Eneken was the first foreign national contractor at the MITRE Corporation (2012–2016), where her work focused on analyzing and advising national cyber security strategy processes and the US cyber diplomacy. Before joining IISS, Eneken worked at the NATO Cooperative Cyber Defence Centre of Excellence (CCD COE) in Tallinn, Estonia, where she established and led the Legal and Policy Branch and initiated the Tallinn Manual project. Eneken is an attorney in the field of information technology law at Ellex Raidla, the leading law firm in Estonia. She has consulted Estonian public authorities on legal and policy issues related to deploying and managing national information systems and services. Eneken holds a Ph.D. in law from the University of Tartu in Estonia. She has conducted post-doctoral studies on Internet of Things and emerging technologies at Cardiff University (2016) and international cyber norms at Leiden University (2017) and international cyber security at University of Toronto (2012). Dr. Tikk has long teaching experience at Tallinn Technical University and the University of Tartu.

Mag. Walter J. Unger Oberst des Generalstabsdienstes, Theresianische Militärakademie 1979–1982, seit 1982 Kommandanten- und Leiterfunktionen in der Truppe und der Zentralstelle des BMLVS; 1988–1991 Generalstabsausbildung; 1998–1999 Führungskräftelehrgang des Bundes, 1999–2000 Kommandant des Panzerabwehrbataillons 1; 2001–2009 Leiter Elektronische Abwehr, 2006–2008 Leiter der Interministeriellen Arbeitsgruppe Strategie „IKT-Sicherheit", 2009 Leiter der Abteilung IKT-Sicherheit, seit Mai 2013 Leiter der Abteilung Cyber Defence & IKT-Sicherheit im Abwehramt, derzeit Leiter Cyber-Verteidigungszentrum (Cyber Defence Centre).

Gérald Vernez ist Delegierter für Cyber-Defence beim Eidg. Departement für Verteidigung, Bevölkerungsschutz und Sport (VBS) hat Geologie, Meteorologie und Sicherheitspolitik studiert. Nach einem ersten Karierenanteil in der Industrie trat er 1996 im Generalstab der schweizerischen Armee ein. Nach einer zentralen Rolle bei der Vorbereitung des Krisenstabes für den „Jahr 2000-Wechsel" hat er die Führungsorganisation der Armee geplant und später die Informations-Operationen der Armee aufgebaut. 2009 wurde er Stabschef des Führungsstabes der Armee und in 2011 stellvertretender Direktor für die Ausarbeitung der Nationalen Strategie für den Schutz der Schweiz gegen Cyber-Risiken. In 2013 wurde er Delegierter des Chefs der Armee für Cyber-Defence und leitete diesen Bereich ab 2015. Seit 2017 ist er Delegierter für Cyber-Defence des Verteidigungsdepartements.

Dieter Warnecke Generalleutnant Dieter Warnecke, Jahrgang 1956, ist seit 2015 Abteilungsleiter Strategie und Einsatz im Bundesministerium der Verteidigung (BMVg) in Berlin. Er war Teilnehmer am 33. Generalstabslehrgang Heer an der Führungsakademie der Bundeswehr in Hamburg. Von 2005 bis 2008 war er Kommandeur der Luftlandebrigade 31 in Oldenburg. Anschließend war Generalleutnant Warnecke von 2008 bis 2011 stellvertretender Leiter des Einsatzführungsstabes im BMVg in Berlin sowie von 2011 bis 2012 Chef des Stabes 1. Deutsch/Niederländisches Korps in Münster. Danach war er von 2012 bis 2015 Abteilungsleiter Einsatz im Kommando Streitkräftebasis in Bonn. Im Jahre 2013 war er als stellvertretender Kommandeur ISAF Joint Command in Kabul/Afghanistan und von 2007 bis 2008 als Regionalkommandeur Nord in Mazar-e-Sharif/Afghanistan im Einsatz. Generalleutnant Warnecke wurde mit diversen Ehrenabzeichen ausgezeichnet, u.a. Ehrenkreuz der Bundeswehr in Gold, Einsatzmedaille der Bundeswehr in Bronze (ISAF), Einsatzmedaille der Bundeswehr in Silber (ISAF), Non-Article 5 NATO-Medal, Verdienstkreuz am Bande des Verdienstordens der Bundesrepublik Deutschland.

Michael Weatherseed has been Director of the IT & Security Business Unit of Comexposium since 2006. Comexposium is one of the world's leading event organisers and Michael's unit is responsible for a number of events: the Milipol homeland security exhibitions (Paris, Qatar, Singapore); TRUSTECH covering trust-based technologies for payment, identification and authentication; and the Finaki "think tank" meetings for senior CIO's and CISO's for the DACH region. Before Comexposium, Michael was Head of the Television Events for Reed Midem and Managing Director EAME for FORTUNE Magazine.

Bastien Wanner is a researcher and a teaching assistant at the University of Lausanne. His research has focused on human failure in information security, competitive intelligence and cyberdefence. His recent area of academic analysis concentrates on the governance of countermeasures as a response to cyber attacks targeting critical infrastructures. He has participated in a range of international workshops on defensive cyber operations. Prior to joining the University of Lausanne, he worked as an IT auditor and security consultant in the financial sector in Geneva and Zurich. He holds a B.Sc. in Business Administration and a MLaw in Legal Issues, Crime and Security of Information Technologies. At the European Cyber 9/12 Student Challenge – an international cyber policy competition – he was a member of the Swiss winning team in the 2015 edition.

Dr. Andreas Wespi is a Research Staff Member at IBM Research – Zurich working on multiple Cyber Security research projects. From 2011 to 2013 he was on assignment to the CTO Office, IBM Software Group Europe, supporting customers in Cyber Security and related areas. From 2002 to 2011 he was managing the Security and Privacy Research team at IBM Research – Zurich. He was leading projects in the areas of security analytics, intrusion detection, data security, cloud security, security policy management, and privacy. In the mid 90s he was a member of IBM's Global Security Analysis Lab (GSAL). The GSAL has made substantial contributions to

IBM's security product and service offerings. Among others it has developed the technology behind IBM Tivoli Risk Manager, the first commercial Security Information and Event Management (SIEM) product. Andreas Wespi is a steering committee member of the International Symposium on Research in Attacks, Intrusions and Defenses. He holds a Ph.D. in Computer Science from the University of Basel, Switzerland, and a M.Sc. in Computer Science from the University of Bern, Switzerland.

Stefan Wunderlich zog es nach seinem Studium in der Literurwissenschaft/Philosophie nach der Jahrtausendwende als Redakteur in die Welt der IT. Als Chefredakteur verantwortete er die Publikationen „dot.net magazin" und „XML & Web Services Magazin", bevor er von 2004 bis 2017 in der Marketing-Kommunikation für Microsoft Deutschland tätig war. Seit Herbst 2017 verstärkt er das Team der Allianz für Cyber-Sicherheit beim Bundesamt für Sicherheit in der Informationstechnik (BSI) in Bonn.

How to Eliminate the Prevailing Ignorance and Complacency Around Cybersecurity

Stefanie Frey

Abstract

The increased digitization, automation and interconnectedness of all spheres of life have resulted in many innovations and improvements, such as Internet of Things, Industry 4.0, Robo Advisor of FinTechs, Smart Home, etc., but it also brings with it great risks and challenges. In this article, I shall highlight the challenges of the twenty-first century and explain why there is what I like to call a prevailing ignorance and complacency about cybersecurity. One of the main reasons why we seem to be ignorant and complacent is that we have never experienced a major and damaging cyber incident that has disrupted essential services and led to a loss of life. In the last few years, we have been faced with disturbing and potentially devastating cyberattacks, but we have always, seemingly, managed to contain them. However, this successful containment of cyberattacks has not been achieved, thanks to our technical and organizational cyber capabilities, but rather to the fact that cyber criminals can attain their goals well below the threshold of a cyber Armageddon. This problem is compounded by a massive increase in technological and organizational complexity that is challenging for governments and industries to manage. I will attempt to give best practice examples of how we can overcome this problem and gain a better overview of this increasingly complex world of cyber friends and foes.

S. Frey (✉)
Deutor Cyber Security Solutions Switzerland GmbH, Bern, Switzerland
e-mail: stefanie.frey@deutor.ch

© Springer Fachmedien Wiesbaden GmbH, ein Teil von Springer Nature 2018
M. Bartsch, S. Frey (Hrsg.), *Cybersecurity Best Practices*,
https://doi.org/10.1007/978-3-658-21655-9_1

1.1   The Challenges of the Twenty First Century

The world is becoming increasingly digitized and interconnected, resulting in a degree of technological and organizational complexity that poses immense challenges for governments and businesses alike. This phenomenon has brought about great innovations and opportunities, but it also entails risks that are becoming increasingly difficult to manage. As Gut and Wespi state in their article in this book "new technologies often introduce new security problems...it is reported that between 75 and 80 percent of the top free apps on Android and iPhone smart phones were breached." (see also Chap. 26 by Gut and Wespi).

Cyber risks have been rated by the World Economic Forum, Global Risks Report 2017 [1], as among the top five risks alongside terrorist attacks, involuntary migration, natural disaster and extreme weather events. Given this changed cyber threat landscape, it is imperative that we are protected by a reliable and efficient cybersecurity. Without a robust and structured approach to cybersecurity, cyber criminals, terrorists, states and totalitarian regimes will continue to abuse the increased digitization to fulfil their goals.

The world has always been dominated by insecurity and wars. Peace and stability have come at a very high price, as history has taught us. Emerging technologies have added to the complexity. Just consider the industrial revolution or the advent of nuclear weapons. These two events transformed the face of the world, entailed irreversible consequences for society as a whole and necessitated an adaptation of our economic and security policies. The Internet, digitization and automation will bring about similar if not more radical changes to our lives. So we need to remain vigilant and prepare for innovations, new technologies and emerging threats. As the ancient Roman poet Vegetius pointed out as long ago as the fourth century, "If you want peace prepare for war" [2].

We have witnessed an increase in the quantity and quality of cyberattacks that have reached into all spheres of life – economical, political, military, diplomatic and private. The methods used by cyber criminals depend on their overarching goal. The main goals are usually financial, economic, political or defence-related, and the methods used range from cybercrime, cyber espionage, cyber sabotage or cyber hacktivism. In recent years these cyberattacks, whether random or targeted, have become much more professional, and their targets manifold, ranging from states and public authorities to global enterprises, SMEs, critical infrastructures and individuals. A worrying fact is that the perpetrators do not necessarily need profound technological specialized know-how, but can penetrate, intrude and invade your computer network with tools that are readily available on the Internet. Among those standardized tools are, for instance, "Crime as a Service"- or "Malware as a Service." These tools are then customized to fit their modus operandi and then used in a highly professional manner.

With the Internet and information technology now dominating all spheres of life, everybody is using and perfecting it, including criminals and governments. This fact has fundamentally changed the profile of perpetrators; we are no longer dealing solely with individual offenders, but with states and professionally organized groups that often have a clear division of labour. Not surprisingly, organized crime and the Mafia are also using information technology to conduct their business.

Example

- **Financially motivated crime** includes all criminal offences that yield a direct financial benefit for the attacker. This includes, for example, the theft of credit card numbers and identities, changing or manipulating data or information and the use of ransomware and DDoS attacks on websites for the purposes of blackmail.
- **Economic or industrially motivated crime** includes gaining a competitive advantage (industrial espionage) or a state-level economic advantage (economic espionage) by gaining illegal access to data and information (espionage) or destroying and manipulating data, information, IT architecture, infrastructures and systems (sabotage). In recent times this has been conducted by using malicious codes such as Trojans and hacking tools.
- **Politically** motivated **crimes** are a more recent trend and are on the rise. Mainly this has to do with state-sponsored crime in order to destroy or manipulate data and information (sabotage) to influence political decision-making and hence the political landscape and our prevailing secuirty policy. The most common examples are fake news, leakage/publication of illegally obtained data and manipulation of political processes through targeted digital media campaigns through social media.

1.2 Current Situation

Against this background, it seems evident that cybersecurity should be the top priority alongside state security and overall business strategy for governments and businesses alike in today's world. As pointed out in our book *Cybersicherheit für Unternehmen und Behörden: Massnahmen zur Erhöhung der Cyberresilienz* [3] and my article in this book *Was Unternehmen von Staaten lernen können: Cyber Strategieentwicklung*, governments have realized the necessity of developing a cyber strategy, but businesses are still not there yet. According to the second Global Cybersecurity Index (GCI), released by the UN telecommunications agency International Telecommunication Union (ITU), about half of all 193 ITU members have a cybersecurity strategy or are in the process of developing one [4]. Clearly, the aim is to increase this number over time, in particular for the developing countries.

Background Information
The GCI is a survey that measures the commitment of member states to cybersecurity in order to raise awareness. It advocates five pillars:

- Legal
- Technical
- Organizational
- Capacity building
- Cooperation

The GCI 2017 states:

"For each of these pillars, questions were developed to assess commitment. Through consultation with a group of experts, these questions were weighted in order to arrive at an overall GCI score. The survey was administered through an online platform through which supporting evidence was also collected.

One-hundred and thirty-four Member States responded to the survey throughout 2016. Member States who did not respond were invited to validate responses determined from open-source research. As such, the GCI results reported herein cover all 193 ITU Member States.

The 2017 publication of the GCI continues to show the commitment to cybersecurity of countries around the world. The overall picture shows improvement and strengthening of all five elements of the cybersecurity agenda in various countries in all regions. **However**, there is space **for further improvement in cooperation at all levels, capacity building and organizational measures**. As well, the gap in the level of cybersecurity engagement between different regions is still present and visible. The level of development of the different pillars varies from country to country in the regions, and while commitment in Europe remains very high in the legal and technical fields in particular, the challenging situation in the Africa and Americas regions shows the need for continued engagement and support…" [5].

In the world of business, the picture looks different, and we are faced with a large "dark" number regarding cybersecurity. Many companies are reluctant to reveal what their level of cybersecurity is, whether they have already developed or are planning to develop a cyber strategy. During the writing of our book *Cybersicherheit für Unternehmen und Behörden: Massnahmen zur Erhöhung der Cyberresilienz*, we approached several companies with a basic survey in order to shed some light on this murky issue. Sadly, we did not find a single company that was willing to give either a best-practice example or indeed any kind of information on the state of their cybersecurity.

There are not many representative studies that give an overview for the business world. One notworty study is the study by the German Association of Information Technology (Bitkom) [6], which compiled representative numbers that give us a glimpse into the state of cybersecurity in the business world. The study, which is based on interviews with 1069 companies, revealed the following:

- 53% of companies in Germany were the victim of cybercrime, cyber espionage or cyber sabotage in 2016 compared to 51% in 2015.
- The cost to the German economy was 55€ bn in 2016, compared to 51€ bn in 2015.
- 31% reported cyber incidents to governmental bodies out of fear of reputational damage [7].

These figures are indicative of the immensity of the challenges we face. Cyberattacks on small- and medium-sized companies are on the increase, and many of the victims are reluctant to notify the incident and get help out of fear of reputational damage (see article by Teresa Ritter and Marc Bachmann). We are also witnessing an increase in targeted cyber espionage attacks carried out by state actors and weak corresponding organizational, physical and staff cybersecurity measures [8]. This opaque, yet very challenging state of cyber (in)security in the business world needs to be addressed; cybersecurity is a global issue that transcends national borders. Governments and businesses of all sizes need to make sure that they increase their cybersecurity and become more resilient; otherwise, they will constitute the weakest link in the global cybersecurity architecture.

As Bitkom president Achim Berg stated in 2017:

"we need to develop a concept of 'need to share,' if we want to make the German economy more resilient against cyber espionage. Only if companies notify cyber attacks against their company or organization, can the security authorities carry out a realistic situational analysis and develop corresponding security and defense measures and mechanisms".

▶ It is good news that governments are beefing up their security and serve as a best-practice example for companies, but what is really needed is a commitment to overall and sustainable cybersecurity and to the respective cyber strategies that either have already been developed or are being developed. Cyber strategies are not worth the paper they are written on unless they are accompanied by an implementation/action plan with actionable and measurable milestones and a timeline and, most importantly, a commitment to engage budget, resources and relevant technologies (see article by Stefanie Frey, Was UNternehmen von Staaten lernen können).

The above analysis shows that there would appear to be a common understanding of and consensus on the overall magnitude and severity of the threat that cyberattacks pose to economies, societies and individuals alike. However, if there is so much awareness with regard to cyber threats, risks and vulnerabilities, how come we are faced with such a dismal situation, with states dragging their feet to develop and implement national cyber strategies and assist developing countries in learning from their best practices, and companies reluctant to engage, share and notify, leaving us in the process in the dark? Personally, I would call this a state of prevailing ignorance and complacency, stemming from:

- The absence of a cyber 9/11 and our boundless confidence in our cyber capabilities
- The increased complexity of IT systems

1.2.1 We Have Not Had a Cyber 9/11

I believe strongly that one of the main reasons for this prevailing ignorance and complacency is that there has not (yet) been a massive and global cyberattack resulting in the disruption of essential services, loss of life or unsustainable financial impacts. Some people like to call it the absence of a cyber Titanic, cyber Armageddon or cyber 9/11. However, do we really need a cyber 9/11 for us to finally wake up and beef up our security? The answer is simple, we do not need a cyber 9/11 – the cyber threats and attacks of today, as emphasised above, are detrimental enough and have both immediate and long-lasting implications.

Cyberattacks are happening on a daily basis and causing devastating economic and political damage. They are either conducted widespread, which means that the attacker does not have a particular target in mind, i.e. they are called mass phenomena, or the attack is targeted with a clear focus on one particular target with a very specific goal. The technical methods used are more or less the same in both approaches, but what distinguishes them is the motivation of the attacker.

For example, criminals who are financially motivated mostly use the mass phenomena approach. They use malware, such as crypto Trojans (Locky, TeslaCrypt, CTB-Locker, GPCode) or banking Trojans (Zeus) among others, to unleash multiple spam waves. Targeted attacks to make a financial gain are also on the rise, as evidenced by the cyberattacks on Walt Disney, Netflix and Sony. Politically and religiously motivated attacks mostly use a combination of the two approaches, depending on the attacker's goal. Examples are the manipulation of digital information sources, such as websites and social media to spread fake news and launch protests for religious or political reasons. Recent examples are the manipulation and meddling in the US and French elections.

Increased state involvement in cyber espionage is another worrying development and is on the rise. A good example is the cyberattack on Lockheed Martin 2011. Let us consider the worldwide cyberattack WannaCry as an illustration of the complexity of targeted versus widespread attacks and state involvement versus criminal organizations (individuals and groups).

Example WannaCry

WannaCry was launched in May 2017 and had a tremendous worldwide impact. This widespread attack targeted everything from critical infrastructures to global enterprises, SMEs and individuals. It is estimated that some 100,000 computers across more than 100 countries were affected, with total damage costing billions of dollars. According to Kaspersky Lab, the most affected countries were Russia, Ukraine, Taiwan and India [9]. The ransom demand to decrypt the data was USD 300–600.

The initial analysis suggested that this was a widespread attack with the goal of making a financial gain, as in the Locky case. However, preliminary attribution efforts lead to North Korea, and this was confirmed in late 2017 by Kaspersky Lab. This demonstrates the complexity of the problem, as an apparently financially motivated attack is suddenly attributed to a state actor.

Therefore, we have to ask the crucial question namely what was the motivation of the cyberattack? Why would a state launch a worldwide attack to make a financial gain? It seems unlikely that a state would embark on such an elaborate cyberattack only for financial reasons. However, it seemingly happened. Therefore, we must consider perhaps alternative motives or a combination the attack was launched under the pretext of a financially motivated criminal act to reach a much higher more dangerous goal. This is extremely worrying. Elaborating on the reasons would go beyond the scope of this article, but suffice it to say at this point that we should all think more about the background and motive of an attack. Appearances can be deceptive.

The attack was stopped within a few days of its being discovered, thanks to a kill switch (Markus Hutchins, Malware Tech. Block) and patches released by Microsoft. However, does this mean that the danger is over and the problem has been contained? Can we afford to be complacent and believe that the situation was contained thanks to our excellent security efforts and cyber capabilities? The answer seems clear; we cannot afford to be complacent, but must keep in mind that there will be another WannaCry and probably a more sophisticated one with even greater implications.

The other reason is the increased complexity of IT systems.

1.2.2 Complexity

▶ **Tip**
Cybersecurity is *not only* IT security: It includes organizational, personal and physical security measures.
   In cybersecurity we are dealing with an innovative and highly motivated third party with malicious intent.
   In IT security we are dealing with regulations, compliance and technical security architectures.

▶ It must be noted that the lines between cybersecurity and IT security are not clear-cut and are becoming increasingly more blurred.

Increased interconnectivity of business models and processes has heightened the complexity and dependency to the extent that they are no longer comprehensible, thereby creating hitherto unknown technical problems with ripple effects that even security experts find hard to predict, analyse and solve.

Whilst new technological innovations, such as cloud computing and mobility, have increased efficiency and created new business opportunities on a company-wide level, they have also led to increased security risks. One of the biggest problems of today's interconnectivity and data processing is the fact that the concepts, architectures and protocols date back to the 1970s when closed networks and stand-alone computer systems and functional requirements were in the forefront. Today these structures and protocols still form the basis of the Internet, and the majority of IT systems rely on them. This has created a security problem, as these underlying technologies have not been developed to deal with the increased digitization and interconnectivity of the twenty-first century. They were devised solely to meet functional demands and are not sufficient in this digitized world.

Moreover, these closed networks and stand-alone computer systems have now been replaced by a web of interconnected systems. There are countless devices and systems, as well as technology vendors, and consequently the task of gaining an overview of the existing systems, their interconnectivity and vulnerabilities has become highly complex. Indeed, the problem of defining and devising security measures and solutions has now become almost insurmountably complex, as nobody seems to know what the IT landscape is today.

This problem is compounded by a few additional crucial factors:

- **Loss of sovereignty in the development of IT products leads to unwanted dependencies**: The global market for IT products has developed rapidly in recent years, and countries with large domestic markets were able to develop new national technologies faster and more effectively, making them cheaper to sell on the world market. This has led to the birth of global market leaders such as Amazon, Cisco, Microsoft, Google and Apple, which are dominating the market and destroying the competitive edge of European IT product manufacturers. China and South Korea have also entered the race and are competing with the USA in the global market with their own IT giants, such as Huawei, ZTE and Samsung. This leads to a geopolitical technology dependency between state-regulated technology providers and international customer structures. Consequently, countries and companies alike are no longer able to independently assess what security vulnerabilities exist in these products. These security vulnerabilities are commonly referred to as "backdoors" because they give unauthorized access to data and functionality of the product to everyone that knows the backdoor exists and can therefore be exploited.

- **Innovation and accelerated product cycles are often incompatible with security**: Information technology systems are being developed under tremendous cost pressure; global standards are forcing vendors to accelerate product cycles; and user demand for innovation and short integration cycles leaves little time for the sustainable development of inherent security approaches.
- **Source lines of code have bugs:** The software installed in large companies requires several billions of source lines of code, and we can safely assume that in each 1000 source lines of code there is a bug which can be used by skilled hackers for a cyberattack. Certified and safer alternatives are usually too expensive for most business and are therefore not implemented.

Source Lines of Code (SLOC) [10]	
Microsoft Office 2001:	25 m SLOC
Windows 2000:	30 m SLOC
Microsoft Office 2013:	45 m SLOC
Facebook (incl. backend code):	60 m SLOC
Mac OS X Tiger:	85 m SLOC
Car Software (modern high end car):	100 m SLOC
Google (all Internet services):	2 bn SLOC

1.3   Conclusion

In a nutshell, the prevailing ignorance and complacency stem from the fact that most people do not understand the complexity of the interconnected IT systems and have lost the overview of "who is who and what is what and who is what to whom in the zoo." There is a general acceptance of the current situation. In short, this prevailing ignorance needs to be addressed. There is also a prevailing complacency in the sense that people have boundless confidence in their own cyber capabilities to solve cyberattacks on a technical and organizational level. This complacency entails a lack of transparency of the overall IT systems, processes and vulnerabilities. It is also responsible for insufficient investment in relevant technologies and other much-needed security-related resources.

One step in the right direction would be to shed some light on this opaque landscape, by knowing your entire IT architecture, cyber vulnerabilities, cyber threat landscape and cyber risks. I would like to suggest a few steps that could be taken to ameliorate the situation:

- Get to know your systems (networks, hard and software) and their interdependencies.
- Conduct regular simulation exercises to evaluate your technical and organizational processes and structures. Single out the cyber risks and cyber vulnerabilities and address them.
- Develop and implement a cyber strategy and adapt it continuously to the changed threat landscape. Regular simulation exercises will help identify new cyber risks and cyber vulnerabilities.
- Adapt your entire business portfolio (product and services) to fit the current cyber threat landscape.
- Adapt your IT operation to fit the new cyber threat landscape.
- Implement an empowered CISO organization.

Cyberattacks are detrimental to our economical, political, diplomatic and private life, are putting a great strain on international relations and are threatening the stability of a hitherto stable world order. We all need to face the problem, without fear of reputational damage; accept the limitations of our cyber capabilities; be open to new ideas, approaches and alliances; and invest in a robust cybersecurity strategy and policy and relevant technologies.

Let us all start now; the Internet is here to stay!

References

1. http://www3.weforum.org/docs/GRR17_Report_web.pdf
2. Vegetius, „de re militari", book 3, 4th or 5th century.
3. Frey, S. und Bartsch, M. (2017) *Cybersicherheit für Unternehmen und Behörden: Massnahmen zur Erhöhung der Cyberresilienz*, Springer Verlag.
4. https://www.itu.int/en/ITU-D/Cybersecurity/Pages/National-Strategies.aspx.
5. Global Cybersecurity Index (GCI) 2017, ITU 2017: https://www.itu.int/dms_pub/itu-d/opb/str/D-STR-GCI.01-2017-PDF-E.pdf.
6. Bitkom steht für Bundesverband der IT-Industrie.
7. Wirtschaftsschutz in der digitalen Welt, Bitkom Präsident Achim Berg and Präsident des Bundesamtes für Verfassungsschutz Dr. Hans-Georg Maaßen, Berlin, 21. Juli 2017: https://www.bitkom.org/Presse/Anhaenge-an-PIs/2017/07-Juli/Bitkom-Charts-Wirtschaftsschutz-in-der-digitalen-Welt-21-07-2017.pdf.
8. Spionage, Sabotage, Datendiebstahl: Deutscher Wirtschaft entsteht jährlich ein Schaden von 55 Milliarden Euro, Presseinformation Bikom 21.07.2017: https://www.bitkom.org/Presse/Pres-

seinformation/Spionage-Sabotage-Datendiebstahl-Deutscher-Wirtschaft-entsteht-jaehrlich-ein-Schaden-von-55-Milliarden-Euro.html.
9. Kaspersky Lab 16.05.2017: https://www.kaspersky.com/blog/wannacry-ransomware/16518/
10. http://www.informationisbeautiful.net/visualizations/million-lines-of-code/

Teil I

Beispiele aus der Praxis

Angriff aus der Dunkelheit: Cyberattacke auf das Lukaskrankenhaus Neuss

2

Ulla Dahmen und Nicolas Krämer

Zusammenfassung

Am Aschermittwoch ist alles vorbei: Diese im Rheinland wohlbekannte Prämisse bewahrheitete sich für das Lukaskrankenhaus in Neuss bei Düsseldorf am Aschermittwoch des Jahres 2016. Ein Hackerangriff traf die IT-Infrastruktur der hochdigitalisierten Klinik. Mit der radikalen Entscheidung, sämtliche IT-Systeme sofort herunterzufahren, konnte ein Ausbreiten der hochaggressiven Schadsoftware und eine Verschlüsselung der Patientendaten verhindert werden. Die Klinik nutzte die Krise als Chance und stellte die gesamte IT-Infrastruktur neu auf. Im Gegensatz zu anderen betroffenen Institutionen verfolgte das Lukaskrankenhaus nach dem Leitgedanken „Transparenz schafft Vertrauen" konsequent einen offenen Umgang mit dem Hackerangriff und seinen Folgen auch den Medien gegenüber. Auf die Digitalisierung setzt man in dem Neusser Krankenhaus weiterhin.

Am Aschermittwoch ist alles vorbei

Das Rheinland kennt die fünfte Jahreszeit. Zu ihrem Ende hin wird es ausgelassen, zumeist fröhlich, und Schlafmangel ist in den letzten Tagen ein wiederkehrendes Phänomen. In Neuss geht das so: Kappessonntag mit dem großen Zug, Rosenmontag, man fährt nach Düsseldorf oder Köln, Veilchendienstag, gefeiert wird noch mal daheim. Dann Aschermittwoch, der Tag, an dem „alles vorbei" ist.

Lukaskrankenhaus in Neuss, Aschermittwoch 2016. Am Morgen merken zuerst die Radiologen, dass etwas nicht stimmt, dann sind es die Ärzte und Pflegekräfte in der

U. Dahmen (✉) · N. Krämer
Städtischen Kliniken Neuss – Lukaskrankenhaus GmbH, Neuss, Deutschland
E-Mail: udahmen@lukasneuss.de; nkraemer@lukasneuss.de

Abb. 2.1 Die Arbeit im Krisenstab

Zentralen Notaufnahme. Was ist los mit der IT? Dies ist mehr als eine ärgerliche, aber doch harmlose Störung eines Systems, merkt die IT-Abteilung schnell. Schnell: Das ist jetzt das Gebot der Stunde – schnell zu handeln, aber kontrolliert. Die Geschäftsführung ruft den Krisenfall aus (siehe Abb. 2.1). Im Krisenstab sitzen vom Chef der Notaufnahme über die Leiter der IT, des Labors, die Pflegedirektorin bis zur Justiziarin und den beiden Pressesprechern diejenigen zusammen, die betroffen sind, Verantwortung tragen und Entscheidungen fällen müssen. Und das schnell. Zeit, die Lage ausgiebig zu analysieren, zu diskutieren und diverse Szenarien für alle möglichen Gegenmaßnahmen auszuarbeiten, ist nicht.

Erpressung 2.0
Denn es wird klar: Dies ist ein Hackerangriff, da versucht jemand, Daten zu verschlüsseln [1]. Auf einigen Rechnern ist in geschliffenem Englisch eine Botschaft zu lesen: Derjenige, der da entgeistert auf den Bildschirm schaut, soll über eine E-Mail-Adresse Kontakt zum großen Unbekannten aufnehmen. Keine Zahlungsaufforderung, keine Drohung, was passieren wird, nur: Kontaktaufnahme.

Der Krisenstab trifft die ersten Entscheidungen, es sind exakt die richtigen. Keine Kontaktaufnahme! Und: Alle IT-Systeme werden sofort heruntergefahren. Nur so, ahnen die Beteiligten, sind die sensiblen Patientendaten zu schützen und kann ein Ausbreiten der Schadsoftware verhindert werden. Diese Entscheidung ist radikal. Den Stecker zu ziehen ist mutig und zunächst einmal einfach. Das Wiederhochfahren der Systeme und der zahlreichen Subsysteme, die Vernetzung und Verknüpfung, die Wiederherstellung der vollen Funktionalität wird Monate dauern. Das weiß an diesem Vormittag noch niemand. Schließlich beschließt die Geschäftsführung, die Polizei hinzuzuziehen, Anzeige zu erstatten. Bange Frage: Werden die Cyber-Cops des LKA Düsseldorf den Versorgungsauftrag des

Krankenhauses behindern, mit ihren Ermittlungen den Weiterbetrieb unter Krisenbedin-
gungen noch weiter erschweren? Sie werden es nicht, das zeigt sich schnell, im Gegenteil:
Kenntnisreich und engagiert helfen die Experten des Cyber Security Center des LKA, die
völlig neuartige Ransomware nach drei Tagen aufzuspüren.

Und noch ein weiterer Beschluss fällt an Tag 1 der Krise. Das Krankenhaus wird die
Cyberattacke öffentlich machen. Transparenz schafft Vertrauen, wird es aus der Geschäftsführung später heißen, und rasch wird das Lukaskrankenhaus für eben diese Transparenz
landesweit viel Anerkennung in den Medien und von Experten erfahren. Die Resonanz auf
die erste Pressemitteilung ist gewaltig. Mehr als 250 Berichte in Printmedien allein in den
ersten 14 Tagen, zahllose Beiträge in Radio und Fernsehen, Interesse vom Boulevard bis
zur Fachpresse, von der BBC bis zu den Tagesthemen.

Zurück in die Zukunft: Automatisierte Klinik im Handbetrieb
Zu berichten ist Ungewöhnliches. Das Neusser Krankenhaus gilt als ein Vorreiter der Digitalisierung: Gerade einmal vier Wochen vor dem Angriff informieren sich Bundesgesundheitsminister Hermann Gröhe und der stellvertretende Vorstandsvorsitzende der Deutschen Telekom, Reinhard Clemens, über das Projekt Visite 2.0 [2]. Mit iPads ausgestattete
Ärzte und Pflegekräfte nutzen die digitale Krankenakte mit zahllosen Vorteilen. Jetzt aber
ist der Klinikbetrieb auf Handbetrieb umgestellt (siehe Abb. 2.2). Ohne Vorankündigung,
an einem Mittwochmorgen. Patientenaufnahme mit Papier und Bleistift, Bettenbelegung
auf überdimensionalen Bögen an der Wand. Die Laborbefunde können nicht mehr elektronisch übermittelt werden, das bedeutet Verzögerungen, und ebenso wenig die Daten der
Radiologie. Die Strahlentherapie muss eine Zwangspause einlegen, die Sekretariate haben
keinen Zugriff auf Terminkalender und Kontakte. Und so weiter.

Abb. 2.2 Die Rechner blieben aus: Das Lukaskrankenhaus im Handbetrieb

Die Patienten merken von der Krise kaum etwas. Nur für drei Tage hat sich die Notaufnahme bei der Kreisleitstelle abgemeldet, dann fahren die Rettungswagen bis auf Transporte mit Polytraumata wieder das Lukaskrankenhaus an, und kurz darauf können auch diese wieder behandelt werden. Große elektive Operationen werden verschoben – die Patienten zeigen Verständnis: Fast alle OPs können nachgeholt werden. Doch an einem Punkt wird der IT-Ausfall für alle Patienten unübersehbar: Statt aus fünf Gerichten auszuwählen, was dann per iPad übermittelt wird, bleibt nur die Wahl zwischen zwei Angeboten. Ein Thema, das dann doch nachrangig erscheint [3].

Denn der Krisenstab, der in der ersten Phase mehrmals täglich zusammenkommt, ist mit immer neuen Problemen konfrontiert. Wie ist die Kommunikation im Haus sicherzustellen, ohne E-Mail? Über einen alten Nadeldrucker werden Informationen für die Mitarbeiter erstellt und auf Rundgängen in den Häusern und auf den Stationen verteilt. Wie schnell finden sich externe Berater und zusätzliche Hilfskräfte, die beim Aufspüren der Schadsoftware, der Erstellung der Antivirensoftware und der Reinigung der mehr als 800 Endgeräte helfen? Drei Tage dauert es, bis die Ransomware identifiziert ist. Die bange Frage, ob Patientendaten geschädigt wurden, ob sie abgeflossen sind oder zumindest einige doch verschlüsselt wurden, kann mit „nein" beantwortet werden.

Wiederaufbau der Systeme

„Sicherheit vor Funktionalität" ist die Maxime jetzt, beim Wiederhochfahren der ersten Systeme. Das klingt schlüssig, ist ohne Alternative und stößt doch auf Widerstand. „Offline" heißt es noch für Wochen, als dann die E-Mails wieder verfügbar sind, bleiben Anhänge zunächst noch tabu. „Sicherheit vor Funktionalität": Doch die Zeit drängt.

Nur kurz kann zum Beispiel die Behandlung von Tumorpatienten in der Strahlentherapie unterbrochen werden. Die Medikamentenbestellung stockt, niemand liefert auf eine Fax-Anfrage hin. Und nicht zuletzt bedeutet „offline" auch: keine Abrechnung mit den Krankenkassen. Es gilt, Prioritäten zu setzen. Der Krisenstab entscheidet sich in enger Abstimmung mit den medizinischen Leistungsbereichen für die Reihenfolge Labor, SAP, Strahlentherapie und weitere Bereiche.

Es macht einen gewaltigen Unterschied aus, ob ein Stationsarzt in der digitalen Welt eine Stunde auf einen angeforderten Laborbefund wartet oder einen ganzen Tag im Handbetrieb. Das SAP-System folgt an zweiter Stelle nicht etwa, weil der kaufmännische Geschäftsführer Buchhalter und Controller schnell wieder arbeitsfähig sehen will. Nein, nach fünf Krisentagen drohen die Medikamentenbestände auszugehen. Die Bestellung von Arzneien ist heutzutage ein ausschließlich webbasierter Prozess. Dritte Priorität: die große Strahlentherapie des Lukaskrankenhauses mit modernster Linearbeschleunigertechnik. Krebspatienten dürfen ihre Bestrahlung für maximal eine Woche unterbrechen, sonst drohen signifikante Beeinträchtigungen der Behandlungsqualität. Für etwa 100 Patienten hätte das eine Einweisung in andere Einrichtungen bedeutet. Die Wiederinbetriebnahme entwickelt sich zu einem Wettlauf gegen die Zeit, der per Zielfotoentscheid gewonnen wird.

Der schwierige Übergang funktioniert. Der Klinikbetrieb im Handbetrieb schweißt nicht zuletzt die so titulierte „Lukasfamilie" zusammen. Die Berichte in den Medien sind fair, die

Patienten verlieren das Vertrauen nicht. Später wird man mit Erstaunen registrieren, dass das Patientenaufkommen in den Krisenwochen sogar über dem des Vorjahres liegt.

Die Frage des Lösegelds

In einer großen gemeinsamen Pressekonferenz berichten die Staatsanwaltschaft Köln, Zentralstelle für Cyberkriminalität, die Cybercrime-Spezialisten des LKA sowie das BSI am 8. März 2016 über den „Fall Lukaskrankenhaus". Zentrale Aussage: Dieser Cyberangriff war keine gezielte Attacke auf eine Kritische Infrastruktur. Ein Fall aber ist sehr gut mit dem des Neusser Lukaskrankenhauses vergleichbar. Das Presbyterian Medical Center in Hollywood wird zeitgleich Opfer einer heftigen Cyberattacke. Anders als in Neuss entscheiden sich die amerikanischen Klinikverantwortlichen auf Anraten des FBI, das geforderte Lösegeld zu zahlen – unterschiedlichen Medienberichten zufolge drei Millionen oder 15.000 US-Dollar, umgerechnet in Bitcoins [4]. Seit Mai folgt das FBI übrigens den deutschen Amtskollegen und rät nunmehr von Zahlungen ab.

In Neuss kommt eine Lösegeldzahlung für die Verantwortlichen zu keinem Zeitpunkt infrage – aus mehreren guten Gründen. Was wäre nach einer Kontaktaufnahme mit dem Täter geschehen? Eine von ihm zur Verfügung gestellte Software hätte nach dem Einspielen vielleicht einen noch viel größeren Schaden verursacht. Außerdem war nach der großen medialen Aufmerksamkeit die Gefahr, Trittbrettfahrer auf den Plan zu rufen, sehr wahrscheinlich. Und schließlich ging es darum, keinerlei Zahlungsbereitschaft unter Beweis zu stellen. Denn Hackerkreise lieben Franchise. Die Ransomware wird weitergegeben, ganz nach dem Motto: Das Lukaskrankenhaus hat gezahlt, versuch Du Dein Glück in sechs Wochen. Nein, aus dem Neusser Krankenhaus fließt kein Geld. Übrigens: Im Darknet lässt sich mit vertraulichen Gesundheitsdaten mehr Geld verdienen als mit geheimen Kontoinformationen von Bankkunden. Weltweit wird mit Cyberkriminalität mehr Geld umgesetzt als im internationalen Rauschgifthandel.

Mit Datenschutz zum Datenschatz

Am 5. Dezember 2015 titelt das Nachrichtenmagazin „Der Spiegel": „Total vermessen – wir werden gläserne Patienten und hoffen auf ewige Gesundheit" [5]. In dieser Ausgabe geht es um die elektronische Patientenakte, die hierzulande nach wie vor kontrovers diskutiert wird. Die Einstellung in anderen Ländern ist weniger kritisch, so zum Beispiel im angelsächsischen Bereich oder in den Niederlanden, wo sämtliche Gesundheitsdaten eines Menschen „von der Wiege bis zur Bahre" auf einer elektronischen Karte gespeichert werden. In Deutschland aber herrscht nach wie vor eine abwartende Haltung vor. Immer wieder wird der Datenschutz – eine Keule, mit der jede gute Idee vernichtet werden kann – als Hauptargument angeführt. Und das, obwohl die Vorteile aus ärztlicher Sicht überwiegen: Deutlich leichter wird dem Mediziner die Diagnose, wenn er einen Blick auf die gesamte Krankengeschichte eines Patienten werfen kann und nicht nur mit akuten Symptomen konfrontiert wird.

Fraglich ist, ob die Daten in der analogen Welt besser geschützt sind als in der digitalen. In Deutschland besteht eine gesetzliche Aufbewahrungsfrist für Patientenakten von 30

Jahren. Einer der beiden Autoren des vorliegenden Artikels hat fünf Jahre im Health-Care-Bereich einer große Wirtschaftsprüfungs- und -beratungsgesellschaft gearbeitet und in dieser Zeit zahlreiche Krankenhäuser als Mandant betreut. Er weiß, wie das typische Patientenaktenarchiv in einem Krankenhaus aussieht: Das ist der feuchte Keller, das ist der Dachboden, das ist das Logistikzentrum in der Peripherie – ohne Wärter, ohne Kameraüberwachung, ohne einbruchsichere Schließsysteme. Wer kriminelle Energie hat, könnte dort ohne große Mühe eindringen, die Akten mit seinem Smartphone abfotografieren und sich im Darknet eine goldene Nase verdienen. Das interessiert hier niemanden. Wenn es aber um Big Data geht, bricht in Deutschland regelmäßig Paranoia aus.

Paradigmenwechsel durch die Digitalisierung
Allen Verunsicherungen zum Trotz: Die Digitalisierung macht auch vor dem Gesundheitswesen nicht halt. Schenkt man Zukunftsforschern Glauben, steht im Gesundheitswesen durch die Digitalisierung ein echter Paradigmenwechsel bevor. Mit 3-D-Druckern werden künstliche Kniegelenke und menschliche Organe reproduziert. 20 Prozent aller ärztlichen Diagnosen sind falsch [6]. Mithilfe des Supercomputers IBM Watson (siehe Abb. 2.3) kann diese Lücke geschlossen werden. Er enthält das Lehrbuchwissen aller medizinischen Fachbücher dieser Welt und sein Wissen verdoppelt sich alle paar Wochen. So kann der Rechner Ärzte bei der Diagnosestellung unterstützen. Bereits in wenigen Jahren wird es möglich sein, für unter 100 Euro einen DNA-Test durchzuführen, der aufzeigt, wie hoch die Wahrscheinlichkeit ist, in einem gewissen Lebensalter an einer bestimmten Krankheit zu erkranken. Und nicht nur das. Es wird möglich sein, den Bakterienmix zu benennen, den der Betroffene in sein Essen mischt, damit diese Krankheit nicht ausbricht. Täglich wird ihm sein Smartphone das Delta zwischen Istzustand und gefordertem Bakterienmix aufzeigen, so dass eine signifikante Steigerung von Lebensqualität und Lebensdauer ermöglicht werden [6].

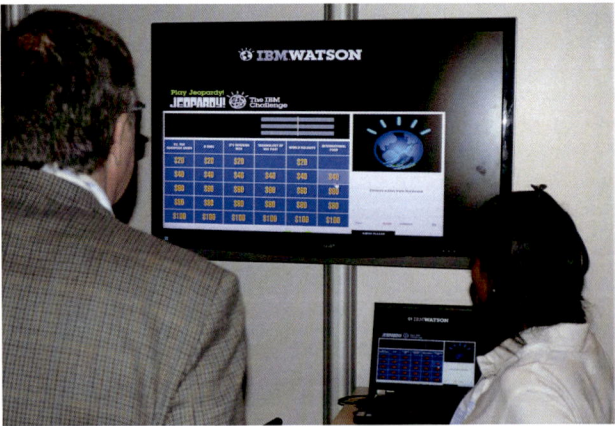

Abb. 2.3 Künstliche Intelligenz unterstützt bei der ärztlichen Diagnose (IBM Watson)

Unabhängig davon, dass hier keine medizinethische Debatte über ein mögliches Recht auf Nichtwissen geführt werden soll, eröffnen sich durch den Einsatz von Informationstechnologie Möglichkeiten, die noch vor wenigen Jahren als Science Fiction gegolten hätten. Es wäre fatal, würden diese fantastischen Zukunftstrends durch fehlende IT-Sicherheit in die falschen Bahnen gelenkt.

Krise und Chance

Zwei Jahre nach dem Angriff sind Spätfolgen der Cyberattacke im Lukaskrankenhaus immer noch zu spüren. Die Mitarbeiter haben neue Wörter gelernt, Sandboxing-Verfahren zum Beispiel: Alle Mailanhänge landen in einem virtuellen Sandkasten, verdächtige Dateien werden zunächst von der IT überprüft. Oder Awareness. Eine Kampagne über Monate informiert zu Security-Themen von Passwort-Sicherheit bis Gefahren von USB-Sticks und dubiosen Anhängen. Die IT-Infrastruktur ist eine andere geworden, die Netzwerk-Segmentierung ist stärker ausgeprägt als vor dem Crash.

Die Cyberkrise hat dem Image des Hauses nicht geschadet. Das Lukaskrankenhaus hat vom ersten Tag an auf Transparenz gesetzt und fühlt sich auf diesem Weg bestätigt. Mitarbeiter und Patienten wurden ebenso informiert wie Behörden und nicht zuletzt die Öffentlichkeit. Transparenz schafft Vertrauen: Das hat sich in der Cyberkrise Tag für Tag erwiesen. Und ein wenig Stolz kommt auch auf, wenn Andrea Vosshoff, Bundesbeauftragte für den Datenschutz und die Informationsfreiheit, im Frühjahr 2017 im Deutschen Bundestag von der „Best Practice Lukaskrankenhaus" spricht (siehe Abb. 2.4).

Abb. 2.4 Best Practice Lukaskrankenhaus. (Quelle: Katrin Neuhauser I Zukunftsforum öffentliche Sicherheit (Deutscher Bundestag))

Abb. 2.5 Präsident Arne Schönbohm und co. Von links nach rechts: BSI-Präsident Arne Schön-bohm, WP StB Prof. Dr. Volker Penter, KPMG, Bundesgesundheitsminister Hermann Gröhe und Dr. Nicolas Krämer im Lukaskrankenhaus Neuss

Das chinesische Schriftzeichen für Krise und Chance ist ein und dasselbe. Im Lukas-krankenhaus hat man viel aus der Krise gelernt, die Umsetzungsphase ist noch nicht abge-schlossen. Übrigens hat Bundesgesundheitsminister Hermann Gröhe das Lukaskranken-haus auf seiner Deutschland-Tour im Sommer 2017 wieder besucht, begleitet vom Präsidenten des BSI (Bundesinstitut für Sicherheit in der Informationstechnik), Arne Schönbohm (siehe Abb. 2.5). Das Thema: Digitalisierung. Darauf setzt die gebeutelte Kli-nik auch weiterhin, offensiv, mit allen gebotenen Vorsichtsmaßnahmen.

▶   Die Täter des Aschermittwochs 2016 sind nicht gefasst. Noch nicht.

Literatur

1. Vgl. DAHMEN, U.: IT-Krise im Lukaskrankenhaus Neuss, in: KU Gesundheitsmanagement, 85. Jg. (2016), Ausgabe April 2016, S. 73–73.
2. Vgl. KRÄMER, N.; PURWIN, U.: Stationsvisite 2.0, in: KU Gesundheitsmanagement, 83. Jg. (2014), Ausgabe November 2014, S. 64–66 und KRÄMER, N.; DAHMEN, U.: Digitale Visite als Voraussetzung für Medizin 4.0: E-Health-Projekt in Neuss bietet entscheidende Vorteile für Pati-enten und Klinik, in: Stoffers, C. (Hrsg.): Krankenhausmarketing 4.0, Kulmbach 2016, S. 67–72.

3. Vgl. DAHMEN, U.; KRÄMER, N.: Angriff aus der Dunkelheit: Erfolgreiches Krisenmanagement nach der Cyberattacke im Lukaskrankenhaus Neuss, in: Verband der Krankenhausdirektoren Deutschlands e.V. (Hrsg.): Praxisberichte zu aktuellen Fragen des Krankenhausmanagements 2016: Projekte, Positionen, Perspektiven, Berlin 2016, S. 51–54 und DAHMEN, U.; KRÄMER, N.: IT-Sicherheit: Angriff aus der Dunkelheit, in: Verband der Krankenhausdirektoren Deutschlands e.V. (Hrsg.): Geschäftsbericht 2016, Berlin 2017, S. 50–53.
4. Vgl. http://www.tagblatt.de/Nachrichten/Klinik-in-Hollywood-zahlt-Hackern-Loesegeld-277691.html, Abruf vom 3. August 2017.
5. Vgl. http://www.spiegel.de/spiegel/print/d-140273569.html, Abruf vom 3. August 2017.
6. http://onlinelibrary.wiley.com/doi/10.1111/jep.12747/full, http://m.spiegel.de/gesundheit/diagnose/fehldiagnosen-zweitmeinung-beim-arzt-kann-wichtig-sein-a-1142733.html
7. Vgl. O.V.: IT-Sicherheit: „Digital ist sicherer als analog", f&w führen und wirtschaften im Krankenhaus, 4. Jg. (2017), Ausgabe Oktober 2017, S. 926–927, hier: S. 926.

Literaturverzeichnis

DAHMEN, U.: IT-Krise im Lukaskrankenhaus Neuss, in: KU Gesundheitsmanagement, 85. Jg. (2016), Ausgabe April 2016, S. 73–73.

DAHMEN, U.; KRÄMER, N.: Angriff aus der Dunkelheit: Erfolgreiches Krisenmanagement nach der Cyberattacke im Lukaskrankenhaus Neuss, in: Verband der Krankenhausdirektoren Deutschlands e.V. (Hrsg.): Praxisberichte zu aktuellen Fragen des Krankenhausmanagements 2016: Projekte, Positionen, Perspektiven, Berlin 2016, S. 51–54

DAHMEN, U.; KRÄMER, N.: IT-Sicherheit: Angriff aus der Dunkelheit, in: Verband der Krankenhausdirektoren Deutschlands e.V. (Hrsg.): Geschäftsbericht 2016, Berlin 2017, S. 50–53

KRÄMER, N.; DAHMEN, U.: Digitale Visite als Voraussetzung für Medizin 4.0: E-Health-Projekt in Neuss bietet entscheidende Vorteile für Patienten und Klinik, in: Stoffers, C. (Hrsg.): Krankenhausmarketing 4.0, Kulmbach 2016, S. 67–72

KRÄMER, N.; PURWIN, U.: Stationsvisite 2.0, in: KU Gesundheitsmanagement, 83. Jg. (2014), Ausgabe November 2014, S. 64–66 und

O.V.: IT-Sicherheit: „Digital ist sicherer als analog", f&w führen und wirtschaften im Krankenhaus, 34. Jg. (2017), Ausgabe Oktober 2017, S. 926–927, hier: S. 926.

http://www.spiegel.de/spiegel/print/d-140273569.html, Abruf vom 3. August 2017

http://www.tagblatt.de/Nachrichten/Klinik-in-Hollywood-zahlt-Hackern-Loesegeld-277691.html, Abruf vom 3. August 2017.

Audrey and Reto Gfeller People Like You and Me

3

Audrey and Reto Gfeller

Abstract
PHISHING Attacks and identity theft have become part of everyday life. This chapter tells the story of Audrey and Reto Gfeller, people like you and me who were the victims of a PHISHING attack in 2008. In July 2008, 206 cars and 35 other items worth almost CHF 2 million were acquired on their behalf on the Ricardo Online Platform. The Gfellers take us on their journey of disappointed and angry sellers, attacks on their house, lawyers, and ricardo.ch, who was unwilling to take responsibility and was very unhelpful in resolving and analyzing the case.

3.1 The Storyline

The Gfeller family, people like you and me registered with the Ricardo Online Platform in July 2008 and created their account. During the month of July 2008, they successfully sold some items. As every year, the Gfeller family is taking their annual summer vacation. The five month pregnant Ms Gfeller, her husband, and their 1 year old child decided to go to Croatia on 29 July 2008.

Shortly after their arrival on 31 July 2008, the telephone rings and Ms. Gfeller, who is of Canadian-French origin, takes a call from a Swiss-German caller, who first of all congratulates her on the successful purchase of a car and secondly wants to discuss how to

A. a. R. Gfeller (✉)
Bournens, Switzerland
e-mail: azuttel@yahoo.com

M. Bartsch, S. Frey (Hrsg.), *Cybersecurity Best Practices*,
https://doi.org/10.1007/978-3-658-21655-9_3

proceed in the matter. Mrs. Gfeller, who is not fluent in German, let alone Swiss-German, is not sure if she understood everything correctly and immediately logs into her Ricardo account. To her great horror, she learns that hundreds of cars and other items have been bought on her behalf.

From the list of Emails on the Ricardo Online Plattform, she could see that the first chapter had been purchased on 30 July 2008 at 23h57 and the last purchase was done on 31 July 2008 at 02h41. During this time 243 chapters had been purchased, of which 206 where cars including a Mercedes Benz SL600 for CHF 159,900: The total amount of purchases amounted to CHF 1,958,521.65. See Figs. 3.1 and 3.2 Snapshot from Ricardo Online Platform.

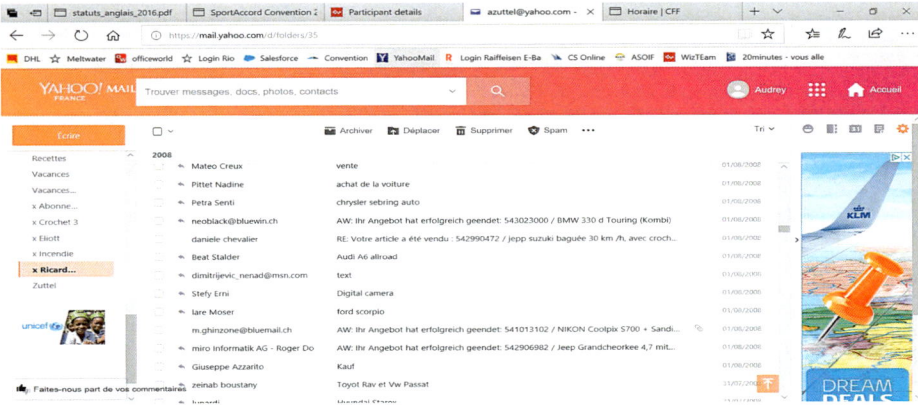

Fig. 3.1 Snapshot of chapters from the Ricardo Online Platform (page 2 from 14)

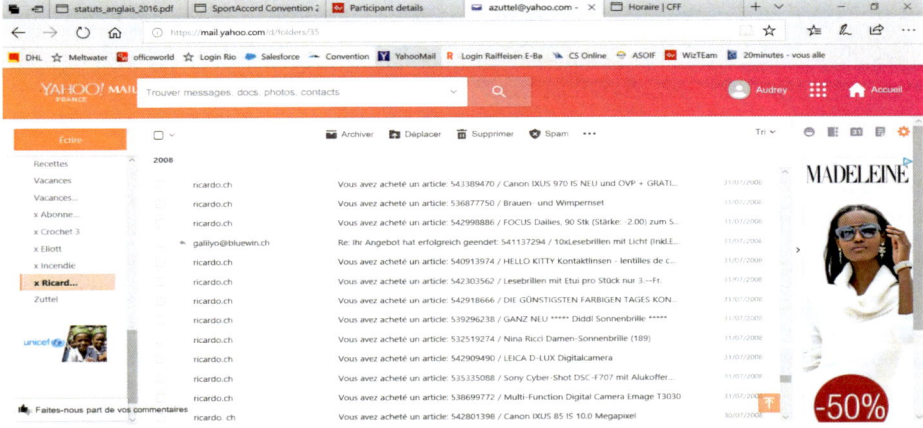

Fig. 3.2 Snapshot of chapters from the Ricardo Online Platform (page 3 from 14)

3.2   Emails Received After the Alleged Purchase

For the purpose of illustration, we picked emails of two disgruntled sellers of second hand cars (out of 100):

Email (Translated from German and French) from a Disgruntled Seller

Emails from Mr. T:

2008/7/31,

Hello, Congratulations on your purchase of your Volvo. When do you want to pick up the car? We are home all weekend, if you want to come by at the weekend. There is no problem, I just need to know today before 15 o'clock, so that I can return the number at the Road Traffic Office.

With kind regards
Mr. T. (the name was changed).

Message d'origine ---- De : xxxxxxxxx@gmail.com> À : azuttel@xxxxxx.com Envoyé le : Jeudi, 31 Juillet 2008, 14h57mn 54s Objet : Re: Ricardo 541855232 Top gepflegter Schwedenpanzer Volvo 745 GL

Hello, as you have not responded until today, is there a possibility for you to pick up the car on Monday, 4 August 2008. Please call me and let me know when you want to come. As from now, I will until 9pm tonight be reachable only on my mobile.

Kind regards
Mr. T (the name was changed).

De : (xxxxxxx@gmail.com) À : Audrey Zuttel Date : Mercredi, 6 Août 2008, 20h47mn 57s Objet : Re: Re : Ricardo 541855232 Top gepflegter Schwedenpanzer Volvo 745 GL

Dear Mrs. Gfeller, Ricardo accounts are not easily hacked, you have to do something for this to happen, such as clicking on the link in the email and then enter your user data. You or someone who knows your Ricardo account details has entered the data. Therefore, you are at least partly responsible for the transfer of your data. You did not become a victim of identity theft, but you are to be blamed, if you enter your details without any prior confirmation. If you had carefully read the mail (I also got the mail by the way), you would have noticed that the mail was not from Ricardo. The grammar of the text alone makes your hair stand in all directions. I assume that you have received my registered letter and I continue to insist on the legally binding purchase agreement. What you do with the car is your business. I expect the car to be picked up and paid for in cash by Wednesday, 13 August 2008. I reserve the right for further legal action without prior notice.

Regards
Mr. T.

----- Message d'origine ---- De : xxxxxxxxx@hotmail.com> À : azuttel@xxxxx.com Envoyé le : Jeudi, 31 Juillet 2008, 11h50mn 02s Objet : Ricoardo Auktion Opel Corsa

Dear Ms. Gfeller

Many thanks for the successful purchase of the Opel Corsas. When do you want to pick up the car?

Many regards

Mr. R (name was changed).

De : xxxxxxx@hotmail.com) À : Audrey Zuttel Date : Mercredi, 6 Août 2008, 18h18mn 24s Objet : RE: Re : Ricoardo Auktion Opel Corsa

Hi Audrey Gfeller

You are responsible for protecting your PC. I find it an impertinence that I have worries now because of your naivety. Maybe without you! someone else would have bought my car and I would not have to pay extra for an additional month for a garage for the amount of CHF 140!

I am seriously considering sending you a bill for my trouble!

Kind regards

Mr. R

3.3 Continuation of Events After Returning from Vacation

The Gfeller family, still in shock, that someone bought chapters worth almost CHF 2 million on their behalf, send an email to all buyers to clarify the situation and are at first reassured, as they have done nothing wrong and have become victims of a great deception. Ricardo is also informed about what had happened.

The following email has been sent to over 200 buyers:

Background Information

Am 06.08.08 schrieb Audrey Zuttel <azuttel@yahoo.com>:

Dear Madam and Sir

We have returned from abroad today. While we were on our trip, we were victims of an identity theft on the Ricardo.ch website. More than 200 cars were bought in our name in our absence. We have filed a criminal complaint with the police and have entered criminal proceedings. Ricardo is aware of what happened and has to pay the sales costs. We would like to draw your attention to the fact that false emails are circulating on the internet in the name of Ricardo. These emails require confirmation of your username and password. Please be vigilant and in case of doubt, do not answer the email. We thank you in advance for your understanding and ask us not to contact us (by email or by phone) anymore. We have received hundreds of calls and are currently overwhelmed and cannot answer.

Audrey Gfeller

Unfortunately, the story does not take the desired course and the explanatory email does not result in the understanding of the sellers. Moreover, Ricardo is unwilling to take responsibility for what happened. The situation escalates.

When returning from vacation, the Gfellers are met by over 20 packages on the doorstep, which must consequently all be returned at the expense of the Gfellers. Some of the sellers resort to extensive threats and gather in front of the Gfeller's house demanding their money back. The Gfellers inform the police and their lawyer.

Email from Ms M from Ricardo with Regard to the Purchase (Email was Translated from French)

----- Message d'origine ---- De : xxxxxx@ricardo.ch> À : "azuttel@yahoo.com" <azuttel@yahoo.com> Cc : xxxx@bluewin.ch" <xxxxxx@bluewin.ch> Envoyé le : Lundi, 4 Août 2008, 10h03mn 39s Objet : Avertissement 543005394

Good day

We have learned from the seller of the deposit No. 543005394 that the sale poses a problem. Hereby we would like to remind you once more about our general terms and conditions, according to which the publication of an offer on our side equals a contractual obligation. By bidding on the starting price set by the seller, which is not exceeded, you are obliged to pay the amount offered and to take over the item. This contractual obligation is also applicable, if you have an offer for a fixed price position.

Freundliche Grüsse/Meilleures salutations/Kind regards

Frau M

xxxxx@ricardo.ch

ricardo.ch AG

Email from Ms. B from Ricardo with regard tot he identity theft (Email was transated fro French)

-----Original Message----- From: xxxxxx@ricardo.ch] Sent: lundi, 4. août 2008 11:28 To: concept@rgdesign.ch Subject: AW: Usurpation d'identite

Dear Sir

Thank you for your email. The account has already been shut down upon your request and we have forwarded the information not to contact you anymore, but rather the person ho misused your address. We also advise you to file a complaint. Contact the police with any documents and evidence on this case.

You can also ask sellers to contact you if they have any questions. Since we do not know who has contacted you and who has not, it is difficult for us to inform the seller. The easiest would be if the sellers get in touch with us. The person who used your address must have left trace.

At the request of the judge handling the case, we may submit all personal information about that person.

Kind regards

Frau B

xxxxx@ricardo.ch

ricardo.ch AG

3.4 The End

Even 10 years after the incident no one knows what had happened and who was behind this PHISHING attack. The Gfellers had to move away from their family home to a remote location for a while, as some sellers threatened with violence and posed a danger to this young family. After lots of email and postal correspondence between the Gfeller's lawyer and Ricardo, Ricardo offered the Gfeller family a petty amount of hush-money tied to the condition that they were not allowed to talk about the incident over the next 10 years. The Gfellers thankfully rejected the offer and decided today to take the opportunity to share their story by making a contribution to this Cyber Security Best Practice Book. This incident poses even after 10 years still a great threat to companies as well as individuals who do not take cyber security seriously. Today everyone involved can laugh about the incident, except perhaps Ricardo.

The case Gfeller shows that people like you and me can be greatly affected and their lives turned upside down, just by a few clicks on the Internet.

3.5 List of All Bought Items

See Table 3.1 for a complete list of all items purchased.

Table 3.1 List of all bought chapters

Date	Time	Bought Item	Value	Category
31.07.2008	02h33	Audi S3	CHF 12.500,00	Cars
		Smart	CHF 7.900,00	Cars
		Alfa 147	CHF 7.100,00	Cars
		Hyundai Atos	CHF 6.500,00	Cars
		Mercedes E410	CHF 10.000,00	Cars
		Mazda 323	CHF 3.700,00	Cars
		Hyundai Starex	CHF 5.000,00	Cars
		Renault Clio	CHF 3.800,00	Cars
		VW LT 35	CHF 18.000,00	Cars
		Mini Cooper	CHF 24.999,00	Cars
		GMC pick-up	CHF 9.000,00	Cars
		Ford Mondeo	CHF 3.500,00	Cars
		Mercedes Benz	CHF 4.000,00	Cars
		Audi A8	CHF 7.850,00	Cars
		Nissan 300ZX	CHF 4.500,00	Cars
		Suzuki Vitara cabrio	CHF 5.000,00	Cars
		VW Golf	CHF 800,00	Cars
		BMW 330 d	CHF 37.900,00	Cars
		Hyundai Trajet	CHF 20.000,00	Cars

(continued)

Table 3.1 (continued)

Date	Time	Bought Item	Value	Category
		Mercedes E320	CHF 32.000,00	Cars
		Renault Espace	CHF 7.000,00	Cars
		Renault Mégane	CHF 21.000,00	Cars
		Toyota MR2	CHF 12.500,00	Cars
		Touran 2.0	CHF 22.000,00	Cars
		Fiat Punto gt	CHF 11.000,00	Cars
31.07.2008	02h29	Mazda 626	CHF 5.386,30	Cars
		Mitsubishi	CHF 7.500,00	Cars
		Alfa Romeo 164	CHF 4.500,00	Cars
		Nissan Primera	CHF 3.000,00	Cars
		Opel Corsa	CHF 1.500,00	Cars
		VW Golf GTI	CHF 4.100,00	Cars
		Toyota Aygo	CHF 16.500,00	Cars
		Bus Diesel	CHF 4.500,00	Cars
		Lancia 2.0	CHF 1.250,00	Cars
		Subaru Justy	CHF 3.500,00	Cars
	02h27	Toyota Corolla	CHF 3.000,00	Cars
		Peugeot 206	CHF 5.500,00	Cars
		Ford Scorpio	CHF 1.000,00	Cars
		BMW 330 d	CHF 11.500,00	Cars
		VW Golf V2,0	CHF 24.500,00	Cars
		BMW 318	CHF 5.900,00	Cars
		Opel Astra	CHF 4.150,00	Cars
		BMW Z3	CHF 24.000,00	Cars
		Opel Corsa	CHF 5.000,00	Cars
		Lancia Y	CHF 2.200,00	Cars
		Nissan Sunny	CHF 2.650,00	Cars
		Opel Calibra	CHF 6.500,00	Cars
		VW Golf 1	CHF 5.500,00	Cars
		Fiat Uno	CHF 1.000,00	Cars
		Pick up	CHF 42.900,00	Cars
		Passat 1.9	CHF 15.500,00	Cars
		Astra	CHF 1.999,50	Cars
		Willys Jeep	CHF 7.500,00	Cars
		Opel Frontera	CHF 6.500,00	Cars
		Oldtimer Wolseley	CHF 6.200,00	Cars
		BMW	CHF 3.600,00	Cars
		Fiat Punto gt	CHF 9.000,00	Cars
		Mercedes Benz	CHF 17.300,00	Cars
		Astra Cabrio	CHF 6.500,00	Cars
		Fiat Fiorino	CHF 3.440,00	Cars
		Passat 1.9	CHF 4.900,00	Cars

(continued)

Table 3.1 (continued)

Date	Time	Bought Item	Value	Category
		Fiat Bravo	CHF 3.600,00	Cars
		Opel Corsa	CHF 4.500,00	Cars
		Ford Escort	CHF 3.500,00	Cars
		Jeep Suzuki	CHF 7.000,00	Cars
		Alfa Romeo	CHF 6.500,00	Cars
		Mercedes 315	CHF 42.000,00	Cars
		Opel Calibra	CHF 5.000,00	Cars
		Peugeot 106	CHF 3.000,00	Cars
		Fiat Punto gt	CHF 2.500,00	Cars
	02h12	Nissan Almera	CHF 5.500,00	Cars
		BMW Z3	CHF 21.000,00	Cars
		BMW 530	CHF 2.900,00	Cars
		Mini Cooper	CHF 12.500,00	Cars
		VW Sharan Syncro	CHF 6.500,00	Cars
		Seat Terra	CHF 2.000,00	Cars
		Chrysler Grand	CHF 9.800,00	Cars
		Jaguar Xtype	CHF 22.500,00	Cars
		Ford Mondeo	CHF 19.500,00	Cars
		Jaguar Sovereign	CHF 4.800,00	Cars
		Peugeot 806	CHF 5.300,00	Cars
		Mini cooper	CHF 21.000,00	Cars
		BMW 330 d	CHF 17.000,00	Cars
		Audi A6	CHF 35.000,00	Cars
		Audi 100	CHF 4.500,00	Cars
		Toyota Celica	CHF 5.100,00	Cars
		Nissan Terrano	CHF 4.900,00	Cars
		Jeep CJ7	CHF 12.000,00	Cars
		Honda Accord	CHF 25.000,00	Cars
		Toyota Celica	CHF 1.700,00	Cars
	01h58	BMW 323 si	CHF 4.800,00	Cars
		Volvo	CHF 3.499,00	Cars
		BMW 330xi	CHF 14.500,00	Cars
		Pontiac Firebird	CHF 15.000,00	Cars
		Chrysler PT Cruiser	CHF 14.500,00	Cars
		Alfa Romeo 156	CHF 7.700,00	Cars
		Opel Astra	CHF 20.500,00	Cars
		Toyota Starlet	CHF 1.600,00	Cars
		VW Passat	CHF 7.500,00	Cars
		Mercedes Benz	CHF 7.770,00	Cars
		Audi V8	CHF 5.000,00	Cars
		Alfa Romeo	CHF 1.000,00	Cars

(continued)

Table 3.1 (continued)

Date	Time	Bought Item	Value	Category
		Cars	CHF 3.000,00	Cars
		Ford Focus	CHF 5.700,00	Cars
		Cars	CHF 4.200,00	Cars
		VW Golf 2	CHF 700,00	Cars
	01h45	Cars	CHF 12.900,00	Cars
		Mazda MX	CHF 6.500,00	Cars
		Opel Corsa	CHF 6.200,00	Cars
		Alfa Romeo	CHF 5.999,00	Cars
		Mercedes Benz	CHF 11.500,00	Cars
		Lexus	CHF 13.000,00	Cars
		VW Polo	CHF 1.700,00	Cars
		Alfa 156	CHF 5.500,00	Cars
		Subaru Legacy	CHF 7.490,00	Cars
		Zu Verkaufen	CHF 1.950,00	Cars
		Daewoo	CHF 3.900,00	Cars
		Seat Ibiza	CHF 2.240,00	Cars
		Chevrolet	CHF 7.500,00	Cars
		Alfa Romeo 147	CHF 10.800,00	Cars
		Toyota Rav4	CHF 4.600,00	Cars
		Renault Master	CHF 5.800,00	Cars
		VW Golf 3	CHF 6.800,00	Cars
		Seat Ibiza	CHF 9.000,00	Cars
		Renault Megane	CHF 10.899,15	Cars
		VW Golf Rallye	CHF 7.400,00	Cars
		VW Lupo	CHF 5.500,00	Cars
	00h41	Ford 1962	CHF 12.800,00	Cars
		VW Golf	CHF 2.600,00	Cars
		BMW	CHF 12.000,00	Cars
	00h40	Fiat Cinquecento	CHF 3.200,00	Cars
		Nissan Patrol	CHF 3.500,00	Cars
		Alfa Romeo	CHF 3.500,00	Cars
		Mazda	CHF 1.150,00	Cars
		Ford KA	CHF 3.200,00	Cars
		Golf II	CHF 1.800,00	Cars
		Porsche Cayenne	CHF 1.200,00	Cars
		BMW	CHF 14.500,00	Cars
		VW Caddy	CHF 3.000,00	Cars
		Mercedes 350	CHF 10.800,00	Cars
		DFW F89	CHF 1.600,00	Cars
		Cars	CHF 16.000,00	Cars
		Alfa Romeo	CHF 7.000,00	Cars

(continued)

Table 3.1 (continued)

Date	Time	Bought Item	Value	Category
		Alfa romeo	CHF 9.900,00	Cars
		Mercedes Benz SL600	CHF 159.900,00	Cars
	00h31	Kia Sorento	CHF 25.000,00	Cars
		NSU Prinz	CHF 11.800,00	Cars
		Subaru	CHF 3.800,00	Cars
	00h30	Audi A6	CHF 23.500,00	Cars
		Audi 90	CHF 6.900,00	Cars
		BMW 328i	CHF 5.900,00	Cars
	00h29	Ford Taunus 12	CHF 9.800,00	Cars
		Astra	CHF 1.500,00	Cars
		BMW X5	CHF 69.900,00	Cars
		BMW	CHF 20.500,00	Cars
		Opel Manta	CHF 5.600,00	Cars
		Opel Vectra	CHF 6.500,00	Cars
	00h25	Peugeot 406	CHF 5.800,00	Cars
		Peugeot 106	CHF 3.200,00	Cars
		Skoda Octavia	CHF 19.200,00	Cars
		Subaru Impreza	CHF 2.950,00	Cars
	00h25	Peugeot 306	CHF 7.800,00	Cars
		BMW 735i	CHF 7.000,00	Cars
		Golf GTI	CHF 8.500,00	Cars
		Chevrolet Malibu	CHF 10.500,00	Cars
		Pontiac Firebird	CHF 14.500,00	Cars
		Opel Corsa	CHF 2.000,00	Cars
		Cars	CHF 3.000,00	Cars
		Peugeot 406	CHF 10.000,00	Cars
		Chrysler Neon	CHF 5.200,00	Cars
		Fiat Brava	CHF 2.300,00	Cars
	00h24	Audi S6	CHF 8.998,00	Cars
		BMW 320i	CHF 7.800,00	Cars
		Jeep Grand	CHF 16.900,00	Cars
		VW Bus	CHF 3.500,00	Cars
		Renault Espace	CHF 5.500,00	Cars
		Renault Twingo	CHF 1.400,00	Cars
		VW EOS	CHF 934,00	Cars
		Saab 900i	CHF 4.000,00	Cars
		VW Golf IV	CHF 10.500,00	Cars
		VW Golf 2	CHF 1.200,00	Cars
		VW Vento	CHF 4.000,00	Cars
		Ford Fiesta	CHF 19.400,00	Cars
		Wohnmobil Hobby	CHF 1.800,00	Cars
		Renault Twingo	CHF 3.600,00	Cars

(continued)

Table 3.1 (continued)

Date	Time	Bought Item	Value	Category
		Opel Corsa		Cars
		Audi A6	CHF 22.500,00	Cars
		Stretch Limousine	CHF 29.000,00	Cars
		Wohnmobil Ford	CHF 7.800,00	Cars
		Citroen	CHF 2.600,00	Cars
		Ford Fiesta		Cars
	00h18	BMW 540	CHF 15.000,00	Cars
		Chrysler Sebring		Cars
		Audi A4	CHF 21.000,00	Cars
		Ford Mondeo		Cars
		Audi S4	CHF 2.500,00	Cars
		Seat Ibiza		Cars
		Volvo V40		Cars
		Iveco Demowagen		Cars
		Nissan 200	CHF 5.400,00	Cars
		Alfa Romeo	CHF 17.000,00	Cars
		Opel Astra	CHF 4.490,00	Cars
	00h13	Ford Mondeo	CHF 650,00	Cars
		Camper	CHF 14.500,00	Cars
		VW Polo	CHF 3.500,00	Cars
		Elta 92220 Aircooler	CHF 159,00	Ventilator
		Ventilator TAble Ventilator		Ventilator
		Ventilator		Ventilator
		Ventilator		Ventilator
		Ventilator Tristar		Ventilator
		Digital Camera	CHF 120,00	CameraCamera
		10x Reading glasses with light		SunglassesSunglasses
		Reading glasses	CHF 10,00	SunglassesSunglasses
	00h10	VW Golf	CHF 2.200,00	CarsCar
		Air Humidifier	CHF 449,00	Humidifier
		Sunglasses		SunglassesSunglasses
		Lacoste Sunglasses	CHF 130,00	SunglassesSunglasses
		TAbleVentilator	CHF 15,00	SunglassesSunglasses
		Contact lenses	CHF 22,00	Contact lenses
		Canon Ixus970		CameraCamera
		Eye lash set		
	00h05	Focus Daylies	CHF 49,00	Contact lenses
		Hello Kitty Kontaktlinsen		Contact lenses
		Lesebrillen mit Ètui		SunglassesSunglasses
		Kontaktlinsen		Contact lenses
		Sunglasses	CHF 15,00	Sunglasses
31.08.2008	00h03	Nina Ricci Sunglasses	CHF 185,00	Sunglasses
		Leica digital Camera		Camera

(continued)

Table 3.1 (continued)

Date	Time	Bought Item	Value	Category
		Sony Cyber Shot Memorystick	CHF 500,00	Camera
		Multi Function Digital Camera		Camera
		Canon Camera		Camera
		Canon Ixus		Camera
		Digital Camera	CHF 129,90	Camera
	23h59	Ricoh	CHF 450,00	Camera
		Tchnaxx X9	CHF 99,90	Camera
	23h58	Digital Camera	CHF 59,90	Camera
		Nikon Coolpix	CHF 420,00	Camera
		Digital Camera	CHF 65,00	Camera
		Mini Camera		Camera
		Digital Camera	CHF 249,00	Camera
30.07.2008	23h57	Samsung Digimax	CHF 150,00	Camera
			CHF 1.958.521,65	

Gesamtwert 1.958.521,65 Schweizer Franken

Teil II

Staaten und Behörden

States and Authorities

Vorworte

4

Arne Schönbohm und Udo Helmbrecht

Zusammenfassung

Leistungsfähige und sichere Kommunikationssysteme sind das zentrale Nervensystem der Gesellschaft im 21. Jahrhundert. Sie schaffen die Voraussetzung für Mobilität, Datenaustausch sowie Kapital-, Waren- und Dienstleistungstransfer. Sie sorgen für die Vernetzung von medizinischen Geräten in einem Operationssaal und sind Voraussetzung für die Industrie 4.0, die Energiewende oder den Betrieb von kritischen Infrastrukturen. Gleichzeitig bieten täglich auftretende neue Sicherheitslücken und Schwachstellen Angreifern immer wieder neue Möglichkeiten, Informationen auszuspähen, Geschäfts- und Verwaltungsprozesse zu sabotieren oder sich auf Kosten Dritter kriminell zu bereichern. Welche Auswirkungen dies haben kann, haben Cyber-Attacken der jüngeren Vergangenheit wie WannaCry oder NotPetya eindrucksvoll gezeigt.

A. Schönbohm (✉)
Bundesamt für Sicherheit in der Informationstechnik, Bonn, Deutschland
E-Mail: arne.schoenbohm@bsi.bund.de

U. Helmbrecht
ENISA, Athens, Greece
E-Mail: Udo.Helmbrecht@enisa.europa.eu

© Springer Fachmedien Wiesbaden GmbH, ein Teil von Springer Nature 2018
M. Bartsch, S. Frey (Hrsg.), *Cybersecurity Best Practices*,
https://doi.org/10.1007/978-3-658-21655-9_4

4.1   Integrierte Wertschöpfungskette der Cyber-Sicherheit

Vorwort von Arne Schönbohm, Präsident des Bundesamtes für Sicherheit in der Informationstechnik (BSI)

Leistungsfähige und sichere Kommunikationssysteme sind das zentrale Nervensystem der Gesellschaft im 21. Jahrhundert. Sie schaffen die Voraussetzung für Mobilität, Datenaustausch sowie Kapital-, Waren- und Dienstleistungstransfer. Sie sorgen für die Vernetzung von medizinischen Geräten in einem Operationssaal und sind Voraussetzung für die Industrie 4.0, die Energiewende oder den Betrieb von kritischen Infrastrukturen. Gleichzeitig bieten täglich auftretende neue Sicherheitslücken und Schwachstellen Angreifern immer

Arne Schönbohm

wieder neue Möglichkeiten, Informationen auszuspähen, Geschäfts- und Verwaltungsprozesse zu sabotieren oder sich auf Kosten Dritter kriminell zu bereichern. Welche Auswirkungen dies haben kann, haben Cyber-Attacken der jüngeren Vergangenheit wie WannaCry oder NotPetya eindrucksvoll gezeigt. Wenn wir die Widerstandsfähigkeit Deutschlands gegen Cyber-Gefahren erhöhen wollen, dann müssen Staat, Wirtschaft und Gesellschaft die damit verbundenen Herausforderungen gemeinsam angehen. Die 2016 beschlossene Cyber-Sicherheitsstrategie der Bundesregierung gibt auch deshalb als Ziel vor, eine gesamtstaatliche Cyber-Sicherheitsinfrastruktur zu schaffen, die leistungsstark und nachhaltig ist.

Als nationale Cyber-Sicherheitsbehörde ist das BSI das Kompetenzzentrum für Fragen der IT-Sicherheit, dessen fachliche Expertise weit über den Bereich der öffentlichen Verwaltung hinaus anerkannt ist. Aufgrund der Bündelung und internen Vernetzung von IT-Sicherheits-Expertise in einer Behörde kann das BSI eine integrierte Wertschöpfungskette der Cyber-Sicherheit anbieten. Darum können Erkenntnisse aus der Cyber-Abwehr ohne Zeitverzug in die Prävention, in die Standardisierung und Zertifizierung eingebracht werden. Darum fließen neue Erkenntnisse aus der Grundlagenarbeit der Kryptografie in die Abwehrfähigkeiten des BSI ein. Darum können Best Practices, Empfehlungen und Sicherheitslösungen entwickelt werden, von denen IT-Anwender in Staat, Wirtschaft und Gesellschaft unmittelbar profitieren.

Verwaltung und Unternehmen etwa profitieren vom aktuell modernisierten IT-Grundschutz des BSI sowie von Kooperationen, wie sie das BSI jüngst mit dem Zentralverband des Deutschen Handwerks (ZDH) geschlossen hat. Ziel der Zusammenarbeit ist es, rund einer Million Handwerksunternehmen die Relevanz der IT-Sicherheit zu verdeutlichen und sie in der Prävention sowie in der Abwehr von Cyber-Angriffen durch konkrete, praxisorientierte Empfehlungen und Hilfestellung zu unterstützen.

Mit der 2012 gegründeten Allianz für Cyber-Sicherheit (www.allianz-fuer-cybersicherheit.de) verfolgt das BSI das Ziel, die Widerstandsfähigkeit des Standortes Deutschland gegenüber Cyber-Angriffen zu stärken. Insbesondere kleine und mittelständische Unternehmen profitieren vom fachlichen Austausch mit anderen Unternehmen und von der Bereitstellung zahlreicher Best Practices und IT-Sicherheitsempfehlungen. Die Allianz für Cyber-Sicherheit ist ein Erfolgsmodell, derzeit gehören ihr mehr als 2500 Institutionen an.

Eine erfolgreiche Digitalisierung kann nur gelingen, wenn die Aspekte der Informationssicherheit von vornherein ganzheitlich betrachtet und kooperativ umgesetzt werden. Denn Vertrauen in neue Technologien entsteht nur durch das notwendige Maß an IT-Sicherheit. Als die nationale Cyber-Sicherheitsbehörde kümmert sich das BSI um diese Aspekte und gestaltet auch weiterhin die Informationssicherheit in der Digitalisierung für Staat, Wirtschaft und Gesellschaft.

4.2   Cyber Security Is a Shared Responsibility

Udo Helmbrecht

Preface by Prof. Dr. Udo Helmbrecht, Executive Director European Union Agency for Network and Information Security (ENISA)

ENISA welcomes the joint effort presented in this book and the best practices made available to the public. For ENISA, cybersecurity is a shared responsibility.

A few years ago, cyber and cyber incidents were unknown to the wider public. Now they are part of our everyday life. Massive hacks, data leaks, and cyber influence operations are becoming larger and more frequent [1], while technologies ranging from the Internet of things (IoT) to self-driving or autonomous vehicles will be adding significantly to the vulnerabilities. The dangers are no longer "merely" criminal, because even our most cherished democratic institutions are now threatened, and the emergence of cyber terrorism in the future is inevitable.

Some time ago a huge ransomware attack [2] caused outages in critical services in many Member States; institutions vital to society, such as hospitals rail stations and airports had to close down their business for hours or days. Eventually this resulted in millions of citizens being affected, a phenomenon that is likely to become very common in the years to come.

We are not 100% secure and it is impossible to be so. The trust in the digital ecosystem is at risk now and even if experts expressed their concerns in the past, their opinions were not listened to. Today we need to do more. The EU is already working towards this direction in many ways: however, now it is the **time to streamline and synchronize all efforts**. In 2013, the EU set out a Cybersecurity strategy launching numerous work streams to improve cyber resilience. The main goals of this strategy were to foster a reliable, safe, and open cyber ecosystem for all, goals that still remain valid. But the continuously evolving threat landscape calls for more effective measures.

In September 2017, the EU announced the Communication on resilience, deterrence, and defense for building a strong cybersecurity for the EU. The EU Member States have the tools and policies required to address cybersecurity; but even though cybersecurity still remains a national priority, the scale and the cross border nature of the threats (like WannaCry) show that cybersecurity is better considered as a joint responsibility. All actors – the EU, the Member States, industry, and individuals – should work together to give cybersecurity the priority it needs to deliver a better EU response to cyber-attacks.

The proposed Communication provides for a comprehensive set of measures that build on previous actions and foster mutually reinforcing specific objectives:

- Increasing capabilities and preparedness of Member States and businesses
- Improving cooperation and coordination across Member States and EU institutions, agencies, and bodies
- Increasing EU level capabilities to complement the action of Member States, in particular in the case of cross-border cyber crises
- Increasing awareness of citizens and businesses on cybersecurity issues
- Increasing the overall transparency of cybersecurity assurance of ICT products and services to strengthen trust in the digital single market and in digital innovation
- Avoiding fragmentation of certification schemes in the EU and related security requirements and evaluation criteria across Member States and sectors

In 2016, the European Union adopted the Network and Information security directive. It is the first piece of EU legislation specifically aimed at improving cybersecurity throughout the Union, a very significant step towards more secure EU information systems. The Directive focuses on protection for Critical Information Infrastructures or national essential services, namely, through setting baseline security measures and implementing cyber incident notification.

Among other measures, the NIS Directive requires the EU Member States to adopt and implement a national strategy on the security of network and information systems (national NIS strategy). National cybersecurity strategies are the main documents used by the Member States to set strategic principles, guidelines, and objectives and in some cases specific measures in order to mitigate risk associated with cyber security. Following a high-level top-down approach, national cybersecurity strategies set the strategic direction for subsequent actions, such as a national cybersecurity roadmap. Based on the priorities set on this roadmap, the states establish agencies, public entities, action plans, academic curricula, and many other activities to achieve making the state more cyber resilient.

ENISA has a key role in the implementation of the NIS Directive. In particular, the Agency has a major role in supporting the Member States to create their national strategy and to implement it. In 2012, only 12 Member states had developed a NCSS. Currently, all 28 Member States have published a national cybersecurity strategy. ENISA is supporting the EU Member States and EFTA countries since 2012 to develop, implement, and evaluate their National Cyber Security Strategies. With the NIS Directive in place, a lot of Member States are considering revising their strategies with the goal to create new versions that will include the provisions of the NIS Directive into their strategic objectives. ENISA is also the secretariat at the CSIRT network created under the NISD.

ENISA is also facilitating the implementation of the GDPR offering recommendations to key stakeholders, as we already did with the ePrivacy Directive. The upcoming Electronic Communication Code will add up to ENISA's agenda, as bringing together the Member States under a common goal is important to achieve harmonization.

Policies and strategies are just preparing the ground; actual hands-on experience is gravely required in this cyber hostile environment. The first Pan European exercise that brought 30 European countries against a common enemy that wanted to bring chaos in the Information systems in the EU was organized in 2010 by ENISA. Since then a major exercise is organized every 2 years. Cyber Europe is testing standard operating procedures on cross border information exchange focusing each time on a different crisis scenario, like, for example, targeting the energy sector or air transport. Experience from these drills resulted into the recently announced EU Blueprint [3] that **explains how cybersecurity is addressed in existing Crisis Management mechanisms** and sets objectives and modes for cooperation between MS.

Cybersecurity is a shared responsibility and ENISA, together with the community, is stepping forward and working towards making collaboration and information and knowledge sharing stronger and more reliable. The multifaceted efforts of ENISA across the cybersecurity spectrum are supporting and empowering a more cyber secure and safe Europe.

References

1. https://www.symantec.com/security-center/threat-report
2. https://www.enisa.europa.eu/news/enisa-news/wannacry-ransomware-first-ever-case-of-cyber-cooperation-at-eu-level
3. http://eur-lex.europa.eu/legal-content/EN/TXT/?uri=JOIN:2017:450:FIN

ENISA's Contribution to National Cyber Security Strategies

Dimitra Liveri, Anna Sarri and Eleni Darra

Abstract

National Cyber Security Strategies (NCSS) are the main documents of MS to set strategic principles, guidelines, and objectives and in some cases specific measures in order to mitigate risk associated with cybersecurity. To encounter existing and emerging cybersecurity threats, EU Member States and EFTA countries are required to evolve and adapt their cybersecurity strategies frequently. In July 2016, the European parliament voted the adoption of the Directive on Security of Network and Information Systems (the NIS Directive). Among other measures, the NIS Directive requires the EU Member States to adopt and implement a national strategy on the security of network and information systems (national NIS strategy). Member States may request the assistance of ENISA in developing national NIS strategies.

ENISA is supporting the EU Member States and EFTA countries since 2012. For this reason, ENISA has published several studies regarding the development, implementation, and evaluation of the NCSS. ENISA has also created several tools like online tutorial videos and an online interactive map that stores all the developed NCSS of EU MS together with their strategic objectives and examples of good practices. More information regarding ENISA's work on NCSS will be further analyzed in Chap. 5 "ENISA's Contribution to National Cyber Security Strategies" of this book.

D. Liveri (✉) · A. Sarri · E. Darra
ENISA, Athens, Greece
e-mail: Dimitra.Liveri@enisa.europa.eu; Anna.Sarri@enisa.europa.eu; Eleni.Darra@enisa.europa.eu

© Springer Fachmedien Wiesbaden GmbH, ein Teil von Springer Nature 2018
M. Bartsch, S. Frey (Hrsg.), *Cybersecurity Best Practices*,
https://doi.org/10.1007/978-3-658-21655-9_5

5.1 Introduction

In July 2016, the European parliament voted the adoption of the Directive on Security of Network and Information Systems [1] (the NIS Directive). The NIS Directive is the main legislative proposal under the 2013 EU Cybersecurity Strategy. It is the first piece of EU legislation specifically aimed at improving cybersecurity throughout the Union. This is a very significant step to secure EU information systems.

By laying down a certain number of obligations across the EU, the Directive ensures a consistent approach to cybersecurity *"with a view to achieving a high common level of security of networks and information systems within the Union so as to improve the functioning of the internal market."*

Among other measures, the NIS Directive requires the EU Member States to adopt and implement a national strategy on the security of network and information systems (national NIS strategy). On this task, the Directive requires ENISA to support Member States by providing expertise and advice and by facilitating the exchange of good practice. Thus, Member States may request the assistance of ENISA in developing national NIS strategies.

In September 2017, the European Commission presented the joint Communication on resilience, deterrence, and defense: building strong cybersecurity for the EU. This Communication aims at building a strong single market through an EU cybersecurity certification framework, through a blueprint plan for operationalizing cybersecurity response through investing in strong encryption and protection of fundamental rights, through strengthening ENISA's role and developing international cooperation for EU leadership on cybersecurity. The Communication recognizes ENISA's role in the implementation of the NIS Directive and addresses a stronger role for the Agency through a proposal for a permanent mandate.

ENISA is supporting the EU Member States and EFTA countries since 2012 to develop, implement, and evaluate their National Cyber Security Strategies (NCSS). In 2012, only 12 Member states had developed a NCSS. Currently, all 28 Member States have published a national cybersecurity strategy. With the NIS Directive in place, a lot of Member States are considering revising their strategies with the goal to create new versions that will include the provisions of the NIS Directive into their strategic objectives.

ENISA has published several studies regarding NCSS. The first guide published in 2012 "National Cyber Security Strategy: An implementation Guide" [1] describes the steps and provides advice and recommendations on how to develop and implement a NCSS. After that, ENISA focused on Phase 3, the evaluation and adjustment of strategies for continuous improvement. Thus, an evaluation framework for cybersecurity strategies was published in 2014 [2]. This publication aims to be a pragmatic evaluation tool and presents a set of possible key performance indicators (KPIs).

In 2016, ENISA published an updated version of a "Good Practice Guide on NCSS" [3]. This guide complements the findings of the 2012 report with current examples and good practice. It also includes information on the evaluation and adjustment. The evaluation part is more concrete as it analyses and evaluates existing NCSS of EU Member States and EFTA countries. Moreover, ENISA has created online tutorial videos [4] and an online interactive map [2] that lists all the NCSS in the EU. The map presents all the developed NCSS of EU MS together with their strategic objectives and examples of good practices.

In the following chapters, we present the core elements based on the experience and knowledge shared throughout all these years.

5.2 A Resilient National Strategy

To encounter existing and emerging cybersecurity threats, EU Member States are required to evolve and adapt their cybersecurity strategies frequently. NCSS are the main documents of MS to set strategic principles, guidelines, and objectives, and in some cases specific measures in order to mitigate risk associated with cybersecurity. Following a high-level top-down approach, NCSS set the strategic direction for subsequent actions.

ENISA's work around NCSS focuses on a lifecycle model that consists of four steps: the development phase, the implementation phase, the evaluation phase, and the maintenance phase. Fig 5.1 depicts this lifecycle.

To build, validate, and update this information, ENISA is collaborating and advising with experts from all EU MS and a couple of EFTA countries.

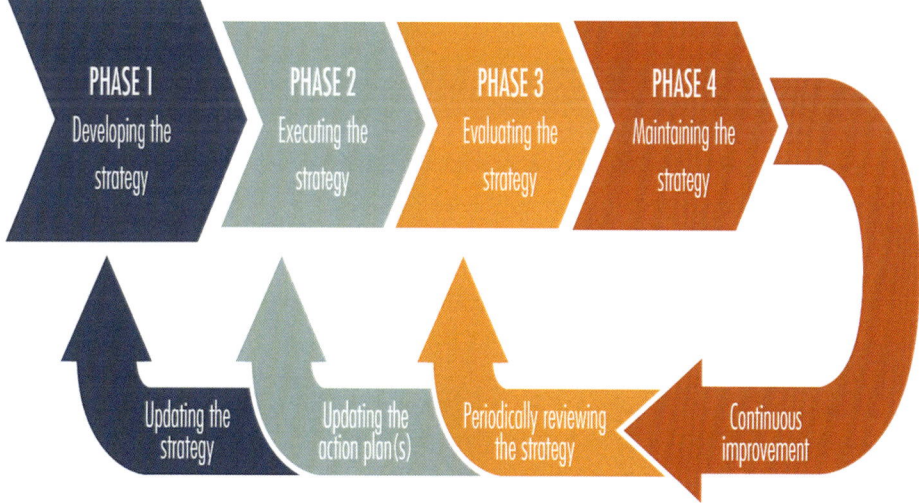

Fig. 5.1 NCSS Lifecycle of ENISA

ENISA's "Good practice Guide on NCSS" presents six steps for the design and development of NCSS and fifteen objectives for the implementation of NCSS. ENISA has identified six steps for the design and development of NCSS:

- Set the vision, scope, objectives, and priorities
- Follow a risk assessment approach
- Take stock of existing policies, regulations, and capabilities
- Set a clear governance structure
- Identify and engage stakeholders
- Establish trusted information-sharing mechanisms

In addition, fifteen objectives for the implementation of NCSS:

- Develop national cyber contingency plans
- Protect critical information infrastructure
- Organize cybersecurity exercises
- Establish baseline security measures
- Establish incident reporting mechanisms
- Raise user awareness
- Strengthen training and educational programs
- Establish an incident response capability
- Address cybercrime
- Engage in international cooperation
- Establish a public-private partnership
- Balance security with privacy
- Institutionalize cooperation between public agencies
- Foster R&D
- Provide incentives for the private sector to invest in security measures

To support the Member States to overcome some barriers, the report presents gaps and challenges identified regardless of the status of implementation of NCSS among EU Member States:

- Establish effective cooperation between public stakeholders
- Establish trust between public and private stakeholders
- Ensure adequate resources
- Promote a common approach and awareness for privacy and data protection
- The implementation of vulnerability and risk analysis

Cybersecurity is still a relatively new problem area for nation states, and while some EU Member States are already drafting their second or third edition, others have just started.

5.2.1   Member State's Objectives

In this section, a few examples of good practices regarding MS's implemented objectives are described. More information about such examples is also listed and ENISA's interactive NCSS map [2].

5.2.1.1   Objective 1: Develop National Cyber Contingency Plans

A national cyber contingency plan (NCP) is an integral part of a NCSS. NCPs are the interim structures and measures for responding to, and recovering services following, major incidents that involve critical information infrastructures (CIIs) [3]. A national cybersecurity contingency plan should be part of or aligned with overall national contingency plans.

An example is the National Crisis Management Plan in Poland:

Example

The Polish National Crisis Management Plan lays out the general roles and responsibilities during a crisis situation. The Council of Ministers holds the political responsibility and will be advised by a Government Crisis Management Team in case of national emergency. The Team shall be composed of different ministers relevant to the kind of crisis. In case of an emergency related to CII, the Ministry of Administration and Digitization will take a leading role in advising other Ministries and the Council of Ministers in crisis situations.

5.2.1.2   Objective 2: Protect Critical Information Infrastructure

Critical information infrastructure protection (CIIP) is an integral part of many cyber and information security strategies. Cybersecurity covers a broad spectrum of ICT-related security issues, of which the protection of CII is an essential part.

An example is The German IT-Security Act:

Example

The IT Security Act provides a definition of critical infrastructure. A methodology for the identification of critical infrastructure has been developed. The German federal ministry of the interior is applying this methodology in an administrative order (BSI-KRITIS-Verordnung) that further defines which infrastructures are critical and affected by the IT Security Act [5].

5.2.2   Objective 3: Organize Cybersecurity Exercises

Exercises enable competent authorities to test existing emergency plans, target-specific weaknesses, increase cooperation between different sectors, identify interdependencies, stimulate improvements in continuity planning, and generate a culture of cooperative effort to boost resilience. Cyber exercises are important tools to assess preparedness of a community against natural disasters, technology failures, cyber-attacks, and emergencies.

An example is the Cross-sectoral cyber exercises in Austria:

Example

Cross-sectoral cyber exercises for SMEs will be organized and held at periodic intervals. Specific sectors of SMEs should be allowed to participate in governmental cross-sectoral cyber exercises upon request [6].

5.2.3   Objective 4: Establish Baseline Security Measures

All relevant public and private organizations should take necessary measures to protect their information infrastructure from threats, risks, and vulnerabilities identified after the completion of the national risk assessment. Baseline security requirements for a given sector define the minimum security level that all organizations in that sector should comply with. Such requirements can be based on existing security standards or frameworks and good practices widely recognized by the industry. Defining a minimum set of security measures is a complex exercise that should take into account the following aspects: the different level of maturity among the stakeholders, the differences in terms of the operational capacity of each organization, and the different standards existing in each critical sector under consideration.

An example is the CIIP law in France:

Example

All Operators of Vital Importance (OIVs) are required to comply with the obligations listed in Article 22 of the French CIIP law ("Loi de programmation militaire 2014–2019"). These obligations include compliance with rules for the protection of information systems set by ANSSI on behalf of the Prime Minister. These rules can be technical or organizational.

According to the CIIP law, OIVs are obligated to report cybersecurity incident notifications to ANSSI. The nature of incidents to be notified will be specified by sectorial orders.

During major crisis that threaten the security of information systems of critical infrastructure, the Prime Minister may decide on additional measures that OIVs would have to implement.

According to the CIIP Law, OIVs are obligated to undergo cybersecurity audits, performed either by ANSSI or a service provider qualified by ANSSI. Audit reports are classified and provided to ANSSI [7].

5.2.4   Objective 5: Establish Incident Reporting Mechanisms

Reporting security incidents plays an important role in enhancing national cybersecurity. The more a person knows about major incidents the better they can understand the threat environment. Incident reporting and analysis helps in adjusting and tailoring the list of security measures, mentioned in the previous objective, to the changing threat landscape. This way, the national preparedness, response, and recovery capabilities are enhanced.

An example is the Incident reporting in Croatia:

Example

In Croatia, information sharing of important incidents is mandatory for systems, which are essential for proper functioning of a critical service.

Sharing information about incidents for all other systems is voluntary. The separate sector authorities will answer the question about what an "important incident" is within their own sector.

The different Croatian sector authorities also define the set of data that has to be shared. The general approach is to share a minimum set of data, depending on the purpose. This can be statistical data or more specific data (e.g., data shared between a CERT and the police in cases of cybercrime).

5.2.5   Objective 6: Raise User Awareness

Raising awareness about cybersecurity threats and vulnerabilities and their impact on society has become vital. Through awareness-raising, individual and corporate users can learn how to behave in the online world and protect themselves from typical risks. Awareness activities occur on an ongoing basis and use a variety of delivery methods to reach broad audiences [8]. Security awareness activities may be triggered by different events or factors, which may be internal or external to an organization. Major external factors could include: recent security breaches, threats and incidents, new risks, updates of security policy, and/or strategy. Among the internal factors are new laws, new governments, etc. [9].

An example is the Raising awareness campaigns by the Information Systems Authority (RIA) in Estonia:

Example

RIA holds periodic events and media campaigns for raising awareness. In addition, it organizes technical and end-user training. It is organizing regular awareness rising and technical trainings for governmental authorities and vital service providers. In addition to trainings, RIA organizes annual CIIP Seminar in every autumn.

5.2.6   Objective 7: Strengthen Training and Educational Programs

Increased investments in cybersecurity-related education programs as well as general education about information security threats for end users is an important pillar to decrease risks for businesses and society [11]. Unfortunately, universities and R&D institutions in many countries do not produce enough cybersecurity experts to meet the increasing needs of the private sector. Cybersecurity is usually not a separate academic topic but part of the computer science curriculum. Cybersecurity is also a continuously changing topic that requires constant training and education.

An example is the knowledge, skills, and R&D&I in Spain:

There Are Several Projects On-Going for This Issue

- Cybercamp (cybersecurity event that INCIBE organizes with the aim of identifying, attracting, managing, and, in short, helping to generate cybersecurity talent that can be transferred to the private sector, in line with its demands).
- Network of excellence on cybersecurity Research, Development and Innocation (R&D+I): In the context of the Trust in the Digital Domain Plan (derived from the Digital Agenda for Spain), INCIBE in cooperation with the cybersecurity research ecosystem is promoting the creation of a network of centers of excellence on cybersecurity research and innovation.
- Grants for advanced cybersecurity research team excellence. The initiative to launch these grants for advanced cybersecurity research team excellence has emerged to meet the current need to retain and attract cybersecurity-research talent.
- Different Masters in Cybersecurity delivered by Universities.
- Public administrations: specific training courses in cybersecurity delivered by the National Cryptologic Centre and focused for civil servants.

5.2.7 Objective 8: Establishment of Incident Response Capability

National/governmental CSIRTs play a key role in coordinating incident management with the relevant stakeholders at national level. In addition, they bear responsibility for cooperation with the national/governmental teams in other countries [12]. According to article 12 of the NIS Directive, a CSIRTs network is established with the role to contribute to the development of confidence and trust between MS and to promote swift and effective operational cooperation. Some of the tasks of the CSIRTs network include the exchange and availability on a voluntary basis of nonconfidential information concerning incidents, the sharing among MS noncommercially sensitive information related to incidents, support in addressing cross border incidents on a voluntary mutual assistance basis, etc.

An example is the community of CERTs in Poland:

In Poland No Institution Is Designated as the National CERT. Instead, a Community of Different Response Teams Exist

- CERT.gov.PL is the main institution for public agencies, but also offers its services to CI operators based on formal agreements. Its tasks are to publish security notifications, to detect incidents in public networks, and to resolve and analyze of incidents. It has been established in 2008.
- The first CERT in Poland was CERT Polska, which is part of the NASK. It holds special expertise in the analysis and research of security incidents and provides information on threats and incidents. Information is available on a database that can be used by private and public entities.

- CERT.gov.PL and CERT Polska also operate a database on honeypots. The latter response team and the IT Security Department of the Polish Internal Security Agency have developed and jointly maintain ARAKIS-GOV, an early warning system for government IT-systems.
- In addition, there exist a number of sectoral institutions such as MilCERT and CERT Orange (telecommunications sector).

5.2.8 Objective 9: Address Cyber Crime

The fight against cybercrime requires the collaboration of many actors and communities to be successful. In this respect, it is important to address and counter the rise of cybercrime and to prepare a concerted and coordinated response with relevant stakeholders.

An example is the legislation and cybercrime units in Estonia:

Example

Estonia has ratified the Budapest Convention and included cybercrime in the penal code (amendments were made after the 2007 large scale cyber attacks in Estonia). It includes components for cybercrime and elaborates on different types of cybercrime.

Furthermore, Estonia has established cybercrime units in the police forces. At the regional level, designated police officers are responsible for cybercrime

At different social media portals, web constables (which are part of the police) are available and can be contacted to report crimes.

5.2.9 Objective 10: Engage in International Cooperation

Engaging in cooperation and information sharing with partners abroad is important to better understand and respond to a constantly changing threat environment.

An example is Denmark as a strong international partner:

Example

Denmark's National Cyber Security Strategy names "Denmark as a strong international partner" as one of six focus areas.

There are three initiatives in this area:

- 18. Strengthening of Danish cyber diplomacy
- 19. Promotion of Denmark's stance in international cyber and information security cooperation forums
- 20. Nordic cooperation on research and education in cyber and information security [13]

5.2.10   Objective 11: Establish a Public-Private Partnership

In the majority of countries, private companies own critical infrastructure and critical services are provided by the private sector. Therefore, a high degree of communication and cooperation can be an effective way for governments to understand the needs and challenges of private companies, but also to ensure that the necessary measures are implemented to achieve a sufficient degree of security.

Public-private partnership can be an effective tool, to pool expertise and resources of the private and public sector. It establishes a common scope and objectives and uses defined roles and work methodology to achieve shared goals [14].

An example is the private sector cooperation in Bulgaria:

Example

Public-Private Partnership: Improving cybersecurity requires a combined, multisector, comprehensive approach that focuses on building a "whole-of-government" cyber organization that includes cooperation with private enterprises and places an emphasis on educating the citizen. Opportunities to enhance the involvement of the private sector and to ensure that we capitalize on their expertise should include jointly exploring best practices and procedures to ensure that no part of the critical infrastructure, whether in public or private hands, would become a weak link and vulnerability.

5.2.10.1   Objective 12: Balance Security with Privacy and Data Protection

A cyber security strategy should seek for the right balance between these two concepts. Moreover, the European Commission has provided the regulatory tools to support the Member States in facing this challenge. For this reason, every Member State should take seriously into account the right of citizens' privacy. Finally, privacy is a horizontal issue that cuts across most of the activities relevant to cybersecurity strategy.

An example is the Finish Data Protection Ombudsman and FICORA:

Example

- The Data Protection Ombudsman: guides and controls the processing of personal data and provides related consultation. The Ombudsman exerts power in issues related to the implementation of the right of verification and the correction of personal data. The Ombudsman also follows the general development in the processing of personal data, launching initiatives if necessary. The Ombudsman sees to the distribution of information related to the field of operation and participates in international co-operation.
- The Finnish Communications regulatory Authority (FICORA) supervises the data protection of electronic communications in the operations of telecommunications operators, corporate or association subscribers, and in other communications providers' operations. FICORA supervises, for example, processing of identification

data, protection of communications and decoding, and compliance with the provisions on the information service of communications services. FICORA is the competent national authority referred to in article 2 of the Commission Regulation 611/2013; hence, it receives telecommunications operators' notifications of personal data breaches. Information collected through these notifications is used in directing FICORA's steering and supervision of telecom operators.

The Data Protection Ombudsman and FICORA collaborate with each other regularly and if needed, also case by case.

5.2.11   Objective 13: Institutionalize Cooperation Between Public Agencies

Cybersecurity is a problem area that spans across different sectors and across the responsibilities of different public agencies. Therefore, close cooperation between these entities is an important pillar for the successful implementation of NCSS.

The institutional setting for an institutionalized form of cooperation can range from advisory boards, steering groups, forums, councils, cyber centers, or expert meeting groups. In addition, the purpose of the institution can vary between consultation, sharing information, or the coordination of actions between the different agencies. In order to set up an institution for coordination, governments either can develop new kinds of cooperation mechanisms for the specific purpose of cybersecurity or extend the scope of existing institutions.

An example is the Swedish Cooperation Group for Information Security (SAMFI):

Example

In order to coordinate the actions between the different agencies and public entities, the Swedish government has developed a cooperative network comprised of authorities "with specific societal information security responsibilities." This Cooperation Group for Information Security (SAMFI) consists of representatives of the different authorities and meets several times a year to discuss issues related to national information security. SAMFI's subject areas are mainly to be found in political-strategic areas and cover topics such as technical issues and standardization, national and international development in the field of information security, or management and prevention of IT incidents [15].

5.2.11.1   Objective 14: Foster Research and Development (R&D) in Cybersecurity

Research and development in cybersecurity is needed in order to develop new tools for deterring, protecting, detecting, and adapting to and against new kinds of cyber attacks.

An example is from the Swedish framework program on information security 2011-2016:

> **Example**
>
> The framework-program on information security 2011–2016 is themed on organization's ability to create a culture of security that involves a high security awareness among management and employees.
>
> The Swedish Government funds different research programs (some of them through the Swedish Civil Contingencies Agency). There is currently a 4-year program running, involving three million Euro, which are provided to different research activities. Furthermore, the government is cooperating with the Royal Institute of Technology regarding a 5-year program in the area of SCADA/ICS systems. In addition, Sweden is cooperating with the USA for R&D.

5.2.11.2 Objective 15: Provide Incentives for the Private Sector to Invest in Security Measures

There are different ways how governments can ensure that businesses implement appropriate security measures. One way is to make certain standards mandatory by law. However, governments can also apply softer steering measures, for example, by giving incentives to businesses to invest in certain security measures.

An example is the incentives given to the private sector to invest in security measures in Finland:

> **Example**
>
> In order to ensure cybersecurity development, Finland will see to it that appropriate legislation and incentives exist to support the business activities and their development in this field. Basic know-how in the field is gained through business activity [16]. For example, a key project of the Government is the creation of a growth environment for digital business operations in Finland. One of the principal measures under this key project is the preparation and implementation of a national information security strategy for increasing the level of trust in the Internet and in digital practices. The strategy was prepared in close cooperation with private sector. A development group for information security in business was set up to support the preparation of the strategy.
>
> The strategy is intended to focus on ensuring competitiveness and the right conditions for exports, developing the EU's digital single market and safeguarding privacy protection and other fundamental rights. The strategy aims to bring about change whereby information security will be an integral part of different systems, terminal devices, and services. The strategy also deals with matters that damage trust, such as information security violations and large-scale infringements of privacy protection in networks.

5.3 Governance Structures in the EU

For the cybersecurity strategy to be successful, a clear governance framework needs to be defined. Specific roles and responsibilities should be assigned for all relevant stakeholders. A clear governance framework provides a platform for dialogue and coordination of the various activities undertaken in the lifecycle of the strategy.

A public body or an interagency/inter-ministerial working group should be defined as the coordinator of the strategy with the overall responsibility for the strategy lifecycle implementation and monitoring. The structure of the coordinating entity, its exact responsibilities, and its relationships with the other stakeholders should be clearly defined.

Different governance structures are possible to govern cybersecurity. In the study "Stocktaking, Analysis and Recommendations for the protection of CIIs" [17] that was published by ENISA in 2016, different profiles of governance structures are analyzed.

A centralized approach is usually characterized by a central cybersecurity authority with wide responsibilities and competencies across sectors. Decentralized approaches are characterized by a strong degree of cooperation between public agencies. This approach is often motivated by the principle of subsidiarity. Countries have also developed different relationships with the private sector. Some countries have established co-regulation in the issue area of cybersecurity through institutionalized forms of cooperation such as public-private partnerships. Other countries have developed new laws in order to regulate the private sector.

The three different governance approaches are described in detail below:

5.3.1   Centralized Approach

The centralized approach is characterized by:

1. Central Authority Across Sectors:
   Member States that follow a centralized approach have developed authorities with responsibilities and wide competencies or have extended the powers of existing authorities. These main authorities combine several tasks such as contingency planning, emergency management, regulatory tasks, and supporting private operators.
2. Comprehensive Legislation:
   A comprehensive legislation creates obligations and requirements across sectors. This can be achieved through new comprehensive laws or through complementing existing sector-specific regulations. See Fig. 5.2.

Fig. 5.2 Centralized approach

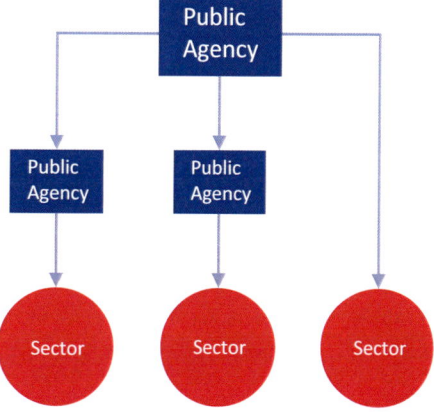

Example

France is a good example for an EU Member State with a centralized approach. France's ANSSI has been declared the main national authority for the defense of the information systems in 2011. ANSSI has a strong supervisory role for "operators of vital importance" (OIVs): The agency can order OIVs to comply with security measures and is authorized to perform security audits on them. Furthermore, it is the main Single Point of Contact for OIVs, which are obligated to report security incidents to the agency.

In cases of security incidents, ANSSI acts as a contingency agency and decides on the measures that operators must take to respond to the crisis. The government's actions are coordinated within ANSSI's operations center. Detection of threats and incident response on an operational level is performed by CERT-FR, which is part of ANSSI.

Among the analyzed EU Member States, the centralized approach is the exception. Most countries are following a cooperative, decentralized approach. However, France is not the only country, which displays characteristics of a centralized approach. Other examples of countries with characteristics of the centralized approach are the Czech Republic (central authority) and Germany (comprehensive legislation).

5.3.2 Decentralized Approach

The decentralized approach is characterized by:

1. Principle of Subsidiarity/Sector-Responsibility:
   Instead of establishing a strong agency with responsibility across all or several critical sectors, the decentralized approach follows the principle of subsidiarity. This means that the responsibility is either in the hands of a sector-specific authority or the companies and operators themselves.

   Therefore, many Member States that fit this profile are lacking a centralized authority, but have placed the responsibility on the sector-specific authorities.
2. Strong Cooperation Between Public Agencies:
   In addition, many Member States have developed cooperation schemes in order to coordinate the work and efforts of the different stakeholders. These cooperation schemes can take the form of informal networks or more institutionalized forums or councils. However, these cooperation schemes only serve the purpose of information exchange and coordination between the different public agencies, but have no authority over them.
3. Sector-Specific Legislation:
   The countries that follow the decentralized approach often refrain from drafting legislation across critical sectors. Instead, the adoption of laws and regulations remains sector-specific and therefore can vary greatly between sectors. See Fig. 5.3.

Fig. 5.3 Decentralized approach

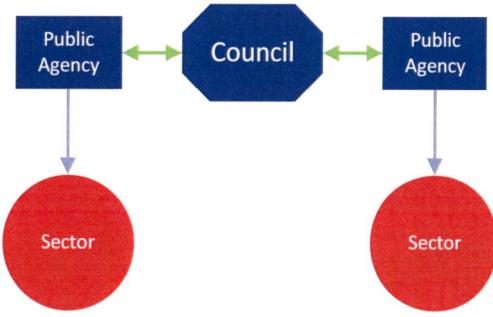

Example

Sweden is a good example for a country that follows a decentralized approach. The country uses a "system perspective," which means that main tasks, such as the identification of vital services and critical infrastructures, the coordination and support of operators, regulatory tasks, as well as measures for emergency preparedness are the responsibility of different agencies and municipalities. Among these agencies are the Swedish Civil Contingencies Agency (MSB), the Swedish Post and Telecom Agency (PTS), and several Swedish Defence, Military and law enforcement agencies (2015c).

In order to coordinate the actions between the different agencies and public entities, the Swedish government has developed a cooperative network comprised of authorities "with specific societal information security responsibilities." This Cooperation Group for Information Security (SAMFI) consists of representatives of the different authorities and meets several times a year to discuss issues related to national information security. SAMFI's subject areas are mainly to be found in political-strategic areas and cover topics such as technical issues and standardization, national and international development in the field of information security, or management and prevention of IT incidents (Swedish Civil Contingencies Agency (MSB) 2015).

Another example for a country that displays characteristics of this profile is Ireland. Ireland follows a "doctrine of subsidiarity," where each Ministry is responsible for the identification of CII and risk assessment within its own sector. Legislation remains sectorial and exists mainly for the energy and telecommunications sector. Other examples are Austria, Cyprus, Finland, and Switzerland.

5.3.3 Co-regulation with the Private Sector

The co-regulation approach is characterized by:

1. Institutionalized Cooperation with the Private Sector:
   A typical form of institutionalized cooperation between the public and private sector is public-private partnerships (PPPs) which are usually based on contractual agreement between the parties. Public and private actors can provide different resources to the

Fig. 5.4 Co-regulation with the private sector

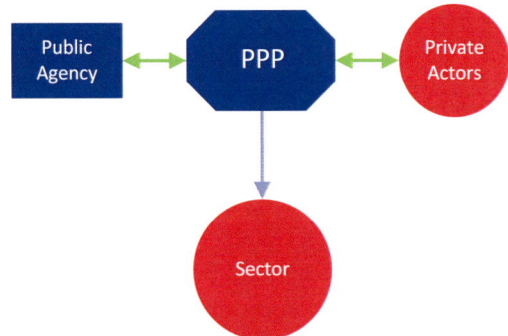

partnerships: For example, the government can offer political legitimacy and funds, while private actors can add special expertise and efficiency. Through PPPs, governments have the possibility for regulation in areas where it is lacking expertise.

2. Horizontal Relationship between Public and Private Parties:

Although not exclusively, PPPs are often characterized by a horizontal relationship between the public and private parties, meaning that both are on equal footing and make joint decisions. The decision making process is based on negotiations rather than hierarchical command structures [18].

In some cases, this kind of relationship is also reflected in a compliance structure which is not based on a strong regulatory framework and enforcement mechanisms but is based on voluntary action and trust. See Fig. 5.4.

Example

An example for co-regulation can be found in the Netherlands. The major cybersecurity agency is the National Cyber Security Centre (NCSC). It is set up as a central information hub and a center of expertise for cybersecurity within the National Coordinator for Security and Counterterrorism (NCTV). The NCSC consists of several partnerships between public and private actors, such as various Information Sharing and Analysis Centres (ISACs) and the ICT Response Board which analyses the situation during a large-scale IT crisis or threat. The NCSC emphasizes that cooperation with private stakeholders is based on equality and trust.

In addition, the Dutch Cyber Security Council offers advice on a strategic and political level. The council is comprised of representatives from different Ministries, academia, and the private sector and has a strong public-private character. Participation in the various Information Sharing and Analysis Centres is based on confidentiality, meaning that members are not forced or obligated to share information with the other participants but do so on a voluntary basis. All representatives are expected to respect the mutual agreement and treat information on threats, risks, and other sensitive issues in a confidential manner. Legal obligations and requirements in the Netherlands tend to be stronger for the telecommunications and nuclear sector. However, Dutch companies are not obliged to report security incidents and a lot of incident notification is done voluntarily.

The different profiles illustrate specific forms of governance, which are defined by their shared characteristics. The profiles are not exclusive types, but are rather points on a spectrum. For example, the centralism of governance displayed by a country will vary, and while some countries can be described as either centralized or decentralized, others fall in between these two points. The same is true for the degree of private-sector involvement. Thus, the selected approach and the relating governance structure should be clearly defined and reflected in the national cybersecurity strategy together with the expected benefits.

5.4 Challenges

Based on the Good Practice Guide on NCSS, this section presents a few of the main challenges and obstacles that countries were facing during the development and implementation of their NCSS.

Establishing effective cooperation between public stakeholders was named by many countries as one of the major challenges they were facing during the implementation of their NCSS. Cooperation in the area of cybersecurity is new for some public stakeholders in many cases and requires a change of habits. A major challenge for cooperation are different interests and competencies between the relevant public stakeholders. In addition, the problem is often caused or compounded by the lack of a clear governance structure.

Establishing trust between public and private stakeholders was named by many countries as one of the main obstacles in the implementation of core objectives, such as establishing baseline and security requirements, incident reporting, or establishing public private partnerships. The establishment of trust is a process, which requires extensive dialogue as well as time and effort. Companies are reluctant to report security incidents, because of potential loss of reputation. In addition to general trust issues, cultural factors can add to the problem. In countries with liberal market policies and a negative perception of security issues, this can lead to a reluctance of stakeholders to take advice from professional bodies. Because of the lack of knowledge, no actions are taken to increase cybersecurity.

Ensuring adequate resources. An important obstacle in the implementation of NCSS can be a lack of resources. Some of the cybersecurity public authorities named the lack of funding and financial resources as a problem for the execution of measures. Resource-intensive objectives, for example, the development of cryptographic algorithms, require adequate financial and personal resources. In addition, some public agencies named a general lack of skilled personal as a main challenge.

Promotion of a common approach and awareness for privacy and data protection is lacking and is a major obstacle in countries where the NCSS is focused around business and growth for digital business. Furthermore, the lack of a joint approach regarding the flow of data inside the EU and towards the situation of the confidentiality of communication of citizens and business is perceived as a hurdle. Furthermore, gaining awareness for information security proved difficult in countries, in which the public perceives security as intrusive surveillance and an unwanted intrusion on personal rights and liberties. This can lead to a lack of understanding of the cross-cutting nature of digital services and of pervasiveness of cybersecurity and insufficient cooperation and coordination between national data protection authorities and information security authorities.

The implementation of vulnerability and risk analysis was challenging for certain countries, because in the beginning the focus was set too broad and the approach was focusing on an integral risk management, which proved to be too challenging as well as resource and finance intensive. The scope of risk analysis needs to be chosen carefully; otherwise, the design can be too comprehensive and cover too many risk areas. This can result in too capital and resource intensive measures.

5.5 ENISA's Contribution to NCSS

ENISA has published several studies regarding the steps of each phase. The first guide published in 2012, "National Cyber Security Strategy: An implementation Guide" [19] describes phase 1 and phase 2 of the lifecycle and provides advice and recommendations on how to develop and implement a NCSS. After that, ENISA focused on Phase 3, the evaluation and adjustment of strategies for continuous improvement. To this end, ENISA published an evaluation framework for cybersecurity strategies in 2014 [20]. The guide aims to be a pragmatic evaluation tool and presents a set of possible key performance indicators (KPIs).

In 2016, ENISA published an updated version of a "Good Practice Guide on NCSS" [21]. This guide complements the findings of the 2012 report with current examples and good practice. It also includes information on the evaluation and adjustment. The evaluation part is more concrete as it analyzes and evaluates existing NCSS of EU Member States and EFTA countries. Moreover, ENISA has created online tutorial videos [22] and an online interactive map [23] that lists all the NCSS in the EU. The map presents all the developed NCSS of EU MS together with their strategic objectives and examples of good practices.

5.6 The Next Steps for NCSS

The European Commission understands that there are still gaps across the EU, notably in terms of national capabilities, coordination in cases of incidents spanning across borders, and in terms of private sector involvement and preparedness. Below we present some recommendations on how to overcome the emerging challenges, based on knowledge obtained all these years working on the topic.

Include the Provisions of the NIS Directive into the NCSS
The European Parliament adopted the Network and Information Security Directive in July 2016 and one of its objectives is to improve EU Member States' national cybersecurity

capabilities. For this purpose, EU Member States are required to develop and adopt a NCSS and implement several additional measures.

Consider Prioritizing Certain Critical Sectors

The NIS Directive names seven critical sectors, which EU Member States should consider when planning and implementing cybersecurity measures. We recommend that EU Member States, which are in an early stage of development or implementation of their NCSS, should consider whether certain sectors could be prioritized. Reasons to prioritize certain sectors are an already high degree of awareness for cybersecurity or available resources. A focused approach rather than a "cover everything" approach can provide several advantages. EU Member States can make fast progress by rolling out cybersecurity measures in sectors, which are already in an advantageous position. These sectors can provide a positive example, when approaching stakeholders of other critical sectors at a later stage.

Promote Innovation Through the NCSS

Many MS have already started creating strategies on emerging technologies like Big Data, Internet of Things (IoT- Industry 4.0), Cloud Computing as they could support critical systems. The NCSS should not only cover the existing landscape but also have a vision for a secure use of ICT in the borders of the country. Moreover, cybersecurity is not only a priority for the public or the private sector; start-ups and SMEs (the backbone of the EU economy) are also affected from the national strategy. Thus, it would be beneficial to include this long-term vision and need for investment early on in the strategy.

Align or Integrate CIIP with NCSS and National Emergency Management Structures

Critical information infrastructure protection is an integral part of a NCSS. With regard to incident and emergency response, there is also a conceptual and often organizational overlap between CIIP and existing national emergency management structures. We recommend aligning CIIP with the national cybersecurity strategy and the national emergency management structures to avoid ambiguities relating to lines of responsibilities, duplication of structures and measures, and waste of resources. Roles and responsibilities of public agencies and private entities in case of cybersecurity incidents should be clearly defined.

Extend the Scope of International Cooperation Beyond International Exercises

Currently, international cooperation between EU Member States is mostly limited to joint cybersecurity exercises. International cooperation in other areas, such as sharing of threat information, early warning systems, research and development, or training and education programs are less developed. However, since cybercrime is a transnational problem, member states can highly benefit from cooperation in these areas. In addition, multinational corporations can benefit from standardized baseline requirements across the European Union. Therefore, it is recommended to extend the scope of international cooperation beyond cybersecurity exercises.

Create a Common Understanding of Concepts and Terminology

A lack of cooperation between public sector agencies and between the public and the private sector has been named as one of the major obstacles for effective implementation of NCSS. One of the main barriers for cooperation between the different entities is different understandings of concepts and definitions with regard to cybersecurity. Therefore, it is recommended for convergence of concepts to create a common terminology across public and private sector entities. ENISA has conducted several studies [24] around the development and use of security classification taxonomies to enhance cooperation both between the EU MS and the Network and Information Security communities.

Approach and Involve Stakeholders at an Early Stage of Development

Certain EU Member States were successful in increasing the willingness of private actors for future collaboration by approaching them at an early stage of development of their NCSS, new laws, or measures. When drafting new legislation or developing a new or updated NCSS, it is recommended to engage private stakeholders at an early stage of the process.

Gain Situational Awareness

Situational awareness with regard to cybersecurity includes knowledge about the current threat situation, activities of relevant public agencies, and the overall status of the implementation of measures with regard to the NCSS. In order to gain a comprehensive overview of the national cybersecurity situation, close collaboration and input is needed from relevant public agencies, such as cybersecurity agencies, law enforcement units, CSIRTs, ministry of interior, ministry of defense, and sector-specific regulatory authorities.

Develop Requirements and Measures Per Critical Sector

EU Member States need to ensure that operators of critical infrastructure, and providers of essential services take necessary measures to secure their information systems in appropriate manners. Member States can guide the efforts of the private sector by developing generic requirements and measures for critical sectors. Generic requirements provide private companies with the flexibility to tailor measures to their specific needs and conditions.

Enhance Capabilities of Public and Private Actors

After baseline requirements for public and private actors have been defined, existing capabilities need to be evaluated in order to identify gaps and deviations. Where existing capabilities do not conform to national or EU requirements, they need to be developed or enhanced. When evaluating and enhancing capabilities, all four areas from prevention, detection, reaction, and deterrence should be considered. Capabilities do include operational measures and technical means but also extend to management systems and necessary resources such as manpower, knowledge, financial resources, and a legal foundation.

Governments can actively support capacity building by publishing national standards, designing cybersecurity capability maturity models, promote, and encourage the exchange of knowledge and best practices, providing support and assistance through official agencies or through state subsidies.

5.7   Conclusions

Currently all 28 European Union Member States have published an NCSS. Of these, several have also updated their strategies since their first edition. National Cyber Security Strategies aim to ensure that Member States are prepared to face serious risks, are aware of their consequences, and are equipped to appropriately respond to breaches in the network and information system.

On September 13th 2017, Jean-Claude Juncker in his State of the Union Speech confirmed a European Commission proposal for a regulation on the future of ENISA called the "Cybersecurity Act."

In this context, the newly proposed mandate reinforces ENISA role and enables the Agency to better support the Member States in implementing the NIS Directive and to counter particular threats more actively by becoming a center of expertise on cybersecurity certification.

It is proposed that the current role of ENISA should be strengthened in the many areas where the Agency is already providing added value, and new areas where support is needed will be added, in particular the NIS Directive, the review of the EU Cybersecurity Strategy, the creation of sectorial ISAC, the upcoming EU Cybersecurity Blueprint for cyber crisis cooperation and ICT security certification.

References

1. Directive (EU) 2016/1148: http://eur-lex.europa.eu/legal-content/EN/TXT/?uri=uriserv:O J.L_.2016.194.01.01.ENG&toc=OJ:L:2016:194:TOC.
2. NCSS map: https://www.enisa.europa.eu/topics/national-cyber-security-strategies/ncss-map.
3. ENISA (2012): Good Practice Guide on National Contingency Plans for CIIs, available on request.
4. https://www.enisa.europa.eu/topics/trainings-for-cybersecurity-specialists/online-training-material
5. IT-Security Act (2015).
6. Federal Chancellery of the Republic of Austria (2013): Austrian Cyber Security Strategy. Available online at https://www.enisa.europa.eu/activities/Resilience-and-CIIP/national-cyber-security-strategies-ncsss/AT_NCSS.pdf.
7. French Senate (2013): *Loi de programmation militaire 2014–2019.*
8. ENISA (2010): The new user's guide: How to raise information security awareness. Available online at http://www.enisa.europa.eu/activities/cert/security-month/deliverables/2010/new-users-guide.
9. See, for instance, the proposal for a regulation 'on electronic identification and trusted services for electronic transactions in the internal market'.
10. http://ec.europa.eu/information_society/policy/esignature/eu_legislation/regulation/index_en.htm.
11. McKinsey Quarterly (2014): The rising strategic risks of cyberattacks. Available online at http://www.mckinsey.com/business-functions/business-technology/our-insights/the-rising-strategic-risks-of-cyberattacks.
12. ENISA's web page on baseline capabilities for national / governmental CERTs: http://www.enisa.europa.eu/activities/cert/support/baseline-capabilities.

13. Center for Cyber Security (2015): The Danish Cyber and Information Security Strategy. Available online at https://www.enisa.europa.eu/topics/national-cyber-security-strategies/ncss-map/national-strategy-for-cyber-and-information-security/at_download/file.
14. ENISA (2011): Cooperative Models for Effective Public Private Partnership – Good Practice Guide. Available online at https://www.enisa.europa.eu/publications/good-practice-guide-on-cooperatve-models-for-effective-ppps/at_download/fullReport.
15. ENISA (2016): Stocktaking, Analysis and Recommendations on the protection of CIIs. Available online at https://www.enisa.europa.eu/publications/stocktaking-analysis-and-recommendations-on-the-protection-of-ciis.
16. Secretariat of the Security and Defence Committee (2013): Finland's Cyber security Strategy. Available online at https://www.enisa.europa.eu/activities/Resilience-and-CIIP/national-cyber-security-strategies-ncsss/FinlandsCyberSecurityStrategy.pdf.
17. Stocktaking, Analysis and Recommendations on the protection of CIIs: https://www.enisa.europa.eu/publications/stocktaking-analysis-and-recommendations-on-the-protection-of-ciis.
18. For a good practice guide on Cooperative Models for Effective PPPs see: https://www.enisa.europa.eu/activities/Resilience-and-CIIP/public-private-partnership/national-public-private-partnerships-ppps/good-practice-guide-on-cooperatve-models-for-effective-ppps.
19. National Cyber Security Strategies: An Implementation Guide: https://www.enisa.europa.eu/publications/national-cyber-security-strategies-an-implementation-guide.
20. ENISA (2014): An evaluation framework for Cyber Security Strategies. Available online at https://www.enisa.europa.eu/publications/an-evaluation-framework-for-cyber-security-strategies.
21. ENISA (2016): NCSS Good Practice Guide. Available online at https://www.enisa.europa.eu/publications/ncss-good-practice-guide.
22. NCSS Training Tool: https://www.enisa.europa.eu/topics/national-cyber-security-strategies/national-cyber-security-strategies-training-tool.
23. ENISA (2017): National Cyber Security Strategies Map. Available online at https://www.enisa.europa.eu/topics/national-cyber-security-strategies/ncss-map.
24. ENISA Report on Information Sharing and Common Taxonomies between CSIRTs and Law Enforcement Agencies: https://www.enisa.europa.eu/news/enisa-news/enisa-report-on-information-sharing-and-common-taxonomies-between-csirts-and-law-enforcement-agencies.
25. ENISA study into taxonomies for incident detection and prevention: https://www.enisa.europa.eu/news/enisa-news/enisa-study-into-taxonomies-for-incident-detection-and-prevention.

Die Allianz für Cyber-Sicherheit: Netzwerke schützen Netzwerke

6

Stefan Wunderlich

Zusammenfassung

Die rasante technologische Entwicklung der letzten Jahre und das ebenso dynamische Fortschreiten der Digitalisierung aller Lebensbereiche von Smart Home bis zu Industrie 4.0 eröffnen Wirtschaft und Gesellschaft enorme Chancen. Damit einher gehen neue und immer komplexere Herausforderungen in Sachen Informationssicherheit, denen einzelne Unternehmen oder Organisationen letztlich nicht mehr allein wirksam entgegentreten können. Vor diesem Hintergrund verfolgt die Allianz für Cyber-Sicherheit, eine 2012 begründete Initiative des Bundesamtes für Sicherheit in der Informationstechnik (BSI), das Ziel, einen offenen Informations- und Erfahrungsaustausch unter allen wichtigen Akteuren im Bereich der Cyber-Sicherheit in Deutschland zu ermöglichen, um im Zusammenschluss die Widerstandsfähigkeit des Wirtschaftsstandorts Deutschland gegenüber Cyber-Angriffen zu stärken.

6.1 Warum eine Allianz für Cyber-Sicherheit?

Wie der aktuelle Bericht des BSI zur Lage der IT-Sicherheit in Deutschland [1] zeigt, bleibt die allgemeine Gefährdungslage hierzulande weiterhin auf hohem Niveau angespannt. Nicht nur bleiben die bekannten Einfallstore für Cyber-Angriffe wie Sicherheitslücken in Softwareprodukten, Malware oder Phishing unverändert kritisch bestehen. Bedingt durch das rasante Fortschreiten der Digitalisierung und die damit einhergehende zunehmende Vernetzung entsteht zudem eine ganz neue Qualität der Gefährdung, nicht zuletzt durch Entwicklungen wie das Internet der Dinge und Industrie 4.0. Hierdurch

S. Wunderlich (✉)
Bundesamt für Sicherheit in der Informationstechnik (BSI), Bonn, Deutschland
E-Mail: stefan.wunderlich@bsi.bund.de

© Springer Fachmedien Wiesbaden GmbH, ein Teil von Springer Nature 2018
M. Bartsch, S. Frey (Hrsg.), *Cybersecurity Best Practices*,
https://doi.org/10.1007/978-3-658-21655-9_6

65

entstehen für Cyber-Angreifer immer neue Angriffsflächen und Möglichkeiten, Informationen auszuspähen, Geschäfts- und Verwaltungsprozesse zu sabotieren oder sich auf Kosten Dritter kriminell zu bereichern.

Unternehmen bewegen sich dabei in einem Spannungsfeld zwischen Innovationsdruck und Sicherheitsbedürfnis. Eine möglichst schnelle Einführung neuer Technologien verspricht nicht nur Wettbewerbsvorteile, sondern in der Regel auch Kosteneinsparungen und höhere Effizienz. Dem steht das erhöhte Risiko von Sicherheitsvorfällen gegenüber, die eine massive Schädigung des Unternehmens bedeuten können – sei es durch Abfluss oder Manipulation von kritischen oder vertraulichen Informationen wie Kunden- oder Entwicklungsdaten oder Ausfallzeiten bei kritischen Geschäftsprozessen oder in Logistik und Produktion. Diesem Dilemma stehen dabei nicht nur große Unternehmen und Betreiber Kritischer Infrastrukturen gegenüber. Die Digitalisierung hat heute alle Branchen von der Automobilindustrie bis zum Handwerk erfasst und betrifft Unternehmen jeder Größe. So liegt gerade im Mittelstand und bei den so genannten „Hidden Champions" als wichtigen Innovationstreibern der deutschen Wirtschaft wertvolles geistiges Eigentum, das diese zu begehrten Zielen potenzieller Cyber-Angriffe macht.

Angesichts der zunehmenden Komplexität von Angriffsmethoden und der Professionalisierung der Angreifer wird es für einzelne Akteure immer schwieriger, wirksame Sicherheitskonzepte zu entwickeln und umzusetzen. Damit die Erhöhung der Cyber-Sicherheit am Standort Deutschland gelingen kann, ist ein kooperativer Ansatz gefordert, der Anwender in der Wirtschaft, IT-Hersteller und Cyber-Sicherheitsexperten aus IT-Branche und Forschung an einen Tisch bringt. Genau zu diesem Zweck hat das BSI 2012 die Allianz für Cyber-Sicherheit als Plattform für den aktiven, offenen Austausch von Expertenwissen und Erfahrungen rund um das Thema Cyber-Sicherheit ins Leben gerufen.

6.2   Die Allianz für Cyber-Sicherheit

Nach einer fünfmonatigen Pilotphase fiel der Startschuss für die Allianz für Cyber-Sicherheit (ACS) im Rahmen der IT-Sicherheits-Leitmesse it-sa im Oktober 2012. Gegründet wurde die Initiative vom Bundesamt für Sicherheit in der Informationstechnik (BSI) in Zusammenarbeit mit dem Bundesverband Informationswirtschaft, Telekommunikation und neue Medien e.V. (Bitkom). Die Allianz für Cyber-Sicherheit erwies sich von Anbeginn als Erfolgsmodell und ist inzwischen auf eine Teilnehmerzahl von über 2700 Unternehmen und Institutionen angewachsen. Die Federführung für die Aktivitäten der Initiative liegt dabei heute beim BSI.

Mit der Allianz für Cyber-Sicherheit löst die nationale Cyber-Sicherheitsbehörde BSI einen zentralen Bestandteil ihres Leitbilds ein, Informationssicherheit in der Digitalisierung durch Prävention, Detektion und Reaktion für Staat, Wirtschaft und Gesellschaft zu gestalten. Das BSI setzt in diesem Zusammenhang auf den offenen Dialog mit Partnern aus der Wirtschaft, um gemeinsam Lösungsstrategien zum Schutz vor Cyber-Angriffen zu erarbeiten und wirkungsvoll umzusetzen. Ausgehend von der Prämisse, dass Cyber-Sicherheit als eine notwendige Bedingung für eine erfolgreiche Digitalisierung verstanden werden muss, unterstützt die Behörde mit den vielfältigen Angeboten der Allianz für Cyber-Sicherheit die deutsche Wirtschaft dabei, das Niveau der Informationssicherheit im Unternehmen zu erhöhen und sich wirksam gegen Cyber-Bedrohungen und IT-bedingte Produktivitätsausfälle zu schützen. Als Grundlage hierfür wird unter anderem der vom BSI entwickelte IT-Grundschutz empfohlen, eine bewährte Methodik für den systematischen Aufbau eines dem individuellen Schutzbedarf angemessenen Managementsystems für Informationssicherheit (ISMS) in Unternehmen und Behörden.

Als herstellerunabhängige, nicht-kommerzielle Institution bietet die Allianz für Cyber-Sicherheit eine neutrale Plattform für den Austausch vertrauenswürdiger Informationen – bereitgestellt von Experten des BSI und ACS-Partnern – und für einen vertraulichen Erfahrungstausch zwischen den Teilnehmern aus Wirtschaft und Forschung. Thematisch werden dabei alle Aspekte der Cyber-Sicherheit von der Awareness bei Mitarbeitern und Geschäftsführung bis zu praktischen Maßnahmen für Prävention, Detektion und Reaktion abgedeckt.

Über die Aktivitäten der Allianz für Cyber-Sicherheit hinaus stellt das BSI zudem noch weitere für Unternehmen relevante Informationsangebote zur Verfügung. Zu nennen sind hier beispielsweise die Ressourcen für Betreiber Kritischer Infrastrukturen (KRITIS) und die an Endanwender gerichteten Informationsangebote im Portal „BSI für Bürger". Die dort veröffentlichten praktischen Empfehlungen können nicht zuletzt bei der Sensibilisierung von Mitarbeitern wertvolle Dienste leisten.

6.3 Struktur der Allianz für Cyber-Sicherheit

6.3.1 Die Teilnehmer

Die Teilnahme an der Allianz für Cyber-Sicherheit steht Unternehmen jeder Branche und Größe mit Sitz oder Niederlassung in Deutschland offen, ebenso wie Verbänden, Hochschulen, Forschungseinrichtungen, Kommunen und kommunalen Einrichtungen sowie Behörden. Voraussetzung für die kostenfreie Teilnahme ist die Unterzeichnung einer Vertraulichkeitsvereinbarung sowie die Benennung eines dezidierten Ansprechpartners. Stellten anfangs die Hersteller von IT-Sicherheitslösungen und Anbieter entsprechender Beratungs- und Dienstleistungen den größten Anteil der Teilnehmer, sind heute die Anwender, die ihre Netzwerke und unternehmenskritischen Daten gegen potenzielle Angriffe absichern müssen, mit einem Anteil von 55 Prozent am stärksten vertreten (siehe Abb. 6.1 und 6.2).

6.3.2 Partner

Einen wichtigen Beitrag zum Erfolg der Initiative leisten die rund 100 Partner der Allianz für Cyber-Sicherheit. Diese engagieren sich in Form von regelmäßigen Partnerbeiträgen aktiv für das gemeinsame Ziel, die Cyber-Sicherheit in deutschen Unternehmen zu erhöhen. Typische Partnerbeiträge sind Fachartikel und Whitepaper zu aktuellen Security-Themen, Workshops, Schulungs- oder Beratungsangebote sowie Penetrationstests und

Abb. 6.1 ACS-Teilnehmer
nach Unternehmensgröße

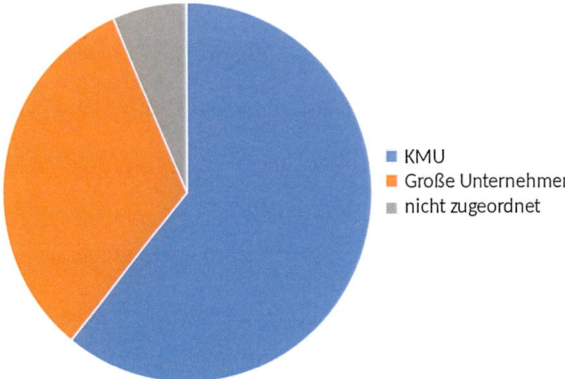

- KMU
- Große Unternehmen
- nicht zugeordnet

Abb. 6.2 Segmentierung
ACS-Teilnehmer

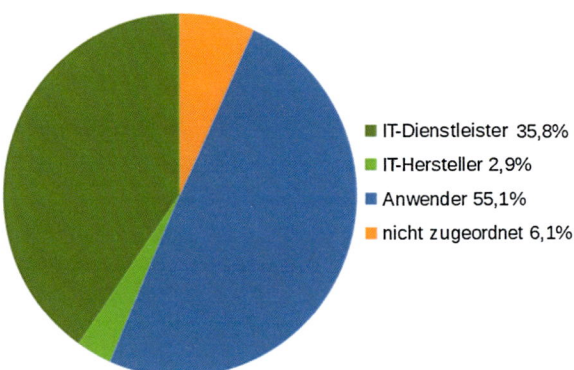

- IT-Dienstleister 35,8%
- IT-Hersteller 2,9%
- Anwender 55,1%
- nicht zugeordnet 6,1%

Sicherheitsanalysen. Alle diese Angebote werden Teilnehmern der Allianz für Cyber-Sicherheit kostenfrei zur Verfügung gestellt.

Bei den Partnern handelt es sich in der Regel um Anbieter von Sicherheitslösungen/-dienstleistungen oder Internet-Infrastrukturbetreiber, die bereits über eine hohe Fachkompetenz im Bereich Informationssicherheit verfügen. Ihre Beiträge ermöglichen es einer breiten Gruppe von Anwendern, von dem bestehenden, praxisnahen Fachwissen der Partner zu profitieren. Gleichzeitig eröffnet sich für den Partner die Möglichkeit, den Austausch über sein Fachthema zu fördern, Feedback zu erhalten und sein Netzwerk zu erweitern.

6.3.3 Multiplikatoren

Um den Bekanntheitsgrad der Initiative zu steigern und zusätzliche Aufmerksamkeit für ihre Aktivitäten und Angebote zu erzielen, arbeitet die Allianz für Cyber-Sicherheit mit einer Gruppe von aktuell rund 55 Multiplikatoren zusammen. Diese verbreiten die Inhalte und Ziele der ACS im Rahmen ihrer Gremien- oder Öffentlichkeitsarbeit und tragen damit zur Erhöhung der Reichweite bei. Multiplikatoren der Allianz für Cyber-Sicherheit sind Institutionen aus dem sogenannten Dritten Sektor wie Verbände, Kammern, Vereine, Initiativen und Netzwerke sowie Vertreter aus der Medienbranche.

6.4   Die Angebote der Allianz für Cyber-Sicherheit

Die Angebote für Teilnehmer der Allianz für Cyber-Sicherheit lassen sich in die drei Bereiche „Informationen erhalten", „Erfahrungen austauschen" und „Know-how erwerben" gruppieren. Eine stets aktuelle Übersicht über die Aktivitäten und Angebote der Initiative bietet die Website https://www.allianz-fuer-cybersicherheit.de/. Neben einem öffentlichen Bereich umfasst diese auch einen geschützten Bereich, über den vertrauliche und exklusiv für ACS-Teilnehmer bestimmte Inhalte bereitgestellt werden. In einem zweiten geschützten Bereich erhalten geheimschutzbetreute Organisationen oder Institutionen im besonderen staatlichen Interesse (INSI) Zugriff auf zusätzliche Informationen mit höherer Vertraulichkeitsstufe. Ankündigungen und Neuigkeiten rund um die Allianz für Cyber-Sicherheit werden darüber hinaus über einen regelmäßigen E-Mail-Newsletter für Teilnehmer, den Twitter-Kanal der Allianz für Cyber-Sicherheit (@CyberAllianz) sowie die XING-Gruppe der Allianz für Cyber-Sicherheit verbreitet (siehe Abb. 6.3).

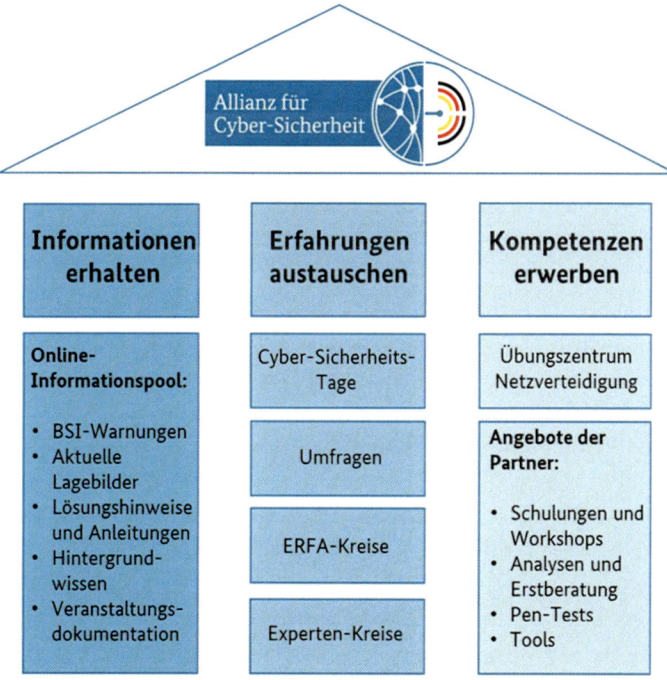

Abb. 6.3 Die Angebote der Allianz für Cyber-Sicherheit

6.4.1 Informationspool

Über die Website der Allianz für Cyber-Sicherheit können Unternehmen auf aktuelle Warnmeldungen des BSI sowie Analysen, Good Practices und Handlungsempfehlungen zu den wichtigsten Aspekten der Cyber-Sicherheit zugreifen. Das Themenspektrum reicht von Empfehlungen zur sicheren Konfiguration verschiedener Betriebssysteme über Netzwerk- und Anlagensicherheit im industriellen Umfeld bis hin zu Empfehlungen zum reaktiven Umgang mit Sicherheitsvorfällen. Der Fokus liegt auf praxisnahen und handlungsorientierten Informationen, die Unternehmen dabei unterstützen, sich auf professionelle Weise gegen aktuelle Cyber-Bedrohungen zu schützen.

Der Informationspool umfasst aktuell rund 350 Dokumente und wird kontinuierlich weiter ausgebaut. Die Inhalte richten sich dabei nicht nur an Techniker, sondern auch an Anwender und Entscheider, da die Erhöhung des Sicherheitsniveaus letztlich nur als ganzheitlicher, unternehmensweiter Prozess gelingen kann.

Informationen des BSI zur Cyber-Sicherheitslage

- **Warnmeldungen**: In besonders relevanten Fällen erstellt das das Nationale IT-Lagezentrum des BSI ausführliche Cyber-Sicherheits-Warnungen. Teilnehmer der Allianz für Cyber-Sicherheit können diese im Warnmeldungs-Archiv im geschützten Bereich der ACS-Website einsehen. Für INSI-Teilnehmer besteht zusätzlich die Möglichkeit mit einem Notfallkontakt in den E-Mail-Verteiler für Warnmeldungen aufgenommen zu werden
- **Regelmässig Lageberichte**: Exklusiv für Teilnehmer der Allianz für Cyber-Sicherheit stellt das BSI die monatlich erscheinenden Lageberichte des BSI IT-Lagezentrums zur Verfügung. Diese beinhalten Statistiken, Hintergrundinformationen und Analysen zu Themen und Vorfällen aus dem jeweiligen Berichtszeitraum.
- **Themen-Lagebilder**: Die vom BSI zusammen mit IT-Sicherheitsexperten erstellten Themenlagebilder stellen die aktuelle Gefährdungslage in Bereichen wie Advanced Persistent Threats, DDoS, Exploit-Kits, Identitätsdiebstahl oder Ransomware dar. Diese geben Sicherheitsverantwortlichen konkrete Handlungsempfehlungen sowie Fakten und Statistiken zur Sensibilisierung und Aufklärung an die Hand.

Fachartikel und Whitepaper von Partnern

Neben den Veröffentlichungen des BSI bringen regelmäßig auch ACS-Partner ihr Fachwissen in Form von Artikeln oder Whitepapers in den Infopool ein. Aktuelle Partnerbeiträge behandeln dabei so vielfältige Themen wie den Schutz vor Ransomware, Tipps zur Datenbanksicherheit, den sicheren Umgang mit Druckern und Multifunktionsgeräten, Empfehlungen zur Entwicklung sicherer Webanwendungen oder IT-Sicherheit in der Produktion für KMUs.

6.4.2   Erfahrungsaustausch

In Unternehmen und Forschungseinrichtungen ist eine Fülle von Fachwissen im Bereich Cyber-Security vorhanden, das häufig im Haus verbleibt. Gleichzeitig fühlen sich viele Organisationen, die vielleicht erst am Anfang der Entwicklung eines IT-Sicherheitskonzepts stehen, von der Komplexität der Cyber-Bedrohungslage überfordert. Eines der Hauptziele der Allianz für Cyber-Sicherheit besteht daher darin, durch verschiedene Veranstaltungs-formate eine Plattform für den Dialog von Experten und Anwendern zu schaffen, damit geeignete Cyber-Sicherheitslösungen gemeinsam und aus dem gegenseitigen Austausch heraus vorangetrieben werden können.

Cyber-Sicherheits-Tage

Seit 2013 bieten die Cyber-Sicherheits-Tage als Leitveranstaltung der Allianz für Cyber-Sicherheit Teilnehmern die Gelegenheit, ihr Wissen zu IT-Sicherheits-Themen auszu-bauen und sich mit Gleichgesinnten zu vernetzen. Die Cyber-Sicherheits-Tage finden mehrmals im Jahr an wechselnden Orten statt. Jeder Termin ist dezidiert einem Themen-bereich gewidmet. Das Themenspektrum reicht dabei von der Sicherheit in industriellen Steuersystemen (ICS), in der mobilen Kommunikation oder im Internet of Things bis zu Cloud-Security oder Cyber-Sicherheit im Handwerk.

Erfahrungs- und Expertenkreise

- **Erfahrungskreise**: ERFA-Kreise unter dem Dach der Allianz für Cyber-Sicherheit bieten interessierten Teilnehmern die Gelegenheit zum zwanglosen fachlichen Aus-tausch. In regelmäßigen Treffen können Teilnehmer in überschaubarer Runde offen Fragen der Cyber-Sicherheit diskutieren und voneinander lernen. Die ERFA-Kreise werden weitgehend von den Mitgliedern selbst organisiert. Bisherige ERFA-Kreise widmeten sich Themen wie Awareness, Distributed Denial of Service (DDoS)-Angrif-fen und Management-Sensibilisierung. Ideen für Erfahrungskreise zu neuen für Unter-nehmen relevanten Themenfeldern können im Dialog mit interessierten ACS-Teilneh-mern entwickelt werden.
- **Expertenkreise**: Die Expertenkreise dienen dem fachlichen Austausch von Expertin-nen und Experten aus Wirtschaft, Forschung und Behörden. Anders als bei den offenen ERFA-Kreisen handelt es sich um ein geschlossenes Format, d. h. die Teilnahme ist nur auf Einladung möglich. Die erarbeiteten Ergebnisse fließen zum Beispiel in Beiträge zur Lagebewertung oder in Veröffentlichungen zur Cyber-Sicherheit ein, die im Rah-men der Allianz für Cyber-Sicherheit veröffentlicht werden und damit von allen Teil-nehmern genutzt werden können.

6.4.3 Praxis

Ein dritter Baustein für die Erhöhung der Cyber-Sicherheit im Unternehmen sind die häufig praktisch oder interaktiv ausgerichteten Angebote, die ACS-Partner für Teilnehmer der Allianz für Cyber-Sicherheit zur Verfügung stellen. Neben Praxisworkshops und Schulungen zu sicherheitsrelevanten Themen können dies auch Beratungen oder Sicherheitstests (Pentests) für Infrastruktur oder Anwendungen sein. Die Angebote sind in der Regel zeitlich limitiert oder auf eine bestimmte Personenzahl begrenzt, in jedem Fall aber kostenfrei für Teilnehmer der Allianz für Cyber-Sicherheit.

Exemplarisch sei hier das begehrte „Übungszentrum Netzverteidigung" angeführt. Ziel dieser fünftägigen Schulung ist es, die Teilnehmer mit dem erforderlichen Grundwissen für die Verteidigung ihrer Infrastrukturen auszustatten. In verschiedenen Modulen lernen sie Sicherheitslücken und Administrationsfehler in unterschiedlichen Komponenten moderner Netzwerke kennen. In Übungen wird das erlernte Wissen anschließend praktisch wiederholt und eingesetzt. Zum Abschluss des Seminars treten die Teilnehmer in zwei Gruppen im „Wettstreit" gegeneinander an und überprüfen ihr Wissen in einer komplexen Netzwerkinfrastruktur als Verteidiger und Angreifer.

6.5 Fazit und Ausblick

Seit ihrer Gründung 2012 hat sich die Allianz für Cyber-Sicherheit, als gelungenes Beispiel einer Public-Private-Partnership, als anerkannte Plattform für das Thema Cyber-Sicherheit in Deutschland etabliert. Durch ihr umfangreiches Angebot an praxisnahen Hilfestellungen unterstützt sie Unternehmen dabei, schneller auf Angriffe zu reagieren und auf diese Weise unternehmensschädliche Auswirkungen zu mindern. Beispiele für eine gelungene proaktive Unterstützung von Unternehmen waren zum Beispiel im Januar 2014 Warnungen vor einem millionenfachen Identitätsdiebstahl und im Juli 2017 die Kontaktaufnahme zu potenziellen Opfern von CEO-Fraud.

Trotz der bisherigen Erfolge bleibt die Erhöhung der Cyber-Sicherheit am Wirtschaftsstandort Deutschland ein drängendes Thema, nicht zuletzt angesichts der durch den technologischen Fortschritt bedingten neuen Bedrohungsszenarien und der sich kontinuierlich weiterentwickelnden und professionalisierenden Angriffsmethoden. Die Allianz für Cyber-Sicherheit strebt daher eine kontinuierliche Ausweitung der Teilnehmerbasis an, vor allem im Segment der kleinen und mittelständischen Betriebe, um noch breiter für das Thema Informationssicherheit zu sensibilisieren. Geplant ist darüber hinaus die Intensivierung der Zusammenarbeit mit anderen Sicherheits-Initiativen in Deutschland sowie perspektivisch mit Organisationen aus europäischen Nachbarländern.

Literatur

1. https://www.bsi.bund.de/DE/Publikationen/Lageberichte/lageberichte_node.html

Polizei – Klotz am Bein oder Partner in der Krise?

Dirk Kunze

Zusammenfassung

Behörden – besonders Strafverfolgungsbehörden – werden häufig als störend und lästiges Übel empfunden. Insbesondere im Falle eines Cyberangriffs sind dies häufig die letzten Stellen, die man währenddessen in der Firma haben möchte. Welche Chancen sich beim Einbinden einer Strafverfolgungsbehörde bieten können, wie diese mit Firmen gemeinsam an der Lösung eines Cyberangriffs arbeiten und welchen Gewinn beide daraus ziehen können, stellt der Autor am Beispiel des Cybercrime-Kompetenzzentrum des Landeskriminalamtes Nordrhein-Westfalen dar. Er beleuchtet dabei auch einige Vorurteile, die ihm in seiner Arbeit immer wieder begegnen, veranschaulicht aber auch die Grenzen der Kooperation.

Die Frage nach einer Einbindung von Sicherheitsbehörden in Fällen von Cyberangriffen, Datenexfiltration und Sabotage wird überwiegend kritisch betrachtet. Eine Studie des Branchenverbandes Bitkom hat ergeben, dass lediglich ein Fünftel aller betroffenen Unternehmen behördliche Unterstützung in Anspruch genommen hat (Bitkom 2015), siehe Abb. 7.1.

Vielmehr wird versucht, die Krise mit eigenen Mitteln oder mit externen Firmen zu bewältigen. Sicherheitsbehörden stören die Bewältigung der Krise. Sicherheitsbehörden behindern die Wiederaufnahme des Wirkbetriebes und beschlagnahmen alles.

D. Kunze (✉)
Leiter des Dezernats 42 – Ermittlungskommissionen Cybercrime, Cyber-Recherche- und Fahndungszentrum des LKA NRW, Landeskriminalamt NRW, Duesseldorf, Deutschland
E-Mail: dirk.kunze@polizei.nrw.de

© Springer Fachmedien Wiesbaden GmbH, ein Teil von Springer Nature 2018
M. Bartsch, S. Frey (Hrsg.), *Cybersecurity Best Practices*,
https://doi.org/10.1007/978-3-658-21655-9_7

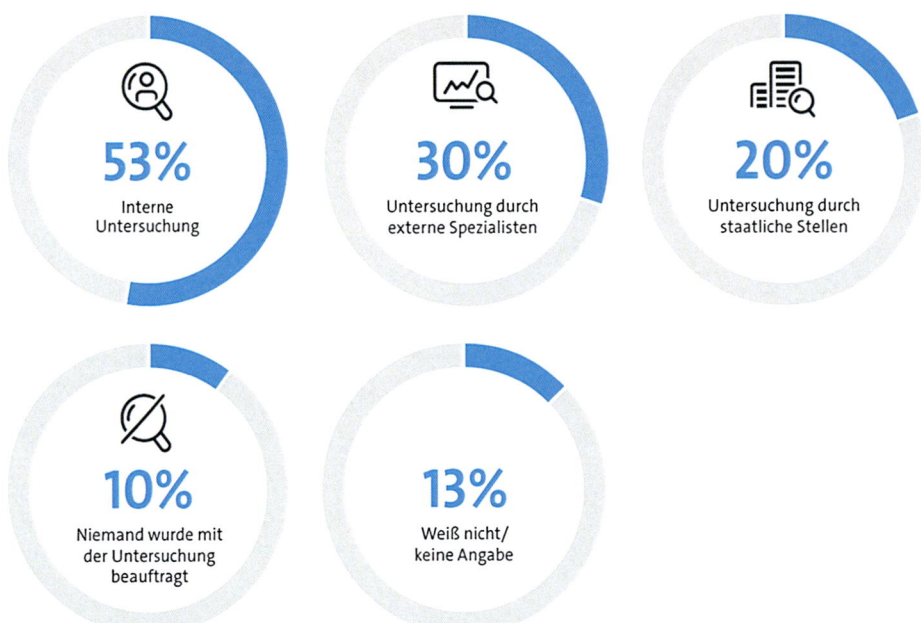

Abb. 7.1   Bitkom Studie Wirtschaftsschutz, 2015

Sicherheitsbehörden tragen zum Imageschaden bei. „Wir sind ein großes Unternehmen mit einem Querschnitt der Bevölkerung als Belegschaft – was wenn einer unserer Mitarbeiter Kinderpornos auf dem Rechner hat?"

Es lassen sich viele Gründe anführen, warum eine Einbindung der Sicherheitsbehörden falsch sein könnte. Aber nicht alle Gründe beruhen auf Tatsachen, andere sind nur Vermutungen und für einige gibt es einfache Lösungen. In diesem Beitrag möchte ich Sie mit der Arbeit der Ermittlungskommissionen des Cybercrime Kompetenzzentrums des Landeskriminalamtes Nordrhein-Westfalen (LKA NRW) vertraut machen und vorstellen, was Sie im Einsatzfall von uns erwarten dürfen – was aber auch nicht.

Cyberangriffe stellen eine größere wirtschaftliche Gefahr dar als Terroranschläge und Staatsbankrotte zusammen und haben ein doppelt so großes Schadenspotential wie Stromausfälle (Lloydd's, 2017). Der Branchenverband Bitkom hat in einer Untersuchung festgestellt, dass 67 Prozent der befragten Unternehmen über 50 Mitarbeitern (n = 609) innerhalb der letzten zwölf Monate Ziel eines Cyberangriffs waren, 14 weitere gaben an, vermutlich betroffen gewesen zu sein. Die restlichen befragten Firmen gaben an, nicht betroffen gewesen zu sein, wobei nicht erkennbar war, ob die Angriffe tatsächlich ausblieben, abgewehrt oder nicht entdeckt wurden. Der frühere FBI-Direktor James B. Comey wird mit den Worten in Verbindung gebracht: Es gibt nur zwei Arten von Firmen – die, die bereits gehackt wurden und die, die es noch nicht gemerkt haben.

Im Fall eines schwerwiegenden Sicherheitsvorfalls ist das Bestreben eines jeden Betreibers von IT-Infrastrukturen, diese schnellstmöglich wieder in Betrieb zu nehmen,

Datenabflüsse zu stoppen und sonstige Auswirkungen möglichst gering zu halten und bei andauernden Bedrohungen diese zu identifizieren und auszuschalten.

Dabei gilt es im Wesentlichen mehrere Szenarien zu unterscheiden:

- Beeinträchtigung von IT-Infrastrukturen, z. B. durch Ransomware
- Datenverluste von Kundendaten
- Datenverluste geistigen Eigentums
- Betrugsversuche
- Manipulation von Produktions- und/oder Qualitätssicherungssystemen (Sabotage)

Diese können sowohl von innen als auch von außen veranlasst sein. Am schwierigsten zu entdecken sind dabei augenscheinlich berechtigte Datenzugriffe. Die Dateizugriffe können durch Mitarbeiter mit den gewährten Berechtigungen, über missbräuchlich erlangte Zugriffsmöglichkeiten oder durch Fehler in der Sicherheitsarchitektur ermöglicht werden. In allen Fällen sind die Datenverluste regelmäßig erst nach der Realisierung auf unterschiedlichen Wegen detektierbar. Dies kann bedeuten, dass man das eigene Produkt plötzlich baugleich auf einer Messe zu einem deutlich günstigeren Preis angeboten bekommt, bei einem Vergabeverfahren scheitert oder gar die eigenen Kundendaten zum Kauf angeboten bekommt.

Insbesondere beim Verlust von Kundendaten ist eine schnelle Reaktion gefragt, um potentielle Folgeschäden und insbesondere einen Reputationsverlust zu vermeiden oder einzudämmen und geltende rechtliche Bestimmungen zu beachten. In diesen Fällen kommen ab dem 26.05.2018 mit Inkrafttreten der Datenschutzgrundverordnung neue Meldeverpflichtungen mit engen Zeitfenstern von 72 Stunden auf Sie zu. Verstöße gegen die Vorschriften der Datenschutzgrundverordnung werden mit bis zu vier Prozent des jährlichen weltweiten Gesamtumsatzes des Unternehmens sanktioniert. Ein weiteres Spielfeld von Angriffen, die häufig mit ausgesprochen effektiver Aufklärung in Social Engineering münden, stellen Betrugsdelikte wie CEO-Fraud, Rechnungsfälschungen, Man-in-the-Middle-Attacken auf (Mail-)Server von Firmen und Firmenkunden dar, die dann dazu genutzt werden, Gelder umzuleiten.

Während diese Vorfälle in der Vorbereitungsphase schwer zu entdecken sind, äußert sich ein Rasomwarebefall durch Anzeigen der Ransomnote und gravierende Funktionsbeeinträchtigungen der betroffenen Systeme sehr deutlich. Häufig ist zu diesem Zeitpunkt der Schaden aber bereits erheblich. In Abhängigkeit von der aufgebrachten Schadsoftware können bereits erhebliche Teile des Netzwerks und weitere Clients befallen und Dateien verschlüsselt sein. Besonders kritisch wird die Situation dann, wenn die Backup-Systeme ebenfalls über das Netzwerk angebunden waren oder die Schadsoftware mit administrativen Rechten im System ausgeführt wurde. In diesen Fällen kann der vollständige Verlust der gesamten Funktionsfähigkeit der IT-Infrastruktur und aller (Kunden-)Daten eintreten. Darüber hinaus stellen Advanced Persistent Threats (APT) oder auch Targeted Attacks eine besondere Herausforderung dar. Ziel dieser Angriffe ist es, so lange wie möglich unentdeckt zu bleiben, sich im Unternehmensnetzwerk auszubreiten und Informationen zu exfiltrieren. Das Eindringen der Täter ins System ist häufig nur schwer oder gar nicht nachzuvollziehen, ebenso die laterale Verbreitung.

Viele dieser Szenarien können Firmen bedrohen. So ist es verständlich, dass die Betroffenen alles daransetzen, den Schaden so schnell wie möglich zu beheben oder im schlimmsten Fall einfach unter den Teppich zu kehren, ohne etwas zu tun außer die Erpresser zu bezahlen. Dass dies wenig erfolgreich ist, musste ein Hotelier in Österreich feststellen. Da ein Austausch oder die Reparatur seiner Systeme teurer war, als andere Maßnahmen, entschloss er sich zu zahlen. Dabei installierten die Täter aber eine Backdoor, über die sie ein weiteres Mal eindrangen, bevor sie zum großen Schlag ausholten und das voll ausgebuchte Hotel übernahmen und alle Schlüsselkarten sperrten (The Local 2017). Mittlerweile hat sich das FBI nach dem Angriff auf das Presbyterian Memorial Hospital am 08.02.2016 dazu entschieden, die deutschen Hinweise zu adaptieren und von einer Zahlung abzuraten.

Diese Informationen, verbunden mit Hinweisen zu einem weiteren Vorgehen und dem effektiven Sichern von Daten können Sie von der Polizei im Rahmen von Vor- und Präventionsgesprächen bekommen, bevor es zu spät ist. Eine enge Kooperation des LKA NRW mit Branchenverbänden wie Bitkom, eco oder „Netzwerker" sollen dazu beitragen, im Rahmen von Präventionskampagnen eine gemeinsame Basis zu schaffen, den persönlichen Austausch zu pflegen und sich kennen zu lernen. Denn eins bewahrheitet sich immer wieder: In der Krise Köpfe kennen! Es wird nicht immer der einzelne Polizist sein, der Ihnen im Falle eines Angriffs helfen wird. Aber sie kennen die Dienststelle und können dort in der Regel die gleiche Hilfe erfahren. Neben diesen Veranstaltungen bieten wir, auch im Rahmen von Messen und Kongressen, immer wieder gerne unsere Unterstützung in Form von Vorträgen an, um am Rande im persönlichen Gespräch eine Basis zu schaffen bzw. Ihnen die Möglichkeit für Fragen zu geben. Es gibt in diesem Rahmen auch Gelegenheit, unerfreuliche Erfahrungen bei der Bearbeitung von IT-Vorfällen zu erfahren. Häufige Ursache dabei ist der Umstand, dass im Krisenfall die falsche Stelle kontaktiert wurde – eine Streifenwagenbesatzung ist in einem breiten Aufgabenbereich hoch qualifiziert, insbesondere was ihre tägliche Arbeit angeht – qualifizierte Angriffe auf IT-Infrastrukturen in Firmen gehören jedoch nicht zum täglichen Aufgabenbereich. Es ist wie in einem großen Konzern: Wenn Sie jemanden aus der Registratur nach einer Fertigungstoleranz Ihres Spitzenprodukts fragen, wird er Ihnen wenig Auskunft geben können. Die Kommissariate Prävention und Opferschutz der 47 Kreispolizeibehörden des Landes NRW sind für Sie gern Ansprechpartner, um Ihnen Hinweise im Umgang mit Angriffen zu geben, aber auch um Ihre örtlichen fachlichen Ansprechpartner im Phänomenbereich Cybercrime zu benennen.

Aber wenn es einmal zu spät ist, wird man diese außerhalb der Bürodienstzeiten nicht erreichen. Aus diesem Grund hat das LKA NRW, wie auch alle anderen Landeskriminalämter, für den jeweiligen Zuständigkeitsbereich eine Zentrale Ansprechstelle Cybercrime (ZAC) eingerichtet. Wir bieten Ihnen den Service einer 24/7 Erreichbarkeit unseres Single Point of Contact. Auch im Falle einer Krise steht Ihnen dieser, genauso wie auch die Mitarbeiter meiner Ermittlungskommissionen, beratend und qualifizierte Erstmaßnahmen treffend zur Seite. Die Besonderheit beim Umgang mit Polizei und Staatsanwaltschaften ist jedoch der Strafverfolgungszwang, dem die Beamten unterliegen. Dies bedeutet, wenn Sie uns eine Straftat schildern, sind wir zum Handeln verpflichtet. Aus diesem Grund bieten wir in Abstimmung mit der für NRW für den Phänomenbereich Cybercrime zuständigen Staatsanwaltschaft Köln und dem BKA (Abteilung 4) eine hypothetische Beratung an – getreu dem Motto: Was würden Sie eigentlich machen, wenn man Ihnen folgenden Sachverhalt antragen würde. Dabei können Sie mit uns den Fall diskutieren, erfahren was wir in diesem konkreten Einzelfall von Ihnen erwarten, welche Informationen wir benötigen und welche Unterstützung wir Ihnen anbieten können und was wir im Falle einer Anzeigenerstattung tun würden. In nahezu 100 % der Fälle erfolgte bislang im Anschluss an eine solche Beratung eine Anzeigenerstattung.

In einem solchen Fall werden wir in der Regel vor Ort mit mehreren Beamten tätig. Um ein Aufsehen bereits zu diesem Zeitpunkt zu vermeiden, fahren wir grundsätzlich mit unauffälligen zivilen Fahrzeugen vor und verabreden mit Ihnen eine Zufahrt/einen Zugang, um nicht bereits zu einem sehr frühen Zeitpunkt unnötige Aufmerksamkeit auf Ihre Firma zu lenken, aber gleichzeitig unsere Spezialausrüstung zu Ihnen transportieren zu können. Ein solcher Einsatz steht in der Regel unter der Leitung eines besonders qualifizierten Beamten im Back-Office, während bei Ihnen vor Ort hoch spezialisierte Beamte und Informatiker aus allen für Ihren Sachverhalt erforderlichen Bereichen tätig werden – Computerforensiker, Netzwerkforensiker, Finanzermittler, Programmierer – um nur eine Auswahl zu nennen. Die Zahl variiert zwischen zwei und mehr als zehn, abhängig vom Sachverhalt. Damit die Einsatzgruppe Ihren Betrieb nicht stört, wird der Einsatzleiter vor Ort unser Vorgehen zunächst mit Verantwortlichen der Geschäftsführung besprechen und ggf. einen Strafantrag einholen. Wissen Sie, wer bei Ihnen in der Firma einen Strafantrag unterschreiben darf?

Anschließend bespricht der Einsatzleiter vor Ort die aufgrund des Schadensbildes erforderlichen Maßnahmen. Darüber hinaus wird er die Geschäftsführung um die erforderlichen Anweisungen an die nachgeordneten Bereiche bitten, die nötig sind, um unsere Arbeit durchzuführen. Ebenfalls hat sich bereits in dieser frühen Phase die Integration in den im Regelfall aufgerufenen Krisenstab der Betroffenen bewährt, da hierdurch Informationsverluste verhindert und zusätzliches Vertrauen aufgebaut wird. Die Teilnahme erfolgt im Regelfall durch maximal zwei Beamte. Die erforderlichen Maßnahmen und im Krisenstab getroffene Entscheidungen werden durch die Mitarbeiter dann in der Regel gemeinsam mit Ihren Technikern oder Verantwortlichen umgesetzt. Sofern die Einschätzung der Situation dies erfordert, werden wir externe Spezialisten zu unserer Unterstützung zuziehen, um möglichst kurzfristig die Ursache Ihres Schadens zu identifizieren und den Zugangs- sowie den Verbreitungsweg festzustellen. Neben der Strafverfolgung hat die Polizei auch immer den Auftrag der Gefahrenabwehr. In Abstimmung mit der sachleitenden Staatsanwaltschaft werden wir Ihnen alle Informationen, die zur Abwehr der Störung als realisierte Gefahr erforderlich sind, unmittelbar zur Verfügung stellen.

Bitte haben Sie Verständnis dafür, dass wir die Angaben Ihrer Mitarbeiter immer auch verifizieren, um Verdeckungshandlungen auszuschließen oder zu erkennen. Dies geschieht vorranging zu Ihrem eigenen Schutz. Es ist schwierig festzustellen, dass eine Firewall nach dem Vorfall neu konfiguriert wurde, wenn alle Protokolle gelöscht wurden. In diesem Fall wird es schwierig, den Zugangsweg festzustellen und bei Ermittlung des Täters nachzuweisen. Dieses Verhalten des Verbergens eigener Fehler ist natürlich und wird durch uns im Einsatz regelmäßig festgestellt, ist aber in diesem Fall wenig sachdienlich, da Beweise im Strafverfahren vernichtet werden und Sie die Sicherheitslücke in Ihrem System nie finden werden und damit eine vollständige Remediation gefährdet wird.

Auch die Angst vor der Sicherstellung Ihrer IT-Infrastruktur und damit vor der Handlungsunfähigkeit Ihres Unternehmens ist unbegründet. Wir benötigen Zugriff auf Ihre IT-Infrastruktur vor Ort, denn wir werden kaum in der Lage sein, Ihr System in unseren Räumen nachzustellen oder wiederaufzubauen. Zudem versuchen wir – sofern möglich – immer, den Schaden im Wirk-Betrieb zu beobachten, zu analysieren, zu dokumentieren und zu sichern sowie Gegenmaßnahmen mit Ihnen zu besprechen. Nur auf diese Art können wir überhaupt gerichtsverwertbar nachweisen, wie der Angreifer in Ihr System eingedrungen ist. Nur so können wir den Ursprung der Infektion, den „Patient 0" finden. Die Sicherstellung einzelner Rechner oder Komponenten zur forensischen Analyse, insbesondere des „Patienten 0", erfolgt in enger Abstimmung mit Ihnen, in der Regel auf Basis einer freiwilligen Herausgabe oder eines Herausgabeverlangens im Sinne der Strafprozessordnung.

Wir arbeiten mit Ihnen zusammen und sind auf Ihre Zusammenarbeit angewiesen. Das bedeutet für Sie gegebenenfalls auch, dass Personalmaßnahmen bis zum Ende der Wiederherstellung unterbleiben müssen. Es erschwert die Arbeit, wenn die einzige Person, die Ihr Netzwerk kennt, weiß, dass sie entlassen werden wird. Und was ist mit Straftaten Ihrer Mitarbeiter, die vielleicht im Rahmen der Ermittlungen aufgedeckt werden? Die werden als genau das behandelt – Straftaten Ihrer Mitarbeiter und nicht der Firma.

Besonders kritisch ist der Verlust von (Kunden-)Daten. Aufgrund der Benachrichtigungspflichten müssen diese ab dem 26.05.2018 innerhalb von 72 Stunden gemeldet werden. Wie schnell ein Unternehmen Opfer eines solchen Innentäters werden kann, zeigt das Beispiel Vodafone aus September 2013 (Focus Online 2013). Damals waren von einem Mitarbeiter eines externen Dienstleisters zwei Millionen Kundendaten entwendet worden. Dem LKA NRW gelang es gemeinsam mit der Staatsanwaltschaft Düsseldorf, die Daten vor einer weiteren Verbreitung in der Schweiz zu sichern und den Täter in wenigen Stunden zu ermitteln. In einem solchen Fall ist die frühzeitige Information der Strafverfolgungsbehörden Ihre einzige Chance, die Verbreitung der Daten zu stoppen. Nur durch das kurzfristige Treffen strafprozessualer Maßnahmen ist es den Strafverfolgungsbehörden möglich, die Daten zu sichern. Solche hoheitlichen Befugnisse stehen privaten Dienstleistern oder Sicherheitsbehörden wie dem Bundesamt für Sicherheit in der Informationstechnik (BSI) oder dem Verfassungsschutz nicht zu. Erfolge aus der jüngsten Zeit zeigen, dass wir – je nach Fallkonstellation und bei uneingeschränkter Kooperation – in der Lage sind, Daten innerhalb von 24 Stunden beweiskräftig sicherzustellen, den Täter zu identifizieren und eine weitere Verbreitung zu verhindern – sofern dies nicht bereits geschehen ist.

Gleiches gilt für abgeflossene Gelder, z. B. im Zusammenhang mit CEO-Fraud oder gefälschten Rechnungen. Insbesondere bei Letzteren werden Sie als Unternehmen in der Regel erst aufmerksam, wenn Sie trotz Zahlung eine Mahnung erhalten. Dann ist es in der Regel auch für die Strafverfolgungsbehörden nicht mehr möglich, die Gelder im Ausland einzufrieren – dafür haben wir in der Regel nur 24 bis 48 Stunden Zeit.

Wie dramatisch die Folgen sein können beweist der Fall der österreichischen Firma FACC AG. Nach dem Abfluss von über 50 Millionen Euro traf die österreichische Finanzaufsicht Maßnahmen gegen die Firma, eine Gewinnwarnung wurde heraus gegeben und sowohl die Finanzchefin als auch der CEO entlassen (Der Standart 2017). Dazu wurde eine Kapitalerhöhung erforderlich. Der Aktienkurs der Firma brauchte 14 Monate, um sich wieder zu erholen (Finanzen.net 2017).

Bei Betrugsdelikten können wir, insbesondere aufgrund unserer guten Kontakte zu Korrespondenzbanken, bei frühzeitiger Anzeige eine Sicherung der abgeflossenen Vermögenswerte initiieren. So ist es dem LKA NRW in enger Zusammenarbeit mit dem Bundeskriminalamt, der Financial Intelligence Unit (FIU), den Korrespondenzbanken und Interpol gelungen, von über 37 Millionen Euro abgeflossenen Geldern im Rahmen eines Ermittlungskomplexes wegen CEO-Fraud über zwei Drittel anzuhalten und zurückzuholen. Dies war nur durch die gesteigerte Anzeigenbereitschaft möglich. Aufgrund der guten und ausgebauten Kooperation war es so auch möglich, mehrere Transaktionen zu stoppen, die der geschädigten Firma bislang nicht aufgefallen waren. Diese Transaktionen im siebenstelligen Bereich konnten nach Anzeige des Geschädigten inzwischen zurückgeführt werden – ohne die Anzeige wären die Gelder innerhalb von 90 Minuten weiter transferiert worden, ohne weitere Chancen der Rückgewinnung.

In diesem Zusammenhang zeigt sich auch ein weiterer wichtiger Bestandteil unserer Arbeit. Sofern Sie uns einbinden, ist eine abgestimmte, gemeinsame Pressearbeit zwischen Ihrem Unternehmen, der sachleitenden Staatsanwaltschaft und dem LKA NRW nicht nur zwingend erforderlich, sie bietet Ihnen im Gegenzug auch die Gewissheit, keine fehlerhaften Informationen zu veröffentlichen, die anschließend revidiert werden müssen. Dabei können Sie auf die Erfahrungen der Staatsanwaltschaft und auf unsere reichhaltigen Erfahrungen auch im Umgang mit den Medien zurückgreifen. Insbesondere im Hinblick auf die Einschränkung von Reputationsverlust konnten wir durch unsere Beratung und abgestimmte Arbeit bislang sehr gute Erfolge erzielen. Der bereits zuvor erwähnte Datenverlust und der Umgang damit sowie die begleitende Öffentlichkeitsarbeit führten zu einer Auszeichnung von Vodafone für den offenen Umgang mit dem Vorfall. Dabei ist uns der Schutz Ihrer Interessen wichtig. Das kann auch bedeuten, dass diese abgestimmte Pressearbeit vorsieht, **keine** aktive Öffentlichkeitsarbeit zu betreiben oder nur abgestimmt und ggf. zeitverzögert auf Presseanfragen zu reagieren.

Deshalb ist es insbesondere zu Beginn eines Incidents wichtig, den Kreis der beteiligten Personen einzuschränken und den Informationsfluss zu kanalisieren. Sie erinnern sich an die Abstimmung über die Anfahrt zu Ihnen vom Anfang meines Beitrages? Dies ist bereits Bestandteil unserer Öffentlichkeitsarbeit bzw. der Kontrolle des Informationsflusses. Wir haben in Abstimmung mit unseren Aufsichtsbehörden Informationskanäle eingerichtet, die es so gut wie ausschließen, dass Informationen unbeabsichtigt in unberechtigte Hände oder an Pressevertreter gelangen. Auch werden wir keine Informationen, die Rückschlüsse auf Sie oder Ihre Firma zulassen, ohne Ihre Zustimmung für Vorträge oder Veröffentlichungen nutzen. Alle hier zitierten Beispiele sind, wie Sie am Quellennachweis sehen können, nur öffentlich zugängliche Daten, die beispielhaft sind und nicht unbedingt von uns bearbeitet wurden. Wir würden uns aber sehr freuen, wenn Sie nach einer erfolgreichen Bewältigung einer Krise Ihre Erfahrungen und Ihren Umgang damit mit uns gemeinsam teilen, damit andere davon lernen können. In der Zeit der fortschreitenden Digitalisierung, des rasanten Wachstums der Technik und hoch entwickelter Angriffsmöglichkeiten haben wir keine Zeit, alle Fehler selber zu machen, wie bereits Winston Churchill in Zeiten analoger Technik feststellte.

Unsere Arbeit ist beendet, wenn im Bereich der Gefahrenabwehr keine unmittelbaren schädigenden Ereignisse mehr drohen und wir auch alle für die Strafverfolgung erforderlichen Informationen erhoben haben. Das heißt auch, dass wir über die Hinweise hinaus, die wir Ihnen aus gefahrenabwehrenden Aspekten geben können, keine Untersuchungen durchführen, die nicht verfahrensgegenständlich sind. Wir werden Sie aber im Rahmen der Zusammenarbeit frühzeitig über alle Schritte informieren und diese mit Ihnen abstimmen. Wir können auch nicht empfehlen, was Sie tun sollen – aber wir können Sie beraten, was wir tun würden. Die Entscheidung liegt dann immer bei Ihnen.

Die Strafverfolgungsbehörden und die Polizei können Ihnen in der Krise wertvolle Unterstützung bieten. Jedoch fußt diese auf Vertrauen und konstruktiver Zusammenarbeit. Diese entsteht nicht auf Zuruf und nicht von jetzt auf gleich. Nutzen Sie die sich bietenden Gelegenheiten und überlegen Sie im Vorfeld, was Sie im Falle eines Falles tun möchten. Denken Sie die Alternativen durch und stimmen Sie die Prozesse und Verantwortlichkeiten firmenintern ab. Auch hierbei können Ihnen die Behörden bereits wertvolle Informationen geben. Wenn Sie sich entschließen, die Behörden einzubinden, stehen wir Ihnen gern beratend und unterstützend zur Seite. Die beste Unterstützung können wir Ihnen bieten, wenn Sie uns schnell einbinden, damit wir frühzeitig Beweise sichern können, echte von Trugspuren unterscheiden und „Verschlimmbesserungen" vermeiden können. Dann können wir Ihnen am besten und am schnellsten helfen und unsere Aufgaben der Strafverfolgung und Gefahrenabwehr erfolgreich wahrnehmen. Je schneller Sie uns einbinden, desto eher können wir Ihnen helfen, den Schaden zu minimieren und gegebenenfalls Geld oder Daten zurückzuholen. In diesem Fall gilt: „Unsere Zeit ist Ihr Geld!"

Literatur

Spionage, Sabotage und Datendiebstahl – Wirtschaftsschutz im Digitalen Zeitalter: https://www.bitkom.org/noindex/Publikationen/2015/Studien/Studienbericht-Wirtschaftsschutz/150709-Studienbericht-Wirtschaftsschutz.pdf abgerufen 09.05.2015

Finanzaufsicht klopft FACC auf die Finger: http://derstandard.at/2000057386938/FACC-muss-fruehere-Bilanzen-aufrollenNach-Brief-der-Finanzaufsicht abgerufen 11.05.2017

Finanzen.net. (29. 10 2017). Von FACC Aktie: http://www.finanzen.net/chart/FACC abgerufen

Focus Online. (12. 09 2013). *Haus nach Hacker-Attacke durchsucht*. Von http://www.focus.de/finanzen/news/tid-33486/cyber-angriff-auf-mobilfunkanbieter-bankdaten-von-zwei-millionen-vodafone-kunden-gestohlen_aid_1098516.html abgerufen

Lloydd's. (30. 11 2017). *Lloyd's City Risk Index 2015–2025*. Von https://www.lloyds.com/cityriskindex/files/8771-city-risk-executive-summary-aw.pdf abgerufen

The Local. (28. 01 2017). *Hotel ransomed by hackers as guests locked in rooms*. Von https://web.archive.org/web/20171006044645/https://www.thelocal.at/20170128/hotel-ransomed-by-hackers-as-guests-locked-in-rooms abgerufen

Comprehensive Cyber Security Approach: The Finnish Model

8

Aapo Cederberg

Abstract

The cyberspace is evolving quickly and becoming a growing challenge for nations, as well as the international community. The key question is how to improve the preparedness of modern societies and how to build new capacities in the cyberspace. Knowledge is crucial to further development, as the weakest links in the chain are the users, be they individuals, companies or governments. Because of the very whole-of-society nature of cyber threats, preparing for and addressing them require strong measures. Multiple countries may enjoy unrivalled power in many of the areas of cyber security, offensive uses included, but may lack the tools necessary to identify in a timely manner threats that nimbly cross all the neat categories and carefully guarded bureaucratic silos. The idea behind a comprehensive security approach is that society's security does not rest on the prowess of traditional security providers such as the police and military alone, but all the key sectors of society have been included in the security planning and implementation process. This whole-of-society aspect of a comprehensive security approach makes the *political leadership* particularly important. Including a wide range of society's players in the security planning and implementation process aims both at increasing capabilities to respond to a wide range of threats, such as cyber threats, that cross sectoral boundaries, but also to secure the vital functions of society that usually demand tight collaboration between several sectors. This efficient collaboration allows wide and efficient mobilisation of society's resources.

A. Cederberg (✉)
GCSP, Colonel (G.S. Ret.), Helsinki, Finland
e-mail: aapo.cederberg@cyberwatch.fi

© Springer Fachmedien Wiesbaden GmbH, ein Teil von Springer Nature 2018
M. Bartsch, S. Frey (Hrsg.), *Cybersecurity Best Practices*,
https://doi.org/10.1007/978-3-658-21655-9_8

8.1   Introduction

The cyberspace is evolving quickly and becoming a growing challenge for nations, as well as the international community. The key question is how to improve the preparedness of modern societies and how to build new capacities in the cyberspace. Knowledge is crucial to further development, as the weakest links in the chain are the users, be they individuals, companies or governments. Cyber threats are now receiving special attention in national security planning circles. This is particularly true in countries that face a current or potential adversary with the necessary capabilities to run hybrid operations. Even further attention should be placed on cyber security if there are major fault lines among the population that can be taken advantage of by the aggressor.

Because of the very whole-of-society nature of cyber threats, preparing for and addressing them require strong measures. Multiple countries may enjoy unrivalled power in many of the areas of cyber security, offensive uses included, but may lack the tools necessary to identify in a timely manner threats that nimbly cross all the neat categories and carefully guarded bureaucratic silos. Smaller countries with less power may have potential in some of the areas of cyber security, such as cyber and information warfare, and key areas of the critical infrastructure like energy, banking etc. However, regardless of their size, all countries can shore up their security against cyber threats. The key in this process is a comprehensive security approach, which aims at intrasocietal security planning instead of settling with a classic intergovernmental approach. The comprehensive security approach demands political leadership, as the whole society should be engaged in security and defensive efforts. This approach needs to be combined with clearheaded vulnerability analysis to understand the potential pressure points in one's own society, access to reliable intelligence and robust counter-intelligence efforts.

While strong and developed autocratic nations may have an advantage on the offensive side of cyber operations, all countries regardless of their position in the international order have an opportunity to organise their cyber security and defences. A credible defensive posture against cyber threats cannot be based solely on military forces and other security providers, because the targets can be located anywhere in society depending on each country's individual vulnerabilities. Thus, cyber defences must be built as a joint action of all stakeholders in society, also including representation from the civil society and the private sector. This model is called a *comprehensive security approach*. The idea behind a comprehensive security approach is that society's security does not rest on the prowess of traditional security providers such as the police and military alone, but all the key sectors of society have been included in the security planning and implementation process. This whole-of-society aspect of a comprehensive security approach makes the *political leadership* particularly important. Including a wide range of society's players in the security planning and implementation process aims both at increasing capabilities to respond to a wide range of threats, such as cyber threats, that cross sectoral boundaries but also to secure the vital functions of society that usually demand tight collaboration between several sectors. This efficient collaboration allows wide and efficient mobilisation of society's resources.

Ensuring the security of society is the key task of every government and the vital functions of our societies must be secured in all situations. As an information society, Finland relies on information networks and systems and, consequently, is extremely vulnerable to disturbances which affect their functioning. An international term for this interdependent, multipurpose electronic data processing environment is the cyber domain. Society's growing information intensity, the increase of foreign ownership and outsourcing, integration between information and communications technologies, the use of open networks as well as the growing reliance on electricity have set totally new requirements for securing society's vital functions in normal conditions, during serious disturbances in normal conditions and in emergency conditions.

In Finland the Cyber Security Strategy is following the main principles of the National Security Strategy, and the Cyber Security Strategy does not change the tasks defined in the Security Strategy for Society. Those strategies are government resolutions which means that the government is having the main responsibility to improve cyber security arrangements in Finland – the whole of government approach is applicable also in cyber security. All ministries have their own role and responsibilities. The Security Committee closely cooperates with other collaborative bodies that coordinate cyber security-related issues as part of their duties. The Cyber Security Centre supports and assists cyber security actors within the scope of its tasking.

The effectiveness of disturbance management will be measured by the successfulness of the pre-emptive measures. Cyber security arrangements in normal conditions will make or break the outcome of cyber incidents in emergency conditions. All administrative branches as well as organisations and companies critical to security of supply are required to make contingency plans against cyber threats. Companies must include cyber preparedness in their normal continuity management planning.

Nevertheless, the cyber domain should also be a possibility and a resource. A safe cyber domain makes it easier for both individuals and businesses to plan and conduct their activities, which in turn boosts the economic activity. A properly working environment also improves Finland's appeal for international investors. In addition to these, cyber security itself is a relatively new and strengthening business area. In addition to the increasing job opportunities and tax revenue, society accrues benefits from this strengthening business sector in many ways. National cyber security is strongly interconnected with the success of Finnish well-being.

8.2   The Cyberworld from the Finnish Perspective

Including only the headlines that we have seen during the last years, we have been witnessing ideologically motivated cyberactivist campaigns launched by individuals, massive online bank breaches by cybercriminal gangs and several alleged cyberespionage operations conducted by state actors. As exemplified by news headlines, the threats against the cyber domain have increasingly serious repercussions for individuals, businesses and society in general. The perpetrators are more professional than before and today the threats even include state actors. Cyber-attacks can be used as a means of political and economic pressure; in a crisis pressure, it can be exerted as an instrument of influence alongside traditional means of military force.

The cyberworld consists of an elaborate and multilayered worldwide information network which comprises ICT networks that are operated by national security authorities, other public authorities, the business community and monitoring and control systems of the industry and critical infrastructure. The increasingly high-speed global cyber domain is bringing states, businesses and citizens ever closer together. While this development has significantly fostered well-being, it has also introduced an entirely new set of risks. When IT equipment and systems are down, the ICT infrastructure crashes or serious cyber-attacks occur; these can result in extremely negative impacts on public services, business life and administration and, consequently, the viability of society as a whole.

Cyber-attacks can seriously disrupt or even paralyse segments of critical infrastructure and society's vital functions. The state or an organisation can be forced to make political, military or financial concessions. The great powers equate cyber-attacks with military action which can be met with any available means. Thus far cyber operations have been interpreted as 'soft measures', for which reason the threshold for using them is estimated to be below that of traditional military operations. The increasing cyber activism, cyber-crime and cyber espionage denote growing activity among states and non-state actors. Consequently, the cyber domain has transformed the traditional power structure, providing even small states and non-state actors with an opportunity to have effectual action. In cyberspace, it is no longer the size and mass that matter; rather, it is expertise. The previously described developments in the cyber domain also impact Finland. Finland is one of the most developed information societies whose functioning relies on various electronic networks and services. Finland has already been the target of cyber operations where the focus was on cyber activism, cybercrime and cyber espionage as well as information manipulation. The international development and especially the hybrid influencing in cyberspace increase the possibilities of new threats being used against us.

The public administration and the business community are continually being targeted by crackers and hackers attempting to exploit system vulnerabilities. That the targets are carefully selected and studied only serves as an indication of the professionalism of the attacks. Sophisticated malware and techniques are increasingly used in these attacks. By exploiting system vulnerabilities, the openness of the cyber domain makes it possible to carry out attacks from all over the world. Such vulnerabilities exist in human action, organisational processes and the ICT technology being used. It is very difficult to protect oneself against complex and sophisticated attacks and to identify or locate the perpetrators.

8.2.1 Cyber as a Game Changer

The rise of a highly interconnected world, involving all walks of life from international politics and global economy to individual citizens, has already proven to be a strategic game changer. Physical world limitations, including the structures and principles that support it, are still in place, but the rules of the cyber domain are bending the old barriers of time and space and changing the structures and the rules of the road. Thus, it can be said that the unfolding world of cyber is very different from the physical world as we know it now. As always, major changes that can be described to be nearly tectonic in their nature will also give a rise to security challenges that the players in the security field from individuals to NGOs and classic security providers such as the police and military need to take into account. The unfolding new connections, interdependencies and ways of operating may bring along many surprises, particularly to those clinging into the old ways of seeing and doing things.

In addition to the newly shaped operating environment, the idea of cyber power can also be considered a global game changer. It can be argued that cyber brings along new asymmetries to power politics. The sheer amount of resources and the size of a country, or established political and military alliances, may not be the most decisive factor when amassing power and applying force in the cyber domain. It becomes increasingly important to be able to efficiently tap into the national and international knowledge pool and get hold of talented individuals. Highly talented individuals can be considered potentially the most dangerous cyber weapon. An ability to amass cyber power, and an understanding how to apply it, offers new possibilities to influence the politics and security in global, regional as well as national levels. Cyber power blurs the traditional concepts of military and civilian security as it also blurs the meaning of national borders. The concept of cyber power is also challenging the traditional administrative lines within societies by having an impact to all sectors and functions of modern societies. The constant process of developing societies also makes them increasingly dependent on digital structures and thus on the world of cyber.

8.2.2 National and International Politics

Cyberspace should not be seen only from a technological perspective but as phenomena that has already had and will continue to have an ever-greater impact throughout our daily lives and functions of our societies. Thus, cyber aspects should be included in an increased manner both in national and international politics. National policies are of the utmost importance in building a solid foundation for the establishment of cyber power and constructing a more cyber-secure society. While the national political manoeuvring space may be limited by international agreements and standards, and most innovation comes from the private sector, national policies still provide the strategic framework for local capability development. National policies and strategies support intergovernmental collaboration and the implementation of educational and industrial policies. National policies are also necessary to support security providers in their work by setting the legal frameworks that define the tools and mandate for security providers. Similarly, national policies define the methods and set the goals for international collaboration. See Fig. 8.1.

Fig. 8.1 Dimensions of cyber security

As the nature of cyberspace is strongly interlinked and international, it is natural that international politics play a major role in defining its functions and uses. While there are various topic areas where cyber-related discussions take place, such as respect for intellectual property rights, innovation and patents; international telecommunications standards; and international law and norms, what is common is that more international, bilateral and multi-stakeholder collaboration is required. All collaboration is based on trust, and at the moment, it appears that genuine globe-spanning trust in cyber matters is lacking. While this will naturally slow down processes to achieve truly international consensus, e.g., on cyber norms, it should not limit more rapid advances taking place in unofficial and official alliances nor bilateral partnerships. The goals for these advances are clear: to increase transparency and build trust among the partners, to improve the exchange of information and to support finding shared goals and agree on common activities to the set goals.

As the financial system and unhindered money flows constitute an important part of the vital functions for both post-industrial and developing economies, it is within the core interests of the governments to ensure the functioning of the financial sector and guard it from external attacks. At the same time, while the global financial system can be seen almost as a global common, there needs to be punitive mechanisms such as sanctions that target the cyber side of financial information networks. These mechanisms allow governments working in collaboration with private organisations to weed out actors that are misusing the global system for criminal purposes.

8.3 The Structure of the Strategy and Main Principles

The government represents the highest level of cyber security management. The government is responsible for providing political guidance and strategic guidelines for cyber security as well as for making the required decisions regarding the resources and prerequisites to be allocated to it. In the Finnish model, each ministry and administrative branch is responsible for cyber security and disturbance management within their mandate.

While the government and its preparedness are of highest importance, it is noteworthy that cyber security relies also on the level of preparedness of the whole society and its elements, such as well-educated citizens, thriving world-class companies and high-quality research and development conducted at universities and other research institutions. Furthermore, in the highly networked world, active international collaboration is necessary to be able to efficiently respond to challenges in the cyber domain. Finnish Cyber Security Strategy defines the key goals and guidelines, which are used in responding to threats against the cyber domain and which ensure its functioning. By following the Cyber Security Strategy's guidelines and the measures required, Finland can manage deliberate or inadvertent disturbances in the cyber domain as well as respond to and recover from them, while ensuring the functioning of society's vital functions at all times.

8.3.1 Cyber Security Strategy: Guiding Vision

We believe that as a small, capable and collaborative country, Finland has excellent chances of rising to the vanguard of cyber security. We have an extensive knowledge base and strong expertise, a long tradition of close public-private cooperation, built on trust, as well as intersectoral collaboration.

The vision of Finland's Cyber Security Strategy states:

Finland can secure its vital functions against cyber threats in all situations. Citizens, businesses and the authorities can effectively utilise a safe and secure cyber domain and the competence arising from cyber security measures, both nationally and internationally. By 2016, Finland will be one of the global forerunners in cyber threat preparedness and in managing the disturbances caused by these threats.

While the vision serves as an overarching long-term term goal, there is a need for managing progress also in a shorter term, particularly because the changes that take place in the cyber domain are constant and fast and their effects are difficult to predict. Cyber threat preparedness, cyber defence and national resilience against cyber threats increasingly require swift, transparent, and well-coordinated action from all parties in society, both individually and collectively.

The cyber domain and the nature of threats highlight the importance of a networked response, which consists of seamless cooperation as well as efficient and flexible coordination of activities. A well-coordinated, distributed response increases the resiliency of society as a whole. See Fig. 8.2.

Threats to society's vital functions and critical infrastructure can emerge independently, concurrently or as a sequential continuum. Whereas their escalation varies in speed and endurance, often they make their impact in a short period of time. Due to the nature of the cyber domain, it is difficult to predict the causes of threats; the actors behind them; their exact targets, goals and scope; or the consequences of their effects. Other risks can also be associated with cyber threats. For example, terrorist strikes causing physical destruction can also incorporate various cyber operations.

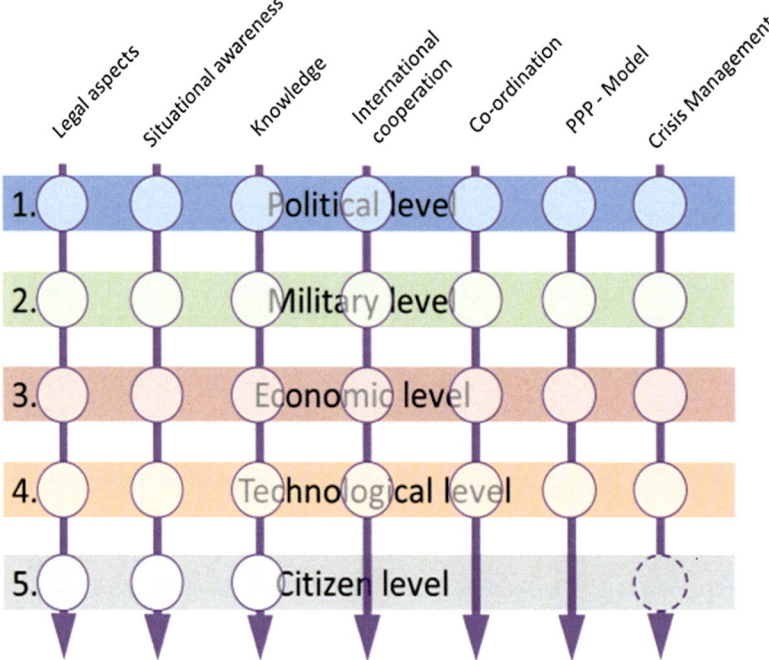

Fig. 8.2 The structure of a comprehensive strategy

For the purpose of preparedness planning, it is helpful if the strategy should include cyber threat models. In the Finnish strategy, they are defined as:

- Cyber activism (cyber vandalism, hactivism)
- Cybercrime
- Cyberespionage
- Cyberterrorism
- Cyber operations: pressure, low-intensity conflict (LIC) or cyber warfare

8.4   Basic Principles of Cyber Security Management

The government comprises the highest level of cyber security management. The prime minister leads the government and is responsible for preparing and coordinating the handling of matters that are the purview of the government. The government is responsible for providing political guidance and strategic guidelines for cyber security, as well as for taking the required decisions regarding the prerequisites and resources allocated to it. In line with the basic principles of the Security Strategy for Society, the competent authorities are responsible for disturbance management and associated contingency planning. Each ministry sees to the legislative process within its administrative domain.

Fig. 8.3 Scope of the cyber security strategy

As the vulnerability of society increases, it is necessary to be able to rapidly start managing sudden disturbances in the cyber domain, aka cyber incidents. Cyber incidents typically have wide-ranging impacts. Therefore, it is necessary to provide the broadest possible inter-sectoral support to the competent authorities, when required. Concurrently, in spite of the disturbances, the viability of society must be secured in an appropriate manner. Cyber incident management will follow the rule of law and the existing division of duties. The same cyber incident management principles that are used in normal conditions will be applied in emergency conditions. The authorities' division of duties and the modi operandi of the cooperation bodies will remain as they are in normal conditions. Situation management will be proactive, and the needed resources will be brought online at once. The competent authority is in charge of operations, supported by intersectoral cooperation bodies.

The other authorities, businesses and organisations will participate in the management of the situation as required. Along with operational activity in situation management, it is essential to ensure the flow of communication and provide sufficient information to the state leadership. Disturbance management will be organised and implemented in accordance with the Security Strategy for Society. In line with the Strategy, the competent authority launches the action needed in managing the disturbance, informs the other authorities and actors as appropriate and brings in the other actors needed for situation management. Cyber incident management encompasses four elements: contingency planning, compilation of a situation picture, countermeasures and recovery. See Fig. 8.3.

8.5 Situational Awareness

The decision-making process of the state leadership and the authorities requires sufficient situational awareness. The various actors need to have reliable, real-time cyber security situation picture on the state of society's vital functions and the disturbances that are affecting them. The real-time cyber security situation picture does not only comprise information from technical monitoring and control, but it also includes an analysis that amalgamates observations, intelligence, other information gathering and previous lessons learned. The National Cyber Security Centre is serving the authorities, the business community and other actors in maintaining and developing cyber security. The Centre's arrangements and services have been implemented as part of the integrated Cyber Security Strategy action plan. The primary service of the Centre will entail the compilation, maintenance and dissemination of the situation picture in close cooperation with its support network. The Cyber Security Centre was founded by merging the functions of the present CERT-FI and the planned GOV-CERT and by earmarking the needed additional resources for its operation. The Centre is supported by a functional network that encompasses all pertinent authorities, businesses and other separately designated actors tasked to prepare and respond to cyber security violations. The planning and implementation of this function have been coordinated with the operations of the Cyber Security Centre.

The Tasks of the Cyber Security Centre:
- Compile and disseminate the cyber security situation picture.
- Compile and maintain a cyber threat risk analysis, in conjunction with different administrative branches and actors.
- Support the competent authorities and actors in the private sector in the management of widespread cyber incidents.

Intensify cooperation and support the development of expertise.

The most important service of the Cyber Security Centre is to compile, maintain and distribute the cyber security situation picture to those who need it. The compilation of the situation picture requires the ability to collect and analyse relevant information and to meet the information requirements of different actors. The integrated situation picture, compiled by the Cyber Security Centre and its support network, comprises a technical situation picture and an evaluation of the total consequences of cyber security violations to the vital functions of society. The Cyber Security Centre and other actors are determining their respective information requirements. The information on vulnerabilities provided to network administrators should become more automatic; whereas, the content of the situation picture intended for the authorities and decision-makers will be developed more towards being an analysis of the consequences of the effects on society's vital functions.

Cyber incident damage control is the responsibility of the authorities and businesses which the disturbance concerns. The Cyber Security Centre can support the lead authority in managing widespread cyber incidents that concurrently impact many authorities or businesses. The Cyber Security Centre generates an overall cyber security situation assessment built on its integrated cyber security situation picture. The purpose of such a briefing is to support the administrative branches in their cyber preparedness arrangements and contingency planning. The Cyber Security Centre monitors and analyses cyber threats and, together with its international partners, generates forecasts on their consequences to Finland. In accordance with its monitoring activities, the threat scenarios of the Security Strategy for Society, the cyber threat scenario and real-time national intelligence information, the Cyber Security Centre alerts businesses and authorities critical to the vital functions of society with intelligence concerning new cyber threats to Finland and heightened cyber threat levels and, upon request, assists them in contingency planning.

8.6   Legal Basis

Cyber security is a new legal phenomenon. Cyber threats are transboundary by nature. The actors behind cyber-attacks may vary and are difficult to identify. Cyber-attack techniques are versatile, rapidly changing and evolving. Cyber security concerns all walks of life, administrative branches and vital functions of society. Basic rights and human rights guarantee the right to privacy and confidentiality of communications. The origin and nature of the cyber threat determine the body of law that will govern the cyber incident. The UN Charter regulates the use of force in state relations. Apart from self-defence in the event of an armed attack or participation in Security Council-mandated military action, the use of force is forbidden. At present, the international community is debating whether cyber-attacks in some situations can rise above the threshold of armed attack, as defined in the UN Charter, justifying a military response by the affected state. Sovereignty also includes responsibility. A state must see to it that its area will not be used in an attack against another state. It must, therefore, also try to prevent attacks beyond its national borders perpetrated by private entities. No rules of engagement exist for cyber operations.

Pursuant to the Constitution of Finland, the public authorities shall guarantee the observance of basic rights and liberties and human rights. Basic rights must also be guaranteed in networks. Increased cyber security may improve, for instance, the protection of the privacy and property of network users. Well-functioning ICT networks can also be seen to promote freedom of speech. More detailed cyber security-related regulation can be found in Chapter 34 of the Criminal Code, the Territorial Surveillance Act, the Readiness Act, the State of Defence Act and the Act on the Defence Forces, the Communications Market Act and the Act on the Protection of Privacy in Electronic Communications. The obligation of the authorities to be prepared to discharge their duties well in all situations, as per the Readiness Act, also includes the development of cyber capabilities. The key requirement for invoking and using the powers of the Readiness Act is subject to the existence of emergency conditions, as provided by law. Pursuant to the justifications of the Act, an attack (according to the definition of emergency conditions) comparable to an armed attack may also mean an attack other than one implemented with traditional means of force. For instance, it can entail an attack against IT systems. An attack can also mean one executed by non-state actors, if it is so organised and wide-ranging that it can be likened to an attack carried out by a state.

Legislation must be developed in such a manner that it adapts to rapidly changing phenomena in cyberspace and makes it possible for the competent authorities in the different sectors to discharge their duties in protecting the sovereignty of the state and the livelihood of the population and in defending society's vital functions against cyber threats. Cyber security must be regarded as an integral element of security. When it comes to the viability of society, it is imperative to find a suitable balance between the legislation and situational awareness, the responsibilities and practices of the authorities and the business community. A stable cyber security situation, for its part, creates a lucrative business environment. In order to repel cyber threats that endanger the security of the state, possible legislative restrictions and hurdles, as well as those arising from international obligations, have been reviewed. Such restrictions and hurdles also include obligations related to data protection and those found to be useful for effective cyber defence purposes that impede the obtainability, disclosure and exchange of information between different authorities and other actors.

When it comes to assessing information gathering and other data processing it has been figured out that the competent authorities should be given better possibilities for gathering information, data processing or being informed of cyber threats and their sources while simultaneously paying attention to basic rights to privacy and confidentiality in electronic communications. With regard to police activities, it is especially important to obtain the powers for intelligence gathering and investigation in order to prevent, identify and fend off cybercrime. The rules on jurisdiction related to cyber warfare and cyber intelligence will be clarified and improved in the near future.

8.7   Education and Awareness of All Societal Actors

Regarding the importance of cyber security to society, the goal has been to improve understanding, competence and skills among the authorities, the business community and the citizens while creating a strong national cluster of cyber know-how. Cyber security research has been developed as part of national top-level research and a strategic cyber security centre of excellence was established in already existing structures. The purpose of the exercises is to improve the participants' ability to identify vulnerabilities in their own activities and systems and to improve their skills and train their personnel. Different sectors regularly test their preparedness when it comes to managing disturbances in vital functions.

The most cost-effective way to advance national cyber security is to improve competence. Increasing cyber risk awareness among the authorities, the business community and the citizens will improve everybody's skills in the implementation of cyber security measures. Top-level research in this field has laid the foundation for developing competence and cyber security systems. The Finnish education system is preserving and developing top-level competence which can be utilised in ensuring and improving the security of society's vital functions in the cyber domain. The learning requirements for cyber security have been included in the curricula of basic education (comprehensive school), vocational upper secondary education, general upper secondary education and higher education. Universities have bolstered the requisites of basic research, applied research and innovation in cyber security, while universities of applied science have improved the preconditions of product development. The level of cyber security research has raised, and its research conditions have been improved so that basic and applied research can continually generate cutting-edge innovation and scientific breakthroughs. Additional cyber/information security courses have been provided by universities and polytechnics. Two professorships in cyber security have been established so far, and, in the long run, the number of professors in cyber security will be increased.

Cyber security skill has also been included to basic military training and special highly skilled cyber units have been set up. They are also utilising the competence of the private sector in their reserve.

8.8   Fighting Against Cybercrime

The police must be able to identify and prevent the planning, financing and directing of terrorist crime and other crimes in networks that endanger society and be able to solve the suspected crimes. Cybercrime has become an extremely noteworthy sector of crime with its consequences extending to states, individuals and businesses alike. IT networks provide an increasingly lucrative and, regarding the risk-benefit and damage ratio, ever more attractive environment for committing crimes that have financial or terrorist goals. Traditional organised crime, too, takes advantage of the vulnerabilities of cyberspace. Cyber-attacks can be employed to endanger society's critical infrastructure and carry out terrorist strikes.

In addition to terrorism, traditional crime, such as fraud, sexual exploitation of children and industrial espionage, is increasing its presence in the cyber domain. The police, being the competent authority in preventing and investigating crime and in taking cases to the prosecutors must improve its cooperation with the other law enforcement authorities. Cybercrime is time and again transboundary in nature and its investigation often demands international police and judicial cooperation. Judicial cooperation is needed, among other things, to obtain evidence or for the extradition of suspects. It must be ensured that the police have sufficient powers, competences and rights to information when it comes to exposing and preventing cybercrime as well as identifying criminals operating in cyberspace and solving these crimes. Also, in Finland new legislation is needed in this regard.

Likewise, it must be ensured that the police have sufficient powers, competences and rights to information when it comes to identifying and preventing the planning, financing and directing of terrorist crime in networks and other crimes that endanger society, including associated propaganda and preparing the ground for criminal activity, and the capability to solve the suspected crimes. The police will establish the competence, capacity and appropriate legal powers to exchange information and cooperate with other law enforcement authorities in preventing, identifying and solving crimes. As part of organised crime prevention, the police shall invest more in cybercrime prevention. The police have developed a national cybercrime prevention centre. In accordance with the order of the National Police Board, the National Bureau of Investigation maintains a situation picture of international and organised crime and is working closely with the National Cyber Security Centre.

8.9   Cyber Defence

Cyber intelligence, cyber warfare and protection capabilities together create a cyber defence capability. The goal has been to customise the capability so that it will best support the Defence Forces' activities in protecting territorial integrity and national defence. Cyber defence have been implemented as an entity which comprises the capabilities of the Defence Forces, other authorities and the rest of society. A credible capability is achieved by cooperating with the other authorities, businesses and universities.

In normal conditions the capability has been improved by networking, exchanging information and participating in joint projects, national and international working groups and exercises. The basic approach will remain unchanged in emergency conditions and during disturbances. Cyber preparedness and threat management are achieved by maintaining and developing various defence and counterattack techniques. Furthermore, an appropriate recovery capability from cyber-attacks has to be established.

Cyber warfare can be used as an instrument of political and economic influence, and in a serious crisis it can be used along with traditional means of military force. The Defence Forces will protect their own systems and networks; they have created and will maintain cyber intelligence and cyber warfare capabilities. The development of these capabilities will be determined by the associated performance requirements and available resources. Emerging cyber threats must be identified early on, and it must be possible to monitor the phenomena and events in cyberspace in real time. This requires the compilation of a cyber situation picture to enable early warning and allow for preparations and the implementation of measures.

The Defence Forces and the Cyber Security Centre are cooperating with each other in the compilation of the cyber situation picture. Intelligence capabilities yield information on networks, including their vulnerabilities, and cyberspace actors, and provide assessments of their ability to carry out cyber operations. The goal of cyber intelligence must establish the kind of situational awareness and intelligence information that protection and cyber warfare require. The national cyber defence capability has been developed by cooperating with other authorities, the business community, the scientific community and other actors. National coordination, the compilation of an integrated situation picture and the provision of the requisites of cooperation demand regularly exchanged information between the different actors.

International cyber defence cooperation has been further intensified between the key actors. Such cooperation is built on bilateral agreements and multilateral collaboration. The purpose of international cooperation is to facilitate the regular exchange of information between different actors and to develop domestic capacities and harmonise procedures. The Defence Forces are providing executive assistance to the other authorities with regard to disturbances caused by cyber incidents. If required, the other authorities will support the Defence Forces in the implementation of cyber defence.

The Defence Forces' capacity to support the other authorities during cyber incidents has been improved. The options and powers related to cyber warfare capabilities have been reviewed. This review has incorporated the applicability and adequacy of existing international law and national regulation and the requirements of cyber defence capabilities. Sufficient powers, competence and the right to information should be given to the Defence Forces for the implementation of national defence, executive assistance, territorial surveillance and crisis management tasks. New legislation is also needed in this area.

8.10   Private-Public Partnership (PPP)

The private sector is having a special role in cyber security. From the standpoint of continuous business growth, it is imperative to retain top-level competence. This will make it possible to take advantage of the cyberworld. Judging by the needs of the business community, one to two educational establishments, together, should retrain at least 10,000 persons in this sector in 2020.

Joint national cyber security exercises are an important tool in improving the resilience of the whole society. Lessons learned from cyber exercises provide concrete information on securing the vital functions of society, including the required level of cooperation. In addition, they provide information on the development needs required by the strategic tasks of administrative branches and organisations and the complete situation of society's preparedness and crisis management capabilities. Exercises help test the basic principles and modi operandi of the Cyber Security Strategy; they also measure the implementation of the Strategy. Preparedness for emergency conditions and serious disturbances in normal conditions must be exercised on a regular basis. This makes it possible to analyse how well cyber security is being achieved in Finland and to continually introduce improvements. Cyber threats have very short mutation cycles and, therefore, all national and international exercises must be frequent and well-organised to effectively support national cyber security.

Successful cyber exercises call for a systematic approach and clear lines of authority. The preparation and implementation of large national cyber exercises must be coordinated in accordance with the principles of the Security Strategy for Society. The implementation of national cyber security entails close public-private cooperation. Businesses and NGOs that are important to society's vital functions should be included in exercises to improve society's comprehensive preparedness.

Public and private sector preparedness for cyber incident management have been trained in national cyber exercises which test the preparedness required by cyber incidents included in the Cyber Security Strategy's threat scenarios and the functioning of management and cooperation arrangements. Exercise themes have incorporated topical challenges caused by changes in the cyber domain. Participation in international multilevel exercises significantly supports the development of national cyber security, know-how in the field, practices, the creation of transnational inter-authority cooperation and a network of experts.

8.11   Critical Infrastructure Protection (CIP)

The functioning of the modern and strongly interconnected global economy is based on an unhindered access to information, energy and financial flows. Unintentional or, in the worst case, intentional disruptions to these flows impact negatively not only the states subjected to the disruptions but the global order as whole. Moreover, as these flows are intertwined, disrupting one of the flows will have a damaging effect on the others, potentially leading to a cascading failure endangering the whole system dependant on the flows. Critical infrastructure protection must be included in every comprehensive Cyber Security Strategy. In the Finnish strategy, the approach is broader when focusing on securing the vital functions of society.

There has been a continuous news stream of cyber-attacks that have included gas pipeline explosions, a disrupted uranium enrichment process, destruction of computing equipment connected to a major energy company and stealing financial information of tens of millions of individuals and companies. These cases exemplify the usefulness of the cyber domain as an attack avenue to the soft underbelly of both societies and private companies alike to further one's political, criminal or other goals. The successful attacks and additional vulnerabilities found during national exercises underline the importance of protecting critical infrastructure and vital streams from cyber threats.

Protecting critical infrastructure from cyber threats is a complicated matter and must be included in national preparedness planning. There are always several open questions that demand to be clarified and solved before cyber threats can be tackled in an organised and efficient manner. Among the core questions are: what are parts of the critical infrastructure that should be specifically prioritised as super critical infrastructure; what are the responsibilities of various actors in the affected space, namely, private sector companies and the governments; and what are the operating areas and mandates of national and supranational entities, such as civilian organisations, the police, military and international regulating bodies?

There are two pressing topics in the field of critical infrastructures (CI). One is to evaluate and develop methods to adequately *identify cross-sector dependencies and interdependencies* and to highlight the potential threats and risks associated to those dependencies. Situational awareness in this context is one of the main goals that will enable further development of risk management and mitigation strategies as well as continuity planning. One of the main enabling factors for situational awareness is an introduction of information sharing platforms that support both national and multinational information sharing in critical infrastructure context. Additionally, overcoming legislative, organisational as well as technological hurdles is necessary to reach this goal.

Another important topic is the *categorisation and prioritisation of the criticality of critical infrastructure services*. Some parts of critical infrastructures are more critical than others to maintain services with reasonable quality or are of special interest in strategic considerations or national security. Some are even called super critical. The risks associated to service failure on these areas of critical infrastructure are exceptionally high. In a crisis or disaster situations, those are the services that require special attention to maintain operations and core functions of the societies. Awareness of the criticality as well as understanding the critical dependencies those services require for operation is a priority to identify and develop adequate measures to have an ability to upkeep operations and reasonably functioning society in all situations, including disasters and man-made crisis.

8.12 International Cooperation

The goal of national cyber security – integrated situation awareness, effective disturbance management and threat prevention – is nationally achieved through active cooperation between different actors. Due to the wide-ranging nature of cyber security, the importance of international cooperation is ever more emphasised. The goal of international cooperation is to exchange information and experiences and to learn from best practices to raise the level of national cyber security.

In the case of Finland, international cyber security cooperation occurs at several levels and fora: in the Nordic context, the European Council and the European Union and in international organisations such as NATO, the OSCE and the UN. Cyber threats are transboundary threats, and, therefore, they require international cooperation in various international fora. Such cooperation provides an opportunity for exchanging information and learning from best practices. Furthermore, it provides benchmarks for the development of national cyber security as part of global cyber security and also increases the interoperability and compatibility of cyber defence. Cooperation is implemented between different organisations and at the international level. When it comes to organisations, the EU and NATO are the key cyber security actors for Finland.

Finland continues its close cooperation with European cooperative organisations such as the European Network and Information Security Agency (ENISA); the European law enforcement agency Europol; the Body of European Regulators for Electronic Communications (BEREC); the European Forum for Member States (EFMS), which is an intergovernmental cooperative forum for the protection of Europe's critical infrastructure; and the European Public-Private Partnership for resilience (EP3R,) which deals with the robustness of ICT systems.

Developing cyber defence cooperation with the EU Military Staff (EUMS), the European Defence Agency (EDA) and NATO will continue. NATO continues to cooperate with its partner countries in responding to new security challenges, supporting NATO-led operations and improving situational awareness. The Organization for Security and Co-operation in Europe (OSCE) aims to improve confidence-building measures for the prevention of cyber conflicts by increasing transparency, cooperation and stability. The goal of this cooperation, built on the OSCE's comprehensive concept of security, is to complement the efforts of other international organisations.

8.13   The Cyber Security Strategy Process

The goal of the national cyber strategy process is to achieve a continuous improvement approach which will make it possible to implement cyber security measures more efficiently and effectively. The strategy process manifests itself as several levels and it includes different phases. The goal was to create a continuous strategy process with parts that regularly repeat and generate continuous improvement. See Fig. 8.4.

Country Analysis
The strategy's analysis phase defines our own position, i.e., our state in relation to the operating environment and its various elements. In the cyber strategy, this translates into an analysis of the cyber threat environment and identification of vulnerabilities in society's vital functions, along with a risk assessment of the ensuing entirety. Moreover, one's own capabilities and shortcomings should be assessed. The operating environment analysis should identify phenomena in cyberspace and assign the necessary definitions for the strategy and catalogue existing national cyber security projects, including related and ancillary projects. Information from other countries' cyber security strategies and best practices

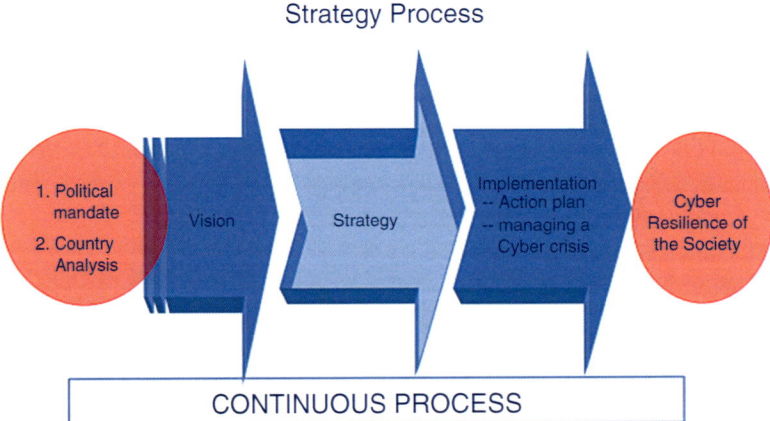

Fig. 8.4 Phases of the strategy process

most suitable for us have been obtained through benchmarking. The analysis resulted in awareness of our standing in both the national and international cyber domain; it also provided further grounds for definitions and reports.

Planning

Planning the cyber security vision, national standards and the cyber security concept was determined in the planning phase. This phase also considered performance requirements, available economic resources and competences. Several options were prepared with regard to achieving the desired end state.

Decision of the Ambition Level

In the decision-making phase several options were compared, and the option leading to the desired end state was selected as well as the national operating concept and the measures it requires. In addition, the desired cyber capabilities and the measures required to create them were defined. Based on country analysis and possible options, the government approved the vision statement which was guiding the rest of the work.

Writing the Strategy

The production phase determines the structure of the Cyber Security Strategy, the way things are presented and the concrete goals and responsibilities of cyber security. The production phase included several iterations in the form of mid-reviews which ensured that the strategic decisions appeared in the text. The drafting of the strategy was completed when it was presented to the commissioning body and was approved by the government.

Implementation and the Action Plan

The strategy must be implemented in a comprehensive manner. For this purpose, an action plan was created which continuously maintains the relevance of the strategy process. In its implementation phase, the strategy must be put into practice by delegating the proposed action of the strategy at the different levels of administration and organisations. A benchmarking and monitoring system for cyber security maturity must be created for the purpose of change management, which can then be used to monitor the success of the process. In Finland the Security Committee is monitoring the implementation of the Strategy. It is also preparing an annual report for the government. The first Implementation Programme for Finland's Cyber Security Strategy, adopted in 2014, comprised all together 74 measures assigned to ministries and partly to individual actors.

The Assessment Identified Significant Impacts Resulting from the Following Measures

- The Government Security Network project and the development of sector-independent ICT tasks
- The National Cyber Security Centre established at the Finnish Communications Regulatory Authority (FICORA) and the development of associated CERT activities

- The Development Project for the Central Government 24/7 Information Security Operations (SecICT) and the related improvement of monitoring and warning
- The Development Project for Jyväskylä Security Technology (JYVSECTEC)
- Cyber security courses organised by the National Defence Training Association of Finland

The new Implementation Programme for 2017–2020 addresses the development of cyber security within the service complex comprising the state, counties, municipalities, the business sector and the third sector in which the individual citizen is the customer. The business community provides most digital services and their cyber security through international service complexes and networks.

Since the publication of the Cyber Security Strategy, the operating environment of the cyberspace has changed because of new service production models and technologies and the new threats directed at them. The Implementation Programme gathers together the public sector's wide-ranging and significant internal projects and actions that aim to improve information and cyber security which are to be implemented together with the business community and NGOs. It also brings them into the public view as coherent and properly delegated processes. When the projects and actions are included in the Implementation Programme, it is possible to regularly monitor and measure their progress, which also provides a better overall situation picture of cyber security development. The measurement methods must be continually developed, especially with regard to monitoring the quality of actions. In addition to the far-reaching measures selected for the Implementation Programme, cyber security is also constantly being improved through other administrative branch-specific actions, as well as by the work associated with developing cyber and information security and continuity management.

8.14   Conclusions

The cyberspace is evolving quickly; it is becoming a growing challenge for nations and the international community. The key question is how to improve the preparedness of modern societies and how to build new capacities in cyberspace. The functioning of the modern and strongly interconnected global economy is based on an unhindered access to information, energy, financial flows etc. Unintentional or, in the worst case, intentional disruptions to these flows impact negatively not only the states subjected to the disruptions but the global order as whole. Moreover, as these flows are intertwined, disrupting one of the flows will have a damaging effect on the others, potentially leading to a cascading failure endangering the whole system dependant on the flows.

The vulnerabilities of modern societies are the main targets of cyber-attacks. In the cyber context, vulnerability is commonly defined as weaknesses related to information technology. The European Union Agency for Network and Information Security (ENISA) specifies vulnerability as "The existence of a weakness, design, or implementation error that can lead to an unexpected, undesirable event compromising the security of the computer system, network, application, or protocol involved." Merriam-Webster describes vulnerability in more general terms as "the quality or state of having little resistance to some outside agent" or "the state of being left without shelter or protection against something harmful."

The security of a modern society in underlining the need to define vulnerabilities and risks in all levels of the whole ecosystem covering people, processes, technology, data, and additionally, governance, where the prerequisite for success or failure initially is laid down. Identifying the need for a common understanding of existing threats, regulations, standards, risks and complexities is essential for securing critical infrastructure and services in the future. It is very much up to the national authorities to decide who is overlooking the security of critical infrastructures and services. Comprehensive situational awareness and understanding, as well as a credible and well-trained action plan, are needed to be able to prevent and defend against cyber-attacks.

Cybercrime has been the trending motivation behind attacks, with hacktivism and cyber espionage being next major motivations. This trend has been continuing also this year. It is interesting to note that a human factor seems to have a much greater role in cyber breaches in the industries. This may indicate problems in security policy compliance, lack of security awareness and training, or simply it may show how strong the existing organisational culture and attitudes in resisting these changes are in the private sector. One can even argue that people are the biggest vulnerability and risk in the critical infrastructure and service ecosystems.

One of the main points is the urgent need for collaboration and need to have coherent **Governance** across the modern societies creating circumstances to support a viable and secure platform for digital future. It must be clear who is overlooking the cyber arrangements comprehensively.

People remain the weakest links. There needs to be an appointed ministry in charge, responsible for cyber security including the coordination among all the stakeholders in the society. An idea of sectoral CERTs could be discussed. The most effective method to improve security is to increase security awareness, education and training, regular audits and penetration testing with social engineering to test real-life security practices and **processes.**

Data is the focal point now and even more in the future in digitalised societies with an advanced utilisation of big data and artificial intelligence (AI). This will require a new approach to data privacy and confidentiality.

Technology and threats keep on developing and only secure-by-design devices and services should be approved to the critical areas of society. There will be new cyber-attacks, new vulnerabilities and threats that are still unknown, which is why a risk-based approach is needed.

Resilience should be emphasised to be able to prevent and quickly recover from any kind of reasonable situations, especially cyber-attacks, even during other **major crises** or when **critical infrastructure** is not fully operating. Despite all countermeasures being in place there remains a residual risk: **insider threats**, unwitting and human errors.

Fig. 8.5 Layers and
dependencies

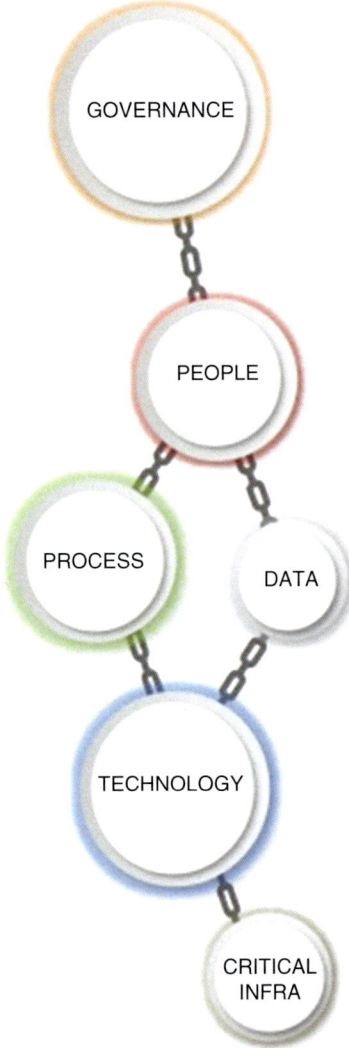

Cyber risks, threat landscapes and vulnerabilities may seem occasionally overwhelming, but well-designed **cyber security is most of all an enabler of reliable and innovative digital environments for people and organisations**. See Fig. 8.5.

Cyberspace is a key domain of hybrid war, and one could even say that without modern cyber capabilities, a full-scale hybrid war would not be possible. Cyber power is indeed a global game changer. It brings along new asymmetries to power politics. All aspects of our lives and functions of our societies will be transformed by all-pervasive and hyperconnected digitalisation. The building of a more resilient society should not be viewed only as an extra burden for already economically struggling Western societies; it is also a wonderful opportunity. The structures that allow a society to respond in an agile manner to hybrid threats also support better understanding and coping with the complex underlying inter-relations that make our modern societies fragile. These defensive structures also help to make our societies more functional, as decision-making processes become more transparent and inclusive.

The "Petnica Group": A Case of Public-Private Partnership for Cyber Security in the Republic of Serbia

9

Irina Rizmal

Abstract

The article presents the case of the development of an informal public-private partnership in cyber security in the Republic of Serbia. Built as a bottom-up initiative and supported by several international organizations working in the field, the public-private framework now poses as a functioning forum for information, knowledge, and experience exchange among key public and private actors. Now officially branded as the *Cyber Security Nexus*, previously known as the informal *"Petnica Group,"* the framework is a recognized body for public-private cooperation. Its regular activities range from debates and consultations on policy development, joint efforts aimed at developing national incident response procedures, and now national cyber security drills as the latest addition. This case of public-private partnership demonstrates how efficient and effective frameworks can be built and how they can contribute to national efforts and capacities even when official, legislative mechanisms are still in their early stages of development.

9.1 Introduction

Public-private partnerships are already recognized as an essential element in establishing and maintaining comprehensive national cyber security frameworks. The necessity of the private sector, academia, and civil society working together is no longer questioned, and only the mechanisms of inclusion of these actors differ from country to country. However, this case study comes from a country that is still in the process of democratic transition from a socialist system and therefore has limited experience with the principles of public-private

I. Rizmal (✉)
DiploFoundation, Belgrade, Serbia
e-mail: irina.rizmal@gmail.com

© Springer Fachmedien Wiesbaden GmbH, ein Teil von Springer Nature 2018
M. Bartsch, S. Frey (Hrsg.), *Cybersecurity Best Practices*,
https://doi.org/10.1007/978-3-658-21655-9_9

partnerships, especially when it comes to matters of national security. The current Law on Public-Private Partnership [1] recognizes such mechanisms merely as cooperation between public and private partners in order to provide: financing, construction, reconstruction, management, and maintenance of infrastructures of public importance.

Normatively, public-private partnerships are thus recognized as serving the purpose of providing services or supporting the public partner with the preconditions needed for providing services to end users within the competence of the public partner. It is precisely for this reason that the establishment of the so-called "Petnica Group," later developing into the Cyber Security Nexus, presented here, deserves to be highlighted and promoted as a notable success story. It has gathered all relevant stakeholders in the national cyber security framework and is already reaping meaningful results.

Now acting as a recognized link between key stakeholders within the national cyber security framework, the informal Petnica Group was primarily established as a result of sheer enthusiasm and will. However, there was also a shared understanding among all the actors involved of the need and benefits that public-private cooperation can foster throughout the process of establishing, developing, and strengthening comprehensive national frameworks. Developing into a more institutionalized body, the Petnica Group has managed to manifest itself in the following three areas: (1) act as a hub for contacts as well as information and experience exchange among key actors, (2) enable strategic planning and testing of coordination, and (3) set forth targeted, feasible suggestions for the legislative and strategic framework of the country governing the field of cyber security. As such, it now poses as a functional public-private endeavor, continuing its efforts in supporting the Republic of Serbia in further establishing, maintaining, and developing the national cyber security framework.

What follows is an overview of the establishment and development phases of the Petnica Group, now institutionalized within the Cyber Security Nexus. Focus areas of action and targeted activities the Group has engaged in over the period since its inaugurtation in 2015 are also listed. Additionally, a glimpse of the legislative and strategic framework in force in the Republic of Serbia and the space it leaves for potential public-private endeavors is provided. Finally, the article underlines general conclusions on the core elements of the Petnica Group's success.

9.2   History: The "Petnica Group"

Following several smaller activities held over the course of 2014, three international organizations commenced a series of joint activities aimed at encouraging the development of a comprehensive framework of cyber security in the Republic of Serbia. To this end, in mid-2015, the Organisation for Security and Cooperation in Europe (OSCE) Mission to Serbia, the Diplo Foundation and the Geneva Centre for the Democratic Control of Armed Forces (DCAF) set up a strategic partnership with the Petnica Science Centre and organized a coordination meeting of stakeholders from both the public and private sector. It soon emerged that Government representatives in charge of the cyber security framework barely knew each other, and communication between representatives of national critical infra-structures and the private sector was sporadic, unsystematic, and in some cases inexistent.

By removing the burden of official institutional settings, the opportunity arose for informal discussion on a variety of pressing issues. This resulted in concrete proposals and recommendations raising ideas for future strategic planning in the field of cyber security policy. The meeting also marked the formation of the so-called "Petnica Group," an infor-mal, multiactor, public-private cooperation group composed of representatives of key national cyber security stakeholders.

In late 2015, the Petnica Group met again at the Petnica Science Centre with the aim of specifically focusing on strategic solutions in terms of establishing a comprehensive, leg-islative national cyber security framework. The discussion was based on conclusions drawn from a foresight scenario planning exercise on the types of Public-Private Partner-ship (PPP) needed and their feasibility in the Republic of Serbia by 2020. Petnica Group members put forward a number of recommendations for institutionalising PPP mecha-nisms in the field of cyber security. These recommendations were compiled by several Group members and presented in the form of a baseline "Guide" on the state of affairs in cyber security in the country [2].

Following the adoption of the Law on Information Security in 2016, the Petnica Group continued its efforts in contributing to the development of a comprehensive national cyber security framework. In late 2016, the Petnica Group met for the third time at the Petnica Science Centre to discuss best practices taking into account expected future trends in cyber security in the Republic of Serbia. The fact that the Petnica Group already has among its members eight out of a total of fourteen members of the working group tasked with developing the country's first national cyber security strategy was a great advantage. They were able to highlight the importance of considering PPPs within the strategic frame-work being developed at the time to relevant decision makers. Eventually, the adopted Strategy for the Development of Information Security embraced the notion of public-private cooperation in cyber security as one of its core priorities.

Building on the contacts and genuine trust developed among its members a myriad of other complementary activities mushroomed since the Petnica Group's establishment. These activities, implemented through cooperation among the Group's members, include:

- Organization of parliamentary hearings on cyber security
- Capacity building programs developed for the Ministry of Interior
- Training programs for young leaders and regional networking events
- Targeted panels on cyber security at the Belgrade Security Forum
- Training and capacity building programs for the Ministry of Foreign Affairs

The Petnica Group members also worked jointly and individually on advocating for resources of donor organizations and institutions to be directed towards filling identified gaps and strengthening the overall capacity of various stakeholders involved in the cyber security framework. Several detailed research reports and policy papers have also been published to date on the state of affairs in cyber security in Serbia and the Western Balkans region. These reports mapped potential solutions based on identified best practice and highlighted possible resources to do so.

Due to its initial success, a private cyber security company, also represented in the Petnica Group, published the second edition of the abovementioned Guide. This is a great example of cross-sector cooperation that has been made possible through the efforts of the Petnica Group. The publication of its third updated edition is in preparation. Finally, the Petnica Group members also actively engaged at each stage of development of the legislative framework governing cyber security, taking part in public hearings and debates on the Law on Information Security itself, as well as submitting suggestions and opinions on draft versions of other relevant normative documents, including complementary bylaws and the Strategy for the Development of Information Security in the Republic of Serbia.

9.3   Legislative Framework and PPP

The Republic of Serbia adopted its first Law on Information Security [3] (hereafter: the Law) on 26 January 2016.

▶   The Law regulates measures for protection against security risks in information and communication systems, responsibilities of legal entities in managing and using information and communication systems and determines the competent authorities for implementation of the prescribed security measures.

Primarily, the Law determines the establishment of a National Centre for the Prevention of Security Risks, which is, according to international practice, a national Computer Emergency Response Team (n-CERT). This body is responsible for rapid response in case of incidents as well as for collection and exchange of information regarding security risks.

▶   The n-CERT is placed within the jurisdiction of the Regulatory Agency for Electronic Communications and Postal Services (RATEL).

Although no official deadline is set for the establishment of the n-CERT, positive steps have already been taken in this direction. The academic sector has been tasked with conducting a comprehensive feasibility study on the establishment of an n-CERT [4], thus recognizing its expertise and potential to contribute to the establishment of national cyber security pillars.

Establishing an n-CERT is also one of the core obligations prescribed by the Directive on Security of Network and Information Systems (NIS Directive) [5] of the European Union. The NIS Directive sets the obligations and principles that all member states of the European Union and all candidate countries, of which the Republic of Serbia is one, should implement.

The Law additionally regulates Information Communication Technology systems (hereafter: ICT) of special importance (operators of essential services) and defines measures for their protection, in accordance with the NIS Directive. It further provides the basis for the regulation of issues pertaining to encryption and compromising electromagnetic emanation which is placed under the jurisdiction of the Ministry of Defence.

The Law also envisions the establishment of an information security inspectorate to oversee the implementation of the Law and complementary regulations by operators of essential services which are placed under the jurisdiction of the Ministry of Trade, Tourism and Telecommunications (MTTT).

Finally, the Law provides for the establishment of a Body for the Coordination of Information Security (hereafter: the Body). This coordinating body is responsible for the cooperation and harmonization of activities aimed at improving information security. Mainly an advisory body, it helps establish a more comprehensive approach to national cyber security by providing for the setting up of expert working groups which may include representatives of public authorities, industry, the academic community, and civil society. As such, the Body represents the political will to establishing PPP in specific aspects of cyber security, a practice generally still approached with caution in the Republic of Serbia.

On 29 May 2017, the Republic of Serbia adopted the Strategy for the Development of Information Security for the period 2017–2020, (thereafter Strategy). The Strategy embraces the need for a more comprehensive approach to national cyber security and lists within its baseline principles the need for establishing permanent cooperation between the public and private sector as a pillar for pursuing strategic priorities. In line with recommendations already previously set forth by the expert community, the Strategy recognizes the possibility for institutionalizing public-private cooperation. The Strategy highlights that establishing public-private cooperation within such a framework enables efficient communication and optimization of planned future activities, that is, timely information exchange and resource sharing. Given the baseline capacities of the public sector, adopting such an approach and understanding as one of the initial priorities for developing the field of cyber security is of great importance.

In addition to creating a comprehensive cyber security framework, such multisector cooperation is also recognized as an opportunity for product, process, and service development aimed at prevention and provision of adequate security levels. In this sense, the Strategy goes as far as to underline the need for institutionalizing cooperation between the competent authorities and academia with active participation of the private sector.

9.4   Continued Efforts: Serbia's "Cyber Security Nexus"

In mid-2017, the establishment of the Serbian Cyber Security Platform – the Cyber Security Nexus was officially announced.

▶ The Cyber Security Nexus is an institutionalized platform for cooperation of a myriad of stakeholders in the field of cyber security in the Republic of Serbia. It aims to support the development of a national strategic, political, commercial, and educational framework through multiactor policy formulation and public-private partnership.

The Nexus builds upon the Petnica Group's efforts. It acts as a permanent cooperation platform enabling dialogue, information, and knowledge exchange, facilitating capacity building and awareness raising, as well as mapping national and international funding opportunities and potential partners from the technical, political, and policy sphere. In addition, through policy research and background studies, the Cyber Security Nexus provides fact-based, tailor-made recommendations, thereby contributing to efforts for improving the overall national policy environment in cyber security. All of these efforts will be in line with global trends and developments. Supported by a standing Secretariat – hosted for the time being at the Diplo Foundation – the Cyber Security Nexus sets out the following key objectives:

• Strengthening the national cyber security framework
• Capacity building of institutions and other actors to enable them to meaningfully contribute to national cyber security
• Developing, organizing, and coordinating specific multi-stakeholder and public-private initiatives in cyber security
• Supporting regional and international cooperation of different types of actors involved in the framework
• Supporting coordination among different CERTs through, for example, the organization of regular cyber drills
• Building academic and professional cyber security competences through the development of academic and research programs and courses
• Nurturing a cyber security culture through awareness raising campaigns and programs targeting all levels of the general public

It was the members of the Petnica Group who agreed that the time was ripe to institutionalize the Group and called for the establishment of a more official framework and a recognizable body. It was jointly agreed on the operational level that targeted, continuous and most importantly, coordinated action was needed in the field of cyber security. It was further concluded that these efforts needed to be directed at higher levels, namely the level of policy decision makers. An officially institutionalized PPP framework was seen as having a stronger voice and greater impact in exerting influence at the political decision making level on cyber security matters.

The Petnica Group, now institutionalized within the Cyber Security Nexus, includes representatives of the:

• Ministry of Trade
• Tourism and Telecommunication (the competent ministry for cyber security)
• Ministry of Interior

- Ministry of Defence
- Ministry of Foreign Affairs
- Office of the National Security Council and Classified Information Protection (NSA)
- Security-Intelligence Agency
- Office of the Prosecutor for High Technology Crime
- Government's Office of Information Technologies and e-Governance
- Regulatory Agency for Electronic Communications and Postal Services (which hosts the n-CERT)
- Innovation Fund
- Telecom providers including Telekom Serbia 'Telenor' and VIP Mobile
- Internet service providers
- Critical infrastructures such as electric power and gas supply and distribution companies
- Serbian National Internet Domain Registry
- Academic institutions including the Faculty of Organisation Sciences and Faculty of Security of the Belgrade University
- International enterprises such as Microsoft and IBM
- Number of representatives of small and medium enterprises and standardization centers as well as several civil society organizations, one of which already hosts its private CERT

Furthermore, Serbia's representatives in both the OSCE Informal Working Group on Cyber Security and the United Nations Group of Governmental Experts on Developments in the Field of Information and Telecommunications in the Context of International Security are among its members.

Thus far, activities within the framework saw over a dozen different national and regional events related to cyber security, gathering over one hundred and fifty participants from key ministries and agencies, members of parliament, representatives of the private sector, academia, civil society organizations, and the media. In addition, international best practice exchange was made possible with partners from Finland, Israel, Montenegro, Poland, Slovenia, Switzerland, and the United States, as well as institutions such as the Belfer Centre for Science and International Relations of the Harvard Kennedy School, Geneva Centre for Security Policy, George C. Marshall Centre's European Centre for Security Studies, European Union Network and Information Security Agency (ENISA) and the International Telecommunications Union.

First National policy-oriented Cyber Drill in the Republic of Serbia

The Cyber Security Nexus gathered its standing members in October 2017 at the Petnica Science Centre to conduct a national cyber drill in order to test existing and developing policies and practice regarding crisis communication in case of a national cyber incident. This tailor-made table-top exercise organized for the Cyber Security Nexus members by its founding organizations, and in cooperation with international consultants, was the first of its kind organized in the Republic of Serbia. The success of the cyber drill has paved the way for further cyber drills in the Republic of Serbia. The results and recommendations gathered throughout the exercise were presented to key government decision makers. It will serve as a basis for their further focus, engagement, and decision making with regard to cyber security.

9.5 Lessons Learnt

PPPs are increasingly recognized in the field of cyber security. A growing number of countries across the globe are embracing cooperative approaches. It has even been discussed to have the private sector taking over certain key elements in the provision of national cyber security in the long term. However, for countries lacking a tradition of public sector openness towards cooperation with the private sector, academia, and civil society, having a functioning public-private partnership at the level of policy proposals is a genuine success. To this end, the now institutionalized Petnica Group is a pioneer of a functional public-private partnership in the Republic of Serbia and the region. It is an exceptional success story for Serbia and a good best practice example in a country with little to no experience in cooperative models, serving as a basis for other countries to replicate the efforts made and establish, or further develop their own national cyber security frameworks. The extent of success it has achieved would not have been made possible without several crucial elements, which are explained below.

Firstly, the main focus of the Petnica Group was on policymaking from the very beginning – an element recognized as lacking attention. It also provided the technical community and operational level staff with the opportunity to highlight normative and policy solutions which can potentially be an obstacle in practice. It served as a bridge between the technical community and policy decision makers, thereby enabling joint solutions. Agreement that this partnership was crucial for the successful development of a comprehensive and functional cyber security framework was vital.

Secondly, the informal nature of discussions encouraged participants to think outside of the boundaries of the institutions they belonged to enabling creative solutions to be found, keeping in mind existing and potential short and long term capacities.

Thirdly, it proved crucial that the operational level staff from institutions and organisations were present during the discussions, which helped highlight the challenges and obstacles they face in everyday operations. This enabled the Petnica Group to put forward joint targeted and plausible policy recommendations. Some of these found their way into the final versions of adopted legislative frameworks.

Fourthly, by understanding other members' jurisdictions and competencies, participants developed a deep knowledge of all key actors in the national cyber security framework. As a result, the Petnica Group acted as a network of potential partners on future projects and an information exchange hub, but also as a potential support network in case of an incident.

Lastly, but perhaps most crucially, continued efforts made within the Petnica Group depended, and still do, on the enthusiasm and openness towards cooperation from all stakeholders involved. As a result, the Petnica Group, now known as the Cyber Security Nexus, is a unique mechanism for a comprehensive, multiactor, and public-private cooperation in the field of cyber security in the Republic of Serbia.

References

1. Law on Public-Private Partnership and Concessions. *"Official Gazette of the Republic of Serbia"* no. 88/2011, 15/2016 and 104/2016.
2. Rizmal, I. Radunovic, V. and Krivokapic, D. 2016. Guide through Information Security in the Republic of Serbia. OSCE.
3. Law on Information Security. *"Official Gazette of the Republic of Serbia"* no. 6/2016.
4. Nešković, A. Krajnović, N. i Nešković, N. 2016. Feasibility study on establishing a national CERT. Department of Telecommunications at the Faculty of Electrical Engineering of the University of Belgrade.
5. Directive (EU) 2016/1148 of the European Parliament and of the Council of 6 July 2016 concerning measures for a high common level of security of network and information systems across the Union. L 194/1.

Nationale Cyber-Strategie: Einbezug der lokalen Ebene in einem föderalen Staat

10

André Duvillard und Melanie Friedli

Zusammenfassung

Dieser Artikel soll anhand des Beispiels des Sicherheitsverbunds Schweiz aufzeigen, wie die lokale Ebene in einem föderalen Staat in die Umsetzung einer nationalen Cyber-Strategie einbezogen werden kann. Dies wird insbesondere am Beispiel des Krisenmanagements im Cyber-Bereich veranschaulicht.

Die Schweiz besteht aus 26 Kantonen, die über eigene politische Institutionen für die Executive, Legislative und Judikative verfügen. Die Kantone sind für alle staatlichen Aufgaben zuständig, die durch die Bundesverfassung nicht ausdrücklich dem Bund übertragen wurden.

10.1 Nationale Cyber-Strategie: 2012–2017

Am 27.06.2012 wurde die Nationale Strategie zum Schutz der Schweiz vor Cyber-Risiken (NCS) durch den Bundesrat verabschiedet. Die Strategie enthält 16 Massnahmen in 7 Handlungsfeldern, die bis Ende 2017 umgesetzt sein müssen. Der Bundesrat verfolgt mit der Strategie die folgenden drei strategischen Ziele:

A. Duvillard (✉)
VBS (Verteidigung, Bevölkerung und Sport), Bern, Schweiz
E-Mail: andre.duvillard@gs-vbs.admin.ch

M. Friedli
Sicherheitsverbund Schweiz, Verteidigung, Bevölkerung und Sport, Bern, Schweiz
E-Mail: melanie.friedli@sif.admin.ch

© Springer Fachmedien Wiesbaden GmbH, ein Teil von Springer Nature 2018
M. Bartsch, S. Frey (Hrsg.), *Cybersecurity Best Practices*,
https://doi.org/10.1007/978-3-658-21655-9_10

- die frühzeitige Erkennung der Bedrohungen und Gefahren im Cyber-Bereich
- die Erhöhung der Widerstandsfähigkeit von kritischen Infrastrukturen
- die wirksame Reduktion von Cyber-Risiken, insbesondere Cyber-Kriminalität, Cyber-Spionage und Cyber-Sabotage.

Die Massnahmen, die umzusetzen sind, richten sich in erster Linie an Behörden der Bundesverwaltung.

Die Umsetzung der Strategie wird durch die Koordinationsstelle NCS, die bei der Melde- und Analysestelle Informationssicherung (MELANI) angesiedelt ist, koordiniert. MELANI ist vom Bundesrat mit dem Schutz der kritischen Infrastrukturen in der Schweiz beauftragt und für die Früherkennung und Bewältigung von Gefahren und die Unterstützung der Betreiber kritischer Infrastrukturen in der Krise verantwortlich.

10.2 Der Sicherheitsverbund Schweiz (SVS)

Der SVS umfasst grundsätzlich alle sicherheitspolitischen Instrumente des Bundes, der Kantone und der Gemeinden. In den Organen des SVS (Operative und Politische Plattform) sind Bund und die Kantone paritätisch vertreten. Der SVS dient der Konsultation und Koordination von Entscheiden, Mitteln und Massnahmen von Bund und Kantonen bezüglich sicherheitspolitischer Herausforderungen, die sie gemeinsam betreffen. Der Fokus liegt deshalb bei Themen im Bereich der Sicherheitspolitik in der inneren Sicherheit. Die Organe des Sicherheitsverbunds Schweiz dienen vor allem der Vermittlung, wenn die Koordination in der Linie nicht zufriedenstellend funktioniert oder keine geeigneten Organisationsformen für die Koordination bestehen. Bei Bedarf setzt die Politische Plattform oder die Operative Plattform temporäre Arbeitsgruppen zur Bearbeitung spezifischer Themen ein. In den Arbeitsgruppen können neben Bundes- und Kantonsvertreter/innen auch Vertreter/innen der kommunalen Ebene sowie aus der Privatwirtschaft Einsitz nehmen.

10.3 Umsetzung der Nationalen Cyber-Strategie mit den Kantonen 2012–2017

Die Nationale Cyber-Strategie ist eine Bundesstrategie und beinhaltet Massnahmen, für deren Umsetzung Bundesbehörden zuständig sind. Sie beinhaltet keine Massnahmen, die Behörden auf lokaler Ebene, wie Kantons- oder Gemeindebehörden, umsetzen müssen, da der Bund den Kantonen in diesem Bereich keine Vorgaben machen kann. Das Thema betrifft die Behörden auf der lokalen Ebene jedoch ebenso, da sie einerseits technisch mit dem Netzwerk des Bundes verknüpft sind und andererseits mit den gleichen Problemen zu kämpfen haben wie Bundesbehörden. Ausserdem steigert die Integration der Kantone die Effizienz der Strategie. Um den Einbezug der Kantone sicherzustellen, beschloss der

Bundesrat, dass der SVS für die Koordination mit den Kantonen bei der Umsetzung der NCS zuständig ist. Der SVS hat 2013 anlässlich seiner jährlichen Konferenz mit den Kantonen Workshops organisiert, um zu besprechen und zu entscheiden, welche Massnahmen der Nationalen Cyber-Strategie mit den Kantonen auf Kantonsstufe umgesetzt werden sollen. Basierend auf den ausgewählten Massnahmen sind vier Arbeitsgruppen gegründet worden, die je etwa zur Hälfte aus Bundes- und Kantonsvertretenden auf operativer Stufe bestehen. Diese vier Arbeitsgruppen werden von einer Fachgruppe gesteuert, die sich aus Kantons- und Bundesvertretenden auf strategischer Stufe zusammensetzt. Ein wichtiges Thema, das sowohl die staatlichen Behörden auf allen Ebenen als auch kritische Infrastrukturen und die Gesellschaft betrifft, ist das Krisenmanagement. Deshalb befasst sich eine Arbeitsgruppe mit dem nationalen Krisenmanagement bei Krisen mit Cyberausprägung. In dieser Arbeitsgruppe nehmen nebst den Bundes- und Kantonsvertretenden auch Vertreterinnen und Vertreter von kritischen Infrastrukturen teil.

10.4   Nationales Krisenmanagement bei Krisen mit Cyberausprägung

Auf Stufe Bund wurde ein Konzept für das Krisenmanagement bei Krisen mit Cyberausprägung erstellt. Dieses Konzept wurde (siehe Abb. 10.1) durch den SVS mit der Ebene der Kantone und kritische Infrastrukturen ergänzt.

In Abb. 10.1 sind auf der linken Seite jeweils die Bundesbehörden und auf der rechten Seite die kantonalen Behörden aufgeführt. In der Mitte befinden sich die kritischen Infrastrukturen. Ergänzend dazu wurde auch eine Struktur für die Ermittlung des Lagebildes im Falle einer Krise mit Cyberausprägung erarbeitet. Siehe Abb. 10.2.

Das Konzept hält fest, welche Organe für welche Aufgaben bei einer Krise mit Cyberausprägung zuständig sind. Nachfolgend werden die wichtigsten Aussagen wiedergegeben.

Ausgelöst durch einen Cyber-Angriff oder Systemfehler oder nicht böswilliges Handeln einer mitarbeitenden Person kann die Integrität und Vertraulichkeit von Informationen verletzt oder die Verfügbarkeit eines Informations- und Kommunikationstechnologie-Systems nicht mehr gewährleistet sein. Das Internet kann als Angriffsvektor missbraucht werden oder selber Ziel des Angriffs sein. Das Spektrum von Cyber-Angriffen reicht von Überlastungsangriffen (Distributed Denial of Service) durch Aktivisten und Erpresser über die Manipulation von Internet-Banking-Vorgängen durch Kriminelle bis hin zur Ausspähung und zu Cyber-Angriffen durch fremde staatliche oder nichtstaatliche Stellen. Denkbar wären etwa Sabotage von kritischen Infrastrukturen oder Angriffe auf die Integrität des Finanzsystems, um das Funktionieren des Systems Schweiz zu beeinträchtigen. Führen diese Herausforderungen im Bereich der Cyber-Sicherheit einzeln oder in Kombination zu einer Eskalation der Lage und bleibt die Cyber-Sicherheit ein wesentlicher Bestandteil der Problembewältigung bei Bund und Kantonen, kann man von einer nationalen Krise mit Cyberausprägung sprechen. Die Beurteilung der Lage, insbesondere der Cyberkomponente, ob es sich um ein technisches Problem handelt oder ob politische Implikationen

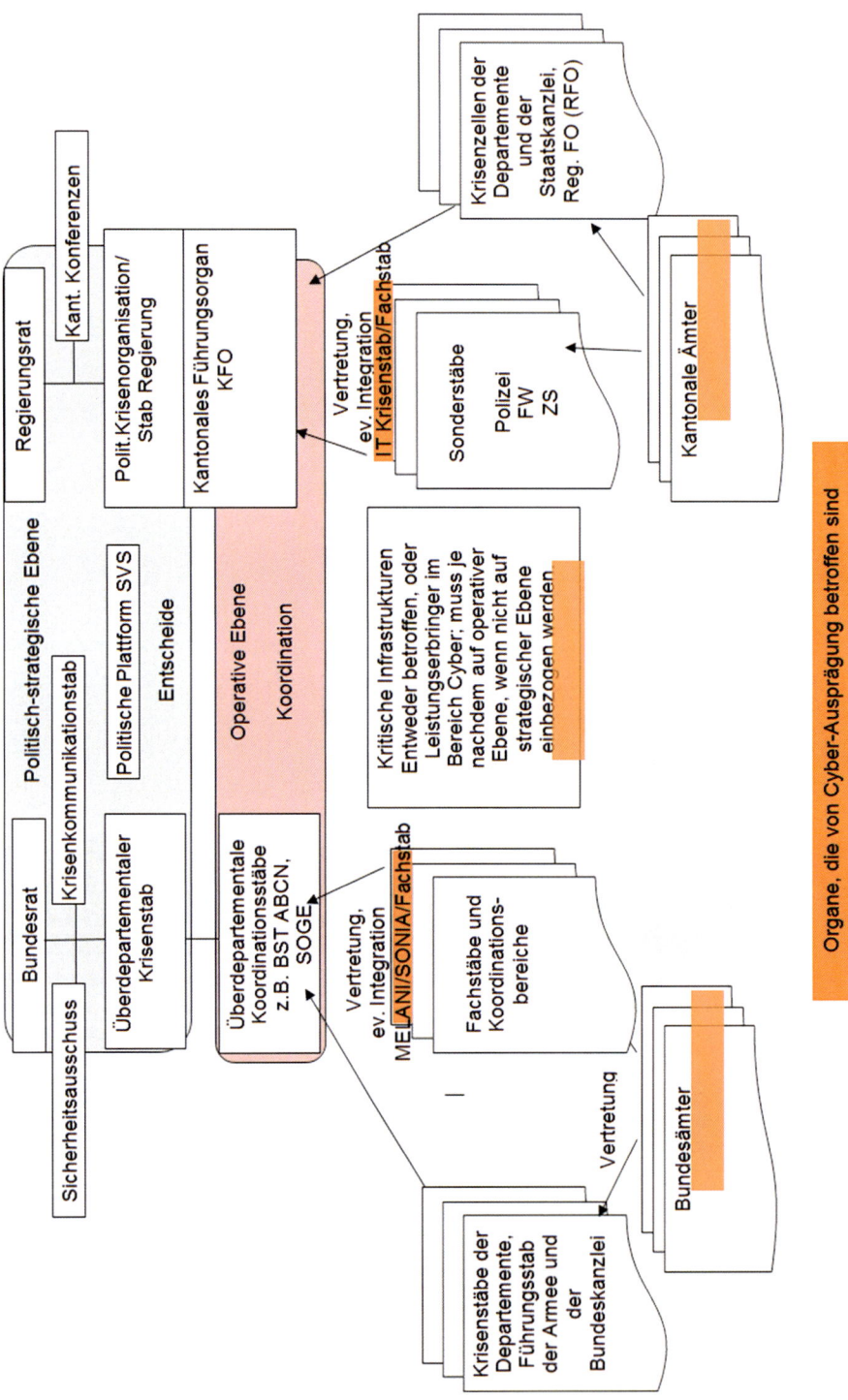

Abb. 10.1 Führungsstrukturen beim Bund und den Kantonen unter Einbezug der kritischen Infrastrukturen

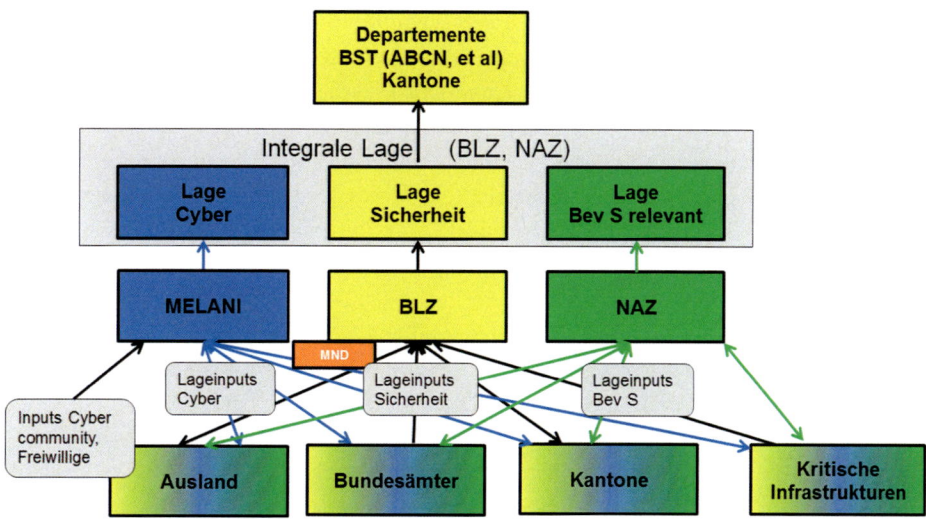

Abb. 10.2 Struktur für die Ermittlung des Lagebildes im Falle einer Krise mit Cyberausprägung

damit verbunden sind und wie gross deren Dimension ist, ist eine erste Herausforderung für die Führung. Ein vollständiges Lagebild zu besitzen ist jedoch wichtig für die Problembewältigung. Gleichzeitig stehen die Führungsverantwortlichen unter hohem Zeitdruck, um adäquate Entscheidungen im Rahmen der Krisenbewältigung zu fällen. Sicherheitspolitisch relevante Krisenszenarien können eine starke Cyberkomponente beinhalten, indem der Missbrauch des Cyberraums wesentlich zur Lageverschärfung beiträgt und die Wiederherstellung der Cyber-Sicherheit zu einer Priorität der Krisenbewältigung werden kann.

Notfall- und Krisenmanagement sind im Gegensatz zum Risikomanagement nicht szenario-, sondern prozessorientiert: Führungsorganisation und Entscheidungsprozesse müssen immer dieselben sein, unabhängig von der Beschaffenheit der Krise. Dies ist insbesondere wichtig, wenn die Reputation, die Handlungsfreiheit oder sogar die Existenz einer Organisation tangiert sind: Es gelten nach wie vor die eingespielten Geschäftsabläufe, und es sind dieselben Personen wie im Alltag, die auf höchster Ebene der Organisation Entscheidungen treffen müssen. Dieser Grundsatz gilt in der Bundesverwaltung, die vom Bundesrat geführt wird, wie auch in den Kantonsverwaltungen, die von den Kantonsregierungen geführt werden. Das allgemeine Krisenmanagement (Führungsabläufe und -prozesse) ist deshalb prinzipiell szenario-unabhängig. Die Führungsstrukturen von Bund und Kantonen bilden aber in einer nationalen Krisenbewältigung einen auf die Bewältigung der Krise zugeschnittenen Führungsverbund, der eine intensive Koordination zwischen beiden Entscheidungsabläufen erfordert. Die an diesem Verbund beteiligten Organe variieren je nach Art der Krise und der von der Exekutive mit der Krisenführung betrauten Instanz.

Prinzipiell szenario-abhängig sind jeweils diejenigen Organe bei Bund, Kantonen und Dritten (insbesondere kritischer Infrastrukturen), die sich mit bestimmten Risiken auseinandersetzen und diese im Alltag überwachen. Sie bilden den themenspezifischen Fachverbund. Die Krisenbewältigung in einer stark vernetzten Gesellschaft erfordert erstens die enge Koordination der Krisenorgane und Entscheidungsträger auf allen Stufen und zweitens die Bündelung des staatlichen und privatwirtschaftlichen Fachwissens. Die Verantwortlichkeiten auf Stufe Bund wie Kantone sind gegeben.

Bei einer Krise mit Cyberausprägung sind die vorhandenen staatlich-privatwirtschaftlichen Partnerschaften zu nutzen, insbesondere sind die Informationen im Rahmen der rechtlichen Möglichkeiten auszutauschen. Ebenso müssen die Fähigkeiten und Mittel der Armee, welche subsidiär zur Verfügung gestellt werden könnten, identifiziert und lagegerecht zur Unterstützung der zivilen Behörden verfügbar gemacht werden.

Eine besondere Herausforderung für das gesamtstaatliche Krisenmanagement bildet der Einbezug der kritischen Infrastrukturen. Diese spielen sowohl bei der Entstehung einer Krise eine Rolle (kritische Infrastrukturen als strategische Ziele) als auch bei den Auswirkungen (Grundversorgung der Bevölkerung und der Wirtschaft).

10.5 Übung POPULA

Das Konzept für das Krisenmanagement bei Krisen mit Cyberausprägung wurde anhand einer vom SVS organisierten Stabsrahmenübung getestet. Das Szenario wurde so gewählt, dass die Schnittstellen und die Führungsfähigkeiten bei Krisen mit Cyberausprägung wie in Abb. 10.1 beschrieben, getestet werden konnten. Das Szenario bildete ein Cyberangriff auf das Schweizer Rentensystem. Rund 2,5 Millionen Personen, davon rund 900.000 Personen im Ausland, beziehen eine Schweizer Rente. Der Angriff führte dazu, dass für mehrere Monate keine Rentenzahlungen mehr möglich waren. Kantonale kritische Infrastrukturen wie ein Spital und Notfallorganisationen in den Kantonen traf es über eine Weiterinfektion in einer zweiten Welle. Die Computersysteme des Spitals wurden infiziert und die Notfallnummern in mehreren Kantonen fielen aus. Die Information über den Cyberangriff wurde über eine Onlinezeitung verbreitet.

Die Übung dauerte eineinhalb Tage und alle involvierten Akteure waren während dieser Zeit vor Ort anwesend. Es konnten die in Abb. 10.1 aufgeführten Organe bis und mit „Operative Ebene" getestet werden. Die politisch-strategische Ebene wurde nicht beübt. Die Teilnehmenden hatten unterschiedliche berufliche Hintergründe (technische, juristische etc.), was sich auch auf die von ihnen gemachte Einschätzung der Lage, Cyberattacke vs. technischer Fehler, auswirkte. Die Teilnehmenden wurden in acht Zellen in acht Räumen aufgeteilt und stellten den Bund, die Kantone und die kritischen Infrastrukturen dar. Diese konnten über E-Mail oder Telefon miteinander kommunizieren. In der Übung fanden auch persönliche Treffen zwischen den Zellen statt, um gewisse Themen direkt zu besprechen. Jeder Zelle wurden eine oder mehrere Beobachterinnen und Beobachter zugeordnet, die die Aufgabe hatten, die Zelle zu beobachten und beratend zur Seite zu stehen. Zusätzlich hatten die Teilnehmenden noch die Möglichkeit, ihre eigenen Beobachtungen zu ihrem Krisenmanagement festzuhalten.

10.6   Lessons learned

Die Validierung des Konzeptes konnte nur teilweise vorgenommen werden, dies vor allem, weil verschiedene Teilnehmende das Problem nicht auf der richtigen Flughöhe angegangen sind und dadurch nur teilweise eine Problemerfassung oder gar keine Problemerfassung durchgeführt haben. Daher konnte insbesondere die Darstellung der integralen Lage nicht beübt werden. Die technische Auswertung anhand der E-Mails und der persönlichen Treffen hat gezeigt, dass der überwiegende Teil der Teilnehmenden Cyberbedrohungen in ihrer gesamten Auswirkung noch nicht genügend wahrnehmen und die technische Komplexität schwierig zu vermitteln ist. Oftmals überwiegt das Vertrauen in die eigene Technologie und Fähigkeiten. Diese Haltung wirkt sich in der Folge auch auf die fachliche Problemerfassung aus. Ein Cybervorfall wird bei der Mehrheit als isoliertes Ereignis analysiert und nicht in einen Gesamtkontext gestellt.

Bei den Teilnehmenden setzte sich die Erkenntnis durch, dass die Ressourcen bei einem Cybervorfall zentral sind, da technisches Wissen vorhanden sein muss und eine Abhängigkeit von Spezialisten besteht. Die Teilnehmenden haben erkannt, dass ein Cyberangriff schnell eine hohe Komplexität annehmen kann, da es durch die Vernetzung viele potenziell Betroffene gibt. Da sich die Lage entwickeln kann, ist eine schnelle Eskalation und Antizipation nötig. Bei einer Cyberkrise ist es schwierig, das Ausmass und die Kettenreaktionen zu evaluieren. Gerade bei einer Cyberkrise bestehen unter Umständen multiple Abhängigkeiten. Hinzu kommt, dass die Forensik ihre Zeit braucht, um die technische Lage zu analysieren und dafür ist viel Spezialwissen nötig. Auch muss die Information verifiziert werden und die Koordination unter den Betroffenen ist essenziell. Die von einem Cyberangriff betroffenen Stellen haben unter Umständen keinen Zugriff auf ein integrales Lagebild des Bundes. Im Ereignisfall muss den Bundesbehörden, den Kantonen und den kritischen Infrastrukturen Zugriff auf ein integrales Lagebild gegeben werden. Diese sind jedoch gleichzeitig auch dazu zu verpflichten, dass sie Informationen an das Lagebild melden. Ein Lagebild ist Bedingung für ein effizientes Krisenmanagement. Übungen im Krisenmanagement sind notwendig, damit mögliche Entwicklungen frühzeitig antizipiert werden können und die Partner bekannt sind.

10.7   Nationale Cyber-Strategie II: 2018–2022

Auch in der neuen Strategie wird das Krisenmanagement behandelt und explizit festgehalten, dass es gemeinsame Übungen zwischen Bund, Kantonen und kritischen Infrastrukturen braucht. Dabei sind sowohl Cyber-Aspekte in generelle Übungen einzubeziehen als auch spezifische Übungen zur Bewältigung von Krisen mit Cyber-Ausprägungen durchzuführen. Aufgrund der Erfahrungen der ersten Cyber-Strategie werden die Kantone enger in die Erarbeitung der zweiten Strategie einbezogen und es wird eine breitere politische Abstützung angestrebt, um die Umsetzung von einzelnen Massnahmen zu erreichen.

…limitem esse delendam – Grenzen sind zu überwinden

Mark A. Saxer

Zusammenfassung

„Cyber" ist inzwischen fast ein Schimpfwort: Der Begriff garantiert Aufmerksamkeit, mehr aber auch nicht. Allzuviel ist allzu technisch. Diese Lehmschicht, die sich durch jede Branche, jede Verwaltungseinheit, ja den Alltag zieht, verstehen zu wollen, ist auf den ersten Blick deutlich aufwendiger als gewinnbringend. Deswegen sind Angriffe nach wie vor einfach. ICT an sich entwickelt sich rasend schnell, Angreifer aber können sich die Mühe sparen, grundsätzlich neue Malware zu entwickeln. Die alte funktioniert „ewig".

Dabei stellt der Mißbrauch des Cyberspace Wirtschaft und Behörden vor sich permanent wandelnde Herausforderungen. Die Bedrohungsfelder sind altbekannt: Spionage, Sabotage und Kriminalität. Dabei beobachtet man seitens der Aggressoren – sie seien unter dem Sammelbegriff „Cybercrime" zusammengefasst – eine zunehmende Internationalisierung, Professionalisierung und Arbeitsteilung. Das allein macht die Aufklärung solcher Fälle hochkomplex. Unternehmen und Behörden sind an Rechtsräume gebunden, der Aggressor ist dies nicht. Die Schweiz ist hier keine Insel: Das Tun von Cyberkriminellen ist zur Kenntnis zu nehmen, vorbeugende wie auch reaktive Maßnahmen tun Not. Die monetären und persönlichen Schäden, die durch Cyberkriminalität verursacht werden, sind gravierend, könnten durch vernetztes Experten-Knowhow jedoch teilweise vermieden werden.

Vor diesem Hintergrund wurden in der Schweiz die Swiss Cyber Experts gegründet. Der privatwirtschaftliche Verein ist durch einen Kooperationsvertrag mit MELANI, der Melde- und Analysestelle Informationssicherung MELANI, zu einer *Public Private Partnership* verbunden. Ein Rückblick auf die ersten drei Aufbaujahre.

M. A. Saxer (✉)
furrerhugi. ag, Bern, Schweiz
E-Mail: mark.saxer@furrerhugi.ch

© Springer Fachmedien Wiesbaden GmbH, ein Teil von Springer Nature 2018
M. Bartsch, S. Frey (Hrsg.), *Cybersecurity Best Practices*,
https://doi.org/10.1007/978-3-658-21655-9_11

11.1 „Cui bono"? (Wem nützt das?)

Am Anfang steht regelmäßig die Frage, warum sich jemand an einer Public Private Partnership (PPP) beteiligen sollte. Die Ausgangslage ist klar:

1. Der primäre Auftrag von MELANI hat den Schutz kritischer Infrastrukturen zum Inhalt. Kritische Infrastrukturen sind ein gut gehütetes Geheimnis, aber man liegt nicht falsch in der Annahme, dass Kraftwerke und Großbanken dazu zählen, ebenso wie Kantone (vergleichbar mit Bundesländern).
2. Eine Kernfrage ist, wie Kantone vorgehen, wenn sie einen Cyber-Incident vermuten. Kantonale Informatiker äußerten sich bei den ersten Sondierungen nach dem mutmaßlichen Nutzen einer PPP deutlich: Sie melden nichts. Die Infrastruktur läuft, die Problembeschreibung aber stellt eine größere Herausforderung dar.
3. Die Eidgenossenschaft („der Bund") ist daran interessiert, Cyber-Incidents analysieren zu lassen. Schon allein, weil fehlende Meldungen das *Lagebild* verzerren. Allerdings liegt der staatliche Beitrag an die Finanzierung der Geschäftsstelle der Swiss Cyber Experts bei einem niedrigen zweistelligen Frankenbetrag. Dem stehen Kosten in achtfacher Höhe gegenüber.

Warum also eine PPP mitfinanzieren, um zugleich auch noch gratis Analyse-Dienstleistungen zu erbringen?

Es ist im Kern eine Frage der Güterabwägung. Oder anders: Wenn wir SCE als *kollektiven Akteur* verstehen, dann muss ein gemeinsames Standard-Interesse vermutet werden.

▶   Es ist im Interesse jedes ICT-Anbieters, dass der „Cyberspace" als sicher gilt –
     oder dass ICT zumindest nur überschaubare Risiken anhaften.

Nach der Lehre der *Rational Choice* führt das gemeinsame Standard-Interesse dazu, ein *Allgemeingut* herzustellen – dies im Wissen um zweierlei:

1. Viele weitere Akteure könnten dies ihrerseits tun und
2. der Anreiz, als *Trittbrettfahrer* abzuwarten, bis das Gemeingut hergestellt wird, ist nicht zu unterschätzen.

Es wurde sogar mehrfach nachgewiesen, dass der erste, der seine Kollektivgut-Präferenzen offenlegt und ergo zu produzieren beginnt, am Ende schlechter dasteht als der Trittbrettfahrer [1]. Die Logik ist einfach: Wer ein Kollektivgut herstellt, hat weniger Ressourcen frei, um sich Privaten Gütern – also etwa der Steigerung des eigenen Umsatzes – zu widmen. Was der Trittbrettfahrer natürlich kann. Wenn das Kollektivgut zudem mit keiner Ausschluss-Klausel behaftet ist, profitiert der Trittbrettfahrer kostenlos.

Ergo liegt es theoretisch nahe, dass sich gar niemand für das Kollektivgut bewegt. Dann wird aber entgegen allen Interessen das Gemeingut produziert, das niemand haben will. In diesem Falle Unsicherheit. Es wird zu zeigen sein, wie geschlossen sich der kollektive Akteur verhält.

Im Wissen um diese Zusammenhänge wurden vor der ersten Übung einige Grundlagen geschaffen.

Den Durchbruch ermöglichte *IBM*, indem der Konzern die Führung des angedachten Vereins übernahm. Dies durchaus aus Gründen der *Rational Choice*, ging es doch darum, von anderen ICT-Firmen zu lernen und im Gegenzug Wissen zur Verfügung zu stellen. Ebenfalls im Sinne der rationalen Wahl öffneten sich danach Türen, war doch der Aufwand, den es bedeutete, einer neuen Idee den Durchbruch zu ermöglichen, zunächst einmal klar allokiert. Die entsprechenden Opportunitätskosten trugen IBM (und die designierte Geschäftsstelle).

Vor diesem Durchbruch waren Sondierungen seitens der Öffentlichen Hand wie auch seitens der Privatwirtschaft in den immer selben Fragen steckengeblieben: „Mit wem sprächen wir" auf der anderen Seite? Und: „Wie ist Kontinuität sichergestellt?" Letztere Frage bezog sich ausdrücklich auf die Privatwirtschaft, da auf dieser Seite die Job- und Funktionswechsel zu Recht als häufiger wahrgenommen werden.

Die Bereitschaft eines Weltkonzerns, dem Ziel „PPP" Kraft seines Namens Schwung zu verleihen, deblockierte fast über Nacht. Dass MELANI der primäre Ansprechpartner seitens des Bundes sei, war von Anfang an klar. Nun allerdings war die Privatwirtschaft schneller als die Verwaltung. Ab 2013 entstanden die Eckwerte der künftigen Statuten und Prozess-Beschriebe und damit auch die Grundlagen des anvisierten Kooperationsvertrages. Mit anderen Worten:

Die Idee zur PPP stammte aus der Privatwirtschaft.

Der Durchbruch der Idee wurde von der Privatwirtschaft ermöglicht.

Die Grundlagen des Kooperationsvertrages entstanden überwiegend auf der Seite der Privatwirtschaft.

▶ Empirische Beobachtung: Wenn „Staat" und „Privat" gemeinsam ein Allgemeingut herstellen wollen, liegt die Last der Aufbauarbeit – liegen die Opportunitätskosten – fast einseitig bei den privaten Initianten.

Diese Grundlagen waren „dem Staat" in verschiedenen Sitzungen zu präsentieren und in eigentlichen Hearings zu diskutieren.

Eckdaten
Gründung SCE: 26. März 2014: Gründungsversammlung Swiss Cyber Experts. Vertreter von sieben Firmen. Wahl des Präsidenten (Alain Gut, IBM) und Unterzeichnung der bereinigten Statuten.

Vertragsunterzeichnung PPP:
Sie erfolgte am 17. Dezember 2014.

11.2 Labor omnia vincit … – Statuten, Prozesse, Vertrag

Zunächst einmal ging es um die ersten *Statuten*: Sie wurden anlässlich der SCE-Gründungsversammlung vom 26. März 2014 unterzeichnet, die Ideen dazu vorher x-fach diskutiert. Der Zweckartikel wurde schließlich auf der SCE-Webseite wie folgt wiedergegeben:

Der Zweck

Swiss Cyber Experts ist rechtlich ein Verein. Er bezweckt laut seinen Statuten die in Tab. 11.1 aufgeführten Punkte.

Man mag in diesem Zweck ein Best Practice Beispiel sehen. Realiter am wichtigsten ist aus Sicht der SCE-Mitgliedsfirmen respektive ihrer Experten jedoch die regelmäßige Gelegenheit zum persönlichen Austausch, ja die Möglichkeit, sich überhaupt kennen zu lernen. Tatsächlich wurde die Erkenntnis gewonnen, dass die Schweiz zwar klein ist, aber doch nicht klein genug, dass sich alle Experts *naturaliter* kennen – eine offenkundige Erfahrungstatsache.

Die Prozesse

Im Kern ging es jedoch nicht um die Statuten, sondern vor allem um die angedachten Prozesse. Dabei standen vier Aspekte im Vordergrund:

1. Die Besetzung der Geschäftsstelle sowie deren Verbindung zu MELANI und die dabei anvisierten Reaktionsfristen: Wie schnell muss die Geschäftsstelle den Eingang eines Falles bei MELANI quittieren und erste Rückfragen stellen? Wie „eskaliert" die Geschäftsstelle den Fall im Verein, und bis wann muss sie die Experten melden können, die sich konkret damit beschäftigen können? Wie oft werden Zwischenberichte abgeliefert?
2. Die Festschreibung des Clearings des Problembeschriebs und der Fragestellungen des Geschädigten durch die staatliche Seite, also MELANI. Sie war zwar immer klar, wurde aber dennoch immer wieder diskutiert.
3. Ebenso die Zusammenarbeit von MELANI und SCE, namentlich das gemeinsame Abstimmen zum Vorgehen.
4. Schließlich ging es darum, dass Vertraulichkeitserklärungen, Kommunikation, Administration und Logistik durch die privatwirtschaftliche Seite zu erbringen seien.

Die Arbeit des Prozess-Designs übernahm ein KMU (abgeschlossen nach zwei Sitzungen in Juni 2014), das sich darauf spezialisiert hat, die e3 AG. Mit anderen Worten lagen hier dieses Mal die überwiegende Mehrheit der Opportunitätskosten. Das Resultat konnte und kann sich sehen lassen, ohne etwas für Schnellleser zu sein (siehe Abb. 11.1).

Tab. 11.1 Der Zweckartikel SCE

–	Die Vernetzung von privatwirtschaftlichem ICT-Know-how zur …
–	… Intensivierung und Systematisierung des Wissenstransfers bei der Bekämpfung schwerer Cyber Incidents, welche die eigenen oder vertraglich gebundenen Mittel der Betroffenen überfordern.
–	Damit bezweckt der Verein auch die Verbesserung der phänomenologischen Erkenntnisse, …
–	die Erweiterung der technischen Kompetenzen seiner Mitglieder durch den Austausch, …
–	und letztlich die Fortentwicklung der Prävention.
–	Zentral ist dabei das Bereithalten einer zentralen Ansprechstelle gegenüber der öffentlichen Verwaltung.

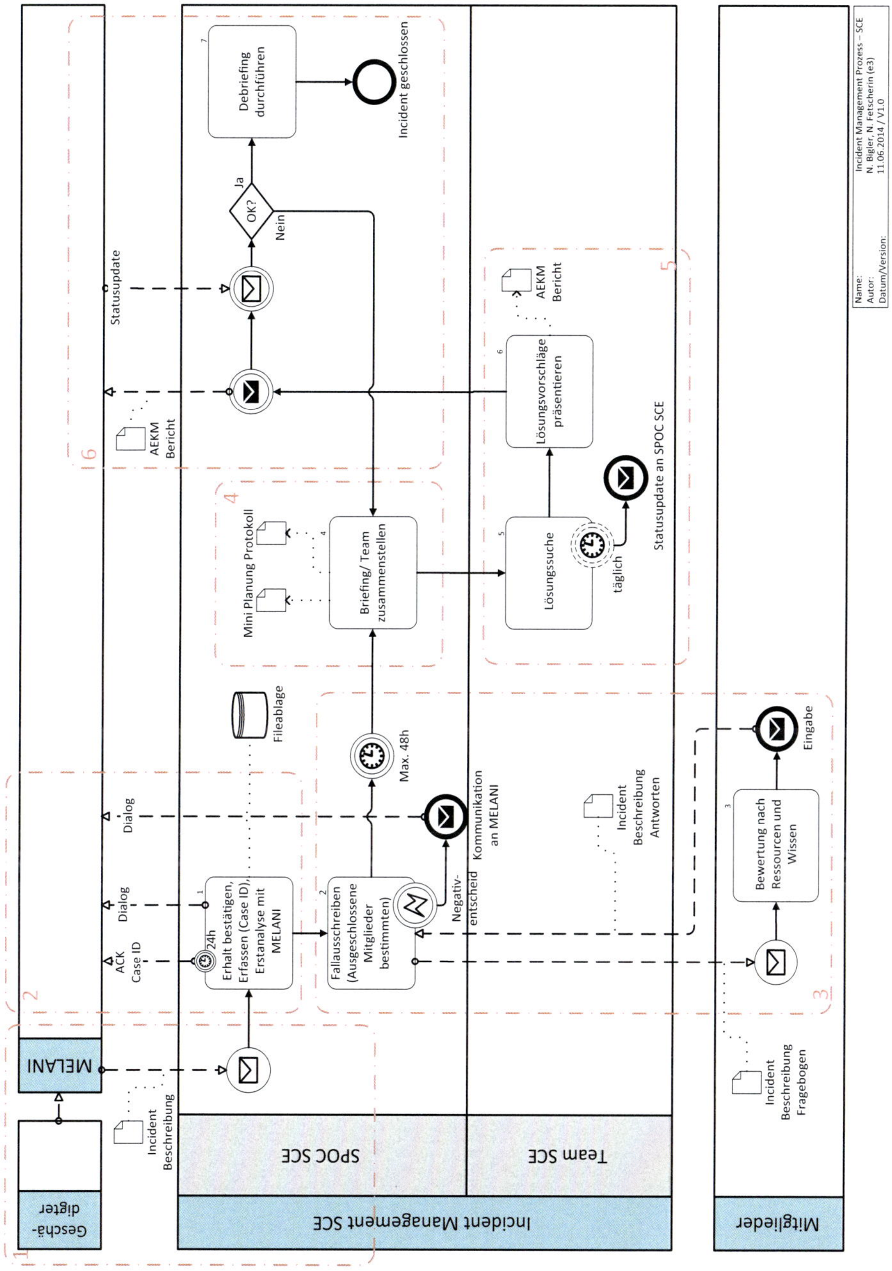

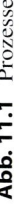

Abb. 11.1 Prozesse

Dieses Dokument und die dazugehörige Prozessbeschreibung ist bis heute ein *Best Practice Beispiel*. Es hat mehreren Übungen und Fällen standgehalten. Allerdings sind die beschriebenen Fristen zu lang angesetzt, sie werden zugunsten der Geschädigten realiter deutlich unterschritten:

1. Die Geschäftsstelle – der Single Point of Contact (SPOC) seitens Privatwirtschaft hat noch nie 24 Stunden benötigt, um den Eingang eines Falles zu quittieren, auch die unmittelbar anschließende Erstanalyse wird entsprechend deutlich schneller erledigt als vorgesehen. Der Denkfehler war: Schwere Cyber Incidents blicken im Falle der Eskalation zu SCE auf eine längere Vorgeschichte seitens des Geschädigten zurück und sind ergo nicht mehr zeitkritisch. Das mag stimmen, die Frist wird in der Realität dennoch klar unterschritten.
2. Analog: Laut Prozessdokument gilt: „Der SPOC schreibt den Incident unter den nicht ausgeschlossenen Vereinsmitgliedern aus. Die Vereinsmitglieder prüfen die Ausschreibung und geben innerhalb von maximal 48 h eine Rückmeldung". Auch diese 48 Stunden werden immer unterschritten. Dies regelmäßig auch auf der Basis technisch klar nicht erschöpfender Lagebeschreibungen – Experts haben bewiesen, dass sie bereit sind, genauer hinzuschauen und die weitere Ausgangslage zu klären.

Auf die Beschreibung der Ausgangslage wird separat einzugehen sein.

Der Vertrag
Auch die eigentliche Ausarbeitung des finalen Kooperationsvertrages fiel in das Jahr 2014, parallel zur Arbeit an den Prozessen. Hier wiederum lagen die Opportunitätskosten bei MELANI, beim SCE-Präsidenten und der Geschäftsstelle – hier wurde das PPP erstmals merklich konkret. Der Vertragsentwurf wurde zuletzt dem Generalsekretariat des Finanzdepartements (EFD) unterbreitet, ebenso die Statuten und die Prozessdokumente. Kerninteresse der Juristin war, seitens MELANI und Geschäftsstelle mündlich zu erfahren, was das Ziel des Vertrags und seiner Bestandteile sein solle. Auf dieser Basis wurden alsdann überarbeitete Versionen vorgelegt. Nach Anhörung der SCE-Anregungen und einer Bereinigung erfolgte die Vertragsunterzeichnung am 17. Dezember 2014.

11.3   „Rheingold": Tit for Tat oder „Quid pro Quo"

„Rheingold" war die Übung „Null". Sie fand statt, bevor der Verein SCE gegründet wurde und war eine reine Trockenübung. Anfänglich stellten sich die grundlegenden Fragen doppelt: Einmal seitens Bund (warum soll sich jemand an einer PPP beteiligen? Kap. 1), dann aber auch innerhalb der SCE-Kerngruppe. Innerhalb dieser Gruppe war die Grundfrage zwar geklärt: Es hatten sich verschiedenste Unternehmen unterschiedlichster Größe und Provenienz zusammengetan, um Experten zur Verfügung zu stellen. Nur:

▶   Ist es tatsächlich möglich, dass Unternehmungen, die teilweise als Konkurrenten am Markt auftreten, zusammenarbeiten und Wissen austauschen?

Getestet wurde genau dies im Rahmen der Übung „Rheingold" (Juli/August 2013).

Ziel war die „Überprüfung, ob die an einer PPP interessierten privatwirtschaftlichen IT-Know-how-Träger effektiv zusammenarbeiten".

Die *Problemstellung*: Der echte Fall eines problematischen Botnet-Takedowns verbunden mit zwei konkreten Fragen: Wie erkennt man rechtzeitig, dass der Aggressor ein neues Botnet aufbaut? Wie kann man sich in dieses Netz einklinken ohne aufzufliegen? Es ging also um eine rein akademische Übung, allerdings mit realem Aufhänger.

Das *Ergebnis*:

1. Es kam tatsächlich Wissen verschiedenster Ausrichtung und von weltweiter Herkunft zusammen. Grosskonzerne zapften ihre weltweiten Netzwerke an, KMUs trugen das ihre bei.
2. Die Firmen legten ihr Wissen sehr transparent offen, es fand ein effektiver Austausch statt. Tatsächlich bestanden alle Firmen, die relevantes Wissen recherchiert respektive zusammengetragen hatten, darauf, die entsprechenden Dokumente allen Teilnehmern zur Verfügung zu stellen – sie seien ja beim (zukünftigen) Verein SCE, um voneinander zu lernen. Damit war die Grundfrage klar beantwortet: *Ja, Konkurrenten arbeiten zusammen und tauschen Wissen aus*. Alltägliche Konkurrenzsituationen spielten keine Rolle in der Sicherheitsfrage.

Was direkt zu Analogien aus der Theorie der (Neuen) Politischen Ökonomie führt. Ein Klassiker ist *TIT FOR TAT*, verwandt mit Quid pro quo. Bekannt geworden ist die Theorie vor allem dank Robert Axelrod (*1943), einem der bedeutendsten Vertreter der *rational choice theory*. Unwissentlich verhielten sich die Spieler beim ersten Zug freundlich (die Übung war in diesem Sinne nicht moderiert) – und tatsächlich wurde der erste freundliche Zug eines Konzerns mit lauter freundlichen Reaktionen der Mitspieler belohnt. Alle legten offen, was sie gefunden hatten und lernten somit dazu. Ein Spieler allerdings verhielt sich am Ende unkooperativ und verweigerte nachdem er allen anderen zugehört hatte seinerseits jegliche Auskunft. Er sollte an der zweiten Runde nicht mehr teilnehmen. (Was nach Axelrod übrigens falsch war: Tit for Tat setzt nicht nur voraus, dass man die nächsten Spielzüge nicht kennt, sondern auch, dass man sich nach einer gegenseitig unkooperativen Runde wieder vergibt).

▸   Erkenntnis:
    Solange sich alle SCE-Spieler (nach Tit for Tat) primär freundlich, also kooperativ, verhalten, gewinnen alle. Es ist statistisch auch unmöglich, nicht zu gewinnen, was x-fach bewiesen wurde. (Die Frage, wie sich wiederholte Kooperationsverweigerung auswirkt, wurde bis Ende 2017 noch nie gestellt)**.**

3. Eine Erkenntnis zum Stand der akademischen Forschung und einer kurz bevorstehenden Publikation (November 2013) führte zu „Rheingold 2" (Februar 2014 [2]) und der weiteren Vertiefung. Der direkte Kontakt zu den Autoren (vom Georgia Institute of Technology sowie Damballa, Inc.) wurde hergestellt. Hier zeigte sich ein erstes Mal der Wert der interdisziplinären Zusammensetzung von SCE: Gefunden hatte diese Spur ein Teilnehmer, der ursprünglich Historiker gewesen war – und folglich wusste, welche Erkenntnisse sich aus Literaturverzeichnissen gewinnen lassen.

„Rheingold": Der empirische Hintergrund

Die SCE Kerngruppe umfasste 2013 (also vor der Gründung) 9 designierte Mitgliedsfirmen sowie MELANI und die designierte Geschäftsstelle.

Davon nahmen 100 % an den Übungs-Workshops teil. Diese Workshops fanden noch „live" vor Ort statt, die Konferenztelefone kamen erst später.

Inhaltlichen Input trugen mit einer Ausnahme alle Firmen bei.

11.4 Übung „Loge" [3] (DHS2015 „iRat")

2015 hätten Fälle an SCE „eskaliert" werden können und aus privatwirtschaftlicher Sicht war es auch angezeigt, dass die staatliche Seite Farbe bekenne. Der Fall-Fluss begann jedoch stockend. Warum?

1. Auf Seiten der Privatwirtschaft – also bei SCE – stand eine Mannschaft, die sich über Monate in konkreter Zusammenarbeit kennen und schätzen gelernt hatte.
2. Auf staatlicher Seite stand eine Mannschaft – die im Wesentlichen aus dem Treiber an der Spitze von MELANI bestand. Dass noch viel in Kommunikation und Teambuilding investiert werden musste, wurde seitens des „Bundes" erst später erkannt.

Oder anders: Auf Seiten SCE schien klar, dass die Zusammenarbeit beginnen konnte. Auf staatlicher Seite war das alles andere als klar. Eine rationale Entscheidung zugunsten der Kooperation war seitens SCE möglich, seitens des „Bundes" eben – nicht.

▶ **Erkenntnis:**
    In der Rückschau ist es sonnenklar, dass beide MELANI-Spitzen beide Teams
    dazu hätten ermuntern müssen, nach Tit for Tat kooperativ zu spielen.

Allerdings ist es eine Erfahrungstatsache, gestützt auch durch ganz alltägliche Erfahrungen mit der Entwicklung von IT-Produkten, dass technische Cracks nicht allzu gerne vorschnell einräumen, es könnte auch noch eine andere, flankierende Idee geben.

Mögliche Ausgänge in einer Tit for Tat Simulation zeigt Tab. 11.2.

Tab. 11.2 Das SCE-Dilemma

Spieler A	Spieler B	Ergebnis
Wissen Teilen,	wenn der andere schweigt	B nutz A aus. In der nächsten Runde wird A schweigen.
Wissen verschweigen,	wenn der andere Wissen teilt	A nutz B aus. Beide haben sich wechselseitig je einmal ausgenutzt. Sie können ewig so weitermachen – Schaden und Nutzen bleiben gering. Oder sie kooperieren.
Wissen teilen	**Wenn der andere Wissen teilt**	**A & B gewinnen**

Kooperieren ist keine Pflicht. Aber es lohnt sich für beide Spieler

Die konkrete Lösung aus Sicht des SCE Vorstandes war: Wir beüben unsere Prozesse selber. Ausgefeilte Angebote, was man tun könnte, lagen ebenso vor wie solche weit jenseits des SCE Budgets. Ergo wurde entschieden, dass die Geschäftsstelle eine Prozess-Übung skizzieren und umsetzen solle.

Zweck

1. Überprüfung der Prozesse
2. Stärkung des Vertrauens in die Organisation

Ziele

1. Überprüfung der Incident-Management-Prozesse
2. Überprüfung der Kommunikationsmittel des Vereins
3. Überprüfung der Teambildung und der Zusammenarbeit
4. Überprüfung der Teamführung und des Führungsrhythmus

Szenario/Aufgabe
Malware: DHS2015/iRat der Gruppe Desert-Falcon

1. Desert Falcon existiert seit 2011, damals bekannter Höhepunkt 2015. Die Spionagegruppe hatte auf mehreren Vektoren 3000 Opfer weltweit in >50 Ländern ausgespäht. Einer der Vektoren ist iRat. In der CH relativ unbekannt.

„Geschädigter": Private Firma/Lebensmittel-Verpackungsindustrie/Hauptsitz: CH/Markt: Weltweit
Aufgabe an SCE:

1. Zusammentragen von Informationen zu iRat, anschl. Information an MELANI (für das Übungsszenario standen keinerlei LogFiles oder echte Daten zur Verfügung)
2. Entwickeln eines Plans für das weitere Vorgehen

Das *Ergebnis*

1. Der Prozess funktionierte. Alle Fristen wurden eingehalten, eine verschlüsselte Dokumentenablage erstellt, Zugriff dazu bestand nur für das Inicident Kernteam.
2. Die Mitglieder stellen tatsächlich Ressourcen bereit.
   – 77,27 % der SCE-Mitglieder reagierten auf die Ausschreibung
   – 40,91 % Aktive Mitarbeit
3. Das heterogene technische Team formierte sich binnen einer Stunde zum Kick-off und lieferte technisch substanzielle Nachfragen & Analysen, einschließlich iRat-Samples.

Die Teamleitung durch ein KMU wurde vom Analyseteam problemlos akzeptiert. Die technische Teamleitung und der nicht mit dem Übungs-Design betraute Teil der Geschäftsstelle vermochten den Führungsrhythmus aufrecht zu erhalten.

4. Ein Plan für das weitere Vorgehen wurde sauber skizziert, protokolliert und kommuniziert.
5. SCE meldete sich dem Staat und dem politischen Beirat am 5. Dezember 2015 „bereit".

11.5   „Claimant Notification B" (Oder: Die Problembeschreibung)

Der erste Echtfall, der zu SCE eskaliert wurde, folgte im Januar 2016. Ein großer Luxusgüterkonzern hatte sich an MELANI gewandt, es ging um Ransomware. Nun handelte es sich um keine kritische Infrastruktur, denen der primäre Fokus von MELANI gilt. Aber: Der Konzern, der seit 1980 auch in der Schweiz produziert, hatte auch in Rom Fälle von Verschlüsselung verzeichnet. Das Operation Information Center – der nachrichtendienstliche Arm von MELANI – entschied sich, dem Geschädigten vorzuschlagen, den Fall an SCE weiterzureichen.

Nach der Einwilligung des Geschädigten landete der Fall auf der SCE-Geschäftsstelle. Allerdings ohne Problembeschreibung. Diese entpuppte sich aus Sicht der Geschäftsstelle als die eigentliche Herausforderung: Das Formular wurde in Zusammenarbeit mit dem Geschädigten ausgefüllt.

Nachdem recherchiert worden war, dass ein typisches in der Schweiz hergestelltes Produkt zum Preis von rund 5000 € zu kaufen war, derweil Fälschungen desselben Produkts ab 35–180 € zu haben waren, stellte sich die Frage nach dem geistigen Eigentum: „Do you have Research and Development activities in Switzerland?" – „Yes." – „Is IP-Data at risk?" – „We send our IP-Addresses with every email". – „True. But „IP" standing for „Intellectual Property"? Is such data at risk"? – „We don't know".

Insgesamt verlangt das Schadenformular nach Auskünften wie:

1. Beschreibung des Incidents/der Situation
2. Vermuteter Angreifer
3. Konkrete Fragen (Hier ging es um die Identifikation der Malware und den Vorschlag möglicher Lösungen und Dienstleister)
4. Was wurde technisch schon unternommen?
5. Andere Maßnahmen (in diesem Falle hatte der Geschädigte zwei Polizeikorps kontaktiert, bevor er sich an MELANI wandte)
6. Technische Details (darunter in diesem Fall die Frage nach der IP-Data)
7. Security und confidentiality requirements, Klassifizierung
8. Erlaubte Zeit
9. Kontakte

Das Ergebnis: Der Fall konnte wegen der Klärung der Ausgangslage über die Feiertage erst unmittelbar nach Jahreswechsel an SCE weitergegeben werden. Dann allerdings hatten die Experten die Lösung rasch gefunden: Die zur Verfügung gestellten Screenshots zeigten zweifelsfrei „TeslaCrypt". Und alle Experten waren sich einig: Diese Ransomware lässt sich sogar entschlüsseln, da sie erstens uralt ist und zweitens auch schon länger geknackt war.

Kurz: Der Geschädigte hatte zuletzt eine Lösung, MELANI konnte diese liefern, SCE hatte funktioniert. Wozu anzumerken ist: Die Vermittlung von Dienstleistern ist keine SCE-Aufgabe. Alle Mitglieder wissen das und stimmen dem explizit zu. Angesichts der sehr spezifischen Fragestellung des Geschädigten kamen SCE-Geschäftsstelle und MELANI im Schlussrapport zur Konklusion, ausnahmsweise mögliche Dienstleister zu „outen". SCE weiß bis heute nicht, wie die eigentliche Lösung von Statten ging, und das ist auch gut so.

11.6   „Cyber Europe 2016" (MELANI und SCE beübt)

2016 veranstaltete die ENISA die Groß-Übung Cyber Europe 2016. MELANI wurde beübt, und zudem ging es darum, Kooperationen staatlicher Institutionen und ihrer privatwirtschaftlichen Partner zu testen (test local-level cooperation processes). Soweit der Autor weiß, fand dies nur in der Schweiz statt, jedenfalls ging es um „technical, operational and more strategic incident-response processes".

Am ersten Tag wurde die SCE-Geschäftsstelle beübt. Ein eindrücklicher Wust von fake BBC-News, fake Tweets und fake Facebook-Meldungen: Der Schreibende konnte allein erkennen, dass weltweit ziemlich grundsätzlich so einiges schief lief. Zuletzt gingen in Asien die Lichter aus. Was fehlte, war die ordnende Lagebeurteilung von MELANI, irgendetwas Konkretes zum Eskalieren. Die Falle: Es ging um ein Linux-Image, auf dem Microsoft laufen sollte, was man seitens Staat (und vereinzelt auch seitens SCE-Experts) sehr rasch und sicher als „unmöglich" taxierte.

Es war das Operation Information Centre von MELANI, das am Abend des ersten Tages den Ausschlag gab. Technisch weniger versiert als das GovCert, dafür nachrichtendienstlich beschlagen, präsentierte das OIC der SCE-Geschäftsstelle am Abend des 13. Oktober drei Fragen:

1. What is the initial infection vector?
2. Potential backdoors: Clean the server.
3. Localise/identify the malware „hosted" by the server.

Ein SCE-Expertenteam hatte alle drei Fragen bis am Mittag des Folgetages geklärt und nach einem Konferenztelephon mit MELANI OIC einen mehrseitigen sehr technischen Bericht bereit. Abb. 11.2 zeigt einen Auszug zu Frage eins.

1. Infection vector

The entry point:

Log & Command extract: <u>Anhang</u>.

Und hier nochmal der Befehl mit Domain separat:

/tmp/dsell 6368696E61495350.ch

Extracted Data: <u>Anhang</u> (pw infected)

dshell IOC:

MD5 838e7fd1c447d2ee585380f47f689ffb

SHA1 BE76102a2f120866578e5010e2716a3e47dec4ae

SHA256 72a52c5oce53a8751179ccoo3b58826fd57584f2d18cad03f62c55eb40cebf9a

An initial, really „dshell"-overview fairly clearly shows a backdoor. It sees to communicate via DNS. The following string can be found in the binary:

dnscat2 v0.05 (client)

Das wird wohl die Basis für die Kommunikation sein

Abb. 11.2 Infection Vector

Also kam eine vierte Frage dazu:

4. Forensic task: Identify deleted data

Hier kam es zu einem kurzen „Kräftemessen" zweier Experten verschiedener Provenienz: Eine kritische Infrastruktur und ein KMU kamen bei ein und derselben Frage zu ein und demselben Image zu diametral verschiedenen Schlüssen. Einmal hieß es: „Da sind keine Deleted Files", andererseits jedoch: „Doch, da sind mindestens deren 14".

▶   **Erkenntnis:** Ein und dasselbe Problem verschiedenen Experten unterschiedlicher Provenienz vorzulegen, führt nicht zwingend zum selben Resultat. Und eine Differenz führt nicht zwingend zum Experten-Streit, jedenfalls tat dies die einzige Differenz unter SCE-Experts nicht.

Zum Schluss zeigt Tab. 11.3 die Tit for Tat-Analyse des empirischen Geschehens während CE 16, gestrafft.

11.7   „…limitem esse delendam" – Grenzen sind zu überwinden

Fazit: Eine Public Private Partnership zu kreieren ist beschwerlich, aber einfacher als ihr Leben einzuhauchen. Sie funktioniert nur, wenn das gemeinsame Grundinteresse gegeben ist, das der Schreibende vorangestellt hat:

Tab. 11.3 Das SCE-Dilemma mit zwei MELANI-Spielern

Spieler A (SCE)	Spieler B (MELANI OIC)	Spieler C (MELANI GovCert)
Warten auf einen klaren Auftrag > Auftragsannahme	Lagebeurteilung > Auftragserteilung	„unmögliches Problem" > Schweigen (Nicht-Kooperation)
Analyse der konkreten Fragen durch mehrere Experten (Kooperation)	Diskussion der Resultate (Offenlegung eigener Erkenntnisse), weitere Einladung an Spieler C, Auftragserteilung an Spieler A (Kooperation)	Reaktiv gesteigerte Bearbeitung der ihnen zugewiesenen Teilaufgaben (Kooperation)
Analyse der zusätzlichen technischen Frage durch mehrere Experten, Offenlegung und Diskussion technischer Differenzen (Kooperation)	Diskussion des letzten Resultats (Offenlegung eigener Erkenntnisse) (Kooperation).	Gesteigerte Bearbeitung der zugewiesenen Teilaufgaben (Kooperation)
Schlussbericht an Spieler B & C (Kooperation)	Schlussbesprechung („Hot Wash") (Kooperation)	Kooperation mit B.

Kooperation ist noch immer keine Pflicht, es haben aber alle drei Spieler davon profitiert. Auffällig ist, dass die Koordination des Einsatzes der technischen Spieler A und C beim Operation Information Center lag

▶   Es ist im Interesse jedes ICT-Anbieters, dass der „Cyberspace" als sicher gilt – oder dass ICT zumindest nur überschaubare Risiken anhaften.

Zweitens ist es unabdingbar, dass sich alle Beteiligten (unbewusst) an die freundliche, kooperative Strategie nach Tit for Tat halten und mindestens in jedem zweiten „Spielzug" kooperieren.

▶   **Kurz:**
Solange sich alle SCE- und alle staatlichen Spieler kooperativ verhalten, gewinnen alle. Alles andere ist statistisch gar nicht möglich.

Es kommen weitere Herausforderungen auf SCE zu, eine ist die (schon angetestete) Kooperation mit fedpol resp. der schweizerischen Bundeskriminalpolizei. Wiederum eine ganz andere Welt, die aber nicht von „major incidents" spricht, sondern von konkreten Phänomenen und Einsatzfällen, in denen sie Unterstützung brauchen könnte. Und die großen Wert auf Nachvollziehbarkeit sämtlicher Schritte legt. Hier wird es um dasselbe gehen: Kooperativ spielen, im Rahmen der klaren Regeln der Strafverfolgung, bringt der staatlichen wie auch der privaten Seite enormen Nutzen.

Die Public Private Partnership ist DAS Zukunftsmodell zur Bekämpfung von Cyber-Risiken. Was zurück zum Titel des Beitrags führt: „…limitem esse delendam". Mit sinngemäß dieser Formulierung betonte Cato der Ältere (234–149 v. Chr.) bei jeder Gelegenheit, Karthago müsse besiegt werden, was schließlich gelang. In unserem Zusammenhang: Grenzen müssen überwunden werden. Und das wird gelingen.

Literatur

1. Kirsch, 1993, S. 139 ff.
2. Yacin Nadji, Manos Antonakakis, Roberto Perdisci, David Dagon und Wenke Lee: Beheading Hydras: Performing Effective Botnet Takedowns.
3. Loki ist die nordische Gottheit des Feuers, der List und der Verwandlung, Name „Loge" nach Richard Wagner, Rheingold.

E-Voting in der Schweiz – Herausforderungen und Schutzprinzipen

12

Christian Folini und Denis Morel

Zusammenfassung

Der Artikel erklärt, wie Wahl und Abstimmungen in der Schweiz praktisch ablaufen und wie E-Voting die bestehenden Stimmkanäle ergänzt. Dabei ist es wichtig festzustellen, dass der Begriff „E-Voting" in der Schweiz im Sinn des Abstimmens und Wählens von zu Hause aus, über das Internet, verwendet wird. Sogenannte Wahlmaschinen respektive Stimmcomputer im Wahllokal werden in der Schweiz keine eingesetzt. In über 200 Versuchen wurde E-Voting in der Schweiz geprüft, verfeinert und nach und nach immer höheren Sicherheitsanforderungen unterstellt. Grundlegende Konzepte wie die individuelle Verifizierbarkeit, die universelle Verifizierbarkeit sowie die Einführung von unabhängigen Kontrollgruppen bieten einen hohen Schutz vor der Manipulation von Stimmen. Die korrekte Umsetzung dieser Techniken und des zu Grunde liegenden E-Voting Protokolls muss jeweils in separaten Zertifizierungen überprüft werden. Die Implementierung, die Einführung und der Betrieb einer sicheren E-Voting Lösung stellen sehr hohe Anforderungen an das Know-How des Personals sowie die Maturität der Prozesse der beteiligten Organisationen. In der Schweiz erfüllen die Schweizerische Post und der Kanton Genf als Anbieter einer Lösung für die elektronische Stimmabgabe die an ein solches System gestellten Anforderungen.

C. Folini (✉)
netnea AG, Liebefeld, Schweiz
E-Mail: christian.folini@netnea.com

D. Morel
Post CH AG, Bern, Schweiz
E-Mail: denis.morel@post.ch

© Springer Fachmedien Wiesbaden GmbH, ein Teil von Springer Nature 2018
M. Bartsch, S. Frey (Hrsg.), *Cybersecurity Best Practices*,
https://doi.org/10.1007/978-3-658-21655-9_12

12.1 Einführung

Die Autoren dieses Artikels arbeiten seit mehreren Jahren für die Schweizerische Post im Bereich E-Voting. Denis Morel ist verantwortlich für den Geschäftsbereich und hat mit seinen Kollegen das System bis zum produktiven Einsatz aufgebaut. Christian Folini besetzte bei der Konzeption und dem Einsatz der Sicherheitselemente der Infrastruktur eine Schlüsselrolle. Die Autoren versuchen mit diesem Artikel, die Herausforderungen für die Sicherheit beim Einsatz eines E-Voting-Systems zu erläutern. Darüber hinaus wird beschrieben, wie die Schweiz diese Herausforderungen adressiert hat.

Der Artikel erklärt zunächst, wie Wahl und Abstimmungen in der Schweiz praktisch ablaufen und wie E-Voting die bestehenden Stimmkanäle ergänzt. Essentiell ist der Zusammenhang mit der brieflichen Stimmabgabe. Zudem ist es wichtig festzustellen, dass der Begriff „E-Voting" in der Schweiz im Sinn des Abstimmens und Wählens von zu Hause aus, über das Internet, verwendet wird. Sogenannte Wahlmaschinen respektive Stimmcomputer im Wahllokal werden in der Schweiz keine eingesetzt.

Nach einer Erläuterung der wichtigsten Herausforderungen und Bedrohungen von E-Voting werden die Antwort der Schweiz in den gesetzlichen Anforderungen erklärt. Insbesondere das Konzept der vollständigen (individuellen und universellen) Verifizierbarkeit spielt hier eine grosse Rolle. Am Ende erklären die Autoren die wichtigsten Schutzprinzipien, die für den Einsatz eines E-Voting-Systems beachtet werden müssen.

12.2 Elektronische Stimmabgabe in der Schweiz

12.2.1 Allgemeine Besonderheiten des politischen Systems

Die Schweiz ist ein Bundesstaat mit drei Ebenen: Bund, Kantone und Gemeinden. Die Verfassung teilt die Kompetenzen der politischen Rechte zwischen Bund und Kantonen auf. Grundsätzlich trägt der Bund die Verantwortung, die Regeln durch gesetzliche Bestimmungen und Anforderungen an eidgenössische Wahlen und Abstimmungen zu definieren und zu überwachen. Die Kantone definieren die Regeln und die Aufteilung der Kompetenzen mit den Gemeinden für kantonale und kommunale Wahlen und Abstimmungen. Dazu kommt, dass der Bund die Kantone mit der Durchführung der Urnengänge auf sämtlichen drei Ebenen betraut. Der Bund fasst danach die Ergebnisse der Kantone für Abstimmungen auf Bundesebene zusammen.

Die Schweiz ist eine direkte Demokratie. Das bedeutet, dass die Schweiz ein Referendums- und ein Initiativrecht besitzt. Das Referendumsrecht erlaubt den Bürgern eine durch das Parlament verabschiedete Gesetzesänderung in Frage zu stellen. Dies geschieht durch eine Sammlung von Unterschriften. Wird das minimale Quorum von 50.000 Unterschriften erreicht, muss der Gesetzestext dem Stimmvolk zur Abstimmung vorgelegt werden. Das Initiativrecht erlaubt Bürgern, Änderungen in der Verfassung vorzuschlagen. Auch hier beginnt der Prozess mit einer Unterschriftensammlung (Quorum von 100.000

Unterschriften bei einer Wohnbevölkerung von 8 Millionen), darauf folgt die Beratung im Parlament und schliesslich die Volksabstimmung. Zu diesen beiden direktdemokratischen Abstimmungsmechanismen kommen alle vier Jahre die eidgenössischen Wahlen. Daneben werden auch kantonale und kommunale Wahlen und Abstimmungen durchgeführt. Das dermassen gestaltete politische System ruft einen Bürger durchschnittlich vier Mal pro Jahr an die Urne. Daraus ergibt sich eine sehr grosse Erfahrung mit Wahlen und Abstimmungen bei den dafür Verantwortlichen, aber auch bei den Stimmbürgern und Stimmbürgerinnen.

Für die praktische Umsetzung hat der Schweizer Bundesstaat in seiner 150-jährigen Geschichte verschiedene Elemente zum Einsatz gebracht. Zentral ist etwa das Stimmregister als Auszug des Einwohnerregisters. Beide Register werden von der Gemeinde gepflegt. Der Bürger erhält automatisch das Stimm- und Wahlrecht in seiner Wohngemeinde. Dazu kommen dieselben Rechte in seinem Kanton und für eidgenössische Wahlen und Abstimmungen. Das Stimmregister wird also laufend gepflegt.

Der primäre Stimmkanal ist die traditionelle „Wahlurne". Sie steht den Bürgern am Abstimmungs- und Wahlsonntag offen. Die Schweizerische Post geniesst in der Bevölkerung ein hohes Vertrauen. Sie garantiert bei der Zustellung eine hohe Qualität und Zuverlässigkeit. Diese Voraussetzungen erlaubte es 1994 als zweiten Stimmkanal die briefliche Stimmabgabe landesweit einzuführen. Dazu füllt der Stimmbürger den Wahlzettel zu Hause aus und steckt ihn in einen Umschlag. Danach unterschreibt er den separaten Stimmrechtsausweis und legt ihn gemeinsam mit der verschlossenen Stimme in einen voradressierten Briefumschlag und bringt ihn zur Post. Je nach Kanton ist der Umschlag vorfrankiert oder der Stimmbürger muss das Porto selbst bezahlen. Bei der Auszählung werden zunächst die Stimmrechtsausweise überprüft und von den verschlossenen Umschlägen mit den Stimmen separiert. Letztere werden erst in einem zweiten Schritt geöffnet (Stimmgeheimnis).

Mit dem Einsatz der brieflichen Abstimmung [1] hat die Schweiz akzeptiert, dass der Bürger den Wahl- und Abstimmungsakt zu Hause in einem ungeschützten Umfeld durchführt. Heute stimmen mehr als 90 % der Bevölkerung brieflich ab. Die komfortable briefliche Stimmabgabe geniesst damit eine hohe Akzeptanz. Gewisse Schwächen (u. a. entzieht sich die Behandlung der eingehenden brieflichen Stimmen der direkten Kontrolle der Bürger) werden akzeptiert und der Stimmkanal wird nicht prinzipiell in Frage gestellt. Daran ändern auch ab und zu vorkommende Betrugsfälle auf lokaler Ebene nichts. Das heisst, die Auswirkungen der Vorfälle beschränken sich in aller Regel auf den kommunalen Rahmen und es ist sehr selten, dass ein Urnengang wiederholt werden muss. Auf nationale Ergebnisse haben die lokalen Unregelmässigkeiten keine Auswirkungen.

12.2.2   E-Voting in der Schweiz

Die Schweiz hat E-Voting (im Sinn des Abstimmens und Wählens über das Internet) 2003 im Gesetz zu den politischen Rechten versuchsweise eingeführt. Der erste Versuch fand bei einer eidgenössischen Abstimmung im Kanton Genf statt. Bis heute sind über 200 Versuche durchgeführt worden. Sie waren alle erfolgreich. In 2014 hat das Parlament eine Gesetzesänderung verabschiedet, welche die Anforderungen an ein sicheres, modernes und überprüfbares System verankert. Dazu kommt die Idee der Beobachtbarkeit. Das bedeutet, dass der digitale Zählvorgang sichtbar werden muss und unter Aufsicht geschehen soll. Am Status der versuchsweisen Durchführung von elektronischen Urnengängen hat sich damit aber noch nichts geändert. Ergänzend hat der Bundesrat (die Schweizer Exekutive) im April 2017 bekannt gegeben, dass die elektronische Stimmabgabe in Zukunft als ordentlicher dritter Stimmkanal verankert werden soll.

Wie oben beschrieben sind die Schweizer Kantone mit der Durchführung von Wahlen und Abstimmungen betraut. Dies schliesst die Bundesebene mit ein und betrifft auch das E-Voting: Das bedeutet, dass jeder Kanton entscheiden kann, ob und wie er die elektronische Stimmabgabe einführen will. Er muss ein System auf dem Markt beschaffen und die Einführung sowie den Betrieb zusammen mit seinem Partner planen und organisieren. Heute gibt es zwei produktive E-Voting-Lösungen in der Schweiz: das System der Schweizerischen Post [2] (in Partnerschaft mit der spanischen Firma Scytl) und das System des Kantons Genf [3] (eine In-house Entwicklung, die der Kanton anderen Kantonen zur Verfügung stellt).

Als Voraussetzung für den Einsatz eines E-Voting-Systems für eidgenössische Wahlen und Abstimmungen müssen die Kantone die eidgenössischen technischen und organisatorischen Gesetzesanforderungen erfüllen. Die Bundeskanzlei – die für die Wahrung der politischen Rechte zuständige Bundesbehörde – führt einen Bewilligungsprozess durch. Am Ende des Prüfprozesses steht die Erlaubnis, das geprüfte E-Voting-System einzuführen.

Zunächst wurde E-Voting primär für Auslandschweizer eingesetzt. Aber mehrere Kantone haben E-Voting auch für Teile ihres Inland-Elektorats zugänglich gemacht (namentlich die Kantone Genf, Freiburg, Neuenburg, Basel-Stadt und St. Gallen). Prinzipiell gelten hierfür dieselben Anforderungen der Bundeskanzlei.

Das Stimmmaterial wird für alle drei Stimmkanäle nach wie vor per Brief in physikalischer Form zugestellt. Die Informationen vom Kanton an den Stimmbürger werden also nicht auf elektronischem Weg übermittelt. Wichtig ist ferner sicherzustellen, dass ein Bürger nur ein einziges Mal auf einem einzigen Stimmkanal abstimmen kann. Die Gemeinden und Wahlbüros setzen dazu eine Doppelstimmprüfung ein. Dabei werden die Nummern der physikalischen Stimmausweise mit den Nummern des digital eingesetzten Stimmmaterials verglichen. Damit stellen sie sicher, dass der Bürger nur einmal abgestimmt hat.

12.3   Prinzipielle Herausforderungen beim E-Voting

IT-Sicherheit beschäftigt sich mit Themen, die sich auf der sogenannten CIA-Triade abbilden lassen: Confidentiality (Vertraulichkeit), Integrity (Integrität), Availability (Verfügbarkeit). Die Herausforderungen mit der Sicherheit von E-Voting passen idealtypisch auf dieses Modell.

Das Stimmgeheimnis lässt sich dem Thema Vertraulichkeit zuordnen. Ausschliesslich im Stimmregister registrierte Personen dürfen Stimmen abgeben und diese Stimmen sind vor Manipulationen zu schützen. Die Integrität der Stimmen muss also garantiert werden. Und schliesslich soll der Zugang zum elektronischen Stimmkanal für die gesamte Abstimmungsperiode verfügbar sein.

Eine grundsätzliche Herausforderung stellt auch der Browser des Stimmbürgers respektive der Stimmbürgerin dar. Diese Geräte unterstehen nicht der Kontrolle der Administration. Die grosse Verbreitung von Malware und die Anfälligkeit von Browsern für Infektionen bringen es mit sich, dass eine gewisse Zahl von Stimmen auf einem infizierten Gerät abgegeben werden. Auch diese Stimmen sind vor einer Manipulation zu schützen.

Neben den Problemen der IT-Sicherheit spielt die Bedienbarkeit und die Barrierefreiheit der E-Voting-Systeme eine grosse Rolle. Dabei muss darauf geachtet werden, dass die verschiedenen Unterstützungssysteme die Sicherheit des Gesamtsystems nicht schwächen.

12.4   Bedrohungen

E-Voting-Systeme unterliegen denselben Bedrohungen, denen auch andere Systeme der elektronischen Datenverarbeitung ausgesetzt sind. Die 2017 neu erschienene Zusammenstellung der OWASP Top Ten Application Security Risks [4] kann als einfacher Einstieg in diese technische Materie gewählt werden. Tatsächlich ist es aber nötig, sämtliche Bedrohungen mit einem sehr systematischen Ansatz zu erschliessen und in einem umfassenden Bedrohungsmodell (Threat Model) zu beschreiben. Dieses Modell der Applikation ergänzt und komplementiert die übrigen Architekturdokumente. E-Voting bringt es aber auch mit sich, dass das Bedrohungsmodell über die Technik hinaus erschlossen werden sollte. Eine Manipulation der Wahl respektive des Resultats erscheint als sehr grosse Bedrohung. Allein, bereits der Verdacht einer Manipulation bringt einen Vertrauensverlust in das Resultat mit sich und stellt deshalb bereits eine bedeutsame Bedrohung dar.

Wer kommt als Angreifer (Threat Actor) in Frage? Im Inland besitzen die Befürworter respektive die Gegner einer Vorlage potenziell ein Interesse an einer Manipulation. Da unterschiedliche politische Lager die zur Verfügung stehenden Wahlkanäle unterschiedlich annehmen und benützen werden, ergibt sich daraus ein weiteres Motiv für die Manipulation eines Wahlkanales respektive ein Angriff auf seine Verfügbarkeit. Auch international ist eine Beeinflussung einer Wahl ein mögliches Thema. Dabei kann die Manipulation des Resultats im Vordergrund stehen, oder aber ein Vertrauensverlust in ein Resultat provoziert werden, um Land und Gesellschaft zu destabilisieren. Handfester ist die Gefahr, die von einer finanziellen Erpressung ausgeht. Es erscheint schwer vorstellbar, dass jemand ein ganzes Land erpressen würde, aber diese Bedrohung sollte nicht vorschnell von der Hand gewiesen werden. Es ist ja auch bekannt, dass nicht alle Opfer von Ransomware gezielt angegriffen wurden. Bisweilen werden auch Fälle von Kollateralschäden publik, in denen Systeme quasi zufällig von Angriffen der organisierten Kriminalität betroffen wurden.

Unabhängig vom Standort sind E-Voting-Systeme prestigeträchtige Ziele für Sicherheitsforscher oder professionelle Angreifer, die sich Ruhm und Ehre erhoffen und weitgehend frei von finanziellen Motiven arbeiten. Weniger aus Erkenntnisinteresse, denn aus destruktiven Motiven dürften Anarchisten und Terroristen vorgehen, denen es einzig um die Störung oder Beeinträchtigung des elektronischen Wahlkanals und damit um eine Störung des demokratischen Prozesses geht. Zwar besteht diese Bedrohung auch bei den übrigen Wahlkanälen, aber die Zentralisierung der elektronischen Wahlurne und der Zugriff über das Internet potenziert die diesbezügliche Bedrohung.

Wo es nur um die Störung eines Wahlvorganges geht, rücken Denial of Service Angriffe ins Augenmerk. Hier geht es nicht um eine direkte Manipulation von Stimmen, sondern um das Unterbinden des Zugangs zur elektronischen Wahlurne. Denial of Service Angriffe werden heute im Internet als Dienstleistung für wenig Geld angeboten. Dabei hat es sich gezeigt, dass die Strafverfolgungsbehörden sich sehr schwer mit der Ahndung dieser Art von Verbrechen tun, da oft keinerlei verwertbare Spuren zum Auftraggeber des Angriffes zurückführen.

12.5   Rechtliche und regulatorische Grundlagen und Richtlinien

12.5.1   Regulation in der Schweiz

Das politische System der Schweiz mit seiner etablierten direkten Demokratie geniesst einen sehr guten Ruf. Die Beschäftigung mit der Ausgestaltung der demokratischen Prozesse und die praktische Umsetzung der durch die Verfassung garantierten demokratischen Rechte besitzt eine lange Tradition. Und auch E-Voting ist kein neues Thema. In über 200 Pilotwahlgängen wurden verschiedene Systeme getestet und die Verfahren und Richtlinien in mehreren Schritten optimiert.

Seit 2014 umfasst die Schweizer Gesetzgebung folgende Instrumente und legislative Elemente, die E-Voting betreffen:

- Das *Bundesgesetz über die politischen Rechte* definiert, dass E-Voting in der Schweiz als Versuch erlaubt ist und dass der Bundesrat für Bewilligung an einzelnen Kantonen zuständig ist.
- Die *Verordnung über die politischen Rechte* definiert die Grundregeln für die Bewilligung des Bundesrats und die prozentuale Grösse des Teils des Elektorats, für den ein Kanton ein E-Voting-System maximal einsetzen darf.
- Die *Verordnung der Bundeskanzlei über die elektronische Stimmabgabe* sowie die zugeordneten *Technischen und administrativen Anforderungen an die elektronische Stimmabgabe* definieren die einzelnen Anforderungen. Dabei unterscheiden sich die Anforderungen je nach dem prozentualen Anteil der zugelassenen Stimmbürger und Stimmbürgerinnen: Je grösser der Teil des zugelassenen Elektorats desto höher die Anforderungen.

Die Kantone, die E-Voting einführten, haben ihre Gesetze und Verordnungen leicht angepasst, damit E-Voting den Anforderungen der Bundeskanzlei genügen kann.

Die im Gesetz definierten prozentualen Limiten können wie folgt zusammengefasst werden:

- Einsatz für bis zu 30 % der Wahlberechtigten eines Kantons: das E-Voting-System erfüllt eine Liste von technischen und sicherheitsrelevanten Anforderungen (insb. BSI Common Criteria), das Hosting geschieht in der Schweiz.
- Einsatz für 30 % bis 50 % der Wahlberechtigten eines Kantons: Zusätzlich zu den Anforderungen an ein System für 30 % der Wahlberechtigten muss das System den Mechanismus der individuellen Verifizierbarkeit implementieren, das Hosting ist nach ISO 27001 zu zertifizieren und die Plattform ist nach den Anforderungen des Gesetzes zu zertifizieren. Das kryptographische Protokoll ist kryptographisch und semantisch zu beweisen.
- Einsatz für über 50 % der Wahlberechtigten: Zusätzlich zu den Anforderungen an ein System für 50 % der Wahlberechtigten muss das System den Mechanismus der universellen Verifizierbarkeit implementieren. Die Stimmabgabe muss End-to-End verschlüsselt erfolgen und die Plattform muss mehrere Kontrollkomponenten besitzen, die unabhängig voneinander betrieben werden.

Im schweizerischen Kontext ist es wichtig zu verstehen, dass die beiden Konzepte der individuellen und der universellen Verifizierbarkeit vom Gesetzgeber leicht anders definiert wurden als in der Wissenschaft gebräuchlich. Sie werden deshalb hier genauer beschrieben.

12.5.2   Individuelle Verifizierbarkeit

Im Schweizer Kontext ist die individuelle Verifizierbarkeit ein Weg, um die Anforderung des sogenannten „cast-as-intended" zu implementieren. Die Wähler erhalten in ihrem (physikalischen) Stimmmaterial eine Liste von Kontrollcodes. Für jede Abstimmungsoption gibt es je einen solchen Code (jede Antwort, jeder Kandidat und jede Liste inkl. der leeren Antwort). Wenn der Wähler seine elektronische Abstimmung beendet, berechnet das System die Kontrollcodes der ausgewählten Optionen und zeigt sie auf dem Gerät des Wählers an. Der Wähler kann dann überprüfen, ob die angezeigten Codes denjenigen entsprechen, die er in seinen Stimmunterlagen erhalten hat. Der Wähler kann damit also überprüfen, ob seine Stimme korrekt übertragen und gespeichert wurde. Falls seine Stimme auf dem Weg der Übermittlung geändert worden wäre (Man-in-the-Middle) würde dies damit auffallen (Siehe [7]).

12.5.3 Universelle Verifizierbarkeit

Mit der universellen Verifizierbarkeit wird das E-Voting-System durch die kantonale Wahlkommission überprüfbar und beobachtbar. Zuerst muss das System durch ein verifizierbares kryptographisches Protokoll definiert werden. Das Protokoll heisst verifizierbar, weil es mathematische Beweise enthält, die erlauben, in jedem einzelnen Schritt zu beweisen, dass die Stimmen in der Urne nicht verändert wurden. Diese Beweise funktionieren selbst mit verschlüsselten Stimmen, also ohne die Stimmen und die Ergebnisse der Abstimmung zu kennen (Zero Knowledge Proof). Diese Beweise werden durch die Wahlkommission geprüft und validiert. Damit kann die Wahlkommission belegen, dass niemand die Urne gefälscht hat.

Zusätzlich sehen die Ausführungsbestimmungen der Schweizerischen Bundeskanzlei als Ergänzung zur universellen Verifizierbarkeit vier Kontrollkomponenten vor. Diese Kontrollkomponenten müssen die elektronische Urne und die Stimmabgabe überwachen. Sie sind unabhängig voneinander zu betreiben und garantieren damit einen zusätzlichen, vierfachen Schutz vor Manipulationen.

12.5.4 BSI Common Criteria

Die Anforderungen der Bundeskanzlei referenzieren direkt das Common Criteria Schutzprofil als Grundlage der Sicherheitsanforderungen an Online-Wahlprodukte (BSI-CC-PP-0037).

In der Einleitung des Dokumentes (siehe [8]) ist das Ziel des Schutzprofiles wie folgt definiert:

„Dieses Schutzprofil definiert einen Basissatz von Sicherheitsanforderungen, den jedes Online-Wahlprodukt zumindest erfüllen muss, um einige Arten von Vereinswahlen, Gremienwahlen, etwa in den Hochschulen, im Bildungs- und Forschungsbereich, und insbesondere nichtpolitische Wahlen mit geringem Angriffspotenzial sicher auszuführen."

Jedes E-Voting-System in der Schweiz muss die kompletten Anforderungen des Schutzprofils erfüllen, soweit sie mit den Gegebenheiten des schweizerischen politischen Systems vereinbar sind.

12.5.5 Zertifizierungen

Das Gesetz zu den politischen Rechten definiert, dass die Kantone und der Betreiber eines E-Voting-Systems ein Management System für Informationssicherheit (ISMS) im Einsatz haben müssen. Es muss konform zum ISO Standard 27001 aufgebaut und zertifiziert sein. Mit dem Management System wird sichergestellt, dass E-Voting sehr hoch in der Organisation verankert ist und dass die beschriebenen Prozesse aktiv gelebt werden. Dazu kommt, dass Entscheidungen auf einem Riskmanagement-System abgestützt werden müssen.

Zusätzlich zu einer Zertifizierung nach ISO 27001 müssen die Kantone und die Betreiber sich durch eine akkreditierte Zertifizierungsstelle prüfen lassen. Damit kann sichergestellt werden, dass das E-Voting-System und sein Betrieb im Detail konform zu den gesetzlichen Anforderungen des Bundes ist und bleibt. Der Scope der Zertifizierung umfasst die folgenden Teile:

- Prüfung des Protokolls: Validierung und Kontrolle der kryptographischen und semantischen Beweise des Protokolls.
- Prüfung der Funktionalitäten: Validierung der Erfüllung der funktionalen Anforderungen inkl. des Schutzprofils.
- Prüfung der Infrastruktur und des Betriebs: Validierung der Erfüllung der betrieblichen und organisatorischen Anforderungen.
- Prüfung der Kontrollkomponenten: Validierung der Erfüllung der Anforderungen für die universelle Verifizierbarkeit.
- Prüfung des Schutzes gegen Versuche in die Infrastruktur einzudringen: Validierung der Sicherheit des Systems, insbesondere. durch Penetrationstests.
- Prüfung der Druckerei: Validierung der Erfüllung der spezifischen Anforderungen an den Druck der Stimmrechtsausweise mit den Kontrollcodes.

12.6   Schutzprinzipien

Ohne moderne kryptographische Methoden wäre es nicht möglich, E-Voting-Systeme adäquat zu schützen. Die Fortschritte der letzten Jahrzehnte auf diesem Gebiet sind damit eine Voraussetzung für die Erfüllung der oben beschriebenen Schutzziele, namentlich Vertraulichkeit und Integrität der Stimmen. Die Public- / Private-Key-Verschlüsselung wie etwa die sogenannte ElGamal-Verschlüsselung ist ein zentrales Element, das in verschiedenen Teilen der Systeme eingesetzt werden kann.

Homomorphe Verschlüsselung erlaubt es, die Stimmen über mehrere Schritte zu anonymisieren, ohne dass die Stimme selbst verändert würde. Die Integrität der einzelnen Stimme wird durch die Verifizierbarkeit garantiert. Auch dahinter stehen kryptographischen Methoden.

Die maximale Sicherheitsstufe eines IT-Systems wird gemeinhin durch das schwächste Element vorgegeben. Die Einbindung der oben angesprochenen Kontrollgruppen hat das Ziel, hier eine höhere Schutzstufe zu etablieren. Der Schutz soll also nicht mehr länger durch das schwächste Element vorgegeben werden können. Vielmehr soll der höchste Schutz erhalten bleiben, solange wenigstens eine der Kontrollgruppen wie vorgegeben arbeitet. Es handelt sich dabei um eine Anwendung von byzantinischer Fehlertoleranz.

Ein wichtiges Grundprinzip beim Bau der E-Voting-Infrastruktur ist die Mandatory Access Control (MAC). Das heisst, jeder Systemzugriff und jede Veränderung von Einstellungen unterliegt einer Prüfung der Zugriffsberechtigungen. Die Berechtigungen selbst werden unterteilt (Separation of Duties) und die Mächtigkeit der einzelnen Akteure und Systeme dadurch limitiert. Es werden immer nur die minimalen Zugriffsrechte, die nötig sind, um eine Arbeit verrichten zu können (Least Priviledge/Need to Have), ausgegeben. Beispielhaft hierfür ist die Aufteilung der Schlüssel zur Dechiffrierung der Wahlurne, die über den gesamten Wahlausschuss verteilt werden. Das bedeutet, dass ein einzelnes Mitglied der Wahlkommission die Urne nicht entschlüsseln kann. Die Betreiber der Wahlurne selbst wiederum besitzen keinen Anteil an diesen Schlüsseln und sind deshalb nicht in der Lage, die Stimmen selbst einzusehen.

Mandatory Access Control bedeutet in der Konsequenz auch eine Trennung der E-Voting-Systeme von anderen Systemen. Diese Separierung der Infrastruktur beim Betreiber stösst allerdings ab einem bestimmten Grad an wirtschaftliche Grenzen und lässt sich nicht mehr finanzieren, so dass bei der Trennung Kompromisse eingegangen werden müssen.

Die Infrastruktur ist durch mehrere Sicherheitsschichten zu schützen (Multi-Tier/Multilayer). Wesentliche Elemente stellen natürlich Netzwerk-Firewalls zwischen den Komponenten aber auch Web Application Firewalls (WAF) dar. Die Open Source WAF ModSecurity erlaubt dabei eine sehr granulare Kontrolle des Verkehrs. Ein Regelwerk wie das OWASP ModSecurity Core Rule Set sorgt für einen Grundschutz und weitere Regelsätze implementieren zusätzliche Schutzmassnahmen welche das MAC Modell respektive das Need-to-Have Prinzip unterstützen (Whitelisting von erlaubten Zugriffen).

Die Transparenz ist ein weiteres Grundprinzip, das die politische Akzeptanz von E-Voting-Systemen erhöhen kann. Die Transparenz bringt aber auch einen administrativen Mehraufwand mit sich, denn Informationen wollen richtig aufbereitet und für die interessierte Öffentlichkeit verständlich kommentiert werden. Die Sicherheit der implementierten E-Voting-Protokolle lässt sich kaum feststellen, solange nicht zumindest die Protokolle öffentlich gemacht und in der Forschungsgemeinschaft diskutiert werden. Bei der Frage der Offenlegung des Quellcodes sind die Interessen der Öffentlichkeit gegenüber den Schutzbedürfnissen des geistigen Eigentums zu prüfen. Die Frage der Transparenz stellt sich auch bei den Berichten zu Zertifizierungen und Penetration Tests, die gegebenenfalls zu publizieren sind. Private Sicherheitstester interessieren sich für E-Voting. Es bietet sich an, diesen die Beschäftigung mit dem E-Voting-System in einem regulierten Rahmen zu erlauben und dadurch öffentliche Penetration Tests zu ermöglichen. Dazu gehört es auch, einen Dialog mit diesen Forschern zu etablieren und auf ihre Befunde gegebenenfalls mit Anpassungen zu reagieren.

Disaster Toleranz und das weiter oben angesprochene Denial of Service Problem verlangen nach eigenen Lösungen. Ein Aufbau über mehrere Server-Standorte hinweg erscheint zwingend. Grosse Denial of Service Angriffe dürften die Infrastruktur dennoch überfordern. Ein Stück weit vermag ein Zusammengehen mit dem Internet Service Provider die Angriffe abzuschwächen, aber die grössten Angriffe werden die Netzwerkkapazität des Providers trotzdem übersteigen. Im Normalfall wird in diesem Moment die Unterstützung eines Content Delivery Networks respektive eines Anti DDoS Services gesucht.

Allerdings bedingen diese Massnahmen, dass man die SSL-/TLS-Schlüssel an den Schutzpartner übergibt, was im E-Voting-Kontext kaum denkbar ist. Das Ausschliessen von fremden IP-Adressen ist ebenfalls eine hilfreiche Massnahme (GeoIP), allerdings schneidet sie Stimmbürgerinnen und Stimmbürger im Ausland vom E-Voting ab, was dem Sinn und Zweck der Lösung zu widersprechen scheint. Effektiver erscheinen deshalb administrative Massnahmen wie die in der Schweiz bis dato favorisierte Schliessung des elektronischen Kanals 24 Stunden vor dem Schliessen des schriftlichen Abstimmungstermins. Das heisst, dass lokale Stimmbürger immer noch an der Urne abstimmen können. Ein DoS-Angriff auf den elektronischen Kanal wäre damit ärgerlich, würde die Stimmbürgerinnen und Stimmbürger aber nicht von einer Stimmabgabe abhalten. Auslandschweizer sind angehalten, ihre Stimme möglichst rasch nach Erhalt der Stimmunterlagen abzugeben.

12.7   Zusammenfassung

Die Schweiz hat ein gut etabliertes politisches System mit starken direktdemokratischen Elementen. Das Stimmvolk wird mehrmals pro Jahr an die Urne gerufen. Die sich daraus ergebende Routine im Umgang mit Abstimmungen und Wahlen sowie das breit akzeptierte briefliche Abstimmen bildet eine gute Voraussetzung zur Einführung der elektronischen Stimmabgabe über das Internet.

In über 200 Versuchen wurde E-Voting in der Schweiz geprüft, verfeinert und nach und nach immer höheren Sicherheitsanforderungen unterstellt. Grundlegende Konzepte wie die individuelle Verifizierbarkeit, die universelle Verifizierbarkeit sowie die Einführung von unabhängigen Kontrollgruppen bieten einen hohen Schutz vor der Manipulation von Stimmen. Die korrekte Umsetzung dieser Techniken und des zu Grunde liegenden E-Voting-Protokolls muss in separaten Zertifizierungen überprüft werden.

Die Implementierung, die Einführung und der Betrieb einer sicheren E-Voting-Lösung stellen sehr hohe Anforderungen an das Know-How des Personals sowie die Maturität der Prozesse der beteiligten Organisationen. In der Schweiz erfüllen die Schweizerische Post und der Kanton Genf als Anbieter einer Lösung für die elektronische Stimmabgabe die an ein solches System gestellten Anforderungen.

Literatur

1. Der Begriff „briefliche Abstimmung" bedeutet in diesem Artikel, dass der Bürger per Brief abstimmen und wählen kann.
2. Siehe https://www.post.ch/evoting (am 24.12.2017 abgerufen).
3. Siehe https://www.ge.ch/vote-electronique/ (am 24.12.2017 abgerufen).
4. https://www.owasp.org/index.php/Category:OWASP_Top_Ten_Project, (am 24.12.2017 abgerufen).

Referenzen

1. Swiss Online Voting Protocol, R&D, Scytl Secure Electronic Voting (2016) https://www.post.ch/-/media/post/evoting/dokumente/swiss-post-online-voting-protocol.pdf (am 24.12.2017 abgerufen)
2. Swiss Post E-Voting Protocol Explained, Scytl Secure Electronic Voting & Post CH Ltd (2016) https://www.post.ch/-/media/post/evoting/dokumente/swiss-post-online-voting-protocol-explained.pdf (am 24.12.2017 abgerufen)
3. Distributed immutabilization of secure logs, Scytl Secure Electronic Voting & Post CH Ltd (2017) https://www.scytl.com/wp-content/uploads/2017/01/Distributed-Immutabilization-of-Secure-Logs_Scytl.pdf (am 24.12.2017 abgerufen)
4. A Secure E-Voting Infrastructure. Implementation by Swiss Post (2017), Second International Joint Conference on Electronic Voting E-Vote-ID 2017, TUT Press (am 24.12.2017 abgerufen)
5. Federal Ordinance on Political Rights, Swiss Federal Chancellery (2014) https://www.admin.ch/opc/de/classified-compilation/19780105/index.html (am 24.12.2017 abgerufen)
6. Federal Chancellery Ordinance on Electronic Voting (VEleS) , Swiss Federal Chancellery (2014) https://www.admin.ch/opc/en/classified-compilation/20132343/index.html (am 24.12.2017 abgerufen)
7. Technical and administrative requirements for electronic vote casting, Swiss Federal Chancellery (2014) https://www.bk.admin.ch/themen/pore/evoting/07979/index.html?lang=en (am 24.12.2017 abgerufen)
8. Common Criteria Schutzprofil für Basissatz von Sicherheitsanforderungen an Online-Wahlprodukte (BSI-CC-PP-0037) https://www.commoncriteriaportal.org/files/ppfiles/pp0037b.pdf (am 24.12.2017 abgerufen)

Teil III

Cyber Defence

NATO: Ein transatlantischer Blick auf die Cybersicherheit

13

Dieter Warnecke und Sorin Ducaru

Zusammenfassung

Cyber-Angriffe auf Staaten und deren kritische Infrastrukturen sind schon lange keine Fiktion mehr, sondern Realität. Die vermeintliche Anonymität von Angriffen und die kostengünstigen Möglichkeiten zur asymmetrischen Wirkung haben Cyber-Angriffe im Informationsumfeld zu einem wirkungsvollen Mittel gemacht. Auch die NATO behandelt schon heute den Cyberraum als einen eigenen Operationsraum. Viele Länder haben Cyber-Fähigkeiten in ihren Strukturen abgebildet. Auch die Bundeswehr baut ihren Beitrag im Rahmen der Sicherheitsarchitektur in Deutschland aus, um die Chancen der Digitalisierung zu nutzen, aber auch um den Bedrohungen aus dem Cyber- und Informationsraum zu begegnen.

D. Warnecke (✉)
Bundesministerium der Verteidigung, Berlin, Deutschland
E-Mail: dieterwarnecke@bmvg.bund.de

S. Ducaru
Hudson Institute, Washington DC, USA
E-Mail: sorin@ducaru.net

© Springer Fachmedien Wiesbaden GmbH, ein Teil von Springer Nature 2018   153
M. Bartsch, S. Frey (Hrsg.), *Cybersecurity Best Practices*,
https://doi.org/10.1007/978-3-658-21655-9_13

13.1   Cyber-Sicherheit geht uns alle an

General Warnecke

Vorwort von Generalleutnant Dieter Warnecke, Abteilungsleiter Strategie und Einsatz im Bundesministerium der Verteidigung

Cyber-Angriffe auf Staaten und deren kritische Infrastrukturen sind schon lange keine Fiktion mehr, sondern Realität. Die vermeintliche Anonymität von Angriffen und die kostengünstigen Möglichkeiten zur asymmetrischen Wirkung haben Cyber-Angriffe im Informationsumfeld zu einem wirkungsvollen Mittel gemacht. Auch die NATO behandelt schon heute den Cyberraum als einen eigenen Operationsraum. Viele Länder haben Cyber-Fähigkeiten in ihren Strukturen abgebildet. Auch die Bundeswehr baut ihren Beitrag im Rahmen der Sicherheitsarchitektur in Deutschland aus, um die Chancen der Digitalisierung zu nutzen, aber auch um den Bedrohungen aus dem Cyber- und Informationsraum zu begegnen.

Die Stärkung der Cyber-Sicherheit und der Ausbau von Cyber-Fähigkeiten sind daher ein essentieller Beitrag zur gesamtstaatlichen Sicherheitsvorsorge und bieten zusätzliche Handlungsoptionen für Konfliktverhütung und Krisenbewältigung einschließlich der Begegnung hybrider Bedrohungen.

Im Nationalen Cyberabwehrzentrum unter der Leitung des Bundesamtes für Sicherheit in der Informationstechnik arbeitet die Bundeswehr eng mit anderen Behörden zusammen. Auf ministerieller Ebene leistet das Bundesministerium der Verteidigung im Cybersicherheitsrat seinen Beitrag zur Stärkung der ganzheitlichen Sicherheitsvorsorge im Cyberraum.

Zur Stärkung des Austausches von Informationen zu Bedrohungen und zur Schaffung gemeinsamer Cyber-Sicherheitsstandards trägt das Bundesverteidigungsministerium in Abstimmung mit dem Auswärtigen Amt und dem Bundesministerium des Inneren in den Gremien der NATO und der EU zur gemeinsamen Strategieentwicklung und gegenseitigen Unterstützung bei.

In der Cyberaußenpolitik beraten die Vertreter des Bundesministeriums der Verteidigung zusammen mit Vertretern des Bundesministeriums des Innern das Auswärtige Amt bei den Bemühungen, Konfliktrisiken zwischen Staaten im Cyberraum zu mindern.

Multilateral oder bilateral gewinnt die Zusammenarbeit getrieben von der gemeinsamen Bedrohung an Momentum. Da zu diesem Buch die Autoren aus Österreich und der Schweiz wesentliche Beiträge geleistet haben, möchte ich die erfolgreichen „D-A-CH"-Gespräche als ein Beispiel der wertvollen multinationalen Zusammenarbeit herausheben.

Vielen Nationen ist gemein, dass das Thema Cyber-Sicherheit immer in einem gesamtstaatlichen Kontext eingebunden ist, zur Fähigkeitssteigerung über die nächsten Jahre erhebliche Anstrengungen im finanziellen und personellen Bereich unternommen werden, die Einbeziehung der Wirtschaft sowie der Wissenschaft einen großen Stellenwert besitzt und personelle Ressourcen durch Rückgriff auf eine Cyber-Reserve im Bedarfsfall schnell und effizient aufgestockt werden sollen. Ebenfalls breites Verständnis ist, dass zur Durchführung wirkungsvoller Cyber-Maßnahmen ein weites Spektrum an Fähigkeiten und an Möglichkeiten des Handelns erforderlich ist.

Neben speziellen technischen Fähigkeiten sind alle staatlichen Instrumente der Krisenbewältigung in Erwägung zu ziehen.

Viele Staaten halten sich die Option offen, im Rahmen der Abschreckung das komplette Spektrum militärischer Mittel gegen Cyber-Angriffe einzusetzen. Diese Haltung spiegelt sich auch in der Erklärung der Regierungschefs anlässlich des NATO Gipfeltreffens in Warschau 2016 wieder. Dadurch zeigt sich die militärische Relevanz des Cyber- und Informationsraums als eigene Dimension neben Land-, Luft-, See- und Weltraum.

Aus operativer Sicht stellen die Besonderheiten des Cyber-und Informationsraums eine große Herausforderung dar:

Der Cyber- und Informationsraum kennt mit Ausnahmen weder physikalische nationale Grenzen noch ein hierarchisches oder institutionelles Gefüge. Er ist hochdynamisch und in Teilen anarchistisch. Trotz der Bemühungen einzelner Staaten, diesen Raum zu kontrollieren, ist der Einfluss von Staaten beschränkt. Selbst die Grenze zwischen offensiver und defensiver Ausrichtung ist fließend. Hat ein Akteur die Fähigkeit zur Verteidigung, besitzt er auch grundlegendes Wissen über Möglichkeiten des Angriffs.

Hierdurch sind die Grenzen zwischen Krieg und Frieden, innerer und äußerer Sicherheit sowie kriminell und politisch motivierten Angriffen schwer erkennbar.

- Die Schwierigkeit der Attribution, also der zweifelsfreien Zurückführung von Angriffen auf Verursacher, verstärkt die gefühlte Grenzenlosigkeit des Cyber-Raums.
- Gleichzeitig sind in den letzten Jahren große Fortschritte sowohl bei technischer Attribution als auch in völkerrechtlichen Fragen und vertrauensbildenden Maßnahmen erzielt worden.

Gleichwohl gelten für den Einsatz von militärischen Fähigkeiten im Cyber- und Informationsraum stets die gleichen völker- und verfassungsrechtlichen Rahmenbedingungen wie beim Einsatz anderer militärischer Fähigkeiten auch.

Cybersicherheit ist ein gesamtstaatliches Konzept der Sicherheitsvorsorge. Dieses Konzept schließt neben dem Zusammenwirken der verantwortlichen Ressorts die Verantwortung von Unternehmen insbesondere der Internetserviceprovider und der Betreiber von KRITIS zur Erhöhung der Sicherheit mit ein. Denn eine Schwäche dort kann die Sicherheit aller gefährden.

Ich hoffe, dass dieses Buch **„Cyberstrategien – Best Practices"** das gemeinsame Verständnis über die Notwendigkeit der Zusammenarbeit zwischen Staat, Industrie und Gesellschaft im Cyberraum erhöht und die hier aufgezeigten Beispiele aus der Praxis unserer gemeinsamen Sicherheit dienen können. Dabei ist der Beitrag jedes Einzelnen wichtig, um Lücken in der Cybersicherheit zu schließen.

Cyber-Sicherheit geht uns alle an.

13.2   Cyber Defense Best Practice: The NATO Experience

Sorin Ducaru

13.2.1   Meeting Challenges in Cyberspace: NATO's Cyber Defense Evolution

Today, you have only to look at the front page of a newspaper to understand the serious nature of cyber attacks. With every headline, it is clear that they are becoming more common, complex, and harmful.

2017 alone had several serious attacks that impacted people's lives, businesses' bottom lines, and governments' operations. In May 2017, WannaCry quickly spread around the globe, taking advantage of a vulnerability not yet patched in all organizations. The UK's National Health Service identified up to 19,000 appointments, including operations, that were affected by WannaCry [1], and FedEx's global delivery platform was also significantly impacted [2]; while the ransom collected was ultimately relatively low, the impacts caused were immediate and acute. About a month later, NotPetya also had multinational effects: malware was introduced into numerous companies through the update of an accounting software popular in Ukraine. NotPetya, however, was able to move through these companies' networks, infecting businesses around the world. Large conglomerates have estimated hundreds of millions of euro – if not more – in losses when NotPetya destroyed data and computers and forced the temporary shutdown of their operations.

While 2017 thus marks a year of widespread and sophisticated attacks that demonstrate the potential for harm on a global scale, this is not the first time, of course, governments, businesses, and individuals have had to confront the impacts of attacks. Over the past 15 years, as the threat environment and geostrategic picture has changed, the North Atlantic Treaty Organization – NATO – has evolved and adapted to meet the challenge of cyber attacks.

In 2002, at the Prague Summit, Allied Heads of State and Government recognized the danger posed by cyber attacks for the first time, stating it was necessary to "strengthen our capabilities to defend against cyber attacks" [3]. NATO took action by establishing the NATO Computer Incident Response Capability, or NCIRC, which protects NATO's networks.

At this stage, NATO's approach to cyber threats was a technical one, focused on traditional network defense. Events in 2007, however, forced a new approach. After the government of Estonia relocated a Soviet-era war memorial from the city center to a cemetery, a series of cyber attacks were launched on Estonia's digital infrastructure, including that supporting political, media, banking, and telecommunications organizations. As Estonia was one of the most digitally interconnected societies, this had a huge impact on the day-to-day functioning of the nation for 3 weeks [4].

These coordinated attacks, undertaken for political purpose, prompted NATO to take a harder look at its cyber defenses, including from a policy perspective. In 2008, NATO adopted its first foundational cyber defense policy – its policy "1.0" – at the Summit in Bucharest. This policy established the objectives, principles, and first organizational elements related to NATO cyber defense. NATO was now moving from purely technical to policy concerns, but it remained focused on its own networks.

The cyber strategic environment changed again in the summer of 2008, when the war in Georgia demonstrated that cyber attacks have the potential to become a component of military operations. Consequently, the NATO Strategic Concept adopted at the Lisbon Summit in 2010 recognized that "cyber attacks can reach a threshold that threatens national and Euro-Atlantic prosperity, security and stability" [5]. This recognition determined the development of a new NATO cyber defense policy in 2011.

This second policy on cyber defense – policy "2.0" – once again took the protection of NATO's own networks as its priority, providing for a centralized protection of all NATO networks. At the same time, however, NATO began to use its established processes to encourage the continued development of Allied capabilities. Using the NATO Defence Planning Process, which will be described in greater detail below, the first cyber defense capability targets were established. With this, the responsibilities of NATO and Allies for improving cyber defense capabilities both increased and balanced.

In 2014, the world witnessed the use of cyber attacks in the context of hybrid operations in Crimea and Eastern Ukraine. NATO itself was also subject to a disruptive Distributed Denial of Service (DDoS) attack, for which a group calling itself "Cyber Berkut" claimed responsibility. As a result of the attack, NATO's main website was unavailable for more than 10 h.

It was against this backdrop that NATO once again stepped up efforts to enhance its cyber defenses at the Summit in Wales. A third policy on cyber defense – "3.0" – was endorsed, representing a significant milestone for NATO cyber defense.

Why Was This the Case?

Firstly, through this policy, Allies acknowledged that "the impact of cyber-attacks could be as harmful to our societies as a conventional attack" and affirmed that cyber defense is part of NATO's core task of collective defense [6]. Secondly, NATO Allies recognized that international law, including international humanitarian law and the UN Charter, applies in cyberspace.

NATO also expanded a number of activities including on training, education, exercises, and information sharing. NATO further decided to create the NATO Cyber Range, introduced cyber aspects into our operational planning, and launched new partnerships, including with industry. This third stage linked cyber defense to NATO's core task of collective defense and established a framework of assistance to Allies.

In 2016, at the Warsaw Summit, NATO's approach to cyber defense continued to adapt. Allied Heads of State and Government adopted a Cyber Defence Pledge to strengthen and enhance the cyber defenses of their national networks and infrastructures as a matter of priority. Allies also recognized cyberspace as a domain of operations in order to enable NATO to defend itself as effectively in cyberspace as it does on land, at sea, or in the air [7]. Finally, NATO continued to take action to strengthen its cyber defense partnerships – with other countries, international organizations, industry, and academia.

While describing this evolution, it is important to highlight that in cyberspace, like in the other domains, NATO's actions are in accordance with its defensive mandate and with international law as well as the fact that the main focus over the years has been to strengthen cyber resilience and defense.

As NATO now enters this phase of operationalizing cyberspace, it is an appropriate moment to reflect on not only what NATO has learned – but how NATO can help other organizations, whether they are private industry, national governments, or other international organizations.

As described, NATO has moved from a narrow, technical approach to cyber defense to one that is broad and policy based, encompassing not only NATO but also Allies. NATO has transformed the way it does cyber business, and it can offer approaches and best practices that it has learned through this experience. Ultimately, NATO is a large organization that has been subject to increasing attacks – what NATO has learned in its own defense can serve directly as best practice for others.

NATO, however, is more than just a unitary organization: by virtue of its Alliance structure, it also serves as a unique platform to discover and share best practices. Through its 29 Allies, as well as through its relationships with Partner nations and industry, NATO has access to a wide variety of best practices that it can make use of as well as share among Allied countries and stakeholders. These practices may be of direct use, as well as provide models for how organizations can increase their own access to best practices.

13.2.2   Best Practices and Lessons Learned

As has been described, NATO has undertaken significant evolution to respond to the changing threat environment. While some of the specific measures and policies that have been implemented are unique to NATO, the reasons for their implementation, as well as their organizational impact, have broad relevance to both public and private sector organizations.

NATO has prioritized three lines of action in order to realize this organizational change: a focus on its *people*, an improved *construct/architecture* for its cyber defense, and more stringent *requirements* for what good cyber defense looks like.

13.2.2.1   Focus on People

Cyber defense is as much about people as it is about technology – even the most advanced technology must be coupled with engaged leadership as well as educated and aware employees.

Large-scale organizational change and investment requires senior leadership buy-in. Cyber challenges must be addressed as a strategic risk, which cannot be done without organizational champions to ensure continued and sustained focus. Over the past decade, NATO has changed the way it manages cyber to achieve this focus.

Cyber defense now starts at the top at NATO with the North Atlantic Council, or NAC. The NAC "is the principal political decision-making body within NATO. It oversees the political and military process relating to security issues affecting the whole Alliance" [8]. The Ambassadors of all the Allies are now regularly briefed on cyber defense issues and are responsible for exercising principal authority in a cyber defense-related crisis management.

The NAC is supported by several different structures. The Cyber Defence Committee "is the lead committee for political governance and cyber defence policy in general, providing oversight and advice to Allied countries on NATO's cyber defence efforts at the expert level" [9]. The Cyber Defence Management Board has responsibility "for coordinating cyber coordinating cyber defence throughout NATO civilian and military bodies. The CDMB comprises the leaders of the policy, military, operational and technical bodies in NATO with responsibilities for cyber defence" [9]. The NATO Strategic Commands – Allied Command Operations and Allied Command Transformation – also now have organizations dedicated to cyber defense issues, ensuring that their leadership is integrating cyber defense considerations into all that they do.

Taken together, these political and military bodies ensure that internal leadership is appropriately coordinated and apprised on cyber issues. With the involvement of the most senior political and military authorities, cyber can be understood from both technical and policy aspect, promoting informed decisions on risks and incidents.

While other organizations are not organized exactly as is NATO, these structures can provide useful insight to others. Private sector organizations could consider, for example, whether their boards of directors are regularly briefed on cyber risks within their enterprises. Do they know what risks their organizations might be accepting, and what the potential impacts could be? Do organizations have standing meetings to bring together stakeholders across the enterprise to ensure that threats and response actions are commonly understood and implemented? In short, NATO has learned the value of regularizing and elevating internal information sharing and decision-making on critical cyber defense issues, which is applicable to any organization.

Leadership, however, cannot be expected to make expert decisions on cyber defense without any training or education – or without informed people at the operational and tactical levels. NATO has invested in several exercises in order to allow political and military leadership, as well as their subordinates, to better understand cyber defense.

The NATO Crisis Management Exercise, for example, allows the Alliance to "rehearse and test its internal and partner consultation and decision making procedures at the strategic political-military level" [10]. This exercise now always includes cyber threats, allowing leaders to respond to developments in cyberspace as part of an integrated and realistic scenario. NATO also hosts its flagship cyber exercise, Cyber Coalition, on a yearly basis. Cyber Coalition is focused on operational personnel, testing their ability to respond to scenarios in a virtual environment.

This sort of exercising is a critical step to improving cyber defense at any organization. It ensures that employees are aware of how cyber could impact their jobs and how they would be expected to react and respond in the event of a real-life incident. Practicing decision-making in a realistic but fictitious environment is crucial to allowing organizations to figure out their strengths and weaknesses – given the prevalence of cyber attacks, organizations will be better positioned by assuming it is only a matter of if, not when, they will experience a cyber incident.

Finally, even as NATO has invested and organized to ensure high-level focus and attention, it has not forgotten about the daily business of cyber defense. We can spend millions on upgrading systems, but if we have not invested adequately in training and educating our people – the users of this technology – then it could be all in vain. We must build security into our systems, and a large part of this is about fostering a culture of security. As the most sophisticated cyber protection products can fail if an employee clicks on a malicious link in an email, NATO has made cyber user awareness training mandatory employees for all employees. NATO has also continued to develop the specialized skills of its cyber defenders. Numerous courses are offered through NATO School Oberammergau, such as those on network security and cyber incident handling and disaster response. Further trainings are also offered through the NATO Cooperative Cyber Defence Centre of Excellence (CCD COE), covering everything from botnet mitigation [11] to international law courses [12].

What is critical for all organizations: how are your employees made aware of cyber threats? Do they understand the basics of cyber hygiene – and do they have opportunities to expand their specialized knowledge as necessary and relevant? Leadership, employees, and technical personnel all must to expand their awareness and skillsets to keep pace with cyber threats.

13.2.2.2 Improved Construct for Cyber Defense

Given the prevalence and persistence of cyber threats, modern network defense no longer assumes that all attacks can be kept out. Instead, detection and remediation must be viewed as equally key parts of cyber protection [13].

In order to ensure consistent, high-level cyber defense, NATO has adopted a model of centralized protection – that is, the NCIRC has responsibility for centrally protecting and defending all networks run by the NATO Communications and Information Agency. This centralized protection spans some 60 sites from United States to Afghanistan, from Iceland to the Indian Ocean. This protection covers a number of services, including:

- Intrusion prevention
- Malware detection
- Analysis and information sharing
- Data loss prevention
- Computer forensics

Over 200 experts are working around the clock with advanced network protection sensors and analytical tools on monitoring sophisticated and persistent threats against NATO networks. NATO also has Rapid Reaction Teams on standby to respond to incidents on NATO networks or to assist Allies, as well as a Cyber Threat Assessment Cell, which carries out post-incident analysis. New cyber defense capabilities are also being considered, including advanced analytics, increased automation, and a broader range of protection to defend against evolving cyber threats. Taken together, this advanced, centralized protection of networks is the very essence of NATO's core cyber business.

This type of construct – a central hub for administration, monitoring, analysis, and response – is a valuable one for any organization with several locations and complex networks to consider. It allows for the broadest insight into all networks, and it provides for critical services to be delivered consistently.

13.2.2.3 More Stringent Organizational Requirements

Even as NATO has thus been striving for a high level of consistent security across all its networks, it has similarly been facilitating the same type of development among its Allies through the NATO Defence Planning Process (NDPP). The NDPP "is the primary means to identify the required capabilities and promote their timely and coherent development and acquisition by Allies" [14]. Through this process, strategy is transformed into capabilities that Allies implement.

As mentioned above, Allies first became responsible for meeting cyber defense targets in the NATO's 2011 cyber defense policy; these targets have continued to mature to promote capability development in all nations. New targets were agreed in 2017, focusing on the protection of deployed networks and enhanced interoperability. This facilitates the coordinated development on national cyber defense capabilities, which assists nations to improve not only in isolation but in harmony, allowing NATO to become more interoperable.

While the NDPP is certainly NATO-specific, the process of and reasons for the NDPP are relevant to all organizations. First, the principle of moving from strategic thought to the means of implementation is key to making cyber defense a part of core business. By translating the mission of an organization into the specific capabilities needed to achieve it, enabling capabilities, such as cyber defense, are no longer viewed as costs to the business, but an integral part of it. Said a different way: IT isn't just a service taking resources from the bottom line, but what is allowing the achievement of profit. Further, the concept of coherent and required capabilities is useful for organizations that might have multiple sites, or several business units, or use third party vendors, for example. If minimum standards are set for all that connect to a company network, the company will be far more confident in its security. Third-party vendors could be required to contractually comply with minimum standards, and if a company acquires a new business, they could be required to meet standards before fully integrating into the enterprise network.

Fundamentally, linking capabilities with organizational goals, then requiring all portions of an organization to have defined, necessary capabilities, is only good and sensible business.

13.2.2.4 Criticality of Implementation

Organizational change is difficult – how an organization achieves change is just as important as what an organization changes. In order to continue to evolve on cyber defense, NATO has created the Cyber Defence Action Plan (CDAP). The CDAP is the master list for all high-level cyber defense tasks that must be completed by different parts of the NATO. To monitor its progress, NATO reports on the status of every CDAP item three times a year to all Defence Ministers of the Alliance.

When other organizations seek to implement significant change, they must focus on how they will manage such change and hold individuals accountable for agreed priorities. Whether that is reports to the board or another mechanism, regular and senior attention is a key part of staying on track.

13.2.3 NATO as a Platform for Developing and Promoting and Best Practice

While NATO's adaptation itself thus offers many practical lessons and best practices for other organizations, NATO is able to further serve as a platform for promoting and discovering best practices. By working with Allies, Partner nations, industry, and other organizations, NATO helps develop and expose others to best practice.

13.2.3.1 The Cyber Defence Pledge

Through the Cyber Defence Pledge made at the Warsaw Summit, Allies have prioritized the continued improvement of their own cyber defenses. At the beginning of 2017, over the course of several months, Allies assessed their cyber defense capabilities using a commonly agreed approach. Based upon these reports and in-depth expert meetings, NATO was able to develop a baseline report of the current state of cyber defenses across all Allies.

This first baseline report highlights that nations have achieved mature national policy, governance, and organizational frameworks for cyber defense, as well as prioritized cyber defense capability development and associated skills. The rapidly evolving cyber threat landscape, however, underscores the importance and urgent nature of this continuing effort to enhance, prioritize, and further invest in cyber defense across the Alliance. Based on the results achieved so far, Allies are continuing to focus on resourcing cyber defense, enhancing information sharing, boosting training, education and exercise, and promoting fundamental cyber hygiene, as well as cyber defense capability development.

In addition to understanding this current state as well as surfacing areas for future focus, a key function and value of the Cyber Defence Pledge is the platform it provides to communicate and share. Allies now have much greater insight into what other nations are doing to improve their cyber defense – and have been able to share and discuss best practice. With this exchange of ideas, nations can now learn new strategies to address some of the most challenging issues in this field.

This type of best practice promotion need not be limited to NATO. Other international organizations, or private sector organizations, can set up similar communities of interest and best practice exchange. Some communities, in fact, already exist: the Financial Services Information Sharing and Analysis Center, for example, already disseminates threat information to its members as well as compiles and shares cyber defense best practices most relevant to financial institutions. Individual organizations can look to join – or collaborate to create – further targeted interest groups.

13.2.3.2 Partnerships and Information Sharing

Cyber defense is a cooperative effort, where no one, however powerful, can go it alone. You cannot build fences that are high enough to keep cyber threats away. NATO believes that it can do a lot more if it works with others, and we are now in continuous contact with industry, other international organizations, and Allies and Partners in order to improve our cyber defense.

Partnering with Industry

Through the NATO Industry Cyber Partnership, or NICP, NATO has adopted a coordinated approach to working with the private sector. The NICP has proven to be a valuable framework for regular consultation between NATO, nations, and industry, enabling NATO to say abreast of industry threat assessments; best practices and demonstration; and technology trends. The exchange of information is facilitated through informal and formal engagements with industry at workshops, events such as NIAS, NATO's annual cyber symposium, and NITEC, which acts on NATO's innovation agenda by bringing high-level defense experts from across NATO, the Allied militaries, industry, and academia together.

Furthermore, the NICP public and private workspaces also enable the virtual exchange of information. To give visibility to industry, Allies, who are driving significant efforts with industry, have provided approved industry points of contact encapsulated in an industry roster available on the NICP website. NATO, through Industry Partnership Agreements, has also formalized cooperation with some industry partners on cyber information sharing. These facilitate rapid and early bilateral exchange of nonclassified information on the nature, scope, prevention, and mitigation of cyber attacks. The NICP Malware Information Sharing Platform (MISP) is also used to share indicators of compromise and other technical characteristics of cyber threats between NATO, industry, and academia, creating better situational awareness, and enabling better protection of NATO and industry networks. This open source platform is also used in NATO to exchange information with nations to enhance situational awareness of cyber threats.

Working with the EU

Just as NATO has focused on increasing its ties with industry, so too has it sought greater cooperation with the European Union (EU). Cyber defense is a priority area for the common set of proposals adopted to implement the 2016 NATO-EU Joint Declaration [15]. Cooperation has been stepped up in the areas of exercises, information sharing, research, and technology. Exercises in particular is a theme for which significant progress has been made in the last year. Earlier this year, the NAC decided to upgrade for the first time the EU cyber defense staff's participation in Cyber Coalition. NATO has also been invited to the EU's Cyber Europe exercise. Exercises help the two organizations to become more interoperable by testing their ability to work together. Moving forward, it will be important to look more broadly at the two organization's respective toolboxes when it comes to managing potential crises, notably in responding to potential large-scale cyber attacks.

NATO and the EU also signed a Technical Arrangement on Cyber Defence between the NCIRC and the EU Computer Emergency Response Team (CERT-EU), which seeks to regularize interaction and create structures and processes for contact to facilitate operational and tactical cooperation. In its nearly 2 years of implementation, the Technical Arrangement is bearing fruit, with the two incident response communities working together on a routine basis. In addition to building trust in regular face-to-face meetings between cyber defenders, a focus has also been placed on deepening automated information exchange. To this end, the CERT-EU has been granted access to NATO's MISP, which facilitates an exchange of indicators of compromise in real-time. The Technical Arrangement also proved its value during recent global cyber attacks WannaCry and NotPetya when "NATO and EU worked closely together, our experts exchanged information and helped each other in our response to these major cyber attacks" [16].

Finally, this cooperation at the technical and operational levels is also complemented by an exchange at the policy level. For example, annual staff talks brings together a number of stakeholders from across NATO and the EU institutions to discuss the more strategic aspects of cyber defense, such as the implementation of the EU's Directive on Network Security and Information Systems or NATO's Cyber Defence Pledge. Briefings to both Allies and Members States of the two organizations also comprise an important part of NATO and the EU's information exchange, providing an opportunity for discussions surrounding the threat landscape and the respective work underway in both policy and operational fields.

Collaborating with Partners

NATO is also engaged actively with partners on a wide range of cyber defense issues, including policy and strategy development, exercises, and training activities. With a network of more than 40 partners countries – from Europe to Asia-Pacific, to the Middle East and North Africa – NATO wants to ensure that our cooperation is beneficial not only to us but to partners as well. Such engagement is tailored and based on shared values and common approaches to cyber defense.

An important driver of cyber defense cooperation with non-NATO nations is the Science for Peace and Security (SPS) Programme. It is an effective policy tool that enhances cooperation and dialogue with all partners, based on scientific research, innovation, and knowledge exchange. The SPS Programme provides funding, expert advice, and support to security-relevant activities jointly developed by a NATO member and partner country. Over the years, the engagement with partner countries has been further enhanced through the support of multiyear projects, workshops, and training courses aiming to strengthen partners' cyber defense capabilities.

The projects approved are diverse in topic and in partners. Allies have agreed to establish a Cyber Defence Laboratory at the Technical University of Moldova, which will serve as a training and research center for cyber defense experts and University students. Furthermore, the ongoing Privacy Preserving Big Data Processing Using Cloud Computing project, developed by the Korea University in Seoul and the University of Houston in Texas, seeks to improve the efficiency to securely process large amounts of data – a key aspect in delivering future defense superiority and security.

NATO also continues to assist partner nations in developing their own cyber defense capabilities by training network administrators working in security-relevant governmental sectors. Notably, a successful series of Advanced Training Courses provided by the Informatics Institute of the Middle East Technical University enabled the training of system and network administrators from Mongolia, Ukraine, Azerbaijan, and Montenegro between 2013 and 2015, and more recently to Iraq in 2016. Additionally, training on network vulnerability assessment and risk mitigation was provided to civil servants of the Moroccan National Defence agency, by the NATO School Oberammergau, Germany, and the Naval Postgraduate School, United States.

The SPS Programme has also sponsored several workshops to better understand cyber issues. One workshop, for example, truly delivered the book on best practices: Best Practices in Computer Network Defence: Incident Detection and Response, edited by Melissa E. Hathaway. As described by the Belfer Center of the Harvard Kennedy School, "The book identifies the state-of-the-art tools and processes being used for cyber defence and highlights gaps in the technology. It presents the best practice of industry and government for incident detection and response and examines indicators and metrics for progress along the security continuum" [17]. SPS workshops also supported the development of the National Cyber Security Framework Manual, a NATO Cooperative Cyber Defence Centre of Excellence Publication edited by Alexander Klimburg [18]. Other workshops have produced books on other critical, specific cyber defense topics, such as Critical Infrastructure Protection Against Hybrid Warfare Security Related Challenges [19] and Meeting Security Challenges through Data Analytics and Decision Support [20].

In all of these partnership situations, NATO always welcomes more and deeper cooperation – initiatives such as the MISP only improve with more participants, and more SPS projects can continue to build capacity and develop research throughout the globe. Industry, governments, and international oragnizations can learn and contribute not only by working with NATO, however, but also by developing similar or new partnership communities. Organizations can, for example, expand on or complement the research done through the SPS workshops, or create tailored communities and platforms for sharing information. Other international organizations and national governments can evaluate how they can build capacity and share the lessons they have learned.

The more people who treat cyber defense as a team sport, the better off the entire ecosystem will be.

13.2.3.3   Multinational "Smart Defense" Projects

Multinational initiatives also help Allies to build capacity and share knowledge on a range of topics. NATO currently has three such "smart defense" projects. Portugal has the lead for a project on education and training, while Belgium steers a group that has developed a multinational malware information sharing platform – that is, the MISP, which has been described above.

Romania and the Netherlands have led the development of a third cyber defense project addressing situational awareness and a system for incident coordination. At this stage, there are 25 Allies and 6 partner countries that participate in NATO's multinational smart defense projects. To help build awareness for the various projects and facilitate the engagement of industry and academia in these activities, an annual conference to take stock of the work for the respective smart defense projects is hosted in Portugal.

Bottom line: developing cyber capability is hard, but it is easier when done in partnership. Industry, nations, and other international organizations can look to create similar platforms and communities of interest for joint development of widely relevant cyber defense tools.

13.2.3.4   NATO Cooperative Cyber Defence Centre of Excellence

The NATO Cooperative Cyber Defence Centre of Excellence, or CCD COE, seeks to "enhance the capability, cooperation and information sharing among NATO, NATO nations and partners in cyber defence by virtue of education, research and development, lessons learned and consultation" [21]. The CCD COE has been very active in pursuing this mission. As has already been described, the CCD COE offers specialized training to the cyber community. The CCD COE has also organized the Locked Shields exercise, the "world's largest and most advanced international technical live-fire cyber defence exercise," every year since 2012 [22]. In 2017, Locked Shields attracted more than 900 participants and focused on real-time network defense. Teams participating in the exercise were put under pressure to handle and report incidents, solve forensic challenges, and respond to legal and strategic communications aspects. As part of the scenario, teams addressed aspects such as attacks on electric power grid systems, drones, and military command and control systems.

Another important effort sponsored by the Centre of Excellence was the development of the Tallinn Manual. A first edition of the Manual published in 2013 addressed International Cyber Law Applicable to Cyber Warfare, while the most recent edition launched in 2017 focused on the International Law Applicable to Cyber Operations. Developed by an independent group of 19 international legal experts from a number of countries, the Manual makes an important contribution to the current debate on applying international law to cyberspace, notably those activities that fall below the level of armed conflict [23].

The CCD COE can be immediately relevant to any organization or individual – much of the extensive work done by the CCD COE is publicly available, and people are encouraged to join and leverage the work being done in this space.

13.2.4 The Way Ahead

NATO has come a long way on cyber defense. We have understood the urgency of the issue, and we are acting accordingly – both on the political and the technical level. Still, we are only at the beginning of what will be a long and difficult journey. Cyber defense blurs traditional patterns of threat and response, military defense and homeland security, and public and private responsibilities. Cyber defense forces us to broaden our understanding of collective defense; to revisit our definition of essential core capabilities; and to explore new ways of doing business with partner countries, other organizations, and, above all, the private sector.

Even as NATO continues to evolve to meet these changing threats, our experiences are already directly relevant to many types of organizations, from the private sector to other international organizations. We will continue to serve as a platform of excellence to discover and promulgate best practices for cyber defense. We hope that other organizations benefit not only directly from NATO's work, but also gain a better understanding of how they, too, can develop or augment platforms to continue to improve the cyber ecosystem for all.

References

1. http://www.bbc.com/news/technology-41753022/
2. http://money.cnn.com/2017/05/12/technology/ransomware-attack-nsa-microsoft//
3. Prague Summit Declaration, https://www.nato.int/docu/pr/2002/p02-127e.htm.
4. https://www.theguardian.com/world/2007/may/17/topstories3.russia/
5. Strategic Concept for the Defence and Security of the Members of the North Atlantic Treaty Organization, https://www.nato.int/strategic-concept/pdf/Strat_Concept_web_en.pdf.
6. Wales Summit Declaration, https://www.nato.int/cps/ic/natohq/official_texts_112964.htm.
7. Warsaw Summit Declaration, https://www.nato.int/cps/en/natohq/official_texts_133169.htm.
8. https://www.nato.int/cps/en/natohq/topics_49763.htm.
9. https://www.nato.int/cps/en/natohq/topics_78170.htm#.
10. https://www.nato.int/cps/en/natohq/news_147373.htm.
11. https://ccdcoe.org/botnet-mitigation-course-may.html.
12. https://ccdcoe.org/international-law-cyber-operations-november-2017.html.

13. http://www.bbc.com/news/business-31048811.
14. NATO Defence Planning Process, https://www.nato.int/cps/en/natohq/topics_49202.htm.
15. https://www.nato.int/cps/ic/natohq/official_texts_133163.htm;   https://www.nato.int/cps/ro/natohq/official_texts_138829.htm.
16. https://www.nato.int/cps/en/natohq/opinions_146642.htm?selectedLocale=en.
17. https://www.iospress.nl/book/best-practices-in-computer-network-defense-incident-detection-and-response/.
18. https://ccdcoe.org/publications/books/NationalCyberSecurityFrameworkManual.pdf.
19. https://www.iospress.nl/book/critical-infrastructure-protection-against-hybrid-warfare-security-related-challenges/.
20. https://www.iospress.nl/book/meeting-security-challenges-through-data-analytics-and-decision-support/
21. https://ccdcoe.org/history.html.
22. https://ccdcoe.org/locked-shields-2017.html.
23. https://ccdcoe.org/tallinn-manual.html

Cyber Defence – eine zwingende Notwendigkeit!

14

Walter J. Unger

Zusammenfassung

Die zunehmende Abstützung aller gesellschaftlichen Bereiche auf vernetzte Informations- und Kommunikationstechnologie (IKT)-Systeme führt zu vitalen Abhängigkeiten von deren Funktionieren. Die Schwachstellen der IKT-Systeme könnten zu Cyber-Angriffen gegen Einzelpersonen, Unternehmen, Behörden und Staaten genutzt werden. Nur eine gemeinsame, gesamtgesellschaftliche Anstrengung und das Setzen eines Bündels von Cyber-Sicherheitsmaßnahmen ermöglichen die Reduktion der Risiken auf ein tolerierbares Ausmaß. Darüber hinaus ist es notwendig, Cyber-Verteidigungsmaßnahmen zur Abwehr großer Angriffe auf die Souveränität Österreichs vorzubereiten.

Informations- und Kommunikationstechnik (IKT) ist die Sammelbezeichnung für technische Mittel in Form von Hard- und Software sowie den Geräten, die der Gewinnung, Übertragung und Verarbeitung von Informationen dienen. Der Begriff IKT umfasst Mittel und Systeme aus den Bereichen Informationstechnik (IT), der Elektronischen Datenverarbeitung (EDV), der Kommunikationstechnik (KT) sowie der klassischen Fernmeldedienste (FM).

14.1 Verteidigung – ein militärischer Begriff

Der Begriff *Cyber Defence* findet zunehmend Eingang in Unternehmensstrukturen. *Cyber Defence Centres* werden zur Abwehr von Cyber-Attacken eingerichtet, *Defence* Software und -Dienstleistungen werden vermehrt angeboten.

W. J. Unger (✉)
Bundesministerium Landesverteidigung und Sport (BMLV), Wien, Österreich
E-Mail: walter.unger@bmlv.gv.at

© Springer Fachmedien Wiesbaden GmbH, ein Teil von Springer Nature 2018
M. Bartsch, S. Frey (Hrsg.), *Cybersecurity Best Practices*,
https://doi.org/10.1007/978-3-658-21655-9_14

Dabei ist *Defence* (Verteidigung) ein typisch militärischer Begriff und bedeutet die Verhinderung der Inbesitznahme eines Raumes (Land, Luft, See) durch eine feindliche Macht. Um Angriffe abzuwehren, werden alle strategisch verfügbaren, besonders militärische, Mittel defensiv und offensiv angewendet. Das Eindringen des Feindes soll verhindert bzw. ein eingedrungener Feind soll vernichtet oder aus dem eigenen Land wieder hinausgedrängt werden. Erfolgreiches militärisches Handeln erfordert neben einer möglichst präzisen Kenntnis des Feindes, der Situation der eigenen Ressourcen sowie der Umfeldbedingungen, vor allem die rasche Umsetzung in militärisches Handeln mittels eines konsequenten Kraft-Zeit-Raum-Kalküles: Welche militärischen Ressourcen können wann und wo zum Einsatz gebracht werden? Dies gilt für alle vier bisher bekannten und genutzten operativen militärischen Dimensionen: Land, Meer, Luft- und Weltraum. Das ursprünglich in den sechziger Jahren des 20. Jahrhunderts zum Zwecke der Sicherstellung der Kommunikation nach einem Atomangriff auf die USA entwickelte Internet hat sich in den letzten 25 Jahren zur größten Maschine der Menschheit entwickelt. Durch die Vernetzung von Computern auf der physikalischen Basis des Internets entstand ein alle Gesellschaftsbereiche umfassender virtueller Raum, der Cyber-Raum [1]. In der Österreichischen Strategie für Cyber Sicherheit wird der Cyber Raum wie folgt beschrieben:

> „Cyber Raum der virtuelle Raum aller auf Datenebene vernetzten IT-Systeme im globalen Maßstab. Dem Cyber Raum liegt als universelles und öffentlich zugängliches Verbindungs- und Transportnetz das Internet zugrunde, welches durch beliebige andere Datennetze ergänzt und erweitert werden kann. Im allgemeinen Sprachgebrauch bezeichnet Cyber Space auch das weltweite Netzwerk von verschiedenen unabhängigen IK-Infrastrukturen, Telekommunikationsnetzen und Computersystemen. In der sozialen Sphäre kann bei Benutzung dieses globalen Netzwerkes zwischen Individuen interagiert werden, Ideen ausgetauscht, Informationen verteilt, soziale Unterstützung gewährt, Geschäfte getätigt, Aktionen gelenkt, künstlerische und mediale Werke geschaffen, Spiele gespielt, politisch diskutiert und vieles mehr getan werden. Cyber Space ist ein Überbegriff für Alles mit dem Internet verbundenem und für die verschiedenen Internet Kulturen geworden. Viele Staaten betrachten die vernetzte IKT und die unabhängigen Netzwerke, die über dieses Medium operieren, als Teil ihrer Nationalen Kritischen Infrastrukturen".

Parallel zur Ausbreitung des Internets wurde über dessen militärische Nutzung nachgedacht. Die steigende Bedeutung dieses Cyber-Raumes gipfelte in der Betrachtung als neue militärische Dimension.

Wie in dieser neuen Dimension eine erfolgreiche Verteidigung sichergestellt werden kann, verlangt einen Blick auf das aktuelle sicherheitspolitische Umfeld und die Betrachtung der Weiterentwicklung des Cyber-Raumes. Anschließend sind aktuelle Cyber-Bedrohungen und erkennbare Trends einschließlich des Szenarios *Angriff auf die Souveränität Österreichs* zu betrachten. Die ableitbaren Konsequenzen auf strategischer Ebene sind den Planungen und aktuellen Maßnahmen zur Verteidigung gegenüberzustellen. Mit der Ausbreitung des Cyber-Raumes zeigten sich auch nach und nach die Schattenseiten dieser riesigen Maschine. Neue Kriminalitätsformen traten auf bzw. die Durchführung alter Formen der Kriminalität mit oder durch Cyber-Mittel wurde insbesondere durch die weitgehende Anonymität im Netz begünstigt.

Die Betrachtungen werden zeigen, dass die Zivilgesellschaft sowie das Militär permanent Angriffen ausgesetzt sind und die Grenzen zwischen Frieden, Krise oder gar Verteidigungsfall sehr unscharf sind. Es stellt sich daher die Frage, in welchem Ausmaß sich auch die Zivilgesellschaft auf die Verteidigung ihrer Cyber-Strukturen vorbereiten muss und welche Maßnahmen sich zum Schutz eigener Cyber-Systeme bewährt haben.

14.2 Sicherheitspolitisches Umfeld und Technologiewandel

Das sicherheitspolitische Umfeld ist durch Vielfalt und Komplexität gekennzeichnet. Interaktionen nehmen permanent zu, neue Elemente, Akteure und Phänomene sind zu beobachten. Die weltweite Verfügbarkeit von Informationen hat enorme Ausmaße angenommen. Gleichzeitig ist die Prüfung der Seriosität der Quellen und des Wahrheitsgehaltes der Informationen kaum noch machbar. Dadurch ergeben sich Möglichkeiten zur Manipulation und Beeinflussung auch von sehr großen Bevölkerungsgruppen. Prognosen werden durch unvorhersehbare Ereignisse, Katastrophen und irrationale Handlungen erheblich erschwert.

Folgende Ereignisse und Trends beeinflussen maßgeblich das sicherheitspolitische Umfeld in Mitteleuropa: Mit Terroranschlägen und Gewalttaten von Einzeltätern muss weiterhin und langfristig gerechnet werden. Krisenhafte Entwicklungen an den Rändern Europas (Ukraine, Türkei) sowie an den Hotspots Syrien, Nordafrika, Subsahara, Afghanistan und Nordkorea verstärken die Migrationsbewegung nach Europa und fordern allfällig auch den Einsatz von militärischen Kräften. Die Spannungen zwischen dem Westen und Russland, speziell das Verhältnis USA/NATO zu Russland kann erhebliche Auswirkungen auf die Sicherheit haben. Schließlich bergen auch Cyber-Angriffe, die auf die durch zunehmende Vernetzung gestiegene Verletzlichkeit unserer Gesellschaft zielen (z. B. gegen die Stromversorgung, gegen GPS/GALILEO, gegen wesentliche IKT-Infrastrukturen), ein hohes Risiko. Als eine wesentliche Konsequenz ergibt sich eine deutliche Verkürzung der Vorwarnzeiten. Damit wird die Überraschung zum dominierenden Faktor.

14.3 Technologiewandel: Digitalisierung, Automatisierung und Vernetzung

Im Jahr 2020 werden mehr als 7 Milliarden Menschen Zugang zum Internet haben und etwa 50 Milliarden *Dinge* mit dem Internet verknüpft sein. Dieser Trend, vom *Internet of Things* [2] zum *Internet of Everything* (Volldigitalisierung; Automatisierung), wird sich weiter fortsetzen, mit dem Ergebnis, dass mittelfristig die gesamte Menschheit und hunderte Milliarden Dinge mit diesem gigantischen Netz verbunden sein werden. Alles, was digitalisiert werden kann, wird digitalisiert, wird automatisiert. Viele physische Systeme werden von der IT erfasst und schrittweise mit dem Internet verbunden. Die Komplexität der IT nimmt durch die vertikale und horizontale Integration in die Wertschöpfungsprozesse erheblich zu. Jedes System wird praktisch zu jeder Zeit und von jedem Ort über das Internet erreichbar sein.

Eng verknüpft mit dieser Entwicklung sind Trends wie Industrie 4.0, Roboter und Drohnen, Künstliche Intelligenz, Blockchain-Technologien, Big Data, Cloud Computing, Methoden der prognostischen Analyse (Predictive/Forecast Analytics) sowie die Mobilität und der Wunsch nach permanenter Erreichbarkeit.

Industrie 4.0 zielt auf die umfassende Verknüpfung industrieller, technischer Prozesse und Technologien mit den dazugehörigen Geschäftsprozessen durch digitale Automatisierung, um den Märkten optimal zu entsprechen und gleichzeitig neue Möglichkeiten der Wertschöpfung in der industriellen Produktion zu schaffen.

Roboter sind universell einsetzbare, frei programmierbare und sensorgesteuerte, stationär montierte oder auch mobile, mittlerweile auch lernfähige Maschinen, die in industriellen Bereichen aber auch z. B. in Haushalten, für die Kranken- und Altenpflege, in Banken, Hotels, im Gastgewerbe und in der Landwirtschaft verwendet werden. Unter *Drohnen* werden funkgesteuerte oder programmierte unbemannte Fluggeräte verstanden, die sowohl für verschiedene militärische als auch zivile und kommerzielle Zwecke eingesetzt werden.

Künstliche Intelligenz, selbst lernende und optimierende Systeme übernehmen bisher von Menschen erledigte Aufgaben in komplexen Umgebungen, weil sie wesentlich schneller reagieren und weniger Fehler machen. Solchen Systemen könnte in der Zukunft eine entscheidende Bedeutung bei der Verteidigung der eigenen Cyber-Infrastruktur zukommen.

Die *Blockchain*-Technologie ist nicht nur die Basis für digitale Währungen. Diese Technologie hat das Potenzial, die Funktion des vertrauenswürdigen Dritten im Umgang mit Behörden und im Geschäftsleben zu ersetzen, mit den Vorteilen hoher Transparenz, sowie Zeit- und Kostenersparnis.

Big Data steht grundsätzlich für die Erfassung, Analyse, Auswertung und Verarbeitung großer digitaler Datenmengen einschließlich der dafür erforderlichen Technologien sowie der Nutzung der Daten mittels neuer Algorithmen für ganz neue Anwendungen. Big Data-Anwendungen finden sich heute in vielen Bereichen, wie z. B. in Suchmaschinen, sozialen Netzwerken, im E-Business, in der Forschung und in der Kriminalitäts- und Terrorismusbekämpfung.

Mit *Cloud Computing* werden IT-Ressourcen (Infrastrukturen, Plattformen, Software) dynamisch zur kostengünstigen Verarbeitung großer Datenmengen zur Verfügung gestellt.

Unter *Predictive Analytics* werden Methoden zur Auswertung großer, z. B. personenbezogener, Datenmengen mithilfe bestimmter Algorithmen zur Prognose der Entwicklung in der Zukunft verstanden. Die modernen Kommunikationsmittel und deren globale Vernetzung erlauben einerseits eine deutlich ausgeweitete Mobilität und führen andererseits zur permanenten Erreichbarkeit von Menschen und vernetzten Dingen.

Mit dieser dynamischen, technologischen Entwicklung geht ein rasanter und dramatischer Wandel bestehender Strukturen in Staat, Wirtschaft und Gesellschaft einher, der mittlerweile weltweit nahezu alle Menschen berührt. Trotz der damit verbundenen Vorteile, wie z. B. enorme Produktivitätssteigerung in vielen wirtschaftlichen Bereichen, eine effizientere Verwaltung oder globale Kommunikationsmöglichkeiten, dürfen die Risiken nicht ausgeblendet werden. Die Digitalisierung und Automatisierung zerstören u. a. bisher sehr erfolgreiche Businessmodelle, verändern die Verwaltung und die Art wie wir leben nachhaltig.

14.4   Strategische Bedeutung der Sicherheit

Seit jeher gilt, dass Staaten von ihren strategischen Infrastrukturen abhängig sind.

Hintergrund
Im European Program for Critical Infrastructure Protection (EPCIP) werden 11 Sektoren kritischer Infrastrukturen angeführt:

- Energie
- Nuklearindustrie
- IKT
- Wasser
- Lebensmittel
- Gesundheit
- Finanzen
- Transport
- Chemische Industrie
- Raumfahrt und Forschungseinrichtungen.

Auf der Basis des Europäischen Programms für den Schutz kritischer Infrastrukturen wurde der Masterplan zur Erstellung des österreichischen Programms zum Schutz kritischer Infrastrukturen (APCIP) auf nationaler Ebene festgelegt. Der Masterplan beschreibt die Grundsätze des Programms, beinhaltet die Auflistung der vorrangig zu untersuchenden Sektoren, definiert Kriterien für die Einstufung kritischer Infrastrukturen, benennt die Risikofaktoren und die Akteure, listet die Maßnahmen zum Schutz kritischer Infrastrukturen auf und entwickelt einen Aktionsplan mit detaillierten Teilzielen. Die Schwerpunkte bei der nationalen österreichischen kritischen Infrastruktur sollen hingegen auch die verfassungsmäßigen Einrichtungen, die Aufrechterhaltung des Sozialsystems und der Verteilungssysteme sowie die Hilfs- und Einsatzkräfte umfassen.

Diese Infrastrukturen oder Teile davon haben eine wesentliche Bedeutung für die Aufrechterhaltung wichtiger gesellschaftlicher Funktionen. Die Digitalisierung und Vernetzung aller Gesellschaftsbereiche führt zu einer massiven Abhängigkeit von der Verfügbarkeit, Vertraulichkeit und Integrität der gespeicherten Daten, der Funktionsfähigkeit der IKT-Infrastrukturen und dem reibungslosen Fluss riesiger Datenmengen über komplexe Netze [3].

Eine Störung oder gar Zerstörung dieser Infrastrukturen kann schwerwiegende Auswirkungen auf die Gesundheit, Sicherheit oder das wirtschaftliche und soziale Wohl der Bevölkerung oder die effektive Funktionsweise von staatlichen Einrichtungen haben. Bisherige

Dependenzen der Teilsektoren

Ausfall de Teilsektors → / Auswirkung auf Teilsektor ↓	Stromversorgung	Telekommunikation	Informationssysteme und -netze
Stromversorgung	–	2	1
Telekommunikation	3	–	3
Informationssysteme und -netze	3	2	–
Internet	3	3	3
	3	3	3
Instrumentations-, Automations- und Überwachungssysteme	3	3	3
Rundfunk und Medien	3	2	3
auf alle 31 Teilsektoren	68	45	45

Bewertet wurden auf einer vierstufigen Skala von 0 (keine Auswirkungen) bis 3 (sehr große Auswirkungen) – unter der Annahme eines Totalausfalls während dreier Wochen in der ganzen Schweiz – die Dependenzen der 31 Teilsektoren voneinander. Quelle: BABS 2009. S. 10. Ausschnitt aus der dortigen Abbildung 4

Abb. 14.1 Abhängigkeiten. (Quelle: Bundesamt für Bevölkerungsschutz 2009, S. 10)

Industriegesellschaften sind auf dem Weg *Informationsgesellschaften* zu werden. Sie basieren (noch immer) auf der industriellen Produktion, aber mittlerweile sind der Wirtschaftsstandort und die Daseinsvorsorge erheblich vom Funktionieren der strategischen Infrastrukturen und der Informations- und Kommunikationsflüsse abhängig. Die strategisch wesentlichen Infrastrukturen sind daher von vitaler Bedeutung für einen technologisch hochentwickelten Staat und können zu vorrangigen Angriffszielen in einem mit Cyber-Mitteln ausgetragenen Konflikt werden.

Die Abhängigkeit von funktionierenden IKT-Infrastrukturen sowie die Bedrohungen durch Angriffe im Cyber-Raum sind in den letzten Jahren so stark angestiegen, dass Cyber-Sicherheit in allen technologisch entwickelten Ländern und zunehmend auch bei vielen Unternehmen strategische Bedeutung erlangt hat (siehe Abb. 14.1) [4].

14.5   Die aktuelle Bedrohung – erkennbare Trends [5]

Zur Veranschaulichung des Bedrohungsbildes ist das Cyber-Risikospektrum sowie ein potenzielles Cyberwar-Angriffsszenario voranzustellen.

Der Cyber-Raum ist die Spielwiese für Script Kiddys, der Aktionsraum für Aktivisten und Wutbürger, der Tatort für Kriminelle, Terroristen und Spione und kann zum Operations-/Kriegsgebiet für staatliche Cyber Warrior werden. Die Akteure unterscheiden sich nach ihrer Motivation, Zielsetzungen, verfügbaren Ressourcen und Fähigkeiten (siehe Abb. 14.2).

Das Cyber-Bedrohungsspektrum (Abb. 14.3) beschreibt Gefahren und Bedrohungen, die den einzelnen Menschen ebenso wie Organisationen, Behörden, Unternehmen und Staaten treffen können. Leider gibt es weder fehlerfreie Soft- noch Hardware, täglich werden neue gravierende Schwachstellen [7] entdeckt. Zudem ergeben sich am Übertragungsweg der Daten zahlreiche Möglichkeiten für Angriffe.

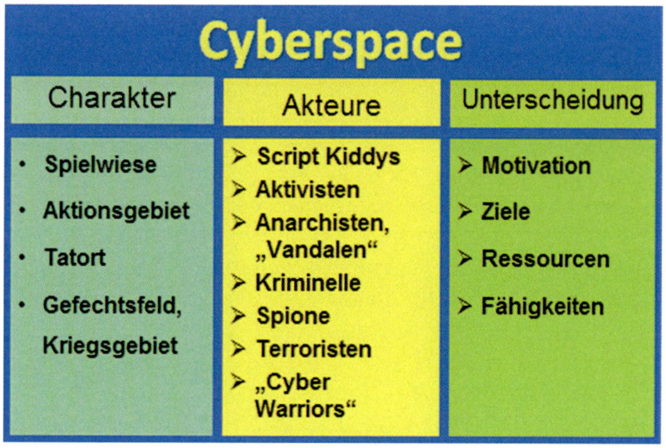

Abb. 14.2 Charakter-Akteure-Motive

Abb. 14.3 Cyber-Bedrohungsspektrum

Daher müssen Staaten, Unternehmen, Organisationen und Einzelpersonen mit folgenden neuen Bedrohungsszenarien rechnen:

Der Risikobogen spannt sich von Datenmissbrauch und subversivem Hacktivismus, über Cyber-Angriffe, um Geld zu ergaunern, und Cyber-, Wirtschafts- und Konkurrenzspionage, bis hin zu Sabotageangriffen gegen strategisch bedeutsame Unternehmen und Behörden und letztlich bis zum digitalen Stillstand eines Staates durch großangelegte Cyber-Attacken [7].

Folgende Trends sind erkennbar: Cyber-Attacken kommen laufend und treffen jeden: Unternehmen, Behörden und Einzelpersonen. Die Angreifer werden immer professioneller und beschäftigen sich intensiv mit den Opfern. Mittels *Ransomware* und *DDoS* werden Unternehmen, Behörden und Spitäler [8] sowie Einzelpersonen erpresst.

Hintergrund

Hacktivismus: (Kofferwort aus Hack und Aktivismus, engl. *Hacktivism*) ist die Verwendung von Computern und Computernetzwerken als Protestmittel, um politische Ziele zu erreichen. Die erste Verwendung erfuhr der Begriff im Juli 2004 von Mitgliedern eines Hacker-Kollektivs namens *Omega* unter http://de.wikipedia.org/wiki/Hacktivismus

Ransomware: (von englisch *ransom* für „Lösegeld"), auch *Erpressungstrojaner*, *Erpressungssoftware*, *Kryptotrojaner* oder *Verschlüsselungstrojaner*, sind Schadprogramme, mit deren Hilfe ein Eindringling den Zugriff des Computerinhabers auf Daten, deren Nutzung oder auf das ganze Computersystem verhindern kann. Dabei werden private Daten auf dem fremden Computer verschlüsselt oder der Zugriff auf sie verhindert, um für die Entschlüsselung oder Freigabe ein Lösegeld zu fordern. Die Bezeichnung setzt sich zusammen aus *ransom*, dem englischen Wort für Lösegeld, und *ware*, entsprechend dem für verschiedene Arten von Computerprogrammen üblichen Benennungsschema (*Software*, *Malware* etc.). https://de.wikipedia.org/wiki/Ransomware

Denial of Service: (*DoS*; engl. für „*Verweigerung des Dienstes*") bezeichnet in der Informationstechnik die Nichtverfügbarkeit eines Internetdienstes, der eigentlich verfügbar sein sollte. Im Fall einer durch eine Unmenge von Anfragen verursachten Dienstblockade spricht man von einer durch Vielanfragen *verbreiteten Verweigerung des Dienstes* (engl. *Distributed Denial of Service*; DDoS). Obwohl es verschiedene Gründe für die Nichtverfügbarkeit geben kann, ist die häufigste Art die Folge einer Überlastung des Datennetzes. Dies kann durch unbeabsichtigte Überlastungen verursacht werden oder durch einen konzentrierten Angriff auf die Server oder sonstige Komponenten des Datennetzes.

BIOS: (von englisch „*basic input/output system*") ist die Firmware bei x86-PCs. Es ist in einem nichtflüchtigen Speicher auf der Hauptplatine eines PC abgelegt und wird unmittelbar nach dessen Einschalten ausgeführt. Aufgabe des BIOS ist es unter anderem, den PC zunächst funktionsfähig zu machen und im Anschluss das Starten eines Betriebssystems einzuleiten.

Angriffe werden indirekt geführt und als Dienstleistungen im Netz angeboten (*Attack-as-a-Service*). Angriffe gegen strategische Infrastrukturen nehmen zu. Schadprogramme werden industriell gefertigt. Täglich tauchen 400.000–500.000 neue Versionen auf. Mittelfristig [9] muss vermehrt mit Angriffen auf Chipebene, gegen das *BIOS* [10] von Computern, auf der Basis von und gegen *IoT* und Industrie 4.0, gegen Cloud-Systeme, gegen Apps und gegen hochsichere Verschlüsselungen [11] gerechnet werden. Weiters sind Cyber-Terrorattacken nicht auszuschließen [12]. Angriffe gegen Betreiber kritischer Infrastrukturen könnten Cyber-Krisen auslösen. Cyber-Angriffe als politisch-militärische Waffe im Vorfeld und in heißen Konflikten werden an Häufigkeit und Intensität noch zulegen.

Daher steht am oberen Ende der Bedrohungsskala der durch großangelegte Cyber-Angriffe verursachte digitale Stillstand. Die strategischen Infrastrukturen [13] sind massiv von deren IKT abhängig und eng miteinander vernetzt.

Ein massiver Angriff auf diese strategisch bedeutsamen IKT-Systeme hat damit unter Umständen ähnliche Auswirkungen wie ein massiver Angriff auf die industrielle Basis eines Staates und könnte zu einem politisch verwertbaren Ergebnis genutzt werden. Zur strategischen Bedrohung für die Souveränität eines Staates werden diese Angriffe, wenn sie einen langfristigen, digitalen Stillstand des gesamten Staates zur Folge haben. Solch massive, großflächige Angriffe mit dem Ziel, einen Staat durch Cyber-Attacken in die Knie zu zwingen, entsprächen einem Cyberwar-Szenario. Davon sieht man im Frieden nicht viel, denn die Entwicklung und Testung von Cyber-Waffen erfolgt in Laborumgebung.

Was man erkennen könnte, sind Handlungen zur Auskundschaftung und Infiltrierung relevanter Ziele.

Österreich ist wie jedes andere Land aktuellen Cyber-Bedrohungen ausgesetzt. Als hoch entwickeltes Land ist es abhängig von funktionierenden Kommunikations- und Informationssystemen. Immer mehr Bereiche des täglichen Lebens, der Wirtschaft oder bspw. des Gesundheitssystems und somit auch der nationalen Sicherheit bedürfen eines möglichst stabilen und sicheren Cyber-Raumes.

Hier ein paar Beispiele für Cyber-Vorfälle in Österreich aus der jüngeren Vergangenheit:

Im Februar 2016 wurde die Telekom Austria (A1 – Österreichs größter Mobiltelefonprovider) Ziel eines DDoS-Angriffes, was dazu führte, dass die mobilen Datendienste über mehrere Stunden für eine große Zahl der Kunden nicht verfügbar waren.

Zwischen **September 2016 und Dezember 2017** gab es zahlreiche politisch motivierte DDoS-Angriffe auf Webseiten österreichischer Institutionen (darunter der Flughafen Wien, das Außenministerium, das Landesverteidigungsministerium, die Nationalbank, das Parlament, die Seite des damals noch Präsidentschaftskandidaten Van der Bellen, die Seite einer politischen Partei etc.). Akteur war (in manchen Fällen bestätigt, in manchen mit hoher Wahrscheinlichkeit anzunehmen) die türkische Hackergruppe Aslan Neferler Tim (ANT). Der Hintergrund dieser Angriffsserie ist das außenpolitische Verhältnis zwischen Österreichs zur Türkei. Die Ransomware- und Sabotage-Kampagnen WannaCry(pt) und NonPETYA [14] im Mai und Juni 2017 betrafen Österreich nur in geringem Ausmaß.

Auch das Österreichische Bundesheer (ÖBH) ist permanent Angriffen ausgesetzt. Pro Tag werden im Durchschnitt etwa 60.000 Events [15] registriert. Nach entsprechenden Analysen verbleibt ca. 1 konkreter Angriff pro Tag. Vielfach handelt es sich um breit gestreute Massenangriffe, einige gezielte Angriffe weisen jedoch die Merkmale von international angesetzten Cyber-Spionagekampagnen auf.

Diese und ähnliche Bedrohungen bestehen nicht erst seit Kurzem. Bereits vor mehr als 4 Jahren hat die österreichische Bundesregierung die Bedrohungen und Herausforderungen Österreichs im Cyber-Raum erkannt. Basierend auf der österreichischen Sicherheitsstrategie, die Cyber-Angriffe als eine der größten Herausforderungen und Bedrohungen unserer Gesellschaft definiert, wurde 2013 die österreichische Strategie für Cyber-Sicherheit verabschiedet.

14.6 Folgerungen aus dem Bedrohungsbild [16] und Herausforderungen

Großangelegte gegen den Gesamtstaat gerichtete Cyberangriffe stellen sowohl die politisch-strategische Ebene als auch die militärische Landesverteidigung vor neue Herausforderungen, auf die im Folgenden näher eingegangen werden soll. Da technische

Vorbereitungsaktivitäten für einen Cyber-Angriff frühzeitig nur schwer bzw. gar nicht direkt erkennbar sind, könnten Attacken überraschend ohne Vorwarnung beginnen. Allenfalls können Indizien für die Aufklärung potenzieller Ziele erkannt werden. Jedoch laufen permanent Aktivitäten zur Ausspähung von Servern und Netzen, wobei die Zuordnung zur Vorbereitung eines kriegerischen Aktes ohne zusätzliche Erkenntnisse aus anderen Bereichen zunächst unmöglich ist [17].

Das Einschleusen von Schadprogrammen, die erst zu einem späteren Zeitpunkt aktiviert werden sollen, kann aufgrund deren technischer Eigenschaften ebenfalls kaum entdeckt und nicht eindeutig zugeordnet werden. Moderne Schadware wird erst nach Nachladung zusätzlicher Elemente auf Befehl aktiv. Bei einem Angriff muss damit gerechnet werden, dass Systeme für eine zeitverzugslose Kommunikation ausfallen oder/und der Abruf von gespeichertem Wissen nicht mehr möglich ist.

Dies bedeutet, dass die Betreiber von strategischen Infrastrukturen auch im tiefsten Frieden permanent Eigenschutz auf dem aktuellen Stand der IKT-Sicherheit gewährleisten müssen. Systeme und Organisationen, die nicht vorbereitet sind, könnten enorme Schäden erleiden. Daraus folgt, dass die erste Verteidigungslinie zunächst einmal präventive Maßnahmen sind. Diese Sicherheitsmaßnahmen müssen regelmäßig auditiert sowie an geänderte Bedrohungslagen angepasst werden (Patch-Management [18], Verstärken physischer Sicherheitsmaßnahmen, etc.). Da diese Infrastrukturen überwiegend in privater Hand sind, muss ein Modell zur Sicherstellung eines erforderlichen Standards entwickelt werden. Verschiedene Ausprägungen wären denkbar [19], z. B. eine freiwillige Selbstverpflichtung. Vorgaben von Standards, regelmäßige Audits und Kontrollen wären die erforderlichen Begleitmaßnahmen. Anreize zur Implementierung und Optimierung von Sicherheitsmaßnahmen könnten die Durchführung kostenloser Sicherheitsberatungen, Unterstützung bei Bedrohungs- und Risikoanalysen und die Entwicklung von Sicherheitskonzepten sein. Die Durchführung von Audits durch eine staatliche Behörde könnte durch die Auszeichnung als „sicheres" Unternehmen mit einem Sicherheitszertifikat („Gütesiegel") honoriert werden. Gemeinsame, von staatlicher Seite vorbereitete Übungen könnten der Verbesserung der Zusammenarbeit, dem Test von Abläufen ebenso wie der Überprüfung von Alarm-, Notfall- und Krisenplänen dienen.

Im kommenden Netzwerk- und Informationssystemsicherheitsgesetz [20] (NIS-G) werden die Aufgaben des Bundeskanzleramtes (BKA), des Bundesministeriums für Inneres (BMI) und des Bundesministeriums für Landesverteidigung (BMLV) geregelt. Es werden Koordinierungsstrukturen unter Leitung des BKA auf strategischer Ebene und unter Leitung des BMI auf operativer Ebene als *Innerer Kreis der Operativen Koordinierung* (IKDOK) eingerichtet. Weiters werden NIS-Behörden beim BKA, BMI und BMLV eingerichtet sowie die Aufgaben des Nationalen CERT und der Branchen-CERTs definiert. Den Unternehmen werden Sicherheitsvorkehrungen vorgeschrieben und Meldepflichten auferlegt, wobei die Sicherheitsstandards durch die Behörden noch erarbeitet werden müssen. Das BMLV erhält als neue Aufgaben die Sicherheitsbetreuung und Zertifizierung von Betreibern wesentlicher Dienste, die für die Erfüllung der Aufgaben zur militärischen Landesverteidigung von besonderer Bedeutung sind. Erstmals wird die

„Cyberverteidigung" als neue Aufgabe des Österreichischen Bundesheeres (ÖBH) gesetzlich normiert.

Darüber hinaus sind Vorkehrungen für eine rasche Warnung und Alarmierung zu treffen. Die Nachrichtendienste sind besonders gefordert, einen Beitrag zur strategischen Frühwarnung zeitgerecht zu liefern. Potenzielle Cyber-Angreifer sind mit nachrichtendienstlichen und Cyber-Mitteln und -methoden zu beobachten, um die allgemeine Lage durch ein konkretes Lagebild zu ergänzen. Diese Aufgaben sind als Schwergewichtsaufgaben von allen Nachrichtendiensten zu betreiben. Im Kontext eines schwelenden oder eskalierenden politischen Konflikts sind politische, diplomatische, wirtschaftliche und militärische Entwicklungen genau zu beobachten und zu analysieren. Hinweise auf einen Konflikt und technische Erkenntnisse müssen in das Lagebild einfließen und sind die Grundlage für ein Cyber-Frühwarnsystem. Ein Verbund der Elemente, die permanent die Cyber-Lage beobachten, und die Zusammenführung zu einem gesamtstaatlichen Lagebild sind zwingend erforderlich. Darüber hinaus muss diese Bedrohungslage permanent mit dem Sicherheitszustand der zu schützenden Systeme korreliert werden.

Da die kritischen, von IKT abhängigen Infrastrukturen überwiegend in privatem Besitz sind, müssen alle Betreiber selbst in hohem Ausmaß für die Sicherheit ihrer Systeme vorsorgen. Darüber hinaus sollten die Betreiber den konkreten Bedarf an Unterstützung durch staatliche Stellen analysieren und bei der zuständigen Behörde einbringen. Nur so können staatliche Stellen in die Lage versetzt werden, eine bedarfsgerechte Ressourcenplanung und -bereitstellung vorzunehmen. Hierzu braucht es eine detaillierte Analyse der Kritikalität, des potenziellen Bedarfs sowie der sonstigen Notwendigkeiten.

Während eines großflächigen Angriffs werden die Sicherheitsorganisationen der kritischen Infrastrukturbetreiber mit der Abwehr bzw. der Wiederherstellung des Betriebs voll ausgelastet oder mutmaßlich sogar überlastet sein. Es ist daher nicht zu erwarten, dass Schlüsselpersonal verschoben werden kann („Nachbarschaftshilfe"). Dies zwingt zum Vorhalten von Reservekräften bei staatlichen Stellen, um überforderten Organisationen rasch Hilfe leisten zu können. Diese Hilfe kann durch Remote-Beratung oder durch die Entsendung von Unterstützungsteams erfolgen.

Nebst der Unterstützung der Sicherheitsorganisationen sind Maßnahmen zur Identifizierung der Angreifer und Unterbindung laufender Angriffe offensiv zu setzen (*Active Cyber Defence*, Aktive Cyber-Verteidigung). Dazu zählen beispielsweise die Identifizierung und Maßnahmen zur Abschaltung bzw. Blockierung von Botmaster-Servern und die Rückverfolgung bis zu den Tätern hinter einem Bot-Netz.

Beispiel

Unter einem Bot (von englisch *robot*, Roboter) versteht man ein Computerprogramm, das weitgehend automatisch sich wiederholende Aufgaben abarbeitet, ohne dabei auf eine Interaktion mit einem menschlichen Benutzer angewiesen zu sein.

Beispiele für Bots sind die Webcrawler von Internet-Suchmaschine, die selbsttätig Webseiten besuchen, wobei sie den vorhandenen Links folgen und dabei ggf. den Inhalt der Seiten auswerten. „Gutartige" Bots halten sich dabei an die Robot Exlusion Standards, mit denen Serverbetreiber das Verhalten eines Bots in Grenzen beeinflussen können. „Bösartige" Bots werden beispielsweise zum Sammeln von E-Mail-Adressen für Werbezwecke sowie für das massenhafte unautorisierte Kopieren von Webinhalten bis hin zum systematischen Ausspionieren von Softwarelücken von Servern mit dem Ziel des Einbruchs in Server eingesetzt. Maßnahmen gegen das unerwünschte Auslesen von Websites durch Bots („spidern") bestehen unter anderem darin, das Verhalten der Bots in einer Falle („Honeypot") zu analysieren und beispielsweise mit einer Sperre der IP-Adresse des Bots zu reagieren. Kommunizieren Bots untereinander, so spricht man von einem Bot-Netz oder Botnet. Gefunden am 02.01.18 unter https://de.wikipedia.org/wiki/Bot.

Hierzu sind IT-forensische Maßnahmen zur Spurensicherung und nachrichtendienstliche Anstrengungen erforderlich. Damit können die Voraussetzungen für Reaktionen im diplomatischen, politischen oder gegebenenfalls militärischen Bereich geschaffen werden. Diese Maßnahmen zur aktiven Verteidigung sind durch entsprechende Rechtsgrundlagen zu ermöglichen. Damit Gegenmaßnahmen nicht Unbeteiligte schädigen, wären handhabungssichere Methoden zu entwickeln. Hierzu sollte die Forschung forciert und Netzwerkanalyse- und Forensik-Spezialisten mit smarter Software zur Just-in-time-Forensik und zur Unterbrechung von Angriffen befähigt werden. Ein ungelöstes Problem ist die Frage der Identifizierung der tatsächlichen Angreifer. Die Zuordnung (Attribution) eines Angriffs zu physischen Angreifern/Tätern [21] ist derzeit technisch nicht gelöst.

Da sowohl kriminelle Täter als auch Terroristen und staatliche Cyber-Krieger mit ähnlichen bzw. gleichen Mitteln und Methoden attackieren, stellt sich zunächst die Frage der Zuständigkeit für die Abwehrmaßnahmen. Gemäß derzeitiger Kompetenzlage ist die Verantwortung für den Schutz kritischer Infrastrukturen beim Bundesministerium für Inneres angesiedelt. Für die Verfolgung der Cyberkriminalität einschließlich des Cyber-Terrorismus sind die Strafverfolgungsbehörden zuständig (Justiz-, Innenministerium). Das BMLV kann zur Unterstützung im Wege der Assistenz oder Amtshilfe beigezogen werden.

Bei einem Angriff von außen auf den Gesamtstaat geht die Zuständigkeit an das Verteidigungsministerium über, wobei die Strafverfolgungsbehörden nicht von ihren Aufgaben entbunden werden. Die Entscheidung dazu ist selbstverständlich auf politischer Ebene zu treffen. Die Aufbereitung der Entscheidungsgrundlagen kann nur auf der Basis eines aktuellen rund um die Uhr verfügbaren, umfassenden Lagebilds erfolgen. Es sind daher Ressourcen für die permanente Lagebeobachtung, -analyse und -aufbereitung zur Verfügung zu stellen.

Da der Wechsel der Verantwortlichkeit während eines laufenden Angriffs eine erhebliche Schwachstelle darstellen würde, sind Vorkehrungen zu treffen, die einen reibungslosen und zeitverzugslosen Übergang ermöglichen. Dazu wird es notwendig sein, schon im Frieden einen Cyber-Krisenstab, bestehend aus Experten aller zuständigen Ressorts, einzurichten und im Anlassfall frühzeitig zu aktivieren.

Nach der Abwehr der unmittelbaren Angriffe sind unverzüglich alle Maßnahmen zur Wiederherstellung des ordnungsgemäßen Betriebs zu treffen und eventuell aktive

Maßnahmen im Sinne der Gesamtstrategie zu setzen. Außerdem sind unverzüglich Maßnahmen zur Härtung der IKT-Systeme umzusetzen. Das Postulat, Angriffe seien nicht wiederholbar [22], stimmt nur dann, wenn beobachtete Angriffe/Schadware mit Reverse-Engineering-Methoden analysiert, die eigenen Systeme gepatcht und das Personal fortgebildet werden. Ein permanenter *Lessons Learned*-Prozess auf der Basis aktualisierter unterstützender Wissensdatenbanken ist unabdingbar.

Eine weitere Herausforderung ist es, die richtigen Ressourcen für den Anlassfall bei staatlichen Organisationen bereit zu halten. Die dynamische Entwicklung der IKT zwingt zu technisch hochqualifiziertem Personal, das permanent fortgebildet werden muss. Dieses Personal ist grundsätzlich Mangelware und kann mit steigender Qualifizierung nur unter erheblichen Anstrengungen bei staatlichen Organisationen vorgehalten werden.

Die Systeme für die Sicherstellung der Regierungstätigkeit und Kommunikation können nicht erst im Anlassfall aufgebaut werden. Diese müssen bereits im Frieden errichtet, routinemäßig betrieben und in Übungen getestet werden. Der Bedarf wäre daher umgehend zu erheben, vorhandene Systeme wären auszubauen und die erforderlichen Ressourcen zuzuordnen.

Außerdem wäre zu klären, wie man Staaten, über deren Cyberspace (Transitländer; wo endet der nationale Cyberspace?) Angriffe laufen, behandeln soll. Sind diese Staaten Mittäter? Welche Pflichten haben Neutrale? [23] Politik und Diplomatie sollten auf die Beantwortung dieser Fragen und die Entwicklung internationaler Instrumente bei der Zusammenarbeit zum Schutz vor Cyber-Angriffen hinarbeiten. Maßnahmen zur Vertrauensbildung (Verbot von Cyberwaffen, Open Cyberspace in Anlehnung an das Open Sky-Abkommen), zur verpflichtenden Zusammenarbeit im Falle von laufenden Angriffen, zur Rückverfolgung sowie bei der Ermittlung von Tätern wären zu entwickeln und vertraglich zu vereinbaren.

14.7   Die Österreichische Strategie für Cyber-Sicherheit (ÖSCS) [24]

Zahlreiche Staaten sahen sich in den letzten Jahren veranlasst, wegen der wachsenden Abhängigkeit und steigenden Bedrohung mit Konzepten auf strategischer Ebene zu reagieren. Auch Österreich hat mit der *Österreichischen Strategie für Cyber Sicherheit* (ÖSCS) [25, 26] 2013 nach einem aufwendigen Analyseprozess reagiert (siehe Abb. 14.4).

Die wesentlichen Inhalte der ÖSCS und deren Umsetzungsstand dürfen wie folgt beschrieben werden (siehe auch Abb. 14.5). Unter der Leitung des Bundeskanzleramtes arbeitet die sogenannte *Cyber-Sicherheit-Steuerungsgruppe* (CSS). Diese Gruppe tagt seit 2013 halbjährlich, berät die österreichische Bundesregierung in Angelegenheiten der Cyber-Sicherheit, sie überwacht die Umsetzung der Cyber Sicherheitsstrategie, sie koordiniert die Cyber-Sicherheitsmaßnahmen auf strategischer/politischer Ebene und verfasst einen jährlichen Bericht zur Cyber-Sicherheit.

Die Struktur zur Koordinierung der Maßnahmen auf operativer Ebene (*Innerer Kreis der Operativen Koordinierung* (IKDOK)) wurde 2014 eingerichtet, hat sich in den Angriffen

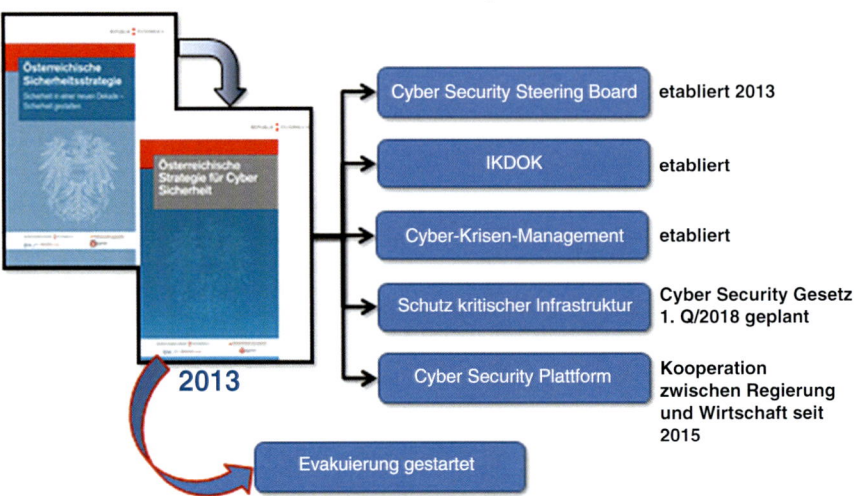

Abb. 14.4 Stand der Umsetzung der ÖSCS (Dezember 2017)

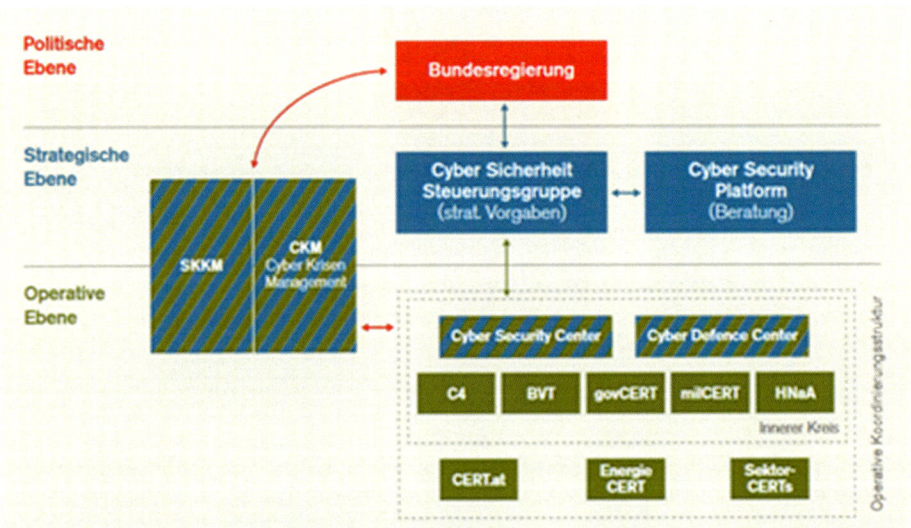

Abb. 14.5 Nationale Akteure und Cyber-Strukturen

des Jahres 2017 bewährt und soll 2018 die volle Einsatzbereitschaft erreichen. Diese Plattform dient zur Aufbereitung und Zurverfügungstellung eines periodischen, aber auch anlassbezogenen Cyber-Lagebildes sowie der Entwicklung von Maßnahmen auf operativer Ebene. Unter Leitung des *Cyber Security Centre* im Innenministerium kooperieren im Rahmen dieser Struktur Vertreter des Bundesministeriums für Inneres, des Bundesministeriums der Landesverteidigung und des Bundeskanzleramtes, CERTs sowie Vertreter von Institutionen, die mit dem Schutz kritischer Infrastruktur beauftragt sind.

Basierend auf der ÖSCS wurde ein Cyber-Krisenmanagement eingerichtet, welches sich aus Vertretern von Behörden und den Betreibern der kritischen Infrastruktur zusammensetzt. Krisenmanagement- und Kontinuitätspläne werden auf Basis von Risikoanalysen für Sektor- spezifische und Sektor-übergreifende Cyber-Bedrohungen ausgearbeitet und laufend aktualisiert. Es werden regelmäßig Cyber-Übungen durchgeführt, um das Cyber-Krisenmanagement sowie die Krisenpläne zu testen. Gemäß der Cyber-Sicherheitsstrategie sollten Betreiber kritischer Infrastrukturen in alle Prozesse des nationalen Cyber-Krisenmanagements eingebunden werden. Viele der prozeduralen Aspekte sind derzeit Gegenstand der Diskussion und werden im künftigen Netzwerk- und Informationssicherheitsgesetz (NIS-G) abgedeckt sein. Mit diesem Gesetz wird die EU-NIS-Richtlinie vom Juli 2016 umgesetzt.

Um die Zusammenarbeit zwischen der Regierung, der Wirtschaft und der Gesellschaft in Cyber-Belangen zu verbessern, wurde 2015 eine sogenannte Cyber-Sicherheits-Plattform (CSP) eingerichtet. Sie bietet als Public-Private-Partnership den institutionellen Rahmen für einen permanenten Informationsaustausch zwischen der öffentlichen Verwaltung und Vertretern der Wirtschaft, Wissenschaft und Gesellschaft. Die Kooperation zwischen Betreibern der kritischen Infrastrukturen und anderer Wirtschaftssektoren mit der öffentlichen Verwaltung ist zweifelsohne von maßgeblicher Bedeutung für Österreichs Cyber-Sicherheit. All diese eben erwähnten Strukturen und Einrichtungen werden selbstverständlich regelmäßig evaluiert und wenn notwendig adaptiert (siehe Abb. 14.5).

Abb. 14.6 gibt einen Überblick über die innerstaatlichen Verantwortlichkeiten der beiden federführenden Ministerien im Bereich der Cyber-Sicherheit und der Cyber-Verteidigung – das Bundesministerium für Inneres und das Bundesministerium für Landesverteidigung. Die erste Eskalationsstufe ist die Ebene der Vorfälle (*Incidents*). Hierbei handelt es sich um hauptsächlich monetär motivierte Cyber-Kriminalität, Wirtschaftsspionage, Erpressung oder Datendiebstahl. Insbesondere Cyber-Awareness und IT-Sicherheitsmaßnahmen sind die geeigneten Mittel, um diesen Gefahren begegnen zu können.

Im Falle von Angriffen auf die kritische Infrastruktur – im Worst-Case-Szenario ein Blackout – erreichen wir Level 2 und sprechen von einer Cyber-Krise (*Cyber Crisis*). Eine Cyber-Krise verlangt stärker ausgeprägte IT-Sicherheits- und Verteidigungsmaßnahmen speziell ausgebildeter und speziell ausgerüsteter Elemente. Sollten derartige Angriffe politisch motiviert sein und eine Bedrohung für die Republik darstellen, dann spricht man von Cyber-Verteidigung (*Cyber Defence*) und dem Schutze der Souveränität Österreichs im Cyber-Raum.

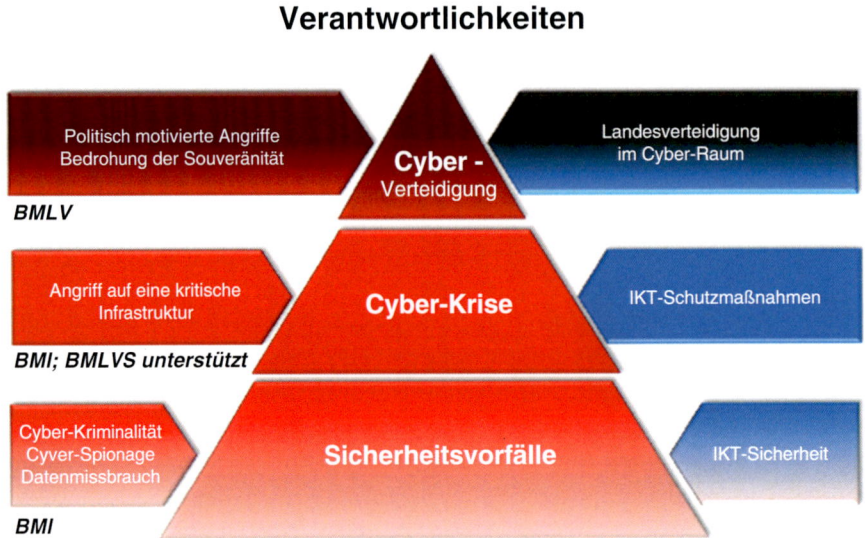

Abb. 14.6 Innerstaatliche Kompetenzverteilung

Wer ist nun auf welcher Ebene zuständig? Da die Vorfälle auf der ersten Ebene einen Akt der Cyber-Kriminalität darstellen, liegt die Verantwortung ganz klar innerhalb der des Bundesministeriums für Inneres. Im Falle einer Cyber-Krise liegt die Koordinierungsverantwortung im Rahmen der eingangs erwähnten operativen Koordinierungsstruktur ebenfalls beim Bundesministerium für Inneres. Es wird in dieser Aufgabe vom Bundesministerium für Landesverteidigung unterstützt. Diese Koordinierungsverantwortung geht im Falle der militärischen Landesverteidigung im Cyber-Raum an das Bundesministerium für Landesverteidigung über. Dann übernimmt das Bundesministerium für Landesverteidigung die leitende Rolle beim Schutz der Souveränität Österreichs. Es wird hierbei aber umgekehrt vom Bundesministerium für Inneres unterstützt.

Insbesondere in der Cyber-Domäne ist eine klare Trennung zwischen innerer und äußerer Sicherheit bzw. Bedrohung kaum vorzunehmen. Angriffe und ihre Angriffsvektoren können dabei ident sein und verlangen dieselben Antworten ohne Unterscheidung des Ursprungs der Bedrohung. Eine tägliche Kooperation zwischen den beiden eben erwähnten Ministerien ist daher unabdingbar.

14.8 Cyber-Sicherheit – sicher Leben im Cyber-Raum

Den Schattenseiten der digitalisierten, vernetzten Welt muss durch ein Bündel von Sicherheitsmaßnahmen auf allen Ebenen begegnet werden. Wichtig ist, dass sich Behörden, Unternehmen und die Bevölkerung dieser Bedrohung bewusst sind. Jeder kann mit einfachen Maßnahmen für PC und mobile Geräte, wie die permanente Aktualisierung aller

Programme, die Verwendung einer Firewall und Anti-Virensoftware, sicherheitsbewusstes Verhalten im Netz und einem sorgsamen Umgang mit den persönlichen Daten, ein Mindestmaß an persönlichem Schutz erreichen und damit einen Beitrag zu mehr Sicherheit im Netz leisten.

Bei Behörden und Unternehmen ist permanent Cyber-Sicherheit/IKT-Sicherheit [27] auf hohem Niveau erforderlich. Das erfordert zwingend eine Sicherheitsorganisation, die eine rasche, professionelle Reaktion (*Incident Management*) bei Sicherheitsvorfällen leisten kann. Dabei ist eine Frühwarnung zur vorbeugenden raschen Reaktion äußerst wertvoll, eine der Hauptaufgaben für staatliche Cyber-Elemente wie z. B. (das Cyber-Verteidigungszentrum, das Cyber Security Centre, das GovCERT). Zur Bewältigung von Angriffen und Minimierung deren Folgen ist es zwingend erforderlich, Redundanzen aufzubauen, Notfalls- und Business Continuity-Pläne vorzubereiten und in Übungen zu testen.

Die militärische Landesverteidigung im Cyber-Raum (Cyber Defence) beschäftigt sich ausschließlich mit dem zuletzt beschriebenen Szenario: Nur bei Vorliegen eines Angriffes auf die staatliche Souveränität und selbstverständlich nach politischer Entscheidung ist das Militär zuständig. Alle anderen Szenarien fallen in die Zuständigkeit des BMI, dem das Militär auf Anforderung Assistenz leisten kann, wenn Ressourcen verfügbar sind.

Das beinahe voll digitalisierte Österreichische Bundesheer (ÖBH) kann den Auftrag, „Schutz und Hilfe" als strategische Reserve Österreichs, nur erfüllen, wenn die Verfügbarkeit, Integrität und Vertraulichkeit der militärischen IKT-Systeme sichergestellt sind. Weiters leistet das ÖBH einen Beitrag zur Resilienz anderer Behörden sowie den strategischen zivilen Infrastrukturen und setzt Verteidigungsmaßnahmen bei großangelegten Angriffen.

14.9   Grundsätze der Sicherheit und Verteidigung im Cyber-Raum

Alles zu schützen ist unmöglich. Eine Verkleinerung der Angriffsfläche ist daher das Sicherheitsgebot der Stunde. Eine präzise Festlegung der zu schützenden Werte auf der Basis einer Risikoanalyse und klarer Entscheidung über die durch eine Versicherung abzudeckenden bzw. in Kauf zu nehmenden Schäden reduziert den Aufwand erheblich. Die physikalische Trennung bzw. die weitgehende Abschottung von Systemen mit einem hohen Schutzbedarf von unsicheren Systemen mag höhere Investitionen erfordern. Die dadurch vermiedenen Schäden übersteigen diese Kosten auf lange Sicht.

Das ÖBH hat in den letzten 25 Jahren mit der physikalischen Trennung der einsatzwichtigen **Systeme von unsicheren Systemen, einschließlich des Internets, sehr positive Erfahrungen** gemacht.

Bei der großflächigen Einführung von Arbeitsplatzcomputern ab 1990 wurden einige noch heute richtungsweisende Entscheidungen zur Sicherheit getroffen und die erforderlichen hohen Budgetmittel zur Verfügung gestellt. So wurde z. B. der Klartextimport/-export durch Verschlüsselung der Daten auf den Clients auf wenige, zentral verwaltete Berechtigte reduziert. Die Verschlüsselung am Übertragungsweg vom Client über die

Server bis zu den redundant ausgelegten Rechenzentren war und ist ein hervorragender Schutz der Vertraulichkeit der Daten. Boot-Schutz und Authentifizierung mit Safecard und Passwort und Adressierung der Computer im Netz verhindern den Zugang für Unbefugte zu PCs sowie die Einbindung fremder Rechner im Netz.

Ab Mitte der 1990er-Jahre entstand der Bedarf an Internetzugängen bei Forschungsabteilungen und bei militärdiplomatischen Dienststellen. Das Internet wurde von Anfang an als unsicheres System betrachtet und physikalisch getrennt von anderen Systemen betrieben. Die Nutzung wurde ausschließlich für Recherchen in offen zugänglichen Quellen sowie für die Kommunikation mit nicht klassifizierten Informationen freigegeben. Dennoch wird ein erheblicher Aufwand in Absicherungsmaßnahmen zur Hintanhaltung von Reputationsschäden an den Internetzugängen investiert. Der Einsatz von Antischadwareprogrammen bis zur Clientebene, der Einsatz von Intrusion Detection-, Intrusion Prevention- und Monitoringsystemen in den Rechenzentren ist selbstverständlich erforderlich. Die regelmäßige Nutzerdatensicherung und die Erstellung von Backups in Verbindung mit Notfallplänen schützen vor großem Datenverlust und stellen die rasche Wiederinbetriebnahme nach einem Schadereignis sicher.

Die schutzwürdigen IKT-Systeme für die Verarbeitung von klassifizierten Daten bzw. mit hoher Bedeutung für die Funktionsfähigkeit des Gesamtsystems werden über den ganzen Lebenszyklus betrachtet. Eine enge Zusammenarbeit beginnend ab der Planungsphase der organisatorisch strikt getrennten planenden, entwickelnden und betreibenden mit den sicherheitsverantwortlichen Stellen liefert den größten Sicherheitsgewinn. Schon in der Planungsphase werden Standards oder *Best practise*-Anforderungen berücksichtigt. Erst nach Genehmigung der Planungspapiere erfolgt die Entwicklung bzw. die Testung. Nach erfolgreichem Abschluss durch ein Abnahmeaudit wird ein System für den Probebetrieb mit nicht klassifizierten Daten freigegeben. Bei entsprechenden Ergebnissen wird der Betrieb freigegeben, eine neuerliche Akkreditierung erfolgt in periodischen Intervallen. Während des Betriebes werden die wichtigen Systeme einem jährlichen IKT-Sicherheitsaudit zur Feststellung des Sicherheitszustandes, zur Entdeckung von Schwachstellen, Einbruchspuren oder laufenden Angriffen unterzogen. Die Auditberichte erzwingen Maßnahmen zur Optimierung der Sicherheit bzw. die Einleitung von Erhebungen einschließlich IT-forensischer Tools und Methoden. Diese Sicherheitsmaßnahmen haben neben der Ausbildung und permanenten Sensibilisierung der Mitarbeiter große Schadprogrammeinbrüche und den ungewollten Abfluss von Informationen verhindert.

Sicherheitsmaßnahmen sind ganzheitlich zu konzipieren. Ineinandergreifende personelle, organisatorische, infrastrukturelle und technische Absicherungsmaßnahmen gewährleisten ein hohes Maß an Sicherheit. Nur verlässliches, gut ausgebildetes und sensibilisiertes Personal darf auf der Basis von klaren Vorschriften mit besonderen Rechten ausgestattet werden. Eine ausreichend große, hochqualifizierte Sicherheitsorganisation entwickelt ein Sicherheitskonzept, passt es permanent den geänderten Umfeldbedingungen an und setzt die angeordneten Maßnahmen durch. Die räumliche Infrastruktur ist einschließlich des Perimeters wertangepasst gut abgesichert und die technischen Absicherungsmaßnahmen sind am neuesten Stand. Redundanzen und Notfallmaßnahmen sind entwickelt und werden regelmäßig in Übungen überprüft.

Von großer Bedeutung für die Sicherheit ist die Sensibilisierung aller User, insbesondere aber der Führungskräfte auf allen Führungs- und Leitungsebenen. Nebst Vorträgen auf allen Akademien, Schulen und Kaderfortbildungstagen wird IKT-Sicherheit regelmäßig in allen militärischen Medien thematisiert. Demnächst geht ein E-Learning-Programm zur Umsetzung der Belehrungspflichten und zur Steigerung des Sicherheitsbewusstseins in den Vollbetrieb. Alle User haben das Programm mit einem Abschlusstest einmal jährlich positiv zu absolvieren.

Die jährliche IKT-Sicherheitskonferenz ist die größte Awareness-Veranstaltung mit den Zielen: Fortbildung des IKT-Sicherheitspersonals aus Wirtschaft, Behörden, Organisationen, Lehre & Forschung; Bewusstseinsschaffung und Sensibilisierung der User aller Ebenen

Vernetzung mit IKT-Sicherheitsrelevanten Behörden, Organisationen, Institutionen und Firmen und Etablierung einer Plattform für einen unabhängigen Erfahrungs- und Informationsaustausch.

Die IKT-Sicherheitskonferenz wurde 2017 zum 17. Mal durchgeführt. Insgesamt waren 2700 Teilnehmer aus 17 Ländern und 565 Organisationen dabei. In mehr als 60 Präsentationen und Live-Vorführungen wurden aktuelle Sicherheitsthemen von Experten aus dem In- und Ausland vorgetragen. Rund 50 Firmen, darunter alle im Cyber-Bereich renommierten, stellten ihre Produkte aus. Parallel wurde das Finale der österreichischen Hacker Challenge, die seit 2012 jährlich durchgeführt wird, ausgetragen. Der Wettbewerb für Schüler und Studenten bezweckt die frühzeitige Entdeckung und Förderung der Fähigkeiten und Stärken junger IT-Talente und den Aufbau von Nachwuchskompetenz. Auch Nachwuchsforscher hatten wieder die Gelegenheit, beim *Young Researchers Day* Projekte zu präsentieren. Mit einem Führungskräfte-Event wurde die Konferenzwoche beschlossen.

14.10 Cyber-Verteidigung

Selbst wenn der Schutz der eigenen Cyber-/IKT-Systeme permanent sichergestellt ist, kann einem Angreifer eine Attacke gelingen. Angriffe können jederzeit starten [28]. Es gibt nur eine sehr kurze Vorwarnzeit oder gar keine. Schäden können sehr rasch sehr hoch sein [29]. Da dies niemals ausgeschlossen werden kann, sind zusätzliche Cyber-Verteidigungsmaßnahmen erforderlich.

Zur Cyber-Verteidigung tragen insbesondere die permanente Verfügbarkeit eines aktuellen Cyber-Lagebildes, die Frühwarnung, die Alarmierung, die Abwehr von laufenden Angriffen einschließlich offensiver Maßnahmen, die Sicherstellung der vitalen Funktionen sowie die rasche Wiederherstellung des Normalzustandes bei.

Die Darstellung eines konsolidierten permanent aktuellen Cyber–Verteidigungslagebildes für den militärischen und als Beitrag für den gesamtstaatlichen Bedarf ist sicherzustellen. Das Cyber-Verteidigungslagebild sollte die globale Cyber-Bedrohungslage, die Situation der militärischen IKT-Systeme, die Ergebnisse der Schnittstellenüberwachungssysteme, nachrichtendienstliche und Erkenntnisse aus der Analyse von Malware und Angriffsmethoden umfassen. Eine Erweiterung um die Systeme anderer Behörden sowie der sonstigen strategischen Infrastruktur sollte möglich sein. Das Lagebild beschreibt alle

Arten von Missbrauchsdaten (*Abuse Data*), neu entdeckte Verwundbarkeiten (*Vulnerabilities*) und Einbruchsindikatoren (*Indicators of Compromise (IoC)*). Die Kenntnis der Ziele, Fähigkeiten, Motive und Ressourcen potenzieller Angreifer/Täter erleichtert die Vorbereitung der Verteidigung. Die Erkenntnisse aus der Analyse des Lagebildes sind einerseits an die Systembetreiber zur Optimierung der Absicherungsmaßnahmen weiterzugeben. Andererseits sind die Leitungsebenen zur Sicherstellung deren Handlungsfähigkeit zu informieren. Lageinformationen haben laufend zu ergehen und der Alarm- und Warndienst schafft die Voraussetzung für ein rasches Hochfahren der Verteidigungsmaßnahmen.

Die Abwehr von konkreten laufenden Angriffen erfordert einen schnellen Aufwuchs der technisch und personell bedarfsgerecht ausgestatteten Verteidigungsorganisation und die Unterstützung der Verteidigungsmaßnahmen. Durch automatisch reagierende und lernende, selbst optimierende Systeme müssen die Verteidiger in die Lage versetzt werden, auf Vorfälle rasch zu reagieren, Unterbrechungen des ordnungsgemäßen Betriebes auf ein Minimum zu reduzieren sowie die Koordination des Incident Management durchzuführen. Methoden wie *Sandboxing* und *Sinkholing* unterstützen die Abwehr und sollten in der erforderlichen Schnelligkeit greifen.

Hintergrund

Die Sandkiste (*Sandbox*) bezeichnet allgemein einen isolierten Bereich, innerhalb dessen jede Maßnahme keine Auswirkung auf die äußere Umgebung hat. Unter Sandboxing versteht man das Verfahren, wie man unbekannte bzw. verdächtige Software überprüft, bevor sie implementiert wird. Dabei gibt es unterschiedlich tief gehende Techniken, die vom Umbiegen eines Dateisystems bis hin zur (kompletten) Simulation eines vollständigen Rechners reichen.

Ein gängiges Verfahren zur Identifikation mit Schadprogrammen infizierter Systeme ist die Umleitung schädlicher Domainnamen auf sogenannte *Sinkholes*. Dabei werden die durch Analyse von Schadprogrammen ermittelten Domainnamen in Zusammenarbeit mit den zuständigen Domain-Registrierungsstellen auf Sinkhole-Server umgeleitet. Die Sinkholes protokollieren anschließend die Zugriffe auf die schädlichen Domainnamen mit Zeitstempel und der Quell-IP-Adresse, von welcher der Zugriff erfolgte. Solche Sinkholes werden von zahlreichen Analysten und IT-Sicherheitsdienstleistern weltweit betrieben. Da sich unter den Domainnamen keine legitimen Internetangebote befinden, werden diese üblicherweise nicht angesteuert. Ein Zugriff auf einen solchen Domainnamen ist daher ein gutes Indiz, dass sich unter der Quell-IP-Adresse, von welcher ein Zugriff erfolgt, mit hoher Wahrscheinlichkeit ein mit einem entsprechenden Schadprogramm infiziertes System befindet.

Die Sicherstellung der vitalen Funktionen (des Staates, eines Unternehmens) erfordert den präventiven Aufbau redundanter Systeme, z. B. um die Regierung bzw. eine Unternehmensleitung handlungsfähig zu halten. Dazu gehören die Notfallkommunikationen ebenso wie die Verfügbarkeit von Rechenzentren und Datenbeständen mit ausreichender Energieversorgung. Gänzlich staatlichen Organen vorbehalten sind Abwehrmaßnahmen in den Tiefen des Internet sowie aktive Gegenmaßnahmen. Die rasche Wiederherstellung des Normalzustandes ist ein wesentlicher Beitrag zur Schadensminimierung und bedarf einer entsprechenden *Business Continuity* Planung und des Einsatzes aller verfügbaren Kräfte.

Die hier beschriebenen Systeme und Methoden überfordern durchschnittliche Behörden und Unternehmen. In Österreich werden nur wenige große Unternehmen und Behörden in der Lage sein, ihre IKT-Systeme bis zum Verteidigungslevel zu schützen. Alle anderen brauchen Unterstützung durch professionelle spezialisierte Sicherheitsdienstleister oder durch staatliche Behörden. Die derzeitig gültige Cyber-Sicherheitsstrategie sieht nur die Unterstützung der kritischen Infrastrukturen durch staatliche Maßnahmen vor. Darüber hinaus können durch das GovCERT und das CERT.at eingeschränkte Unterstützung für kleinere und mittlere Unternehmen geleistet werden.

Das ÖBH definiert Cyber-Verteidigung als eine Kombination aus dem Schutz unserer eigenen militärischen IT-Systeme und der militärischen Landesverteidigung im Cyber-Raum. Die beiden Hauptelemente, die in diesem Feld tätig sind, sind das Kommando Führungsunterstützung und Cyber Defence sowie das Cyber-Verteidigungszentrum.

Das Kommando Führungsunterstützung & Cyber Defence ist für das Betreiben und Schützen aller militärischen IKT-Systeme im Inland wie auch im Ausland zuständig. Zu diesem Zwecke ist im Kommando der Organisationsbereich IKT-Sicherheit eingerichtet, der auch die bereits etablierten Computer Emergency Response Team (milCERT)-Fähigkeiten und Security Operation Centres (SOCs) umfasst.

Das Cyber-Verteidigungszentrum ist für die Vorbereitung und Koordinierung der militärischen Landesverteidigung im Cyber-Raum verantwortlich. In Zusammenarbeit mit dem Kommando Führungsunterstützung & Cyber Defence sowie dem Heeres-Nachrichtenamt stellt es ein aktuelles, operatives Cyber-Lagebild zur Verfügung. Darüber hinaus ist es die einzige Einrichtung, die über offensive Cyber-Kapazitäten zur Durchführung von Cyber-Network-Operations verfügt. Das Cyber-Verteidigungszentrum ist Teil des Abwehramtes.

14.11 Ausblick

General Naumann meinte, dass neutrale Staaten des 21. Jahrhunderts die Bewältigung der überwiegend globalen Gefahren „nur noch durch Bündnisse oder internationale Organisationen" erreichen werden [30]. Verteidigung im 21. Jahrhundert umfasst nicht nur die drei herkömmlichen Dimensionen (Land, Luft, See) sondern zusätzlich auch den Weltraum und den Cyberraum [31]. Verteidigung ist keine Aufgabe der Streitkräfte alleine mehr, sondern „erfordert den Verbund aller Sicherheitskräfte, eine verzugsarm handelnde, interministerielle und die Gesamtheit des Staates erfassende Führung, und sie reicht vom Schutz in humanitären Notfällen und Naturkatastrophen über den Kampf gegen organisierte Kriminalität bis hin zur Abwehr von und zum Schutz gegen die Wirkung von ABC-Waffen, von Luftangriffsmitteln und von Cyber-Angriffen" [32].

Naumanns Ausführungen bestätigen den Weg, den Österreich eingeschlagen hat und sollten Ansporn sein, die Umsetzung der ÖSCS und den Auf- und Ausbau der geplanten Instrumente zum Schutz des Cyber-Raumes zügig voranzutreiben. Im nationalen Verbund aller Cyber-Sicherheits- und -Verteidigungskräfte, eingebettet in der europäischen Union und partnerschaftlich mit der NATO, sollte ein hinreichender und nachhaltiger Schutz des Cyber-Raumes erreichbar sein.

Cyber-Verteidigung ist eine gesamtstaatliche, strategische Aufgabe und für Österreich als Hochtechnologiestandort und als Innovationsweltmeister zwingend erforderlich. Auch Unternehmen müssen sich verteidigen. Es darf empfohlen werden, Cyber-Sicherheit als Chance, als *Business Enabler* zu betrachten und damit einen Standortvorteil zu generieren. Die Basis dafür ist ein angemessener Schutz der eigenen Assets, der Daten der Kunden und der Kommunikation.

Literatur

1. Gem. BKA, Österreichische Strategie für Cyber Sicherheit, (ÖSCS), Wien 2013, S. 21.
2. *Internet of Things*, Kurzform: *IoT*, bezeichnet die Vision einer globalen Infrastruktur der Informationsgesellschaften, die es ermöglicht, physische und virtuelle Gegenstände miteinander zu vernetzen und sie durch Informations- und Kommunikationstechniken zusammenarbeiten zu lassen. https://de.wikipedia.org/wiki/Internet_der_Dinge.
3. Laut einer Studie der BitKom vom 10 04 2013, „WIRTSCHAFT DIGITALISIERT, Wie viel Internet steckt in den Geschäftsmodellen deutscher Unternehmen?", sind 50 % der deutschen Unternehmen vom Internet abhängig. Zuletzt gefunden am 25 12 17 unter https://www.bitkom.org/noindex/Publikationen/2013/Studien/Wirtschaft-digitalisiert-II/wirtschaft-digitalisiert-ii.pdf.
4. Deutscher Bundestag, Bericht des Ausschusses für Bildung, Forschung und Technologiefolgenabschätzung zum TA-Projekt: „Gefährdung und Verletzbarkeit moderner Gesellschaften- am Beispiel eines großräumigen und langandauernden Ausfalls der Stromversorgung", Drucksache 17/5672, 17. Wahlperiode, vom 27. April 2011, S. 37, Tabelle 2, in https://www.bundestag.de/dokumente/textarchiv/2012/37875997_kw09_vorschau/207756
5. Vgl.: Unger Walter, Cyber Defence – eine militärische Herausforderung, ÖMZ 6/2012, S. 698 ff.
6. Vgl. https://www.cert-bund.de/schwachstellenampel und https://nvd.nist.gov/.
7. In diesem Spektrum ist Vandalismus ebenso enthalten wie die Veröffentlichung vertraulicher Daten zur Bloßstellung von Personen oder Organisationen ohne Bereicherungsmotiv oder politischer Aktivismus.
8. Vgl. Bericht NZZ Michael Schilliger vom 13 05 17 gefunden am 25 12 17 in https://www.nzz.ch/digital/globaler-cyberangriff-sieben-antworten-zur-cyberattacke-wanacrypt-20-ld.1292982.
9. Wenn hier von mittelfristig die Rede ist, gilt es zu bedenken, dass mittelfristig im IT-Bereich eine eher kurze Zeitspanne ist. Tatsächlich habt man schon Angriffe auf IoT-Basis gesehen. Wenn es nicht gelingt, die IKT sicherer zu machen, ist ein Cyber-GAU möglich!
10. https://de.wikipedia.org/wiki/BIOS.
11. Ein Quantencomputer würde alle derzeitigen Verschlüsselungssysteme in Frage stellen.
12. Ein Horrorszenario könnte z. B. mit der Störung von Atomkraftwerken oder auch der Sabotage von Luftverkehrskontrollzentren entstehen.
13. Siehe Liste von EPCIP.
14. Siehe Heise online vom 22.09.2017, 09:57 Uhr, Martin Holland, „NotPetya: Auch Fedex kostet die Cyber-Attacke 300 Millionen US-Dollar", gefunden am 25 12 17 unter https://www.heise.de/newsticker/meldung/NotPetya-Auch-Fedex-kostet-die-Cyber-Attacke-300-Millionen-US-Dollar-3838159.html.

15. Unter einem Event wird eine Auffälligkeit in den Systemabläufen verstanden. Diese Auffälligkeiten können verschiedene Ursachen haben. Erst nach entsprechenden Analysen kann festgestellt werden, ob es sich um einen Sicherheitsvorfall handelt.

16. Vgl. ObstdG Mag. Walter J. UNGER/Univ. Prof. Dr. Sigmar STADLMEIER, LL.M./Mag. Andreas TROLL, LL.M. (2014) „Cyber Defence – eine nationale Herausforderung (Teil 1)", in Österreichische Militärischer Zeitung, Ausgabe 5/2014, S. 532–545.

17. Ein potenzieller Aggressor sollte jedoch nicht übersehen, dass auch einfache Maßnahmen der Aufklärung (*Computer Network Exploitation*) tendenziell zur Eskalation eines schwelenden Konflikts beitragen können. Da die verbleibende Reaktionszeit extrem kurz sein könnte, könnten beobachtete Aufklärungsversuche einen „Erstschlag" im Sinne eines präemptiven Vorgehens provozieren.

18. Ein *Patch* ist eine Korrekturauslieferung für Software oder Daten aus Endanwendersicht, um Sicherheitslücken zu schließen, Fehler zu beheben oder bislang nicht vorhandene Funktionen nachzurüsten. Unter http://de.wikipedia.org/wiki/Patch_%28Software%29; zuletzt am 25.01.2014.

19. Ein Beispiel hierfür könnten die Bestimmungen des Telekommunikationsgesetzes sein. Die Rundfunk- und Telekom-Regulierungsbehörde kann demnach Sicherheitsstandards vorschreiben und regelmäßig überprüfen.

20. Mit dem NIS-Gesetz wird die europäische NIS-Richtlinie umgesetzt.

21. Es stellt sich daher die Frage, wie z. B. ein DDoS-Angriff auf der Basis eines großen Bot-Netzes mit Zombie-Rechnern in 150 Staaten oder eines eingeschleusten Schadprogramms (beispielsweise STUXNET) einem konkreten Angreifer zugeordnet werden könnte.

22. Das Schadprogramm „Conficker" verbreitete und verursachte erhebliche Schäden. Beispielsweise wurden die 3.000 PC der Landesverwaltung von Kärnten im Januar 2009 zur Gänze lahmgelegt· obwohl schon Monate zuvor ein Sicherheitspatch mit entsprechenden Warnhinweisen zur Verfügung gestellt worden war.

23. Eine weiterführende Analyse findet sich im Abschnitt „Völkerrechtliche Erwägungen" sowie bei: Sigmar Stadlmeier und Walter Unger, Cyber War und Cyber Terrorismus aus völkerrechtlicher Sicht, in: Kirsten Schmalenbach (Hrsg.), Aktuelle Herausforderungen des Völkerrechts, Beiträge zum 36. Österreichischen Völkerrechtstag (2011), Wien 2012, S. 63 ff.

24. Vgl. BKA, Bericht Cyber Sicherheit vom Mai 2016; gefunden am 25 12 17 unter http://archiv.bundeskanzleramt.at/DocView.axd?CobId=63191.

25. Beschluss der Bundesregierung vom 18. 03 2013; Bundeskanzleramt, Wien März 2013 unter http://www.bundeskanzleramt.at/DocView.axd?CobId=50748.

26. Im Herbst 2017 wurde ein Prozess zur Evaluierung der Strategie Cyber-Sicherheit gestartet. Im ersten Halbjahr 2018 soll eine adaptierte Version vorliegen.

27. Cyber-Sicherheit und IKT-Sicherheit werden in diesem Artikel synonym verwendet.

28. Die DDoS-Angriffe auf die Telekom A1 starteten kurz nach Mitternacht am Samstag den 30 01 16; gefunden zuletzt am 27 12 17 https://www.a1.net/newsroom/2016/02/cyber-angriff-auf-a1-infrastruktur/in

29. Vgl. Die Fa. Maersk beziffert den Schaden, der durch NotPetya verursacht wurde, auf 200 – 300 Mio. Dollar(!); gefunden zuletzt am 27.12.17 https://www.heise.de/newsticker/meldung/NotPetya-Maersk-erwartet-bis-zu-300-Millionen-Dollar-Verlust-3804688.html

30. Naumann, Klaus, Was heißt Verteidigung im 21. Jahrhundert? In: ÖMZ 2/2014, S. 143f.

31. Naumann, S. 145.

32. Naumann, S. 145

Erfahrungselemente erfolgreicher Strategie-Entwicklung und -Umsetzung im Umgang mit existenziellen Risiken im Cyber-Raum

15

Gérald Vernez und Adolf J. Dörig

Zusammenfassung

Best Practices? Ist es überhaupt möglich, den Anderen zu erklären, was richtig ist oder nicht? Die beiden Autoren, jeder mit über 20 Jahren Erfahrung im Bereich von Strategieschöpfungen auf allen Führungsstufen im Bereich Cyber sind der Meinung, dass es die Professionalität des Beraters ist, eine Entität – sei es ein Unternehmen, eine öffentliche Gemeinschaft oder eine Regierung – mittels deren spezifischen Werten, Eigenschaften und Prozessen zu entwickeln und zu betreuen. Dabei handelt es sich prioritär darum Sprache, Kultur und Inhalte der Leistungs- und Systemarchitekturen dieser Entitäten umfassend und präzise zu verstehen. Dies vor allem auch in Bezug auf die Dynamik, Robustheit und Resilienz der vitalen und kritischen Leistungen, welche stark durch digitalisierte Systemkomponenten geprägt werden. Dieser Beitrag verfolgt das Ziel, einige praktische Erfahrungen der Autoren im Umgang mit der Strategieentwicklung und -umsetzung einer integrierten Cyber-Sicherheitsarchitektur zu vermitteln.

G. Vernez
Delegierter Cyber-Defence Verteidigung, Bevölkerung und Sport, Bern, Schweiz
E-Mail: gerald.vernez@gs-vbs.admin.ch

A. J. Dörig (✉)
Präsident Expertengruppe Cyber-Defence Bevölkerung und Sport, VBS (Verteidigung, Bevölkerung und Sport), Bern, Schweiz
E-Mail: adolf.doerig@protonmail.com

© Springer Fachmedien Wiesbaden GmbH, ein Teil von Springer Nature 2018
M. Bartsch, S. Frey (Hrsg.), *Cybersecurity Best Practices*,
https://doi.org/10.1007/978-3-658-21655-9_15

15.1 Komplexität beherrschen – Gleiches verstehen, analysieren und behandeln

Der Cyber-Raum beschreibt die komplexe und multidimensionale Umgebung, in der Daten gesammelt, gespeichert, benutzt und übermittelt werden um Aktionen – und dann Leistungen – zu erlauben. Sind diese Daten verfälscht oder nicht vorhanden, erfolgen falsche oder gar keine Aktionen. Aktivitäten im Cyber-Raum verursachen somit auch physische Auswirkungen, wenn diese Daten für das Funktionieren eines Fahrzeuges oder eines industriellen Prozesses fehlen oder fehlerhaft sind und zu ungewünschten Konsequenzen oder sogar Unfälle führen. Schwerwiegende Angriffe in diesem Raum können zu erheblichen Beeinträchtigungen der gesellschaftlichen Lebensgrundlagen führen. Daher wird die Verfügbarkeit des Cyber-Raums sowie die Integrität, Authentizität und Vertraulichkeit der darin vorhandenen Daten zu einer existenziellen Frage dieses Jahrhunderts.

Im dynamischen Cyber-Raum, geprägt durch rasch ablaufende Entwicklungen, herrscht eine Vielfalt an Begriffen. Dies bietet die praktische Herausforderung, dass es auch unter Experten echt anspruchsvoll wird, ein komplexes und dynamisches System von Systemen wirklich umfassend zu verstehen. Vielfach herrscht in der Praxis ein Zustand, wie er in der indischen Parabel der blinden Weisen und des Elefanten beschrieben wird (siehe Abb. 15.1). In dieser untersucht eine Gruppe von blinden Weisen in völliger Dunkelheit einen Elefanten, um zu begreifen, worum es sich bei diesem Tier handelt. Jeder untersucht einen anderen Körperteil (aber jeder nur einen Teil), wie zum Beispiel die Flanke oder einen Stosszahn. Dann vergleichen sie ihre Erkenntnisse und Erfahrungen untereinander und stellen fest, dass jede individuelle Erfahrung zu eigenen, vollständig unterschiedlichen Schlussfolgerung führt. Wenn Erkenntnisse unter Experten und Verantwortlichen so auseinander gehen, herrscht das Risiko, dass Chancen und Gefahren nicht oder mangelhaft erkannt werden, konfliktäre Situationen auslösen und bei Krisen falsche Entscheidungen getroffen werden.

Wie in der Abb. 15.2 modellhaft ersichtlich, umfasst der Begriff Cyber-Raum weit mehr als Informatik [1] alleine, da diese immer auch Strom, Infrastrukturen und (noch)

Abb. 15.1 Die Blinden und der Elefant. (Quelle: coachtherapy)

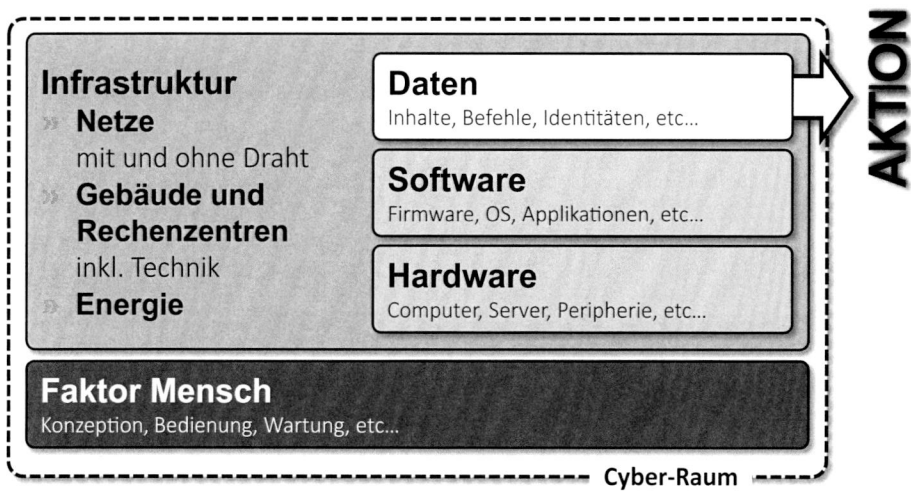

Abb. 15.2 Beschreibung des Cyber-Raumes

Personen benötigt. Der Cyber-Raum entwickelt sich rasant, verändert unsere Lebensweise und sogar die Natur der Konflikte. Er ist zwar ein Schlüsselfaktor des menschlichen Fortschritts, birgt aber in sich viele Verwundbarkeiten, welche manchmal nur Jahre später entdeckt werden. Die Hauptmerkmale des Cyber-Raumes sind die Komplexität, die Verflechtung, der Quasi-Wegfall zeitlicher und geografischer Grenzen, die Anonymität und damit verbunden die Schwierigkeit, Handlungen bestimmten Akteure zuzuordnen.

Als die ersten PCs in den achtziger Jahren auftauchten, waren nur wenige Maschinen miteinander verbunden (Abb. 15.3). Die ersten Sicherheitsvorfälle hatten nur lokale und begrenzte Auswirkungen. Bei der späteren Vernetzung nahmen die Auswirkungen den Aufzug und plötzlich waren ganze Firmen oder Dienste kompromittiert. Mit der heutigen Hyperkonnektivität kann nun eine ganze Gesellschaft von großen Konsequenzen betroffen sein. Mit einer Auswirkung auf Landesebene, Kontinente oder sogar weltweit [2] sowie mit der wachsenden Gefährdung der kritischen Infrastrukturen ist Cyber-Sicherheit [3] eindeutig zu einer der wichtigsten und unmittelbarsten Fragen der Sicherheitspolitik geworden. Es ist mindestens gleich zu stellen mit dem Kampf gegen großräumige Naturkatastrophen oder bewaffnete Konflikte aber ohne Vorwarnzeichen – Entdeckung und Wirkung sind bei Störungen quasi simultan.

Computersicherheit und Netzwerke bleiben zwar voll aktuell, aber die sicherheitspolitischen Dimensionen sind jetzt von erheblicher Bedeutung. Grund dafür sind die Dimensionen der Konsequenzen [4]. Nun können ALLE betroffen werden und bei großflächigen Konsequenzen, zum Beispiel beim Ausfall vitaler Systeme und Infrastrukturen wie Strom [5], werden die daraus resultierenden Krisen alle möglichen Mittel (technisch, physisch, diplomatisch, kommunikativ, rechtlich, usw.) benötigen um diese bewältigen zu können. Die rasche und umfassende Betrachtung aller Dimensionen wird somit sehr bedeutend für die beteiligten Entitäten und deren klare Beurteilung ihrer cyber-physischen Souveränität.

Die verantwortlichen Ebenen der Führung (Governance, Risk and Control) sind herausgefordert, die komplexen Inhalte der betroffenen Systeme wirklich gesamthaft zu

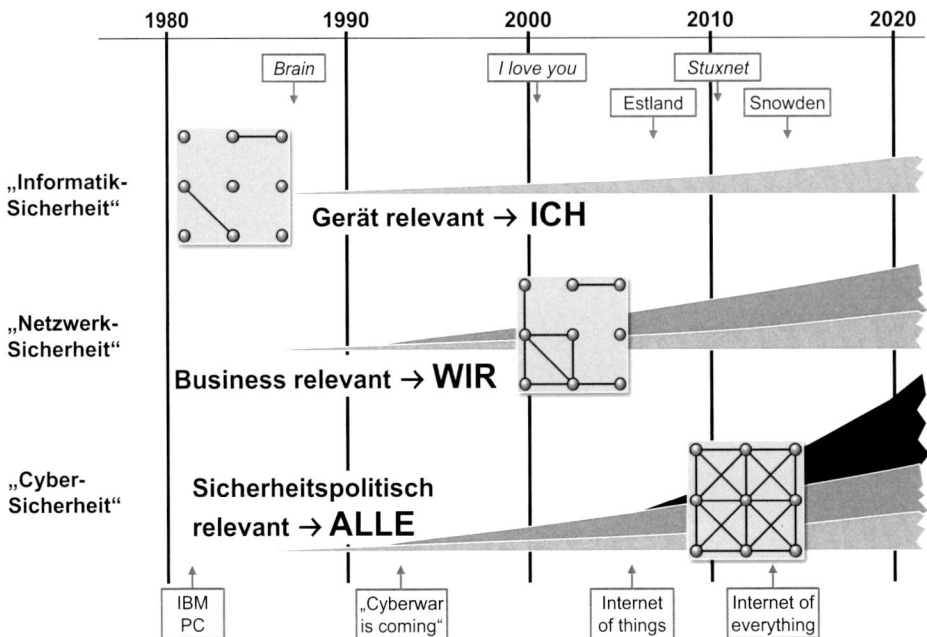

Abb. 15.3 Die Entwicklung und Verkomplizierung des Cyber-Raumes

verstehen und die effektive und effiziente Sicherung des Cyber-Raumes wird zwingend auf oberster Entscheidungsebene geführt.

Vertiefte technische Kenntnisse sind entscheidend, reichen aber alleine nicht mehr aus für eine effektive Führung. Diese handelt somit im Idealfall mit unterschiedlichen Kenntnissen und Fähigkeiten für die gesamtheitliche Sicherstellung der notwendigen cyber-physischen Souveränität. Die oberste Entscheidungsebene schafft dabei das notwendige Vertrauen auch mit einer umfassenden und kompetenten Kommunikation an alle Stakeholder.

15.2 Finden und verknüpfen – Systeme, Prozesse und Technologien verstehen, entwickeln und führen

Unsere moderne Gesellschaft ist unwiderruflich abhängig vom funktionierenden Cyber-Raum geworden. Die Entwicklungen sind volkswirtschaftlich gewünscht, da sie positive Fortschritte bewirken. Gleichzeitig entstehen aber völlig neue Risiken und Konfliktformen.

Die Cyber-Aggressionsformen sind nicht mehr bloss durch Kleinkriminelle und Vandalen mit einfachen Mitteln verursachte geringfügige Störungen kurzer Dauer und geringer Reichweite. Aktuell beobachten wir viel komplexere und vielschichtige Angriffsformen. Dies im Zusammenwirken einer bisher noch nie dagewesenen Vielfalt von immer professionelleren privaten und staatlichen Akteuren. Diese handeln aus den unterschiedlichsten Beweggründen und benutzen das zivile Umfeld für ihre vorbereitenden Aktionen schon in Friedenszeiten.

Seit einigen Jahren entwickelt sich der Bereich Cyber als eigenständige Operationssphäre der Nachrichtendienste sowie der Armeen. Einige Streitkräfte entwickeln sogar massive Kapazitäten im Cyber, auch um ihre Mittel in den Operationssphären Boden, Wasser, Luft und Weltraum strategisch und operationell digitalisiert zu führen. In all den jüngsten Konflikten (Syrien, Korea, Naher Osten, Ukraine, Kampf gegen Terrorismus) gehören die Cyber-Mittel zu den normalen Effektoren der verschiedenen staatlichen und nicht staatlichen Akteure.

Die Cyber-Dimension stellt eine Reihe neuer Herausforderungen für ziviles und militärisches Verhalten dar, die über den rein technologischen Aspekt hinausgehen. Wie in Abb. 15.4 dargestellt, wird jede Technologie irgendwann einmal zu einer neuen Dienstleistung oder einem neuen Geschäft, welche das Verhalten der Anwender/Konsumenten beeinflussen wird. Um sich davon zu überzeugen, genügt eine kurze Selbstbeobachtung unseres Umgangs mit Smartphones. Wenn dieses Gerät aus der Tiefe der Tasche eines Soldaten Daten überträgt, und dies während der Infiltration einer Truppe durch feindliche Linien, kann es seine Position verraten; jeder versteht die Konsequenzen und die sich daraus ergebenden Führungsfähigkeiten, über die militärische Führer neu verfügen müssen. Die Nachlässigkeit eines Mitarbeiters mit einem beschädigten USB-Schlüssel, den er im Rahmen einer Marketing-Aktion erhalten hat, könnte durch Spionage oder Sabotage auch fatale Folgen für ein Unternehmen haben. Es gibt unzählige Beispiele, die zeigen, dass Organisationen und Führungskräfte von KMU's, internationalen Unternehmen und Staaten mit neuen Herausforderungen konfrontiert werden, die sie nicht mehr ignorieren können und dürfen, weil störende Ereignisse im Cyber-Raum den Ausfall von vitalen Leistungen auf kritischen Systemen mit kolossalem Schaden bedeuten kann.

Die Pyramide in Abb. 15.4 zeigt wie wichtig es ist, die Mechanismen und Interdependenzen zwischen Technologien, Diensten, Benutzerverhalten, Führung (Leadership) und schliesslich die Konsequenzen zu verstehen. Kein Problem und keine Krise erfolgt per

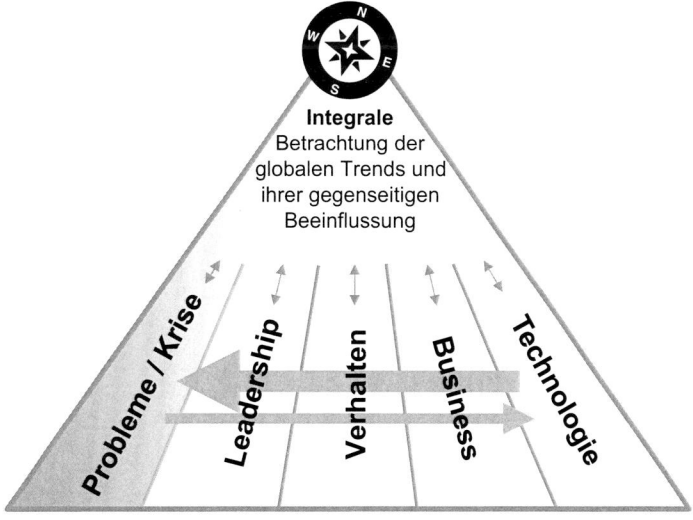

Abb. 15.4 Faktoren zur Schaffung eines Gesamtüberblicks der Cyber-Herausforderungen

Zufall. Jede Entität muss deswegen ihre kausalen Ketten verstehen und sich ein möglichst präzises Gesamtverständnis verschaffen, um rechtzeitig die richtigen Massnahmen zu treffen. Die Erfahrung zeigt, dass zusätzlich zu den Massnahmen zum individuellen Grundschutz eine sorgfältige integrale Beobachtung es ermöglicht, viele Entwicklungen vorherzusehen. Überraschungseffekte, Intensitätslevel und Dauer der Probleme und Krisen können somit deutlich verkürzt oder reduziert werden.

15.3 Strategieschöpfungsprozess – alte Planungsvorgehensweise an neue dynamische Realitäten anpassen

Um eine Strategie erfolgreich zu entwickeln, sollten einige „Fallstricke" vermieden werden, unter denen fünf Klassiker sich hervorheben:

1) *„Spiegelsyndrom"*: Es gibt den berühmten Satz *„Wir haben es immer so gemacht"* von denen, die glauben, dass sie bisher alles richtig machten und sich mit Lösungen aus der Vergangenheit zufrieden geben.
2) *Verteidigung der eigenen Interessen*: Veränderungen führen bei Verantwortlichen immer zu Verlust oder zur Stärkung ihrer Macht. Mögliche Verlierer werden alles tun, um das zu erhalten, was sie als ihre bisherigen Errungenschaften ansehen.
3) *Unsicherheit*: Veränderung bedeutet für Menschen immer, aus der eigenen Komfortzone herauszukommen. Dies kann alle möglichen mehr oder weniger begründeten Ängste und Widerstände hervorrufen, die mit mangelndem Projekt-, Veränderungs- und Kommunikationsmanagement meist noch zunehmen. Vielfach fehlt auch ein projektspezifisches Risikomanagement.
4) *Mangel an Kenntnissen und Fähigkeiten*: Angesichts wachsender Komplexität fehlen die fachlichen Kenntnisse auf den betroffenen Führungsebenen. Entscheidende Schlüsselarbeiten werden Führungspersonen anvertraut, die dafür unzureichend vorbereitet sind.
5) *Zeitdruck*: Mangelndes, prospektives und zeitnahes Vorausschauen kann zu den bekannten *„schon bisher gemachten"* Lösungen führen, von denen man weiss, dass sie leicht akzeptiert werden.

Mit den fünf obigen „Fallstricken" wird die Logik „End – Way – Means" umgekehrt; anstatt nach vorne zu schauen, schaut man zuerst, was am wenigsten stört, damit die Veränderung ohne zusätzliche Ressourcen erfolgen kann. Die Veränderungen sollen für alle budgetneutral wirken. Die Führung kann Auseinandersetzungen bei der Prioritätensetzung vermeiden, die natürlicherweise meistens zu Spannungen führen. Die Fallstricke beinhalten auch verschiedene Risiken, von denen das Grösste darin besteht, sich mit früheren Leistungen in opportunistischer Art zufrieden zu geben. Dies führt zur Unterbindung von kreativen und innovativen Prozessen zur Lösungsfindung in neuen Lagen, Bedrohungen und Herausforderungen.

Zu Form einer allgemeinen Empfehlung schlägt Abb. 15.5 ein Arbeitsvorgehen vor, die mit der rigorosen, präzisen und möglichst automatisierten Auflistung des „IST-Zustandes"

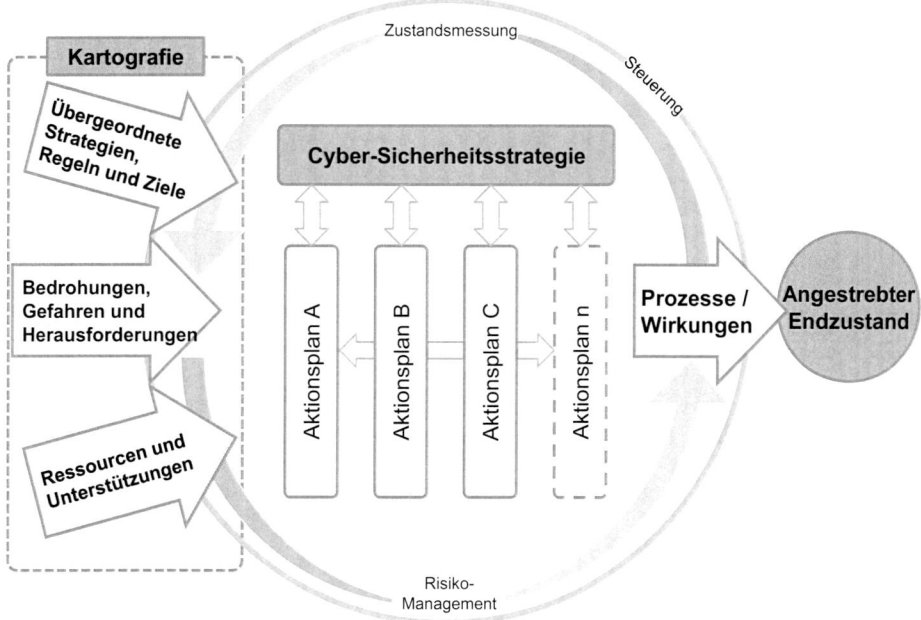

Abb. 15.5 Elemente der Strategieschöpfung

in allen Bereichen beginnt, insbesondere mit einer detaillierten Analyse aller relevanten externen Faktoren, des übergeordneten Umfelds, aller Rechtsgrundlagen, aller Ergebnisse von Strategien oder aus Aktivitäten der Nachbarn und Partner. Ohne diese laufend angepasste auf dem aktuellsten Stand befindliche „Kartografie" bleiben alle nachstehenden Arbeiten meistens blosse Makulatur.

Es ist dann notwendig, den angestrebten Endzustand oder „SOLL-Zustand" zu definieren und eine Strategie zu entwickeln, die nach klar definierten Prozessen und Verantwortlichkeiten messbare Effekte erzeugt. Je nach Komplexität der Strategie kann zudem der Pfad vom IST zum SOLL aus verschiedenen (sektoriellen) Teilaktionsplänen bestehen. Darüber hinaus müssen diese Pläne konsistent miteinander sein und das (dynamische) Risikomanagement der Strategieentwicklung und -umsetzung muss sichergestellt sein. Die Aufgabe der Steuerung besteht insbesondere darin, die Konsistenz auf der Grundlage von zwei Hauptindikatoren, die Zustandsmessung und das Risikomanagement sicherzustellen. Die Teilaktionspläne müssen dann kontinuierlich an die Lage angepasst werden, währenddessen der angestrebte Endzustand und die Strategie nur noch bei grundsätzlichen Veränderungen angepasst werden.

Der angestrebte Endzustand kann jedoch nicht souverän festgelegt werden. Hierin werden die Ambitionsniveaus pro Bereich definiert. Jeder Level hat einen Preis und/oder beinhaltet Risiken, die früh im Strategieschöpfungsprozess identifiziert und von der Führung genehmigt werden müssen. Dies bedeutet, dass die oberste Führungsebene regelmässig über die Fortschritte der Arbeiten informiert werden muss und sich grundsätzlich an der

Strategieentwicklung und -umsetzung dauernd aktiv beteiligen kann. Dies hilft in den wichtigen Entscheidungen zur frühzeitigen Bereitstellung aller relevanten Mittel zur erfolgreichen Umsetzung der strategischen Projekte.

15.4 Architektur – die Meta-Ebene der Organisation und Prozesse

Basierend auf der Erfahrung anderer Nationen sind die Autoren dieses Beitrags von der zwingenden Notwendigkeit überzeugt, jede Strategie mit einer verständlichen Darstellung zu kommunizieren, auf der sich alle Interessengruppen mit ihren Schwerpunkten leicht identifizieren können. So findet jede Umsetzungseinheit ihren konstruktiven Platz, was zu einer verbesserten Zusammenarbeit und zur erheblichen Reduktion von Machtkämpfen führt.

Abb. 15.6 stammt (angepasst) aus dem Aktionsplan Cyber-Defence des VBS, den die Leser online [6] finden und stellt ein mögliches Beispiel dar. Diese Architektur umfasst den Rahmen mit den externen und leitenden Einflussfaktoren und den internen Funktionen der Entität innerhalb ihrer eigenen Kompetenzen und Fähigkeiten, wobei:

- Die *Steuerung* (oder *Governance*, *Risk and Control*), die auf Führungsebene der Entität günstige Bedingungen für die Entwicklung und den Einsatz der Mittel schafft und mit ihren Planungs- und Kontrolltätigkeiten dafür sorgt, dass die angestrebten Ziele erreicht werden;
- Der *Schutz*, wo die originären Leistungen der Entität erbracht oder verändert werden und sich die Betreiber der verschiedenen Systeme und Infrastrukturen (die „Produktion") befinden und die unter auf der Stufe Steuerung genannten Sicherheitsvorschriften umsetzen;
- Die *Verteidigung*, in der alle Leistungen erzeugt werden, die nicht dem Rhythmus des Betriebs untergeordnet sind, um konkrete Cyber-Bedrohungen oder -Aggressionen in den geltenden Rechtsgrundlagen abzuwehren oder entgegenzuwirken; es umfasst (die Auflistung ist nicht umfassend) nachrichtendienstliche Aufgaben, die Überwachung

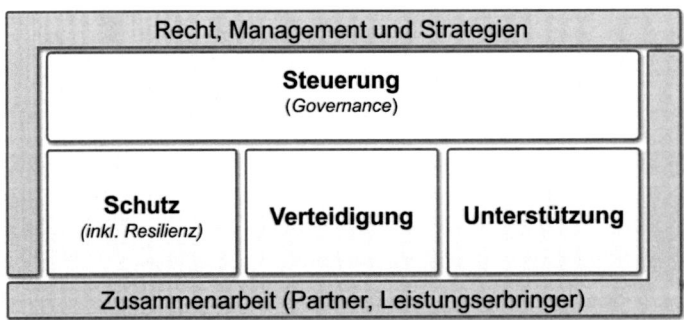

Abb. 15.6 Funktionelle Architektur

der IKT-Systeme und -Infrastrukturen (zum Beispiel mittels eines Security Operation Center) um Anomalien rechtzeitig zu erkennen, forensische Arbeiten bei Vorfällen oder die Durchführung von Stress- und Penetrationstests; offensive Gegenmassnahmen gehören diese Kategorie, sind aber wie bei Gewaltmonopol mit der Armee, einzig eine Aufgabe des Staates;

- Die *Unterstützung*, mit der genügendes und qualifiziertes Personal mit Wissen und Kompetenzen sowie technologische Kapazitäten dynamisch, rasch und flexibel für alle entscheidenden und notwendigen Arbeiten der effektiven Umsetzung der Strategie bereitgestellt werden.

Es liegt an der Entität, diese Funktionen zu definieren, von denen jede unterschiedlich ist. Das von der Geschäftsleitung festgelegte Ambitionsniveau hat einen Preis und/oder bestimmt Restrisiken, die genau zu definieren und zu akzeptieren sind.

Schlussbemerkung

Es wäre anmassend, sich vorzustellen, dass die beschriebenen wenigen Erfahrungen und Beobachtungen die Lösung aller Herausforderungen des Cyber-Raumes sein könnten. Die Erfahrung zeigt jedoch, dass ihre Bedeutung – natürlich nach der Anpassung an den spezifischen Kontext jeder Entität – für den Erfolg der Entwicklung einer Strategie zur Bewältigung dieser Herausforderungen unbestreitbar ist und daraus sich drei wesentliche Effekte erzeugen:

- *Agilität*, weil die Entität in der Lage sein wird, sich kontinuierlich an neue Herausforderungen anzupassen, welche durch die ununterbrochene Schaffung von Neuerungen mittels Big Data, Blockchain, Künstlicher Intelligenz usw. sich permanent weiterentwickeln.
- *Wissen* durch die dynamisch aktualisierte Kartografie, die für die Simulation und Entscheidungsfindung unerlässlich ist und es ermöglicht, Krisen vorauszusehen oder zumindest ihre Eintretenswahrscheinlichkeit und Auswirkung erheblich zu reduzieren.
- *Interoperabilität* der verschiedenen Akteure, so dass sie eine gemeinsame Vision von den zu erreichenden Zielen haben und in der Lage sind, jederzeit kohärent zusammen zu interagieren, insbesondere im Falle eines Ereignisses, bei dem Zeitverlust und Improvisation schädlich sind, auch im Hinblick auf interne und externe Kommunikation.

Für die Autoren ist es wichtig, dass die Cyber-Herausforderungen als umfassende und vielschichtige Kernaufgaben der Geschäftsleitungen verstanden werden. Eine kohärente, werteorientierte Sicherheitspolitik im Cyber-Raum wird somit zu einem Kernelement der digitalen Transformationen. Sie ist deshalb integrierter Bestandteil der bereits bestehenden und vernetzten sicherheitspolitischen Instrumente. Die Anforderungen an die Führungskräfte sind deshalb viel grösser als je zuvor, ... aber äusserst spannend, nicht?

Literatur

1. Es handelt sich um die Vielfalt von Geräten die heute in Milliarden für das Funktionieren aller Facetten unserer Gesellschaft unabdingbar geworden sind. Dazu gehören auch vermehrt Implantate in unsere Körper.
2. Zum Beispiel mit Not-Petya in 2017 oder der DDoS gegen Dyn in den USA in 2016.
3. Der Begriff Cyber-Sicherheit beschreibt den allgemeinen Stand der IKT-Lage, in dem die Risiken durch eine Reihe von passiven und aktiven/offensiven Massnahmen auf ein akzeptables Mass reduziert werden. In der Schweiz sind der Nachrichtendienst des Bundes und die Armee die einzigen Institutionen, welchen durch die Regierung erlaubt werden kann bewilligungspflichtige offensive Gegenmassnahmen zu treffen.
4. Jüngste Schätzungen zeigen, dass die Konsequenzen der Cyber-Kriminalität alleine bereits über ein Prozent des GDP weltweit kostet, steigend.
5. Die *Proof of Concept* sind bereits erfolgt, zum Beispiel in der Ukraine in Dezember 2015 und 2016.
6. https://www.vbs.admin.ch/content/vbs-internet/de/die-schweizer-armee/schutz-vor-cyber-angriffen.download/vbs-internet/de/documents/verteidigung/cyber/Aktionsplan-Cyberdefense-d.pdf

Vorworte

Heinz Karrer und Holger Mühlbauer

Zusammenfassung

Digitalisierung ist in aller Munde. Klar ist mittlerweile, dass es sich beim Thema nicht um eine Modeströmung handelt, sondern dass Digitalisierung vielmehr die Grundlage bildet, auf der Wirtschaft, Wissenschaft und Gesellschaft in Zukunft aufbauen. Noch wissen wir nicht im Detail, wie dieser Prozess ablaufen wird, geschweige denn, wo wir in zehn Jahren stehen werden. Prognosen sind aber durchaus möglich: Einzelne Jobs und Geschäftsmodelle werden verschwinden, gleichzeitig werden aber andere, neue geschaffen. Es gibt für uns gute Gründe, positiv in die Zukunft zu schauen. Die Schweiz ist als wettbewerbsfähiges und innovatives Land gut aufgestellt, um die technologischen Veränderungen zu ihrem Vorteil nutzen zu können.

H. Karrer (✉)
economiesuisse, Zürich, Schweiz
E-Mail: heinz.karrer@economiesuisse.ch

H. Mühlbauer
TeleTrusT, Berlin, Deutschland
E-Mail: holger.muehlbauer@teletrust.de

© Springer Fachmedien Wiesbaden GmbH, ein Teil von Springer Nature 2018
M. Bartsch, S. Frey (Hrsg.), *Cybersecurity Best Practices*,
https://doi.org/10.1007/978-3-658-21655-9_16

16.1   Mit Sicherheit zum wirtschaftlichen Erfolg im Cyber-Raum

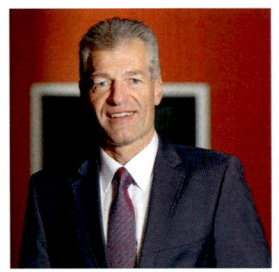

Heinz Karrer

Vorwort von Heinz Karrer, Präsident des Schweizer Wirtschaftsdachverbandes economiesuisse, Switzerland

Digitalisierung ist in aller Munde. Klar ist mittlerweile, dass es sich beim Thema nicht um eine Modeströmung handelt, sondern dass Digitalisierung vielmehr die Grundlage bildet, auf der Wirtschaft, Wissenschaft und Gesellschaft in Zukunft aufbauen. Noch wissen wir nicht im Detail, wie dieser Prozess ablaufen wird, geschweige denn, wo wir in zehn Jahren stehen werden. Prognosen sind aber durchaus möglich: Einzelne Jobs und Geschäftsmodelle werden verschwinden, gleichzeitig werden aber andere, neue geschaffen. Es gibt für uns gute Gründe, positiv in die Zukunft zu schauen. Die Schweiz ist als wettbewerbsfähiges und innovatives Land gut aufgestellt, um die technologischen Veränderungen zu ihrem Vorteil nutzen zu können.

Viele hiesige Unternehmen haben das Potenzial der technologischen Entwicklung denn auch erkannt. Sie treiben digitalisierte Geschäftsmodelle zielstrebig voran und digitalisieren ihre Prozesse, um so im internationalen Wettbewerb weiter an der Spitze mitspielen zu können. Bei anderen Unternehmen geschieht auch einiges, ohne dass sie sich dessen wirklich bewusst sind: Neue Generationen von Geräten bieten eine Vielzahl an zusätzlichen Möglichkeiten und ermöglichen es dadurch, produktiver und präziser zu arbeiten. Auch so wird ein Unternehmen digitalisiert. Von den Veränderungen sind alle Branchen betroffen. So setzt der Laborant beispielsweise ein ferngewartetes Analysegerät ein, die Aussendienst-Mitarbeiterin erfasst Bestellungen mit dem Tablet und der Schreiner nutzt die digitale Fräsmaschine für 3D-Produktionen.

Im Zentrum der Digitalisierung stehen somit nicht nur Daten, Maschinen, Algorithmen oder einzelne Anwendungen, sondern die Menschen. Für uns alle gilt: Wir müssen die Chance packen, die Digitalisierung mitzugestalten.

Die Digitalisierung eröffnet zahllose Möglichkeiten für neue Geschäftsideen. Sie hat aber auch eine Kehrseite: Das Internet ermöglicht dubiosen Organisationen und Individuen mit schlechten Absichten, neue Formen der Kriminalität zu leben. So können über das Internet Daten gestohlen oder abgeändert, Systeme beschädigt und Unternehmen erpresst werden. Damit tun sich neue Gefahren auf, welche in der analogen Welt nicht oder nicht in diesem Ausmass möglich waren.

Wenn die Sicherheit bei der Digitalisierung vernachlässigt wird, kann sie zum existenzbedrohenden Risiko werden. Viele Anwender, Unternehmen wie auch Private, ignorieren heute mögliche Gefahren beim Einsatz neuer Technologien. Dabei muss man klar erkennen: Jedes neue System, das wir mit dem Internet vernetzen – vom Firmenwagen bis zur Fräsmaschine –, vergrössert die Angriffsflächen für Internetkriminelle.

Gegen Angriffe im Cyber-Raum ist letztlich niemand gefeit. So hat es dieses Jahr unter anderem den Internetgiganten Yahoo erwischt. Anscheinend wurden dem US-Konzern Informationen zu rund drei Milliarden Nutzerkonten gestohlen. Falls diese Angaben stimmen, wäre das der grösste Datendiebstahl aller Zeiten. Eine zusätzliche Dimension erhält der Vorfall dadurch, dass er sich offenbar schon im Jahr 2013 ereignet hat, aber das wahre Ausmass erst im Oktober 2017 erkannt wurde. Das Beispiel zeigt, dass auch ein Technologieunternehmen umfassend angegriffen werden kann und gleichzeitig erst sehr spät davon Kenntnis erlangt. Dies unterstreicht ein im Bereich der Cyber-Sicherheit fast schon geflügeltes Wort, dass es heute wohl nur noch zwei Arten von Unternehmen gibt: solche, die bereits gehackt wurden und solche, die dies noch nicht wissen.

Andere Beispiele finden sich leicht: Stichworte sind die jüngsten Wanna-Cry- und Petya-Ransomware-Attacken, bei denen sich zahlreiche Nutzer, deren Systeme befallen wurden, plötzlich vor die Frage gestellt sahen, ob sie für die bösartige Entschlüsselung ihrer Daten Geld bezahlen sollen.

Unternehmen, Private und Behörden sehen sich regelmässig Angriffen ausgesetzt. Im Internet lauern auf die Nutzer und Unternehmen unterschiedliche Gefahren. Es kann jeden treffen, den Grosskonzern, die Privatperson aber insbesondere auch das kleine und mittelständische Unternehmen. Dies wird sich in Zukunft auch nicht bessern, im Gegenteil: Durch die zunehmende Vernetzung von elektronischen Geräten wird sich das Potenzial von Gefährdungen aus dem Cyber-Raum eher noch vergrössern.

Hier ist aber nicht Panik angesagt. Es braucht viel mehr das Bewusstsein, dass diese Gefahren existieren. Darüber hinaus braucht es eine abgeklärte Analyse der Risiken und die Bereitschaft, sich mit den Gefahren auseinanderzusetzen und angemessene Lösungen zu finden.

Eine digitale Unternehmensstrategie muss daher zwingend auch Sicherheitsfragen berücksichtigen. Alle Möglichkeiten, die uns die Technologie heute und in Zukunft bietet – Fernzugriffe, nomadisches Arbeiten, das Internet of Things, die Sharing Economy und vieles mehr –, sind auf eine Anbindung ans Internet angewiesen. Sie sind mit entsprechenden Risiken verbunden, wenn man die Sicherheit bei der Gestaltung des Geschäftsmodelles nicht ernst nimmt. Häufig braucht es nicht viel, um die Sicherheit markant zu verbessern. Bisweilen kann ein Sicherheitsrisiko aber auch zum eigentlichen Geschäftsverhinderer werden. Daher gilt, dass Sicherheit und die damit verbundenen Kosten bei Investitionen von Anfang an einkalkuliert werden müssen.

Dies zeigt auch auf, dass es nicht ausreicht, das Thema einfach an einen Informatik-Verantwortlichen zu delegieren. Es braucht eine Berücksichtigung des Themas auf der Stufe der Unternehmensführung. Fragen um die Sicherheit von Unternehmen sind für den Erfolg und sogar für das Überleben eines Unternehmens von grundlegender Bedeutung. Nicht aus den Augen verloren werden darf schliesslich, dass trotz aller Digitalisierung weiterhin der Mensch im Zentrum steht und gerade dieser auch nach wie vor das grösste Sicherheitsrisiko darstellt. Das Thema ist entsprechend Chefsache.

Wohlverstanden: Ein Management muss sich in der Regel nicht mit den Details zur technischen Ausgestaltung der IT-Security befassen. Es muss aber sicherstellen, dass eine Firmenkultur herrscht, welche das Thema ernst nimmt, dass die internen Prozesse korrekt aufgesetzt sind, dass die Compliance-Anforderungen eingehalten werden und dass qualifiziertes Personal in der Lage ist, die erforderlichen Massnahmen zu ergreifen. Das

Management muss auch wissen, wo besonderer Schutz erforderlich ist und wie im Falle eines Angriffes vorgegangen werden soll.

Gerade hier bieten „Best Practices" willkommene Hilfestellung. Denn auch wenn letztlich jedes Unternehmen sein Sicherheitskonzept selber definieren muss, soll es ihm möglich sein, von der Erfahrung anderer zu profitieren. Das Ziel muss es sein, dass jedes Unternehmen, ob gross oder klein, ein Sicherheitskonzept entwickeln kann, welches angemessen ist, ausreichend Sicherheit bietet und gleichzeitig die operative Handlungsfähigkeit des Unternehmens aufrechterhält.

16.2   IT Security made in Germany

Holger Mühlbauer

Vorwort von Dr. Holger Mühlbauer, Geschäftsführer TeleTrusT – Bundesverband IT-Sicherheit e.V.

Die Bundesrepublik Deutschland darf ihre technologische Hoheit über kritische IT-Anwendungen nicht verlieren. Die Nutzung von IT-Sicherheitstechnologie „made in Germany" muss bei Staat, KRITIS und volkswirtschaftlich wichtigen Produktionsunternehmen Präferenz haben.

Datenschutz „made in Germany" muss ein international wettbewerbsrelevanter Standortfaktor sein. Die Förderung deutscher IT-Sicherheitsunternehmen und Unterstützung bei der Bildung von international wettbewerbsfähigen Marktteilnehmern muss eine Zielsetzung der Politik sein, ebenso die Vergabepolitik in sensiblen Bereichen des Gemeinwesens mit Berücksichtigung nationaler Interessen.

Der deutsche Mittelstand ist bei der digitalen Transformation zu Industrie 4.0 auf politische Unterstützung angewiesen. IT-Sicherheitsprodukte ‚made in Germany' müssen sich auch weiterhin durch besondere Vertrauenswürdigkeit auszeichnen, um in Zukunft die Digitalisierung verlässlich umsetzen zu können. Ohne IT-Sicherheit gelingt keine nachhaltige Digitalisierung. „Security by Design", „Privacy by Design" und nachvollziehbare Qualitätssicherung sind unabdingbar.

Eine der zentralen Herausforderungen beispielsweise von „Industrie 4.0" wird die Absicherung der vernetzten Automatisierungssysteme gegen Risiken aus dem unsicheren Internet sein: IT Security, Datenschutz und Safety müssen auf hohem Qualitätsniveau in deutschen Lösungen für Industrie 4.0 etabliert sein. „IT Security made in Germany", wie sie auch dem gleichnamigen geschützten Zeichen zugrunde liegen, manifestiert sich im Besonderen durch 5 Kriterien:

▶ **5 Kriterien**

1. Der Unternehmenshauptsitz muss in Deutschland sein.
2. Das Unternehmen muss vertrauenswürdige IT-Sicherheitslösungen anbieten.
3. Die angebotenen Produkte dürfen keine versteckten Zugänge enthalten (keine „Backdoors").
4. Die IT-Sicherheitsforschung und -entwicklung des Unternehmens muss in Deutschland stattfinden.
5. Das Unternehmen muss sich verpflichten, den Anforderungen des deutschen Datenschutzrechtes zu genügen.

Eine Kombination aus der werthaltigen Industriemarke „Made in Germany", deutschem Datenschutz und „IT Security made in Germany" kann zum neuen Qualitätszeichen werden und somit den Industriestandort und die Exportnation Deutschland im internationalen Vergleich stärken. Notwendig ist eine politische Allianz zwischen der deutsche IT-Sicherheitswirtschaft und der deutschen Industrie im Rahmen der sog. Digitalen Agenda der Bundesregierung.

Die Sichtbarkeit deutscher Spitzentechnologie und deutscher Unternehmen in Bezug auf IT-Sicherheit sollte staatlich unterstützt werden. Insbesondere vertrauenswürdigere, robuste IT-Systeme, die die Probleme „Softwaresicherheit" und „Malwarebefall" adressieren, sollten gefördert werden. IT-Sicherheitslösungen sollten auf starker Kryptographie basieren und im Kern der IT-Systeme verankert sein. Proaktive IT-Sicherheitslösungen für „Industrie 4.0" sollen direkt umgesetzt werden und Deutschland damit eine weltweite Vorreiterrolle in IT-Sicherheit und Vertrauenswürdigkeit in Bezug auf die Leitindustrien übernehmen.

Was Unternehmen von Staaten lernen können: Cyberstrategieentwicklung

Stefanie Frey

Zusammenfassung

Die Cyberbedrohungen sind in den letzten Jahren stark angestiegen und jeder steht heute im Visier der Täter – Staaten, kritische Infrastrukturen und Unternehmen jeglicher Größe sowie weite Teile der vernetzten Bevölkerung. Je nach Motivation bedienen sich die Täter verschiedener Straftaten wie Cybercrime, Cyberhacktivismus, Cyberspionage oder auch Cybersabotage zur Durchführung des Cyberangriffes. Staaten haben diese Cyberbedrohungen erkannt und von 193 Mitgliedern der International Telecommunication Union (ITU) haben fast die Hälfte bereits Cyberstrategien entwickelt. Die meisten Unternehmen sind noch nicht so soweit. Die Entwicklung einer Cyberstrategie ist der erste Schritt in eine sichere und planbare Zukunft. Simulationsübungen oder auch sogenannte War Games sind eine gute Methode, die technischen und organisatorischen Schwachstellen im Unternehmen zu identifizieren und geeignete Maßnahmen zur Erhöhung der Cybersicherheit zu entwickeln. Die Ergebnisse des War Game dienen auch als Grundlage zur Cyberstrategieentwicklung. In diesem Artikel werden die Methoden und Instrumente des War Game sowie die generischen Schritte zur Cyberstrategieentwicklung beschrieben.

▶ **Cybersicherheit ist nicht nur IT-Sicherheit**
  Viele Unternehmen auf der Anbieter- als auch auf der Anwenderseite stellen die Cybersicherheit immer noch der IT-Sicherheit gleich. Durch die zunehmende Digitalisierung und Vernetzung der Systeme und Netzwerke ist jedoch festzustellen, dass ein reiner IT-Ansatz nicht zielführend ist und die

S. Frey (✉)
Deutor Cyber Security Solutions Switzerland GmbH, Bern, Schweiz
E-Mail: cyberstrategien@deutor.de

© Springer Fachmedien Wiesbaden GmbH, ein Teil von Springer Nature 2018
M. Bartsch, S. Frey (Hrsg.), *Cybersecurity Best Practices*,
https://doi.org/10.1007/978-3-658-21655-9_17

Cyberproblematik über den IT-Ansatz hinausgeht und zusätzlich personelle, physische und organisatorische Aspekte berücksichtigen muss [1].

Bereits getroffene IT-Sicherheitsmaßnahmen sind als Grundlage der Basishygiene zu betrachten, da sie zumeist generisch sind und für die meisten technischen Maßnahmen zutreffen. Die Bewertung der Basishygiene und die bisherigen Aktivitäten werden in den Gesamtkontext integriert und dienen zur Definition der Startpunkte der Maßnahmen. Es sollte bewertet werden, welche bisherigen Maßnahmen und Aktivitäten die Risiken nachhaltig minimieren und welche Anpassungen und Korrekturen vorgenommen werden sollten. Es geht eher darum, die Risikobetrachtung auf Prozessebene zu beschreiben, als auf Basis der darunterliegenden IT-Systeme.

Der erste wichtige Schritt ist die Entwicklung einer Cyberstrategie mit bedarfsgerechten Maßnahmen und Lösungsansätzen, gefolgt von einem Umsetzungsplan und der Bereitstellung von technischen und finanziellen Mitteln zur Reduzierung der Cyberrisiken und Stärkung der Cybersicherheit.

17.1 Cyberbedrohungslage

Das Internet ist zu einem der wichtigsten Wirtschafts- und Handelsräume für alle Staaten, die Wirtschaft und die Gesellschaft geworden und ist heute nicht mehr wegzudenken. Nahezu die Hälfte der weltweiten Wertschöpfung basiert schon heute auf der Informations- und Kommunikationstechnologie (IKT). Die Vernetzung der IKT bringt große Chancen, aber auch Risiken mit sich. Die IKT als solche ist oft unsicher und weist Schwachstellen auf, die für Straftaten missbraucht werden können. Diese Straftaten werden durch staatliche und nicht-staatliche Akteure ausgenutzt, um einen finanziellen, politischen, wirtschaftlichen oder militärischen Vorteil zu erlangen. Die IKT-Systeme sind nicht das Ziel, sie sind lediglich das Mittel zum Zweck und werden dazu benutzt, um entweder Daten zu entwenden, zu manipulieren oder Systeme nachhaltig zu stören (Cybercrime, Cyberhacktivismus Cyberspionage, Cybersabotage). Welche Methode von den Tätern angewandt wird, hängt vom übergeordneten Ziel des Cyberangriffs ab. Wichtig in diesem Zusammenhang ist, dass bei Cyberangriffen ein Täter und somit eine Straftat im Vordergrund steht und daher nicht nur technische, sondern zumeist auch nicht-technische Aspekte berücksichtig werden müssen.

Die Vernetzung, Automatisierung und Digitalisierung durch IKT-Systeme ist in den letzten Jahren rasant vorangetrieben worden und somit sind auch Cyberangriffe, insbesondere von staatlichen Akteuren angestiegen. Es gilt nun diese Cyberrisiken und -bedrohungen zu erkennen und durch geeignete Maßnahmen zu minimieren, damit die Chancen des Cyberraums vollumfänglich genutzt werden können. Cybersicherheit sollte eines der wichtigsten strategischen Ziele von Staaten und Unternehmen sein. Es besteht der Bedarf und die Notwendigkeit, das Bewusstsein und das Verständnis für Cybersicherheit im Rahmen einer „Sicherheitskultur" zu entwickeln und ein besseres Verständnis der Schwachstellen, Bedrohungen und Risiken für die IKT-Systeme und Netzwerke zu etablieren. Dies wird immer wichtiger, da die stetig wachsende Anzahl vernetzter Informationssysteme und Netzwerke einer steigenden Anzahl von Schwachstellen und dadurch auch Bedrohungen ausgesetzt ist.

Cyberkriminelle werden auch in Zukunft diese Schwachstellen vermehrt ausnutzen, was wiederum eine Zunahme der Cyberangriffe mit sich bringen wird. Illegale Aktivitäten im Internet (organisierte Kriminalität), die durch neue Vertriebswege für illegale Daten und Waren im „deep" und „dark" Web entstehen, sind ebenfalls zunehmend zu beobachten. Daraus entstehen zusätzliche Herausforderungen für die Strafverfolgungsbehörden und betroffene Unternehmen, die mit diesen dynamischen und hochgradig technisierten Entwicklungen nur mit größten Anstrengungen Schritt halten können.

17.2   Bedrohungen der Zukunft

In den letzten Jahren konnten enorme Fortschritte in der Entwicklung neuer Technologien beobachtet werden. Man denke nur an die schnellen Entwicklungen im Bereich künstliche Intelligenz und Robotik [2]. Es ist eines der innovativen Themen in der Informationstechnologie und damit eine logische Konsequenz der Nutzung von sehr großen und verfügbaren Datenmengen (Big Data). Durch Big Data stehen erstmalig in der Geschichte der Menschheit Daten in Menge und Qualität zur Verfügung, um daraus neues Wissen zu generieren, bessere Vorhersagen zu treffen und neue Systeme und Anwendungen zu entwickeln. Vom autonomen Fahren über Finanzvorhersagen (RoboAdvisor und FinTech) bis hin zu medizinischen Analysen sind Anwendungsfelder die sich bereits in der Entwicklung befinden und sich stetig weiterentwickeln.

Auch in der Robotik und durch das Internet of Things (IoT) werden diese neuen Algorithmen eingesetzt, damit Roboter selber aus Ihren Fehlern lernen. Künstliche Intelligenz und Robotik umfasst alles von Such-Algorithmen zu IBM Watson zu autonomen digitalisierten Systemen. Diese Entwicklungen und deren Vernetzung werden in der Zukunft noch viel schneller vorangetrieben und was heute als Science Fiction angesehen wird, wird morgen schon Realität sein.

Diese Innovationen bringen jedoch auch Risiken mit sich. Die Hauptrisiken dieser neuen Technologien liegen wie bei allen Kombinationen aus Soft- und Hardware in der Vollständigkeit der Algorithmen oder vielmehr in der Fehlererkennung und in der Manipulierbarkeit von Software und Daten oder ganzer Systeme.

17.2.1 Einige Beispiele

Internet of Things (IoT) bezeichnet eine Querschnittstechnologie zur Vernetzung von Sensoren, Aktoren und spezialisierten Minicomputern, die in vielen neuen Geschäftsmodellen eingesetzt werden. Es ist noch nicht absehbar, wo die technologischen Grenzen von IoT liegen werden. IoT ermöglicht neue Themen wie Industrie 4.0, Smart Home, Wearables, Fitness- und Gesundheitstracker, etc.

Risiken

Die der IoT zugrunde liegende Miniaturisierung lässt nicht genügend Spielraum für die Eigensicherheit der Sensoren und Systeme und bringt oft ungenügende Schutzmechanismen mit sich. Diese können von Cyberkriminellen leicht gehackt, manipuliert oder gestört werden.

Beispiel

Bei Manipulation bieten einfache digitale Schlösser keinen ausreichenden Schutz gegen Einbrecher und können mit einem fremden Smartphone geöffnet werden. Der Schlüssel ist nur noch Software.

Cloud-Computing bezeichnet alle Dienste und Services, die aus einem Rechenzentrum erbracht werden und lokale Technologien ersetzen. Beim Cloud-Computing ist die Sicherheitsarchitektur im Allgemeinen besser als bei klassischen Systemarchitekturen, da die Cloud durch die Anbieter professionell gemanagt, gepatcht und betrieben wird.

Risiken

Sollte ein Cyberangriff auf eine Cloud-Infrastruktur erfolgreich sein, sind sehr viele Kundeninfrastrukturen auf einmal betroffen.

Beispiele

Es wurden bereits Unternehmen angegriffen, die ihre Systeme in einer Cloud betreiben. Die EU regelt mit der NIS-Richtlinie präventiv die Sicherheitsanforderungen von Online-Marktplätzen, Online-Suchmaschinen und Cloud-Computing-Diensten.

Industrie 4.0 [3] bezeichnet die kundenzentrierte und vernetzte Produktion individualisierbarer Produkte. Automatisierte und dezentralisierte Produktionsketten werden die Fabriken und Produktionsstätten revolutionieren. Neue Technologien wie 3D-Druck und IoT-basierte Services wie proaktive Ersatzteilbelieferung werden das Kundenverhalten deutlich verändern, da Individualisierung und Design wie auch Funktion und Verfügbarkeit die Produkte kundenspezifischer werden lassen.

Risiken

Die erhöhte Vernetzung und Automatisierung der Industrie 4.0 kann von Cyberkriminellen missbraucht und manipuliert werden. Manipulationen von Produktionsdaten und Angriffe auf die unterliegenden Systeme führen zu mangelnder Produktqualität oder veränderten Produktionsabläufen.

Beispiele

Manipulation der Konfiguration von Schweißrobotern oder Werkzeugmaschinen mit dem Ziel, ein Endprodukt zu sabotieren, damit Unfälle oder Schäden entstehen.

Autonomes Fahren: Fahrzeuge, die eigenständig am Straßenverkehr teilnehmen, sind auf eine Vielzahl von Sensoren angewiesen und sind vom Informationsaustausch abhängig.

Für die Logistikbranche bedeutet dies ein verändertes Geschäftsmodel, das ohne Personal in den Fahrzeugen auskommt.

> **Risiken**
>
> Werden diese Systeme von außen gestört, entstehen lebensgefährliche Risiken für jeden Teilnehmer im Straßenverkehr und die Logistikketten werden gestört oder unterbrochen.

> **Beispiel**
>
> Lebensgefährliche Unfälle bei teilautonomen Elektrofahrzeugen (Tesla); Unterbrechung der autonomen Logistikketten durch Cyberangriffe mit dem Ziel der Erpressung oder Sabotage.

FinTech ist eine Kombination der Begriffe Finanzdienstleistung und Technologie. FinTechs betreiben datengetriebene Bankgeschäfte. Alle Transaktionen werden nur noch online abgewickelt. FinTechs bedrängen als neugegründete digitale Banken die Filial- und Vollbanken durch kundenbezogene, auf Big Data und Sicherheit ausgelegte Spezialisierungen und ein besseres und individuelleres Service- und Produktportfolio.

> **Risiken**
>
> Durch die Volldigitalisierung der Bank- und Geldgeschäfte durch Einsatz von Big Data, Algorithmen und Online-Systemen entfallen menschliche Kontrollmechanismen. Cyberangriffe haben somit das Potenzial, einen deutlich höheren finanziellen Schaden anzurichten.

> **Beispiel**
>
> Manipulation der Zahlungsdatenströme an der Quelle der Anwendungssysteme.

Health 4.0 – Hightech-Medizin ist eine Bezeichnung für die Digitalisierung des Gesundheitswesens. In allen Bereichen vom Patienten (Überwachung) über Krankenhäuser (automatisierter OP, Telemedizin), Medizintechnik (computergesteuerte Maschinen) bis hin zur Verwaltung und Abrechnung wird die IT-gestützte Medizinbranche in den nächsten Jahren die Digitalisierung vorantreiben. Durch Automatisierung und maschinell erstellte Diagnosen wird jedoch auch eine feinere medizinische Betreuung der Patienten möglich.

> **Risiken**
>
> Durch Vernetzung, Spezialisierung und Digitalisierung steigt das Potenzial von Sabotage und Erpressung. Massenphänomene wie Verschlüsselungstrojaner können eine ganze Klinik lahmlegen und den operativen Betrieb blockieren. Ein externer Eingriff in die Medizin- und Operationstechnik hätte Personenschäden zur Folge.

> **Beispiele**
>
> Nicht gezielte Ransomware-Angriffe, von denen auch Krankenhäuser betroffen waren und dadurch der Klinikbetrieb massiv beeinträchtigt war. Die Möglichkeit von Manipulation bei Insulinpumpen und Herzschrittmachern wurde bereits technisch nachgewiesen.

17.3   Staaten: Cyberstrategieentwicklung

Viele Staaten haben die Notwendigkeit der Cybersicherheit erkannt und darauf reagiert
und Cyberstrategien entwickelt [1]. Unternehmen sind sehr häufig noch nicht so weit.
Unternehmen können von den Arbeiten der Staaten profitieren und anhand deren Erfahrungen ihre eigene Cybersicherheit stärken und daraus abgeleitet eine geeignete Cyberstrategie entwickeln. Eine effektive Cybersicherheit kann langfristig nur etabliert werden,
wenn sie auf einer umfassenden Cyberstrategie aufgebaut ist. Es entsteht ein Bedarf an
übergreifender Zusammenarbeit, internationaler Kooperation sowohl auf regionaler wie
auch auf globaler Ebene und an der Entwicklung eines gesamtheitlichen Ansatzes, um
diesen Herausforderungen zu begegnen („Whole-of-System-Ansatz"). Auch kann die
innere Sicherheit nicht mehr von der äußeren getrennt werden, sondern beide sind heute
weitgehend in der Cyberwelt verschmolzen. Diese Veränderungen führen zu einem Sicherheitsgefälle, das sich über alle Ebenen und Bereiche (staatlich, wirtschaftlich und gesellschaftlich) erstreckt.

Das Sicherheitsgefälle (siehe Abb. 17.1) stellt sich wie folgt dar:

Sicherheitsgefälle
1. Staatliche Vorsorgeplanung (Gesamtstaatliche Sicherheitsarchitektur)
2. Staatliche Cyberstrategie
3. Behörden- und Unternehmens-Cyberstrategie
4. Informations- und Kommunikationstechnologien (IKT)-Strategie
5. IT-Sicherheitsstrategie

Aufgrund der Komplexität und der allgemeinen Abhängigkeiten und Vernetzung der
IT-Systeme haben viele Staaten bereits erkannt, dass Cybersicherheit nicht mit einer rein
technischen Lösung erzielt werden kann, sondern auch politische Implikationen hat, welche die Involvierung der politischen Entscheidungsträger erfordert. Cyberrisiken sind ein
ernst zu nehmendes Problem, zumal sie das Potenzial haben, die nationale Sicherheit zu
gefährden. Dies hat dazu geführt, dass die staatliche Sicherheitsvorsorge in vielen Ländern
um eine Cyberstrategie ergänzt wurde. Die IT-Vernetzung hat die Grenzen zwischen Staat
und Wirtschaft weitestgehend aufgehoben. Alles ist miteinander verbunden, und durch das
Internet existiert nur noch eine gemeinsame Infrastruktur. Somit können der Staat, die
kritischen Infrastrukturen und die Unternehmen nicht mehr technologisch klar voneinander abgegrenzt werden. Auch die zivilen und militärischen Einrichtungen können aufgrund der flächendeckenden Technologisierung nicht mehr klar voneinander getrennt werden. Die Kaskadeneffekte sind heutzutage von einer nicht mehr überschaubaren Dimension,
und ein kleines Problem in einem Teilsystem kann zu einem großen Problem im Gesamtsystem führen und dadurch Auswirkungen auf die nationale Sicherheit, die Bevölkerung
oder im Umweltschutz haben.

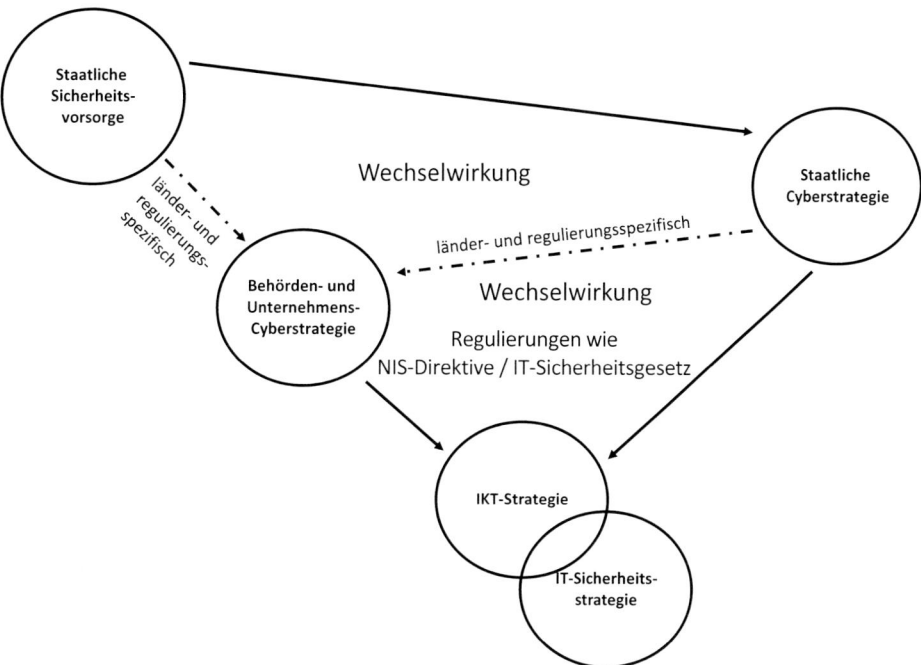

Abb. 17.1 Strategiegefälle und die Wechselwirkungen

Viele Staaten haben eine nationale Cyberstrategie entwickelt und teils schon umgesetzt oder sind dabei, diese umzusetzen. Die meisten Staaten sind sich im Grundsatz einig, dass der Cyberraum der unzählige Chancen bringt, zu schützen ist. Bei fast der Hälfte der ITU Mitglieder [4] wurden bereits Cyberstrategien entwickelt. Ziel der Cyberstrategie ist die Stärkung der Resilienz und eine Reduktion von Cyberangriffen. Dazu müssen Strukturen und Prozesse aufgebaut werden, die auf nationalen und internationalen Kooperationsmodellen basieren, den Informationsaustausch zwischen den Akteuren fördern und die Reaktions- und Durchhaltefähigkeit erweitern, sowie gewisse regulatorische Auflagen und rechtliche Grundlagen entwickeln.

17.3.1 Internationale Gremien und Kooperationen

Staaten sind sich auch einig, dass der Cyberraum nur durch eine enge internationale Zusammenarbeit geschützt werden kann. Dazu wurden wichtige Gremien und Foren ins Leben gerufen, die sich damit befassen, das Internet als offenen, transparenten, freien und sicheren Raum zu gestalten. Darunter sind die Organisation für Sicherheit und Zusammenarbeit in Europa (OSZE), die Organisation für wirtschaftliche Zusammenarbeit und Entwicklung (OECD), die European Union Agency for Network and Information Security (ENISA), die Organisation der Vereinten Nationen (UNO), die Europäische Union (EU), die NATO (NATO Cooperative Cyber Defence Centre of Excellence in Tallinn) – alle haben Cyber-Expertengruppen ins Leben gerufen, die sich mit der Sicherheit im Cyber-raum befassen. So hat man sich mit vertrauensbildenden Maßnahmen, der Einführung von Cyber-Normen und Standardisierungsprozessen unter Staaten, Rechtsgrundlagen, staatli-cher Verantwortung, Schutz der Privatsphäre im Cyberraum und dem Kapazitätsausbau bezüglich der Cybersicherheit im Cyberraum befasst.

Kooperationen finden auf regionaler wie auch auf globaler Ebene statt:

Regionale Ebene:

- Organisation für Sicherheit und Zusammenarbeit in Europa (OSZE).
- Organization of American States (OAS).
- Association of Southeast Asian Nations (ASEAN).
- Shanghai Cooperation Organization (SCO).

Globale Ebene:

- United Nations Governmental Group of Experts (UN GGE).

Es geht darum, ein globales Regelwerk zu entwickeln, da jede regionale Organisation andere Ansätze und Prioritäten hat. Durch die extreme Vernetzung haben Cyberangriffe aus gewissen Regionen globale Auswirkungen. Deshalb muss die internationale Gemein-schaft sicherstellen, dass sie eine globale Cybersicherheitsagenda entwickeln kann, die mithilfe regionaler Ansätze und Organisationen entstehen könnte.

Unternehmen können von den Erfahrungen und Best Practice Beispielen der Staaten lernen und die generischen Grundsätze der Cyberstrategieentwicklung übernehmen. Unternehmen können es sich nicht mehr leisten, keine Cyberstrategie zu entwickeln, da sie ansonsten eine Sicherheitslücke in der Gesamtsicherheitsarchitektur darstellen. Es sollten auch die Grundsätze des Sicherheitsgefälles befolgt werden und Unternehmen soll-ten der IT-Strategie und damit der zugehörigen IT-Sicherheitsstrategie der übergeordneten Cyberstrategie folgen.

▶   Cyber ist kein Teil der IT-Sicherheitsvorsorge, sondern ein übergeordnetes strategisches Ziel innerhalb der Unternehmensstrategie. Jeder Beteiligte in diesem Sicherheitsgefälle muss seine Rolle wahrnehmen und durch geeignete Maßnahmen dazu beitragen, dass die Sicherheit gewährleistet werden kann.

17.4   Grundsätze der Strategieentwicklung

Strategie kann als die planmäßige Vorgehensweise zur Erreichung langfristiger Ziele beschrieben werden. Die Strategie soll beschreiben, was die Vision und übergeordneten stra-tegischen Ziele sind, wie die „Governance" Struktur aussehen soll, wie die Vorgehensweise zur Zielerreichung und wie der Prozess der Zielsetzung gestaltet werden sollen. Auch sollte die Strategie stetig dem sich verändernden Umfeld angepasst werden.

17.4.1 Cyberstrategieentwicklung für Unternehmen

Die Cyberstrategie sollte eine Teilstrategie der übergeordneten Unternehmensstrategie sein und mit den strategischen Unternehmenszielen (Vision und Mission) übereinstimmen. Für die Cyberstrategieentwicklung müssen Unternehmen die strategischen Cyberziele, Handlungsfelder, Maßnahmen und Meilensteine definieren und einen Umsetzungsplan erstellen, damit der Cyberstrategieprozess nachhaltig überprüft und bei Bedarf angepasst werden kann.

Eine Cyberstrategie zu entwickeln ist keine Zauberei, wenn die richtige Methode und die richtigen Instrumente angewendet werden. Unternehmen (insbesondere Kleine und Mittlere Unternehmen – KMU) beschäftigen sich selten mit der Cyberstrategieentwicklung. Die gesamte Energie und Konzentration wird in das operative Tagesgeschäft investiert und nicht in den Cyberstrategie-Planungsprozess.

Abb. 17.2 stellt den ersten Schritt zur Cyberstrategieentwicklung dar. Das Unternehmen sollte zuerst die Ausgangslage analysieren und sein Umfeld kennen. Dann sollten die strategischen Ziele gesetzt und die Cyberstrategie aufgrund der Ausgangslage und den strategischen Zielen entwickelt werden. An diesem Punkt sollte das Unternehmen auch

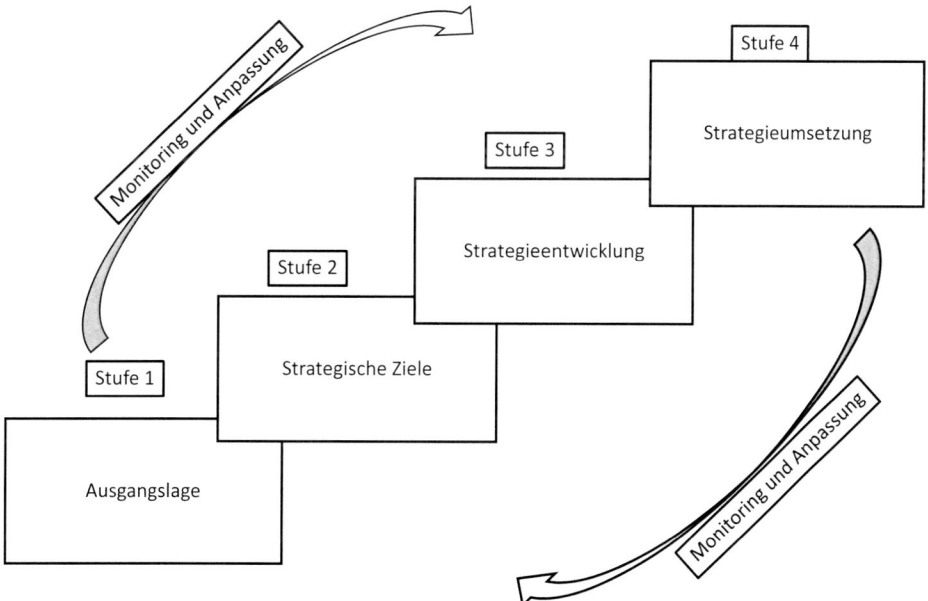

Abb. 17.2 Die vier Schritte zur Cyberstrategie-Entwicklung

planen, wie die Cyberstrategie umgesetzt wird und wer die Verantwortung dafür über-nimmt. Es ist wichtig, dass es eine Struktur gibt, die den Umsetzungsprozess aktiv mitver-folgt und anhand eines Monitorings Anpassungen vornimmt.

1. **Ausgangslage:**
   Auf der ersten Stufe muss die Ausgangslage analysiert werden. Das Unternehmen muss analysieren, wo es steht und welche Herausforderungen bestehen. Die Cyberstra-tegieentwicklung wird im Allgemeinen durch einen der folgenden drei Faktoren ausgelöst:

   – **Nach einem erfolgreichen Cyberangriff. Je höher der Schaden, desto höher die Motivation:** Einige Staaten haben sich nach erst einem erfolgreichen Angriff ent-schieden, eine Cyberstrategie zu entwickeln, um die Abwehrbereitschaft zu erhöhen und sich Methoden anzueignen, die zu einem schnelleren und effizienteren Incident Handling führen. Im Unterschied zu Staaten treffen Unternehmen oft selbst nach erfolgreichen Cyberangriffen nicht die Entscheidung, eine Cyberstrategie zu entwi-ckeln. In den meisten Fällen wird partiell versucht, die IT-Sicherheit zu erhöhen und sich gegen Cyberangriffe zu versichern (Cyber-Risiken-Versicherung). Es werden Sofortmaßnahmen ergriffen, die nicht nachhaltig, aber mit oft hohen Zusatzkosten verbunden sind. Leider wird nur in seltenen Fällen eine Cyberstrategie für das gesamte Unternehmen entwickelt. Die Entwicklung einer Cyberstrategie hängt in den meisten Fällen vom unternehmensrelevanten Schadensausmaß und der Innova-tionsfähigkeit ab.
   – **Regulative Auflagen wie z. B. die NIS-Direktive und das IT-Sicherheitsgesetz:** Wie erwähnt geht es bei der NIS-Direktive um die Gewährleistung einer hohen gemeinsa-men Netz- und Informationssicherheit. EU-Mitgliedstaaten und Unternehmen müssen zukünftig gewisse verpflichtende regulative Auflagen erfüllen. Dazu gehört die Ent-wicklung von Cyberstrategien und Kooperationsplänen für die EU-Mitgliedstaaten.
   – **Präventive Entscheidung für eine Cyberstrategie:** Einige Staaten, die schon früh Opfer von Cyber(-spionage-)angriffen geworden sind, haben eine Cyberstrategie entwickelt. Dies hat dazu geführt, dass weitere Staaten eine präventive Entschei-dung für die Entwicklung einer Cyberstrategie getroffen haben und dies in zum Teil enger Kooperation organisieren. So hat die ENISA eine Cyber Expert Working Group ins Leben gerufen, die aus einigen EU-Mitgliedstaaten und der Schweiz besteht. Der Zweck dieser Arbeitsgruppe besteht darin, in Zusammenarbeit mit Län-dern, die schon eine Cyberstrategie erstellt haben, den Ländern, die noch keine haben, bei der Erstellung ihrer Cyberstrategie zu helfen. Im Gegensatz dazu treffen die meisten Unternehmen keine präventive Entscheidung zur Entwicklung einer Cyberstrategie. Dies resultiert zumeist aus der Unterschätzung des Themas, der Komplexität sowie an gebundenen und nicht entsprechend priorisierten Budgets.

Eine Umfeldanalyse kann zur Beantwortung dieser Fragen hilfreich sein. Kein Unter-nehmen existiert ohne äußere Beeinflussung. Mit der Umfeldanalyse werden diese äußeren Einflussfaktoren (Cyberbedrohungslage, geopolitische Veränderungen, technologische Innovation, neue Kriminalitätsfelder und veränderte Wettbewerbssituationen) aufgezeigt, damit ein Unternehmen eruieren kann, wie sich diese Faktoren zukünftig entwickeln werden.

2. **Strategische Ziele:**

   Im zweiten Schritt müssen auch messbare und langfristige (5 Jahre) strategische Ziele festgelegt werden. Diese muss jedes Unternehmen für sich selbst festlegen. An diesem Punkt muss auch geregelt werden, ob externe Unterstützung benötigt wird und das Budget (Ressourcen und Finanzierung) muss festgelegt werden. Es gibt allgemeine Ziele, die für nahezu alle Unternehmensklassen und -größen identisch sind sowie unternehmensspezifische Ziele, die durch Branche, Größe und die jeweiligen regionalen Tätigkeitsräume bestimmt werden.

   Die Ziele müssen erreichbar, messbar und kontrollierbar sein. Hierbei liegt die größte Herausforderung, da Ziele langfristig stabil und von äußeren Einflüssen unabhängig sein müssen. Falsch definierte Ziele innerhalb einer Cyberstrategie reduzieren weder die Risiken noch erhöhen sie die Widerstandsfähigkeit gegen Cyberangriffe.

3. **Strategieentwicklung:**

   Aufgrund der strategischen Zielsetzung sollen die geeigneten Handlungsfelder und Maßnahmen definiert werden, die bedarfsgerecht auf das jeweilige Unternehmen ausgerichtet werden. Die Handlungsfelder und Maßnahmen können oft generisch dargestellt werden.

Beispiel

- **Säule 1 Prävention:** Risikomanagement, Awareness und Training
- **Säule 2 Reaktion**: Incident- und Krisenmanagement
- **Säule 3 Stabilisation**: Kontinuitätsmanagement

---

4. **Strategieumsetzung:**

   Nachdem die Cyberstrategie entwickelt wurde, sollte ein Umsetzungsplan erstellt werden. Im Umsetzungsplan müssen die Rollen und Zuständigkeiten projektbezogen definiert und eine Roadmap mit Zeitplan enthalten sein. Des Weiteren braucht es ein strategisches Komitee (Lenkungsausschuss) mit den wichtigsten Akteuren und den Umsetzungsverantwortlichen aus allen beteiligten Bereichen sowie ein strategisches Controlling, das den zielorientierten und termingerechten Fortschritt der Umsetzung der Maßnahmen überwacht.

5. **Mögliche Projektorganisation:**

   In Abb. 17.3 werden mögliche Projektorganisationen aufgezeigt. Mittelständische Unternehmen fassen die Ebenen Steuerungsausschuss und Lenkungsausschuss häufig zusammen, wie auch das Programm-Management und die Projektleitung. Somit wird der Projektaufwand der Unternehmensgröße entsprechend angepasst. Das Projekt Cyberstrategieentwicklung sollte organisiert und budgetiert sowie ein Zeitplan dafür festgelegt und in einer Roadmap visualisiert werden.

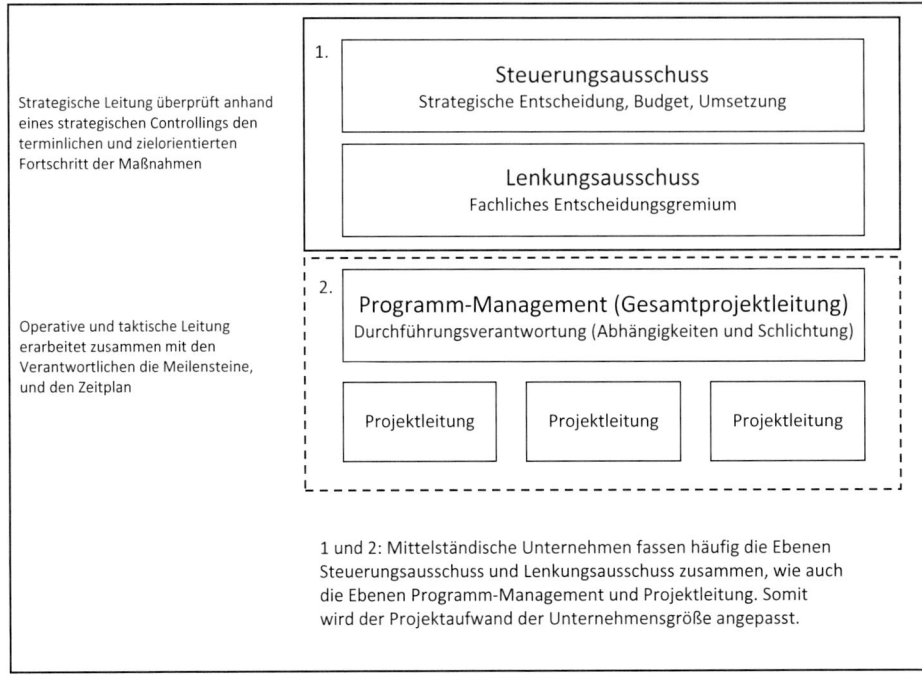

Abb. 17.3 Mögliche Projektorganisation für die Entwicklung und Umsetzung der Cyberstrategie

Mit diesen Schritten haben Sie nun die Strategieentwicklung abgeschlossen und die Strategieumsetzung definiert.

▶ An diesem Punkt fängt die Arbeit erst an, denn die Cyberstrategie muss den Mitarbeitern klar und verständlich vermittelt und konsequent umgesetzt werden.

17.4.2 Maßnahmenentwicklung

Gegen Cyberangriffe, die nach einem generischen Muster ablaufen, sollten vorab geeignete Maßnahmen entwickelt werden, damit bereits bekannte Cyberangriffe nicht durchführbar sind und das Unternehmen auf weitere Cyberangriffe vorbereitet ist. Diesbezüglich gibt es drei generische Phasen, die als allgemeingültig gelten können: die Präventionsphase, die Reaktionsphase und die Stabilisationsphase (siehe Abb. 17.4).

Präventionsphase: Maßnahmen, die verhindern, dass ein Cyberangriff mit erheblichen Folgen stattfinden kann. Dazu zählen Maßnahmen wie Awareness und Training, Detektionsfähigkeit von Angriffen, organisatorische und technische Maßnahmen zur Verbesserung der Sicherheit, Bedrohungsanalysen und Lagebeurteilungen sowie Verwundbarkeitsanalysen der kritischen Geschäftsprozesse und -systeme.

Abb. 17.4 Cyberstrategie als
Bindeglied zwischen
Prävention-Reaktion-
Stabilisation

Reaktionsphase: Maßnahmen zur Schadensminimierung und raschen Vorfallbearbeitung. Dazu zählen ein effektives Incidentmanagement (technisch), Krisenmanagement (organisatorisch) und eine effektive Krisenkommunikation sowie die Umsetzung von Auflagen (gesetzliche Vorgaben, Meldepflicht, polizeiliche und weitere staatliche Schnittstellen).

Stabilisationsphase/Kontinuitätsphase: Maßnahmen zur schnellen Bereinigung und Wiederherstellung des Regelbetriebs. Hierbei muss der Angriff so schnell wie möglich abgewehrt und vermieden werden, dass dieser Angriff erneut stattfinden kann. Dazu zählen Kontinuitätsmanagement, Lessons learned (organisatorisch und technisch), die nachhaltige Weiterentwicklung der Sicherheitsarchitektur zur Vermeidung weiterer Angriffe, Weiterbildung der Forensik und die Anpassung bzw. Weiterentwicklung der Cyberstrategie, damit die neuesten Erkenntnisse einfließen können.

Um sich dem Thema zu nähern, sollten die richtigen Fragen gestellt und beantwortet werden. Mit der Durchführung von Simulationsübungen sogenannte War Games können durch bedarfsgerechte Cyberszenarien die richtigen Fragestellungen aufgeworfen und daraus konkrete Maßnahmen abgeleitet werden.

17.5   Szenariobasierte Übungen als erster Schritt der Cyberstrategieentwicklung

Szenariobasierte Übungen haben sich in der letzten Zeit als wirksames Instrument zur Identifikation von organisatorischen und technischen Schwachstellen und damit zur Cyberstrategieentwicklung etabliert (siehe Abb. 17.5). Staaten führen schon seit einigen Jahren nationale sowie internationale Übungen durch und können anhand der Übungsresultate das Incident- und das Krisenmanagement sowie das Krisenkommunikationsmanagement aufbauen oder verbessern und auch die Maßnahmen zur Prävention anpassen.

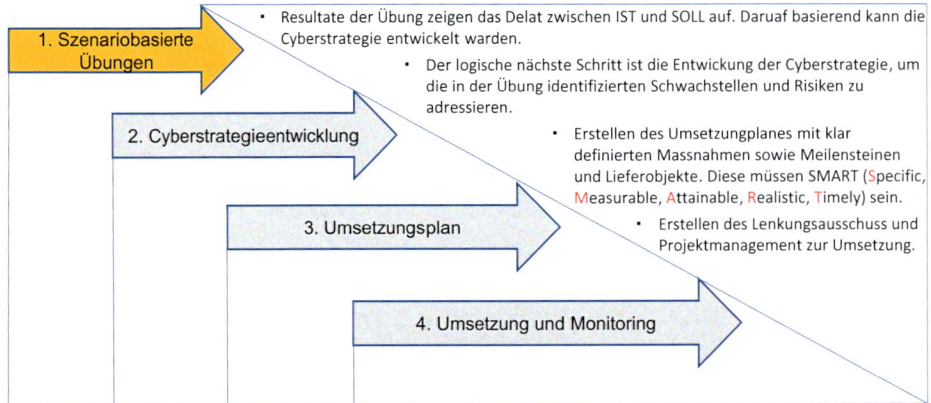

Abb. 17.5 Strategische Simulationsübungen als Basis zur Cyber-Strategieentwicklung

Es folgen einige Beispiele von nationalen und internationale Krisenmanagementübungen. Einige dieser Übungen sind keine per se Cyberübungen, sondern nationale Krisenmanagementübungen. Da Cyberbedrohungen und Cyberrisiken eines der Top 5 Risiken darstellen, können viele Übungen ohne die Cyberkomponente gar nicht mehr durchgeführt werden.

Einige Beispiele für nationale Übungen sind:

- **Deutschland**: LÜKEX länderübergreifende Krisenmanagementübung/Excercise [5].
- **Schweiz**: Strategische Führungsübungen 2013 (SFU13) und 2017 (SFU 2017) [6].
- **Österreich**: Kuratorium Sicheres Österreich (KSÖ) [7].
- **Serbia**: National Cyber Drill 2017 [8].

Einige Beispiele für internationale Übungen:

- **NATO (CCDCOE)** [9]: Locked Shields [10].
- **NATO (CCDCOE)**: Cyber Coalition [11].
- **NATO (CCDCOE):** Crossed Swords [12].
- **ENISA** [13]: Cyber Europe 2016 [14].

Unternehmen sollten ebenfalls darüber nachdenken, regelmäßige auf das Unternehmen zugeschnittene Übungen durchzuführen, um die Cyberresilienz in ihrem Unternehmen zu erhöhen. Die strategischen Simulationsübungen dienen auch als Basis zur Cyberstrategieentwicklung.

Die sogenannte Table-Top-Simulationen und insbesondere die strategischen Simulationsübungen auch War Game genannt haben sich War Gaming haben sich als besonders effektiv erwiesen.

Bei **Table-Top-Simulationen**, auch Konfliktsimulation genannt, wird die Ausgangslage eines Cyberangriffs beschrieben und die Teilnehmer erarbeiten Maßnahmen zur

Problemerfassung, zur Lösungsentwicklung und zu Kommunikationsstrategien, um das Schadensmaß und die Auswirkungen des Angriffs zu minimieren.

Beim **War Game** werden lageverändernde Eskalationen (Injects) eingespielt und somit die Intensität und Komplexität der Übung erhöht. Das War Gaming ist eine strategische Simulationsübung, bei der die Teilnehmer in ihrem Aufgabengebiet agieren und Entscheidungen vor diesem Hintergrund treffen. In der Regel werden für das War Game ein bis zwei aktive Tage eingeplant, da die lageverändernden Eskalationen zeitintensiv in der Bearbeitung sind. Die Vorbereitungszeit für die aktiven Übungstage richtet sich nach der Komplexität und dem Anspruch des durchführenden Unternehmens. Eine Table-Top-Simulation wiederum kann auch in wenigen Stunden geübt werden, da hier spezifische Problemstellungen im Vordergrund stehen wie z. B. das Krisenmanagement im Falle des Ausfalls einer Fachanwendung. Table-Top-Szenarien werden häufig in einem War Game als Teilproblem erkannt und dann gesondert als Übung ausgearbeitet.

Bei beiden Übungsarten geht es darum, den Führungskräften und verantwortlichen Mitarbeitern aus den relevanten Bereichen ein Verständnis der Cyberrisiken zu vermitteln und auf Cyberkrisen vorzubereiten sowie die benötigten Methoden aufzuzeigen, um zukünftig einen Cyberangriff und eine daraus resultierende Krise schneller und effizienter zu bearbeiten.

17.5.1 Ziel und Ablauf des War Game

Auf Basis reeller Szenarien wird ein Planspiel durchgeführt. Durch aufeinander aufbauende Eskalationen werden die Führungskräfte unter Zeitdruck vor Entscheidungen und Maßnahmen gestellt, damit eine Krise durch Cyberangriffe vermieden werden kann. Jeder Teilnehmer wird aktiv an der Simulation beteiligt und muss Entscheidungen vor dem Hintergrund seiner alltäglichen Aufgaben treffen und begründen.

Die War Games basieren auf Erfahrungen, die in echten Cybervorfällen gemacht worden sind und entsprechen weitestgehend der Realität. Dadurch können Rückschlüsse darauf gezogen werden, welche strategischen, organisatorischen, personellen und technischen Maßnahmen getroffen werden sollten, damit Cyberangriffe mit so wenig wie möglich Auswirkungen überstanden werden können. Häufig wissen die Betroffenen nicht, was bei einem Cyberangriff zu tun ist und wo sie Hilfe und Unterstützung bekommen können.

Am Ende sind die Teilnehmer in der Lage die folgenden Punkte einzuschätzen:

- Welche Cyberbedrohungen gibt es und wie sehen mögliche Tätermotivationen aus.
- Beurteilung wie gut das Unternehmen auf Cyberangriffe vorbereitet ist.
- Erkennen von Lücken und ein Verständnis darüber, welche Maßnahmen wichtig sind, um Schäden zu begrenzen und den Normalbetrieb wiederherzustellen.
- Welche Vorbereitungen wichtig sind, damit eine Cybersicherheitsstrategie entwickelt und umgesetzt werden kann.
- Verständnis einer umfassenden Problemerfassung des Cyberangriffs und Zerlegung in Teilprobleme.

17.5.2 Resultate des War Game

Eine Übung dient der Entwicklung von Fähigkeiten und kann sich in folgende Schritte gliedern:

- Problemerfassung (wo stehen wir, wohin wollen wir?)
- Beurteilung der Lage (Fakten, Chancen und Risiken, Konsequenzen)
- Einleiten von Sofort- und Sondermaßnahmen
- Entwicklung von Sicherheitsmaßnahmen
- Krisenkommunikation

Konsequenzen der Übung:

- Anpassung der „Governance" Struktur und Verantwortlichkeiten
- Anpassung des Incident- und Krisenmanagements
- Entwicklung einer Cyberstrategie
- Einführung eines Monitorings und eines strategischen Controllings
- Regelmäßiges Durchspielen von Übungen
- Bei Bedarf Anpassung der Cyberstrategie, der Maßnahmen, der Abläufe und Strukturen entsprechend den Erkenntnissen aus den Übungen.

Reaktionsphase:
Bei der Reaktionsphase braucht es ein Incident- und Krisenmanagement. Beide sind aber nur effizient, wenn Cyberangriffe detektiert werden. Bei vielen Unternehmen und Behörden, die in der Vergangenheit Opfer eines Cyberangriffs geworden sind, hat es trotz guter Schutzmechanismen in der IT-Sicherheit zum Teil lange gedauert, bis ein Angriff entdeckt wurde. Wie viele Angriffe nicht entdeckt werden, ist immer noch unklar. Daher bemühen sich alle staatlichen Organisationen, dieses Dunkelfeld von Straftaten zu verringern. Bei den Massenphänomenen mit dem Ziel, einen finanziellen Vorteil zu erlangen ist ein Incident- und Krisenmanagement zentral, damit der Vorfall schnellstmöglich behoben wird und die Erkenntnisse in die Präventionsphase einfließen können.

17.6 Zusammenfassung

Die Durchführung von strategischen Simulationsübungen/War Games sind ein gutes „Best Practice" Beispiel für Staaten und Behörden, internationale Organisationen, IT-Industrie und Anwender, um ihre Cybersicherheit nachhaltig zu erhöhen. Basierend auf den Ergebnissen kann eine nachhaltige und umfassende Cyberstrategie erstellt werden.

> **Vorteile von strategischen Simulationsübungen/War Games**
> - Entdecken von technischen und organisatorischen Schwachstellen.
> - Überblick und Verständnis der eigenen IT-Sicherheitsarchitektur.
> - Überblick, Kritikalität und Verwundbarkeiten der kritischen Infrastrukturen, Produkten, Systemen und Prozessen.
> - Überblick in welche relevanten Technologien investiert werden soll.
>   Konkrete Lösungsansätze mit klar definierten Maßnahmen und Meilensteinen sowie Lieferobjekten.

Literatur

1. Siehe Artikel von Stefanie Frey in Cybersicherheit – Best Practice Beispiele, Eliminating the Prevailing Ignorance and Complacency about Cybersecurity (Springer 2018).
2. https://www.bosch.com/de/explore-and-experience/kuenstliche-intelligenz-interview-mit-peylo/
3. Dr. Stefanie Frey and Michael Bartsch, Cyberstrategien für Unternehmen und Behörden: Massnahmen zur Erhöhung der Cyberresilienz, (Springer, 2017).
4. Oliver Doleski, Utility 4.0 Herausforderungen für die Energiewirtschaft, Kapitel 16, pp. 301–308.
5. https://www.itu.int/en/ITU-D/Cybersecurity/Pages/National-Strategies.aspx.
6. http://www.claytonhusker.de/archiv/Flyer_Luekex.pdf und https://www.bbk.bund.de/DE/AufgabenundAusstattung/Krisenmanagement/Luekex/TT_Luekex_ueberblick.html
7. https://www.admin.ch/gov/de/start/dokumentation/medienmitteilungen.msg-id-48976.html und https://www.admin.ch/gov/de/start/dokumentation/medienmitteilungen.msg-id-68786.html
8. https://kuratorium-sicheres-oesterreich.at/
9. Siehe für mehr Informationen das Kapitel von Irina Rizmal, The Petnica Group – a case of Public-Private Partnership for cyber security in the Republic of Serbia.
10. Cooperative Cyber Defence Centre of Excellence in Tallinn.
11. https://ccdcoe.org/locked-shields-2017.html
12. https://www.nato.int/cps/ic/natohq/news_149233.htm
13. https://ccdcoe.org/crossed-swords-exercise.html
14. European Netzwerk und Informationssicherheitsagentur
15. https://www.enisa.europa.eu/topics/cyber-exercises/cyber-europe-programme/ce-2016

Weiterführende Literatur

NCSS interaktive Map auf der ENISA-Website unter https://www.enisa.europa.eu/ und ITU Homepage

Offizielle ENISA-Website.

Joint Communication to the European Parliament, the Council, the European Economic and Social Committee and the Committee of the Regions, Cybersecurity Strategy of the European Union: An Open, Safe and Secure Cyberspace, Brussels, 07.02.2013.

Vorschlag für eine Richtlinie des Europäischen Parlaments und des Rates über Maßnahmen zur Gewährleistung einer hohen gemeinsamen Netz- und Informationssicherheit
in der Union, Brüssel 07.02.2013.

European Commission Press Release, Commission welcomes agreement to make EU
online environment more secure, Brussels 8 December 2015, http://europa.eu.

Richtlinie (EU) 2016/1148 des Europäischen Parlaments und des Rates vom 6. Juli 2016
über Maßnahmen zur Gewährleistung eines hohen gemeinsamen Sicherheitsniveaus
von Netz- und Informationssystemen in der Union.

Als Table-Top bezeichnet man ein Strategiespiel, welches auf Baron von Reiswitz zurück-
geht. Im 19. Jahrhundert sollten preußische Offiziere auf strategische Kriegsführung
vorbereitet werden. Diese Art Spiel wird auch Konfliktsimulation genannt.

Teresa Ritter und Marc Bachmann

Zusammenfassung

Tägliche Cyberattacken auf Unternehmen und Organisationen, bei denen Daten gestohlen oder die digitalen Infrastrukturen angegriffen werden, gehören bereits heute zu unserem Alltag. Nicht nur Unternehmen, auch Behörden und staatliche Einrichtungen werden Opfer von Wirtschaftsspionage, Sabotage und Datendiebstahl. Aber gerade in der Wirtschaft wird eine große Dunkelziffer darüber vermutet, wie viele Unternehmen tatsächlich Opfer von Hackerangriffen sind. Bitkom führt alle zwei Jahre eine aufwändige Unternehmensbefragung durch, um trotz der undurchsichtigen Lage Licht ins Dunkel zu bringen. Mit der Studie wird nicht nur ein kleiner branchenspezifischer Teil der Industrie abgebildet, sondern die deutsche Gesamtwirtschaft repräsentiert. Wie ist es also um die Sicherheit der Wirtschaft in Deutschland wirklich bestellt? Der folgende Beitrag stellt die zentralen Ergebnisse der Bitkom Wirtschaftsschutzstudie 2017 vor. Dabei beleuchtet er insbesondere folgende Fragen: Welche Unternehmen sind von entsprechenden Vorfällen betroffen? Wer sind die mutmaßlichen Täter? Schützt sich die Wirtschaft ausreichend? Außerdem werden verursachte Schäden benannt und Gründe für die hohe Dunkelziffer identifiziert. Im Rahmen eines Fazits wird ein Ausblick in die Zukunft gewagt sowie Handlungsempfehlungen sowohl für die Wirtschaft als auch für die Politik gegeben.

T. Ritter (✉) · M. Bachmann
Bitkom, Berlin, Deutschland
E-Mail: t.ritter@bitkom.org; marc-bachmann@gmx.com

© Springer Fachmedien Wiesbaden GmbH, ein Teil von Springer Nature 2018
M. Bartsch, S. Frey (Hrsg.), *Cybersecurity Best Practices*,
https://doi.org/10.1007/978-3-658-21655-9_18

„Cyberangriffe gehören zum Alltag" (Spiegel Online 2016). Nach dem Hacker-Angriff auf die Deutsche Telekom im Jahr 2016 ging dieses Zitat von Bundeskanzlerin Angela Merkel durch die Medien. Tatsächlich sind Unternehmen und Organisationen täglichen Cyberattacken ausgesetzt, bei denen Daten gestohlen oder die digitalen Infrastrukturen angegriffen werden. Das US-amerikanische Technologie-Magazin WIRED berichtete in einem Jahresüberblick über die bedeutendsten Hackerangriffe im Jahr 2017. Beispielsweise haben sich im September 2017 Hacker Zugang zu Equifax verschafft, der größten Wirtschaftsauskunftei der USA. Durch den Angriff wurden persönliche Informationen von 143 Millionen US-Amerikanern entwendet. Diese beinhalten neben Namen, Adressen und Geburtsdaten auch die in den Vereinigten Staaten hoch-relevante Sozialversicherungsnummer (Spiegel Online 2017). Durch die Ransomware WannaCry und ihre Nachfolger wurde die IT von Tausenden Unternehmen weltweit beeinträchtigt oder gar lahmgelegt. Diese spektakulären und medial präsenten Fälle sind aber nur die Spitze des Eisbergs (Wired 2017). Nicht nur Unternehmen, auch Behörden und staatliche Einrichtungen werden Opfer von Wirtschaftsspionage, Sabotage und Datendiebstahl. Im Sommer 2017 wurde bekannt, dass Unbefugte Zugriff auf sensible Daten des schwedischen Militärs und der schwedischen Führerscheinbehörde hatten. Die Folge war eine Umbildung der Regierung durch den Ministerpräsidenten Stefan Löfven (Kurier 2017).

Aber gerade in der Wirtschaft wird eine große Dunkelziffer darüber vermutet, wie viele Unternehmen tatsächlich Opfer von Hackerangriffen sind. Hierfür gibt es verschiedene Gründe: Zum einen werden Angriffe von den Unternehmen oft erst spät festgestellt und zum anderen wird der Schaden in vielen Fällen gar nicht gemeldet – aus Angst vor Reputationsschäden. Bitkom führt alle zwei Jahre eine aufwändige Unternehmensbefragung durch, um trotz der undurchsichtigen Lage Licht ins Dunkel zu bringen. Im Jahr 2017 wurden telefonisch mehr als 1000 Unternehmen aus allen Branchen befragt. Damit bildet die Studie nicht nur einen kleinen branchenspezifischen Teil der Industrie ab, sondern ist repräsentativ für die deutsche Gesamtwirtschaft.

Wie ist es also um die Sicherheit der Wirtschaft in Deutschland wirklich bestellt? In den folgenden Seiten werden die zentralen Ergebnisse der Bitkom Wirtschaftsschutzstudie 2017 vorgestellt. Nach einem kurzen Überblick über die Methodik werden die wichtigsten Ergebnisse aufgeführt: Welche Unternehmen sind von entsprechenden Vorfällen betroffen? Wer sind die mutmaßlichen Täter? Schützt sich die Wirtschaft ausreichend? Außerdem werden verursachte Schäden benannt und Gründe für die hohe Dunkelziffer identifiziert. Im Rahmen eines Fazits wird ein Ausblick in die Zukunft gewagt sowie Handlungsempfehlungen sowohl für die Wirtschaft als auch für die Politik gegeben.

18.1 Methode

Ausländische Geheimdienste und kriminelle Hacker haben die deutsche Industrie aufgrund ihrer innovativen Lösungen und starken globalen Position schon lange als lukratives Ziel von Cyberattacken entdeckt. Der durch die digitalen Angriffe verursachte Schaden beläuft sich mittlerweile auf Milliardenhöhe. Dabei sehen sich gehackte Unternehmen mit dem Diebstahl sensibler Unternehmensdaten, dem Ausfall von IT-Systemen oder gar einer Unterbrechung der Produktion konfrontiert.

In der Wirtschaftsschutzstudie von 2017 untersuchte der Digitalverband Bitkom, welche Unternehmen von entsprechenden Vorfällen betroffen waren, wer die mutmaßlichen Täter sind und ob sich die Wirtschaft ausreichend schützt. Außerdem wurde die Höhe der verursachten Schäden ermittelt.

Befragt wurden im Zeitraum vom 16. Januar bis 17. März 2017 insgesamt 1069 nach Branchen und Größenklassen repräsentativ ausgewählte Unternehmen mit mindestens zehn Mitarbeitern. Interviewt wurden Führungskräfte, die in ihrem Unternehmen das Thema Wirtschaftsschutz verantworten. Dazu zählen Geschäftsführer sowie Führungskräfte aus den Bereichen Unternehmenssicherheit, IT-Sicherheit, Risikomanagement oder Finanzen.

Durch die disproportional geschichtete Zufallsstichprobe wurde gewährleistet, dass Unternehmen aus den unterschiedlichsten Branchen und Größenklassen in für statistische Auswertungen ausreichender Anzahl vertreten sind. Die Aussagen der Befragungsteilnehmer wurden bei der Analyse gewichtet, so dass die Ergebnisse ein nach Branchengruppen und Größenklassen repräsentatives Bild für alle Unternehmen ab zehn Mitarbeitern in Deutschland ergeben.

Es handelte sich um eine computergestützte, mündliche, telefonische Befragung (CATI). Der Digitalverband Bitkom konzipierte den standardisierten Fragebogen gemeinsam mit der Bitkom Research GmbH.

18.2 Ergebnisse der Wirtschaftsschutzstudie 2017

18.2.1 Mittelständische Unternehmen – ein besonders beliebtes Angriffsziel

Zunächst wurden die Unternehmen befragt, ob sie in den vergangenen zwei Jahren Opfer von Datendiebstahl, Spionage oder Sabotage wurden (siehe Abb. 18.1). Mit 53 Prozent entspricht der Wert etwa dem aus der letzten Studie im Jahr 2015. Damals waren mit 51 Prozent auch knapp über die Hälfte der Unternehmen betroffen. Darüber hinaus geben 28 Prozent der Unternehmen an, dass sie vermutlich Opfer solcher Angriffe geworden sind. Ob Daten abgeflossen sind oder Angriffe im Verborgenen blieben, lässt sich nicht immer zweifelsfrei feststellen.

Betroffen waren Unternehmen aller Branchen. Die Ergebnisse machen aber deutlich, dass insbesondere der Mittelstand beliebtes Angriffsziel von Hackern ist. Dafür gibt es zwei wesentliche Gründe: Zum einen ist der Mittelstand in Deutschland besonders innovativ und zugleich stark in die Lieferketten von großen Konzernen eingebunden. Kleine und mittlere Unternehmen (KMU) können also auch als Einfallstor für Angriffe auf Großunternehmen genutzt werden. Der Schutz mittelständischer Unternehmen vor digitalen Angriffen ist in vielen Fällen nicht ausreichend, weshalb sie vergleichsweise leichte Opfer sind.

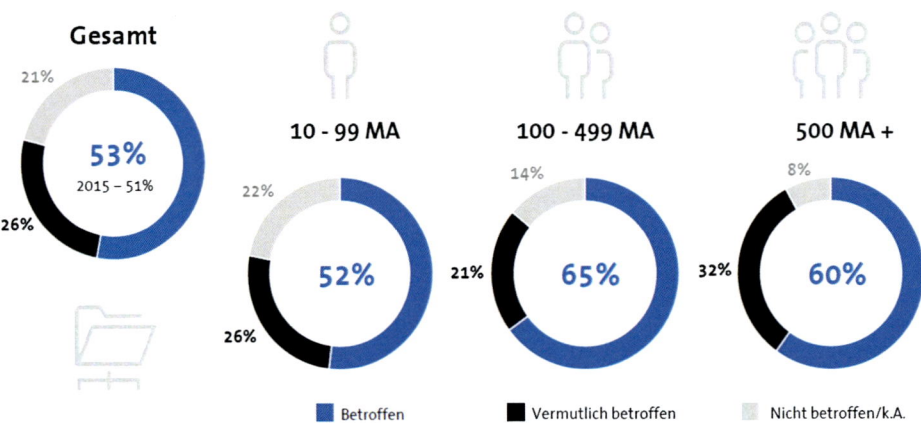

Abb. 18.1 War Ihr Unternehmen in den letzten 2 Jahren von Datendiebstahl, Industriespionage oder Sabotage betroffen? (Quelle: Bitkom Research)

18.2.2 Über Umwege zum Ziel

Ein Teil der Studie beschäftigte sich mit den unterschiedlichen Handlungen, von denen die befragten Unternehmen betroffen waren (siehe Abb. 18.2). Am häufigsten werden IT- oder Telekommunikationsgeräte gestohlen, auf denen sich sensible Daten befinden könnten, also etwa Notebooks oder Smartphones. Hier ist es für die Unternehmen besonders schwer einzuschätzen, ob es den Tätern nur um das Gerät oder um die sensiblen Daten ging. Die zweithäufigste Angriffshandlung ist das Social Engineering. Rund jedes fünfte Unternehmen war davon betroffen. Ziel dieses Angriffs ist das Personal. Die Angreifer versuchen zum Beispiel am Telefon – getarnt als vermeintliche Mitarbeiter eines IT-Dienstleisters oder als Paketbote – Informationen wie Namen und Funktionen von Beschäftigten herauszufinden. Die werden dann genutzt, um persönliche und glaubhaft wirkende E-Mails zu verfassen. Mitarbeiter des Unternehmens sollen dazu verleitet werden, einen mitgeschickten Anhang zu öffnen. Durch den wird dann zum Beispiel ein Trojaner eingeschleust.

Wie Abb. 18.2 zeigt, war in 17 Prozent der Fälle ein Abfluss von sensiblen digitalen Daten oder Informationen die Folge des Angriffs. Die Sabotage von Infrastruktur trat bei 12 Prozent der Befragten auf. In diesem Bereich ist der Anteil derjenigen, die einen Angriff nicht sicher belegen können, ihn aber vermuten, mit 29 Prozent besonders hoch. Das Ausspähen von digitaler Kommunikation wurde bei 8 Prozent der Befragten festgestellt, Abhören von Besprechungen oder Telefonaten bei 7 Prozent.

Betroffene Unternehmen wurden im Rahmen der Studie auch befragt, welche Art von Daten durch die Angriffe entwendet wurde. In 62 Prozent der Fälle wurden laut den Betroffenen unkritische Geschäftsinformationen gestohlen. Mit 41 Prozent ist der Diebstahl von Kommunikationsdaten wie E-Mails am höchsten, gefolgt von 36 Prozent gestohlenen Finanzdaten. Geistiges Eigentum, wie Patente oder Ergebnisse aus Forschung und Entwicklung, wurde in 11 Prozent der Fälle entwendet.

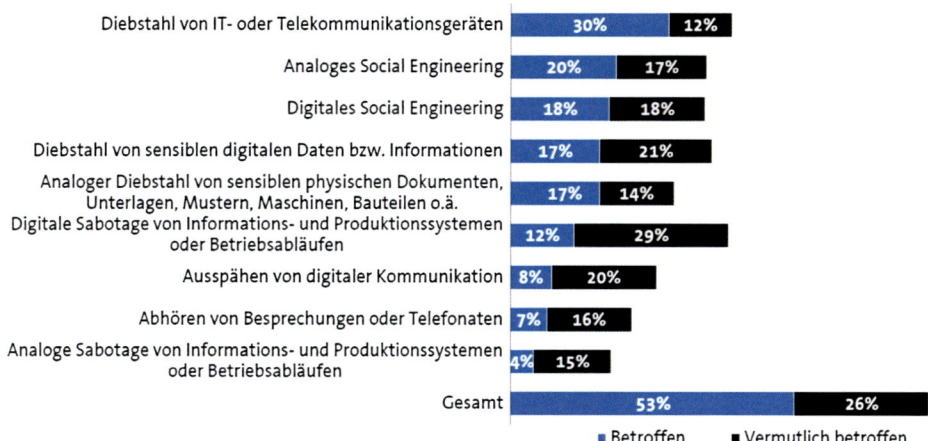

Abb. 18.2 Von welchen der folgenden Handlungen war Ihr Unternehmen innerhalb der letzten zwei Jahre betroffen? (Quelle: Bitkom Research)

	Schadenssummen in Mrd. Euro
Kosten für Ermittlungen und Ersatzmaßnahmen	21,1
Umsatzeinbußen durch Verlust von Wettbewerbsvorteilen	17,1
Patentrechtsverletzungen (auch schon vor der Anmeldung)	15,4
Imageschaden bei Kunden oder Lieferanten/ Negative Medienberichterstattung	15,4
Kosten für Rechtsstreitigkeiten	11,0
Ausfall, Diebstahl oder Schädigung von Informations- und Produktionssystemen oder Betriebsabläufen	10,5
Umsatzeinbußen durch nachgemachte Produkte (Plagiate)	6,9
Datenschutzrechtliche Maßnahmen (z.B. Information von Kunden)	6,4
Erpressung mit gestohlenen Daten oder verschlüsselten Daten	1,3
Sonstige Schäden	4,5
Gesamtschaden innerhalb der letzten 2 Jahre	**109,6**

Abb. 18.3 Schäden in Deutschland nach Delikttyp in Milliarden Euro (Basis: Selbsteinschätzung). (Quelle: Bitkom Research)

18.2.3 Rund 55 Milliarden Euro Schaden pro Jahr

Die Studie beziffert den Schaden auf gut 55 Milliarden Euro pro Jahr (siehe Abb. 18.3). In den Jahren 2016 und 2017 entstand somit ein Gesamtschaden von rund 110 Milliarden Euro. Das ist gegenüber dem Wert von der Studie aus dem Jahr 2015 – ca. 102,5 Milliarden Euro – ein Anstieg um 8 Prozent. In den Bereichen Umsatzeinbußen durch Verlust von Wettbewerbseinbußen, Imageschäden bei Kunden oder Lieferanten, datenschutzrechtliche Maßnahmen und Abwerben von Mitarbeitern sind höhere Kosten entstanden als in den Jahren zuvor. Sehr viel geringer sind aber die Schäden durch Ausfall, Diebstahl oder Schädigung von Informations- und Produktionssystemen oder Betriebsabläufen. Das Durchführen von regelmäßigen Back-ups könnte hierauf positiv gewirkt haben. Auch ist ein deutlicher Rückgang der Kosten durch die Erpressung mit gestohlenen bzw. verschlüsselten Daten zu erkennen. Damit dürfte fast allen Betroffenen klar sein, dass man bei digitalen Erpressungen nicht auf die Forderungen der Täter eingehen sollte.

18.2.4 Täterkreis: Mitarbeiter

In einem weiteren Schritt wurden die unterschiedlichen Täterkreise untersucht (siehe Abb. 18.4). Besonders überraschend ist, dass 62 Prozent der zuvor aufgeführten Schäden durch aktuelle oder ehemalige Mitarbeiter verursacht wurden. Das ist ein Anstieg um 10 Prozent im Vergleich zur Studie aus dem Jahr 2015. Mit 41 Prozent folgen Wettbewerber, Kunden, Lieferanten oder Dienstleister. Jedes fünfte Unternehmen wurde von Hobby-Hackern angegriffen und jedes zwölfte wurde Opfer durch organisierte Kriminalität. Wie im Jahr 2015 wurden auch im Jahr 2017 3 Prozent der Angriffe von ausländischen Geheimdiensten verübt. Positiv zu beobachten ist, dass der Anteil der Unternehmen, die von unbekannten Tätern angegriffen wurden, von 18 auf 7 Prozent deutlich gesunken ist. Das könnte ein Hinweis darauf sein, dass unternehmensinterne Fähigkeiten Angriffe abzuwehren deutlich gestiegen sind.

Die Studie befasste sich nicht nur mit dem Täterkreis der Angreifer, sondern auch mit den Regionen, aus denen die Angriffe vorgenommen wurden. Mit 37 Prozent werden die meisten Taten aus Deutschland selbst begangen. Auffällig ist aber, dass die Spur oft nach Osten – nach Osteuropa, nach Russland und nach China – führt. Der Anteil der Angriffe aus China hat sich beispielsweise innerhalb von zwei Jahren von 6 auf 20 Prozent mehr als verdreifacht. Russland liegt mit 18 Prozent im Mittelfeld, dicht gefolgt von den USA mit 15 Prozent. Die Angriffe aus Westeuropa haben sich innerhalb von zwei Jahren fast

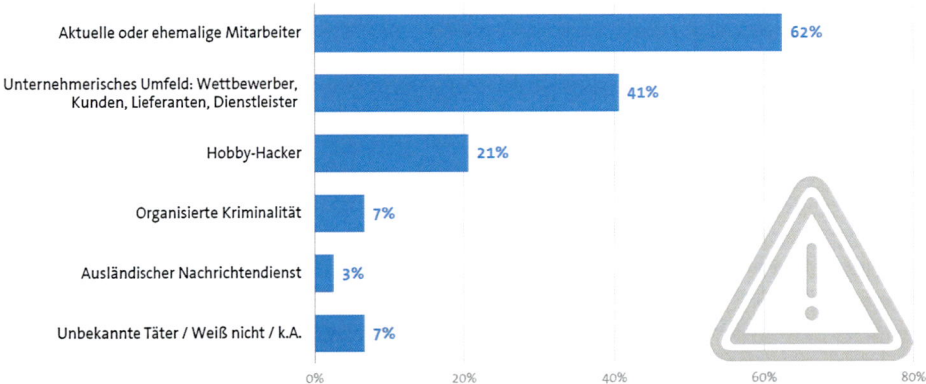

Abb. 18.4 Von welchem Täterkreis gingen diese Handlungen in den letzten zwei Jahren aus? (Quelle: Bitkom Research)

verdoppelt (2017: 12 Prozent, 2015: 7 Prozent), während Japan nur noch für 6 Prozent der Vorfälle verantwortlich gemacht wurde.

18.2.5 IT-Sicherheitssysteme spielen bei der Aufdeckung kaum eine Rolle

Bisher spielen die eigenen IT-Sicherheitssysteme bei der Aufdeckung von Angriffen kaum eine Rolle. Lediglich 1 Prozent der Vorfälle wurde durch Sicherheitssysteme, Virenscanner oder Firewalls erkannt. Bei 37 Prozent der Vorfälle wurde das Unternehmen erstmalig durch Unternehmensinterne (Einzelpersonen) auf die Angriffe aufmerksam gemacht. Eine Vielzahl an Angriffen, nämlich 30 Prozent, werden durch Zufall aufgedeckt.

18.2.6 Jeder dritte Betroffene schaltet staatliche Stellen ein

Die Ergebnisse, die durch Abb. 18.5 verdeutlicht werden, geben einen Hinweis darauf, an wen sich betroffene Unternehmen wenden. Erfreulich ist, dass nur 3 Prozent der Unternehmen, die angegriffen wurden, auf eine Untersuchung der Vorfälle gänzlich verzichten. Vor zwei Jahren waren es noch 10 Prozent. In den Jahren 2016 und 2017 schaltete fast jedes dritte betroffene Unternehmen staatliche Stellen ein. Das ist ein Anstieg um 11 Prozent.

Unternehmen, die staatliche Stellen einschalten (33 prozent), wenden sich meistens an die Polizei (84 Prozent) oder an die Staatsanwaltschaft (57 Prozent). 15 Prozent der Unternehmen nehmen Kontakt mit der Datenschutz-Aufsicht oder dem BSI auf. Der Verfassungsschutz wird nur von rund 3 Prozent der Betroffenen kontaktiert. Dies könnte daran

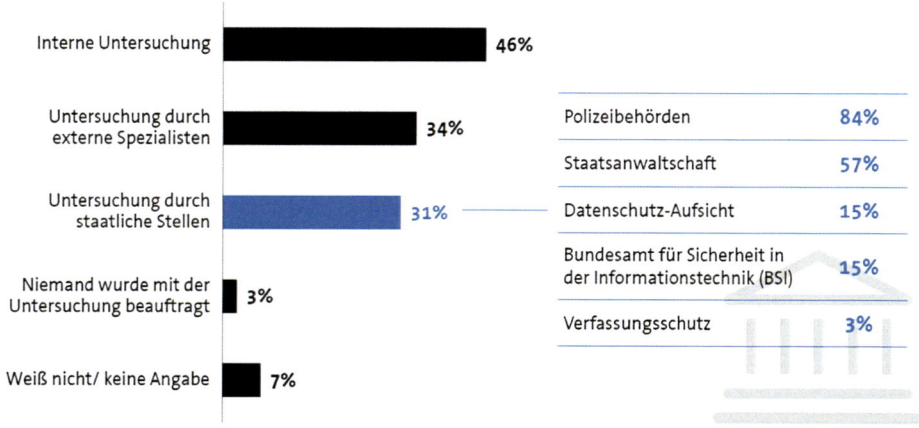

Abb. 18.5 Wer hat diese Vorfälle untersucht? (Quelle: Bitkom Research)

liegen, dass in nur 3 Prozent der Angriffsfälle ausländische Nachrichtendienste als Täter identifiziert wurden.

18.2.7 Angst vor Imageschäden

Zwar ist der Kontakt zu staatlichen Stellen von 2015 auf 2017 deutlich angestiegen, dennoch ist er noch viel zu gering. Die Antwort der Unternehmen auf die Frage, warum sie auf Meldungen verzichten, ist eindeutig. Der Hauptgrund ist die Angst vor Imageschäden: 41 Prozent der Befragten befürchten einen Imageschaden durch eine mögliche Veröffentlichung. Das ist fast eine Verdopplung seit der letzten Untersuchung durch den Bitkom (2015: 23 Prozent). Jedes dritte Unternehmen gibt an, auf Meldungen zu verzichten, weil die Täter ohnehin nicht gefasst würden. Für 29 Prozent der Unternehmen spielt aber auch der hohe Aufwand bei der Einschaltung von staatlichen Stellen eine Rolle.

Dieses Verhalten ist aus Unternehmensperspektive verständlich. Aber nur wenn sich Betroffene an Behörden wenden, kann ein realistisches Lagebild erstellt, neue Angriffswege erkannt und andere Unternehmen rechtzeitig gewarnt und geschützt werden. Deutsche Behörden müssen deshalb aktiver werden, um das Vertrauen der Wirtschaft (zurück) zu gewinnen.

18.2.8 Wie Schutz heute aussieht

Welche Sicherheitsmaßnahmen schon heute in den Unternehmen zum Einsatz kommen untersucht Abb. 18.6. Unterschieden wurde in der Studie zwischen technischer, organisatorischer und personeller Sicherheit. Passwörter auf den Geräten, Firewalls, Virenscanner, regelmäßige Back-ups gelten als technischer Basisschutz und sind in nahezu 100 Prozent

Technische Sicherheit		Organisatorische Sicherheit		Personelle Sicherheit	
100%	Passwortschutz, Firewalls, Virenscanner, Backups	99%	Festlegung von Zugriffsrechten	58%	Background-Checks
20%	Intrusion Detection Systeme	85%	Kennzeichnung von Betriebsgeheimnissen	54%	Bestellung eines Sicherheitsverantwortlichen
17%	Penetrationstests	81%	Festlegung von Zutrittsrechten für bestimme Räume	53%	Schulung der Mitarbeiter
		43%	Sicherheits-Zertifizierung		
		24%	Sicherheits-Audits durch externe Spezialisten		

Abb. 18.6 Welche Sicherheitsmaßnahmen kommen in Ihrem Unternehmen zum Einsatz? (Quelle: Bitkom Research)

der Unternehmen vorhanden. Technisch anspruchsvollere Maßnahmen sind dagegen leider nur die Ausnahme. Dazu gehören Intrusion Detection Systeme (20 Prozent), mit denen Angriffe bemerkt werden können, oder Penetrationstest (17 Prozent), mit denen Schwachstellen systematisch identifiziert werden und Sicherheitslücken geschlossen werden können.

Auch im Bereich der organisatorischen Sicherheit sind Standardmaßnahmen weit verbreitet. 99 Prozent der Unternehmen legen Zugriffsrechte für bestimmte Informationen fest, 85 Prozent kennzeichnen Betriebsgeheimnisse besonders und 81 Prozent beschränken Zutrittsrechte für bestimmte Räume im Gebäude auf begrenztes Personal (81 Prozent). Immerhin 43 Prozent der Unternehmen nutzen Sicherheits-Zertifizierungen. Viel zu selten aber werden regelmäßige Audits durch externe Spezialisten durchgeführt (24 Prozent).

Zu wenig Bedeutung messen die befragten Unternehmen der personellen Sicherheit bei. Backgroundtests der Mitarbeiter sind nur bei 58 Prozent der befragten Unternehmen üblich. Nur 54 Prozent legen einen Sicherheitsverantwortlichen im Unternehmen fest und grademal jedes zweite Unternehmen schult seine Mitarbeiter zu Sicherheitsthemen. Da die zweithäufigste Angriffshandlung – das Social Engineering – es auf die Mitarbeiter absieht, ließe sich hier die Sicherheit in den Unternehmen mit geringem Aufwand und in kurzer Zeit deutlich verbessern.

Neben dem technischen Schutz sollten Unternehmen insbesondere auch die organisatorische und personelle Sicherheit berücksichtigen und fördern. Ein technischer Basisschutz alleine reicht nicht. Die Verschlüsselung von Daten und E-Mails in Kombination mit speziellen Angriffserkennungssystemen wäre der erste Schritt hin zu einem umfassenden technischen Schutz. Im Bereich der organisatorischen Sicherheit sollte jedes Unternehmen einen Notfallplan aufstellen, um in einem Angriffsfall schnell reagieren zu können. Gerade aber im Bereich der personellen Sicherheit kann schnell viel gewonnen werden – durch Schulungen, die Etablierung einer Sicherheitskultur und geeigneten Sicherheits-Zertifizierungen.

18.3   Ausblick in die Zukunft

Mit der Wirtschaftsschutzstudie hat Bitkom ein Instrument entwickelt, das umfassende Erkenntnisse über Cyberangriffe auf die deutsche Gesamtwirtschaft ermöglicht. Die Ergebnisse der Studie unterstreichen, dass in Zeiten der wachsenden globalen Bedeutung des Cyberraums, des Internets und informationstechnischer Systeme ein besonderes Augenmerk auf die Abwehr von Spionageangriffen auf die deutsche Wirtschaft gerichtet werden muss. Ziel muss ein ganzheitlicher und nachhaltiger Wirtschaftsschutz sein, der nicht allein IT-bezogene Maßnahmen, sondern insbesondere auch risikominimierende Pläne in den Bereichen Organisation, Personal und Sensibilisierung umfasst. Insbesondere KMU sind künftig gefordert in einen ausreichenden Schutz zu investieren. Hierbei steht der Faktor Mensch als ein großes Risiko im Fokus.

Für die richtigen Rahmenbedingungen ist die deutsche Politik verantwortlich. Damit unsere Behörden den Unternehmen die richtigen Werkzeuge zum Schutz und zur Aufklärung von Cyberangriffen an die Hand geben können, müssen sie ausreichend personell und finanziell ausgestattet sein. Die Zusammenarbeit zwischen den einzelnen Behörden, aber auch ein enger Austausch zwischen Industrie und Behörden ist zwingend notwendig. Betroffene Unternehmen müssen Vorfälle flächendeckend melden. Nur so kann ein umfassendes Lagebild erstellt werden, das neue Angriffswege erkennt und andere Unternehmen rechtzeitig warnt und schützt. Das vermeintlich verloren gegangene Vertrauen der Unternehmen in die Behörden muss zurückgewonnen werden. Hier sind sowohl Industrie als Politik gefordert, Schritte aufeinander zuzugehen.

Literatur

Bitkom. (21. Juli 2017). Wirtschaftsschutz in der digitalen Welt. Abgerufen am 28. Dezember 2017 von https://www.bitkom.org/Presse/Anhaenge-an-PIs/2017/07-Juli/Bitkom-Charts-Wirtschafts-schutz-in-der-digitalen-Welt-21-07-2017.pdf

Kurier. (27. Dezember 2017). Datenleck in Schweden: Regierungsumbildung nach Skandal. Abgerufen am 28. Dezember 2017 von https://kurier.at/politik/ausland/datenleck-in-schweden-regie-rungsumbildung-nach-skandal/277.340.573

Spiegel Online. (8. September 2017). Hacker erbeuten Daten von bis zu 143 Millionen US-Bürgern. Abgerufen am 28. Dezember 2017 von Spiegel Online: http://www.spiegel.de/netzwelt/netz-politik/hackerangriff-auf-equifax-kriminelle-erbeuten-daten-von-etwa-143-millionen-us-buer-gern-a-1166659.html

Spiegel Online. (29. November 2016). „Cyberangriffe gehören zum Alltag". Abgerufen am 28. Dezember 2017 von http://www.spiegel.de/politik/deutschland/angela-merkel-cyber-angrif-fe-gehoeren-zum-alltag-a-1123612.html

Wired. (31. Dezember 2017). The Worst Hacks of 2017. Abgerufen am 31. Dezember 2017 von https://www.wired.com/story/worst-hacks-2017/

Private and Public Partnership: An Unavoidable Issue

Christian Aghroum

Abstract

The public-private partnership model was not born with the digital revolution. Often presented abstractly as an essential element, it is rarely understood even if the digital revolution gives it all its meaning. This reality had been lived by Christian Aghroum during the last 15 years, while he carried partnership projects both with governments and the private sector or through an academic and associative life, rich of experiences. Based on various concrete examples, this chapter aims to recall the good practices of the public-private partnership; those practices help thankfully to pass from word to act and from the idea to its realization. After a definition of public-private partnership and a study of the progressive decline of the notion of state in Western countries, the author will describe the elements conducive to the recourse of the private sector in a more and more sensitive field, because at the heart of the personal, professional, economic, cultural and social activity of our society. The author will then pragmatically define the means and actions needed to achieve effective partnerships, while advocating the use of common standards and an extension of the number of actors.

19.1 Introduction

Private-public partnership (PPP) is a universal, old-fashioned concept that pre-dates the advent of new technologies and cybersecurity issues. The notion of PPP has been overused in the context of the growing need for cybersecurity and the fight against cybercrime. Concluding all the political speeches and professional presentations, the PPP appears in

C. Aghroum (✉)
CyAN, SoCoA Consultancy Company, Saint Sulpice, Switzerland
e-mail: christian.aghroum@socoa.ch

© Springer Fachmedien Wiesbaden GmbH, ein Teil von Springer Nature 2018

M. Bartsch, S. Frey (Hrsg.), *Cybersecurity Best Practices*,
https://doi.org/10.1007/978-3-658-21655-9_19

many cases as the miracle solution, the opening towards an aspiration, that of a perfect world in which would work together representatives of the state and world of the company, defenders of the public sphere and promoters of the private environment. The digital adventure marks the advent of a new political, economic and social revolution. During the previous stages of evolution, the public and private sector confronted and reconciled civil servants and entrepreneurs, politicians and captains of industry. Couldn't this adventure benefit from the same advances at least? PPP is not born with the digital revolution. However, the digital revolution seems to give it all its meaning. Through various concrete examples, this chapter aims to recall good practices, only conducive to moving from words to action, from the idea to its realization.

19.2 Putting It into Perspective

19.2.1 Defining PPPs

Let's start by recalling what is not the public-private partnership: it is neither a relationship of subordination nor a process of sponsorship: the public can arrogate the skills of the private sector through any contract outsourcing or public service delegation. Nor is it for a company to sponsor a public initiative for the sole purpose of promotion and tax rebate. These modes of action exist for a long time; they are recognized and supervised, but they are not enough to define the public-private partnership. The term partner is important because it introduces all the nuance. Being a partner means acting on an equal footing. Of course, the PPP is contractualized, but it often fails insofar as it introduces a notion of subordination between the actors. Some revealing examples: a prison is built and operated by a private company for the benefit of the prison administration; a road network built entirely by a public works company which will collect the tolls in the coming years up to the clearance of the state debt. These are models that are often presented as illustrating public-private partnership.

For my part, I find them inadequate and see only classical delegations of public service, whatever its legal form. The public-private partnership has real realization only through the respect of the partnership concept of the link which unites state and company. Therefore, each one finds an interest and especially a common interest, guided by an ideal win-win spirit. Cybersecurity offers this field of possibilities.

19.2.2 An Evolution of Realities

The second half of the twentieth century has completely shaken up the organization of states, their respective geopolitical weight and their relationship to their population and beyond the weight of their administrations. The fall of the colonial empires, the advent of the Cold War, the fall of the Berlin Wall, the collapse of the East-West antagonism and the arrival of new health scourges have marked the world of the years of the end of World War II at the end of the millennium. The nascent twenty-first century saw the emergence of a multipolar world, with faltering economies, driven by geopolitical and economic uncertainties. The rise of international terrorism striking both northern and southern countries is shaking up alliances.

New tools, born during the second half of the twentieth century, are imposing and reworking our means of communication, exchange and commerce. They accelerate time and force new paradigms. Computers, smart phones and internet open up surprising potentials and new hopes. Big data, cloud computing, Internet of things and 5G are both dreaming and quivering. Our world has become totally dependent on what I call "always new technologies," because their novelty is permanent, of a constantly repeated topicality, constantly generating new challenges. We live in a science fiction book whose last pages we write as time goes by; the book never ends. It's both magical and scary.

Magical and frightening because the planet, a global village, seeks new benchmarks between consumption and pollution, the need to produce and the labour market, labour and automation, transparency and discretion, democracy and authority and secularism and spirituality. All actors are involved in an interaction at any level: geographical (we can instantly reach anyone on the other side of the planet and send images, films documents), social (digital social networks interpenetrate the social strata with a penetration rate and speed hitherto unparalleled), political (crowd movements are set in motion almost instantaneously), industrial (orders are honoured in record time at prices lower and lower) and cultural (the popular success of self-produced novels and films calls into question the mode of access to entertainment); the examples are infinite.

Magical and frightening because the dependence of our society on digital networks and information systems opens the door to an increase in the risk factor, to the potentiality of diffuse threats whose daily life leads to affirming reality and scope. Cyber insecurity is a portal open to cybercriminals, the gaping window through which the burglar penetrates and the unveiled sleight of hand the rogue uses.

19.2.3   The Decline of the State and the Advent of Capitalism

The state, this incarnation of public authority, remains the guarantor of the social pact, of this desire to live together in the peace and prosperity, security and happiness to which its citizens aspire. The weight of the state tends to dwindle in the recent years. France, for example, sees its centralizing model built around a powerful state, struggling to meet the expectations of its fellow citizens. "The State is me," said Louis XIV. After the French Revolution, the empire built a strong state around a modern administrative organization based on a geographical reality; Napoleon I made his mark on the organization of the French territory and a large part of Europe. Between the end of the eighteenth century and the middle of the twentieth, modern nation-states are organized around the world.

Closer to home, the European Union appears as a structuring of post-war ambition and accompanying the collapse of Empires. She hopes to set up a supranational administration. But the European Union is not a confederation of states, and its administrative impulse is painful in the face of successive economic crises, creeping nationalisms, resuscitated regionalisms. In the same stroke of time, capitalism takes precedence over other socio-politico-economic models and has emerged since the end of the twentieth century: Communist China is largely open to the realities of the global economic market; Cuba is also changing of paradigm. At the same time, the digital revolution is sending back each nation-state to its own doubts in an area where cybercrime, the latest form of cross-border crime, makes fun of borders and their sovereignty.

19.2.4 Sharing the Territory of Data

Public authorities now share the data territory with the private sector. The relationship to the very idea of security has evolved. Technical constraints open up new perspectives. The state no longer has all the data available to its citizens, to which its representatives, civil servants and magistrates must have access. The state is the guarantor of the social pact, of living well together, of the capacity to occupy the field of its sovereign duties: to coin money, to levy taxes, to defend its territory, to ensure the security of its fellow citizens, to render justice. To do this, he must have access to data. The law frames this access, and ultimately this access must be quick and simple when the quest for truth demands it. Direct access to the data themselves held by the state and its officials seems to be an optimal solution. And yet the reality is contrary to this approach. The more democratic a state is, the less direct and free access it has to data.

Security has in parallel considerably evolved. It is leaving the state field to open more and more to the private sector, even in the states least open to the sharing of the field of security. Between mercenaries, subcontracting and the dilution of responsibilities between the various public actors, the actors of the security are diversified. Cybersecurity is just as impacted by this phenomenon, or even more so than the rest of the security partners, as space – as soon as the advent of new technologies – has been left open to the private sector, its software and software developer's hardware.

Cloud computing and big data complicate the rules of access and data processing, especially as they introduce new paradigms, including the crucial one of extra sovereignty. The state is defined by a territory, a nation, a mode of government. From this flow the regal realities of the national language or languages, the currency within a social and cultural environment. Introducing a notion of extra territoriality leads to submission to the extra-national rules of international law, diplomacy and international cooperation.

So many notions that have been shattered since the advent of the digital society, including the rules of transparency, openness, freedom of access combined with massification, the speed and anonymity of exchanges. International law is still in its infancy on cybersecurity and only partially covers what could be the "data cadastre," leaving the field open for private companies to the detriment of most states.

19.3   The Revision of the Relationship Between State and Private Partners

19.3.1   The Public Sector Is Lagging Behind

Cybersecurity has grown beyond state understanding, even though cyber insecurity is one of the main drivers of cybercrime. In the race between police and thieves, the state is always lagging. Most states take a vested interest in cybersecurity only when cybercrime has reached a critical point.

The Ivory Coast has demonstrated that from the moment the country hosted both cybercriminals and cyber victims, both the police force and law enforcement were given the necessary resources to act. In its 2014 annual report, the General Directorate of the National Police of the Republic of Ivory Coast says:

The ratio of victims residing in Ivory Coast is increasingly important, 77.13% in 2014 against 40.94% in 2013. This is always explained by these new scams related to payment services by mobile phone whose victims reside mainly in Ivory Coast. Globally and naturally, residents of French-speaking countries are the main targets of cybercrime perpetrated from the Ivory Coast. Finally, note that the number of those arrested is increasing (+32.86%) compared to 2013. "According to that same report, this awareness has had an immediate effect:" 10 officers animate the laboratory. Compared to 2013, the number rose from 06 to 10, an increase of 65%. This has had a significant impact on business, including the delivery time of investigation results and the management of monitoring and processing requests.

Similarly, Western countries have only recently implemented cyber defence policies, and it means necessary to carry it out. This reality began in the early years of 2010 and is reflected in the first Tallin handbook published in 2013. Until then cybersecurity was left to the good care of software publishers and IT solution providers. The overly technical vision of cybersecurity has long weighed on states' awareness of a managerial, human and procedural need for this same cybersecurity. States, facing the lack of sufficient organisation, have allowed to develop skills in insufficient numbers. The use of private cybersecurity was the inevitable consequence. By analogy, would it have been possible to resort to private policies to fight drug trafficking in the 1970s, during which time this traffic became a global priority?

In the case of cybersecurity, reclaiming this space at the national and international levels will take a lot of effort and cannot succeed without an essential public-private partnership.

19.3.2   Practice Leads to a Revision of Standards

A metamorphosis is revealing of the report of the state with the private companies; it is about the modes of access to the personal data. Until the 1980s, telephone data were held by state operators. These are now private economic actors. This reality has increased with the appearance of new operators. The relationship between state actors (justice, law enforcement agencies, intelligence services) and private actors has evolved. The number of operators has grown since the era of the few state operators in the pre-90 years, coinciding with the democratization of the Internet and mobile telephony.

The General Data Protection Regulation (GDPR: Regulation (EU) 2016/679) and *the NIS Directive* (Directive (eu) 2016/1148 of the European Parliament and of the Council of 6 July 2016 concerning measures for a high common level of security of network and information systems across the Union) are examples of progress made on an intra-European level that benefit member and associated states, including Switzerland. These two European regulations commit to more public-private partnership.

A gap analysis will be necessary after a period of 3–5 years to determine which progress had been made in Europe via this new regulation.

19.3.3 Legal Requests Are Good Examples of This Evolution

The judicial or administrative request, this act which allows a representative of the state to request information from a private enterprise, was based until then on a simple model, that of a response from the private actor, fast, free and non-negotiable. The model has changed over the last 40 years and has accelerated with the advent of the digital world. The requisition is now paying; it is the subject of discussions and questioning. The legal services of the operator question it regularly and ask for more details. There are two main reasons for this: the fear of responding to abusive demands on the one hand and the lack of sufficient internal control procedures in the public services on the other. This can also be translated into two words: mistrust and parity. The private sector is wary of states and their national administrations. Private sector stands as an equal in his ability to question and negotiate. This behavior proves the evolution of the democratic nature of our societies.

This proof of democracy is more flagrant because it often translates, on the other hand, in countries far removed from the democratic model by the following reality: judicial and administrative requisitions are rarely paid for; the discussion is often reduced to nothing.

19.3.4 The Weight of International Actors

The digital world has introduced new players: Internet service providers and other international operators, including GAFAM (Google, Apple, Facebook, Amazon, Microsoft) and their myriad of joint ventures and other affiliates. These companies are governed by US law if their legal address is based in 1 of the 50 US states. GAFAM have gradually imposed a global model, responding to a real need or a consumer based approach. Their virtual absence of competition places them, de facto, in a situation of monopoly. Their ability to juggle legal obligations allows them to optimize taxation in all directions and leads them to settle only in the countries most useful for their growth, also escaping domestic rules of common law.

These Internet access providers have thus imposed their own way of answering the requisitions to many countries of the planet that could be divided in two: those who benefit from a representation of the international provider of access on their territory and the other. For the former, the ability to obtain quick answers is acquired; for others the work is more difficult. For all, a reality is needed. We must question ourselves and "clean our own garden" review its own rules of organization, drafting and recourse to legal and administrative requisitions, even to give up forever some answers. In the absence of reciprocity, certain requests for international requisitions or mutual assistance in criminal matters (mutual legal assistance) fail; the rule is international and is not questionable.

But since the scope of a regulation goes beyond the national limits of fact and not of law, the rule of reciprocity finds its limits. For example, the criminal prosecution of many offences does not succeed in Europe because of the US domiciliation of the sites complained of. Indeed, the first amendment to the US Constitution guarantees freedom of religion, ideas and the press. As a result, many of the offences commonly prosecuted in Europe are not recognized in the USA (neo-Nazism, incitement to racial hatred); then, the possibilities of identification and therefore prosecution of perpetrators disappear. Extra US countries cannot pursue many offences targeting their own citizens. US law is beginning to be a global legal system! Fortunately, there are other, more traditional, methods of identifying offenders.

Questions

Will the almost monopolistic position of GAFA leads to an Americanization of criminal law? This is another debate and yet it is also one of the challenges of international public-private partnerships.

States are therefore forced to negotiate individually with international companies, whose turnover sometimes exceeds their GDP; this is to say, international companies that are more powerful than states themselves economically. Individual private-state bargaining is giving way to diplomatic relations by international institutions and other non-governmental organizations. Only the recourse to a geopolitical power of a level different from that of the state and the support of a relay media then allow to fight with "equal arms." Only the European Union and the public within and outside Europe are able to sell GAFAM futures in the tax negotiations conducted since the mid-2010.

Regarding cybersecurity and the fight against cybercrime, international organizations and agencies, such as the Council of Europe, ICANN, ITU, the World Bank, ENISA, alongside the UN, or the European Union are the promoters of public-private partnerships.

19.4 Persistent Constraints

The restraints on PPPs are numerous, but two are recurrent: the diversion of legal rules and mutual ignorance.

19.4.1 Lack of Legality

As we have seen previously, PPP only makes sense through the achievement of a contractual agreement through which each of the two parties can be considered equal. Each party is a partner. This legitimacy of the PPP guarantees its duration and purpose. The lack of domestic regulation limits the actual implementation of PPPs in most of countries. These PPPs then turn into mock contracts and eventually reveal the meanders of rampant corruption. Active or passive bribery, real or supposed, is a brake on private-public partnership even in the states in which it is supposed to be slaughtered. The relation to money varies from one country to another according to history and cultural, social and religious traditions. Many institutional partners currently resist the PPP for fear of being confronted with a phenomenon of corruption.

19.4.2 Mutual Ignorance

This approach is not guided by moral reflections; it is the result of an observation. Two worlds meet and do not necessarily know each other. From often different schools and schools, the representatives of the public and the private sector often defend with so much obstinacy two different objectives: for some it is about the defence of the public service, the nation and the state, and for others to work for the benefit of their company whose ambition is above all profit. Despite all the goodwill of private and public sector, their common feeling of working for the well-being of humanity, the reality is obvious: the fundamental objectives are different and the relationship to money is different, splitting the two sectors. Finally, the two sectors are rarely encountered on a daily basis.

Does this statement really apply to the world of cybersecurity? In part and because of the primary objectives of the partners : for some serving public service and for the others looking after profit. The actors of cybersecurity find themselves more easily through a common subculture in which the internal rules are split around a search for information sharing. This subculture is often confronted with a world which answers paradoxical rules (respect for privacy, state secrets versus transparency, whistle-blowers). Thus, among other motives are born perfect misunderstandings with heavy consequences illustrated by Snowden and WikiLeaks cases. Learning to know each other, training each other are the bases of a successful PPP. For a complete success, those basics need to be remembered.

19.5 The Best Conditions for Founding a PPP

A public-private partnership regarding cybersecurity will be practised all the better if certain best practices have been respected.

19.5.1   Judicial Framework

A legal framework known to all guarantees the realization of a sustainable and effective public-private partnership. Rules are mainly stemming from the international law. The international literature abounds in examples of doctrine and in jurisprudence especially because, if the digital world is new, the tradition of PPP is former.

The basics are highly relevant: the most quoted examples could be the *Recommendation of the Council on Principles for Public Governance of Public-Private Partnerships* from OECD or at a regional level *Guidelines for Ssuccessful Public-Private Partnerships* from European Commission but also *ASEAN Public Private Partnership Guidelines*.

In 2008, The Council of Europe provided *Guidelines for the cooperation between law enforcement and internet service providers against cybercrime* shared by the European Union in its *Conclusions du Conseil (de l'Union Européenne) relatives à une stratégie de travail concertée et à des mesures concrètes de lutte contre la cybercriminalité* enhancing countries to create national frameworks and to share best practices. ENISA also go through this item publishing a model of public-private partnerships (PPPs), *"essential for the Security and Resilience of Critical Information Infrastructures (CII), since a large part of them belongs to private sector stakeholders."*

The consideration of the issue by the World Economic Forum in 2017 calls back how much the action of companies and implication of their governance is a guarantee of success in the fight against the cybercrime and for the cyber safety.

19.5.2   Governance Involvement

To ensure efficiency in any project, the involvement of governance is essential. This reality also concerns the founding of PPPs in cybersecurity. The latest waves of cyberattacks in 2016 and 2017 proved that many companies and states were poorly or not prepared.

Rob Wrainwright, Director of Europol stated in preface to Europol's annual activity report on the fight against cybercrime, the so-called Internet Organized Crime Threat Assessment the following:

The assessment confirms that cybercrime remains a real and significant threat. It also highlights how those criminal techniques and methods which have traditionally been associated with cybercrime are extending into other crime and threat areas.

James Stavridis, a retired four-star US Navy Admiral and NATO Supreme Allied Commander, stated in 2017:

Here in the United States, despite billions of dollars invested by both the government and the private sector, we are still behind the curve in preparing for major cyberattacks.

And according to Microsoft CEO Satya Nadella:

The battle between private cloud and public cloud has ended with neither emerging victorious.

For Mark Hughes, CEO of BT Security, after BT has signed an agreement to exchange data with INTERPOL as part of a new initiative to tackle cybercrime around the world stated:

Threat intelligence sharing between law enforcement agencies and the private sector is essential in the fight against cyber-crime, which is increasingly borderless in nature. Tackling cyber-crime therefore requires a collective, global response where the public and private sectors work together. BT's security expertise will help INTERPOL to identify cyber-criminals and hold them to account, as we jointly develop our understanding of the challenges that we and other organisations face in the battle against cyber-attacks.

19.5.3   Involving All Actors

None project should begin without a good brainstorming meeting. The kick-off of the project, in which each speaker can give his opinion, mark his territory or even try to impose himself, is not a lost meeting. It is a human constant that launching meetings in which everyone tries to mark his territory. To understand it, to know how to manage this moment, is also an instrument of success of the project. This "rat race" often illustrates the fears and misunderstanding of each other and the desire to impose each point of view. Time will be saved at the second meeting to introduce mutual organizations and skills and to invite each to receive the other. It is also good that the places are known and identified. The project takes shape; the asperities become smooth; and the ambition becomes common.

19.5.4   An Ongoing Challenge

It has already been said how much the definition of PPP matters. The partnership must be clearly remembered from the beginning of the project until its completion; each party must find his account. Most often the public sector earns money, sparing taxpayers' money, and the private sector is also rewarded for the access to research and development and awareness. Partnership only works through an objective clearly understood by all, the common ideal of a cause and this without any announcement effect. Some examples are enlightening. The fight against cyber child pornography is a "buoyant" subject in this area, as is the fight against terrorism or the fight against drug trafficking. Since the beginning of the twentieth century for the first, the 1970s for the second, these last two subjects have brought legal progress, judicial reforms and police reinforcements in men, materials and techniques. The fight against terrorism has been intensified since 9/11 and in the fight against Al Qaeda and Daesh. These are high-profile subjects that are easily understandable at the state level.

The cyber proselyte involvement and some denial of service attacks have introduced the notion of cyber terrorism. The significant indignity of cyber child pornography and the ease with which video and photo material can be obtained via the Internet also provide easy understanding of the public and policy makers. The subjects are, and for good reason, sensitive, mediatic and easy to apprehend. For cyber terrorism, the use of intelligence services and armies is acquired; for cyber child pornography, the support of family associations ensures a sufficient echo. The PPP in this area is therefore relatively easy to implement, and its benefits will be gained for the entire field of cybersecurity.

19.5.5   Enlarging the Circle of Actors

Restricting PPP to two parties would be far away from the reality of cybersecurity.

A good example of a successful PPP in the fight against cyber child pornography is the Child Exploitation and Online Protection Command, the famous British CEOP under the command of the NCA (National Crime Agency). The first challenge identified is that it is a national tool, in a country where the policies are mainly regional and local, in partnership with the Irish and Scottish police. Since its creation in 2006, the CEOP has benefited from the support of Microsoft, Vodafone or AOL but also from the National Society for the Prevention of Cruelty to Children, sports association and other ministries. A partnership tool (public-public, public-private, non-profit/private) is fabulous. This PPP is lokking for a clear objective, it is "Child Protection". All the involved actors work on this same ideal; they share the fruits of their success but also the gains of knowledge and good practices. Cybersecurity skills, still rare in 2017, must also be shared through partnership solutions. Associating in the same partnership, state, local authorities (regions, states, cantons), multinationals and SMEs guarantees the success of a modern PPP. We will add universities and associations, it goes without saying. Great Britain practices KTP (knowledge transfer partnership) to ensure the transmission of knowledge between universities and SMEs. The symbiotic role of the German Association of the Internet Industry (ECO) is thus considerable at both federal and *Länder* level.

In December 2017, the famous Swiss High School EPFL (Ecole Polytechnique Fédérale de Lausanne) created a new "digital trust" complex in association with the university hospital of Lausanne (CHUV), the International Red Cross and some companies (ELCA, Sicpa, Swisscom, Swissquote, SGS and Swiss Re).

19.5.6   Shared Standards

Using the same tools allows workers to work together more easily. This lesson is well known, from the construction of pyramids to those of cathedrals. It is also perfect for the world of cybersecurity. By nature, the cultural difference encourages the private and public sectors to work with different methods. And yet, experience shows that both, even if they use differently named processes, work identically. Few administrations, for example, are ISO certified, and yet many of them use quality management systems that would quickly enable them to obtain a 9001 qualification. The same applies to the 27K standard: public administrations often tend to do so without requiring it. A same language is possible: it is provided by ISO 15'408 and called common criteria:

It defines two forms for expressing IT security functional and assurance requirements. The protection profile (PP) construct allows creation of generalized reusable sets of these security requirements. The PP can be used by prospective consumers for specification and identification of products with IT security features which will meet their needs. The security target (ST) expresses the security requirements and specifies the security functions for a particular product or system to be evaluated, called the target of evaluation (TOE). The ST is used by evaluators as the basis for evaluations conducted in accordance with ISO/IEC 15408.

The same is true for risk management: ENISA lists all the methods used by European countries, all methods of great similarity.

Of course, it is not a question of pushing for an all-round standardization of processes. Too much uniformity would eventually spoil the spirit of initiative and progress. The need for common working methods should be considered right from the start of a PPP. It is in this state of mind that the founders of Signal Spam, for example, had worked since 2008 in France, as "a public-private partnership that allows users to report anything that they consider to be spam in their e-mail client or webmail in order to assign it to the public authority or the professional that will take the required action to combat the reported spam".

19.6 Conclusion

Cybersecurity and the fight against cybercrime are fields of activity still to plough as their field of activity is young, prosperous and vast. The public-private partnership in this area is indispensable; the stake of society is real; the implication of the companies is increased. Our digital world is changing the way we operate the economy, the factor and the "work" resource. Bridges are to be created at the national level (where the issue of critical infrastructure makes sense), at the supranational level (in Europe, e.g., in the interest of each member state but also of the partners of the political Europe) and at international level (e.g., from a humanistic perspective and in the context of global projects, such as the ecological defence of the planet).

The methods are known to all: it goes beyond the technical aspects that matter imposes, to put the human in front. Recipes as simple as they are, without naïveté but on the contrary with the hindsight of the experiment, lead to the success of the projects since the will of all is proved. Without angelism, some verbs are enough to define the assets of a successful PPP: manage, exchange, reflect together, know each other, meet, understand its priorities, define rules of exchange, speak the same language (literally as in figured) and train and train each other. It will also be necessary to know how to "clean one's own garden", review one's models, recognize one's mistakes and let it know. And then also, share a fair remuneration (sometimes no compensation sometimes), to be an incentive on both sides. Finally make sure to maintain the link, continue to pay once the project is committed and register in the long term.

In a world in which crime and security, and thus cybercrime and cybersecurity, are essentially extraterritorial, public-private partnerships are indeed a vital tool that guarantee the expression of need, respect and mutual understanding at each level. The public-private partnership in cybersecurity is thus a guarantee of moderation between the economic model and the social model, between capitalism henceforth dominant and the social pact necessary for a good living together. The digital world, as we approach 2020, is entering a pivotal period, the meeting of private interests and public understanding. The interdependence of sectors is acquired; there will be no turning back without significant disaster. No one can do without computer tools and the use of the Internet. Only a confident future, i.e., secure cyber, will guarantee the passage to the next generation, that of smart connected objects and its counterpart, the advent of a robotic world.

It is also through the public-private partnership that this transition will succeed.

References

Christian Aghroum, Olivier Hassid "Les entreprises et l'État face aux cybermenaces" L'Harmattan, 2013.

Bernard Batet, "S'enrichir en dormant, l'argent et les religions", Desclées de Brouwer, 1998.

Germà Bel, Trevor Brown, Rui Cunha Marques "Public-Private Partnerships: Infrastructure, Transportation and Local Services", Taylor and Francis Group, 2015.

Madeline Carr, "Public–private partnerships in national cyber-security strategies", Chattam House, Volume 92, Number 1, January 2016.

Eric Müller, "Les instruments juridiques des partenariats public-privé", l'Harmattan, 2011.

Tatiana Tropina, Cormac Callanan, "Self- and Co-regulation in Cybercrime, Cybersecurity and National Security", Springer, 2011.

Jean Ruegg, Stéphane Decoutère, Nicolas Mettan "Le partenariat public-privé: un atout pour l'aménagement du territoire et la protection de l'environnement", Presses Polytechniques et Universitaires Romandes, EPFL, 1994.

Best Practices in Cybersecurity from Intergovernmental Discussions and a Private Sector Proposal

20

Richard Hill

Abstract

This paper comments on the best practice norms presented in the 2015 Report of the UN Intergovernmental Group of Experts in the Field of Information and Telecommunications in the Context of International Security (UN document A/70/174) (https://daccess-ods.un.org/access.nsf/GetFile?Open&DS=A/70/174&Lang=E&Type=DOC).

In Sect. 20.1, we comment on the best practices outlined in the proposed norms. In Sect. 20.2, we make additional recommendations.

20.1 The Eleven Norms of Paragraph 13 of the UN GGE 2015 Report

A best practice to be considered in the context of the 11 norms includes the 2012 International Telecommunications Regulations (ITRs) [1], a treaty of the International Telecommunication Union (ITU) [2], and the following scholarly comments [3] on that instrument:

- Hill, Richard (2013), "WCIT: failure or success, impasse or way forward?", *International Journal of Law and Information Technology,* vol. 21 no. 3, p. 313, https://doi.org/10.1093/ijlit/eat008
- Hill, Richard (2013), *The New International Telecommunications Regulations and the Internet: A Commentary and Legislative History,* Schulthess/Springer

R. Hill (✉)
Hill & Associates, Genf, Switzerland
e-mail: rhill@hill-a.ch

© Springer Fachmedien Wiesbaden GmbH, ein Teil von Springer Nature 2018
M. Bartsch, S. Frey (Hrsg.), *Cybersecurity Best Practices,*
https://doi.org/10.1007/978-3-658-21655-9_20

We list each of the proposed norms and then comment as to how to best understand and implement it.

(a) Consistent with the purposes of the United Nations, including to maintain international peace and security, States should cooperate in developing and applying measures to increase stability and security in the use of ICTs and to prevent ICT practices that are acknowledged to be harmful or that may pose threats to international peace and security.

The proposed norm is, in our view, a relevant and justified best practice.

Article 6 of the ITRs states:

> Member States shall individually and collectively endeavour to ensure the security and robustness of international telecommunication networks in order to achieve effective use thereof and avoidance of technical harm thereto, as well as the harmonious development of international telecommunication services offered to the public.

This treaty provision would appear to implement the proposed norm. Consequently, it is suggested that all states should agree to be bound by this article of the ITRs [4].

In order to more closely align with the proposed norm, Article 6 of the ITRs could be modified to read as follows:

> Member States shall endeavour [5], individually and in cooperation, to develop and apply measures to increase stability and security of international telecommunication networks and in the use of ICTs in order to achieve effective use thereof and avoidance of technical harm thereto, as well as to maintain international peace and security, the harmonious development of ICTs, and to prevent ICT practices that may pose threats to international peace and security.

(b) In case of ICT incidents, States should consider all relevant information, including the larger context of the event, the challenges of attribution in the ICT environment and the nature and extent of the consequences.

The proposed norm is, in our view, a relevant and justified best practice.

This norm could be implemented by agreeing an additional provision for Article 6 of the ITRs, for example:

> In case of ICT incidents, Member States shall endeavor to consider all relevant information, including the larger context of the event, the challenges of attribution in the ICT environment and the nature and extent of the consequences.

(c) States should not knowingly allow their territory to be used for internationally wrongful acts using ICTs.

The proposed norm is, in our view, a relevant and justified best practice.

This norm could be implemented by agreeing an additional provision for Article 6 of the ITRs, for example:

> Member States shall endeavour not knowingly to allow their territory to be used for internationally wrongful acts using ICTs.

(d) States should consider how best to cooperate to exchange information, assist each other, prosecute terrorist and criminal use of ICTs and implement other cooperative measures to address such threats. States may need to consider whether new measures need to be developed in this respect.

The proposed norm is, in our view, a relevant and justified best practice.

This norm could be implemented by agreeing an additional provision for Article 6 of the ITRs, for example:

> Member States shall endeavor to consider how best to cooperate to exchange information, assist each other, prosecute terrorist and criminal use of ICTs, and implement other cooperative measures to address such threats.

(e) States, in ensuring the secure use of ICTs, should respect Human Rights Council resolutions 20/8 and 26/13 on the promotion, protection and enjoyment of human rights on the Internet, as well as General Assembly resolutions 68/167 and 69/166 on the right to privacy in the digital age, to guarantee full respect for human rights, including the right to freedom of expression.

The proposed norm is, in our view, a relevant and justified best practice.

This norm is covered by the Preamble of the ITRs, which states:

> Member States affirm their commitment to implement these Regulations in a manner that respects and upholds their human rights obligations.

(f) A State should not conduct or knowingly support ICT activity contrary to its obligations under international law that intentionally damages critical infrastructure or otherwise impairs the use and operation of critical infrastructure to provide services to the public.

The proposed norm is, in our view, a relevant and justified best practice.

This norm could be implemented by agreeing an additional provision for Article 6 of the ITRs, for example:

> Member States shall endeavor not to conduct or knowingly support ICT activity contrary to their obligations under international law that intentionally damages critical infrastructure or otherwise impairs the use and operation of critical infrastructure to provide services to the public.

(g) **States should take appropriate measures to protect their critical infrastructure from ICT threats, taking into account General Assembly resolution 58/199 on the creation of a global culture of cybersecurity and the protection of critical information infrastructures, and other relevant resolutions.**

The proposed norm is, in our view, a relevant and justified best practice.

This norm could be implemented by agreeing an additional provision for Article 6 of the ITRs, for example:

> Member States shall endeavor to take appropriate measures to protect their critical infrastructure from ICT threats, taking into account General Assembly resolution 58/199 on the creation of a global culture of cybersecurity and the protection of critical information infrastructures, and other relevant resolutions.

(h) **States should respond to appropriate requests for assistance by another State whose critical infrastructure is subject to malicious ICT acts. States should also respond to appropriate requests to mitigate malicious ICT activity aimed at the critical infrastructure of another State emanating from their territory, taking into account due regard for sovereignty.**

The proposed norm is, in our view, a relevant and justified best practice.

This norm could be implemented by agreeing additional provisions for Article 6 of the ITRs, for example:

> Member States shall endeavor to respond to appropriate requests for assistance by another State whose critical infrastructure is subject to malicious ICT acts.
>
> Member States shall also endeavor to respond to appropriate requests to mitigate malicious ICT activity aimed at the critical infrastructure of another State emanating from their territory, taking into account due regard for sovereignty.

(i) **States should take reasonable steps to ensure the integrity of the supply chain so that end users can have confidence in the security of ICT products. States should seek to prevent the proliferation of malicious ICT tools and techniques and the use of harmful hidden functions.**

The proposed norm is, in our view, a relevant and justified best practice.

This norm could be implemented by agreeing additional provisions for Article 6 of the ITRs, for example:

> Member States shall endeavor to take reasonable steps to ensure the integrity of the supply chain so that end users can have confidence in the security of ICT products.
>
> Member States shall endeavor to prevent the proliferation of malicious ICT tools and techniques and the use of harmful hidden functions.

(j) States should encourage responsible reporting of ICT vulnerabilities and share associated information on available remedies to such vulnerabilities to limit and possibly eliminate potential threats to ICTs and ICT-dependent infrastructure.

The proposed norm is, in our view, a relevant and justified best practice.

This norm could be implemented by agreeing an additional provision for Article 6 of the ITRs, for example:

> Member States shall endeavor to encourage responsible reporting of ICT vulnerabilities and share associated information on available remedies to such vulnerabilities to limit and possibly eliminate potential threats to ICTs and ICT-dependent infrastructure.

(k) States should not conduct or knowingly support activity to harm the information systems of the authorized emergency response teams (sometimes known as computer emergency response teams or cybersecurity incident response teams) of another State. A State should not use authorized emergency response teams to engage in malicious international activity.

The proposed norm is, in our view, a relevant and justified best practice.

This norm could be implemented by agreeing additional provisions for Article 6 of the ITRs, for example:

> Member States shall endeavor not to conduct or knowingly support activity to harm the information systems of the authorized emergency response teams (sometimes known as computer emergency response teams or cybersecurity incident response teams) of another State.
>
> A Member State shall endeavor not to use authorized emergency response teams to engage in malicious international activity.

20.2 Additional Recommendations

A well-known software company has recently called for steps to be taken to address the very real cybersecurity threats that the world is facing [6]. In essence it is proposed that states agree to certain treaty-level provisions (a Digital Convention) that an Attribution Organization be created to investigate cyberattacks and to attempt to determine their source and that industry voluntary adhere to certain best practices.

Those proposals [7] are, in our view, relevant and justified best practices.

The proposals regarding a Digital Convention and an Attribution Organization could be implemented by agreeing additional provisions for the ITRs. Some of the proposals in question are covered by the proposals in Sect. 20.1. The following additional proposals could be considered:

Member States shall endeavor to refrain from hacking personal accounts or private data held by journalists and private citizens involved in electoral processes.

Member States shall endeavor to refrain from using ICTs to steal the intellectual property of private companies, including trade secrets or other confidential business information, to provide competitive advantage to other companies or commercial sectors.

Member States shall endeavor to refrain from inserting or requiring "backdoors" in mass-market commercial technology products.

Member States shall endeavor to agree to a clear policy for acquiring, retaining, securing, using, and reporting of vulnerabilities that reflects a strong mandate to report them to vendors in mass-market products and services.

Member States shall endeavor to exercise restraint in developing cyber weapons and ensure that any that are developed are limited, precise, and not reusable; Member States shall also endeavor to also ensure that they maintain control of their weapons in a secure environment.

Member States shall endeavor to agree to limit proliferation of cyber weapons; governments shall endeavor not to distribute, or permit others to distribute, cyber weapons and to use intelligence, law enforcement, and financial sanctions tools against those who do.

Member States shall endeavor to limit engagement in cyber offensive operations to avoid creating mass damage to civilian infrastructure or facilities.

Member States shall endeavor to assist private sector efforts to detect, contain, respond, and recover in the face of cyberattacks; in particular, enable the core capabilities or mechanisms required for response and recovery, including Computer Emergency Response Teams (CERTs); intervening in private sector response and recovery would be akin to attacking medical personnel at military hospitals.

Member States shall endeavor to facilitate the establishment of an international cyberattack attribution organization to strengthen trust online.

That organization shall be independent of Member States; it could be modelled on the International Federation of Red Cross and Red Crescent Societies; its membership could consist of CERTs [8].

The proposals regarding a voluntary industry agreement are:

No assistance for offensive cyber operations: Global technology companies should pledge that they will not assist any government in attacking the information infrastructure of any customer anywhere in the world. They should similarly agree that they will not help any government to adversely impact commercial, mass-market technology products and services.

Assistance to protect customers everywhere: Global technology companies should issue patches to protect all users and refrain from leaving any customers at risk.

Collaboration to bolster first-response efforts: Global technology companies should collaborate to proactively defend against cyberattacks and to minimize the duration and impact of such attacks. Increased collaboration across companies will make responses to cyberattacks more effective and make the technology ecosystem more secure for users.

Support for governments' response efforts: Global technology companies should assist public sector efforts to identify, prevent, detect, respond to, and recover from events in cyberspace. As part of a two-way collaboration effort, the tech industry could support states in defending against, and recovering from, cyberattacks.

Coordination to address vulnerabilities: Global technology companies should work together to address security issues ("vulnerabilities"). Reporting and handling vulnerabilities in a coordinated way will help best protect users while minimizing the risk of vulnerabilities being exploited.

Fighting the proliferation of vulnerabilities: Global technology companies should not traffic in cyber vulnerabilities for offensive purposes, nor should technology companies embrace business models that involve proliferation of cyber vulnerabilities for offensive purposes. To counter the threat posed by undisclosed, "zero-day" vulnerabilities available on the black market, the tech industry should leverage publicized bug bounty programs, which provide recognition and compensation for individuals who report bugs, especially those which relate to security vulnerabilities.

References

1. http://www.itu.int/en/wcit-12/Pages/default.aspx
2. http://www.itu.int/en/Pages/default.aspx
3. For more information, see: http://www.hill-a.ch/wcit
4. A number of states refused to sign the ITRs in 2012. The reasons given, in particular that article 6 might justify violations of freedom of speech, are not valid from a legal point of view, see the cited scholarly works. For greater clarity, states acceding to the ITRs could make a formal declaration along the lines of the proposal at: http://www.hill-a.ch/ITR%20accession.doc
5. During the negotiations of the ITRs, the point was made that it might be impossible for a state to ensure certain aspects of cybersecurity, so the use of the term "shall" did not achieve consensus. On the other hand, it point was made that the term "should" is too weak. As a compromise, it was agreed to use the term "shall endeavor", which means that states must make efforts to implement the provision. See the discussion on pp. 95-96 of Hill, Richard (2013), *The New International Telecommunications Regulations and the Internet: A Commentary and Legislative History,* Schulthess/Springer.
6. See   https://blogs.microsoft.com/on-the-issues/2017/02/14/need-digital-geneva-convention/#sm. 00017arazqit2faipqq2lyngzmxx4   https://www.wired.com/2017/05/microsoft-right-need-digital-geneva-convention/
7. The proposals were available at the following web sites in November 2017, but may no longer be available there: https://mscorpmedia.azureedge.net/mscorpmedia/2017/05/Digital-Geneva-Convention.pdf https://mscorpmedia.azureedge.net/mscorpmedia/2017/05/Attribution-Organization. pdf https://mscorpmedia.azureedge.net/mscorpmedia/2017/05/Tech-Accord.pdf
8. This proposal is not part of Microsoft's proposal. It is a proposal by the author of this paper.

Woher nehmen, wenn nicht stehlen – oder wo haben Sie Ihren CISO her?

21

Michael Bartsch

Zusammenfassung

CISO werden ist nicht schwer, CISO sein umso mehr. Frei nach diesem Motto durfte ich einigen Unternehmen helfen, die Jung-CISOs bzw. Neu-CISOs dabei zu unterstützen, die CISO Agenda und die (Cyber-) Sicherheitsstrategie aufzubauen. Gerade die Positionierung des CISO als Funktion im Unternehmen spielt dabei eine wesentliche Rolle. CISOs sind normalerweise das Sammelbecken für allerlei technische Problemlagen, um die sich keiner kümmern möchte.

21.1 Der CISO Dein Freund und Helfer

Was heute über Cyberbedrohungen bekannt ist, ist nur ein kleiner Teil dessen, was wirklich geschieht. Das liegt zum einen daran, dass wir nicht richtig hinschauen und zum anderen daran, dass, wenn etwas passiert, es meist unter den Teppich gekehrt wird. Daher ist die weitläufige Meinung, dass alles ja gar nicht so schlimm ist und die IT-Industrie den Cyberhype als Verkaufsargument ausnutzt. Aber die Cyberangriffe aus dem Jahr 2017 haben mal wieder deutlich gemacht, dass jeder getroffen werden kann und die Auswirkungen sind für die Betroffenen enorm. Je mehr passiert, je höher der Schaden ist, desto schneller fangen Unternehmen an, über ihre Sicherheitsarchitektur nachzudenken. Normalerweise ist der CIO für die IT-Sicherheit mitzuständig, dabei stehen auf der Prioritäten-Liste des CIO im Unternehmen immer noch ganz viele andere und zumeist, aus seiner Sicht, wichtigere Themen oberhalb der Sicherheitsproblematik: Schlagworte wie Digitalisierung, die neuerdings alles an der Schnittstelle vom Business zur IT zu einem Oberbegriff zusammenfassen. Die

M. Bartsch (✉)
Deutor Cyber Security Solutions GmbH, Bern, Schweiz
E-Mail: cyberstrategien@deutor.de

© Springer Fachmedien Wiesbaden GmbH, ein Teil von Springer Nature 2018
M. Bartsch, S. Frey (Hrsg.), *Cybersecurity Best Practices*,
https://doi.org/10.1007/978-3-658-21655-9_21

IT-Strategie mit Themen wie Cloud, Mobility, Konsolidierung, irgendwas mit SAP!, Legacy Migration, Two-Speed-Architecture, etc. dominieren den CIO-Alltag. Dabei sind die Geschwindigkeit und der Kostendruck die wesentlichen Hausaufgaben die ein CIO zu erledigen hat. Dazu kommt jetzt noch die Sicherheitsthematik als solche hinzu. Das Sicherheitsthema kommt aber nicht alleine, sondern es bringt eine Reihe an Gesetzen und Verordnungen mit, die unter Androhung von Strafe auch noch umzusetzen sind. Der CIO kann durch die gegebenen Rahmenbedingungen all diese Themen gar nicht mehr alleine bewältigen.

Was aber ist der Ausweg aus der Sicherheitsmisere? Viele Unternehmen denken daher über einen Chief Information Security Officer – einen CISO – nach, wissen aber nicht, wie dieser zu implementieren ist, welche Aufgabenbeschreibung er haben sollte, welches Budget er bekommen müsste und vor allem: Woher soll man ihn nehmen, wenn nicht stehlen? Große Konzerne haben schon vor einiger Zeit angefangen, einen CISO zu implementieren, einige haben eine CISO-Organisation, die allumfänglich für die Sicherheitsthemen verantwortlich ist. Aber Richtlinienkompetenz und Durchsetzungskraft haben die wenigsten.

Nun ist guter Rat teuer und häufig werden Berater eingesetzt. Zuerst kommen die Unternehmensberater und erstellen ein Organisationskonzept, dann kommen die Personalberater und erstellen eine Aufgabenbeschreibung, dann wird das Suchprofil in Stein gemeißelt und geeignete Kandidaten werden gesucht. Vielleicht hat man Glück und findet einen CISO, der würdig genug ist, diesen Titel zu tragen. Da kommen dann gleich die etablierten Abteilungen um die Ecke und sagen C-Level? Muss das denn sein? Der CIO ist ja auch nicht wirklich C-Level. Also wird der CISO dann Leiter IT-Sicherheit, Direktor Cybersicherheit oder Leiter Informationssicherheit. Er gehört zum CIO und darf sich nun um die Sicherheit in der IT kümmern.

Fragen

Jedes Unternehmen sollte sich fragen, ob es überhaupt in der Lage ist, die Anforderungen an einen CISO so zu beschreiben, dass der jeweilige Kandidat zur Erhöhung der Sicherheit beitragen kann. Wenn Unternehmen dazu nicht in der Lage sind, sollten sie wissen, wo sie Hilfe bekommen.

21.2 Wie wird man eigentlich CISO?

Bevor man CISO werden möchte, sollte man wissen, was der CISO können muss. Hier liegt nämlich genau das Problem. Denn der CISO ist das Mädchen für alles geworden und muss zu viel mitbringen und wissen und somit ist bei vielen Anforderungsprofilen eine Wunschvorstellung der fachlichen Überqualifikation entstanden. Unternehmen verlassen sich häufig dabei auf Personalberater, dennoch werden die meisten Personalentscheidungen in der IT-Sicherheit subjektiv getroffen, da es im IT-Sicherheitsbereich kaum Menschen gibt, die andere Menschen bezüglich Ihrer IT-Sicherheitsfähigkeiten beurteilen können.

Die Grundqualifikation eines CISO ist in fast allen Anforderungsprofilen eine Sammlung von IT-Sicherheitsfachwörtern, die von einer Person nie alleine fachlich vertreten werden können. Diese fachliche Überqualifikation ist am Personalmarkt schlicht weg nicht verfügbar. Der CISO muss gewisse Grundanforderungen mitbringen, wie ein abgeschlossenes Studium, IT-Sicherheitsaffinität, Kenntnisse der einschlägigen Verfahren, Methoden, Architekturen und Sicherheitsprodukte. Dazu muss er Erfahrungen im Bereich Recht und Compliance, aber auch Grundlagen der Forensik sowie der allgemeinen Cyberbedrohungslage mitbringen. Dazu verlangen die meisten Unternehmen noch methodische Zusatzqualifikationen wie CISSP, CISM, T.I.S.P, T.P.S.S.E, zertifizierter Pen-Tester, Certified Ethical Hacker etc. Die Liste ist lang und dazu gibt es noch diverse Herstellerqualifikationen zu Produkten und Services. Die möglichen Zusatz-Qualifikationen eines CISO sind häufig damit verknüpft, die Grundstrukturen der IT sicherer zu machen, was aber eher eine passive Rolle ist, da der CISO das sicherheitstechnische Ende der digitalen Nahrungskette ist. Er kann weder Produkte auf echte Sicherheit prüfen, noch kann er großen Anbietern Vorgaben machen. Er muss sich nach bestem Wissen und Gewissen auf Produkte und Systeme verlassen. Immer in der Hoffnung, dass ein Angreifer nicht doch schlauer ist als die Hersteller, die Systeme und Produkte herstellen.

Aus dieser passiven Rolle ergeben sich für einen CISO im Allgemeinen folgende Aufgaben:

* Planung und Entwicklung der Cyber- und IT-Sicherheitsstrategie;
* Entwicklung und Umsetzung von Konzepten, Standards und Richtlinien für die Cyber- und Informationssicherheit;
* Implementierung technischer Maßnahmen zur Erhöhung der IT-Sicherheit;
* Erstellung von Konzepten zu Trainings und der Awareness für Führungskräfte, Mitarbeiter und des IT-Personals (intern/extern);
* Vorfalls-Bearbeitung (Incident Management)
* Kontinuierliche Verbesserung der IT-Sicherheit bzgl. der geschäftlichen Weiterentwicklung durch neue Geschäftsfelder, Märkte, Produkte und der Digitalisierung;
* Aufbau und Überwachung der Cyber- und IT-Risiken;
* Unterstützung der Auditabteilung bzgl. Sicherheitsfragen;
* Überprüfung, Analyse und Sicherheitsbewertung von technischen Architekturen, Systemen und Projekten;
* Schnittstelle zur Strafverfolgung, Behörden und Regulatoren bei Melde- bzw. anzeigepflichtigen Vorfällen.

Zusammengefasst muss der CISO von heute ALLES können!

In dem man alle diese Qualifikationen mitbringt, sich für das Thema Cyber- und IT-Sicherheit interessiert, muss man jetzt nur noch jemanden finden, der einen CISO sucht und ihn davon überzeugen, dass man der Richtige ist. Laut Bitkom dem Digitalverband in Deutschland, fehlen auf der Anwenderseite 6300 Sicherheitsspezialisten und bei den Anbietern 6580 Sicherheitsspezialisten. Das sind zwar nicht alles CISO-Positionen, aber immerhin ist es ein guter Einstieg in die IT-Sicherheitsbranche.

21.3 Jetzt hat man einen CISO und was nun?

Viele Unternehmen, die in die technische und organisatorische Sicherheit investiert haben und trotz den vielen Hürden einen qualifizierten CISO ins Haus geholt haben, stellen sich bei einem erfolgreichen Cyberangriff trotzdem die Frage:

Fragen

Haben wir die richtige Person eingestellt, haben wir ihr die nötigen Kompetenzen eingeräumt, war das Budget hoch genug? Oder besser gesagt stellt man sich die Frage: Wer ist schuld, dass es doch passiert ist?

Die Antwort liegt in der Erwartungshaltung an den eigenen Sicherheitsanspruch. Es ist falsch zu denken, dass der CISO alles kann und vor allem, dass er alle Cyberangriffe verhindern kann. Ein CISO kann viele Arten von Cyberangriffen nicht vermeiden. Er hilft dabei, eine Basishygiene in die IT zu implementieren, die Risiken zu beschreiben und vor allem hilft er, Cyberangriffe zu entdecken, um diese dann besser bearbeiten zu können.

Mittlerweile haben einige Unternehmen erkannt, dass Sicherheit ein wichtiges Thema ist und dass Unternehmen sich mit dem Thema beschäftigen sollten. Dabei werden weitere sicherheitsrelevante Funktionen neben dem CISO implementiert, die eigentlich zusammenwirken sollten aber meist mit unterschiedlichen Zielen und Verantwortungen ausgestattet werden. Neben dem CISO sind Teilbereiche der Sicherheit auf den Datenschutzbeauftragten, die Audit Abteilung, den Rechtsbereich, den Produktionsbereichen und manchmal noch auf einen Informationssicherheitsbeauftragten verteilt. Eine solche organisatorische Verteilung der Sicherheit funktioniert einigermaßen bei regulatorischen, gesetzlichen und branchenspezifischen Auflagen. Einen professionellen, innovativen Gegner mit einem strategischen Ziel hält das jedoch nicht auf. Aber am Ende wird immer der CISO gefragt, warum der Cyberangriff so überhaupt hat passieren können.

Abb. 21.1 zeigt die Themenfelder und Zuständigkeiten eines CISO. Die Abgrenzung zu weiteren Funktionen und Zuständigkeiten im Unternehmen richtet sich meist nicht nach dem Geschäftsmodell, sondern orientiert sich an gewachsenen Strukturen, die in Zeiten von zunehmenden Cyberrisiken nicht immer optimal zur Cyberbedrohungslage passen.

Daher ist es umso wichtiger eine (Cyber-) Sicherheitsstrategie zu entwickeln, die auf das jeweilige Unternehmens- und Geschäftsmodell zugeschnitten ist und für die der CISO bzw. die CISO-Organisation zuständig ist. Jeder CISO, der nicht innerhalb eines Jahres eine Cyberstrategie entwickelt, hat zumeist nur eine reaktive bzw. intern beratende Funktion.

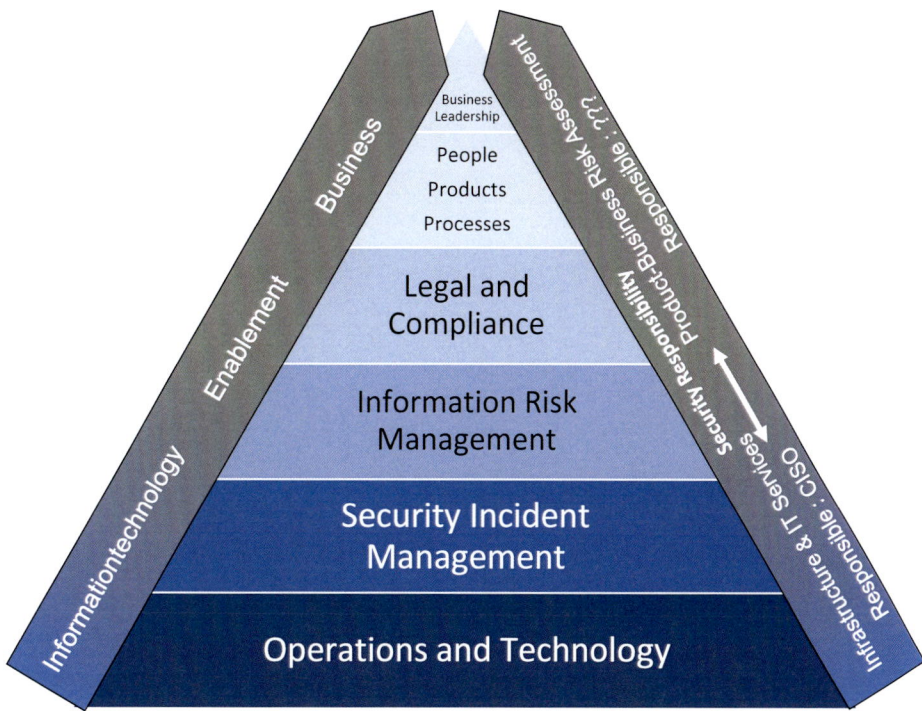

Abb. 21.1 Zuständigkeiten und Aufgaben eines CISO

21.4   Positionierung des CISO im Unternehmen

So langsam fangen Unternehmen an, den CISO als direkte Berichtslinie zur Geschäftsleitung zu etablieren. Dies geschieht zumeist in Branchen, die als kritische Infrastruktur [1] wie
z. B. Energieversorger und Finanzdienstleister durch einen Regulator verpflichtet werden
eine hohe Sicherheit zu gewährleisten. In den meisten Fällen berichtet der CISO an unterschiedliche Funktionen innerhalb des Unternehmens. Personell wird der CISO häufig in der
CIO-Organisation geführt und mit einer zusätzlichen, sogenannten „dotted-line" berichtet er
bedarfsweise an die Geschäftsleitung. Sehr häufig berichtet der CISO aber direkt an den
CIO. Durch diese Organisation kommt es häufig zu Spannungen, die aufgrund der Hierarchie und den unterschiedlichen Zielen begründet sind. Der CISO wird dann häufig als Inno-
vationsbremser angesehen, der mit paranoiden Sicherheitsvorstellungen die Budgets nach
oben treibt oder aufgrund übertriebener Sicherheitsanforderungen die Zeitpläne gefährdet.

▷   Jedes Unternehmen, das einen CISO implementiert, sollte sich überlegen, wel-
    che Governance Struktur für die CISO-Organisation gewählt wird und mit welchen
    Kompetenzen der CISO gegenüber der IT, dem Business, der Auditabteilung,
    der Revision und dem Datenschutz ausgestattet wird. Und am allerwichtigsten
    ist das Vertrauen gegenüber dem CISO. Ein CISO, sei er noch so gut, kann Cyber-
    angriffe und Sicherheitsvorfälle nicht vermeiden. Er kann aber zur Früherken-
    nung beitragen, Risiken minimieren und die Auswirkungen verringern.

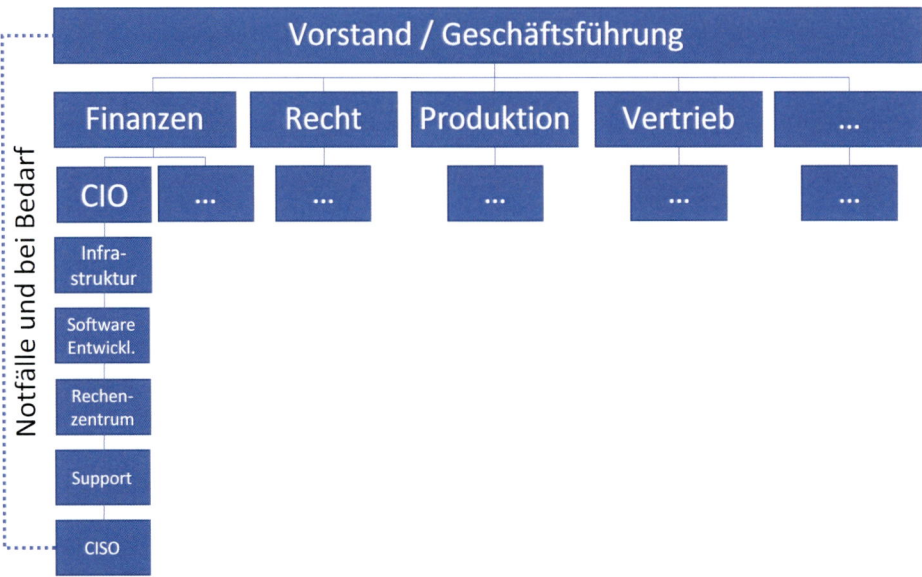

Abb. 21.2 Der CISO im Unternehmensmodell

Abb. 21.2 zeigt, wie der CISO im Allgemeinen im Unternehmen positioniert ist. Für die Zukunft dürfte dieses Modell nicht mehr tragfähig sein. Der CISO wird in der Hierarchie aufsteigen, wie und wo seine Position dann sein wird, hängt von der Innovationsfähigkeit und vom jeweiligen Geschäftsmodell ab. Der CISO wird auf jeden Fall eine wichtigere Rolle spielen müssen.

21.5   Warum es trotz CISO zum Cyberangriff kommt

▶   Der CISO implementiert im Tagesgeschäft grundlegende Systeme der IT-Si-
     cherheit. Diese sind für die IT-Sicherheit zwar wichtig, aber die Praxis zeigt, dass
     sie gegen gezielte Cyberangriffe nur bedingt helfen [2].

Die Bedrohungslage im Internet ist komplex und die Anzahl der eingesetzten Systeme sind unüberschaubar und nur in den gängigsten Systemen wird systematisch nach Schwachstellen gesucht. Das führt dazu, dass sich CISOs im Tagesgeschäft um die Einführung von allgemeinen Sicherheitsmaßnahmen wie Information Security Management Systeme (ISMS), Security Incident and Event Management (SIEM) oder um ein Security Operations Center (SOC) kümmern dürfen. Diese grundlegenden Systeme der IT-Sicherheit sind für die IT-Sicherheit zwar wichtig, helfen gegen gezielte Cyberangriffe aber nur bedingt.

Die Rolle des CISO ist heute zumeist eine operativ taktische, sollte aber eine strategische Rolle sein, die frühzeitig die Cyberbedrohungslage erkennt, das Problem für das

Unternehmen analysiert, eine klare Risikoabschätzung durchführt und diese in geeignete Lösungsansätze überführt und damit langfristig Sicherheitsvorfälle minimiert und deren Folgen mindert.

Als bestes Beispiel seien hier die Sicherheitslücken „Meltdown" und „Spectre" [3] genannt

Meltdown und Spectre haben dazu geführt, dass fast alle aktuellen Computersysteme und darauf implementierten Sicherheitssysteme durch gezieltes Suchen nach Passwörtern oder Verschlüsselungs-Schlüssel kompromittierbar sind. Fast alle CISOs waren hier vor ein unlösbares Problem gestellt und wussten nicht, wie damit umzugehen ist, da es lange dauert, bis die Hersteller Lösungen zu diesem Problem anbieten. Durch die Aufwertung des CISOs zu einer strategischen Rolle wäre er in der Lage, geschäftsrelevante Entscheidungen zu treffen. Ist das Problem im Vorfeld zu verstehen, zu analysieren, eine klare Risikoabschätzungen zu treffen und mit allen beteiligten Lieferanten, Herstellern und Betreibern (Cloud-Provider, Outsourcing-Partnern) nach Lösungen zu suchen, wären die Unternehmen besser vorbereitet gewesen. Bei der heutigen Ausrichtung ist der CISO, bis eine Lösung zum Problem gefunden wird, in Alarmbereitschaft (oft auch über einen längeren Zeitraum hinweg) und agiert als Krisenmanager zu einem Problem, wozu er die Lösung nicht kennt.

Der CISO muss empowered und enabled werden, seine Rolle als strategischer Krisenmanager wahrzunehmen.

21.6   Der CISO als Krisenmanager

Sicherheitsvorfälle sind heutzutage keine Seltenheit mehr und viele Vorfälle werden im Rahmen der Regelprozesse durch Softwareupdates (Patchen) oder durch bessere Konfigurationen behoben. Was aber passiert, wenn man Ziel von höherwertigen Cyberangriffen ist? Zum einen sind die Auswirkungen von sogenannten Massenphänomenen wie Crypto- bzw. Ransomware-Trojanern zu nennen. Im Jahr 2017 waren die prominentesten Schadsoftwares Locky, Wannacry, Petya und Not-Petya, die zusammen einen erheblichen Schaden angerichtet haben. Auf der anderen Seite stehen gezielte Angriffe auf einzelne Branchen, Unternehmen, Staaten und Behörden, die zu Spionage- oder Sabotagezwecken durchgeführt werden, die sehr schwer erkennbar sind.

Der Schaden ist hierbei für die Betroffenen deutlich höher und meistens ist das Schadensausmaß erst langfristig feststellbar. Jeder CISO sollte sich auf unterschiedliche Szenarien vorbereiten und Maßnahmen ergreifen, die Cyberkrisen planbar, vorhersehbar und erkennbar machen. Dazu ist eine grundsätzliche Cyberstrategie hilfreich, die langfristig die Umsetzung von technischen und organisatorischen Maßnahmen definiert und diese Anhand vorausgedachter und aktueller Szenarien dauerhaft überprüft. Sollte es dennoch zu unvermeidbaren und ernsthaften Cyberangriffen kommen, sollte der CISO fachlich und organisatorisch in der Lage sein, den Krisenstab führen zu können.

► In den meisten Unternehmen ist es nicht vorgesehen, dass ein CISO im Krisenstab eine führende Rolle einnehmen kann. In vielen Unternehmen sind IT-
und Cyberkrisen nicht ausreichend definiert und die Strukturen entsprechend
der Risiken nicht festgelegt bzw. standardisiert. Hierbei besteht ein erheblicher
Nachholbedarf, denn den meisten Führungskräften ist nicht wirklich klar, dass
ohne eine funktionierende IT gar nichts mehr geht.

21.7 Der CISO als „Enabler" im Unternehmen

Der CISO sollte nicht nur eine passive Rolle haben, sondern aktiv die Sicherheit im Unternehmen gestalten. Nur in der aktiven Rolle kann der CISO auch die Verantwortung und
Sicherheit für die eigenen Produkte übernehmen und so mit seinem Wissen neue Produkte
und Services und damit neue Marktchancen für seinen Arbeitgeber „enablen".

Was war die Digitalisierung der Musik eine Erleichterung

Die Digitalisierung macht aus physikalischen bzw. haptischen Produkten Daten. Immer
mehr Produkte werden digitalisiert und ihre Vorgänger verschwinden oder werden von
Nostalgikern oder Technologieverweigerern als das einzig Wahre beschworen. Die
Digitalisierung der Musik ist ein gutes Beispiel hierfür:

Keine verkratzen Schallplatten aus Vinyl mehr, sondern silberne runde Scheiben mit
besserer Klangqualität, die ein paar Kratzer vertragen konnten und dann brauchte man
auch noch nur einen Viertel des Platzes im Wohnzimmerregal, da die CDs viel kleiner
waren. Die ewig Gestrigen haben gesagt, die Qualität ist schlecht. Dann kam das MP3-
Format, man brauchte keine CDs mehr, sondern nur eine Internetverbindung und ein
MP3-Abspielgerät. Da haben die CD-Nutzer gesagt, die Klangqualität sei schlecht.
Heute hört jeder auf dem Smartphone Musik und man hat im Streaming Abo 40 Mio.
Musiktitel im Zugriff. An diesem kleinen Beispiel, das nun wirklich jeder kennt,
erkennt man das Ziel der Digitalisierung: „weg mit dem „alten Kram" der nur Platz
braucht und teuer ist".

Dieses Beispiel zeigt auf, wie schnell die erste Welle der Digitalisierung vorangeschritten
ist. Die Geschwindigkeiten sind heute in der globalen Geschäftswelt deutlich höher. Hat
es bei der Musik 20 Jahre gedauert, bis die Plattenindustrie quasi fast ausgestorben ist,
reden wir heute von 20 Monaten, in denen sich ganze Geschäftsmodelle und Anbieter
wandeln können. Sicherheit wird somit eines der wesentlichen Qualitätsmerkmale digita-
lisierter Produkte.

Der CISO als gutes (sicheres) Gewissen der Digitalisierung wird meistens nur zur passiven Digitalisierung genutzt, das bedeutet, dass der passive CISO nur die eigene IT absichern und beschützen soll. Diese Aufgabe ist aufgrund der Komplexität und der Vielzahl
der Systeme und Komponenten schon kaum zu schaffen. CISOs sind somit Verwalter
eines Restrisikos gepaart mit der Eintrittswahrscheinlichkeit eines Cyberangriffs. Jede

Firma sollte erkennen, dass ein CISO nur so gut ist, wie der Wille und die Fähigkeiten des gesamten Unternehmens – von der Geschäftsleitung bis hin zu jedem Mitarbeiter.

Ein aktiver CISO ist auch dafür verantwortlich, die eigenen Produkte, die heutzutage fast nicht mehr ohne Informationstechnologie auskommen, sicher zu machen. Er „enabled" somit mit seinem Wissen neue Produkte und Services und damit neue Marktchancen für seinen Arbeitgeber. In diesem speziellen Fall ist der CISO für die Qualität der digitalen Anteile eines Produktes (mit-)verantwortlich. Sicherheit wird in naher Zukunft eines der hauptsächlichen Qualitätsmerkmale von Produkten sein, die in irgendeiner Form Hardware- und Softwarekomponenten oder IoT[1]-Module beinhalten. Daher sollten sich Unternehmen sehr gut überlegen, ob der CISO eine Person, eine Organisation oder nicht besser eine Unternehmensphilosophie sein sollte. Daraus ergibt sich für den CISO ein noch sehr viel komplexeres Tätigkeitsfeld, welches sich von der strategischen Ebene über alle operativen Ebenen der internen IT, zu Kunden und Lieferanten bis hin zum Produktdesign, Serviceprozessen und bis zum Daten- Spionage- und Sabotageschutz erstreckt.

21.8   Fazit

Das Aufgabengebiet eines CISOs bzw. einer CISO-Organisation wird sich in den nächsten Jahren stark wandeln. So wie der Chief Digital Officer (CDO) anfängt, den Chief Information Officer zu überholen, ist es nur eine Frage der Zeit, wann der CISO den CDO überholt. Denn für viele Unternehmen wird die Frage der Sicherheit in einer digitalisierten Welt überlebenswichtig werden. Durch die stetig ansteigende Nutzung von Cloud-Computing, Mobility und immer höher integrierte, vernetzte Systeme und Prozesse bleibt dem Unternehmen am Ende nur noch das eigene Business und die damit verbundene Security. Der Rest kommt aus der Cloud, nutzt künstliche Intelligenz und steuert standardisierte Prozesse selbstständig. Der Weg dorthin ist noch weit, aber er wird schnell gegangen werden. Der CISO wird bleiben, denn er ist ein wichtiger Teil in einer zukünftigen Unternehmensstruktur, der einen direkten Anteil am Geschäftsmodell und am Erfolg des Unternehmens hat.

Literatur

1. https://www.kritis.bund.de/SubSites/Kritis/DE/Einfuehrung/Sektoren/sektoren_node.html
2. Cybersicherheit ist nicht nur IT-Sicherheit, siehe Michael Bartsch und Stefanie Frey, Cyberstrategien für Unternehmen und Behörden, Springer 2017.
3. https://www.bsi-fuer-buerger.de/BSIFB/DE/Service/Aktuell/Informationen/Artikel/Meltdown_Spectre_Sicherheitsluecke_10012018.html;jsessionid=216E8608AA22BFD13BEF61A33C1C4137.2_cid351#IoT: Internet of Things – Internet der Dinge.

---

[1] IoT: Internet of Things – Internet der Dinge.

Einbindung Datenschutz und Betriebsrat beim Aufbau eines SIEM

22

Matthias Drodt, Ludger Pagel und Thomas Biedorf

Zusammenfassung

Die zunehmende Gefährdung durch professionelle Cyberangriffe erfordert einen Paradigmenwechsel: Ergänzung der Prävention durch Detektion und Reaktion. SIEM-Systeme („Security Information and Event Management System"), in denen systematisch und umfassend Logdaten zusammenlaufen und ausgewertet werden, sind hierbei unverzichtbar.

Vor dem Aufbau eines SIEM gilt es einen umfassenden Abstimmungsprozess mit allen relevanten Bereichen durchzuführen. Hierfür sollte man hinreichend Zeit einplanen. Nicht nur technische Aspekte gilt es beim Aufbau zu berücksichtigen. Immens wichtig sind eine frühzeitige Einbindung von Datenschutz und Betriebsrat sowie ein offener und transparenter Dialog. Abzuwägen ist die Notwendigkeit zur Erhebung, Speicherung und Verarbeitung von personenbezogenen Daten mit dem berechtigten Unternehmensinteresse zur Erkennung und Analyse von Cyberangriffen. Hilfreich hierbei sind klare und enge Zweckbindung der Datenspeicherung, geeignete Löschfristen sowie ein stringent eingeschränkter Kreis der Zugriffsberechtigten.

Ein SIEM kann – richtig eingesetzt – Cyberangriffe erkennen und zugleich alle Anforderungen von Datenschutz und Betriebsrat erfüllen.

M. Drodt (✉) · T. Biedorf
Deutsche Bahn AG, Frankfurt, Deutschland
E-Mail: matthias.drodt@deutschebahn.com; thomas.biedorf@deutschebahn.com

L. Pagel
DB Systel GmbH, Frankfurt, Deutschland
E-Mail: ludger.pagel@deutschebahn.com

© Springer Fachmedien Wiesbaden GmbH, ein Teil von Springer Nature 2018
M. Bartsch, S. Frey (Hrsg.), *Cybersecurity Best Practices*,
https://doi.org/10.1007/978-3-658-21655-9_22

Technische Fragestellungen stehen zumeist im Vordergrund beim Aufbau eines SIEM. Vielfach vernachlässigt, aber nicht minder wichtig ist die notwendige Berücksichtigung der Anforderungen von Datenschutz und Betriebsrat. Vorausgesetzt, es findet eine zeitnahe Einbindung statt und entsprechende Anforderungen sind bereits frühzeitig in den Konzepten berücksichtigt, kann eine erfolgreiche Abstimmung in wenigen Monaten erfolgen. Ansonsten drohen unweigerlich langwierige Verzögerungen oder Verstöße gegen gesetzliche Vorgaben.

Weltweit ist eine stetige Zunahme der professionellen und teilweise erfolgreichen Cyberangriffe zu verzeichnen. Die Schlagzeilen der letzten Jahre, in denen kaum eine Woche ohne Meldung über erfolgreiche Cyberattacken, gestohlene Passwörter und Kundendaten oder Angriffe auf IT-Infrastrukturen verging, belegen dies eindrucksvoll. Finanzielle Interessen spielen hierbei eine immer stärkere Rolle. Waren es vor Jahren noch sogenannte „Skript-Kiddies", hat sich mittlerweile die Cyberkriminalität zu einem professionellen Geschäft entwickelt. Die Cyberkriminalität ist hierbei selbst zum „Business" geworden und wird als „Cybercrime as a Service" auf internationalen Marktplätzen professionell angeboten. Hierdurch sinken die Einstiegshürden für zielgerichtete Cyberangriffe stetig. Ein mehrstündiger Distributed Denial of Service Angriff (DDoS) oder das gezielte Ausspionieren von Computersystemen können zum Beispiel für wenige 100 $ käuflich und teilweise mit Erfolgsgarantie erworben werden. Spezialwissen ist hierfür kaum mehr nötig.

22.1 Cyberangriffe bekommen ein immer breiteres Spektrum und werden für Unternehmen zunehmend kritischer

Die Digitalisierung und die ihr zugrunde liegenden Informations- und Kommunikationstechnologien (IT) sind von zentraler Bedeutung für Gesellschaft, Staat und Wirtschaft. Dies gilt für Deutschland ebenso wie für jedes andere Land der Welt. Wir erleben eine vollständige Durchdringung von IT in nahezu alle unsere vorhandenen Strukturen und Lebensbereiche. Keine Gesellschaft und kein Geschäftsprozess kommen heute ohne den Einsatz von professioneller IT aus. Die Digitalisierung ist eine notwendige Voraussetzung für gesellschaftliches und wirtschaftliches Wohlergehen und für politische Stabilität und den Schutz unserer Grundwerte geworden. Cybersicherheit und Privatsphärenschutz stellen hierbei unabdingbare Voraussetzungen für eine erfolgreiche Digitalisierung als auch für das Business dar. Oder anders formuliert: eine nicht angemessene Umsetzung von IT-Sicherheit mit einer professionellen Erkennung und Abwehr von Cyberangriffen gefährdet die Digitalisierung der Gesellschaft und das wirtschaftliche Überleben von Unternehmen.

Einige konkrete Cybervorfälle der jüngeren Zeit belegen die Breite dieser Bedrohungen:

* **Politische Einrichtungen** werden ausspioniert: 2015 wurde bekannt, dass Angreifer über längere Zeit Zugriff auf praktisch alle Daten des Deutschen Bundestages hatten [1].
* **Personenbezogene Daten** sind oft nur unzureichend geschützt: vor kurzem wurde bekannt, dass Hacker bei Yahoo ab 2013 Daten von mehr als 3 Milliarden Nutzern erbeutet hatten [1].
* Die **Wirtschaft** wird im großen Stil ausspioniert: Bitkom schätzte 2015, dass bereits mehr als 51 % aller Firmen Opfer von Industriespionage waren [2].

- Betroffen sein können ebenfalls **Betreiber kritischer Infrastrukturen:** 2016 führte ein Computervirus im Lukaskrankenhaus in Neuss zu erheblichen Serviceeinschränkungen [3].

Wie bei den meisten Unternehmen auch existiert bei der Deutschen Bahn eine hohe Abhängigkeit des Business von der IT. Zusätzlich ist die Deutsche Bahn Betreiber kritischer Infrastrukturen und fällt somit teilweise unter das IT-Sicherheitsgesetz.

Überblick Deutsche Bahn AG: Business, Governance, IT, Datenschutz und Betriebsrat

Der Deutsche Bahn Konzern ist ein internationaler Anbieter von Mobilitäts- und Logistikdienstleistungen und agiert weltweit in über 130 Ländern. Über 300.000 Mitarbeiter, davon rund 187.000 in Deutschland, setzen sich täglich dafür ein, Mobilität und Logistik für die Kunden sicherzustellen und die dazugehörigen Verkehrsnetze auf der Schiene, der Straße, zu Wasser und in der Luft effizient zu steuern und zu betreiben. Kern des Unternehmens ist das Eisenbahngeschäft in Deutschland mit über 5,5 Millionen Kunden täglich im Schienenpersonenverkehr und rund 558 Tausend Tonnen beförderter Güter pro Tag. Rund 2,1 Millionen Kunden sind täglich mit den Bussen der DB in Deutschland unterwegs. Insgesamt fahren auf dem modernen, über 33.400 Kilometer langen und für Wettbewerb geöffneten Streckennetz täglich rund 40.000 Züge. Die Anzahl der Personenbahnhöfe beträgt 5662.

Die Digitalisierung gehört heute zu den zentralen strategischen Themen der Deutschen Bahn AG. IT wird immer mehr zur Lebensader und zum Treiber der Digitalisierung. Ohne IT sind weder die eisenbahnbetrieblichen Prozesse, noch die Planungs-, Dispositions- oder Verwaltungsprozesse denkbar. Kunden, Beschäftigte und Lieferanten müssen sich hierbei auf zuverlässige, performante und auch sichere IT-Services verlassen können. IT-Sicherheit dient innerhalb der Deutschen Bahn AG dem Schutz der IT-gestützten Geschäftstätigkeiten vor Bedrohungen und Schäden sowie der Einhaltung von datenschutzrechtlichen Vorgaben.

Das Business der Deutschen Bahn AG wird von aktuell 18 eigenständigen Geschäftsfeldern (z. B. DB Fernverkehr, DB Regio, DB Fahrweg und DB Cargo) verantwortet und diese werden bezüglich IT fachlich geführt von der zentralen IT-Governance (verankert in der Konzernleitung). Diese Führungsaufgabe erfolgt u. a. über konzernweit einheitliche Vorgaben, Grundsätze sowie über einheitliche Strategien. DB Systel ist der zentrale Digitalisierungspartner und deckt den gesamten Lebenszyklus von IT-Lösungen ab: von der Planung über Entwicklung und Betrieb bis zu ihrer Optimierung. CSIRT (Cyber Security Incident Response Team, siehe Definition in Abschn. 22.1.1) und SIEM sind ebenfalls bei DB Systel operativ angesiedelt und sind zentrale Bestandteile der Cyber Defense der DB. Die zentrale Governance zum Datenschutz wird von dem Bereich Konzerndatenschutz wahrgenommen, welcher ebenfalls in der Konzernleitung verankert ist. Der Konzerndatenschutz unterstützt und berät die Geschäftsfelder hinsichtlich der Einhaltung von datenschutzrechtlichen Vorgaben. Die Konzerndatenschutzbeauftragte ist ebenfalls hier verortet und ist zugleich in den meisten Geschäftsfeldern als Datenschutzbeauftragte bestellt. Die Interessen der Beschäftigten der Deutschen Bahn werden zentral vertreten vom Konzernbetriebsrat, den Betriebsräten vor Ort und den Gesamtbetriebsräten, die auf die Einhaltung der gesetzlichen Vorgaben des Betriebsverfassungsrechts achten. Der Konzernbetriebsrat ist das zentrale Organ innerhalb der Deutschen Bahn zur Mitbestimmung und Vertretung der Arbeitnehmerinteressen, das auch an betrieblichen Entscheidungen mitwirkt.

Auch bei der Deutschen Bahn ist festzustellen, dass die Cyberangriffe sowohl quantitativ als auch qualitativ zunehmen. Die Angriffe erfolgen gezielter, diskreter und systematischer. Waren vor wenigen Jahren noch hauptsächlich DDoS-Attacken auf die IT-Infrastrukturen zu verzeichnen, ist in jüngster Zeit ein Trend in Richtung zielgerichteter Angriffe erkennbar. Sowohl die Angriffstechnik selbst als auch die „Wucht" lassen keinen Zweifel zu, dass zunehmend kriminelle und/oder finanzielle Beweggründe hinter diesen Angriffen stehen.

Diese zielgerichteten Angriffe haben vielfach das Ziel, unbemerkt in die IT-Systeme des Opfers einzudringen, um dort einen spezifischen Schaden anzurichten oder unbemerkt an vertrauliche/wertvolle Informationen zu gelangen. Hierbei spricht man auch oftmals von APT-Angriffen [5]. Das Angriffsschema läuft hierbei immer ähnlich ab:

- In einem ersten Schritt **recherchiert** der Angreifer in öffentlich zugänglichen Quellen nach nutzbaren Informationen (wie IP-Adressen, E-Mail-Adressen von Mitarbeitern oder Zugangsdaten).
- Anschließend erfolgt die **Infiltration** in die internen Kommunikationsnetze, zum Beispiel über Missbrauch von Zugangsdaten oder über Social Engineering [6].
- Als nächstes versucht der Angreifer, in der Phase **Discovery,** sich unbemerkt in den internen Kommunikationsnetzen lateral auszubreiten auf der Suche nach den gewünschten Informationen.
- Hat er das „Ziel" erreicht oder die Daten gefunden, wird er die IT-Systeme oder die Informationen **übernehmen** bzw. **kapern.**
- Im Rahmen der **Exfiltration** erfolgt der unbemerkte Abzug der gefundenen Informationen.

Da eines der wesentlichen Ziele des Angreifers ist, unentdeckt zu bleiben, bedarf es einer grundlegenden Überarbeitung der vorhandenen Abwehrmaßnahmen. Schutzmaßnahmen zur **Prävention** sind nicht mehr ausreichend. Es sind zusätzliche Maßnahmen hinsichtlich **Detektion** und **Reaktion** notwendig. In Deutschland entfällt ein Großteil der Ausgaben für IT-Sicherheit auf präventive Maßnahmen. Hier ist in den nächsten Jahren eine Angleichung der Ausgaben notwendig (ohne die präventiven Maßnahmen zu vernachlässigen). Oder anders formuliert: wir müssen akzeptieren, dass der in der Vergangenheit gewählte Weg – all unsere Zeit und Ressourcen dahingehend einzusetzen, die Netzwerke abzuschotten, um Angreifer fernzuhalten – nicht mehr ausreichend sein wird. Das klassische „Burgen bauen" hat als alleinige Abwehrstrategie ausgedient. Denn es ist nicht die Frage, ob ein professioneller Angreifer in die internen Kommunikationsnetze eindringen wird (die errichteten „Türme und Mauern" überwinden wird), sondern nur wann und wie. Zukünftig entscheidend wird sein, die Angreifer möglichst frühzeitig zu erkennen sowie schnell angemessene reaktive Maßnahmen zu ergreifen, um Schäden gering zu halten oder vollständig abzuwenden.

Auch die DB verfügt über ein Cyber Security Incident Response Team (CSIRT) inkl. der notwendigen technischen Systeme. Besondere Bedeutung hat hierbei die Einführung eines Security Information and Event Management Systems (SIEM), ohne dass ein CSIRT quasi blind ist – sowohl bezüglich der Detektion akuter Security Incidents wie auch bei der notwendigen forensischen Nachanalyse zur Erkennung und Beseitigung der Infektionswege. Laut einer Studie von Verizon [7] erkennen nur 5 % der Unternehmen einen Angriff, obwohl in 90 % der Fälle Hinweise in den Logdaten vorhanden waren. Sehr hilfreich für einen erfolgreichen und effizienten Start war und ist auch der sehr intensive und fruchtbare Erfahrungsaustausch mit anderen Unternehmen aus dem Dax30-Kreis.

▶ **CSIRT Definition der Europäischen Informationssicherheitsbehörde ENISA** Ein CSIRT ist ein Team von IT-Sicherheitsexperten bzw. -sachverständigen, deren Hauptaufgabe darin besteht, auf Computersicherheitsverletzungen zu reagieren. Dieses Team bietet die zu ihrer Behandlung notwendigen Dienstleistungen und unterstützt seine Klientel bei der Wiederherstellung nach derartigen Sicherheitsverletzungen. [...]

Damit ein CSIRT effektiv arbeiten kann, ist es notwendig, dass das CSIRT Kenntnis von Vorgängen/Ereignissen auf den einzelnen IT-Systemen und im Kommunikationsnetz erlangt, die einen Bezug zu potenziellen Security Incidents haben können. Nicht effektiv wäre es, die Logdaten eines jeden IT-Systems manuell und isoliert durch zu schauen. Genauso ist es auch nicht ausreichend, sich auf klassische Systemmanagement-Systeme zu beschränken, da hier „nur" rein technische Statusmeldungen wie Auslastung, Verfügbarkeit, Performance, Hardwarefehler usw. sichtbar sind. Im Umfeld der IT-Security gehören auch andere Ereignisse dazu, wie z. B. erfolgreiche wie auch nicht erfolgreiche Anmeldeversuche an IT-Systemen, unerwarteter Netzverkehr oder unerwartete Zugriffsversuche auf IT-Systeme. Ein weiterer wichtiger Faktor ist die Korrelation von Ereignissen, die Hinweise auf laufende Angriffe geben können. So sind z. B. Administratoren einzelner IT-Systeme bei der Beobachtung lokaler nicht erfolgreicher Anmeldeversuche noch relativ gelassen. Beobachtet man dies aber bei mehreren IT-Systemen gleichzeitig von einer Quelle ausgehend, so ist das eine gezielte Untersuchung wert. Um hier effektiv diese ganzheitlichen wie auch detaillierten Sichten für ein CSIRT ermöglichen zu können, setzt man auf Security Information and Event Management (SIEM) Systeme. Die Funktionsweise und insbesondere die datenschutzrechtlichen und mitbestimmungsrelevanten Themen werden im Folgenden vorgestellt.

Die Behandlung von Ereignissen durch ein SIEM kann durch zwei wesentliche Arbeitsschritte beschrieben werden:

- Auf der Quellsystem-Ebene werden von den relevanten IT-Systemen, Infrastrukturelementen und Endgeräten Loginformationen bereitgestellt und in einem zentralen Logdatenmanagement (Loghost-Ebene) aggregiert.
- Auf der nachfolgenden SIEM-Ebene werden diese zunächst normalisiert und priorisiert. Hierdurch wird erreicht, dass aus einer Vielzahl von Logdaten die Ereignisse vorgefiltert werden, die relevante sicherheitsbezogene Inhalte aufzeigen. Im weiteren Verlauf werden die Logdaten auf Auffälligkeiten bezüglich sicherheitsrelevanter Ereignisse oder im Rahmen einer forensischen Nachanalyse von Sicherheitsvorfällen automatisiert oder manuell analysiert. Das SIEM ist hierbei – je nach Vorgaben und Möglichkeiten – auch in der Lage, Ereignisse/Informationen verschiedener Quellen in Relation zu setzen (Korrelation). Hierdurch können sowohl akute Cyberangriffe als auch die eingetretenen Schäden durch Nachanalysen erkannt und ggfs. minimiert werden.

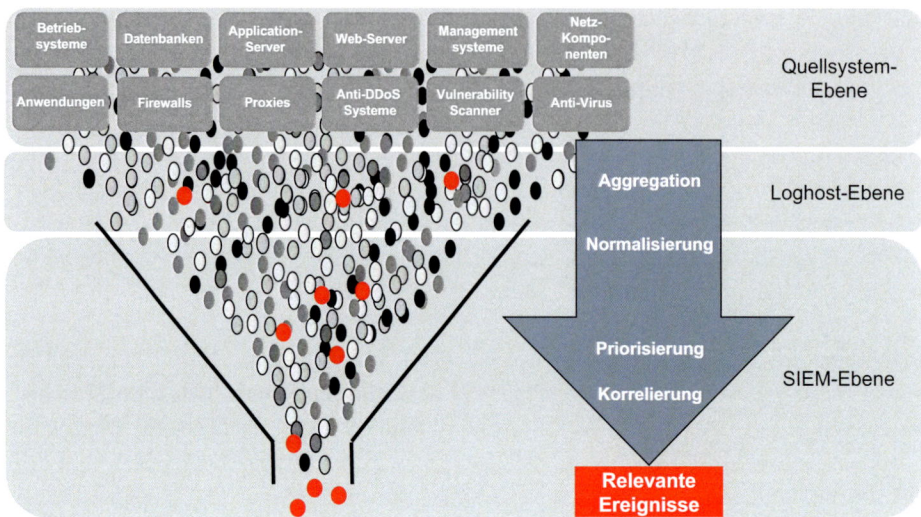

Abb. 22.1 Zusammenspiel Logdatenmanagement und SIEM: Schematische Darstellung

Damit liefert das Logdatenmanagement (siehe Abb. 22.1) gemeinsam mit dem SIEM die Grundlage für eine umfassende Protokolldatenbewertung bzw. Verwaltung von Sicherheitsinformationen und -ereignissen mit folgenden konkreten Zielen:

- Erkennung und Abwehr von Bedrohungen und zielgerichteten Cyberangriffen in Echtzeit
- Indiziensicherung als Basis für die Aufklärung und Bearbeitung von Sicherheitsvorfällen
- Forensische Nachanalysen zur Feststellung der Infektionswege sowie zur Analyse und Eingrenzung des möglicherweise bereits eingetretenen Schadens
- Kapazitätsplanung der genutzten IT-Systeme
- Aufklärung von Fehlerzuständen
- Erkennung und Vermeidung von Datendiebstahl/Wirtschaftsspionage
- Bei Cyberangriffen: Minimierung der Auswirkungen für das Business (finanzielle Auswirkungen, Reputationsschäden, Strafzahlungen, Datenpannen)
- Behebung von System- und Netzwerkproblemen

Neben rein technischen Daten fallen auch personenbezogene Daten an. Im Einzelnen sind dies:

- IP-Adressen,
- E-Mail-Adressen,
- Servernamen,
- Clientnamen,
- Benutzerkontodaten/Ereignisdaten (z. B. Benutzernamen, Zeitpunkte der Anmeldung an IT-Systemen, Anzahl fehlgeschlagener Anmeldeversuche, Lokalitäten der Benutzer, Einrichtung oder Sperrung von Berechtigungen)

Diese personenbeziehbaren Daten erlangen erst im Zusammenhang mit technischen und/oder Ereignisdaten eine besondere Brisanz.

Ein Beispiel zur Verdeutlichung ist ein typisches Angriffsszenario über Phishing-Mails mit dem Ziel, einen Empfänger zur Herausgabe von Informationen oder unbewusstem Nachladen von Schadsoftware zu verleiten. Hierzu veranlasst der Inhalt der Phishing-Mail den Empfänger dazu, einen Link zu öffnen, der ihn auf eine Seite im Internet lenkt, um dort, in unserem Beispiel auf Basis einer gefälschten Firmenseite, interne Daten zu hinterlassen. Wird nun z. B. über einen zentralen eigenen Internetproxy festgestellt, dass Aufrufe auf eine als bekannt gefälschte Internetseite vorhanden sind, so ist zu prüfen:

- Was wird auf dieser Seite angezeigt und abgefragt? (Angriffsmotivation und Schadenspotenzial bestimmen)
- Wer hat auf diese Seite zugegriffen? (Betroffene ermitteln, Unterstützungsleistung für Betroffene)
- Wer hat dort welche Daten hinterlassen? (Schadenseinschätzung)
- Wieso haben Beschäftigte diese Seite aufgerufen („Infektionsweg")? (Ursachenermittlung, Bestimmung Abwehrmaßnahmen)
- Wer hat alles diese Phishing-Mail bekommen und wer hat hier noch nicht aktiv gehandelt? (Schadenseindämmung, Angriffsumfang ermitteln)
- Welche Clients/IT-Systeme müssen bereinigt werden (wenn auch Schadsoftware beteiligt ist)? (Bereinigung, Abwehrmaßnahme)

Für die Beantwortung dieser Fragestellungen werden die aggregierten Logdaten – in unserem Beispiel vom Internetproxy, Mailgateway, Virenscanner, Anti-SPAM-Filter, netzbasierte Anomalieerkennung – im SIEM zentral, effektiv und übergreifend gemäß des benötigten Informationsbedarfes analysiert und ggfs. in Korrelation gesetzt. Diese Fragenstellungen sind ohne personenbeziehbare Daten nicht zu lösen, und die notwendige Unterstützungsleistung für die Beschäftigten zur Schadensbegrenzung und Bestimmung von Abwehrmaßnahmen sind nicht oder nur sehr begrenzt möglich. Siehe Abb. 22.2.

Wie zu erkennen ist, erlaubt die Kombination der personenbeziehbaren Daten mit Ereignisdaten ein großes Maß an Analysen im Allgemeinen wie aber auch auf Einzelpersonen bezogen. Deshalb ist hier bei der Erhebung, Speicherung, Auswertung und Ergebnisweitergabe der Spagat zwischen der notwendigen Erkennung von Security Incidents, der Bestimmung zusätzlicher präventiver Maßnahmen und einem Höchstmaß an Sorgfalt und Vertraulichkeit bezüglich der Daten von potenziell involvierten Personen zu beachten.

Um hier beiden Anforderungen Rechnung zu tragen, müssen bei der Planung, Aufbau und Einsatz eines SIEM frühzeitig Aspekte des Datenschutzes und der betrieblichen Mitbestimmung berücksichtigt werden. Folgende Aspekte sind hierbei besonders relevant:

- Klare Definition, welche Daten erhoben und verarbeitet werden. Dabei ist der Grundsatz der Erforderlichkeit zu berücksichtigen.
- Klare und stringente Bestimmung der Zweckbindung

- Festlegung der Speicherfristen (Löschkonzept) und Begründung der zugehörigen Notwendigkeiten
- Begrenzung des Personenkreises, der Einblick in die Daten und Auswertung haben darf (Berechtigungskonzept)
- Spielregeln für die Weitergabe von Ergebnissen mit Personennennung
- Ausschluss einer Verhaltens- und Leistungskontrolle (Mitbestimmung)

22.2   Entscheidend zur Angriffserkennung ist die Zeitdauer der Datenspeicherung

Eine anfallende Thematik sind die Speicher- bzw. Löschfristen, wobei dies bezüglich der rein technischen Daten lediglich eine Frage der Kapazitäten ist. Bei den personenbezogenen Daten sind aber die Belange des Datenschutzes und der Interessenvertretungen zu berücksichtigen.

Aus Sicht der Aufgabenstellung, Erkennung und Nachverfolgung von Angriffen ist sicherzustellen und zu beachten, dass speziell bei Wirtschaftsspionage oder langfristig geplanten Sabotageangriffen der Angreifer sich zunächst einen Zugang zu den IT-Systemen des Opfers verschafft mit der wesentlichen Zielstellung nicht entdeckt zu werden. Erst nach einer gewissen Zeitspanne wird der Angreifer aktiv. Im Falle von Datendiebstahl möchte er auch nicht direkt auffallen – geht also nach Möglichkeit „still" vor. Verizon hat in 2014 berichtet, dass die mittlere Zeit bis zur Erkennung eines solchen Angriffes 243 Kalendertage dauert [8]. Im Gegenzug bedeutet dies, dass eine Zeitspanne der Speicherung der Logdaten es ermöglichen muss, auch langlaufende Angriffe zu erkennen und nachverfolgen zu können. Angriffsweg und ggfs. Betroffene lassen sich nicht mehr ermitteln, wenn der Speicherzeitraum zu kurz definiert wurde und die erforderlichen Logdaten bereits gelöscht wurden. Eine nachhaltige Beseitigung der erfolgten Infektionen ist dann nicht mehr möglich (die Infektion kann erneut immer wieder unkontrolliert auftreten). Siehe Abb. 22.3 zur Bedeutung der Speicherfrist von Daten zur Analyse von Cyberangriffen.

Das vom Bundesverfassungsgericht in seinem berühmten Volkszählungsurteil [9] formulierte Recht auf „Informationelle Selbstbestimmung" bildet den Grundstein unseres heutigen Datenschutzverständnisses: Jeder einzelne soll in die Lage versetzt werden, grundsätzlich selbst über die Preisgabe und Verwendung seiner personenbezogenen Daten zu bestimmen. Dieses Recht wird hergeleitet aus Art. 2 Abs. 1 in Verbindung mit Art. 1 Abs. 1 Grundgesetz („Allgemeines Persönlichkeitsrecht"). Die Richter erkannten so schon damals die Gefährdungen, die sich aus der automatisierten Verarbeitung personenbezogener Daten für den Einzelnen ergeben könnten. Die Entscheidung des Einzelnen über die Verwendung seiner personenbezogenen Daten bedarf dabei heutzutage eines besonderen Schutzes, da mit Hilfe automatisierter Verfahren zum einen in Sekundenschnelle die ihn betreffenden Daten abgerufen werden können und zum anderen diese nahezu unbegrenzt gespeichert werden können. Beim Zusammenführen verschiedener Datenquellen könnten so Persönlichkeitsprofile und Verhaltensmuster erstellt werden, ohne dass der Betroffene

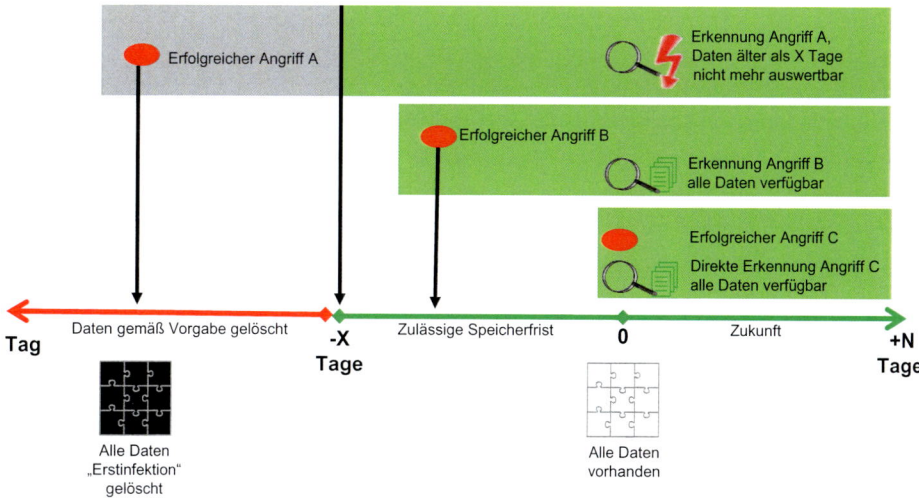

Abb. 22.2 Analyseoptionen abhängig vom Erkennungszeitpunkt (hier: Angriff und ereignisnahe Erkennung)

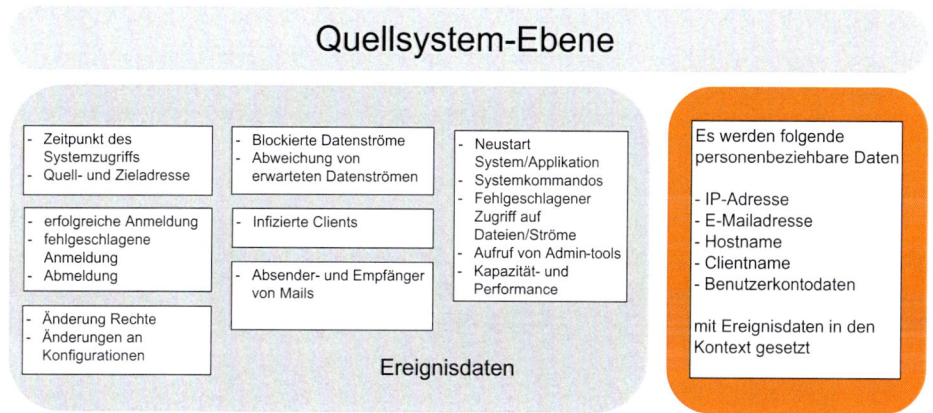

Abb. 22.3 Quellsystem Ebene

davon Kenntnis erlangt und ohne, dass er ggfs. dagegen intervenieren könnte. Der Einzelne ist also vor unbegrenzter Erhebung und Verarbeitung, Speicherung und Verwendung seiner personenbezogenen Daten zu schützen. Im Rahmen einer bestehenden Rechtsgrundlage kann dies eingeschränkt werden, wenn die Rechte anderer verletzt oder gegen die verfassungsmäßige Ordnung oder das Sittengesetz verstoßen wird. Es müssen zudem technische und organisatorische Maßnahmen getroffen werden, die einer Verletzung des Persönlichkeitsrechts entgegenwirken. Sie sollen personenbezogene Daten der Beschäftigten, Kunden und Lieferanten z. B. gegen unbefugte Weitergabe und Verwendung schützen. Dabei wird man sich immer im Spannungsfeld zwischen Erhebung, Speicherung und Verarbeitung und den datenschutzrechtlichen Vorgaben bewegen müssen. Eine enge Zweckbindung und geeignete Löschfristen helfen, dieses Spannungsfeld zu lösen.

Das Schreiben von (technischen) Protokollen ganz allgemein ist eine Grundvoraussetzung, um die Integrität von personenbezogenen Daten zu gewährleisten. Dieses Schutzziel ergibt sich unter anderem aus der Anlage zum § 9 des Bundesdatenschutzgesetzes (BDSG), im Rahmen derer u. a. sicherzustellen ist, dass der Zugang zu personenbezogenen Daten, die Zugriffe auf und die Weitergabe von personenbezogenen Daten und deren Veränderung zu protokollieren sind. Bei der Protokollierung werden nicht nur technische Parameter zur Systemüberwachung, sondern auch die Tätigkeiten von externen wie internen Nutzern und Administratoren erfasst. Auch wenn das SIEM primär geschaffen wurde, externe Angriffe zu delektieren, so können natürlich auch Daten von Beschäftigten in den Logdaten anfallen. Es ist grundsätzlich also immer von Personenbezug in Protokollen auszugehen [10], so dass man im Anwendungsbereich des BDSG bzw. der ab 25. Mai 2018 geltenden Datenschutzgrundverordnung (DSGVO) landet. Im Rahmen eines SIEM werden, gerade in einem Konzernumfeld, erhebliche Mengen an Protokolldaten erfasst und ausgewertet, so dass eindeutige Regelungen, die allen Beteiligten Handlungs- und Rechtssicherheit geben, gefordert sind.

Die Verarbeitung personenbezogener Daten erfordert wie erwähnt zwingend eine Rechtsgrundlage. Im Rahmen eines SIEM muss dies regelmäßig der § 28 Abs. 1 Satz 1 Nr. 2 BDSG (Verarbeitung für eigene Geschäftszwecke im Rahmen des berechtigten Interesses) in Verbindung mit § 31 BDSG [12] sein. Dieser ist sehr eng auszulegen, da die Datenspeicherung nur für die Sicherstellung des ordnungsgemäßen Betriebs, die Datensicherungskontrolle und die Datenschutzkontrolle erlaubt ist. Speicherung auf Vorrat ist dabei unzulässig. Der § 31 BDSG gibt insofern nur den Rahmen für den Betrieb eines SIEM vor. In einer zu erstellenden Verfahrensmeldung (siehe Konzerndatenausschuss in Abschn. 22.1.3) müssen daher die Zwecke der Verarbeitung sehr detailliert beschrieben sein, wenn die Protokolle sinnvoll genutzt werden sollen. Die Zwecke dürfen sich nur auf die Zwecke Datenschutzkontrolle, Datensicherung und Aufrechterhaltung des Betriebs beziehen [12]. Da die Deutsche Bahn ein Betreiber kritischer Infrastrukturen ist, kann dies auch nur im Rahmen des § 8a Abs. 1 BSIG (Gesetz über das Bundesamt für Sicherheit in der Informationstechnik) [13] geschehen, der als weitere Rechtsgrundlage hinzuzuziehen ist und den Betrieb eines SIEM für solche Betreiber vorsieht. So sind am Ende drei Normen einschlägig: § 28 Abs. 1 Satz 1 Nr. 2 BDSG in Verbindung mit § 31 BDSG sowie § 8a BSIG, die eine sehr enge Zweckbindung vorsehen.

22.3   Kernpunkte sind enge Zweckbindung und stark eingeschränkter Kreis der Zugriffsberechtigten

Den Tätigkeiten der SIEM-Administratoren und -Nutzer sind dabei sehr enge Grenzen zu setzen. Der Zugriff auf personenbezogene Daten in Protokollen, um automatisiert gemeldete Anomalien zu überprüfen, ist in diesem Rahmen zu regeln. Dabei ist grundsätzlich die automatisierte Verarbeitung und Meldung vorzuziehen, auf ein Durchsuchen ohne Anlass durch die Administratoren ist zu verzichten. Weiterhin sollte der Personenkreis, der bei Verdachtsmomenten Zugriff erlangen kann, sehr klein sein. Bei der DB ist dieser klar auf die CSIRT-Mitarbeiter eingeschränkt. Dies alles ist detailliert festzulegen, ein einfaches „Sicherstellen des Betriebs" als Zweck wird hier grundsätzlich nicht reichen. Der Zugriff auf die Protokolle durch andere Protagonisten, wie z. B. die interne Revision oder das Management, ist dabei regelmäßig ausgeschlossen und die Protokolle entziehen sich einer eventuellen Leistungs- und Verhaltenskontrolle, da damit die Zweckbindung eklatant verletzt würde.

Wenn ab dem 25. Mai 2018 die Datenschutzgrundverordnung gilt, wird es keine entsprechende Regelung mehr für den § 31 BDSG geben. In den Erwägungsgründen (ErwG) ist jedoch entsprechendes formuliert. Sie sind Bestandteil der Verordnung und haben insofern Gültigkeit. ErwG 49 erlaubt grundsätzlich die Verarbeitung personenbezogener Daten im Rahmen eines CSIRT (oder CERT), „wie dies für die Gewährleistung der Netz- und Informationssicherheit unbedingt notwendig und verhältnismäßig ist." Er geht dabei explizit auf die Arbeit eines CSIRT ein, denn „Ein solches berechtigtes Interesse könnte beispielsweise darin bestehen, den Zugang Unbefugter zu elektronischen Kommunikationsnetzen und die Verbreitung schädlicher Programmcodes zu verhindern sowie Angriffe in Form der gezielten Überlastung von Servern („Denial of Service"-Angriffe) und Schädigungen von Computer- und elektronischen Kommunikationssystemen abzuwehren." Der ErwG 49 entspricht so den Vorgaben des § 31 BDSG, er bedarf keiner Ergänzung. Die von der Deutschen Bahn getroffenen Maßnahmen im Rahmen des BDSG werden dem ErwG 49 der DSGVO bereits gerecht.

Konzerndatenausschuss der Deutsche Bahn

Im DB Konzern gibt es seit 2002 ein besonderes Gremium, das 10 Mal im Jahr tagt: Der sog. Konzerndatenausschuss. In ihm sitzen Vertreter des HR-Bereiches, der IT-Sicherheit, des Konzernbetriebsrates und des Konzernsprecherausschusses. Geleitet wird er von der Konzerndatenschutzbeauftragten. Dem Ausschuss werden alle die Beschäftigen der Deutschen Bahn betreffenden, konzernrelevanten Verfahren zur Prüfung und Empfehlung vorgelegt. Die Unterlagen umfassen die Verfahrensmeldung [14], eine Verfahrensbeschreibung und ein Datenflussdiagramm. Änderungen und Modifikationen an bestehenden Verfahren werden ebenfalls als sog. „Änderungsmeldung" zur weiteren Empfehlung vorgelegt. Grundsätzlich muss außerdem jedes Verfahren nach 5 Jahren re-evaluiert und dem Ausschuss vorgelegt werden. In der Sitzung erläutert der jeweils zuständige Datenschutzberater die datenschutzrechtlichen Aspekte, die vom Ausschuss dann nochmals detailliert diskutiert werden können. Meist wird auch ein Vertreter der verantwortlichen Stelle eingeladen, der ggfs. weitere Hintergrundinformationen liefern kann. Der Ausschuss kann Auflagen aussprechen und Verfahren auch nicht empfehlen, diese können dann in der nächsten Sitzung nachgebessert wieder vorgelegt werden. Der Ausschuss muss seine Empfehlung einstimmig aussprechen. Nach der Empfehlung (ggfs. mit Auflagen) gibt der Personalverantwortliche das Verfahren frei. Mit dem Ausschuss ist sichergestellt, dass alle Stellen, die für Beschäftigtendaten eine wichtige Rolle spielen, informiert und involviert sind.

Relevante Betriebsvereinbarungen bei der Deutschen Bahn

Die Betriebsparteien im DB Konzern haben zwei wesentliche Konzernbetriebsvereinbarungen (KBV) geschlossen, die für die Datenverarbeitung von Beschäftigtendaten im Rahmen des SIEMs zu betrachten sind: Die KBV Beschäftigtendatenschutz (KBV BDS) und die Rahmen-KBV Beschäftigtendatenverarbeitung (RKBV Beschäftigten DV).

Die KBV BDS bildet das Rahmenwerk, wie und unter welchen Umständen Daten der Beschäftigten verarbeitet werden dürfen. Gerade im Hinblick auf eventuelle Gesetzesverstöße oder Straftaten regelt sie in den §§ 18 und 19, wie bei der Ermittlung von eventuellen Innentätern im Rahmen einer doppelten Verhältnismäßigkeitsprüfung vorzugehen ist. Diese unterliegt zum einen einem arbeitsrechtlichen Prüfschritt. In ihm wird die arbeitsrechtliche Komponente (mindestens abmahnfähig?) beurteilt. Sollte diese Prüfung zu dem Ergebnis gelangen, dass es sich mindestens um einen abmahnfähigen Sachverhalt handelt, folgt zum anderen der zweite, datenschutzrechtliche Prüfschritt (Verhältnismäßigkeit der Maßnahme). In ihm wird entschieden, ob die vorgesehenen Maßnahmen verhältnismäßig sind. Bagatelldelikte werden nicht weiter verfolgt. Im Rahmen des SIEM unterliegen grundsätzlich die Protokolldaten mit den Beschäftigtendaten diesem Prozess, sollten Auffälligkeiten im Rahmen des Beschäftigungsverhältnisses auftreten. Beide Prüfschritte erfolgen unter Beteiligung der Interessensvertreter.

Die RKBV Beschäftigten DV regelt die frühzeitige Einbindung der Datenschutzorganisation und der Interessensvertreter bei der Einführung von Verfahren, die Beschäftigtendaten verarbeiten, sowie das Genehmigungsverfahren solcher Verfahren. In der RKBV ist die Arbeit des Konzerndatenausschusses (KDAS) verankert. Die im Betriebsverfassungsgesetz verankerten Rechte der Arbeitnehmervertreter bleiben dabei unberührt.

Betriebsräte haben gemäß Betriebsverfassungsgesetz (BetrVG) in vielen die Beschäftigten betreffende Maßnahmen ein umfangreiches Mitspracherecht. Sie müssen gemäß § 80 Abs. 1 Nr. 1 BetrVG nicht nur die Einhaltung der Gesetze kontrollieren, sie sind auch mitspracheberechtigt bei der Einführung technischer Verfahren, die dazu geeignet sind, das Verhalten und die Leistung von Beschäftigten zu kontrollieren (§ 87 Abs. 1 Nr. 6 BetrVG). Im Rahmen der Ausübung ihrer Mitbestimmungsrechte können die Betriebsräte die Bedingungen festlegen, unter denen Daten der Beschäftigten verarbeitet werden können. Dies geschieht meist mit Hilfe einer Betriebsvereinbarung, deren Inhalt dann meist viele datenschutzrechtliche Komponenten aufweist. Auch beim SIEM war die Einbindung des Betriebsrates von Nöten, da in den Protokolldaten auch personenbeziehbare Daten von Beschäftigten enthalten sind und hierdurch prinzipiell eine Leistungs- und Verhaltenskontrolle möglich ist – was auszuschließen ist.

22.4   Für den Weg durch die Instanzen ist eine zeitnahe Einbindung nötig

Es war frühzeitig klar, welche Bedeutung der Datenschutz und die Mitbestimmung für den erfolgreichen Einsatz eines SIEMs im DB Konzern haben. Aus diesem Grund wurde frühzeitig und vor der Beschaffung der Weg durch die Instanzen des DB Konzerns gestartet. Hierbei spielt keine Rolle, dass das SIEM beim internen IT-Dienstleister DB Systel aufgebaut und im Auftrag des DB Konzerns betriebsgeführt wird. Entscheidend ist, dass die personenbezogenen Daten in Verantwortung der Geschäftsfelder (aus Sicht DB Systel: interne Kunden) liegen und dass damit die Interessen der Beschäftigten des DB Konzerns (und nicht nur von DB Systel) betroffen sind. Zuständig auf Konzernebene sind der

Konzerndatenschutz sowie der Konzernbetriebsrat. Als verantwortliche Stelle wurde der Bereich der IT-Governance festgelegt, da er die zentrale Steuerung verantwortet und die Konzernvorgaben für sichere IT regelt.

Der Weg durch die Instanzen konnte aufgrund der intensiven und guten Vorbereitung und aufgrund der frühzeitigen aufgenommenen Abstimmung mit Konzerndatenschutz und Konzernbetriebsrat innerhalb von wenigen Monaten erfolgreich umgesetzt werden. In enger Abstimmung mit dem Konzerndatenschutz erstellte die verantwortliche Stelle die Verfahrensmeldung und reichte diese zur Empfehlung beim Konzerndatenschutz ein. In der Diskussion im Konzerndatenausschuss wurde die Notwendigkeit eines SIEM nie in Frage gestellt. Die Rechtsgrundlagen im Rahmen des § 28 Abs. 1 Satz 1 Nr. 2 BDSG i. V. m. § 31 BDSG und § 8a BSIG waren eindeutig, da zwei entscheidende Bedingungen beim Aufbau des SIEMs von Anfang an beachtet wurden:

1. Aufbau eines separaten eigenständigen Logdatenmanagements ausschließlich für die Belange des SIEMs sowie
2. der ausschließliche Zugriff der SIEM-Administratoren und CSIRT-Mitarbeiter auf diese Daten.

Größeren Diskussionsbedarf gab es lediglich bei den Aufbewahrungsfristen der Logdaten. Hier galt es, die im Gesetz geforderte Datensparsamkeit mit dem berechtigten Unternehmensinteresse abzuwägen, die sog. Vorratsdatenspeicherung galt es zu vermeiden. Langfristige Angriffsmuster sollten jedoch erkennbar bleiben, da dies für ein effektives SIEM erforderlich ist. Nach intensiven Diskussionen und Abwägungen wurde die Speicherdauer auf 12 Monate festgelegt. Entscheidend war hierbei die Notwendigkeit von Nachanalysen, um die Infektionswege feststellen und beseitigen zu können. Gerade dies dient auch dem Schutz der Beschäftigten. Diese Vorgehensweise überzeugte letztendlich den Ausschuss, so dass das Verfahren ohne größere Auflagen empfohlen wurde.

Im nächsten Schritt erfolgte die Aufbereitung der Unterlagen – angereichert mit praktischen Beispielen und der Vorstellung eines theoretischen Vorfalles mit einer Ende-zu-Ende Betrachtung, d. h. vom Angriff über die Entdeckung bis zur Abwehr/Eindämmung – und Einreichung beim betreffenden Ausschuss des Konzernbetriebsrats zur betriebsverfassungsrechtlichen Behandlung. Hierbei wurde Wert darauf gelegt, zu zeigen, dass es nicht nur um den Schutz des Unternehmens, sondern auch um den Schutz und Unterstützung der Beschäftigten bis hin zur Entlastung von Beschäftigten bei Security Incidents geht. Dies wurde anhand von konkreten praktischen Beispielen gemeinsam diskutiert und ein gemeinsames Verständnis erarbeitet. Auch für diese, sehr intensiv geführten Diskussionen, hat sich gezeigt, dass die strukturellen Elemente des zentralen Logdatenmanagements für das SIEM sowie der ausschließliche Zugriff der SIEM-Administratoren und CSIRT-Mitarbeiter sehr hilfreich für eine positive Entscheidung waren. Als eine Auflage wurde gefordert, dass regelmäßig über den weiteren Ausbau und insbesondere über hoffentlich erfolgreiche Analyseergebnisse informiert werden sollte.

Nach nun erfolgter Freigabe durch alle notwendigen Gremien der Deutschen Bahn wurden die Beschaffung und der Aufbau des SIEM gestartet.

Epilog

Das Projektteam zur Sicherstellung der datenschutzrechtlichen und mitbestimmungsrelevanten Anforderungen bei der Einführung eines SIEM wurde 2016 bei der Vergabe eines Datenschutz-Awards der Deutschen Bahn honoriert.

Literatur

1. https://www.n-tv.de/politik/Cyber-Angriff-kam-per-E-Mail-article15285896.html
2. Heise Security; „Rekordhack bei Yahoo war drei Mal so groß"; 04.10.2017.
3. BITKOM: „Spionage, Sabotage und Datendiebstahl – Wirtschaftsschutz im digitalen Zeitalter", 2015.
4. RP-Online: „Computer-Virus legt das Lukaskrankenhaus lahm".
5. APT (Advanced Persistent Threat): Angriffe, die, um unerkannt zu bleiben, in kleinen Schritten und über sehr lange Zeiträume vonstattengehen.
6. Social Engineering: gezielte Beeinflussungen von Personen mit dem Ziel, bestimmte Verhaltensweisen hervorzurufen (z. B. Preisgabe von vertraulichen Informationen oder unbewusste Aktivierung eines Schadprogramms über Anhänge in E-Mails).
7. Verizon's Data Breach Investigations Report 2014.
8. Verizon's Data Breach Investigations Report 2014.
9. BVerfG, Urteil vom 15.01.1983.
10. Ganz abgesehen davon, dass der EUGH auch IP-Adressen als personenbezogenes Datum beurteilt. EUGH – Rechtssache C-582/14.
11. „Personenbezogene Daten, die ausschließlich zu Zwecken der Datenschutzkontrolle, der Datensicherung oder zur Sicherstellung eines ordnungsgemäßen Betriebes einer Datenverarbeitungsanlage gespeichert werden, dürfen nur für diese Zwecke verwendet werden."
12. Vergleiche auch Plath (Hrsg.), BDSG DSGVO, 2. Auflage 2016.
13. „Betreiber Kritischer Infrastrukturen sind verpflichtet, spätestens zwei Jahre nach Inkrafttreten der Rechtsverordnung nach § 10 Absatz 1 angemessene organisatorische und technische Vorkehrungen zur Vermeidung von Störungen der Verfügbarkeit, Integrität, Authentizität und Vertraulichkeit ihrer informationstechnischen Systeme, Komponenten oder Prozesse zu treffen, die für die Funktionsfähigkeit der von ihnen betriebenen kritischen Infrastrukturen maßgeblich sind. Dabei soll der Stand der Technik eingehalten werden. Organisatorische und technische Vorkehrungen sind angemessen, wenn der dafür erforderliche Aufwand nicht außer Verhältnis zu den Folgen eines Ausfalls oder einer Beeinträchtigung der betroffenen Kritischen Infrastruktur steht."
14. § 4d BDSG – Meldepflicht und § 4e BDSG – Inhalt der Meldepflicht.

Divide et Impera: Sicherheit durch Separation

23

Dirk Loss und Magnus Harlander

Zusammenfassung

Das bewährte Prinzip der Separation (die Aufteilung eines Systems in Sicherheitsdomänen und Kontrolle der Kommunikation zwischen ihnen) sollte bei der Umsetzung einer Cyber-Sicherheitsstrategie als Best Practice rekursiv auf alle Ebenen eines Informationssystems angewandt werden. Es ist nicht nur für die Abgrenzung von Netzbereichen sinnvoll (z. B. mit Firewalls und VPN-Gateways), sondern auch zur Aufteilung unterschiedlich kritischer Komponenten innerhalb einzelner IT-Systeme – insbesondere solcher, die Sicherheitsfunktionen übernehmen und daher besonders vertrauenswürdig, korrekt und nachvollziehbar gestaltet sein müssen. Das Kapitel stellt das MILS-Konzept als übergreifenden Ansatz zur Entwicklung einer separierten Systemarchitektur vor und gibt einen Überblick über die wichtigsten betriebssystemnahen Mechanismen zu deren Realisierung.

23.1 Sicherheitsprobleme durch Komplexität

Die hohe Komplexität heutiger Informationssysteme macht es schwierig, sie geeignet abzusichern. Bereits eine einzige Schwachstelle in einer einzelnen Software-Komponente kann die Kette ineinandergreifender Sicherheitsmaßnahmen durchbrechen und einen Angriff oder einen Sicherheitsverstoß ermöglichen. Und das Problem nimmt zu: Die Anzahl der vernetzten Hard- und Software-Komponenten und die Abhängigkeiten

D. Loss (✉) · M. Harlander
genua GmbH, Kirchheim, Deutschland
E-Mail: dirk_loss@genua.de; harlan@harlan.de

© Springer Fachmedien Wiesbaden GmbH, ein Teil von Springer Nature 2018   285
M. Bartsch, S. Frey (Hrsg.), *Cybersecurity Best Practices*,
https://doi.org/10.1007/978-3-658-21655-9_23

zwischen ihnen steigen stark an. Der Umfang an Programmcode in den einzelnen Software-Komponenten wächst stetig und damit statistisch auch die Anzahl sicherheitsrelevanter Bugs. Dies wird sowohl von Malware-Autoren als auch von gezielten Angreifern ausgenutzt. Weil Informationstechnik längst nicht mehr nur Office-IT heißt, sondern auch Produktionsumgebungen und kritische Infrastrukturen mit dem Internet verbunden werden, wächst nicht nur die Angriffsfläche, sondern auch das Schadenspotenzial. Nicht in allen Umgebungen lassen sich regelmäßig Software-Updates einspielen, um Schwachstellen zu beheben. Die Komplexität steht der gewünschten Beherrschbarkeit und Verlässlichkeit der Systeme entgegen.

23.2 Mehr Beherrschbarkeit durch Separation

Um der zunehmenden Komplexität entgegenzuwirken und die Systeme wieder nachvollziehbar und beherrschbar zu machen, empfiehlt sich ein Prinzip, das bereits die alten Römer erfolgreich angewandt haben: *Divide et impera* (teile und herrsche). Unterteile dein Land in mehrere Bereiche und kontrolliere den Informationsfluss zwischen ihnen. Im Imperium Romanum ging es um den Informationsfluss zwischen den unterworfenen Provinzen; sie durften nicht direkt miteinander kommunizieren bzw. Verträge abschließen, sondern nur vermittelt über die Zentrale in Rom. So wollte man verhindern, dass sich die Provinzen zusammenschließen, zu mächtig werden und sich den Regeln Roms widersetzen. Bei der Umsetzung einer Cyber-Sicherheitsstrategie geht es nicht um Provinzen, sondern um Software, IT-Systeme und Netzwerke; das Prinzip ist allerdings das gleiche: Aufteilung in Sicherheitsdomänen und strikte Kontrolle der Kommunikation zwischen ihnen. Das klassische Beispiel hierzu in der IT ist die Separation von Netzen mit Sicherheitsgateways. Firewalls trennen das interne Netz vom Internet und prüfen alle übertragenen Daten gegen ein konfiguriertes Regelwerk, so dass definierte Sicherheitsvorgaben (Security Policies) eingehalten werden.

Die klare und sorgfältige Trennung der Sicherheitsdomänen bietet einige Vorteile in Bezug auf die Sicherheit: Der Informationsfluss zwischen den Sicherheitsdomänen kann strikt kontrolliert werden, um zu verhindern, dass geheime Daten ungewollt in die andere Sicherheitsdomäne gelangen (Schutz der Vertraulichkeit). Die Limitierung des Datenflusses verringert die Gefahr von Datenlecks. Zum anderen lässt sich verhindern, dass Systeme manipuliert werden (Schutz der Integrität) oder dass durch Angriffe oder Überlast die Nutzung von Systemen beeinträchtigt wird (Schutz der Verfügbarkeit). Dies ist insbesondere relevant für Systemkomponenten mit sicherheitskritischen Funktionen.

Durch die Kontrolle des Informationsflusses und die Konzentration auf klare Schnittstellen zwischen den Sicherheitsdomänen wird die Angriffsfläche minimiert und damit zugleich die Gefahr, dass ein System erfolgreich angegriffen werden kann. Sollten Angriffe erfolgreich sein oder sonstige Fehlfunktionen auftreten, ist zunächst nur eine Sicherheitsdomäne betroffen. Die Informationsflusskontrolle verhindert, dass die Störung bzw. der Angriff sich auch auf Systeme in anderen Sicherheitsdomänen ausbreitet.

Tab. 23.1 Einige Normen und Standards, die Domänentrennung/Separation fordern

Norm/Standard (Anwendungsbereich)	Relevante Abschnitte
IEC 62443 (Sicherheit industrieller Anlagen):	IEC 62443-3-2 Zones & Conduits
ISO/IEC 15408 Common Criteria (Zertifizierung von IT-Sicherheitsprodukten	ADV_ARC Definition von Sicherheitsdomänen
SP 800-27 Rev A (Engineering Principles for Information Technology Security)	Principle 21 Boundary mechanisms, Principle 31 Information Domains
IT-Grundschutz (Standardsicherheitsmaßnahmen für normalen Schutzbedarf):	B 3301 Sicherheitsgateways, M 2.70, M 5.62
NERC CIP (Energiesektor):	CIP-005-5 Elektronischer Perimeter
PCI DSS (Payment Card Industry Data Security Standard):	Restrict connections between untrusted networks and any system components in the cardholder data environment.
IEC 61508 (Safety)	Part 3, Annex F (F2, F4, F5): Independence of execution, non-interference
DO-178C (Luftfahrt)	Section 2.4.1 Software Partitionierung
IEC 61508 Part 3 (Safety Zertifizierung)	Non-Interference
ISO 26262 (Safety für den Automobilsektor)	Part 6, Annex D: freedom from interference

Eine geeignete *Separation* vorausgesetzt, lassen sich weniger vertrauenswürdige Elemente mit vertrauenswürdigeren Elementen in einem System kombinieren. Im besten Fall lassen sich sogar einzelne, ausreichend separierte Systemkomponenten als Module ändern oder hinzufügen, ohne dass dies Auswirkungen auf Komponenten in anderen Sicherheitsdomänen hat. Zertifizierungen bzw. Prüfverfahren müssen dann nicht neu durchlaufen werden oder werden zumindest vereinfacht. Dies erlaubt eine flexible Anpassung von Systemen im Feld.

Domänentrennung bzw. Separation wird bereits in einigen Normen und Standards gefordert (s. Tab. 23.1). Andererseits lässt sich mit einer Aufteilung in Sicherheitsdomänen umgekehrt ggf. der Geltungsbereich von Compliance-Vorgaben begrenzen.

23.3 MILS als Vorgehensweise zur Konzeption einer angemessenen Separierung

Wie geht man nun am besten vor, um eine geeignete Separation zu konzipieren? Einen Rahmen bietet der *MILS*-Ansatz (Vanfleet et al. 2005; Alves-Foss et al. 2006), der auf Überlegungen britischer Sicherheitsforscher aus den frühen 1980er-Jahren basiert (Rushby und Randell 1983) und um die Jahrtausendwende zunächst beim Militär und in der Flugzeugindustrie eingesetzt wurde. MILS – ehemals eine Kurzbezeichnung für Multiple Independent Levels of Security, heute ein feststehender Ausdruck – sieht vor, das Problem auf zwei Ebenen zu betrachten: zunächst auf der Policy-Ebene und erst danach auf Implementierungsebene (s. Abb. 23.1).

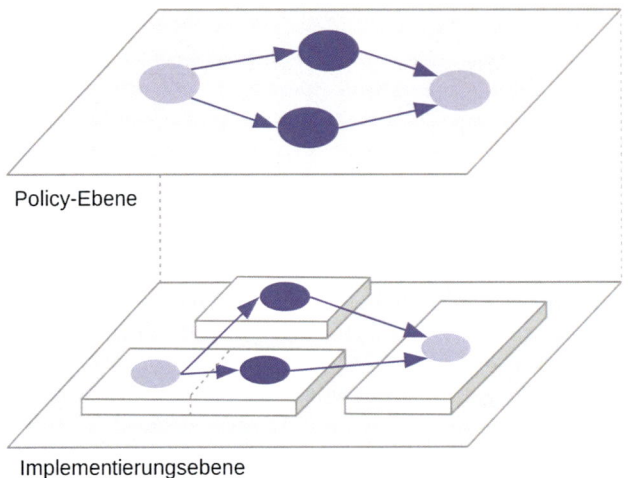

Policy-Ebene

Implementierungsebene

Abb. 23.1. MILS-Ebenen

Auf der Policy-Ebene wird ganz abstrakt ein Graph erstellt aus Komponenten und erlaubten Kommunikationsverbindungen zwischen ihnen. Knoten symbolisieren die Komponenten, gerichtete Kanten die direkten Kommunikationsverbindungen bzw. Informationsflüsse. Um die gewünschte Security Policy durchzusetzen, müssen in der Regel manche Knoten als vertrauenswürdig angenommen werden, andere jedoch nicht. Ziel ist es, dass System so zu entwerfen, dass die Komplexität der vertrauenswürdigen Knoten minimiert wird (Rushby und Randell 2007). Damit wird es später einfacher, diese für die Sicherheit entscheidenden Komponenten korrekt zu implementieren und ihre Funktionsweise nachzuvollziehen. Die Modellierung sollte so gewählt werden, dass jeder vertrauenswürdige Knoten eine möglichst einfache Funktionalität und eine klare Security Policy hat. Ist die Funktionalität oder die Security Policy komplex, wird der Knoten in mehrere Unterknoten aufgeteilt. In der Regel sind dann auch zusätzliche Kommunikationsverbindungen einzufügen.

Durch die geschilderte Vorgehensweise werden bereits beim Entwurf des Systems die Elemente mit Sicherheitsrelevanz (in Abb. 23.2 dunkel dargestellt) von denen ohne Sicherheitsrelevanz getrennt. Wenn es im entstehenden Diagramm zwischen zwei Knoten keine Kante gibt, bedeutet dies, dass es zwischen den entsprechenden Komponenten keinen direkten Informationsfluss geben darf. An diesen Stellen ist auf Implementierungsebene ein geeigneter Separationsmechanismus erforderlich, um diesen Informationsfluss zu unterbinden. Komponenten, die überhaupt keine Kanten haben, können völlig isoliert werden.

Die für die Umsetzung benötigten Ressourcen und ihre Kosten bleiben auf der Policy-Ebene noch völlig unberücksichtigt. Dies geschieht erst in einem zweiten Schritt auf der Implementierungsebene: Zunächst geht es dabei darum, wie die Komponenten auf physische Ressourcen verteilt werden. Hier ist eine Abwägung zu treffen: Konzeptionell am

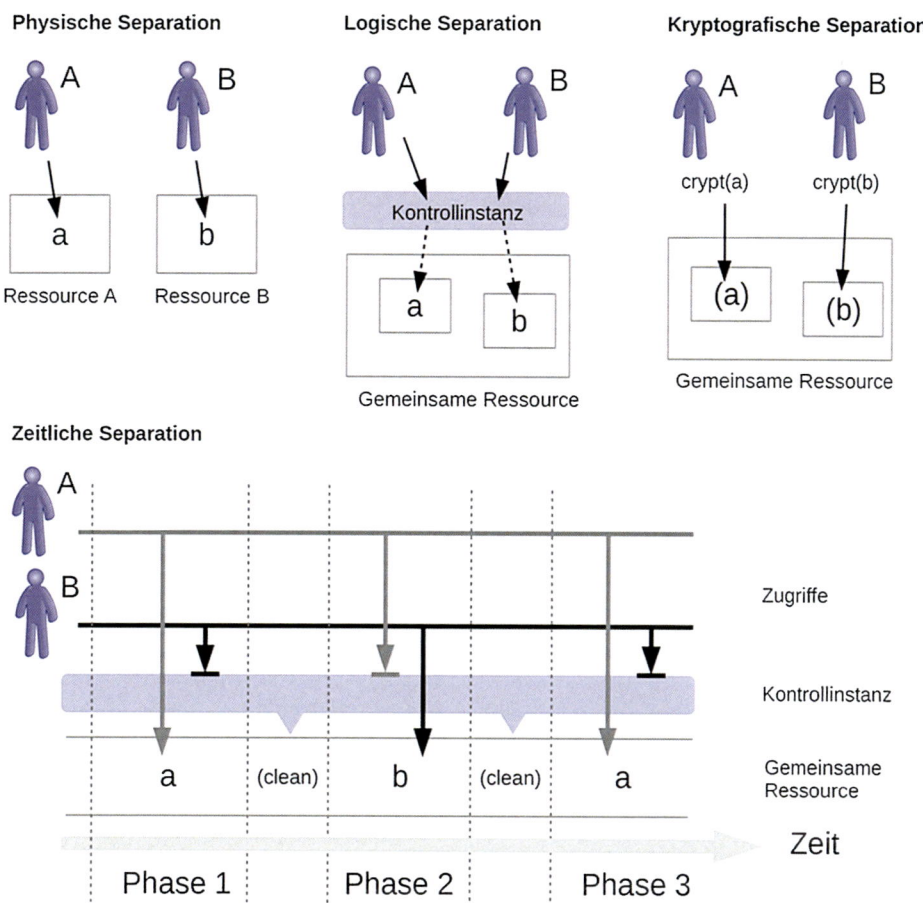

Abb. 23.2 Varianten der Separation: physisch, logisch, zeitlich, kryptografisch

einfachsten ist die Bereitstellung eigener Ressourcen für jede Komponente. Diese physische Separation ist sehr stark, führt aber zu hohen Kosten. Werden dagegen Ressourcen von mehreren Komponenten gemeinsam genutzt, steigt die Wirtschaftlichkeit, aber es muss durch besondere Mechanismen für eine geeignete Separation gesorgt werden. Diese Separation kann logisch, zeitlich oder kryptografisch realisiert werden (Rushby und Randell 1983, vgl. Abb. 23.2).

Logische Separation bedeutet, dass zwischen den Komponenten (den Subjekten) und der Ressource (dem Objekt) eine Instanz eingefügt wird, die alle Zugriffe der Komponenten auf die gemeinsame Ressource kontrolliert. Diese Art von Kontrollinstanz wurde bereits in einer der ersten Veröffentlichungen zur IT-Sicherheit (Anderson 1972) beschrieben und dort als Referenzmonitor bezeichnet. Ein Referenzmonitor soll für alle Zugriffe verwendet werden (always invoked) und nicht umgehbar sein (non-bypassable). Er soll nicht manipulierbar (tamperproof) und klein genug sein, dass man seine Funktionalität untersuchen und nachvollziehen kann (evaluable).

Bei *zeitlicher Separation* (engl. periods processing) wird die gemeinsame Ressource von einer Kontrollinstanz abwechselnd jeweils genau einer Sicherheitsdomäne zugeteilt. Separation bedeutet hier, dass die Informationsverarbeitung der einen Sicherheitsdomäne nicht die Verarbeitung einer nachfolgend aktiven Sicherheitsdomäne beeinflussen kann. Dazu muss die Ressource jeweils vor dem Wechsel der Sicherheitsdomänen in einen definierten Zustand zurückgesetzt, d. h. gesäubert werden.

Kryptografische Separation bietet sich an, wenn die gemeinsam genutzte Ressource eine Kommunikationsverbindung bzw. ein Netz ist. Die zu übertragenden Daten werden dann vor dem Versand mit einem für die Sicherheitsdomäne spezifischen Schlüssel verschlüsselt und vor dem Empfang wieder entschlüsselt. So ist gewährleistet, dass die Daten nicht von Komponenten einer anderen Sicherheitsdomäne gelesen oder verändert werden können und Komponenten aus unterschiedlichen Sicherheitsdomänen können sich eine gemeinsame Kommunikationsinfrastruktur teilen (s. Abb. 23.3).

Eine vollständige *Isolation* von Sicherheitsdomänen, ohne jede Kommunikationsmöglichkeit zwischen ihnen, ist in aller Regel nicht nützlich. Das heißt in einem nächsten Schritt ist festzulegen, welche Daten zwischen den Komponenten ausgetauscht werden dürfen und auf welche Weise dies geschehen soll. Aus Sicherheitssicht ist es wünschenswert, die Kommunikation möglichst minimal zu gestalten. Für die Implementierung ist es ferner günstig, wenn die Kommunikation einem wohldefiniertem Kommunikationsprotokoll folgt und Datenformate benutzt, die sich einfach und mit hoher Zuverlässigkeit prüfen lassen.

Die geschilderte Aufteilung eines Systems in Sicherheitsdomänen kann rekursiv auf jede einzelne Sicherheitsdomäne bzw. Komponente angewendet werden. Netze oder Subnetze werden dabei z. B. in weitere Subnetze aufgeteilt. Aber auch für einzelne IT-Systeme kann eine interne Separation in unterschiedliche Bereiche sinnvoll sein. Insbesondere empfiehlt sich dies für Komponenten mit Sicherheitsfunktion, z. B. Firewalls oder Kryptokomponenten. So entsteht eine ganze *Separationshierarchie* (s.Abb. 23.4), in der auf verschiedenen Ebenen sicherheitskritische Komponenten voneinander getrennt und nur über definierte Kommunikationskanäle miteinander verbunden sind. Wie sich innerhalb von IT-Systemen Sicherheitsdomänen voneinander abgrenzen lassen, wird im folgenden Abschnitt genauer beschrieben.

Abb. 23.3 Verschlüsselung von Netzwerkverbindungen als Beispiel für kryptografische Separation

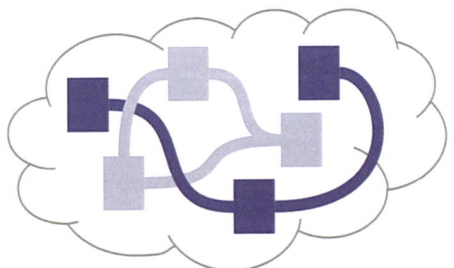

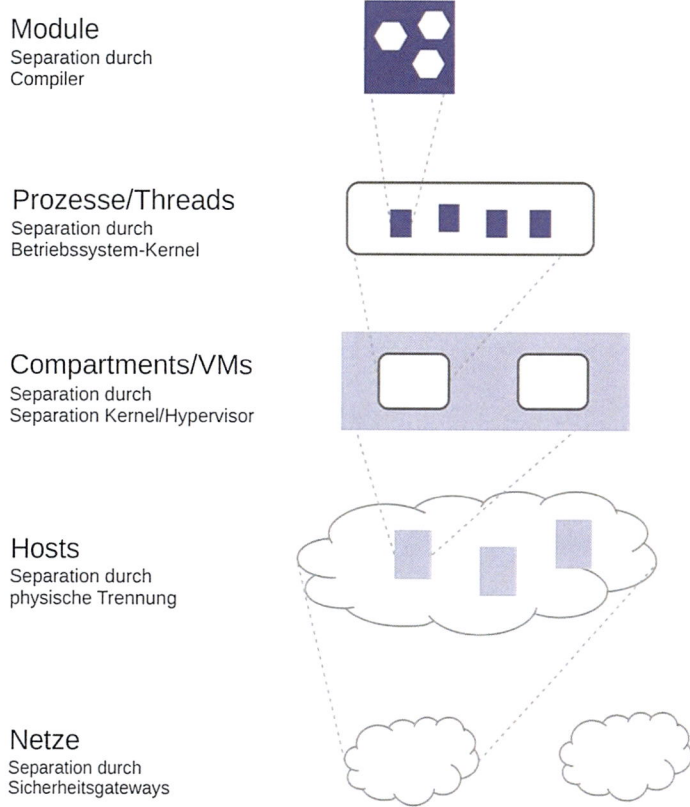

Module
Separation durch
Compiler

Prozesse/Threads
Separation durch
Betriebssystem-Kernel

Compartments/VMs
Separation durch
Separation Kernel/Hypervisor

Hosts
Separation durch
physische Trennung

Netze
Separation durch
Sicherheitsgateways

Abb. 23.4 Separationshierarchie

23.4 Mechanismen für die Separation innerhalb von IT-Systemen

Die Forderung nach Domänentrennung innerhalb von IT-Systemen mit Sicherheitsfunktionen findet sich bereits im Orange Book (Department of Defense 1985), dem ersten US-amerikanischen Kriterienwerk zur Prüfung und Zertifizierung von IT-Systemen. Die Kurzbezeichnung der Evaluierungsstufe B3 nimmt den Begriff *Security Domains* sogar in ihren Titel auf. Auch das aktuelle internationale Kriterienwerk (Common Criteria 2017) fordert *Domänentrennung* (domain separation) für IT-Systeme.

Im Laufe der Jahrzehnte wurden zahlreiche Mechanismen entwickelt, um innerhalb eines IT-Systems verschiedene Sicherheitsdomänen zu unterscheiden und sie technisch voneinander abzugrenzen. Der folgende Abschnitt gibt einen Überblick (vgl. Abb. 23.5).

Klassisch und in fast allen gängigen Betriebssystemen implementiert ist die Aufteilung der Anwendungen in *Prozesse*. Jeder Prozess hat seinen eigenen Speicherbereich; Kommunikation mit anderen Prozessen ist nur über Mechanismen des Betriebssystems möglich.

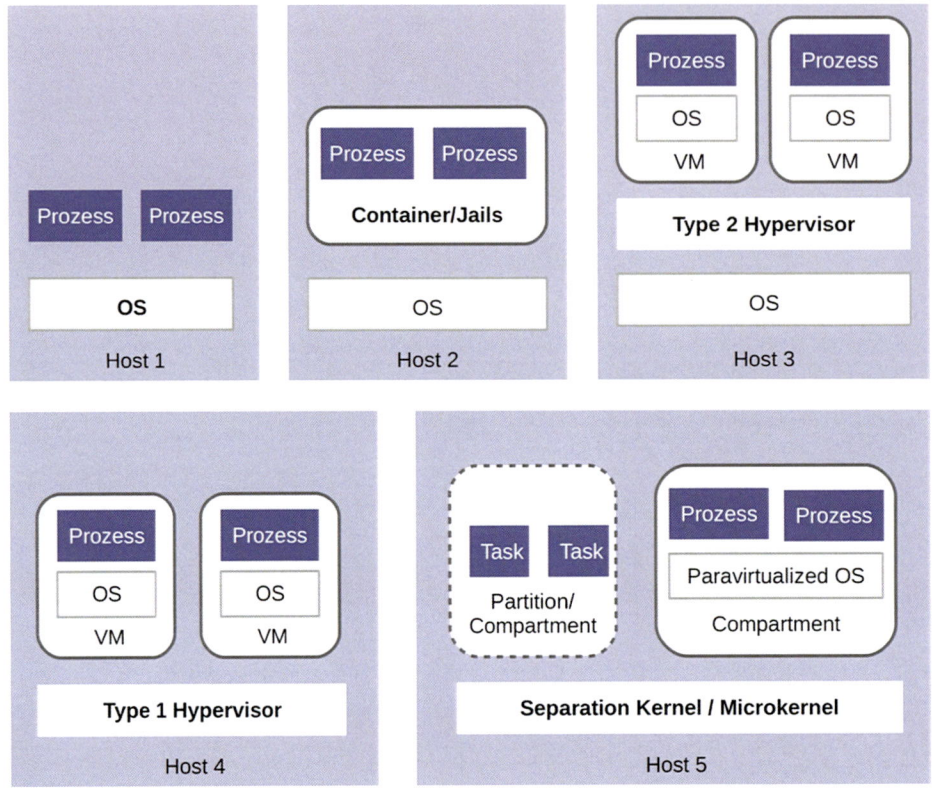

Abb. 23.5 Betriebssystemnahe Separationsmechanismen innerhalb von IT-Systemen

Der Betriebssystemkern fungiert hier als Kontrollinstanz. Er läuft in einem privilegierten Hardwaremodus (für Intel-Prozessoren: Ring 0) und ist daher besonders privilegiert, so dass die Kontrolle nicht umgangen werden kann.

Über die Jahre wurden dann einige weitere Techniken entwickelt, die es erlauben, abgegrenzte Ablaufumgebungen für Prozesse zu realisieren:

In UNIX-Betriebssystemen gibt es schon seit Anfang der 1980er-Jahre einen System-aufruf *chroot(2)*, der es nur erlaubt, Prozessen eine eingeschränkte Sicht auf das Dateisystem zu geben. Dieser Mechanismus ließ sich jedoch von Angreifern leicht aushebeln und war daher kein wirklicher Separationsmechanismus, sondern nur für Entwicklungszwecke und vertrauenswürdige Umgebungen zu gebrauchen.

Unter dem Betriebssystem FreeBSD wurde ein erweitertes chroot Konzept namens *Jails* entwickelt, das es erlaubt, auch User, Prozesse und Netzwerkzugriffe zu separieren (FreeBSD 2017). Das Betriebssystem Solaris bietet mit *Zones* einen ähnlichen Mechanismus (Oracle 2014). Für Linux gab es schon längere Zeit die Projekte OpenVZ (SWsoft 2005) und Linux VServer. Allerdings wurden die für sie nötigen Patches lange Zeit nicht oder nur eingeschränkt in den offiziellen Kernel aufgenommen. LXC (Linux Containers 2017) nutzt neue Features des Linux Kernel (Namespaces und Control Groups).

Namespaces stellen dabei für jede Sicherheitsdomäne einen eigenen Namensraum für Ressourcen bereit. Mit Control Groups lässt sich die Nutzung von Ressourcen (Zugriffe auf Dateisystem, Geräte, Speicher, Netzwerk, CPU) für eine Gruppe von Prozessen begrenzen. Mit diesen Mechanismen werden sogenannte *Container* gebildet, um Ablaufumgebungen voneinander abzugrenzen. Jeder Container teilt sich den Kernel (und gegebenenfalls auch andere Teile des Dateisystems) mit dem Host und mit anderen Containern. Dies bedeutet, dass die Container das gleiche Betriebssystem verwenden wie der Host. Außerdem heißt es, dass der Kernel sichere Mechanismen beinhalten muss, um die Container voneinander zu separieren. Gelingt es einem Angreifer, durch Ausnutzung einer Schwachstelle im Kernel eigenen Programmcode im Kernel auszuführen, kann er auch auf andere Container zugreifen und die Separation ist umgegangen. Da die Schnittstelle zwischen Container und Kernel sehr groß ist (bei Linux mehrere hundert Systemcalls), ist die Gefahr, dass solche Schwachstellen existieren, recht groß.

Bei Virtualisierungslösungen stellt der *Hypervisor* oder *Virtual Machine Manager* (VMM) eine Ablaufumgebung bereit, die einer vollständigen Hardware gleicht (Vollvirtualisierung, z. B. VMware, Linux KVM, Microsoft Hyper-V) oder speziell für Virtualisierungszwecke angepasste Hardware-Schnittstellen bietet (Paravirtualisierung, z. B. Xen). In jeder Sicherheitsdomäne läuft eine virtuelle Maschine (VM) mit ihrem eigenen Kernel. Die VMs können also andere Betriebssysteme einsetzen als der Host. Type 1 Hypervisoren laufen direkt auf der Hardware, Type 2 Hypervisoren dagegen auf einem Betriebssystem (OS).

Ein Problem der Separation durch Virtualisierungstechnologie ist, dass ein typischer Hypervisor sehr komplex ist und daher viel Programmcode umfasst. Daher gibt es immer wieder Schwachstellen in der Implementierung, die ein Ausbrechen aus der VM (einen sogenannten „Virtual Machine Escape") und Zugriff auf den Host bzw. andere VMs erlauben. In den letzten Jahren wurden in vielen bekannten Virtualisierungslösungen für PCs (KVM, Xen, Hyper-V, Virtual Box) entsprechende Schwachstellen gefunden (z. B. Mitre 2014; Geffner 2015; Xen Project 2016; Microsoft 2017).

Insbesondere für sicherheitskritische Anwendungsfälle muss daher das Ziel sein, die Separationsfunktionalität in möglichst wenig Code zu implementieren. Dies verringert die Wahrscheinlichkeit für Bugs und erleichtert es, den Code nachzuvollziehen und auf Schwachstellen zu überprüfen. *Microkernel* führen diese Idee der Minimalisierung ins Extrem: Ein Microkernel soll nur solche Funktionen enthalten, die sich nicht außerhalb des Kernels implementieren lassen (Liedtke 1995).

Weil Microkernel so extrem klein sind und sich daher gut evaluieren lassen, wurde in diesem Jahrtausend damit begonnen, sie im Sinne eines Separation Kernels (Rushby 1981) als Separationsplattform für sicherheitskritische Anwendungen einzusetzen. Ihre Möglichkeiten der Interprozesskommunikation werden dabei genutzt, um erlaubte Kommunikationsverbindungen zwischen den einzelnen Sicherheitsdomänen (einzelne Tasks oder Compartments als Gruppen von Tasks) zu definieren.

Ein *Separation Kernel* erlaubt keine Interaktion zwischen einer Komponenten und einer anderen, außer über konfigurierte Kanäle. Er ist ausschließlich verantwortlich für die

Separation (der Komponenten und Kanäle) und die Einhaltung der festgelegten Konfiguration (der Verbindungen). Welche Policy durchgesetzt wird, lässt sich hier, wie im vorhergehenden Abschnitt geschildert, flexibel für den jeweiligen Anwendungszweck des Systems festlegen. Die Policy ergibt sich durch die Funktionen der einzelnen Komponenten sowie durch die möglichen Kommunikationsverbindungen zwischen ihnen (vgl. Abb. 23.1). Will man beispielsweise sicherstellen, dass alle zwischen zwei Komponenten übertragenen Daten kontrolliert werden, fügt man einfach dazwischen eine zusätzliche Prüfkomponente ein und konfiguriert das System so, dass die beiden äußeren Komponenten nur über die Prüfkomponente miteinander kommunizieren können.

23.5   Anwendungsbeispiel Datendiode

Separation Kernel erlauben die Schaffung von sogenannten *Mixed Criticality Systems*, bei denen einzelne Partitionen bzw. Compartments, die einen hohen Schutzbedarf aufweisen, mit anderen gekoppelt werden, die nur einen niedrigen Schutzbedarf haben. Ein Beispiel für ein solches System ist eine sogenannte logische Datendiode.

Datendioden sind spezielle Sicherheitsgateways, die Datenverkehr nur in eine Richtung erlauben. Sie werden einerseits im Geheimschutzbereich eingesetzt, um Daten von außen beziehen zu können, aber keine vertraulichen Informationen preiszugeben, andererseits in Industrieumgebungen, um Status- und Maschinendaten für Auswertungen nach außen zu leiten, aber gleichzeitig Maschinen und Anlagen zuverlässig vor Angriffen von außen zu schützen. Bei klassischen Datendioden erfolgt die Separation auf physischer Ebene; der Rückkanal der Glasfaserverbindung zwischen den verbundenen Netzen ist durchtrennt. Dadurch können jedoch keine Informationen übertragen werden, ob die Daten korrekt beim Empfänger angekommen sind. Auch eine Flusskontrolle zur Ermittlung einer optimalen Sendegeschwindigkeit ist nicht möglich. Dies führt zu Problemen mit der Zuverlässigkeit und der Performance der Datenübertragung. Logische Datendioden dagegen kontrollieren den Datenfluss auf höheren Ebenen des OSI/ISO-Schichtenmodells und bieten einen minimalen Rückkanal für Empfangsbestätigungen und Flusskontrolle.

Abb. 23.6 zeigt beispielhaft, wie eine logische Datendiode unter Berücksichtigung des Separationsprinzips implementiert werden kann, sodass die zentrale

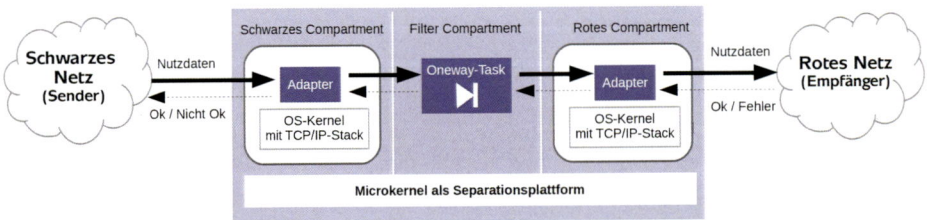

Abb. 23.6 Separation interner Sicherheitsdomänen innerhalb einer logischen Datendiode

Sicherheitsfunktionalität gut nachvollziehbar und evaluierbar ist. Die Datendiode ist eine Appliance aus Hard- und Software, die zwischen zwei Netze eingebaut wird und eine unidirektionale Datenübertragung von der schwarzen auf die rote Seite ermöglicht. Basis der Software ist ein Microkernel, der die vorhandenen Hardware-Ressourcen aufteilt und dadurch drei Compartments voneinander separiert. Der Microkernel stellt sicher, dass eine Kommunikation zwischen den äußeren Compartments nur über den OneWay-Task möglich ist.

Die beiden äußeren Compartments bilden die Schnittstelle zum schwarzen bzw. roten Netz und nehmen die Daten vom Sender an bzw. leiten sie an den Empfänger weiter. Sie beinhalten jeweils ein komplettes Betriebssystem (OS) mit Kernel, Netzwerkkartentreibern und TCP/IP-Stack. Außerdem enthalten sie Adapter, um die nach außen gesprochenen Kommunikationsprotokolle an den Einweg-Transfer anzupassen.

Im Filter Compartment in der Mitte läuft ein OneWay-Task, der die zentrale Sicherheitsfunktionalität übernimmt. Er kopiert die Daten im Arbeitsspeicher von einem äußeren Compartment ins andere und stellt dabei sicher, dass Nutzdaten nur von Schwarz nach Rot übertragen werden und in Gegenrichtung ausschließlich eine 1-Bit Empfangsbestätigung (Ok/Nicht Ok) am Ende der Datenübertragung durchgelassen wird. Der OneWay-Task läuft direkt auf dem Microkernel, umfasst nur wenige Hundert Programmzeilen und hat selbst keinen Zugriff auf Netzwerkschnittstellen oder andere Geräte.

Sicherheitskritisch sind in dieser logischen Datendiode nur der Microkernel und der OneWay-Task; eventuelle Fehler in den eher komplexen Software-Komponenten der äußeren Compartments gefährden nicht die zentrale Filterfunktionalität. Gelingt es beispielsweise einem Angreifer, über eine Schwachstelle eigenen Code in einem der äußeren Compartments auszuführen, kann er immer noch nicht den OneWay-Task umgehen oder manipulieren. Aufgrund der strikten Separation wird die Datendiode besonders resistent gegen Angriffe. Zudem kann sich eine Sicherheitsevaluierung des Systems auf die wenigen Tausend Programmzeilen des Microkernels und die nur wenigen Hundert Programmzeilen des OneWay-Tasks konzentrieren. So lässt sich leichter das nötige Vertrauen in die Korrektheit und Zuverlässigkeit der Datendiode gewinnen.

23.6   Separation innerhalb einzelner Programme

Die rekursive Verfeinerung der Separation lässt sich von der Ebene der Betriebssysteme auch bis auf die Ebene einzelner Programme weiterführen.

23.6.1   Privilege Separation

Ein Beispiel für die Separation auf der Ebene von Programmen ist die sogenannte *Privilege Separation* für Serverprozesse. Sie erfordert eine besondere Strukturierung des Programms und ist daher bereits bei der Entwicklung zu berücksichtigen: Der Server wird aufgeteilt in zwei Prozesse, einen Monitor, der alle Aktionen ausführt, die besondere

Privilegien benötigen und einen Slave für alle restlichen Aktionen – insbesondere solche, die Daten unbekannter Herkunft bearbeiten. Der Slave läuft in einer eingeschränkten Umgebung (z. B. chroot) und kann nur über Nachrichten an den Monitor mit dem System interagieren. Der Master erlaubt bestimmte Nachrichten des Slaves nur in bestimmten Phasen der Sitzung. Sobald sich ein Benutzer authentisiert hat, läuft der Slave mit dessen Benutzerrechten, davor als unprivilegierter System-User.

23.6.2 Module

In der Software-Entwicklung ist das Separationsprinzip bereits seit den 1970er-Jahren unter dem Begriff *Modularisierung* bekannt (Parnas 1972). Modularisierung meint die logische Aufteilung eines Gesamtsystems (z. B. eines Programms) in mehrere relativ abgeschlossene Einheiten (Module), die jeweils bestimmte Funktionalitäten realisieren und nur über definierte Schnittstellen miteinander interagieren. Dass nur die gewünschten Interaktionen möglich sind, wird hier bereits zur Entwicklungszeit vom Compiler durchgesetzt, der Programmcode generiert, welcher die gewünschten Eigenschaften bzw. Beschränkungen hat oder der Komponenten besitzt, die die Prüfungen zur Laufzeit des Programms durchführen. Relevant sind hier sowohl die Struktur der Abhängigkeiten zwischen den Modulen (wer kommuniziert mit wem) als auch die übertragenen Daten (z. B. die Datentypen von übergebenen Argumenten). Die Modularisierung erleichtert es, die Funktionsweise des Gesamtsystems nachzuvollziehen, weil sie erlaubt, zunächst jedes Modul für sich zu analysieren. Anschließend kann das Zusammenwirken der Module betrachtet werden. Dabei reicht es, die aufgerufenen bzw. angebotenen Dienste an den Schnittstellen zu untersuchen. Wie die Implementierung innerhalb jedes Moduls aussieht, muss auf dieser Ebene dann nicht mehr betrachtet werden.

23.7 Zusammenfassung

Separation sollte als allgemeines Strukturierungsprinzip zur Entwicklung sicherer und nachvollziehbarer Systeme verstanden werden. Es lässt sich rekursiv auf allen Ebenen eines Informationssystems anwenden, von der Aufteilung von Netzen in einzelne Zonen mit Hilfe von Sicherheitsgateways oder VPN-Gateways über die Aufteilung von Funktionen auf physisch separate Hardwarekomponenten und die Bildung unterschiedlich kritischer Compartments innerhalb einzelner IT-Systeme bis hin zur Modularisierung einzelner Programmteile.

Immer geht es darum, die einzelnen Bereiche bzw. Sicherheitsdomänen mit Kontrollmechanismen geeignet zu kapseln, die Angriffsfläche zu minimieren und die Nachvollziehbarkeit zu erhöhen. Zur Verfügung stehen dabei vier grundsätzliche Varianten der Separation: physisch, logisch, zeitlich oder kryptografisch. Welche Variante und welche Implementierungsmechanismen im Einzelfall geeignet sind, hängt vom Anwendungsfall ab. Für hochsichere hostbasierte Separation eignen sich insbesondere Microkernel, da sich aufgrund der minimalen Größe und Funktionalität ihre Sicherheitseigenschaften gut nachvollziehen und verifizieren lassen.

Literatur

Alves-Foss J, Oman PW, Taylor C, Harrison WS (2006) The MILS architecture for high-assurance embedded systems. International Journal of Embedded Systems, vol. 2. no. 3/4, pp. 239-247

Anderson JP (1972) Computer Security Technology Planning Study. http://seclab.cs.ucdavis.edu/projects/history/papers/ande72.pdf. Zugegriffen: 2017-11-14

Common Criteria (2017) Common Criteria for Information Technology Security Evaluation. Part 3: Security assurance requirements. ADV_ARC. Version 3.1. Revision 5. http://www.commoncriteria.org. Zugegriffen: 2017-11-14

Department of Defense (1985) Trusted Computer System Evaluation Criteria. DoD 5200.28-STD. https://csrc.nist.gov/publications/history/dod85.pdf. Zugegriffen: 2017-11-14

FreeBSD (2017) FreeBSD Handbook. Chapter 17: Jails. https://www.freebsd.org/doc/handbook/jails.html. Zugegriffen: 2017-11-14

Geffner J (2015). VENOM. Virtualized Environment Neglected Operations Manipulation. CVE-2015-3456. http://venom.crowdstrike.com. Zugegriffen: 2017-11-14

Liedtke J (1995) On micro-kernel construction. Proceedings of the fifteenth ACM symposium on Operating systems principles.

Linux Containers (2017). LinuxContainers.org Infrastructure for container projects. https://linux-containers.org. Zugegriffen: 2017-11-14

Microsoft (2017). Hyper-V Remote Code Execution Vulnerability. CVE-2017-0109. http://www.cvedetails.com/cve/cve-2017-0109. Zugegriffen: 2017-11-14

Mitre (2014). Oracle VirtualBox 3D acceleration multiple memory corruption. CVE-2014-0983. https://cve.mitre.org/cgi-bin/cvename.cgi?name=cve-2014-0983. Zugegriffen: 2017-11-14

Oracle (2014) Hard Partitioning With Oracle Solaris Zones. http://www.oracle.com/technetwork/server-storage/solaris11/technologies/os-zones-hard-partitioning-2347187.pdf. Zugegriffen: 2017-11-14

Parnas DL (1972) On the Criteria To Be Used in Decomposing Systems into Modules. Communications of the ACM. Volume 15, number 12

Rushby J (1981) Design and Verification of Secure Systems. 8th ACM Symposium on Operating System Principles (SOSP). ACM Operating Systems Review, Volume 15, Number 5, pp 12–21. http://www.csl.sri.com/users/rushby/abstracts/sosp81. Zugegriffen: 2017-11-14

Rushby J, Randell R (1983) A distributed secure system. IEEE Computer, Vol. 16, No. 7

Rushby J, Randell R (2007) Distributed Secure Systems: Then and Now. In: Proceedings of the Twenty-Third Annual Computer Security Applications Conference. Seite 177–198. www.csl.sri.com/~rushby/papers/DSS-Then-Now.pdf. Zugegriffen: 2017-11-14

SWsoft (2005) OpenVZ User's Guide. Version 2.7.0-8. https://download.openvz.org/doc/OpenVZ-Users-Guide.pdf. Zugegriffen: 2017-11-14

Vanfleet WM, Luke JA, Beckwith RW, Taylor C, Calloni B, Uchenick G (2005) MILS: Architecture for High-Assurance Embedded Computing. Crosstalk: The Journal of Defense Software Engineering, Aug 2005

Xen Project (2016). Xen Security Advisory. CVE-2016-7092 / XSA-185 version 3. http://xenbits.xen.org/xsa/advisory-185.html. Zugegriffen: 2017-11-14

Die Komplexität der IT-Security meistern

Ramon Mörl

Zusammenfassung

In diesem Beitrag verfolgen wir zuerst die überspitzt formulierte These, ob wir als Gesellschaft zu dumm sind für adäquate IT-Sicherheit, die wie Umweltschutz eine nachhaltige Planung und eine Regulierung mit Fingerspitzengefühl benötigt. Dabei arbeiten wir verschiedene Themen heraus, die dazu führen, dass die IT-Sicherheit immer komplexer wird und als vielköpfige, monsterähnliche Hydra wahrgenommen wird, der nach dem Abschlagen eines Kopfes sofort mehrere nachwachsen. Wir stossen dabei auf viele in der IT-Sicherheit als querschnittliche Disziplin intrinsisch verankerte Problemkreise, die in den folgenden Kapiteln jeweils einzeln adressiert und einer Lösungsmöglichkeit gegenübergestellt werden.

So wird zuerst die Möglichkeit einer Sicherheitsarchitektur diskutiert, der Problemkreis des Fachkräftemangels beleuchtet und schliesslich ein Vorschlag erarbeitet, wie – trotz der hohen Komplexität der IT-Sicherheit – Beschaffungsvorgänge mit der einfachen Frage „wie bekomme ich den besten Schutz für mein Geld und welche Folgen für den Betrieb meiner IT Landschaft in kommerziellen und organisatorischen Aufwänden resultieren daraus". In dem ganzen Beitrag schwingt zwischen den Zeilen mit, dass sich eine demokratische Gesellschaft damit beschäftigen könnte, wie der Schutz, den der Bürger auf der Strasse und die angesiedelten Unternehmen im Wirtschaftsraum geniessen auch für alle Teilnehmer im Cyber-Informationsraum (kurz CIR) etabliert werden könnte. Aus dieser Betrachtung entsteht ein kurzer Ausflug in das Thema Medienkompetenz und ein Vorschlag, wie eine auf drei Säulen basierende Informationsaustauschplattform die Gesamtsicherheit deutlich verbessern könnte und welche Herausforderungen dabei noch in der Forschung gelöst werden müssten.

R. Mörl (✉)
Geschäftsführer, itWatch GmbH, München, Deutschland
E-Mail: marketing@itwatch.de

© Springer Fachmedien Wiesbaden GmbH, ein Teil von Springer Nature 2018
M. Bartsch, S. Frey (Hrsg.), *Cybersecurity Best Practices*,
https://doi.org/10.1007/978-3-658-21655-9_24

24.1   Sind wir zu dumm für IT-Sicherheit?

▶   IT-Sicherheit ist zweifelsohne ein komplexes Thema, da es selten um sichtba-
re, einfach prüfbare Funktionen und hübsche, ergonomische Oberflächen
geht, sondern darum eine höhere Robustheit und einen verbesserten Schutz
gegen aktuell bekannte und vorstellbare Angriffe zu erreichen. Der Schutz
sollte von allen Beteiligten komfortabel und selbstverständlich wahrgenommen werden. Weder für den Schutz noch für den Komfort gibt es eine Metrik,
wie diese Parameter vergleichbar gemessen werden können. Zertifizierungen
bieten eine Hilfestellung, deren Verfahrensweise man aber genau verstehen
muss, um die Ergebnisse zu beurteilen. Zulassungen beurteilen meist gesamte genauer definierte Umgebungen und erfordern intensive Prüfungen. Der
Know-how Mangel zur IT-Sicherheit ist bekannt und an diesen und vielen
weiteren Stellen bemerkbar. Aktuelle Zahlen gehen davon aus, dass ca. 1 %
der in der ITK Beschäftigten Spezialwissen in IT-Sicherheit besitzen.

24.1.1   Fachkräftemangel und Fehlendes Know-how in der
IT-Sicherheit

Die IT-Sicherheitshersteller in Deutschland beklagen einen Fachkräftemangel bei vielen
Positionen in der Herstellung sicherer IT-Produkte von der Planung über Produktion, Qualitätssicherung und Marketing bis in den Vertrieb. Dieser Fachkräftemangel soll zunehmend
durch neue Ausbildungsprogramme behoben werden. Häufiger ist zu hören „IT-Sicherheit
ist nicht alles, aber ohne IT-Sicherheit ist alles nichts". In der Tat werden bei vielen Themen
und Technologien wie Cloud, Industrie 4.0, Outsourcing und sogar dem Abschluss von
Außenhandelsvereinbarungen Themen der Datensicherheit und des Datenschutzes als
blockierende, weil komplex und häufig Situations- und Technologie-abhängig, Faktoren
genannt.

Betreiber von IT-Systemen, Beschaffer von IT-Produkten, IT-Dienstleister und Anwender
stehen vor dem Problem, ihren individuellen Schutzbedarf oder den ihrer Kunden und Daten
gegen Bedrohungen durchzusetzen, wobei ihnen die Bedrohungen im Detail zumeist unver-
ständlich sind. Der Schutzbedarf wird nicht nur durch eigene Schutzziele, sondern auch
durch von extern auferlegte Regularien und Gesetze definiert, die häufig lokal unterschiedliche Ausprägungen haben (z. B. die Landeskrankenhausdatenschutzgesetze in Deutschland,
die Länderrecht sind). Dazu wählen die Verantwortlichen Vorgehensmodelle und Lösungen
und müssen sichere von weniger oder sogar unsicheren Lösungen unterscheiden, um den
individuell als adäquat betrachteten Schutzbedarf umzusetzen und das investierte Geld zielorientiert einzusetzen. Softwareprojekte sollen nur noch unter dem Credo Security-by-De-
sign und Privacy-by-Design arbeiten und so sicherstellen, dass die Implementierungen von
Anfang an sicher sind – wieder werden hier ähnliche oder gleiche Skills in einer frühen

Projektphase begleitend benötigt. Nicht nur der ehemalige Datenschutzbeauftragte Deutschlands, Herr Schaar, sagte auf der Bonner Future Security am 05.09.2012 in der Plenum Session I „Cloud and Law", welche von Fraunhofer VVS veranstaltet wurde: „eine Applikation kann nicht sicherer sein, wie das zugrunde liegende Betriebssystem" – die Entwicklung von sicherheitsbewussten Anwendungen wird dadurch noch komplexer. Medienkompetenz soll schon im frühen Kindesalter geschult werden. Lehrer und Professoren mit geeigneten Skills sind Mangelware. Trainingsmodelle und Lerninhalte sind unscharf, da z. B. die Diskussion um den sinnvollen Datenschutz und die Vorteile von großen Datensammlungen noch keinen gesellschaftlichen Konsens gefunden hat.

Während wir nun der Frage nachgehen, wie wir in 10 oder 20 Jahren die Know-how-Engpässe überwinden können, ist es zwingend notwendig, aktuell Strategien zu leben, die trotzdem echten Schutz ermöglichen. Eine der wenigen Möglichkeiten ist es, das Know-how zu bündeln, indem vertrauenswürdige Kommunikationskanäle – also Vertrauensketten – etabliert werden. Entscheidungen und Informationen sollten dann auf standardisierten, konsolidierten Ergebnissen aufbauen – keine einfache Aufgabe.

Unbestritten gibt es täglich viele Angriffe – die Tendenz ist in Quantität und vor allem Qualität zunehmend. Viele hundert Seiten Text über die intendierte Sicherheitsarchitektur, die gesetzten Sicherheitsziele, das Commitment der CXO zu diesen Zielen und die verabschiedeten Sicherheitsregeln werden die Cyber-Attacken nicht abwehren, sind aber, wenn sie professionell aufgebaut sind – also überschaubar, pragmatisch und zielorientiert – eine notwendige Voraussetzung für sinnstiftendes Handeln.

In einer zukunftsweisenden Rede in kleiner Runde fordert ein Mitarbeiter der Inneren Sicherheit Deutschlands [1], dass wir uns als Gesellschaft auch kulturell damit auseinandersetzen sollten, welche Abbildung der gesellschaftlich etablierte Schutzbedarf und die dazu akzeptierten Schutzvorrichtungen der traditionellen, analogen Welt in den Bedrohungen und IT-Sicherheitsvorrichtungen der digitalen Welt finden sollten. Dazu braucht es Know-how an verschiedenen Stellen, denn der aus Sicht der Betroffenen adäquate Schutz entsteht erst durch die Robustheit des eingesetzten Verfahrens; diese Robustheit richtig einzuschätzen erfordert aber gute Kenntnisse. In der analogen Welt glaubt sich „die demokratische Gesellschaft" in Deutschland adäquat geschützt und die Steuergelder für den Schutz geeignet investiert – Landesgefälle in den Statistiken sollen hier als eine Art Rundungsfehler als nebensächlich gesehen werden, wohingegen es viele Länder gibt in welchen der analoge Schutz bereits auf niedrigerem Niveau liegt. Deutschland gilt als sehr sicher, ein positiver Aspekt für den Standort Deutschland. Zweifelsohne wäre es ein Wettbewerbsvorteil, wenn Deutschland und in der Folge Europa „die Sicherheit in der digitalen Welt" als attraktiven Standortfaktor besetzen könnte – erste Schritte sind ja erkennbar. Wie kann nun die IT-Sicherheit besonders befördert werden, wo doch an vielen Stellen das Know-how um die IT-Sicherheit fehlt. IT-Sicherheit ist überall notwendig, Know-how ist aber nicht überall vorhanden.

Deshalb soll dieser Artikel der Frage nachgehen, an welchen Stellen welches Know-how der IT-Sicherheit benötigt wird, wie es aktuell darum bestellt ist und wie eventuelle Defizite behoben werden können.

24.1.2 Vertrauensketten sind mehrdimensional

Geeignete Vertrauensketten sind eine gute Lösung für den aktuellen Engpass der Know-how-Ressourcen, da das Ergebnis der Vertrauenskette einfach genutzt werden kann und wenig Know-how beim Nutzer des Ergebnisses voraussetzt. Um die Kette und das Vertrauen in die Handlungsträger in der Kette, das für einen konkreten Vorgang benötigt wird, herzustellen, muss der „Endabnehmer" nicht nur überzeugt sein, dass die von ihm gewünschte Robustheit des Verfahrens bzw. der Vertrauenskette gegeben ist, sondern das Ergebnis muss auch nach dem State of the Art „sein Geld wert sein" und keine Mogelpackung darstellen. In analogen Produkten haben sich verschiedene Organisationen wie z. B. die Stiftung Warentest, aus Sicht der Verbraucher, die TÜVe und andere der Frage nach der Qualität im intendierten Einsatzspektrum und dem Aufdecken von Mogelpackungen gewidmet. In der IT-Sicherheit funktioniert das noch nicht so gut, da die Schutzziele nicht so einfach zu artikulieren sind und das Know-how für geeignete Verfahren wie z. B. Penetrationstests und White-Hat Hacking nicht so verbreitet ist.

Eine Vertrauenskette muss, um es einem Fachmann zu ermöglichen sich von ihrer Robustheit zu überzeugen, zumindest in fünf Dimensionen vollständig und nachweisbar sein: **Technik, Organisation, Rechtssicherheit, Haftung** und **Lieferkette. Technik** wird bereits häufig diskutiert und ist eigenständig schon sehr komplex. Neu in der Betrachtung der **Technik** sind hauptsächlich der „letzte Meter" und die Betrachtung der Schnittstellen zwischen den Sicherheitslösungen (siehe Abb. 24.1).

Unter **Organisation** ist mehr zu verstehen als nur eine Sicherheitsrichtlinie, die aufgeschrieben wird und mit asynchronen Security-Awareness-Maßnahmen versucht, den Anwender mit in die Verantwortung einzubinden. Die Organisationseinbindung muss alle Elemente der Sicherheitsrichtlinie entweder technisch umsetzen oder in Echtzeit in konkrete Handlungsanweisungen, die der Anwender versteht, „übersetzen". Zwingend gehört

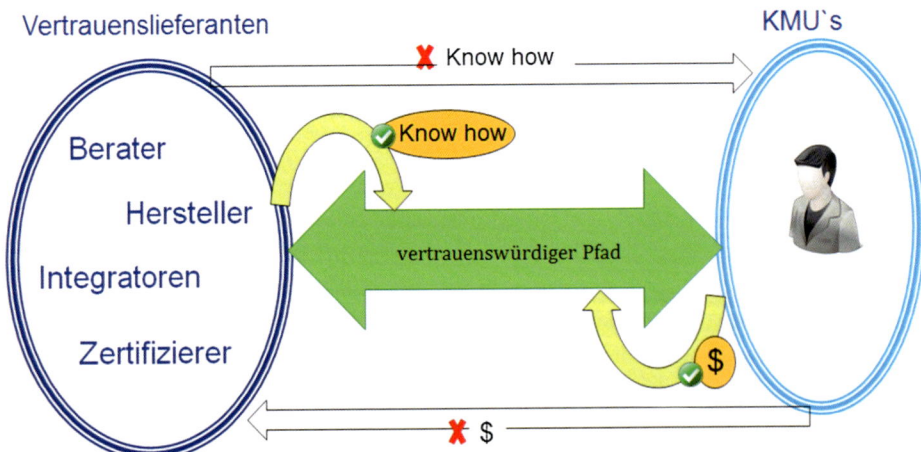

Abb. 24.1 Vertrauenswürdiger Pfad

auch das Monitoring des Verbotenen zur organisatorischen Einbettung, wenn das Verbotene aus anderen Gründen nicht vollständig geblockt werden kann (siehe Abb. 24.2).

Rechtlich wird in Deutschland häufig die Auffassung vertreten, dass organisatorische Verbote, deren Einhaltung nicht begleitend geprüft wird oder technisch umgesetzt ist, insgesamt unwirksam sind.

Vollständige Rechtssicherheit entsteht aber erst, wenn die verschiedenen Rechtsräume, die Anwendung finden, sich in den wesentlichen Fragen widerspruchsfrei überlagern. Die Überlagerung kann durch verschiedene Orte der Datenhaltung aber auch durch unterschiedliche Orte der Produktion von Teilen der Lösung bzw. Services entstehen. Zurzeit ist kaum eine **Haftung** für die Robustheit der Einsatzziele in der IT-Sicherheit gegeben. Ein AntiVirus-Produkt haftet nicht dafür, alle Viren, die älter als n Tage sind, sicher zu erkennen und sicher abzuweisen. Die Durchsetzbarkeit einer eventuell in einem Rechtsraum bestehenden Haftung mit Durchgriff in einen anderen addiert zusätzliche Komplexität – digitale Prozesse sind häufig global, ohne dass der Nutzer davon Kenntnis hat oder den relevanten Rechtsraum steuern kann.

Die **Lieferketten** sind nicht nur bezüglich der Rechtssicherheit und Haftung eine wesentliche Komponente zur Einschätzung der Robustheit, sondern auch durch die TQM (Total Quality Management) Prozesse der einzelnen eingesteuerten Komponenten. Soft- und Hardware ist zumeist aus verschiedensten Komponenten mit unterschiedlichen Lieferwegen zusammengesetzt. Zum einen können nun auf dem Weg Hintertüren eingebaut worden sein oder zusätzliche Komponenten z. B. zur remote-Administration eingebaut worden sein, die sich im gesamten Produkt für den Einsatz in schützenswerter Umgebung als problematisch herausstellen. Zum anderen muss aber insbesondere bei Produkten, die direkt die IT-Sicherheit fördern sollen aber auch bei Produkten, die den Cyber-Angriffen ausgesetzt sind, die Handlungsgeschwindigkeit gegen neue Angriffe als eine wesentliche Qualität betrachtet werden. Besteht eine Lösung aus vielen verschiedenen Komponenten, die aus Open Source und Komponenten von Drittanbietern zusammengesetzt sind, dauert

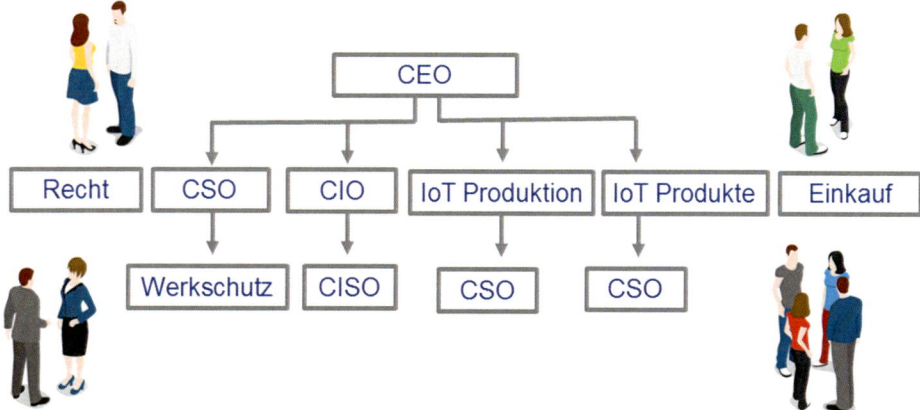

Abb. 24.2 Spannungsfeld in einer Organisation

es natürlich wesentlich länger für einen Lieferanten oder Hersteller die gesamte integrierte Liefereinheit gegen aktuelle Angriffe zu prüfen und – noch wesentlicher – die verbauten Komponenten im Falle einer Verletzbarkeit verlässlich nachbessern zu lassen, da
die Nachbesserung nicht in Eigenregie durchgeführt werden kann, sondern evtl. mehrere
Teilnehmer der Lieferkette koordiniert aktiv werden müssen. Aktuell sind noch nicht
einmal die verbauten Komponenten mit ihrer jeweiligen Lieferkette auszuweisen, weder
der Endkonsument noch die Akteure innerhalb einer Lieferkette haben notwendigerweise
Kenntnis über alle verbauten und mitgelieferten Komponenten, was weder der Sicherheitseinschätzung dienlich ist noch die nötige Transparenz herstellt und ein Qualitätsmanagement des Endproduktes aus Sicht der IT-Sicherheit nahezu unmöglich macht. Hierzu
sei noch eine Klarstellung erlaubt: bei der Betrachtung der gesamten Sicherheit – also des
erreichten Schutzgrades einer Gesamtumgebung – ist es nicht notwendig, dass jedes einzelne Element den gleich hohen Sicherheitsstandard erreicht. So kann beispielsweise
durch die verschlüsselte Kommunikation über Kupferkabel der Angreifbarkeit des Kabels
bezüglich der Vertraulichkeit sehr gut entgegengesteuert werden – aber es ist absolut
notwendig, diesen Angriffsvektor zu kennen, um ihm geeignet begegnen zu können
(siehe Abb. 24.3).

Detailliert dargestellte Lieferketten dienen dem Integrator/Käufer nicht nur dabei,
Ziele der digitalen Souveränität umzusetzen, sondern auch der besseren Einschätzung
der notwendigen Handlungsgeschwindigkeit falls Exploits gegen verbaute Einzelelemente bekannt werden. Die Cyber-Attentäter sind sehr innovativ im Auffinden neuer
Schwachstellen oder noch einfacher dem Ausnutzen alter bekannter Schwachstellen in
Systemen, von welchen der Betreiber noch nicht einmal weiß, dass sie in seinem
Betrieb vorhanden sind. Gut ist es, wenn der Lieferant oder Hersteller eines IT-Sicherheitsproduktes eine hohe Handlungsgeschwindigkeit auf dem im Einsatz befindlichen
Produkt nachweisen kann, denn die Verteidigung ist immer auch ein Kampf gegen die
Zeit.

Abb. 24.3 Mit der Lupe auf die Schnittstellen

24.1.3 Geeignete Sekundärindikatoren bei der Entscheidungsfindung

Bereits 2004 erzählte der Hersteller einer für VS-NfD (Verschlusssache Nur für den Dienstgebrauch – definiert in der Verschlusssachenanweisung, kurz VSA, des Bundesministerium des Innern – **Allgemeine Verwaltungsvorschrift des Bundesministeriums des Innern zum materiellen und organisatorischen Schutz von Verschlusssachen**) und Nato-restricted zugelassenen Verschlüsselungslösung, dass es zunehmend komplizierter wird, die höhere Robustheit – also den höheren Schutz – seiner Lösung im Markt darzustellen, weil auf Kundenseite auch bei großen Unternehmen kaum jemand die Unterschiede und deren Auswirkung auf die Sicherheit des Gesamtsystems der im Markt verfügbaren Produkte versteht. Auf der Seite der Entscheider ist das Know-how, die höhere Robustheit der gleichen „Funktion", wie z. B. einem Firewall-System, zu erkennen, nicht vorauszusetzen. Die Bundesregierung und die zuständigen Verbände möchten Privatpersonen und kleinere und mittlere Unternehmen (KMU) in die Lage versetzen, im Internet und den digitalen Welten sicher zu handeln. Wenn in den großen Unternehmen schon kaum Kompetenz vorhanden ist zu unterscheiden, welche Lösung „besser schützt", also wie viel Sicherheit man für wie viel Geld erreicht, wie soll das dann für KMU und Privatpersonen gehen. Es wird keine andere Möglichkeit geben, als gute und verlässliche Sekundärindikatoren einzurichten – also verlässliche Entscheidungshilfen. Solche Sekundärindikatoren können aber trügerisch sein. So haben Einkäufer z. T. sehr komplexe Mechanismen erarbeitet, wie sie sicherstellen können, dass sie immer nur von Unternehmen beziehen, die in den verschiedensten IT-Produkten über längere Zeiträume immer die günstigsten Preise und Konditionen bieten. Der Transferschluss, dass diese Lieferanten auch die sichersten Produkte liefern, ist natürlich falsch. Auch wenn die sichersten Produkte nicht die teuersten sein müssen, geben sie häufig nicht die höchsten Margen für den Zwischenhandel, da sie häufig auf einen kleineren Insidermarkt abzielen und marketingseitig nicht so breit aufgestellt sind.

Wie können nun geeignete Sekundärindikatoren für die relevanten Märkte so etabliert werden, dass geeignete Entscheidungen auch ohne tief gehendes Know-how getroffen werden können? Bei Privatanwendern und KMU lassen sich im Wesentlichen drei Gruppen unterscheiden:

1. *Teilnehmer, die bereits etwas für ihre Sicherheit tun und willens sind, mehr zu tun, wenn sie die richtigen Möglichkeiten dazu aufgezeigt bekommen.*
2. *Teilnehmer, denen die Thematik eigentlich egal ist, die eher als Mitläufer handeln – sogenannte „Follower".*
3. *Teilnehmer, die aus konkreten Gründen, also absichtlich keine oder nur geringe Sicherheit umsetzen möchten.*

Die IT-Sicherheit ist ähnlich wie der Umweltschutz organisiert. Die Belohnungen für Bemühungen sind erst nach längerer Zeit sichtbar und bestehen zu einem großen Teil im nicht sichtbaren Nicht-Eintreten von Schadensereignissen. Ähnlich wie im Umweltschutz ist es auch nötig, eine durchgehende Kette von Mindestmaßnahmen einzuhalten, weil sonst die Maßnahmen generell gefährdet oder insgesamt kostenintensiver sind. Im Umweltschutz ist es beispielsweise von keinem Wert, wenn Haushalte den Abfall trennen, in der Sammelstelle aber alles wieder zusammenkommt. Einzelne und deren richtiges, nachhaltiges Handeln ist die Keimzelle, die unbedingt nötig ist, das Fortsetzen dieses Handelns ist oft nötig, um einen sichtbaren Effekt zu erzielen. Wesentliche Schwellwerte der Sicherheit kann man also nur überschreiten, wenn viele oder sogar alle in einer „Community" oder in einer Handlungskette ihre ähnlichen Schutzziele vergleichbar robust umsetzen oder einen gemeinsamen Mindestschutz einhalten, da sich Kommunikation und Prozesse in solchen Handlungsgemeinschaften immer enger aufeinander abstützen (Abb. 24.4).

Für das Ziel einer verbesserten Gesamtsicherheit gilt also für die erste der genannten Gruppen gute Lösungen bereitzustellen und vor allem über verlässliche Sekundärindikatoren von neutralen Stellen Entscheidungssicherheit herzustellen. Die Follower werden, sobald keine Einbußen im Komfort festzustellen und die Preise annehmbar sind oder größere Schäden in der Presse so angesprochen werden, dass sich die Handelnden persönlich angesprochen fühlen, nachziehen.

Die dritte Gruppe wird nur handeln, wenn eine mit Sanktionen belegte Regulierung für sie greift – aber auch im Falle von sanktionierter Regulierung kann die frei werdende Kapazität und Investition nur dann in echte Sicherheitsverbesserung fließen, wenn Blaupausen mit Vorbildcharakter bestehen – also real in Betrieb sind, von denen durch neutrale Stellen bestätigt ist, dass sie die regulatorischen Anforderungen sanktionsbefreiend erfüllen.

Abb. 24.4 IT-Sicherheit verlangt nach Spielregeln, „Gemeinsam stark gegen Cyber Angriffe"

Fragen

Wie sieht also nun die Praxis im Bereich der KMU der ersten Gruppe und auch vielen größeren Organisationen aus? Wo liegen Defizite auf ihrem Weg zu echter Sicherheit und wie können diese aus dem Weg geräumt werden?

Kosten und Ergonomie, also die Praktikabilität im Einsatz, sind die Hauptgründe, die aktuell gegen einen Einsatz von IT-Sicherheit genannt werden. Die Kosten und Ergonomie beziehen sich dabei nicht nur auf die Beschaffung, sondern auch auf die gesamte Handlungskette wie Beschaffung, Inbetriebnahme und den Betrieb. Es kann davon ausgegangen werden, dass der Markt der *Teilnehmer, die bereits etwas für ihre Sicherheit tun und willens sind, mehr zu tun, wenn sie die richtigen Möglichkeiten dazu aufgezeigt bekommen* (oben als 1. aufgelistet) eine führende Rolle für alle weiteren spielt. Deshalb soll in diesem Artikel hauptsächlich dieser Markt untersucht werden. Welche Stakeholder sind daran beteiligt, dass die IT dort wirklich sicherer wird? Dabei gilt es die gesamte Handlungskette von Bedarf über Herstellung, Marketing, Vertrieb, Kauf, Installation und Betrieb in ihrer Einbettung in regulierende Faktoren zu betrachten. In dieser Handlungskette soll an realen Beispielen der letzten Zeit aufgezeigt werden, dass jeder Stakeholder spezifisches Know-how benötigt, welches im beschriebenen Fall nicht verfügbar war oder aus anderen Gründen nicht „zum Tragen kam". Es soll erwähnt werden, aber hier nicht mehr detaillierter ausgeführt werden, dass auch im „begleitenden Markt", also Berater, Tester, Pen-Tester, Zertifizierer, Testierer etc. eine begleitende Handlungskette entsteht, die unter ähnlichen Problemen leidet.

24.1.4   Anforderungen an IT-Sicherheit in der Beschaffung

In modernen IT-Systemen wird – auch getrieben durch die 27000er Serie – die Klassifikation von Daten gefordert. Das Ziel der Klassifikation oder des „Labelings" ist es, eine bestimmte Information (dauerhaft) mit einem Sicherheitsmerkmal wie z. B. „firmenvertraulich – Nur für den Dienstgebrauch" oder „vertraulich" zu verbinden. Viele Lösungen auf dem Markt binden nun die Klassifikationsinformation in den sogenannten „Alternate Data Stream", kurz ADS. Der ADS ist wie eine Art Dateieigenschaft, also ein Attribut einer Datei, den das zugrunde liegende Dateisystem (z. B. NTFS) als Standard kennt. Diese Eigenschaft einer Datei geht bei der Übertragung per Mail oder auf bestimmte Dateisysteme (z. B. Dateisysteme, die auf USB-Sticks angewendet werden) einfach verloren, weil das Dateisystem keine ADS-Formate kennt. In der Anforderungsliste nach der Klassifikation von Daten findet sich aber selten eine Anforderung, die das sichere, nachhaltige und dauerhafte Koppeln der Klassifikationsinformation – also das Sicherheitsmerkmal mit dem zu schützenden Inhalt einfordert, obwohl die Klassifikation später als Sicherheitsmerkmal verwendet werden soll. Auf konkrete Nachfrage wird in diesen Fällen entweder gesagt, dass dieser Zusammenhang unbekannt war oder dass man die Projektierung, die ohnehin komplex ist, nicht noch schwieriger gestalten wollte. Beide Antworten sind Signale von Know-how-Defizit, welches in der sehr frühen Phase der Anforderungen evtl. auch der Marktsichtung hätte behoben werden können, wenn es Vorlagen geben würde, was aus einer Labeling-Funktion eine echte Sicherheitsfunktion macht, die man später auch als Grundlage für DLP-Projekte einsetzen kann.

Lieferkette des IT-Sicherheitsproduktes: Viele IT-Sicherheits-Produkte greifen auf weit verbreitete de-facto Standards zurück und integrieren diese. SSL und TLS sind solche de-facto Standards. Heartbleed [1] war eine Schwachstelle, die lange nach der Implementierung dem Einsatz der Implementierung in einer gängigen SSL-Implementierung gefunden wurde, die auch häufig in Drittprodukten verbaut war, ohne dass das den Endkunden bekannt war. Die Endkunden hatten aber zum großen Teil auch nicht danach gefragt, welche Technik in welcher Version real in den angebotenen Produkten verbaut ist.

Heartbleed hat gezeigt, dass es sinnvoll sein kann, zu wissen, in welchem System welche Open Source oder welches Drittprodukt z. B. als OEM verbaut ist. Ein Grund ist schneller handeln zu können, da man frühzeitig weiß, wenn man betroffen ist, wenn neue Angriffe bekannt werden und dadurch geeignet handeln kann. Ein weiterer Grund ist beim Kauf besser einschätzen zu können, auf was man sich „einlässt". Dieser Punkt ist mehrdimensional, denn sowohl die rechtlichen Abhängigkeiten, Fragen der Haftung als auch technische wie juristische Hintertüren können die eigene Einschätzung der „digitalen Souveränität" des Käufers verändern – siehe auch zu Anfang des Artikels.

Insofern macht es mehr als Sinn die zugekauften bzw. mitgenutzten Komponenten in einem Produkt per Herstellererklärung listen zu lassen, den Lieferanten für die Echtheit der Eigenerklärung Haftung übernehmen zu lassen und damit vom Lieferanten die Lieferkette offen legen zu lassen.

Die Anforderungen bezüglich einer Transparenz in der Lieferkette für eine robuste vertrauenswürdige IT sind nur in Teilen bisher bekannt und werden kaum umgesetzt. Folgendes Know-how ist nur spärlich vorhanden:

Fragen

Welche positiven Auswirkungen hat die Transparenz der Lieferkette von IT-Sicherheitsprodukten für den Betreiber?

Welche Fragen sind deshalb auf Basis der Lieferkette vor dem Kauf sinnvoll?

Bei welchen der Aussagen zur IT-Sicherheit und der Lieferkette ist gegebenenfalls die Echtheit der Aussagen mit Haftung zu unterlegen, weil die Entscheidung für den Kauf und den Einsatz eines IT-Sicherheits-Produktes unter bestimmten – nicht notwendig offen gelegten – KO-Kriterien getroffen wurde?

Die Fähigkeit, die Informationen zur Lieferkette aller eingesetzten Produkte im Sinne einer Gesamtsicherheit im Unternehmen zu managen, erfordert weiteres Know-how, welches ebenfalls selten ist. Sobald eine flächige Aufmerksamkeit entsteht und die haftungsunterlegte Angabe der vollständigen Lieferkette in großen Beschaffungen berücksichtigt würde, würde dieser Punkt zum gelebten Standard werden und könnte so, mit einfachen Kriterien unterlegt, eine Entscheidungshilfe für KMU darstellen. Eine von neutraler Stelle kommentierte Vorlage für einen „Lieferketten-Fragekatalog" würde helfen, dieses Know-how zu bündeln.

Zielerfüllung von robusten Verfahren über Ausschreibungen: In einer Ausschreibung, in der eine Verschlüsselungslösung beschafft werden sollte, wurden weit über einhundert funktionale und ergonomische Kriterien gelistet, die eine potenzielle Lösung zur Verschlüsselung von Dateien erbringen muss. Insgesamt konnten 1000 Punkte erreicht werden. Eine der Fragen zu dem System war die Frage: „Kann das kryptographische System umgangen oder gebrochen werden?" Die möglichen Ergebnisse: „mit einfachen Mitteln" ergibt 0 Punkte „nicht möglich" ergibt 10 Punkte – also 1 % der erreichbaren Punkte für die Vergabe.

D. h. in einer Ausschreibung, welche nur zum Ziel hatte, die IT-Sicherheit zu verbessern, konnte ein Produkt, welches mit einfachen Mitteln umgangen oder gebrochen werden kann, 990 von 1000 Punkten erzielen und die Ausschreibung gewinnen. Dieses Produkt wäre das Geld und den Aufwand ersichtlich nicht wert.

24.1.5 Schwellenwerte/Minimalanforderung

In diesem letzten Fall fehlte das Know-how, dass Ausschreibungen für IT-Sicherheit anders verlaufen müssen, wenn sie die Sicherheit verbessern sollen. Wenn man Geld für mehr Schutz ausgeben will, muss ein unterer Schwellwert der Robustheit definiert werden, so dass z. B. durch einen Teilnahmewettbewerb sichergestellt ist, dass jede der angebotenen Lösungen, die es bis zur Preisauswahl schafft, diese Minimalanforderung erfüllt. Nur Produkte, die nachweislich diesen Schwellwert überschreiten, können später mit den Standardkriterien (z. B. Funktionale Erfüllung/Preisparameter, Anforderungen an die Administrationsoberfläche) verglichen werden. Bei der Robustheit von Verschlüsselungsverfahren wird aber sofort sichtbar, dass das reine Verschlüsselungsverfahren also Zufallszahlen-, Schlüsselgenerierung, Schlüsselverwaltung, -lagerung, Algorithmus und andere Parameter nicht ausreicht. Vielmehr geht es ja auch um die Einbettung in das Zielsystem, denn wenn jeder laufende Prozess von remote die Entschlüsselung anfordern kann oder viele den Schlüssel kennen oder herleiten können, dann ist zwar möglicherweise das Verschlüsselungssystem in sich robust, aber das Gesamtsystem hat keinen oder geringen Schutz.

Problematisch bei diesem Vorgehen, wenn ein vorgeschalteter Teilnahmewettbewerb für die Robustheit durchgeführt wird, ist, dass der zeitliche Verzug und die nicht unerhebliche Investition in die Penetrationstests zu Lasten des Auftraggebers gehen. Es gibt aber auch aktuelle Beispiele, wie mittels eines „Gesamtauftrages" das Problem gelöst werden kann. Eine Ausschreibung im Sommer 2017 hat beispielsweise eine Securitylösung inklusive Integration, Training, Betriebskonzept, Übergabe und abschliessender Sicherheitsprüfung durch das Fachpersonal als ein nicht teilbares Paket ausgeschrieben. Rechnungsstellung ist hierbei an die Vollständigkeit der Leistung gekoppelt gewesen, wodurch nur Lösungen angeboten wurden, die nach Meinung der Bieter auch am Schluss halten was gefordert wurde – nämlich nach der Integration eine Verbesserung des Schutzes.

24.1.6 Informationsaustauschplattform

Ein großes Problem stellt hier die Definition des unteren Schwellwertes für die Robustheit des Gesamtverfahrens dar, denn es gibt keine Maßeinheit/Metrik für die Robustheit. Hier ist vielfältiges Know-how nötig, welches nur sehr spärlich in der ITK vorhanden ist. Hilfreich wäre es, wenn Organisationen mit höherem Schutzbedarf ihre Ergebnisse beim Testen der Robustheit von Produkten und ihre Erfahrungen beim Betrieb detailliert beschreiben und veröffentlichen könnten, so dass diese Erfahrungen bis hin zu einer Liste von empfehlenswerten Produkten, den geeigneten Betriebskonzepten, vertrauenswürdigen Integratoren und Beratern mit diesem Kompetenzfeld andere Organisationen bei deren Entscheidungen unterstützen würden. Höherer Schutzbedarf ist häufig bei Organisationen der öffentlichen Hand und deren Zulieferern im Geheimschutz gegeben. Diese haben verständlicherweise kein Interesse offen zu legen, welche Produkte mit welchen Betriebskonzepten im Einsatz sind. Deshalb benötigt man eine Art Tauschbörse, welche es auf der einen Seite ermöglicht, die praktischen Erfahrungen zu kommunizieren, ohne dass der Sender publik wird, auf der anderen Seite aber auch sicherstellt, dass die Qualität und Integrität der Information prüfbar ist, denn ein kurzer Test von einem Tag Dauer wird andere Einsichten bringen als eine Marktuntersuchung mit praktischen Tests mit mehreren Personenjahren, die parallel in kurzer Zeit durch ein großes Team mit breitem Know-how abgearbeitet wurden.

Ein weiteres wesentliches Hindernis zur Veröffentlichung sind Fragestellungen der Haftung und der Wettbewerbsverzerrung, die ebenfalls durch eine neutralisierende Plattform gelöst würden. Heutige Plattformen zum Austausch von Informationen verteilen hauptsächlich Informationen zu Bedrohungen, aber nicht zum adäquaten Schutz vor diesen Bedrohungen (Threat Landscape vs. Protection Landscape).

24.1.7 Bewertung von IT-Sicherheitslösungen – mangels Metrik

Die praktische Nutzbarkeit einer Lösung ist von wesentlicher Bedeutung und steht dem Einsatz von IT-Sicherheit häufig entgegen. Trotzdem ist es in der IT-Sicherheit noch wichtiger, dass die implementierte Lösung tatsächlich einen besseren Schutz darstellt als das System ohne diese Lösung, da sonst gar nicht investiert werden sollte. Stellen Sie sich vor, eine Organisation zwingt ihre Mitarbeiter zu komplexeren Passworten, indem sie die Passwortkomplexität für den Systemzugang spontan auf 12 Zeichen mit komplexen Nebenanforderungen und wöchentlichem Wechsel des Passwortes setzt, ohne dafür Sorge zu tragen, dass die vergebenen Passworte nicht gegen die Klartextausspähung z. B. mit Soft- oder Hardware-Keyloggern oder Angriffen mit Dictionary Attacken und Rainbow-Tables geschützt sind. Die Mitarbeiter würden sich zu Recht gegängelt vorkommen und der Aufwand der betrieben wird und zu signifikanten Kosten im Help-Desk führen kann, wäre nicht gerechtfertigt. Eine parallele Maßnahme zum Schutz der Passworte gegen Ausspähen hingegen würde die Maßnahme sinnvoll begleiten und man könnte die Häufigkeit des Passwortwechsels reduzieren, was zu einer höheren Benutzerakzeptanz führt.

In verschiedenen Bewertungen wird aus praktischen Gedanken für jede IT-Lösung standardmäßig ein komfortables remote-Management gefordert – zumeist, da es aus Fachanwendungen heraus als State of the Art betrachtet wird. Dass das remote-Management aller Systemeigenschaften von außerhalb – evtl. sogar noch über unsichere Betriebssysteme oder BYOD Elemente – praktische Vorteile in der Handhabung hat, ist evident. Handelt es sich aber um Schutzsysteme und Sicherheitseigenschaften, überwiegen die Nachteile für die IT-Sicherheit. Ebenso evident sollte deshalb das remote-Management von IT-Sicherheit sein und eben in der Bewertung eines Schutzsystems negativ bewertet werden, denn die Erhöhung des Schutzes ist ja der einzige Investitionsgrund und remote Interfaces zur Verwaltung aus beliebigen Drittsystemen senken die Sicherheit und sind selbst wieder aufwändig zu bewachen. Genauso wie die remote-Zugänge müssen natürlich die eigentlichen Konfigurationsdaten und administrativen Einstellungen der IT-Sicherheitssysteme vor Manipulation geschützt werden. Sind diese z. B. in einer einfachen marktüblichen Datenbank gelagert, die über Angriffe von dritten leicht manipuliert werden kann, so muss der zusätzliche Aufwand, den man in den Schutz der Datenbank steckt, in der Gesamtkalkulation – auch bezüglich des erreichbaren Schutzes – berücksichtigt werden.

Weitere Betrachtungen dieser Art sind die Entwicklungswerkzeuge, mit welchen das IT-Sicherheitsprodukt hergestellt wurde und wie es dann im System verankert ist. C#, .Net, Interpretersprachen etc. sind leichter angreifbar als auf gut geprüften, also einige Jahre alten, Compilern erstellter C-Code. Systeme, die im Applikationskontext oder als Dienste laufen, sind leichter angreifbar als Systeme, die mit einem im Betriebssystem-Kern verankerten Treiber (kernel-mode-driver) arbeiten.

Am Ende stellt man fest, dass die Ergonomie für die Endanwender wichtig ist, in der Ergonomie der Administration und der Einbettung der Schutzsysteme aber Wert auf wirkliche Sicherheit gelegt werden sollte. Denn wenn die Administrationskonsole von jedem parallel laufenden Prozess aus angreifbar ist, dann ist der Schutz des administrierten Systems dadurch auch reduziert.

Besonders komplex wird die Problematik dadurch, dass man ein Defizit einer Lösung (z. B. geringe Robustheit des Compilers des Produktes gegen Angriffe) auch durch andere Sicherheitsmaßnahmen wieder wettmachen kann, hier z. B. Isolation des Produktes auf einem stark gehärteten System. Das Betriebskonzept kann also ebenso positive wie negative Auswirkungen auf die Sicherheit des Gesamtsystems haben. Das dafür benötigte Know-how über solche IT-Risiken zu halten und bei Einführung neuer Produkte die potenziell neu entstehenden Risiken zu erkennen und zu reduzieren, ist wieder sehr selten im Markt zu finden.

Wieder – wie oben schon beschrieben – sind all diese Aspekte (und noch mehr) für hochsichere Umgebungen schon vorgedacht, aber noch nicht mit einfachen Checklisten und prüfbaren Kriterien-Listen oder sogar schon fertigen Prüfberichten für die KMU oder Integratoren der KMU verfügbar.

Die Bestätigungen über die Herstellungsprozesse erweitern die Fähigkeiten zur Sicherheitseinschätzung und können zusammen mit dem Fragenkatalog zur Lieferkette als Herstellerfragen in die Beschaffung mit aufgenommen und beantwortet werden. Sowohl für das Erstellen der richtigen Fragen (ein einfaches Kopieren der 27001 ist nicht zielführend) als auch für deren Auswertung ist aber ein anderes Know-how erforderlich und im Fragenkatalog ist zu berücksichtigen, dass ein Hersteller nicht jedem KMU direkt Einblick in die Sicherheitsüberprüfung seines Personals und seiner Prozesse geben wird oder in manchen Fällen sogar geben darf.

Auch hier wäre deshalb eine Art Vertrauensbörse wichtig, welche die Ergebnisse der Prüfung verbindlich darstellt ohne die Anonymität der handelnden Personen und die Vertraulichkeit der Inhalte der Herstellung zu gefährden. In Verschlusssache-Umgebungen gibt es für diesen Zweck eine Sicherheitsüberprüfung eines Herstellers oder relevanter Teile des Herstellers und der Lieferanten. Diese Unternehmen unterliegen nach Prüfung dann dem Geheimschutz. Hat ein Hersteller diese Prüfung positiv hinter sich gebracht, darf aber darüber nicht öffentlich gesprochen werden – für KMU bleibt die Information, welche Unternehmen geheimschutzgeprüft sind also unsichtbar. Der Hersteller darf mit dieser Information auch keine Werbung betreiben und sie veröffentlichen. Wesentliche bereits geleistete Anstrengungen, um eine vertrauenswürdige IT bzw. ein vertrauenswürdiges Unternehmen identifizieren zu können, bleiben somit ungenutzt. Wieder wäre es hilfreich diese bereits erreichte Qualität so zu veröffentlichen, dass auch die Interessen aller Stakeholder – also auch der öffentlichen Hand, die den Aufwand des Geheimschutzes betreibt – geeignet berücksichtigt würden, aber KMU von den Ergebnissen in deren Entscheidungsfindung profitieren können.

24.1.8   Relevante Strukturen in der Herstellung von IT-Sicherheit

Welcher Interessent zeigt sich an der Kostenstruktur zwischen Forschung, Entwicklung, Marketing und Vertrieb interessiert? Dabei geben diese Kostenstrukturen klare Indikatoren, dass die Produkte mit den teuersten Marketingprozessen und den meisten Vertriebsstandorten nicht unbedingt die robustesten IT-Sicherheitsverfahren implementieren, weil evtl. wenig Ressourcen in die Forschung und Entwicklung von Schutzmechanismen fließen. Auch bei den Produkten, die unter der Flagge „IT-Sicherheit" vertrieben werden, verbergen sich schwarze Schafe, sogar wenn legitimer Weise „IT-Security made in Germany" [BAN 15] als Label verwendet wird. Dass erheblicher investigativer Rechercheaufwand nötig ist, um solche schwarzen Schafe zu erkennen, zeigt, dass nicht jedes KMU diesen Aufwand wieder neu und für sich alleine treiben kann. Der Konsument kann – meist mangels geeigneter Informationen – gar nicht beurteilen, welche Komponenten wo gebaut wurden und welche Personen evtl. sogar ausländischen, nachrichtendienstlichen Hintergrund haben (siehe auch Lieferkette).

Natürlich kann ein Produkt nur dann gekauft werden, wenn es beworben und vermarktet wird. Ausgaben in Marketing und Vertrieb sind also zwingend notwendig, häufig aber für die besten, weil sichersten Lösungen nicht so intensiv, dass diese auch für KMU und die Handelsketten, die KMU bedienen, sichtbar wären. Häufig ist auch die Annahme vorhanden, dass große Firmen, weil sie überall bekannt und präsent sind, stabile und sichere Produkte mit nachhaltigen Strategien anbieten. Dass das nicht der Fall sein muss, zeigen viele reale Beispiele: der Cisco Security Agent wurde aufgekündigt, Check Point hat seine nach dem Kauf von pointsec und DiskNetPro entwickelte Endpoint-Strategie mehr oder weniger ganz aufgegeben, die in Deutschland recht bekannten Produkte von utimaco sind nach der Übernahme von Sophos z. T. aufgekündigt, z. T. durch ein Wechselbad der Strategien gegangen.

Zu guter Letzt ist auch die Frage nach dem Geld wesentlich. Ein Händler wird ein Produkt, auf welches er mehr Marge, also einen höheren Anteil an dem Verkaufserlös erhält, aus einsichtigen Gründen lieber verkaufen. Produkte mit geringer Marge oder kleinen Absatzmärkten werden gar nicht erst in das Portfolio genommen, da ja verständlicherweise auch die internen Kosten mit einem neuen Produkt gedeckt werden müssen. Jeder an der Handelskette Beteiligte muss entweder über Quantität der abgenommenen Stückzahlen oder über hohe Marge beim einzelnen Verkauf seine internen Kosten decken. Beides spricht dagegen, dass sogenannte „best-of-the-breed"-Lösungen, also Lösungen, die technologisch z. T. nur in einem kleinen Zielbereich führend sind, auch in die weitverbreiteten Handelsketten aufgenommen werden, da bei den „best-of-the-breed"-Lösungen zumindest zu Beginn der Vermarktung für gewöhnlich geringe Margen und kleine Absatzmärkte die Regel sind. Hilfe bietet dann Kapital für die Vermarktung, welches über Venture-Kapital (VC) aufgenommen wird. VC-Gesellschaften geben Kapital nur gegen Beteiligung an den Patenten und der Intellectual Property (IP) des Unternehmens her, wodurch die Eigenständigkeit und z. T. die Innovationskraft leidet und im schlimmsten Fall die Nachhaltigkeitsstrategie bei den Kunden ins wanken kommt, wenn die Produkte nicht mehr wie gekauft weiter geführt werden.

Auch dieser Punkt zeigt, dass Konsumenten ohne das nötige Know-how eher zu einer vom Marketing gepushten Lösung greifen, anstatt sich für eine eventuell noch unbekanntere aber dafür nachhaltig robuste Lösung mit strategischen Vorteilen zu entscheiden. Die handelnden Marktteilnehmer sind notwendigerweise umsatzgetrieben. Ähnlich wie beim Umweltschutz wird aber ein völlig frei entwickelter Markt wenig in echte IT-Sicherheit und mehr in gut verkaufte Scheinsicherheit investieren. Im Markt fehlen Dirigenten, die das gesamte Orchester mit der geeigneten Information versorgen und so auch den KMU den Zugang zu neuen Informationen barrierefrei und leicht konsumierbar (also frei von IT-Fachbegriffen und langen Detailtexten) aber von vertrauenswürdiger neutraler Stelle beglaubigt, ermöglichen. Wie schon beschrieben wäre eine geeignete Vertrauenskette oder Vertrauensbörse ein mögliches Medium, um die Erfahrungen und nötigen Informationen zu transportieren und dann auch in die geeigneten, konsumierbaren Informationspakete zu übersetzen.

In einer Untersuchung des KMU-Marktes hat sich ergeben, dass viele KMU gerne in IT-Sicherheit investieren würden, wenn der Zugang für sie barrierefrei und kalkulierbar wäre. Das heißt, dass eine von neutraler Stelle beglaubigte Zusammenstellung von verschiedenen

Produkten mit einem geeigneten Betriebskonzept, zusammengefasst zu einem einzigen „Mach-mich-sicher"-Paket zu einem festen Preis als adäquat empfunden wird. Natürlich dürfen die Verfügbarkeit und die Ergonomie des Gesamtsystems nicht leiden und der Anbieter muss für dieses Paket auch in diesen Aspekten eine Haftung übernehmen, die er an die Hersteller durchreichen muss.

Integratoren und Berater haben aber keine verlässlichen Informationen, mit welchen Lösungen sie die Pakete aus welchen Gründen für welche Märkte schnüren sollten und müssen deshalb die Zusammenstellung auf eigene Untersuchungen abstellen, die sich auch kommerziell tragen müssen und deshalb begrenzte Ressourcen zur Verfügung haben. Statt also punktuell IT-Sicherheitsprodukte zu verkaufen, sollte im Markt ein Handlungsversprechen auf dauerhaften Schutz ins Angebot kommen.

24.1.9 Herstellung von Schutzverfahren – make or buy

Bei der Herstellung von Schutzverfahren stehen viele Unternehmen vor der Frage „make or buy". Durch die Doktrin „Security by Design" soll die IT-Sicherheit bereits im Produktdesign berücksichtigt werden, also einer sehr frühen Phase der Produktplanung. Diese Doktrin ist sehr wünschenswert. Sie führt zu Ende gedacht dazu, dass jeder Softwarehersteller und jedes Systemhaus in der IT auch IT-Security-Know-how braucht und zwar eines der teuersten und seltensten, nämlich das in der Planung von Architekturen und dann in der Umsetzung. Prinzipiell kann natürlich diese Expertise zugekauft werden – man steht also wieder vor der Entscheidung „make or buy".

Am konkreten Beispiel aus der Vergangenheit stellt sich das z. B. so dar: Die Firma Gartner empfahl in ihren Strategieberatungen für Hersteller von Softwareverteilverfahren einzelne Komponenten der Endpoint Security mit zu liefern – in diesem Fall vor allem Device Control Software.

Deshalb begannen viele Firmen große und kleinere Nischenanbieter und auch deutsche Firmen eigene „Sicherheitslösungen" herzustellen. Vor der Frage „make or buy" stehend, entschieden sich die meisten Unternehmen natürlich für make, da die Wertschöpfungstiefe größer und die Handlungsgeschwindigkeit auf einem eigenen Produkt größer ist. Aber das Produkt muss erst einmal fertig werden und natürlich mit den „best-of-the-breed"-Lösungen bezüglich der Robustheit einigermaßen mithalten können.

In der Konsequenz bewegen sich Hersteller von „Non-IT-Security"-Produkten in den IT-Security-Markt, weil „das ja auch nur IT ist und so schwer kann das nicht sein". IT-Architekten werden dann zu Security-Architekten und Entwickler zu IT-Security Entwicklern umdefiniert. Wesentlich ist es zu erkennen, dass hier im Entscheidungsverfahren „make or buy" die Robustheit der Lösung kein wesentliches Ziel darstellt, weil es keine Metrik auf der Robustheit gibt und es deshalb auch gar nicht in den Köpfen präsent ist, dass zu der Funktion noch Robustheit, also Schutzwirkung gegen Angriffe, dazukommt. „Time to Market" und Produktionskosten stellen dagegen wesentliche Entscheidungsparameter dar, die auch aus der klassischen IT bekannt sind. Als Resultat gibt es dann

Produkterweiterungen und Sicherheitsfunktionen mit fraglicher Robustheit, weil kein langjähriges Know-how zur IT-Sicherheit in den „make or buy"-Entscheidungsprozess eingeflossen ist. In den oben genannten Fällen hat ein deutscher Hersteller die Entwicklung nach vielen Monaten wieder aufgegeben und ein Weiterer ein eigenes Produkt auf den Markt gebracht, welches z. B. immer dann, wenn eine neue Sicherheits-Richtlinie geladen wird, weder die alte noch die neue durchsetzt, also im IT-Sicherheitsjargon einfach „offen" ist und während dieser Zeit überhaupt keinen Schutz bietet. Aus Systemmanagement-Sicht ist das erlaubt – aus Sicht eines robusten Schutzes absolut verboten.

Die resultierende Problematik ist mehrdimensional. Zum einen verbrennt ein Hersteller Geld für Produkte, die die Marktziele nicht erfüllen. Viel schlimmer sind aber Verwerfungen im Markt, die dadurch entstehen, dass der Vertrieb natürlich versucht, das langjährige Vertrauen des Marktes in die bisherigen Non-Security-Produkte in die neuen Scheinsicherheitsprodukte zu transportieren und darüber diese zu verkaufen.

Natürlich wird ein guter Vertrieb Käufer finden, denn es gibt ja keine Metrik für die Robustheit. Die angebotenen Non-Security-Funktionen, wie remote Management, einfache Integration, Administrationsoberfläche etc., kann aber jeder miteinander vergleichen. D. h. es werden die berühmten Äpfel mit Birnen verglichen, wenn ein nicht robustes Produkt, welches die gleichen Funktionen anbietet wie ein robustes, mit einem robusten Produkt verglichen wird.

Hier wäre der Rückgriff auf neutrale Vertrauensketten zu jedem Zeitpunkt in der Planung, der Herstellung und der Markteinführung extrem wertvoll, denn man kann auch IT-Security als Infrastruktur oder als Basiskomponente zukaufen – leider gibt es für diese Phase keine neutralen, beratenden Institutionen.

Kommen wir auf den Punkt „Security by Design" zurück, dann stellen wir fest, dass sich das Problem multipliziert, denn alle Produkte sollen ja ihre Security im Design berücksichtigen. Da man z. B. beim Herstellen einer Applikation für die elektronischen Bankgeschäfte einer Privatperson zweifelsohne mit sensiblen Daten umgeht, sollte man also hier schon im Design die adäquate Sicherheit einplanen.

Da, wie Herr Schaar schon mehrfach öffentlich betonte, eine Anwendung nur so sicher sein kann wie das Betriebssystem auf dem sie läuft, kommen also auf einen Hersteller sehr viele für ihn „fachfremde" Aufgaben zu – nämlich das Härten der verschiedenen Betriebssysteme und das bauen eines Sicherheitsankers, um die Anmeldedaten lokal gegen das Ausspähen von Taschenlampenapps und auf dem Weg gegen weitere Angriffe wie z. B. SMS-Umleitung zu schützen. Für solche Zwecke gibt es z. B. IT-Sicherheitsbaukästen (SDK – Software Development Kits), die man in die eigenen Programme einbinden könnte – was aber selten getan wird, weil die Doktrin „make or buy" eben oft in Richtung make entschieden wird. Wieder wäre es wünschenswert, wenn dieser Markt orchestriert würde, da man die Qualität und Robustheit so eines SDK nicht einfach erkennen kann und wieder die Frage nach „make or buy" je nach dem einzelnen Vorhaben begleitet werden sollte. Es könnte also eine sehr plausible Lösung in einer Sicherheits-Börse und den zugehörigen Vertrauensketten liegen.

24.1.10   IT-Security– eine unsichtbare Investition?

Angriffe auf IT-Systeme sieht man nicht. Die Verfahren für die IT-Sicherheit werden oft als Verhinderer wahrgenommen – im besten Fall sind sie ebenfalls unsichtbar. Was also motiviert ein Unternehmen, Geld in etwas zu investieren, was es potenziell behindert und vor unsichtbaren Dingen potenziell in der Zukunft bewahrt, wo es doch das Geld heute in sinnvolle Dinge investieren kann, mit denen es morgen mehr Umsatz macht?

Das ist im Wesentlichen eine häufige Argumentation der oben erwähnten dritten Gruppe im Markt der KMU, die an IT-Sicherheit nicht interessiert ist. Dazu kommen noch Argumente wie „100 % Sicherheit gibt es ohnehin nicht, also brauche ich doch nicht in 50 % oder 80 % investieren, wenn ich dann immer noch nicht geschützt bin".

Es ist ein langer Weg, der auch sanktionierte Regulierung miteinbeziehen muss, um in solchen Umgebungen zumindest eine Basissicherheit zu etablieren, damit andere Kommunikationspartner nicht durch diese ungeschützten Unternehmen gefährdet werden. Das von einem Mitglied der Piratenpartei einmal geforderte freie Recht sich selbst mit Schadcode zu infizieren, muss auf einen demokratischen Konsens hin überprüft werden.

Wenn das nicht der Fall ist, muss der Markt sich so weiterentwickeln, dass die Marktdurchdringung mit einem Basisschutz ähnlich nahe an 100 % liegt wie heute schon die Durchdringung mit Anti-Viren-Programmen.

Der einfache Zugang zu einfach zu nutzenden Schutz-Technologien ist eine wesentliche Voraussetzung hierfür. Diese Technologien sind in Ansätzen schon erkennbar. So hat beispielsweise Microsoft in dem Betriebssystem Windows 10 das automatische Anschalten des Plattformeigenen Antivirus-Programmes implementiert, wenn das potenziell installierte Zusatzprodukt nicht mehr lizenziert ist oder aus anderen Gründen seinen Dienst einstellt.

24.1.10.1   Installation

Ein Produkt nützt nichts, wenn es nicht sicher installiert ist, eine sichere Organisation nützt nichts, wenn sie nicht gelebt wird. Dass man nahezu jedes IT-Sicherheitsprodukt auch so installieren kann, dass es keine Sicherheitsziele erfüllt, ist klar. Es empfiehlt sich also, vor der Installation zu untersuchen, welche Schutzziele erreicht werden sollen und wie der Einsatz des neuen Werkzeuges evtl. mit den Schutzzielen von bereits etablierten Produkten harmonisiert werden muss. Eine sehr hochwertige Aufgabe. Mal eben schnell nebenbei geht das nicht und unter den Fehlern bei der Installation kann man gegebenenfalls lange leiden (ohne es zu merken).

Auch hier wäre es sehr hilfreich, wenn die Expertise von großen IT-Organisationen beim sicheren Betrieb für KMU zugänglich gemacht würde. Auch solche Versuche sind bereits unterwegs. So haben einige DAX-Unternehmen in der DCSO eine IT-Security-Firma gegründet, die auch dritten mit gebündelten Erfahrungen helfen soll. Der CIO-Verband VOICE hat ebenfalls eine Anlaufstelle für ihre Mitglieder organisiert und in einer eigenen Service-Dienstleistungs-Organisation gebündelt.

Optimal wäre es, wenn auch die Expertise des Bundes – insbesondere bei der Konsolidierung der IT-Sicherheit – mit für die Länder und Kommunen eingesteuert werden würde und dadurch die mit Steuermitteln erarbeiteten Ergebnisse für alle Steuer-konsumierenden Organisationen multipliziert werden könnten.

24.1.10.2 Betrieb

Bei Systemen, die dem Schutz dienen, sollte man mit der Fähigkeit, diese in Echtzeit umzukonfigurieren oder deren durch die Installation erreichte Sicherheitsziele in Echtzeit manuell zu reduzieren, vorsichtig umgehen. Eine remote-Administration vom Urlaubsort, wie sie in den verschiedenen Werbebroschüren der Produkte visualisiert wird, ist mehr als bedenklich. Notwendig ist also ein die erreichte Sicherheit erhaltendes Betriebskonzept, welches auch geprüft wird oder noch besser mittels technischer Maßnahmen eingehalten werden muss. Zusätzlich gilt: je mehr unterschiedliche Systeme man betreibt, umso wahrscheinlicher sind menschliche Fehler. Insofern ist es zwar manchmal sinnvoll, zwei Technologien für ein Thema zu nutzen, die Zusatzkosten in Know-how und abgestimmtes Betriebskonzept müssen aber dabei berücksichtigt werden.

Damit keine Defizite an den Schnittstellen zu anderen Produkten entstehen, empfiehlt es sich, vorab in einem „Proof of Concept", kurz POC, die Installation UND den Betrieb zu testen und gegebenenfalls nachzubessern.

Diese Verfahren kosten Zeit und Geld. KMU können sich das nicht leisten. Optimal wäre deshalb eine generische Blaupause einer Sicherheitsarchitektur, welche in mehreren Implementierungen (also unterschiedlichen Produktzusammenstellungen) im Betrieb mit dieser Schnittstellenproblematik beschrieben wird. Diese Produktzusammenstellungen ergeben dann im besten Fall eine Gesamtlösung, die mit einer monatlichen Miete bezogen werden kann, ohne dass innerhalb des KMU eigene Expertise aufgebaut werden muss. Investitionen des KMU, die bereits getätigt sind, könnten berücksichtigt werden, indem die einzelnen Komponenten des KMU in die Architektur integriert werden, wodurch wiederum neue Produktzusammenstellungen entstehen können, deren Robustheit dann im Echtbetrieb geprüft werden kann.

24.1.11 Verfügbarkeit und Integrität – gegenläufige Ziele

In einer Diskussion um die beste Robustheit von IT-Sicherheitsverfahren wurde deutlich, dass sich die Ziele von Verfügbarkeit auf der einen Seite und Integrität und Vertraulichkeit auf der anderen Seite zum Teil entgegenstehen. Für die Verfügbarkeit von Systemen ist es prinzipiell gut, alle Technologien parallel von möglichst verschiedenen Herstellern auf möglichst unterschiedlichen Betriebssystemen und Hardwareplattformen zu betreiben und dadurch redundant zu halten. Bei einem erfolgreichen Angriff würden dann nicht alle Systeme gleichzeitig ausfallen. Durch die verteilte Plattform reduziert sich die Ausfallwahrscheinlichkeit. Für die Ziele Integrität und Verfügbarkeit nutzt der Angreifer dann natürlich die am schwächsten geschützte Plattform für seinen Angriff – die Schwächen der genutzten Systeme addieren sich sozusagen auf. Für die Integrität und Vertrauenswürdigkeit wäre es also sinnvoll, die verschiedenen Technologien hintereinander zu schalten, so dass ein erfolgreicher Angriff auf das erste System im zweiten oder dritten hängen bleibt.

Weil sich die drei Grund-Ziele der IT-Sicherheit – Verfügbarkeit, Integrität und Vertraulichkeit – hier schon gegenseitig widersprechen ist es wesentlich, dass die Anforderungen subjektiv und in feiner Granularität definiert werden. Dieser Vorgang ist zeitintensiv und kann von KMU zumeist nicht geleistet werden. Deshalb ist es wichtig, Best Practices für die verschiedenen Branchen zu erarbeiten. Hier ist über die im KRITIS-Bereich diskutierten Mindeststandards schon Bewegung im Markt. Die Branchenverbände können hier in der Vertrauenskette gute Arbeit leisten, um die komplexen Themen der IT-Sicherheit für ihre Branche zu vereinfachen.

24.1.12 Medienkompetenz und Wertewandel

Galt es im letzten Jahrhundert noch als Inbegriff von Freiheit, wenn ein 18-jähriger sein erstes Auto kaufte, so gibt es heute Gesellschaftsgruppen, die sich durch ein eigenes Auto zu stark angebunden fühlen. Sie nehmen es als Freiheit wahr, am Carsharing teilzunehmen und eben keine Verantwortung für ein eigenes Auto zu übernehmen.

In einigen Communities ist bezüglich des geltenden bzw. gelebten Datenschutzes und des Wunsches nach Schutz in der digitalen Umgebung in Deutschland ebenfalls ein Wertewandel wahrzunehmen, so dass ein bewegliches Ziel bezüglich der zu schützenden Information und vielen anderen Parametern entsteht. Dieser Wertewandel führt dazu, dass die gesellschaftlichen Ziele bezüglich der Vertraulichkeit z. B. von personenbezogenen Daten auf der einen Seite und den Möglichkeiten des „Big Data" aktuell keiner klaren demokratisch gesamtgesellschaftlich anerkannten Linie unterliegen, wodurch natürlich auch der Transport von Lerninhalten an Schulen weichen, z. T. persönlichen Auslegungen unterliegt.

Für die besondere Stellung z. B. des BDSG kann man auch mehrere Beispiele finden:

Das Unabhängige Landeszentrum für Datenschutz Schleswig-Holstein (ULD S-H) stellte in einem Bericht fest, dass die AGB von iPhone und iPad in mehreren Punkten gegen das BDSG verstoßen, was niemanden wirklich verblüfft hat. Interessant ist, dass diese formale Feststellung keine Reaktion auslöst, die dazu zwingt, das Problem zu heilen.

Mit deutschen Steuergeldern finanzierte Projekte in Entwicklungsländern nutzen immer auch IT und bauen z. T. auch IT-Infrastrukturen in den Entwicklungsländern auf. Das BDSG wird dabei nicht verpflichtend mit implementiert, weder in den eigenen Systemen noch in den Systemen vor Ort.

Während man den Verlust an Verfügbarkeit von Information sofort bemerkt, werden der Verlust der Integrität erst im Problemfall und der Verlust der Vertraulichkeit spät oder sogar nie bemerkt. Die Beweisbarkeit von Schutzverletzungen, also erfolgreichen Angriffen, folgt ebenfalls dieser Reihenfolge. In der IT-Sicherheit ist dieser Zusammenhang seit Langem bekannt. Der Transport solcher einfachen Informationen – und davon gibt es ja viel mehr wesentliche Entscheidungsfaktoren – und ihrer Konsequenzen an die gesamte Bevölkerung, um eine sogenannte Medienkompetenz herzustellen, scheitert aber aus verschiedenen Gründen:

Die Communities mit reduziertem Datenschutz-Empfinden ziehen sich durch alle Bevölkerungsgruppen und alle Altersstrukturen, weshalb es nicht den einen definierten Kommunikations-Kanal gibt, um die Hintergründe und Vorteile von „der Privatheit von Daten" zu kommunizieren. Ziel müsste es ja sein, dass jeder Bürger seine Entscheidung über die Privatheit bzw. Vertraulichkeit seiner Daten, so er ein geeignetes Alter bzw. eine geeignete Kompetenz hat, selbst treffen kann.

Für die Ausbildungseinrichtungen wie Schule, Universität, Erwachsenenbildung etc. lässt sich kein klarer Lerninhalt erkennen, der wirklich demokratisch konsolidiert ist, da die gesellschaftliche Diskussion noch offen ist. Insofern bleibt nur der praktische Umgang nach bestem Wissen und Gewissen der Lehrer und Ausbilder im digitalen Wandel, was im Normalfall deren persönlicher Meinung entspricht. Die persönlichen Meinungen zu den sinnvollen Datenschutz-Zielen unterliegen aber auch bei den Lehrern und Ausbildern der oben bereits erwähnten breiten Varianz.

Werden in der Ausbildung hohe Datenschutz-Ziele als wertvolle Inhalte transportiert, so müssen diese Ziele natürlich auch praktisch umsetzbar sein. Es gälte also, die Robustheit des Schutzes ebenso zu unterrichten. Das würde aber dazu führen, dass entweder jeder Bürger ein IT-Sicherheitsexperte wird oder klare, einfache Aussagen zu der Robustheit von Produkten und Lösungen von einer geeigneten neutralen Stelle gemacht werden. Mit der Seite „BSI für Bürger" ist im Internet hier schon eine Informationsquelle geschaffen, diese beschäftigt sich aber nur mit kostenfreien Produkten nicht mit Kaufprodukten.

Konkrete Angaben zu konkreten Lösungen von neutralen anerkannten Stellen scheinen der einzige Weg zu sein, der es ermöglicht, der Komplexität des Themas und den Know-how-Engpässen gerecht zu werden. In vielen Produktlandschaften sind schriftlich belegte Qualitätskriterien ein wesentlicher Faktor im Markt – in der IT-Sicherheit noch nicht. Albert Einstein wird zugeschrieben, dass er die Dummheit darin sah, bei dauerhaft gleichbleibender Handlungsweise andere Ergebnisse zu erwarten. In vielen Branchen wie z. B. Automotive, Gesundheit und Ernährung hat man nach dem Erkennen des Problems gehandelt, indem striktere Kontrollen, geforderte Merkmale, Nachweise über Lieferketten, Nachweise über verwendetes Material etc. und darauf basierende Haftung eingeführt wurden. Es bleibt zu hoffen, dass auch in der IT-Sicherheit bald die adäquaten Mechanismen etabliert werden, nach welchen sich jeder Lehrer, jeder Bürger, jedes KMU und jedes Unternehmen auf seine Kernkompetenzen bzw. Kernaktivitäten im digitalen Raum richten kann und die Robustheit des Schutzes für sein IT-System nach klaren, einfachen Mechanismen für jeden Teilnehmer durch belegte, neutrale Aussagen nachgewiesen wird und so der Kauf bzw. die Nutzung von IT-Sicherheit ähnlich einfach, standardisiert und unauffällig wird wie eine TÜV-Plakette an jedem Auto in Deutschland.

Abschließend ist noch einmal festzustellen, dass es sich nicht jedes kleine oder mittelgroße Unternehmen (KMU) leisten kann eine eigene Abteilung zu unterhalten, welche die Leistungen des BSI, eines TÜV oder anderer Organisationen nachbildet, welche die

Robustheit von IT-Sicherheit entlang akzeptierter Standardverfahren beurteilen. Bestehende Zertifikate, z. B. nach den Common Criteria, lösen das Problem überhaupt nicht, da in der Zertifizierung nur gegen die für die Prüfung definierten Protection Profiles geprüft wird und bereits das Verständnis für die Inhalte der Protection Profiles und damit die „Aussagekraft des Zertifikates für die eigene IT" Know-how erfordert, welches in KMU nicht vorhanden ist. Know-how zur Bewertung der Robustheit, des Schutzgrades von Lösungen ist also vorhanden – es handelt sich aber um ein Spezial-Know-how, welches nicht beliebig multiplizierbar ist. Wie kann also dieses Spezial-Know-how so eingesetzt werden, dass alle darauf zugreifen können und die Ergebnisse selbst verbindlich und vertrauenswürdig sind? Es wird kein Weg daran vorbei führen, die Handlungsketten vollständig und vertrauenswürdig zu gestalten. Z. B. ist es bei Alarmanlagen üblich, dass es Listen von vertrauenswürdigen Alarmanlagen gibt und Listen mit Unternehmen, welche diese adäquat verarbeiten und einbauen können. Lieferketten und Handlungsketten sind für die Sicherheit des entstehenden Gesamtsystems wesentliche Parameter. Stand heute lassen wir den Bürger und die KMU bezüglich der Auswahl von Prozessen, kommerzieller Produkte auf Basis der Robustheit und deren sicherer Integration und dem sicheren Betrieb allein, obwohl es Kenntnisse dazu gibt. Selbst die Annahme, dass sich Behörden und Kommunen – allein schon um die Kosten durch die Abnahme großer Mengen zu senken – auf einige standardisierte Produkte einigen und die Erfahrungen bei Installation und Betrieb in User-Communities austauschen, ist deutlich zu optimistisch. So gibt es zwar z. B. bei der Bundeswehr durch die sogenannte „Technische Architektur der Bundeswehr" (TA-Bw) Standards, die bis auf Produktniveau gehen – diese haben aber keine Auswirkung in anderen Ressorts und sind für viele Organisationen der öffentlichen Hand gar nicht sichtbar, selbst wenn man danach fragt, weil die TA-Bw selbst eingestuft ist.

24.1.13   Fazit zum Status der KMU

In einem Umfeld mit beweglichen Schutzzielen und fehlenden Vertrauensketten ist es für KMU nahezu unmöglich, echte, robuste IT-Sicherheit zu kaufen und zu implementieren.

KMUs benötigen dazu einfach befolgbare Handlungsabläufe und konkrete Empfehlungen für vertrauenswürdige Integratoren, Berater und Produkte und Sekundärindikatoren (z. B. in Form von Herstellereigenen Erklärungen über Lieferketten mit Haftungsübernahme bei Fehlinformation) entlang derer sie prüfen können, ob die dargestellten Vertrauensketten und Lösungen für sie adäquat sind. Ein konstruktiver Vorschlag folgt weiter unten im Text.

Die Empfehlung, dass jeder einzelne Anwender selbst so viel „Security Awareness" bekommen kann, dass alle Personen in der IT im privaten wie im geschäftlichen Umfeld sicher handeln, geht teilweise am Thema vorbei, denn gute Angriffe sind immer unsichtbar. Wenn wir uns allerdings intelligent aufstellen und die bei einzelnen Marktteilnehmern durchgeführten Analysen und bereits erreichten Schutzziele in adäquaten, verlässlichen Vertrauensketten kommunizieren könnten, dann könnten diese Maßnahmen mit geringerem Aufwand multipliziert werden und so mit geringeren Kosten und vor allem geringerem

Know-how auch eingeführt und betrieben werden. Wir sind also eigentlich nicht zu dumm für die IT-Sicherheit, aber wir benutzen die Ressourcen – also unser kollektives Know-how – nicht effizient, weil wir den Experten nicht das geeignete Vertrauen schenken und die dafür notwendigen vertrauenswürdigen Infrastrukturen nicht anlegen.

Dafür gibt es wieder viele Gründe, warum es sich in den letzten 20 Jahren so entwickelt hat, wie es nun einmal ist. Wichtig ist aber, dass wir die Chancen, die gerade durch zentralisierte Organisationen wie DCSO, VOICE, ITZBund, BWI und viele andere entstehen und die Konsolidierungsvorhaben in diesen Organisationen auch wirklich nutzen. Die Konsolidierung der Bundes-IT im Leistungsverbund ITZBund und BWI könnte hier Vorbild werden, wenn die formulierten Ziele in die Tat umgesetzt werden und nicht in Organisation, Papier und Willen hängen bleiben, sondern bis in die Konsolidierung von Plattformen und Lösungen durchgreifen und die Ergebnisse dann auch so kommuniziert werden, dass die Ergebnisse auch für andere Teilnehmer nutzbar sind – also z. B. von Branchenverbänden für deren jeweilige Branche „übersetzt" werden. So würden Vertrauensketten entstehen, welche die Erfahrungen aus unterschiedlichen Umgebungen bündeln und über vertrauenswürdige Informationsketten bis in die KRITIS Unternehmen oder die KMU weiterleiten und dabei jeweils das für den Teilnehmer konsumierbare Format zur Verfügung stellen.

24.2   IT-Sicherheitsarchitektur, was ist das, wem nutzt das, wie geht das – ein nicht ganz fiktives Beispiel

▶   **Trailer**
Das Ziel von IT-Sicherheit ist Schutz vor bestimmten, manchmal explizit benannten, manchmal auch nur abstrakt vorhandenen Risiken und Bedrohungen. Eine einzelne Maßnahme allein – z. B. der Ende-zu-Ende-verschlüsselte Datenaustausch ist nur ein Baustein für die IT-Sicherheit. Denn, wenn jeder die verwendeten Schlüssel kennt oder einfach ableiten kann, dann ist die Verschlüsselung ja kein Schutz, sondern nur ein Feigenblatt, um zu sagen man hätte ja etwas getan.

Das Zauberwort heißt IT-Sicherheitsarchitektur, also der Versuch das Thema wie beim Hausbau auch planerisch und vollständig anzugehen und dann bei der Umsetzung zuerst den Keller zu bauen und erst am Schluss das Dach aufzusetzen, weil es nun mal in der Luft schlecht hält. Wie beim Hausbau auch kommt es aber nicht nur auf den Rohbau, sondern auch auf die detaillierte Ausgestaltung der Details an – eine Dusche funktioniert nun mal ohne Wasserzuleitung nicht und wenn kein geeigneter Druck auf dem Wasser ist, dann kommt das Wasser auch nicht in den 2. Stock. Bei einem Bau ist das jedem klar – bei der IT-Sicherheit gibt es Nachholbedarf, der hier an einem nicht ganz hypothetischen Beispiel, nämlich der Konsolidierung der IT-Sicherheit über mehrere hunderttausend Arbeitsplätze mit seinen Vorteilen, Problemen und möglichen Lösungen vorgestellt wird.

24.2.1 Schutzräume für Services und Daten

Eine Sicherheitsarchitektur beschäftigt sich also zuerst mit den Risiken, gegen welche primär geschützt werden soll und welche Schutzziele dabei verfolgt werden sollen. Dabei fällt sofort auf, dass die Daten und Services rund um eine elektronische Verkaufsplattform wenige vertrauliche Elemente, aber ein hohes Maß an Integrität und Verfügbarkeit benötigen. Personaldaten hingegen benötigen – auch gesetzlich unterlegt – ein hohes Maß an Vertraulichkeit. Mit dieser Erkenntnis entwickelt man das Ziel unterschiedlicher Schutzräume für Services und Daten, meist werden diese aus Business-Sicht dann „geclustert", also in einzelne Segmente aufgeteilt, denn das Business muss später ja auch die Kosten für die Umsetzung der funktionalen Ziele und der Schutzziele tragen. Nach dieser Betrachtung stellt man fest, dass man im Unternehmen im Normalfall immer von allen Anforderungen ein bisschen was hat, also für manche Information einen hohen Vertraulichkeitsbedarf, für manche intensive Integrität und an vielen Stellen hohe Verfügbarkeit. Die erste Überlegung ist nun, man verlangt in jeder Dimension (Verfügbarkeit, Integrität und Vertraulichkeit) jeweils das höchste bei irgendeiner Information geforderte Niveau – daran muss man aber scheitern – warum?

Man kann allgemein sagen, Integrität und Vertraulichkeit auf der einen Seite und Verfügbarkeit auf der anderen Seite stehen in einem starken Spannungsverhältnis, weshalb es die eine Lösung für alles nicht geben kann. Diese Erkenntnis motiviert also dazu, eine IT-Sicherheitsarchitektur zu bauen, welche alle abstrakt notwendigen Funktionen zum Schutz vor allen Risiken enthält und diese Funktionen dann jeweils falltypisch auf die geeigneten Maßnahmen abbildet – wir werden später sehen, dass eine Abbildung auch situationsbezogen in Echtzeit sinnhaft ist.

24.2.2 Ordnung im Dschungel des Möglichen

Ein kurzer Blick ins Internet und die Themenlisten der IT-Sicherheitskonferenzen und Messen zeigt, dass es eine schier nicht endende Liste von Produktgruppen gibt: Web-Application-, Personal-, Firewalls, AntiVirus, Advanced Persistant Threat, Unified Threat Management, VPN, V-LAN, Multi Purpose Sandbox, Full-Disk-, File-, Folder-, Hardware-Encryption, PKI, CA, RA, White-, Grey-, Black-Pen-Testing… Viele der IT-Security-Funktionen werden in Software, Hardware, On-Premise, in der Cloud oder als Managed Service angeboten, enthalten aber immer im Beipackzettel, dass der Provider des Services nicht die Haftung des Daten- bzw. Service-Eigentümers übernehmen kann.

Es gilt also zu allererst den Dschungel zu ordnen und sich bei jeder Lösung die Frage zu stellen, auf welchem Sicherheitsanker, auf welcher Sicherheitsannahme beruht der Schutz der Lösung und dann nachzuvollziehen, ob in der eigenen Struktur der Schutz dieses Sicherheitsankers gewährleistet werden kann oder die Sicherheitsannahme hält und welche Seiteneffekte beim Betrieb der Lösung entstehen. So ist es z. B. ein schlechter Plan für eine Verfügbarkeit von 99,9 % einen hohen Preis zu bezahlen, wenn diese Verfügbarkeit unter

Betriebsbedingungen (also Erreichbarkeit von den vordefinierten Orten) nicht beweisbar gemessen wird. Das Messen von Vertraulichkeit ist wesentlich schwieriger – weshalb die Planung und akademische und praktische Untersuchung der Lösung auf ihre Robustheit bei diesem Schutzziel wesentlich ist.

Die Annahme, dass bei der Lösung nur eine technische Lösung mit adäquater Wirksamkeit ausgewählt und installiert werden muss, ist natürlich auch zu kurz gedacht. Auch Lösungen mit hohem Schutzgrad können falsch installiert sein oder durch administrative Fehler im Betrieb ihre Schutzwirkung einbüßen. Die sichere Inbetriebnahme und der sichere Betrieb erfordern also ein geeignetes Betriebskonzept, welches erstellt und organisatorisch oder technisch verifiziert werden muss. Im Betriebskonzept ist besonderer Wert darauf zu legen, dass die Sicherheitsanker der einzelnen Lösung durch den Betrieb anderer Maßnahmen abgesichert sind und bleiben.

24.2.3 Kosteneffizienz mit durchdachter Architektur

Ein Vorteil einer gut durchdachten Architektur in der IT-Sicherheit ist also die Wiederverwendbarkeit und der bessere Skaleneffekt, der durch die häufigere Anwendung entsteht. Dieser Skaleneffekt hat mehrere Facetten: zum einen benötigt es einiges an Know-how und generiert Kosten, eine stabile und dauerhaft „haltende", also robuste Sicherheitsarchitektur zu erstellen, so dass man diesen Vorgang nicht häufig und vor allem nicht für jeden Bedarf und jede Umgebung neu durchführt. Diese Kosten verteilen sich aber im Fall einer Wiederverwendung auf mehrere Kostenträger. Der eigentliche Skaleneffekt wird aber durch die Kosten im Betrieb deutlich. Täglich gibt es Meldungen zu neuen Angriffen und Schwachstellen in Produkten.

Die Untersuchung, ob und wie und in welcher Stückzahl man betroffen ist, ist als Teil des Risikomanagements viel effizienter, wenn standardisierte Lösungen und Betriebskonzepte vorliegen, die dann auch das Vorgehensmodell bei der Minimierung der tagesaktuellen Risikomeldungen deutlich erleichtern. Hinzu kommen Kosteneffizienz bei Einkauf, Know-how und Betrieb, wenn die Sicherheitsarchitektur, was sinnhaft ist, bis auf Produkt und Betriebskonzept standardisiert ist (Tab. 24.1).

Tab. 24.1 Vertrauensketten

	Durchgehende, lückenlose Vertrauenskette
Technik	Zusammenfügen der Sicherheitsprodukte zu einer sicheren, durchgehenden Vertrauenskette – von der Tastatur bis zu den Services und Daten
Organisation	Brückenschlag zwischen Security Awareness und technischer Lösung
Rechtssicherheit	Verfolgen der Lieferkette unter Berücksichtigung von überlagernden Rechtsräumen (z. B. patriot act)
Haftung	Wenn die Haftung für erfolgreiche Angriffe nicht durchgesetzt werden kann, muss der proaktive Schutz erhöht werden
Lieferkette	Integritätskontrolle der fertig integrierten Produkte bis in ihren produktiven Einsatz hinein

24.2.4   Unmöglichkeit einer gültigen Rechtssicherheit

Jedes der Themen hat eine eigene „Agenda", die z. T. durchaus komplex ist. Es folgt ein beliebiges Beispiel aus dem Bereich der Rechtssicherheit. Nach nationalem und auch durchaus kontinentaleuropäischem Verständnis darf ein Arbeitgeber seine Mitarbeiter nicht ohne weiteres durch das Erfassen personenbezogener Daten protokollieren. Die aktuelle Rechtslage macht es bei einer elektronischen Nachfrage, ob der Anwender in einer konkreten Situation elektronisch und rechtsverbindlich einer teilweisen Protokollierung zustimmt, notwendig, dass die Nicht-Zustimmung des Anwenders auch nicht protokolliert werden darf. Berücksichtigen die technischen Lösungen das nicht, so ist ein Einsatz im kontinentaleuropäischen Umfeld nicht rechtssicher bzw. zustimmungspflichtig. Gleichzeitig kann es sein, dass die AGB bei der Nutzung eines Services zur Anwendung kommen und dem lokal geltenden Recht widersprechen. Ist die Vertraulichkeit der Daten betroffen, so heilt natürlich die Rechtsansicht, dass die betroffene Passage der AGB nicht gültig ist, den Bruch der Vertraulichkeit nicht. Wer sich schon einmal damit beschäftigt hat, wie schwierig es ist, einen konkreten Schaden durch den Bruch der Vertraulichkeit in der elektronischen Welt in einem Rechtsverfahren von einem konkreten Dritten zu beziffern und einzufordern, wird zustimmen, dass es der einzig gute Plan ist, die Vertraulichkeit der Daten bereits vorab so sicherzustellen, dass auch Grauzonen in der Liefer- und Servicekette und der jeweils geltenden Rechtsräume nicht zu einem Datenverlust führen können. Wären also in den Snowden-Daten, die er von seinem Auftraggeber illegal mitgenommen hat und über eine „Leak-Plattform" im Internet veröffentlicht hat Teile Ihrer vertraulichen Unternehmensdaten dabei gewesen, so sind Fragen der Rechtssicherheit und Haftung extrem komplex und wahrscheinlich ist juristisch kein adäquater Schadensersatz durchsetzbar. Also gilt es, die Daten von Anfang an gut zu beschützen.

24.2.5   Sicherheit der Anwendung hängt an der Sicherheit des Systems

Zu diesem Zweck sehen wir uns die Handlungskette an, welche Daten „nutzbar" macht. Zum einen kommen die Daten irgendwoher und werden dann über Services meist auch über Netzwerke zugegriffen und über Anwendungen oder Apps dann dem Anwender dargestellt. Peter Schaar, zur damaligen Zeit Bundesdatenschutzbeauftragter, formulierte auf einer Veranstaltung treffend: „eine Anwendung kann nur so sicher sein wie das darunterliegende Betriebssystem", so dass auch dieses in die Gesamtbetrachtung einfließen muss. Wie in den Unterlagen des BSI-Kongress [2] aufgezeigt, können auf den meisten Betriebssystemen alle unter einer Kennung laufende Prozesse gegenseitig auf ihre Daten zugreifen. Deshalb müssen auch die Anwendungen, die gleichzeitig laufen, darauf betrachtet werden, ob sie schädlichen Code enthalten oder selbst über Hintertüren oder fehlerhafte Implementierungen zu Einfallstoren werden können. Der Anwender kann dann, nachdem er Daten dargestellt bekommen hat, die Daten meist mit anderen Anwendungen weiterverarbeiten, speichern, drucken verschicken etc. Prinzipiell kann man davon ausgehen, dass, wenn der Anwender beliebige Freiheit bei der weiteren Verarbeitung hat, man die Daten später elektronisch nicht wiedererkennen kann, da sie zu Bildinformation oder verschlüsselt oder in andere Formate gewandelt werden können. Für die Ziele der Integrität und Vertraulichkeit gilt es also die gesamte Handlungskette so zu organisieren, dass ein adäquater Schutz in allen Lebenslagen für die Daten besteht – das klingt noch relativ einfach, wenn man die wirklich sensiblen Daten in geeignet geschützten Datenräumen unterbringt und die Anwender und Services in diesem Datenraum einer strikten Kontrolle unterliegen, also die erarbeitete IT-Sicherheitsarchitektur dort nach den Zielen der Integrität und Vertraulichkeit vollständig und mit hoher Mechanismus-Stärke/Robustheit durchgesetzt wird. Zur Betrachtung der vollständigen Handlungskette müssen wir uns aber den „gesamten Lebenszyklus" und die ganze Handlungskette beginnend mit dem Booten und der Anmeldung ansehen.

24.2.6 Angriff auf den Deutschen Bundestag

Warum ist ein Anwender zu einer bestimmten Aktivität berechtigt und ein anderer nicht? Warum kann jemand, der physikalisch im Besitz eines Zugangsgerätes, z. B. eines legitimierten Notebooks, ist, auf die Daten und Services zugreifen, ein anderer über das gleiche Gerät aber nicht? Generell ist dieser Aspekt als IAM (Identity and Access Management) in der IT-Sicherheit adressiert. Angriffe auf die Passworteingabe mittels „über die Schulter schauen" und Soft- oder Hardware-Keylogger sind bekannt und können mit guten Awarenessmaßnahmen (auch gegen Kameras) und einigen Endpoint Security Lösungen verhindert werden. Der Angriff auf den Deutschen Bundestag in 2015 hat aber gezeigt, dass auch über andere Angriffe wie PassTheHash und Mimikatz die Identität eines Anwenders gestohlen werden kann, ohne dass man dessen Passwort und Username benötigt. Das Problem des Identitätsdiebstahls ist also viel komplexer als dem Anwender seinen Besitz (Smartcard oder Zugangstoken) und sein Wissen (Passwort/PIN) zu stehlen. Viele Sicherheitsberater gehen heute davon aus, dass man nicht jede Umgebung „sauber" halten kann und in manche IT-Umgebungen wenig Vertrauen setzen sollte – insbesondere in solche, welche über viele Services notwendigerweise mit dem Internet verbunden sind und dazu auch wirklich Nutzdaten austauschen. Wird also eine Kennung für diese „unsicheren" Umgebungen verwendet und gleichzeitig (ohne Zusatzschutz) für die sicheren Datenräume, dann passt die Umsetzung der Architektur nicht. Prinzipiell ist – auch durch die AGB-Betrachtung oben – jetzt klar, dass die Eingabe eines mehrfach nutzbaren Passwortes oder einer solchen PIN auf der Tastatur eines mobilen Endgerätes (IOS oder Android machen dabei keinen Unterschied) als nicht sicher betrachtet werden muss, diese Identität aus Sicht der Sicherheit also als „einfach zu stehlen" anzusehen ist und deshalb keine Sicherheitsanker darstellen kann. Wenn aber die Identität gestohlen ist, greifen alle nachfolgenden Sicherheitsmaßnahmen, die auf den Rechten einzelner beruhen, nicht mehr. Gleiches gilt natürlich für die Übernahme von Benutzerrechten durch schadhafte, parallel laufende Anwendungen auf einem IT-System, mit welchem der Anwender tatsächlich arbeitet.

Einem Benutzer sind aber meist mehrere Kennungen für unterschiedliche Datenräume nicht zuzumuten. Wichtig ist hier also die Vertrauensstellung der einzelnen Systeme untereinander. Ein System mit hoher Vertrauensstellung kann ein automatisches Login in ein niedrigeres System durchführen – umgekehrt darf das nicht passieren. Prinzipiell gilt also, dass die Tastatur zur Eingabe eines mehrfach verwendbaren Passwortes oder einer solchen PIN im „Sicherheitsraum" der genutzten Daten und Services liegen muss. Um lokale Angriffe sicher zu vermeiden, gilt es auch bestimmte Vorkehrungen bei der Kommunikation der Tastatureingaben zu treffen, wenn Passwort oder PIN betroffen sind.

24.2.7   Erwartungshaltung für mobile Sicherheit

Bereits früher haben wir auf die „Echtzeitfähigkeit" einer Sicherheitsarchitektur hingewiesen. Lassen Sie uns dazu noch ein praktisches Beispiel verfolgen. Ein Notebook ist über eine Dockingstation über Ethernetkabel mit dem Hausnetz verbunden. Alle Funkfähigkeiten des Notebooks sind ausgeschaltet, weil kein Bedarf gesehen wird. Jetzt nimmt der Anwender das Notebook aus der Dockingstation und geht auf Reise. Die Erwartungshaltung ist gleiche Sicherheit im mobilen Betrieb, da ja der gleiche Anwender auf die gleichen Daten zugreifen kann. D. h. Themen wie VPN, Personal Firewall, „Friendly Net Management" sollen also – um den Betrieb im Hausnetz nicht zu verlangsamen – erst jetzt „zugeschaltet" werden. Die Sicherheitsarchitektur kennt also den abstrakten Bedarf sicherer Kommunikation und unterscheidet diesen je nach IT-Element. Ein Webserver wird mehr auf Verfügbarkeit ausgerichtet sein. Das Tablet eines Vorstandes auf Ergonomie und Vertraulichkeit. Bei multipler Nutzung in verschiedenen Netzen ist der Übergang technisch unterstützt und spontan, sollte aber evtl. aus Sicht der User-Awareness mit einer Echtzeitinformation begleitet werden, die z. B. in Erinnerung ruft, dass bei der Eingabe von Passworten auch eine Kamera auf dem Flughafen über die Schulter schauen kann und der Nutzer sich an sein Briefing erinnern möchte.

Mitarbeiter des Fraunhofer SIT haben gezeigt, dass ein Notebook über eine Browserschwachstelle angegriffen werden kann, wenn es im gleichen WLAN angemeldet ist, in welchem sich auch der Angreifer befindet. Wenn also die auf dem Notebook laufenden Anwendungen nicht auf solche Schwachstellen intensiv geprüft wurden und die VPN-Verbindung nicht hohe Schutzanforderungen erfüllt, sollte man in fremden WLAN-Umgebungen auf besonders sensible Datenverarbeitung verzichten. Man sollte also die Security Policy in Echtzeit an die Netzsituation anpassen – ein Themenfeld, welches auch unter dem Namen friendly net detection bekannt ist.

24.2.8   Bewertung des erreichten Schutzes

Wir haben jetzt also erarbeitet, dass eine IT-Sicherheitsarchitektur immer unterschiedliche Komponenten aufweist, die aus Betriebssystemen und deren Härtung, der Netzkommunikation, der Klassifikation von Daten und Services, Kryptosystemen, Sicherheitsankern in Technik und Organisation und vielen weiteren Elementen bestehen, die dann jeweils auf technische und organisatorische Lösungen abgebildet werden, wobei insbesondere die Mehrfachnutzung von Betriebskonzepten und des Know-hows zu einer Standardisierung der Produkte führt. Ein wesentlicher, wirklich schwieriger Schritt ist jetzt die Bewertung des erreichten Schutzes durch eine konkrete Implementierung der Architektur. Praktisch gibt es heute leider noch keine Metrik für den Schutzgrad. Ein Zertifikat nach Common Criteria schützt nur vor den im Protection Profile definierten Gefahren in einer meist als ideal angenommenen Betriebslandschaft. Zwingend sind also Tests der Robustheit des Gesamtsystems. Das Suchen nach Schwachstellen ist um mindestens den Faktor 10 in vielen Fällen sogar 100 bis 1000 teurer als das Verifizieren der fachlichen Korrektheit, da nicht nur positive Tests, sondern eben auch beliebig strukturierte Angriffe durchzuführen sind, die auf das Fehlverhalten einzelner Komponenten abzielen. Umso wichtiger ist es, die Erkenntnisse in diesem Umfeld auszutauschen und die Barrieren gegen den Austausch zu beseitigen.

Aktuell geht die Bundesregierung mit dem Projekt der Konsolidierung der IT des Bundes einen wesentlichen Schritt, der – wie oben dargestellt – extreme Einsparungsmöglichkeiten bei gleichzeitiger Verbesserung des Schutzes ermöglicht, wenn es gelingt die Barrieren zu beseitigen. Einige der Ressorts sind bezüglich ihrer eigenen IT-Sicherheitsarchitektur – auch dem inneren Schutzbedarf geschuldet – natürlicherweise weiter als andere. Das „Quermultiplizieren" einer fertig implementierten Architektur in eine andere Umgebung stößt aber auf natürliche Widerstände in Organisation und Technik. Für den Schutz der IT in der Industrie und der Wirtschaft wäre es also sehr hilfreich, die Erfahrungen und Ergebnisse der einzelnen Ressorts und vor allem der Konsolidierung kennen zu lernen, da man dadurch einen hohen Schutz bei geringen eigenen Vorlaufkosten erwarten kann. Nachdem der Konsolidierungsprozess gerade im Laufen ist, empfehlen wir hier, die wesentlichen Stakeholder und deren Ergebnisse bezüglich der fertig implementierten IT-Sicherheitsarchitektur als Vorbildfunktion zu sehen und sich eine geeignete IT-Landschaft bezüglich Größe, Schutzbedarf, Verteilung etc. herauszusuchen und zu verfolgen, welche Empfehlungen und Ergebnisse dort ankommen.

24.3   Was läuft falsch in der Cyber-Sicherheit?

▷   **Trailer**
Die Vorteile einer IT-Sicherheitsarchitektur wurden bereits in Abschn. 24.2 „IT-Sicherheitsarchitektur – Was ist das, wem nutzt das, wie geht das?" beschrieben. Höhere Robustheit bei gleichzeitiger Kostensenkung sind dabei die Treiber.

Viele größere Unternehmen die mittels Zukäufen gewachsen sind, kennen das Problem der inhomogenen IT-Landschaft genauso gut wie die Generäle, die jetzt im CIR unter General Leinhos nicht nur versuchen müssen in jedem Projekt auf dem Wasser zu Lande und der Luft eine Vergleichbarkeit der Robustheit des Schutzes herzustellen, sondern auch noch den Auftrag bekommen haben Deutschland im Cyber Informationsraum (kurz CIR) zu verteidigen – das Bundesmnisterium des Innern geht dem gleichen Auftrag bei anderen Bedrohungslagen nach. Natürlich kann man zuerst versuchen zu klären, wer hat welche innere und wer welche äußere Verantwortung, was ist der deutsche CIR überhaupt, welche Schlüsseltechnologien benötigen wir, in welchen Fällen dürfen wir aktiv verteidigen, wie sehen die Mandatierungsprozesse dafür aus, wenn klar ist, dass es im CIR um Sekunden geht. Wir finden noch viele weitere Fragen, deren Klärung uns aber auch nicht besser schützt, weil zwar die Prozesse und Zuständigkeiten dann geklärt sind, aber das operative Geschäft des aktiven Schutzes noch nicht durchgeführt wird. Deshalb wird an dieser Stelle von den Mandatsträgern auf die neuen Aktivitäten verwiesen, die alle an der Stärkung des aktiven Schutzes beteiligt sein werden: das Cyber Abwehrzentrum [3], das weiter ausgebaute BSI, zentrale Stelle für Informationstechnik im Sicherheitsbereich (kurz ZITIS) etc.

Ende Mai 2017 hat Frau Dr. v. d. Leyen auf dem Bitkom politischen Abend in Berlin (siehe Abb. 24.5) überzeugend dargestellt [4], dass die Fähigkeiten der Bundeswehr und das dazu benötigte Material auf dem Wasser, in der Luft und auf dem Land viele Milliarden Euro kosten, die Nutzung der Fähigkeiten aber eigentlich alle IT-abhängig sind. Dass also der Schutz der IT erst die Grundvoraussetzung dafür schafft, die Fähigkeiten auch im

Abb. 24.5 Bitkom politischer Abend Sicherheitspolitik 4.0 mit Verteidigungsministerin Dr. Ursula von der Leyen

Fall der Fälle wirklich nutzen zu können. In der Bundeswehr ist klar, dass die IT-Sicherheit eine mehrdimensionale Aufgabe darstellt. Diese Situation ist auf fast alle Unternehmen übertragbar. Der Maschinenbauer muss seine inneren Prozesse wie bisher schützen (z. B. auch DLP), seine Produktionsumgebung davor schützen, dass keine unbekannten, unerwünschten Funktionen in seine IT-gestützten Maschinen vordringen können und dem Kunden die „Sicherheit" geben, dass die produzierten Waren, Maschinen, Autos, Flugzeuge etc. bezüglich der in den Waren verbauten IT gut geschützt ausgeliefert werden und sich selbst (Security by Design) in der fremden Umgebung vor Angriffen schützen – und natürlich nicht selbst schon in ihrer Hard-, Firm- oder Software schädliche Elemente tragen, die im Produktionsprozess oder innerhalb der Lieferkette „angereichert" wurden. Je weiter fortgeschritten das Unternehmen in der Digitalisierung ist, je digitaler die Produkte sind und je kritischer die Produkte in der Verwendung später sein können, umso wichtiger wird also dieses mehrdimensionale Verständnis von Schutz und Sicherheit.

> **Fragen**
>
> Was sind nun die begrenzenden Faktoren bei dem Versuch, die richtige IT-Sicherheit „an allen Fronten" mit einer guten durchgängigen IT-Sicherheitsarchitektur adäquat zu etablieren – was also läuft noch falsch?

Know-how: Alle Welt beklagt den Fachkräftemangel. Im öffentlichen Bereich kommt hinzu, dass die Gehaltsstrukturen nicht immer identisch zu den Strukturen der freien Wirtschaft sind. Betrachten wir aber das klassische Vorgehensmodell im öffentlichen Sektor, so stellen wir fest, dass einiges von diesem Problem hausgemacht ist.

IT-Sicherheit ist komplex und in vielen Stellen einer Organisation zu verankern. Bildet nun jede Organisation den gesamten Zyklus der IT-Sicherheit in der eigenen Organisation ab, so entsteht Bedarf an IT-Sicherheitsarchitekten, Penetrationstestern, die in der Lage sind, die Robustheit von Lösungen im Markt zu bewerten Beschaffern mit Cyber-Security-Kenntnissen, Administratoren, die verstehen was man wann warum nicht tut sowie Personal, welches die Kosten-Nutzen-Rechnung adäquat im Management darstellen kann, einer Rechtsabteilung, die zu würdigen versteht, wie die neue Rechtslage in technischen oder organisatorischen Schutz umgesetzt werden kann. Unter den Schlagworten „Security by Design" und „Privacy by Design" werden noch ganz neue Know-how-Gruppen gefordert. Ob das ein Web-Service im Zuge des E-Gouvernements ist, der personenbezogene Daten trägt, oder sensible Daten, die für Angreifer besonders interessant sind wie z. B. der erfolgreiche Angriff auf die Daten bei der US-Börsenaufsicht [5] im September 2017, der es den Angreifern ermöglichte, hohe Spekulationsgewinne an den Börsen einzufahren, jede öffentliche Verwaltung hat IT, hat personenbezogene Daten und sensible Daten (und seien es auch nur die Login-Daten ihrer Anwender), die es zu schützen gilt.

Alleine im Raum Koblenz bis Köln sind mit vielen sicherheitsrelevanten Stellen der Bundeswehr, dem BSI, dem Bundesamt für Verfassungsschutz, der Bundespolizei und der operativen IT von einigen Bundesbehörden schon so viele Organisationen angesiedelt, die die IT-Sicherheit wirklich ernst nehmen, dass nicht nur mit den vielen privatwirtschaftlichen Unternehmen am Arbeitsmarkt ein Wettbewerb um die richtigen Personen entsteht. Es bestehen zwar Arbeitsgruppen und Kooperationen, aber keine vollständige Vertrauenskette, welche die Ergebnisse der einen Stelle direkt in die nächste übernimmt. Warum kann man sich nicht zusammentun und „das beste von allem" gemeinsam entwickeln und so im Sinne einer gemeinsamen IT-Sicherheitsarchitektur Kosten sparen und Ressourcen inkl. Know-how schonen.

Plakativ gesprochen fehlen für dieses Vorgehen nicht nur das Vertrauen zwischen den Organisationen, ja zum Teil sogar das Vertrauen zwischen zwei Standorten der gleichen Organisation,

sondern auch die Grundlagen und der Prozess, der diese gemeinsame Planung und Umsetzung ermöglichen würde – denn man weiß ja nicht genau was dort gemacht wird. Zwar ist mit dem BSI-Gesetz [6] ein formaler Schritt in die Richtung der Zentralisierung der Kompetenzen gemacht, aber die Praxis sieht noch anders aus.

An erster Stelle werden hier Punkte angeführt wie: „Behörden können keine konkreten Aussagen zu Produkten weitergeben, da das eine Marktverzerrung wäre und dem Wettbewerb entgegen steht" und natürlich darf die Herkunft eines Produktes kein Kriterium einer Ausschreibung sein. Sehr wohl muss aber die gewünschte Robustheit des Schutzes über das Beschaffungsverfahren so transportiert werden, dass im Ergebnis nicht nur auf einem Formular ausgefüllt wird, dass eine bestimmte beschriebene Schutzqualität gegeben ist, sondern dieser Schutz auch real geleistet wird. Es muss also in Ausschreibungen möglich sein einen gewissen technischen Schutz so zu beschreiben, dass er als KO-Kriterium mindestens eingehalten wird – im Sinne des Schutzes nicht der Funktionalität.

Eine Aussage wie „das kryptografische Verfahren darf nicht mit einfachen Mitteln gebrochen werden können" muss also notwendig mit Penetrationstests von unabhängigen Dritten oder kompetentem Personal aus dem eigenen Haus unterlegt werden, die nicht nur versuchen das verschlüsselte Ergebnis anzugreifen, sondern eben auch den Schutz der gespeicherten Schlüssel, der Herleitung der Schlüssel und vieler weiterer Verfahren, die zur Gesamtsicherheit beitragen. Solche Prüfungen sind zum einen wirklich schwer klar in Ausschreibungen zu formulieren und zum anderen ist die Prüfung, wenn sie sachgemäß durchgeführt wird, sehr aufwändig, zeitintensiv und teuer.

Wie früher schon im Text dargestellt, lohnt es sich noch zu verstehen, wie die beiden Themen Qualität und Schutz, bzw. Robustheit des Schutzes (früher auch Mechanismus Stärke genannt) miteinander verwandt sind. IT-Sicherheitsprodukte schützen vor etwas, das man nicht sieht, schmeckt, fühlt oder messen kann, nämlich konkreten Bedrohungen durch Angriffsvektoren.

In der IT-Sprache sind das Bedrohungen auf die Verfügbarkeit, z. B. DDoS, die Integrität, z. B. Fake News oder die Vertraulichkeit, z. B. der Angriff auf die Börsenaufsicht [7] als Basis oder dann im weiteren auf die Authentizität, z. B. im Dt. Bundestag durch den Diebstahl von User Accounts [8], die Verbindlichkeit, z. B. elektronische TANs über SMS-Umleitung im elektronischen Bankverkehr und viele weitere abgeleitete Bedrohungen. Das prinzipielle Vorgehen, wenn man sich vor solchen Bedrohungen schützen möchte, ist es, in organisatorische oder technische Maßnahmen zu investieren. Was, wenn diese nicht schützen, sondern sogar durch eigene Schwachstellen neue Bedrohungen ermöglichen, wie das z. B. bei einem Sicherheitsprodukt über die letzten Jahre mehrfach passiert ist.

24.3.1 Beispielhafte Schwachstellen in einem Sicherheitsprodukt im zeitlichen Verlauf:

Beispiel

- 2014: Update für kritische Lücken im Endpoint Protection Manager [9]
- 2015: Endpoint Protection: Gefährlicher Sicherheitslücken-Cocktail [10]
- 2016: Kritische Lücke gefährdet Antiviren-Produkte [11]
- 2016: Angreifer können Endpoint Protection Code unterjubeln [12]

Ob hinter diesen Schwachstellen der Sicherheitsprodukte eine höhere Strategie liegt, das Know-how bei der Entwicklung fehlte (Security by Design), die geforderte Geschwindigkeit der Freigabe (Time to Market) nicht genug Zeit zum Testen ließ, die Gründe können vielfältig sein. Es sei explizit erwähnt, dass das Produkt nur beispielhaft mit Zitaten unterlegt ist und der Leser auch bei anderen – zweifelsohne nicht bei allen – Sicherheitsprodukten eine solche Liste von zeitlich immer wiederkehrenden Schwachstellen findet. Für die Betrachtung hier ist wichtig, dass es sich bei diesen Schwachstellen nicht um technische Probleme im eigentlichen Sinn handelt. Eine Software, die nach Kauf nicht „verteilt" werden kann, nicht installierbar ist oder deren Einsatz aus anderen technischen Gründen nicht möglich ist, wird entlang der üblichen Beschaffungsverfahren wie z. B. einer Ausschreibung einfach rückabgewickelt. Bei IT-Sicherheit ist das anders. Zum einen gibt es keine Metrik, die die Robustheit des Verfahrens „beweist", zum anderen gibt es auch keine Haftung auf Schutz, der mit dem Einsatz verbunden sein sollte, auch wenn dieser konform zum Manual war. Und natürlich gibt es niemanden, der in die Lösungen „ganz durchdringend" hineinschauen kann, denn nur derjenige, der alles was „drin" ist ganz verstanden hat, kann beurteilen wie es um die innen mitgebrachte Sicherheit aussieht und welcher Schutz von außen für dieses Teilsystem noch nötig ist. Das Handlungsversprechen „Sicherheit" wird also in der IT ganz anders vermarktet, verkauft, bewertet, beschafft und eingesetzt, als klassische funktionale Anforderungen in der IT.

Vielleicht ist dieser besondere Umstand in der IT-Sicherheit ein Grund dafür, dass das Department of Homeland Security als zentrale Stelle für alle nationalen Behörden in den USA den Einsatz der Produkte der Firma Kaspersky Labs [13] verbietet, wenig später zieht Großbritannien [14] nach. In Deutschland wird die Situation „liberaler" bewertet. So macht der Artikel „Warum benutzt Brandenburgs Polizei russische Software" [15] klar, dass der Einsatz von Sicherheitssoftware einer Firma, die Natalja Kaspersky [16] gehört, bei einer Landespolizei in Deutschland in den Medien durchaus problematisch gesehen wird, aber die Landespolizei keine Probleme bei dieser Situation sieht. In Abb. 24.6 wird dargestellt warum es nötig sein kann sehr genau hinzuschauen und dabei auch die „Verpackung" zu öffnen, wenn man unterscheiden will ob etwas Gutes oder gefährliches in einer Lieferung enthalten ist.

Das Sicherheitsgesetz in Deutschland beleuchtet diese Frage von einer Seite für sogenannte kritische Infrastrukturen (kurz KRITIS) und führt den Begriff der Mindeststandards

Abb. 24.6 „Whitelisting/Blacklisting allein ist chancenlos". (Quelle: it Watch 2012)

als das Bindemittel zwischen Bedrohung und Schutz ein; sozusagen als Feststellung wie viel Schutz muss in welchem System mindestens bestehen, wenn man eine bestimmte Bedrohungslage betrachtet. Eine der Fragen zu Metrik und gemeinsamem Verständnis des Schutzes ist also, wer kann bei den gesetzten Mindeststandards beurteilen, ob bei konkreten IT-Systemen diese Mindeststandards eingehalten werden. Sobald technische Lösungen für das Erreichen des Schutzes notwendig sind, also organisatorische und Awareness-Maßnahmen nicht ausreichen, muss also notwendigerweise einer konkreten Lösung mit einem konkreten Betriebskonzept auch eine Mechanismusstärke beim Schutz zugewiesen werden, um zu beurteilen, ob die minimalen Schutzbedingungen erreicht sind. In Abb. 24.7 ist anschaulich dargestellt, dass der Anwender als menschliche Firewall keine geeignete Mechanismusstärke gegen Bedrohungen über Funkwellen ist.

Abb. 24.7 Kein Zugriff – Funkwellen verboten. Vortrag: Benutzerzentrierte IT-Sicherheit, senkt Kosten und ist „praktisch". (Quelle: Mörl 2015)

24.3.2   Unterstützung organisatorischer Verfahren durch technische Aspekte

Dass es bei realen Systemen immer notwendig ist organisatorische Verfahren durch Technische zu unterstützen, wird an einigen Beispielen sofort deutlich. Ein Anwender kann nicht bei Funkwellen prüfen, ob diese „gut" sind – es gilt technisch den Sender zu authentisieren und dann die Protokolle geeignet zu schützen. Ein USB-Device kann ganz genau so aussehen, wie das, welches der Anwender jeden Tag verwendet, aber im inneren sind während seines Urlaubs andere Firmware, Hardware oder Software-Komponenten verbaut worden – von außen kann das niemand sehen. Für den kriminellen Umbau von Originalgeräten gibt es im Darknet gegen Bezahlung perfekten Service [17]. Seine Maus und Tatstatur während des Urlaubs im Safe einzusperren erscheint eine unrealistische Lösung. Nachdem die vorhandenen Standards zur Authentisierung von Mailadressen nicht weltweit umgesetzt wurden, kann der Anwender nicht entscheiden, ob die Mail wirklich von der im Senderfeld angezeigten Person stammt. Insofern ist es für den Anwender bei guten Mailangriffen nicht möglich zu sagen, welche Attachments zu öffnen sind und welche nicht. Gerade bei Mitarbeitern im Personalbereich ist klar, dass sich Unbekannte melden und den Kontakt über E-Mail und Attachments unterschiedlicher Objektstruktur (Word, pdf, jpg, Links auf Videos) suchen – ebenso geht es Bankmitarbeitern im Immobilienvertrieb und vielen anderen immer digitaleren Prozessbeteiligten an der Kunden- oder Bürgerschnittstelle. Im E-Governement wird die „Bürgerschnittstelle" immer stärker digitalisiert. Jede Kommune hat sensible personenbezogene Daten. Aber hat die Kommune auch das Know-how, die Beschaffungsverfahren, die finanziellen Mittel etc., um eine IT-Sicherheitsarchitektur selbst zu entwickeln, zu beschreiben, auszuschreiben, zu beschaffen und dann nachhaltig zu implementieren, so dass bestimmte zentral beschriebene Mindestanforderungen erfüllt sind? Neben den eigenen ‚hausinternen' Anforderungen gibt es immer auch externe regulierende Faktoren, wie z. B. die europäische Datenschutzgrundverordnung.

Hier einige statistische Daten: während der Bund für IT etwas über 1 Mrd. Euro ausgibt, liegen die Ausgaben deutschlandweit in Ländern und Kommunen bei ca. 30 Mrd. Euro. Der Koalitionsvertrag der letzten Legislatur geht von einem Zielwert von 10 % der IT-Ausgaben für IT-Sicherheit aus. Es sollte also genug Volumen vorhanden sein, um den erforderlichen Schutz umzusetzen und so zu testieren, dass eine Vorbildfunktion für andere Marktteilnehmer wie z. B. KMU entsteht. Noch besser wäre es natürlich, wenn die Architektur und der Bebauunggsplan, der zur positiven Testierung geführt haben, ebenso kommuniziert würden und damit als Blaupause für andere gelten könnten. Bevor ein Resultat erkennbar wird, gilt es noch zu überprüfen, ob denn bei dem Schutzziel klarer Konsens besteht. Es darf nämlich nicht verheimlicht werden, dass es mittlerweile viele Menschen in Deutschland gibt, die die hohen Anforderungen des Datenschutzes als überholt sehen und am liebsten auch die Anforderungen aus der Europäischen Datenschutzgrundverordnung als „antik" und nicht relevant betrachten würden. Im Wahlkampf hat beispielsweise die FDP mit dem Slogan „Digital first, Bedenken second" [18] geworben, von einer Staatssekretärin im Verkehrsministerium des Bundes war auf der Cyber-Security-Konferenz in München zu dem Thema

Digitalisierung zu hören „nutzt die Chancen, vergesst die Risiken" [19]. Dieser Aspekt sollte nicht vernachlässigt werden, denn es stellt sich ja auch die Frage, wie geht der Schutz des nationalen Cyber-Informationsraumes auf demokratischem Boden. Sollten wir also feststellen, dass die Demokratie sich von bestimmten Grundwerten wegentwickelt, dann muss das auch die geeigneten Auswirkungen haben.

So lange aber die Datenschutzwerte gesetzlich so geregelt sind, wie es sich in Bezug auf personenbezogene Daten aktuell darstellt, müssen sich auch alle Beteiligten an die Gesetze halten. Leider ist die Strafverfolgung ausserhalb Europas schwierig bis unmöglich, je nachdem in welchem Zielland der Verstoß erfolgt. Dadurch haben in Bezug auf Werbung und Marketing Unternehmen mit Sitz in bestimmten Ländern große Vorteile. Es gilt also gleiche Chancen für alle herzustellen, zumindest für kontinentaleuropäische Unternehmen die gleiche reale Wettbewerbssituation herzustellen, indem eben auch Lösungen für die Verfolgbarkeit von Datenschutzthemen nationaler personenbezogener Daten bei Unternehmen außerhalb Europas mit der gleichen Wirksamkeit etabliert werden.

Von verschiedenen Marktteilnehmern wird oft beklagt, dass es schwierig sei, Industrie 4.0 auf der Basis einer Gesetzgebung 1.0 nachhaltig aufzubauen. Für die Strafverfolgung sieht die Sachlage nicht besser aus. Wenn aber der Schutz im Cyber-Informationsraum (noch) nicht durch den Staat mit den bezahlten Steuermitteln vollständig wahrgenommen werden kann, dann bleibt dem einzelnen nur den aktiven Schutz seiner Daten, Services und digitalisierten Prozesse zu erhöhen oder eben die Risiken zu vernachlässigen.

24.3.3 Geeignete Maßnahmen

Was sind nun die notwendigen Maßnahmen, um die erkannten Probleme aus dem Weg zu räumen. Zuallererst müssen die qualifizierten Kräfte, die vorhanden sind, gebündelt werden und nicht weiter zersplittert. Heute zeigt sich eine Tendenz, dass sich jede Region, jede Behörde, jeder Verband, jede Branche, jede Unternehmensgröße ihr eigenes Cyber-Security-Cluster bildet, wodurch sich die Kräfte der Know-how-Träger nicht bündeln, sondern weiter zersplittern, weil keine Orchestrierung der Maßnahmen und Gruppen stattfindet. Regulierung, so sie auf demokratischem Boden gewünscht ist, kann nur vom Staat ausgehen. Die Erfahrungen aus dem Projekt der Konsolidierung der IT des Bundes, in welchem notwendig auch die IT-Sicherheit als ein Teilbereich der IT konsolidiert wird, sind eine hervorragende Möglichkeit Know-how zu bündeln.

Das Know-how zu Lösungen für den Schutz, welches es zu bündeln gilt, hat mindestens drei Säulen: Eigenerklärungen der gesamten Lieferkette, Beurteilungen des erreichten Schutzes durch unabhängige Dritte und Berichte über qualifizierte Betriebserfahrungen. Lieferanten müssen bei Lieferungen in der IT-Sicherheit zumindest gegenüber dem interessierten Kunden transparent machen, welche Komponenten in dem ausgelieferten Produkt verbaut sind. Diese Liste muss vollständig sein und die Vollständigkeit muss mit signifikanter Haftung des CEOs des Lieferanten bestätigt sein. Es darf z. B. nicht sein, dass bei einem Exploit, wie Heartbleed, in einer Open Source Komponente, die in vielen

Lösungen verbaut ist, der Kunde aber gar nicht weiß, wo er überall reagieren muss, weil er gar nicht weiß, was alles verbaut ist.

Im besten Fall beschafft der Lieferant von allen im Fertigprodukt verbauten Lieferungen identische Eigenerklärungen und reicht die Haftung an den Endkunden durch. Prüfungen der Robustheit von Produkten/Lösungen/Verfahren und der Verlässlichkeit von Beratungsleistungen auf den jeweiligen Kernsektoren müssen, wenn sie mit Steuermitteln erstellt wurden, an alle anderen steuerkonsumierenden Stellen weitergegeben werden, die ähnliche Investitionen durchführen wollen oder müssen. Die Qualität des Prüfungsergebnisses kann dabei geeignet nivelliert werden, da die Qualität der Prüfung sicher nicht die gleiche ist, wenn Prüfungen von kleinen Kommunen mit wenig Mitteln und andere aufwändig gestaltete Prüfungen von großen Bundesbehörden mit IT-Sicherheitshintergrund gemeinsam einfliessen. Hier ist signifikante Forschungsarbeit zu leisten, um zu verstehen wie die Anonymität des Informationsgebers gewährleistet werden und gleichzeitig der oben beschriebene Qualitätsparameter geeignet eingebracht werden kann. Schutz der zwar sicher wäre, sich aber nicht betreiben lässt, ist nicht empfehlenswert.

Daher ist es wichtig, dass die Betriebserfahrungen der Betreiber der öffentlichen Hand in einer anonymisierten Form an andere Betreiber der öffentlichen Hand (denn alle bezahlen ihre IT mit Steuermitteln) verfügbar gemacht werden. Es ist dabei wichtig, dass man nicht Äpfel mit Birnen vergleicht, denn eine Hochsicherheitsumgebung mit wenigen hundert Usern hat natürlich andere Betriebsaspekte als eine gemeinsame Infrastruktur für hunderttausend Anwender.

Diese drei Säulen wären ein erster Schritt, um sowohl eine echte Vertrauensbasis zwischen den öffentlichen Auftraggebern und im Weiteren zu ihren Lieferanten zu schaffen. Diese Vertrauensbeziehung kann dann nachhaltig bewirtschaftet werden. Dadurch bilden sich ganz natürlich Know-how-Schwerpunkte heraus, die das Vertrauen weiter stärken und sukzessive zu intensive Mehrfach-Besetzungen der gleichen Themen überflüssig machen. Die IT-Sicherheit könnte durch dieses Vorgehensmodell vom „Glauben" und den Bauchschmerzen wegen der Angst vor vagen Bedrohungen mehr in Richtung einer transparenten auf Fakten basierenden Entscheidung wachsen. Der Schutz des Cyber-Informationsraumes kann dann mit weniger Aufwand auf demokratischem Boden gemeinsam entwickelt werden.

Quellenverzeichnis

Literatuverweis

1. Eilsers, Carsten, „OpenSSL – Der Heartbleed Bug und seine Folgen", https://www.ceilers-news.de/serendipity/483-OpenSSL-Der-Heartbleed-Bug-und-seine-Folgen.html, Zugriff am 01.12.2017.
2. Mörl, Ramon itWatch GmbH: „BadUSB, vergleichbare Exploits – sinnvolle Verteidigungsstrategie", 2015, Augsabe 1.
3. (Unknown, „Enge Kooperation, klare Trennung der Befugnisse", https://www.bsi.bund.de/DE/Themen/Cyber-Sicherheit/Aktivitaeten/Cyber-Abwehrzentrum/cyberabwehrzentrum.html; Zugegriffen: 28.09.2017).

4. (Unknown, „Politischer Abend des Bitkom: Sicherheitspolitik 4.0", https://www.bitkom.org/Themen/Datenschutz-Sicherheit/Sicherheit/Inhaltsseite-2.html; Zugriff am 29.09.2017).

5. (Unknown, „Hacker knackten US-Börsenaufsicht ";http://www.handelsblatt.com/-finanzen/geldpolitik/offenbar-insiderhandel-hacker-knackten-us-boersenaufsicht/20356712.html; Zugegriffen: 21.09.2017).

6. (BSI Gesetz; Bundesgesetzblatt Jahrgang; 2009 Teil I Nr. 54).

7. (Beutelsbacher, Stefan; „Angriff auf die Schatzkammer der US-Börsenaufsicht"; https://www.welt.de/wirtschaft/article168951707/Brisanter-Angriff-auf-die-Schatzkammer-der-US-Boer-senaufsicht.html, Welt N24; 22.09.2017)

8. (Tanriverdi, Hakan; „Hackerangriff auf Bundestag", http://www.sueddeutsche.de/digital/netz-sicherheit-hackerangriff-auf-den-bundestag-1.3440215; Süddeutsche Zeitung; Zugegriffen: 28. März 2017)

9. (Scherschel, Fabian A., „Update für kritische Lücken im Symantec Endpoint Protection Mana-ger", https://www.heise.de/security/meldung/Update-fuer-kritische-Luecken-im-Symantec-End-point-Protection-Manager-2114834.html; 14.02.2014, Zugegriffen: 11.10.2017)

10. (Schirrmacher,Dennis; „Symantec Endpoint Protection: Gefährlicher Sicherheitslücken-Cocktail", https://www.heise.de/security/meldung/Symantec-Endpoint-Protection-Gefaehrlicher-Sicherheits-luecken-Cocktail-2768461.html; 04.08.2015, Zugegriffen: 11.10.2017)

11. (Schirrmacher, Dennis, „Angreifer können Symantec Endpoint Protection Code unterjubeln", https://www.heise.de/security/meldung/Angreifer-koennen-Symantec-Endpoint-Protecti-on-Code-unterjubeln-3143338.html; 18.03.2016, Zugegriffen: 11.10.2017)

12. (Schirrmacher,Dennis; „Kritische Lücke gefährdet Antiviren-Produkte von Symantec und Norton", https://www.heise.de/security/meldung/Kritische-Luecke-gefaehrdet-Antiviren-Produkte-von-Sy-mantec-und-Norton-3208967.html; 17.05.2016, Zugegriffen: 11.10.2017)

13. (Volz, Dustin; „Trump administration orders purge of Kaspersky products from U.S."; https://www.reuters.com/article/us-usa-security-kaspersky/trump-administration-orders-purge-of-kas-persky-products-from-u-s-government-idUSKCN1BO2CH; Reuters; Zugegriffen: 13.09.2017)

14. (Reuters, „Britische Behörde warnt vor Kaspersky-Software", http://www.spiegel.de/netzwelt/netzpolitik/kaspersky-britische-regierungsbehoerde-warnt-ministerien-vor-anti-viren-soft-ware-a-1181417.html, Zugegriffen: 04.12.2017)

15. (Unknown, „Warum nutzt Brandenburgs Polizei russische Software?", https://www.welt.de/wirtschaft/article149395147/Warum-nutzt-Brandenburgs-Polizei-russische-Software.html; 29.11.2015, Zugegriffen: 21.09.2017)

16. Natalja Kaspersky hat entsprechend der Informationen der Redakteure dieses Artikels eine ver-gleichbare Ausbildung und einen ähnlichen politischen Werdegang wie ihr Ex-Ehemann Eugene Kaspersky.

17. (Mörl, Ramon, „itWatch GmbH: [2]BadUSB, vergleichbare Exploits – sinnvolle Verteidigungs-strategie", 2015, Augsabe 1)

18. (Piech, Guido, „Digital first, Bedenken second.", https://www.it-zoom.de/mobile-business/e/digital-first-bedenken-second-17640/, Zugegriffen: 28.09.2017)

19. (Proll; Behördenspiegel; 06.11.2014).

Internetquellen

Beutelsbacher, Stefan; „Angriff auf die Schatzkammer der US-Börsenaufsicht"; https://www.welt.de/wirtschaft/article168951707/Brisanter-Angriff-auf-die-Schatzkammer-der-US-Boersenauf-sicht.html, Welt N24; 22.09.2017

Eilsers, Carsten, „OpenSSL – Der Heartbleed Bug und seine Folgen", https://www.ceilers-news.de/serendipity/483-OpenSSL-Der-Heartbleed-Bug-und-seine-Folgen.html, Zugriff am 01.12.2017

Piech, Guido, „Digital first, Bedenken second.", https://www.it-zoom.de/mobile-business/e/digital-first-bedenken-second-17640/, Zugegriffen: 28.09.2017

Reuters, „Britische Behörde warnt vor Kaspersky-Software", http://www.spiegel.de/netzwelt/netzpolitik/kaspersky-britische-regierungsbehoerde-warnt-ministerien-vor-anti-viren-software-a-1181417.html, Zugegriffen: 04.12.2017

Scherschel, Fabian A., „Update für kritische Lücken im Symantec Endpoint Protection Manager", https://www.heise.de/security/meldung/Update-fuer-kritische-Luecken-im-Symantec-Endpoint-Protection-Manager-2114834.html; 14.02.2014, Zugegriffen: 11.10.2017

Schirrmacher, Dennis; „Symantec Endpoint Protection: Gefährlicher Sicherheitslücken-Cocktail", https://www.heise.de/security/meldung/Symantec-Endpoint-Protection-Gefaehrlicher-Sicherheitsluecken-Cocktail-2768461.html; 04.08.2015, Zugegriffen: 11.10.2017

Schirrmacher, Dennis; „Kritische Lücke gefährdet Antiviren-Produkte von Symantec und Norton", https://www.heise.de/security/meldung/Kritische-Luecke-gefaehrdet-Antiviren-Produkte-von-Symantec-und-Norton-3208967.html; 17.05.2016, Zugegriffen: 11.10.2017

Schirrmacher, Dennis, „Angreifer können Symantec Endpoint Protection Code unterjubeln", https://www.heise.de/security/meldung/Angreifer-koennen-Symantec-Endpoint-Protection-Code-unterjubeln-3143338.html; 18.03.2016, Zugegriffen: 11.10.2017

Tanriverdi, Hakan; „Hackerangriff auf Bundestag", http://www.sueddeutsche.de/digital/netz-sicherheit-hackerangriff-auf-den-bundestag-1.3440215; Süddeutsche Zeitung; Zugegriffen: 28.03.2017

Unknown, „Enge Kooperation, klare Trennung der Befugnisse", https://www.bsi.bund.de/DE/Themen/Cyber-Sicherheit/Aktivitaeten/Cyber-Abwehrzentrum/cyberabwehrzentrum.html; Zugegriffen: 28.09.2017

Unknown, „Hacker knackten US-Börsenaufsicht ";http://www.handelsblatt.com/-finanzen/geldpolitik/offenbar-insiderhandel-hacker-knackten-us-boersenaufsicht/20356712.html; Zugegriffen: 21.09.2017

Unknown, „Politischer Abend des Bitkom: Sicherheitspolitik 4.0", https://www.bitkom.org/Themen/Datenschutz-Sicherheit/Sicherheit/Inhaltsseite-2.html; Zugriff am 29.09.2017

Unknown, „Warum nutzt Brandenburgs Polizei russische Software?", https://www.welt.de/wirtschaft/article149395147/Warum-nutzt-Brandenburgs-Polizei-russische-Software.html; 29.11.2015, Zugegriffen: 21.09.2017

Volz, Dustin; „Trump administration orders purge of Kaspersky products from U.S."; https://www.reuters.com/article/us-usa-security-kaspersky/trump-administration-orders-purge-of-kaspersky-products-from-u-s-government-idUSKCN1BO2CH; Reuters; Zugegriffen: 13.09.2017

Literaturquellen

BSI Gesetz; Bundesgesetzblatt Jahrgang; 2009 Teil I Nr. 54

Mörl, Ramon itWatch GmbH: „BadUSB, vergleichbare Exploits – sinnvolle Verteidigungsstrategie", Augsabe 1; 2015

Mörl, Ramon; „Whitelisting/Blacklisting allein ist chancenlos"; kes – Sonderdruck für itWatch; 2012

Mörl, Ramon; „Vortrag: Benutzerzentrierte IT-Sicherheit, senkt Kosten und ist praktisch"; It-Sa 2015

Proll; Behördenspiegel; Auflage 06.11.2014

Progressing Towards a Prescriptive Approach on Cyber Security – Adopting Best Practices and Leverage Technical Innovation

Jörg Eschweiler

Abstract

Buzzwords like artificial intelligence, big data analytics, predictive operations support and cyber threat intelligence emerged over the last years, being appraised as game changers. Several evangelists and vendors are still claiming to "solve" the Cyber Security challenge by those. This article compiles some thoughts about influential factors, critical success factors as well as lessons learned from other domains and conceptual limits of feasibility when taking the endeavor to implement and leverage the next level of Cyber Security operational capabilities. The article seizes some thought leadership and concepts promoted by the Atos Scientific Community embracing the insights and experience of the author towards making new methods and technologies actionable – comprehensibly and result driven.

25.1 Motivation

When reviewing the lessons learned from Cyber Incidents over the last years approx. 3 years – when the term Cyber Incident started to become "on vogue" – it seems like the situation is a bit devastating. Basically technology keeps being vulnerable, new products bring new and keep some old vulnerabilities … of course those and other vulnerabilities might get be discovered and exploited "from time to time" by adversaries either obviously or clandestine, sooner or later – pending on the adversaries goals and capabilities.

Chances that, e.g., paste of deployment of new technologies esp. in end user mass markets will run at reduced speed to ensure proper level of security assurance before spreading in the field are rather low and most probably will stay limited to certain regulated

J. Eschweiler (✉)
Atos Information Technology GmbH, Köln, Germany
e-mail: joerg.eschweiler@atos.net

© Springer Fachmedien Wiesbaden GmbH, ein Teil von Springer Nature 2018
M. Bartsch, S. Frey (Hrsg.), *Cybersecurity Best Practices*,
https://doi.org/10.1007/978-3-658-21655-9_25

sectors. Finding the right balance between effective regulation, technical feasibility and socioeconomical applicability is a challenge by itself. Even if decisively addressed within the next years, it will need years to adopt and hence show effects- seen from a global perspective.

Though organizations did make some progress by protecting their information domain/ information technology/Cyber domain footprint by preventive and operational measures, this does and will not provide "perfect" protection. Beside the technology life cycle keeping paste, the threat landscape changes. Business models and underlaying technologies will adopt and the level of digitalization fuels will disrupt those as well.

This of course leads to the fact that assessment of exposure, amount of events and triggers to monitor and hence analytic work to be done to make sense out of this grows likely more in an exponential than linear way. In a world that becomes more networked and business models relying on this approaches like isolation and disconnection most probably won't be feasible for mass use.

Further the fact of shortage on skilled staff and challenge to keep staff up-to-date with technical skills and capability to perform networked operations covering complex information technology infrastructures does not look like a "golden hammer" will solve it - especially when looking at geopolitical situations nations and economies are constrainted by and demographic development applying to those.

Besides human resources the amount of monetary fundings and other tangible resources available to be spent on Cyber Security is limited as well. While nowadays it is accepted that the Cyber Security is a "Must Have" there are and most likely always will be constraints towards availability and applicability of resources. Of course the question of cost-effectiveness proportionality still has to be figured out by every organization.

Also – like in physical security – organizations must recognize that effective Cyber Security protection involves a proactive approach to prevention, capability for as timley as possible detection and counter-action, but as well recovery from compromise are crucial.

In the digital economy, the grim reality will stay that organizations must accept that it's no longer a matter of "if" but "when" a Cyber Security incident like, e.g. a security breach, will occur. Traditional IT security technology nor "security by obscurity" technologies will sustainably protect against sophisticated Cyber adversaries who are increasingly successful and operating without obligations to comply with regulations nor being measured against a KPI to stay within boundaries of resource planning.

25.2   Relevance of Threat Intelligence

Once recognizing that perfect protection will most likely neither be feasible nor affordable as well as threat landscape and risk exposure will evolve continuously (maybe even disruptively), one could draw the conclusion that – although it's Cyber – the paradox on itself is also known from the physical world. Security and safety have always been a known issue there as well, of course with other constraints, parameters, and vectors.

So probably when facing the challenge to protect against Cyberattacks or technology-driven failures, a good start could try to answer the question: "Are you aware of how your organization is already or could be targeted today?"

With industrial and governmental organizations as well as end users relying more and more on IoT-like devices and loosely integrated technology this question becomes even more important as the perimeter line becomes more and more obsolete regarding action-ability of measures and ability to enforce.

With approximately 7 billion devices connected to the Internet worldwide today and 20 billion estimated to be connected by 2020 [1], risk of information leakage, targeted infiltration/exfiltration and the organization's "adressable" attack surface will increase. Recent research [2] has identified that, globally, the average total cost of a data breach is above 2Mio. €. This does not account for the introduction of General Data Protection Regulation (GDPR) in May 2018, which will command stricter controls around the governance and protection of sensitive data. However, security concerns relating to the Internet of Things (IoT) span much further than purely unauthorized access to data. Most IoT devices are still in their infancy when it comes to security, which makes them easier to target due to vulnerabilities such as software reconfiguration and default passwords.

The growth of IoT has led to a notable increase in cybercriminal activity and capability. Malicious actors have capitalized on the ability to quickly establish large-scale botnets. These are wide-scale, coordinated attacks that use the IoT to spread through IT networks and can result in major disruption called "distributed denial-of-service" (DDoS). Sometimes known as "DDoS of Things" attacks, they have become commonplace, with the most notorious being Mirai and Brickerbot in recent times. Industry analysts predict [3] that ransomware will increasingly migrate to IoT and become a primary threat, potentially leading to significant impact on both commercial and critical national infrastructure.

The typical types of adversaries like hacktivists, short-term money-driven cybercriminals, state-sponsored actors and insider threats combine to form a dangerous threat landscape for organizations. Combining this with nowadays ease of access to "off-the-shelf" attacks (such as malware distribution and phishing campaigns as a service) available in dark web marketplaces lowers the barrier of applying those attacks.

This plethora of threats emphasizes the importance of maintaining awareness by effectively using threat intelligence. Conceptually seen Threat intelligence is not new and in relation to Cyber Security means "evidence-based knowledge, including context, mechanisms, indicators, implications and actionable advice, about an existing or emerging menace or hazard to assets that can be used to inform decisions regarding the subject" response to that menace or hazard' [4].

What is new, is the emerging ability to derive actionable intelligence from the sheer volume of threat intelligence now available. The value of threat intelligence is in helping organizations to prioritize actions in proportion to the threat and an analysis of overall risk. Over the years, organizations have attempted to introduce threat intelligence into their Cyber security tooling in order to detect and protect against known malicious domains, blacklisted internet addresses and other identifiers. The problem was, this intelligence consisted of millions of indicators that needed filtering and prioritizing, was soon out of date and most usually not even contextualized.

So some lessons are learned:

- Cyber threat intelligence must not be seen isolated form real world threat intelligence.
- Collecting and leveraging intelligence demands resources and skills with context of the organization; suppliers can of course support with some parts but unlikely provide a full picture nor the full intelligence cycle.
- Before starting to invest in intelligence collection, a clear purpose on what shall be achieved by the intelligence should be stated and operationalized.
- When deciding to get into threat intelligence a critical mass of resources to be able to succeed shall be provided: people, technology, sources and processes to leverage those.

25.3 From Security Operations to Cyber Defense: Changing Roles and Approach

A (Cyber) security operations center (aka. CSOC), also sometimes referenced as a Cyber Defense Center, is first of all a secured facility equipped to perform as the hub to host operations and provide capabilities needed to prevent, detect, and respond to Cyber incidents. Those are usually operational 24 h a day, 7 days a week, and 365 days a year incl. needed staff which are by minimum connected analysts (usually organized in competence levels 1–3) and incident response experts. In order for the CSOC to perform its duties a close uplink with IT infrastructure operations, business IT, and other functions within an organization like legal, compliance, works council, and communications as well as the appropriate levels of management is vital. When operating globally, it is has been proven useful to still have a central hub but also deploy operational cells as part of the overall CSOC into local geographies to be in the same time zone as the supported business as well as to be able to communicate in local language, understand local regulation and context, and in case of crisis, provide a trusted and reliable interface.

As the world transforms into a virtual bubble of information domains with fuzzy boundaries, investing in digital defense has become an essential common practice that in many cases can only be done collaboratively. While being a Cyber Security Operation Center analyst means being on the front lines of an organization's "digital fortress," it also means being reliable on internal and external sources of information and functions performing their duties. The group of analysts performs many duties which include not only being on watch to protect the perimeter but also to contribute to advancement of protection measures and ensure monitoring capabilities deliver what's needed. Over the years it appeared to be useful to rotate staff between analyst, incident response and architecture teams. Besides job enrichment and skill development, this especially enables a more thorough understanding as a vital ingredient to daily business, and by understanding each other better, this smoothens joint operations in case of incident, emergency, or even durable crisis.

With most businesses relying on their IT infrastructure to function, the IT infrastructure operations is not necessarily manned 24*7*365. Over the last years – driven by cost reduction or just agile use of shared services and new cloud offerings – it turned out that most IT infrastructure ops rarely have an integrated asset and config repository anymore nor are ITSM processes connected to Cyber Incident Response to the needed amount, technology- and process-wise. In case of an incident, this makes it even harder to precisely detect, determine, and timely react properly.

Taking an educated guess on the growth of the digital ecosystem, it has been predicted that by 2020, our digital universe will hold ~44 trillion gigabytes of data, which is the equivalent of 6.6 stacks of iPads between the Earth and moon [5]. The exponential rate of data growth means that Cyber Security Operation Centers face the challenge of being swarmed by a plethora of potential security alerts; analysts can easily become overloaded by alert management tasks rather than fulfilling their job of a proactive defender and target-oriented and effective analyst. This challenge has a volume that cannot be solved by classical automation and professional process hygiene factors. Besides the sheer volume, it has also to be taken into account that the IT infrastructure itself will become more and more dynamically.

Taking scientifical and technical progress regarding artificial intelligence, machine learning, and cognitive analytics that has been achieved over the last years into consideration Prescriptive Security – the application of Prescriptive Analytics for Cyber security – is seen as a promising approach to relieve, enabling intelligent analytics and automation to a degree that enables analysts to better utilize their time as an advanced threat hunter and security specialist again. Further this opens up chances to tackle the challenge of automating responsive and or corrective actions, step by step not to create additional issues.

The modern growth of connectivity and business infrastructure quickly impacted the role significantly. The vast amounts of data and alerts caused the thinly spread specialized analyst to prioritize their responsibilities, meaning actively seeking and researching threats took a back seat. What should have been a partly proactive role suddenly became a heavily reactive one. Prescriptive Security is based on automating simple threat analysis. Sophisticated machine learning can identify threats, even initiate remediation, and clean up actions in significantly quicker time. Automating the basic tasks of the analyst frees them to combine the brilliance of a human mind with the supercomputing power of Prescriptive Security. Under this new model, analysts are returning to detailed malware analysis, researching the latest exploits, and spending more time on stopping attacks before they even happen. As advanced technology can draw meaning from huge quantities of seemingly random data, complex patterns and trends emerge which were before unseen, unlocking further potential for accurate foresight to keep organizations one step ahead. Once enabling this level of leverage, Prescriptive Security can even be leveraged to support more sophisticated analytical task within, e.g., malware permutation analytics, lateral movement detection and analytics as well as estimating appropriate measures to achieve maximum effectiveness with least possible risk and minimal invasion to IT infrastructure when fighting incidents.

While not all CSOCs work in the same way, they share a common need to mature and maintain regular efficiency and scalability in order to provide an effective service while efficiently leveraging available ressources. It is no surprise that the more advanced security organizations are embracing the need for change, and realizing the requirement to adapt its people as well as technology is becoming equally important. The role of a CSOC Analyst is maturing within the community as well as first standardized curricula are available to enable a more structured and predictable way of building and maintaining skills. Same paradigm applies inside Cyber as outside Cyber: true value of people powerplays through enabling them to excel. In this case by integration of big data analytics and machine learning techniques with Cyber Security, domain-specific context is needed.

Cyber Security progressions are driven by the boardroom, with leading organizations in all industries setting the de facto standards, in turn affecting how CSOCs operate. Organizations who invest in intelligent Cyber Security will advance their level of Cyber Security capabilities by enabling a proactively focused defense strategy. This way the CSOC analysts should become enabled to invest their time and passion into the work and research of a true security practitioner which at the end also becomes a significant factor to keep those people motivated and this way the organization can leverage their invest in recruitment, people development, etc. as well more effectively and sustainably.

25.4 Prescriptive Security: Using the Haystack to Find the Needle

In an increasingly data-driven world, organizations engage into gathering all kinds of operational and customer data and apply analytics with the aim to transform that data into valuable business insights and actionable results. At most organizations this is done within several business departments from manufacturing to customer services. Yet one important application that is still rarely addressed is Cyber Security.

Hearing regularly about major Cyber Security incidents or breaches, most mindful people start wondering whether they were preventable or even if not preventable why detection and mitigation could not happen at an earlier stage.

Prescriptive Security is about exactly preventing such incidents from happening, or hitting their target with full impact, by leveraging big data analytics and machine learning – fueled by high-performance computing capabilities to enable processing vast amount of raw data and deriving results in near-real-time. As technologies advance and risk exposure becomes more and more dynamic, Cyber Security must shift to the next stage from a purely reactive model with some proactive to a prescriptive model that can reliably analyze across silos and detect weak patterns in order to identity the next threats and to automate security control responses in an adjustable way while being context aware and transparent for operators like analysts and incident responders.

While the Cyber Security analyst's work (similar to intelligence analyst work) has been focused on finding the needle in the haystack, the shift must be done toward using the haystack to find the needle by leveraging big data and machine learning analytics and utilizing all available data within the organization and outside the organization, in order to bring full security visibility and eliminate all potential blind spots. Of course this has to be done in accordance with privacy regulation, industry regulation and algorithms, etc., which need to be scientifically proven and not "next generation security by obscurity."

Prescriptive Security operations shall enable organizations to:

- Face the ever-evolving threat landscape: The threat landscape has been increasing exponentially as the adoption of new technologies such as Internet of Things (IoT), big data and cloud computing are expanding the attack surface. Several analysts say that every 3 months, over 18 million new malware samples are captured, being partly machine-generated themselves. Zero-day exploits expected to rise from one per week in 2015 to one per day by 2021. With Prescriptive Security, threat intelligence is no longer a separate process "just" acquiring information through external sources like alert bulletins and social media, but becoming an integrated vital part of the Cyber Security Operations giving actionable input and enabling detection of yet unknown threats – in best case before they hit the organization.
- Significantly improve detection and response times: Time is on the side of any adversary who is patient, persistent, and creative. We're fighting human ingenuity and attackers aren't playing by the same rules as the defenders. Prescriptive CSOCs can sustainably progress current operational models and considerably improve detection times and response times. Instead of thinking in days and months to detect and mitigate threats, with machine learning, artificial intelligence and automation neutralization of emerging threats in real time, time should become "state of the art" to prevent from future attacks.
- Optimize use and leverage of Cyber Security resources: While cyberattacks are growing in volume, complexity, and pervasiveness, organizations will still have to counter these using their limited set of resources. Some latest research estimates that by 2020, over 1.8 million Cyber Security jobs will not be filled due to a shortage of skills. Prescriptive Security, by introducing and maturing artificial intelligence and (semi-) automatic response, will optimize the use of professionals who will be able to supervise automation and response against threats in order to focus on the more complex and persistent ones. It will most likely also introduce new roles, such as Cyber Security Data Scientists to integrate statistical and mathematical models and provide innovative mechanisms to detect future cyberattacks. Further this will enable Cross Domain Threat analytics combining Cyber domain, Physical domain, and e.g., commercial activities or constraints.

Prescriptive Security will help advance the known paradigm by increasing detection surface and increasing paste of response while decreasing mitigation time. By using big data, analytics, machine learning, artificial intelligence and high-performance computing, it shall also effectively help to optimize the cost factors of limited resources. With this in place, organizations will be able to more effectively protect their business assets including valuable business and customer personal information as well as vital business processes and though support the goals of their organization.

25.5 Simplification in Cyber Security by Emerging Technologies?

In nowadays more and more hyperconnected times, almost every device can be considered part of some information technology ecosystem. They interact in dynamic ways without strict supervision, giving rise to new challenges and threats in the context of Cyber Security and esp. human awareness and control. In addition more and more opportunities are provided to offer deeper integrated and open solutions aimed at improving overall situational awareness and increasing organizational and system resilience.

A number of upcoming technologies will probably combine within the next years to become important drivers of simplicity and context-aware automation in Cyber Security engineering and operations. Those technologies should concept for the security of interconnected value chains – like trusted brokers, dynamic access control, application shielding, or Cyber ecosystems – use-cases that were introduced in Atos Ascent Journey 2018 [6].

Software-defined security architectures implement layers of abstraction and intelligence that cross traditional boundaries, like network topology, security domains, and business process management. All security mechanisms such as network segmentation, intrusion detection, data loss prevention, and identity and access management are interoperating in a business process contextual manner. These mechanisms will be under the governance of dedicated policy-driven software that ensures the orchestration of dynamic security controls which can automatically adapt over time to changes in system configuration, underlying infrastructure or risk situations.

Cyber-resilient systems have the ability to independently adapt to changing threat or impact levels as a result of dynamic business processes. Evolving business requirements have to be fulfilled using dynamically reconfiguring infrastructure and connectivity. This requires protective, detective, reactive, and – if possible – prescriptive controls within the respective Cyber physical system, while at the same time dealing with the challenge of limited performance and storage capacities.

Real-time security analytics allow interrogation of large volumes of data in near-real-time to quickly reverse-engineer attacks to their source and neutralize them accordingly – or even preempt attacks via target threat intelligence. Such an approach allows the storing and access of security information at a fast pace to detect abnormal behavior, predict security threats, and prescribe countermeasures before any incidents are able to have an impact. Correlation and observation of huge amount of data will be simplified through such analytic engines.

The next-generation cryptography encompasses the innovative technologies in trusted computing to stay trusted even though hardware base might be untrusted or proven compromised that are expected to mature by 2020. It includes such topics as Blockchain or homomorphic encryption. Allthough neither one will be the "golden hammer" nor "end hunger and suffering" of the world.

Blockchain might enable a new form of distributed, secure, and accountable cooperation without the need to trust a central intermediary. This also eliminates the tactical risk of operational failure once a central hub is temporarily or permanently offline.

Homomorphic encryption on the other hand is a technology still very much in a research stage that allows the processing of encrypted data without the need to decrypt it. This is particularly interesting to implement privacy-compliant processing and allows not only for transition and storage but also for the operation of data in untrusted or third-party environments.

References

1. Gartner 2015.
2. Ponemon 2017 Cost of Data Breach Study, based on 419 companies across 11 countries and 2 regions who had each suffered a loss of between 2,600 and 100,000 records.
3. McAfee Labs 2017 Threat Predictions Report.
4. Gartner Analyst Rob McMillan.
5. https://www.emc.com/leadership/digital-universe/2014iview/executive-summary.htm
6. Atos Ascent Journey https://atos.net/content/mini-sites/journey-2020/index.html

Increasing the Efficiency of Security Analysts

26

Alain Gut and Andreas Wespi

Abstract

Security monitoring and analytics are widely deployed technologies supporting enterprises to cope with the multitude of security challenges they are facing. The proliferation of methods and techniques demands a systematic approach to cover the various aspects of security monitoring and analytics. Security 360° is both a comprehensive operational security model integrating the many aspects of security monitoring and analytics as well as a vision for bringing security to the next level of quality. It represents a contextual, cognitive, and adaptive approach for protecting enterprises' mission-critical assets. Security technology is steadily evolving by making use of advances in related fields. Cognitive systems possess the potential to further improve the detection capability of today's security systems. Based on a specific realization of a cognitive security system, we demonstrate how cognitive technology eases the work of security analysts and increases their efficiency.

26.1 Introduction

As the IT industry is embracing new computing paradigms, the attackers are the first to exploit the platform shifts and launch attacks against business-critical assets. We have witnessed such attacks through the mainframe era, the personal computing era, and the

A. Gut (✉)
IBM Schweiz AG, Zürich, Switzerland
e-mail: alain.gut@ch.ibm.com

A. Wespi
IBM Schweiz Research, Rüschlikon, Switzerland
e-mail: anw@zurich.ibm.com

© Springer Fachmedien Wiesbaden GmbH, ein Teil von Springer Nature 2018   349
M. Bartsch, S. Frey (Hrsg.), *Cybersecurity Best Practices*,
https://doi.org/10.1007/978-3-658-21655-9_26

web era [1]. Furthermore, advanced persistent threat (APT) type of attacks is able to circumvent traditional preventive security measures. Security monitoring and analytics is one possible response to highly sophisticated attacks. In particular cognitive security systems whose functions are not expressed in well-defined rules but which are adaptive and learn over time have the potential to detect and defend against such attacks.

While security monitoring and analytics technologies are steadily evolving, a sound basis is needed that helps to move away from point solutions and develop an integrated security framework. The Security 360° model aims at systematically exploring the security analytics space and providing the foundation for a comprehensive, contextual, and adaptive security monitoring and analytics framework.

There is a need for analyzing data sources holistically which obviously also increases complexity due to the massive amount of data to be analyzed. Cognitive technologies have the potential to handle the increasing complexity and detect security issues early and accurately. The objective of this paper is to systematically review the capabilities of cognitive security solutions. Additionally, a first realization of a cognitive security system is presented.

This paper is organized as follows. In Sect. 26.2, we introduce the Security 360° concept of contextual, cognitive, and adaptive security monitoring and analytics. Section 26.3 discusses the potential of cognitive technologies for security, and Sect. 26.4 presents a concrete realization of the cognitive computing paradigm in form of the Watson for Cyber Security solution. Cognitive technologies are steadily evolving. Sect. 26.5 discusses enhancements we can expect to see in the future. Some conclusions are drawn in Sect. 26.6.

26.2 Security Monitoring and Analytics

IT security is an unsolved problem. We are witnessing a high number of successful attacks despite of all efforts to secure computing systems. There are various explanations for this unbroken trend. Legacy systems with their known vulnerabilities are still in use. The attack sophistication is increasing. There are organizations that have the means of putting nearly unlimited resources in the preparation and execution of targeted attacks, i.e., attacks against a well-defined and specifically chosen target. While security is a technical discipline, it still also relies on humans to defend against potential attacks. For example, humans sharing passwords, responding to phishing mails, or getting tricked by social engineering attacks represent a security risk that cannot be addressed with current technology alone. Surprisingly there is yet another threat factor to be considered: innovation. As history teaches us, new security problems get introduced with new technologies. As an example, it is reported that between 75% and 80% of the top free apps on Android and iPhone smartphones were breached [2]. In many cases, providing new functionality is more important – at least from a business perspective – than securing applications right from the beginning.

Given all these observations, we cannot assume that the attack landscape will change soon. Therefore, increasing efforts are needed on the defender side.

26.2.1 Principles

While it does not seem to be possible – at least with today's security technologies – to build secure systems that cannot be penetrated, complementary solutions are needed that may not cure the problem per se but at least help to detect any misuse. Ideally already first steps of an attack get detected. A security monitoring and analytics solution has to cover all phases of an attack, from the reconnaissance over the real attack to the exploitation phase. Security monitoring and analytics cover a wide space of technologies, and many approaches are being explored. Therefore, a systematic approach to security monitoring and analytics is required. In [1], three principles underlying an operational security model are discussed.

Focus on Secure Service Outcomes

A holistic approach to security is closely connected to the business needs. Therefore, instead of a bottom-up approach that consists of a heterogeneous set of security controls, a top-down approach is needed that focuses on secure services outcomes. This also means that the security architecture evolves over time and adapts not only to the threat level but also to the business needs.

Use Analytics First to Derive Executable Security Intelligence

Given the risk of systems getting penetrated, an additional layer of security is needed. Security monitoring and analytics provide situational awareness and can help to identify ongoing attacks. Very often security monitoring and analytics solutions are fragmented. Security tools focus on specific, siloed data sources. For example, host-based intrusion prevention systems analyze logs and activities observed on a server, whereas network-based intrusion prevention systems analyze network traffic. Each of these monitoring systems has its own benefit but also limitation due to its limited view. Therefore, the traditional approach is to correlate the output of dedicated security systems. The objective is to get a more accurate security statement based on the combined output of security tools.

Today's enterprise boundaries are no longer well defined. Cloud computing and BYOD (bring your own device) pose new challenges from a security monitoring and analytics point of view. Innovative approaches are required to complement on-premise with off-premise security monitoring.

Provision Adaptive, Optimized, Risk-Based Responses

Security monitoring and analytics also require the capability to respond to observed threats. Adaptive, risk-based approaches take into account not only the IT but also the business context when responding to threats and attacks. The business value of the impacted assets determines the response priority.

26.2.2 Security 360°

The three principles presented in Sect. 26.2.1 lead to a new operational model for security called Security 360°. It is depicted in Fig. 26.1. The model goes beyond the security monitoring and analytics approaches typically deployed in enterpises today. It realizes a contextual, cognitive, and adaptive approach to security as described hereafter. It can be universally applied to any environment in scope, be it, e.g., a cloud or a smartphone.

Monitor and Distill

Simply put we can state that the more security-relevant data is available, the more accurate the security assessment is. Data collection covers but is not limited to data from the network, the devices, the users (privileged and non-privileged), the applications, and the business processes to gain an end-to-end view. There are different methods of data collection ranging from passively gathering data that is already available up to actively probing systems to getting the specific data one is interested in. Depending on the business context, it may be possible to actively instrument a system and get new data that is typically not monitored. This can go as far as, e.g., modifying an application and adding new logging and auditing capabilities. On the other hand, there are also environments where the security monitoring must be as least intrusive as possible. Industrial Control Systems (ICS) are optimized for the interactions between digital systems and physical components. Because ICS operators are concerned that by instrumenting the ICS unwanted side effects could occur, only passive security monitoring of the network traffic is allowed. This certainly

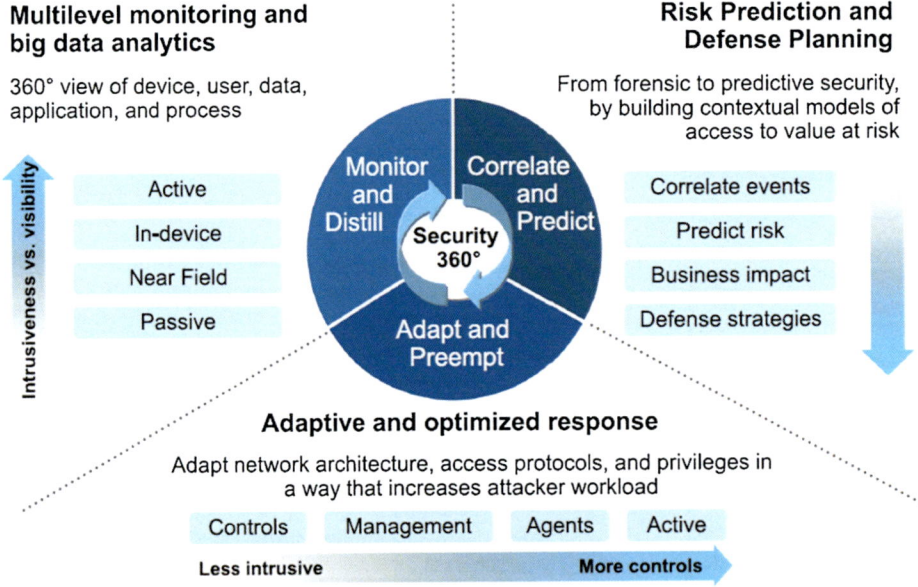

Fig. 26.1 Security 360° A contextual, cognitive, and adaptive approach to security. (Quelle: IBM)

limits the overall security monitoring and analytics capabilities, but it reflects the adaptive approach: make the best out of the information available.

Not only typical security data is relevant from a comprehensive security monitoring and analytics point of view, also other data such as system resource utilization data or software change logs can be of value.

Traditional security monitoring and analytics approaches focus on single data sources. This allows to build security solutions that are optimized for the given data source. However, such an approach quickly gets to a point where the system cannot determine with high accuracy whether there is a security problem or not. Therefore, it is a widely deployed approach to bring all events of the deployed security solutions to a central location for further, overall assessment.

The objective of comprehensive data collection and analysis also demands an appropriate infrastructure. Big Data technologies as they have evolved over the past few years provide the framework for scalable data processing. New, evolving technologies such as edge computing will offer interesting extensions to current security analytics frameworks.

Correlate and Predict

Making best use of the collected data and extracting the security-relevant information is the objective of the second phase. We differentiate between knowledge- and behavior-based security analytics approaches [3]. The knowledge-based approach looks for well-known signs of attacks, whereas the behavior-based approach is a data-driven technique that can detect security problem with no a priori knowledge. A wide variety of Artificial Intelligence technologies is deployed for behavior-based security analytics.

The advantages of both technologies are well known. Knowledge-based systems can only detect known security issues, while behavior-based systems have the potential to detect attacks never seen before. However, behavior-based systems tend to generate false alarms. By analyzing the collected data in a cross-domain fashion, the assumption is that a more accurate statement about the overall security state can be made. For example, based on the user system access logs, it may not be possible to differentiate between good and malicious activities. However, when the system access log analysis is extended with the analysis of application logs, there may be better chances to make an accurate security statement.

Ideally a security monitoring and analytics system can make some predictive statements, i.e., warn about security attacks before the attack has succeeded. While there is ongoing work in the area of predictive security breach detection, one has to admit that the technology has not yet reached a good level of maturity. However, what is possible is to make some business risk prediction based on an observed activity. By knowing the IT infrastructure not only from a technical but also a business perspective, one can determine the implications of hacked components on the related business processes. The business risk prediction allows one to set the right priorities and trigger the appropriate responses.

Adapt and Preempt

Responding to detected security attacks is still quite labor intensive. The problem needs to be fully understood before concrete countermeasures can be launched. The increasing accuracy of correlation and risk prediction technologies allows one to consider automated responses. For example, a response system can "pre-compute" possible responses and present them to the security analyst. Based on his complementary assessment, the analyst can select the response that gets executed automatically.

The emergence of software-defined environments allows an increased level of agility. Defense mechanisms can get activated dynamically. Moving Target Defense (MTD) is such a dynamic defense method. At the compute layer, e.g., MTD allows the dynamic migration of workloads. At the network layer, IP address and port randomization can be applied. The MTD mechanisms are transparent to internal users but make it difficult for an attacker to perform a successful attack. It has to be mentioned that such variable defense strategies have to be rooted in a good understanding of the security threats and their implications on an organization. In particular, it is important to know the critical assets of an organization. Adaptive security techniques take this information into account.

26.3   Security in the Cognitive Computing Era

The increasing amount of security data requires new technologies for processing them. Cognitive technologies have the potential to assist the human security analyst, allowing him to make more timely and accurate decisions. To understand the potential of the technology, it is helpful to put it in historical context [4]. In the Tabulating Era (1900s–1940s), computers were single-purposed mechanical systems that performed the well-defined tasks they were developed for. The Programming Era (1990s–present) brought a shift from mechanical tabulators to electronic systems whose instructions could be coded in software. With the underlying hardware, the software developed rapidly. Everything we currently call a computing device – from mainframe to personal computer to smartphone – is a programmable computer and hence belongs to the Programming Era. The Cognitive Computing Era (2011–) introduces a new way of how humans and computers interact and collaborate. It realizes the vision predicted by J.C.R Licklider as far back as 1960 [5]. Licklider pointed out that the cooperation between man and machine will overcome the inflexible dependency on predetermined programs.

Cognitive computing supports the Security 360° vision. The "monitor and distill" phase benefits from cognitive technologies particularly when it comes to analyzing unstructured data such as text documents. Cognitive technologies provide the next generation of analytics tools to be applied in the "correlate and predict" phase. The "adapt and preempt" phase requires a holistic view on IT and business processes. Cognitive systems excel in processing heterogeneous data sources and hence are expected to make key contributions also in this third phase. As a summary, Security 360° provides the framework for integrating cognitive technologies. It ensures a holistic and coordinated approach to current and future security monitoring and analytics challenges.

Cognitive systems are characterized by several properties. We discuss four main properties that we consider highly relevant from a security perspective.

Natural Language Sources and Processing

The world produces over 2.5 quintillion bytes of data every day, 80% of it being unstructured [6]. Even if we assume that security data may contain more structured data than other domains, there is still a large portion of unstructured data such as advisories, blogs, technical reports, or scientific papers. While human security experts aim at being up-to-date with the latest security information, it is impossible to know all the information produced. Security experts have to rely on their ability to quickly find the information they need when working on a specific security topic.

As demonstrated already in other domains, be it the Jeopardy playing IBM Watson system or the IBM Watson for Oncology [8] solution, a core capability of a cognitive system is to process large volumes of unstructured data in order to be able to answer domain-specific questions.

Initially a curated corpus of knowledge, i.e., security data, has to be given to the cognitive security system. The information is turned in an internally maintained security knowledge graph. While initially the creation of the knowledge graph has to be supported by humans who manually label the data, after a while the cognitive system can extend its knowledge base on its own.

In a next phase, the cognitive system needs to be trained by being fed a series of question-and-answer pairs. The machine "knowledge" is enhanced as security professionals interact with the system, providing feedback on the accuracy of the system's responses. A cognitive system is not just a large data lake, it is a system that steadily expands by the data ingested and the collective usage.

Human-Centric Communication

A cognitive system cannot only process natural language data, it can also interact with humans in a natural way. It can respond to questions asked by a human, and it can engage in a discussion to get more specific input and to further refine the results of the initial query. Furthermore, advanced visualization eases the task of the security analyst, helping him to quickly detect high-risk security issues.

Continuous Machine Learning

As discussed in Sect. 26.2.2, novel techniques are needed to process all the security data produced in an IT environment. Applying Artificial Intelligence technologies to security is not a new field. However, the steadily increasing data volumes ask for new approaches. The objective is to gain new insights by investigating data holistically as opposed to analyzing data sources separately. While Machine Learning and also Data Mining are established security analytics technologies, applying Deep Learning methods such as Neural Networks for security gets a lot of interest these days.

The technologies to be used typically depend on the type of task to be accomplished. As experience shows, there is no "one size fits all" solution.

Evidence-Based Reasoning

A challenge with Artificial Intelligence systems is that the system may produce some result, e.g., flag some activities as malicious, but is not able to specify the reason. This also means that it is difficult to act on the provided result. An evidence-based reasoning system can communicate how it got to a specific result. If the result is not clear or there are several possible results, the system can engage in a conversation with the security analyst and ask for additional input. The additional input can help to get to a clear ranking of the answers, this way empowering the analyst to initiate the right response.

As the discussion of the cognitive system properties shows, there is enormous potential to apply cognitive technologies for security. They enhance the Security 360° model with novel capabilities and support the realization of the Security 360° vision.

26.4   Watson for Cyber Security

We present Watson for Cyber Security[1] [9] as an example of a system that implements the cognitive security concepts. Cognitive computing and with it cognitive security is at the beginning of a journey. While we describe current capabilities, obviously there are many ideas for future extensions.

26.4.1 Architecture

In Fig. 26.2 the main components of the Watson for Cyber Security solution are depicted. In a traditional security monitoring and analytics solution, there are two main components: the security system and the security analyst sitting in front of the security system's console. The security analyst investigates the offenses, i.e., the correlated security events that specify security-critical situations. He has to decide whether a reported offense requires some action such as contacting a system owner or triggering a technical response such as disconnecting a machine from the network. While analyzing the problem, the analyst may also analyze the raw events that triggered an offense. However, digging deeper and collecting more context information is quite some effort. Furthermore, there may also be external information available on the Internet that needs to be consulted and helps to better understand the security situation.

---

[1] This section refers to an IBM product for technical illustration purposes but not for any business reason.

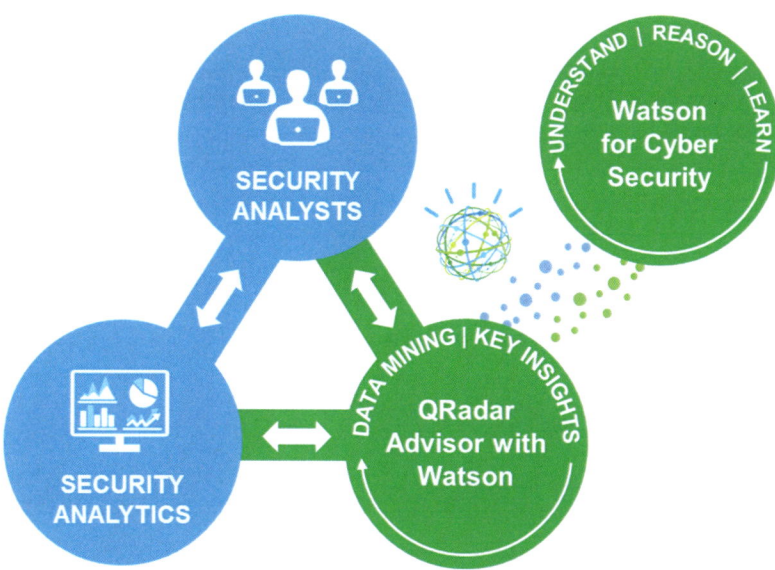

Fig. 26.2 Watson for Cyber Security – main components. (Quelle: IBM)

Therefore, the traditional security monitoring and analytics setup is extended with two components:

IBM® QRadar® Advisor with Watson for Internal Data Retrieval
The QRadar Advisor with Watson component gathers automatically the information relevant to the reported offense in the internal event history. The available relevant information is preprocessed and presented to the security analyst.

IBM® Watson™ for Cyber Security for External Data Retrieval
While the collection and presentation of internal historical events helps to better understand the local context, some more information may be needed. Watson for Cyber Security represents the global security knowledge. Callouts to the Watson for Cyber Security component provides more context information that helps to better understand the offenses and decide on appropriate countermeasures.

26.4.2 Security Threat Investigation

Based on the architectural components described in Sect. 26.4.1, we describe the security threat investigation cycle. The main objectives of the integrated solution are to improve the accuracy of the investigation result as well as to decrease the investigation time.

The following steps as shown in Fig. 26.3 are part of the threat investigation process:

1. The security monitoring and analytics solution reports an offense that requires some investigation by the security analyst.
2. To support the investigation, QRadar Advisor with Watson provides local context information by collecting related information from the event history. For example, if the offense shows an internal device that seems to be infected by a malware, QRadar Advisor with Watson may display the external destinations the device has communicated with in the past.
3. QRadar Advisor with Watson maintains a set of observables such as source and destination IP addresses of connections or hashes of detected malware. The observables – or a subset of them – can be sent to Watson for Cyber Security for further analysis.
4. The received observables get enhanced with additional information. For example, an IP address may have been listed in a blacklist, an advisory, or a blog entry. The value proposition of Watson for Cyber Security is that this information is immediately available and no lengthy searches on the Internet have to be performed.
5. The local knowledge graph gets extended with the relevant portion of the Watson for Cyber Security knowledge graph. By doing so, the research results are being made available to QRadar Advisor with Watson.
6. Both the information provided by QRadar Advisor with Watson and the information provided by Watson for Cyber Security are visually presented to the security analyst and allow him to easily explore the data.

26.4.3 Operational Efficiency

Watson for Cyber Security realizes the symbiosis between human and machine. Each - the human and the machine - contributes their strengths toward the solution of a problem, in this case the assessment of the reported security offense. The machine presents the technical context information and makes a first assessment of the root cause of an offense; the human can review the presented data and combine it with his own expertise. He is given all the information to quickly decide on the actions to be taken.

The value of the presented approach is accuracy and time saving. Decisions are made under consideration of all relevant information. A large volume of public security knowledge is available at the fingertips of the security analysts. Furthermore, because time intensive searches are not needed, security analysts can focus on what they are good at. They can decide on the best reaction based on the collected facts and their implicit knowledge of the monitored computing infrastructure.

The time factor is another important aspect. Security analysts are shielded from the time-consuming task of searching and collecting information about vulnerabilities and attacks. This saves the security analysts time. They can focus on their core work. If we consider the case

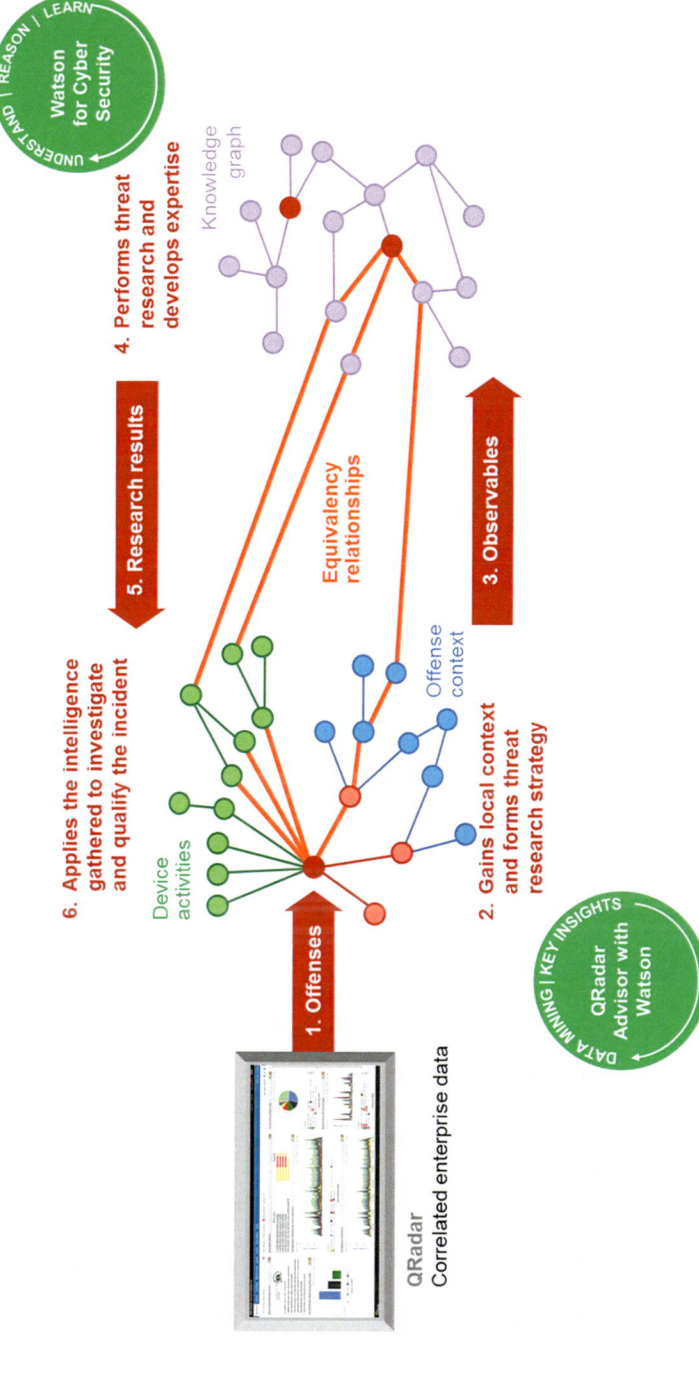

Fig. 26.3 Cognitive security threat investigation. (Quelle: IBM)

of a security operations center (SOC) that offers 24 × 7 services, there is a tremendous scalability effect. The globally reported lack of security professionals can be addressed by empowering the available professionals to do their job more efficiently.

26.5   Future Cognitive Security Enhancements

As discussed in Sect. 26.3, we are at the beginning of the Cognitive Computing Era. New Artificial Intelligence technologies are being developed that help us to solve the most challenging problems. There is no doubt that security is such a challenging topic. Watson for Cyber Security is a first and important step toward a cognitive security solution. More steps will follow. There are various areas where advances are possible.

Incorporation of Local Customer Data

To exploit the full power of a cognitive security solution, also non-security information is relevant. For example, information about business processes or regulatory compliance requirements should be integrated in the data analysis process.

Incorporation of Security Analyst Feedback

To support the self-learning concept, feedback from security analysts should be incorporated in the knowledge graph and be available for future analysis. The feedback can be as simple as the positive or negative assessment of a response but as complex as any free text description of the analysts knowledge about the IT and business infrastructure.

Advanced Cognitive Security Analytics

On the Artificial Intelligence side, there are many new and evolving technologies. The security community can benefit from this trend and explore the applicability of new analytics technologies to the security domain.

Remediation Planning

The analysis and the assessment of security offenses is the focus of the presented cognitive security solution. The collected and analyzed data is also an excellent basis for the planning of remediation actions. The data contains a lot of context information that can be used to define concrete actions to cure the observed problem.

While cognitive systems offer many advantages, we also have to be aware of their risks. As other security solutions, also cognitive systems can become the target of attacks. A concrete attack scenario is the ingestion of poisoned data into the data corpus from which the cognitive system learns. Various approaches are explored to address this challenge, ranging from data protection methods to improved methods for data curation. Data poisoning is one example of an attack against cognitive systems, other attack scenarios are possible. It is important that early on the risks of cognitive systems are discussed and mitigation actions explored.

26.6   Conclusion

Security monitoring and analytics are important and widely accepted technologies that complement other security technologies. It is known that traditional security monitoring and analytics solutions are not free of generating false positives. In order to improve the accuracy, new approaches are needed. By realizing the Security 360° model, security can be elevated to the next level of quality. However, there is a price for it in terms of larger data volumes that have to be analyzed. This is the area where cognitive computing can help. First cognitive technologies have been successfully applied to the IT security domain and help not only to process large data volumes but also to increase the quality of the analytics solution. This represents the starting point of an interesting journey that will bring forward new cognitive security solutions to the never-ending battle between attacker and defender.

References

1. J.R. Rao et al., "Security 360°: Enterprise security for the cognitive era", IBM Journal of Research and Development, vol. 60, July/Aug. 2016, pp. 1:1 – 1:13, July/Aug. 2016.
2. CBS NEWS, "Beware downloading some apps or risk "being spied on", Feb. 24, 2016, https://www.cbsnews.com/news/mobile-phone-apps-malware-risks-how-to-prevent-hacking-breach/
3. H. Débar et al., "A revised taxonomy for intrusion-detection systems", Annales des télécommunications, volume 55, issue 7–8, pp. 361–378, July 2000.
4. J. E. Kelly III, "Computing, cognition, and the future of knowing", IBM, 2015.
5. J.C.R. Licklider, "Man-Computer Symbioses", IRE Transactions on human factors in electronics, 1960.
6. IBM, "Cognitive security white paper", Feb. 2016.
7. IBM, "QRadar Advisor with Watson", June 8, 2017, https://www-01.ibm.com/events/wwe/grp/grp308.nsf/vLookupPDFs/QRadar Watson Advisor Overview 201705 Sec Event/$file/QRadar Watson Advisor Overview 201705 Sec Event .pdf
8. IBM, "Watson for Oncology", https://www.ibm.com/watson/health/oncology-and-genomics/oncology/
9. IBM, "Watson for Cyber Security", https://www.ibm.com/security/cognitive/

Intelligence and Cyber Threat Management

27

Applying Foresight and Analytical Techniques to Mitigate Cyber Risks

Martin Dion

Abstract

In a world where technology advancements are only outpaced by the growth of the attack surface we are trying to defend, the use of the intelligence cycle and its associated techniques is of primordial importance to safeguard both the public and private sector in the virtual world. This chapter focuses on how to build a coherent strategy to implement and leverage an apparatus that has proven invaluable many times over to governments when ensuring national security and sustaining economic growth in the physical world.

"If you know the enemy and know yourself, you need not fear the result of a hundred battles. If you know yourself but not the enemy, for every victory gained you will also suffer a defeat. If you know neither the enemy nor yourself, you will succumb in every battle." – Sun Tzu, The Art of War

27.1 Introduction

It seems that nobody can write about matters of security without referring to Sun Tzu (722-481 BCE). I, for one, was thinking "oh no, not me, not again…." But in all honesty, I can't figure out who, if not the great Chinese strategist, cornered so efficiently the value

M. Dion (✉)
Kudelski Security, Cheseaux-sur-Lausanne, Switzerland
e-mail: martin.dion@kudelskisecurity.com

© Springer Fachmedien Wiesbaden GmbH, ein Teil von Springer Nature 2018
M. Bartsch, S. Frey (Hrsg.), *Cybersecurity Best Practices*,
https://doi.org/10.1007/978-3-658-21655-9_27

of intelligence to defend one's organization (no offence to Clausewitz)! I won't add insult to injury by outlining the essential victory principles that leads into this quote, but one thing is sure, without understanding both your internal strengths and weaknesses, and your adversary capabilities and motivations, it will be almost impossible to successfully defend the digital front of your organization.

Unfortunately, the logic behind the reflection that leads to this situation is implacable given our seemingly unstoppable movement toward digital transformation. Our postulate is that given all technologies bare a certain amount of vulnerabilities, the never-ending race to adopt more technologies to digitalize our organization and to bridge our physical self with our virtual self leads to an accumulation of vulnerabilities. Such being exploited by adversaries therefore augments the attack surface available to them and the size of the digital wall we try to defend.

This is where cyber intelligence becomes invaluable and why Sun Tzu's position on knowing both oneself and the enemy makes so much sense. Equipped with the right information, at the right time, the leaders at all level of the organization can make better decisions. Ideally, they will be more focused and unbiased and will support proper alignment of goals, resource investments and generate a shared understanding of what is valuable to the organization when defending the digital terrain at a precise point in time. From now on, this chapter will explore the concept of both traditional and cyber intelligence, as well as the distinctions between strategic, operational, and tactical intelligence products. Moreover, it proposes you with an innovative and structured approach to build your own cyber intelligence management system (CIMS).

We hope that the foundational knowledge presented and the approach we developed to build your own cyber intelligence capabilities will allow you to more efficiently manage and mitigate the threats you face within the fifth domain, the cyber terrain.

27.2 Part 1: Intelligence and the Cyber Domain

The first part focuses on defining what intelligence is as well as its production cycle. We will shortly explain how cyber intelligence differs from traditional intelligence and present you with some key definitions in the context of cyber. Afterwards, we'll further explore the intelligence production cycle and introduce the OODA loop (Boyd 1977) originally developed in the 1950s. Finally, we will provide you with an overview of the three types of intelligence products and their relevance to the different audiences tasked with making impactful cybersecurity decisions.

27.2.1 Intelligence: Its Traditional Use and Value

To define what Intelligence is, its use, and value, let me first start by stating that intelligence is not the art of spying. For the purpose of this chapter, we'll focus on a NATO-derived definition (NATO 2016) where intelligence is about threats, what you want to know about them, helping you prepare, respond, and avoid hazardous consequences. In other words, intelligence focuses on acquiring foreknowledge of an adversary or of a threat. To put things in perspective, spying is only one of the craft used for the collection phase of the intelligence full cycle and is not an aspect that we will further explore in this chapter.

To further enhance our understanding of intelligence, we must also distinguish the difference between two meanings that are often used interchangeably where in the first case, intelligence is defined as a series of activities to acquire information that will later be analyzed to produce the other type of intelligence, the product itself. The intelligence product is an actionable piece of analysis that informs the customer and helps him make the best unbiased decision leveraging the currently and most reliable information available. It usually includes an interpretation by a subject matter expert providing an opinion on a specific challenge or is trying to forecast possible outcomes to support an informed decision-making process by the recipient.

Furthermore, it is also important to understand that a national intelligence apparatus is usually divided in two segments, the intelligence and the counterintelligence. The intelligence side is often tasked with supporting preparedness when it comes to tackling issues originating from outside the nation and acquiring foreknowledge of adversaries from the military, political, and critical economic sectors. Counterintelligence on the other hand focuses on protecting valuable and exposed personnel and both national and key private sector assets against the incursion of foreign intelligence services within the country. Remember that embassies on foreign soil are also usually considered to be part of the country.

Without limiting the value of each segment or the various use cases of intelligence and counterintelligence, let us briefly explore a few classical scenarios where they have been used efficiently in the past. Some of the most common scenarios are the following.

Military Campaign Preparedness

When comes the time to deploy valuable men and women to defend the values and interests of a country, one wants to make sure that loss of life, who are often inevitable, are limited to a number that will never be small enough. To do so, various means can be used to determine the terrain we'll be confronted with, the types of obstacles, the strength of the adversary position, or of the means he'll deploy against our offense and defenses. Those pieces of information are used to make all sorts of logistical decision, that if made without, would expose those valuable beings like sitting ducks in enemy's territory or equip them with knifes when joining a gun fight.

Geopolitical Analysis and Risk Assessment

When entering a large negotiation or deciding to invest in a foreign region to support some national trade imperatives, a government must be fully aware of the situation on the terrain. As an example, a targeted region might be infested with corruption whilst the potential investors' motherland has very strong anti-bribery regulation in place. This would create an almost unmanageable situation for the national companies who would take a grant to develop in the target region and be confronted with local practices that are criminal offences in their country of origin. Moreover, that same government might invest into an emergency relief or peace effort in a region that is controlled, at the street level, by gangs or local warlords. Without "boots on the ground," and reliable information to support risk management, local population who deserve our compassion and support might not get access to it if other measures are not negotiated and implemented in parallel.

Competitive Intelligence

Although often seen as the private sector equivalent to spying practices or associated to enterprise stealing secrets from each other, competitive intelligence can be a very valuable tool where none of that needs to happen. As an example, knowing that our primary competitor is massively investing into energy cell technologies might be the signal we were missing to launch our own electric car investment program. Monitoring the amount of new job posts might be indicative of growth or interest in a given region. If only to prevent bad investment strategy, competitive intelligence is both an effective and important activity. It must be noted that counterintelligence agencies are often tasked with helping R&D-oriented companies and sensitive contractors against foreign, private or national, competitive intelligence campaign.

Profiling of Individuals

Profiling has been used in various contexts, the two most obvious might be when used by various police forces to track down an unknown individual and to link him back to a series of crimes (i.e., criminal profiling and serial offender tracking). Another case would be to better understand how our counterpart thinks, so we could modulate a negotiation strategy in accordance to his own, and probably predictable, cognitive decision-making biases. To a larger extent, psychologists have been using some level of profiling to classify challenges one might be faced with personally or at an enterprise level and to determine what is the best treatment or action plan given a series of parameter that will help or impede the resolution of the situation.

Foreign Power Threat Assessment

Not all threats deserve military response; even military threats do not all deserve military response, and this is why diplomats have been using intelligence in various manners to better understand how to de-escalate situations for centuries. Better understanding the threats, its nature, the motivations, and the people behind it, as well as the execution timeline, has helped countless conflict peaceful resolution by finding alternate pressure point. By using the full apparatus of international law, various pacts and agreements, international treaties, and in some case economic trade leverage points, those diplomats were able to thwart those situations with shedding a single drop of blood.

The previous examples tried to demonstrate that intelligence is used in all sort of manners, and we hope that those examples helped you better understand and contextualized how part of those situations are similar to your own challenges. As an example, an entrepreneur can easily make parallel with a military campaign when comes the time to expand into a new region where fierce competition might exist.

From now on, to help readers' comprehension and avoid confusion for those exposed for the first time to such a detailed level of the field, we will no further distinguish between intelligence and counterintelligence and will refer to it all as "intelligence." As well, we will focus on elements that support the defense of your security posture given that most organizations do not have an offense or aggressor agenda. Ultimately, the goal of the cyber intelligence management system is to help you increase your security posture and to yield the most efficiency out of your defensive measures.

Such will be apparent as we will narrow our efforts to focus on supporting the development of the situational awareness concept as there is a strong argument about the fact that intelligence should first focus at better understanding oneself. Doing so enables organization to better assess the risks of adverse consequences coming our ways and to direct the mitigation plan accordingly.

27.2.2 Cyber Intelligence: How Does It Differ?

What is fundamentally different between traditional intelligence and its cyber counterpart is the complexity of the problem. To simplify a problem, the first step is usually to define its boundaries but what if the attackers don't have to travel distance to deliver an attack? What if, when he steals something from you, it is still there? What if he is able to penetrate your network and spend an average of more than 6 months on the inside by avoiding detection? What if his attack toolkit accounts for more than 8000 active vulnerabilities (CVE. ORG 2017) he can potentially exploit against you?

Those are not "if" but facts that you will have to deal with when you think about cybersecurity. You also have to remember and acknowledge that there is no cyber equivalent to the army or the police to defend you and no surgeon or emergency doctor if you are bleeding out valuable data. From a security standpoint, the Internet well known WWW actually stands for the Wild Wild West and the legal apparatus coupled with transboundary lack of isolation makes you responsible for your own protection. Given that those are simple and mostly undisputable facts, we must face reality and make the best out of the cards we are dealt with.

Being positive in nature, this is also where and when I can look up to the problem and see it has an opportunity and so should you. If you tackle the challenge first hand, and before your competitors, you are already one step ahead and more resilient in case of turbulence. The other aspects that make things uniquely challenging is the pace of change and the speed to which business is conducted within the digital realm. Today, almost everything operates 24/7, and you are on the opposite side of the planet in milliseconds; no need to sleep; the computer is running and is never tired. Again, one's tormented sea brings to another plenty of opportunities. Just think about it; if you are given 24 h to do something, it will take you (as a human) an average of 3 business days to do the work, but if that same task could be automated by the computer, then you can deliver three times as much work in the same period, simply brilliant.

Although the challenges of cybersecurity can't be solely addressed by technology, in this case, it is our friend, and we must consider and leverage it as much as we can when designing our cyber intelligence program. In fact, in the second part of this chapter, we will focus on building the tactical aspects of the cyber intelligence program, and we will spend the better part of our time together discussing the use of technology and automation. But let's not get ahead of ourselves just yet. Regardless of the fact that we might have what seems to be a low-hanging fruit with technology use for tactical intelligence, we are of the opinion that people and process aspects are what are most difficult with cybersecurity and intelligence today.

Case in point, most people simply do not understand what they are stepping into when they dip their toes in the technology pool, and this is why both strategic and operational intelligence are of utmost relevance. When a cyber security officer talks to his management and all they hear is blah blah blah, how can the organization move forward? Both strategic and operational intelligence focus on bridging the gap that both parties are faced with as they sit at opposite ends of the spectrum; only then they'll be able to work the best out of the resources they are respectively accountable for.

27.2.3 The Intelligence Cycle

First things first, when it comes to intelligence, we must understand what is its production cycle. It starts with the need for a specific piece of actionable intelligence down to the consumption of a final product. Ideally, it will be complemented by a feedback loop that will support the increase in quality and accuracy of the intelligence products. The good news is that almost every organization already generates some sort of intelligence on an ongoing basis. What we are proposing is to consolidate it into a management system to derive maximal value out of it and to fill up the blanks you currently have.

Let us start with a visualization of the intelligence cycle (see Fig. 27.1) and remember that our objectives are to facilitate well-informed and unbiased business and security decisions

Fig. 27.1 The intelligence cycle. (Quelle: Lowenthal 2015)

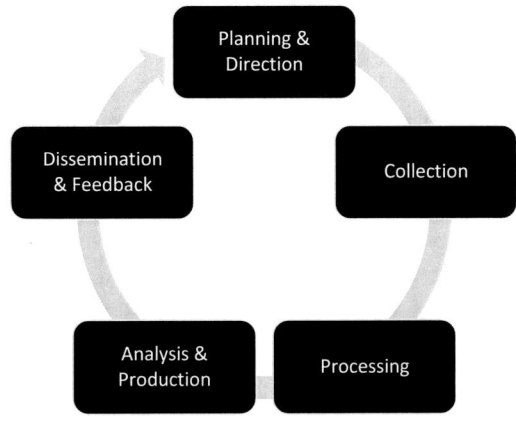

about risks related to your brand, reputation, people, infrastructure, and the partners within your ecosystem. In this section, we'll introduce to the key concepts using high-level definitions as more details and implementation steps are presented in the second part of the chapter.

High-level explanation of the various aspects of the intelligence cycle (Collective P. U. 2017):

Planning and Direction: The step where the elicitation of goals and intent from the customer is conducted (the intelligence problem), where priorities are set (Priority Intelligence Requirement (PIRs)), and where resources are provided to support and direct the collection process and efforts. In short: What do we need and how much are we willing to spend to get it?

Collection: The management process where potential sources of information are identified, interpreted, and evaluated and from which information is extracted in preparation for processing. In short: Getting the information input and make sure it's timely, aligned with PIRs, specific to our needs, and accurate.

Processing: The phase where collation and correlation and where transformation and enrichments happens, so the analyst can consume it and assess if we have access to all of the required information and in sufficient quantity to conduct our analysis with the expected degree of precision. In short: Transform, normalize, translate, and enrich and make sure we have everything we need.

Analysis and Production: This is where the analysts or algorithm ingests the information that was collected and processed to integrate supplemental data and derive a customer-consumable intelligence product applying proper methods and subject matter expertise to answer the customer's question. In short: This is the work output expected to be disseminate to the customer.

Dissemination and Feedback: This is where the information is transmitted to the customer in a written form (report or brief), orally, or electronically and where feedback is collected to determine if further analysis is required or quality adjustment needed (human-to-human dissemination). Human-to-cyber or cyber-to-cyber dissemination happens in some operational context and in almost all tactical context and usually leverages some sort of automation, machine interpretable format, and electronic transmission. In short: Information gets transmitted to customer using agreed upon means, and quality gets measured via some sort of feedback loop.

27.2.4 The OODA Loop

Another way of looking at the intelligence production cycle is through the OODA Loop (see Fig. 27.2), a model that was developed by Colonel John Boyd, a military strategist from the United States Air Force in the 1950s. Although originally designed to provide a

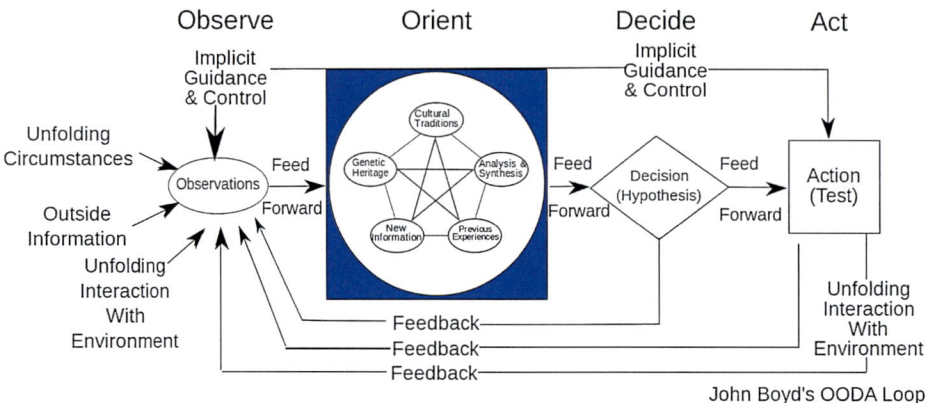

Fig. 27.2 John Boyd's OODA Loop Model. (Quelle: Boyd 1995)

rapid decision-making framework for combat situation, you will be able to see many simi-
larities with the intelligence lifecycle presented earlier.

Moreover, when it comes to cyber and given the speed at which things are constantly
unfolding, one can probably appreciate even more how this model provides further value
on top of the classical model, especially for high-speed decision-making cycle relying on
tactical intelligence products.

A key difference in this model comes from the *observe* phase where instead of using a
directing and collecting approach, there is an assumption that a given context is getting
flooded with a lot of potentially useful information that might or not influence the decision-
making process for the next steps. When observed and recognized as potentially valuable,
the information gets *oriented* (disseminated) and further enriched (processing) before
making its way to the *decide* steps in which a person or algorithm will test a hypothesis
and drive an *act*ion. What is also interesting with Boyd's model is the fact that feedback
is constant and happens at different stages of the process, shortening and constantly
improving both the intelligence product and the iteration cycle. To conclude on the OODA
Loop, when it comes to operational and tactical intelligence for cybersecurity purposes,
looping out of the classical intelligence model and adopting Boyd's proposal would be our
favored model. To learn more about John Boyd and his fascinating lifework, we suggest
you read "Science, Strategy and War – The Strategic Theory of John Boyd" by Frans
Osinga (2005).

27.2.5 Cyber Intelligence: The Three Pillars and Product Family

Now that we discussed both intelligence and cyber intelligence and the elements that com-
pose the production cycle, please take the time to review Table 27.1 as we take a closer
look at the three types of intelligence (INSA 2017) that are needed to improve enterprise
resilience through the implementation of a cyber intelligence management system.

Table 27.1 The three pillars of intelligence

Intelligence pillars	Customers	Goals
Strategic	Senior leadership (CxO and Board)	To provide upper management with information to effectively assess, quantify the risk to the business, and explain it to senior management. This will help determine objectives and guidance based on what is known of potential adversaries, adverse terrain, and the current security posture of the organization in order to successfully mitigate threats. The ultimate goal is to reach a common understanding of the cyber threat landscape and its impact on the business in order to drive the organization's cybersecurity strategy and investments
Operational	Risk, Technology and Security Leadership	These bridges the broad, nontechnical nature of strategic cyber intelligence and the narrow, technical nature of tactical intelligence. It supports the organization's executive managers in the development of strategy-based plans and policies to protect the organization against potential adversaries. In short, it helps operationalize the mitigations to defend against adversaries and difficulties of the operational theater
Tactical	SOC and NOC people, cyber threat hunters	Tactical intel is directed at efforts to detect and respond to adversaries already operating at the perimeter and within the organization's network by facilitating predictive analysis of specific threat actors before they gain access to an organization's network. It provides context and relevance to a tremendous amount of data and empowers organizations to develop a proactive cybersecurity posture and bolster its overall risk management policies. It supports better decision-making during and following the detection of a cyber intrusion and drives momentum toward a cybersecurity posture that is predictive, not just reactive

27.2.6 Bringing It All Together

Before moving into the second part which focuses on building your cyber intelligence management system, we would like to wrap up this first part with a few supplemental definitions and concepts that will be valuable to your understanding afterward.

As introduced earlier, the CIMS should bring your organization with cybersecurity situational awareness which combines both knowledge of yourself and of your adversaries. Such is attained when you acquire the ability to obtain and maintain foreknowledge of the threats you are faced with and when you are capable of determining your level of exposure to such threats. To do so, you will also need to be able to put in perspective your own capabilities to mitigate the potentially adverse impacts of an attack.

To understand the threats, you need to understand your potential adversaries (SRI 2002); Table 27.2 presents you with an overview of industry agreed upon categories most organizations are faced with.

Table 27.2 The six types of cyber adversaries

Risks	Potential adversary	Overview and motivation
High	Organized crime	This group is all about business and very dangerous. They are independent or collective groups of hackers that collect information to be sold for profit or used directly to conduct fraud and extortion. Those illegal activities are conducted independently, under more traditional criminal organization or under sponsorship of various states. We see them at the top of the pyramid as some are operational units of existing criminal organization with access to massive financial means. They can conduct industrialized global extortion campaign with little to no physical risks and limited jurisdiction exposure; they are usually patient, and some can even engage in cyber-kinetic attacks using local muscle for hire or private contractors
	Hacktivist and advocacy groups	They are decentralized individuals or groups that targets sectors of interest to disrupt productivity and cause reputational damage or advance specific causes through information gathering and sharing it back in the court of public opinion. Like other forms of activism, they usually idealize and impersonate a cause. They usually expose confidential information but also actively engage in misinformation or injection of partisan information into the news stream using website defacement or large denial of service campaign to promote their message. In this area, most digital self associate or belong as an official member to a real physical organization, not necessarily in an official capacity, but at least from an ideological perspective creating also a risk for cyber-kinetic or coordinated actions
Medium	State-sponsored entity	Usually well resourced; they are professional teams directly managed by governments or are privately operating under the sponsorship of a nation. Such private contractors are used in cyber warfare to promote national interests whilst ensuring a certain level of deniability. Usually, they target specific enterprises with the goal to acquire technologies or otherwise nonpublicly available information to advance the national interests of their sponsor or home nation. Since 2015, they have been involved in various information campaigns to promote and support indirectly more "interest compliant" politicians get into office
	Disgruntled employees and contractors	Might be used by other adversaries; they usually have some sort of personal vendetta against your organization or what it represents. They try to damage your organization or its reputation by using more or less advanced techniques related directly to their technical skills and motivation to learn (usually correlated with the size of the grunge). They might cause major disruption causing productivity and data losses or leak sensitive information back into the public space

(continued)

Table 27.2 (continued)

Risks	Potential adversary	Overview and motivation
Low	Competitors	Companies in your sector or in similar parallel businesses that might benefit from acquiring particular knowledge, trade, or production secrets at a much lower cost and much faster than if they had to research and finance a solution on their own. They rarely conduct the attack on their own and would usually hire a specialized contractor, a "future ex-employee," or an insider to get access to the privileged information
	Opportunists	Unaffiliated hackers looking for bragging rights and hacker's community recognition. They might target information that might be valuable on the black market. They usually take advantage of more or less advanced security gaps in your infrastructure and have a tendency to explore for a long period once they are in

To conclude this section and explain why we spend some time exposing you with the various types of adversaries, we would like to introduce a last concept which is the Threat Indicators. Also known as indicators of attack (IOA) or indicators of compromise (IOC), they are the equivalent of a digital DNA evidence, a cyber fingerprint of some sort. They can usually be liaised back, if not to a specific adversary, to a specific type of tools or attack campaign that you can use to determine the best course of action when defending your enterprise.

So without further ado, let's move on to Part 2 to understand how to build your own cyber intelligence management system.

27.3 Part 2: Building the Cyber Intelligence Management System (CIMS)

Based on more than two decades of experience and readings on the subject, I can attest that I was never really able to read anything on "building" an end-to-end intelligence apparatus that included the aspects related to cyber, people, processes, and technologies to handle strategic, operational, and tactical requirement. Most of my readings were around very specific aspects, but few recommended a step-by-step and end-to-end approach, and this is what I tried to summarize, at a high-level, within a single paper. The second part of this chapter presents you with an innovative approach to build what we have been referring to as a cyber intelligence management system (CIMS). We start by explaining the core difference between program management versus a management system. We'll then move on to an implementation program with components overview, followed by the three classical phases of initiating a program, building the management system, and measuring the outcome of the intelligence products.

▶   Before we dive in further in this section, I would like to offer you with an advice:
       Think big but start small!

The time when people were asking permission and resources to build something, then disappear for 24 months, and come back victorious is gone. We currently live in a micro-financing era where people will expect you to deliver regular evolutions upon your initial iteration demonstrating progress and increase mastery of your craft before giving you more resources. To put things in perspective, I suggest that you adopt the minimal viable product approach (MVP, Robinson, 2001) to launch your phase 1 so you can start showing result fast. Don't be afraid to fail, it is part of the learning process, but do so in a controlled fashion, and do it quickly so you can pivot and readjust to deliver something better and more impactful next time. Don't fall into paralysis due to analysis, and keep in mind that basic results are far better than no result at all. If you want to learn more on MVP and lean product management concepts, the book Lean Startup (Ries 2011) is a great reference.

27.3.1 Program Management Versus Management System

Without dwelling too much into the past failure of traditional intelligence (Jervis 2011), one can argue that there is a fundamental design flaw in the way it has been operated up to now. Words and their meaning have deep value and the following definitions explain why I strongly feel that calling what must be done an "intelligence program" is a mistake and that what we must refer to and build is an "Intelligence Management System." As defined by the Project Management Institute (PMI 2017), a program is "A group of related projects managed in a coordinated manner to obtain benefits not available from managing them individually. Program management is the application of knowledge, skills, tools, and techniques to meet program requirements." Whilst this definition sounds almost inspiring, we can recognize that its nature focuses on specific outcomes, time bound (the nature of projects), and touch points under known conditions. Again, sounds great, but we must see that here is little to no space for accountability of both the consumer and the producer nor are there clear roles and responsibilities on the collector or receiver ends in this definition. In other words, if we voluntarily make a cognitive shortcut, and because "program" focuses on the what instead of the how or the why, there is a huge potential for misunderstanding, quality issues, finger pointing, and little space for efficient root cause analysis leading to better performance when the program fails to deliver the expected outcome.

On the other hand, the International Organization for Standardization (ISO 2017) defines a management system as a series of organized and structured means for ensuring that an organization can achieve and maintain high standards of performance. It is a comprehensive system that is both proactive and preventive in nature requiring visible management leadership and commitment. It involves employees in a meaningful way and uses both reactive and proactive measures to continuously improve. It is a process that holds management accountable for achieving performance through goal setting, defining roles and responsibilities, developing proactive performance measures, and holding individuals accountable for their responsibilities within the management system. Finally, it is a continuous management process that, through time, increases efficiency and production quality and prevents incidents.

Furthermore, ISO management systems are based on eight principles that lead to proven knowledge management practices and provision for third-party risks which are both part of the very nature and motivation behind the operation of an intelligence apparatus:

1. **Improve Customer Focus:** The primary focus is to meet customer requirements and exceed expectations in terms of the quality of products and services.
2. **Enhance Leadership Involvement:** The leadership team is expected to be highly committed to strengthening the outcome, that every business unit understands and accepts the changes to ensure a unified commitment to quality and provide the required resources and training.
3. **Improve Engagement of People:** People are engaged in delivering value as there is clarity on the role and responsibilities which contribute to organizational synergy and success whilst capturing regular feedback.
4. **Adopt a Process-Based Approach:** Documentation is available to implement processes, resources, methods, and controls defining and supporting quality objectives at the relevant function and process levels whilst keeping track of ongoing activities.
5. **Enable People and Process Improvement:** Persistent focus on improvement, both in terms of organizational efficiency and effectiveness. Organizations should focus on the improvement of products and processes enabling growth and organizational goals attainment.
6. **Facilitate Evidence-Based Decision-Making:** Emphasizes evidence-based decision-making, indicating that decisions based on the analysis and evaluation of data and information are more likely to produce the desired results. The evidence collected should be accurate, reliable, and easily accessible to those who need it for decision-making.
7. **Ensure Relationship Management:** To ensure high standards of quality, organizations need to be able to effectively manage their relationships with third parties such as suppliers and partners to enable sustained growth. By sharing their knowledge, vision, and values with each other, organizations and their third parties can enhance their relationship.
8. **Establish a Systematic Approach to Risk Management:** Inculcate risk management into an organization's day-to-day activities. The end goal is to make business processes seamless to ultimately deliver customer satisfaction in a timely fashion. Risks are implicit, but "risk-based thinking" makes preventive actions part of one's daily routine.

27.3.2 Understanding the Management System Components

Management systems are a set of tools for strategic planning and tactical implementation of policies, practices, guidelines, processes, and procedures that are used in the development, deployment, and execution of plans and strategies and all associated management activities. They provide a foundation for successful implementation of both strategic and tactical business decisions regarding current activities, processes, procedures, and tasks for the purpose of meeting existing goals and objectives of an organization whilst satisfying customer

Table 27.3 The three pillars of intelligence

Pillars	People	Processes	Technologies
Strategic	• CEO and board • Executive managers • Intelligence manager • Senior Analyst(s) with understanding of geopolitics and business	• Identification of business risks and challenges • Direction and observation requirement definition and operation	• Business, competitive, legal, geopolitical, and social monitoring services and information sources • Knowledge sharing and management platform
Operational	• CIO, CISO, and other IT executive managers • Mid-management from the operational side of the business • Analyst(s) with understanding of IT and cyber security	• Collection to dissemination requirement definition and operation • Measurement and feedback requirement definition and operation • Risk assessment and management	• Business risk assessment and management automation platform • Translation software • Business asset repository and graph analytics
Tactical	• Security and Network Operation People • Analyst(s) with deep understanding of cyber security	• Identification of technical security risks and challenges • Asset management and protection baselining • Direction and observation requirement definition and operation • Collection to dissemination requirement definition and operation • Measurement and feedback requirement definition and operation • Risk assessment and management	• Technical information feeds and sources • Threat Intelligence Platform (TIP) • Integration components to internal detection, prevention, and response systems • Data exchange and service bus • Vulnerability scanning and management • Asset discovery and management, risk assessment automations • Risk and knowledge management

needs and expectations. At a high level, those elements can be classified under three categories of resources: people, processes, and technologies. As organization evolves and their operating ecosystems complexifies, "people" can be either internal or external to the organization, "processes" will govern tasks that can be totally or only partially realized by the organization, and "technologies" describe the various layers of the information systems from data to network and from databases to applications.

Please take the time to review Table 27.3 that aggregates and resumes some of the elements under each category that you will have to plan for; we have also distinguished within which pillar they are focused. More details on each aspect will be provided later on within the implementation section of each intelligence cycle components.

27.3.3 Initiating the Cyber Intelligence Management System Program

Although it might seem confusing, since we proposed to position intelligence as a management system instead of a program in a previous section, we must remember that building the management system is effectively a program. The reason why we formalize this initiative as a program goes back to the PMI definition offered earlier: "A group of related projects managed in a coordinated manner to obtain benefits not available from managing them individually...." In this section, we won't review all the elements specific or success factors associated with launching a program; rather, we will keep our focus on the elements specific to initiating an intelligence production program. We recommend that your initiation phase formalize the following elements:

1. Identify a project leader and a business champion.
2. Define the cyber intelligence management system objectives and program scope.
3. Clarify how the business is expecting to crystalize the value of intelligence products.
4. Document use of cases and categories of risks the business is trying to tackle with the program.
5. Identify the various stakeholders of the *strategic*, *operational*, and *tactical* pillars on both the production and reception side of the intelligence product.
6. Establish the expected timeline and phases from the program launch to the delivery of an operational capacity.
7. Identify the high-level people, processes, and technology requirements along with the budgetary line from an investment, operation, and full-time equivalent perspective.
8. Propose a project team and conduct internal kickoff.
9. Formalize the program and project risk management strategy, performance monitoring, and communication plan.
10. Conduct a formal program kickoff meeting with all the relevant stakeholders.

If you step back and think about it, each phase of the intelligence cycle implementation is a project of their own, and as identified in the previous sections, *strategic* and *operational* pillars are sufficiently different from the *tactical* pillar to be further split in two unique sub-project streams.

Depending on your own project management practices, it means you will have between six and twelve unique projects to manage under your program.

27.3.4 Building the Cyber Intelligence Management System

Now that the project has been successfully initiated, launched, and resourced, we will focus on the elements specific to each capability you need to build up, so you can enrich your own project plans.

Before moving on to the capability building, the first steps you should probably undertake is hiring your first analyst (ideally a senior) as they will positively influence the next steps you will have to go through to build, launch, and operate your CIMS.

27.3.4.1 Direction

The goal of this phase of the intelligence cycle is to get valuable business inputs that will direct the work of the team(s) from collection to dissemination (FAS 2017). The following elements need to be clarified to a greater extent and with much finer level of details than we did during the initiation phase.

At a minimum, we suggest that you undertake the following steps:

1. Identify and define your customer(s) and understand their mission(s).
2. Agree on the roles, responsibilities, and expectations of the producer and the receiver.
3. Define what the customer needs to protect or be protected from, extending to geopolitical and regulatory elements that might influence collection and sources.
4. Assign the customer priorities, also known as the priority intelligence requirements.
5. Agree on an answer to the question "What is an actionable piece of Intelligence?"
6. Reach consensus on the definition of "situational awareness."
7. Agree on the form, update frequency and the content of the intelligence products they expect to receive and how they should be communicated back to them.
8. Define the expectations with regard to analytical products. Do they expect analysis, signals, warnings, forecasts…?
9. Define products and services, acceptance criteria, as well as performance metrics.
10. Formalize those requirements and get sign-off from the various customers among your stakeholders.
11. Use them as the foundation input to build your collection to dissemination capacities.
12. Identify from a people perspective the workload (FTE) and the skills you need to acquire or to develop within your analytical team based on your customers' expectations, and start hiring as soon as possible.

Both business and the threat environment are far from being static; therefore, we suggest that you review and revisit those requirements at least on a yearly basis with your stakeholders to determine if the premises have changed and if the outputs meet or still meet. As well, make sure you set time aside for impromptu subject analysis in your yearly schedule; priorities are influenced by the news cycle, and questions will come; don't worry.

To conclude, we would recommend splitting the requirement definition between two distinct initiatives, one managerial and one technical. The managerial one should be business-oriented to meet strategic and some of the operational stakeholder's goals, and the technical one will be more specific to the pure cybersecurity technical subject area with a narrower focus on potential automations and expected speed of transition from collection to dissemination due to the volume of information that will need to be processed.

27.3.4.2 Collection

The goal of this phase of the intelligence cycle is to build upon customers' requirement elicitation to implement the collection processes and technologies that you will need to harvest the required information. Where direction is more of a human-driven process you launch at the beginning of your program, and that you would update on a regular basis afterwards, collection is a continuous process that will rely heavily on technology and automation.

For those of you who are more familiar with intelligence collection practices, I would like to state that the purpose of the chapter is to provide the reader with the overarching view that will allow an organization to build their CIMS. Hence, we will not dive in the details or best practices specific to each collection disciplines. Effectively, complete books have been written on each of those disciplines (HUMINT, OSINT, GEOINT, SIGINT, SOCMINT…), and some of them are presented in the bibliography and within the "further reading" list at the end of the chapter.

For this reason, one must also recognize that collection of information in support of strategic and operational (STRATOP) intelligence product is very different from the collection of information for tactical products. STRATOP collection relies heavily on open-source intelligence (NATO 2002) and potentially some closed-source intelligence. They will be collected in the form of free text like emails, newspaper chapters, patent releases, academic papers, or social network communications, and the lack of structure is a challenge because you need to build your own taxonomy and semantic to be able to process them in an organized way. The other challenge comes from the source language, as the information of interest to you might need to come from Japan, for example, extracting an early warning will only be possible if you can process Kanji. Otherwise, you will have to wait until it becomes so "big" that all media outlet will have to translate it in English making it much less valuable. Moreover, with some language, a lot of dialects or regionalisms might influence the meaning of a text making it a bit more difficult to translate and interpret by both human and machines. The advantage of this type of information is that it is often a self-contained piece of information providing both context and meaning that can be read by almost anybody who can read it.

TAC collection on the other hand often relies on very structured feeds of information that might be available from open sources but also from commercial sources via subscription. It might be an RSS feed, a Common Vulnerability Exposure database extraction, indicators of compromise (IOC) or Attack (IOA) in JSON, or some other proprietary formats. Those usually rely on structured protocols for data exchange, automation, and integration like the widely used STIX and TAXII protocols (Collective C. T. 2017). Most of the information is exchanged in a machine readable/interpretable format and is usually not structured in a way to be humanly interpreted unless you have been technically trained. One of the strong advantages of structured information is that you can use graph analysis to process and correlate massive amounts of information and to discover previously unknown liaison and leverage algorithmic interpretation and processing to derive secondary and meaningful intelligence products.

In both cases, one should not neglect the value of the meta data that is included or that can be generated out of the source information. As examples, character map might point to a region of origin even if the wording is English, concentration of electronic activities within a certain timeslot might suggest a time zone, and less communications in a specific time frame, let's say Friday afternoon, might suggest even more precise region of the world and so on.

Although very different in nature and subject to separated project streams, we propose that you use the following steps to build your two collection capabilities:

1. Have the analyst teams review both requirement documents from the direction phase and establish a high-level delivery and build up plan.
2. Identify what are the collection automation tools currently or soon to be available and their built-in sources extraction capabilities.
3. Identify any gaps between the current capabilities and the extraction requirements to determine if we should challenge the direction guidelines.
4. In terms of sources, identify not only the known-known but also the known-unknown as they might further enhance your capability to deliver quality and accurate products.
5. Establish an information source reliability index to classify in order of credibility the incoming data sources. Information originating from a low-reputation source will probably need a second confirmation or further analysis before raising an alarm.
6. Identify retention period based on trend analysis and or legal requirements. Do not overstep this activity; collecting massive amount of information and archiving it can be a massive endeavor and might even cripple the processing and searching speed of the overall platform if wrongly designed.
7. Formalize the technical requirements of the solution that will host the information you need to process and further analyze once collected.

8. Consider if the outsourcing part or most of the collection is a viable option. The collection efforts might be very consequent, and the relative value small within the overall cycle for your specific threats and challenges. Maybe you don't need the raw information; maybe you need a curated feed.

9. Document the flow of information and execution from data to analysis and dissemination to make sure you are not shortcutting something.

10. Resist the geek fever that turns you into an animal seeking to implement a new system!!! Conduct a tabletop end-to-end (collection to dissemination) simulation before acquiring any feeds or implementing any systems. You need to determine if the information you need is available from your sources and if the potential automation you foresee mimic or improve the manual process, if not, you might be aiming in the wrong direction.

11. Then and only then you should start implementing the technical layers, and we suggest you conduct a proof of concept.

12. Last but not the least, make sure you also collect the information you need from your internal systems. People when building the collection mechanisms tend to focus on external source of information and are missing a big part of the required data need for situational awareness.

We would like to conclude this section by circling back to the last step we have proposed you with. In the field of operational and tactical intelligence, the data about your own assets, their value, security posture, and weaknesses are as important as, if not more than, the data you will get externally about potential adversaries, threats, or vulnerabilities. What is the value of knowing that a new dangerous vulnerability just got published if you can't confirm that your system is protected against it?

This is why we feel it's so important for analysts to review the output expectation (step 1) and to further think about how the result will be attained (Step 3 and 10). Doing so will help pinpoint gaps in value that we need for the equation to be computed properly. You might also end up in a situation where the internal system or the relevant data is simply not available, preventing you from meeting some of your customers' expectations as set in the direction phase.

27.3.4.3 Processing

Many scholars and practitioners represent the intelligence cycle as four steps where they merge processing and analysis and dissemination and feedback together. In our model, we have split those two in four and consider them as unique elements.

The reasons behind this are twofold; first, in a world where automation is a necessity, you will notice that processing can and should be vastly automated and that analysis is still very human in nature. Second, as we are proposing a management system instead of a program or a model, the feedback is a mandatory step that closes the loop of the management system ensuring continuous improvement. Ideally it should automatically follow dissemination which, in our proposal, is a stand-alone activity between humans or automated and transparent in a cyber-to-cyber context.

Going back to processing, the goal of this phase of the intelligence cycle is to take the collected information and apply various methods to collate, correlate, translate, enrich, and prepare the information for presentation for the analysis phase including monitoring and alarm automation.

Hence, to build up your processing capacity, we suggest the following steps:

1. Formalize the requirement around information transformation, collation, and correlation.
2. Implement a unified data dictionary and data transformation engine.
3. Implement the collation and correlation algorithms.
4. Implement data scoring automation and evaluation algorithm and methods to enrich the data including those specific to the generation of metadata.
5. Automate any translation or transformation that you can.
6. Implement automatic threshold monitoring for certain conditions.
7. Analyze and implement information monitoring, warning, and signaling mechanisms
8. Implement automated testing protocols to detect any failure of elements 2–7.
9. Implement data analysis and workflow design tools to simplify and support autonomy of the analysts when further enhancing information processing.
10. Conduct design session with analysts focusing on ergonomics to ensure optimal production work.
11. Analyze and implement visualization and collaboration tool requirements to ensure complete and efficient presentation to the analyst for the next phase.
12. Conduct a dry run with the analyst teams before scaling up the system.

27.3.4.4   Analysis

This is where the proverbial rubber hit the road in terms of intelligence production. In this section, you will find information on building the analysis capability, more details on intelligence products, an overview of structured analytic techniques, and information on the analyst and his development.

As it relates to the building of this capability, like we suggested previously, there are profound differences on how analysis is conducted for strategic and operational purposes versus the tactical pillar. Most of the steps we will present you with in the first part of this section will be focused on the analysis and production of human consumable intelligence products with a heavy emphasis on situational awareness and risk management.

As an example, one of the burning questions that most customers have around cybersecurity is a forecast tinted one: Does this new thing/attack will have an impact on us, or are we ready to face this in our business? In this particular case, it will require the analyst to leverage a lot of technical information collected internally and compare it with what is happening outside the organization. In other words, it is an input from the tactical pillar transformed into an output in the operational pillar.

Before moving on to our proposed steps to build your analysis capability, I think it is worthwhile to present you more formally with some of the intelligence products that are usually expected from the analyst team. We will review the most common to help you put in perspective the various types of intelligence product (Major 2014) you might be requested to produce.

- **Analysis:** By far the most common product type; it refers to the unbiased and factual presentation of the analysis based on historical or current events research and/or scientific and technical analysis of information collected and processed around a given matter of interest to the customers. They might include options and even recommended path of action and alternative. Those will be produced by subject matter expert as potential ways of handling a challenge or problem of interest.
- **Signal:** Refers to collected, either pre- or post-processed, pieces and element of information aligned with customer's interest that would trigger a specific escalation or emergency analysis. Signals are often unqualified by subject matter experts other than for the reliability of its source.
- **Warning:** Refers to a piece of information that usually needs to be promptly escalated or delivered to the customer and that has been qualified by a subject matter expert. The warning usually confirms that the information is of interest and is usually part of a greater monitoring scenario. Usually when warnings get released, an action or next step definition is expected.
- **Forecasts/Anticipation/Horizon Scanning:** Refers to a more advanced intelligence product that tries to assess the validity and probability of various outcomes and possible future alternatives based on current and unfolding events. They usually rely on foresight techniques and combine various quantitative techniques like statistical analysis to define future possibilities within a given timeline on a specific question. They may also rely on scenario planning and storytelling technique to imagine what are the possible chain of events, dependencies, and/or synergies that might warn us in the future that what we have foreseen is currently unfolding and that a specific action should be triggered to either capture the opportunity or mitigate the adverse consequence.
- **Situational Awareness:** Refers to a capability that permanently maintains a snapshot containing the latest information about our own security and risk posture as well as our vulnerabilities and defense capability readiness. This status is to be kept up to date so it can be quickly compared to unfolding events that might threaten our capability to reach the organizational goals. It helps both subject matter experts and decision makers to take position and to adopt the best course of action when handling a potential disruption efficiently.

On a general note, most of the analytical work happens in the brain of the analyst and on his desktop computer; most of the tools and technology you would need here provide support for research, content creation, and collaboration between the analyst team members. Here are the steps we suggest you go through to build the analytical capability:

1. Identify the structured analytic tools and practice you need to implement.
2. Formalize the special request/new incoming request for intelligence product management process.
3. Formalize definition and production guidelines for analysis, signal, warning, and forecasts.
4. Formalize the intelligence product drafting and peer review processes.
5. Formalize the intelligence product delivery process.
6. Document the requirement for the tactical pillar in terms of human-to-cyber interface if specific types of information can't be automated or if sensitive enough to require human approval before automating a response.
7. Document the integration of feedback in future product creation.
8. Formalize the process to regularly iterate on enhancement and automate during the processing.
9. Formalize the process to identify knowledge gaps and possible integration in regular collection.
10. Formalize the process to identify competence gaps and training requirement for the analyst team.
11. Formalize the situational awareness production process including scope, information inputs and outputs, and production frequency.
12. Formalize the situational awareness segmentation and dissemination process.

Now that we share an understanding of what the intelligence products are and what the analysis capability will contain, one of the first question I usually got asked is: How do we build them in terms of forms and content? In his book *Communicating with Intelligence*, James Major does a fantastic job of laying out the structure, sequence, and form of the content so we won't spend more time on this aspect. Rather, we will focus on the second question that should come to your mind: How does the analyst distill knowledge out of data, think about the problem, test the hypotheses, and provide the essence of the document?

My take on the answer is: structured analytic techniques (Pherson 2014). Over and above subject matter expertise, the analysts are expected to use various methods to support the development of their content in a systematic manner to identify and eliminate a wide range of cognitive biases and other shortfalls of intuitive judgment. As an example, AIMS (audience, issue, message, and storyline) prompt the analyst to consider up front who the paper is being written for, what key question(s) it should address, and what is the key message the reader should take away and best to present the analysis in a compelling way.

Again, due to the constraint in terms or chapter length, we will suggest that you further research this topic which addresses the following key techniques available to the analyst when producing quality work:

1. Decomposition and visualization
2. Idea generation
3. Scenarios and indicators
4. Hypothesis generation and testing
5. Assessment of cause and effect
6. Challenge analysis
7. Conflict Management
8. Decision support

To conclude this section on Analysis, we would like to spend some time on its real engine, the analysts, his training, and development. After all, technology and processes are only supporting tools that enable the analyst to strive, so it is legitimate to reflect on what are the characteristics of good analysts. The Software Engineering Institute of Carnegie Mellon University has produced high-quality researches on this topic within the Cyber Intelligence Tradecraft Project (Ludwick 2013) and defines the personality traits and skills of a cyber security analyst as shown in Table 27.4.

When selecting your analysts, some of the traits will be stronger than other, but it is important to understand that you can't compromise on some fundamental elements. As an example, linear thinkers would be very challenged by the complexity of the problems they usually are faced with versus a system thinker who would perform much better. Curiosity and thirst for knowledge are key qualities, and although one might develop methods to cope with lack of certain personality traits, transforming or coping with the inner nature of an individual have its limits. On the other hand, core competencies and skills deficiencies can be dealt with given you have the patience to train the person and that the analyst is a motivated learner and is capable of quickly evolving. From that standpoint, my recommendation would be not to wait to get the perfect candidate but to be realist in the selection process with regards to your own timeline and requirements. It would be unfair to expect and expose who would be considered a junior analyst to advanced topics that only experience and subject matter expertise can tackle.

Table 27.4 Analyst personality traits, core competence, and skills

Personality traits	Core competences and skills
• Inquisitive	• Computing and computer fundamentals
• Persistent	• Information security
• Self-motivated team player	• Technical exploitation
• Quick learner	• Communication and collaboration
• Open minded	• Data collection and examination
• Generalist	• Critical thinking

To conclude and as a general advice, don't be seduced by a candidate who has very strong core competencies in the field of security but lacks in character or critical thinking skills; cyber security knowledge is only a part of a balanced equation.

27.3.4.5 Dissemination

This phase of the intelligence cycle starts when the product is completed. Finished intelligence products take many forms depending on the needs of the decision maker and reporting requirements. The level of urgency of various types of intelligence is typically established by the customers of the intelligence organization. Dissemination is the part of the cycle that delivers products to consumers, and dissemination management refers to the process that encompasses the organization of the dissemination of finished intelligence.

When building your CIMS, you will have to plan for two distinct dissemination paths, one targeting human consumption of product and the other one targeting computer systems. Dissemination is synonymous to communication which suggests bilateral interaction. In this case, we refer to it as a push/pull model where we often push information to primary customers, but secondary and tertiary customers might be more in a pull mode, and to complete the comparison, communication is completed when the reception is acknowledged as satisfactory to both parties. Until now, we have not mentioned the sensibility or security classification of the intelligence product, but it is important to put that dimension in perspective when we build the dissemination capability as well to ensure the right level of authentication, integrity, and protection of potentially sensible content.

To build this capability, we propose you to consider the following steps:

1. Establish a communication matrix to regulate content distribution.
2. Categorize the various products for human versus computer system consumptions.
3. Document what will be the repositories, retention mechanisms and period, and access conditions to the intelligence products.
4. Agree with your customers on a "service-level agreement" that will set timeline expectations from collection to publication. This is even more critical for tactical intelligence when they might be consumed by computer system and should be integrated as quickly as possible to support your detection and defense mechanisms.
5. Document the authorized communication channels and methods. The obvious example is classified or very sensitive information that might need encryption, or might not be prudent to transmit via public email. A less obvious example but very important one is the data source integrity checking, imagine a scenario where you automate the injection of blacklist IP address and automated blocking measures in your firewalls and that somebody is able to pollute your vendor feeds blocking access to legitimate clients or your organization.
6. Conduct an asset inventory of your technical detective and protective technologies to determine which one can and would benefit from receiving cyber threat intelligence products such as feeds, IoC, and IoA. Usually, a stand-alone technical architecture of the solution integration in your security operations center is preferable.

7. Establish a reference architecture to ensure that future product acquisitions account for the various protocols you will be supporting in terms of information distribution and sharing automation.
8. Document a rollout and testing plan for the technical integration aspects.
9. Ensure monitoring controls are in place supporting the integrity of incoming products (especially when automation is present after ingestion) to prevent contamination or wrongful distribution.
10. Plan for a reception acknowledgement mechanic that will also trigger the feedback gathering and integration process.
11. Formalize a TLP protocol (FIRST.ORG 2017) to label products and to ensure that recipients do not share inadequately the product they receive and to inform them that some others are safe for distribution in certain contexts.
12. Consider that your dissemination platform might be part of your monitoring apparatus to detect early in the collection process that some signals need to shortcut further processing and analysis and prioritize immediate and raw distribution.

Dissemination, especially in the context of cyber intelligence, is a highly technical subject that is worth investigating further. Implementing the dissemination process from a cyber intelligence standpoint is greatly facilitated by the use of Threat Intelligence Platform (TIP). TIP solutions usually automate most of the collection, process, and dissemination of technical and tactical information and come out of the box with multiple integrations to detective and responsive technologies. They usually already embed mechanics like the TLP to ensure that you can receive and share back information within trusted communities.

In the field of cyber intelligence, and cybersecurity in general, one should not forget the asymmetric nature of the threats we are faced with. Hackers work together and share information globally when they discover new vulnerabilities or develop new attack tools and methods. On the other hand, most organizations are alone when it comes to defending themselves. This is the reason why you should consider joining an ISAC or Information Sharing and Analysis Center (Wikipedia 2017) pertinent to your business line or even join a Cyber Fusion Center (Forsyth 2005) that would basically expand your own analytic capabilities by joining a trusted community.

Think of this as a problem between good guys and bad guys, not as a competitive advantage or disadvantage. By joining a group of good guys, what you are effectively doing is extending your immune system. Before triggering actions to defend your body, your immune system basically detects particular conditions and then tries to fight them. When joining an ISAC or a CFC, you are basically extending your digital immune system outside your organization boundaries. You become part of a massive network of sensors globally. Sometimes you might be hit first, but statistically, you will get heads up on attack more often than being its first victim. Moreover, with proper TLP, no internal or confidential information about your own organization should flow back into the community or the public space.

To conclude this section, it is worth mentioning that we can extend the dissemination part to further discuss the presentation and consumption of intelligence products, specially for products targeted for human consumption. Again, both James S. Major (2014) and Randolph H. Pherson (2014) extensively wrote on those subjects, and it would not make them justice to try to boil it down to a few paragraphs.

27.3.5 Production Measurement and Continual Improvement

Like any management systems, a CIMS must be monitored, its performance measured, and the related investment should yield better results over time. Otherwise, it's not a management system; it's just you, throwing money at a problem with the hope that your bet will send back benefits your way.

This last section of the chapter will briefly focus on the feedback loop that should conclude your intelligence cycle and improve the deliverables and quality of the management system.

27.3.5.1 Feedback

As stated before, we would not be able to talk about the CIMS as a management system without a proper performance measurement and feedback capabilities to support continual improvement. Even if, at one point in time, our products are almost perfect on their own, a good management system should try to deliver as much value for less production costs. The intelligence cycle does not end once the product is delivered to the customer. It rather continues in the same manner in which it began: with interaction between producers and customers. For the product to be useful, the analyst and policy maker need to hear and share feedback from one another, with the goal of refining both the analysis and its requirement and to be more impactful.

Feedback procedures between producers and customers include key questions, such as:

- Is the product usable?
- Is it timely?
- Was it in fact used?
- Did the product meet expectations?
- If not, why not?
- What are the next areas of interest or shall we dig deeper?

The answers to these questions lead to refined production, greater use of intelligence by decision makers, and further feedback sessions. Thus, the customer of intelligence generates more, or at least clearer, requirements, and the analyst generates better products in an iterative process.

It is worth mentioning that on the tactical side, the evaluation of the quality of our product is a bit more empiric as we can measure how accurate is the information we received. By conducting technical analysis, we can answer questions such as: Was it used to block an attack? Did we detect intruders' due to this new rule? Do we have less incidents now that we spent time and money on those aspects?

To build this capability, we suggest considering the following steps:

1. Document a continual improvement charter that describes what you are trying to achieve and how it will be measured.
2. Document what "good looks like" and what are the potential source of improvement opportunities.
3. Document what would be considered a failure of your intelligence production unit.
4. Document a root cause analysis process and the guidelines on how it will be independently executed in time of important failure or major customer dissatisfaction.
5. Build and document the feedback process to engage more clearly with your customers.
6. Build a technical analysis process for intelligence products targeted toward computer systems.
7. Implement both a face-to-face and anonymous feedback mechanism to capture as much of it as possible and compare trends or variance between both.
8. On top of peer reviews during the analysis process (during which some level of feedback should be captured as well), consider having an observer in the room when delivering the intelligence product to the customer to observe what are the questions and feedback that are raised.
9. Take time to formally analyze those results to determine if recurrent problems, questions, or types of question comes toward your production unit or if you can observe recurring patterns for specific analysts. Also, try to identify recurring questions or advice that you ask or deliver to your customers to determine if some systematic education should occur on the customer side as well.
10. Define some metrics to determine skill alignment and adequacy of the analysis team in comparison with direction guidelines. Validate it on a regular basis and observe macro-trends to determine if training should occur rather sooner than later.
11. Accumulate data on production cycle time in the various areas of your apparatus and analyze improvement opportunities.
12. Make sure everyone on the team understands the PDCA cycle and principles and the details of Deming's postulates on continual improvement.

27.4 Conclusion

As Louis Pasteur said, "fortune favors the prepared mind." As it relates, intelligence and cyber intelligence are in my opinion fascinating fields as they focus at helping you prepare against potentially adverse consequences. I stand small at the feet of the giants who preceded me when it comes to developing ideas and writing on this topic. Although this chapter is a high-level introduction to the topic, I hope it was up to your expectations and that it captured your interest.

I am respectful of your time and grateful to you, the readers, to be given the opportunity to spark your curiosity on the subject. Should you want to learn more about the topic, please be aware that tens of thousands of pages were written on the subject over the past few decades. There is a variety of books that are available out there on matters related to intelligence; some are general, but many are also very specific. If you look around, you will be able to find some who cumulate hundreds of pages of knowledge on each of the phase of the intelligence cycle, or on more specific topics like structured analytic techniques or communicating and writing intelligence products.

As a thank you to the reader, I have included at the end of this chapter a list of books and publications which have inspired me over the years and a complete bibliography of the chapters and books which have been used to support the development of this chapter. As well, I have included a list of technology vendors and solutions both commercial and open-source that I have worked with in the past to address some of the technical challenges that you will be faced with when building your own intelligence management system.

The last quote I would like to share with you is one from Ray Dalio:

▶   "He who lives by the crystal ball, will eat shattered glass" (Dalio 2017).

My interpretation and contextualization of this quote is that the information you need is out there to help you formulate answers and strategies to the cybersecurity problems you are faced with. Diligently searching for it and fighting cognitive biases is for me the essence of good cyber intelligence.

Reference Books and Further Readings

 1. Katherine H. Pherson: Critical Thinking for Strategic Intelligence and
 2. Randolph H. Pherson: Structured Analytics Techniques for Intelligence Analysis
 3. Taylor & Francis: International Journal of Intelligence and Counter-Intelligence
 4. Taylor & Francis: Intelligence and National Security
 5. Royal United Services Institute: The RUSI Journal
 6. Henley-Putnam University: Journal of Strategic Security
 7. George & Bruce (Editors, 2008/2014): Analyzing Intelligence 1 & 2 – Origins, Obstacles, and Innovation/National Security Practitioners' Perspectives
 8. Allen W. Dulles (2006): The Craft of Intelligence
 9. Robert M. Clark (2013): Intelligence Collection (CQ Press)
10. Mark M. Lowenthal (2016): Intelligence – From Secrets to Policy 7th edition (CQ Press)
11. James S. Major (2014): Communicating with Intelligence – Writing and briefing for national security (R&L Publishers)

12. Daniel Kahneman (2013): Thinking, Fast and Slow
13. Stella Cottrell (2011): Critical Thinking Skills – Developing Effective Analysis and Argument (Palgrave)

Intelligence-Related Product Vendors and Open-Source Solutions

1. Digimind, a commercial OSINT and Social Media collection and processing solution
2. Recorded Future, a commercial intelligence collection and processing platform
3. Palantir, a high-end full intelligence cycle solution used by governments
4. EclecticIQ, a commercial Threat Intelligence Platform (TIP) used by both the private and public sector
5. Maltego, an open-source and commercial OSINT investigation and collaboration platform
6. I2 Analyst, an environment to help investigators and intelligence analyst coordinate their efforts
7. Cambridge Intelligence/KeyLines, a commercial and very powerful visualization development toolkit
8. MISP (Malware Information Sharing Platform), an open-source TIP platform
9. STIX/TAXII/MAEC, open-source threat intelligence characterization and exchange protocols
10. COGITO Intelligence API, a powerful commercial translation and semantic analysis engine
11. Oxford Analytica, a geopolitically inclined top-shelf intelligence products and consulting provider
12. The Economist Intelligence Unit, the commercial intelligence analysis branch of the magazine
13. Cyber Threat Intelligence feeds varies a lot in nature and are available from vendors like Crowdstrike, F5, Trendmicro, FireEye, Cisco, Kaspersky, EcleticIQ, Anomali and Cymon just to name a few.

References

Boyd, J. (1977). *Patterns of Conflict.* U.S. Army Command and General Staff College.
Boyd, J. (1995). *The Essence of Winning and Losing.* Retrieved from Defense in the National Interest: https://www.danford.net/boyd/essence4.htm
Collective, C. T. (2017). *Sharing threat intelligence.* Retrieved from Structured language and transport mechanism for sharing cyber threat intelligence: https://oasis-open.github.io/cti-documentation/
Collective, P. U. (2017). *Intelligence Cycle and Process.* Retrieved from The Learner's Guide to Geospatial Analysis: https://www.e-education.psu.edu/sgam/node/15

CVE.ORG. (2017). *Common Vulnerability Exposure Database.* Retrieved from CVE.ORG: https://cve.mitre.org/

Dalio, R. (2017). *Principles: Life and Work.* Simon & Schuster.

FAS, F. o. (2017). *Intelligence Cycle.* Retrieved from CIA Factbook on Intelligence: https://fas.org/irp/cia/product/facttell/intcycle.htm

FIRST.ORG. (2017). *Standards Definitions and Usage Guidance – Version 1.0.* Retrieved from TRAFFIC LIGHT PROTOCOL (TLP) – Forum of Incident Response and Security Teams: https://www.first.org/tlp/

Forsyth, W. A. (2005). *STATE AND LOCAL INTELLIGENCE FUSION CENTERS: AN EVALUATIVE APPROACH IN MODELING A STATE FUSION CENTER.* U.S. Naval Postgraduate School.

INSA, I. a. (2017). *Collected Publications.* Retrieved from INSA: https://www.insaonline.org/resources/publications/

ISO. (2017). *Management system standards.* Retrieved from International Organization for Standardization: https://www.iso.org/management-system-standards.html

Jervis, R. (2011). *Why Intelligence Fails: Lessons from the Iranian Revolution and the Iraq War.* Cornell Studies in Security Affair.

Lowenthal, M. M. (2015). Intelligence: From Secrets to Policy. In M. M. Lowenthal, *Intelligence: From Secrets to Policy* (p. 85). CQ Press.

Ludwick, M. K. (2013). *Cyber Intelligence Tradecraft Project.* SEI Emerging Technology Center. Retrieved from Cyber Intelligence Tradecraft Project: https://www.sei.cmu.edu/about/organization/etc/citp.cfm

Major, J. S. (2014). *Communicating with Intelligence – Writing and briefing for national security .* R&L Publishers.

NATO. (2002). *OSINT Handbook.* SACLANT Intelligence Branch.

NATO. (2016). *Glossary of Terms and Definition.* NATO STANDARDIZATION AGENCY.

Osinga, F. (2005). *Science, Strategy and War – The Strategic Theory of John Boyd.* Eburon Academic Publishers.

Pherson, R. H. (2014). *Analytic Writing Guide.* Pherson Associates, LLC.

Pherson, R. H. (2014). *Structured Analytics Techniques for Intelligence Analysis 2nd* Edition. CQ Press.

Project Management Institute (2017) Program definition retried from https://www.pmi.org/learning/featured-topics/program

Ries, E. (2011). *The Lean Startup: How Today's Entrepreneurs Use Continuous Innovation to Create Radically Successful Businesses.* Currency.

Robinson, Frank (2001) MVP definition retrieved from https://en.wikipedia.org/wiki/Minimum_viable_product

SRI, I. (2002). *Insider Threat, SRI 2002 Cyber Adversary Spectrum.* Menlo Park: SRI International.

Tzu, S. (722-481 BCE). *The Art of War.* Translation and interpretation of original manuscripts.

Wikipedia. (2017). *Information Sharing and Analysis Center.* Retrieved from https://en.wikipedia.org/wiki/Information_Sharing_and_Analysis_Center

Die digitale Transformation

28

Michael Kranawetter

Zusammenfassung

Der Handlungsbedarf bei der Umsetzung von Compliance-Anforderungen wächst unaufhaltsam, nicht zuletzt getrieben durch die fortschreitende Verlagerung von Geschäftsprozessen und Workflows in die digitale Welt. Die digitale Transformation und der damit einhergehende verstärkte Einsatz von Cloud-Lösungen hat nicht nur Auswirkungen auf Geschäftsprozesse, die Einbindung von Mitarbeitern oder das Verhältnis zu Kunden, sondern bringt eine Dynamik ins Spiel, die die Erfüllung von Compliance-Anforderungen vor neue Herausforderungen stellt.

28.1 Compliance als Nutzbringer für den Geschäftserfolg

Die Erfüllung von Compliance-Anforderungen ist bei der fortschreitenden Verlagerung der Geschäftsprozesse und Workflows in die digitale Welt, längst mehr als nur eine lästige Pflicht. Die im Zusammenhang mit Compliance umgesetzten Maßnahmen haben auch einen positiven Effekt für den eigenen Geschäftserfolg. Die Frage stellt sich:

Wenn Regularien ohnehin umgesetzt werden müssen, wie kann aus dieser Umsetzung ein maximaler Nutzen für das eigene Geschäft gezogen werden?

M. Kranawetter (✉)
Microsoft, München, Deutschland
E-Mail: michael.kranawetter@microsoft.com

© Springer Fachmedien Wiesbaden GmbH, ein Teil von Springer Nature 2018   393
M. Bartsch, S. Frey (Hrsg.), *Cybersecurity Best Practices*,
https://doi.org/10.1007/978-3-658-21655-9_28

Dabei stehen regulatorische und geschäftliche Anforderungen nicht im Widerspruch zueinander. Im Gegenteil: Beide lassen sich auf gemeinsame Zielsetzungen und Intentionen zurückführen. Unternehmen können regulatorische Vorgaben als Ausgangspunkt nutzen, um Synergie Effekte zwischen den vorgegebenen Pflichten und den eigenen Zielsetzungen zu realisieren.

Welche Schritte müssen unternommen werden, um dieses Ziel zu erzielen?

Zur Vereinfachung haben wir ein Compliance-Modell entwickelt, das die Komplexität des Themas stark reduziert und zu einem besseren Verständnis beiträgt. Dabei verfolgen regulatorische und geschäftliche Anforderungen – mit Blick auf Informationen – sechs gemeinsame Ziele: Schutz, Verfügbarkeit, Nachvollziehbarkeit, Transparenz, Sorgfalt und Dynamik. Diese Ziele basieren auf gesetzlichen und regulatorischen Grundwerten und liegen in der einen oder anderen Form den meisten Regelungen zugrunde. Lediglich die Ausprägung unterscheidet sich von Land zu Land und von Regelung zu Regelung.

Diese geschäftlichen und regulatorischen Vorgaben und Ziele können in der Regel über Prozesse aus den folgenden sechs Kernbereichen erfüllt werden:

- Informationssicherheit und -schutz;
- Umgang mit Risiken;
- Informations- und Kommunikationsmanagement;
- Bilanztheorie, Prüfungswesen und Organisation;
- Transparenz- und Informationspflicht;
- Globalisierung und Transformation.

Das sind die gemeinsamen Themenfelder, die sich aus den gesetzlichen und betriebswirtschaftlichen Anforderungen herauskristallisieren.

Ein Unternehmen, das in diesen Kernbereichen gut aufgestellt ist, kann künftige Compliance Anforderungen besser umsetzen. Wer sich also auf die sechs genannten Bereiche konzentriert, nutzt Compliance auch als Treiber für eine dynamische IT-Infrastruktur. Außerdem werden für geschäftliche Anforderungen zusätzlich Nutzenpotenziale geschöpft, darunter die Kalkulierbarkeit und Reduzierung von Geschäfts- und IT-Risiken, die Vermeidung von Betrugsfällen, mehr Effizienz und Transparenz durch die Automatisierung und Optimierung von Prozessen, die erhöhte Reputation des Unternehmens insgesamt und letztlich auch die Optimierung von Investitionen in Schutzmaßnahmen siehe Abb. 28.1.

Die Auseinandersetzung mit diesem Thema hilft, dein Verständnis für die Problematik zu entwickeln. Jedoch müssen auch konkrete Schritte für die Umsetzung unternommen werden, die abhängig von der bestehenden Ist-Situation sind. Die Frage stellt sich, wie ein Unternehmen überhaupt seinen aktuellen Compliance-Zustand und das angestrebte Ziel erkennen kann. Durch die Analyse des Ist-Status eines Unternehmens bezüglich der Umsetzung der Ziele und Kernbereiche des Compliance-Modells können Handlungsfelder identifiziert werden, über die sowohl Compliance umgesetzt als auch der eigene Geschäftserfolg vergrößert werden. Ein Unternehmen, das sich umfassend und bereichsübergreifend mit

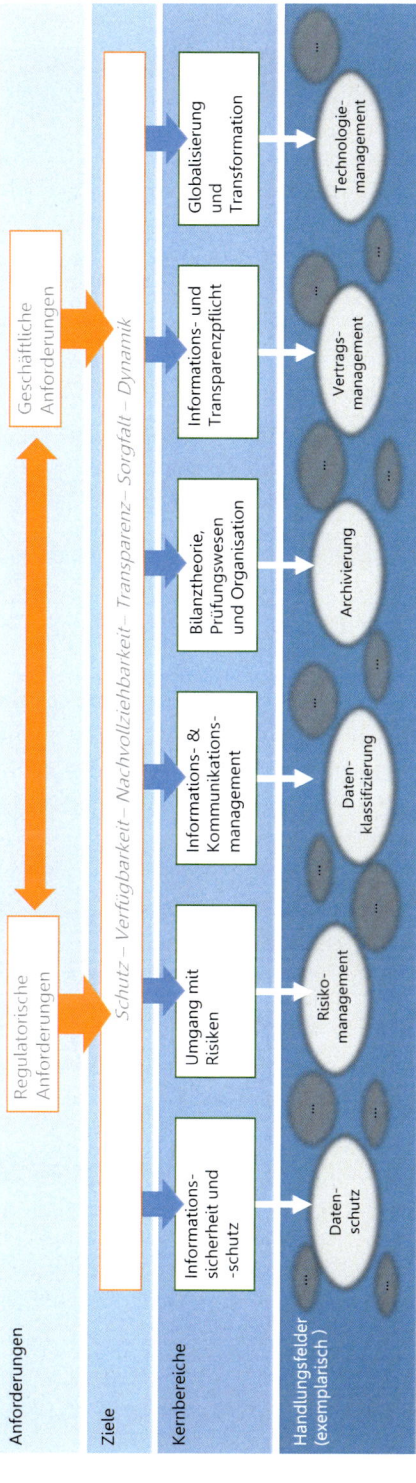

Abb. 28.1 Zusammenfassung des Compliance-Modells

der Analyse der eigenen Prozesslandschaft auseinandersetzt, erhält auf diese Weise einen Überblick über all jene Bereiche, in denen die Erreichung regulatorischer und geschäftlicher Ziele verbessert werden kann.

Das beschriebene Compliance-Modell holt Ihr Unternehmen dort ab, wo es momentan steht. Das Modell zeigt einfache Schritte, um sich dem Thema Compliance anzunähern und eine gemeinsame Kommunikationsebene zu schaffen. Dabei ist klar, dass ein vereinfachtes Modell keinen Anspruch auf Vollständigkeit erhebt. Jedoch wird das Modell helfen, eine Grundlage für das Verständnis von Compliance und deren Beitrag zur Geschäftsoptimierung zu schaffen. Naturgemäß muss bei einer vertieften Betrachtung auf die jeweilige individuelle Situation des Unternehmens eingegangen werden, auch wenn sich die grundlegenden Strukturen immer wieder gleichen. Über die qualitative Einordnung von Prozessen, mit denen bestimmte Handlungsfelder in den sechs Kernbereichen umgesetzt werden, ist die Bestimmung des Reifegrades der eigenen Compliance-Anstrengungen möglich. Dies erleichtert es dem Unternehmen, den eigenen Standort zu bestimmen und seine aktuelle Risikosituation darzustellen. Es wird transparent, welcher Status vorliegt und wie ein übergreifendes Zusammenspiel der Beteiligten zur Verbesserung beitragen kann.

28.2 Entwicklungen der digitalen Transformation

Die Entwicklung immer neuer Technologien geht mit fortlaufenden Veränderungen in Unternehmen und Organisationen einher und ebnet den Weg für die Digitalisierung. Das bedeutet, dass immer mehr bisher analoge Prozesse und Abläufe auf IT-Technologien basieren, was die Effizienz in Organisationen beträchtlich steigern kann. Dass die digitale Transformation einen enormen strategischen Nutzen für Organisationen und Unternehmen haben kann, zeigen die zahlreichen bestehenden Anwendungen, etwa im Bereich Cloud Computing, mobiles Arbeiten und dem Internet der Dinge. Nach wie vor entstehen in diesen und anderen Bereichen stetig neue, innovative Geschäftsideen. Die Trends und Technologien der digitalen Transformation bedeuten aus Sicht von Unternehmen und Organisationen also vor allem auch fortlaufenden Wandel.

28.2.1 Technologien, Trends und Ziele

Ausgehend von den technischen Möglichkeiten lassen sich für Anbieter, Mitarbeiter und Kunden neue Ziele definieren, die mit der digitalen Transformation erreicht werden können:

- Ganz neue Produkte und Dienstleistungen werden entwickelt oder bereits bestehende Produkte und Dienstleistungen werden vereinfacht, verschlankt, um neue Funktionen erweitert oder in ihrem Ablauf optimiert.
- Produktion und Abläufe werden komplett automatisiert, auch so weitgehend, dass sich Prozesse über Unternehmensgrenzen hinweg selbsttätig durch die Kommunikation zwischen Maschinen steuern und Ereignisse auslösen.

- Kunden werden stärker in Produkte und Dienstleistungen eingebunden. Dies führt zu einem verbesserten Kundenerlebnis, schnelleren Prozessen und einer verbesserten Kundenbindung.
- Kosten werden verringert, weil überflüssige manuelle Anteile von Workflows von IT-Systemen übernommen und Fehler verringert werden.

Nutznießer der digitalen Transformation sind dabei alle Beteiligten: Unternehmer können schnell auf die Wünsche ihrer Kunden reagieren und ad hoc innovative Produkte und Dienstleistungen in den Markt bringen und skalieren, aufbauend auf einer automatisierten Wertschöpfungskette. Mitarbeiter werden von lästigen und zeitfressenden Tätigkeiten entlastet und können sich um die wesentlichen Dinge, die Optimierung und Weiterentwicklung ihrer Arbeit kümmern. Und die Kunden profitieren von den auf ihren Bedarf zugeschnittenen Angeboten, möglicher Individualisierung („build to customer order") sowie einer verbesserten Interaktion mit dem Anbieter. Das alles ist möglich bei sinkenden Kosten und höherem Durchsatz, also einer Anhebung der Gesamtgeschwindigkeit. Im Folgenden werden die wichtigsten Trends und Entwicklungen im Zusammenhang mit der digitalen Transformation diskutiert.

28.2.2   Digitalisierung von Geschäftsprozessen

Eine besonders deutlich zu erkennende Veränderung durch die digitale Transformation betrifft Geschäftsprozesse (Workflows), also Vorgänge und Abläufe innerhalb von Unternehmen und Behörden. Allgemeine Geschäftsprozesse und ihre durch die Ablauforganisation definierten Arbeitsabschnitte und Arbeitsschritte wurden bisher durch die IT-Technologie nur bedingt unterstützt. Viele Geschäftsprozesse, insbesondere auch in der Interaktion mit Dritten, hatten viele Brüche und auch Nicht-IT-Anteile, die dann oft manuell bearbeitet werden mussten. Ein einfaches Beispiel dafür sind E-Mails, die zwar optimiert durch die IT transportiert werden, dann aber so lange im Eingangskorb eines Benutzers verbleiben, bis dieser sie liest und bearbeitet. Eine weitere, aber auch entscheidende Dimension manueller Vorgänge sind deren Fehleranfälligkeit und Sicherheitsrisiken, beispielsweise durch Phishing-Mails, Betrugs- oder Erpressungs-Trojaner. Zudem führt ein immer größer werdendes E-Mail-Aufkommen zur Überlastung von Mitarbeitern, was eine steigende Fehlerquote mit sich bringen kann. Der Ablauf der Verarbeitung von E-Mails ist folglich nicht effizient.

Bei der Digitalisierung von Geschäftsprozessen geht es darum, zu teure, überflüssige, fehleranfällige oder sicherheitskritische manuelle Anteile am Workflow nicht nur durch die IT zu unterstützen, sondern durch die IT abzubilden und somit zu automatisieren. Das ist eine neue Qualität. Durch die IT werden standardisierte Abläufe sowie benutzerfreundliche und eingabenplausibilisierende Schnittstellen zur Verfügung gestellt, die auch nicht-IT-affine Mitarbeiter und Kunden ansprechen. Ferner können diese Interfaces durch weitgehende Automatisierung und Autonomisierung so optimiert werden, dass die oben aufgezählten Schwächen einfach wegfallen. Wichtig dabei ist, dass die neue Technik Akzeptanz bei Anwendern und Kunden findet, denn wenn die Wünsche, die sich mit der digitalen Transformation verbinden, unerfüllt bleiben, bleibt auch der wirtschaftliche Erfolg aus. Klar ist jedoch auch, dass Unternehmen und Organisationen gerade durch die neuen technologischen Ansätze dazu in die Lage versetzt werden, geräteunabhängige Lösungen mit situationsangepassten und sicheren Schnittstellen zu Menschen und Maschinen bereitzustellen. Wer sich strategisch mit dem Mehrwert der unterschiedlichen neuen Technologien auseinandersetzt, kann frühzeitig die Weichen für eine prosperierende Zukunft stellen.

28.2.3 Digitaler und mobiler Workspace

Mit der digitalen Transformation ändern sich nicht nur Geschäftsprozesse und Work-flows, sondern auch die Arbeitsplätze der beteiligten Mitarbeiter. Bei einer zentralen Datenhaltung, den notwendigen Benutzerschnittstellen sowie gesicherten Verbindungen mit rollenbasierten Zugriffen besteht kein Grund mehr, seine Arbeit im Büro oder im Homeoffice zu erledigen. Prinzipiell können Mitarbeiter an jedem Ort der Welt mit jedem denkbaren Endgerät ihren Teil der Arbeit erledigen, genauso wie Partner und insbesondere Kunden. Benutzerfreundliche Schnittstellen, die es Kunden ermöglichen, selbst in Prozesse einbezogen zu werden, sind gerade eine Grundlage der Digitalisierung.

Solche Kundenschnittstellen und digitalen Arbeitsplätze werfen aus Sicht von Sicherheit und Compliance entscheidende Fragen auf, insbesondere bei Auswahl und Absicherung von Endgeräten. Prinzipiell sollten neben Desktop-Systemen und Laptops, deren Sicherheit man mit klassischen Methoden gut in den Griff bekommen kann, auch Smartphones und Tablets eingesetzt werden können, inklusive BYOD-Geräten. Die Anforderungen an das Endgeräte-Management und die Endpunkt-Security steigen unter diesen Vorgaben stark an. Kunden- und Benutzer-Interfaces, mit denen die manuellen Workflow-Anteile abgewickelt werden, müssen sich an diese digitalen Arbeitsplätze anpassen lassen. In der Regel werden die Schnittstellen über webbasierte Applikationen zur Verfügung gestellt. Da gerade im Bereich der Darstellung von Webinhalten viel Erfahrung mit der Skalierung auf unterschiedliche Endgeräte besteht, sollten sich hier keine großen Anpassungsprobleme ergeben.

28.2.4 Veränderte Arbeitstechniken

Digitale Arbeitsplätze führen zu anderen Arbeitstechniken. Standardisierte, webbasierte Benutzerschnittstellen werden anders bedient als typische Anwendungen, wie man sie aus dem Büroalltag kennt. Natürlich wird von den betroffenen Mitarbeitern erwartet, dass sie sich an die neuen Arbeitstechniken gewöhnen und die gewohnte Leistung für das Unternehmen erbringen. Durch die Standardisierung fallen aber auch „Rüstzeiten" beim Wechsel von einer Anwendung in eine andere weg, etwa durch zentrale Bereitstellung oder Updates. Durch eine kontextbezogene Plausibilisierung wird zudem die Fehlerquote bei der Eingabe gesenkt.

Bei den Themen Sicherheit und Compliance sind solche Standardisierungen ein großer Vorteil. Richtlinien müssen nicht mehr an jede Applikation angepasst werden. Zudem ergeben sich Synergieeffekte bei der technischen Erzwingung der Umsetzung von Richtlinien, da die Technik im Hintergrund weniger Plattformen als bisher bedienen muss. Ein gutes Beispiel in dieser Hinsicht ist das Single-Sign-on (SSO), bei dem in klassischen Büroumgebungen eine Unzahl von Plattformen und Anwendungen bedient werden muss. Bei webbasierten Anwendungen lässt sich SSO viel einfacher und zuverlässiger implementieren.

28.2.5 Internet der Dinge

Das Internet der Dinge (IoT) ist ein ganz bedeutender Antrieb für die digitale Transformation. Wenn sich Geräte untereinander verständigen, also Maschinen mit Maschinen, so setzt das voll automatisierte Workflows voraus. Das IoT ist somit Paradebeispiel und Testfeld für neue Technologien zugleich. Am IoT kann auch gesehen werden, wohin die Reise bei der digitalen Transformation führt. IoT-Lösungen sind in der Regel cloudbasiert, d. h. die einzelnen Systeme halten nur wenige Daten lokal vor und sind über das Internet erreich- und steuerbar. Die Verarbeitung der Signale von IoT-Geräten über zentrale Datenspeicherung unter Mithilfe von selbstlernenden Systemen und künstlicher Intelligenz macht die Zukunft des IoT aus.

Über die Cloud und standardisierte Schnittstellen können die unterschiedlichsten Geräte in ein IoT eingebunden werden und miteinander sowie mit zentralen Stellen kommunizieren. Die übergeordneten Workflows sind in der Regel relativ starr vorgegeben, denn einen großen Entscheidungsspielraum wird den angeschlossenen Geräten nicht gegeben. Die eigentliche Intelligenz sitzt in den Workflows in der Cloud. Die Geräte haben nur eine lokale Sicht auf die Vorgänge und arbeiten ausschließlich mit den für sie relevanten Daten, die sie über eine abgesicherte Kommunikation untereinander und über die zentrale Steuerung erhalten.

Um die digitale Transformation umzusetzen, kommen moderne Technologien wie mobiles Computing, plattform- und geräteübergreifende Applikationen und Kommunikation, Big-Data-Analysen, selbstlernende Systeme sowie künstliche Intelligenz zum Einsatz. Diese Technologien sind mit ihrem Anspruch an Kapazität, Skalierbarkeit, Flexibilität, Funktionalität und Rechenleistung in einem wirtschaftlich vertretbaren Ausmaß nur noch über Cloud-Angebote realisierbar. Man kann die Cloud daher geradezu als Basistechnologie für die digitale Transformation bezeichnen.

28.3   Herausforderungen der digitalen Transformation

Durch die digitale Transformation entstehen ganz neue Anforderungen, etwa an die Einhaltung von Regularien. Der schnelle technologische Wandel muss dabei auf strategischer, technologischer und organisationaler Ebene erkannt und berücksichtigt werden. Vor allem Unter nehmen und Behörden, die sich bisher nicht mit der Digitalisierung beschäftigt haben, müssen umlernen und sich auf schnell veränderliche technische und organisatorische Rahmenbedingungen einstellen. Die Einhaltung regulatorischer Anforderungen (Compliance) spielt eine besondere Rolle, um Fortschritt und Wandel unter Berücksichtigung potenzieller Risiken umzusetzen. Im Detail wird das Zusammenspiel von Compliance und der digitalen Transformation Gegenstand späterer Kapitel sein. Im folgenden Abschnitt werden zunächst Herausforderungen aus Compliance-Sicht für die bereits aufgegriffenen Technologien und Trends der digitalen Transformation diskutiert.

28.3.1   Kooperation durch übergreifende Workflows

In vielen Fällen erstrecken sich Workflows über den Einflussbereich einer Organisation hinaus. Beispiele sind hier Just-in-time-Beziehungen zwischen Automobilherstellern und ihren Zulieferungen oder Self-Service-Portale von Stadtverwaltungen. Unter Compliance-Gesichtspunkten können sich hier Überschneidungen oder Widersprüche auftun, etwa wenn die beiden Partner unterschiedliche Anforderungen erfüllen müssen oder der Status von Compliance-Umsetzungen des Partners unbekannt ist. Bei den beiden Beispielen aus der Automobilindustrie oder öffentlichen Portalen kann die Erfüllung von Compliance-Anforderungen mittels SLAs oder Nutzungsbestimmungen erzwungen werden. Schwieriger wird es, wenn beide Seiten inkompatible Anforderungen haben – etwa wenn ein Unternehmen einen Lieferanten in China hat und zu den Compliance-Anforderungen des deutschen Unternehmens der Einsatz bestimmter zertifizierter Verschlüsselungsverfahren gehört.

28.3.2   Mobilität, Flexibilität, Sicherheit

Mit digitalen und mobilen Arbeitsplätzen werden klassische Perimeterschutzkonzepte außer Kraft gesetzt. Daten, Systeme und Arbeitsplätze befinden sich nicht mehr in Bereichen, die unter der (vermeintlichen) Kontrolle eines Unternehmens oder einer Behörde stehen. Die Arbeitsplätze können überall auf der Welt sein, etwa in öffentlichen Hotspots oder in fremden Kundennetzwerken. Die Verbindung zu den eigenen Systemen, also der Transport der Daten zu den Arbeitsplätzen, erfolgt über Netze, die ebenfalls nicht der Kontrolle der eigenen Organisation unterliegen und über deren Sicherheit meist keine Aussage möglich ist.

Die Arbeitsplätze selbst wandeln sich kontinuierlich. Natürlich wird es immer noch die klassischen Firmenarbeitsplätze geben, die gemäß strengen Richtlinien vorkonfiguriert und mit sehr beschränkten Benutzerrechten ausgeliefert werden. Doch es werden in zunehmendem Maße auch privat angeschaffte Tablets, Smartphones oder andere Geräte angebunden werden, bei denen die Firma oder die Behörde nur eingeschränkte Konfigurationsmöglichkeiten hat. Damit geht einher, dass sich das Augenmerk immer mehr auf die Daten, deren Klassifizierung und deren angepassten Schutz verlagert. Infrastruktur und Geräte selbst werden zweitrangig. Zudem wird die Unterscheidung zwischen privaten und geschäftlichen Daten immer mehr an Relevanz gewinnen, insbesondere bei einer parallelen Verarbeitung in verschiedenen Endgeräten und Anwendungen (Kommunikation, Social Media, Adressdaten etc.).

Trotz dieser Randbedingungen müssen unsichere Netzwerke und Geräte die eigenen Compliance-Anforderungen erfüllen. Die Compliance und die betriebswirtschaftliche Aufgabe, geschäftseigene Daten und die Verfügbarkeit von Diensten zu schützen, befruchten sich dabei gegen seitig. Wenn etwa als Compliance-Vorgabe die Umsetzung des Informationssicherheitsstandards ISO 27001 erforderlich ist, sind beispielsweise verschlüsselte Verbindungen und die ausreichende Absicherung von Endgeräten nicht nur eine lästige Erfüllung der Pflicht, sondern dienen dem Schutz relevanter sensibler Geschäftsdaten und damit dem eigenen Geschäftszweck.

28.3.3   Schnelle und automatisierte Kommunikation

Zum Wesen von voll automatisierten Workflows gehört die schnelle, automatisierte und kontinuierliche Kommunikation. Lediglich bei den manuellen Workflow-Anteilen wird dieser Prozess für die Zeit der Bearbeitung angehalte, um nach der Interaktion wieder fortgesetzt zu werden. Schnelle und automatisierte Kommunikation schafft unter Sicherheitsgesichtspunkten Herausforderungen. Wenn in der Automatik ein Fehler auftritt, ist es kaum noch möglich, diesen manuell zu korrigieren und Folgeerscheinungen zu unterbinden. Dies bedeutet, dass in automatisierten Workflows die Fehleranfälligkeit und -wahrscheinlichkeit extrem geringgehalten und Sicherheitsmaßnahmen entsprechend ganzheitlich angewendet werden müssen. Diese geringen Fehlerraten kann man nur erreichen, wenn an vielen Stellen des Workflows automatische Überprüfungen auf Plausibilität und Einhaltung von Vorgaben stattfinden. Die Sicherheitsmaßnahmen müssen eine durchdachte Architektur haben und Möglichkeiten zur Überwachung und Reaktion umfassen.

In diesem Punkte gehen Sicherheit und Compliance Hand in Hand. Denn auch die Einhaltung von Compliance-Anforderungen muss weitgehend automatisiert werden. Dazu sind Mechanismen nötig, mit denen die Umsetzung von Richtlinien entweder erzwungen wird oder zumindest eine Kontrolle mit der Möglichkeit zum Abbruch des Workflows im Falle von Compliance-Verletzungen gegeben ist.

28.3.4   Die Welt der Maschinen

Das Internet der Dinge stellt eine der größten Herausforderung für die Compliance dar. Denn hier geht es um eine Welt, in der Maschinen und Geräte Workflows weitgehend selbstständig abwickeln und der menschliche Einfluss – abgesehen von der initialen

Konfiguration – gering ist. Das gilt besonders bei selbstlernenden autonomen Systemen. In dieser rein technischen, von Maschine zu Maschine gesteuerten Welt müssen Compliance-Vorgaben in technische Vorgaben übersetzt und im IoT an die beteiligten Systeme verteilt werden. Eine Welt, in der Roboter, intelligente Stromzähler, Router und Switches, Heizungsthermostate, Kameras, Kühlschränke und fast beliebige andere Systeme zu Hause sind, ist mit ihren Sensoren, Akteuren und Events extrem heterogen. Die Übersetzung von Vorgaben in gerätespezifische Richtlinien stellt deshalb eine Herausforderung dar, die noch nicht ansatzweise gelöst ist. Dies gilt ebenso für Kontrollen, ob die Richtlinien tatsächlich auch umgesetzt worden sind. Die Erzwingbarkeit von Regeln muss daher zukünftig integraler Bestandteil von IoT-Geräten sein.

Da Logik, Systeme und Daten von IoT-Netzwerken in aller Regel zentral in einer Cloud gehalten werden, lassen sich einige Compliance-Anforderungen in der Cloud bündeln. Dies trifft etwa in den Bereichen Sicherheit und Datenschutz zu, da sämtliche Aspekte der physischen und logischen Datensicherheit sowie die Umsetzung von Datenschutzrichtlinien in der Cloud umgesetzt werden können, also beispielsweise der Perimeterschutz, der Einsatz von Verschlüsselungstechnologien und die Klassifizierung von Daten. Leider existieren bisher für die große Masse an möglichen und bereits verfügbaren IoT-Geräten kaum Regularien und Standards, was eine flächendeckende Durchsetzung sicherer und zuverlässiger Technologien und die strategische Planung für Anbieter erschwert.

28.4 Strategische Aspekte der digitalen Transformation

Bei der Betrachtung der Vorteile und Herausforderungen wurde bereits angedeutet, dass die digitale Transformation aus strategischer Sicht eine hohe Relevanz für Unternehmen und Organisationen hat. Im nun folgenden Abschnitt soll dieses grobe Bild weiter verfeinert und um konkretere Erkenntnisse ergänzt werden. Am Ende steht eine klare Übersicht darüber, welche Technologien die digitale Transformation prägen und welche strategischen Implikationen dies für Unternehmen und Organisationen mit sich bringt.

28.4.1 Technologische Entwicklungen

In der Praxis bietet es sich an, Anwendungen und Daten zentral zu halten und die Zugriffsvergabe und Handhabung an zentral definierbare Richtlinien zu knüpfen. Diese Richtlinien müssen bereits bei der Prozessgestaltung berücksichtigt werden, damit ein Anwender Zugriff nur auf die Daten und Systeme erhält, die er für seine Workflows auch wirklich braucht. Eine Voraussetzung hierfür ist die zentrale Definition und Überwachung von Sicherheitsrichtlinien. Außerdem muss eine zentrale und automatisierte Steuerung der Vergabe von Zugriffsberechtigung und Handhabung für die angepasste Verwendung von Ressourcen wie Geräten und Diensten möglich sein.

28.4.2   Cloud als Basistechnologie

Auf zahlreichen Anwendungsgebieten hat sich Cloud Computing in den letzten Jahren insbesondere aufgrund der kostengünstigen und skalierbaren Bereitstellung virtualisierter Ressourcen als Schlüsseltechnologie für die zentralisierte Bereitstellung von Daten und Systemen etabliert. Cloud-Anbieter stellen ihren Kunden ein immer größer werdendes Portfolio an Diensten bereit, was die Möglichkeiten in Bezug auf Anwendungsszenarien, aber auch im Hinblick auf die individuelle Konfiguration und Steuerung der Daten- und Systemlandschaft stetig erweitert.

Die digitale Transformation kann getrost als „Killer-Applikation" für die Cloud bezeichnet werden. Ohne die Cloud in ihrer Funktion als zentrale und standardisierte Plattform für Daten und Systeme sind zentrale Anliegen der digitalen Transformation nur schwer umsetzbar. Hierzu zählen nicht nur automatisierte Workflows und das Internet der Dinge, sondern auch die Durchsetzung von Sicherheitsrichtlinien und ein nachhaltiges Gerätemanagement. Hierdurch wird etwa ein nachhaltiges Konzept zur mobilen Arbeit überhaupt erst möglich. Auch Institutionen oder Organisationen, die sich eine Nutzung der Cloud bislang gar nicht vorstellen konnten, müssen sich die Frage stellen, ob sie die digitale Transformation ohne Cloud-Technologie überhaupt durchführen können.

Ob die Daten in einer öffentlichen, privaten oder hybriden Cloud abgelegt sind, spielt für die Funktionalität eines automatisierten Workflows zunächst keine Rolle. Unter Compliance-Gesichtspunkten, wie zum Beispiel Sicherheitsanforderungen, kann die Auswahl eines bestimmten Cloud-Modells allerdings eine große Bedeutung haben. Im folgenden Kapitel wird das Thema Compliance zunächst allgemein analysiert. Anschließend wird das Thema im Zusammenhang mit den Entwicklungen und Chancen der digitalen Transformation und des Cloud Computings betrachtet.

28.5   Compliance und die digitale Transformation

28.5.1   Compliance – eine Einführung

Sprach man in der Vergangenheit über Compliance im Kontext von IT, so gab es einen relativ breiten Konsens darüber, welche Arten von Regularien gemeint waren. In vielen Fällen ging und geht es bis heute um Themen wie Sicherheit und Datenschutz. Die digitale Transformation erweitert den Fokus, da immer mehr bisher kaum oder gar nicht IT-gestützte Prozesse durch IT-Technologien erfasst werden. Es lohnt sich also, vor der inhaltlichen Auseinandersetzung mit Compliance im Kontext der digitalen Transformation eine terminologische Auseinandersetzung mit den unterschiedlichen Compliance-Begriffen vorzunehmen. So fällt es im Anschluss leichter, ein Verständnis für die Veränderungen zu entwickeln, die sich im Zuge der digitalen Transformation auch für den strategischen Wert von Compliance aus geschäftlicher Sicht ergeben.

Begriffe und Definitionen

Dazu soll zunächst eine Definition des Begriffs „Compliance" im Spannungsfeld der digitalen Transformation vorgenommen werden. Eine Spezifizierung von allgemeinen und IT-spezifischen Compliance-Begriffen ist da hilfreich. Die folgenden Begriffe finden so auch in vielen anderen Werken Anwendung:

Compliance im Allgemeinen bezeichnet Aktivitäten, um ein regelkonformes Verhalten zu erlangen und Hilfsmittel zur Abbildung der Unternehmenslage bereitzustellen. Dabei geht es nicht nur um Gesetzeskonformität, sondern auch um das Einhalten von unternehmensinternen Richtlinien, die wiederum auf Best Practices – also empfohlenen Richtlinien und Standards – basieren können. Das schafft einen Verhaltenskodex, der dem Aufbau einer Vertrauensbasis im geschäftlichen Umgang dient. Dieser Kodex gilt zwischen Geschäftspartnern, im Verhältnis zu Kunden, innerhalb des Unternehmens sowie als Vorgabe für Dienstleister jeglicher Art.

IT-Compliance beschäftigt sich als Teilbereich der Compliance schwerpunktmäßig mit denjenigen Compliance-Anforderungen, welche die IT-Systeme eines Unternehmens oder einer Organisation betreffen.

Der Begriff **Corporate Compliance** soll im Rahmen dieses Handbuchs zur Abgrenzung von der IT-Compliance dienen. Mit Corporate Compliance sind also die Compliance-Anforderungen gemeint, welche vom Begriff der IT-Compliance nicht erfasst werden.

Wie wirken sich digitale Transformation und Cloud Computing auf den strategischen Umgang mit dem Themenkomplex Compliance aus und wie kann Compliance in Anbetracht größerer technologischer und organisatorischer Umbrüche in Unternehmen und Organisationen erfolgreich gestaltet werden? Im folgenden Teil dieses Kapitels wird ein strategischer Ausblick auf Herausforderungen und Chancen der digitalen Transformation in Bezug auf Compliance gegeben.

28.5.2 IT-Compliance und Corporate Compliance – Grenzen verschwimmen

Man könnte meinen, dass es sich bei der digitalen Transformation um ein Thema primär im Spannungsfeld der IT-Compliance handelt. Die in Kap. 5 beschriebenen Anwendungsfälle der digitalen Transformation zeigen aber, dass diese Annahme zu kurz greift. Im Zuge der Digitalisierung bisher analoger Geschäftsprozesse und Workflows werden auch Anforderungen wichtig, die bisher der Corporate Compliance zugeordnet wurden. Mit der digitalen Transformation wandert auch die Umsetzung von Corporate-Compliance-Anforderungen zusammen mit den Geschäftsprozessen mehr und mehr in die digitale Welt. Die IT muss Geschäftsprozesse und Compliance-Anforderungen abbilden und umsetzen. Das betrifft auch Geschäftsprozesse, die bisher keinen oder nur einen minimalen Anteil an IT hatten.

Der Wandel, von dem die IT und Corporate Compliance im Zuge der digitalen Transformation erfasst wird, hat auch größere Auswirkungen auf die Aufgaben der Compliance-Verantwortlichen in Unternehmen und Behörden. Die Einhaltung regulatorischer Anforderungen scheint in Anbetracht tief greifender technologischer und organisatorischer Veränderungen also primär eine Frage des Managements und der Prozessgestaltung zu sein. Da Compliance-Anforderungen in Form von Regeln automatisch in die Benutzerschnittstellen integriert werden, befindet sich der Anwender bereits in einem Compliance-Rahmen, in den die Umsetzung eines großen Teils der Regeln bereits eingearbeitet ist.

28.5.3   IT-Compliance – eine Frage der Sicherheit?

Derzeit lässt sich ein kontinuierlicher Anstieg der Anforderungen an Sicherheit und den Schutz von Informationen erkennen, der sich nicht auf Cloud-Anbieter und -Infrastrukturen beschränkt. Seit dem Inkrafttreten des IT-Sicherheitsgesetzes im Juli 2015 (NIS Verweis) gelten nicht nur für Betreiber kritischer Infrastrukturen, sondern auch für Betreiber von Webangeboten erhöhte technische und organisatorische Sicherheitsmaßnahmen zum Schutz von Kundendaten und IT-Systemen. Das Bundesdatenschutzgesetz verlangt zudem konkret die Umsetzung technischer und organisatorischer Maßnahmen zum Schutz von Kundendaten bei der IT-gestützten Verarbeitung. 2018 wird mit der General Data Protection Regulation (GDPR) auf EU-Ebene eine einheitliche Regulierung zum Datenschutz aller EU-Bürger getroffen werden, die auch den Datenexport in Länder außerhalb der EU reguliert.

Das Thema der IT-Compliance hängt daher nach wie vor stark mit Fragen des Datenschutzes und der Informationssicherheit zusammen. Gerade beim Einsatz von Cloud-Lösungen ist Sicherheit ein zentrales und viel diskutiertes Thema. Dies unterstreichen auch die Ergebnisse einer auf Microsoft Insights publizierten Studie zur Zukunft der Informationssicherheit, für die 365 führende IT-Manager aus der Wirtschaft befragt wurden. Die Studie schlägt den Bogen von aktuellen Angriffen über die Nutzung von Cloud-Diensten bis hin zu Anforderungen an Cloud-Anbieter.

Die Ergebnisse besagen, dass fast ein Viertel aller befragten Unternehmen in den vergangenen zwölf Monaten von einer Cyberattacke betroffen war. In diesem Zusammenhang gibt die Studie auch Aufschluss darüber, welche Bedrohungen für den Schutz von Daten von besonderer Bedeutung sind. Auf den vorderen Plätzen landen dabei Phishing-Angriffe, Social Engineering, Malware mit Zugriff auf schützenswerte Daten und sogenannte Advanced Persistent Threats (APT), also raffinierte, zielgerichtete und technologisch hoch entwickelte Angriffe, die mit großem Aufwand betrieben werden.

Abb. 28.2 stellt das aktuelle Bedrohungsszenario deutlich dar. Die weiteren Fragen der Studie ermitteln unter Berücksichtigung dieser Bedrohungen, wie es mit der aktuellen Nutzung von Cloud-Diensten aussieht und welche Anforderungen an die Anbieter gestellt werden. Die Ergebnisse der Studie besagen, dass aktuell 31 % der Befragten die Cloud für mehr als 50 % und 48 % der Befragten die Cloud für weniger als 25 % ihrer operativen Aktivitäten verwenden.

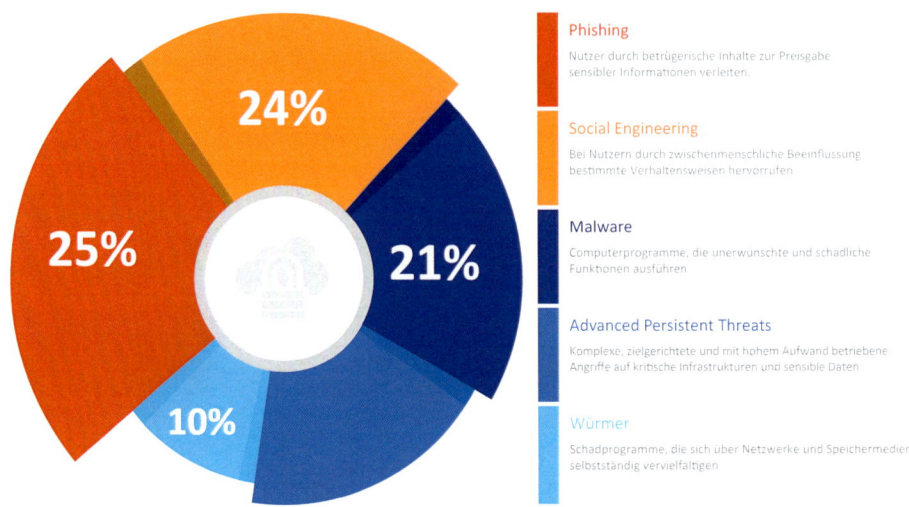

Abb. 28.2 Bedeutung von Cyberbedrohungen. (Quelle: Microsoft Insights Studie)

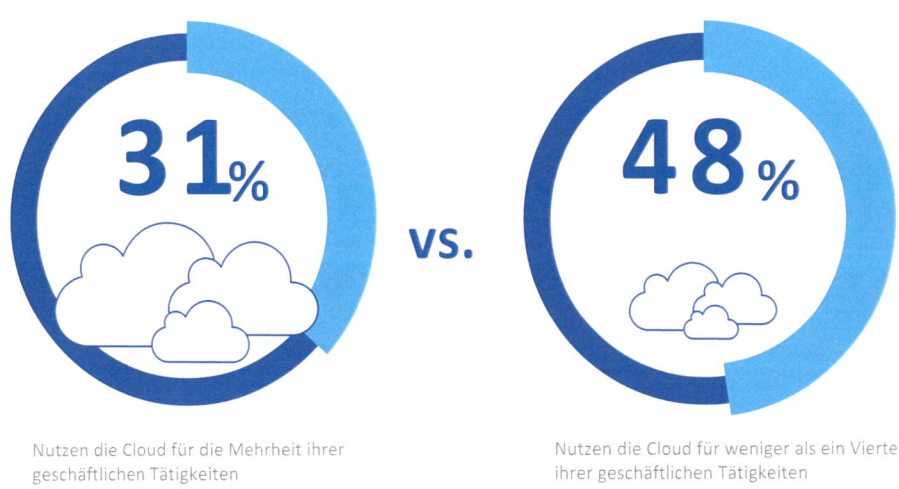

Abb. 28.3 Nutzung von Cloud Computing. (Quelle: Microsoft Insights Studie)

In knapp einem Drittel der befragten Unternehmen leistet die Cloud also bereits einen erheblichen Anteil bei Erbringung und Bereitstellung von IT-Infrastruktur und Diensten. In knapp der Hälfte der befragten Unternehmen wird immerhin für weniger als ein Viertel der operativen Aktivitäten auf Cloud-Dienste zurückgegriffen. Die Nutzung von Cloud-Diensten ist also bei den meisten Befragten Bestandteil des normalen Tagesgeschäfts (siehe Abb. 28.3). Auf welche Eigenschaften legen die befragten Unternehmen bei der Wahl des Cloud-Anbieters in Folge besonderen Wert? Die Frage nach den wichtigsten Qualitäten eines Cloud-Anbieters liefert recht aussagekräftige, eindeutige Ergebnisse.

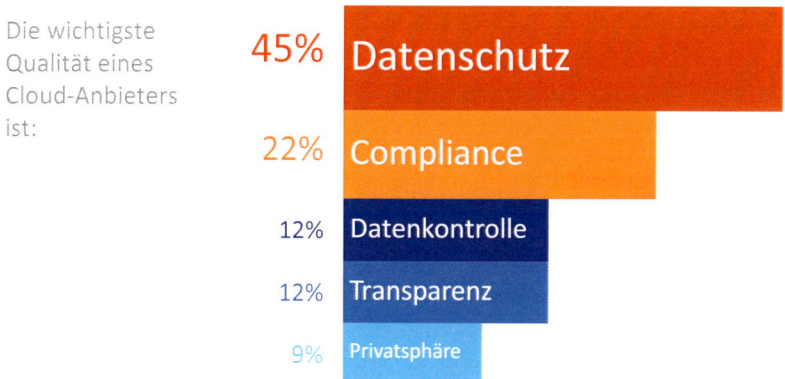

Abb. 28.4 Bedeutung von Qualitäten eines Cloud-Anbieters. (Quelle: Microsoft Insights Studie)

Mit einer hohen Zustimmung von 45 % überragt das Thema Datenschutz die Diskussion. 22 % der befragten Unternehmen messen zudem dem Thema Compliance eine hohe Bedeutung bei. Mit jeweils 12 % runden die Themen Datenkontrolle und Transparenz das Feld der Kriterien ab. Für Unternehmen und Organisationen, die den Schritt in Richtung digitale Transformation gehen wollen, haben diese Fragen einen hohen Stellenwert (siehe Abb. 28.4). Es sind Kriterien erforderlich, nach denen Anbieter verglichen und auf Kompatibilität mit den eigenen IT-Compliance-Anforderungen geprüft werden können. In der Regel werden Referenzkunden, eigene Erfahrungen mit dem Anbieter, vor allem aber Zertifizierungen nach anerkannten Standards als Entscheidungskriterien genutzt. Mittlerweile gibt es einige Standards und Zertifizierungen, die sich an den Einsatz von Cloud-Lösungen richten und über die sich cloudspezifische Compliance-Anforderungen abbilden lassen.

Einige Beispiele
- Der Cloud Computing Compliance Controls Catalogue (C5), ein Prüfschema des Bundesamtes für Sicherheit in der Informationstechnik (BSI).
- ISO 27001 spezifiziert Anforderungen an die Einrichtung, Umsetzung, Aufrechterhaltung und fortlaufende Verbesserung eines dokumentierten Informationssicherheitsmanagementsystems unter Berücksichtigung des Kontexts einer Organisation.
- ISO 27017, ein Maßnahmenkatalog für Informationssicherheit in Cloud-Diensten.
- ISO 27018, ein Maßnahmenkatalog für den Schutz personenbezogener Informationen, die im Rahmen einer Auftragsdatenverarbeitung in öffentlichen Cloud-Diensten verarbeitet werden.

Auch aus Anbietersicht spielen Einhaltung, Zertifizierung und regelmäßige Auditierung von Standards bei der Erreichung geschäftlicher Ziele eine wichtige Rolle. Solche Maßnahmen schaffen Transparenz im Hinblick auf das Sicherheitsniveau der Cloud-Dienste und spielen somit eine wichtige Rolle beim Gewinnen des Vertrauens potenzieller Kunden. Im Wettbewerb um Kunden stellen die Einhaltung von Standards und die fortlaufende und frühzeitige Bereitstellung transparenter und unabhängiger Belege in Form von Audits und Zertifizierungen einen wichtigen Differenzierungspunkt dar. Abgesehen davon liegt es auch im Interesse von Cloud-Anbietern, ihre eigene Infrastrukturen und die verarbeiteten Daten vor teuren und geschäftsschädigenden Angriffen zu schützen. Der Erfolg der Cloud steht und fällt also mit den Antworten, die Cloud-Anbieter auf die Sicherheits- und Datenschutzanforderungen ihrer Kunden finden, basierend auf entsprechenden Maßnahmen. Compliance stellt also – gerade im Bereich Sicherheit und Datenschutz – mitnichten nur eine kostspielige, aber strategisch irrelevante Notwendigkeit dar. Vielmehr muss die Frage erlaubt sein, ob und wie Kunden bei der Nutzung von Cloud-Diensten Synergien nutzen, ihren Umgang mit Compliance effizienter gestalten und so auch einen Beitrag zur Steigerung des Geschäftserfolges leisten können.

28.6 Compliance und Cloud: Risiko oder Chance?

Aus Sicht von Cloud-Anbietern stellt die Umsetzung der Compliance-Anforderungen von Kunden einen wichtigen Wettbewerbsfaktor dar. Gleichzeitig gelten zahlreiche Regularien für vom Anbieter betriebene Cloud-Systeme und für kundenbetriebene On-Premises-Systeme gleichermaßen. Es besteht also nicht nur die Möglichkeit, die Umsetzung von Compliance-Anforderungen durch bestimmte Cloud Services zu unterstützen. Die Umsetzung, Auditierung und Zertifizierung von Compliance-Anforderungen kann in einigen Fällen sogar direkt in die Zuständigkeit des Anbieters fallen. Die folgenden Abschnitte geben Aufschluss über die Chancen, welche mit einer Cloud-Nutzung für die Compliance einhergehen.

28.6.1 Compliance als Strategie für Cloud-Anbieter

Eine Voraussetzung für die Erzielung von Synergieeffekten ist, dass zwei Akteure in einer Art und Weise zusammenwirken, die für den Gesamtnutzen förderlich ist. Im Kontext der Themen Datenschutz und Informationssicherheit wurde bereits verdeutlicht, dass die Einhaltung von Kundenanforderungen aus Anbietersicht einen wichtigen Wettbewerbsfaktor darstellt. Setzt man nun einen generischen, übergreifenden Blickwinkel auf das Verhältnis zwischen Anbieter- und Kundenanforderungen in Bezug auf Compliance voraus, so lassen sich zunächst zwei Feststellungen treffen:

1. Auf dem Markt der Cloud-Anbieter existieren zahlreiche Angebote, die Lösungen für die umfassenden geschäftlichen und regulatorischen Anforderungen von Kunden aus unterschiedlichen Branchen versprechen.
2. Viele IT-Compliance-Anforderungen, die Cloud-Anbieter erfüllen müssen, müssen in gleicher Weise auch von IT-Systemen und IT-Diensten anderer Unternehmen erfüllt werden – ganz egal, ob es sich dabei um On-Premises- oder On-Purpose-Dienste handelt.

Was bedeutet das für Unternehmen und Organisationen, die Cloud-Dienste nutzen oder nutzen möchten und dabei ihre eigenen Compliance-Anforderungen umsetzen müssen? Zum einen unterliegen Cloud-Anbieter – als Anbieter von IT-Diensten – selbst hohen Compliance-Anforderungen. Darüber hinaus messen Cloud-Anbieter dem Thema Compliance als Verkaufsargument eine immens hohe Bedeutung bei. Dies zeigt sich nicht nur in den bereits erwähnten ständig wachsenden Dienstportfolios, mit denen Cloud-Anbieter ihre Kunden bei der Einhaltung allgemeiner wie branchenspezifischer Anforderungen unterstützen möchten. Auch beständige hohe Investitionen, etwa im Bereich Sicherheit und Datenschutz, verdeutlichen dieses Interesse der Anbieter. Aus Kundensicht bedeutet dies, dass die Cloud Nutzenpotenziale bei der Einhaltung von Compliance-Anforderungen freisetzt. Anbieter setzen das technologische Innovationspotenzial der Cloud in Dienste um, welche den Compliance-Anforderungen von Unternehmen und Organisationen gerecht werden. Dabei orientieren sich Cloud-Anbieter an technischen und organisatorischen Standards, welche auch für Kunden eine hohe Relevanz haben können.

In den folgenden Abschnitten des Kapitels wird thematisiert, welche Chancen die Cloud in Bezug auf die Einhaltung regulatorischer Compliance-Anforderungen bietet und wie Kunden das Potenzial der Cloud für die Einhaltung regulatorischer Anforderungen und letztlich auch zur Steigerung des Geschäftserfolges nutzen können.

28.6.2   Wie unterstützt die Cloud die Umsetzung von Compliance?

Durch die digitale Transformation werden vermehrt Workflows etabliert, welche unternehmens- bzw. organisationsübergreifend gestaltet sind und somit die Einhaltung von Compliance-Anforderungen unterschiedlicher Unternehmen bzw. Organisationen notwendig machen.

Cloud Computing und die daraus hervorgehenden Technologien schaffen ein breites und stetig wachsendes Spektrum an Lösungen zur Festlegung und Umsetzung von Compliance Anforderungen. Ein Ansatz, der es erlaubt, Compliance-Anforderungen an zentraler Stelle zu definieren, umzusetzen, zu erzwingen und zu überwachen, wird im Folgenden grob skizziert:

- Über ein zentrales Repository werden Compliance-Anforderungen definiert. Das kann in Form von abstrakten Vorgaben („muss dem deutschen Datenschutz genügen") oder auch mittels detaillierter Richtlinien bzw. technischer Vorgaben erfolgen.
- Daten können in der Cloud nach ihrem Schutzbedarf klassifiziert und in unter schiedlichen Zonen verarbeitet werden. Ihre Verwendung kann dann in den verschiedenen Workflows gesteuert und kontrolliert werden.
- Die Umsetzung von Compliance-Anforderungen erfolgt in der Cloud durch die Erzwingung der Richtlinien gemäß der Definition im Repository.

Das Leistungsspektrum von Cloud-Anbietern beinhaltet häufig Prozesse und Tools, die Unternehmen bei der Erfüllung regulatorischer Anforderungen unterstützen und sie damit von der Eigenentwicklung derartiger Lösung befreien. Hierzu zählen beispielsweise das Managment von Vorfällen, die Risikobeurteilung, die rollenbasierte Zugriffsverwaltung oder die Überwachung von Zugriffen auf Daten und Systeme. Cloud-Anbieter können häufig auch Ressourcen oder Best Practices zum Erhalt weiterführender Zertifizierungen auf Basis eines Cloud-Dienstes bereitstellen. Nicht zuletzt tragen auch die Technologien der digitalen Transformation selbst zur Verbesserung der Einhaltung von IT-Compliance-Anforderungen bei. Sogenannte Managed Security Services unterstützen gerade kleinere Unternehmen mit skalierbaren Sicherheitslösungen aus der Cloud, mit denen das Schutzniveau von Daten und Systemen beträchtlich gesteigert werden kann. Auch Big-Data-Analysen leisten bei der Suche nach Schwachstellen oder der Analyse von Vorfällen einen wichtigen Beitrag. Durch Machine Learning-Algorithmen können Angriffsmuster erkannt und Abhilfe geleistet werden.

Durch Cloud-Technologie bereitgestellte Dienste versetzten Unternehmen in die Lage, die Umsetzung und Überwachung technischer und organisatorischer Compliance-Anforderungen zu automatisieren und somit effizient und effektiv zu gestallten. Wenn Unternehmen untereinander und auch Cloud-Anbieter vergleichbare oder gleiche Compliance-Anforderungen einhalten müssen, dann lassen sich Synergieeffekte freisetzen, da durch die Cloud-Nutzung die technischen und organisatorischen Umsetzungen vom Cloud-Anbieter sichergestellt und nachgewiesen werden. Im folgenden Abschnitt werden die Chancen solcher Nutzenpotenziale diskutiert.

28.6.3   Compliance as a Service? Leichter als gedacht!

In den vorherigen Abschnitten wurde offensichtlich, warum für Cloud-Anbieter die Abbildung wichtiger Regularien und Standards in ihren Diensten ein für den eigenen geschäftlichen Erfolg wichtiges Anliegen darstellt. Audits und Zertifizierungen kommt in diesem Kontext sowohl für Cloud-Anbieter als auch für Unternehmen, die ihre Dienste in die Cloud verlagern, eine sehr wichtige Rolle zu. In vielen Fällen endet der Nutzen, den die Auslagerung von Diensten in die Cloud für die Einhaltung von Regularien bietet, noch nicht an dieser Stelle. Während beim On-Premises-Betrieb von IT-Diensten gerade im Zuge der technischen Bereitstellung auf Software- und Hardwareebene zahlreiche Standards erfüllt und Zertifizierungen abgelegt werden müssen, obliegt die Zuständigkeit hierfür bei der Cloud-Nutzung meist dem Anbieter. Zwar findet kein direkter Transfer der Verantwortung für die Einhaltung von IT-Compliance-Anforderungen vom Cloud-Kunden zum Cloud-Anbieter statt. Allerdings fällt die Umsetzung der relevanten technischen und organisatorischen Anforderungen dem Cloud-Anbieter zu, welche beim On-Premises-Betrieb in die Zuständigkeit des Kunden fallen würden. Das Ausmaß dieses Transfers von Zuständigkeiten hängt in erster Linie vom Cloud-Dienstmodell ab. Eine umfassende Darstellung dieser Zusammenhänge in den unterschiedlichen Modellen wird in Kap. 7 gegeben.

Aus Kundensicht ergibt sich hieraus der Vorteil, dass nicht nur die Aufgabe der Umsetzung des eigentlich eingekauften Dienstes selbst, sondern auch zahlreicher technischer und organisatorischer Schutzmaßnahmen an den Cloud-Anbieter abgegeben wird, die er sonst selbst in seiner eigenen Umgebung erfüllen müsste. Auch die regelmäßigen Audits müssen vom Cloud-Anbieter angestoßen werden und dienen dem Kunden sowohl als Grundlage für die Akzeptanz des Anbieters als auch seinem eigenen Nachweis. Der Kunde erspart sich damit fortlaufende Kosten für die Bereitstellung und Instandhaltung einer aktuellen technischen Sicherheitsinfrastruktur. Organisatorische Aufgaben wie die Bereitstellung von Notfallprozessen oder Schulungen für Mitarbeiter werden ebenfalls verlagert. Gerade bei kleineren Unternehmen bedeutet dies nicht nur eine starke Entlastung von kosten- und arbeitsintensiven Aufgaben sowie dediziertem Personal, sondern oft auch die Erzielung eines höheren Schutzniveaus. Datenschutz und Sicherheit stellen für Cloud-Anbieter sehr wichtige Differenzierungsmerkmale dar, weshalb diese in der Regel signifikante Investitionen in diesem Bereich tätigen.

Aus Sicht von Cloud-Kunden entfällt zudem die Notwendigkeit neuer Zertifizierungen bei Ausweitung oder Veränderung des Portfolios der IT-Dienste. Während bei einer On-Premises-Bereitstellung von IT-Diensten die Einhaltung von Anforderungen über Audits und Zertifizierungen stets neu sichergestellt werden muss, führen Cloud-Anbieter diese Audits und Zertifizierungen grundsätzlich für einen Großteil ihrer Dienste durch. Möchte nun ein Kunde das Portfolio seiner IT-Dienste ausbauen oder umstrukturieren, entfällt beim Cloud-Bezug der Dienste der erneute Nachweis der Erfüllung der Anforderungen, da dieser fortlaufend vom Cloud-Anbieter erbracht wird. Veränderungen am IT-Dienstportfolio können also auch deswegen aus der Cloud deutlich effizienter und flexibler durchgeführt werden. Nicht zuletzt ergibt sich zudem der Effekt, dass gerade bei Unternehmen, die in einer Wertschöpfungskette zusammenarbeiten und Compliance-Vorgaben des Herstellers unterliegen, diese einfach und direkt über den Cloud-Anbieter nachweisen können. Gegebenenfalls hat der Hersteller auch Cloud-Anbieter vorselektiert, die die Einhaltung der Vorgaben nachweisen können.

28.7 Resümee: Compliance wird digitaler und standardisierter

Neben den bereits erörterten technischen Möglichkeiten ergeben sich auch organisatorische Vorteile und strategische Chancen. Compliance-Maßnahmen auf Anbieterseite, aber auch die Bereitstellung immer besserer und innovativerer Dienste zur Umsetzung der technischen und organisatorischen Compliance auf Kundenseite stellen für Cloud-Anbieter einen wichtigen Wettbewerbsfaktor dar. Zudem bietet die Cloud, wie im vorigen Abschnitt beschrieben, weitere Synergieeffekte zwischen Anbieter und Kunden, wenn sich deren Compliance-Anforderungen überschneiden. Die Umsetzung von Standards, Audits und Zertifizierungen fallen dann in den Zuständigkeitsbereich des Anbieters.

Festhalten lassen sich also abschließend nicht nur fortlaufende Verbesserungen der technischen und organisatorischen Umsetzung von Compliance durch die digitale Transformation und speziell die Cloud. Unternehmen können zusätzlich Synergien durch das Auslagern der Zuständigkeit für Standardisierung, Auditierung und Zertifizierung von Prozessen und Infrastrukturen erzielen. All das geschieht vor dem Hintergrund,

dass immer neue Compliance-Anforderungen und Anwendungsszenarien von der Inno-
vationsspirale der digitalen Transformation erfasst werden. Denn wie in Abschn. 4.1
beschrieben wurde, profitieren auch Anforderungen, Prozesse und Workflows der Corporate Compliance immer mehr von IT-Unterstützung – basierend auf Technologien und
Trends der digitalen Transformation.

28.8   Compliance und Geschäftserfolg verbinden – Ein Modell

28.8.1   Compliance als strategischer Ansatz

Die vorhergehenden Kapitel haben Aufschluss darüber gegeben, wie sich Entwicklungen
und Trends der digitalen Transformation auf Organisationen und Unternehmen auswirken.
Das Verhältnis zum zweiten großen Themenkomplex – der Compliance – stellt sich dabei
ambivalent dar: Zum einen wirkt sich die digitale Transformation auf die Art und Weise
aus, wie regulatorische Anforderungen erfüllt werden. Zum anderen ergeben sich aus den
neuen Technologien, Trends und Geschäftsmodellen neue Anforderungen, die auch für die
IT bisher wenig relevante Bereiche erfassen. Governance, Risk Management und Compliance stellt einen bekannten Ansatz dar, der Compliance sowohl strategisch als auch operativ einordnet. Dieser Ansatz stellt, wie schon in der Vorgängerversion des Handbuchs, die
Basis für die Entwicklung eines Modells dar, das die gemeinsamen Ziele von Compliance
und Geschäftserfolg unter Beachtung aktueller Entwicklungen strukturiert darstellt.

28.8.2   Compliance aus Governance-Sicht

Auf der anderen Seite steht die Betrachtung von Compliance aus Governance-Sicht.
Compliance wird dabei als Mittel zur Führung einer Organisation verstanden, mit dem
Ziel, die Compliance kontinuierlich zu verbessern. Damit trägt sie direkt zum Geschäftserfolg des Unternehmens oder der Behörde bei. Diese Verbesserung beschränkt sich
nicht nur auf die beteiligten Informationssysteme, sondern hilft gleichzeitig, Transparenz und Verfügbarkeit von Informationen zu erhöhen sowie die Kosten für Beschaffung
und Auswertung von Informationen zu senken. Damit wird die Effizienz von Geschäftsprozessen sowie der gesamten Organisation gesteigert. Das Management kann schneller
auf Geschäftsdaten zugreifen und seine Aufgaben bei der Lenkung der Organisation
besser wahrnehmen.

Ein Ansatz, der geschäftliche und regulatorische Aspekte der Compliance verbindet,
schlägt zwei Fliegen mit einer Klappe. Neben der Erfüllung externer Anforderungen trägt
Compliance direkt dazu bei, Geschäftsprozesse zu optimieren und letztlich die eigene
Organisation zum Erfolg zu führen. Diese doppelte Funktion von Compliance spielt in
diesem Handbuch eine wichtige Rolle. Das im Folgenden vorgestellte Compliance-Modell
berücksichtigt beide Aspekte und hilft, die regulatorischen und geschäftlichen Anforde-

rungen zu erfassen und umzusetzen. Diese strategische Funktion der Compliance lässt sich besonders gut im Kontext von Governance und Risk Management aufzeigen. Die konkrete Anwendung des Modells wird dann in Kap. 6 beschrieben.

28.8.3 GRC – Governance, Risk Management und Compliance

Das Einhalten von Regelungen (Compliance im allgemeinen Sinn) ist keine isolierte Maßnahme, sondern fällt in den größeren Zusammenhang von Governance, Risk Management und Compliance (GRC). GRC bildet die strategische Klammer für verschiedenste Aufgaben, die die Lücke zwischen Unternehmensstrategie und -zielen einerseits und dem operativen Tagesgeschäft auf der anderen Seite schließt. GRC ist keine Technologie, sondern Ansatz und Prozess, um Synergien zwischen Geschäftszielen und Regularien zu realisieren.

Governance dient als Oberbegriff für die verantwortungsvolle Führung von Unternehmensbereichen oder eines ganzen Unternehmens. Dazu gehören das Festlegen von Zielen und Verantwortlichkeiten, die Definition von Aktivitäten und Kontrollmechanismen sowie die Ressourcenplanung und das Einbetten in einen Risikomanagementprozess. Im Rahmen der Steuerung auf allen Ebenen liegt dabei ein besonders starkes Gewicht auf dem Ausrichten der Zielsetzungen an der Unternehmensstrategie – etwa im Bereich der IT Governance.

Risk Management ist ein systematischer, prozessorientierter Ansatz, um Risiken zu identifizieren, zu analysieren, zu bewerten, zu behandeln und zu überwachen. Eine wichtige Zielsetzung liegt daher im Verständnis von Bedrohungen, Schwachstellen und Risiken für das Unternehmen, im Abbau von Risiken durch entsprechende Maßnahmen oder der Anstrengung, das Restrisiko so gut wie möglich einzuschätzen. Die Liste potenzieller Risikobereiche ist lang und reicht von der Sicherheit für Mitarbeiter, Gebäude, Produktionsanlagen und Informationen über Technologie- und Projektrisiken bis hin zu Risiken im Umfeld von Compliance und Kriminalität, Ethik und Kultur, Geopolitik und Klima – um nur eine Auswahl zu nennen.

Ein mit Blick auf GRC gut aufgestelltes Unternehmen

- Erhöht die Effizienz und Wirksamkeit von organisatorischen und technischen Prozessen.
- Schützt die Reputation und die Werte des Unternehmens.
- Schafft Transparenz gegenüber externen Parteien wie Investoren, Analysten, Gesetzgebern, Regulierungsbehörden, Kunden und Mitarbeitern.
- Übernimmt gegenüber Mitarbeitern und der Gesellschaft Verantwortung.
- Ist auf Krisen und deren Bewältigung besser vorbereitet.
- Vergrößert die Sicherheit von unternehmens- und kundenspezifischen Informationen.
- Senkt das Risiko von Betrugsfällen.

Über IT-Technologien lassen sich vermehrt Aspekte von GRC automatisieren und umsetzen. Auch hier hinterlässt die digitale Transformation ihre Spuren. Viele Unternehmen setzen deshalb IT-Komponenten ein, die für GRC genutzt werden.

28.9 Mit Compliance zum Geschäftserfolg

Regulatorische und geschäftliche Anforderungen stehen bei Anwendung von GRC nicht im Widerspruch zueinander, sondern beruhen auf gemeinsamen Intentionen. Es lassen sich überlappende Ziele zwischen äußeren Vorgaben und dem eigenen geschäftlichen Erfolg ableiten. Wenn etwa der Gesetzgeber von Informationsschutz spricht, spiegelt sich dies aus geschäftlicher Sicht im Schutz vor Betrug, Industriespionage oder im Wahren einer guten Reputation wider. Aus diesen Zielen lassen sich Kernbereiche ableiten, die Verantwortungsbereiche in Organisationen abbilden (siehe Abb. 28.5).

28.9.1 Nutzenpotenziale resultieren aus gemeinsamen Zielen

Vergleicht man die Absicht regulatorischer Vorgaben mit der Motivation geschäftlicher Anforderungen, so kristallisieren sich folgende gemeinsame Ziele heraus:

- **Schutz** von Informationen.
- **Verfügbarkeit** von Informationen.
- **Nachvollziehbarkeit** von Prozessen und der Verarbeitung von Informationen.
- **Transparenz** gegenüber Dritten.
- **Sorgfalt** im Geschäftsleben und die Unterstützung der **Dynamik** moderner Geschäftsprozesse, besonders im Hinblick auf die schnelllebigen Entwicklungen im Zuge der digitalen Transformation.

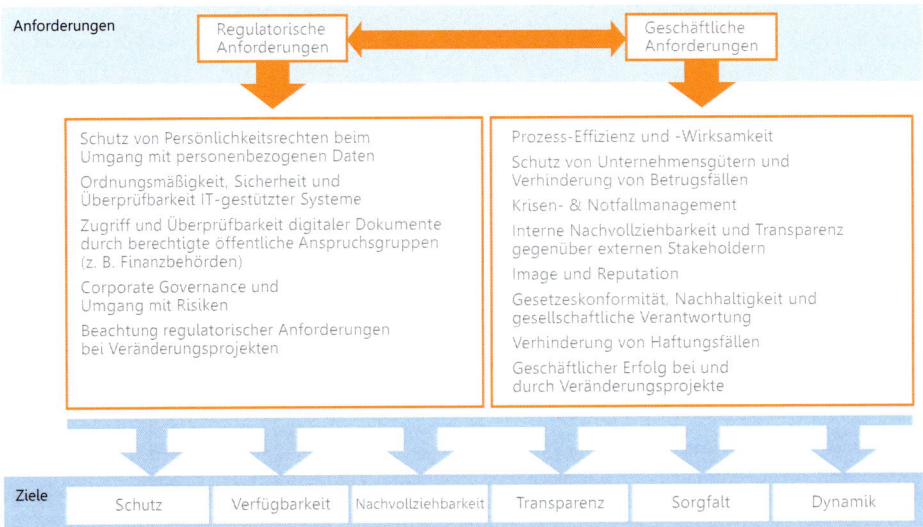

Abb. 28.5 Compliance-Modell – Gemeinsame Ziele regulatorischer und geschäftlicher Anforderungen

Schutz von geistigem Eigentum, personenbezogenen Informationen, von Geschäftsstrategien sowie Finanz- und Vertriebsinformationen ist eine essenzielle Voraussetzung für das Fortbestehen und die Konkurrenzfähigkeit eines Unternehmens. Aus Sicht einer IT-basierten Verarbeitung dieser Informationen stellt die Gewährleistung von Vertraulichkeit und Integrität von Daten die grundlegenden Anforderungen dar. Diese Schutzaspekte finden sich in verschiedenen Regularien wieder:

- Bundesdatenschutzgesetz (BDSG, EU-DSGVO) und BDSAuditG.
- GoBS.
- Telekommunikationsgesetz (TKG).
- §§ 203 und 353b Strafgesetzbuch über den Umgang mit personenbezogenen Informationen.
- Zahlreiche Standards, die technische, organisatorische und Notfallmaßnahmen im Hinblick auf den Umgang mit Daten und Informationen festlegen, z. B. ISO27001/18, ISO 22301, Verschlusssachenanweisung (VS, VS-nfD), BSI-IT-Grundschutz oder der Cloud Computing Compliance Controls Catalogue (C5) des BSI.

Verfügbarkeit stellt in einer weitgehend digitalisierten Arbeitswelt eine Grundvoraussetzung für das Funktionieren von geschäftskritischen Prozessen dar, sei es die Verfügbarkeit von Systemen, Diensten, Daten, Geräten oder Konnektivität. Ein weiterer Aspekt der Verfügbarkeit ist die Archivierung, also die mittel- bis langfristige Aufbewahrung von Informationen. Damit werden Unternehmen und Behörden vor Datenverlusten beim Ausfall von Systemen geschützt, und die Erfüllung gesetzlicher Vorgaben bezüglich des Zugriffs auf relevante Informationen wird gesichert. Dies umfasst etwa:

- Grundsätze zur ordnungsmäßigen Führung und Aufbewahrung von Büchern, Aufzeichnungen und Unterlagen in elektronischer Form sowie zum Datenzugriff (GoBD).
- Grundsätze ordnungsgemäßer DV-gestützter Buchführungssysteme (GoBS).
- Krankengeschichtenverordnung (KgVO).

In Cloud-Diensten wie beim Outsourcing wird eine definierte Leistungserbringung an Verfügbarkeit über **Service Level Agreements (SLAs)** garantiert. So kann die den regulatorischen und geschäftlichen Anforderungen entsprechende Sicherstellung der Verfügbarkeit an einen externen Dienstleister weitergereicht werden.

Nachvollziehbarkeit bezieht sich – in Abgrenzung zum externen Blickwinkel der Transparenz – auf die unternehmensinterne Sicht auf Abläufe und Strukturen. Sie umfasst Möglichkeiten der Prüfung und Auditierung von Geschäftsprozessen und Systemen sowie auch die kontinuierliche Verbesserung auf Basis der gewonnenen Erkenntnisse. Aus Unternehmenssicht ist von essenzieller Wichtigkeit, dass der Zugriff auf Informationen und deren Abruf jederzeit reproduzierbar sind, auch für forensische oder e-Discovery-Zwecke. Außerdem müssen den Geschäftsabläufen autorisierte Rollen zugeordnet und diese von entsprechend autorisierten Personen wahrgenommen werden.

Auch beim Wissensmanagement in Unternehmen schafft ein hohes Maß an Nachvollziehbarkeit eine Struktur, die Genauigkeit und Konsistenz im Umgang mit Informationen
und deren Lebenszyklus gewährleistet.

Transparenz bezieht sich auf externe Anforderungen in Bezug auf die Dokumentation
von Geschäftsabläufen, die Orientierung an anerkannten Standards und die Einführung
von Überwachungssystemen. Die Transparenzpflicht gegenüber externen Anspruchsgruppen kann auch unterstützend auf Geschäftsziele einwirken, wenn die Daten auch zur Optimierung verwendet werden. So können interne Entscheidungsprozesse verbessert und die
Geschäftsagilität gesteigert werden. Darüber hinaus schafft Transparenz Vertrauen bei
Kunden und Partnern und wirkt sich positiv auf die Reputation aus. Folgende Regularien
gelten unter anderem in Bezug auf Transparenz:

- **Gesetz zur Kontrolle und Transparenz im Unternehmensbereich (KonTraG)**: Früh-
  erkennungssystem für potenzielle Risiken und Aussagen über Risiken und Risiko-
  struktur eines Unternehmens.
- **Handelsgesetzbuch (HGB)**: Einhaltung von Vorschriften bei der Abschlussprüfung
- **Telekommunikationsgesetz (TKG)**: Transparenzverpflichtung für Betreiber öffentli-
  cher Telekommunikationsnetze, Offenlegung etwa von Informationen zur Buchführung
  oder technischen Spezifikationen.

Sorgfalt ist ein entscheidender Faktor für die Sicherung der Wirtschaftlichkeit und Wirksamkeit der Geschäftstätigkeit eines Unternehmens. Dies umfasst die ausreichende
Beschaffung von Informationen, eine adäquate Situationsanalyse und eine verantwortungsvolle Risikoeinschätzung, um zu fundierten und gesetzeskonformen Geschäftsent-
scheidungen zu kommen. Die Sorgfaltspflicht tangiert somit auch die Zielsetzungen der
anderen Bereiche, Schutz, Verfügbarkeit, Nachvollziehbarkeit, Transparenz und Flexibilität. Die einzelnen Sorgfaltspflichten sind überwiegend nicht schriftlich dokumentiert.
Sorgfalt als Grundsatz der Unternehmensführung findet sich allerdings in einigen Regularien wieder, etwa im Aktiengesetz bzw. im GmbH-Gesetz, die beide die ordnungsgemäße
Unternehmensführung unter Einhaltung von Gesetzen, Satzungen und Verpflichtungen
beinhalten. Branchenspezifische Sorgfaltspflichten ergeben sich darüber hinaus aus den
Anforderungen von Basel II oder dem Kreditwesengesetz (KWG) für das Finanzwesen.
Diese umfassen Sorgfaltspflichten bezüglich wirksamer interner Kontrollen zur Vermei-
dung einer Kreditrisikokonzentration oder von Haftungsfällen. Aus Sicht der IT gehören
insbesondere die Entwicklung und Etablierung von IT-Richtlinien dazu. Dabei sollten
Branchenstandards und gesetzliche Vorgaben eingehalten und kontrolliert werden. Interne
Trainings, Zertifizierungen und Audits können hierbei helfen.

Dynamik ist ein Ziel, das vor allem durch die Digitalisierung und Automatisierung von
Geschäftsprozessen und Workflows entsteht. Dabei geht es um den Grad der Adaptierbarkeit
bzw. Anpassbarkeit von Compliance-Anforderungen im Kontext von Digitalisierungspro-
jekten in einem Unternehmen oder einer Behörde. Aus Sicht neuer und alter regulatorischer
Anforderungen ist Dynamik notwendig, um im Zuge der Transformation von Unternehmen

die Erfüllung aller relevanten Compliance-Anforderungen zu gewährleisten. Aus geschäftlichem Blickwinkel führt die Dynamik zu einer höheren Zielerreichung hinsichtlich der anderen gemeinsamen Ziele: Schutz, Verfügbarkeit, Nachvollziehbarkeit, Transparenz und Sorgfalt. Darüber hinaus legt Dynamik den Grundstein dafür, dass interne Abläufe fortlaufend, effizient und flexibel an neue Technologien angepasst beziehungsweise Trends auch zeitnah agil und wirtschaftlich vertretbar zum Nutzen des Geschäftsziels umgesetzt werden können, ohne dabei die Einhaltung der Compliance-Vorgaben zu übergehen (siehe Abb. 28.6).

28.9.2 Kernbereiche regulatorischer und geschäftlicher Anforderungen

Nahezu alle regulatorischen und geschäftlichen Anforderungen haben einen Zusammenhang mit den genannten sechs gemeinsamen Zielen. Aus den Zielen lassen sich sechs Kernbereiche ableiten, auf die sich ein Unternehmen konzentrieren sollte, um den Anforderungen und Zielen erfolgreich gerecht zu werden. Diese Kernbereiche fallen in der Regel in jedem Unternehmen in die Verantwortung einer Person oder eines Bereichs. Es ist sinnvoll, die Aktivitäten unternehmensweit, also bereichs- und rollenübergreifend, wahrzunehmen, zu koordinieren und umzusetzen.

Informationssicherheit und -schutz
Aus Unternehmenssicht sind Informationssicherheit und -schutz in mehrfacher Hinsicht wichtig. Dies betrifft vor allem Vertraulichkeit und Integrität von Informationen – bei kritischen und für das Fortbestehen des Unternehmens wichtigen Informationen, dem Schutz geistigen Eigentums, aber auch bei vom Gesetzgeber als schützenswert eingestuften Informationen. Neben der Erfüllung juristischer Anforderungen sind Informationssicherheit und -schutz auch zur Nachvollziehbarkeit und Transparenz von Geschäftsprozessen notwendig, unter anderem im Sinne der Unveränderbarkeit von Protokollen. Datenabwanderungen aufgrund von unzureichenden Schutzmaßnahmen können sich zudem negativ auf die Reputation von Unternehmen auswirken. Maßnahmen, um Informationssicherheit und -schutz zu gewährleisten, werden beispielsweise in den Standards COBIT (Control Objectives for Information and Related Technology), ITIL (IT Infrastructure Library), BSI-IT-Grundschutz, ISO 27001 sowie im IDW PS 330 des Instituts der Wirtschaftsprüfer in Deutschland e. V. (Prüfungsstandard) definiert.

Umgang mit Risiken
Der Umgang mit Risiken ist ein systematischer Ansatz und Prozess zur Identifikation, Analyse Bewertung, Behandlung und Überwachung von Risiken (siehe GRC). Damit erkennen Unternehmen Bedrohungen, Schwachstellen und letztlich Risiken für das eigene Geschäftsmodell. Risiken werden so weit wie möglich kalkuliert, die Höhe der Risikoakzeptanz festgelegt und Prioritäten bei angepassten Maßnahmen gesetzt. Das rechtfertigt auch Investitionen in Sicherheitsmaßnahmen und führt letztlich zu einem höheren Sicherheitsbewusstsein im Unternehmen – auch und insbesondere beim Management. Eine wichtige

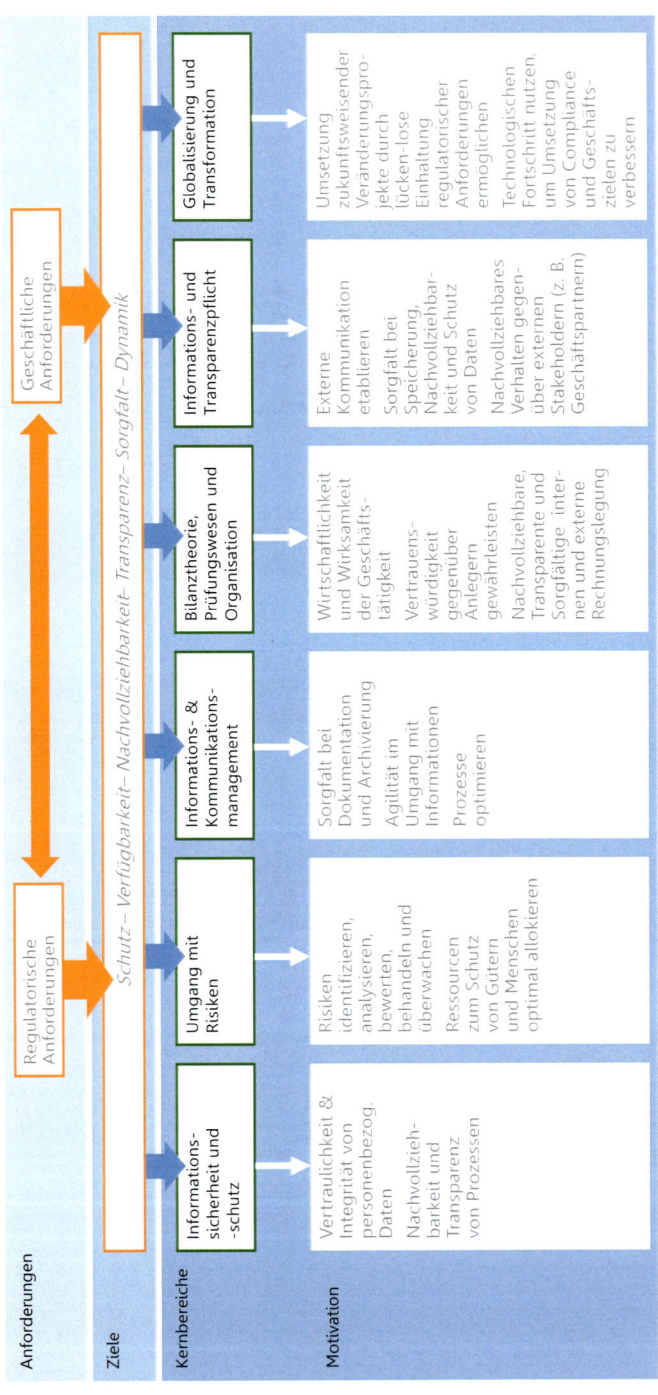

Abb. 28.6 Compliance Modell – Kernbereiche regulatorischer und geschäftlicher Anforderungen

Motivation beim Umgang mit Risiken liegt in der Verbesserung der Zuweisung von Ressourcen zum Umgang mit Bedrohungen und der Reduktion des Risikos auf ein akzeptables Maß.

Die generischen Ziele beim Umgang mit Risiken liegen im Schutz und der Verfügbarkeit von Daten, der Nachvollziehbarkeit von Prozessen und dem Erfüllen der Sorgfaltspflicht insgesamt. Zwar ist der Umgang mit Risiken Gegenstand zahlreicher Regularien und Standards, etwa dem Gesetz zur Kontrolle und Transparenz im Unternehmensbereich (KonTraG), Basel III und COBIT. Nichtsdestotrotz liegen die Nutzenpotenziale aus geschäftlicher Sicht auf der Hand: Ein systematischer Ansatz zum Umgang mit Risiken ist notwendig, um Risiken korrekt einzuschätzen und entsprechende Maßnahmen zur Vermeidung von Verlusten zu ergreifen.

Informations- und Kommunikationsmanagement

Im Rahmen des Informations- und Kommunikationsmanagements erfolgt das Planen, Gestalten, Überwachen und Steuern von Informationsflüssen. Für diese Aktivitäten werden nachvollziehbare und reproduzierbare Geschäftsprozesse benötigt, die auf einer sicheren und effizienten IT-Infrastruktur aufbauen. Trotz permanenten Datenwachstums und zunehmender Flexibilisierung von Geschäftsprozessen müssen Unternehmen spezifische Informationen bei Bedarf schnell finden und abrufen. Dies fordern beispielsweise die GoBD und die Regelungen des Bilanzrechtsmodernisierungsgesetzes (BilMoG). Weitere rechtliche Regelungen, welche die Aufbewahrung von Daten betreffen, lassen sich im Bereich der Produkthaftung und der Prozessordnung finden. Beim Umsetzen dieser Forderungen hilft etwa der standardisierte ITIL-Prozess.

Über das Informations- und Kommunikationsmanagement erreichen Unternehmen auch strategische Ziele durch methodische Informationssteuerung und Kommunikation. Um diese effektiv anzuwenden, ist es unumgänglich, bei Dokumentation und Archivierung mit angemessener Sorgfalt vorzugehen. Die Schnittmenge zwischen geschäftlichen und regulatorischen Anforderungen liegt hier also insbesondere im Erreichen von Verfügbarkeit, Nachvollziehbarkeit und letztlich der Sorgfaltspflicht im Informationslebenszyklus. Dabei ist ein Lösungsansatz zur Klassifizierung von Daten nötig, um Informationen gemäß den rechtlichen und unternehmensinternen Anforderungen differenziert zu verwalten.

Bilanztheorie, Prüfungswesen und Organisation

Dieser Kernbereich umfasst mit der Bilanztheorie die Bewertung der Vermögensgegenstände eines Unternehmens sowie die von diesen erzielten Erträgen. Damit werden Compliance-Vorgaben aus dem Steuer- und Handelsrecht umgesetzt. Das Prüfungswesen überwacht Effizienz und Effektivität bei der Umsetzung der Kernelemente und dient der Sicherung von Wirtschaftlichkeit und Wirksamkeit der Geschäftstätigkeit eines Unternehmens. Dieser Kernbereich ist zudem notwendig, um Nachvollziehbarkeit, Transparenz und Sorgfalt der internen und externen Rechnungslegung sowie die Einhaltung der maßgeblichen rechtlichen Vorgaben zu garantieren. Dies erfolgt in der Regel durch ein internes Steuerungs- und Überwachungssystem, ergänzt durch ein Risikomanagement. Die Notwendigkeit dieser gesetzlichen Forderungen entsteht durch länderspezifische Prüfungsstandards, wie etwa dem IDW PS 330 – Abschlussprüfung bei Einsatz von Informationstechnologie. Diese haben für einen Abschlussprüfer rechtliche Bindung und müssen somit vom Unternehmen indirekt befolgt werden.

Transparenz- und Informationspflicht

Die Informations- und Transparenzpflicht eines Unternehmens hängt eng mit Datenschutz, Informations- und Risikomanagement sowie internen Kontrollsystemen zusammen. Zu ihren Voraussetzungen zählen entsprechend verfügbare Daten, die nachvollziehbar und transparent sind und mit Sorgfalt erhoben und gepflegt wurden. Die Informations- und Transparenzpflicht ist sowohl ereignisgetrieben als auch ein kontinuierlicher Prozess. Ersteres trifft beispielsweise auf das Bundesdatenschutzgesetz und die dort festgehaltenen Betroffenenrechte bei Datenschutzverletzungen zu. Die Richtlinie 2004/39/EG über Märkte für Finanzinstrumente (MiFID), die Geschäftsprozesse für den Lieferantenwechsel im Gassektor (GeLi Gas) und die GoBD sind weitere Beispiele für die Informations- und Transparenzpflicht. Auch das IT-Sicherheitsgesetz setzt hier Akzente, etwa bei der für Telekommunikationsunternehmen verpflichtenden Warnung von Kunden bei einem Missbrauch eines Kundenanschlusses. Auch wenn viele Unternehmen die Informations- und Transparenzpflicht als unangenehm empfinden, ermöglicht sie auch Synergien in Bezug auf geschäftliche Ziele. Hierzu gehört die externe Kommunikation, optimierte Prozesse, die Pflege und Wahrung der eigenen Reputation, der verantwortungsbewusste Umgang mit Daten und vor allem die Einführung eines Kontrollsystems, das kritische Ereignisse zeitnah erkennt und eine adäquate Reaktion anfordert und überwacht.

Globalisierung und Transformation

Dieser letzte Kernbereich widmet sich der steigenden Dynamik, welche Unternehmen im Zuge der digitalen Transformation vor schnelllebige technologische und organisatorische Veränderungen stellt. Geschäftsprozesse fußen – wie erläutert – immer stärker auf der IT. Auch Unternehmensbereiche, die bisher vornehmlich durch analoge Workflows geprägt waren, greifen immer stärker auf innovative IT-Technologien zurück. Die Cloud steht dabei im Zentrum dieser Entwicklung als Garant für die mobile Verfügbarkeit und die Vereinheitlichung von Datenflüssen über technologische, organisatorische und Landesgrenzen hinweg. Um dieses Potenzial abzurufen, müssen Unternehmen und Behörden ein hohes Maß an Flexibilität im Umgang mit Technologien und im Hinblick auf die eigene Organisationsstruktur an den Tag legen.

Der Compliance kommt im Kontext der digitalen Transformation auch deshalb eine Schlüsselfunktion zu, weil die Erfüllung regulatorischer Anforderungen eine Voraussetzung für die Adaption von Technologien und Veränderungen im Allgemeinen ist. Compliance-Anforderungen, die sich aus Veränderungen ergeben, müssen in allen Unternehmensbereichen bekannt und umgesetzt sein. Wer das Thema Compliance im

Hinblick auf Veränderungen also frühzeitig angeht, verbessert seine Chancen auf Effizienzsteigerungen und Wettbewerbsvorteile durch Innovation und erhöht somit auch seinen Geschäftserfolg.

28.10 Anwendung des Compliance-Modells: Vom Verständnis- zum Anwendungsmodell

Im vorherigen Kapitel wurde ein Verständnismodell eingeführt, das die Anforderungen regulatorischer und geschäftlicher Ziele in sechs Kernbereichen abbildet. Das ist ein notwendiger Schritt, um einen vereinheitlichten Umgang und eine gemeinsame Sprache in Bezug auf die komplexe Thematik zu entwickeln. Unternehmen, die sich bereichsunabhängig und systematisch mit den Kernbereichen auseinandersetzen, erlangen über das Modell nicht nur Kenntnis über die wesentlichen regulatorischen Anforderungen, sondern auch über konkrete Handlungsfelder, in denen Synergien zwischen Compliance und Geschäftserfolg erzielt werden können.

28.10.1 Verfeinerung des Modells

Wie kann eine solche Auseinandersetzung effektiv und im Kontext einer bestehenden Prozesslandschaft stattfinden und wie können passende Maßnahmen für das eigene Unternehmen getroffen werden? Die Lösung liegt in der Identifikation von Handlungsfeldern, mit denen das Modell verfeinert wird und die konkrete Notwendigkeiten für die Einhaltung von Anforderungen beschreiben. Auf Basis solcher Handlungsfelder können Prozesse definiert werden, die einen Beitrag zur unternehmensweiten Umsetzung der Anforderungen der Kernbereiche leisten. Die zur Ermittlung von Handlungsfeldern benötigten zentralen Prozesse müssen Maßnahmen definieren, die es trotz rascher organisatorischer und technologischer Veränderungen ermöglichen, alle Compliance-Anforderungen zu erfüllen, und zwar vor, während und nach Veränderungen. So wird verhindert, dass Änderungen an Geschäftsprozessen zu Einbrüchen bei der Compliance führen, und seien diese auch nur temporär. Ein Unternehmen kann Handlungsfelder bestimmen, indem es einen kritischen Abgleich der eigenen Prozesslandschaft mit den Anforderungen der Kernbereiche durchführt. Jedem Kernbereich werden Handlungsfelder zugeordnet, aus denen sich konkrete Verbesserungsmaßnahmen für die jeweils relevanten Prozesse generieren lassen. Gegebenenfalls kann sogar die Notwendigkeit der Etablierung eines neuen Prozesses aus der Bestimmung eines oder mehrerer Handlungsfelder erwachsen. Es empfiehlt sich, eine zentrale, prozessübergreifende Steuerung der Handlungsfelder zu etablieren, um Synergien zu erreichen und damit potenziell multiplizierten Aufwand zu reduzieren. Die zentrale Organisation der Nutzung von Maßnahmen und Kontrollen ermöglicht die Identifizierung von wiederholbaren Einsatzmöglichkeiten, eben für die Erfüllung von Compliance-Anforderungen und die Unterstützung von betriebswirtschaftlichen Geschäftszielen.

28.10.2   Analyse als Basis für unternehmerisches Handeln

Das Compliance-Modell dient also nicht nur als Verständnismodell, sondern ist als Anwendungsmodell ein Rahmenwerk für die Bewertung der eigenen Prozesslandschaft und die Bestimmung potenzieller Verbesserungen. Um dies konkret darzustellen, wird das Modell in Abb. 28.7 um je zwei exemplarische Handlungsfelder erweitert.

Während die Kernbereiche regulatorischer und geschäftlicher Anforderungen also im Groben reglementierte Aspekte der IT-Nutzung umfassen, stellen die den Kernbereichen zugeordneten Handlungsfelder konkrete Ansätze und Bereiche unternehmerischen Handelns zur Umsetzung der Ziele dar. Die Handlungsfelder müssen dabei durch Prozesse und Workflows umgesetzt werden. Ein Unternehmen, das sich umfassend und bereichsübergreifend mit der Analyse der eigenen Prozesslandschaft auseinandersetzt, erhält auf diese Weise einen Überblick über all jene Bereiche, in denen die Erreichung regulatorischer und geschäftlicher Ziele notwendig ist und gegebenenfalls verbessert werden kann. Die Gestaltung bzw. Verbesserung der Compliance-Prozesse kann dann basierend auf den individuell bestimmten Handlungsfeldern unternehmensweit durchgeführt werden, wobei auch eine Wiederverwendung von Maßnahmen möglich ist.

28.10.3   Handlungsfelder zur Verbesserung des Geschäftserfolges

Nachdem im vorherigen Abschnitt der strategische Nutzen von Handlungsfeldern beschrieben wurde, stellt sich nun die Frage, welche konkreten Zielsetzungen mit Hilfe der Handlungsfelder abgedeckt werden können. Im folgenden Abschnitt findet eine detaillierte Auseinandersetzung mit je einem Handlungsfeld pro Kernbereich statt. Zwar deckt diese Darstellung nur einen sehr kleinen Teil aus der großen Menge möglicher Handlungsfelder für Organisationen und Unternehmen ab. Dennoch machen die Beispiele deutlich, dass die Verbesserung von Prozessen, welche auf die Einhaltung regulatorischer Anforderungen abzielen, auch für den Geschäftserfolg Nutzen bringt (siehe Abb. 28.8).

28.10.3.1   Informationssicherheit und -schutz

Beim Thema Informationssicherheit und -schutz greifen Handlungen mehrerer Kernbereiche ineinander. Zur Festlegung sinnvoller IT-Sicherheits- und Datenschutzrichtlinien sowie zum Management von Identitäten und Zugriffsrechten muss die Klassifizierung von Daten nach ihrem Schutzbedarf umgesetzt werden, etwa hinsichtlich branchen- und eigentümerspezifischer Anforderungen. Auch die Identifikation und Bewertung von Risiken spielt in diesem Kontext eine wichtige Rolle, um Schutzbedarfe festzustellen und Maßnahmen zu motivieren. Im Allgemeinen muss die IT-Landschaft einer Organisation im Hinblick auf logische und physische Schwachstellen überwacht werden. Zudem ist ein sauber definierter Prozess für den Umgang mit Vorfällen und Sicherheitsverletzungen erforderlich. Die Handlungen konzentrieren sich auf die Einhaltung spezifischer Regularien (z. B. Datenschutz). Gleichzeitig leisten Maßnahmen der Informationssicherheit einen

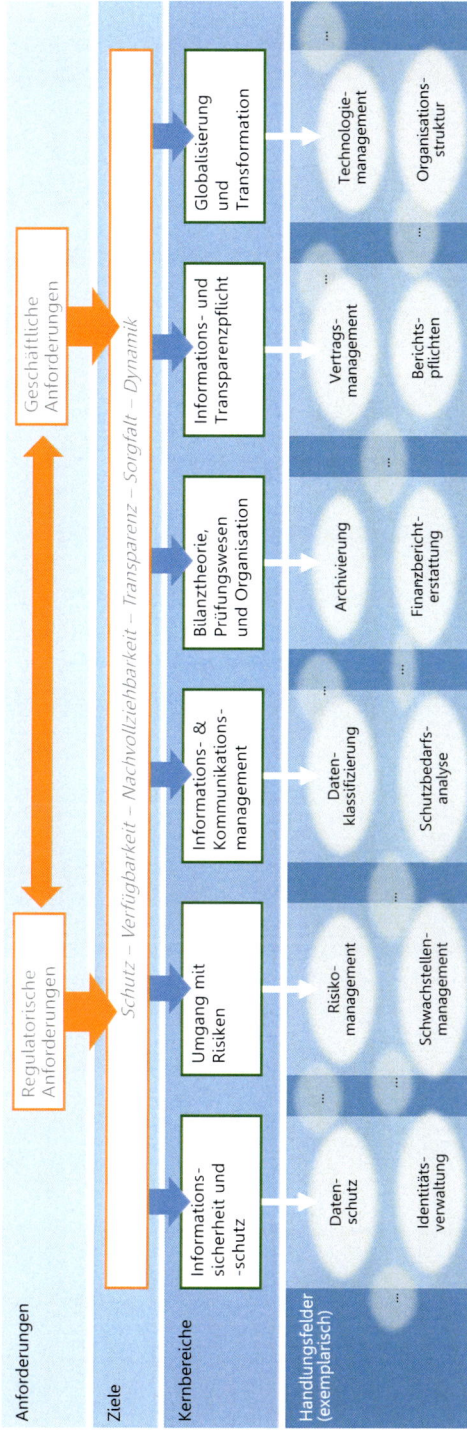

Abb. 28.7 Compliance-Modell – Exemplarische Handlungsfelder

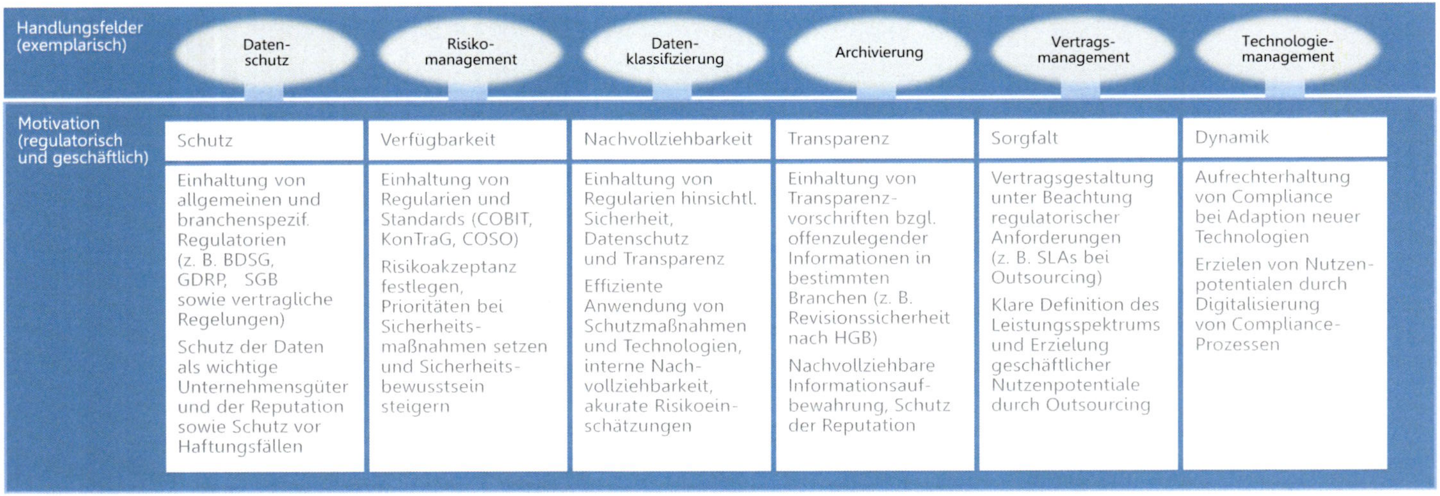

Abb. 28.8 Compliance-Modell – Motivation exemplarischer Handlungsfelder

entscheidenden Beitrag zum Schutz wichtiger Unternehmensgüter sowie der Reputation und beugen Haftungsfällen durch Nichteinhaltung vor.

Die beiden exemplarischen Handlungsfelder **Datenschutz** und **Identitätsverwaltung** werden im Folgenden weiter konkretisiert:

Das Handlungsfeld **Datenschutz** umfasst alle Prozesse und Maßnahmen zur Umsetzung regulatorischer Anforderungen zum Schutz sensibler Daten. Sensible Daten enthalten beispielsweise personenbezogene (Kunden-)Informationen. Auch und gerade infolge der zunehmenden Automatisierung der Datenverarbeitung muss der Schutz solcher Daten vor unbefugten Zugriffen sichergestellt werden, um gesetzlichen und ggf. auch branchenspezifischen Anforderungen zu genügen. Unternehmen müssen relevante Daten schutzvorgaben identifizieren, umsetzen und die Einhaltung fortlaufend überprüfen. Änderungsprozesse an Richtlinien und Prozessen müssen wahrgenommen und hinsichtlich möglicher Auswirkungen auf die eigenen Prozesse evaluiert werden. Gegebenenfalls können so notwendige Anpassungen in Prozessen, der Organisation und der IT-Infrastruktur frühzeitig umgesetzt werden.

Im Handlungsfeld **Identitätsverwaltung** wird ein Sicherheitskonzept angestrebt, welches die große Anzahl an Benutzern, Systemen, Daten und anderen IT-Ressourcen umfasst, Zugriffsmöglichkeiten auf Ressourcen auf ein notwendiges Minimum reduziert und Aktivitäten und Zugriffsversuche nachvollziehbar macht. Hierzu ist ein einheitlicher und dokumentierter Prozess erforderlich, der Identitäten sowie die Zugriffe auf relevante Systeme und Kommunikationskanäle verwaltet und überwacht. In vielen Systemen hat sich das Modell der rollenbasierten Zugriffskontrolle (RBAC) durchgesetzt, welches Benutzerrechte auf Basis einer den Benutzern zugeordneten Rolle sowie Gruppen vergibt.

28.10.3.2   Umgang mit IT-Compliance-Risiken

Grundsätzlich stehen im Umgang mit Risiken vier Ansätze zur Auswahl:

- Eine häufige Vorgehensweise ist das Reduzieren von Risiken durch geeignete **technische und organisatorische Maßnahmen (TOM)** sowie Kontrollmechanismen.
- Zweitens lassen sich Risiken zum Teil auf externe **Parteien übertragen**, z. B. auf Versicherungen oder (mit Einschränkungen) auf Dienstleister.
- Das Vermeiden von Risiken durch **Einstellung von Aktivitäten**, die zu Risiken führen, z. B. durch Re-Design von Geschäftsprozessen oder Vermeidung neuer, unsicherer IT-Systeme, ist eine weitere Option.
- Zu guter Letzt besteht die Möglichkeit, **Risiken zu akzeptieren**, wenn die Gegenmaßnahmen in keinem Verhältnis zum Wert des Geschäftsgutes stehen. Wichtige Handlungsfelder im Umgang mit Risiken stellen unter anderem das Risikomanagement und das Schwachstellenmanagement dar.

Egal, für welchen Ansatz man sich entscheidet – für die Umsetzung ist in jedem Fall ein klar geregeltes Risikomanagement erforderlich, welche Maßnahmen zur Erkennung, Analyse und Überwachung sowie Kriterien zur Bewertung von Risiken in Bezug auf konkrete Güter festlegt und die individuellen Rahmenbedingungen der getroffenen Entscheidung dokumentiert.

Bei der Identifikation und Bewertung von Risiken werden alle im Unternehmen vorhandenen Güter, also etwa Systeme, Informationen, Produktionsanlagen etc., berücksichtigt. Wichtig ist auch die Definition von Rollen im Risikomanagement sowohl auf übergeordneter Ebene als auch im IT-Risikomanagement. Unternehmensweite Abstimmungsprozesse zwischen den Beteiligten sind ebenso zu etablieren, wie die Ausrichtung auf ein gemeinsames unternehmensweites Risikomanagementrahmenwerk. Hierzu zählen Bewertungsverfahren für Risiken und die Integration von Risiken unterschiedlicher Bereiche, etwa IT-, Vertrags- und Unternehmens Risiken, in ein einheitliches Konzernrisikowesen.

Dem **Schwachstellenmanagement** kommt speziell beim Management von IT-Risiken eine wichtige Rolle zu, da auf diese Weise die aktuelle Bedrohungslage für wichtige digitale Unternehmensgüter bestimmt wird und entsprechende Gegenmaßnahmen ergriffen werden können. Sollten kritische Informationen durch Schwachstellen bedroht sein, so wird das betroffene Unternehmen schnellstmöglich die Behebung der Schwachstelle, beispielsweise durch Updates oder neue Sicherheitsmaßnahmen, veranlassen. Hier zeigt sich auch die Bedeutung des Umgangs mit Risiken für andere Kernbereiche – in diesem Fall der Informationssicherheit und des -schutzes.

28.10.3.3 Informations- und Kommunikationsmanagement

Die Gestaltung von Geschäftsprozessen und Infrastrukturen, die den Umgang mit Informationen beeinflussen und steuern, ist für verschiedene Unternehmensbereiche und -funktionen von zentraler Bedeutung. Das Informations- und Kommunikationsmanagement ermöglicht die Verarbeitung und Haltung von Daten auf Basis einer zentralen und einheitlichen Infrastruktur und schafft somit die Grundlage für die Steuerung von Datenhaltung und Kommunikation nach rechtlichen und geschäftlichen Vorgaben. Auf Anwendungsebene stehen vor allem Enterprise Content Management (ECM) und Geschäftsprozess-Management (BPM) als Querschnittsdisziplin im Fokus. Enterprise Resource Planning (ERP) und Business Intelligence (BI) sind weitere Applikationen, die das Informations- und Kommunikationsmanagement berühren.

Handlungsfelder, die sich aus dem Informations- und Kommunikationsmanagement herleiten, sind beispielsweise die **Klassifizierung** und die **Bestimmung des Schutzbedarfs von Daten**. Diese beiden Handlungsfelder hängen stark voneinander ab und werden mit der Unterstützung technischer Analyseverfahren und unternehmensweit einheitlicher Prozesse, Kriterien und Regeln bearbeitet. Beide Handlungsfelder sorgen für die Erfüllung von Sicherheits-, Datenschutz- und Transparenzanforderungen und führen zu einer effizienteren Zuweisung von Schutzmaßnahmen, einer besseren Einschätzung und Nachvollziehbarkeit des Schutzbedarfs unterschiedlicher Datenarten und infolgedessen zu genaueren Risikoeinschätzungen.

28.10.3.4 Bilanztheorie, Prüfungswesen und Organisation

Das Bilanz- und Prüfungswesen beschäftigt sich im weitesten Sinne mit der Umsetzung regulatorischer Anforderungen aus dem Steuer- und Handelsrecht über länder- und branchenspezifische Standards. Unternehmen richten ihre Prozesse an gemeinsamen Standards aus (beispielsweise COSO) und etablieren ein internes Kontrollsystem (IKS) zur Steuerung und Überwachung. Hierbei gelten in der Regel vier Prinzipien:

- Das Prinzip der vier Augen erfordert eine gegenseitige Kontrolle jedes Workflows durch einen anderen Mitarbeiter, sodass für jeden kritischen Prozess mindestens zwei Mitarbeiter verantwortlich sind.
- Das Prinzip der Funktionstrennung („segregation of duties") sorgt für die Trennung zwischen Auftragserfüllung und Auftragskontrolle.
- Das Prinzip der Transparenz besagt, dass Konzepte für Unternehmensprozesse nachvollziehbar und verständlich sein müssen. Über Kontrollziele kann objektiv und von Außenstehenden geprüft werden, ob die Mitarbeiter mit dem Sollkonzept konform agieren.
- Beim Prinzip der Mindestinformation („need to know") geht es darum, dass Mitarbeiter nicht mehr Informationen erhalten sollen als genau jene, die sie für ihre Arbeit benötigen.

Diese Prinzipien spiegeln sich nicht nur in den Prozessen wider, sondern auch in der Basis-IT-Infrastruktur und bei Applikationen wie ERP. Das Pendant zu IKS auf Geschäftsebene heißt im IT-Bereich COBIT (Control Objectives for Information and Related Technology). Handlungsfelder aus dem Kernbereich Bilanztheorie, Prüfungswesen und Organisation sind beispielsweise die Archivierung und die Bereitstellung erforderlicher Informationen für die Finanzberichterstattung.

Die Archivierung beschreibt die unveränderbare, vollständige, sichere, nachvollziehbare und langfristige Aufbewahrung und Wiederherstellung von Informationen. Dies geschieht anhand von Methoden, Techniken und Tools des Enterprise Content Managements (ECM), das organisatorische Prozesse zur Verwaltung unterschiedlich strukturierter Informationen unterstützt. Die in diesem Kontext eingesetzten Prozesse und Systeme müssen regulatorische Transparenzanforderungen erfüllen, die sich häufig aus dem Handels- und dem Steuerrecht ergeben. Hierzu zählt etwa die Einhaltung der Revisionssicherheit durch elektronische Archivsysteme. Aus geschäftlicher Sicht ermöglicht die Archivierung eine nachvollziehbare Aufbewahrung wichtiger Informationen und den Schutz der Reputation des Unternehmens.

Aufbauend auf der Archivierung relevanter Dokumente kann in Unternehmen die regelmäßige Bereitstellung von Rechnungslegungsunterlagen im Rahmen der Finanzberichterstattung erfolgen. Ein hohes Maß an Effizienz wird auch hier durch die Nutzung entsprechender Prozesse und Systeme erzielt. Anforderungen an die Finanzberichterstattung müssen durch diese Prozesse und Systeme umgesetzt und deren Einhaltung fortlaufend überprüft werden. Generell gelten wie schon bei der Archivierung hohe Anforderungen an die Transparenz des Transfers und der Haltung relevanter Daten.

28.10.3.5 Informations- und Transparenzpflicht

Die Erfüllung der Informations- und Transparenzpflicht umfasst verschiedene Aspekte. Aus interner Sicht stellt diese Pflicht hohe Anforderungen an die Prozesse und die bereichsübergreifende Zusammenarbeit im Unternehmen. Je nach Branchen können besondere Berichts- und Offenbarungspflichten gelten, welche Unternehmen bei der Gestaltung ihrer Infrastruktur und Prozesse berücksichtigen müssen. Auch Kunden- und Lieferantenverhältnisse ziehen spezielle Anforderungen nach sich. Ein wichtiges Handlungsfeld der Informations- und Transparenzpflicht ist das Vertragsmanagement. Um Anforderungen, die aus Kunden- und Lieferantenvereinbarungen entstehen, nachvollziehbar und effizient zu verwalten und letztlich umzusetzen, müssen klare Richtlinien und gegebenenfalls einheitliche Vorlagen zur Vertragsgestaltung vorliegen. Im Hinblick auf Outsourcing-Vorhaben etwa hat eine einheitliche Gestaltung von Sourcing-Verträgen den Vorteil, dass allgemein geforderte Leistungsmerkmale an ausgelagerte Dienste einheitlich und transparent gehalten werden (zum Beispiel die Verfügbarkeitsquote von Cloud-Diensten).

Ein weiteres Handlungsfeld besteht in den Berichtspflichten, welchen Unternehmen je nach Branche oder für bestimmte Märkte unterliegen. Als allgemeines Beispiel kann hierfür die **Finanzberichterstattung** genannt werden, die im Rahmen des Bilanz- und Prüfungswesens eine wichtige Rolle spielt. Für die regulierten Bereiche sollten klare Zuständigkeiten existieren, mit denen die Erfüllung der Berichtspflichten abgedeckt wird. Auch hier gilt der Grundsatz, dass die Umsetzung und Überprüfung der Berichtsanforderungen anhand dokumentierter Prozesse und Systeme erforderlich und wichtig sind, um Transparenz gegenüber externen Anspruchsgruppen und Nachvollziehbarkeit der internen Abläufe zu gewährleisten.

28.10.3.6 Globalisierung und Transformation

Um das Innovationspotenzial der digitalen Transformation und der Erschließung globaler Märkte abzurufen, müssen Unternehmen ein hohes Maß an Flexibilität im Umgang mit Technologien und im Hinblick auf die eigene Organisationsstruktur an den Tag legen. Um Infrastruktur und Organisationsstruktur schnell an neue Technologien und notwendige Veränderungen anzupassen, müssen Verfahren etabliert sein, welche für die fortlaufende Einhaltung regulatorischer Anforderungen sorgen. Wichtige Handlungsfelder stellen dabei das **Technologiemanagement** und das **Management der Organisationsstruktur** dar. Das Technologiemanagement beinhaltet die Analyse und Bewertung bestehender und neu aufkommender Technologien, unter anderem hinsichtlich ihres Nutzens, des Aufwands der Umsetzung sowie bei der Umsetzung zu beachtender regulatorischer Anforderungen (Stand der Technik). So muss beispielsweise vor dem Einsatz von Cloud Computing oder von Big Data-Analyseverfahren geklärt werden, welche Auswirkungen der Einsatz auf die Einhaltung bestehender Regularien hat und ob sich aus dem Einsatz neue Verpflichtungen ergeben. Im Gegensatz zu konventionellen IT-Abteilungen, die sich mit Infrastrukturfragen beschäftigen, steht hier das Informationsmanagement im Zentrum. Das Management der Organisationsstruktur beschäftigt sich in vergleichbarer Weise mit der Analyse und Bewertung anvisierter organisatorischer Veränderungen im Hinblick auf Nutzen, Aufwand und Compliance.

Beide Handlungsfelder sollten nicht ad hoc, sondern auf Basis klarer und unternehmensweiter Prozesse und Verfahren umgesetzt werden, um die Einhaltung regulatorischer

Anforderungen fortlaufend sicherzustellen und um die infolge der hohen Dynamik der digitalen Transformation notwendige Handlungsschnelligkeit und Flexibilität zu erreichen. Damit werden Unternehmen befähigt, Transformations- und Globalisierungsvorhaben im globalen Wettbewerb schnell, effizient und unter Beachtung aller relevanten Regularien durchzuführen.

28.10.3.7 Compliance-Prozesse beurteilen und verbessern

Mit dem oben dargestellten Modell lassen sich zwei unterschiedliche Ansätze verfolgen. Beide dienen dazu, den Status der Compliance in der eigenen Organisation zu erfassen, zu bewerten und letztlich zu verbessern. Der Ansatz verfolgt das in der ersten Ausgabe dieses Handbuchs vorgestellte Reifegradmodell. Bei diesem werden die „Reife" und damit die Umsetzungsqualität der mit Compliance befassten Prozesse bestimmt. Je höher der Reifegrad, desto besser sind die sechs Ziele des Modells umgesetzt.

Nutzung eines qualitativen Reifegradmodells

In der Literatur gibt es verschiedene Reifegradmodelle, die manchmal auch als Prozessbefähigungsmodelle bezeichnet werden. Mit diesen Modellen lässt sich die Güte von Prozessen messen. Die Grundidee stammt ursprünglich aus dem Bereich der Softwareentwicklung. Mittels Reifegraden lässt sich überprüfen, wie gut der Prozess der Softwareentwicklung und damit letztlich auch die Software selbst ist. Das Modell lässt sich aber auch gut für die Messung der Qualität anderer Prozesse einsetzen – etwa für den Umgang mit Compliance-Anforderungen. Im Folgenden soll das weit verbreitete Reifegradmodell Capability Maturity Model Integration (CMMI) eingesetzt werden. Abb. 28.9 und 28.10 zeigen die fünf Stufen des Modells.

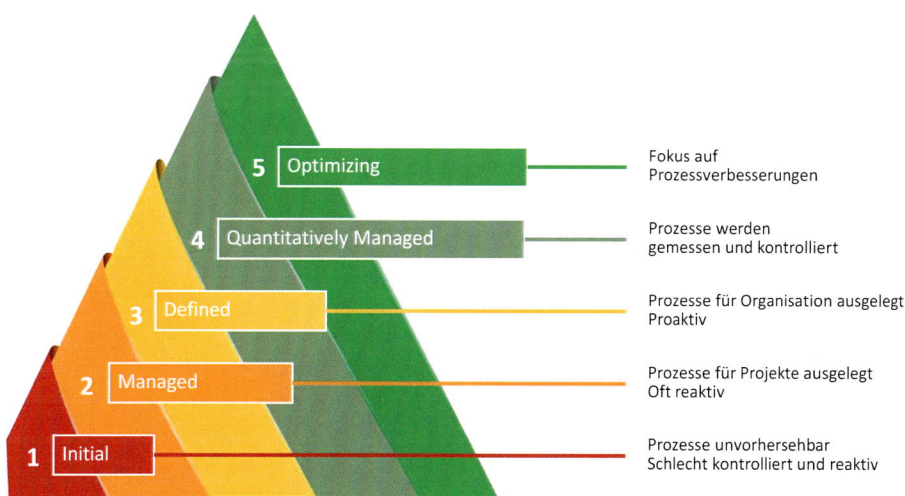

Abb. 28.9 CMMI-Reifegradmodell

Stufe	Bedeutung
1	Die niedrigste Reifegradstufe, die es zu erreichen gilt, ist die 1 (Initial). Die Prozesse werden ad hoc abgewickelt. Projekterfolge beruhen in erster Linie auf den Fähigkeiten des Projektleiters. Bei einem anderen Projektleiter könnte dasselbe Projekt ein Misserfolg werden. Planungen sind unvollständig, eine konsequente Erfolgskontrolle gibt es nicht.
2	Stufe 2 bringt gegenüber Stufe 1 einige Fortschritte in Bezug auf das Projektmanagement. Stufe 2 wird erreicht, wenn die grundlegenden Projektmanagementprozesse zur Planung und Steuerung von Zeit und Kosten etabliert sind. Dabei reicht es aus, wenn diese Prozesse rudimentär implementiert sind. Wichtig ist, dass die Prozesse auch tatsächlich „gelebt" werden.
3	Ab Stufe 3 geht es nicht mehr um einzelne Prozesse, sondern um die Organisation als Ganzes. Innerhalb der Firma oder Behörde müssen die Prozesse einheitlich standardisiert werden. Darüber hinaus ist eine Dokumentation der Prozesse erforderlich.
4	Für Stufe 4 müssen die Prozesse innerhalb der Organisation vereinheitlicht werden. Zudem ist es erforderlich, dass die Qualität der Prozesse über KPIs (Key Performance Indices) gemessen und daraus Vorhersagen für den Projektverlauf getroffen werden.
5	In der höchsten Stufe 5 müssen die Prozesse kontinuierlich verbessert werden. Ein Hilfs mittel dazu ist die regelmäßige Suche nach Schwachstellen in den Prozessen.

Abb. 28.10 Beschreibung der CMMI-Reifegradstufen

Es stellt sich die Frage, welchen Reifegrad Prozesse haben müssen, um im täglichen Geschäftsablauf akzeptabel zu sein. Das Endziel ist natürlich ein Reifegrad von 5 für alle Prozesse, doch diesen Zielwert wird man in der Praxis kaum erreichen. Ein Beispiel für praxisgerechte Reifegrade ist die Zertifizierung eines Managementsystems – beispielsweise ein Informationsmanagementsystem nach ISO 27001. Für eine Erstzertifizierung müssen dessen Prozesse einen Reifegrad von 3 oder höher aufweisen. Bei jeder Re-Zertifizierung wird dann ein Reifegrad angestrebt, der höher liegt als beim letzten Audit. Dabei lässt sich über eine Automatisierung von Workflows mit vergleichsweise kleinem Aufwand ein höherer Reifegrad erreichen – einer der Vorteile der digitalen Transformation. Ein angenehmer Nebeneffekt bei der Erhöhung von Reifegraden ist die Verringerung von Kosten für einen Prozess. Allerdings ist die Beziehung zwischen Reifegrad und Prozesskosten nicht linear. Im Gegenteil: Soll der Reifegrad erhöht werden, muss zunächst Geld in die Hand genommen werden, etwa für entsprechende Projekte oder für den Kauf einer Software. Im Endeffekt wird jedoch Geld gespart, wie Abb. 28.11 verdeutlicht.

Auch die Definition von Compliance-Anforderungen und deren Umsetzung umfasst Geschäftsprozesse, deren Qualität sich mit einem **Reifegradmodell** messen lassen. Entscheidungsträger stellen sich dabei einerseits die Frage nach dem Status quo – also dem aktuellen Reifegrad der Compliance-Prozesse in ihrem Unternehmen – und nach möglichen Handlungsfeldern, also konkreten Verbesserungsmöglichkeiten und daraus resultierenden Aufgaben, die das Erreichen eines höheren Reifegrades ermöglichen sollen.

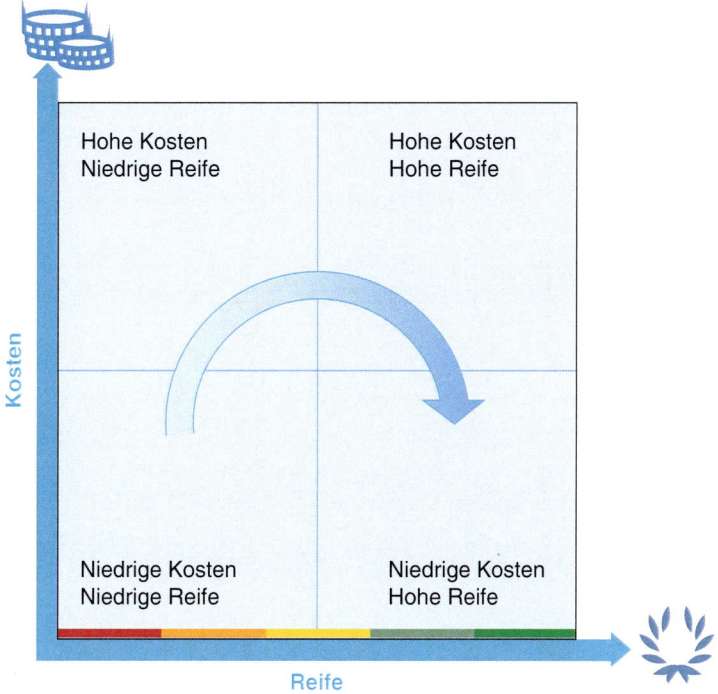

Abb. 28.11 Prozessreife und Prozesskosten

Das beschriebene Reifegradmodell kann wie folgt zum Einsatz kommen:

1. Im ersten Schritt werden die für die eigene Organisation wichtigen Handlungsfelder ermittelt. Dabei können die im Modell angegebenen Beispielhandlungsfelder als Vorgaben und Inspirationsquellen genutzt werden. Es ist darauf zu achten, dass jeder der sechs Kernbereiche durch mindestens zwei Handlungsfelder repräsentiert wird bzw. dass sich existierende Organisationseinheiten im Handlungsfeldmodell wiederfinden.
2. Anschließend sind die Prozesse zu ermitteln, durch die diese Handlungsfelder bearbeitet werden. Dabei sollte jeder Prozess mit seinen Schnittstellen zu anderen Prozessen beschrieben werden. Außerdem muss neben Zuständigkeiten und Rollen ebenso dokumentiert werden, welche Informationen im Prozess verarbeitet werden und wie der Datenfluss über die Schnittstellen ist.
3. Dann wird jeder Prozess dahingehend bewertet, wie sein Reifegrad ist. Diese Bewertung findet qualitativ nach den Kriterien des **CMMI-Reifegradmodells** statt. Die Reifegradstufen jedes Prozesses werden mit der Begründung für die Einstufung in die Dokumentation aufgenommen.
4. Der Reifegrad jedes Kernbereichs wird durch das arithmetische Mittel der Reifegrade aller Prozesse ermittelt, die die Handlungsfelder des jeweiligen Kernbereichs bearbeiten.

5. Kernbereiche mit einem Reifegrad von 3 oder weniger sind dahingehend zu untersuchen, wie die den Handlungsfeldern zugeordneten Prozesse verbessert werden können.

6. Befinden sich innerhalb eines Kernbereichs Prozesse mit stark unterschiedlichem Reifegrad, so besteht ebenfalls Handlungsbedarf. Im Idealfall haben alle mit Compliance befassten Prozesse einen sehr ähnlichen Reifegrad. Zurückgebliebene Prozesse sind mit Priorität zu verbessern und in ihrem Reifegrad zu steigern.

28.11 Beitrag der Cloud zu Compliance und Geschäftserfolg

Mit der Verlagerung von Geschäftsprozessen in die digitale Welt nimmt die Bedeutung der Informationstechnik zwar zu, die der klassischen Betreiber-IT jedoch ab. Die technischen Lösungen werden durch Cloud-Anbieter bereitgestellt, die interne IT wird sich eher mit der digitalen Gestaltung von Geschäftsprozessen beschäftigen und damit, ein Informationsmanagement abzubilden und zu unterstützen sowie Cloud-Dienste zu überwachen. Das gilt auch insbesondere für die mit Compliance zusammenhängenden Prozesse, bei denen cloudbasierte Ansätze Teil des internen Kontrollsystems werden.

28.11.1 Cloud-Service-Modelle im Vergleich

Wie bereits beschrieben wurden mögliche Nutzenpotenziale der Cloud-Nutzung aus Sicht der Compliance erläutert. Dabei wurde insbesondere der Transfer der Zuständigkeit für die Auditierung und Zertifizierung technischer und organisatorischer Sicherheitsmaßnahmen vom Kunden zum Anbieter und die damit einhergehende höhere Flexibilität von Unternehmen bei der (Um-)Gestaltung ihrer Prozesse und Systeme hervorgehoben. Im folgenden Abschnitt werden zunächst gängige Cloud-Dienstmodelle erläutert und mit klassischen Modellen der IT-Bereitstellung verglichen. Im Anschluss wird dargestellt, inwiefern Zuständigkeiten für die technische und organisatorische Umsetzung von Compliance zum Anbieter transferiert werden können und welche Vorteile sich daraus aus Compliance-Sicht ergeben.

28.11.1.1 Übertragung von Zuständigkeiten

Bei der eigenständigen Inhouse-Bereitstellung einer Anwendung liegen die Zuständigkeiten für Implementierung, Umsetzung und Instandhaltung von Kontrollen beim Unternehmen selbst. Bei einer cloudbasierten Bereitstellung teilen sich Cloud-Anbieter und Kunde diese Zuständigkeiten. Maßgeblich für den Grad der Abgabe derartiger Zuständigkeiten an den Anbieter ist das angewendete Cloud-Dienstmodell. IT-Leistungen werden immer mehr durch externe Dienstleister erbracht. Dazu zählen bereits klassische Hosting-Dienste, welche die Bereitstellung von Servern für ihre Kunden übernehmen. Eine wichtigere Rolle spielen jedoch Cloud-Dienste, die ihren Kunden je nach Cloud-Modell Infrastrukturdienste, Plattformdienste oder gleich gesamte Softwareapplikationen

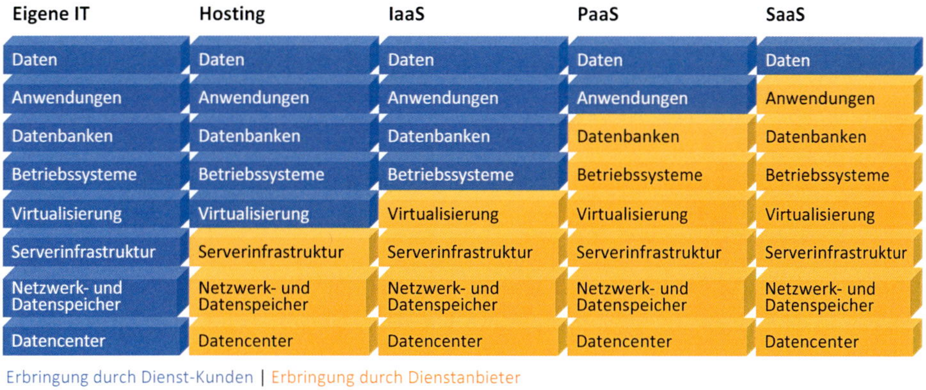

Eigene IT	Hosting	IaaS	PaaS	SaaS
Daten	Daten	Daten	Daten	Daten
Anwendungen	Anwendungen	Anwendungen	Anwendungen	Anwendungen
Datenbanken	Datenbanken	Datenbanken	Datenbanken	Datenbanken
Betriebssysteme	Betriebssysteme	Betriebssysteme	Betriebssysteme	Betriebssysteme
Virtualisierung	Virtualisierung	Virtualisierung	Virtualisierung	Virtualisierung
Serverinfrastruktur	Serverinfrastruktur	Serverinfrastruktur	Serverinfrastruktur	Serverinfrastruktur
Netzwerk- und Datenspeicher	Netzwerk- und Datenspeicher	Netzwerk- und Datenspeicher	Netzwerk- und Datenspeicher	Netzwerk- und Datenspeicher
Datencenter	Datencenter	Datencenter	Datencenter	Datencenter

Erbringung durch Dienst-Kunden | Erbringung durch Dienstanbieter

Abb. 28.12   Aufteilung der Zuständigkeiten zwischen Cloud-Anbieter und -Kunde

bereitstellen. Die Wahl des Cloud-Modells stellt dabei für Unternehmen keine rein technische, sondern eine strategische Entscheidung dar, die entscheidende Auswirkungen auf Infrastruktur, Prozesse und nicht zuletzt auch auf die Umsetzung von Compliance hat. In Abb. 28.12 werden die drei verbreitetsten Cloud-Modelle erläutert und der internen Inhouse-Bereitstellung sowie dem klassischen Hosting hinsichtlich der Verteilung technischer Zuständigkeiten zwischen Dienstanbieter und -kunde gegenübergestellt.

Vom klassischen Server Hosting unterscheidet sich die Cloud in erster Linie durch den Einsatz von Virtualisierungstechnologien. Im Gegensatz zu Hosting-Anbietern stellen Cloud-Anbieter also keine dedizierten Server mehr bereit, die physisch vom Kunden genutzt und konfiguriert werden. Kunden erhalten vielmehr Zugriff auf virtuelle Instanzen, die über ein oder mehrere Datencenter verteilt betrieben und zentral angesteuert werden können. Während Systeme und Daten beim Hosting also auf einem physisch vorhandenen Server verweilen und an dessen Kapazitäten gebunden sind, können Ressourcen wie Speicher, Hardware oder auch verfügbare Instanzen in der Cloud nahezu beliebig skaliert werden.

Der Einsatz von Virtualisierung stellt eine der wesentlichen technischen Innovationen der Cloud gegenüber klassischen Outsourcing-Vorhaben wie Hosting oder Collocation dar. Durch den Einsatz von Virtualisierung werden nicht nur verbesserte Infrastrukturdienste im IaaS-Modell, sondern auch deutlich komplexere Plattform- und Softwaredienste im PaaS- bzw. SaaS-Modell ermöglicht.

- Im **IaaS-Modell** erfolgt die Bereitstellung einer sicheren und überprüfbaren Server-, Netzwerk und Hostinfrastruktur innerhalb des Datencenters durch den Cloud-Anbieter. Diese Infrastruktur ermöglicht die Bereitstellung von Rechenkapazitäten, Netzwerkanbindung und der nötigen Hard- und Softwarekomponenten zur Datenablage und zur Implementierung virtueller Maschinen.
- Im **PaaS-Modell** stellt der Cloud-Anbieter nicht nur die Hardware-Infrastruktur bereit, sondern darüber hinaus grundlegende Software in Form von Entwicklungsumgebungen

und Schnittstellen. Auf deren Basis können Kunden eigene Systeme installieren, Software entwickeln und bereitstellen.

- Im **SaaS-Modell** wird eine Software vom Anbieter auf seiner Cloud-Infrastruktur betrieben und vom Kunden als Dienstleistung – in der Regel über das Internet – bezogen. Für die Nutzung der Software reicht in vielen Fällen ein Internetbrowser aus.

Die unterschiedlichen Leistungsmerkmale der drei Cloud-Modelle gehen einher mit einer unterschiedlichen Aufteilung der Zuständigkeiten für die Gestaltung der Dienste unter Einhaltung regulatorischer und geschäftlicher Anforderungen. Auch wenn nach wie vor der Cloud-Kunde die Verantwortung für die Nutzung der Dienstleistung mit allen Konsequenzen trägt, birgt der Transfer technischer und organisatorischer Zuständigkeiten gerade aus Compliance-Sicht viele Vorteile.

28.11.2   Steuerung des Anbieter-Kunden-Verhältnisses

Bei der Betrachtung der Vereinbarungen über die Cloud-Nutzung, die Kunde und Anbieter in aller Regel treffen, werden bereits erste Nutzenpotenziale deutlich. In Service Level Agreements (SLAs) und Dienstleistungsbedingungen („Service Terms") werden Leistungsmerkmale und -kontrollen fixiert. Über diese Vereinbarungen kann der Cloud-Kunde steuern, in welcher Qualität und Intensität ein Cloud-Anbieter Dienste erbringt. Bestandteile dieser Vereinbarungen sind etwa:

- Verfügbarkeitsgarantien seitens des Anbieters.
- Vorgaben für den Datenschutz.
- Vorgaben für den Ort der Datenhaltung und -verarbeitung.
- Vorgaben zur Überprüfbarkeit und Auditierung von Diensten und Infrastruktur.
- Vorgaben für die korrekte Nutzung von Diensten.
- Verantwortlichkeiten bei der Nutzung von Diensten sowie Haftungsübernahmen und -begrenzungen.

Die Aufteilung der Verantwortlichkeiten wird erleichtert, wenn die beteiligten Partner ihre unternehmensinternen Prozesse an gängigen Standards ausrichten. Das können beispielsweise COSO, COBIT oder die Informationssicherheitsstandards ISO 27001 oder 27002 sein. Damit spricht man eine gemeinsame Sprache und hat ein gemeinsames Verständnis. Übergangspunkte von Prozessen und die dazu benötigten Protokolle lassen sich dann leichter definieren, umsetzen und kontrollieren.

Anwendungsbeispiele

Betrachtet man die Eigenschaften und Leistungsmerkmale der Cloud unter Berücksichtigung der drei unterschiedlichen Cloud-Modelle, so wird deutlich, dass gerade die Nutzung von Plattform- und Softwarediensten (PaaS bzw. SaaS) zur Einhaltung regulatorischer

Anforderungen und zur Erreichung eines hohen Maßes an Flexibilität im Hinblick auf zukünftige Veränderungen beiträgt. Warum dem so ist, soll im Folgenden beispielhaft anhand zweier Kernbereiche beschrieben werden.

Compliance, Informationssicherheit und -schutz

Die Sicherheit von Daten, Systemen und Informationen muss organisatorisch und technisch für Hardware, Software und die zugrunde liegende Infrastruktur sichergestellt werden. Dazu existieren regulatorische Anforderungen und Standards, deren Einhaltung überwacht werden muss. Betrachtet man zunächst die einfache On-Premises-Bereitstellung, so wird schnell klar, dass alle Sicherheits- und Schutzmaßnahmen vom Unternehmen selbst getroffen, koordiniert, umgesetzt, überwacht und fortlaufend gemäß der Bedrohungslage und dem Stand der Technik aktualisiert werden müssen. Besonders für kleinere und mittelständische Unternehmen stellt dies eine große finanzielle und organisatorische Herausforderung dar. Wie würde sich die Nutzung eines der drei Cloud-Modelle für das Unternehmen bezahlt machen?

Das IaaS-Modell:

Mit dem IaaS-Modell delegiert ein Unternehmen die Aufgabe der Bereitstellung einer sicheren, zertifizierten und sich auf dem Stand der Technik befindlichen Datencenter-, Server-, Netzwerk- und Hostinfrastruktur an einen Cloud-Anbieter. Die Einhaltung von Normen, Regularien und Standards zum Betrieb des Rechenzentrums, der Server und der Netzwerkanbindung wird also vom Cloud-Anbieter übernommen. Notwendige Aktualisierungen werden vom Cloud-Anbieter durchgeführt, ohne dass auf Kundenseite beispielsweise neue Hardware angeschafft oder neues Sicherheitspersonal eingestellt oder geschult werden muss. Auch bei Datenwiederherstellung und Notfallmanagement profitiert der Cloud-Kunde von der Infrastruktur des Anbieters. Viele Cloud-Anbieter bieten hier mehrere Optionen an, etwa die lokale redundante oder die georedundante Speicherung von Daten in Datencentern in verschiedenen Regionen. Da der im Wettbewerb mit Konkurrenten stehende Cloud-Anbieter selbst ein großes Interesse daran hat, sich nach etablierten Sicherheitsstandards zertifizieren zu lassen, profitiert der Cloud-Kunde zudem von der fortlaufend überprüften Einhaltung gängiger und hoher Sicherheitsstandards durch den Cloud-Anbieter.

Das PaaS-Modell:

Beim PaaS-Modell werden neben der Infrastruktur auch die Sicherheit der für den Betrieb einer Plattform notwendigen Software – etwa Betriebssysteme und Datenbanksysteme – durch den Cloud-Anbieter bereitgestellt. Hierdurch werden Umsetzung und Überprüfung softwareseitiger Sicherheitsmaßnahmen an den Cloud-Anbieter delegiert. Dies gilt etwa für die Umsetzung eines Identitäts- und Zugriffsmanagements, die Bereitstellung sicherer Verschlüsselungsprotokolle und die Forcierung der Einhaltung guter Entwicklungspraktiken. Das PaaS-Modell ermöglicht einem Kunden also den Aufbau eigener Applikationen auf einer fortlaufend überprüften und vertrauenswürdigen Infrastruktur- und Softwareplattform. Dadurch erhalten Entwickler auf Kundenseite eine standardisierte und fortlaufend überwachte Basis für die Implementierung eigener Applikationen. Oft können PaaS-Kunden dabei bereits auf Sicherheitszertifizierungen des Anbieters aufbauen. Auf Plattformebene stellen viele Cloud-Anbieter zudem spezielle Tools und Dienste bereit, die dem Kunden die Möglichkeit geben, ein höheres Maß an Sicherheit zu erzielen. Dazu zählen beispielsweise Tools zur Schwachstellenanalyse oder zur Analyse und Klassifizierung von Daten nach ihrem Schutzbedarf.

Das SaaS-Modell:

Die Nutzung des SaaS-Modells bedeutet den weitreichendsten Transfer von Zuständigkeiten vom Cloud-Kunden zum Anbieter. Da die gesamte Anwendung vom Anbieter bereitgestellt wird, entfällt auf Kundenseite sogar die Entwicklung der Applikation. Damit gehen weiterführende Sicherheits- und Compliance-Kontrollen bezüglich der Software in den Aufgabenbereich des Anbieters über. Unter anderem zählen hierzu etwa die kostspielige Überprüfung der Software auf Sicherheitslücken sowie die Bereitstellung fortlaufender Aktualisierungen und Updates. Nutzer von SaaS-Anwendungen erreichen ein sehr hohes Maß an Flexibilität, da das Portfolio an IT-Diensten, welche über SaaS bezogen wird, sehr einfach skaliert oder ergänzt werden kann, ohne dass dabei weitere Investitionen in Infrastruktur, Entwicklung oder Zertifizierungen anfallen. Audits und Zertifizierungen, die sich direkt auf die Sicherheit der Hardware- und Softwarekomponenten beziehen, werden vom Cloud-Anbieter erbracht.

Cloud-Dienste für mehr Dynamik und Flexibilität

Der Kernbereich Globalisierung und Transformation zielt auf eine hohe Flexibilität der Organisation sowie der technischen Infrastruktur ab, um schnelle Anpassungen an technische Innovationen vorzunehmen. Dies bedeutet auch, dass die vorhandene Infrastruktur anpassbar und skalierbar sein muss und sich die Änderungskosten in Grenzen halten. Hierin liegt eine der Schlüsselkompetenzen der Cloud, da Hardwareleistung und Softwarekomponenten von der zugrunde liegenden Infrastruktur abstrahiert und als Dienst bereitgestellt werden.

Der Beitrag der Cloud beschränkt sich nicht nur auf die Bereitstellung skalierbarer Hardwareressourcen. Denkt man den Grundgedanken von Cloud Computing konsequent zu Ende, so gelangt man zu der Erkenntnis, dass gerade in der Bereitstellung standardisierter Entwicklungsumgebungen oder ganzer Software-Pakete „as a Service" eine große Chance für Unternehmen liegt. Diese können die technologische Basis ihres Erfolges wandelbar und ohne zusätzlichen Kostenaufwand gestalten. Die Nutzung der drei Cloud-Modelle macht sich dabei schon unter Gesichtspunkten der Transformierbarkeit aufgrund von Innovationen und Globalisierungsbestrebungen bezahlt.

Das IaaS-Modell:

Die eigenständige On-Premises-Bereitstellung einer IT-Infrastruktur bremst die Anpassbarkeit der Organisation hinsichtlich neuer Technologien in vielerlei Hinsicht aus. Ändern sich die Anforderungen an die IT-Infrastruktur, mündet dies oft in teuren und zeitaufwendigen Investitionen. Technologische Anpassungen oder regulatorische Vorschriften können auch dazu führen, dass angeschaffte Hardware obsolet wird, Kapazitäten nicht ausreichen oder Standards nicht oder nur unzureichend erfüllt werden. Bereits die Nutzung der Cloud im IaaS-Modell ermöglicht es, Hardwareressourcen als beliebig skalierbaren Dienst in Anspruch zu nehmen. Kosten und Zeitaufwand für die Bereitstellung und Wartung der Infrastruktur entfallen. Die infrastrukturelle Grundlage für IT-Innovationen wird also im wahrsten Sinne des Wortes „per Mausklick" durch die Buchung von IaaS-Ressourcen geschaffen. Die Einhaltung von Regularien in Bezug auf die Hardware-Infrastruktur wird dabei, wie bereits beispielhaft für die Anforderungen des Informationsschutzes beschrieben, in den meisten Fällen vom Cloud-Anbieter umgesetzt.

Das PaaS-Modell:

PaaS-Anbieter unterstützen Kunden durch eine einheitliche Plattform, die häufig eine Vielzahl an Softwarekomponenten wie Betriebssysteme oder Datenbanksysteme umfasst. Gleichzeitig werden oft Dienste bereitgestellt, die Kundenvorhaben unterstützen und einzeln gebucht werden können. Neben den Vorteilen durch die Bereitstellung der Infrastruktur ermöglicht das PaaS-Modell den Kunden eine effizientere Entwicklung und Implementierung eigener Lösungen auf Basis allgemeingültiger Standards. Regulatorische Anforderungen und Standards unterschiedlicher Branchen werden von PaaS-Anbietern häufig durch Dienste und in der Architektur der Plattform selbst umgesetzt, so etwa Überwachungs-, Diagnose- oder Analysetools. Dies beschleunigt die Entwicklung individueller Kundenlösungen und vereinfacht Compliance durch die Standardisierung der Softwarelandschaft. Insgesamt wird im PaaS-Modell sowohl im Hinblick auf die eingesetzte, eigenständig entwickelte Software als auch hinsichtlich der Anpassbarkeit der Softwarelandschaft an veränderte Anforderungen ein hohes Maß an Flexibilität erreicht.

Das SaaS-Modell:

Da im SaaS-Modell komplette Softwarekomponenten als Cloud-Dienst bezogen werden, bietet dieses Modell das höchste Maß an Anpassbarkeit hinsichtlich veränderter Anforderungen. Ändern sich die Anforderungen an eine Softwarekomponente, so besteht keinerlei software- oder hardwaretechnischer Veränderungsbedarf mehr. Die SaaS-Nutzung kann einfach skaliert werden, etwa hinsichtlich Rechenleistung oder Benutzeranzahl. Ferner können einfach und bedarfsgerecht Dienste hinzugebucht oder abbestellt werden. Da die Software als Ganzes vom Anbieter bereitgestellt wird, obliegt auch deren Auditierung und Zertifizierung dem Anbieter. Während Änderungen an eigenständig bereitgestellter On-Premises-Software häufig neue Auditierungen und Zertifizierungen notwendig machen, entfällt dieser Aufwand im SaaS-Modell. Sofern ein Cloud-Anbieter über ein passendes Portfolio an SaaS-Diensten verfügt, können Unternehmen ihre Softwarelandschaft bequem um adäquate Standardlösungen für allgemeine oder branchenspezifische Fälle ergänzen. Cloud-Kunden können darauf verzichten, eigene aufwendige Investitionen zu tätigen, die unter funktionellen und regulatorischen Gesichtspunkten fortlaufend Veränderungen unterliegen.

28.12   Die Cloud als Win-win-Strategie

Für ein Unternehmen, das sich zum Einsatz einer Cloud-Lösung entschließt, ergibt sich ein großer Nutzen. Man profitiert von den Vorteilen der digitalen Transformation, gleichzeitig werden Compliance-Anforderungen besser erfüllt, und als Folge davon wird der Reifegrad der eigenen Geschäftsprozesse erhöht. Zudem kann in einer Cloud ein höherer Grad an Informationssicherheit erreicht werden, als dies in einem normalen Rechenzentrum eines kleinen oder mittleren Unternehmens der Fall sein kann. Damit ergeben sich Vorteile auch für Prozesse, die nicht oder nur indirekt von der Cloud betroffen sind. Der Nutzen liegt aber auch beim Anbieter von Cloud-Leistungen. Je mehr Kunden seine Dienste in Anspruch nehmen, desto besser können diese standardisiert werden. Dies führt zu Synergieeffekten, die sich aus dem Verkauf gleicher oder ähnlicher Leistungen an mehrere Kunden ergeben. Die gleiche Leistung kann dann effizienter angeboten werden. Cloud-Anbieter profitieren aber auch beim Thema Compliance und Informationssicherheit. Schon aus Gründen der Konkurrenz muss jeder Anbieter für ein hohes Niveau an Compliance und Sicherheit sorgen und dies mittels Audits und Zertifizierungen nachweisen. Der Reifegrad der Geschäftsprozesse steigt beim Anbieter von Audit zu Audit ebenfalls an, mit denselben Vorteilen wie bei seinen Kunden. Die obligatorischen Audits und Zertifizierungen haben dann wieder direkte Vorteile für die Cloud-Kunden. Den Nachweis, dass Compliance, Daten- und Informationsschutz im eigenen Unternehmen ausreichend umgesetzt werden, kann ein Cloud-Kunde mit Verweis auf die Zertifizierung seines Anbieters leicht erbringen. Nur in Ausnahmefällen muss der Kunde eigene Lieferanten-Audits bei seinem Cloud-Dienstleister in die Wege leiten. Insgesamt entsteht durch die digitale Transformation und die Cloud als ihre Basistechnologie eine Win-win-Situation für alle Beteiligten. Das umfasst Cloud-Kunden und -Anbieter, aber auch Endkunden und Endnutzer, die von digitalisierten Prozessen profitieren und ihre privaten Ansprüche besser mit den Erfordernissen der Informationstechnik in Einklang bringen können.

28.13   Epilog

Ziel dieser Ausführungen ist es, aufzuzeigen, dass sich jedes Unternehmen – vom Start-up über den Mittelstand bis zum Global Player – und jede Behörde mit dem Thema Compliance konstruktiv und auch zum eigenen wirtschaftlichen Nutzen auseinandersetzen sollte und muss, denn faktisch ist es für jede Organisation eine Pflicht, gesetzliche und regulatorische Anforderungen zu erfüllen. Aber Compliance ist nicht nur eine Pflicht, sondern eine Verpflichtung.

Compliance gibt Maßnahmen vor, die garantieren, dass gesetzliche oder auch regulatorische Mindestanforderungen erfüllt werden, die auch in den Bereichen greifen, die gerne Sparmaßnahmen oder anderen Faktoren zum Opfer fallen oder einfach nicht berücksichtigt werden. Ein Grund hierfür ist beispielsweise der zusätzliche oder kostenintensive Aufwand, der sich unternehmensintern nur schwer rechtfertigen lässt. So steht beispielsweise im Niedrigpreissegment des IoT zu vermuten, dass aufgrund von Sparmaßnahmen einige wichtige Aspekte des Funktionsumfangs vernachlässigt würden, wenn nicht Compliance-Vorgaben dafür sorgten, dass ein bestimmtes Qualitätsniveau gehalten wird.

Setzen Organisationen ein Compliance-Modell um, können sie erreichen, dass Normen und Regeln einheitlich definiert und auch umgesetzt werden. Die Regulierungen bzw. Standardisierungen stellen sicher, dass der Ablauf wirtschaftlicher Prozesse transparent, kontrollier- und nachvollziehbar wird. Dies vereinfacht auch das Zusammenspiel der Unternehmen sowie den Aufbau von unternehmensübergreifenden Produktionsketten und erweiterten Serviceorganisationen. Die Basis einer Kooperation beruht damit nicht mehr nur auf Vertrauen und Selbstverständnis, sondern auch auf Klarheit und Wissen. Wird ein Compliance-Modell in einer Organisation zentral und einheitlich aufgebaut und umgesetzt, ist auch sicher gestellt, dass alle Workflows regelkonform ineinandergreifen – und hierbei spielt Cloud-Technologie eine tragende Rolle.

Compliance-Informationen sind heute wichtige Metadaten zu Geschäftsdaten. Diese begleitenden Informationen geben den Geschäftsdaten einen zusätzlichen Wert, da sie eine automatisierte und rechtskonforme Weiterverarbeitung erst möglich machen. Mit dem gezielten und situationsgebundenen Austausch von Compliance-Informationen zwischen den Unternehmen können sie automatisierte Workflows abbilden, die der notwendigen Dynamik heutiger und künftiger Prozesse entsprechen. Ein Ausbau dieser Möglichkeiten – auch über die Grundlagen der Compliance hinaus – wird eine Voraussetzung für den Erfolg dieser vierten Wirtschaftsperiode sein.

Unternehmen und Behörden sollten jedoch nicht nur die Compliance-Anforderungen umfassend erfüllen, sondern ihre Investitionen auch nutzen, um ihre Unternehmensziele optimal erfüllen zu können. Dann greifen die Maßnahmen auch in nicht-regulierten Bereichen und schützen so den gesamten Wert von Forschung und Entwicklung, Produktion, Dienstleistung und Transaktionen und anderen wertschöpfenden Leistungen des Unternehmens.

Die Bedeutung von Compliance wird auch weiterhin zunehmen. Die Umsetzung und die Einhaltung von Compliance-Vorgaben sind wichtige strategische Aufgaben einer jeden Organisation. Ein entscheidender Erfolgsfaktor hierbei ist es, frühzeitig eine IT-Umgebung bereitzustellen, die anpassungsfähig und flexibel ist und die die Compliance-Maßnahmen dynamisch und automatisiert umsetzen kann.

Moderne digitale Kooperationen und Verbundkonzepte mit sensiblen Daten

Jörg Kebbedies

Zusammenfassung

Kooperation und Zusammenarbeit innerhalb und zwischen Behörden auf Bundes-, Landes- und kommunaler Ebene sind wichtige Aspekte des täglichen Behördenlebens. Digitale Prozesse erfordern vertrauliche Grundprinzipien und sichere Architekturen, wenn es um den Austausch von Dokumenten geht, die als VS-NfD oder sogar GEHEIM gekennzeichnet sind. Der behördliche Alltag zeigt, dass fehlende sichere digitale Raumstrukturen dem klassischen, d. h. dem papierbezogenen Weg, immer noch den Vorzug geben. Der Beitrag führt systematisch in die Kernkonzepte vertrauenswürdiger digitaler Kooperationen ein. Im Mittelpunkt stehen qualifizierende Prinzipien, sodass Informationsprozesse mit hohen Ansprüchen an Vertraulichkeit und einer zugesicherten Nachweisführung umsetzbar werden. Eine koordinierte Zusammenarbeit ist eng verknüpft mit der Thematik einer hoheitlichen normativen Verhaltenssteuerung. Das vorgestellte Prinzip abgegrenzter, jedoch bedarfsgerecht integrierbarer digitaler Raumstrukturen gewährleistet eine hohe kooperative Dynamik.

29.1 Grenzen Digitaler Strukturen

Soziale Strukturen repräsentieren gesellschaftlich verteilte Verantwortungsbereiche. Prozesse der sozialen Welt sind mit Kommunikationen außerhalb digitaler Methoden verbunden. In Bezug auf notwendige Verhaltensformen und Aufbaustrukturen konstituieren sich soziale Strukturen über eine Bandbreite rechtlicher Regelungen.

J. Kebbedies (✉)
secunet Security Networks AG, Dresden, Deutschland
E-Mail: joerg.kebbedies@secunet.com

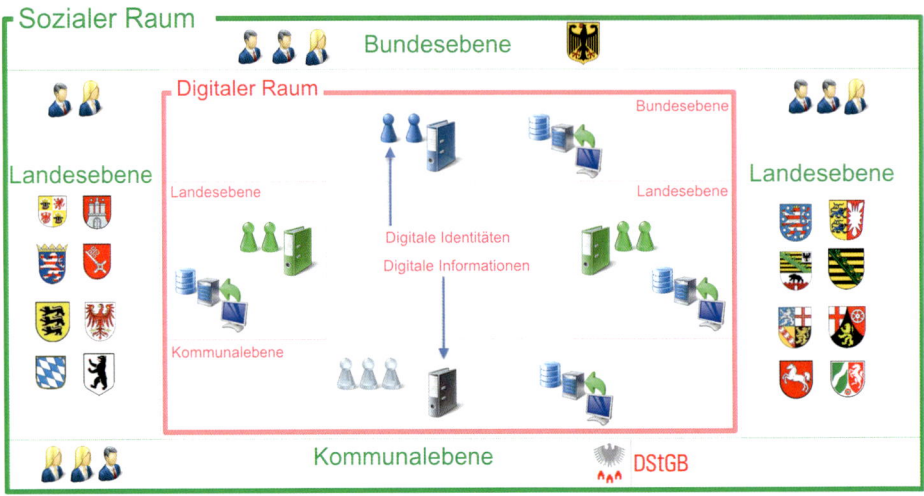

Abb. 29.1 Strukturdefinition moderner Organisationen

Kooperationen im sozialen Kontext unterliegen ausgereiften Mechanismen und zeich-
nen sich durch hohe Erfahrungswerte aus. Der Handlungsrahmen zur Erfüllung von
Aufgaben erweitert sich erst in der Öffnung neuer kooperativer Beziehungen unter Einbeziehung von Strukturbereichen außerhalb des eigenen Verantwortungsbereiches. Die
dafür notwendigen Vertrauensgrundlagen entwickeln sich aus den spezifischen Ausfüh-
rungsformen selbst heraus, denn handelnde Akteure sind zweifelsfrei identifizierbar und
ausgeübte Handlungsmuster gut nachvollziehbar.

In Abb. 29.1 wird deutlich, dass sich vollständig komplementär zu einem sozialen Kontext, zunehmend digitale Strukturen herausbilden und sich als differenzierte IT-
Architekturen, Domänen- und Betriebsmodelle manifestieren.

Die digitale Transformation vollzieht sich als fortschreitende Verlagerung bestehender
sozialer Kommunikationen und geistiger Wertschöpfungen in Strukturen verteilter *digitaler Räume*. Digitale Identitäten für die Verarbeitung digitaler Informationen innerhalb
hoheitlich abgegrenzter IT-Konzepte kennzeichnen *digitale Räume* als paralleles und
transformiertes Strukturkonzept.

Unter dem Aspekt einer adäquaten Abbildung bestehender Organisationsstrukturen,
schafft die Digitalisierung qualitativ neue Bereiche effektiver Kommunikationen und digitaler Fachprozesse und vergrößert somit den Handlungs- und Einflussbereich bestehender
Verantwortlichkeiten. Eine Effizienzsteigerung in der Ausübung strukturbezogener Prozesse lässt sich durchaus nachweisen und begründet die enormen Anstrengungen im Aufbau digitaler Strukturen.

Setzt man den Betrachtungswinkel jedoch größer, so zeigen sich die begrenzenden
Faktoren dieser Entwicklung, da sich der Radius digitaler Erweiterungen an bestehenden
Konzepten sozialer Strukturen ausrichtet, ohne jedoch die bestehenden, sozial geprägten
Beziehungsmodelle zu berücksichtigen.

Föderal geprägt, entwickelten sich behördliche digitale Strukturen als eigenständige, zum Teil völlig separierte, digitale Hoheitsbereiche heraus. Richtet sich die Betrachtung auf die Aspekte Sicherheit, Geheim- und Datenschutz, IT-Sicherheitsmanagement und nicht zuletzt auf die infrastrukturelle Komplexität und Compliance, so zeichnet sich in der Bewertung eine große qualitative Diversität ab.

Digitale Diversität führte zunehmend zu einer Abgrenzungspolitik, denn der Begriff *Vertrauen* in Bezug auf digitale Partner, Informationen und Prozesse fand bisher keine Grundlage, auf die er sich herausbilden konnte. Das Fazit, *Stacheldraht, hohe Mauern und schmale Tore – so schützen wir heute* [1], als Ergebnis einer repräsentativen Bestandsanalyse zum Zukunftskongress 2017, veranschaulicht die *digitale Sackgasse*.

29.2   Strategie Digitaler Prozessformen

Die bundesweite digitale Strukturentwicklung [2] sieht sich im Zuge zunehmender Cyberbedrohungen, bei stetig wachsenden Erfordernissen flexibler regulierter Informationsprozesse, mit der Frage konfrontiert, wie sich eine Strategie für die übergreifende Zusammenarbeit und Informationsverteilung zwischen föderativen digitalen Domänen gestalten lässt.

Es geht nicht allein um die technische Vereinheitlichung und Harmonisierung komplexer IT-Systeme und Dienstleistungen [3]. Große Anstrengungen werden auch im Bereich der Netzinfrastrukturen unternommen, um bestehende Differenzen im Bereich der Sicherheitsniveaus anzugleichen [4].

Im Mittelpunkt steht jedoch ein mehrschichtiges, ineinander verzahntes Konzept, eine qualitative Neuordnung und Erweiterung bestehender digitaler Strukturen zur Übertragung sozialer Prinzipien und Paradigmen auf den *digitalen Raum*.

Bestehende soziale Konzepte wie

- Hoheitsbegriff, Autorität,
- Rechtliche Regulierung,
- Vertraulichkeit, Verbindlichkeit,
- Vertrauensbeziehungen,
- Objekt- Subjekt-Authentizität und
- Governance[1]

benötigen für deren adäquate digitale Transformation moderne Technologien.

Ein architekturelles Re-Design in Richtung flexibler, sicherer und vertrauenswürdiger IT-Prozess-, Dienstleistungs- und offener Kooperationsfähigkeiten erfordert die Anwendung infrastruktureller Sicherheits- und Funktionsmuster. Damit entsteht ein funktional

---

[1] Formen und Mechanismen der Koordinierung zwischen mehr oder weniger autonomen Akteuren.

und qualitativ abgestimmter Unterbau, um darauf aufsetzend die erweiterten Konsolidierungsziele hinreichend zu erfüllen.

Eine unvollständige Sicht auf die Gesamtkonsolidierung birgt das Risiko, dass die Bereiche der infrastrukturellen Architektur nur unzureichend die technischen Grundlagen für übergreifende Sicherheits- und Regulierungsstrategien etablieren. Konzepte, die später keine Grundlage finden könnten, sind z. B. eine policy-gestützte Steuerung zur Separierung bzw. Begrenzung von Ressourcen auf Netzwerkebene, die vertrauenswürdige Attestierung von Infrastruktureigenschaften oder Mechanismen zur kontrollierten Informationsverteilung zwischen separierten Netzwerkbereichen unterschiedlicher Sicherheitsniveaus unter Anwendung verifizierbarer Datenkennzeichnungen (Datenlabel).

Gegenwärtige Sicherheitsprobleme und Verwundbarkeiten staatlicher IT-Dienstleistungen und Verfahren resultieren aus fehlenden oder unzureichend transformierten Konzepten der höheren Ebenen. Allein die Tatsache, dass der im Zuge der Digitalisierung für die Architektur und Normungen von Software der Netzkommunikation maßgebende sog. *Code* noch keiner rechtlichen Regulierung unterzogen ist [5, S. 41], begründet die mangelnde Qualitätspolitik, das fehlende Vertrauen in der Anwendung von Soft- und Hardwaresystemen und eine erfolgreiche Cyberangriffspraxis [6].

29.3   Digitaler Kooperationsraum

Für die Wahrung eigener Interessen und zum Ausgleich der föderalen Diversität aktueller IT-Strukturen sind erweiternde Konzepte zur Harmonisierung und vor allem zur Steuerung übergreifender Prozessstrategien erforderlich. Die Analyse von Pasternak [1] verdeutlicht, dass die Risiken in den Bereichen Vertraulichkeit und Datenschutz enorm steigen, wenn sich behördliche übergreifende Informationsverteilungen auf eine nichtkontrollierbare Kommunikation, wie z. B. den Austausch über E-Mail, USB-Stick oder Webdienste stützen.

Im Mittelpunkt steht die Anforderung nach regulierenden Maßnahmen, die nur unter Einbeziehung einer grundlegenden Konzeption, der *Datenhoheit*, effektiv gelöst werden kann. Die Konzeption impliziert ein digitales Hoheitsgebiet (Digital Territory – DT), als einen festgelegten, normierenden bzw. rechtlich verbindlichen Geltungs- und Anwendungsbereich, mit kontrollierten Grenzen zur Außenwelt.

Obwohl sich die digitale Entwicklung als Erweiterung sozialer Konzepte erklären lässt, wird diesem Thema bisher eine noch zu geringe technologische Aufmerksamkeit geschenkt. Aus der Perspektive der Rechtsprechung führte die Digitalisierung zu einem *Wandel der Staatlichkeit* [7, S. 25] und verweist auf das Problem, dass *neue Räume* eine begrenzte Staatlichkeit vorfinden, die zu Schwierigkeiten im Bereich der *Governanc*e führt.

Einen ersten Lösungsansatz für die Entwicklung hoheitlich normierender IT-Bereiche bietet das Konzept des *kooperativen Raums* Abb. 29.2. Das Konzept findet seine

Anwendung innerhalb digitaler Infrastrukturen auf Bundes-, Landes- und Kommunal-
ebene und ist für die Einbeziehung weiterer Ebenen vorbereitet. Der Begriff beschreibt aus
Technologiesicht eine kooperative Plattform, die sich administrativ und operativ in verschiedene Ebenen der Vertraulichkeit und Verantwortlichkeit als regulierendes Prozessele-
ment integriert. Der digitale *kooperative Raum* ist ein Instrument zur Gestaltung
bedarfsgerechter übergreifender Informationsprozesse.

Effektive Kooperationen müssen nicht zwangsläufig einem zentralen Strukturansatz
folgen. Auch bewährte, aus dem sozialen Kontext stammende föderative Verfahren und
Beziehungen, können sich unter Bedingung einer selbstbestimmten Anwendung *kooperativer Räume* auf den digitalen Bereich ausdehnen. Der eigenverantwortliche Betrieb
erzeugt eine vorher nicht gekannte Handlungsflexibilität.

Kooperationen werden geöffnet (z. B. auf Bundesebene in Abb. 29.2), die Handlungs-
bedingungen nach Prinzipien bekannter, aber auch neuer Muster der Zusammenarbeit
bestimmt und miteinander verknüpft. Im Ergebnis bilden *kooperative Räume* ein Instrument für das Design erweiterter Kommunikationen um ein gewolltes, aber geregeltes
Anschlusshandeln im Bereich externer Zuständigkeiten (z. B. auf Landes oder Kommunal-
ebene) zu bewirken.

Sind die Zielstellungen einmal erfüllt, schließen sich technisch *kooperative Räume* in
der Weise, wie die Ergebnisse sich dem Prinzip einer elektronischen Aktenmäßigkeit
unterziehen.

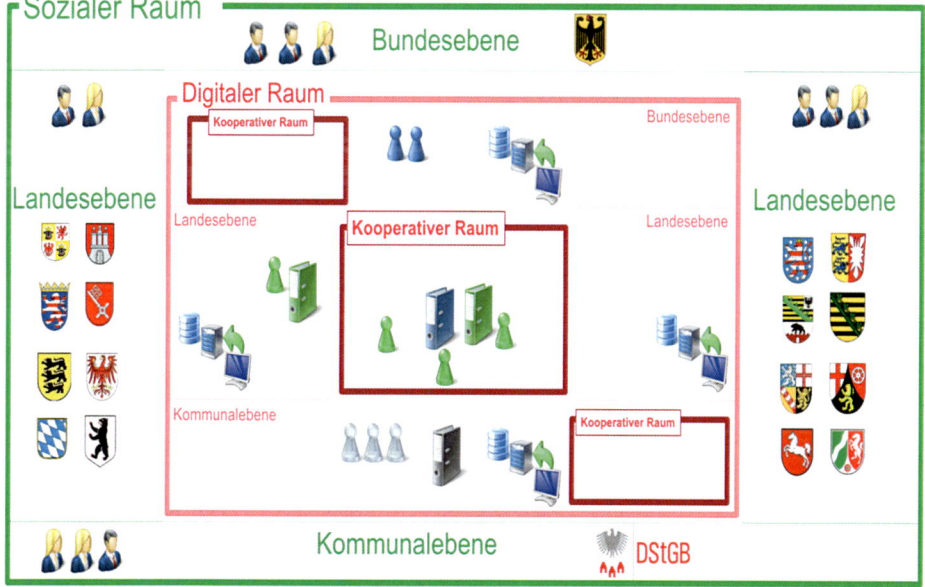

Abb. 29.2 Konzept kooperativer Räume

29.3.1   A. Konzept vertrauenswürdiger Kooperation

Ausgezeichnete und verifizierbare Qualitätseigenschaften begründen den *kooperativen Raum* als ein digitales gesichertes Hoheitsgebiet. Es handelt sich um einen Bereich zur Anwendung und Durchsetzung normierender Verfahren mit höchsten Ansprüchen an die Vertraulichkeit und die Zusicherung von Compliance-Grundsätzen.

Eine der wichtigen Grundlagen bildet das aus dem sozialen Kontext stammende Konzept einer Autorität (siehe Abb. 29.3). *Autoritäten* als soziale Struktur geben Handlungsprinzipien vor, stellen Regeln auf und repräsentieren Herrschaftsbeziehungen über ihre Fähigkeit, diese verbindlich durchzusetzen und deren Einhaltung zu kontrollieren. Autoritäten schaffen Vertrauensgrundlagen und stehen in der Verantwortung für einen klar begrenzten Hoheitsbereich.

Das Eintreten in einen *kooperativen Raum* ist mit der Formulierung von Regeln verbunden. Die Übertragung von Prinzipien einer auf den *kooperativen Raum* hoheitlich wirkenden *digitalen Autorität* (siehe Abb. 29.4) schafft die notwendige Grundlage. Die Einführung einer *digitalen Autorität* qualifiziert den *kooperativen Raum* für Grundsätze einer vertrauenswürdigen digitalen Praxis.

Ein wesentlicher Grundsatz besteht in der Absicherung von Funktionen zur sicheren Bindung *digitaler Identitäten* an natürlich handelnde Personen (Benutzer-Entität). Die Sicherstellung vertrauenswürdiger Entitäten im Konzept vertrauenswürdiger Kooperation gewährleistet zurechenbare Handlungsmuster im Rahmen regulierter Verhaltensvorgaben.

Die Außenverhältnisse *kooperativer Räume* sind kontrolliert und orientieren sich an Regeln zur Steuerung zugelassener, qualifizierter und verifizierbarer Daten als

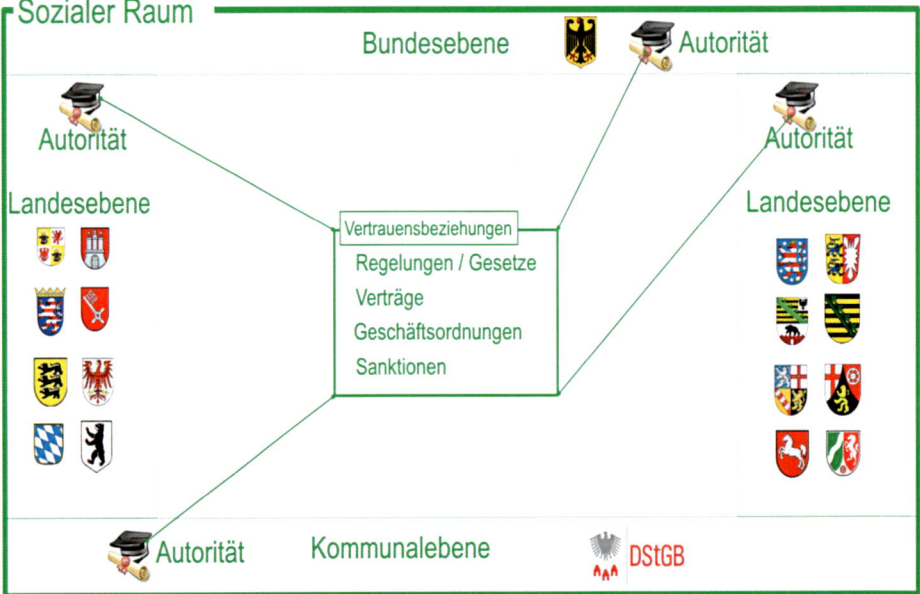

Abb. 29.3 Normierende soziale Prinzipien

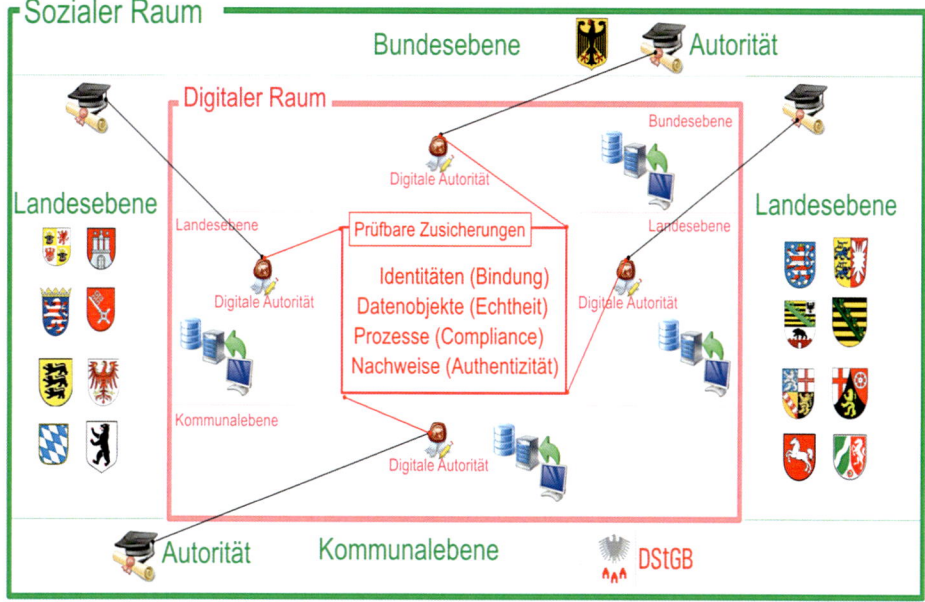

Abb. 29.4 Normierende digitale Prinzipien

Informationsträger. Im Mittelpunkt steht der Echtheitsnachweis, d. h. eine Qualifizierung von Informationsobjekten mit kryptografisch verknüpften *Datenlabel*. Das Prinzip findet gleichermaßen Anwendung innerhalb regulierender Funktionen für die Übernahme und Anwendung von Softwarekomponenten (digitale Komponenten-Entität), deren Echtheit als Qualitätssiegel maßgeblich die Ausführungssicherheit im *kooperativen Raum* bestimmt.

Das Konzept vertrauenswürdiger Entitäten in Bezug auf Softwarekomponenten ist eine Antwort auf die zunehmende Verwundbarkeit gegenwärtiger IT-Architekturen. Die regulierte operative Behandlung und Bewertung von IT-Ressourcen ist Teil eines holistischen Ansatzes für den Aufbau vertrauenswürdiger verteilter IT-Architekturen, [8, 9].

Im Bereich der Nachweisführung vollzieht sich die hoheitliche Kontrolle über den ausgeführten kooperativen Handlungsrahmen. Jede einzelne Aktivität verlangt einen nachweisbaren Bezug als gewollte und zurechenbare Entscheidung des betroffenen Akteurs und erlaubt eine belastbare *Compliance*-Bewertung. Der Nachweis qualifiziert sich als vertrauenswürdig über die *Authentizität* der bestätigenden Kontrollinstanz als Teil der *digitalen Autorität*.

29.3.2   B. Konzept vertraulicher Kooperation

Die Fähigkeit, *kooperative Räume* in separierte Vertraulichkeitszonen aufzuteilen, erlaubt die Umsetzung von Grundsätzen zur Geheimhaltung und die geregelte Informationsverteilung konform zu den Bestimmungen der Verschlusssachenanweisung (VSA) [10].

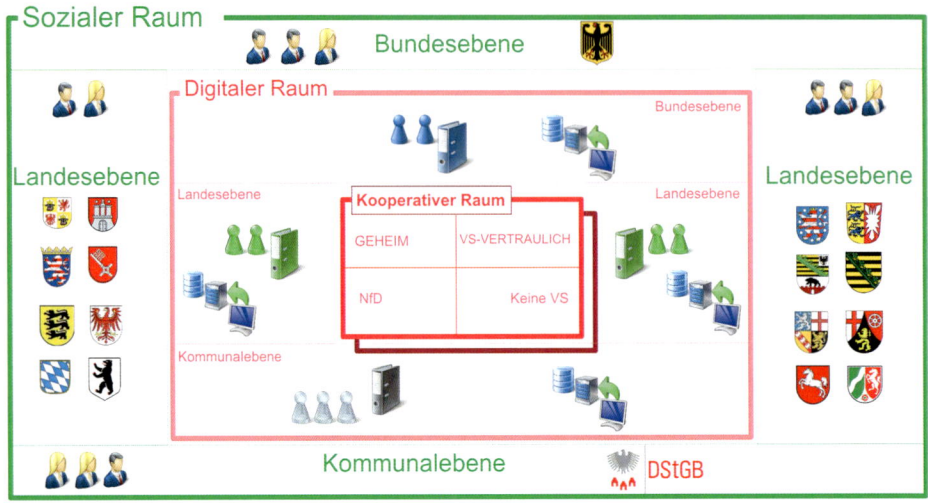

Abb. 29.5 Konzept regulierter Vertraulichkeit

Die Anwendung von einem *Geheimhaltungsgrad* für Daten legt ein Klassifikationskennzeichen fest und ist Ausdruck eines Schutzbedarfs der damit verbundenen Information. Die sichere Kennzeichnung von Informationen ist Ausgangspunkt einer nachweisgeführten Verwaltung vertraulicher Informationen im *kooperativen Raum* (siehe Abb. 29.5).

Pasternak et al. [1, S. 38] bezeichnet dieses Schutzprinzip von Informationen als *Information Rights Management* [11] und begründet die Notwendigkeit einer schutzbedarfsgerechten Informationsverarbeitung.

Der *kooperative Raum* beschreibt ein Hoheitsgebiet und qualifiziert sich als Sicherheitsdomäne für ein festgelegtes maximales Vertraulichkeitsniveau. Ein strenges Separierungskonzept von Informationsbereichen bestimmt die notwendige Sicherheitsarchitektur, um trotz sehr hoher Vertraulichkeitsanforderungen notwendige kooperative Fähigkeiten steuern zu können.

Der Zu- und Abfluss und die Nutzung klassifizierter Informationen im *kooperativen Raum* sind vollständig kontrolliert. Die Bestandsverwaltung setzt Grundprinzipien der elektronischen Registrierung um – immer in Verbindung mit einer transaktionsorientierten kryptografischen Audit-Trail-Chaining-Technologie zur Nachweisführung und Dokumentation. Bei Wahrung der Vertraulichkeit ist ein schnelles Auffinden von Informationen im registrierten Bestand möglich. Jede Information enthält Nachweise darüber, welche Verarbeitungs- und Verwaltungsschritte damit ausgeführt wurden.

Zugangspunkte für den *kooperativen Raum* sind Arbeitsplatzsysteme mit kryptografischen Fähigkeiten [12], die eingehende Informationen unmittelbar benutzerbezogen verschlüsseln. Die Sicherheitseigenschaften der Arbeitsplätze richten sich nach dem maximalen Geheimhaltungsgrad und stehen mit Zulassungen des BSI[2] abgestuft,

---

[2] Bundesamt für Sicherheit in der Informationstechnik.

beginnend mit *Nicht-VS* über *NfD* bis zu *GEHEIM*, zur Verfügung. Die Zugangswege zwischen Arbeitsplatz und *kooperativem Raum* sind gemäß dem Schutzbedarf über regulierte verschlüsselte Sicherheitsverbindungen [9] abgesichert.

Akteure, die einen *kooperativen Raum* beitreten können, besitzen *kryptografische Credentials*[3] zum sicheren Nachweis ihrer Identität und für die nutzerbezogene Verschlüsselung. Das Prinzip *Kenntnis nur, wenn nötig* (Need-to-Know – NTK) umfasst einen zweistufigen Sicherheitsprozess für die Bereitstellung notwendiger kryptografischer Schlüssel.

In einem ersten Schritt (*grant NTK*) wird der Schlüssel zur Entschlüsselung der Metadaten übergeben. Der betreffende Akteur entscheidet auf Grundlage der Beschreibungsinformationen, ob er sich mit dem eigentlichen *geheimen* Inhalt belasten möchte. Die Kenntnisnahme einer vertraulichen Information repräsentiert sich über den Besitz des zweiten Schlüssels, den kryptografischen Schlüssel zur Entschlüsselung der vertraulichen Information. Das Verfahren für die Schlüsselübergabe fordert eine nicht-umgehbare Willensbekundung[4] des Akteurs (*accept NTK*) und sichert die *Nicht-Abstreitbarkeit* seiner bewussten Kenntnisnahme.

29.4 Schutz der E-Akten

Behördliche Schriftgutverwaltung und Verfahren zur Geheimhaltung (Verschlusssachen) haben sich historisch unabhängig voneinander entwickelt. Mit dem Einzug elektronischer Aktensysteme (e-Akte) verlagert sich der Geltungsbereich behördlicher Verwaltungskonzepte [13] und Geschäftsordnungen noch stärker in den digitalen Bereich. Anwachsende Kommunikations- und Austauschbeziehungen führen zu vielschichtigen Anwendungsszenarien, die eine teilweise oder vollständige vertrauliche Behandlung nach den Grundsätzen der VSA [10] verlangen. Der *kooperative Raum* bietet die Möglichkeit, dass die vorher differenziert behandelten Verwaltungskonzepte über die e-Akte-Fachebene komplementär zusammenwirken.

Das Modell einer e-Akte-Integration mit einem vertraulichen *kooperativen Raum* zeigt Abb. 29.6. Das Integrationskonzept stellt Schnittstellen bereit, um klassifizierte Schriftstücke oder Vorgänge in den *kooperativen Raum* zu überführen und im Bestand als Verschlusssache (Datenlabel) zu kennzeichnen. Die Trennung zwischen klassifizierten und nicht-klassifizierten e-Akte-Inhalten ermöglicht eine separierte Behandlung von Schriftstücken. Während nicht-klassifizierte Schriftstücke den Prinzipien behördlicher Schriftgutverwaltung folgen, unterliegen klassifizierte Schriftstücke den Vorschriften der VSA.

Für Verteilungs- und Verwaltungsaufgaben mit klassifizierten Informationen erfüllt der *kooperative Raum* allein die Anforderungen an die Vertraulichkeit und Nachweisführung.

---

[3] Gespeichert auf einer Smartcard oder USB Security-Token.

[4] Unter Anwendung einer elektronischen Signatur.

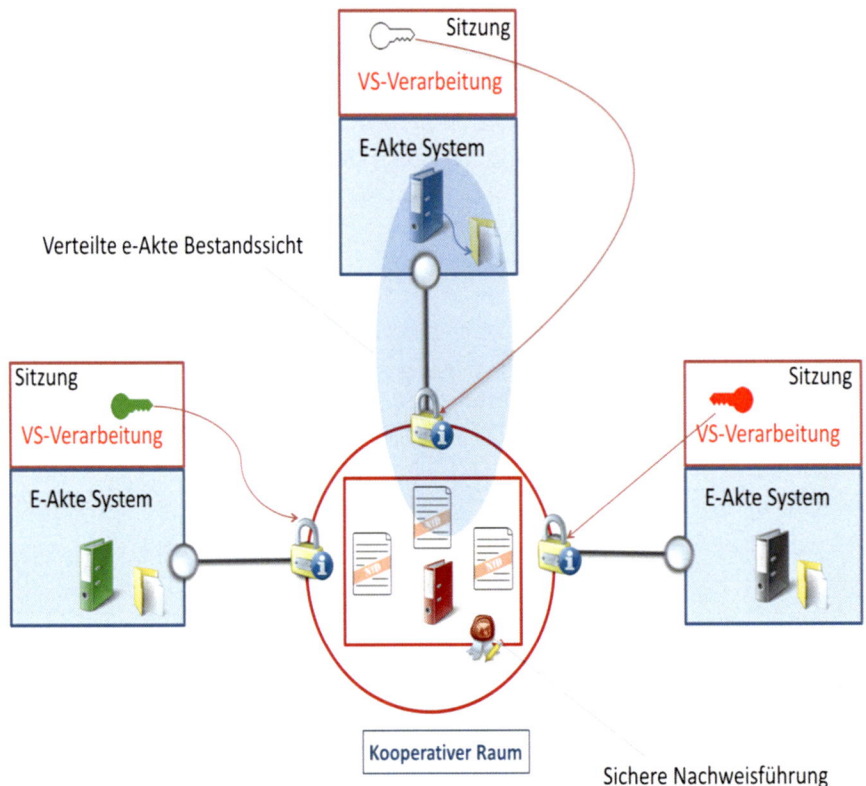

Abb. 29.6 Verteilte e-Akte mit VS-Schriftgut

Sämtliche Inhalte von e-Akte-Schriftstücken und der dazugehörigen Metadaten sind verschlüsselt. Administrative Rollen besitzen ebenfalls keine Zugriffsrechte.

Für den Zweck der Verarbeitung vertraulicher Inhalte stehen separierte Verarbeitungssitzungen (*VS Verarbeitung*) zur Verfügung. Entkoppelte Sitzungen sichern die Nachweisführung über Operationen, die im *kooperativen Raum* zur Anwendung kommen, und erzwingen die Informationsverteilung nur in diesem Bereich, denn es bestehen keine Verbindungen zu anderen Netzen. Akteure mit einem Need-to-Know sind im Besitz des entsprechenden Dokumentenschlüssels und können kryptografisch autorisierte Inhalte öffnen und diese vollständig separiert von nicht-klassifizierten Informationen verarbeiten.

Solange sich eine Information im Zustand *klassifiziert* befindet, erfolgt die Verarbeitung und Verteilung im *kooperativen Raum*. Eine übergreifende Verteilung zwischen verschiedenen *kooperativen Räumen* ist möglich. Eine Einstufung als *Nicht-VS* erlaubt die Rückführung der Informationen in einen e-Akte-Bestand für nicht-klassifizierter Schriftstücke.

29.5 Ausblick

Der Beitrag unterbreitet mit dem Konzept *kooperativer Raum* einen Architekturvorschlag, um flexibel spezifische Formen digitaler Zusammenarbeit gestalten zu können. Flexibel steht für effektive und einfache Planung und Ausführung selbstbestimmter Kooperationen, unabhängig von digitalen strukturellen Besonderheiten.

Das vorgestellte Prinzip einer bedarfsgerechten und sicheren Kooperation ist nicht allein auf behördliche Interessen oder dem Geheimschutz zugeschnitten. Es bildet ein allgemeines vertrauenswürdiges Prozessparadigma, das auch in Kommunikationskonzepten der Industrie, in Forschung und Gesundheitswesen eine Bedeutung erlangen kann.

Der *kooperative Raum* beschreibt einen ganzheitlichen Ansatz eines regulierten digitalen Hoheitsbereiches. Die Fähigkeit, regulierend Daten zu qualifizieren, Handlungsmuster durchzusetzen und vertrauenswürdig nachzuweisen, erfüllen für moderne digitale Prozesse Rahmenbedingungen zur Sicherstellung einer hohen Vertraulichkeit und einer verifizierbaren Governance im Umgang mit sensitiven Daten.

Die Struktur und der regulierende Charakter setzen hinreichende Bedingungen, um auch datenschutzrechtliche Interessen in die Betrachtung aufzunehmen. Die Aufrechterhaltung von Vertraulichkeitsansprüchen allein erfüllt noch nicht den Anspruch, die Persönlichkeitsrechte betroffener Akteure nachvollziehbar zu berücksichtigen, deren Daten in Verfahren der Informationsverteilung und Zusammenarbeit eingebunden sind. Die Konzepte einer *digitalen Autorität* und einer *Willensbekundung* bilden z. B. regulierende Kernelemente in der neuen EU-Datenschutz-Verordnung [14].

Das Plattformdesign für einen *kooperativen Raum*, die Methoden zur Implementierung geforderter Zuverlässigkeit, Betriebs- und Sicherheitseigenschaften und die Verfahren zur Evaluierung gesetzter Sicherheitsziele, etablieren einen hohen Qualitätsstandard. Als infrastruktureller Grundbaustein steht ein technisches Potenzial zur Verfügung, um alternative geschlossene Verfahren zur Informationsverteilung aufzubauen, die sich einer Überwachung durch externe Dienstleister entziehen und vollständig auf die Bedürfnisse der Kommunikationspartner abgestimmt sind.

Für eine erfolgreiche Einführung und Anwendung der e-Akte-Verfahrensformen sind dringend Konzepte für die differenzierte Behandlung von Inhalten unterschiedlicher Klassifikationen zu berücksichtigen. Dazu gehören u. a. digitale Arbeitsplätze zur Absicherung differenzierter Sicherheitsniveaus.

Der Beitrag stellt nicht nur Forderungen nach angemessenen Sicherheitskonzepten für die e-Akte-Einführung, sondern zeigt strukturelle Wege für eine erfolgreiche Umsetzung dieser strategischen Ziele. Die vorgestellten Grundkonzepte sind den Planungen aktueller Konsolidierungsziele vorzustellen und in die architekturelle Bewertung einzubeziehen.

Literatur

1. T. Pasternak, "Information Rights Management – zentralisierter Schutz der Information," In: Jahrbuch innovativer Staat 2017. S. 38–39., 2017. [Online]. Available: http://www.cassini.de/fileadmin/user_upload/Pasternak_Cassini.pdf
2. Der Beauftragte der Bundesregierung für Informationstechnik. "Projekt ït-konsolidierung bund". [Online]. Available: http://www.cio.bund.de/Web/DE/Innovative-Vorhaben/IT-Konsolidierung%20Bund/it_konsolidierung_bund_node.html
3. Der Beauftragte der Bundesregierung für Informationstechnik. "Bündelung der it-beschaffung". [Online]. Available: http://www.cio.bund.de/Web/DE/IT-Beschaffung/Buendelung-der-IT-Beschaffung/buendelung_der_it_beschaffung_node.html
4. Der Beauftragte der Bundesregierung für Informationstechnik. "Netze des Bundes". [Online]. Available: http://www.cio.bund.de/Web/DE/Innovative-Vorhaben/Netze-des-Bundes/netze_des_bundes_node.html
5. W. Hoffmann-Riem, Innovation Und Recht – Recht Und Innovation:Recht Im Ensemble Seiner Kontexte (German Edition). Mohr Siebeck, 5 2016.
6. "Zahlreiche Sicherheitslücken im Netzwerk desBundestags," Süddeutsche Zeitung, April 2017. [Online]. Available: http://www.sueddeutsche.de/digital/it-sicherheit-zahlreiche-sicherheitsluecken-im-netzwerk-des-bundestags-1.3462578
7. G. F. Schuppert, "The world of rules: Eine etwas andere vermessung der welt," 2015.
8. secunet AG. (2017) SINA Technologie (Sichere Inter-Netzwerk Architektur). [Online]. Available: https://www.secunet.com/de/themen-loesungen/sina/
9. secunet AG. (2017) SINA – Skalierbares Sicherheitsniveau für höchste Ansprüche. [Online]. Available: https://www.secunet.com/de/themen-loesungen/hochsicherheit/sina/
10. Bundesministerium des Innern, "Allgemeine verwaltungsvorschrift des bundesministeriums des innern zum materiellen und organisatorischen schutz von verschlusssachen (vs-anweisung – vsa) vom 31. märz 2006," 2006.
11. "Information Rights Management – Begriffsbestimmung," 2017. [Online]. Available: https://de.wikipedia.org/wiki/Information_Rights_Management
12. secunet AG. (2017) Sina workstation. [Online]. Available: https://www.secunet.com/de/themen-loesungen/hochsicherheit/sina/sina-workstation/
13. Bundesministerium des Innern, "Organisationskonzept elektronische Verwaltungsarbeit," 2017. [Online]. Available: http://www.verwaltung-innovativ.de/DE/E_Government/orgkonzept_everwaltung/orgkonzept_everwaltung_artikel.html
14. "Regulation (EU) 2016/679 of the European Parliament and of the Council (General Data Protection Regulation)," Official Journal of the European Union, April 2016. [Online]. Available: http://eur-lex.europa.eu/legal-content/EN/TXT/?uri=CELEX:32016R0679

Mehr Cyber-Sicherheit geht uns alle an

Wolfgang Schwabl

Zusammenfassung

Rasch denkt man an Science-Fiction-Filme, Roboter und Computer, die allgegenwärtig erscheinen, sowie an Bösewichte, die listig und gewaltsam ihre Macht ausbreiten und alles kontrollieren wollen. Diese großteils der Fantasie entsprungenen Geschichten dienen vor allem der Unterhaltung, in der Realität sieht die Welt zwar viel nüchterner, aber nicht einfacher aus. Wenn Fachleute vom Begriff „Cyber" reden, dann meinen sie eine Vielzahl von informationsverarbeitenden Maschinen, die untereinander direkt oder indirekt kommunizieren können. In diesem Artikel werde die Cyber-Herausforderungen sowie Cyber-Sicherheit bei A1 und Konsument dargestellt.

30.1 Die Cyber-Herausforderung

Fragen

Was ist „Cyber"?

Cyber bedeutet das Zusammenwirken von IKT (IKT = Informations- und Kommunikationstechnologien) Systemen in Netzwerken, wobei meistens das Internet damit gemeint ist. Aber auch andere digitale Netzwerktechniken gehören dazu, wie z. B. SCADA-Systeme für die Prozessautomation in der Industrie, CAN-Bus-Systeme in der KFZ-Technik, Mobilfunkstandards unterschiedlicher Generationen (GSM, UMTS, LTE), SS7-Signalierung für Steuerbefehle in internationalen Telekommunikations-Netzwerken, WiFi-Netze,

W. Schwabl (✉)
A1 Telekom Austria, Wien, Österreich
E-Mail: wolfgang.schwabl@a1telekom.at

© Springer Fachmedien Wiesbaden GmbH, ein Teil von Springer Nature 2018
M. Bartsch, S. Frey (Hrsg.), *Cybersecurity Best Practices*,
https://doi.org/10.1007/978-3-658-21655-9_30

die Datenübertragung bei Bezahlautomaten oder die Datenübertragung bei unterschiedlichen Sperrsystemen (z. B. in Hotels). Einfacher gesagt: jede Elektronik, die Daten verarbeitet und jede Technologie, die Daten überträgt, gehört zum Cyber-Raum. Somit drückt der Begriff „Cyber" auch eine enorme Komplexität aus, die durch die technischen und wirtschaftlichen Entwicklungen geprägt ist. Die vielen Netze, die untereinander in Wirkung treten können, werden auch Cyber-Raum genannt.

Fragen

Was ist ein System?

Unter System ist jede Art einer informationsverarbeitenden Elektronik zu verstehen, von der einfachen digital steuerbaren LED-Birne, dem Smart-TV über das Handy, den Laptop/PC bis hin zum Geldautomaten, den Webservern, zu Datenbanken und großen Routern und Kommunikationsnetzen.

▶ Die Begriffe „Datenschutz", „Datensicherheit", „Informationssicherheit" und „Cyber-Sicherheit" werden oft untereinander verwechselt, sie haben jedoch eine unterschiedliche Bedeutung.

„**Datenschutz**" ist eine gesetzliche Anforderung, die den richtigen und angemessenen Umgang mit personenbezogenen Daten regelt. Besondere Schwerpunkte sind das Führen eines Verarbeitungsregisters, eine konsequente Zweckbindung, das Einhalten einer Auftragskonformität, das Einholen von Zustimmungen, die Richtigstellung, die Löschung und die Meldepflicht bei Schutzverletzungen.

Die Aufgabe der „**Datensicherheit**" ist es, technische Mechanismen anzuwenden, um Daten und Computer zu schützen. Dazu gehören z. B. Implementieren von Zugriffskonzepten, -autorisierungen, -aufzeichnungen, deren Kontrolle der zweckgemäßen Anwendung sowie regelmäßige Backups und Computerwartungen.

Unter „**Informationssicherheit**" verstehen wir einen ganzheitlichen und korrekten Umgang mit Informationen.

Die Ziele der Informationssicherheit sind:

1) Vertraulichkeit. Sie bedeutet nicht nur den Schutz von personenbezogenen Daten, sondern auch den Schutz von Geschäfts- und Betriebsgeheimnissen.
2) Verfügbarkeit. D. h. Informationen sind verfügbar, werden verarbeitet und/oder bewirken etwas, wenn man das braucht.
3) Integrität. Integrität bedeutet, dass die ordnungsgemäße Erfassung, Verarbeitung, Übertragung, Speicherung und Löschung von Informationen systematisch mit den dafür vorgesehenen Methoden gewährleistet wird.

▶ Das Ziel der „Cyber-Sicherheit" ist die Anwendung von Informationssicherheit in großen Netzwerken, so einem, wie es eben der Cyber-Raum ist. Die Cyber-Sicherheit kann man kaum auf den eigenen Wirkungsraum begrenzen.

Die Problemfelder der Cyber-Sicherheit sind:

1. Die Komplexität der in die Systeme eingebrachten und benutzten Software ist so groß, dass keine Fehlerfreiheit garantiert werden kann.
2. Die Funktionalität der Systeme nimmt ständig zu. Es gibt immer mehr Möglichkeiten, von überall aus etwas mit dem Handy oder über das Internet zu steuern, sei es das Haustor zu öffnen, das Auto aufzusperren, das Licht abzudrehen, sein Heim zu überwachen, bestimmte Daten abzufragen, Geld zu überweisen, Genehmigungen zu erteilen oder Server aus der Ferne zu warten. Wegen der ständig wachsenden Zahl an neuen Funktionen und Möglichkeiten entsteht ein Sicherheitsrisiko. Haben wir alle Neben- und Wechselwirkungen im Griff?
3. Immer mehr digitale Netze werden ungewollt durch das Einbringen neuer Hard- oder Software überbrückt, sodass vermeintlich getrennte Netzwerke überraschend zusammengeschaltet sind. Sicherheitsannahmen der Netze, wie z. B. „die sind ja vollkommen getrennt", haben keine Gültigkeit mehr.
4. Kriminelle haben den Cyber-Raum für ihre Betrügereien, Erpressungen und andere kriminelle Handlungen längst entdeckt. Solange illegale Geldbeschaffung im Cyber-Raum möglich und ertragreich ist, nützen Kriminelle dies aus. Die Steigerungsraten bei Cyber Crime sind erschrecken. In Österreich wurden im Jahr 2016 insgesamt 13.103 Cyber-Straftaten angezeigt, das sind ca. 30,9 % mehr als im Vorjahr [1].
5. Finanzierung der Cyber-Sicherheit wird zur Glaubensfrage. Die Frage der Angemessenheit von Investitionen und Kosten für Cyber-Sicherheit wird zur Meinungsfrage, die so schwierig zu beantworten ist, weil die Erfahrungen in diesem Bereich sehr unterschiedlich sind.

30.2   Cyber-Sicherheit bei A1

Als größter Telekommunikationsnetzbetreiber und Internet Service Provider in Österreich sind wir uns unserer Verantwortung bewusst, da die Kunden sich darauf verlassen, dass unser Netz funktioniert. Wir unternehmen sehr viel, damit unser Netz auch sicher ist.

Sicherheit ist keine Mode-Frage, ob man den letzten Schrei einer immer ausgefeilteren Angriffstechnik mit dem super-modernen „Verteidige-Auch-Diesen-Angriff-Server" bereits abwehren kann. Würde man nur den Marktschreiern folgen, so wären die Rechenzentren vollgepfropft mit viel unnützem oder uneffektivem Zeug. So wie auch vieles andere in der IKT-Branche werden Produkte manchmal gehyped. Die Sicherheitsprodukte müssen in ein Gesamtkonzept passen und systematisch eingearbeitet werden, sodass ein Nutzen für Kunden und das Unternehmen vorhanden ist und alle Beteiligten mit den Systemen richtig umzugehen verstehen.

Bei A1 beruht die Cyber-Sicherheit auf 3 Säulen:

1. MitarbeiterInnen:

   Alle MitarbeiterInnen müssen beim Unterschreiben ihres Dienstvertrages ihren Straf-registerauszug vorlegen. Vorstände und Prokuristen müssen dies sogar quartalsweise tun. Manche Mitarbeiter, die in besonders sicherheitsrelevanten Bereichen (z. B. Wartung der kritischen Infrastruktur) arbeiten, werden einer polizeilichen und/oder militärischen Sicherheitsüberprüfung unterzogen.

   Alle Mitarbeiter bekommen Awareness-Trainings, damit sie die Systeme richtig bedienen können, die wesentlichen Vorschriften kennen, die Informationen mit den zur Verfügung stehenden Methoden richtig schützen, Fahrlässigkeit im Umgang mit Daten, Laptops und Handys vermeiden und gebräuchliche Tricks der Betrüger kennen.

2. Prozesse:

   Sicherheit ist kein Zustand, sondern ein Vorgang, an dem ständig zu arbeiten ist. Jede Sicherheitsanlage ist nur so gut wie ihre Wächter. Beide Aussagen gelten für alle Sicherheitssysteme. Deshalb werden vor Anschaffung und Inbetriebnahme von Sicherheitssystemen zunächst die beabsichtigte Wirkung und dazugehörigen Prozesse im Unternehmen geplant und trainiert. Die Prozesse haben deshalb eine zentrale Bedeutung für die Sicherheit. Die, die am meisten zur Cyber-Sicherheit beitragen, sind:

   a. Festlegen der Regeln und Richtlinien

      Die firmeninternen Sicherheitsrichtlinien sind auf mehreren Ebenen geregelt. Auf oberster Ebene sorgt eine „Information Security Policy" für einen einheitlichen Rahmen der Informationssicherheit in allen Konzernunternehmen der A1 Telekom Austria Gruppe. Diese Policy fordert generelle Sicherheitsprozesse von den Unternehmen, z. B.: Was ist beim Eintritt oder Austritt von Mitarbeitern zu beachten? Wie sind Informationen zu klassifizieren und wie wird damit richtig umgegangen? Wann braucht man ein Non-Disclosure-Agreement?

      Jedes Konzernunternehmen hat eigene, dem Land bzw. Markt angepasste Sicherheitsrichtlinien zu beschließen, die strenger als die Konzern-Vorgabe sein können, sie dürfen jedoch nicht schwächer sein. Der Konzern überprüft die Einhaltung der Vorgaben.

   b. Errichten eines Information Security Management Systems (ISMS)

      Darunter versteht man das professionelle Entscheiden über risiko-minimierende Maßnahmen bei erkannten Bedrohungen oder Mängeln der Informationssicherheit im eigenen unternehmerischen Wirkungsbereich. Das könnte man vergleichen mit dem Abarbeiten der Mangelliste bei Routine-Kontrollen eines Kraftfahrzeuges. Zwar ist klar, dass die für Betriebssicherheit oder Verkehrssicherheit erforderlichen Maßnahmen sofort erledigt werden müssen, aber wie ist es mit der ausgefallenen Glühbirne der Kofferraumbeleuchung oder dem Kratzer am Kotflügel? Aus ökonomischen Gründen wird man das Fahrzeug vielleicht doch nicht neu lackieren lassen. Die Zusammenhänge in Computersystemen sind wesentlich komplexer und oft ist es in IT-Systemen unklar, ob ein Problem nur ein „harmloser Rostfleck" oder eine

„die Tragfähigkeit gefährdende Durchrostung" ist. Es ist sehr schwierig, die richtige und ökonomisch vertretbare Entscheidung zu treffen. Wesentlich ist die Dokumentation über getroffene Entscheidungen.

Es gibt international genormte Standards für ISMS, nämlich ISO-27001. A1 erfüllt als erster Netzbetreiber Österreichs seit 2005 diesen Standard.

c. Zur Verfügung stellen eines Helpdesks

Der interne Helpdesk ist die zentrale Anlaufstelle, wo die Mitarbeiter die aufgetretenen IKT-Probleme melden, unabhängig davon ob es ein Problem mit dem Dienst-PC gibt oder ein Problem im Festnetz oder der Mobilfunkinfrastruktur auftritt. Der interne Helpdesk leitet das Problem zur richtigen Stelle im Unternehmen weiter.

d. Betrieb eines Service Operation Centers

Die Verfügbarkeit des Netzes ist der höchste Wert eines Telekommunikationsunternehmens. Deshalb wird das Netz und die gesamte, dazugehörige Infrastruktur rund um die Uhr überwacht. Sobald eine Störung auftritt, wird unverzüglich die dafür vorgesehene Entstörungsprozedur eingeleitet. Täglich treten mehrere Störungen auf, das ist in einem großen Netz normal. Die meisten Störungen sind harmlos, wie z. B. durch unachtsame Bautätigkeit abgerissene Leitungen, die meist nur eine geringe Auswirkung haben. Bei katastrophalen Unwettern jedoch kann das Kabelnetz schon erheblich beschädigt werden, deshalb gibt es das Krisen- und Katastrophen-Management.

e. Krisen- und Katastrophen-Management

Die Behebung von Störungen großen Ausmaßes erfordert eine professionelle Koordinierung. Um einen Überblick über die Lage zu bekommen, die Handlungsoptionen zu kennen, die Geschäftsleitung, die Kunden, die Mitarbeiter und die Öffentlichkeit zu informieren werden die notwendigen Informationen rasch beschafft und aufbereitet. Dafür sorgt ein Krisenstab, dessen Mitglieder den Kontakt mit den staatlichen Stellen, wie z. B. Bundesministerium für Inneres, Landeswarnzentralen etc. pflegen. So leistet A1 einen Beitrag zum österreichischen staatlichen Krisen- und Katastrophen-Management (SKKM).

f. Einrichten des A1 CERT

A1 hat ein eigenes Computer Emergency Response Team (CERT). Speziell geschulte Mitarbeiter sorgen dafür, dass die eigene Infrastruktur bei einem Cyber-Angriff verteidigt, Beweise gesichert, PCs und Server ggf. „entseucht" und wieder in einen sicheren Normalzustand zurückgeführt werden.

Das A1 CERT ist Mitglied im Austrian Trust Circle (ATC). Das Bundeskanzleramt betreut diesen Vertrauens-Verbund von staatlichen und privaten CERTs, der vor allem dem österreichischen Erfahrungsaustausch auf Techniker-Ebene dient.

Mitglieder des A1 CERTs nehmen regelmäßig an Cyberübungen teil.

g. Einberufen eines Security Steerings

In allen Fachbereichen des Unternehmens gibt es Mitarbeiter, die mit der Informationssicherheit besonders vertraut sind. Sie treffen sich regelmäßig, meist 1x pro Monat. Bei diesen „Security Steerings" werden aktuelle Themen der Sicherheit behandelt, über Vorkommnisse berichtet, neu aufgetretene oder erkannte Probleme angesprochen sowie Lösungsvarianten diskutiert und entschieden. Diese Steerings tragen wesentlich zur ständigen Verbesserung der Sicherheit bei.

h. Externe Mitarbeit für mehr Cyber-Sicherheit

A1 hält es für richtig, dass viele Cybergefahren nur gemeinsam mit anderen Organisationen und Institutionen zu bewältigen sind. Deshalb beteiligt sich A1 an verschiedenen Initiativen, wie z. B. der Cyber-Sicherheits-Plattform (CSP) des Bundeskanzleramtes (ich bin selbst Co-Leiter dieser Plattform), des Cyber-Sicherheitsforums im Kuratorium Sicheres Österreich, der Sektor-Risikoanalyse der Regulierungsbehörde RTR, und nimmt an einschlägigen Sicherheitsveranstaltungen in Österreich teil, wie z. B. der IKT-Sicherheitskonferenz des BMLVS.

Im internationalen Umfeld pflegt A1 einen Erfahrungsaustausch betreffend Sicherheit mit ETIS (the trusted community for telecom professionals) und der GSMA (GSM Association).

Vertrauensvoller Erfahrungsaustausch auf allen Ebenen ist von großer Bedeutung.

3. Technische Einrichtungen:

Sobald die Prozesse festgelegt sind, können technische Sicherheitseinrichtungen in Betrieb genommen werden. A1 hat viele technische Einrichtungen, jedoch nur einige wenige tragen wesentlich zur Sicherheit bei. Die folgende Liste erhebt keinen Anspruch auf Vollständigkeit, ich bin jedoch von ihrer Nützlichkeit überzeugt:

a. Antimalware

Ein Virenschutz, der ständig Updates erfährt, gehört zum Basisschutz. Wichtig ist es, unterschiedliche Produkte zum Einsatz zu bringen, d. h. PCs/Laptops haben einen anderen Schutz als die Proxy-Server für das dienstliche Surfen und diese haben wiederum einen anderen Schutz als z. B. die File-Server im Büro-Netzwerk. Der Sinn der Unterschiedlichkeit liegt in den erhöhten Verteidigungschancen, falls ein Computervirus eine bestimmte Schutzmaßnahme zu umgehen weiß.

b. Backup

Ein Backup, das nicht nur die Daten, sondern auch die Programme und Konfigurationen (Images) umfasst, wehrt zwar nicht unmittelbar einen Angriff ab, doch ist es sehr wertvoll bei der Schadensbeseitigung und Wiederherstellung eines integren Zustandes der IT bzw. des Netzwerkes.

c. Computerwartung

Nur ordnungsgemäß lizenzierte Software darf verwendet werden, Software muss jedoch regelmäßig gepatched werden. Bei A1 gibt es Patch-Management-Systeme, die für einen geordneten Rollout auf tausende PCs und Laptops sorgen.

Die ersten 3 Punkte sind die essenziellen Elemente eines technischen Basisschutzes, die jeden PC und jeden Server betreffen, egal ob diese privat verwendet werden oder Teil einer großen Organisation sind. Das ist das Cyber-Security-ABC. Es wäre grob fahrlässig, diese Punkte zu ignorieren.

d. Data Leakage Prevention (DLP)

DLP reduziert bei A1 das Risiko des Entwendens vertraulicher Daten durch illoyale Mitarbeiter. Auch wenn es nicht der ursprüngliche Anschaffungszweck war, so hat

DLP eine sehr nützliche Nebenwirkung. Bei der Abwehr von Ransomware haben wir die Erfahrung gemacht, dass DLP auch zur Cyberverteidigung beiträgt. Erstaunlich gut gelingt die Erkennung von versteckter Malware in betroffenen PCs, manchmal sogar besser als es die Antimalware-Lösung vermag.

e. AntiSPAM

Nach wie vor beginnen viele Cyber-Betrugsversuche mit SPAM-Methoden. Deshalb kommt einer effizienten SPAM-Abwehr besondere Bedeutung zu. Jeder Mitarbeiter bei A1 verfügt über persönlich konfigurierbare SPAM-Filter, sodass unerwünschte E-Mails seinen dienstlichen Posteingang und sein Diensthandy nicht erreichen.

f. Anti-CEO-Fraud

Oft bekommt A1 einen Betrugsversuch der CEO-Fraud Methode, d. h. mit gefälscher E-Mail im Namen des CEOs wird ein anderer Mitarbeiter dazu verführt einen Geldtransfer zu veranlassen. Unsere Mitarbeiter sind diesbezüglich geschult. Zusätzlich zur Bewusstseinsbildung haben wir folgende technische Maßnahme implementiert: Sämtliche E-Mails, die von außen kommen und den Namen eines Vorstandes tragen, werden zum A1 CERT umgelenkt. Bis jetzt waren fast alle umgelenkten E-Mails nur Betrugsversuche.

g. Anti DDoS

Die Abwehr erpresserischer DDoS-Angriffe gehört zu unserem Sicherheits-Standard. Nachdem A1 im Jänner/Februar 2016 den heftigsten DDoS-Angriff in der Geschichte des österreichischen Internets hatte (6 Tage, 150 unterschiedliche, stundenlange Angriffe, durchschnittliche Angriffslast rund 100 Gbit/s), wurden unsere Abwehrsysteme entsprechend hochgerüstet. Die derzeitige DDoS-Verteidigungskapazität ist höher als 300 Gbit/s. Diesen Schutz bieten wir auch unseren Großkunden an.

h. SIEM (Security Incident and Event Monitoring)

Tausende Systeme erzeugen Protokolldaten, auch Logfiles genannt. Darin wird festgehalten, was im System gerade passiert. Die meisten Ereignisse sind harmlos, manche jedoch können auf ein ernsthaftes Problem hinweisen. Das SIEM sammelt all diese Logfiles, korreliert diese und schlägt Alarm, wenn sich ein Sicherheitsproblem zeigt. Viel Erfahrung und Sachkenntnis ist notwendig, um das SIEM so abzustimmen, dass falsche Alarme unterdrückt und wichtige Alarme richtig hervorgehoben werden.

i. Redundanzen

Hohe Verfügbarkeit kann nur durch geplante und bereitgestellte Reserve-Systeme sprich Redundanzen erreicht werden. Das beginnt bei der Stromversorgung, geht über Mehrwegverbindung im Netzwerk und endet bei mehrfach redundanter, fehlertoleranter Hard- und Software. Wartung ohne Betriebsunterbrechung muss in großen Teilen möglich sein. Redundanz muss testbar sein (z. B. Stromausfalls-Test). Das Vertrauen in redundante Systeme kann man nur bestehen, wenn die Ausfallssicherheit durch echte Tests im laufenden Betrieb bestätigt wurde.

Natürlich hat A1 auch viele weitere, notwendige Systeme, wie z. B. zahlreiche Firewalls um die Netzwerkzonen abzuschotten, Intrusion Detection Systeme, Ticketsysteme, Datenbankmonitore, Benutzerverwaltungssysteme und viele weitere Systeme, die dem

Geschäftszweck (z. B.: Kundenportal, Einkauf, Verkauf, Verrechnung, Service) und der Betriebsführung dienen. Selbstverständlich werden auch diese Systeme von der Cyber-Sicherheit in ihrer alltäglichen Anwendung umfasst.

30.3 Cyber-Sicherheit für Konsumenten

Wieviel kann und soll der Staat, ein Betreiber, ein Dienstleister und jeder Konsument zu Cyber-Sicherheit beitragen? Diese Diskussion beschäftigt viele Gremien und Experten. Klarerweise hat der Staat für rechtliche Rahmenbedingungen zu sorgen. Die EU hat bereits eine neue Verordnung für den Datenschutz [2] und Richtlinien für die Netzwerksicherheit [3] erlassen. Es wäre sehr wünschenswert, wenn sich die EU dazu entschließen würde, nur noch sichere IKT-Systeme und -Dienste im digitalen Markt zuzulassen. Vorschläge für solche Minimum-Sicherheitsvorschriften gibt es bereits von der ENISA [4].

IKT-Betreiber und -Dienstleister haben ein besonderes Eigeninteresse, gegen Gefahren des Cyberraumes gewappnet zu sein. Das ist gut für deren Kunden, schützt aber die Kunden nicht vor Cyberkriminalität. Jeder Internetbenutzer ist den Gefahren des Internets ausgesetzt, so wie jeder Verkehrsteilnehmer den Gefahren des Straßenverkehrs ausgesetzt ist. Jeder Teilnehmer hat eine gewisse Eigenverantwortung und entscheidet selbst, wie viel Sicherheit er haben möchte. Unzählige Bewusstseins-Kampagnen und Broschüren weisen auf die Gefahren und fehlerhaftes Verhalten im Internet hin.

Fragen
Was kann nun jeder Einzelne tun, um noch mehr Cyber-Sicherheit für alle zu erreichen?

Die folgenden praktischen Tipps sollen dabei helfen.
ABCD des Computer- und Handybesitzers:

A) Antimalwareschutz ist unerlässlich
    Jeder Computer (d. h. PC/Laptop/Tablet/Handy) braucht eine Schutzsoftware gegen schädliche Programme. Jedes Qualitätsprodukt ist empfehlenswert, Gratis-Angebote sind eher zu vermeiden, insbesondere, wenn unklar ist, wie der Anbieter einen fortwährenden Support dafür leistet und finanziert.

B) Backup
    Ein regelmäßiges Offline-Backup der Daten und Programme hilft nach einem Angriff enorm. Offline ist deshalb wichtig, weil eine Ransomware-Infektion auch alle Daten auf Netzwerklaufwerken beschädigen kann, egal ob es ein lokaler Server oder ein Cloud-Dienst ist. Ein einziger infizierter Computer reicht, um die Daten für alle berechtigten Teilnehmer am Server unbrauchbar zu machen. Programmbackups sind nützlich. Ich empfehle eine Sammlung von Installationssoftware samt Lizenzschlüssel, um einen vom Angriff beschädigten Computer neu aufzusetzen.

C) Computer/Handy regelmäßig warten

Wer kennt es nicht? Nach dem Einschalten oder beim Ausschalten braucht der Computer viele Minuten, um scheinbar unnötige Updates zu installieren. Lassen Sie ihren Computer diese Tätigkeit zu Ende führen. Das zu ignorieren oder fortwährend zu unterdrücken wäre grob fahrlässig! Mit der Selbstverständlichkeit eines Autobesitzers, sein Auto regelmäßig zu waschen, brauchen auch die eigenen Computer ihre Software-Pflege. Nur so wird gewährleistet, dass behebbare Schwachstellen im eigenen Computer und Handy auch tatsächlich beseitigt werden.

D) Delete

Apps, Programme und Daten, die nicht oder nur selten verwendet werden, empfehle ich zu löschen. Diese könnten ja bei Bedarf ohnedies rasch wieder installiert werden. Das vermeidet Gefahren und Schwachstellen, die die selten gebrauchte Software möglicherweise beinhaltet. Zusätzlich hält es den eigenen Computer und das Handy „schlank", wodurch er/es schneller reagiert.

30.3.1 Wie kann Digitalisierung zu mehr Cyber-Sicherheit führen?

Digitalisierung ist ein neuer Begriff für die Verarbeitung von elektronischen Informationen aus fast allen Bereichen unseres Lebens. Dank der Digitalisierung sind die elektronischen Informationen überprüfbar geworden. Es ist leichter geworden festzustellen, ob sie authentisch oder gefälscht sind.

• Richtige Webseite prüfen?
Woher weiß ein Internet-Benutzer, ob er auf der richtigen Webseite gelandet ist? Das ist eine Sorge, die beim Online-Banking angesichts der zahlreicher Phishing-Vorfälle berechtigt ist. Ein Schloss-Symbol im Browser zeigt eine verschlüsselte (sogenannte SSL-) Verbindung an. Mit einem einfachen Click auf das Schloss-Symbol lässt sich prüfen, ob das die richtige Webseite ist und für die gewünschte Webadresse auch ausgestellt wurde.
• Gute Verschlüsselung einer Webseite prüfen?
Wie gut ist tatsächlich die Verbindung mit einer Webseite verschlüsselt? Man muss kein Verschlüsselungsexperte sein, um das zu beantworten. Es gibt interessante, kostenlose Dienste im Web, ich empfehle nach „SSL Server Test" zu suchen.
• Ist eine E-Mail authentisch?
Besonders leicht und oft werden Absender von E-Mails gefälscht und mit SPAM-Methoden verschickt. Viele Cyberbetrugsarten beginnen mit einer gefälschten E-Mail. Deshalb ist es sehr nützlich, wenn der E-Mail-Absender auch eine digitale Bestätigung seiner Adresse mitschickt. Zwei Standards existieren dafür im Internet: S/MIME (für Anwender) und PGP (PGP = Pretty Good Privacy, eher für IT Experten). Mein Tipp lautet: Internet-Benutzer sollten sich ein S/MIME Zertifikat besorgen (es gibt viele Anbieter) und ihre E-Mails stets signiert versenden (Einstellung im E-Mail-Programm). So kann jeder Empfänger prüfen, ob die E-Mail tatsächlich von Ihnen stammt und der Inhalt unverfälscht ist.

E-Mails von Dienstleistern an ihre Kunden sollten ebenfalls immer mit S/MIME signiert sein.

- Wie unterschreibt man digital?

  Durch die e-Government Initiative von Österreich wird jeder in Österreich sesshafter Person eine kostenlose „Bürgerkarte" in elektronischer Form [5] angeboten, die zumeist als „Handy-Signatur" genutzt wird. Jeder Besitzer einer österreichischen Bürgerkarte kann digitale Dokumente im PDF-Format unterschreiben und seine elektronische Unterschrift ist rechtsgültig [6] in der EU. Um die digitale Unterschrift zu leisten, gibt es mehrere offizielle und kostenlose Onlinedienste[7].

- Wie überprüft man ein digital unterschriebenes Dokument?

  Bei einem Papierdokument, das händisch unterschrieben ist, wird das kompliziert. Banken benutzen für den Vergleich der vorliegenden Unterschrift ein Unterschriftsprobenblatt. Privatpersonen könnten einen behördlichen Ausweis des Unterzeichners für einen Vergleich heranziehen. Bei wichtigen Verträgen wird eine notariell beglaubigte Unterschrift benötigt. Bei einem Fax oder einem gescannten Dokument ist es praktisch unmöglich, die Authentizität des unterschriebenen Dokuments zu prüfen, es könnte genauso gut mit einem Foto-Editor zusammengestellt worden sein.

  Viel leichter ist es, digital unterschriebene Dokumente zu prüfen. Ich verwende dafür die offizielle Webseite http://www.signatur-pruefung.gv.at/, die mir nach dem Hochladen der zu prüfenden Datei sofort das Ergebnis präsentiert.

30.4 Abschliessende Worte

Es ist nicht einfach in einem Beitrag zu „Best Practice" den Bogen von Herausforderungen zu praktikablen Tipps zu spannen. Dennoch hoffe ich, mit diesem Artikel zu mehr Cyber-Sicherheit beigetragen zu haben, sei es durch Nachdenken über die Herausforderungen oder Anwendung der einen oder anderen Empfehlung. Ich hoffe, dass der geneigte Leser etwas Brauchbares diesem Artikel zu entnehmen vermag und stehe gerne für Fragen zur Verfügung.

Literatur

1. „Sicherheit 2016 – Kriminalitätsentwicklung in Österreich", Bundeskriminalamt, Josef-Holaubek-Platz 1, 1090 Wien.
2. Verordnung (EU) 2016/679 – Datenschutz Grundverordnung (DSGVO).
3. Richtlinie (EU) 2016/1148 – Netz- und Informationssystemsicherheit (NIS).
4. "Indispensable baseline security requirements for the procurement of secure ICT products and services", ENISA, Dec. 2016.
5. Siehe auch www.buergerkarte.at
6. Gemäß Verordnung (EU) Nr. 910/2014 – eIDAS-VO.
7. Siehe www.buergerkarte.at/pdf-signatur-handy.html

Tobias Glemser

Zusammenfassung

Eine spannende Frage ist und bleibt, warum Unternehmen für Cybersicherheit motiviert werden. Bei vielen Unternehmen ist Compliance eine große Triebfeder. Sie werden zum Beispiel durch gesetzliche Vorgaben gezwungen, sich an Standards zu halten. Für andere Unternehmen wiederum gelten Vorgaben ihrer Großkunden in der Lieferkette. Auch hier wird die Einhaltung spezifischer Standards meist erzwungen. Wie ist es jedoch bei Unternehmen, die keine konkreten Vorgaben haben? Diese haben häufig kein Informationssicherheitsmanagementsystem (ISMS) vorzuweisen. Sie kennen den Zustand ihrer Cybersicherheit nicht. Meist aufgeschreckt durch Presseberichte oder gar Ereignisse im eigenen Haus rufen diese Unternehmen und Organisationen bei einem Berater an. Häufig haben die Unternehmer oder deren IT-Leiter (ein IT-Sicherheitsbeauftragter oder gar Informationssicherheitsbeauftragter ist dort sehr selten zu finden) bereits von Penetrationstests gehört. Für die Fragestellung „wie sicher bin ich denn eigentlich?" ist ein Penetrationstest jedoch denkbar ungeeignet. Insbesondere bei Unternehmen, die über ihre Prozesse nicht Bescheid wissen. Alternativ wäre ein Audit nach zum Beispiel ISO 27001 oder gar BSI-Grundschutz denkbar. Allerdings würden diese Audits allein schon an fehlenden formalen Dokumenten scheitern. Eine Aussage zur Cyber-Sicherheit ist auch hier nicht von einem durchaus umfänglichen Projekt zu erwarten. Einen pragmatischen Ansatz für Unternehmen ohne definierte Sicherheitsprozesse nach einem spezifischen Standard bietet der „Cyber-Sicherheits-Check".

T. Glemser (✉)
secuvera, Gäufelden, Deutschland
E-Mail: tglemser@secuvera.de

© Springer Fachmedien Wiesbaden GmbH, ein Teil von Springer Nature 2018
M. Bartsch, S. Frey (Hrsg.), *Cybersecurity Best Practices*,
https://doi.org/10.1007/978-3-658-21655-9_31

31.1 Einleitung

Viele Unternehmen, die den Zustand ihrer Cybersicherheit nicht kennen holen sich Berater die einen Penetrationstest durchführen sollen. Ein Penetrationstest ist jedoch denkbar ungeeignet bei Unternehmen, die über ihre Prozesse nicht Bescheid wissen. Darüber hinaus ist ein Penetrationstest stets selektiv. Eine umfassende Berichterstattung über den Zustand der Cybersicherheit mithilfe von Penetrationstests, insbesondere in kleinen und mittelständischen Unternehmen bei gleichzeitiger Blindheit für Prozesse, ist daher nicht zu empfehlen. Alternativ wäre ein Audit nach zum Beispiel ISO 27001 oder gar BSI-Grundschutz denkbar. Allerdings würden diese Audits allein schon an fehlenden formalen Dokumenten scheitern. Eine Aussage zur Cyber-Sicherheit ist auch hier nicht von einem durchaus umfänglichen Projekt zu erwarten.

31.2 Entstehungsgeschichte

Der Leitfaden Cyber-Sicherheits-Check[1] ist vom ISACA Germany Chapter e.V. Ressort Facharbeit und Arbeitskreise (Fachgruppe Informationssicherheit) in Kooperation mit Experten des BSI entwickelt worden. Der Leitfaden wurde als Partnerbeitrag für die Allianz für Cyber-Sicherheit konzipiert und steht kostenfrei zum Download zur Verfügung. Erstmals vorgestellt wurde er auf dem Mitgliedertreffen des ISACA Germany Chapter im April 2014. Die entsprechende Fachgruppe tagt weiterhin regelmäßig und arbeitet an stetigen Verbesserungen des Cyber-Sicherheits-Checks. Mitglieder der Fachgruppe erarbeiten auch die Schulungen zum „Cyber Security Practitioner" (CSP). Im Rahmen dieser eintägigen Schulung können Experten für Cyber-Sicherheit ihre Kenntnisse unter Beweis stellen.

31.3 Üblicher Ablauf

Der Leitfaden stellt eine Methodik bereit, mit der ein Experte sowohl die Cyber-Exposition eines Unternehmens feststellen, als auch die Abwehrfähigkeit gegenüber Angriffen vor dem Hintergrund von Basis-Maßnahmen bewerten kann. Üblicherweise wird ein CSP beauftragt, einen solchen Check unabhängig durchzuführen.

Dennoch ist der Leitfaden auch für die interne Anwendung geeignet. Die meisten IT-Leiter in mittelständischen Unternehmen sind Allrounder und verfügen über jahrelange, vertiefte Kenntnisse vieler unterschiedlicher (Sicherheits-)Technologien und Anforderungen. Selbst wenn diese bei einigen Fragestellungen vielleicht zu kurz greifen, ist der Check in seiner Gesamtheit geeignet, bei einer Selbstprüfung das Bauchgefühl zu

---

[1] https://www.bsi.bund.de/SharedDocs/Downloads/DE/BSI/Publikationen/Broschueren/Leitfaden-Cyber-Sicherheits-Check.pdf?__blob=publicationFile

objektivieren und daraus geeignete Folgemaßnahmen abzuleiten. Dies können konkrete organisatorische oder technische Maßnahmen sein oder doch die Hinzuziehung eines CSP. Sofern die personellen Ressourcen intern bereitstehen, kann der Cyber-Sicherheits-Check daher auch rein intern durchgeführt werden. Weniger internen, dafür entsprechend externen Aufwand verursacht die Durchführung durch einen Berater.

31.4 Methodik

31.4.1 Verteidigungslinien

Die drei Verteidigungslinien sind Linie 1 Management, Linie 2 Risk Management und Linie 3 Internal Audit, die in Abb. 31.1 aufgezeigt werden.

31.4.1.1 Linie 1: Das Management

Völlig zu Recht steht das Management als erste Linie der Verteidigung im Fokus des Cyber-Sicherheits-Checks. Jeder Berater hat in der Vergangenheit Projekte nach kurzer oder in gar tragischen Fällen langer Zeit scheitern sehen, weil das Management am Ende doch nicht hinter einer stringenten Umsetzung einer Cyber-Sicherheitsstrategie gestanden hat.

In der Praxis werden Maßnahmen nicht durch das Management selbst umgesetzt. Für den Informationssicherheitsbeauftragten ist es daher wichtig, dass das Management hinter seinen Maßnahmen steht. Nur das schafft Akzeptanz bei den Mitarbeitern. Insbesondere, wenn auch einmal auf den ersten Blick unbequeme Maßnahmen anstehen.

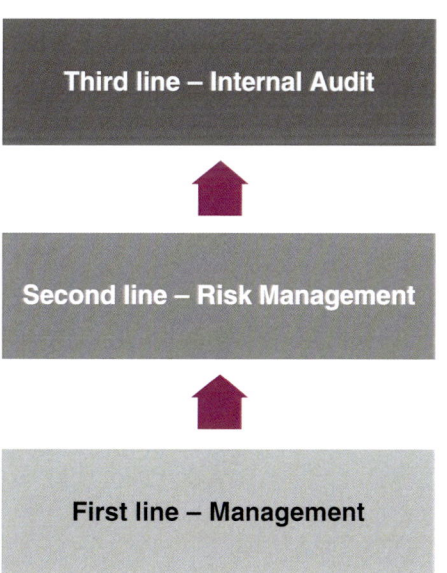

Abb. 31.1 Drei Verteidigungslinien. (Quelle: ISACA, Leitfaden Cyber-Sicherheits-Check)

In Ableitung gilt es, interne Kontrollen – z. B. des Rollenkonzepts – einzuführen. Des Weiteren sollten in regelmäßigen Abständen Funktionstests der wichtigen Anwendungen durchgeführt werden. Die korrekte Umsetzung der genannten Prozesse ist durch das Management zu überprüfen.

In der Praxis hapert es insbesondere bei der Durchführung der Kontrollmaßnahmen. Eine weitere lästige Aufgabe im Kalender eines Managers. Positiv ist, dass für alle Abläufe sowohl interne als auch externe Unterstützung möglich ist, sodass das Management am Ende meist nur mit Beschlussvorlagen konfrontiert wird. Es ist nicht empfehlenswert, dass das Management jede kleine Entscheidung selbst treffen muss. Dies ist für den Informationssicherheitsbeauftragten immer ein Spagat zwischen transparenter Informationspolitik und Mikro-Management durch den Vorgesetzten.

31.4.1.2 Linie 2: Das Risko-Management

Die nächste Verteidigungslinie fordert eine formale Risikountersuchung der Institution sowie der dazugehörigen kritischen Geschäftsprozesse. Zusätzlich kann es sinnvoll sein, eine Business Impact Analyse (BIA) durchzuführen. Die Entscheidungen der Leitungsebene werden bezüglich der Risikofaktoren durch das Risk Management untersucht. Das Ergebnis wird anschließend der Leitungsebene zur Verfügung gestellt, die über die Umsetzung der vorgeschlagenen Maßnahmen entscheidet.

31.4.1.3 Linie 3: Das interne Audit

Die dritte Verteidigungslinie fordert die Konformität mit den Cyber-Sicherheits-Vorgaben sowie die Durchführung einer formalen Risiko-Akzeptanz, welche in diesem Schritt durch die Durchführung des Checks erledigt wird. Des Weiteren sollten bei Sicherheitsvorfällen forensische Untersuchungen durchgeführt werden. Es ist zu prüfen, ob die internen Kontrollen an den richtigen Stellen durchgeführt werden und einen Mehrwert für die Erreichung der Unternehmensziele haben.

31.4.2 Die Phasen des Cyber-Sicherheits-Checks

Der Cyber-Sicherheits-Check durchläuft sechs Phasen. In der ersten Phase muss zunächst sichergestellt werden, dass der Auftrag durch die Leitungsebene genehmigt wird und die entsprechenden Personalressourcen zur Durchführung bereitgestellt werden.

Dann wird der Informationsverbund, sprich Anwendungsbereich, gegebenenfalls abgegrenzt. Sofern wesentliche IT-Systeme von der Betrachtung ausgenommen werden sollen, kann auch nur ein definierter Informationsteilverbund den Cyber-Sicherheits-Check durchlaufen. Um ein umfassendes Ergebnis zu erhalten, sollte jedoch versucht werden, die Gesamtheit des Unternehmens mit einzubeziehen.

Sind die Formalitäten einmal erledigt, kann im nächsten Schritt eine erste Risikoeinschätzung – diese wird „Cyber-Sicherheits-Exposition" genannt – durchgeführt werden. Ist eine Risikoeinschätzung im Unternehmen bereits erfolgt, können mit deren Hilfe der zeitliche Horizont, die Beurteilungstiefe und eine Auswahl an Stichproben festgelegt werden. Der Cyber-Sicherheits-Check empfiehlt, wie in den Verteidigungslinien beschrieben, eine regelmäßige Bestimmung der Cyber-Sicherheits-Exposition. Dies erfordert zwar einen initialen Aufwand, ist aber im Gegensatz zur Durchführung von Penetrationstests langfristig ressourcenschonender, ganz zu schweigen von den Kosteneinsparungen und dem nicht vorhandenen Risiko, physikalische Systeme für einen gewissen Zeitraum außer Betrieb zu setzen.

Die Exposition basiert auf den drei Grundwerten der IT-Sicherheit: Vertraulichkeit, Integrität und Verfügbarkeit. Für jeden Grundwert werden folgende Kriterien angesetzt, um die Exposition zu bestimmen:

- Wert der Daten & Prozesse
- Attraktivität für Angreifer
- Art der Angreifer (Hobbyisten, Forscher, Kleinkriminelle, professionelle Kriminelle, Hacktivisten, staatliche Akteure)
- Zielgerichtetheit des Angriffs (von Flächenangriff bis gezielter Angriff)
- Angriffe in der Vergangenheit

Nach der Risikoeinschätzung erfolgt die Dokumentensichtung. Die Dokumentensichtung dient dazu, einen Überblick über die vorhandenen Prozesse, das Unternehmen und die enthaltenen IT-Infrastrukturen zu schaffen. Dabei werden, sofern vorhanden, das IT-Rahmenkonzept, die Liste der kritischen Geschäftsprozesse, die Sicherheitsleitlinie sowie das Sicherheitskonzept inklusive Netzplan überprüft. Die Dokumentensichtung dient ebenfalls dazu, die Stichproben und den Schwerpunkt der Beurteilung zu identifizieren. Sollten die Dokumente noch nicht vorhanden sein, müssen die Informationen in Form von Gesprächen mit den relevanten Ansprechpartnern aus den zuvor identifizierten Bereichen eingeholt werden.

Im Gegensatz zu bereits angesprochenen anderen Standards müssen die Dokumente hierbei keine im Standard vorgesehenen Sprachkonstrukte bedienen. Sie müssen die Inhalte und Forderungen aus den Maßnahmen des Cyber-Sicherheits-Checks erfüllen.

In der darauffolgenden Phase muss auf Basis der gesammelten Informationen ein Ablaufplan für die Durchführung eines Workshops am Arbeitsplatz erstellt und gegebenenfalls unter den Mitarbeitern kommuniziert werden, damit die entsprechenden Personen bzw. deren Vertreter sich darauf einstellen können und die Ressourcen wie z. B. ein Besprechungsraum organisiert werden können.

Am Tag der Durchführung des Workshops bietet es sich an, zunächst ein Eröffnungsgespräch mit dem Management zu führen und die Hintergründe nochmals zu erläutern.

Während der Vor-Ort-Phase bzw. Durchführungsphase werden Interviews auf Basis der Maßnahmenziele des Cyber-Sicherheits-Checks mit den Ansprechpartnern der identifizierten Objekte geführt und die dazugehörigen IT-Systeme bzw. Dokumente eingesehen. Gegebenenfalls kann auch nur einer dieser Schritte durchgeführt werden. Stehen keine Ansprechpartner zur Verfügung bzw. kann der Prüfer die Fragen ohne die Hilfe

Dritter beantworten, werden die Maßnahmenziele durch den Prüfer selbst beurteilt. Die Wahl der Beurteilungsmethoden (Interview, Aktenanalyse, Datenanalyse, Fragebogen, Beobachtung oder Inaugenscheinnahme) obliegt dabei dem Prüfer. Dieser kann im Einzelfall auch mehrere Methoden zur Erfassung eines Sachverhalts kombinieren. Die erhaltenen Informationen sind für die Berichterstellung festzuhalten. Sowohl im Eröffnungs- als auch beim Abschlussgespräch sollte die Leitungsebene informiert werden. Beim Abschlussgespräch werden bereits erste Hinweise auf die Einschätzung des Sicherheitsniveaus und ggf. schwerwiegende Sicherheitsmängel (siehe folgender Abschnitt) benannt, welche zeitnah behoben werden sollten. Alternativ kann die Information zur Einschätzung des Sicherheitsniveaus natürlich auch im Nachgang durch Abgabe des Berichts geschehen.

Im letzten Schritt des Cyber-Sicherheits-Checks wird der Beurteilungsbericht erstellt. Dieser ist so zu erstellen, dass die während des Audits festgestellten Mängel reflektiert werden. Genaue Hinweise zur Erstellung des Beurteilungsberichts gibt es im Leitfaden Cyber-Sicherheits-Check Kap. 4.6 „Erstellung des Beurteilungsberichts". Auf den Internetseiten der Allianz für Cyber-Sicherheit ist weiterhin ein Muster für den Beurteilungsbericht[2] zum Download bereitgestellt. Der Beurteilungsbericht enthält grundsätzlich nur die festgestellten Mängel, kann demnach also auch als Mängelbericht interpretiert werden. Des Weiteren ist erwähnenswert, dass zu jedem Beurteilungsergebnis in dem Bericht ein Maßnahmenziel definiert werden sollte.

31.4.3 Ergebnis

Wie bei jeder Prüfung ist das Ergebnis auch ein Stück weit von der Expertise des jeweiligen Prüfers abhängig. Insofern sind leichte Unterschiede bei Bewertungen durchaus normal. Dennoch wurde bei der Erstellung des Leitfadens großer Wert darauf gelegt, möglichst vergleichbare Ergebnisse zu erhalten. Durch verbindliche Maßnahmenziele, welche anhand der Basismaßnahmen der Cyber-Sicherheit (siehe „Basismaßnahmen der Cyber-Sicherheit") erstellt wurden, soll ein Cyber-Sicherheits-Check stets eine konsistent hohe Qualität erzielen, selbst bei unterschiedlichen Prüfern. Die verbindlichen Maßnahmenziele sind im Leitfaden Cyber-Sicherheits-Check in Kap. 7 „Maßnahmenziele" hinterlegt. Abb. 31.2 stellt einen Auszug der verbindlichen Maßnahmenziele dar.

Die Maßnahmenziele sind immer nach dem Schema Maßnahmen, Basismaßnahmen und Referenzen in drei Spalten aufgebaut. Die Maßnahmen beschreiben dabei, um welches Maßnahmenziel es sich handelt.

Die Basismaßnahmen in Spalte zwei beschreiben die einzelnen Aspekte, um gegen Angriffe gewappnet zu sein. Dabei ist in oben genanntem Beispiel wichtig, dass sowohl

---

[2] https://www.allianz-fuer-cybersicherheit.de/ACS/DE/_downloads/materialien/schulung/muster.pdf?__blob=publicationFile.

Maßnahmen	Basismaßnahmen	Referenzen
B **Abwehr von Schadprogrammen** Im Sinne einer gestaffelten Verteidigung gegen Angriffe durch Schadprogramme (Viren, Würmer und Trojanische Pferde) muss die Abwehr über eine große Zahl von IT-Systemen einschließlich der Sicherheitsgateways verteilt werden. Der eigentliche Client als Arbeitsplatzsystem ist dabei die letzte Verteidigungslinie.	» Schutzsoftware gegen Schadprogramme kommt durchgängig zum Einsatz und wird fortlaufend aktuell gehalten. » Verteilt über die verschiedenen IT-Systeme kommen mehrere Lösungen unterschiedlicher Anbieter zum Einsatz (gestaffelte Verteidigung). » IT-Systeme ohne angemessenen Schutz vor Schadprogrammen sind in speziellen Netzsegmenten isoliert.	**BSI IT-GSK 13. Erg.-Lieferung:** B 1.6 **COBIT 5:** DSS05.01 **ISO/IEC 27001:2005:** A.10.4 **ISO/IEC 27001:2013:** A.12.2.1 **PCI DSS 3.0:** 5.1, 5.1.1, 5.1.2, 5.2, 5.3, 5.4

Abb. 31.2 Auszug verbindliche Maßnahmenziele. (Quelle: ISACA, Leitfaden Cyber-Sicherheits-Check)

die Anti-Viren-Patterns als auch die Schadsoftware aktuell gehalten werden. Außerdem sollte eine Staffelung der Virenschutzsoftware zum Einsatz kommen, sodass beispielsweise auf dem Proxy-Server, dem Mail-Gateway und dem Sicherheitsgateway Virenschutzsoftware von unterschiedlichen Herstellern zum Einsatz kommt. Sollten einzelne IT-Systeme nicht kompatibel mit einer Virenschutzsoftware sein, so sollten diese in einem separierten Netzsegment eingerichtet werden. Diese Maßnahmen sind stets konkret, praxisorientiert und meist ohne weitere Recherche verständlich.

Die Spalte Referenzen enthält mehrere Verweise auf einzelne Bereiche der Standards, in denen diese Maßnahmenziele ebenfalls vorhanden sind. Referenziert wird stets auf die IT-Grundschutzkataloge des Bundesamts für Sicherheit in der Informationstechnik (BSI IT-GSK), Cobit 5, ISO 27001 2005 und 2003 sowie den „Payment Card Industry Data Security Standard" (PCI DSS).

Der Leitfaden Cyber-Sicherheits-Checks bietet weiterhin Informationen in Form eines Bewertungsschemas, wie kritisch einzelne Sicherheitsmängel einzustufen sind. Dabei werden drei Kategorien (Sicherheitsempfehlung, Sicherheitsmangel und Schwerwiegender Sicherheitsmangel) ähnlich der Einstufung in einem Basissicherheitscheck entlang der Methodik des BSI-Grundschutzes definiert. Des Weiteren werden Informationen zum Aufbau und Inhalt des Beurteilungsberichts geliefert. Der Beurteilungsbericht besteht aus den folgenden Teilen.

31.4.3.1 Rahmendaten

Im ersten Teil werden Details des geprüften Informationsverbunds dokumentiert. Dabei wird zum Beispiel auch festgehalten, falls bestimmte IT-Systeme vom Cyber-Sicherheits-Check ausgeschlossen wurden.

31.4.3.2 Management-Summary

Das Management-Summary dient dazu, in komprimierter und verständlicher Form eine Zusammenfassung für die Leitungsebene zu erstellen. Sollte der Cyber-Sicherheits-Check durch Mitarbeiter mit Management-Funktionen durchgeführt werden, ist dieser Abschnitt als optional anzusehen. In der Management-Summary werden neben der Zusammenfassung die Cyber-Sicherheits-Exposition und eine Übersicht der Beurteilungsergebnisse festgehalten.

31.4.3.3 Detailbeurteilung

Im letzten Teil des Berichts werden die Maßnahmenziele erläutert, sowie die Ergebnisse zusammen mit der Bewertung und ggf. durchgeführten Stichproben dokumentiert. Letztlich werden noch die festgestellten Mängel zusammen mit der entsprechenden Maßnahmenempfehlung beschrieben.

Durch die formalen Aspekte, welche im Leitfaden Cyber-Security-Check dargestellt werden, ist außerdem der äußere Rahmen eines Beurteilungsberichts stets derselbe.

31.5   Praxis und Fazit

In der Praxis konnte der Cyber-Sicherheits-Check problemlos auch bei kleinen Unternehmen mit 20 Mitarbeitern angewendet werden. Es ist jedoch auch möglich den Check bei größeren Mittelständlern anzuwenden. Dies ist im Rahmen von Projekten mit einem noch einstelligen Aufwand sogar standortübergreifend grundsätzlich möglich.

Der Cyber-Sicherheits-Check stellt damit eine im Vergleich zu anderen Methoden äußerst kostengünstige, etablierte und tief in Technik und Prozesse Einblick nehmende Methodik dar. Insbesondere die Rückmeldung von Geschäftsführern und Vorständen war sehr positiv. Das Bauchgefühl, dass sowohl die Unternehmer als auch die IT-Leiter bzw. Administratoren zur Cyber-Resilienz haben, wird mit dem Cyber-Sicherheits-Check objektiviert.

Durch die regelmäßige Durchführung eines Cyber-Sicherheits-Checks können Unternehmen auch ohne ein formales Informationssicherheitsmanagementsystem den Reifegrad ihrer Cybersicherheit regelmäßig bewerten. Insbesondere die Praxisnähe der Maßnahmen wird von den IT-Leitern geschätzt.

IT-Sicherheit in Industrienetzen – IoT und IIoT

Sascha Herzog

Zusammenfassung

In Zeiten von Industrie 4.0, „Internet of Things (IoT)" und einer zunehmenden Internetvernetzung von Industriesystemen bieten sich natürlich für Hacker neue Möglichkeiten, Industrienetzwerke direkt aus dem Internet anzugreifen. Im Folgenden gehen wir jedoch davon aus, dass das Zielunternehmen seine kritischen Systeme gut gesichert und deshalb nicht direkt an das Internet angeschlossen hat. Da wir in unserer Tätigkeit schon viele Industrieunternehmen aus diversen Branchen (Automation, Energie, Fertigung, Chemische Industrie etc.) auf Sicherheitslücken in ihrer Unternehmensinfrastruktur untersucht haben, ist uns etwas aufgefallen: Die gleichen Angriffsmuster und Angriffsmöglichkeiten ergeben sich immer wieder, selbst, wenn das Unternehmen keine direkt aus dem Internet erreichbaren Industriesysteme besitzt. Die fast immer gleiche Angriffsmethodik wollen wir hier grob skizzieren. Die Auswirkungen solcher und ähnlich erfolgter Angriffe hängen natürlich stark von der kontrollierten Umgebung, dem Industriesektor und weiteren physischen Schutzmaßnahmen des Unternehmens ab. Sie können jedoch von der Zerstörung einzelner Maschinen über den Know-how-Diebstahl bis hin zur Destabilisierung von ganzen Ländern durch die Zerstörung kritischer Infrastrukturen führen. Das gefährliche bei Industriesteuerungen ist grundsätzlich, dass durch mechanische Komponenten immer auch Menschen zu Schaden kommen können.

S. Herzog (✉)
NSIDE ATTACK LOGIC GmbH, München, Deutschland
E-Mail: sh@nsideattacklogic.de

© Springer Fachmedien Wiesbaden GmbH, ein Teil von Springer Nature 2018　　　471
M. Bartsch, S. Frey (Hrsg.), *Cybersecurity Best Practices*,
https://doi.org/10.1007/978-3-658-21655-9_32

32.1   Wie gehen Angreifer und auch unsere Analysten (als erlaubte Angreifer) vor?

Das Vorgehen der Angreifer folgt oft einem generischen Muster. Abb. 32.1 zeigt die wichtigsten Schritte des Angriffs dar.

▶ **Schritte des Angriffs (siehe Abb. 32.1):**
   Schritt 1 – Taktische Informationsbeschaffung
   Schritt 2 – Auswahl des geeigneten Angriffspfads
   Schritt 3 – Planung und Vorbereitung des Angriffs
   Schritt 4 – Einbruch ins Office-Netzwerk
   Schritt 5 – Kontrollübernahme des Office-Netzwerks
   Schritt 6 – Identifikation von Schnittstellen zum Industrie- oder Produktionsnetzwerk
   Schritt 7 – Einbruch ins Industrienetz über Schnittstellensysteme
   (Schritt 8 – Sabotage und Spionage)

Da jeder der aufgeführten Schritte für sich alleine genommen ganze Bücherregale füllen könnte, möchte ich mich in diesem Artikel auf die Schritte 6 und 7, die Identifikation und Kompromittierung von Schnittstellensystemen konzentrieren.

Anhand der zahllosen öffentlich verfügbaren Informationen und technischen Möglichkeiten, die sich einem versierten Angreifer heutzutage bieten, ist der Einbruch auf mindestens einem Mitarbeiter-PC oder einem IoT (Internet of Things) Gerät im Zielunternehmen so gut wie sicher. Dieses Gerät kann dann als Basisstation für weitere Vorstöße des Hackers in das Office-Netzwerk und zu guter Letzt auch in das Industrienetz fungieren (siehe Abb. 32.2). Meistens wird hier mit Malware gearbeitet, die mittels gezielter Phishing-Angriffe (Spear-Phishing) auf einzelne Personen eingeschleust wird. Dazu beschäftigt sich der Hacker im Vorfeld länger mit der Zielperson und erstellt ein psychologisches Profil, um die Erfolgsaussichten des Angriffs zu verbessern.

Ein Beispiel

Die Personalabteilung eines Industrieunternehmens im Energiesektor hat eine Stellenbeschreibung für einen „Field-Engineer" auf ihrem Jobportal geschalten. Ein Angreifer sucht mit einer einfachen Google-Suche nach einem perfekt wirkenden Lebenslauf (siehe Abb. 32.3). Er kopiert und passt den echten Lebenslauf, ein Word-Dokument, an und integriert einen eigenen, schwer zu entdeckenden Trojaner in das Dokument, welches er im Anschluss direkt an die Personalabteilung verschickt. Als der Mitarbeiter des Industrieunternehmens das Dokument öffnet, wird der Trojaner im Hintergrund aktiviert und erlaubt dem Angreifer aus dem Internet die Kontrolle des Mitarbeiter-PCs.

Nach der Kontrollübernahme des Mitarbeiter-PCs identifiziert der Angreifer Möglichkeiten, das Office-Netzwerk auf Grund von Fehlkonfigurationen einzelner Systeme oder von vorhandenen Softwareschwachstellen vollständig unter seine Kontrolle zu bekommen. Dieser Schritt gelingt uns in simulierten Angriffen bei Kunden (leider) in über 90 % aller Fälle. Dieses

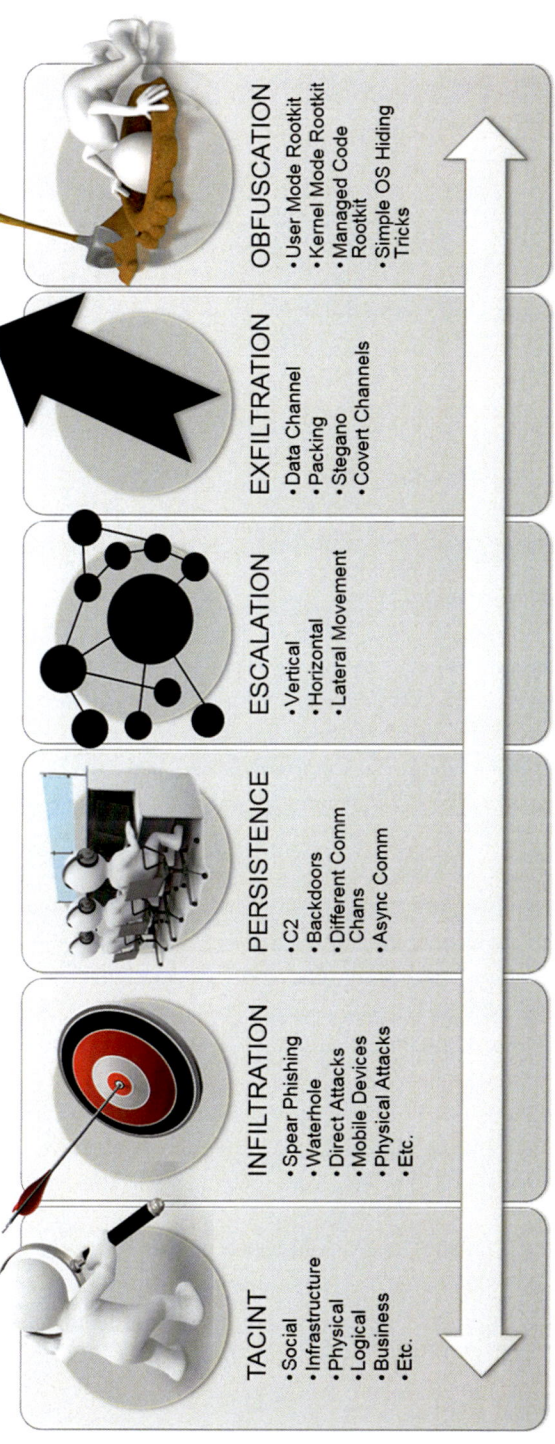

Abb. 32.1 Schritte des Angriffs

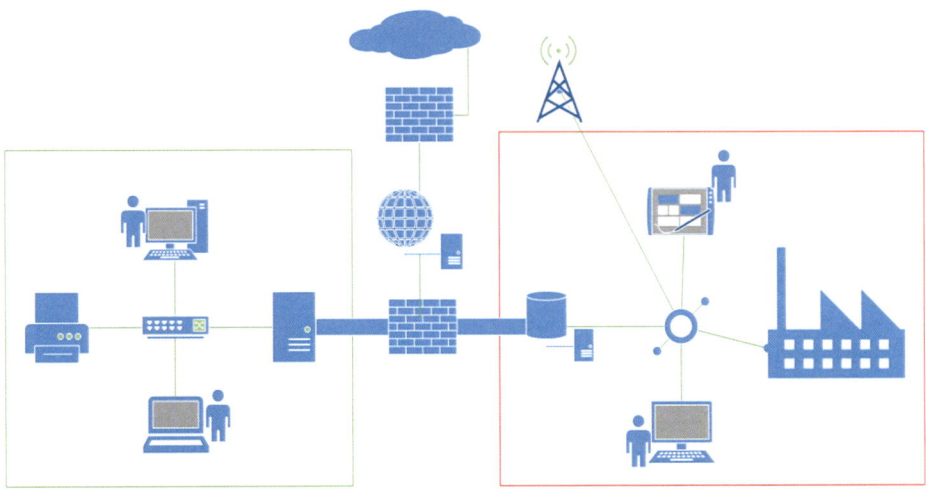

Abb. 32.2 Benachbartes Office- und Industrienetz – Theoretische Trennung durch Firewall

Abb. 32.3 Gezielte Google-Suchanfrage

Vorrücken dauert meist zwischen 1–5 Tage und wird als „Lateral Movement" bezeichnet. Eigentlich sollte dieser Umstand keine Gefahr für das Industrienetzwerk bedeuten, da, wie wir alle wissen, Industrienetzwerke komplett abgeschottet und getrennt zu nicht vertrauenswürdigen Netzwerken wie WLANs und Office-Netzwerken arbeiten, der sogenannte „Air Gap".

Leider entspricht dieses idealistische Bild, selbst in Unternehmen die zur kritischen Infrastruktur zählen, meistens nicht im geringsten der Realität (***Disclaimer: Wir können natürlich nur von Unternehmen berichten, die wir in unserer langjährigen Karriere selber getestet haben und Aussagen uns bekannter Spezialisten einbeziehen!***).

Es geht also sowohl beim Angriff als auch bei der Verteidigung aus unserer Sicht stets um Schnittstellen zu anderen Netzwerken! Wir suchen nach Systemen, die ein Bein im Office-Netzwerk (oder einem anderen unsicheren Netzwerk) und das andere in unserem eigentlichen Zielnetzwerk, dem Industrie-/Fertigungsnetz haben. In einigen Fällen tauchen die von uns identifizierten Systeme weder im Konzept, noch in den Netzwerktopologiezeichnungen auf und wurden deshalb bei vorangegangenen konzeptionellen Risikobetrachtungen übersehen.

Systeme mit zwei oder mehr aktiven Netzwerkschnittstellen zu finden ist sehr einfach für Angreifer, die in einem Microsoft-Netzwerk (Active Directory) die höchsten Benutzerrechte (Domain/Enterprise Admin) erreicht haben. Von uns oft identifizierte Systeme sind diverse Datenbanken (Warehouse-DB, Werkstück-DB etc.), MES-Systeme, SAP-Server, FTP-Server, Security-Produkte (wie Firewalls) und Workstations von Technikern (Administratoren, Ingenieuren, Operatoren).

Sind diese Systeme erst einmal identifiziert, ist es oft ein Leichtes diese als weiteren Sprungpunkt vom Office-Netzwerk in das Industrienetz zu verwenden, da diese Systeme ja schließlich auch vom „*Chef*" des Office-Netzwerks (Domain-Admin) verwaltet werden. Da der Angreifer diese Rechte erlangt hat, schaltet er sich über das neu ergatterte System nun eine Weiterleitung ins Industrienetz (siehe Abb. 32.4).

Der Rest wäre dann nur noch Formsache. Befindet sich ein Angreifer erst mal im Industrienetz, Fachkenntnisse vorausgesetzt, bieten sich ihm oft zahlreiche Möglichkeiten, die Maschinensteuerungen und Industrieanlagen zu übernehmen. Oftmals finden sich zahlreiche Schwachstellen in veralteten Betriebssystemen (WinXP etc.) sowie fehlenden oder schwachen Authentisierungsmechanismen (Zugang ohne Passwort, Klartextprotokolle, fehlender zweiter Faktor etc.) und Verschlüsselungen.

Wie die Übernahme von Industriesteuerungen und Industrierobotern stattfinden kann, zeigen wir auch exemplarisch in einzelnen Live-Hacks:

- CEBIT 2017.
- IKT Sicherheitskonferenz 2017 Villach, Österreich.
- SPS IPC Drives 2017.

Die Auswirkungen solcher und ähnlich erfolgter Angriffe hängen natürlich stark von der kontrollierten Umgebung, dem Industriesektor und weiteren physischen Schutzmaßnahmen des Unternehmens ab. Sie können jedoch von der Zerstörung einzelner Maschinen über den Know-how-Diebstahl bis hin zur Destabilisierung von ganzen Ländern durch die Zerstörung kritischer Infrastrukturen führen. Das gefährliche bei Industriesteuerungen ist grundsätzlich, dass durch mechanische Komponenten immer auch Menschen zu Schaden kommen können.

Abb. 32.4 Einbruch ins Industrienetz mittels Malware aus dem Office-Netzwerk

32.2   Mögliche Schutzmaßnahmen

Im Folgenden haben wir die aus unserer Sicht wichtigsten Möglichkeiten aufgelistet sich vor diesen Angriffen bestmöglich zu schützen, falls eine komplette physikalische Trennung der Netze („Air Gap") aus Unternehmenssicht nicht möglich ist:

- Schnittstellen auf ein Minimum reduzieren
- Funktionale Gruppen und Enklaven einrichten
- Regelmäßige Penetrationstests und Sicherheitsanalysen durchführen
- Grenzen der Enklaven schützen und überwachen
- Unidirektionaler Datenverkehr an Enklavengrenzen
- Produktionsnetze nicht an das Corporate AD koppeln
- Multifaktor-Authentisierung an Enklavengrenzen
- Verbot/Whitelisting von Wechselmedien wie USB-Sticks
- Sichere Fernwartungkonzepte (Opt-In)
- Endpoint Protection auf Systemen im Produktionsnetz
- Whitelistings von Anwendungen, Benutzern, IPs, Assets, Uhrzeiten etc.

Cyber Governance: Knowing and Doing What's Important for making Smart Cities resilient

33

Lars Minth

Abstract

CYBER GOVERNANCE should be regarded as the *implicit* steering level of all of the CYBER activities. It sets principles and legal baselines and enforces them, respectively, by the power of convincing through guidelines, standards, and procedures to be followed.

Since CYBER GOVERNANCE has its own scope and definition per industry or even organizations, it's up to you to declare accountability and responsibility for certain ICT problems.

We will have a look at the ingredients of a proper CYBER GOVERNANCE, and you get aware of traps and errors the author experienced in order to reach a working CYBER GOVERNANCE.

At the end we will have a look at the diesel engine of CYBER GOVERNANCE, the cyber security management system, which serves as the melting pot of all relevant information of CYBER.

33.1 Daring to Give Advice?

I have just two actually used accounts in today's social media channels where I learn, share, and discuss topics around security, including cyber issues.

In these discussions though, I can rarely feel a definition of CYBER which matches even a third of the discussing participants – worldwide. So, if all the participants are talking and recommending about cyber security, cyber warfare, reactive cyber measures, cyber

L. Minth (✉)
Quantusec, Heimenschwand, Switzerland
e-mail: l.minth@quantusec.com

© Springer Fachmedien Wiesbaden GmbH, ein Teil von Springer Nature 2018
M. Bartsch, S. Frey (Hrsg.), *Cybersecurity Best Practices*,
https://doi.org/10.1007/978-3-658-21655-9_33

threats, and a myriad of other cyber "things," finally the scope and definition of each of them are heavily dependent of the participants' country, culture, academic background, political influence, and even applied marketing techniques and personal aims to succeed as a well-paid consultant.

Therefore, every cyber expert may be correct in her/his own inertial system of cyber specialties but lacks sometimes the knowledge and background of the others. The result of these circumstances is an international discussion that seems to be very often controversial and lacks mostly "deep inspection" (not the one within A.I. these days) and empathy concerning opinions, recommendations, and scopes.

So if I search the Internet for CYBER, I get totally different directions and recommendations how to behave and where to spend my money in order to adhere to the requirements of my company's board (if I really know these requirements).

By the way, searching for CYBER GOVERNANCE gives me a total different result: very few sources are investigating into the steering of all these technical countermeasures.

Realizing and accepting the above, I gave up to search for the real definition and scope of CYBER and instead concentrated on understanding the *value chain of security* itself, sometimes also called "return of security investment" (ROSI).

These epiphanies in mind I nevertheless dare to give you, the reader of this book, some advice based on my experiences, failures, success stories, and hopes.

Due to the fact that I worked for 15 years until today in the world of CYBER serving more than 35 nations and their critical infrastructures plus additionally being disenchanted by reading so many guidelines from "cyber gurus," I feel honored to pass my experiences and my way to cope with cyber challenges, especially the governance of cyber security which I will explain step by step in the next chapters.

Keep reading to the end and you will find out how I developed a management system that serves as the central diesel engine in order to find out what's important for knowing and doing by establishing a realistic CYBER GOVERNANCE, at least from my perspective and my working environment.

▶   I like Bob Ross. My wife loves his techniques of painting, and I, well, am not so persuaded by his paintings but by a more than often used verbal phrase of him explaining how the scenery shall be painted:

   It's up to you!

   So Bob leaves it to his pupils how to set the trees and bushes and shores in their paintings. He just explains the technique to succeed.

   Just remember the content of Chap. 1 and always think of this motto. You are responsible for yourself what to believe, adopt, learn, and promote concerning all the cyber discussions. Believe in yourself and do listen to the others. Read the "source codes," not the triple interpreted versions of an act or a reference model or a definition.

   With this motto I gained very precious insights and fundamentals in order to succeed in difficult political discussions, especially in topics like CYBER which, for a good amount, still are unknown for most of the politicians and CxOs.

33.2 Setting the Foundation

Which aspects are important to establish a CYBER GOVERNANCE that will be accepted by the board, the whole company, the complete government, and even the whole country or state?

I listened and read a lot in articles and theories and ended up with very few frameworks which seem to be very useful for my work and now do represent my personal *cyber security toolbox*.

Adapted these frameworks for my work, I just can recommend you at least to know these documents which represent the "source code" for me.

Later it's up to you to understand, accept, adopt, adapt, or maybe deny the single contents of your toolbox in order to find the best way in your environment.

▶ **Cyber Security Toolbox of Lars Minth**

- The Updated Good Practice Guide on NCSS published by the European NIS Agency
- The Enterprise Security Architecture published by the Open Group
- The Information Security Management Maturity Model published by the Open Group
- The Sherwood Applied Security Architecture published by the SABSA Institute
- The Reference Model of Information Assurance and Security published by the University of Cardiff (RMIAS)
- The Cyber Security Framework v1.1 published by NIST (under development)

These single guides and models represent "internationally recognized best practices" for itself in their very own scope.

During this writing I am working for the Swiss federal government and being delegated to establish an information security strategy, an information security management system, with its security countermeasures and a proposal for an institute of information security plus price tags for the Swiss public authorities.

Parallel to this work, the establishment of an information security act for the federal government helps me to gain management attention and supports my work at board/ministerial level.

Background Information
For the topics of "information security," "data protection," and even "electronic identity," the Swiss government mandated its respective ministries to bring acts into being.

The topic CYBER, although predominant in press and social media channels, could just reach the level of a legal ordinance and regulation. At its broadest point, there is a national strategy for the protection against CYBER RISKS plus a small amount of personnel.

The challenge is obvious: there is still a lack of accepted definition and also interface between the distinct security topics especially "information security" and "CYBER" and "ICT."

33.3 Let's Start

Before telling you my story, I need to admit that the single success factors for me are quite overlapping, not mathematically combinable, and for sure a personal experience. For you, dear reader, to have a learning and/or consuming effect, I try to structure my approach for establishing a CYBER GOVERNANCE as followed below as you can look up relatively easy to apply this or that hint from me to establish your own CYBER GOVERNANCE.

Normally I will hold lectures on this topic which makes it way easier to avoid a "sender-receiver" problem in communication. I promise I do my best.

Here comes the minimalistic structure:

- Definitions – including several embeddings
- Framework for the governance of cyber security
- Circle of CYBER GOVERNANCE
- Circle of CYBER management
- Circle of CYBER architecture
- Circle of operational security countermeasures
- Bringing together the distinct CYBER fragments
- Bringing together second try

33.3.1 Definitions: Including Serval Embeddings

What is the scope of your CYBER GOVERNANCE? Do you have exclusions of distinct organizations, and do you compete with the INFOSEC people or the ICT security for the interpretive of the one business security?

It's up to you! Remember?

For Switzerland the definition is published straight in the "National Strategy for the Protection of Switzerland Against Cyber Risks" [1] (see Fig. 33.1).

Is the Swiss definition clear? Well, take care of the footnotes when reading, and you will recognize that the pronunciation of protection is concentrated on the technical aspects, which means data centers, racks, servers, and telecommunication channels are under protection, not the information itself or even physical buildings.

Integrity or possession of information is explicitly excluded which makes a huge differentiation to the scope of another discipline: information security.

The protection of technical equipment for reaching information security is dealt with as one of six "general countermeasures" of the upcoming Swiss information security act.

Thinking straightforward I would say that CYBER SECURITY, respectively, the protection of CYBER RISKS, is an integral part of the second general countermeasure of information security following the respective act: "Security when using Information and Communication Technology."

▶   We are all not living in a green field to set up CYBER GOVERNANCE. Therefore, we will find existing areas of security-related action (ICT, today's cyber ambitions, data protection, infosec, compsec, etc.) in every single business unit.

    Would be your environment (and the people within) ready to accept organizational shifts like the one above? Would you be heard and accepted by the other security disciplines if it turns out like stated above?

Fig. 33.1 Definition and scope of todays "Swiss Cyber"

Think of Bob! It's up to you to define your own CYBERSPACE! The biggest challenge is overcoming silos. After succeeding logical thinking has a chance to gain momentum. I wish you reach solid accreditation with your board level to be heard.

I faced similar challenges when establishing one of the core countermeasures of information security. In order to pursue the gained capability of governing/steering, I realized quite late that exactly these traditional silos are an imminent threat concerning the ever-changing world of security and especially all of the results of my program. Without a logical embedding into something bigger plus board-level sponsors that trust in you, I would never had a chance to bring the conceptual results into life.

I like and do understand the upcoming Swiss information security act and do have a first challenge:

Although CYBER, as the protecting countermeasure for the ICT being an integral part of information security, is well embedded into the information security strategy, the ISMS, and also its security countermeasures of the public authorities, some parliament members still are of the opinion that everything is CYBER concerning security. Therefore, today it is hard to explain to them the symbiotic relationship between information security, cyber security, and ICT security.

Guilty in the name of business! How can this be? We do have employed very well-paid external and internal security consultants, and everybody has an excellent expertise. Do you remember Chap. 1?

I dare to say that we, the sec guys,

- Did very often not yet learn to speak the right language and become hilarious when talking about our topics.
- Act on our own in our security silo (predominantly in the pure technical area) and like to isolate and safeguard our security shop when new organizational threats arise on the horizon.
- Listen solely to others instead reading and understanding the personal "source codes" of our specific business and THEN discuss in a critical way.
- Follow our own goals in terms of marketing and personal revenue.

Pushing all the negative impressions away, the topic itself is motivating, thrilling, and absolutely necessary for the business, hence a good working area to spend studies and development in order to become an accredited security person.

Just be open-minded, have a sound amount of self-criticism, and do never lose your humor. It's just business!

33.3.2 Framework for the Governance of Cyber Security

Based on my personal toolbox, I have chosen the ENISA paper to structure my steps to establish a proper and logically structured CYBER GOVERNANCE since I do not want to invent another wheel:

1. Setting the vision, scope, objectives, and priorities adopting and adapting the ISM3 notion of "security in context"
2. Following a risk assessment approach adopting the RMIAS of the University of Cardiff plus the fundamentals of the federal risk management
3. Taking stock of existing policies, regulations, and capabilities based on empirical investigations
4. Setting a clear governance structure adopting the experience inside the Swiss public authorities

5. Identifying and engaging stakeholders according to the given circumstances
6. Establishing a trusted information-sharing mechanism both personnel and materiel

These steps I could proof to be good by using them prior for the establishment of a federal IAM system for which I was responsible as head of program. Well, since I did not take care too much for point 5, the establishment of point 6 was and still is harsh and stoney. With the upcoming information security act, I lastly found a possibility to do it better and have an immense lesson learnt. So please take care about a working stakeholder management!

It also comes to the point that you need to trust such structuring papers and road maps at the very first time before you can expect your board of directors to trust YOU. At this point the discipline of "trust modeling" is one of the most precious subjects to follow in academic (or empirical) education.

So if you are trying to stem a burden like establishing a CYBER GOVERNANCE the first time, be sure you have a trusted and believing mentor at board level and be prepared to face the resistance of several security silos!

At this point we do have the challenge by defining the scope, the spheres of activity, and the embedding into information security which forms part of the definition of CYBER.

Drawing the experiences from my toolbox, I derived the following spheres of activity in which the CYBER GOVERNANCE can be completely projected:

The structure itself is derived from Open Group's ESA, but I needed to adapt the contents and priorities of the model in order to satisfy the requirements of a CYBER GOVERNANCE in my working environment plus I added my gained experiences. It would be possible to map these activities into the NIST CSF, CobIT, ISO 27, or other models. So just feel free to adapt my toolbox in order to get a working one for yourself.

As you can see the CYBER GOVERNANCE level comprises the other three circles, respectively, spheres of activity: CYBER management, CYBER architecture, and operational security countermeasures.

▶   Accountability
     It does not matter how perfect your CYBER GOVERNANCE is set up and even undersigned from the board of directors. The ultimate responsibility just goes up the circles.
     Therefore, CYBER GOVERNANCE is responsible to set the frame for all of the other activities in order to enable them to succeed. Any failure in the inner circles can easily be shuffled off to the GOVERNANCE level.

Best practice means we are talking about the real problems and challenges. Comparing to the original Open ESA, you will find out that I changed the outer two circles. Now governance is encompassing management, not vice versa. Here I had many discussions which led me to set governance on top of the management. Again, it's up to you whether this suits to your environment. Being more a regulator than a market-oriented enterprise, my employer needs legal baselines, compliance assessments, and fixed roles in order to manage properly.

33.3.3 Circle of CYBER GOVERNANCE

Cyber principles are the start of a policy-driven approach to CYBER GOVERNANCE. How do you formulate these high-level principles in order to steer the management, the business analysts, the architects, and finally the ICT service centers?

You could have a good glass of wine and draft some trials on your home desk, you could invite your stakeholders for a 2-day workshop "Guiding Principles for our Cyber Security," or you could send an email asking your stakeholders for their requirements regarding cyber principles. Good luck!

Does this sound familiar for you? I pay tremendously respect to the pioneers of setting principles and rules since this is one of the toughest tasks. You are a changer, a revolutionist, and a person whose reputation will be questioned because you are tearing down walls of wealth and comfort.

Best example is George Washington whose success story cannot be denied. Nevertheless, his masterpiece *Rules of Civility and Decent Behavior* was questioned exactly the way I described above, but it sets the ground for a good governance. Take your time and read that masterpiece. You will gain precious insights for writing useful CYBER principles.

I did not copy Washington's rules for cyber principles. I just used his technique in order to reach my own goal. Please remember Bob's approach!

Now you are trapped: writing the high-level CYBER principles can just happen context-sensitive. This means you have to concentrate on the requirements and dependencies of your working environment.

For example, the financial sector just published in 2016 the "Principles for International Cybersecurity, Data and Technology." Among the authors are the European Banking Federation, the Securities Industry and Financial Markets Association (SIFMA), and the Asia Securities Industry and Financial Markets Association (ASIFMA).

The pharmaceutical industry does have different aims, business goals, and compliance frameworks (e.g., HIPAA). It is quite obvious that the cyber security principles for this kind of industry will differ from the financial industry.

It is obvious that for me, working for a public authority, that all of these principles could be partly interesting since the Swiss government also regulates the financial sector via the FINMA institute. A simple copy wouldn't do it.

My approach to succeed in the important step of establishing CYBER principles is a blending mix of:

- Looking at the others (searching the Internet incl. social media channels should be sufficient)
- Knowing the requirements and the pain points of my stakeholders (a decade experience plus bilateral interviews are helping)
- Drafting two sets of principles in order to feel the acceptance to be ruled (empathy is necessary)

- Evangelizing and embedding the topic CYBER in order to overcome political and silo thinking
- Presenting the business value of these principles (not easy but doable, at least essential!)

I hesitate to give you a list of CYBER principles of the Swiss public authorities since I am still in the process to establish these with the stakeholders, but if you follow my approach, you cannot go wrong.

A last word to CYBER principles: the development is more time-consuming than setting the legal baseline or the necessary architectures since acceptance and trust are more fragile than anywhere else.

Have a second look at the ESA figure. You realize that **legal baselines** (acts, ordinance, regulations) are listed opposite "standards, guidelines, and procedures" on the governance level. Have you ever heard of regulators publishing standards, guidelines, and even processes to follow? Neither do I.

But I saw quite often that some kind of legal baselines and issued principles have been published, and nobody really knew how to fulfill these regulations.

The result of such a problem is really easy: one by another disregard the rules since nobody has an answer how to fulfill them, and in the end, the principles and legal baselines are obsolete and just made for the satisfaction of the ivory tower of governance. This would be just useless, and without consequences if additionally, a **continuous compliance assessment** is not in place!

Another brilliant example of this wrong situation is the European General Data Protection Regulation (GDPR). I have hold a couple of speeches informing Fortune 500 companies that their knowledge what to do and what is not necessary is quite superficial. All of them have put the burden onto the shoulders of external consulting companies and let them interpret how the GDPR is meant.

I was urged to tell them to take the time and read the GDPR for themselves since the European Union did not provide guidelines or standard procedures how to comply with the new GDPR from May 2018 on. Today we do have a huge mess with this GDPR, and I do hope that the Union members will do their job within their role as DATA PROTECTION GOVERNANCE owner.

If you really want the people live your CYBER GOVERNANCE, you have to show them how they need to interpret and use your CYBER principles and legal baselines. For that you can choose from a myriad of possibilities, depending what you prefer or what your recipients are capable of understanding:

- Procedures in form of standard operating procedures, use policies, or processes
- Guidelines in every color of your corporate identity
- Promotion and use of industrial standards that are used broadly, at best internationally and at least with your B2B partners

You may see here is another trap to fail when conceptualizing and establishing CYBER GOVERNANCE. It is quite time-consuming to develop, write, and pedagogically deduct these helping tools to fulfill, enable, and enforce the mandatory legal baselines and principles within your organization. Connected tightly to the activity of "training and development," you can easily calculate a full position for a specialist transferring your "ivory tower" down to the consumers.

I already mentioned a "continuous compliance assessment" on the governance level. This would be happening in the ideal world, and I would be glad to enforce such an assessment at least periodically. Without such an assessment, you will never have the chance to show whether your CYBER security countermeasures have been set right in order to demonstrate the effectiveness of all the CYBER actions.

Concerning the assessment there are a lot of possibilities depending on your companies' maturity and stringent wish to maintain a strong CYBER GOVERNANCE.

The weakest form of assessment is a self-declaration of compliance without any external check. Every department or business unit has to fill out a prepared questionnaire that in turn will be evaluated and maybe published on the corporate websites or to the shareholders.

A little bit more stringent would be the "informal compliance assessment," whereas the CISO or head of CYBER GOVERNANCE would pursue an assessment in order to delegate the responsibility to close detected gaps to the respective departments or business units.

A real and effective compliance assessment can only be connected to the corporate risk management which is located in the next circle.

At governance level, it is important to select the level of assessment at best in the form of a regulation so that management has not the chance to circumventing all the efforts of securing the business.

Last point to take care of are the acting people within CYBER GOVERNANCE. You need to define roles and boards in order to fulfill all the activities and decisions made in the circle of governance.

Here I just can give you the advice to know very well the opinion of the executive board and the existing boards since it is very difficult to establish "yet another board" next to the ICT security board, the CISO board, the ICT board, and the risk management board, you know what I mean?

During the lifetime of my IAM program, I had a federal board just dealing with governance issues concerning IAM. Within a few months, the board developed itself to a swimming pool of technical IAM-related question for which the departmental delegates would have not been chosen. Corrected this wrong direction back to real governance issues, it was just another board the board level and I decided to skip it in order to put more effort into the stakeholder management instead of fighting for board which is regarded a "dead horse."

33.3.4 Circle of CYBER Management

The complete management needs to fulfill the obligations of the governance level. This can be a very tricky task to fulfill since the management sometimes has the competence to set the governance rules into force. To restrict yourself does not represent the behavior of a human being, and therefore your task as revolutionist and second George Washington is to prioritize points 5 and 6 of my steps to establish a CYBER GOVERNANCE. You need to gain trust that your cyber security goals support also the companies' goals.

It is obsolete to discuss every single point at this level. Basically, I have chosen the "reference model for Information Assurance and Security" of the University of Cardiff as the guiding model, added the result of my federal-wide IAM program and got the distinct tasks you can see in Fig. 2.1 "CYBER GOVERNANCE: Spheres of activity."

The reason to use RMIAS is its simplicity of explaining the connection between the requirements of the business via typical risk management approaches down to selected security countermeasures.

Although the definition and scope of cyber security differs from company to company, it is necessary to learn what the executives regard as "protectable." In our time, being an "information society," "information" is seldom wrong, and so just follow the RMIAS by defining a proper information taxonomy in order to prioritize the companies' security goals.

Once the security goals are agreed upon with the help of a well-defined risk analysis, it is just a small step to select appropriate security countermeasures to reach not just the defined security goals but also show cost-effectiveness and efficiency with the right selection.

All of these steps can be written down in digestible pieces we call business requirements, CYBER strategy, CYBER planning, and CYBER risk management. It is clear that these results need to be enforced and a continuous compliance assessment could be the right tool for this.

Please have a straight look at the circle of CYBER management, and you will find a very small word with a huge impact on money, human resources, and complexity: ISMS.

As I mentioned before, we need a very strong diesel engine in order to cope with all the distinct activities and issues to be dealt with in all spheres of activity. The information security management system is exactly this diesel engine. As you got aware about my embedding of CYBER into information security, we can call the ISMS also CSMS, but the content, the result, the activities, and the challenges remain the same.

Having had the honor to learn and study at the oldest academic security group, I wrote my master thesis about information security managements systems and found out that two pain points have been disastrous for implementing an ISMS in the real world: (a) lacking a proper maturity model and (b) a control-based approach instead of a process-oriented.

Both requirements have been met with the "information security management maturity model" ISM[3]. Hence, I added this model to my toolbox and now feel being enabled to set up also a cyber security management system since it's embedded into information security, at least in my environment.

Additionally, the ISM[3] is defining "security as the result of the continuous meeting or surpassing of a set of objectives." This is the core of the "security in context" approach of that model and shows in best practice style how to formulate security goals and security targets following business goals, very helpful!

Embedding all of these characteristics into a "cyber security management model" enables your diesel engine to be the right means for managing the CYBERspace. As I have seen a couple of ISMS projects being nearly successful, I feel urged to remember you to take care of point 5 of my steps mentioned above.

33.3.5 Circle of CYBER Architecture

> …box of Pandora…never-ending story…philosophical discussion in the ivory tower…

Don't get me wrong. I also was an architect before and I do respect the precise thinking of architects at all levels. Very often the problem here is a wrong requirements definition from the managerial circle and missing barriers.

Ok, being an architect means being artistic in its own way. Basically, there is a waterfall progress if you follow the typical architecture tools like TOGAF, FEA, NAF, or SABSA.

For my toolbox I have chosen "Sherwood's Applied Business Security Architecture" to cover the central aspects of that circle. But before starting any architectural work, it is necessary to define the right security service (security countermeasure).

Once this decision is set, the CYBER GOVERNANCE controls this circle solely by compliance assessments. If the architectural work of a security countermeasure is very specific, this work becomes very critical for the overall success of the CYBER GOVERNANCE. Lack of knowledge, few personnel and also egocentric ambitions can lead the architectural work to a disaster.

Remember the accountability of that circle!

Once the architectural contract is signed, I never had any problems at this level and could be excited about the outcome when it comes to deployment and integration into the existing ICT infrastructure. One failure I have overseen is an electron jump over two architectural layers which means that the physical architect has too few barriers and requirements in order to build a physical instance of the conceptual work. The logical architecture is just missing. Sustainability is more often used in other areas of work, but if it comes to a review of the architecture and just a few business requirements have changed, the architectural cycle needs to start from scratch without lessons learnt. To avoid this threat, the CYBER GOVERNANCE need to take care for a proper documentation of all architectural layers and is responsible for a sufficient staffing of this level.

33.3.6 Circle of Operational Security Countermeasures

Here we are: the tangibles of CYBER GOVERNANCE.

Sometimes I saw the following scenario (please hold in mind Fig. 33.1):

Tech company A meets two executive board members at an ICT networking party and created enough trust to sell their security product suite in order to fulfill the business requirements the board member has in mind. After a financial bargaining, the security countermeasure has been installed, and the CISO, the head of cyber security, and the architects did not know anything until migration.

Cyber threats are similar to other threats: maybe they will become true or not. From the governing perspective, this scenario is quite worse, since we have no clue whether the security goals are met or the technical bargain is really mitigating the risks and threats. Additionally, it is very unclear whether the integration into the existing ICT landscape has been successful without functional consequences of the other systems.

CYBER GOVERNANCE is responsible to set principles and regulations so that the ICT service providers just integrate, deploy, and manage the CYBER services and show compliance to all the spheres of action up to the business requirements.

Dear ICT service provider: do not hesitate. The CYBER GOVERNANCE and its team are responsible to clarify it for you.

According to that CYBER GOVERNANCE got another stakeholder group: the ICT service providers.

When you have outsourced security countermeasures to external companies, it becomes more and more difficult to steer them. At this point CYBER GOVERNANCE needs to be familiar with data protection, contract management, and compliance checks at technical level.

For doing this efficiently and cost-effectively, it would be helpful if the staff of CYBER GOVERNANCE not only has deep insights into international threat scenarios but also in ITIL, IT4IT, and other systematic structures in order to understand the provider of their tangibles.

33.3.7 Bringing Together the Distinct CYBER Fragments

Next to the "dashboard" of CYBER GOVERNANCE (the "spheres of activity" model), we need to have a useful, simple, and effective management system that shows easily and understandably the causal connections between information, respectively, the business requirements concerning information, CYBER risks, CYBER threats, CYBER security goals, and CYBER security countermeasures.

I was asked quite often if we just can skip such immense exercises to document and formulate things to be done within security nobody is really interested in. But the times when "security by obscurity" was working now are over. *"Need to know" is history, "need to share" is just there.*

Some of the new security goals next to "confidentiality," "integrity," or "non-repudiation" are "cost-effectiveness," "transparency," and "auditability." In order to additionally demonstrate the performance and efficiency of a CSM/ISM system, we exactly need to realize this. Once the necessity for a management system is given, you need to know who and what to follow in order to succeed: copying the sec-process of the ISO 27k-series is quite popular since "everybody is doing it and it works they say."

Does it really work? Or does it work just in the eyes of people earning money with strictly formalized questions to tick off? Remember the ISO 9001 dilemma! The framework is not bad and assures you a certain standardized process that is not too chaotic. Nevertheless, you can produce life jackets made from concrete and still comply with the ISO 9001. So, I have a tested product that will barely help when needed.

It's an old comparison but still valid. The same applies with an ISO 27k certification. You will have a good baseline of security and have gained a 3 years valid certification based on discrete controls. What the ISO standard does not advise you is how you reach these goals.

With the selection of ISO 27k, you did step 2 of showing the required expectations of your board level. But if you do not mind, we will go back to step 1: building a management system that is feasible to map all of the abovementioned topics into a system that can be interpreted, read, and understood based on collected facts around the topic CYBER.

33.3.8   Bringing Together: Second Try

As a mathematician and programmer, you could program a complex table with five dimensions or a "lot" of distinct and simple 2D tables with referral points, a similar challenge you have with the topics to deal with when you decide to establish a management system for CYBER security.

However, such a management system is basically needed for the circle of CYBER management although very often the CYBER GOVERNANCE team initializes such developments by setting the rules. So careless who establishes a CSMS/ISMS at least there needs to be a security process that reports to the strategical level whatever is done, spent for what reason and if the things done are supporting the expectations of the board members. It's existentially!

It is relatively easy, isn't it?

Let's think about it: what is important, what is absolutely necessary to manage, and what needs to be demonstrated to the senior line management or the board level? A couple of years ago, I wrote about the establishment of an ISMS for military forces with Royal Holloway, University of London. The conclusion from this work was a useful blend of distinct ISMS frameworks in order to fulfill military requirements.

Today still I am using this work because it gives hints and checklists to think about. The toughest overcoming in the useful CSMS/ISMS is to forget about the necessity of "control first."

People are doing something: they open VPNs, they let you pass the doors, they cut your net access, they misconfigure your laptop remotely, they ask you for permission to gain access, and so on. All of these activities can and should be described in processes in order to gain oversight and control of it.

These process descriptions do help us to understand if there is a deviation from normal behavior or not. Maybe you also establish KPIs. Transferring this to our CSMS/ISMS, we do have a first process by putting the reporting to the management into a suitable process: "report to strategical management." When you now try to put all of the other CYBER topics and doings into processes, it is way easier to look around if other people faced the same challenge instead of reinventing the wheel.

During my works with Royal Holloway, I came across a Spanish mastermind who solved exactly the above described challenge by structuring security processes in order to fulfill the expectations of management. You do not need OSINT to find out who this person is. From this moment on, I skipped the old ISO structure and conceptualized security processes on three levels taking care to be able to map to the famous ISO27k controls, just in case I ought to be able to show compliance with ISO (greetings to the old security world). Now the work begins in order to collect all the CYBER actions and press them into distinct processes with its inputs, outcomes, and added values.

> It is very important for the existence of these processes to show the added value. Please do never forget this small fragment of work since it is guaranteeing your budget the next year.

That's it. You are there. You established your management system and everybody is happy, while you have all under control.

No way! It is nearly impossible to establish such a system from scratch. It is even worse if there are some reminiscents looking like context-free security processes and you have a low maturity concerning process management.

And exactly this "not so perfect situation" is helping you to establish a well-accepted CSMS/ISMS: integrate "maturity"!

Nothing in business is simple or even perfect. It is obvious that a cross-discipline like CYBER needs to be developed and tailored to the specific needs of your company/working environment.

Use this situation and create just a boot-up from your CSMS/ISMS.

The approach could be realized easier with the following points to be in mind:

(a) Establish a holistic approach (so that the board members can and will support you if they are capable of following your way).
(b) Create the absolute necessary boot-up processes (so that you can call it a CSMS/ISMS with the necessary maturity level (here you can define your own or use a maturity model from one of the frameworks).
(c) I have used ISM[3] and tailored it for my purposes since it embeds maturity and is process-oriented.

33.3.9 The Other Ingredients

We now looked from different perspectives onto CYBER GOVERNANCE and learnt that a proper CSMS/ISMS plus a governance framework are essential fragments to survive the CYBER business and stay on top.

Within all of the distinct details I was just mentioning, disciplines like risk analysis, stakeholder management, political correctness, trust modeling, process management and process establishment, requirements engineering with its main topic requirements analysis, knowledge of different security frameworks and even principles' writing, and technical knowledge about IAM, COMPSEC, NETSEC, etc. are necessary to succeed.

Do you feel what I want to say to you? It is not possible just to go to university, succeed in a reputationally perfect study course, and hope to be successful. I spent my time and money in three different MScs in order to gain understanding in a holistic way plus served a lot of nations. Now I am asked to establish all the things I told you above, and sometimes I am just thinking: "gladly there is a huge community I can use as sparring partners. But hey! I am confident that I can bring my employer/customer at least to the next maturity level...."

This is the last recommendation to you: do not stop learning and think you are done. Never ever will you be perfectly ready for such huge venture called CYBER GOVERNANCE, so please do yourself a favor and stay hungry for new horizons, challenges, and intellectual discussions with the ancient security crew.

Conclusion

I hate these conclusion sections. Everything is said and in the abstract, you can read a highly condensed summary of the important facts. This is also best practice.

If I can conclude something, then just learn from my personal failures and success stories.

I do hope that you can derive enough facts from my story in order to create a proper CYBER GOVERNANCE at your company or at least understand how such a GOVERNANCE should be established and with which activities this GOVERNANCE shall deal with. Challenge your head of CYBER with the right questions, and you will find out if the CYBER GOVERNANCE in your environment operates in a realistic dimension or resides in the ivory tower of insignificance.

References

1. The contents and scope could change with the second version of the strategy to by planned somewhere in 2018

How Blockchain Will Change Cybersecurity Practices

Claudio Di Salvo

Abstract

While the entire business world is trying to make sense of the ascent of cryptocurrencies, Bitcoin being the forefront, the promise of Blockchain's distributed open ledger format to be an "unhackable" network able to record and verify data transactions without typical third-party validation holds the potential to change the cybersecurity practice long before its promise to change the way value is exchanged over the Internet. Globally, sophisticated cyberattacks are compromising organizations at an unprecedented rate and with devastating consequences. Today's hackers are motivated by a wide range of objectives that include financial gain, industrial espionage, cyberwarfare, and terrorism. The Blockchain not only has a place in cryptocurrency exchanges but could also be used to improve security solutions, this article claims. By itself Blockchain provides little in terms of threat detection and defense, but its strength comes from creating an infrastructure trusted by all transaction participants, decentralized by nature. Blockchain builds more transparent and decentralized systems that offer event tracking and cryptography: threats can be tracked and dealt with before they spread.

Can Blockchain deliver on its promise? The potential is clear. Blockchain technology could constantly check and validate data communication flow with no single point of failure and offload authentication to a decentralized layer of security.

C. Di Salvo (✉)
International Air Transport Association (IATA), Le Grand Saconnex, Switzerland
e-mail: disalvoc@iata.org

© Springer Fachmedien Wiesbaden GmbH, ein Teil von Springer Nature 2018
M. Bartsch, S. Frey (Hrsg.), *Cybersecurity Best Practices*,
https://doi.org/10.1007/978-3-658-21655-9_34

34.1   A New Approach to Cybersecurity Is Required

In the past years, the digital transformation has altered not only the corporate business models, but the very nature of their asset has significantly changed: 80% of the value of Fortune 500 companies now consists of intellectual properties (IP) and other intangible assets. The rapid digitization of assets has come with an increased risk due to data breach, compromised authorizations, and other cyberattacks: recent research shows that corporations worldwide are losing hundreds of billions USD annually from loss of IP, trading algorithms, altered financial and consumer data, diminished reputation, as well as risk of increased regulatory and legal exposure. 2017 will be probably remembered as the year cybersecurity became mainstream due to the high-profile cyber-related incidents which occurred, including big data breaches, physical infrastructure tampering, Internet of Things (IoT) devices turning on their owners, Ransomware, and even allegations of election hacking that captured the public's attention. Sometimes the feeling that there's only so much that enterprises and governments can effectively do to stop the rising tide of cyberattacks may have crossed you.

Digital systems have been designed without security in mind, the fundamental protocols that have made the Internet possible have themselves not been designed with authentication or digital identity in mind, and the explosion of mobile devices and the networked connection of almost every physical asset from security cameras to refrigerator – as much as any IoT devices – is increasing the risks.

The traditional approach to cybersecurity has been to use a prevention-centric strategy focused on blocking attacks, borrowing the concept of building an impenetrable fortress from physical security and defense. Many of today's advanced and motivated threat actors are circumventing these defenses with creative, stealthy, targeted, and persistent attacks that often go undetected for significant periods of time. The sort of sophisticated cyberattacks we saw only between nations a few years ago (Stuxnet and alike) are not being practiced by common criminals.

34.2   The Economics of Cybersecurity Favors the Attackers

Cybersecurity economics favor the attackers: cyberattack tools are relatively cheap, and profit margins are extremely generous, while defense tends to be a generation behind the attackers due to the fact that it's always harder to show return on investment for attacks that are prevented and law enforcement is almost nonexistent, when we consider that less than 2% of criminals are actually prosecuted.

The often-overlooked imbalance in economic incentives between cyberattack and defense is exacerbated by the fact that many of the technologies and business practices that have recently driven corporate growth, innovation, and profitability also undermine cybersecurity.

Technologies such as cloud computing and VoIP bring tremendous cost efficiencies but dramatically complicate security. Efficient, even necessary, business practices such as the use of long supply chains and BYOD (bring your own device) are also economically attractive but extremely problematic from a security perspective.

Corporates are faced with the conundrum of needing to use technology to grow and maintain their enterprises without risking their crown jewels or hard-won public faith in the bargain.

As pointed out by Moore and Anderson (2011), there are three major economic barriers that plague cybersecurity:

- Misaligned incentive
- Information asymmetries
- Externalities

34.2.1 Misaligned Incentives

Misaligned incentives between those responsible of the security and those who benefit from the protection are rife in cybersecurity; consequently, any analysis of cyber risks should begin with an analysis of stakeholders' incentives. There is a natural tension between efficiency and resilience in the design of an information system: this is best exemplified by the push to the network convergence of the past few years. Many critical infrastructures used to rely on incompatible network protocols, devices, and operations. The convergence on the Internet protocol has greatly reduced operating costs, leading to an increase in long-term vulnerability.

Since perfect security is impossible, the trade-off between security and efficiency has also another implication; it implies an optimal level of insecurity, where the benefits of efficient operations outweigh any reduction in risk brought by additional security measures. For instance, consumers greatly benefit by online banking efficiency, which introduces a risk of fraud for the banks that are taken to balance between quantifying the new risk and the reduced branch cost involved by providing digital banking services. When those misaligned incentives arise, it is very common to make suboptimal choices about where to make the trade-off.

34.2.2 Information Asymmetries

Many corporations report a deluge of data; some of them are actually overwhelmed. In spite of that abundancy to drive cybersecurity investments, there's a deep scarcity of relevant data on which making a call. Reported incidents draw a perfect picture of the past, while the future attacks are alike stochastic events, difficult to predict with certainty. And although there are many estimates of the size of cybercrime annual profits, these are likely overestimates: in fact, we don't know the true cost of cybercrime as there is no incentive for corporations to make this data available. We know that most of the cybercrime is financial in nature, but most banks aren't revealing their loss due to online fraud.

There is an incentive to underreport cybersecurity incidents and even cooperate with the police, for fear their reputation (and stock price) may take a hit. Such reticence is more than offset by the overenthusiasm of the participants in the cybersecurity industry, to hype up the threats. This is a dangerous combination; as demonstrated by George Akerlof (1970), a market with asymmetric information will lead to products of lower quality.

Buyers will refuse paying a premium price for a quality (security) they cannot measure, therefore disincentivizing vendors to invest into quality of their products. A similar effect is triggered by refusing to disclose data on losses due to security incidents: a lack of reliable data on the cost of information security makes it difficult to manage the risk. The existence of this information asymmetry does not necessarily mean that society isn't pouring enough cash into security; it rather means that we may not be investing in ideal proportion to the threat.

Most corporations would be happy to know that they acquired firewall devices and antivirus software for themselves but would probably be ignoring that any other cybersecurity breach, data loss, or fraud in any other company in their supply chain would render them compromised as well. What about Cloud computing: when moving your data and applications to the cloud, you're in your provider's hands in terms of confidentiality, data integrity, malware protection, and the like.

34.2.3 Externalities

Digital business is characterized by many types of externalities, where individual's actions have an effect on others. A compromised computer that has been recruited to a botnet is a negative network externality; it can pollute the Internet, harming others more than the host. Botnets send spam, phishing scams, and denial-of-service attacks and provide anonymous cover for attacker. In each case, the target of the malicious activity is someone other than the host computer.

The software industry tends toward dominant firms, thanks in large part to the benefits of interoperability; this is a network externality: a larger network of users is more valuable than each of its members. Microsoft PowerPoint users benefit not only by the features of the software but also by the interoperability with a large number of people who made the same choice when using a presentation software. That explains also the rise and dominance of Windows operating systems or Facebook social network, but it also explains the typical pattern of a security flaw. As a software platform is building market dominance, it must appeal to vendors of complementary products as well as its own customers. A secure product becomes more difficult for other vendors to extend or to develop on; therefore, security is not emphasized until market dominance has not been stably achieved. That provides the economic justification for which insecure – or shall we call it imperfect – software is readily pushed on the market and why today's software is issued in perpetual "beta" version.

34.3   The Cybersecurity Problem in the Cloud

Cloud computing is one of the latest innovations of the modern Internet and technological Landscape. With everyone from the major online technological leaders like Amazon and Google to local governmental administrations using or offering cloud computing services, this technology truly presents itself as an exciting and innovative method to store and use data online. By offering software, applications, storage, and other services online account, cloud providers can greatly reduce costs for small/large businesses and startups by giving them access to advanced features that used to be a domain of few large corporations who could afford large capital expenditures. Today cloud computing and its paradigm like SaaS (Software-as-a-Service) can simplify a company's IT infrastructure by providing turnkey solutions to nontechnical staff such as a CRM or ERP as well as telephony, payment services, accounting tools, and other databases in one affordable account seized upon the customers' needs.

While this is great news from a business point of view, in spite of these advantages, there are unfortunately some drawbacks and security issues that can arise when using these computing paradigms: from a cybersecurity economics perspective, while the reliance on cloud computing providers might sound as risk mitigating due to the incentive for cloud provider to keep their systems updated, sound, and secure, it introduces a new element of risk based on trust that can be discussed as due to asymmetry of information.

An attacker who might be able to break into a public or private cloud computing environment can steal – unnoticeably from an end-user perspective – sensitive information from many different users and either use or sell that information, information such as credit card numbers, bank coordinates, financial records, reports, trading agreements, IP, till the most inauspicious case that the attacker can gain logical access to any customer application and perform undesirable changes.

At an unprecedented pace, cloud computing has then simultaneously transformed business and government and created new security challenges. The development of the cloud service model delivers business-supporting technology more efficiently than ever before. The shift from traditional client/server to service-based models is transforming the way technology departments think about designing and delivering computing technology and applications. However, the improved value offered by cloud computing advances has also created new security vulnerabilities, including security issues whose full impacts are still emerging.

Cloud and SaaS undeniably provide savings and advantages for the business; the shift from traditional client/server to service-based models is transforming the way technology departments think about designing and delivering computing technology and applications. However, the improved value offered by cloud computing advances has also created new vulnerabilities, emphasizing the spectrum of possible cyberattacks.

The first step in minimizing the risk in the cloud is to identify the top security threats; the Cloud Security Alliance (CSA), a business-driven organization, chartered with promoting the use of best practices for security within cloud computing compiled a list of 12 recognized threats.

CSA: Top 12 Cloud security threats

- Threat No. 1: Data breaches
- Threat No. 2: Compromised credentials and broken authentication
- Threat No. 3: Hacked interfaces and APIs
- Threat No. 4: Exploited system vulnerabilities
- Threat No. 5: Account hijacking
- Threat No. 6: Malicious insiders
- Threat No. 7: The APT or parasitical forms of attacks
- Threat No. 8: Permanent data loss
- Threat No. 9: Inadequate diligence
- Threat No. 10: Cloud service abuses
- Threat No. 11: DoS attacks
- Threat No. 12: Shared technology, shared dangers

Fig. 34.1 CSA: Top 12 cloud service threats

As you can see in Fig. 34.1, together with traditional security problems, a new typology arises from the cloud adoption – CSA warns – due to the shared, on-demand nature of cloud services that enable users to bypass organization-wide security policies and setup their own accounts. Data breaches are a much as a threat as in traditional corporate networks; cloud makes data a more attractive target for an attacker, due to the vast amounts that you can store in a cloud environment.

A data breach can result in some very high costs for business from the investigation to the remediation, and their impact can last in an organization for years; cloud providers typically deploy security controls and practices to protect their environment, but ultimately, data are assets that organizations are responsible to control by themselves.

Every cloud service and application nowadays offers API connectivity; interfaces and APIs are used to manage and interact with cloud service; the security and availability of those services – from authentication, access control, encryption, provisioning, and monitoring – depend on the security of APIs, as those are usually accessible from the open Internet.

System vulnerabilities or exploitable program bugs are also offering a larger surface of attack within the multitenancy of cloud computing; organizations in fact share databases, programs, storage, and other resources in close proximity; the weakness of one is the risk of another. Fortunately, in this case the vulnerability risk mitigation has a lower cost and relies on basic IT practices like prompt patch management and regular vulnerability scanning. Vulnerabilities in shared technology pose a significant threat to cloud computing. Cloud service providers share infrastructure, platforms, and applications, and if a vulnerability arises in any of these layers, it affects everyone.

In the most recent years, though, attackers have also been able to use the cloud application to launch other attacks: these services can be commandeered to support nefarious activities, such as using cloud resources to break an encryption key or launching a DDoS attacks, sending spam and phishing emails for ransom attacks, or hosting malicious content.

A good portion of the most recent outbreaks in cybersecurity has stressed the importance of considering the human factor when building an effective threat prevention strategy. Human factor exposes the vast majority of companies to cyberattacks more than they have to be; poor password management, lack of procedural compliance, lack of awareness, and malicious insiders, these are all making businesses vulnerable from within.

The recent Ransomware epidemic wave of attacks has used phishing email as a vector for the attack with non-IT personnel being the weakest link, for example, employees with local administrator rights who disabled security solutions on their computers and let the infection spread from their computer onto the entire corporate network.

34.4   What Should a Business Do Then?

IT practices, technologies, and policies can mitigate the risk of cyberattacks, but threats are becoming increasingly sophisticated, and there's only so much you can do to reduce the dependency on stochastic events like an attack and human errors. Technologies and practices are expensive to deploy, and they're not very often in proportional measure to the perception of risk. How can an organization define what is at stake and what should be measured to quantify an organization's exposure to cyber risk? IT incidents logged are a reliable deterministic parameter, but they only give you a picture of the past; the exposure to risk has the behavior of a set of random variables, not precisely easy to define and measure.

Which metrics should then be considered to put together a cybersecurity plan, given the limited resources any organization can pull together on it, especially in today's economic climate? The right metrics will help to justify and allocate security spending. Rainer Böhme (2012) has developed a framework to justify any investment in security programs that aims to quantify the costs, as well as the benefits of undertaking a cybersecurity program based on three variables: the security costs, the security level, and the security benefits.

The result is the security productivity function illustrated in Fig. 34.2: the productivity of a cybersecurity program is graphically represented by the solid line in the figure. Spending a certain amount of resources will get you a certain security level; however, the exponential

Fig. 34.2 Security cost-benefit

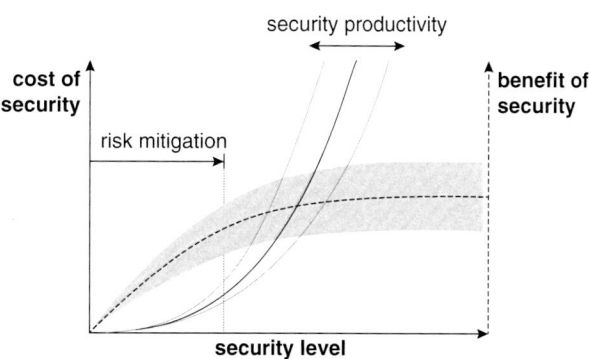

shape of this function expresses that there are decreasing returns on investment. Simply put, spending more and more will get you smaller and smaller improvement in security.

The dashed-line shows the second relationship between security level and security benefits. How do the benefits evolve when the security level changes? This function also sees decreasing returns: after a certain point, further increasing the security level only provides marginal benefits.

The security level can have deterministic and stochastic indicators: the latter are able to capture uncertainty produced by the attacker's behavior, while deterministic don't. Deterministic indicators include patch level, existence of intrusion detection systems, firewalls, antivirus systems, etc. On the other hand, stochastic indicators are the incidents reported by intrusion detection systems, known vulnerability reports, the number of phished passwords, or the number of compromised server hosts.

We can always come up with approximate calculation of the cost – directly or indirectly – related to a successful cyberattack, i.e. a computation of the cost of social impact due to the cyberattack and the operational costs to bring back the business to run, but as described, the economics of cybersecurity leads to disincentives to large investments and eventually does not facilitate the role of those who bear the responsibility to mitigate cybersecurity risks.

34.5 Blockchain Can Reengineer Cybersecurity

Where cyber investments should be placed then, given that no cyber defense or information system can be regarded as 100% secure, and what is deemed safe today won't be tomorrow given the lucrative nature of cybercrime and the criminal's ingenuity to seek new methods of attack.

The traditional approach to cybersecurity has been to use a prevention-centric strategy focused on blocking attacks, while a shift from perimetral prevention to detection and response seems needed. The Blockchain is regarded as a possible technology overhaul as it addresses the fundamental flaws of security by taking away the human factor from the equation, which is usually the weakest link while constantly checking and validating data communication flow with no single point of failure. A Blockchain purposely facilitates secure online transactions, by leveraging a distributed ledger and taking away the risk of a single point of failure; Blockchain technology provides end-to-end privacy and encryption while still ensuring convenience for users: a perfect solution for the cloud computing era with a zero-trust policy for each network device.

Blockchain technologies are, after all, the culmination of decades of research and breakthroughs in cryptography and security; it offers a totally different approach to storing information, making transactions, performing functions, and establishing trust, which makes it especially suitable for environments with high security requirements and mutually unknown actors.

34.5.1 What Is a Blockchain?

A Blockchain is a decentralized and distributed digital ledger that is used to record transactions across a network of the peer-to-peer computers so that the record cannot be altered retroactively without the alteration of all subsequent blocks and the collusion of the network. While Blockchain was designed with banking and finance in mind to create a secure and unstoppable peer-to-peer network to exchange a value in the form of a digital asset (e.g., the Bitcoin), its technology has an inherent connection to cybersecurity. Thus, while cryptocurrencies like Bitcoin sometimes experience rocky fluctuations in value, its Blockchain underpinnings have so far successfully withstood cyberattacks for more than 9 years. The Blockchain offers, in fact, safer transactions, protection against certain hacking attacks, and even, to a certain extent, obviates the need for passwords.

Its distributed ledger is made up of block strings (Fig. 34.3 below is admittedly a naïve representation of a Blockchain, whose structure is in fact a Merkle tree, but its simplicity helps giving the idea of how the hash pointers are linked together; if one transaction is tampered, the link gets broken; therefore, the Blockchain is secure and immutable) designed to avoid any kind of after-the-fact modification. Once data has been published on it, using a reliable time stamping technique and a link to a previous block through cryptographic function hash value, there is no going back and making alterations to the record.

Its potential has been analyzed with respect to the services offered by DNS servers to deflect cyberattacks. Due to the inviolability and decentralization of the Blockchain, if this technology were used to replace the domain name system, denial of service (DDoS) attacks would be made impossible. The consequence of such attacks has been seen time

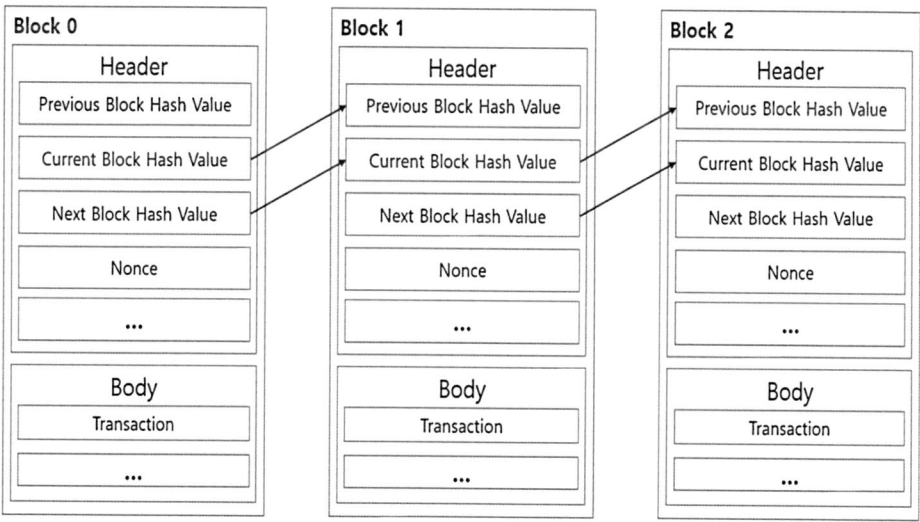

Fig. 34.3 Blockchain architecture

and again, with DDoS attacks cutting off users' access to such mainstream websites like PayPal, Twitter, and Spotify. The problem is that current DNS servers lack in security because they keep the access key on a single server and rely too much on caching. The advantage is clear: Blockchain technology could constantly check and validate data communication flow with no single point of failure, like a distributed notarization service.

Cybersecurity is undoubtedly on course to adopt Blockchain technology: the fundamental difference in the technological approach allows to go beyond the endpoints, including the security of the user's identity, the transaction of information, and the protection of critical infrastructure. It is a complex and sophisticated paradigm shift, but we are already seeing the first results of its application.

Bottom line: Blockchain delivers a secure ecosystem that any business network may benefit from; the distributed ledger it provides is an append-only log that can record business transaction as well as code the conditions for the transactions to occur (smart contracts) as it was a third-party arbitrator on whose rules all the participants have foreknowledge. It provides business with a technology breakthrough that locks transactions and their participants in a single trust system that can be used as a compliance-driven transaction processing vehicle for business rules, regulatory requirements, and data formats.

Blockchain core features for the business network participants are:

- *Consensus*: all network participants agree to network verified transactions.
- *Provenance*: enabling every digital and physical product or piece of information to come with a digital "passport" that proves authenticity and origin.
- *Immutability*: all past transaction information are unchangeable, therefore cannot be counterfeited or tampered.
- *Privacy*: appropriate visibility if granted to the participants; transactions are secure, authenticated, and verifiable.
- *Finality*: single source of truth for each transaction, it can be regarded as an "invisible" enterprise chain infrastructure that provides foundations for other business to connect via APIs or connectors.

34.6 Rethinking Cloud Security with a Zero Trust Security Model

34.6.1 The BeyondCorp Story from Google

When a highly sophisticated APT attack named "Operation Aurora" occurred in 2009, Google began an internal initiative called BeyondCorp to reimagine their security architecture with regards to how devices and employees access internal applications.

Unlike the traditional perimeter security models with their inner vulnerability to attacks, BeyondCorp dispels the notion of network segmentation as the primary mechanism for protecting sensitive resources. On the contrary, all applications are deployed to the public

Internet, behind no special security perimeter, accessible through a user and device-centric authentication and authorization workflow. The guiding principles set forth by Google help pave the path for other organizations to realize their own implementation of a so-called Zero Trust network.

Zero Trust is then a security model conceived on the premise – quite intuitive – that economic incentives are so high for an attacker and attack tactics and technologies are so pervasive for a network, with all the many different mobile devices, applications, and platforms today interconnected that the only way to mitigate your cyber risk is by removing completely the element of trust in your network, your employees, and your partners: trust nothing and no one in your environment, which sounds a very simplistic approach but has profound implications in the architecture and the security of applications. Zero Trust was originally developed as part of the BeyondCorp architecture (see Fig. 34.4)and assumes that all assets are untrusted, and there's no distinction between the inside and the outside of the firewall, because no areas are safer than another.

It praises a data-centric approach to security, and as we'll be discussing, it requires a detailed and dynamic asset inventory, which is probably its biggest hurdle for its implementation, as it's not often what you find in most of organizations' IT, as well as the other primitive that requires authentication, authorization, and access control at every level. This letter is a shift up in expectations compared to the current network access control that defines policies on what devices can connect to your network; it requires an authentication, authorization, and access control for each microservice that access your cloud environment that call each other. A firewall in this security model is not any longer the

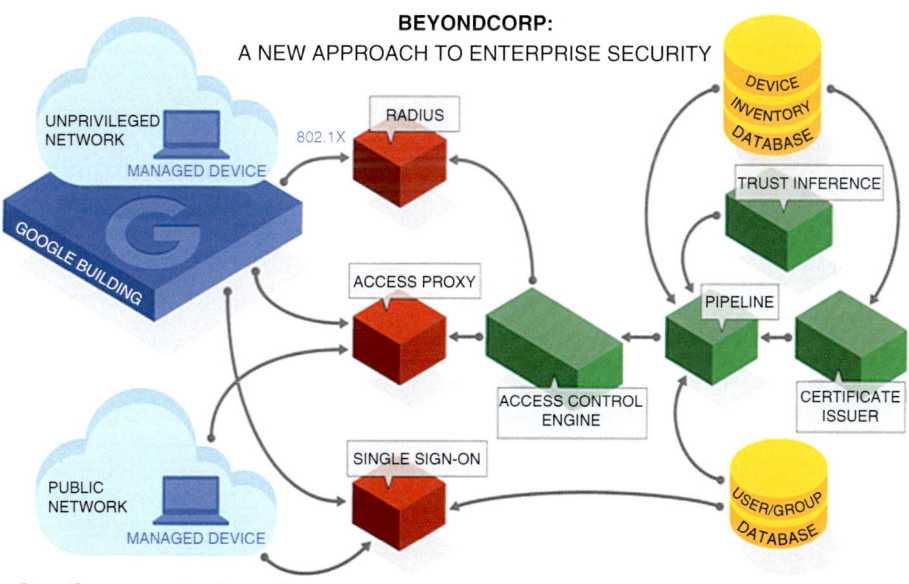

BeyondCorp components and access flow

Fig. 34.4 Beyond corp

perimeter; it does not delimit good from bad, which is quite an interesting evolution to face the risks we have been talking about. Encryption is the final primitive that must be utilized in a Zero Trust model; all data, identities, and communications have to be encrypted. If that sounds not too different from just applying a new philosophical approach and some new primitives, let us see what is different when trying to migrate to a Zero Trust network: fundamentally, implementing a Zero Trust network is about removing perimeter around servers and creating a logical distinction between data sources and Access Intelligence from Gateways and Resources (see Fig. 34.5).

Resources are those elements that people need access to: the network, the applications, the code repositories, and all the micro-services, while the logical opposite side of the network is comprised of the data sources, the assets, and the information that people need to consume through the Access Intelligence layer, which is essentially a set of access policies and controls that get layered on that complex inventory service that we had introduced, placed as a blue box in the picture above; a kind of a God's box, the database that knows everything of your environment and the Access Intelligence is the rule checker that decides who can talk to what. The gateways are the points where those controls can actually be applied to the entities in the resources box.

The key thing is then inventory service that is supposed to keep track of lots of items: from the certification authorities to trust, the configuration management changes, the patch management information, access management, directory services, network infrastructure, vulnerability scanners, inventories of microservices, etc. Very elegant design but – in practice – a source of frustration, tribulation, and trials for Google to implement in practice, this is how they had described the migration in their project documentation.

A recent survey from Nemertes Research showed that a successful security initiative to migrate to a Zero Trust concept had high performance on operational matrix; those

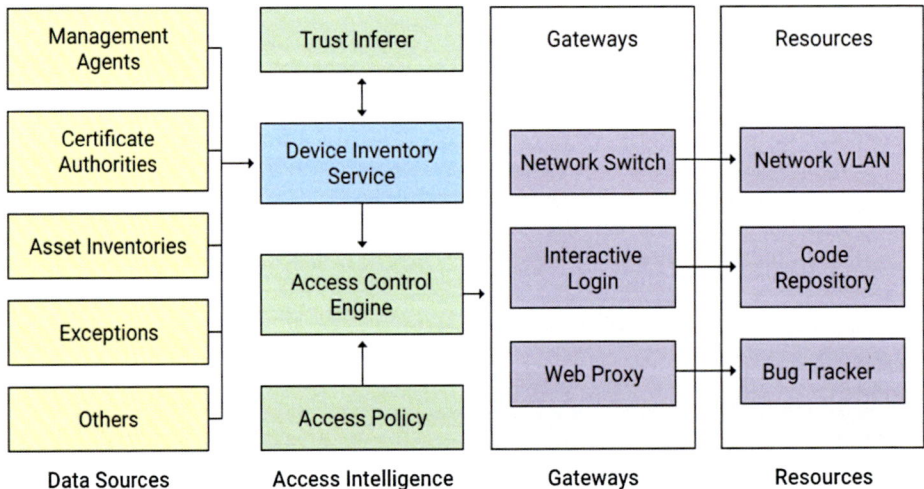

Fig. 34.5 Data sources and access intelligence from gateways and resources

organizations who had a successful move were able to objectively detect threats, respond to threats, and remediate against attacks much faster than those companies that were unable to migrate or had unsuccessful initiatives. In terms of enabling practices, not software you can buy but initiatives needed to adopt a Zero Trust security model, the key practice is a data classification campaign: if you want to decide who should get access to what, then you have to review how important is each type of data you own. The same research shows that successful adopters of Zero Trust had implemented some particular enabling technology, particularly an Advanced Endpoint Security (AES) software. So AES have been a key component of adoption, which should come as no surprise, since the peculiar functionality of an AES is to compress any piece of code capability and let it do only a limited set of functions that are necessary. Another enabling technology turned out to be Application Security Testing (AST) for those companies who develop internally a large amount of code, and network access control (NAC) are tools that even though you are not building perimeters of confidence in your network, it can help you to apply those Access Intelligence policies that are critical for Zero Trust adoption.

The Zero Trust security approach isn't new music for the ears of cybersecurity specialists, yet organizations are spending millions of dollars while witnessing successful breach of their defenses, and the consensus appears to be that IT industry – despite its sets of sophisticated best practices, compliance, and guidance – might be losing the game to smarter and innovative groups of dispersed threat actors; there is evidence that IT departments looking for a future proof organizational models are turning back to Zero Trust models, despite the initial concern over implementation complexity, ease of administration, and the necessity to reset of all end-user access registers.

Ten years ago, the Zero Trust security approach would have meant a strict "corporate device only" usage policy, while other technologies and improvements have released the stress on the primary device nature, and today a Zero Trust security approach does not reject the flexibility of personal choice of devices awarded to end users through the BYOD policy. Another argument often made in the past was the delays in user access and reductions of user productivity due to system and network infrastructure latencies and non-responsiveness. However, today compute latency is a nonissue, while network latency is now better controlled through service level agreements with cloud providers.

But it does mean that whichever device is being used, verification of access to data by the device will be much more rigorous; any end-user device will not be trusted till they explicitly establish their identity before any requested access, through multiple layers of security credentials. Vigorous authentication of end users and their devices and their entitlement to access corporate data will soon become the norm in the years ahead.

Zero Trust is also particularly suitable for digital transformation as it applies micro-segmentation for growing multi-cloud access that is responsible for driving digital transformation and development of innovative and new business processes. Once a Zero Trust policy has been pursued, the organization will be better equipped to move to the next level of enablement and implementation: these include working with managed security service providers and the adoption of Blockchain technologies.

34.6.2   Software Defined Perimeter

Before we put all together in a final use case to strengthen Cloud cybersecurity, let's intro-duce the Software Defined Perimeter or SDP or otherwise referred as Black Cloud. SDP is a new technology that was built to tackle a few challenges of IP network protocols; the first and foremost is that you can make a layer 3 connection through IP protocol before you get authenticated, and any server decides whether you'd have access to a resource or not. This is a common issue with IoT devices connecting to a cloud service: you don't want your servers to syndicate the two services first and then decide whether they should talk to each other. An SDP will force the authentication first and then open the connection afterward.

Connectivity is then reinvented in an SDP based on a need-to-know model, in which device posture and identity are verified before access to application infrastructure is granted. Application infrastructure is effectively "blacked out," which means that the infrastructure cannot be detected, without visible DNS information or IP addresses. The claim for SDP adoption is that building a Software Defined Perimeter mitigates the most common network-based cyberattacks, including server scanning, denial of service, SQL injection, operating system and application vulnerability exploits, man in the middle, and few others.

It is easy to show the potential risk mitigation on data breaches: data loss or compro-mised when it comes to intellectual property, financial information, HR, and other digital assets available within an enterprise network is quite a dramatic event; an attacker is nor-mally obtaining access to internal network by compromising a computer, or its owner identity, and then moves laterally to get access to high-value information. An SDP use case could be partitioning the network and isolating high-value applications, somewhat in the same way network segmentation used to realize, with the additional feature of rendering those high-value applications invisible, thus mitigating the lateral movements of an attacker.

A Software Defined Perimeter consists of two components (see Fig. 34.6), in its sim-plest form: a Software Host and a Software Controller. The SDP Host can either initiate connections or accept connections; in both cases these are managed by the SDP Control-ler. The first architectural element that comes at sight is that in SDP, the control level is separated by the data flow, to enable great scalability.

While useful for protecting physical machines, the software overlay nature of the SDP also allows it to be integrated into private clouds to leverage the flexibility and elasticity of those environments. In that context, SDPs can be used by enterprises to hide and secure their public cloud instances in isolation or as a unified system that includes private and public cloud instances and/or cross-cloud clusters.

Software as a service vendor can use an SDP to protect their services; in this context, the software service would be an Accepting SDP Host, and all users desiring connectivity

Fig. 34.6 Software defined perimeter

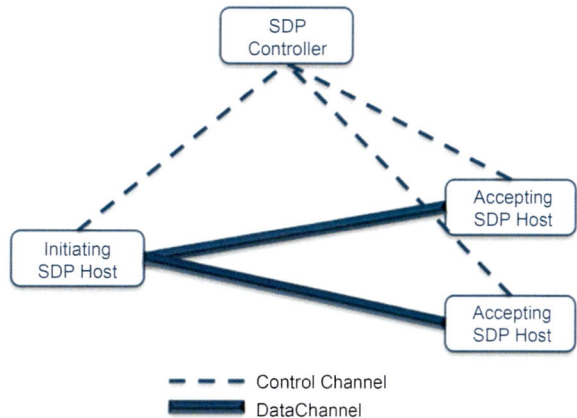

to the service would be the initiating hosts. This allows a SaaS to leverage the global reach of the Internet without enabling the Internet's global attack surface.

34.7 Putting All Together: A New-Gen Cybersecurity Model with Zero Trust, SDP, and the Blockchain

A well-reviewed and prepared cybersecurity policy can also be enhanced by the usage of Blockchain technologies; their distributed ledger of identified transactions cannot be altered and are accessible and visible across an open platform of a network of systems. This backbone can be used to keep a record of user authentication and access requests, resulting in a huge leap into path-breaking standards of compliance and audits. No longer can log data go missing or be compromised by accidental or intentional efforts of cover-ups, but everything is traced and available for IT department, auditors, and business perusal.

Now, given all the technologies and policies that we have introduced, we can answer the business demand for a cybersecurity use case that is cloud-native and future proof, ideally suited for a business network like any supply chain. Knowing the constraints, the restrictions and the economic incentives of the current security models, how could we completely overhaul the traditional approach to cybersecurity architecture and address the fundamental flaws and economic failures such as the human factor and information asymmetry that natively provide end-to-end privacy and encryption while still ensuring convenience for users and – finally – shift cybersecurity model from prevention to detection and response?.

Well, if the readers have followed me up to this point, presumably they are able to anticipate the conclusions of this article and hopefully are now standing in front of an

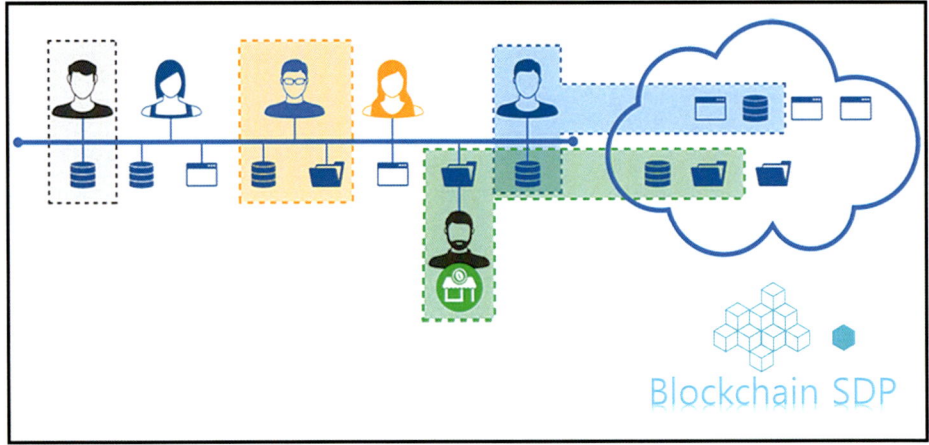

Fig. 34.7 Putting all together: new-gen cybersecurity model

important discovery that directly concerns the future of their organizations: a new gen cybersecurity (see Fig. 34.7.) implementation model built on Zero Trust model with a Software Defined Perimeter defined by a Blockchain set of services. This "Blockchain Defined Perimeter" would then become a maximum cybersecurity for critical systems and cloud infrastructure that would replace the centralize fortress model in favor of a distributed fortress. The Blockchain Defined Perimeter would then provide:

- *Digital identity* services using Blockchain-based digital signature to authenticate humans, devices, and data
- *Black Cloud* access type: invisible locked-down access to critical systems, assets, and devices
- *Best-in-class encryption* for secured access to critical resources
- *Tamper-proof immutable logging* to identities and accesses stored on the Blockchain

If introduced, those features would make the IT infrastructure resilient to compromised passwords and identities. When combined with a policy of multi-authentication (two- or three-factor based) that perimeter would render any critical service (servers, databases, IoT devices, microservices and APIs) completely invisible to attackers, reagardless the type on cloud architecture, be it private, hybrid, or public.

Another great consequence is that your organization will not depend only by a mature patch management policy; a ransom attack like WannaCry or Petya would find difficult the lateral move and attack a critical application, even if its patch level would make it inherently vulnerable to the attack. Equivalently, a phishing attack targeting a user identity would fail because the authentication process would not rely on username and password credentials only, but it'd be more robust with the use of multifactor authentication and digital signature for both users and devices.

Monitoring for attacker activity would also be a new weapon: as we know an intruder may be able to spend a significant time on a corporate network, after being able to penetrate. Attackers are also quite sophisticated; they are normally able to alter their traces modifying the logs, if they can find them. The Blockchain software perimeter would not just lock-down high-value targets but also encrypt and notarize each system log and trace that would give an organization sufficient information to detect the attack or its failed attempt and take countermeasures.

Another element of trust that concerns cloud providers is removed by the picture with a Blockchain Defined Perimeter: imagine the case that a cloud service provides is compromised by an attacker or one of their administrators is gone rogue; likewise all the logs of their activities will be safely stored in the Blockchain, minimizing the incentive and discouraging anyone to create damage to your organization.

BDP prevents most of the traditional attacks, like IP spoofing and DoS, and even if you log on an encrypted http connection to a cloud service, still the communication will be encrypted by the BDP. BDP can also be a catalyst to adopt technologies which, in the past, have requested a significant overhead of activity for IT departments, like authentication with secure certificate. The maintenance of the certificates' validity has been a reason for non-adoption; in many cases, Blockchain allows the creation of an ecosystem where key-based or certificate-based authentication can be used without any administration overhead. See Fig. 34.8 for the benefits for this technology.

In conclusion, the economic incentives for an implementation of Zero Trust security policy with Blockchain Defined Perimeter are multiple; you obtain a future proof, cloud-native, security infrastructure, it will facilitate the adoption of new cloud services and

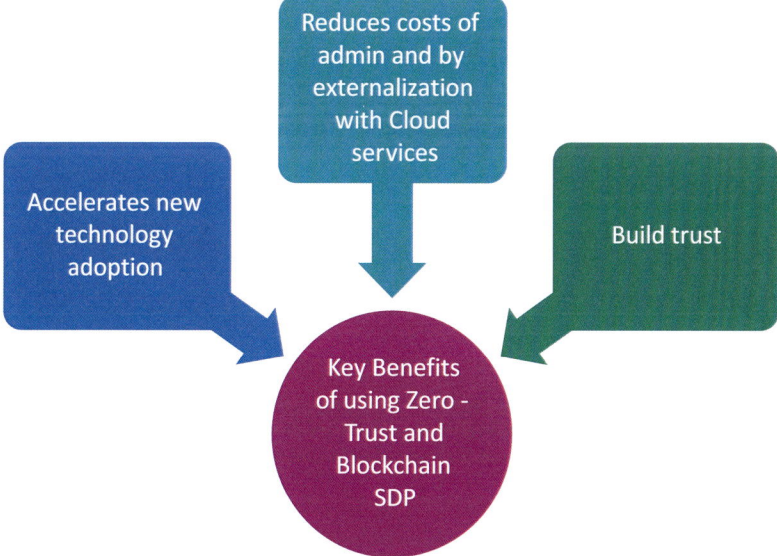

Fig. 34.8 Final picture of benefits for this technology

therefore lower the total cost of ownership of your software assets, it will reduce the administration effort in provisioning secure services to your users (you can centralize on a single-user interface all the provisioning/revoke of authorizations for any type of application), and most importantly it will reduce the risk on the weakest element on the security chain: the human behavior prone to errors. Commonly, an IT insfrastructure you will depend from a mix of services which are on premise, on a private and/or hybrid cloud; imagine removing yourself form the need of Firewalls, VPNs, layer of complexity and adminsitration overhead: sound like a hazardous move, isn't it!? The strong encryption, the automation and transparency of a Blockchain SDP would actually let you achieve the stark opposite: top-notch security level and fine granularity control over your data and services. Finally, it helps building trust with your partners in the supply chain.

References

Tyler Moore and Ross Anderson – Computer Science Group Harvard University – "Economics and Internet Security: a Survey of Recent Analytical, Empirical and Behavioral Research" 2011 https://www.cl.cam.ac.uk/~rja14/Papers/moore-anderson-infoeconsurvey2011.pdf

Rainer Böhme – Universität Innsbruck, Austria – "Measuring the cost of cybercrime" (2012) – https://link.springer.com/chapter/10.1007/978-3-642-39498-0_12

George A. Akerlof "The Market for Lemons: Quality Uncertainty and the Market Mechanism" – The Quarterly Journal of Economics Vol. 84, No. 3 (Aug., 1970), pp. 488–500 (MIT Press) – https://www.sas.upenn.edu/~hfang/teaching/socialinsurance/readings/fudan_hsbc/Akerlof70(2.1).pdf

Axel Allerkamp

Zusammenfassung

Die Anhäufung der Überschriften „Ransomware verhindert Operationen, Millionen von Kundendaten wurden veröffentlicht, die Produktion stand für Wochen still, Neuinstallation von 3000 Servern in 5 Tagen, durch Dataleak Verlust des Aktienwertes, Kühlschränke legen das Internet lahm" macht deutlich, es kann trotz fortschrittlicher Sicherheitsarchitektur jederzeit zu einer (Cyber-)Krise kommen. In diesem Kapitel werden keine konkreten Maßnahmen oder wiederverwendbare Rezepte vorgestellt. Um die eigene Vorbereitung oder Sichtweise zu diesem Thema zu reflektieren, werden Impulse gegeben und ausgewählte Zusammenhänge aufgezeigt.

Durch die häufige und teilweise inflationäre Verwendung des Begriffs Krise wird im Weiteren dieser Begriff für operative Krisen in Unternehmen oder Organisationen verwendet.

Eine Krise ist eine objektive Gegebenheit und sie wird von subjektiver Wahrnehmung und Interpretation begleitet. Im Allgemeinen kann davon ausgegangen werden, dass eine Krise die Konsequenz von verschiedensten Ereignissen ist, welche die Organisation in ihrer Gesamtheit bedroht. Ein zentrales Element ist die Einzigartigkeit der Situation. Standardprozesse und die alltäglichen Verantwortlichkeiten versagen.

Jede Krise ist dadurch gekennzeichnet, dass eine Vielzahl der folgenden Merkmale in unterschiedlicher Ausprägung aufeinandertreffen – unerwartet eskalierende Entwicklung, Zeitdruck, Entscheidungsdruck unter stark ausgeprägter Informationsasymmetrie (fehlende – falsche – zu viele Informationen).

A. Allerkamp (✉)
Berater und Sicherheitsexperte in IT/Cyber-Sicherheit und Krisenmanagement
Potsdam, Deutschland
E-Mail: allerkamp@cyber-crisis.de

© Springer Fachmedien Wiesbaden GmbH, ein Teil von Springer Nature 2018
M. Bartsch, S. Frey (Hrsg.), *Cybersecurity Best Practices*,
https://doi.org/10.1007/978-3-658-21655-9_35

Fakt ist, dass eine Krise handlungsbedürftig ist. Nichts zu tun, kann weitreichende Folgen nach sich ziehen. Nicht vorbereitet zu sein, verringert die Möglichkeit einer Schadensreduktion.

Eine Cyberkrise ist eine Krise, deren primäre Ursache oder Wirkung im digitalen Umfeld einzuordnen ist. Reproduzierbarkeit und Interaktion in einem Netzwerk mit einer Vielzahl an schwer identifizierbaren Entitäten sind ergänzende Merkmale.

Eine Cyberkrise muss sich vom Leitgedanken „Es ist möglich ein Gesamtsystem zu verstehen, jede einzelne Entität im Detail jedoch nicht oder die Entität in ihrer Bedeutung wird im Detail verstanden, dann jedoch ist ein Gesamtüberblick nicht möglich" tragen lassen.

Für das Thema „Notfallvorsorge und Krise" gibt es zahlreiche Normen und unterstützende Rahmenwerke. Diese sind in ihrer Grundaussage auch unter dem Aspekt Cyber gültig. Anhand einiger ausgewählter Szenarien wird deutlich, dass eine intensive und spezielle Auseinandersetzung erforderlich ist. Die Beispiele sind geeignet, strategische Entscheidungen im Rahmen einer Digitalisierungsstrategie zu bewerten. Alle Beispiele sind gleichgewichtig, mit ihnen soll die Komplexität und die Wechselwirkungen im Detail erörtert werden. Zu allen exemplarischen Beschreibungen wird grundsätzlich eine europäische Sichtweise eingenommen.

Eine Vielzahl der Internet of Things (IoT) Geräte sind billig produziert und verwenden unpatchbare oder minimal konfigurierbare Software. Die aktuell gelebte Praxis zeigt, dass die IoT-Software für Sicherheitsexperten als „unsicher" einzustufen ist. Verwendete Software, Bibliotheken, (weitere) Accounts und Protokolle sind nur minimal dokumentiert und beschreiben nur auszugweise den Zustand aus einer Security Perspektive. Es gibt diverse Gründe, warum für diese Geräte auf „security by design"-Ansätze verzichtet wird.

Nach einer erfolgreichen Kompromittierung können solche Systeme sich zu einem Albtraum entwickeln. Zusätzlich zu den beschriebenen Eigenschaften fehlt in großen Organisationen der Überblick, an welchem Ort sich derartige Geräte befinden und welchen Formfaktor diese haben. Eine zeitnahe Identifikation und Einleitung weiterer Maßnahmen ist sehr aufwendig. Eine Abstimmung mit dem Hersteller ist eine besondere Herausforderung. Die Identifizierung des eigentlichen Herstellers einer Software in einem IoT-Gerät ist fast unmöglich. In diesem Umfeld ist es üblich, dass Produkte für einen Kunden gebrandet werden und ganz tief im Maschinenraum ist doch vieles auf eine begrenzte Anzahl von Produzenten zurückzuführen. Grundsätzlich ist davon auszugehen, dass der Produzent nur ein geringes Interesse hat, dass Problem aus der Welt zu schaffen. Im günstigen Fall könnte eine neue Version des IoT-Gerätes ohne diese Schwachstelle bereitgestellt werden. Spekulativ werden zwischen Lieferung und Nutzung mehrere Tage vergehen. Der Vollständigkeit halber sei erwähnt, dass auch namenhafte Hersteller von embedded Geräten diese Strategie verfolgen. Beschrieben sind Situationen, in denen ein Hersteller einer Software für ein IoT-Gerät zweifelsfrei identifiziert wurde. Die Realität ist auch, dass eine Vielzahl von Open Source Komponenten auf diesen Geräten vorzufinden ist.

Auch wenn eine Organisation keine IoT-Geräte im Kontext des Kerngeschäftes einsetzt, wird diese mit dem Thema in Berührung kommen. Diverse IoT-Geräte sind bereits heute als Sensor oder Aktor verbaut. Das Augenmerk soll exemplarisch auf derartige Geräte im Umfeld von Gebäudetechnik gerichtet werden. Klimaanlage, Zutrittssysteme und Videokameras sind prominente Beispiele. Eine unberechtigte Nutzung durch Dritte kann so zum zeitweisen Erlöschen einer Betriebserlaubnis führen. Die direkte Folge ist eine Kombination aus digitalen und analogen Aspekten, die sowohl eine Gefahr für die Unversehrtheit der Mitarbeiter als auch einen Produktionsausfall zur Realität werden lassen.

Die Fortsetzung des Gedankens verlangt eine Auseinandersetzung mit public cloud Services oder Software as a Service Angeboten. Vorausgesetzt wird, dass vor Nutzung derartiger Angebote eine Risikoabschätzung erfolgte und die Verantwortlichkeiten abgestimmt sind. Unabhängig wie die Sicherheitsarchitektur ist, sind Services der Kategorie „public cloud oder Software as a Services" für Angreifer ein lohnendes und wertvolles Ziel. Die Vielzahl der unterschiedlichen Kunden und Daten innerhalb einer Infrastruktur macht es sehr attraktiv. Die Ausnutzung bereits einer Schwachstelle ermöglicht eine breite und mannigfaltige Schädigung bzw. die Durchführung von erfolgreichen Angriffsoperationen. Die eigene Organisation war zu dem ursprünglichen Zeitpunkt nicht das primäre Ziel eines Angriffs. Trotz des Kollateralschadens befindet sich die Organisation im Zustand einer Krise. In der Anfangsphase der Krise und der vorhandenen Abhängigkeit sind die Handlungsalternativen begrenzt. Betroffene Kunden der eigenen Organisation haben kein Interesse, die Abhängigkeiten zu verstehen. Im Fokus steht die eigene Organisation. Der vorhandene Vertrag hilft in der Situation nur bedingt, das Kernproblem ist beim Diensteanbieter zu lösen und die Organisation ist vom Fortschritt oder Erfolg abhängig.

Die Auswertung aus öffentlich zugänglichen Statistiken zeigt, dass branchenunabhängig mehr als 150 Tage vergehen vom Zeitpunkt eines erfolgreichen, gezielten Angriffs bis zum Wahrnehmen dieses Angriffs. Diese Zahl verlangt eine Betrachtung unter dem Gedanken „Ein Angreifer bestimmt Ort, Zeit und Geschwindigkeit eines Angriffs". Wird der Sicherheitsvorfall erkannt, können eigentlich die IT-Infrastruktur und die Daten als nicht vertrauenswürdig eingestuft werden. Sofern es nicht um einen quick hack geht, wird ein primäres Ziel sein, ein „goldenes Ticket" (Secupedia) zu erlangen. Mit einem „goldenen Ticket" bleibt der Angreifer unverändert in der Situation, die IT-Infrastruktur zu kompromittieren. Auch wenn das primäre Ziel nicht erreicht werden kann, bleibt die Frage „Welche Systeme, Konfigurationen und Daten sind seit welchem Zeitpunkt nicht mehr vertrauenswürdig?". Die Beantwortung verlangt eine forensische Analyse. In Filmen sind die Ergebnisse forensischer Analysen innerhalb von wenigen Minuten verfügbar. Aus dramaturgischen Gründen ist das akzeptabel. In der Realität hängt das Ergebnis von Anzahl der Datenquellen, Güte der Log-Datei, Einzigartigkeit des Angriffs und weiterer Faktoren ab. Mehrere Wochen werden für eine umfängliche Analyse und Bewertung erforderlich sein. Dieser Zeitraum steht im Widerspruch zu einer kurzfristigen Behandlung der eskalierten Situation.

Digitalisierung oder auch Cyber müssen losgelöst von geografisch referenzierten Betrachtungen erfolgen. Dennoch treffen unterschiedlich geografisch geprägte Rechtsnormen aufeinander, deren Abwägung gegeneinander im Einzelfall zu erfolgen hat. Typische Konstellationen, die aufeinandertreffen können: Öffentliche Bekanntgabe vs. Strafverfolgung oder Verbot des Datenexports vs. Erfüllen einer Anzeige- oder Transparenzpflicht.

Ein Massenproblem stellen die Kundendaten dar. Gerade in einem B2C-Umfeld ist die Wahrscheinlichkeit hoch, dass die Organisation über eine sehr hohe Anzahl von Kundendaten verfügt. Für dieses Beispiel schaffen wir ein fiktives Unternehmen mit insgesamt

5 Mio. Kunden. Durch ein internes Audit wurde festgestellt, dass 1 Mio. Kundendaten durch Unberechtigte aus den zentralen Systemen kopiert wurden. Im Idealfall ist eine genaue Trennung in betroffen und nicht-betroffen möglich. Gemäß aktueller Rechtsnormen (u. a. Datenschutz) sind die Betroffenen über diesen Missbrauch in einem engen zeitlichen Zusammenhang zu informieren. Die Verbreitung dieser Information wird bereits viel Synchronisierung benötigen und eine erhebliche Anzahl von Ressourcen binden. Spätestens zum Zeitpunkt der Veröffentlichung dieser Information an die betroffene Person werden sich die nicht-informierten Personen an das Unternehmen wenden. Das Bedürfnis seine individuelle Unsicherheit durch Informationen zu befriedigen, wird weitere Ressourcen des Unternehmens binden. Beide Gruppen „vom Datendiebstahl betroffen" und „nicht betroffen" sind ihren Ansprüchen und Erwartungen entsprechend zu behandeln. Die Kommunikation an die Mitglieder der entsprechenden Gruppen darf nicht mit der Genauigkeit der Erkenntnisse im Widerspruch stehen. Die Zuordnung von Personen in die falsche Gruppe hat erhebliches Eskalationspotenzial.

Spätestens zum Zeitpunkt des Datenmissbrauchs wird dieses ein öffentliches Thema sein. Je bedeutender oder sichtbarer die Organisation zu diesem Zeitpunkt ist, desto größer wird die Anzahl derer sein, die sich berufen fühlen, zu diesem Thema eine Meinung abzugeben. Bereits die Masse bestimmter Meinungen kann zu einer Meinungsführerschaft führen. Organisationsbekannte Realität und in der Öffentlichkeit wahrgenommene Realität driften mit zunehmender Dauer auseinander.

Bereits die wenigen Beispiele haben gezeigt, dass die Abgrenzung von Sicherheitsvorfall/Notfall zu Krise sich nicht an allgemeinen Maßstäben orientieren kann, sondern eine organisationsspezifische Regelung verlangt. Auch wenn diese Regelung vorhanden ist, wird eine ungewisse Zeit vergehen bis eine Organisation sich formal in einer Krise befindet. Es hat sich bewährt, den Zustand formal festzustellen. Die Veränderung von Verantwortlichkeiten, Abläufen, Rechten und Pflichten ist mit dieser Feststellung eindeutig.

In einer analogen Krise sind Parameter beschreibbar, die den Wechsel in den Zustand „Krise" hinreichend genau ermöglichen. Viele vernetzte Akteure, viele scheinbar zusammenhanglose Ereignisse und oft ein technisches Vokabular verzögern die Bewertung der Situation, Abschätzung der Folgen und formale Feststellung einer Cyberkrise. Das Spannungsfeld, in dem innerhalb von Minuten sich ein Security Incident zu einer Krise entwickeln kann und das Treffen der wegweisenden Entscheidung „die Organisation befindet sich in der Krise" verlangt schnelle und verlässliche Entscheidungsprozesse. Ziel sollte es sein, das „Chaos" schnell zu überwinden und selbst wieder die Handlungsfähigkeit zu erlangen.

Eine Frage, die vor einer Krise beantwortet werden kann, ist die folgende: „Auf welchen Wegen soll im Fall einer Cyberkrise, d. h. die Vertrauenswürdigkeit oder Verfügbarkeit der bisher genutzten IT-Infrastruktur ist fragwürdig, mit Partnern, Mitarbeitern und Betroffenen kommuniziert werden?" Besonderes Augenmerk ist auf die Wechselwirkung zu Awarenesskampagnen zu richten. Die Kernaussage in der Sensibilisierung ist, dass E-Mails o. ä. von unbekannten Absendern ignoriert werden sollen.

Eine ad hoc Möglichkeit ist immer, bestehende und verfügbare Kommunikationsplattformen für sich nutzbar zu machen.

Sollte dieses für die Organisation eine Option sein, um in der Cyberkrise kommunizieren zu wollen, so verlangt dieses eine vorbereitende und begleitende Information an die Partner, Führungskräfte und Mitarbeiter. Sollte diese vorbereitende Kommunikation nicht erfolgen, so ist davon auszugehen, dass nur ein Bruchteil der Empfänger reagieren, da sie erfolgreich an Awarenesskampagnen teilgenommen haben. Eine direkte Folge ist, dass geplante Maßnahmen in ihrem Zeitpunkt oder Umfang ihre Wirkung verlieren. Die zielgerichtete Erreichbarkeit der Empfänger ggf. unter Aspekten einer Vertraulichkeit verlangt eine hohe Datenqualität von Kommunikationsdaten. Diese Daten zu erheben ist im Fall der Fälle nur begrenzt möglich und führt unweigerlich zu Verzögerungen.

In der Vorbereitung auf mögliche Cyberkrisen ist ein Aspekt die Identifizierung von Experten. Aufgrund der Komplexität und auch erwarteten Detailtiefe werden Cyberkrisen nur durch den synchronisierten Einsatz einer Vielzahl von unterschiedlichen Experten gelöst werden können. Bei herkömmlichen Krisen konnten die Maßnahmen oft durch mehr oder umfangreicheren Einsatz von Ressourcen erfolgreich umgesetzt werden. In der Cyberkrise wird auch die Qualität ein Erfolgsfaktor sein. Die Identifizierung geeigneter Experten und die Art der Zusammenarbeit sind frühzeitig zu klären. Wichtig ist, eher einen breiten Ansatz zu wählen. Die Poolbildung von Experten schafft Flexibilität für die Krise.

Die Erfahrung von konventionellen Krisen zeigt deutlich, dass ein gutes Informationsmanagement das Fundament ist, um diese eskalierten Situationen zu einem Erfolg zu führen. Im Fall der Cyberkrise in der die Verlässlichkeit der Systeme und Daten zweifelhaft ist, kommt es auf entsprechende erprobte und alternative Verfahren an. Die zeitlich und logische Abhängigkeit bzw. Kausalketten sind oft für das menschliche Gehirn nicht greifbar. Das gilt sowohl für Ursache als auch die Wirkungen von ergriffenen Maßnahmen. So können kleine Maßnahmen bereits erfolgreich sein und große Maßnahmen ihre Wirkung vollständig verfehlen oder erst zeitlich verzögert bemerkbar sein.

Ein wirkungsvolles Hilfsmittel ist die Visualisierung. Ein Bild sagt mehr als tausend Worte – dieses Prinzip gilt unverändert insbesondere in kritischen Situationen. Granularität und in sich vorhandene Komplexität von Informationsmanagement und Visualisierung sind außerhalb dieses Artikels. Der Appell ist: Der investierte Aufwand vor einer Krise macht sich bereits in den ersten Minuten einer Krise bezahlt.

Krisen im Allgemeinen und Cyberkrisen im Besonderen verlangen Entscheidungen unter Unsicherheit. Keine Entscheidung ist auch eine Entscheidung. Jede Entscheidung und jede resultierende Maßnahme verändern die Situation. Komplexität, Dynamik und Informationsasymmetrie werden auch Entscheidungen produzieren, welche in der Reflexion sich als unzweckmäßig herausgestellt haben. Jede Entscheidung beinhaltet die Elemente: Maßnahme – Effekt – Ziel. Wenn diese Elemente formuliert werden können, so können abweichende Entwicklungen zu einem frühen Zeitpunkt erkannt und korrigiert werden. Die Wirkungsmessung einer Maßnahme kann oft nur über den Effekt wahrgenommen und interpretiert werden. In der Interaktion der Entitäten in einem Netzwerk können bereits kleine ungewöhnliche Maßnahmen zu einer erheblichen Wirkung führen (Schmetterling – Sturm). Die Fähigkeit eigene Entscheidungen zeitnah zu treffen, die Wahrnehmung der Wirkung und eine fokussierte Reflexion verlangen Erfahrung.

Situationen zu erfahren ist die beste Vorbereitung für die nächste Krise. Unabhängig der eigenen Vorbereitung oder Überlegungen zu den beschriebenen Aspekten ist eine Cyberübung immer richtig und wichtig. Die Ziele und die Intensität von Übungen sind sehr organisationsspezifisch. Ein Effekt wird aber immer erreicht: Es wird Bewusstsein für die Komplexität und Dynamik in der Cyberkrise geschaffen. In Abb. 35.1 ist der Artikel visuell dargestellt.

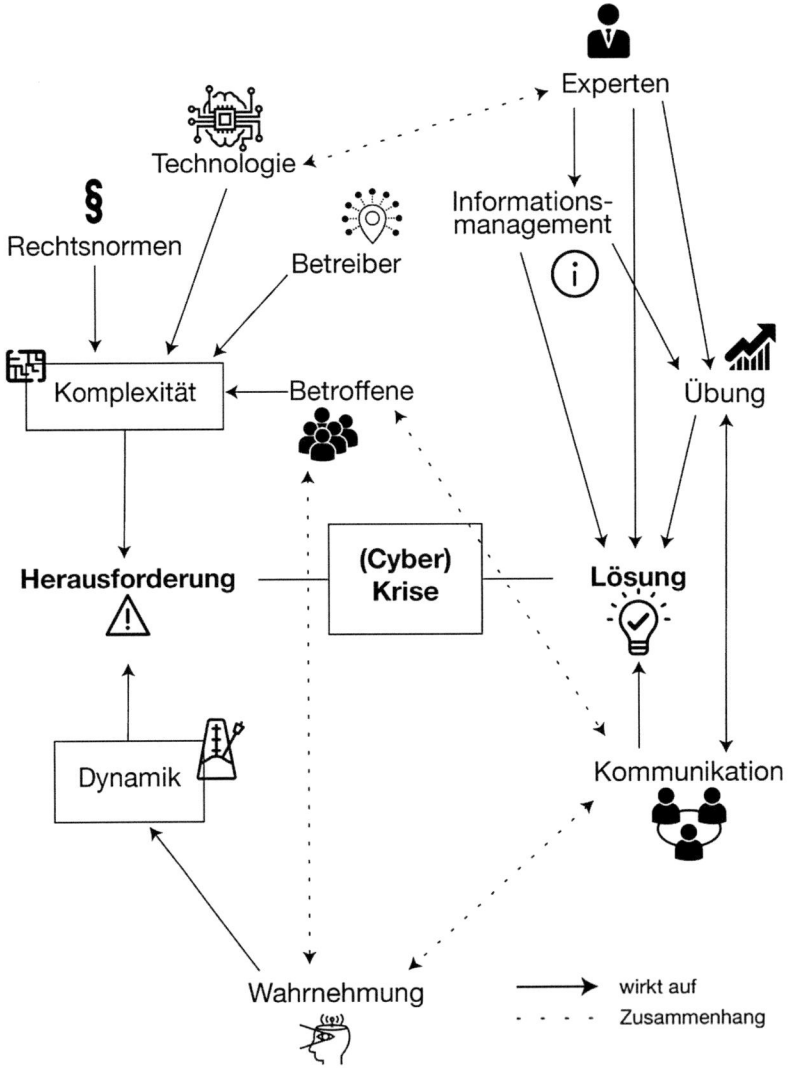

Abb. 35.1 Artikel als Bild zusammengefasst

Being More Effective Through Information Sharing and Cooperation

Michael Weatherseed

Abstract

Often there is great reluctance to share information about security issues. This chapter looks at the different types of professional events currently being organised and how they can be used to learn, exchange best practices and lead to optimisation of protection against, and reaction to, cyber threats.

Executives with responsibility for cybersecurity do not need to be told by anybody else that they have a challenging role to play. Organisations are becoming increasingly dependent on data and information systems, and the volume of data is ever growing. Data has a value and therefore is an attractive target for competitors and cyber criminals. Cyberattacks are growing in volume, in frequency and in sophistication, and organisations both large and small are already targets. The challenges will get bigger rather than diminish. It is a race to keep one step ahead and to be able to recognise a cyber threat, to prevent a cyberattack and to repair the damage after the cyberattack and not forgetting having to work within allocated (i.e. limited) budgets.

To optimise cybersecurity effectiveness in these circumstances, an executive that has responsibility for cybersecurity (CISO) needs to be equipped with the best available information and tools to do the job. To do this, means benefiting from the experience of others and especially from those outside one's own organisation. As soon as the term "security" is mentioned, there is often a reluctance to talk about one's own issues with external people. However, the sharing of information, intelligently and for very selfish reasons, should be encouraged.

M. Weatherseed (✉)
COMEXPOSIUM, Paris La Defense, France
e-mail: michael.weatherseed@comexposium.com

© Springer Fachmedien Wiesbaden GmbH, ein Teil von Springer Nature 2018
M. Bartsch, S. Frey (Hrsg.), *Cybersecurity Best Practices*,
https://doi.org/10.1007/978-3-658-21655-9_36

36.1 What Should Be Shared?

Companies often concentrate on internal threats, which in today's world are not enough. The increased digitization with shared and interconnected infrastructures and supply chains means that cyber threats can target systems upon which the entire organisation is dependent. It is therefore imperative to "Think outside the box!" and consider the entire organisation and not only components of it. It is also important to know the current and future cyber threat landscape and cyberattacks that happen to others, as they could hit your company as well. Information available in the public domain tends to concentrate on the problem and cyber threat rather than discussing possible solutions and possible defence systems. Furthermore, it is important to examine solutions and defence systems that do not work as much as those that do work.

36.1.1 Challenges to Sharing Information: Choose What You Share

Information sharing outside one's own organisation is a sensitive topic. In the case of cybersecurity, the information could cover not only technical and operational subjects but also corporate and commercial ones. Such information has the potential to be harmful to one's organisation but also give competitive advantage to other companies. Information sharing therefore has to be used intelligently and be based on a cost benefit analysis.

▶   **TRUST is key!**

For really valuable information to be shared, there needs to be TRUST between the different parties. Trust needs to be built by:

- Sharing of cybersecurity incidents, best practices, threat information – giving and receiving of value. It has to be two-way street.
- Building long-term, regular relationships and not just in the case of an immediate problem.

Trust is best built on face-to-face meetings. Often the most effective meetings are based on social occasions – dining and wining, conferences and networking meetings.

36.1.2 Support from the Top

The CISO also needs to be supported from top management in order to be able to share what could be perceived as confidential information. The above mentioned need for cost benefit analysis is key for potentially reluctant management.

36.1.3   Choose with Whom You Share

- **With peers:** CISOs have the same objectives – protecting their information systems and data. A peer might work for a company that is competing commercially, but sharing cyber solution strategies and information about cyber threats will benefit everybody and should not be withheld due to commercial rivalry.
- **With solution providers:** Solution providers not only have tools and strategies, to protect and react against cyberattacks, but they also have practical experience, much of which can be shared.
- **With specialist government departments:** Organisations such as BSI in Germany, ANSSI in France and the National Cyber Security Centre in the UK all have in their remit to improve general cybersecurity with advice to citizens and organisations.

36.2   What Are the Options?

So, if as a CISO I want to share information and best practices, what options do I have apart from ringing up another CISO I know or trawling through LinkedIn or Xing for individuals whose profile mentions the term "cybersecurity?"

36.2.1   CISO Associations

In many countries there are associations that group together cybersecurity professionals. They aim to create a community of executives who have similar challenges and objectives. Knowledge is shared, a help network is created and workgroups are formed to address particular challenges, the results of which can then be shared with the community; the association can often be an effective lobbying group. These associations often organise evening or day meetings and an annual members' conference. Examples of such associations are the CESIN, le Club des Experts de la Sécurité de l'Information et du Numérique, in France, and the SASIG, the Security Awareness Special Interest Group, in the UK.

These associations are currently essentially organised by country. However cybersecurity knows no borders, and links to professionals from other countries should be encouraged to increase the sharing of knowledge and best practices. Experience has shown that national associations welcome input and interest from professionals from other countries.

36.2.2   Exhibitions

A trade show offers the opportunity to meet and talk to solution providers and discover what is available on the market. The exhibitors rent stands where they present their products and services and hold presentations. It is the format that can offer the largest number of solution providers in one place, but also the largest number of visitor-participants. Usually the exhibition will take place over a 3 or 4 day period. In most cases, there is also a conference programme (either with a delegate fee or free of charge) and exhibitor workshops (usually free to attend in small "theatre spaces" on the exhibition floor, where companies present their products in presentation format). Some exhibition organisers also provide a matchmaking software that enables visitors to make appointments with exhibiting companies. Examples of professional cybersecurity exhibitions are it-sa in Nuremberg and Infosecurity in London.

36.2.3 Conferences

The growth in the public and professional profile of cyber threats has been accompanied by a huge growth in the number of conferences covering the different subjects of cybersecurity. Some conferences do have a small exhibition element with a few stands for solution providers, but the main attraction is content. The quality of the content in such events can vary enormously. Therefore, potential delegates should check in advance that the subjects treated are useful and interesting for them and that the speakers have a relevant expertise.

Often the disadvantage of the pure conference format is that the information is in one direction, from the speaker to the audience. There are usually only limited opportunities to ask questions, let alone exchange in any depth on a pressing subject or particular issue for the delegate. A conference is usually a 1 or maximum 2 day format. For delegates, the most interesting conferences have a mixture of different session types that range from single keynotes, keynotes interviewed, round-tables and real debates.

36.2.4 "Business Meetings"

"Business meetings" is a term that can be used for different types of events. The details given below are based on an event in Monaco called Les Assises de la Sécurité et des Systèmes d'Information that has been bringing together French CISOs and solution providers for 17 years.

The event has several elements that appeal to CISOs:

- Keynotes from the world of cybersecurity and associated fields.
- Solution provider workshops where their innovations are presented. The clever companies bring along a customer to present a real user case, explaining how and why they chose a particular solution and give feedback on its implementation and effectiveness.
- A matchmaking system where CISOs can choose to meet on a one-to-one basis a number of solution providers, either to update themselves on product developments or to discuss a particular need. Such an event enables a CISO to meet a wide range of companies from the cybersecurity ecosystem in a limited period of 3 days.

- Numerous networking opportunities – lunches, dinners, cocktails and meetings over a cup of coffee – where CISOs can exchange information and experiences between themselves in a relaxed environment.

The main advantage of such an event is the opportunity to exchange best practices and solutions with the key ecosystem players over a 3-day period.

36.2.5   "Think-Tank Meetings"

There also exist events where participants spend 3 days together, they split into different working groups (often each of 10–15 people) and the groups discuss a particular issue for CISOs in general. The group will work over 2 days on their selected subject and then present to all the other groups in a final plenary session. The participants are a mix of CISOs and solution providers. The general rule is that the event is for discussions and exchanging best practices and views; it is not an environment where selling takes place. An example of such an event is SEKOP organised by Finaki.

The key elements for success for such an event are that the participants have the correct profile – a position and experience that enable everyone to contribute and share during the working group sessions – and that the subjects chosen are interesting, relevant and useful. The subjects are chosen by a programme committee of experienced CISOs, and then each working group is prepared and moderated by one or two CISOs to ensure that each group's objectives are met.

The following hold major appeal to CISOs in this type of event:

- The work group conclusions give concrete advice regarding the topics examined.
- The small numbers involved (between 50 and 150 participants) enable CISOs to really get to know their peers present.
- Breakfasts, lunches, dinners and social events all provide effective networking opportunities.

36.3   Conclusion

Specialised events such as those mentioned in this chapter are useful tools that give opportunities to executives with cybersecurity responsibility to build and expand their expert network, learn about and exchange best practices, discover potential solutions in a time-efficient manner and generally enable them to optimise threat identification, prevention and reaction.

Cybersecurity Capacity Building: A Swiss Approach

Laura Crespo, Bastien Wanner and Solange Ghernaouti

Abstract

For states and societies to increase international cyber-realm stability, they must first develop capacities to recognize the relevant risks. The relation between capacity building and cybersecurity has been recognized by a wide range of international organizations and states. This article aims to illustrate the Swiss approach to increasing global cyberspace stability, at the core of which lies the Geneva Internet Platform (GIP). The use of the GIP quickly emerged as a best practice to empower both states and non-state actors to acquire the requisite skills and knowledge to comprehend and participate in global digital debates. While the GIP is certainly a success, the authors argue that it is not enough to address challenges such as cybercrime, data breaches, and malicious operations targeting critical infrastructures. Switzerland needs a comprehensive, harmonized capacity building program rather than a patchwork of related activities.

L. Crespo (✉) · B. Wanner
Université de Lausanne, Lausanne, Switzerland
e-mail: laura.crespo@unil.ch; bastien.wanner@unil.ch

S. Ghernaouti
Université Lausanne, Lausanne, Switzerland
e-mail: sgh@unil.ch

© Springer Fachmedien Wiesbaden GmbH, ein Teil von Springer Nature 2018
M. Bartsch, S. Frey (Hrsg.), *Cybersecurity Best Practices*,
https://doi.org/10.1007/978-3-658-21655-9_37

37.1   Introduction

Since the appearance of the Internet connectivity, information and communication technologies (ICTs) have had a significant catalyzing impact on economic growth, prosperity, social progress, and development. Today, only two decades later, it is difficult to imagine the world without the Internet and the ICTs that underpin it. Almost daily, the new technologies enable us to do things that would previously have been impossible. New information technologies have changed not only the way we communicate, interact, and conduct our business but the way we live.

ICT connectivity is now integral to social and economic development. It is estimated that the digital economy in the G20 area amounted to $ 4 trillion in 2016, with an annual growth rate of 10% (World Economic Forum, 2015). Growth rates are even higher in developing countries, at 15–20% annually (The Boston Consulting Group, 2012). The current growth and spread of ICTs are unprecedented: by 2020, it is estimated that 50 billion devices and 5 billion people will be connected to the Internet (Evans, 2011). And yet, the surface has only been scratched: the Internet constitutes young technology that is still developing.

The downside of this information revolution is that – alongside the digital domain's new functionalities – new risks have arisen: around the globe, individuals, corporations, and governments are exposed to an increasing number of ICT-based vulnerabilities, including threats originating from malicious cyber activities. And at the state level, in industrialized nations, as ICTs have become the central nervous systems of societies and economies, cyberspace has evolved into a realm of political and military conflict.

As a matter of fact, the opportunities and benefits generated by cyberspace are only possible if the digital environment is stable and secure. That means, for societies and economies to benefit from ICTs' positive effects, cybersecurity is essential. However, coping with cyber threats, such as cybercrime, cyber espionage, and cyber sabotage, depends on national capacities to address them. It comes as no surprise that the international community has acknowledged the importance of building capacities to minimize the risks that stem from the use of ICTs. In fact, as capacity building is now recognized as an effective instrument of cyber stability, it is also accepted as a tool of foreign policy (Pawlak, 2016). However, states have only recently begun to understand the extent to which cyberspace threats and limited capacities entail risks not only regarding communications but also in such fields as critical infrastructures (Pawlak, 2014).

Parallel to the development of national cybersecurity strategies, governments have begun to fund the creation of programs and centers designed to enhance overall "cyber readiness" (Hathaway, 2015). During the 2015 Global Conference on Cyberspace, for instance, the Netherlands launched the Global Forum on Cyber Expertise, a platform for countries, international organizations, and private companies to pool and share best practices and expertise on capacity building. Another example is the International Telecommunication Union (ITU) which has defined capacity building as an element of its Global Cybersecurity Agenda and developed the Global Cybersecurity Index (2017).

Switzerland has also supported a series of international capacity building initiatives, most aiming to ensure states' participation in global cybersecurity discussions. At the same Global Conference on Cyberspace, Didier Burkhalter (2015), the former head of the Swiss Federal Department of Foreign Affairs, announced his government's willingness to enhance its efforts to "bridge the digital divide and enable ever more people to benefit from the opportunities of cyberspace." The previous year, to broaden international cyber expertise and strengthen small and developing countries' participation in the debate on digital cybersecurity and Internet governance, Switzerland launched the Geneva Internet Platform (GIP).

This article aims to illustrate the Swiss approach to increasing global cyberspace stability, at the core of which lies that platform. The use of the GIP quickly emerged as a best practice to empower both states and non-state actors to acquire the requisite skills and knowledge to comprehend and participate in global digital debates. Designed to facilitate the exchange of experiences and build knowledge and expertise, it operates as a neutral, independent, and inclusive platform for policymakers, practitioners, and experts around the world.

▶ While the GIP is certainly a success, the authors argue that it is not enough to address challenges such as cybercrime, cyber espionage, and malicious operations targeting critical infrastructures. Switzerland needs a comprehensive, harmonized capacity building program rather than a patchwork of related activities.

37.2   Context, Approaches, and Definitions

For states and societies to increase international cyber-realm stability, they must first develop their abilities to recognize the relevant cyber threats. The relation between capacity building and cybersecurity has been recognized by a wide range of international organizations and states. Following broad agreement at the 2013 Seoul Conference for Cyberspace and again at the 2015 Global Conference on Cyberspace in The Hague, capacity building has evolved into one of the least controversial cyber issues (Tiirmaa-Klaar, 2013). In its 2015 consensus report, the United Nations Group of Governmental Experts in the Field of Information and Telecommunications in the Context of International Security (UN GGE) concluded that "different levels of capacity for ICT security among states can increase vulnerability in an interconnected world" (UN GA, A/70/174, p. 7). Disparities between national laws, regulations, and practices related to the use of ICTs amplify the possibilities for malicious actors to exploit networks independently of their location. Consequently, the UN GGE consensus reports of 2013 and 2015 both recognized that capacity building is of "vital importance" and an effective tool to "bridge the divide in the security of ICTs and their use" (UN GA, A/68/98, p. 10). They also recognized that assisting states in their efforts to improve the security of critical ICT infrastructure might increase international cyber stability as a whole.

In response, scholars have focused on the interplay between capacity building and cybersecurity and analyzed methodologies and measures that can be employed to combat the abusive and criminal uses of ICTs (e.g., *Cyber Power: Crime, Conflict and Security in Cyberspace*, Ghernaouti, 2013). Also, individual governments, international organizations, and private sector actors have allocated funds to reduce the cybersecurity capacity gap. For example, the Global Cyber Security Capacity Centre at Oxford developed a framework, "The Cyber Security Capacity Maturity Model for Nations" (CMM) (University of Oxford, 2016). The framework allows governments to self-assess their capacities in dealing with threats.

The CMM Encompasses Five Dimensions

- Cybersecurity education, training, and skills
- Cybersecurity policy and strategy
- Cyber culture and society
- Legal and regulatory frameworks
- Standards, organizations and technologies

According to the CMM model, the five areas illustrated in Fig. 37.1 should be considered when planning to increase a nation's capacity to address cybersecurity issues. As the figure implies, the areas are overlapping and interdependent.

- The first dimension, **cybersecurity policy and strategy**, refers to a state's capacity to devise a strategic document that discusses cybersecurity as a high-priority policy area, defines roles and responsibilities across government agencies, and allocates resources. Capacities regarding incident response teams, crisis management, redundancy, and critical infrastructure protection capacities are also included. This dimension further addresses the level of cybersecurity coordination not only across government but also

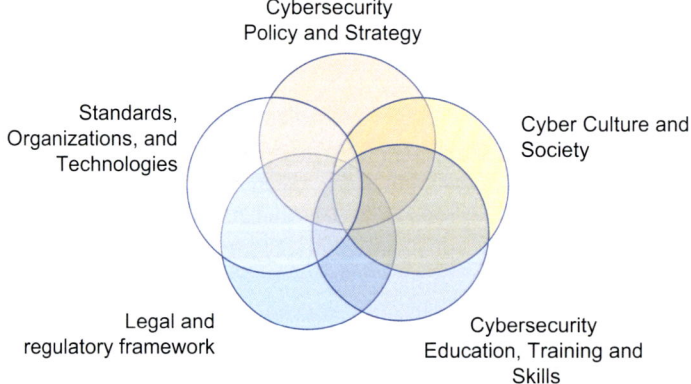

Fig. 37.1 Dimensions of the CMM (University of Oxford, 2016)

between the public and private sectors. Lastly, it relates to strategies to enhance cyber-security, e.g., raising public awareness or mitigating cybercrime.

- **Culture and society** refers to a societies' comprehension of cyber-related threats, the degree of confidence in ICT services and products and individual users' understanding with respect to online safety. The provision of reporting mechanisms for users to report ICT-related crimes is an element of this dimension.
- **Education, training, and skills** monitor cybersecurity initiatives designed to raise awareness both in the public and in management structures. Furthermore, this dimension includes an evaluation framework to assess the availability and quality of education and training delivered to a broad range of stakeholders.
- The fourth dimension, **legal and regulatory frameworks**, assesses a nation's ability to enact legislation to deal effectively with issues relating to privacy, data protection, and cybercrime.
- **Standards, organizations, and technologies** analyze the implementation of standards and good practices, the implementation of processes and controls, and the development of technologies and products.

The European Union Institute for Security Studies offers another approach to measuring a country's capacity-related readiness (Pawlak, 2014). Applying their model, capacity building is arranged around four scales of security goals Fig. 37.2.

- Activities scaled within the **prevention** field include awareness raising regarding threats associated with cyberspace, i.e., the root causes of cyber risks. This dimension includes all efforts to enhance the overall understanding of cyber threats and vulnerabilities and to promote the coordination of national preventive policies.
- Under **protection**, the European Union Institute for Security Studies names activities designed to protect individuals and infrastructures from attacks. Protective measures include, inter alia, the development of Computer Emergency Response Teams (CERTs); the adoption of adequate legislation, standard setting, development of models for public/private sector cooperation, and risk assessment; and participation in joint cyber defense exercises.

Fig. 37.2 Based on the European Union Institute for security studies' four pillars of cybersecurity capacity building (Pawlak, 2014)

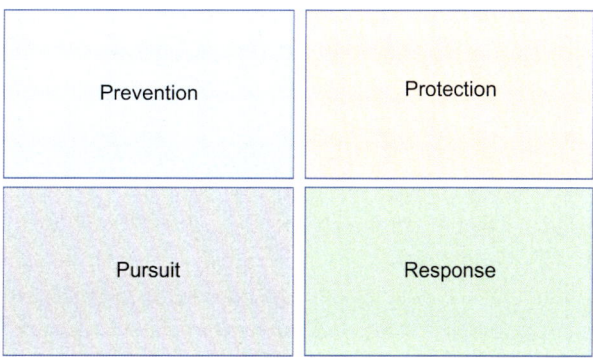

- Following a cyberattack, **pursuit** measures include assessment and attribution of responsibility – necessary steps regarding liability, sanctions, and countermeasures. Capacity building programs must be constructed on frameworks conducive to effective information sharing, increased understanding of threats, cooperation between authorities, and the adoption and implementation of international legal instruments (e.g., the Budapest Convention).
- The last category, **response**, includes actions to minimize and manage the consequences of a malicious cyberattack. Capacity building activities could include the establishment of a CERT, forensics, and the nomination of 24/7 points of contact, along with any necessary interagency cooperation.

In addition to the abovementioned dimensions to enhance cybersecurity capacities, Neil Robinson (2014) proposes another building block, namely, **implementation**. Once concepts and strategies, laws, and policies have been devised, achieving their objectives demands that they be integrated within all necessary national structures. Implementing cybersecurity capacity building programs and initiatives requires the allocation of funding and other resources. Furthermore, achieving the objectives laid out in the previous pillars will require specialized skills, which, in turn, require awareness, education, and training. Moreover, building cybersecurity capacity depends on a high degree of physical infrastructure and equipment, such as cyber ranges, labs, and data centers. Lastly, the involvement and coordination of a range of private organizations are essential, since it is commonly held that critical infrastructures are operated and owned by the private sector. Thus, public-private information-sharing partnerships and analysis centers acting as information clearinghouses are essential for implementing the necessary policies, laws, and organizational structures.

As with many ICT-related concepts, cybersecurity capacity building lacks a universally accepted definition. However, capacity building is generally understood to include programs designed to empower and assist individuals, organizations, and social structures to achieve their cyber development goals and enhance existing capacities, i.e., to narrow the gap between current and desired performance (Walters, 2007). The United Nations (2002) provided a definition on the broader notion of capacity building that was enshrined in the "United Nations system support for capacity-building" report to the Secretary General. In that context:

"[Capacity building is regarded as a crucial aspect of the UN's] overall efforts to achieve the goals of poverty eradication, economic growth and sustainable development, and to devote more attention and resources to strengthening the national capacities necessary to make progress in achieving the millennium development goals (p. 1)."

Usually acknowledged as a set of guidelines to address the challenges of poor governance and define a minimal acceptable level of state capacity to deliver essential functions, the UN report defines capacity building as an instrument to "invent, develop and maintain institutions and organizations that are capable of learning and bringing about their own continuing transformation, so that they can better play a dynamic role to sustain national

development processes" (p. 4). With this in mind, capacity building addresses the development of human resources (enhancing understanding and increasing expertise and skills) and organizational structures as well as institutional and legal frameworks (Pawlak, 2016).

Applying this notion of empowering a multitude of stakeholders to the cybersecurity realm, cybersecurity capacity building could be understood as a "way to empower individuals, communities and governments to achieve their developmental goals by reducing digital security risks stemming from access and use of Information and Communication Technologies" (Pawlak, 2014). Recognizing the interplay between cybersecurity and capacity building, this definition acknowledges the importance of capacity building vis-à-vis mitigating technical risks that threaten to destabilize international peace and security. Against this backdrop, capacity building programs are implemented by international stakeholders not only to facilitate technical undertakings that will enhance economic and social development or overall global cyber resilience; they are also intended to align positions between donors and beneficiaries and to export values. As a result, capacity building has evolved into a foreign policy tool to advance national (ideological, security-based, and economic) interests and export standards of appropriate state behavior in the cyber domain (Pawlak, 2016). It is important to note that cybersecurity capacity building is the result of multi-stakeholder engagement involving a multitude of governmental and nongovernmental actors.

37.3 The Swiss Approach to Cybersecurity Capacity Building

On 27 June 2012, the Swiss Federal Council (Bundesrat) adopted a "national strategy for Switzerland's protection against cyber-risks" (Federal Council, 2012). Along with a number of states that developed and published national cybersecurity strategies from 2009 to 2017, Switzerland recognizes the need for a comprehensive and society-wide approach to coping with current and emerging cyber threats. With this in mind, its national strategy pursues three main goals: the timely identification of threats emanating from ICTs, the improvement of critical infrastructures' robustness and resilience, and the reduction of cybercrime and sabotage (Federal Council, 2012). The key assumptions upon which the strategic document is based include various shared needs, for example, for a culture of cybersecurity, for the sharing of responsibility among all participants, and for a risk-based approach.

While the Swiss cybersecurity strategy postulates a holistic approach including 16 measures within 7 spheres of actions, the paper lacks a clear link between capacity building and the reduction of cybersecurity challenges. Even though the national cybersecurity strategy entitled one of the seven spheres of action "competence building," both measures developed under this category seem to be rather toothless. Both involve a pair of core objectives: providing an "overview of existing competence building options" and identifying gaps in the set of possibilities at Switzerland's disposal to deal with cyber-related risks (Federal Council, 2012, p. 36). Unfortunately, while acknowledging its options and needs is an important initial step, Switzerland lacks a well-concerted approach to cybersecurity capacity building.

Despite this fact, former Swiss Federal Department of Foreign Affairs head Didier Burkhalter (2015) emphasized Switzerland's intention to help "bridge the digital divide and enable ever more people to benefit from the opportunities of cyberspace." This policy on building capacities differs significantly from those of other countries: none of the above-analyzed frameworks mentioned states' participation in the general global digital debate as an element conducive to cyber stability. Switzerland's stance acknowledges a special need to make digital policy discussions more inclusive and to allow more states to engage effectively in these debates. This is not least due to the digital environment's new status as the "premier league of global politics" (DiploFoundation, 2017).

It was with this core objective in mind that the Swiss government launched the GIP in 2014. With the launch of the GIP, Switzerland has certainly found a niche in addressing cybersecurity capacity building gaps. The platform's initiative is supported by the Federal Department of Foreign Affairs (FDFA) and the Federal Office of Communications (OFCOM) and is operated by DiploFoundation. Understood as a center for general digital policy debate, it includes an online observatory, a capacity building center, and, of course, a platform for discussion. At its opening event, held at the DiploFoundation, Ambassador Alexandre Fasel (2014) – former Deputy Permanent Representative of Switzerland to the UN in Geneva – said the initiative was developed in response to the "urgent need for the international community to address growing risks and vulnerabilities faced by governments, corporations, and citizens while still ensuring digital growth and innovation."

The GIP observatory was developed to provide a comprehensive overview of international developments and actors related to the policy areas of Internet Governance and cybersecurity. To accompany it, DiploFoundation has developed its Digital Watch tool – a "one-stop shop" for overviews on issues, events, actors, instruments, and processes, including explanations and live updates. With the aim of assisting governments, civil society, technical communities, and other stakeholders, and focusing particularly on small and developing countries, the GIP's developers have also devised a dedicated capacity building program. Available both online and in situ, its function is to empower and encourage them to participate more efficiently in the global policy processes of Internet governance and cybersecurity. Concurrently, through its discussion forum, where diverse voices and opinions can be heard, the platform provides a neutral and inclusive area for broader digital policy debates.

As the birthplace of the World Summit on Information Society, Geneva has always played a key role in engaging digital actors, fostering digital governance and monitoring digital policies. Today, a number of international organizations focusing on Internet governance, including the Internet Governance Forum, are based in Geneva. In fact, at the Internet Governance Forum held there in December 2017, Krystyna Marty Lang – the Swiss Deputy Secretary of State of the Federal Department of Foreign Affairs – announced Switzerland's plan to launch a Geneva Model for responsible behavior in cyberspace, indicating Switzerland's continuing efforts to strengthen Geneva as a cyber hub.

Since its launch less than 4 years ago, the GIP has grown from one among many Internet governance-related platforms to a center poised to break open policy silos and affect real change. By encouraging meaningful discussion of cybersecurity-related topics, it informs the diplomatic community about ICT-related threats and vulnerabilities. It organized and hosted a series of cyber-related events, including the Cybersecurity Days and the Geneva Digital Talks, and has fostered research, including Radunović and Rüfenacht's (2016) study on cybersecurity competence building trends. As a contribution to Switzerland's participation in the UN GGE process in 2016 and 2017, it also organized a side event in Geneva to discuss the roles of regional security organizations such as the Organization for Security and Cooperation in Europe.

Switzerland has opted to foster capacity building by means of a platform where a broad range of stakeholders from a variety of fields can convene. In fulfilling this aim, the GIP has also contributed to the development of vital expertise and skills in its participants. However, Switzerland's capacity building efforts are not limited to the GIP. It has also supported a series of selective initiatives to increase not only its own national capacities to mitigate cyber-related risks but those of other countries as well. In order to facilitate the engagement of states, especially developing countries, in bilateral, regional, and global cooperation within multilateral processes, Switzerland has partnered with think tanks and specialized organizations such as the Geneva Centre for Security Policy and the ICT-4Peace Foundation.

One more project is worth mentioning, as it tackles states' incapacities to keep pace with the diplomatic agenda on cybersecurity: the international cybersecurity capacity building workshops. Organized by the ICT4Peace Foundation with joint support from, inter alia, the governments of the United Kingdom, Germany, and Switzerland, these seek to enhance the understanding of practitioners, diplomats, and civil society regarding ongoing international processes promoting confidence-building measures, norms of responsible state behavior, and international cooperation in cyberspace. The ICT4Peace capacity building program further envisages broadening participation in international cybersecurity debates, negotiations at regional and global levels, and multilateral fora such as the OSCE and the UN GGE. The workshops that were held with the help of regional organizations, such as the Organization of American States and the African Union, also aimed at increasing the understanding of cybersecurity threats and regional concerns while sharing best practices and institutional arrangements to cope with ICT-related risks (ICT4Peace, 2014).

Switzerland is also a member of the Meridian process, a collective multilateral effort to address issues related to the protection of critical information infrastructure. This platform is conducive to exchanging ideas and initiating actions for cooperation between governmental bodies on this policy area. Opportunities for cooperation between governments are also examined and best practices shared. The Meridian process is open to all countries and has evolved into a community of senior government policymakers discussing the issue of critical information infrastructure protection.

At the technical-operative level, Switzerland also increases its own national capacities through membership in the Forum of Incident Response and Security Teams (FIRST) and in the European Governmental Computer Response Teams (EGC). These technical platforms are important venues for the exchange of information, e.g., on ICT vulnerabilities.

37.4   Recommendations

The authors of this article have argued that cybersecurity capacity building is an effective instrument to foster and enhance the stability of the digital ecosystem. Combined with the growing number of malicious or otherwise hostile cyber operations, their increasingly sophisticated nature has had a destabilizing effect on international peace and security. It is essential to develop the necessary human skills and expertise, the organizational structures, and the legal frameworks to address the threats such activities pose. Broad international and regional disparities in cybersecurity maturity exacerbate the challenge.

In order to fully seize the opportunities and benefits the digital environment provides and to close down safe havens for online extremists (Pawlak, 2016), international organizations and various states have invested in cybersecurity capacity building programs. This article has shed light on various frameworks, such as the CMM (University of Oxford, 2016) and the dimensions defined by the European Union Institute for Security Studies (2014). Most of the models scrutinized by the authors stressed the importance of devising cybersecurity policies and strategies, of promoting a societal cybersecurity culture, of developing dedicated cybersecurity entities (e.g., CERTs), and of creating legal frameworks.

However, not one of the frameworks examined emphasized the need to improve the effective participation of states within the multilateral cybersecurity agenda, such as within the UN and regional security organizations (e.g., the OSCE), as a means of increasing their capacities to cope with cyber risks.

And yet, this is the Swiss approach to cybersecurity capacity building. Noting the lack of a well-concerted cybersecurity capacity building program considering all relevant dimensions (human skills, organizational structures, and legal frameworks), Switzerland has focused on developing human skills and expertise and on ensuring states' participation in global cybersecurity discussions. It was to pursue these goals that it launched in the GIP in 2014. As a venue where the diplomatic community can share and learn from all Internet-related questions, the GIP is a uniquely Swiss success story and a best practice in itself. As a neutral and impartial forum, it allows digital actors from diverse disciplines to convene and discuss current and future trends.

Still, the authors argue that more needs to be done to address cybersecurity capacity building efforts in a holistic manner. With almost 90% of its population Internet users, making it a world leader in Internet use, Switzerland has a strong interest in stepping up its promotion of concerted and effective cybersecurity capacity building. A piecemeal approach and a patchwork of selected activities will have only a limited effect and will not be conducive to sustainable cybersecurity resilience. Since the Swiss national cybersecurity strategy is currently being revised, the authors recommend that the new version afford closer attention and a more systematic approach to cybersecurity capacity building.

In the current context, Switzerland is well positioned to develop a dedicated cybersecurity capacity building approach that could be aligned with the newly adopted cybersecurity strategy (Federal Council, 2018). Source: https://www.admin.ch/gov/de/start/dokumentation/medienmitteilungen.msg-id-70482.html. The first step would be to define who needs which capacities and for which purposes. This would place pressure on governmental actors in the triangle of diplomacy, security, and development as well as nongovernmental entities (academic researchers and civil society) to participate in the process. Clarification of these actors' roles and responsibilities would require a concerted institutional setup plan. With a clearly delineated mandate, the Swiss national cybersecurity strategists could nominate a governmental agency to coordinate all relevant capacity building projects while collaborating with developmental offices, cybersecurity-related organizations, the private sector, and academia. Each member of the resulting consortium could make full use of existing cybersecurity capacity building models and frameworks, e.g., the CMM (University Oxford, 2016), to shed light on its capacities vis-à-vis cyber risks. Their findings would then help the decisionmakers prioritize the full range of capacities in terms of investment value.

This means Switzerland's efforts to build cybersecurity capacity need to go well beyond enhancing individual or even local expertise, skills, and knowledge. It should also increase its efforts to help beneficiary states develop legal frameworks and legislation to combat cyber-related crime. This would be a productive use of the expertise Switzerland gained through its participation in the Budapest Convention on Cybercrime. In addition, regarding the handling of cyber incidents (e.g., via CERTs), Switzerland's institutional setup could serve as a best practice model for other states' implementation of similar structures.

As safe, stable Internet connectivity is increasingly recognized as vital to economic growth and development, the Swiss Directorate for Development and Cooperation should focus on systematically aligning cybersecurity capacities with development projects. At the Seoul Conference for Cyberspace in 2013, Magdy Martinez-Soliman, Assistant Secretary-General and Assistant Administrator of the United Nations Development Programme's Bureau for Policy and Programme Support, posited that the "growth of cyberspace helps close the digital divide between rich and the poor. By boosting the number of 'digital natives' it offers many new opportunities for advancing human development." However, he also warned that "greater reliance on cyberspace introduces new risks and vulnerabilities, " underlining the necessity for countries to "develop governance capacities and individual skill sets to run and manage sophisticated technologies that run global cyberspace" (Martinez-Soliman, 2013).

Unfortunately, to date, a very limited amount of projects on cybersecurity and development have been run (Hohmann, Pirang and Benner, 2017). Switzerland's dispatch on international cooperation, valid from 2017 until 2020, lays out its aims to reduce poverty and global risks, alleviate suffering, and promote peace and respect for human rights (Federal Council, 2016). Unfortunately, its efforts to encourage sustainable development do not include cybersecurity-related initiatives. It is important to stress that, as the focus of Swiss capacity building engagement has evolved exclusively around cybersecurity, cyber defense has not yet been systematically, coherently, and consistently examined as a capacity building priority. This is because the Swiss national cybersecurity policy's scope of application is limited to peacetime: it "explicitly excludes war" (p. 28). Therefore, all responses to cyber threats are nonmilitary, i.e., every one of the 16-named measures is meant to handle cyber incidents that occur below the threshold of armed conflict. Consequently, as outlined in the Swiss cyber strategy, the roles and capacities of the Swiss

Armed Forces are limited. Further, the Swiss Armed Forces are specifically exempt from the civil steering mechanism of the Federal IT Steering Unit's 2013 implementation plan (Federal Council, 2013), according to which the Armed Forces' core task is to "protect and defend their own infrastructure and systems in all situations" (p. 5).

However, as no clear boundaries delineate civilian from military domains, particularly regarding the protection of critical infrastructures, the development of active defensive capacities needs to be addressed. Luckily, the Federal Department of Defence, Civil Protection and Sports published an action plan on cyber defense on 9 November 2017 to meet the cyber defense capacity building demand. Specifically, a strong collaboration is necessary between all relevant agencies of the Swiss Federal Administration (civil and military) and the private sector. Among other arguments in favor of such collaboration, the legal framework to develop active defensive measures was created in response to the Intelligence Service Act, which came into force on 1 September 2017. As a next step, all relevant staff need to be educated and trained in cyber defense (e.g., exercises such as Locked Shields). Furthermore, organizational structures and governance have to be developed to integrate these new cyber defensive measures into existing structures and processes.

References

Burkhalter, D. (2015). Promoting trust and globally shared rules to ensure an open, free and secure cyberspace. In: https://www.news.admin.ch/message/index.html?lang=de&msg-id=56892 (30 May 2015).

DiploFoundation (2014). Report of the official launch of the GIP. https://www.giplatform.org/events/official-launch-geneva-internet-platform (4 December 2017).

DiploFoundation (2017). The Future of Diplomacy: Between Continuity and Change. https://15years.diplomacy.edu/wp-content/uploads/2017/11/Thefutureofdiplomacy-finalreport.pdf (30 November 2017).

Evans, D. (2011). *The Internet of Things. How the Next Evolution of the Internet is Changing Everything*. Cisco Internet Business Solutions Group (IBSG). https://www.cisco.com/c/dam/en_us/about/ac79/docs/innov/IoT_IBSG_0411FINAL.pdf (8 December 2017).

Fasel, A. (2014). Official Launch of the Geneva Internet Platform https://www.giplatform.org/events/official-launch-geneva-internet-platform (1 December 2017).

Federal Council (2012). National strategy for the protection of Switzerland against cyber risks. In: https://www.isb.admin.ch/isb/en/home/ikt-vorgaben/strategien-teilstrategien/sn002-nationale_strategie_schutz_schweiz_cyber-risiken_ncs.html (2 December 2015).

Federal Council (2013). Implementation plan NCS. In: http://www-temp.isb.admin.ch/themen/01709/01711/index.html?lang=en (1 January 2016).

Federal Council (2016). Botschaft zur Internationalen Zusammenarbeit 2017-2020. https://www.admin.ch/opc/de/federal-gazette/2016/2333.pdf (10 December 2017).

Federal Department of Defence, Civil Protection and Sports. (2017). Aktionsplan Cyber-Defence des VBS. https://www.vbs.admin.ch/de/verteidigung/schutz-vor-cyber-angriffen.html (5 December 2017).

Ghernaouti, S. (2013*). Cyber Power: Crime, Conflict and Security in Cyberspace*. EPFL Press.

Hathaway, M. (2015). Cyber Readiness Index 2.0. *Protomac Institute for Policy Studies*. http://www.potomacinstitute.org/images/CRIndex2.0.pdf (4 December 2017).

Hohmann, M. Pirang, A. and Benner, T. (2017). *Advancing Cybersecurity Capacity Building: Implementing a Principle-Based Approach*. Global Public Policy Institute. http://www.gppi.net/publications/data-technology-politics/article/advancing-cybersecurity-capacity-building-implementing-a-principle-based-approach/ (4 December 2017).

ICT4Peace (2014). International Cyber Security Capacity Building Workshops. Promoting Openness, Prosperity, Trust and Security in Cyberspace. http://ict4peace.org/wp-content/uploads/2017/10/Outline-Capacity-Building-2017811.pdf (4 November 2017).

International Telecommunication Union (2017). Global Cybersecurity Index (GCI). https://www.itu.int/dms_pub/itu-d/opb/str/D-STR-GCI.01-2017-PDF-E.pdf (7 December 2017).

Martinez-Soliman, M. (2013). United Nations Development Programme. http://www.undp.org/content/seoul_policy_center/en/home/presscenter/articles/2013/10/18/-seoul-framework-could-make-cyberspace-safer-more-accessible-.html (4 November 2017).

Pawlak, P. (2014). Riding the Digital Wave: The impact of cyber capacity building on human development. *European Union Institute for Security Studies*, Report Nr. 21. https://www.iss.europa.eu/sites/default/files/EUISSFiles/Report_21_Cyber.pdf (6 November 2017).

Pawlak, P. (2016). Capacity Building in Cyberspace as an Instrument of Foreign Policy. *Global Policy*, Vol. 7, Issue 1.

Radunović, V. and Rüfenacht, D. (2016). Cybersecurity Competence Building Trends. Research Report. DiploFoundation. https://www.diplomacy.edu/sites/default/files/Cybersecurity%20Full%20Report.pdf (3 December 2017).

Robinson, N. (2014). Building blocks for strengthening cybresecurity capacities. In: Pawlak, P. (2014). Riding the Digital Wave: The impact of cyber capacity building on human development. *European Union Institute for Security Studies*, Report Nr. 21. https://www.iss.europa.eu/sites/default/files/EUISSFiles/Report_21_Cyber.pdf (6 November 2017).

The Boston Consulting Group (2012). The Internet Economy in the G-20. The $ 4.2 Trillion Growth Opportunity. https://www.bcg.com/documents/file100409.pdf (2 November 2017).

Tiirmaa-Klaar, H. (2013). *Cyber Diplomacy: Agenda, Challenges and Mission*. In: Ziolkowski, K. (2013). *Peacetime Regime For State Activities in Cyberspace; International Law, International Relations and Diplomacy*. NATO Cooperative Cyber Defence Centre of Excellence. https://ccd-coe.org/sites/default/files/multimedia/pdf/PeacetimeRegime.pdf (4 December 2016).

United Nations Economic and Social Council (2002). United Nations system support for capacity-building. Report of the Secretary General. http://www.un.org/documents/ecosoc/docs/2002/e2002-58.pdf (4 December 2017).

United Nations, General Assembly, A/68/98, (2013). Group of Governmental Experts on Developments in the Field of Information and Telecommunications in the Context of International Security. In: http://www.unidir.org/files/medias/pdfs/developments-in-the-field-of-information-and-telecommunications-in-the-context-of-international-security-2012-2013-a-68-98-eng-0-578.pdf (3 December 2017).

United Nations, General Assembly, A/70/174, (2015). Group of Governmental Experts on Developments in the Field of Information and Telecommunications in the Context of International Security. In: http://www.un.org/ga/search/view_doc.asp?symbol=A/70/174 (3 March 2016).

University of Oxford (2016). Global Cyber Security Capacity Building Centre. Cybersecurity Capacity Maturity Model for Nations (CMM). https://www.sbs.ox.ac.uk/cybersecurity-capacity/system/files/CMM%20revised%20edition_09022017_1.pdf (7 November 2017).

Walters, H. (2007). Capacity Development, Institutional Change and Theory of Change: What do we mean and where are the linkages. http://portals.wi.wur.nl/files/docs/successfailuredevelopment/Walters_CapacityDevelopmentConceptPaperFIN.pdf (5 December 2017).

World Economic Forum (2015). Expanding Participation and Boosting Growth: The Infrastructure Needs of the Digital Economy. http://www3.weforum.org/docs/WEFUSA_DigitalInfrastructure_Report2015.pdf (5 November 2017).

Research and Education as Key Success Factors for Developing a Cybersecurity Culture

38

Solange Ghernaouti and Bastien Wanner

Abstract

The development and deployment of a cybersecurity culture and best practices among all stakeholders are a crucial issue for the information society. Based on two innovative initiatives in the field of education and research issued by the University of Lausanne, this chapter points out mains stakes, challenges and constraints encountered by research activities in the field of cybersecurity and the fight against cybercrime, to improve skills, competences and measures that will contribute to obtain an effective cybersecurity culture.

38.1 Needs and Context

The information economy, among other elements, heavily depends on cybersecurity. Without the latter, the former is unlikely to develop. On the other hand, cybersecurity is the result of technological development, organisational structure, legal frameworks and international cooperation. As a matter of fact, cybersecurity is a precondition for overall performance in the information society. Without a secure cyber environment, desired outcomes, such as innovation, growth and prosperity, could become wishful thinking. Developing and less-developed

S. Ghernaouti (✉)
Université Lausanne, Lausanne, Switzerland
e-mail: sgh@unil.ch

B. Wanner
Université de Lausanne, Lausanne, Switzerland
e-mail: bastien.wanner@unil.ch

© Springer Fachmedien Wiesbaden GmbH, ein Teil von Springer Nature 2018
M. Bartsch, S. Frey (Hrsg.), *Cybersecurity Best Practices*,
https://doi.org/10.1007/978-3-658-21655-9_38

countries may face significant challenges in meeting the requirements of the global market place without cybersecurity.

The lack of know-how in all the dimensions of cybersecurity, namely, technical, legal, organisational and human dimensions, may lead to serious deficiency of vital national infrastructures and could enlarge and widen the digital divide.

Against this backdrop, developing a global cybersecurity culture has been on the international agenda since at least the UN General Assembly adopted resolution 58/199 in 2004 [1]. The cybersecurity culture deals with key economic, legal and social issues related to information security in order to help countries get prepared to face issues and challenges linked to information and communication technologies (ICT) deployment, uses and misuses [2].

Information protection is a crucial task to take into consideration when developing an information society. At the crossroads of technological, legal, sociological, economic and political fields, cybersecurity is an interdisciplinary domain by nature. Depending on the country, it must reflect the vision, the culture and the civilisation of a nation as well as meet the specific security needs of the local context in which it is introduced. Because cybersecurity has a global dimension and deals with a large range of issues as ICT uses or misuses, technical measures and economic, legal and political issues, it is important to develop a global cybersecurity culture in order to raise the level of understanding of each member of the cybersecurity chain.

Specific actions should be taken at a national level, to raise or build cybersecurity capacities of various members in order to be able to deal with national and international cybersecurity issues. Awareness raising is time-consuming and costly and necessitates political leadership. This holds true for education programmes, as well as they are difficult to develop and require funds. As capacity building activities most of the time take place at the national level, appropriate resources should be allocated to national actors. For that, financial, technical, organisational and human resources designed to build a cybersecurity culture should be developed.

Raising awareness is an important first step. However, it is not enough to empower the end-user in a way that he or she would be able to adopt a safe and responsible behaviour when dealing with ICT technologies. Specific educational programmes should aim at enabling all stakeholders, such as policymakers, justice and police practitioners, managers, information technology professionals and end-users (including children and the elderly). At the very beginning of these programmes, cybersecurity training courses should be mainstreamed into different levels of educational courses, from school to university, and integrated into education in the legal, scientific and social science disciplines. Developing an interdisciplinary approach to cybersecurity will be a real added value activity, permitting people to deal with a large range of cybersecurity issues. Continuous training should not be omitted, in order to prepare professionals to face the evolving and dynamic context of technology and threats [3]. Investments need to be made available to educate and train all the members of the information society, from decision makers to citizens, and including children and the elderly.

38.2 Some Stakes and Recommendations for Developing a Cybersecurity Culture

The use of the Internet varies from country to country, and even if cybersecurity problems are similar, the way to deal with those problems will depend, for example, on the local culture, contexts and national legal frameworks. Even if countries are different, they might be exposed to a set of similar cybersecurity-related challenges. Thus, regional solutions and answers to these similar problems could be ideal in an appropriate context. Consequently, any approach to develop a global cybersecurity culture has to take into account local needs and has to be adapted to regional contexts.

When developing and designing a cybersecurity culture, one of the main challenges is to correctly identify what the global and international issues are and what the local specific needs are for a cybersecurity culture. International standards can only contribute to identifying the global and generic main issues related to a cybersecurity culture because cultures rely upon local and temporal factors. A unique and exclusive cybersecurity culture could be prejudicial to specific information society environments and visions. It could fail to adequately respond to the multitude of end-user backgrounds, points of views and needs [4].

Promoting a culture of cybersecurity that will touch the entire population needs to rely upon an appropriate political vision and will as well as efficient private and public partnerships. Several awareness and educational initiatives have been developed at different levels (e.g., information security programmes in companies or awareness campaigns for online child protection).

There are no real theories or methodologies related to the design, the communication, the validation or the control of the adequacy of a cybersecurity culture. Evaluating the effectiveness of cybersecurity culture, from policies and guidelines to practice, is very difficult. But at the same time, if the public and private sectors do not support such initiatives together as soon as possible, there will be a long-term negative effect on economic development and the ability to ensure the security of goods and people.

The OECD's 2002 guidelines for the security of information systems and networks – "Towards a culture of security" [5] – firstly focus on awareness and responsibility. It is necessary to emphasise the need to offer citizens the appropriate information on cybersecurity that they need to be effective and responsible cybercitizens. Awareness raising and education will contribute to prevent incompetent and incorrect behaviours as well as to develop trust and confidence in digital infrastructures, services and also in cybersecurity mechanisms and controls.

People should be able to develop their own approaches to cybersecurity and the use of ICT. It is everyone's responsibility to promote a safe and reliable cyberspace environment in the context of an emerging information society. A minimum level of cybersecurity must be provided at an affordable cost. In addition cybersecurity must not become an obstacle for anyone who would like to conduct private or business activities over the Internet.

Presently, most ICT end-users (individuals or organisations) simply do not understand cybersecurity issues and do not have the skills or the tools to correctly protect their assets. They do not have the objective means to build confidence in digital infrastructures and services. They must rely on products and mechanisms they do not master and on solutions that have been imposed on them for commercial reasons.

In the context of information security, some basic recommendations could be proposed:

- Educate the end-user.
- Increase public awareness to enhance users' behaviour in respect of security.
- Give the end-user the required tools and means to be responsible.
- Design an end-user-centric security model within a given technical and legal framework whereby the user can decide what is judicious based on his/her own resources.

So, to empower human resource in a global perspective, a general, modular and flexible educational framework in cybersecurity should exist to answer the needs of increased public awareness and provide a tailored educational curriculum for specific professionals. This concerns both well-developed countries and less-developed ones.

Education on cybersecurity is the key factor in becoming an actor in the information society, and it constitutes the cornerstone of a knowledge-based society. Thanks to education, the digital divide and the cybersecurity gap could be reduced.

Therefore, to enhance confidence and security in the use of ICTs, education should not be considered merely as an option or even worst, as an afterthought. Education is the cornerstone for both, a well-functioning information society and security. Education constitutes a real human capacity building challenge that governments have to face. Human capacity building should address in particular the process of enabling individuals to understand as well as to access information, knowledge and training. In fact, every citizen should:

- Understand the cyberthreats for the end-user (e.g., viruses, spam, identity theft, fraud, swindle, privacy offence) and their impacts.
- Understand how to adopt and adapt behaviour conducive to cybersecurity.
- Be able to promote a cybersecurity culture based on well-recognised good practices.

With the Global Cybersecurity Agenda [6], the ITU proposed a framework to consider cybersecurity issues in a holistic and systemic approach in 2008 – a model designed to deal with the global challenges of building confidence and security. Awareness and education are at the heart of this model.

ITU proposes an innovative and efficient interdisciplinary framework from which global, schedulable and specific answers could be developed by relevant players in order to be effective in international collaboration and well prepared to face the challenge of building an inclusive information society.

Considering cybersecurity education is a long-term approach which is efficient for a sustainable information society.

38.3   An Innovative Master Programme

The University of Lausanne has set up a Master of Law (MLaw) in Legal Issues, Crime and Security of Information Technologies in 2001 [7]. This Master is the result of a collaboration between the Law School and the School of Criminal Justice of the Faculty of Law, Criminal Justice and Public Administration and the Faculty of Business and Economics. Flexible in terms of its architecture, this multidisciplinary course carries on from basic studies in law, economic, risk management, cybersecurity, the fight against cybercrime and forensic science. Its aim is to allow to acquire the necessary skills to understand problems posed by information technologies generally, be it in a legal sense or in relation to information technology, management or crime detection techniques.

Avant-gardist and pioneer in 2001 [8], this interdisciplinary educational programme is still unique in Switzerland and continues to address the needs of the private and public sectors to rely upon competent professional people assuming several types of jobs needed by the information society.

Moreover, this university programme develops, in addition to specific academic skills, cross-cutting competences such as oral and written communication; critical, analytical and summarising faculties; abilities to research; learning and transmission of knowledge; independence; and the ability to make critical judgements in the field of specialisation and overlapping areas. This panoply of skills, combined with specialised knowledge acquired in the course of studies, is an excellent preparation for a wide range of employment opportunities.

This university programme has also contributed to disseminate the basic culture of cybersecurity in private and professional spheres among all kinds of actors belonging to the political, legal, organisational, technical and social dimension of the digital ecosystem.

38.4   Lessons Learned from the European Research Project E-Crime

E-crime [9] – a European Union-funded research project – aims to minimise the spread and development of cybercrime in non-ICT sector from a legal and economic perspective. This 3-year project (2014–2017) has been conducted by an international consortium of 10 partners from law enforcement, private sector, research institutes and academia. The University of Lausanne, represented by a team under the leadership of Professor Ghernaouti, was among the partners along with Interpol that provided a link to the international law enforcement community.

The main objectives of the E-Crime project are:

- Measuring the economic impact of cybercrime – after gaining an understanding of the current picture of cybercrime, the E-Crime project will use available information and new data to develop a multilevel model to measure its economic impact.
- Assessing existing counter-measures against cybercrime – to include current technology, legislation, best practices, policy, enforcement approaches and awareness and trust initiatives.

- Developing concrete solutions – the E-crime project will integrate its findings to identify and develop diverse, effective counter-measures, including enhancement for crime-proofed applications, legislative proposals, risk management tools, policy, best practices and trust and confidence measures.

In fact, one of the more valuable and long-term impacts of this project is to be able to raise awareness among policymakers, legislators and law enforcement, in a national and international context.

It could also allow the development of targeted educational programme that contributes to fight against cybercrime. Moreover, E-Crime has contributed to the development of legal recommendations regarding the need for updated investigative tools and mutual legal assistance procedures. In addition, the result of the project has contributed to a more in-depth understanding of cybercrime to improve prevention and enforcement measures.

Taking into account the legal dimension and specific needs for justice and police professionals, global understanding of legal issues related to ICT technologies and misuses should be apprehended, which means the understanding of:

- Legal requirements at national and international levels.
- Computer investigation and forensic methodologies and tools.
- How to interpret and implement existing international regulation as the Cybercrime Convention of the Council of Europe that could be considered as an international reference model to develop legal frameworks and international cooperation.
- Enhance the level of report of technical incidents.
- Define a whistleblower status.

This requires a common understanding of computer-related crime and of international collaboration in order to fight against cybercrime and deals with global cyberthreats. They should be able to define a legal framework, appropriate laws enforceable at national level and compatible at the international level. In addition, specific measures to fight against cybercrime and to collaborate at international level should be developed.

38.5   Constraints and Challenges Encountered in Researching Cybersecurity and the Fight Against Cybercrime

The question of building human capacities is essential, especially in the struggle against cybercrime. This struggle is a true challenge at the national and global level and cannot be disassociated from the way in which research is carried out in the field of information and technological crime. The quality of teaching, be this formal education, awareness building, education aimed at the general public, school or university teaching, depends to a certain extent on the quality, maturity and relevance of research.

In fact, there are some difficulties in carrying out cybersecurity and cybercrime-related research with the aim of contributing to stimulating further interdisciplinarity as well as interaction and cooperation between diverse actors and stakeholders. Being able to understand what has changed with the extensive use of ICT and how criminals use and misuse digital technologies to obtain power and profit, who the cybercriminals are, how they are organised and how they operate is fundamental in order to develop effective countermeasures. For that, we have to identify the critical factors for success of research in the fields of cybercrime – the word cybercrime should be understood in the broadest sense, taking into consideration that, at present, there is no internationally accepted definition of cybercrime.

However, the European Convention on Cybercrime [10] provides a good reference as this legal instrument offers a definition on computer crime and cybercriminality that is accepted by the signatory parties. Currently, the Budapest Convention is the only legal instrument to tackle cybercriminality. Unfortunately, the Budapest Convention cannot be treated as an international standard since not all countries have signed and ratified this treaty. The challenge is that this treaty dates back to 2001, long before the era of social platforms and cloud computing, to name just two revolutions in the use of ICT, and before the massive take up of the Internet by the man and woman in the street. By their very nature, however, cybercriminality is a cross-border, international phenomena, and this needs to be reflected in both definitions and targeted research.

Developing and defining appropriate research agenda and projects in the fight against cybercrime will necessarily have to include major issues in fields related to the social and technical sciences. The following elements have to be addressed as part of an integrated and global research agenda:

- Politics (security studies (national security, public safety, diplomacy, etc.)
- Economics and finance
- Law and law enforcement
- Sociology, anthropology, criminality and psychology
- Cryptography, computer sciences, information systems and network and telecommunication

One major complication added by such a multidisciplinary approach is that each field is studied separately by individuals and teams from diverging backgrounds, using differing languages, tools and methodologies, and possessing varying visions on the topic. It is a matter of real urgency to decompartmentalise the disciplines so as to allow an effective approach in studying cyber issues related to crime in a transdisciplinary way. Therefore, it will require systematic efforts to work together, to standardise vocabulary and methodologies, to share results and to identify areas of strength and weakness for specific disciplines.

Innovation in research in these fields begins with the understanding of these questions in an integrated way by opening up these disciplines. This has not yet been performed and represents a major gap in research and also in the way to organise, finance and evaluate research. As long as this subject remains unaddressed, we will only have partial studies and solutions that will be insufficient and inefficient when attempting to define the nature of cybercrime and their potential to cause harm.

Fundamentally, then, we need to propose a framework that could enhance and promote an interdisciplinary approach to research and then be used to structure and direct enforce research activities in respect of cybercrime. The greatest difficulties in understanding the phenomenon of cybercrime come from the fact that it is necessary to possess, simultaneously, skills in technology, law, human relations, economics and management.

In respect of technical skills, it is necessary to know the means of operation of information technologies and telecommunications and have a good understanding of information security mechanisms taking into account the needs to understand how cyberattacks are carried out, how technical and security weaknesses and vulnerabilities are used and how security tools are bypassed by cybercriminals.

From a legal and a political point of view, it is necessary to know, most notably, the limits of existing legal frameworks, judicial systems and international cooperation. Political issues should also be addressed from geopolitical and conflictual perspectives.

In respect of human relations, it is necessary to understand criminals' approach to exploit users in order to entice them into carrying out or participating in cybercrimes (e.g. as a mule in a money-laundering process on the Internet) or to trick them into lending their technical resources or characteristics to crime without their consent (e.g., installing a Trojan Horse, using their machine as part of a botnet, using their login details, identity theft, etc.). From an academic research perspective, it is very difficult to have access and to study what is going on inside the dark web where everything could be sold and bought (competences, personal data, malwares, 0-day vulnerabilities, etc.).

Moreover, in respect of economics and management skills, it is necessary to understand how the profitability of cybercrimes is organised, how money circulates (including crypto money), who are the actors and the processes and the organisation of black markets in the dark web. It has become fundamental and urgent to put in place research mechanisms that will allow a greater understanding of how the Internet is being used to optimise the profitability of criminal activities and the financing of terrorist activities, in order to develop strategic and operational measures to counter these. Among the specific research challenges that should be addressed, we should emphasise the challenge relating to those financial transactions manipulated by criminals, most notably money laundering, that are used by criminals and help them extend their power, spheres of influence and ranges of activities.

Another significant challenge facing society is related to understanding the differences in the various approaches that have been and are being adopted to combatting cybercrime across the globe. Some countries have been making structured and systematic efforts to identify and eliminate cybercrime prepared or carried out from within their own territories, while others have been less motivated and effective at doing so.

As a result of this, it is imperative that the research community creates a summary of common points and divergences between countries and regions in order to identify common denominators from which attributes, parameters and factors can be identified; then going on to use this as a basis for defining strategies and policies and defining the framework for the effective cooperation of bodies involved in the fight against cybercrime. How can we free up the necessary means to fight against cybercrime if we do not know the real scale of the problem? In fact, not all cybercrimes are reported to the police and the judicial authorities. In addition, in cyberspace it is easier to steal one Euro from each of one hundred million people or entities than it is to steal one hundred million Euros from one single entity. The great majority of cybercrimes concern small amounts and are seldom reported. Moreover, it is difficult to identify and hence to quantify the impact and cost of the illegal copying of data.

Studies of businesses' security in respect of cybercriminality published by service companies and security specialists give a certain perspective on the situation but cannot provide an overall and objective view. They are more frequently to be treated as communicating tools designed to increase awareness. Different sources exist and different groups monitor, but none offer a consolidated global view of the reality of cybercrime. This is also a result of the fact that today, there remains a great difficulty in sharing data between the private sector which owns part of the Internet infrastructure and observes the problems that arise and between the businesses that have fallen victim to cybercrimes and possess data useful for the later analysis of the phenomenon by, potentially, public sector and the scientific community.

It is difficult to find a model for organising and operating such a partnership, because deep down the culture of sharing information and knowledge – in real time – about the reality of vulnerabilities, cyberthreats and security incidents and their impacts is not yet very widespread. These kinds of information are still seen by some as assets not to be shared, because some companies build their businesses upon these, while other companies fear for their reputations. All of this contributes to a bad collective and global understanding of the problem.

So far, the fact-finding aspect of research has been discussed. It is true that because of the very nature of cybercrime activities carried out in the shadows, with care taken not to leave any traces and not to share any information with outsiders, and in the case of certain cybercrimes specifically trying even to hide the fact that a crime has been committed, researchers, both on the academic and justice sides, have for a long time been struggling to gain any idea of the scope, size and range of activities. Gathering statistics on road accidents, say, is procedurally straightforward. Gathering statistics on bank fraud, by way of contrast, is far more difficult, because the perpetrators are unlikely to brag about doing it and the victims – individuals or the institutions themselves – are very often extremely reluctant to publicly admit that they have been subject to an attack.

Nevertheless, there comes a point in which better use must be made of the information that has been gathered. A clear idea of what is being done where, by whom and with what frequency and impact will allow identifying the types of generic measures (political, economic, organisational, legal, judicial and technical) that can contribute to developing pragmatic measures for protecting the cyberspace. The output could, potentially, also include an action plan, a reference framework for defining roles and responsibilities, some key factors of success of private and public partnerships (PPP) or some recommendations for digital privacy and the protection of fundamental rights in cyberspace.

It is needed to create and maintain a practical cybersecurity ecosystem that allows legitimate users to go about their daily activities unhindered while protecting them from the activities of malicious actors of the same infrastructures. Cybersecurity should not be a pretext for abusive surveillance, even if some surveillance measures are necessary to detect weak signals which, if they are correctly analysed, correlated and interpreted, might allow cyberattacks to be anticipated and appropriate actions to be undertaken. Cybersecurity can be viewed as a framework of interlocking pieces connecting together a variety of actors. Many participants have a role to play in this structure, with the weakest link in the chain always proving to be the most significant.

Individuals have their share of the burden, needing to protect their own data and systems through passwords, encryption, good ICT access habits and appropriate physical security measures. Clearly this will always be an area of great potential weakness, as many users do not possess the resources, the education or the experience to be able to implement and maintain good security practices and perhaps also because ICT security solutions are not sufficiently easy to understand, to implement or to manage or are too expensive for real value they provide. Typical end-users and consumers will not know to what kinds of risks they are exposed, where their key data and information might be stored, or whether their security has actually been compromised at any moment, or that their digital identities have been stolen.

At a very fundamental level, the traditional triad of CIA – the confidentiality, integrity and availability of information – is always relevant. This applies to all users and providers of systems and data, from the least significant individual to the largest corporation and the most powerful state. The impacts of these risks being exploited can range from purely personal (data lost, websites or mail accounts compromised, individual financial losses) to corporate losses or inaccessibility to systems and to national and critical infrastructures being damaged or forced offline, with potentially very significant impacts in such domains as power generation and supply, logistics, communications, diplomacy and military or strategic command and control.

It is commonly known that the criminal world is opportunist and one in which existing vulnerabilities are exploited. Digital environments should be less vulnerable, more secure and better managed. It is not enough to have access to good security solutions from a technical perspective if end-users are unable to apply and manage them correctly. This means that it is very important to perform high-quality risk management and to manage security measures in a coherent way. It is part of the responsibility of the owners of infrastructures to ensure that all cyberrisks are under control. This does not mean eliminating all risks, which would be impossible, but ensuring that the impact of the residual risks will be tolerable for society as a whole.

The cybersecurity ecosystem is complex, and it is more or less impossible to have an exhaustive view of it or to understand all the political, economic, technological or societal implications of its development. At the same time, the operational requirements for more security and stability in cyberspace should not be allowed to hide the far wider problem of dependency on digital infrastructures and on service providers.

When considering cybersecurity and cybercrime issues, we cannot avoid making the effort to understand the geostrategic environment within which the information society is evolving and which currently finds itself in a context of a general and long-lasting economic crisis.

In fact, it is now a question of finding a collective answer to the need to protect digital infrastructures. This need is increasingly urgent as technological evolution is moving towards ever greater and permanent interconnectivity via Internet technologies (Internet of everything, the integration into the living body of technological prosthetics, as is already the case with the pacemaker controllable at a distance over the Internet). Everything that is connectable is hackable and will be hacked. Not to forget the miniaturisation of components, of RFID chips and of intelligent chips that are becoming so tiny, thanks to nanotechnologies that they are invisible but which are being integrated everywhere and will participate of all our activities.

38.6 Conclusion

Technology and security are the fruit of our society. It happens in a given political and cultural environment. For that, cybersecurity should be studied from a transdisciplinary approach and not only from a technical point of view. It is necessary to cross-fertilise different disciplinary fields, that is, to analyse the interplay between the political, economic, social, legal and technical realms. That means that the academic community needs to adapt its research structure and organisation to support it. So evaluation of research programmes and projects should be improved to this new way of doing research.

So far when governance and strategy have been addressed by academia, the focus lights primarily on national strategies regarding cybersecurity and cyberdefence issues. In addition, research should also analyse how these cybersecurity policies could be put in place through organisational structures of public and private entities in order to make cooperation and collaboration more efficient, coherent and effective. These issues have not been very well addressed by the research community.

There is a real need to shorten the delay between innovations and solutions. That could have impacts on:

- The way research is financed
- How researchers collaborate and are able to disseminate their results
- How private sector can collaborate with academia
- How to balance the financial risk between long-term and short-term research and between public and private sectors

ICT-related risks have become complex with multiple cascading effects in our daily life, with deep impacts on the individual, organisational and state levels. Hence, it is very important to address risk management issues, with a research and education perspective and agenda, in order to be able to produce more robust and resilient cybersecurity measures and to improve security practices in complex environments. Complexity means fragility and generates more insecurity.

The level of risk complexity rises with the level of dependencies within critical infrastructures, in particular with those related to energy and electricity. Complexity is also linked to the level of imbrication between the digital world and the physical one and between technology and life.

Moreover, research and development activities have an urgent need to find a way to reduce the asymmetry that exists between the attacker and the defender, which could be a branch of research that could be delved into.

We have to think cybersecurity through the prism of risk management, taking into consideration the human aspect, in particular, the human dimension of the adversaries, the human dimension of those in charge of protection and defences and the human aspects of users that will circumvent security measures or rules if they are burdensome or not well understood.

Technology relies mainly upon science, engineering and mathematics, but it needs to serve a political vision of our society as well. Technical innovations and progresses should drive social progress for the benefit of everyone in an inclusive society. In this context, there is an urgent need to address these considerations within any research and development plan in cybersecurity. When considering research in an era where everything is "smart", security has to be integrated by design. Consequently, research should focus on the following:

- How to deter and discourage malicious cyber activities
- How to raise the level of situational awareness from a user point of view
- How to identify weaknesses
- How to protect users, systems and infrastructures against cyber incidents and how to preserve fundamental security and safety needs
- How to detect misuses and incidents
- How to adapt and recover after problems, crisis or disasters and manage them
- How to address privacy risk and human rights protection at the very beginning and throughout all the life cycle of any new smart something or security measures

Cybersecurity is a shared responsibility. That means that a cybersecurity research agenda has to be complemented by a cybersecurity industrial and development plan. Transforming ideas and research innovations into products and commercial solutions, which the market would adopt, in order to be able to have some return on investments, constitutes critical issues. Research needs a global vision also in order to quickly design, develop, implement, manage and use new security technologies and services.

Accelerating the transition from research innovation to practice supposes that the workplace is able to take advantage of the digital evolution and is educated for that. It is still a huge effort to do to reduce the gap between today's reality and cybersecurity requirements, as well as the gap between research objectives and cybersecurity practices. Investments have to be done not only in fundamental research but also in education and also in actions that could optimise the transition from innovation to best practices among all stakeholders.

References

1. United Nations General Assembly (2004). Creation of a global culture of cybersecurity and the protection of critical information infrastructures. https://www.itu.int/ITU-D/cyb/cybersecurity/docs/UN_resolution_58_199.pdf.
2. S. Ghernaouti-Hélie - "Information Security for Economic and Social Development" UNESCAP – 2008 – Link http://www.unescap.org/icstd/policy/.
3. Solange Ghernaouti; ITU Regional Cybersecurity Forum for Europe and CIS, Sofia, Bulgaria, 07-09 October 2008.
4. S. Ghernaouti; "Cyberpower, crime, conflict and security in cyberspace" EPFL Press 2013.
5. http://www.oecd.org/sti/ieconomy/oecdguidelinesforthesecurityofinformationsystemsandnetworkstowardsacultureofsecurity.htm.
6. https://www.itu.int/en/action/cybersecurity/Pages/gca.aspx.
7. www.unil.ch/dcs This master is a result of a strong vision and deep understanding of the ongoing digital transformation of the society that have been carried out by professors P. Margot, L. Moreillon and by S. Ghernaouti who has been the first director of the Master.
8. This master is a result of a strong vision and deep understanding of the ongoing digital transformation of the society that have been carried out by professors P. Margot, L. Moreillon and by S. Ghernaouti who has been the first director of the Master.
9. Collaborative Project. FP7-SEC-2013.2.5-2. Grant Agreement Number 607775. http://ecrime-project.eu/.
10. Convention on Cybercrime ETS No.185: https://www.coe.int/en/web/conventions/full-list/-/conventions/treaty/185

Bibliography

"The Fight against Cybercrime. Cooperation between CERTs and Law Enforcement Agencies in the fight against cybercrime" ENISA, 2012.
"Give and Take. Good Practice Guide for Addressing Network and Information Security". ENISA, 2012.
"Aspects of Cybercrime Legal, Regulatory and Operational Factors Affecting CERT Co-operation with Other Stakeholders" ENISA, 2012.
"The Directive on attacks against information systems, A Good Practice Collection for CERTs on the Directive on attacks against information systems" ENISA, 2013.
Akhgar Babak**, Brewster** Ben (Eds.) "Combatting Cybercrime and Cyberterrorism Challenges, Trends and Priorities", Springer 2016.
Solange Ghernaouti; "Cyberpower, crime, conflict and security in cyberspace" EPFL Press 2013.

Solange Ghernaouti "Cyberpower: stakes and challenges for Europe" The European files, January 2016.

Solange Ghernaouti; "La cybercriminalité, les nouvelles armes de pouvoir" Lee savoir suisse, PPUR 2017.

Thomas A. Johnson (editor); "Cybersecurity: Protecting Critical Infrastructures from Cyber Attack and Cyber Warfare", CRC Press 2015.

Report on the opportunities for deterring and fighting cybercrime across non ICT sectors. Deliverable D7.1 submitted in May 2016 in fulfilment of the requirements of the FP7 project, E-CRIME grant agreement n° 607775.

Christopher Hadnagy; "The Art of human hacking" Wiley Publishing Inc. 2011.

Kevin D. Mitnik; "The art of Deception: Controlling the human element of security", Wiley Publishing Inc. 2002.

Eine vertrauenswürdige Zusammenarbeit mit Hilfe der Blockchain-Technologie

Norbert Pohlmann

Zusammenfassung

Die „Blockchain" ist eine spannende und faszinierende IT-Technologie, die das Potenzial hat, Politik, Verwaltung und Wirtschaftszweige gewaltig auf den Kopf zu stellen. Die Blockchain-Technologie ist eine Querschnittstechnologie mit hohem disruptiven Potenzial für viele Wirtschaftsbereiche. Die Blockchain-basierten Systeme könnten in vielen Bereichen zentrale Instanzen ablösen, wie Banken, Notare oder Treuhänder. Das ist möglich, weil die Validierungsalgorithmen der Blockchain-Technologie ganz ohne solche Intermediäre die Vertrauenswürdigkeit der aufgezeichneten Transaktionsdaten garantieren. In der Zukunft werden zunehmend sogenannte Smart Contracts im Rahmen der Blockchain-Technologie umgesetzt, die eine vorprogrammierte, selbstausführende Vertragsabwicklung möglich machen. Die Blockchain-Technologie wird unsere IT-Systeme im Laufe der Digitalisierung effektiver und sicherer machen. Damit neue Geschäftsideen mit der Blockchain-Technologie positiv gestaltet werden können, soll dieser Artikel helfen, die komplizierte Technologie besser zu verstehen und mit Hilfe von Anwendungsfällen die Nutzungsmöglichkeiten aufzuzeigen.

39.1 Einleitung

Die verschiedenen Disziplinen können die Blockchain-Technologie aus sehr unterschiedlichen Blickwinkeln betrachten. Für einen Informatiker ist die Blockchain grundsätzliche eine einfache Datenstruktur, die Daten als Transaktionen in einzelnen „Blöcken" verkettet

N. Pohlmann (✉)
Instituts für Internet-Sicherheit an der Westfälischen Hochschule Gelsenkirchen
Aachen, Deutschland
E-Mail: pohlmann@internet-sicherheit.de

© Springer Fachmedien Wiesbaden GmbH, ein Teil von Springer Nature 2018
M. Bartsch, S. Frey (Hrsg.), *Cybersecurity Best Practices*,
https://doi.org/10.1007/978-3-658-21655-9_39

und in einem verteilten Netz redundant verwaltet. Die Alternative wäre z. B. eine konventionelle Datenbank, die kontinuierlich repliziert wird. Für die IT-Sicherheitsexperten hat die Blockchain den Vorteil, dass die Daten als Transaktionen in den einzelnen „Blöcken" manipulationssicher gespeichert werden können, das heißt, die Teilnehmer an der Blockchain sind in der Lage, die Echtheit, den Ursprung und die Unversehrtheit der gespeicherten Daten zu überprüfen. Die Alternative wäre hier z. B. ein PKI-System als zentraler Vertrauensdienstanbieter. Für den Anwendungsdesigner bedeutet die Nutzung der Blockchain-Technologie eine vertrauenswürdige Zusammenarbeit zwischen verschiedenen Organisationen, ohne die Einbindung einer zentralen Instanz. Die Alternative könnte hier z. B. ein kostenintensiver Treuhänder sein.

Grundsätzlich sind Blockchains fälschungssichere, verteilte Datenstrukturen, in denen Transaktionen in der Zeitfolge protokolliert nachvollziehbar, unveränderlich und ohne zentrale Instanz abgebildet sind. Damit lassen sich mit Hilfe der Blockchain-Technologie Eigentumsverhältnisse direkter und effizienter als bislang sichern und regeln, da eine lückenlose und unveränderliche Datenaufzeichnung hierfür die Grundlage schafft.

Die Blockchain-Technologie stellt mit unterschiedlichen Sicherheitsmethoden ein „programmiertes Vertrauen" zur Verfügung.

Nach einer Studie, die der eco-Verband in Auftrag gegeben hat, glaubt der Mittelstand an die Blockchain-Technologie. Die Blockchain setzt sich für bestimmte Anwendungsfälle und Branchen in der Breite durch – das denken 44 Prozent der Mittelständler. Neun Prozent der befragten Unternehmen planen bereits konkret den Einsatz einer Blockchain im eigenen Unternehmen. 17 Prozent der Befragten denken immerhin über den Einsatz in ihrem Unternehmen nach. Drei Prozent der Mittelständler nutzen die Blockchain bereits. Nur 26 Prozent glauben nicht an diese Technologie, 30 Prozent sind unschlüssig oder machen keine Angaben [1].

Die IT-Marktführer in den USA bauen ihre IT-Systeme und Dienstleistungen in der Regel auf zentrale Dienste auf. Dazu passt das Konzept der Blockchain-Technologie nicht wirklich! Da wir in Deutschland und in der EU sehr viel mehr KMUs haben, ist die Blockchain eine ideale IT-Technologie, die eine vertrauenswürdige verteilte Zusammenarbeit ermöglicht. Aus diesem Grund werden wir mit Hilfe der Blockchain-Technologie in vielen Bereichen den Digitalisierungsprozess beschleunigen, aber auch sicherer und vertrauenswürdiger umsetzen können.

Damit neue Geschäftsideen mit der Blockchain-Technologie positiv gestaltet werden können, soll dieser Artikel helfen, die komplizierte Technologie besser zu verstehen und mit Hilfe von Anwendungsfällen die Nutzungsmöglichkeiten aufzuzeigen.

„Geschichte" der Blockchain Als „Satoshi Nakamoto" an der Bitcoin-Kryptowährung arbeitete, benötigte er eine dezentrale, öffentliche und vor Manipulationen geschützte Datenstruktur, auf welcher die einzelnen Transaktionen gespeichert werden konnten und dabei noch öffentlich einsehbar waren. Sozusagen ein öffentliches Transaktionsbuch (Distributed Ledger). Da dies mit traditionellen relativen Datenbanken nicht möglich war, entwickelte er die Blockchain [2].

39.2   Elemente, Prinzipien und Struktur der Blockchain-Technologie

In diesem Kapitel werden die Elemente, Prinzipien und Struktur der Blockchain-Technologie als Grundlagen beschrieben.

Element: Daten Die Blockchain ist eine einfache Datenstruktur, wie eine Datenbank (Siehe Abb. 39.1). Daten werden in der Blockchain in einzelnen, chronologisch miteinander verketteten Blöcken als Transaktionen verwaltet. Die Daten werden in Transaktionen vor Manipulationen gesichert in der Blockchain gespeichert, siehe auch Abschnitt Transkationen. Die Blockchain ist bei jeder Node (Teilnehmer) und damit verteilt und redundant vorhanden, d. h. es besteht eine sehr hohe Verfügbarkeit der Daten und alle Nodes müssten gleichzeitig manipuliert werden. Eine Blockchain kann sehr groß werden, wie z. B. die Bitcoin-Blockchain etwa 115 GByte groß ist, Stand: Mai 2017.

Element: Block Ein Block in einer Blockchain ist ein strukturierter Datensatz, der beliebige Transaktionen mit Daten enthalten kann und vor Manipulationen gesichert ist (Siehe Abb. 39.2). Was die Blockchain interessant macht, ist der sogenannte *Blockheader*. In diesem wird z. B. der jeweilige Hashwert des Blockheaders vom Vorgänger-Block gespeichert. Dieser Hashwert, *HashPrev*, wird dabei über den gesamten letzten Blockheader – inklusive des Hashwertes des Vorgänger-Blockes – generiert, wodurch die Verkettung der Blöcke manipulationssicher umgesetzt werden kann.

Jeder Block in der Blockchain kann im Prinzip gelesen und überprüft werden. In den Blöcken finden sich die verschiedenen Daten als Transaktionen vor, die in der Blockchain gespeichert werden. Blöcke können auf ihre Integrität geprüft werden, indem der aktuelle Hashwert eines Blockes des gespeicherten Hashwertes im Folgeblock (HashPrev) übereinstimmen muss. Dies ist für jede Node ohne weiteres möglich, da jede Node im Normalfall alle Informationen innerhalb eines Blockes lesen kann. Soll ein neuer Block hinzugefügt werden, so kann dieser nicht einfach an die Blockchain angehängt werden. Für jeden neuen Block muss die Richtigkeit des Blockes geprüft werden und mit Hilfe

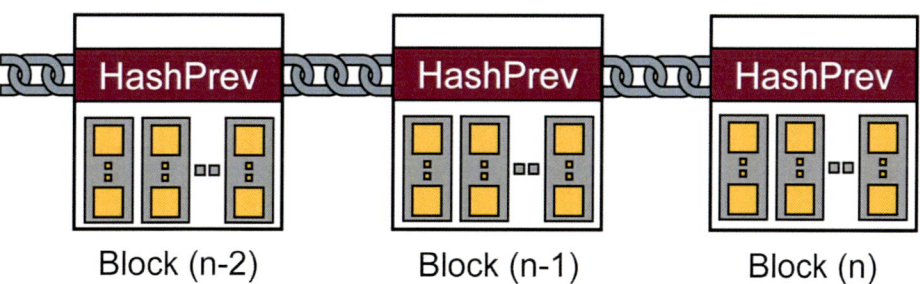

Abb. 39.1 Datenstruktur einer Blockchain

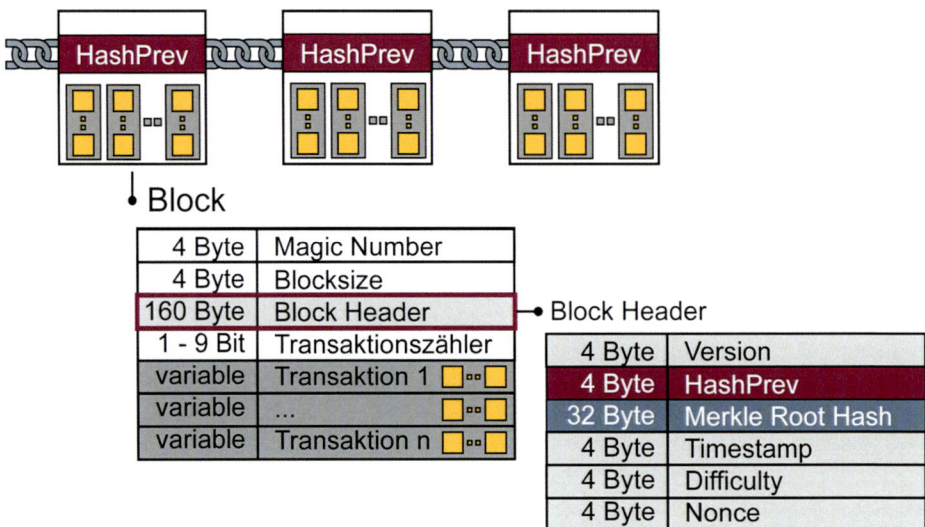

Abb. 39.2 Inhalt eines Blocks

Abb. 39.3 Aufbau einer
Transaktion

eines Konsensfindungsverfahrens bestimmt werden, welche Node einen Block hinzufügen darf, damit es nicht möglich ist, die Blockchain zu manipulieren.

Element: Transaktionen Alle Daten innerhalb der Blöcke, werden als „Transaktionen" bezeichnet. Transaktionen enthalten Daten, die in der Zeitfolge protokolliert (chronologisch), nachvollziehbar, unveränderlich und ohne zentrale Instanz abgebildet sind (Siehe Abb. 39.3.). Die Daten können Kontostände, Werte, Attribute, Quelltexte, Merkmale, usw. oder allgemein „digital Assets" sein. Eine Transaktion enthält auch immer den Public-Key (Adresse) der Node, der die Transaktion erstellt und signiert hat.

Jede Transaktion, die hinzugefügt werden soll, muss zunächst von der erstellenden Node mit dem Private-Key aus der eigenen Wallet signiert und an alle Nodes über das P2P-Blockchain-Netzwerk gesendet werden. Jede Node im P2P-Blockchain-Netzwerk kann die Identität der Node, welche die Transaktion erstellt und abgesendet hat, und den Inhalt der Transaktion verifizieren.

Element: Node Jeder, der an der „Blockchain" teilnimmt, wird als „Node" beziehungsweise „Teilhaber" bezeichnet. Jede Node erhält eine aktuelle Kopie der Blockchain, die fortlaufend aktualisiert wird. Jede Node, die zu einer „Blockchain" gehört, falls diese nicht eingeschränkt ist, hat im Prinzip die gleichen Rechte, die Blockchain zu speichern und neue Blöcke hinzuzufügen (validieren). Jede Node hat eine eigene Wallet und kann Transaktionen mit Daten erstellen, signieren und im Peer-to-Peer-Blockchain-Netzwerk verteilen (Siehe Abb. 39.4).

Element: Wallet Jede Node verfügt über eine „Wallet". Eine Wallet ist dabei eine Datenstruktur, in der die eigenen Private- und Public-Keys der Node sicher gespeichert sind. Aus dem Public-Key wird mit Hilfe einer Funktion die eindeutige Kennung (Adresse) einer Node berechnet. Mit dem Private-Key signiert eine Node eine Transaktion, die sie erstellt hat (Siehe Abb. 39.5). Mit Hilfe des Public-Keys ist es möglich zu verifizieren, dass die Transaktionen von einer bestimmten Node erstellt wurden.

Abb. 39.4 Inhalt einer Node

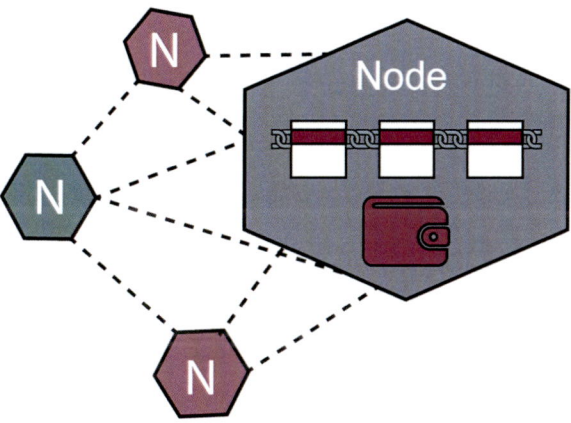

Abb 39.5 Inhalte einer Wallet

Angriffe auf eine Blockchain passieren sehr häufig auf die Wallet der Node, da mit den Private-Keys manipuliert werden kann. Wallets können in verschiedenen Formen existieren bzw. gespeichert werden. Dazu zählt zum Beispiel eine einfache Datei auf der Node. Es ist aber auch möglich, eine Wallet auf einem Sicherheitsmodul, wie z. B. USB-Stick, für Personen oder High-Level-Sicherheitsmodule für Server zu realisieren. Eine weitere Möglichkeit ist es, die Wallet auf einem Papierzettel in Form eines QR-Codes zu halten.

Prinzip: Keine „zentrale Instanz" Eine Blockchain besitzt keine „zentrale Instanz", sondern ist auf all ihren Nodes (Teilhabern) in einem Peer-to-Peer-Netzwerk verteilt (Siehe Abb. 39.6). Jeder kommuniziert z. B. über das Internet direkt miteinander. Damit gibt es keinen „Single Point of Failure" mehr und Logs bzw. Backups müssen nicht besonders berücksichtigt werden, da die Datenstruktur sich selbst regeneriert.

Jeder Block wird mit dem vorherigen Block über den Hashwert (HashPrev) des Blockheaders „verkettet". Wird versucht innerhalb eines Blockes Daten in Transaktionen zu ändern, so würden die gesamten Hashwerte ab diesem Block „falsch" werden.

Struktur: Unterschiedliche Arten von Nodes In der Praxis gibt es unterschiedliche Ausprägungen von Nodes (siehe Abb. 39.7). Nodes, die die gesamte Blockchain speichern, werden als „Full Nodes" bezeichnet.

Für ein portables Gerät, wie zum Beispiel ein Smartphone oder IoT-Geräte, wie Autos, ist es allerdings nicht umsetzbar, eine eventuell mehrere Gigabyte große Blockchain zu speichern. Solche Nodes werden auch als „Lite Node" bezeichnet. Sie speichern nur die aktuellsten bzw. für sich „relevantesten" Blöcke wie z. B. Blöcke, an welchen die Node selber teilhatte. Die Wallet ist sicher im Geräte gespeichert. Zudem gibt es auch noch sogenannte „Service Nodes", welche keine direkten Teilhaber sind. Endgeräte wie Smartphones nutzen einen Dienst, der virtuelle Nodes anbietet. Die Aktivierung der Dienste müssen bei den Service Nodes sicher umgesetzt werden, um Missbrauch zu vermeiden.

Abb. 39.6 Verteilung der Nodes untereinander

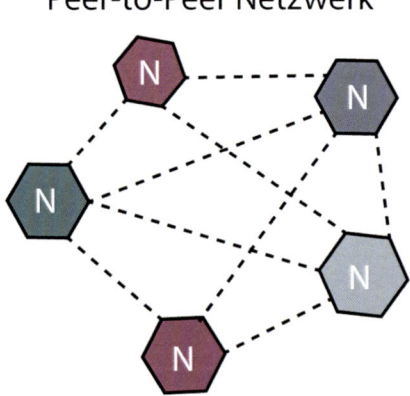

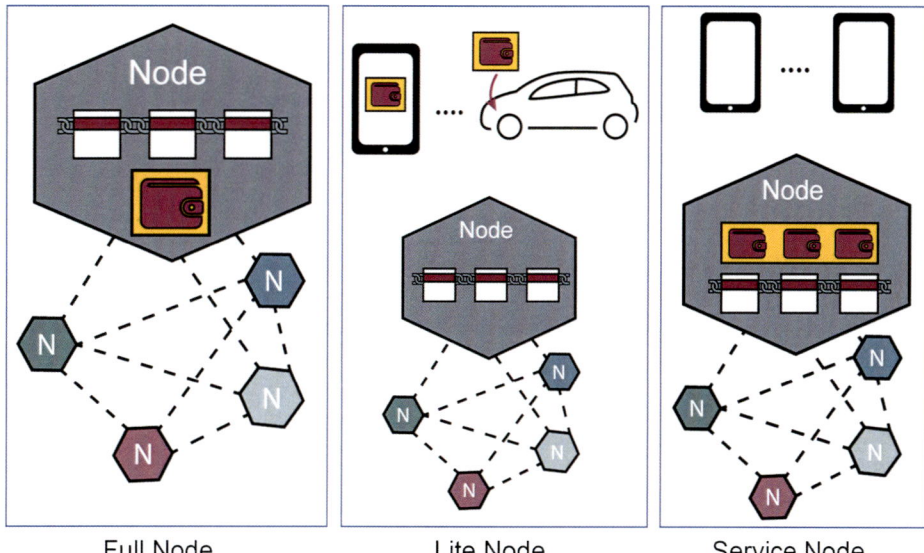

Abb. 39.7   Verschiedene Arten von Nodes/Wallets

Struktur: Konsensfindungsverfahren   Alle Transaktionen werden von den entsprechenden Nodes signiert, die für die Daten in der Transaktion verantwortlich sind und an alle anderen Nodes über das Peer-to-Peer-Netzwerk verteilt. Ein Konsensfindungsverfahren bestimmt, welche Node einen neuen Block validieren und an die Blockchain „hängen" darf [3]. Diese Node überprüft, ob die Transaktionen von Semantik und Syntax her richtig sind und ob die digitalen Signaturen des Initiators der Transaktionen mit der Adresse übereinstimmen. Dann wird ein neuer Block mit HashPrev und Merkle Root Hash generiert und an alle Nodes verteilt. Jede Node hat dadurch jederzeit eine Kopie der aktuell gültigen Blockchain.

Dieses Prinzip des Distributed Consensus macht die Konsistenzprüfung der Transaktionen vollkommen unabhängig von einer einzelnen vertrauenswürdigen Instanz. Für die Herstellung des Konsenses zwischen den Nodes, wer für den Abschluss neuer Transaktionen und das Hinzufügen eines bestimmten Blocks an die Blockchain verantwortlich ist, gibt es verschiedene Verfahren.

Proof of Work-Konsensfindungsverfahren   Proof of Work ist die aktuell gebräuchlichste Methode zur Konsensfindung und wird z. B. aktuell von der Bitcoin-Blockchain genutzt.

Hier konkurrieren die einzelnen Nodes als sogenannte „Miner" untereinander, indem sie jeweils ein mathematisches Problem – dessen Schwierigkeit sich dynamisch ändern lässt – lösen müssen. Jeder Miner einer Node muss einen Hashwert für einen Block finden, der einem bestimmten vorgegebenen Muster entspricht. Dieses Muster wird vom Netzwerk eigenständig festgelegt, wobei die Schwierigkeit sich mit der Anzahl der vorgegebenen Stellen des Musters erhöht. Zum Beispiel soll ein Hashwert 5 führende Nullen als Muster besitzen.

Die einzige Möglichkeit für die Nodes, einen anderen Hashwert zu erzeugen, ist es, den NONCE-Wert eines Blockes, ein bestimmter Wert, welcher jede Zahl enthalten kann, zu verändern. Somit wird die Konsensfindung eines Blockes zu einem Glückspiel für die Miner in einer Node, da diese nun einen NONCE-Wert finden müssen, der den zu suchenden Hashwert ergibt. Der Miner, der dieses Problem als erstes gelöst hat, darf den Block an die Blockchain anhängen. Die Komplexität des Problems wird in der Praxis so gewählt, dass die Aufgabe im Schnitt 10 Min. dauern soll. Das bedeutet, dass die Transaktionen nur alle 10 Min. in einen Block der Blockchain hinzugefügt werden und gültig sind Abb. 39.8.

Die Berechnung des mathematischen Problems beim Proof of Work-Konsensfindungsverfahren kostet sehr viel Energie. Bei Bitcoin werden pro Tag Stromkosten von 2,8 Mio. US-Dollar verbraucht, 1,3 Giga-Watt, das sind ca. 10 US-Dollar pro Transaktion. Solange eine Node nicht die Mehrheit an Miner-Kapazitäten besitzt (mehr als 50 %), ist das Mining-Prinzip robust und nicht zu kompromittieren. Ein weiteres Problem ist, dass der Zeitraum der Validierung sehr hoch ist.

Proof of Stake-Konsensfindungsverfahren Bei dieser Methode der Konsensfindung wird z. B. die Node gewählt, die die meisten Anteile an Blöcken einer Blockchain hinzugefügt hat. Dieses Verfahren merzt einige Sicherheitslücken aus, die bei Proof of Work-Problemen vorhanden sind. Es ist zum Beispiel für einen Angreifer nicht mehr möglich, eine beliebige Anzahl an „Pseudo Miners", welche falsche Blöcke als richtig validieren, dem Netzwerk ungesehen hinzuzufügen. Zudem hätte z. B. die Node mit den meisten Coins das größte Interesse an einer stabilen und sicheren Blockchain. Zudem müsste ein Angreifer erst einmal so viele Coins besitzen, dass er Blöcke erstellen darf. Mit einer Attacke würde er sich also im Grunde selbst angreifen. Da der Konsensmechanismus sehr auf „Vertrauen" basiert, wird dieses Verfahren eher bei privaten Blockchains genutzt.

Alternative Konsensfindungsverfahren Neben den beiden Grundmethoden gibt es noch weitere, sich aktuell in der Probephase befindliche Methoden zur Konsensfindung. Ein Verfahren ist das sogenannte „Byzantine Fault Tolerance" Verfahren, das eigentlich zur

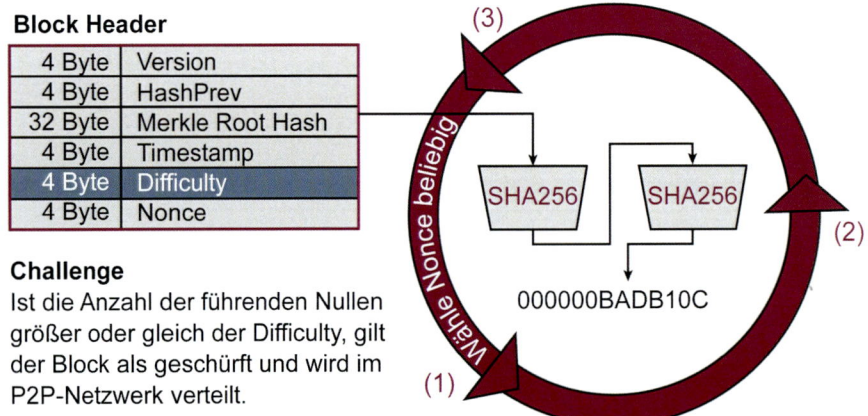

Abb. 39.8 Mining (Proof of Work)

Ermittlung von defekten Sensoren genutzt wird. Damit soll ermittelt werden, welche Node in einer Blockchain versucht, kompromittierte Blöcke an die Blockchain anzuhängen.

Struktur: Berechtigungsarchitektur Eine Blockchain kann sowohl für jeden zugänglich, als auch nur für bestimmte Nodes (Teilnehmer) einsehbar und nutzbar sein. Es wird zwischen den Zugriffsberechtigungen der Nutzung einer Blockchain und der Validierungsberechtigung, Blöcke hinzufügen, unterschieden (Abb. 39.9). Bei den Zugriffbeschränkungen wird festgesetzt, wer überhaupt auf eine Blockchain zugreifen darf. Bei einer Public Blockchain darf jede Node uneingeschränkt die Blockchain nutzen. Bei einer Private Blockchain dürfen nur klar definierte Nodes zugreifen. Die Validierungsberechtigungen sagen dagegen aus, welche Nodes Blöcke einer Blockchain hinzufügen dürfen. Auf „Permissioned"-Blockchains dürfen nur bestimmte Nodes, wohingegen auf „Permissionless"-Blockchains alle Nodes Blöcke einfügen dürfen.

Public permissionless Diese Struktur ist die zurzeit am besten erprobte Blockchain-Struktur. Eine solche Blockchain kann jeder einsehen und auch jede Node im Prinzip Blöcke hinzufügen. Dabei ist die Identität der Node, welche die Blockchain einsieht und/oder Blöcke dieser Blockchain hinzugefügt hat, nicht mehr nachzuweisen. Dieses Modell wird unter anderem für die Blockchain der Kryptowährung Bitcoin verwendet. Hier kann jeder von der Blockchain lesen und jede Node als Miner Blöcke der Blockchain hinzufügen, wenn sie die Challenge gewinnt.

Private permissionless Diese Art der Blockchain verpflichtet die Nodes sich zunächst zu registrieren, um Zugriff auf die eigentliche Blockchain zu erlangen. Danach kann jedoch jeder registrierte Node Blöcke zu der Blockchain hinzufügen. Diese Art der Blockchain ist die am wenigsten genutzte Art.

Private permissioned Die restriktivste Blockchain Variante ist eine private permissioned Blockchain, die nicht öffentlich lesbar und auch nicht für alle Nodes beschreibbar ist. Die einzelnen Blöcke dürfen nur die Nodes einer Transaktion und eventuell eigens dazu berechtigte Nodes einsehen. Ansonsten ist es unmöglich für außenstehende Nodes, die Blöcke der Blockchain einzusehen.

		Validierung	
		Permissionless	Permissioned
Zugriff	Public	„Jeder darf lesen und validieren."	„Jeder darf lesen, nur Berechtigte validieren."
	Private	„Nur Berechtigte dürfen lesen, jeder darf validieren."	„Nur Berechtigte dürfen lesen und validieren."

Abb. 39.9 Berechtigungsarchitektur

Dieses mehr lokalisierte Modell eignet sich vor allem für Unternehmen, die die Vorteile der Blockchain nutzen wollen, jedoch keine öffentliche Einsicht in ihre Trankaktionen bzw. Daten geben möchten.

Zum Beispiel möchte eine Bank nicht unbedingt, dass die gesamten Transaktionsdaten ihrer Kunden für jeden (auch für Nicht-Kunden der Bank) öffentlich einsehbar sind. Zudem besitzt eine Bank immer noch eine „zentrale Instanz" und überlässt das Verifizieren und Hinzufügen von Blöcken lieber den eigenen Nodes, denen sie mehr vertrauen kann, als anderen Nodes, welche zu den Kunden gehören.

Public permissioned Bei einer solchen Blockchain sind die Blöcke zwar für jeden einsehbar, allerdings haben nur durch die Organisation ausgewählte Nodes das Recht, Blöcke der Blockchain hinzuzufügen.

Dabei wird die „Wahl zur vertrauenswürdigen Node" zwar nicht dauerhaft festgelegt, allerdings muss diese deutlich klar sein, warum wurde gerade diese „Node" zur „vertrauenswürdigen Node" gewählt. Da in der Regel den Nodes vertraut wird, werden zur Konsensfindung Verfahren, wie zum Beispiel das „Byzatine Fault Tolerance" Verfahren genutzt.

Wird eine Node als kompromittiert angemahnt, so gibt es eine Gruppe an Entscheidern, die die Node überprüfen und darüber entscheiden, ob der Block, den diese Node einfügen möchte, kompromittiert ist oder nicht. Diese „Entscheider" werden „Konsortium" („Consortium") genannt, weswegen eine solche Blockchain auch als „Consortium Chain" bezeichnet wird.

39.3   Anwendungsformen und Anwendungen der Blockchain

Mit Hilfe der Blockchain-Technologien können verschiedene Anwendungsformen und Anwendungen realisiert werden. Im Folgenden werden einige exemplarisch dargestellt.

Anwendungsform „Smart Contracts" In den Blöcken einer Blockchain lassen sich nicht nur Werte, sondern beliebige Elemente in den Transaktionen speichern. So ist es möglich, Quelltext, also ausführbaren Programmcode, abzulegen, der bei einem bestimmten definierten Ereignis ausgeführt wird. Der in einem Block abgelegte Quelltext ist dabei Blockchain-charakteristisch unveränderlich. Diese Idee wird auch als Smart Contracts bezeichnet (Siehe Abb. 39.10.).

Smart Contracts sind Verträge zur „automatisierten" Umsetzung von Vertragsbedingungen über Programmcode. Damit sollen in der Zukunft z. B. Juristen überflüssig werden. Ein Jurist hat bisher die Aufgabe, bei jedem Vertrag die Bedingungen, die dieser Vertrag stellt, nachzuprüfen. Soll beispielsweise für den Kauf eines Autos ein Betrag von einem auf das andere Konto fließen, so muss dies ein Jurist nachvollziehen, bevor der Schlüssel übergeben werden kann. Durch einen Smart Contract soll es nun möglich sein, die Vertragsbedingungen in „Wenn-Dann-Funktionen" einzuteilen. Wenn zum Beispiel eine Node einen

Abb. 39.10 Smart Contracts

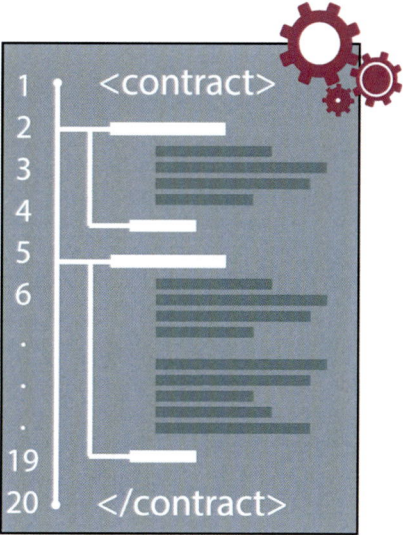

bestimmten Betrag auf das Konto einer anderen Node überweist, würde dies der entsprechende Smart Contract merken und beispielsweise den elektronischen Autoschlüssel des Verkäufers für den entsprechenden Käufer freischalten oder – falls es sich bei dem Kauf um ein älteres Auto handelt – den Verkäufer per E-Mail darüber informieren, dass sein Auto verkauft wurde. So kann der Verkäufer dem Käufer den Schlüssel des Autos übergeben.

Smart Contracts stellen eine Kontroll- oder Geschäftsregel innerhalb eines technischen Protokolls dar und helfen, die Zusammenarbeit zwischen verschiedenen Organisationen vertrauenswürdig und vor allem automatisiert umzusetzen.

Anwendungen, die eine Blockchain-Technologie nutzen Da es in vielerlei Hinsicht Bemühungen gibt, Firmen und Entwickler für die Blockchain zu begeistern, stellt sich die Frage, was mit der Blockchain-Technologie alles gemacht werden kann.

Kryptowährung Angefangen hatte alles mit der Realisierung der Bitcoin-Kryptowährung, die Banken als dritte Instanz, also als Vermittler zwischen zwei Parteien, überflüssig macht.

Idee und Verfahren von Bitcoin:

Bitcoin ist eine Internetwährung, die verteilt, dezentral und unabhängig von einer Zentralbank ein globales Zahlungsnetzwerk zur Verfügung stellt. Die Funktionsweise des Bitcoin-Systems stellt sicher, dass es in ein paar Jahrzehnten maximal 21.000.000 Bitcoins weltweit geben wird. Die Node, die beim Mining gewonnen hat, bekommt 12,5 Bitcoins als Belohnung (Stand 2017). Jede Person hat eine Wallet und der Public-Key entspricht der Kontonummer. Mit dem Private-Key werden Transaktionen signiert, um Guthaben auf diesem Bitcoin-Konto an eine andere Adresse zu überweisen (public permissionless Blockchain).

Bitcoin hat in Deutschland zurzeit keine gesetzliche Grundlage für die Verwendung eines Zahlungssystems. Der schwankende Kurs ist ein weiterer Grund, warum sich Bitcoin nicht als globales Zahlungssystem im Alltag durchgesetzt hat. Bitcoin ist aber dennoch eine sehr relevante Währung, vergleichbar mit z. B. Gold. Am 07.12.17 um 21:45 Uhr waren ca. 16,65 Mio. Bitcoins vergeben und ein Bitcoin hatte einen Wert von **12.559,45 €**. Damit sind alle Bitcoin zusammen, d. h. die Bitcoin-Blockchain, über 209 Mrd. € wert.

Weitere Zahlungssysteme Die Banken gingen nach dem ersten Schock selbst in die Offensive und stellten Forscherteams zusammen, mit dem Ziel, die Blockchain-Technik für sich selber nutzbar zu machen.

Die Schweizer Bank UBS möchte beispielsweise ihre eigene digitale Währung entwickeln, den sogenannten „Utility Settlement Coin", kurz USC. Zum Einsatz kommen soll die Währung beim Handel an der Börse mit dem Ziel, Clearinggesellschaften zu ersetzen, die sich bisher um die Geld- und Wertpapiertransfers gekümmert haben. So lassen sich Tage beim Transfer einsparen, da sich Geld und Wertpapiere sofort durch einen neu hinzugefügten Block austauschen lassen. Smart Contracts regeln dabei die automatische Überweisung der USC des Käufers an den Verkäufer. Nach Angaben der UBS ist der Utility Settlement Coin keine parallele Währung wie der Bitcoin, sondern basiert auf realen Werten. 2018 soll das Projekt in die Tat umsetzt werden. Einige Banken haben ihre Beteiligung an dem Projekt zugesichert, unter anderem die Deutsche Bank. Die Bundesbank arbeitet zusammen mit der Deutschen Börse an einem ähnlichen Prototyp, der noch mehrere Jahre Entwicklungszeit benötigt. Eine private permissioned Blockchain wird für Wertpapiere und den Transfer von USC eingesetzt. Full Nodes befinden sich bei den Banken, die mit den Wertpapieren handeln. Für Kunden würden Light Nodes infrage kommen, die nur die für den Kunden wichtigen Blöcke mit den entsprechenden Wertpapieren abspeichern.

Der RSCoin wurde von Forschern für die britische Zentralbank entworfen und ist eine Kryptowährung, die zentral verwaltet werden soll. Die Blockchain ist immer noch dezentral, jedoch weist die Zentralbank das Recht auf Einträge in diese mit Hilfe von kryptographischen Schlüsseln anderer Parteien, wie zum Beispiel Geschäftsbanken, zu. Begrenzte Geldmengen, sieben Transaktionen pro Sekunde und das Proof-of-Work-Problem, wie es bei Bitcoin zum Einsatz kommt, fallen weg. Zweitausend Transaktionen pro Sekunde sollen verarbeitet werden. Was bleibt, ist die Pseudoanonymität des Nutzers. Werden keine zusätzlichen Maßnahmen für den Schutz der Privatsphäre getroffen, entsteht ein transparenter Nutzer, dessen Transaktionen immer und überall nachverfolgt werden können. Zudem ist, wie bei der Schweizer Bank UBS, eine private permissioned Blockchain vorstellbar, damit nicht in bestehende Transaktionen eingesehen werden kann. Andere Parteien, die die Blockchain verändern wollen, können Light Nodes oder Service Nodes einrichten.

Im Bereich rund um die Bezahlung von Dienstleistungen, Inhalten und Rohstoffen werden ebenfalls Überlegungen und Lösungen präsentiert.

Das Startup-Unternehmen Pey möchte Firmen auf einfachem Wege ermöglichen, ihren Mitarbeitern Teile des Gehalts in Bitcoin auszuzahlen. Pey arbeitet mit dem Dienst „PayrollAPI" von Bitpay, der den Umtausch von Euro in Bitcoin und die Auszahlung an die Arbeitnehmer übernimmt. Das Geschäftsmodell sieht vor, die Nutzung zunächst kostenlos anzubieten und später eine Gebühr von einem Euro pro Mitarbeiter pro Monat einzuführen. Die Mitarbeiter müssen sich zunächst auf der Pey-Plattform anmelden und den Wert, den sie von ihrem Gehalt umwandeln wollen, eintragen.

Ein Ärgernis für Inhalte-Anbieter sind Ad-Blocker. Viele finanzieren sich durch die auf ihrer Seite gezeigte Werbung. Für Ad-Block-Nutzer, aber auch um allgemein mit den bereitgestellten Informationen Geld zu verdienen, gibt es Paywalls. Gegen Bezahlung wird ein Inhalt für den Leser freigegeben. Das deutsche Bitcoin-Startup „Satoshipay" möchte die Zahlung für Paywalls leichter machen. An den Browser wird ein Online-Wallet angedockt, worüber die Inhalte mit einem Klick bezahlt werden. Den Dienst von Satoshipay zahlt der Inhalte-Anbieter mit 10 % seines Verdienstes. Gefördert wird das Startup von Axel Springer und Visa. Das Wallet soll zukünftig auch mit der Visa-Karte aufgeladen werden können. Zudem sind Bezahlungen in die andere Richtung geplant, sprich der Anbieter zahlt seinen Nutzern für die Teilnahme an Umfragen oder Tests Geld.

Große Energiekonzerne wie RWE wollen gleich mehrere Probleme mit der Blockchain-Technologie lösen. Bei der Elektro-Mobilität gibt es zum einen kein einheitliches Bezahlsystem für das Aufladen von E-Autos und zum anderen ist die Reichweite dieser im Vergleich zu Autos mit Verbrennungsmotoren geringer.

Ladesäulen werden von verschiedenen Energiekonzernen angeboten. Jedes Unternehmen hat eine andere Art der Bezahlung. Bei längeren Fahrten, bei denen öfter an einer Ladestation haltgemacht werden muss, ist es also schwierig, eine Säule passend zum eigenen Bezahlsystem zu finden. RWE hat sich an dieser Stelle mit dem Startup „Slock.it" zusammengesetzt und an einer Blockchain-basierten Lösung mittels Smart Contracts gearbeitet. Ladesäulen sollen nur noch mit dem Auto kommunizieren und die Bezahlung automatisch abwickeln. Diese Entwicklung würde RWE auch bei einem anderen Projekt helfen. Micropayments sind Bezahlungen z. B. im Cent-Bereich und sind in großen Massen sehr aufwändig und teuer. Durch Smart Contracts wäre dies wiederum einfach und schnell. Es kann genutzt werden, um Ladungen an Ampeln für E-Autos zu ermöglichen, wie RWE es für die Zukunft plant. Dadurch würde auch die Reichweite von E-Autos verbessert, da die Aufladung automatisch und problemlos während der Rotphase an einer Ampel geschieht und so weite Strecken zurückgelegt werden können.

Da es unsinnig ist, eine komplette Blockchain in einem Auto zu speichern, sind betreffende E-Autos Light Nodes.

Manipulationssicherheit von Zuständen Eine weitere Idee ist, das Manipulieren von Tachometern bei Autos zu erkennen und damit einen Betrug zu verhindern. Das Verfahren könnte dabei wie folgt funktionieren: Wird ein Auto gestartet, so wird eine Transaktion mit dem Kilometerstand gesendet. Dies ermöglicht, eine Manipulation des Tachometers zu erkennen. Aber auch Versicherungen können so einfach die gefahrenen Kilometer berechnen und den Vertrag entsprechend anpassen.

Elektronische Auktion In der Ukraine wurde im Februar 2016 die erste elektronische Auktion mit einer Blockchain durchgeführt. Dies geschah testweise und soll die Welt der Auktionen einfacher und vor allem sicherer machen. Ein Block der Kette fungiert hierbei als eine private Handelsplattform, die eine Schnittstelle für Interessenten und Auktionäre bereitstellt. Hier kann nun für das Objekt der Wahl geboten werden. Es können auch feste Anfangsgebote gesetzt werden. Durch das Zahlen einer Teilnahmegebühr ist ein Teilnehmer mit seinem Bankkonto oder einem Konto für Kryptowährungen mit einer API des Systems verbunden und kann bei einem Kauf sofort das ersteigerte Objekt bezahlen.

Der Code, um nach diesem Prinzip elektronische Auktionen zu starten, ist frei erhältlich. Denkbar ist für Auktionshäuser, dass eine private permissonless Blockchain erstellt wird, damit jeder, der registriert ist, unkompliziert mitbieten kann.

Supply Chain Hier ist z. B. die Idee, eine automatische 3D-Druck-Produktions-, Bezahl- und Lieferkette umzusetzen. Nach der Bestellung wird die Konstruktion des gewünschten Teils an die Blockchain gesendet (one time use only). Die Produktion druckt dann automatisch das gewünschte Teil (pay per use). Nach dem 3D-Druck läuft die Zahlung automatisch. Das gedruckte und bezahlte Teil ruft den Versanddienst automatisch (Siehe Abb. 39.11).

Identity Management Große Vorteile können auch für das Identity-Management gefunden werden. Jeder Mensch trägt seinen Personalausweis oder andere Ausweisdokumente mit sich. Die persönlichen Informationen liegen schriftlich wie digital vor. Im Grunde genommen haben wir keine Kontrolle darüber, wer was sehen darf. Kauft ein Jugendlicher einen Film oder ein Spiel, der erst ab sechzehn oder achtzehn freigegeben ist, muss er seinen Personalausweis vorzeigen, um zu bestätigen, dass er das betreffende Alter erreicht hat. Einzusehen sind aber auch andere Daten, wie der vollständige Name und die Adresse. Das Unternehmen ShoHei bietet ein Konzept zu einer Blockchain-basierten Lösung an. Alle persönlichen Daten werden in einem Block gespeichert. ShoHei nutzt dazu den

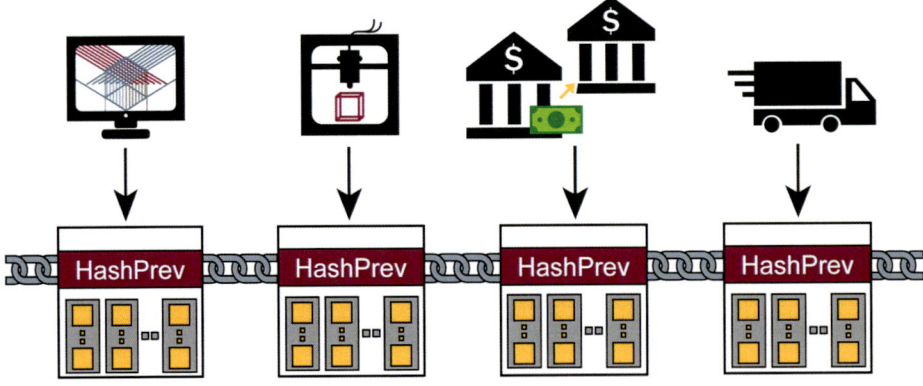

Abb. 39.11 Supply Chain

Abb. 39.12 Diamantenhandel

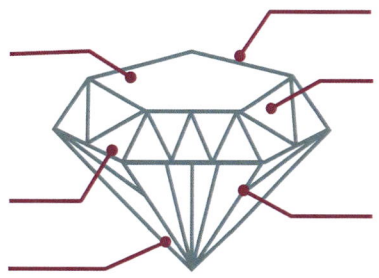

BlockCypher Blockchain Service. Es soll unter anderem möglich sein, sich mit dem Handy auszuweisen. Der Identifikationsnachweis geschieht dabei biometrisch. Nach der Identifikation kann festgelegt werden, welche Daten gezeigt werden sollen. Da die Blockchain nicht manipuliert werden kann, ist diese Technologie zum Identifizieren von Personen in vielen Lebensbereichen hilfreich, nicht zuletzt für die EU und die Anforderung nach mehr Sicherheit beim Überprüfen von auffälligen Flüchtlingen.

Da vertrauliche Daten verwaltet werden, sollten Full Nodes nur in den entsprechenden Ämtern stehen und die genutzten Smartphones als Light Nodes dienen, die nur die eigenen Blockdaten speichern.

Diamantenhandel Im Diamantenhandel werden alle Edelsteine zertifiziert. Unter anderem wird vermerkt, wem diese gehören und was für eine Qualität vorliegt. Es ist kaum zu glauben, aber so ist eine Zettelwirtschaft entstanden, die Kriminellen in die Hände spielt und es Behörden nicht leicht macht, Fälschungen oder Betrüger schnellstmöglich in Kontrollen zu entlarven. Selbst Datenbanken wurden gehackt und Tausende von Informationen verändert. Bei der Diamantenhandel-Blockchain werden alle Diamanten aufgenommen mit Informationen über den Besitzer, die Qualität und mehr als vierzig Merkmalen, die diesen Diamanten auszeichnen (Siehe. Abb. 39.12).

Wird der Diamant X von Person A an Person B verkauft, wird an die Blockchain einfach ein neuer Block gehängt mit den Informationen von Diamant X, nur dass als Besitzer Person B eingetragen ist. Mehr als 800.000 Diamanten wurden bereits eingetragen. Minengesellschaften, Händler und Versicherer unterstützen diese Art der Verwaltung.

39.4   Blockchain-as-a-Service

Da die Blockchain-Technologie nicht nur in der IT-Branche große Fortschritte bringen soll, sondern in möglichst vielen Arbeitsbereichen, die jedoch das nötige Wissen für den Umgang mit einer solchen IT-Technik nicht mitbringen, wird die Blockchain-Technologie auch „Blockchain-as-a-Service" angeboten.

Hierbei handelt es sich um vorgefertigte Blockchain-Lösungen, die bei Unternehmen eingepflegt werden. Zwei große Anbieter sind IBM und Microsoft.

Microsoft widmet sich unter dem Projektnamen „Bletchley" der Verkettung und bietet in seinem Clouddienst „Azure" den Aufbau einer eigenen Blockchain und deren Verwaltung an. Nodes können einfach festgelegt und entweder mit einem Passwort oder einem SSH Key gesichert werden. Zusätzlich können bestimmte Pakete eingebunden werden, wie zum Beispiel das „Ethereum Studio" für 0,001$ je Stunde zuzüglich der Kosten für die Azure Infrastruktur. Hiermit können Smart Contracts erstellt und getestet werden. Die Einbindung ins Netzwerk geschieht nach Abschluss aller Tests einfach mit einem Klick. Microsoft möchte mit seinem Angebot besonders Entwicklern entgegenkommen. Für Visual Studio gibt es Erweiterungen, die es erlauben, Smart Contracts zu erstellen, wodurch später der Umstieg auf Ethereum vereinfacht werden soll.

IBM bietet seine Blockchain-Lösung ebenfalls im eigenen Clouddienst „Bluemix" an. Mit mehr Sicherheit und einer schnelleren Verwaltung richtet sich das Angebot gezielt an Unternehmen. Die Blockchain-Technologie kann zunächst mittels vier bereitgestellter Nodes und einer Zertifizierungsstelle in einer virtuellen Umgebung getestet werden. Zudem werden Beispiel-Code und Beispiel-Apps zur Verfügung gestellt. Entscheidet sich ein Unternehmen, den Dienst in Anspruch zu nehmen, wird eine einzelne isolierte Umgebung aufgebaut, deren Miete 10.000 Dollar im Monat kostet. Smart Contracs stehen hier ebenso im Fokus wie bei Microsoft. Informationen von IoT-fähigen Geräten sollen integriert werden, um als Auslöser der Verträge zu dienen. Als zusätzliche Hilfe sollen in Großstädten wie New York, London und Tokyo Anlaufstellen entstehen, in denen Unternehmen und Entwickler Hilfestellungen zu verschiedenen Problemstellungen bekommen.

IBM ist Teil des von der Linux Foundation ins Leben gerufenen „Hyperleger" Projekts. Das Projekt kümmert sich um die Festlegung von Standards im Umgang mit der Blockchain-Technologie.

39.5   Sicherheit und Vertrauenswürdigkeit von Blockchains

Damit eine Blockchain sicher und vertrauenswürdig langfristig genutzt werden kann, müssen z. B. die folgenden Aspekte berücksichtigt werden.

Das verwendete *Public-Key-Verfahren* und *Hashfunktionen* müssen dem *Stand der Technik* genügen und die passenden Schlüssellängen müssen verwendet werden. Außerdem müssen langfristig Post-Quantum Kryptoverfahren berücksichtigt und genutzt werden. Die Lebensdauer einer Blockchain muss von Anfang an berücksichtigt werden. In der BSI – Technische Richtlinie „Kryptographische Verfahren: Empfehlungen und Schlüssellängen" steht z. B. beschrieben, welche kryptographische Verfahren und Schlüssellängen genutzt werden sollten, damit sie für die nächsten 10 Jahre als sicher gelten: Für Hashfunktionen SHA-2/SHA-3 mit einer Mindestschlüssellänge von 256 Bit. Für Public-Key-Verfahren bei RSA mit einer Schlüssellänge von mindestens 3000 Bit und für elliptische Kurven mit einer Mindestschlüssellänge von 256 Bit.

Die Sicherheit der Blockchain-Technologie hängt auch von der *Geheimhaltung der privaten Schlüssel* der Public-Key-Verfahren in der Wallet ab. Der private Schlüssel muss geheim bleiben. Wer immer den privaten Schlüssel einer Wallet besitzt, ist in der Lage, über die gesamten Transaktionen der Wallet zu verfügen. Ein Verlust des privaten Schlüssels bedeutet gleichermaßen, dass sämtliche in der Adresse gespeicherten Transaktionen für immer „verloren" sind. Gefahren bei nicht ausreichendem Schutz des privaten Schlüssels sind z. B.: Der private Rechner des Nutzers wird gehackt (Malware), IoT, z. B. Auto (Light Node) wird gehackt, die Website der Online Wallet (Service Node) wird gehackt, ein nicht ausreichend gesichertes Smartphone wird gestohlen (Light Node). Der Schutz des privaten Schlüssels in der Wallet sollte mit Hilfe von Hardware-Security-Module realisiert werden (SmartCards, Sec-Token, High-Level-Sicherheitsmodule) und unberechtigte Nutzung muss aktiv verhindert werden!

Außerdem müssen bei den Konsensfindungsverfahren die *Randbedingungen überprüft* werden, damit keine Manipulation bei den unterschiedlichen Konsensfindungsverfahren durchgeführt werden kann.

Ein weiterer wichtiger Punkt ist die *vertrauenswürdige Anzeige der Transaktionen.* Hierzu werden einfache und vertrauenswürdige *Blockchain-Viewer* benötigt. Aber auch die Blockchain-Anwendung muss manipulationssicher sein, damit keine erfolgreichen Angriffe umgesetzt werden können.

Wenn die Blockchain an sich eine hohe Sicherheit bietet, werden die Angreifer über die eigentliche Anwendung, die die Blockchain nutzt, angreifen. Daher muss auch die Blockchain-Anwendung manipulationssicher sein, damit keine erfolgreichen Angriffe umgesetzt werden können.

39.6 Zusammenfassung

Die Blockchain-Technologie schafft eine Basis für eine verteilte und vertrauenswürdige Zusammenarbeit und stellt damit ein hohes Potenzial für neue Geschäftsmodelle und Ökosysteme dar. Die Elemente, Prinzipien und Struktur der Blockchain zeigen den technischen Hintergrund und die interessanten Möglichkeiten auf. Für Deutschland und die EU mit sehr vielen KMUs ist Blockchain eine ideale Technologie für eine vertrauenswürdige verteilte Zusammenarbeit. Vertrauensdienste spielen eine immer wichtigere Rolle in der Zukunft! Die beschriebenen Anwendungen der Blockchain zeigen deutlich, dass die Blockchain-Technologie in der Zukunft ein hohes Potenzial für interessante Anwendungen hat.

Literatur

1. https://www.eco.de/2017/pressemeldungen/eco-und-yougov-mittelstand-glaubt-an-die-block-chain.html – letzter Aufruf 07.12.2017
2. C. Kammler, N. Pohlmann: „Kryptografie wird Währung – Bitcoin: Geldverkehr ohne Banken". IT-Sicherheit – Management und Praxis, DATAKONTEXT-Fachverlag, 6/2013
3. R. Palkovits, N. Pohlmann, I. Schwedt: „Blockchain-Technologie revolutioniert das digitale Business: Vertrauenswürdige Zusammenarbeit ohne zentrale Instanz", IT-Sicherheit – Fachmagazin für Informationssicherheit und Compliance, DATAKONTEXT-Fachverlag, 2/2017

Cybersecurity for Everyone

Jan van den Berg

Abstract

The rapid development of cyberspace in the recent two decades has introduced the new term *cybersecurity* as a follow-up of information security or IT security. Despite the rapid adoption of this new term, there exists a lot of confusion about its precise meaning, while – due the societal importance of it – there is a high need for a *common understanding* of what cybersecurity entails. This paper discusses a new framework of thinking where (*i*) *cyberspace* is being defined as the *space of cyber activities* (i.e., *IT-enabled activities*) and (*ii*) *cybersecurity* as the multidisciplinary *(cyber) risk management* challenge of *securing cyberspace*. As is argued, this new *holistic conceptualization* enables a common understanding and participation of all stakeholders in the current cybersecurity challenge.

40.1 Introduction

Around 20 years ago, due to the popularization of the Internet, the term *computer security* hit in vogue – next to *information security* applied to technology – meaning "the practice of preventing unauthorized access, use, disclosure, disruption, modification, inspection, recording or destruction of information" [1]. Within this view, *IT* or *information* is considered to be the key asset, the *confidentiality, integrity,* and *availability* (CIA) of which have to be secured. This conceptualization reflects a technological perspective on information security, which has been the typical approach in those days and also the starting point of many "best practices" in the field like the BS7799 standard [2] and the ISO27000 series [3]

J. van den Berg (✉)
Delft University of Technology and Leiden University, Delft, Netherlands
e-mail: j.vandenberg@tudelft.nl

© Springer Fachmedien Wiesbaden GmbH, ein Teil von Springer Nature 2018
M. Bartsch, S. Frey (Hrsg.), *Cybersecurity Best Practices*,
https://doi.org/10.1007/978-3-658-21655-9_40

showed. And despite various developments around the definitions and elaborations of these best practices, this technological perspective – which is difficult to understand for non-IT specialists – is still *the* starting point of thinking for many information security experts.

Meanwhile however, roughly speaking around the year 2000, the application of IT started to grow fast, first in the e-commerce domain [4], followed by many other applications that support nearly all activities we currently execute, at home, at work, and on the move. The mobile revolution [5] pushed the number of IT-enabled activities further ahead enabling people to read, listen, calculate, view, search, communicate, game, translate, book a holiday, and execute financial transactions (just to name a few IT-enabled activities), at any place, at any time.

The mentioned trend of growing use and dependence on IT does not seem to stop: discussions in modern society touch upon topics like smart city, smart (renewable) energy, autonomous cars, smart water supply, intelligent robots, Internet of Things (IoT), cybercrime, cyber warfare, and so on, and so forth. In the context of these developments, the term *cyberspace* is used more often, being a new, manmade space (deeply embedded in the four physical domains of land, water, air, and space) and denoted as the fifth domain [6], in which around three billion persons through over the world are active. In other words, we continue to create a modern society that, due to its complexity, is, in the words of Ulrich Beck, in a permanent state of risk and which is denoted as a *society at risk* [7]. Since we wish to live in a safe and secure society, an important goal in modern society is to create a *risk society* [7], i.e., a society that adequately deals with its risks. That is, of course, easier said than done: many people, and not only the non-IT persons, feel overwhelmed by the current technological push of IT.

Observing the mentioned IT revolution, we understand that new "cyber risks" are emerging. But how can we adequately deal with them? For example, what should we do if our computer at home is affected by a virus (e.g., ransomware), what is the appropriate cyber crisis management if a company suffers from a serious cyber incident (like a successful DDOS attack), how should the police work on cyber law enforcement in the "dark web," what rules and regulations should be put in place by politicians (e.g., related to cybercrime), how to keep our critical infrastructures safe and secure while making them more IT-dependent every day, what are effective countermeasures against severe information warfare attacks executed by hostile states, and how to develop and deploy effective cyber weapons?

The above-given sketch illuminates that we have created and still continue to further shape the complex fifth domain of cyberspace, that this space is in a permanent state of risk, but that the best practices to deal with the risks are still mostly rooted in a classical conceptualization that takes IT or information as key assets and starting point of thinking. Illustrative for this is that in many organizations the responsibility of cybersecurity is still in the hands of just the IT department. As a consequence, many people do not feel themselves attached to the discussion on cybersecurity and, thus, not directly responsible for it. This thwarts the creation of a *cyber risk society*, i.e., a society that adequately deals with its cyber risks.

There is an urgent need to change this: we have to learn how to behave properly in cyberspace and to secure it to acceptable risk levels.

To do so, which coincides with the goal of this paper, we first need to create a better understanding, that is, a *better conceptualization of what cyberspace entails* and, related to that, what the *key assets of cyberspace* are, in terms that everybody can understand. Having developed this new view on cyberspace, we also need to define what the related *cybersecurity challenges* are and *what methods and methodologies* can be used to effectively and sufficiently secure cyberspace.

The remainder of this paper is structured as follows. Section 40.2 further explores the current limitations of information security approaches. In Sect. 40.3 we provide a new conceptualization of cyberspace, while Sect. 40.4 deals with the related cybersecurity challenges. In Sect. 40.5, we provide a reflection on our achievements, and finally in Sect. 40.6, we draw our conclusions.

40.2 Limitations of Existing Information Security Approaches

40.2.1 Computers, the Internet, and Information Security

Computers or, more generally spoken, computing devices (which include laptops, smartphones, tablets, IoT [8] items, among others) are basically generic data processing devices. Due to the current availability of all kinds of applications for these devices, we can use them for all kind of purposes. For end users the underlying complexity is completely hidden, which is, of course, very convenient for them. Most computing devices are currently also connected to the Internet, which provides the ability to connect to other computing devices and exchange data. This basic facility of data exchange is also applied for all kinds of purposes, the complexity of which is hidden to the end user as well. This convenience however has its price: if for whatever reason the laptop, smartphone, or tablet of an average user fails to function properly, he or she often experiences great difficulties in repairing it. At ICT level, the nonfunctioning of the device can be expressed in terms of non-*availability* in case the desired service is fallen apart. If the data are being corrupted, their *integrity* is at stake, while if the data have become available for non-authorized persons, their *confidentiality* is being broken. This CIA terminology is typically used by IT experts working in the domain of information security. And it is his or her task to guarantee sufficient levels of confidentiality, integrity, and availability.

Actually we observe two very different perspectives here. The first one is the perspective of the end user applying the IT for all kind of purposes. The *functionality* of the specific application is key and should be adapted to the goal she/he wishes to achieve. Also the *semantics* of the data being processed is essential. The second perspective is that of the technical information security specialist who is *not* interested in the precise *functionality of the application of the end user* nor *in the semantics of the data* being processed. He or she focuses on possibilities to keep the IT running properly (availability) and applies IT solutions that try to guarantee the confidentiality and integrity of the data. For the latter, cryptographic algorithms are applied. Note that also these algorithms have a generic character and work independent of the semantics of the data being processed.

40.2.2 Information Security Developments in the Twenty-First Century

The rapid emergence of Internet applications and hereby the creation of cyberspace have, as a matter of fact, also attracted the attention of other stakeholders. Within many organizations (especially those strongly depending on IT), it soon became clear that cybersecurity (the new term for information security) should also be a responsibility for nontechnical people including the board. And due to recent cyber incidents where it became clear that employees of organizations are directly targeted in order to create access to the internal IT infrastructure of the organization for criminal attackers (see, e.g., the Carbanak case [9]), the need for nontechnical measures like awareness raising and adequate cyber crisis management is crucial. Moreover, in various countries, so-called ISACs [10] were created to effectively exchange data and information between organizations working in the same cyber sub-domain about upcoming cybersecurity trends.

In addition, scientists from all kinds of disciplines started to execute research around all kinds of (emerging) phenomena taking place in cyberspace. Social scientists, for example, started to research the interaction of people on social network sites, criminologists research around new forms of cybercrime, and experts in law research about the applicability of the rules of law around privacy and security, counter attacking, and cyber warfare. Economists started to study issues like return on information security investment, market structures that stimulate competition between ISPs, and cybersecurity-related issues around information asymmetries and externalities.

The abovementioned list of new initiatives by direct stakeholders and scientists is far from complete but provides a basic understanding of the fact that society starts to deal with the upcoming cybersecurity risks, although often not in a very systematic manner.

We further observe a limited influence of these initiatives on the existing cybersecurity standards with best practices. Considering the 27000 series [3], we see certain changes like the adoption of business continuity management and compliance in the 27002 version, that of risk management in the 27005, and that of information security governance in the 27014. But overall the perspective remains to have very technical focus.

The ISO 27032 on "guidelines for cybersecurity" was introduced in 2012 and offers an interesting definition of cyberspace being "the complex environment resulting from the interaction of people, software and services on the Internet, supported by worldwide distributed physical information and communications technology (ICT) devices and connected networks." What is made explicit here is that (*i*) ICT is an enabling technology and that (*ii*) the interaction of people with this technology and related services creates a complex environment termed cyberspace. What this complex environment precisely entails is however not made explicit.

The same standard (27032) also provides a definition of cybersecurity being "the preservation of confidentiality, integrity and availability of information in the cyberspace." Unfortunately this definition returns to the old paradigm of information security with its technical focus and with information considered to be the key asset. Actually, a relatively easy opportunity has been missed here to update the definition of cybersecurity and to align it with the new definition of cyberspace.

40.2.3   Summarizing the Current Limitations of Information Security

Summarizing the observations done above, we notice that (*i*) the classical technical focus of information security does not pay attention to the semantics of the interaction between people and IT, (*ii*) a lot of new approaches to securing cyberspace emerged in the twenty-first century as put forward by scientists and practitioners in the field of cybersecurity but miss an overarching framework of thinking, and (*iii*) new definitions of cyberspace and cybersecurity include interesting starting points but are not sufficiently elaborated to create a common understanding. Putting these elements together, we might say that a proper conceptualization of what cyberspace and cybersecurity entail is actually still missing. In the next sections, we will try to fill in this knowledge gap.

40.3   Conceptualizing Cyberspace

The definition of cyberspace mentioned above describes it as "the complex environment resulting from the interaction of people, software and services on the Internet, supported by worldwide distributed physical information and communications technology (ICT) devices and connected networks." Reformulating this more concretely, we may say that cyberspace concerns the *space of cyber activities* as executed by people while making use of ICT services. So, cyber activities are *ICT-enabled activities*. Since they are based on the interaction between people and a technology (here ICT), we are an example of so-called *socio-technical* [11] activities, which describe *behavior of people* using complex technology.

  People execute cyber activities to achieve certain goals like personal goals, organizational goals, business goals, and societal goals. Considering the various ways, ICT devices are used nowadays; it is easy to come up with a list of a variety of cyber activities:

Basic cyber activities related to *communication* (SMS, email, chat, WhatsApp, Skype, VoIP, Twitter, etc.), *information retrieval* (news, weather forecast, public transportation, crisis information, etc.), *listening* and *watching* (radio, movies, music, television, videos, etc.), and *calculating* (spreadsheets, cloud computing, (big) data analytics, etc.)

More advanced cyber activities related to *searching* (Google, Wikipedia, route planning, translating, etc.), *transacting* (e-shopping, e-trading, e-payments, e-procurement, holiday planning, tax returns, e-marketplaces, e-voting, crowdsourcing/funding, etc.), *social gathering* (Facebook, LinkedIn, e-dating, 2nd love, sexting, gambling, etc.), *educating* (MOOCs, e-learning, e-coaching, etc.), *monitoring and surveillance* (monitoring, detecting, applying drones, etc.), *controlling critical infrastructures* (energy and water supply, transport, chemical processing, flood defense, etc.), *protesting* (activism, lobbying), *fundraising*, etc.

Less favorable cyber activities related to *cybercrime* (e.g., in dark markets with activities like financial fraud, theft, hacking, child pornography, e-espionage, cyberbullying, sale of drugs, guns, etc., illegal downloads, etc.), *cyber warfare* (intelligence, defense, attack), *information warfare*, etc.

This list of cyber activities is certainly not complete but meant to show how many different things we currently execute in cyberspace. We further observe here that many cyber activities are executed by people in *complex interaction with IT*, where smart ICT processes make all kind of smart and autonomous decisions (e.g., around transactions and control of critical infrastructures). So in fact, the actors of cyber activities are *both people and intelligent systems/processes* hereby creating a complex ecosystem.

Cyber activities have become so common nowadays, and we have become so dependent on their proper functioning in almost everything we do that they may be considered as the *critical assets of cyberspace.* Due to their complexity, they are in a permanent state of risk (remember U. Beck [3]), so we have to secure them. This is the basic challenge of cybersecurity and concerns the complex tasks of (*i*) defining acceptable risk levels and (*ii*) taking measures that together reduce existing risk levels to the desired ones. For that we need governance (to be elaborated in more detail below).

Cyber activities are being executed in all kinds of *cyber sub-domains* (like, e.g., the financial sector, the transport sector, the food sector, the chemical industry sector, the healthcare sector) and can be very different in nature. As a consequence, the related risks are also very diverse, and we have to deal with these differences.

Based on this analysis, we can make a *model of cyberspac*e, which we have visualized in Fig. 40.1. In the heart of it (layer 1), we place the ICT, the *enabling* technology. In this

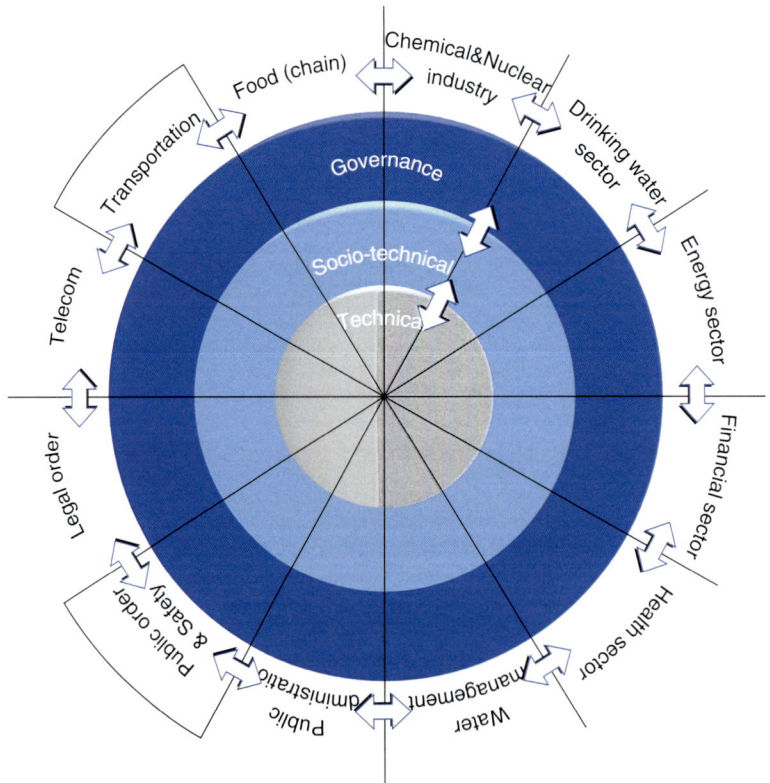

Fig. 40.1 Conceptualization of cyberspace in three layers (rings) and (cyber) sub-domains

technical layer, the key assets are the *IT services,* the CIA of which has to be secured, so this concerns *IT security.*

In layer 2 termed the *socio-technical layer,* we draw the key assets of cyberspace, i.e., the *cyber activities.* The security of these cyber activities, we define as the principle challenge of *cybersecurity.*

Finally layer 3 concerns the *governance layer*: here acceptable risk levels should be fixed and appropriate measures taken to reduce the identified *cyber risks to acceptable levels,* taking ethical issues and compliance into account.

In order to include cyber sub-domains in the same figure, we have divided the three layers in sectors as well, each sector representing an important cyber sub-domain (again, not meant to be complete).

The big advantage of this conceptualization of cyberspace is that it puts the applications of IT in a *context* by making an explicit distinction between (*i*) cyber activities (as executed by people in interaction with (smart) ICT) and (*ii*) the enabling ICT. Cyber activities are the key assets of ICT users, and people executing them understand their functionality (semantics) and can explain how important they are for them (also if they have no single clue about the working of the underlying ICT). Therefore, this distinction also enables a fruitful discussion on what the cybersecurity challenges are of a given set of cyber activities.

40.4   4   Cybersecurity Challenges

Having defined cyberspace, time has come to elaborate on the related cybersecurity challenges. Within our conceptualization, cybersecurity is about *securing the cyber activities* we execute. This concerns a *risk management* challenge, and therefore we can borrow ideas from safety and security science here. Risk management is often executed in a continuous *risk management cycle* [13], which in our context of thinking can be framed as:

"Repeat forever
Identify the *critical cyber activities*;
Identify and assess their *cyber risks*;
Define *acceptable* cyber risk levels;
Decide way(s) of *dealing with the risks*;
Design and implement *cyber risk measures*;
Monitor effectiveness."

Let us in short discuss every step of this risk management cycle:

1. People and organizations usually execute all kinds of cyber activities, some of which might be critical, others just helpful, and still others of little importance. It is key for appropriate cyber risk management that in the first place the critical cyber activities are being defined (and are known to the board). Sometimes they are denoted as the "crown jewels" of an organization.

2. The second step concerns the identification and assessment of the related risks. This entails a challenging task for which "bowtie thinking" is a good starting point. The origin of the bowtie model [14] is in the 1960s of the previous century and became the company standard of Shell for analyzing and managing risks in the early 1990s. Within bowtie thinking, risk is being operationalized as the product of (*i*) the probability (or likelihood) of an incident and (*ii*) its impact. Incidents occur as a result of a threat that can be intentional (security) or non-intentional (safety). How threats can lead to incidents can be modeled in various ways: well-known methods include fault trees [15], attack trees [16], and Bayesian networks [17]. Incidents can lead to all kinds of impacts, which can be modeled using event trees, among others [18]. Note that the impact of a given cyber incident may have all kinds of forms and can be expressed in, e.g., economical, social, political, or environmental terms.

A visualization of the bowtie model is provided in Fig. 40.2.

There exist all kinds of ways to elaborate this bowtie approach, and the best way to go strongly depends on the precise cyber activity at stake. For example, the assessment of the probability of a possible cyber incident is very much dependent on whether historical data are being present or not. Note further that cyber incidents are the result of certain threats for the related cyber activity. These threats are partly rooted in failing ICT, partly in other failures. A simple example illuminates this. Consider the cyber activity of tele-surgery. The risks related to a tele-surgery operation are, of course, partly rooted in failing ICT (if, e.g., the communication channel stops to function, the impact of the failing operation might be catastrophic) but also related to the conditions in the surgery room (if the nurse of the patient does not act properly, the surgery operation might also fail). Actually, when applying our three-layer model of cyberspace, we observe that an *ICT breach/incident at the technical layer* is a *threat for the* (related) *cyber activity at the socio-technical layer.*

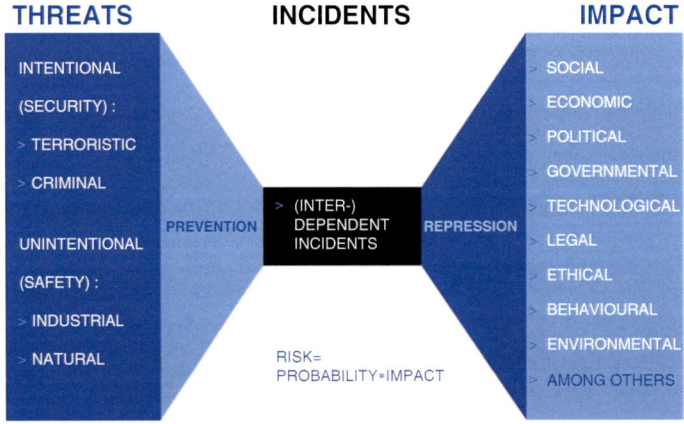

Fig. 40.2 Cyber risk management using the "bowtie model"

In addition and explained above, the impacts of cyber incidents in different sub-domains often show very different characteristics that have to be taken into account.

3. The fixation of what acceptable risk levels are concerns a personal, organizational, or societal *choice*, which mostly lies outside the scope of science. It is more related with politics and culture.

4. In principle there exist four ways of dealing with identified risks, namely, *accept, avoid, mitigate,* or *transfer* [13]. "Accept" does not require any follow-up, "avoid" implies the cancelation of the related cyber activity, "mitigate" implies that countermeasures have to be taken (see below), and "transfer" implies that others take over the responsibility to dealing with the identified cyber risk.

5. To mitigate cyber risks, all kinds of measures can be taken that together should reduce the cyber risks to acceptable levels. Within bowtie thinking, this concerns *preventive* measures to reduce the likelihood of occurring incidents and *repressive* measures to detect and response to occurring incidents in order to reduce their impact. It should be clear that these types of measures should be balanced depending on the concrete cyber activities. If prevention is difficult or very costly, the emphasis on repression is a natural choice.

Note also that cybersecurity *measures* can be taken *in all three layers of our cyberspace model*. A simple example may illustrate this. Consider the threat of a virus attack by means of a USB stick (as happened in the famous Stuxnet case [19]). A simple countermeasure at the technical layer would be to disable all USB ports of the IT system. At the socio-technical layer, all users of the system may decide not to use any USB anymore (which concerns a behavior change of risk-aware users). At the governance layer, a strict rule might be announced to forbid the use of all USB sticks at the IT system. The preferred (combination of) countermeasures to be taken of course strongly depend on the cyber risks and cyber risk appetite related to the concrete case.

In line with this distinction between possible countermeasures at the three layers of cyberspace, we mention two related approaches from literature. The first one concerns the *four modalities of regulating behavior* in cyberspace as proposed by Lawrence Lessig [20]. The first one concerns *regulation by law*, which steers people's behavior through the threat of punishment. This modality is, of course, typically used to regulate cybercriminal activities but is also applicable to regulate cyber behavior of employees according the interest of a company. The second modality concerns *social norms* and regulates behavior of people "by threatening ex post." For example, behavior on social network sites is regulated this way: if someone publishes a message with content not according to the norms of the group, such a person might be forced to apologize, might change his or her behavior, or might even be shut out. The third modality concerns *regulation by the market*. According to Lessig, markets regulate by price. For example, if market prices of certain IT services are high, people may look for alternatives, even if these alternative services are less secure. The final modality Lessig puts forward concerns *architecture*. In cyberspace, this concerns the functionality of the ICT services to the end users: next to enabling end users their cyber activities, the functionality of them also constrains their activities

to a certain degree. For example, an end user might not be allowed to use a certain financial transaction service unless he or she uses a strong password.

In summary, Lessig describes four modalities of regulation that *constrain cyber
behavior*, i.e., they constrain activities in the socio-technical layer of cyberspace. The
three first ones described above (law, norms, markets) concern modalities of regulation in
the governance layer, while the fourth modality (architecture) is one in the technical layer.

A second very interesting approach of designing effective cybersecurity measures in
line with the three layers of the cyberspace model can be found in Ross Anderson's
book *Security Engineering* [21]. Although the book's title suggests a technical focus,
he argues that "*cross-disciplinary expertise* is needed ranging from (…) computer
security (…) to a knowledge of economics, applied psychology, organizations and the
law." In his approach, *incentives of people* play an important role to influence their
behavior, both behavior of designers of the system (needing an incentive to design a
secure system, e.g., more secure than that of their competitors) and that of the end
users. The economic perspective, for example, helps to understand how incentives can
be influenced: he discusses how *information asymmetries* may create failures of markets for developing secure Internet services and may create too high prices of
cybersecurity insurance contracts, and he also discusses how strong *externalities may*
let people connect lots of insecure devices to the Internet "dumping costs on others."

6. Monitoring effectiveness of the cybersecurity measures taken concerns the final step of
   continuous cyber risk management. In the complex domain of cyberspace also, this is
   not an easy challenge. To assess their effectiveness, we need to understand in detail
   what occurs in cyberspace or, more conceptually, we need to create *cyber situational
   awareness* [22], in all cyber sub-domains. In practice it requires precise monitoring and
   data analytics to induce relevant cybersecurity information. Examples of this approach
   include the real-time monitoring and analysis of financial transactions, control of critical infrastructures, cyber activities at the dark web, and cyber intelligence activities by
   state actors. Based on the insights collected, certain measures can be taken to improve
   the security of the cyber activities at stake. The creation of cybersecurity awareness
   however is not without societal implications: understanding precisely what is going on
   in cyberspace relates to, e.g., privacy issues. Without going in depth here, we would
   like to express that the discussion on the privacy-security dilemma can only be held
   successfully in the context of the identification and assessment of related cyber risks. If
   the risks turn out to be high (e.g., society disruptive), then the outcome of this dilemma
   will be much different from a case where the risks are low.

40.5   Reflections

Above we have sketched a framework of thinking about cybersecurity at a high conceptual
level. The first ideas of this framework emerged when a group of scientists and practitioners with very different backgrounds worked on the design of a new cybersecurity MSc

program for professionals [23]. A common vision on the underlying security challenge was a prerequisite in order to arrive at a successful design. The first ideas that resulted from this work have already been published in 2014 [24]. In discussions, assignments, and MSc theses, the framework of thinking (especially the cyberspace model and bowtie model) is often used, tested, validated, and polished. It helped a lot to create a common terminology that everybody can grasp.

In the first place, the new framework of thinking makes an explicit distinction between the technical domain of ICT (layer 1 of cyberspace) and the domain of activities we execute *using* ICT (layer 2 of cyberspace). This strongly facilitates the participation of everyone in the discussion on cybersecurity since the things we do using the ICT (the cyber activities) are the things that truly count to the end user. In different words we may say that making this distinction puts the use of ICT in context; it adds semantics to our cyber activities.

In the second place, we added a governance layer to cyberspace to make clear that this complex new fifth domain needs steering. In this way, the participation of all stakeholders in cybersecurity is guaranteed: the technical specialists feel at home in the technical layer, the end users in the socio-technical layer, and the remaining stakeholders in the governance layer. Based on these starting points, it can be tried to create a secure cyberspace with contributions by everyone while everybody understands the importance of the contributions of him-/herself and others. This also is of importance for cybersecurity education: everybody gets a common understanding using the proposed framework of thinking but can also specialize in his or her preferred sub-topic of cybersecurity without forgetting the overarching picture.

Next to proposing the new cyberspace model, we introduced a bowtie model in the context of cybersecurity. Basically, cybersecurity concerns a cyber risk management challenge in the huge cyberspace domain. Generic risk management approaches can only be useful in case they are adapted to the context in which the cyber activities are being executed while looking at the specific involved cyber risks. The precise risk management approach to be selected should be adapted to the context. In the end the gap between the existing and desired cyber risk levels determines which balanced set of risk mitigation measures will be most effective.

A final reflection concerns the observation that the proposed framework of thinking is actually just a starting point. Going back to the cyberspace model proposed, we strongly believe that within specific sectors new cybersecurity standards of best practices have to be elaborated having as starting the key cyber activities (crown jewels) being executed in that sector (not the ICT!).

40.6 Conclusions

In this paper a new framework of thinking has been introduced around the realization of a secure cyberspace that everyone can understand and everyone can contribute to in his or role as end user, as ICT specialist, or as another stakeholder. Within this view, *cyber activities* (defined as ICT-enabled activities) are the key assets of cyberspace we need to secure sufficiently. While *information* or *IT security* focuses on the *technical layer* of cyberspace, *cybersecurity* takes the relevant *cyber activities* in layer 2 as starting point: they should be sufficiently secured by taking a *balanced set of technical and nontechnical countermeasures*. Governance issues around cybersecurity are covered by the third layer.

The *bowtie model* and *cyber risk management cycle* introduced can be used as *starting point* for adequate cyber risk management. In practice, all kinds of methodologies, methods, and tools should be used to make detailed proposals for effective cyber risk management. In terms of standards of best practices, we propose to elaborate sector-based cybersecurity approaches.

Acknowledgments Many thanks go to my colleagues and students at TUDelft, Leiden University, and the Cyber Security Academy The Hague with whom I had so many discussions on the fascinating subject of cybersecurity. I'm very grateful to all of you.

References

1. https://en.wikipedia.org/wiki/Information_security#cite_note-1 (last access April 10, 2017)
2. BSI, Information Technology – Code of Practice for Information Security Management. BS7799, part 1 (1995) and part 2 (1999).
3. ISO/IEC 27k-series: for an overview see Gary Hinson: http://www.iso27001security.com/ISO27k_Standards_listing.docx.
4. E-commerce, the dot,com bubble: see https://en.wikipedia.org/wiki/Dot-com_bubble (last access April 14, 2017)
5. https://en.wikipedia.org/wiki/History_of_mobile_phones (last access April 14, 2017)
6. Larry D. Welsch, Cyberspace the fifth operational domain, IDA Research Notes, 2011.
7. U. Beck, Risk Society: Towards a New Modernity, New Delhi, Sage, 1992.
8. Internet of Things (IoT): https://en.wikipedia.org/wiki/Internet_of_things, (last access April 14, 2017)
9. Kaspersky Labs' Global Research & Analysis Team (GReAT),. The Great Bank Robbery: the Carbanak APT., 2015.
10. NCSC, ISAC's, https://www.ncsc.nl/english/Cooperation/isacs.html (last access April 14, 2017)
11. Socio-technical system: https://en.wikipedia.org/wiki/Sociotechnical_system (last access April 14, 2017)
12. Cyberspace as ecosystem: http://itlaw.wikia.com/wiki/Cyber_ecosystem (last access April 14, 2017)
13. ISO 31000 series of risk management: https://en.wikipedia.org/wiki/ISO_31000 (last access April 14, 2017)
14. The Bowtie Method: https://www.cgerisk.com/support-a-downloads/support/bowtie-method-support/56-the-bowtie-method (last access April 14, 2017)
15. Fault tree analysis: https://en.wikipedia.org/wiki/Fault_tree_analysis (last access April 14, 2017)
16. Attack tree: https://en.wikipedia.org/wiki/Attack_tree (last access April 14, 2017)
17. Bayesian network: https://en.wikipedia.org/wiki/Bayesian_network (last access April 14, 2017)
18. Event tree analysis: https://en.wikipedia.org/wiki/Event_tree_analysis (last access April 14, 2017)

19. Stuxnet: https://en.wikipedia.org/wiki/Stuxnet (last access April 14, 2017)
20. L. Lessig, The Law of the Horse: What Cyberlaw Might Teach, 1999.
21. R. Anderson, Security Engineering, a guide to building dependable distributed systems, 2nd edition, Wiley, 2008.
22. Jajodia et al., Cyber Situational Awareness, Springer, 2010.
23. Executive MSc Program Cyber Security: https://www.csacademy.nl/en/education/education (last access April 14, 2017)
24. Jan van den Berg, Jacqueline van Zoggel, Mireille Snels, Mark van Leeuwen, Sergei Boeke, Leo van de Koppen, Jan van der Lubbe, Bibi van den Berg and Tony de Bos, On (the Emergence of) Cyber Security Science and its Challenges for Cyber Security Education, Proceedings of the NATO STO/IST-122 symposium in Tallinn, October 13–14 2014. (winner best conference paper award)

Learning from the Past: Designing Secure Network Protocols

41

Tobias Fiebig, Franziska Lichtblau, Florian Streibelt,
Thorben Krüger, Pieter Lexis, Randy Bush and Anja Feldmann

Abstract

Network protocols define how networked computer systems exchange data. As they define all aspects of this communication, the way they are designed is also security sensitive. If communication is supposed to be encrypted, this has to be outlined in the protocol's specification. If services implementing the protocol should allow for authentication, this has to be defined in the protocol. Hence, the way a protocol is designed is elemental for the security of systems later implementing it. Security by design starts with the protocol definition. Especially in today's fast-moving environment, with cloud services and the Internet of Things, engineers constantly have to develop new protocols. In this chapter, we derive guidelines for designing new protocols securely, as well as recommendations on how existing protocols can be adjusted to become more secure. We base these recommendations on our analysis of how – historical – protocols were designed and which underlying design decisions made their corresponding implementations susceptible to security issues.

T. Fiebig (✉)
Department of ESS, TU Delft, Delft, The Netherlands
e-mail: t.fiebig@tudelft.nl

F. Lichtblau · F. Streibelt · T. Krüger · A. Feldmann
Saarbrücken, Germany
e-mail: rhalina@mpi-inf.mpg.de; fstreibelt@mpi-inf.mpg.de; tkrueger@mpi-inf.mpg.de; anja@mpi-inf.mpg.de

P. Lexis
PowerDNS.COM BV, Den Haag, The Netherlands
e-mail: pieter.lexis@powerdns.com

R. Bush
Internet Initiative Japan research, Tokio, Japan

© Springer Fachmedien Wiesbaden GmbH, ein Teil von Springer Nature 2018   585
M. Bartsch, S. Frey (Hrsg.), *Cybersecurity Best Practices*,
https://doi.org/10.1007/978-3-658-21655-9_41

41.1   Introduction

A protocol is a series of rules that describe how two parties are supposed to interact. Our world knows a multitude of protocols, for example, the diplomatic protocol, detailing how diplomatic interaction between two states should happen.

Similarly, when computers communicate over a network, they have to follow protocols. Protocols ensure that both (or a multitude of) computers can actually understand each other. These protocols exist for various "layers" of the Internet. There are protocols that tell computers how to exchange information, in general, with each other and protocols that describe how applications on top of this information exchange can be implemented. For example, SMTP (Simple Mail Transfer Protocol) is such a protocol, detailing how emails can be send around on the Internet. Such application protocols are commonly implemented in programs called Internet services.

Today's Internet utilizes a multitude of different protocols. While some of these protocols were first implemented and used and later documented, others were first specified and then implemented. Regardless of how protocols came to be, their definitions can contain traps that lead to insecure implementations or deployments. Insufficiently strict authentication requirements in a protocol specification are a prime example of this.

This leads to problems in practice, e.g., not enabling strong authentication in an Internet service are common root causes for Internet security incidents. Indeed, Internet protocols have been commonly designed without sufficient security in mind. While this obviously leads to a multitude of security traps, strict security considerations can have a similarly bad effect. Due to complex implementations and insufficient documentation, security features may remain unused, leaving deployments vulnerable. Given the newest Internet trends, services in the cloud; Internet of Things including Industry 4.0; autonomous systems, e.g., self-driving cars; and mobile applications, we expect a constant need for designing new protocols.

While there is a large community that supports the development of protocols, e.g., within the IETF (Internet Engineering Task Force), protocols are regularly needed in a proprietary context as well. For example, when creating a new, distributed IoT device, a company may want to specify how these specific devices interact with each other. Even though communication may happen over an established channel, e.g., HTTP, what is requested and designed at this point is a form of a protocol.

Condensed and comprehensible literature for engineers tasked with developing new protocols, especially in such situations, is sparse. Literature on how to do it securely is even sparer. Similarly, when auditing the protocol design efforts in a company, a CISO may want to have a set of guidelines, on how to evaluate the basic security posture of the engineers' efforts. Similarly, a product manager may be wondering, why the design of a new protocol for a product constantly leads to regressions due to overlooked security issues.

This chapter should provide all of the concerned shareholders in that situation with a first impression on how to securely design protocols. We do this by actually learning from the security issues people faced in the past when handling protocols and how these were induced by certain design choices made for specific protocols. Hence, in this chapter we look at the security pitfalls protocol designers fell for in the past to derive recommendations for improving existing and designing new protocols – without introducing security-sensitive traps for operators, implementers, and users.

41.2   RFCs: Engineering-Driven Standardization

Thousands of Internet protocols have been proposed, developed, and deployed on the Internet. Those most relevant in practice have been documented in so-called Requests for Comments (RFCs). RFCs are, in comparison with documents from other standard bodies, far more applied and result driven. As this chapter aims at providing a practical view on protocol design, we extract essential features from different eras of protocol design in RFCs to base our recommendations on them.

Since 1992, each RFC must address the topic of security, according to IETF processes (RFC1311 (Postel 1992), RFC1543 (Postel 1993), RFC2223 (Postel and Reynolds 1997), RFC7322 (Flanagan and Ginoza 2014)), which document what an RFC must contain. Indeed, RFC1311 (Postel 1992) states: "All STD RFCs must contain a section that discusses the security considerations of the procedures that are the main topic of the RFC."

Over time, the community realized that this statement by itself is not sufficient and the specification of the security requirements have gotten stricter; see RFC3552 (Rescorla and Korver 2003) from 2003, the Best Current Practices for "Writing RFC Text on Security Considerations." The goal of this requirement is to make all protocol designers and implementers aware of possible security implications. Given that this basic requirement existed in 1992, we conclude that the importance of security has been recognized for at least 23 years.

41.3   Threat Modeling

One of the motivations for including a security section in each RFC is to make the protocol designer consider the following two questions: (i) against whom to defend and (ii) how to defend. We find that protocol designers consider different kinds of attackers, ranging from very weak to very strong. The weak attacker is either unskilled or is resource limited. The strong attacker is very skilled and has all necessary resources in their hands. Defining how to defend is more difficult as it depends on the eyes of the beholder. Some argue that the cost of breaking security should be larger than the value of the protected asset. This goes back to Pfleeger and Pfleeger (2002) and specifies that one should put up a wall against threats at least high enough that most attacks will not break the wall. Moreover, the wall should not cost more than the protected asset. We call this the "good enough" approach to security. Others, especially the field of cryptography (Krämer 2015), follow the approach of "perfect security." Perfect security refers to using every possible mean to achieve security. We refer to these two approaches as the defense paradigm.

Thus, we have two dimensions, namely, the capabilities of the attacker and the defense paradigm. Using these dimensions, we classify our selected set of protocols and identify four major clusters. These clusters correspond to the four quadrants of the two-dimensional space. We refer to them as Early Internet, Emerging Threats, Complex Security, and A New Simplicity.

41.3.1   Weak Attacker: Good Enough

This class contains those protocols that are designed for a friendly, collaborative environment, the Internet, when security was not yet a major concern. This class, in particular, contains those protocols that initially were designed under the assumptions that there is no attacker or still carry artifacts from that idyllic time. Such an attacker is the weakest one possible. We refer to this class as Early Internet.

41.3.2   Weak Attacker: Perfect Security

This class no longer assumes that the environment is entirely friendly. Rather it recognizes that there are threats, but not yet by sophisticated attackers. However, since significant assets can be at stake, even attacks that are only theoretically possible are considered. We refer to this class as Emerging Threats.

41.3.3   Strong Attacker: Perfect Security

This class captures the protocols that consider security a necessity at all costs. As a result, the protocols in this class are designed to handle strong attackers and be safe against all, even theoretically conceived, attack vectors. However, as a result, they are often complex and hard to deploy, maintain, and difficult to use. We refer to this class as Complex Security.

41.3.4   Strong Attacker: Good Enough

This class contains those protocols whose designers recognize that strong attackers exist but also value protocols that "just work" out of the box. Therefore, the designer does not try to defend the asset against every possible attack by reducing the attack surface. In this class we see a conscious choice between security and operational ease, favoring the latter. We refer to this class as A New Simplicity.

Interestingly, when one considers when most protocols in each of the above classes were designed, we find that Internet protocol designers have started with protocols in the Early Internet category and moved to ones from Emerging Threats when they realized that

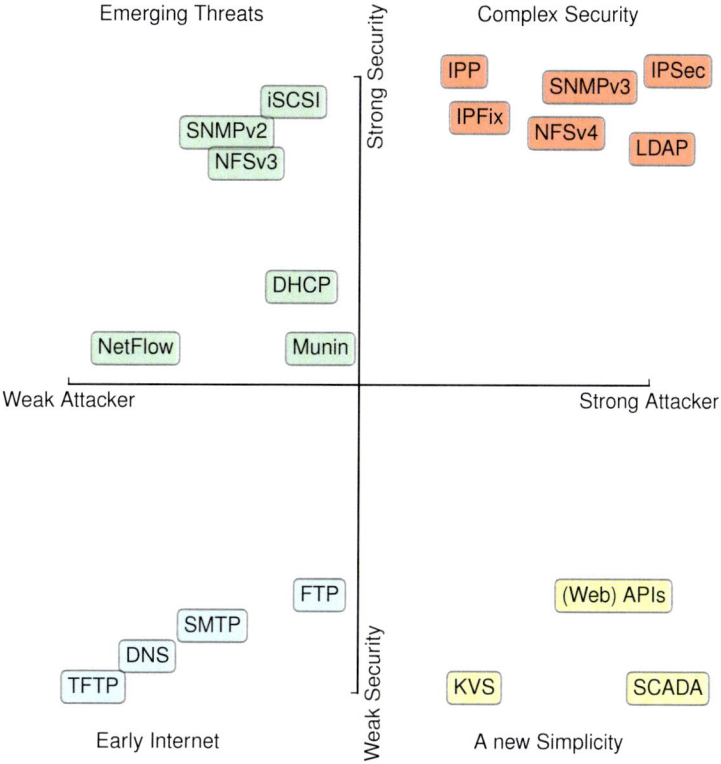

Fig. 41.1 Example protocols used in this chapter, arranged based on their underlying threat models

the Internet was no longer nice. However, while the core ideas did not change, the protocols were hidden behind fences such as DMZs. Since this did not suffice, they moved to Complex Security. As these were hard to maintain or difficult to use, we see a new trend toward A New Simplicity. Please see Fig. 41.1 for a visualization of where the example protocols we discuss in the remainder of this chapter can be found in that two-dimensional plane.

41.4   Protocol Design in the Early Internet

This class includes those protocols that were designed in the context of the Early Internet, roughly from 1960 to 1988, where attacks had yet to be considered, and therefore protocols were designed without security considerations. The paper by David Clark about "The Design Philosophy of the DARPA Internet Protocols" (Clark 1988) does not even contain the term security even though availability in the sense of survivability is a major goal. After all, the main goal of the Internet was to interconnect existing networks with the implicit assumption that all participants worked toward the common goal of communication.

As a result, attacks were not yet common. Hence, the need for security either did not exist or was extremely limited. Toward the end of the era, attacks against operating systems became more prominent, and the first major Internet worm, namely, the Morris worm, was let loose (Spafford 1989; Orman 2003).

Most popular protocols from that era have been updated to remain usable in today's hostile Internet. However, this does not remove all security challenges. Today many protocols still have artifacts of their design for a friendly Internet.

Thus, the threat model of this class is "weak attacker" with "good enough" (or rather none at all) security. The representative protocols we examine are SMTP and DNS. Other protocols in this class include TFTP, FTP, Finger, rexec, Chargen, NIS, RIP, NTP, WHOIS, Ident, XDMCP/X11, Syslog, rsync, and IRC.

41.4.1 Example Protocols

41.4.1.1 SMTP

The objective of the Simple Mail Transfer Protocol (SMTP) as documented in 1982 in RFC821 (Postel 1982) and most recently updated by RFC5231 (Segmuller and Leiba 2008) is to reliably and efficiently transfer email. Among the important features of SMTP is the ability to relay email across multiple networks.

The base architecture of SMTP used open relays for forwarding messages between mail transfer agents (MTAs) without authentication or authorization; see RFC822 (Crocker 1982). Authentication was suggested by an Internet draft in 1995 and finally added with RFC2554 (Myers 1999) in 1999. TLS was also added in 1999 with RFC2487 (Hoffman 1999).

Attackers realized early on that open relays are great for amplifying the effects of worms, viruses, and in particular SPAM (Klensin et al. 1995). Even with the newly added features to improve confidentiality, integrity, and availability, SPAM is a major daily annoyance.

These problems are usually mitigated by providing strict and well documented default configurations (Jung and Sit 2004). In today's deployments, almost all SMTP servers only accept emails for their configured domains. Thus, the possibility of amplification has been reduced. If MTA to MTA relay is allowed, it is only with credentials and TLS.

Another problem with SMTP is that an attacker may take over an SMTP server and send rogue data which is not easily mitigated. The defense here is blacklisting, whitelisting, sender verification, etc.; see, e.g., Cormack (2007).

However, it is still possible – in an attempt to "make things work" – to misconfigure SMTP servers. After all, problematic configurations do still have applicable use cases on the Internet, e.g., an outbound email relay for a large network which every machine should use. In the wild, open SMTP relays are still observed from time to time. But most are quickly found and closed down.

41.4.1.2 DNS

Since the early 1980s the domain name system (DNS), RFC882 and RFC883 (Mockapetris 1983a, b), is used to map hostnames to IP addresses and vice versa.

DNS is a hierarchical distributed database organized in independently administered DNS zones. These zones are implemented as subtrees in the hierarchy of the DNS. Each zone has at least one "authoritative" DNS server, while one server can be authoritative for multiple zones. In addition, a nameserver can also be queried by client hosts and provide name resolution for arbitrary domains for which it is not necessarily authoritative. Most non-authoritative DNS servers only serve clients within their administrative domain, e.g., an Internet service provider (ISP), providing name resolution for its customers. However, services like OpenDNS and the Google public DNS provide public available nameservers.

While some services are intentionally open to the public, there is a large mass of misconfigured servers unintentionally providing public name resolution. DNS by default uses connectionless UDP, and usually the responses are larger than the queries as the query is contained in the response. Thus, DNS, by design, can be abused for amplification attacks, in particular both with open resolvers (Rossow 2014) and resolvers that return large answers.

Mitigation strategies against amplification attacks exist and are usually deployed by the large providers of open DNS servers. Nevertheless, this kind of abuse cannot be completely prevented due to inherent protocol limitations (Rossow 2014). While DNSSEC is currently being discussed as mitigation for various other problems in the DNS protocol suite, it exacerbates this abuse as it often produces very large answers (van Rijswijk-Deij et al. 2014).

Another attack vector is information disclosure in reverse DNS lookups. Using these, an attacker may infer which hosts offer which services, even inside a firewalled network, or disclose the organizational structure. Some misconfigured systems may still allow zone transfers of full DNS (Kalafut et al. 2008), which was historically the default (Bernstein).

Currently, we find more than 10,000,000 DNS servers on the Internet. A substantial fraction, more than 5,000 (Streibelt et al. 2013), of these are open DNS servers of which it is unclear to what extent they deploy even the available limited amplification mitigation.

41.4.2 Discussion

A common issue for security in this class is the assumption that neither client authentication nor encryption is needed as the services are in a trustworthy environment. Indeed, access without authentication is considered a feature (FTP, SMTP, and DNS). Other abuse opportunities are stateless amplifications attacks (TFTP, DNS) where the root cause is that the server sends data without checking if the client wants it.

Based on these observations, one would presume that protocols in this class have seen the end of their live cycle. However, almost all of the above protocols are still very popular. The main reasons are (i) the Internet's reliance on these services (DNS, SMTP), (ii) their convenience (FTP), (iii) the fact that there is no good alternative (TFTP), and (iv) that the service happen to be running in legacy systems. Worse, the implementation of, e.g., TFTP requires a small code base which makes it common in millions of customer premise equipment (CPE). Indeed, these protocols are unlikely to disappear as they are the foundation of the Internet.

The reason why such services are still in operation is twofold: Either it is presumed possible to hide the services behind firewalls (TFTP, NIS, RIP) or work on alternative protocols has started, but these protocols are not yet in Internet-wide use (DNS, SMTP). But, security issues occur if either the firewall fails or the protocols are not used as originally designed.

The first major security incident based on this was an email amplification attack: The Morris worm in 1988 (Spafford 1989). At about the same time, the community started to realize that major security issues can occur and its security is not taken seriously during protocol design. For this, see RFC1122 (Braden 1989b) and RFC1123 (Braden 1989b) that "provide guidance for vendors, implementers, and users of Internet communication software" (Braden 1989b).

41.5   Protocol Design Facing Emerging Threats

Security incidents such as the Morris worm changed the way that Internet protocols are perceived. Instead of designing them for the Internet at large, they became explicitly designed with firewalls in mind. Thus, network firewalls, more precisely packet filters (Chapman 1992), became the typical way of fencing off network services.

Bellovin and Cheswick (1994) state that the motivation for network firewalls is "Computer security is a hard problem. Security on networked computers is much harder. Firewalls (barriers between two networks), when used properly, can provide a significant increase in computer security." In addition, the approach from 1988 onward is, according to Bellovin and Cheswick (1994), "Everything is guilty until proven innocent. Thus, we configure our firewalls to reject everything, unless we have explicitly made the choice – and accepted the risk – to permit it."

Protocol designers find network firewalls to be a convenient way to handle security. In their minds, firewalls enable them to basically ignore security threats as they presume that the firewall rejects everything that is "untrusted." The design assumption of most protocols is that since the attacker is not strong enough to get passed the firewall, the protocol itself can be designed for a trusted environment.

However, as stated by Wool (2004): "The protection that firewalls provide is only as good as the policy they are configured to implement. Analysis of real configuration data shows that corporate firewalls are often enforcing rule sets that violate well established security guidelines." His conclusion is to keep firewall configurations simple but efficient to avoid misconfiguration.

Thus, the threat model for this class is "weak attacker" with attempted "perfect security." The representative protocols we take a closer look at are NetFlow, SNMPv2, and iSCSI. Other protocols in this class include DHCP, Munin, NFSv3, Wake-on-LAN, remote DMA, NBD, rsyslog, SCADA, early versions of CIFS/SMB, and Mapping of Airline Traffic over Internet Protocol (MATIP).

41.5.1 Example Protocols

41.5.1.1 NetFlow

Services implementing Cisco Systems' NetFlow allow network administrators to collect IP flow information from their network. A flow is a summary of a set of packets that pass through a device that have some common property. NetFlow uses UDP as its transport protocol. NetFlow is widely used in many ISP and enterprise networks. Indeed, many resource accounting and security incident systems are built on this data source. Early versions are documented as Cisco white papers. Version 9 is documented in RFC3954 (Claise 2004).

NetFlow itself does not provide authentication, authorization, or encryption support. This was a conscious choice by the protocol designers, to cite RFC3954 (Claise 2004): "The designers of NetFlow Version 9 did not impose any confidentiality, integrity or authentication requirements on the protocol because this reduced the efficiency of the implementation and it was believed at the time that the majority of deployments would confine the Flow Records to private networks, with the Collector(s) and Exporter(s) in close proximity." Indeed, RFC3954 specifically redirects the issue of security to the subsequent IPFix security requirements in RFC3917 (Quittek et al. 2004).

RFC3954 outlines possible attacks including disclosure of flow information data, forgery of flow records or template records, and DoS attacks on NetFlow collectors. The latter enables an attacker to exceed the collector's storage or computational capacity and, thus, can disable the monitoring of the network. Using forgery, an attacker can inject flow information that (i) may redirect network-forensic investigations by incriminates another party or (ii) lead to illicit financial charges if NetFlow is the basis for billing.

These attacks can, in principle, be mitigated by, e.g., moving to TCP and enforcing TLS/DTLS and mutual authentication. An example of such a mitigation strategy is the proposal in the IPFIX security requirements RFC3917 (Quittek et al. 2004).

The documentation of NetFlow is given mainly by Cisco white papers and Cisco device configuration examples. We observe that the documentation does not even mention how to secure NetFlow or that it is necessary. It does, however, point out that NetFlow data can be used as security enhancement to investigate network anomalies.

In summary, NetFlow's main security trap is insufficient fencing. Since NetFlow is a stateless write-only protocol, it is unfeasible to estimate the misconfigured number of NetFlow collectors by active scans.

41.5.1.2 SNMPv2

The Simple Network Management Protocol (SNMP) dates back to 1988, when it was first specified in RFC1067 (Case et al. 1988). It is the standard protocol for managing IP network devices, including routers, switches, and workstations. It is typically shipped on the device. Small command extensions led to community-based SNMPv2 (Case et al. 1996), the version supported by most vendors, e.g., Cisco and Juniper. While other versions of SNMPv2 already support extensive security features, most became prominent with SNMPv3 (Wijnen et al. 1999; Case et al. 2002), which we discuss in Sect. 41.5.1. The only authentication mechanism of SNMPv2c is the so-called community string. Moreover, SNMPv2c does not support transport layer security.

Common issues are the use of weak (default) credentials, e.g., the community string public for read access and string private for the read/write access (Moonen 2012). While SNMP-enabled devices should be shielded by proper firewall configurations, they often are not. Moreover, SNMP proxies which are designed to handle ACLs can easily be misconfigured as well. Note, weak credentials can lead to disclosure of information. With the private community, it is possible to take over the device. Moreover, open SNMPv2 servers have been used for amplifications attacks (Rossow 2014).

By default, a lot of devices come with communities pre-configured, e.g., public or/and private. Even if the operator configures their own communities, they often forget to remove the pre-configured ones – leaving the door open to attackers. Moreover, with a network sniffer, it is possible to extract community strings. Depending on the class of the device, the documentation differs significantly from good for high-end devices to almost none for low-end customer premise devices. This is, in particular, problematic as the customer premise devices are often directly connected to the Internet. The potential number of devices that may be subject to this issue is, according to Shodan's[1] scans, more than 3,800,000 devices with their community string set to "public."

41.5.1.3 iSCSI

The Internet Small Computer System Interface (iSCSI) is a protocol for remotely accessing block devices over the Internet using SCSI commands first documented 2004 in RFC3720 (Satran et al. 2004). Since iSCSI was designed for a hostile Internet, a dedicated RFC3723 (Aboba et al. 2004) exists, that spells out the security requirements for iSCSI and similar network accessible block storage protocols. This RFC has been updated most recently in April 2014 by RFC7146 (Black and Koning 2014).

These RFCs require iSCSI to include authentication and authorization but delegate encryption and integrity to IPSec. Moreover, RFC3723 (Aboba et al. 2004) acknowledges

---

[1] http://shodan.io/

common threats for iSCSI deployments under the assumption that authentication and authorization are working, i.e., that the attacker is not able to initiate a valid connection. Moreover, the base security assumption is that there is no monkey in the middle either due to IPSec or an isolated network segment.

However, if due to a misconfiguration the iSCSI target is reachable via the Internet without authentication, iSCSI becomes a severe security liability. An attacker with access to an iSCSI volume can tamper with all data thereon and can take over all machines with root file systems on those volumes.

Indeed, it is easily possible – and many large enterprise applications and how-tos for setting up UNIX-based targets recommend – to configure iSCSI without any authentication, neither for the whole target set nor the individual targets. Usually, this is done to cater to operational needs, especially in the cases where iSCSI volumes are used as boot devices or if a dynamic set of virtual machines has to have access to a volume. In contrast to the above common malpractice, the Payment Card Industry Data Security Standards (PCI-DSS) (Industry 2014) explicitly requires client authentication; in particular, it requires it for each volume individually. Nevertheless, the common security trap for iSCSI is missing authentication coupled with reliance on fencing.

So far, these security issues have been recognized in the industry (Dwivedi 2005) but not necessarily in academic references. With a quick ZMap (Durumeric et al. 2013) scan, we find roughly 9,000 iSCSI targets reachable via the Internet of which 1,000 do not require authentication. Among these are various major organizations as well as academic institutions.

41.5.2 Discussion

The base assumption of all protocols/services in this class is that the local LAN is safe. Thus, a common misconception is that they can be used with "convenient" security settings. This often leads to major security incidents when the fencing mechanisms fail. This is the major security trap for all protocols in this class.

NetFlow is a blatant example of the low security considerations within this class. Its security concept relies entirely on fencing. SNMPv2 is one of the protocols in this class that first added security but then reduced it. NFSv3 does do authorization using OS ACLs, but without authentication. This means that anyone can impersonate anyone. While iSCSI, in principle, supports authorization and authentication, some deployments do not enable it as iSCSI should be restricted to the storage network and, if used as boot device, is difficult to supply the clients with secured credentials for the iSCSI volume. However, if fencing breaks down, this is a major misconfiguration as large amounts of sensitive data are leaked.

However, the assumption that everything can be fenced in does not necessarily hold as specifying security policies is difficult and realizing them in a firewall is rather difficult and prone to errors (Mayer et al. 2000; Al-Shaer and Hamed 2003; Cuppens et al. 2005;

Yuan et al. 2006; Garcia-Alfaro et al. 2013). Among the complications are that the designer of the security policies are not necessarily the ones that configure the firewalls and those are not necessarily the ones that deploy the network services. Moreover, updating and maintaining such rules is quite error prone. This opens up the network service for all kinds of attacks that bypass firewalls or access services that are thought to not be reachable from the Internet.

Other means of fencing include (i) not connecting the service to the Internet at all (air gap/segmentation), (ii) VLANs and sub-networks, and (iii) virtual routing and forwarding (VRF) tables. However, all of these techniques tend to fail in practice. Firewalls are circumvented via VPNs, hidden dialups/UMTS, and other covert channels, as, e.g., described in the Maroochy water breach discussion (Slay and Miller 2008). Stuxnet (Falliere et al. 2011) is the prime example for bypassing an air gap. One example for breaking a VRF is accidentally announcing a BGP full table into the VRF engine. Overall, the industrial lore states, for example, in the Security Issues and Best Practices for Water/Wastewater Facilities (Hayes 2013): "Industrial networks are often shared with the business side of the operation. VLANs, sub-networks, firewalls all help to create a layer defense, but are not impervious."

This is particularly the case for services that were first envisioned for enterprises and then commonly used in small office/home office (SoHos) and home networks. In these settings, security by default configurations are essential as the users often lack the knowledge and means to properly address security and network challenges.

41.6   Complex Security Solutions in Protocol Design

At the end of the twentieth century, the awareness that firewalls were not "the" security solution became prominent. For example, RFC3365 (Schiller 2002) dated 2002 states: "History has shown that applications that operate using the TCP/IP Protocol Suite wind up being used over the Internet. This is true even when the original application was not envisioned to be used in a "wide area" Internet environment. If an application isn't designed to provide security, users of the application discover that they are vulnerable to attack."

As a result, protocol designers realized that (i) there was a need for improved protection architectures, e.g., the work on SANE (Casado et al. 2006) or DoS-limiting network architecture (Yang et al. 2005), and (ii) that security had to be an essential feature of future protocols and services. Moreover, just adding another component to ensure security to existing protocols, e.g., firewalls, did not suffice. This fits the increased need for security in the society due to the increasing economic relevance of the Internet (Mahadevan 2000).

At the same time, the diversity of the scenarios also increased with home users, SoHos, enterprises, infrastructure providers, company mergers and splits, etc. Indeed, road worriers started to appear. As a result, more assets were at stake which had to be accessible in many different ways. Thus, versatile security solutions to model complex organizational structures, e.g., via role-based access control (RBAC), were needed.

Indeed, the Danvers Doctrine (Schiller 2002) stated that the "IETF should standardize on the use of the best security available." Thus, the threat model for this class is "strong attacker" with "perfect security." The representative protocols we take a closer look at are IPSec, IPP, SNMPv3, and IPFIX. Other protocols in this class include LDAP, NFSv4, AFS, Postgresq, FTPs, RADIUS and WPA2Enterprise, s/MIME encryption, SSL/TLS, and PGP. On the side of system security, SELinux is a good example.

41.6.1 Example Protocols

41.6.1.1 IPSec

IPSec, first introduced in RFC1825–1829 (Atkinson 1995a, b, c; Karn et al. 1995; Metzger and Simpson 1995) and updated by RFC4301–4309 (Eastlake 2005; Hoffman 2005; Housley 2005; Kaufman 2005; Kent 2005a, b, c; Kent and Seo 2005; Schiller 2005), is a suite of protocols that promise to seamlessly extend IP with authentication, data integrity, confidentiality, non-repudiation, and protection against replay attacks.

To cite Ferguson and Schneier (2000): "Our main criticism of IPsec is its complexity. IPsec contains too many options and too much flexibility; there are often several ways of doing the same or similar things. This is a typical committee effect." Thus, this is a prime example of this class. However, IPSec is often used as an argument why it is possible to leave out certain security features in other protocols (Aboba et al. 2004; Romanow et al. 2005).

IPSec is in use for corner cases such as LTE backend network security (Bikos and Sklavos 2013). Indeed, as Ferguson and Schneier state (Ferguson and Schneier 2000): "Even with all the serious criticisms that we have on IPsec, it is probably the best IP security protocol available at the moment." Still, IPSec has not yet seen widespread deployment, e.g., Richter et al. (2015). One possible reason is usability. Here we cite Gutmann (Gutmann and Grigg 2005) "If we consider security usability at all, we place it firmly in second place, and anyone wishing to dispute this claim is invited to try setting up an IPsec tunnel via a firewall or securing their email with S/MIME."

41.6.1.2 IPP

The Internet Printing Protocol (IPP) is documented in RFC2565 (Herriot et al. 1999) dated 1999 and its companion RFCs. IPP is an application level protocol suite for distributed printing using Internet tools and technology. It uses HTTP, namely, 1.0 or 1.1, as its transport protocol.

IPP itself implements the relevant mechanisms to perform strong authentication by default against members of a local UNIX group via PAM (pluggable authentication module) and supports the use of transport encryption. For IPP (Herriot et al. 1999) authentication and authorization are critical due to an unrelated security topic, accounting. Printing, or, rather, use of paper and ink, must be accounted for in most companies as well as universities. Thus, it is not surprising that the most prominent UNIX-based IPP server, CUPS, currently uses TLS for all connections containing credentials. Moreover, authentication is required by default for all administrative actions.

The main security trap with IPP is that printing on a device is – by default – allowed for unauthenticated clients (Institute 2003). Thus, a remote attacker can print on all printers they learn about. While this is usually not a major security problem, it may become an interesting basis for social engineering attacks. In addition, it enables DoS attacks, e.g., if an attacker prints endless numbers of fully black pages. Lastly, it is a nasty way of large-scale resource waste. Keep in mind that the IPP service is offered by most major network-attached printers by default as well as Apple devices if they share their home printer.

41.6.1.3 SNMPv3

SNMPv3 (Stallings 1998; Case et al. 1999, 2002) is the successor to the Simple Network Management Protocol v2; see Sect. 41.4.1. The motivation for SNMPv3, RFC3410 (Case et al. 2002), was to fix: "The unmet goals included provision of security and administration delivering so-called 'commercial grade' security with: authentication …, privacy …; authorization and access control; and suitable remote configuration and administration capabilities for these features." Thus, SNMPv3 makes few changes to the protocol aside from adding the option of on-the-wire encryption. Rather, it focuses on two main aspects, security and administration (Corrente and Tura 2004). SNMPv3 supports the notion of users and authorization.

The main security trap with SNMPv3 is using SNMPv2 – falling victim to its security traps – instead or in parallel. Indeed, SNMPv2 and SNMPv3 are not exclusive. A host offering SNMPv2 can also offer SNMPv3 even on the same port. Today many hosts indeed offer SNMPv2 and SNMPv3 simultaneously (Frye et al. 2000, 2003). Since SNMPv2 is often enabled by default, the hosts remain vulnerable even though they support SNMPv3. Therefore, it is not surprising that we still see more than 3,800,000 hosts with SNMPv2 enabled. Indeed, this is supported by data from Cisco Advanced Services from May 2013 (Bollinger 2015) which reports on the SNMP configuration status of 1,724,827 device configurations in 2013; see Table 41.1. Even though the adoption of SNMPv3 has increased, it has been at a lower rate than SNMPv2. Part of the reason is the complexity of SNMPv3 as outlined, e.g., by Cisco training material (Bollinger 2015).

However, even if SNMPv3 is correctly deployed, the corresponding RFCs come with another security trap. The original RFCs, RFC2264 (Blumenthal and Wijnen 1998) to RFC3414 (Blumenthal and Wijnen 2002), only specify DES as a cipher. AES was added significantly later, RFC3826 (Blumenthal et al. 2004). Similarly, the only supported digest algorithms are MD5 and SHA1. This leads to implementations with weak crypto and,

Table 41.1 #M

Protocol version	Customers	Devices	Change 2012–2013
SNMPv2	98.5%	88.2%	Up 9%
SNMPv3	34.6%	10.4%	Up 4%

Adoption of SNMPv3 among Cisco's customers following (Bollinger 2015)

thus, are susceptible to advanced attacks (Lawrence and Traynor 2012). Note that the (obsolete) SSHv1 suffers from similar problems as CRC32 is fixed in the protocol specification (Barrett et al. 2005).

41.6.1.4   IPFIX

The purpose of the IP Flow Information Export (IPFIX) protocol (please see RFC5101 (Claise 2008)) is to transfer IP Traffic Flow information from an exporter to a collector. IPFIX is the vendor-independent successor of NetFlow version 9, Sect. 41.4.1. IPFIX supports flexible definitions of network flows via a template-based extensible information model. The design goal was to make the protocol future proof as well as applicable to all network protocols.

Given the inherent insecurity of NetFlow, the goal of IPFIX was to incorporate strong security in its design; see RFC3917 (Quittek et al. 2004). This resulted in RFC5101 (Claise 2008) which states that IPFIX must ensure confidentiality and integrity of the transferred IPFIX data and authentication for the exporter and collector.

However, none of the major vendors, including Alcatel, Cisco, and Juniper, implement any of the CIA mechanisms of the IPFIX RFC. Thus, the same exploits and security issues that apply to NetFlow also apply to IPFIX, Sect. 41.4.1. Hence, the major security trap remains insufficient fencing, even though the protocol was initially planned and designed with security in mind.

41.6.2   Discussion

The common design of all protocols within this class is that they are designed according to the Danvers Doctrine (Schiller 2002). Therefore, they all offer full CIA support. Unfortunately, when looking at the deployment base, we either find few indications of actual use of the protocol or that the deployed instances do not utilize or implement the full CIA support.

Among the reasons are difficult setup (LDAP, NFSv4) or limited perceived benefit of latest version of the protocol (NFSv4, SNMPv3). Also, they are often used within the SoHo, rather than the enterprise, where there is a lack of required security infrastructure (IPP without Kerberos). Furthermore, implementations do not support required protocol security features (IPFIX). Furthermore, third-party documentation may recommend simpler solutions, e.g., Postgres.

Another aspect is that the system administrator and the IT security professionals are typically not the same person, e.g., Botta et al. (2007) and Furnell et al. (2009). Moreover, these systems come with substantial complexity which leads to many misconfiguration opportunities. For example, Xu et al. (2013, 2015) in their papers "Do Not Blame Users for Misconfigurations" and "Hey, You Have Given Me Too Many Knobs! Understanding and Dealing with Over-Designed Configuration in System Software" point out that major causes of today's system failures are misconfigurations due to complexity. However, it is not necessarily the user or the system administrator who is to blame, but rather the inherent complexity and mismatch of the tools (Barrett et al. 2004; Haber and Bailey 2007) as well as poor usability for system operators (Xu et al. 2013, 2015).

Given the above complexity, let's review what might or might not motivate a system operator to deploy the latest secure protocol suites, see, e.g., the discussion of West as well as Schneier in their papers on "The psychology of security" (Schneier 2008; West 2008): (i) No or little reward for secure behavior. Indeed, there are hardly any monetary incentives for deploying the secure versions. Some claim that such incentives might change this (Greenwald et al. 2004). (ii) The misconception of operators that there is a low risk of being attacked. (iii) The "laziness" of the operator that wants to get the main service working first and then worry about security if there is time left. (iv) The time pressure by management that forces the operator to get a service working in no time. (v) The presumption that no one is likely to get caught for not deploying the secure version of the service. (vi) The insufficient maintainability of complex security infrastructures.

41.7 A New Simplicity in Protocol Design

The inherent complexity of protocol suites of the previous class provided the motivation for trade-off-based security. This class is about "strong attackers" and "good enough" security. As noted by Schneier (2008): "Security is a trade-off. This is something I have written about extensively and is a notion critical to understanding the psychology of security. There's no such thing as absolute security, and any gain in security always involves some sort of trade-off."

The protocol designs in this class must be seen in the context that we now have clouds as well as many start-up companies with various (mobile) applications. Indeed, the Internet is experiencing yet another growth explosion in terms of services (Armbrust et al. 2010; Pallis 2010). In terms of infrastructure, we are now in a "world of HTTP everywhere," virtualization, the cloud, large-scale as well as microservice architecture, and configuration orchestration.

Let us consider Internet application developers. Among the easiest ways to develop new applications is to do it in the cloud using a microservice architecture. They can rely on "Node.js" or similar programming languages and reuse existing code. The reuse of existing code has been made easy by the equivalent of App Stores. As transport protocol, they will most likely use HTTP/HTTPs. Moreover, the application grows as the feature sets and/or user base increases. A common observation is that the security review of such services is often lacking and the assumption is that it is possible to fence the service in a private cloud as it is just another Web service.

With "simplicity," we refer to the security concept rather than the feature sets of the protocols or, rather, protocol suites. The threat model for this class is "strong attacker" with "good enough." The representative protocols/protocol suites we examine are key-value stores, the reuse of Telnet, and the many incarnations of (HTTP/Socket) APIs. Other protocols in this class include VNC, PulseAudio's, and Systemd's internal protocols as well as control protocols for tools such as Nessus, Aircrack, etc. Since most of these use HTTP as transport layer protocols, the same security traps apply as discussed in the API subsection.

41.7.1 Example Protocols

41.7.1.1 Key-Value Stores

A useful Internet service is provided by key-value stores which are widely used by companies such as Amazon, Facebook, Digg, and Twitter (Atikoglu et al. 2012). Key-value stores provide a mapping between keys and their associated data and can, if implemented In-memory, avoid classic I/O bottlenecks. Thus, they allow quick nonrelational data storage. Examples include Dynamo, MongoDB, Redis, and Memcached. Initial development started around 2004. A first paper (DeCandia et al. 2007) reporting on "Dynamo, Amazon's highly available key-value store" appeared in 2007. While not a protocol in themselves, key-value stores are an almost universal network service and often rely on HTTP/ HTTPs or JSON for their communication.

Initially, most of the key-value services did not support authentication, authorization, and/or encryption. However, over time most were augmented with support for authentication, authorization, and encryption.

To highlight the underlying assumption of the design of all of key-value stores, we cite the Dynamo paper (DeCandia et al. 2007): "Other Assumptions: Dynamo is used only by Amazon's internal services. Its operation environment is assumed to be non-hostile and there are no security related requirements such as authentication and authorization."

Most key-value stores allow for transitive attacks. When an attacker can access a central Web session storage, they can impersonate users and/or administrators. When using key-value stores for caching, e.g., of SQL requests or of pre-compiled just-in-time byte code, access to the cache can result in information disclosure or even attack code execution.

Next we give a few examples, using Memcached, of the defaults when deploying key-value stores. For Memcached, strong authentication on the basis of SASL was introduced in 2009. Moreover, Memcached now supports transport layer encryption. However, this support is lacking by default in most UNIX derivatives as the implementation of SASL was flaky in Memcached and led to bugs. We surveyed the following distributions for SASL support: Gentoo, Debian Wheezy, Ubuntu 14.04.1 LTS, Arch Linux, CentOS 6, OpenBSD 5.6, and FreeBSD 10. We found that only since 2014 Debian Wheezy and Ubuntu 14.04.1 LTS started to link against SASL by default.

There are two options regarding the configuration of the listen socket, restrictive or global.

Restrictive means a specific IP, e.g., the localhost IP 127.0.0.1, or nonrestrictive using 0.0.0.0. We find that for Memcached, only Debian Wheezy and Ubuntu 14.04.1 LTS use the restrictive default.

We find, not surprisingly, that the documentation is large given the feature set of the services. Instructions for enabling the optional security features are hidden in Dynamo, misleading in Memcached, and clear and simple in Redis. It seems that initially, the security documentation of MongoDB was also hidden. On the 10th of February 2015, more than 40.000 MongoDB databases were unprotected on the Internet. Since then a major update effort on the documentation took place (website 2015).

Indeed, the weaknesses in the security models of NoSQL databases are known. While Srinivas and Nair (2015) conclude that they are on a good path forward with regard to providing CIA, Okman et al. (2011) point out that "Clearly the future generations of such DBMSs need considerable development and hardening in order to provide secure environment for sensitive data which is being stored by applications (such as social networks) using them."

BinaryEdge (Edge 2015) finds that there are still more than 175K unprotected Redis/MongoDB/Memcached instances in the Internet that can be contacted from any host. This is also supported by the data Fiebig et al. analyze a year later, painting a more temporal picture of the issues of key-value stores (Fiebig et al. 2016).

41.7.1.2 Telnet

Back in 1969, the idea of the Telnet protocol, e.g., RFC15, RFC137, RFC854, and RFC5198 (Carr 1969; O'Sullivan 1971; Postel and Reynolds 1983; Klensin and Padlipsky 2008), was to make a terminal usable by a remote host as if it was local. The result was a bidirectional, byte-oriented communication protocol. Since SSH (Ylonen and Lonvick 2006a, b, c, d) was designed in 1995 as a secure replacement for Telnet, rlogin, etc. (Ylönen 1996), Telnet usage should have declined to almost zero. Therefore, one would think if at all we should have discussed Telnet in Sect. 41.3.

Unfortunately, today for many application and infrastructure systems, e.g., customer premise equipment (CPEs), storage area network (SAN) devices, and what is now the Internet of Things (IoT) and Industry 4.0, Telnet is again the default choice for accessing devices (Foster et al. 2015) – with attacks skyrocketing in the past 18 months (Pa et al. 2015). After all, Telnet is relatively simple. Thus, most of these devices already come with a built-in daemon from the original design/equipment manufacturer (ODM/OEM) that supports a subset of the Telnet protocol in their firmware templates (Costin et al. 2014). This is the reason we discuss Telnet in this section.

The original versions of Telnet did not offer authentication/authorization or encryption. Telnet authentication defaulted to the operating system's login. Various authentication and authorization mechanisms including Kerberos and RSA were added to Telnet in 1993; see RFC1409 (Borman 1993). Adding TLS to Telnet was suggested by an Internet draft in 2000 (Boe and Altman 2002). A recent publication on vulnerabilities in telematic systems found that for all investigated devices, authentication was not enabled for the Telnet interface (Foster et al. 2015).

CPEs differ from operator equipment in the sense that they are actually operated by the end users. They also differ from the typical end-user equipment in the sense that they are often pre-configured and directly reachable via the Internet. Given vendors pre-provisioning their products with known default credentials, these CPE devices can be vulnerable as soon as they are accessible over the Internet. The extent to which this can be a problem was demonstrated in 2012 by the Carna botnet (Botnet 2013; Krenc et al. 2014). Another major attack used these devices to change the DNS settings of the end users and, thus, did a monkey in the middle attack (Assolini 2012).

Mitigation is relatively easy. Vendors should rethink if Telnet access is necessary at all. Even if it is, it should be possible to physically turn it on/off with a small dip switch on the device – with default off. Furthermore, they should not come with no, default, or guessable credentials. Indeed, the initial credentials should be unique for each device and should not be computable from anything that is also related to the device. Various vendors already use this approach (Lorente et al. 2015).

The documentation of the Telnet service is usually very limited as the documentation usually focuses on the devices themselves and only mentions that Telnet is supported. In the past most CPE services used default configurations with weak credentials.

Today, we find more than 10,600,000 devices with an open Telnet port according to Shodan. Indeed, the Carna botnet exploited about 1,200,000 of these devices (Botnet 2013). Furthermore, a recent study by Pa et al. (2015) finds that the attack volume on Telnet-enabled IoT devices has increased by many orders of magnitude since 2014.

41.7.1.3   APIs and Microservices

Remote procedure calls (RPCs) are a fundamental concept introduced before 1981, with the goal to make execution of code on a remote machine as simple and straightforward as on the local machine (Nelson 1981; Birrell and Nelson 1984). Today RPCs are everywhere but often hidden behind a different name; examples include JSON-RPC, XML-RPC, Java-RMI, SOAP, and REST. Indeed, one often refers to them as application programming interfaces (APIs).

APIs are commonly used in, e.g., (i) microservices, (ii) configuration interfaces, (iii) mobile application services, and (iv) Web applications. Microservices (Pratistha et al. 2003; van Halteren and Pawar 2006; Newman 2015) reuse the traditional UNIX philosophy of combining "small, sharp tools" (Hunt and Thomas 2000). The communication is delegated to APIs. An example of a configuration interface is the Docker API which allows operators to orchestrate applications built-in Docker containers via Web services (Docker.com 2015). Examples of mobile applications are the various APIs used in a multitude of Android and iOS apps (Masse 2011; Fiebig et al. 2013; Polakis et al. 2015). Web applications often rely on client-based JavaScript code that calls back to APIs on the server-side (Charland and Leroux 2011; Cantelon et al. 2014). While APIs often use RPCs, they do not have to. Some use HTTP as a transport protocol and are either REST-full or use JSON or XML as basis. Others use plain JSON or plain XML-RPC. Yet another group defines their own protocol often using binary encoding.

Some APIs provide some form of authentication, authorization, and encryption. However, APIs are often used in what the application designer thinks is a fenced environment. Hence, the typical use case has most security elements disabled (van Halteren and Pawar 2006; Alarcón and Wilde 2010). This is the reason that APIs are in this class as they basically repeat the misconceptions of Early Internet, namely, to trust every client.

Most attacks against APIs are ones that "just" use the service. This can result in unintended side effects due to missing authentication and authorization, e.g., abusing the Docker API, or information leakage, e.g., in mobile application APIs (Fiebig et al. 2013; Polakis et al. 2015), or using the backend API rather than the client interface to overcome rate limits against brute force attacks on the original service (Fallon 2015). These attacks are enabled by misconfigurations such as APIs that are Internet-wide accessible due to (i) holes in the firewall, (ii) a misconfigured bouncer applications, and (iii) inside attacks via another compromised microservice (Breen 2015).

We again find that, as with almost all new cool ideas, security aspects are the ones that are considered last. Thus, many APIs come with unclear documentation and/or global binds for their management APIs, e.g., Docker, tomcat, and JBoss (Breen 2015). Even though the meta documentation tells reasonably well that APIs have to be secured, the practice does not adhere to this goal. Indeed, the problems are known for microservices since 2003 (Pratistha et al. 2003). Moreover, good practices are known but hardly followed (Newman 2015).

41.7.2 Discussion

In this class, we often do not have a single protocol but concepts that are realized by different protocols that all suffer from the same security issues, e.g., key-value stores and APIs. Overall, we observe a clear trend toward using HTTP as application layer protocol, likely because HTTP allows middlebox traversal (Qazi et al. 2013). In theory, this opens up the possibility of "just securing HTTP" rather than having to secure a large number of Internet protocols (Richter et al. 2015). Still, the problem of missing authentication remains. Even if an API uses SSL for encryption, it can still be abused by an attacker (Breen 2015) to disclose information. The origin of this trend is the need for complex yet easy to deploy services.

Apart from delegating security issues to HTTP, these modern services again rely on fencing. During software and system development, the main focus is on getting the service ready and not necessarily on security. Hence, "[…] Its operation environment is assumed to be non-hostile […]" as stated in the Amazon Dynamo paper (DeCandia et al. 2007).

The underlying misconception is that services can be securely fenced off as they are only used within "internal systems." That this can lead to security incidents has already been shown in previous discussions. Nevertheless, many recent security incidents have led to prominent examples of data leakage (key-value stores, APIs) (Edge 2015; Fiebig et al. 2016).

The motivation for delegating security to a fenced environment is the notion that security without fencing is a complex and time-consuming task, impossible to achieve, and making the (backend) services unusable. Hence, the spirit during the development follows the start-up culture, which includes reusing available protocols as they are (Telnet/VNC).

Fencing techniques have advanced as well and, since 2013, include the concept of containers (Kim and Zeldovich 2013). A common security issue is captured by the following idea: "If we put a service in its own container in its own dedicated VM in its own VLAN behind a firewall nothing can happen." However, since services have to be reachable, they have to allow some access. This access often turns out to be the entry point for attacks.

Containers, e.g., Docker, are a deployment and testing mechanism. The motivation is that traditional means of software distribution do not scale to the cloud as traditional testing/release procedures do not fit the rapid development cycle. This often leads to monolithic deployment of formerly modular software components. This is unmanageable if some component has to be updated, e.g., to patch a security hole. Furthermore, containers usually come pre-configured which adds additional security traps.

Due to their experience with Complex Security, several developers state that one should not be too strict about security and that security is "in the way" of innovation. This goes as far as, e.g., Ren et al. (2012) claiming that: "Security and privacy is one fundamental obstacle to cloud computing's success."

Old mistakes are redone as the default assumption of the software developer is again "this is an esoteric scenario and not the intended use case." APIs may release more information than intended (Fiebig et al. 2013; Polakis et al. 2015). Moreover, the cloud adds the complexities of multiparty trust and the need for mutual auditability (Chen and Zhao 2012). Additionally, developer guidelines with a focus on security are hard to find even if they exist.

Overall, we note that, after having had too complex security and unusable systems, we are now in a world with easily deployable solutions. However, security is often outsourced – not in the business sense but to other layers of the network. This results in many security traps.

41.8   Lessons Learned

From our observations in this chapter, we can compile a set of action points and requirements protocol designers should consider when they create new or update old protocols.

41.8.1   The Early Internet

The major lesson from this class is that security requirements and environments change. However, this class also demonstrates that such issues can be tackled. *Hence, when updating a protocol, one MUST purge problematic use cases and design choices.* Only then can appeals for fixing bad configurations combined with sanctioning of insecure practices lead to improved overall security (see, e.g., Jung et al. 2002; Kührer et al. 2014). While the community succeeded with SMTP, the Internet still suffers from, e.g., DNS and NTP amplification attacks. In addition, other protocols from this era still linger and urgently require revisiting.

41.8.2 Emerging Threats

Given that the non-hostile Internet is gone, a new paradigm emerged. Instead of adjusting the protocols to the new insecure environment, the environment is redefined to be fenced. Thus, the assumption is that the service is behind a firewall or that lower layers offer security guarantees. Yet, it is common knowledge that firewalls tend to fail eventually and lower layers do not hold up to their promises. Thus, when designing a protocol, one MUST not assume that it will only be used in the environment it was designed for. Moreover, *when designing a protocol, one MUST include authentication, authorization, and confidentiality preserving methods.*

41.8.3 Complex Security

Here the community tried to address some of the above recommendations. However, the resulting protocols come with other complications. Security features designed for an enterprise setup may not be appropriate in SoHo scenarios, e.g., recall IPP. IPSec is so complex that it is not in widespread use. Moreover, implementations do not necessarily interoperate. In an attempt to ensure good cryptographic algorithms, SNMPv3 and SSHv1 specified algorithms that were good then but not necessarily now. Hence this class provides us with the following three lessons. First, *when designing a protocol, one MUST ensure that the security is scalable.* Scalable in the sense that it is applicable to large as well as small setups. Even the simplest setup should provide confidentiality, integrity, and availability by default. Second, *when designing a protocol, one MUST keep it simple and concise*, to allow multiple parties to implement interoperable solutions. Third, *when designing a protocol, one MUST not mandate the use of specific ciphers but instead MUST exclude plain and weak algorithms in an open and extendable list* since cryptographic algorithms become obsolete over time.

41.8.4 A New Simplicity

Protocol designers MUST be strict in mandating that all security features are included in implementations and this must be reflected in the RFCs or related standards. Even if there are external implications that restrict the applicability of a security feature, it should be used opportunistically. For example, to advance the use of TLS, a decent infrastructure, e.g., DANE (Barnes 2011; Hoffman and Schlyter 2012), is necessary. If such an infrastructure is unavailable, encryption should at least be performed opportunistically (Ylönen 1996; Roth et al. 2005).

Opportunistic encryption raises the question of usability. Usability has to become a key part of the protocol design process: The goal has to be to make the protocol secure while designing the system such that it is simple to comprehend and use. The correct way is either the only way or at least the most straightforward one (Balfanz et al. 2004; Roth et al. 2005; Bernstein et al. 2012).

Good examples of such design practices exist in the context of user centric protocols, e.g., SSH (Ylönen 1996) and the large set of encrypted (mobile) messaging protocols (Unger et al. 2015). The rise of the latter is motivated by the – emotional – demands of end users (Kraus et al. 2015) and professionals (McGregor et al. 2015) for easy but secure communication. Important security features include strong mutual authentication and opportunistic encryption. The same kind of protocol design is needed for all Internet protocols and, in particular, those used within the infrastructure.

41.9   Summary

Our systematization of security pitfalls in Internet protocols and services is based on assumptions about the attackers, weak vs. strong attacker, as well as security trade-offs – good enough vs. perfect security – in the protocols. We find that, based on certain security pitfalls, Internet protocols and their services fall into one of our four classes: Early Internet, Emerging Threats, Complex Security, and A New Simplicity. We observe that protocol design and service development have come full circle with regard to security. In the sense that initially the Internet was a cooperative environment, see Early Internet. Once it was realized that the Internet was hostile, it was presumed that it was possible to fence of services; see Emerging Threats. However, attackers are getting stronger and assets more valuable, and, thus, there is the attempt to get security "right"; see Complex Security. The drawback is complexity, and, thus, we complete the circle back to a simple security model in a presumed friendly environment guaranteed by enhanced fencing mechanisms; see A New Simplicity. Overall, we find many security traps in all of the above classes.

Fencing is seen as a major security solution and often used as only barrier protecting major assets. However, fencing is a major (potential) security trap in itself. After all, with regard to fencing, there is the statement from RFC3365 (Schiller 2002): "History has shown that applications that operate using the TCP/IP Protocol Suite wind up being used over the Internet. This is true even when the original application was not envisioned to be used in a 'wide area' Internet environment."

In summary, we can make specific observations for the different players involved. We find that protocols that are easily deployable are appreciated by operators. Having to configure security mechanisms can lead to frustration in operators, if they are unable to deploy a service due to their complexity. Hence, not including security measures reduces the chance that an operator becomes frustrated with a service implementation.

Hence, we observe that protocol/service designers move from strong but too complex security to hardly secure but easily deployable software that works "out of the box." Moreover, for many decision-makers (i.e., managers), the operational focus is on fulfilling business needs and generating revenue. However, in contrast to a conveniently deployed but insecure service, frustrated operations personnel that is unable to deploy services does not provide a business benefit. This is only true in the short term, as in the long term a security incident commonly proves to be more costly than proactive security considerations would have been. Nevertheless, these costs are not immediately visible and, hence, are often overlooked.

In summary, we find that the considerations taken into account during the design of a protocol do indeed inflict upon how easily implementations of a protocol can be operated in a secure manner. We propose various practices that can reduce the impact of this for existing as well as newly developed protocols. We hope that these guidelines can help engineers as well as management in designing more secure Internet protocols.

References

Aboba, B., et al. (2004). Securing Block Storage Protocols over IP, IETF.

Al-Shaer, E. S. and H. H. Hamed (2003). *Firewall policy advisor for anomaly discovery and rule editing*. Proc. IFIP/IEEE Symposium Integrated Network Management.

Alarcón, R. and E. Wilde (2010). *RESTler: Crawling RESTful services*. Proc. World Wide Web Conference.

Armbrust, M., et al. (2010). "A view of cloud computing." *Communications of the ACM* **53**(4): 50–58.

Assolini, F. (2012). The Tale of One Thousand and One DSL Modems.

Atikoglu, B., et al. (2012). *Workload analysis of a large-scale key-value store*. ACM SIGMETRICS Performance Evaluation Review.

Atkinson, R. (1995a). IP Authentication Header, IETF.

Atkinson, R. (1995b). IP Encapsulating Security Payload (ESP), IETF.

Atkinson, R. (1995c). Security Architecture for the Internet Protocol, IETF.

Balfanz, D., et al. (2004). "In search of usable security: Five lessons from the field." *Proc. IEEE Security & Privacy* (5): 19–24.

Barnes, R. (2011). Use Cases and Requirements for DNS-Based Authentication of Named Entities (DANE), IETF.

Barrett, D. J., et al. (2005). *SSH, The Secure Shell: The Definitive Guide: The Definitive Guide*, O'Reilly Media, Inc.

Barrett, R., et al. (2004). *Field studies of computer system administrators: analysis of system management tools and practices*. Proc. ACM Conference on Computer Supported Cooperative Work.

Bellovin, S. M. and W. R. Cheswick (1994). "Network firewalls." *IEEE Communication Magazine* **32**(9): 50–57.

Bernstein, D. J. How the AXFR protocol works.

Bernstein, D. J., et al. (2012). The security impact of a new cryptographic library. *Progress in Cryptology – LATINCRYPT 2012*: 159–176.

Bikos, A. N. and N. Sklavos (2013). "LTE/SAE security issues on 4G wireless networks." *Proc. IEEE Security & Privacy* **11**(2): 55–62.

Birrell, A. D. and B. J. Nelson (1984). "Implementing remote procedure calls." *ACM Trans. Computer Systems* **2**(1): 39–59.

Black, D. and P. Koning (2014). Securing Block Storage Protocols over IP: RFC 3723 Requirements Update for IPsec v3, IETF.

Blumenthal, U., et al. (2004). The Advanced Encryption Standard (AES) Cipher Algorithm in the SNMP User-based Security Model, IETF.

Blumenthal, U. and B. Wijnen (1998). User-based Security Model (USM) for version 3 of the Simple Network Management Protocol (SNMPv3), IETF.

Blumenthal, U. and B. Wijnen (2002). User-based Security Model (USM) for version 3 of the Simple Network Management Protocol (SNMPv3), IETF.

Boe, M. and J. Altman (2002). TLS-based Telnet Security, IETF.

Bollinger, G. (2015). "Securely Managing Your Networks With SNMPv3." *CiscoLIVE! BRKNMS-2658.*

Borman, D. (1993). Telnet Authentication Option, IETF.

Botnet, C. (2013). Internet census 2012: Port scanning/0 using insecure embedded devices.

Botta, D., et al. (2007). *Towards understanding IT security professionals and their tools.* Proc. ACM Symposium on Usable Privacy and Security.

Braden, R. (1989a). Requirements for Internet Hosts – Application and Support, IETF.

Braden, R. (1989b). Requirements for Internet Hosts – Communication Layers, IETF.

Breen, S. (2015). What Do WebLogic, WebSphere, JBoss, Jenkins, OpenNMS, and Your Application Have in Common? This Vulnerability.

Cantelon, M., et al. (2014). *Node.js in Action*, Manning.

Carr, C. S. (1969). Network subsystem for time sharing hosts, IETF.

Casado, M., et al. (2006). *SANE: A Protection Architecture for Enterprise Networks.* Proc. Usenix Security Symp.

Case, J., et al. (1996). Introduction to Community-based SNMPv2, IETF.

Case, J., et al. (1999). Introduction to Version 3 of the Internet-standard Network Management Framework, IETF.

Case, J., et al. (2002). Introduction and Applicability Statements for Internet-Standard Management Framework, IETF.

Case, J. D., et al. (1988). Simple Network Management Protocol, IETF.

Chapman, D. B. (1992). *Network (In) Security Through IP Packet Filtering.* Proc. Usenix.

Charland, A. and B. Leroux (2011). "Mobile application development: Web vs. native." *Communications of the ACM* **54**(5): 49–53.

Chen, D. and H. Zhao (2012). *Data security and privacy protection issues in cloud computing.* Proc. IEEE Computer Science and Electronics Engineering (ICCSEE).

Claise, B. (2004). Cisco Systems NetFlow Services Export Version 9, IETF.

Claise, B. (2008). Specification of the IP Flow Information Export (IPFIX) Protocol for the Exchange of IP Traffic Flow Information, IETF.

Clark, D. (1988). "The design philosophy of the DARPA Internet protocols." *ACM Computer Communication Review* **18**(4): 106–114.

Cormack, G. V. (2007). "Email spam filtering: A systematic review." *Foundations and Trends in Information Retrieval* **1**(4): 335–455.

Corrente, A. and L. Tura (2004). *Security performance analysis of SNMPv3 with respect to SNMPv2c.* Proc. IFIP/IEEE Network Operations and Management Symposium (NOMS).

Costin, A., et al. (2014). *A large-scale analysis of the security of embedded firmwares.* Proc. Usenix Security Symp.

Crocker, D. (1982). STANDARD FOR THE FORMAT OF ARPA INTERNET TEXT MESSAGES, IETF.

Cuppens, F., et al. (2005). *Detection and removal of firewall misconfiguration*. Proc. IASTED Conference on Communication, Network and Information Security.

DeCandia, G., et al. (2007). *Dynamo: Amazon's highly available key-value store*. ACM SIGOPS Operating System Review.

Docker.com (2015).

Durumeric, Z., et al. (2013). *ZMap: Fast Internet-wide Scanning and Its Security Applications*. Proc. Usenix Security Symp.

Dwivedi, H. (2005). "iSCSI Security." *Black Hat*.

Eastlake, D. (2005). Cryptographic Algorithm Implementation Requirements for Encapsulating Security Payload (ESP) and Authentication Header (AH), IETF.

Edge, B. (2015). Data, Technologies and Security – Part 1.

Falliere, N., et al. (2011). "W32. stuxnet dossier." *White paper, Symantec Corp., Security Response* **5**.

Fallon, R. (2015). Celebgate: Two Methodological Approaches to the 2014 Celebrity Photo Hacks. *Internet Science*: 49–60.

Ferguson, N. and B. Schneier (2000). "A cryptographic evaluation of IPsec."

Fiebig, T., et al. (2016). *A One-Year Perspective on Exposed In-Memory Key-Value Stores*. Proc. ACM Workshop on Automated Decision Making for Active Cyber Defense (SafeConf), ACM.

Fiebig, T., et al. (2013). Grindr application security evaluation report.

Flanagan, H. and S. Ginoza (2014). RFC Style Guide, IETF.

Foster, I., et al. (2015). *Fast and Vulnerable: A Story of Telematic Failures*. Proc. USENIX Workshop on Offensive Technologies (WOOT).

Frye, R., et al. (2000). Coexistence between Version 1, Version 2, and Version 3 of the Internet-standard Network Management Framework, IETF.

Frye, R., et al. (2003). Coexistence between Version 1, Version 2, and Version 3 of the Internet-standard Network Management Framework, IETF.

Furnell, S. M., et al. (2009). "An integrated view of human, organizational, and technological challenges of IT security management." *Information Management & Computer Security* **17**(1): 4-19.

Garcia-Alfaro, J., et al. (2013). "Management of stateful firewall misconfiguration." *Elsevier Computers & Security* **39**: 64–85.

Greenwald, S. J., et al. (2004). *The user non-acceptance paradigm: INFOSEC's dirty little secret*. Proc. ACM Workshop on New Security Paradigms.

Gutmann, P. and I. Grigg (2005). "Security usability." *Proc. IEEE Security & Privacy* **3**(4): 56–58.

Haber, E. M. and J. Bailey (2007). *Design guidelines for system administration tools developed through ethnographic field studies*. Proc. ACM Symposium on Computer Human Interaction for the Management of Information Technology.

Hayes, J. (2013). "Security Issues and Best Practices for Water/Wastewater Facilities." *Proceedings of the Water Environment Federation* **2013**(8): 6442–6461.

Herriot, R., et al. (1999). Internet Printing Protocol/1.0: Encoding and Transport, IETF.

Hoffman, P. (1999). SMTP Service Extension for Secure SMTP over TLS, IETF.

Hoffman, P. (2005). Cryptographic Suites for IPsec, IETF.

Hoffman, P. and J. Schlyter (2012). The DNS-Based Authentication of Named Entities (DANE) Transport Layer Security (TLS) Protocol: TLSA, IETF.

Housley, R. (2005). Using Advanced Encryption Standard (AES) CCM Mode with IPsec Encapsulating Security Payload (ESP), IETF.

Hunt, A. and D. Thomas (2000). *The pragmatic programmer: From journeyman to master*, Addison-Wesley Professional.

Industry, P. C. (2014). Payment Card Industry Data Security Standards, Abril.

Institute, S. A. N. S. (2003). Printer Insecurity: Is it Really an Issue?

Jung, J. and E. Sit (2004). *An empirical study of spam traffic and the use of DNS black lists.* Proc. ACM Internet Measurement Conference.

Jung, J., et al. (2002). "DNS Performance and the Effectiveness of Caching." *IEEE/ACM Trans. Networking (TON)* **10**(5): 589–603.

Kalafut, A. J., et al. (2008). *Understanding implications of DNS zone provisioning.* Proc. ACM Internet Measurement Conference.

Karn, P., et al. (1995). The ESP DES-CBC Transform, IETF.

Kaufman, C. (2005). Internet Key Exchange (IKEv2) Protocol, IETF.

Kent, S. (2005a). Extended Sequence Number (ESN) Addendum to IPsec Domain of Interpretation (DOI) for Internet Security Association and Key Management Protocol (ISAKMP), IETF.

Kent, S. (2005b). IP Authentication Header, IETF.

Kent, S. (2005c). IP Encapsulating Security Payload (ESP), IETF.

Kent, S. and K. Seo (2005). Security Architecture for the Internet Protocol, IETF.

Kim, T. and N. Zeldovich (2013). *Practical and Effective Sandboxing for Non-root Users.* Proc. Usenix.

Klensin, J., et al. (1995). SMTP Service Extensions, IETF.

Klensin, J. and M. Padlipsky (2008). Unicode Format for Network Interchange, IETF.

Krämer, J. I. (2015). Why cryptography should not rely on physical attack complexity, Springer.

Kraus, L., et al. (2015). "Analyzing End-Users' Knowledge and Feelings Surrounding Smartphone Security and Privacy." *Proc. IEEE Security & Privacy Workshops – Mobile Security Technologies (MoST).*

Krenc, T., et al. (2014). "An Internet census taken by an illegal botnet: A qualitative assessment of published measurements." *ACM Computer Communication Review* **44**(3): 103–111.

Kührer, M., et al. (2014). *Exit from Hell? Reducing the Impact of Amplification DDoS Attacks.* Proc. Usenix Security Symp.

Lawrence, N. and P. Traynor (2012). *Under New Management: Practical Attacks on SNMPv3.* Proc. USENIX Workshop on Offensive Technologies (WOOT).

Lorente, E. N., et al. (2015). *Scrutinizing WPA2 Password Generating Algorithms in Wireless Routers.* Proc. USENIX Workshop on Offensive Technologies (WOOT).

Mahadevan, B. (2000). "Business models for Internet-based e-commerce." *California management review* **42**(4): 55–69.

Masse, M. (2011). *REST API design rulebook*, O'Reilly Media, Inc.

Mayer, A., et al. (2000). *Fang: A firewall analysis engine.* Proc. IEEE Security & Privacy.

McGregor, S. E., et al. (2015). *Investigating the computer security practices and needs of journalists.* Proc. Usenix Security Symp.

Metzger, P. and W. Simpson (1995). IP Authentication using Keyed MD5, IETF.

Mockapetris, P. V. (1983a). Domain names: Concepts and facilities, IETF.

Mockapetris, P. V. (1983b). Domain names: Implementation specification, IETF.

Moonen, R. (2012). "Digitale achterdeuren in de Nederlandse internet infrastructuur." *Itsx bv.*

Myers, J. (1999). SMTP Service Extension for Authentication, IETF.

Nelson, B. J. (1981). "Remote procedure call."

Newman, S. (2015). *Building Microservices*, O'Reilly Media, Inc.

O'Sullivan, T. C. (1971). Telnet Protocol – a proposed document, IETF.

Okman, L., et al. (2011). *Security issues in NoSQL databases.* Proc. IEEE Trust, Security and Privacy in Computing and Communications (TrustCom).

Orman, H. (2003). "The Morris worm: A fifteen-year perspective." *Proc. IEEE Security & Privacy* (5): 35–43.

Pa, Y. M. P., et al. (2015). *IoTPOT: Analysing the Rise of IoT Compromises*. Proc. USENIX Workshop on Offensive Technologies (WOOT).

Pallis, G. (2010). "Cloud computing: the new frontier of Internet computing." *IEEE Internet Computing* (5): 70-73.

Pfleeger, C. P. and S. L. Pfleeger (2002). *Security in computing*, Prentice Hall Professional Technical Reference.

Polakis, I., et al. (2015). *Where's Wally?: Precise User Discovery Attacks in Location Proximity Services*. Proc. ACM Conference on Computer and Communications Security (CCS).

Postel, J. (1982). Simple Mail Transfer Protocol, IETF.

Postel, J. (1992). Introduction to the STD Notes, IETF.

Postel, J. (1993). Instructions to RFC Authors, IETF.

Postel, J. and J. Reynolds (1997). Instructions to RFC Authors, IETF.

Postel, J. and J. K. Reynolds (1983). Telnet Protocol Specification, IETF.

Pratistha, I. M. P., et al. (2003). *A Micro-Services Framework on Mobile Devices*. ICWS.

Qazi, Z. A., et al. (2013). *SIMPLE-fying middlebox policy enforcement using SDN*. ACM Computer Communication Review.

Quittek, J., et al. (2004). Requirements for IP Flow Information Export (IPFIX), IETF.

Ren, K., et al. (2012). "Security challenges for the public cloud." *IEEE Internet Computing* (1): 69–73.

Rescorla, E. and B. Korver (2003). Guidelines for Writing RFC Text on Security Considerations, IETF.

Richter, P., et al. (2015). *Distilling the Internet's Application Mix from Packet-Sampled Traffic*. Proc. Passive and Active Measurement (PAM).

Romanow, A., et al. (2005). Remote Direct Memory Access (RDMA) over IP Problem Statement, IETF.

Rossow, C. (2014). *Amplification hell: Revisiting network protocols for DDoS abuse*. Symposium on Network and Distributed System Security (NDSS).

Roth, V., et al. (2005). "Security and usability engineering with particular attention to electronic mail." *International Journal of Human-Computer Studies* **63**(1): 51–73.

Satran, J., et al. (2004). Internet Small Computer Systems Interface (iSCSI), IETF.

Schiller, J. (2002). Strong Security Requirements for Internet Engineering Task Force Standard Protocols, IETF.

Schiller, J. (2005). Cryptographic Algorithms for Use in the Internet Key Exchange Version 2 (IKEv2), IETF.

Schneier, B. (2008). The psychology of security. *Progress in Cryptology – AFRICACRYPT 2008*, Springer: 50-79.

Segmuller, W. and B. Leiba (2008). Sieve Email Filtering: Relational Extension, IETF.

Slay, J. and M. Miller (2008). *Lessons learned from the maroochy water breach*, Springer.

Spafford, E. H. (1989). "The Internet worm program: An analysis." *ACM Computer Communication Review* **19**(1): 17–57.

Srinivas, S. and A. Nair (2015). *Security maturity in NoSQL databases-are they secure enough to haul the modern IT applications?* Proc. IEEE Conference on Advances in Computing, Communications and Informatics (ICACCI).

Stallings, W. (1998). "SNMPv3: A security enhancement for SNMP." *IEEE Communications Surveys* **1**(1): 2–17.

Streibelt, F., et al. (2013). *Exploring EDNS-client-subnet adopters in your free time*. Proc. ACM Internet Measurement Conference.

Unger, N., et al. (2015). *SoK: Secure Messaging*. Proc. IEEE Security & Privacy.

van Halteren, A. and P. Pawar (2006). *Mobile service platform: A middleware for nomadic mobile service provisioning*. Proc. IEEE Wireless and Mobile Computing, Networking and Communications (WiMob).

van Rijswijk-Deij, R., et al. (2014). *DNSSEC and Its Potential for DDoS Attacks: A Comprehensive Measurement Study*. Proc. ACM Internet Measurement Conference.

website, M. (2015).

West, R. (2008). "The psychology of security." *Communications of the ACM* **51**(4): 34–40.

Wijnen, B., et al. (1999). An Architecture for Describing SNMP Management Frameworks, IETF.

Wool, A. (2004). "A quantitative study of firewall configuration errors." *IEEE Computer* **37**(6): 62–67.

Xu, T., et al. (2015). *Hey, you have given me too many knobs!: Understanding and dealing with over-designed configuration in system software*. Proc. ACM Meeting on Foundations of Software Engineering.

Xu, T., et al. (2013). *Do not blame users for misconfigurations*. Proc. ACM Conference on Symposium on Operating Systems Principles (SOSP).

Yang, X., et al. (2005). *A DoS-limiting network architecture*. ACM Computer Communication Review.

Ylönen, T. (1996). *SSH: Secure Login Connections over the Internet*. Proc. Usenix Security Symp.

Ylonen, T. and C. Lonvick (2006a). The Secure Shell (SSH) Authentication Protocol, IETF.

Ylonen, T. and C. Lonvick (2006b). The Secure Shell (SSH) Connection Protocol, IETF.

Ylonen, T. and C. Lonvick (2006c). The Secure Shell (SSH) Protocol Architecture, IETF.

Ylonen, T. and C. Lonvick (2006d). The Secure Shell (SSH) Transport Layer Protocol, IETF.

Yuan, L., et al. (2006). *Fireman: A toolkit for firewall modeling and analysis*. Proc. IEEE Security & Privacy.

National Cybersecurity Legislation: Is There a Magic Formula?

42

Eneken Tikk

Abstract

Cybersecurity has, without doubt, become a global issue. There is hardly a State that has not experienced a cyberattack, disruption of national or corporate networks, loss of data, or various forms of cybercrime. Moreover, with the deepening and widening penetration of information and communication technologies (ICTs) penetrating in the society, there is an element of "cyber" to every crime, conflict and civil unrest.

To this global problem, not all fixes need, or can, be international. Alongside the heavily debated status and scope of international law and regional coordination of confidence-building measures, the key to international, and national, cybersecurity lies with individual States.

Research on comprehensive national cybersecurity legislation has been less prominent than the scholarship on above-mentioned international law discourse or national cybersecurity strategies. Current research focuses mostly on individual jurisdictions and limited issue areas. As "cyber" has become a new dimension in all societal affairs, a comprehensive approach to developing national cybersecurity regulation requires due attention by not just national policy-makers but the legislature and judiciary alike.

42.1 The Notion of "Cyber" in National Legislative Process

Although it can be argued that many countries do not yet have "cybersecurity legislation," it is essential to remember that the very term "cyber" only entered national policy discussion about a decade ago, designating the convergence, on top of technologies, of personal,

E. Tikk (✉)
ICT4Peace Foundation, Geneva, Switzerland
e-mail: enekentikk@ict4peace.org

© Springer Fachmedien Wiesbaden GmbH, ein Teil von Springer Nature 2018
M. Bartsch, S. Frey (Hrsg.), *Cybersecurity Best Practices*,
https://doi.org/10.1007/978-3-658-21655-9_42

corporate and political risk in the use of ICTs. Accordingly, the paradigms of information security, information technology security and cybersecurity all denote the increasing centricity of ICTs in societal affairs, and all are accompanied by characteristic national legislation.

The classical information security approach, focusing on preservation of the confidentiality, integrity and availability of information [1], mainly focused on the various forms and characteristics of information itself. The early regulatory issues in information security became the many ways in which information could be obtained, stored or disseminated. Accordingly, in information security era, the focus was on technical protection of information and the systems and hardware used to store and transmit it [2].

A parallel, information and communication technology security paradigm acknowledged the interconnection between various systems and services, therefore emphasizing the need to define, achieve and maintain the above-mentioned functions of information across information resources and demanding additional focus on non-repudiation, accountability, authenticity and reliability [3]. These two paradigms of information and ICT security ran in parallel, one focusing on information itself and the other on ways in which information was transmitted across and between various information infrastructures and resources.

The role of law in this epoch was to emphasize the categories and functions of information that needed to be protected and set a normative expectation to the technical community to provide relevant protections [4].

As the use of computers and networks evolved, the process of securing ICTs had to extend beyond technical tradecraft and beyond any one organization's capacity. The focus on information and networks alone became insufficient to address the outbreak of data and network services and, more importantly, the mix of individual, corporate and political risk that attached to ICTs as now an underpinning element of all societal affairs, governmental functions and personal self-determination. Cybersecurity is a concept that emphasizes the prevalence of ICTs in modern societal and world order. From social media to home automation to criminal and terrorist use of ICTs to the employment of military cyber capabilities, it calls for a comprehensive and all-encompassing cognizance of vulnerabilities that the development and proliferation of ICTs have introduced in the modern society. The object of protection in this discourse is no longer just information or its carrier technologies. It is the person itself, the information society, the State and public international order. Personal, corporate and political risks converge alongside with technological convergence and increasing dependence on ICTs.

Accordingly, the challenges posed to legislation in this stage of still relative maturity of the information society are profound. They relate to fundamental values and developmental goals of respective societies. They call for inter-agency, multi-stakeholder, interdisciplinary responsibilities and remedies. They highlight the question of accountability in the widest sense – how to distribute and assign responsibility across all relevant stakeholders, processes and assets? The law, in the current phase of ICT development, must help distil vital national interests, balance the many, and often conflicting, expectations and stabilize national cyber affairs.

42.2 Trends and Developments in National Cyber Legislation

Given the elevation of cyber risk, reports of updated cybersecurity legislation pour from all over the world. Evident in these reports is the very uneven landscape of cybersecurity legislation. However, embedded in these diverging national approaches and reactions is a logical model of national cybersecurity legislation.

Heavily invested into an ICT-immersed way of life, EU countries offer some very advanced case studies of cybersecurity legislation. The recent EU cybersecurity reform is an advanced example of a deliberately comprehensive regulatory approach and compelling intervention. Despite being at the forefront of information and ICT security regulation over the past decades, the EU has considered it necessary to up the level of intensity and scope of its cybersecurity regulation. Evident in this move is the determination to abolish a stovepiped attitude towards cybersecurity as a complex societal issue and the acknowledgement of the potential value of a strong regulatory involvement.

The EU regulatory approach to cybersecurity is firmly grounded in the previous experience and phases of the EU information security regulation. It consolidates the goals of the EU Digital Agenda, with considerations outlined in the 2013 Cybersecurity Strategy. The current reform will build on the experience of earlier personal data protection reforms and add new requirements to network and information system protection. Although latest improvements focus mainly on personal data protection and general network and information protections, the EU has, over a relatively short period of time, created a rather comprehensive and systemic regulatory framework for cybersecurity and information society building.

Table 42.1 offers a selection of the EU ICT regulations. It is construed as a thematic overview to highlight the topics, rather than format, or detailed contents, of their regulation. The reader will note that in the recent years, rather than adopting entirely new instruments, the EU regulatory efforts have focused on providing updates and adding legal force to pre-existing instruments.

Table 42.1 Selected themes in EU information society and cybersecurity regulation

1991	Legal protection of computer programs [5]
1995	Protection of personal data [6]
1996	Legal protection of databases [7]
1997	Protection of consumers in respect of distance contracts [8]
1998	Protection of services with conditional access [9]
1999	Electronic signatures [10]
2000	e-Commerce [11]
2002	The "Telecoms Package" [12]
2005	Attacks against information systems [13]
2006	Data retention [14]
2008	Critical infrastructure protection [15]
2016	Network and information systems security [16]

Another group of countries offering ambitious and fresh approaches to cybersecurity legislation comprises the world's leading cyber powers – the USA, China and Russia. While these countries have a rather different history of, and considerations for, levelling up their national cyber law, they all offer examples of national legislation put into the service of essential national interests and societal developments. For instance, in 2017, Russia passed three new cybersecurity and Internet laws that support its policy of strong governmental controls over national information space [17]. China has used national legislation to put stricter obligations on personal data processing, critical infrastructure security and domestic control over data [18]. The USA has, over the past years, invested into legislation that supports information sharing, breach notifications and private-public partnerships in the field of cybersecurity [19].

Several States have preferred to mount the dimension of cybersecurity to national legislation by way of a dedicated legal instrument. Latvia was one of the first countries to introduce a Law on the Security of Information Technologies in 2010 [20]. Japan adopted a Cybersecurity Basic Act in 2014 [21]. Estonia and Singapore are in the process of adopting national cybersecurity acts [22].

Meanwhile, many countries of the world still do not possess the very baseline legislation needed to support information society ambitions. These elementary pieces include laws on cybercrime, personal data protection, regulation of telecommunication infrastructure and intellectual property protection.

Despite these very different approaches and structures, there is a logical approach to cybersecurity-related regulation. All stages of information society development require legislative building blocks that reflect and support the particular strategic goals and interests of the society. Various issues need to be considered as the information society matures. First of all, depending on the direction and goals related to employment of ICTs in State and societal functions, there is a need for routine consideration of issues like privacy and access to information, e-commerce, information society services, e-government, intellectual property protection and the functioning of national networks. With the adoption of ICTs in various affairs comes the need to adjust deviations of behaviour and the corresponding requirement for adequate criminal law. National security considerations, in turn, add tension to the guarantees of privacy and freedom of information by requiring special provisions on evidence gathering, data retention and forensics. In the interest of international cybersecurity and stability, States are also expected to form views as to the national implementation of public and private international law.

42.3   Regulating Information Society in Estonia

To further illustrate some of the observations above, mainly the need for an organic approach and the ideally tailored nature of national regulatory approaches, this chapter explains the system of regulating information society interests and goals in Estonia. Choosing Estonia as a case study is not to suggest that the Estonian regulatory approach to cybersecurity is optimal or excellent. However, the Estonian framework is sufficient to illustrate some of the considerations and challenges the States may have when tackling the issue of cyber law.

Estonia was one of the countries fully embracing the Clinton-Gore call for joining the international information highway in the early 1990s. A newly re-independent, fragile State with a very young government, Estonia saw ICTs as a way to overcome some of the State-building challenges. The Foundations of Information Policy from 1998 thoroughly chart the Estonian considerations and goals vis-a-vis the use of ICTs. Acknowledging that the path towards the information society would likely result in fundamental changes of the world and societal order, Estonia decided to adopt ICTs as a central element in its societal development [23]. ICTs were seen as a way to compensate the limited economic opportunities and to support the Estonian integration in the EU [24].

Estonia was successful in founding the initial approach to information society on a strong culture of coordination between the private and public sector. Already in the very early phase of information society development, modernization of legal instruments was one of the key areas of emphasis, alongside with the promotion of the development of the private sector, designing a process of interaction between the State and citizens and raising awareness of the information society and related challenges [25].

The Estonian government set the goal of transforming Estonia into a cordial State strongly based on democracy. The government set the course towards investments into national information infrastructure, e-commerce and digital services [26].

To support these goals, the Parliament identified initial directions for a sustainable legal environment supporting the information society. The two main baskets for developing an advanced information society were the creation of a competitive and innovative economic environment and the shaping of information society relations [27]. In the first basket, legal instruments were to predispose competition, support frugal economic growth, promote standardization and provide for protection of intellectual property [28]. In the second basket, the Parliament requested gradual improvements in equal access to communication technologies and a whole-of-a-society communication service. Such connectivity, it was emphasized, needs to be established in a way that upholds the privacy of individuals and the security of data. Accordingly, the first wave of legislation in the field of ICTs was expected to master this balance.

In line with these considerations, Estonia adopted a regulatory approach rather typical to European countries during the 1990s. During the 1990s, Estonia adopted a number of legal acts to frame and sustain a strong information society: the 1992 Copyright Act [29], the 1996 Personal Data Protection Act, the Databases Act of 1997 and the Telecommunications Act of 2000. Estonia was also an early adopter of the Budapest Convention, integrating the provisions of cybercrime in the Penal Code.

At the turn of the millennium, developments in the Estonian information society legislation run in parallel with relevant developments in the EU law, with a strong emphasis on specific Estonian aims and realities. The Digital Signature Act of 1999 followed the examples of Germany, Italy and France and supported the very Estonian ambition for a strong and functioning information society. The rather unique Public Information Act of 2001 was a decisive move towards transparency in the relationship between citizens and the State, mandating a wide range of information generated in public functions to be made available on dedicated websites.

The period between 2000 and 2007 was the one of adjusting national legislation to the next ambitions in Estonian information society development while incorporating in national legislation further EU instruments. The information policy instrument for the period of 2004–2006 noted that the goals set 5 years ago had been largely achieved. Meanwhile, the Estonian access to the EU had actuated the need for better coordination and integration of EU and Estonian information policy and legislation [30]. The keywords for the second phase of the Estonian information society development became integration and the role of ICTs in societal economics [31].

Assessing the progress so far, it was noted that Estonia had developed a commendable legislative basis for its information society goals and that in close cooperation between various stakeholders the country had been able to build a wide-based and modern telecommunication infrastructure that facilitated providing public services and modernizing public administration [32].

The next key goals for information society development were set to root e-services across the private sector, keeping up with the information society indicators of other EU countries, and to create the preconditions for Estonian ICT sector export [33]. These tasks included considerations of public administration efficiency, e-democracy, incorporation of ICTs in education, health and other sectors, as well as the ambition of becoming an internationally acknowledged information society [34].

This epoch of Estonian cyber legislation comprised few entirely new legal instruments. The Information Society Services Act of 2004 was to incorporate certain provisions of the EU e-Commerce Directive, while the Electronic Communication Act of the same year replaced the Telecommunication Act in the spirit of the EU telecommunication reform. Meanwhile, several adjustments were made in pre-existing legal instruments to support new services and functions online. Among other things, these amendments made possible electronic voting at national elections, the e-health system and the Estonian access to the Schengen Information System. A comprehensive legal reform was conducted to organize and optimize national registries and databases, leading to the incorporation of the Databases Act into the Public Information Act.

Year 2007 notes the beginning of the third period of Estonian information society regulation. Although it was anticipated that the Estonian emphasis on information society would necessitate attention on security, little had been done to date to consider the security of information processes and services beyond rather basic technical and organizational measures. True, the Estonian access to NATO opened a separate inquiry into the topic of military cyber defence – something that became a political interest in conjunction with offering to NATO the Estonian contribution of establishing a Cooperative Cyber Defence Centre of Excellence in Tallinn [35].

The 2007 cyberattacks against Estonia left little room for deliberating the next course of action. In line with its international ambitions, Estonia took lead in calling for upgrades in relevant EU legislation as well as discussions of how to apply international law to issues of cybersecurity. Since 2007, Estonia has revised its cybercrime provisions of the Penal Code to consider politically motivated cyberattacks. The 2009 Emergency Act incorporated the concept of vital information services, while the establishment of the Estonian Cyber Defence League was accompanied with changes in the Defence League Act. Characteristic to the current era of information security regulation in Estonia is, where possible, avoid new cyber-specific instruments and, instead, normalize the dimension of ICTs and cyber across the normative spectrum.

Over time, many cyber-specific provisions have been added to numerous other Estonian laws – such as the Financial Services Act, Statistics Act, State Secrets Act and many others. Annex A of this paper provides a schematic overview of the Estonian ICT law and policy.

The above case study highlights the very tailored approach to information society and relevant legislation in just one country. It should be considered that the Estonian approach, and experience, has been contoured by very specific circumstances – the size of the population, the unique path of transferring from a Soviet republic into an *über*-democratic society and the relative coherence, among all members of society, in embracing ICTs as means of societal development, a rather rare (and early) culture of cooperation and coordination between government, the private sector and NGOs in achieving the set information society goals.

42.4 Best Practices in Regional and International Instruments

When shaping national responses to cybersecurity issues, experience of other countries is but one source of valuable inspiration. No matter what the point of departure, or destination of particular national efforts, there is valuable guidance available from international and regional organizations.

Various organizations have over the years adopted dozens and dozens of instruments that guide or codify normative considerations on various aspects of information society development and cybersecurity. While, again, the word "cyber" is not present in most of the titles, regional and international instruments also offer a logical and systemic approach to issues related to the development and use of ICTs. They also allow analysis of regional and international trends in regulation. Table 42.2 shows the main themes in international and regional instruments addressing aspects of cybersecurity.

Particularly on the question of international information security, OSCE and UN GGE have recently provided a framework that States can apply in developing their legislation and strategies. The guidance of the GGE is particularly valuable as it constitutes consensus between both instruments. They emphasize the role of the rule of law in achieving an open, free, secure and stable cyberspace and elaborate on some of the key steps in promoting cybersecurity considerations and practices worldwide. See Table 42.3 for the cybersecurity recommendation provided by the OSCE and UN GGE.

Table 42.2 Main themes in international and regional instruments addressing aspects of cyber security

Theme	Number of instruments
Personal data protection (including privacy) [36]	17
Freedom of information (including public information and public services online) [37]	7
Telecommunications (including electronic communications) [38]	11
Computer/cybercrime [39]	12
Information security (including cryptography and general cybersecurity) [40]	11
Electronic commerce (including electronic payments, digital signatures, consumer protection and information society services) [41]	11
Critical infrastructure protection [42]	3

This list and numbers are not conclusive, yet offer the baseline

Table 42.3 Cybersecurity Roadmap provided by OSCE and UN GGE

	OSCE [43]	GGE [44]	
Upholding the rule of law	Have in place modern and effective national legislation to facilitate exchange and cooperation #6	States should not knowingly allow their territory to be used for internationally wrongful acts using ICTs (13 c)	A repository of national laws and policies for the protection of data and ICT-enabled infrastructure and the publication of materials deemed appropriate for distribution on these national laws and policies (16 d i)
		States should respect resolutions on the pro-motion, protection and enjoyment of human rights on the Internet (13 e)	Establish focal points and cooperation for the provision of assistance in investigations (17 b)
		States should intensify cooperation against criminal and terrorist use of ICTs, harmonize legal approaches and strengthen practical collaboration between law enforcement and prosecutorial agencies (22)	Cooperate, in a manner consistent with national and international law, with requests from other States in investigating ICT-related crime or the use of ICTs for terrorist purposes or to mitigate malicious ICT activity emanating from their territory (17 e)

(continued)

Table 42.3 (continued)

	OSCE [43]	GGE [44]	
		States should consider how to best cooperate to exchange information, assist each other, prosecute terrorist and criminal use of ICTs and implement other cooperative measures to address such threats (13 d)	Enhanced mechanisms for law enforcement cooperation to reduce incidents that could otherwise be misinterpreted as hostile State actions (26 f)
Exchange of views and information	National views of national and international threats #1		Voluntary sharing of national views and information on various aspects of national and transnational threats to and in the use of ICTs (16 c)
	Information in relation with security of and in the use if ICTs #2		
	Measures that they have taken to ensure an open, interoperable, secure, and reliable Internet #4		
	Effective responses to threats to and in the use of ICTs #5		
	Best practices, awareness-raising, information on capacity-building #5	Prevent practices that are acknowledged to be harmful or that may pose threats to international peace and security (13 a)	Voluntary sharing of national views and information on best practices for ICT security (16 c)
	Information on their national organization; strategies; policies and programmes – including on cooperation between the public and the private sector #7		Voluntary sharing of national views and information on national organizations, strategies, policies and programmes relevant to ICT security (16 c) (26 a)
	Provide a list of national terminology: terms and definitions or explanations #9		

(continued)

Table 42.3 (continued)

	OSCE [43]	GGE [44]	
	Exchanges in different formats: workshops, seminars, roundtables at regional and sub-regional level, to investigate further areas for cooperation #12		The creation of bilateral, regional and multilateral consultative frameworks for confidence-building, which could entail workshops, seminars and exercises to refine national deliberations on how to prevent disruptive incidents arising from State use of ICTs and how these incidents might develop and be managed (26 b)
	Between competent national bodies #2	In developing and applying measures to increase stability and security in the use of ICTs (13 a)	Establishment of focal points and cooperation for the exchange of information on malicious ICT use (17 b)
	Consultations to reduce the risks of misperception, and possible emergence of pol-mil tension or conflict #3		The development of and support for mechanisms and processes for bilateral, regional, sub-regional and multilateral consultations to enhance inter-State confidence-building and reduce the risk of misperception, escalation and conflict that may stem from ICT incidents (16 b)
CI protection	To protect critical national and international ICT infrastructures, including their integrity #3	A State should not conduct or knowingly support ICT activity contrary to its obligations under international law that intentionally damages CI or otherwise impairs the use and operations of CI to provide services to the public (13 f)	Voluntary provision of national views of categories of infrastructure that they consider critical and national efforts to protect them, including information on national-level laws and policies for the protection of data and ICT-enabled infrastructure (16 d)
	Facilitate cooperation between authorized authorities responsible for securing critical infrastructures #15	States should take appropriate measures to protect their CI from ICT threats (13 g)	States should seek to facilitate cross-border cooperation to address CI vulnerabilities that transcend national borders (16 d)

(continued)

Table 42.3 (continued)

	OSCE [43]	GGE [44]	
		States should respond to appropriate requests for assistance by another State whose CI is subject to malicious ICT acts (13 h 1)	The development or mechanisms and processes for consultations on the protection of ICT-enabled CI (16 d ii)
			The development of technical, legal and diplomatic mechanisms to address ICT-related requests (16 d iii)
			The adoption of national arrangements to classify ICT incidents in terms of the scale and seriousness of the incident, for the purpose of facilitating the exchange of information about incidents (16 d iv)
Incident prevention and handling	Measures to ensure rapid communication at policy levels of authority, to permit concerns to be raised at the national security level #8	In case of ICT incidents, States should consider all relevant information, including the larger context of the event the challenges of attribution in the ICT environment and the nature and extent of the consequences (13b)	Strengthen cooperative mechanisms between relevant agencies to address ICT security incidents (17 a)
	Provide and update contact data of national structures that manage ICT-related incidents and coordinate responses #8	States should respond to appropriate requests to mitigate malicious ICT activity aimed at the CI of another State emanating from their territory, taking into account due regard for sovereignty (13 h 2)	Establish a national computer emergency response team and/or cybersecurity incident response team or officially designate an organization to fulfil this role (17 c)
			Expand and support practices in computer emergency response team and cybersecurity incident response team cooperation, such as information exchange about vulnerabilities, attack patterns and best practices for mitigating attacks, including coordinating responses, organizing exercises, supporting the handling of ICT-related incidents (17 d)

(continued)

Table 42.3 (continued)

	OSCE [43]	GGE [44]	
	Nominating contact points to facilitate communications and dialogue #8	States should not conduct or knowingly support activity to harm the information systems of authorized emergency response teams of another State (13 k 1)	The identification of appropriate points of contact at the policy and technical levels to address serious ICT incidents (16 a)
		A State should not use authorized emergency response teams to engage in malicious international activity (13 j 2)	Consider categorizing CERT as critical infrastructure (17 c)
			Enhanced sharing of information on ICT security incidents, involving the more effective use of existing channels or the development of new channels and mechanisms to receive, collect, analyze and share information related to ICT incidents, for timely response, recovery and mitigation actions (26 c)
			States should consider exchanging information on national points of contact, in order to expand and improve existing channels of communication for crisis management, and supporting the development of early warning mechanisms (26 c)
			Exchanges of information and communication between national CERTs bilaterally, within CERT communities, and other forums, to support dialogue at political and policy levels (26 d)
			Increased cooperation to address incidents that could affect ICT or CI that rely on ICT-enabled industrial control systems, including guidelines and best practices among States against disruptions perpetrated by non-State actors (26 e)

(continued)

Table 42.3 (continued)

	OSCE [43]	GGE [44]	
Other	Regular meetings each year #11	States should take reasonable steps to ensure the integrity of the supply chain so that end users can have confidence in the security of ICT products (13 i 1)	
	Coordination through OSCE platform #10	States should seek to prevent the proliferation of malicious ICT tools and techniques and the use of harmful hidden functions (13 i 2)	Voluntary sharing of national views and information on vulnerabilities and identified harmful functions in ICT products (16 c)
	Responsible reporting of vulnerabilities affecting the security of and in the use of ICTs and sharing available measures, also with ICT business and industry #16	States should encourage responsible reporting of ICT vulnerabilities (13 j 1)	
		States should share information about available remedies to vulnerabilities to limit and possibly eliminate potential threats to ICTs and ICT-dependent infrastructure (13 j 2)	
	Promote PPPs #14	States should encourage the private sector and civil society to play and appropriate role to improve security of and in the use of ICTs, including supply chain security for ICT products and services (24)	
		State should consider how to best cooperate in implementing the above norms and principles, including the role that may be played by the private sector and civil society organizations (25)	

42.5   Information Society and Cybersecurity Regulation in Estonia

National Cyber Policy and Strategy	Foundations of Estonian Information Policy 1998 Foundations of Estonian Information Policy 2004–2006 Broadband Strategy 2005–2007 Information Society Development Agenda 2013 Digital Agenda 2020 for Estonia National Cyber Security Strategy 2008 National Cyber Security Strategy 2014	
International Obligations and International Cyber Policy (examples)	The UN Charter The Budapest Convention EU NATO	
Supported International and Regional Working Formats (examples)	UN GGE OSCE CBMs	
Main Legal Instruments	Copyright Act (1992) Data Protection Act (1996) Databases Act (1997) Telecommunications Act (2000) Electronic Signatures Act (2000) Public Information Act (2001) Electronic Communications Act (2004) Cybersecurity Act (draft) Penal Code (2001) Emergency Act (2009)	
Administrative Regulations	Information Systems' Security Measures (ISKE) State Information System's Management System (RIHA) Information Management Measures CII security measures Risk Analysis Instructions Use of Cyber Defence League in National Cyber Security Statutes of National Databases	

42.6   Conclusion

When we accept that ICTs, or cyber, have become a dimension of our way of life, we accept that the legal environment for accommodating relevant opportunities and challenges needs to be comprehensive and adaptive. Determining not just gaps but also redundant norms in our regulatory frameworks and the ability to create coherence between the goals of justice, security and the information society are essential goals in national cyber regulation preparedness and proficiency. There are aspects of information society and cybersecurity that require due attention of legislature and judiciary, especially when it comes to accommodating considerations of security in public expectations of privacy and freedom of information, as well as balancing, more broadly, between private and public interests. At the same time, regulatory steps should not become steered by trends and sentiments. Regulatory frameworks must remain clear and logical, safeguarding the stability of legislative developments.

Like in any other area of national legislation, it is essential that decisions to regulate follow an issue-based, evidenced necessity of supporting, sustaining or re-defining particular societal preferences and goals. Given the prevalence of the issues for all stakeholders and members of the society, national regulatory initiatives would benefit of inclusive processes (consultations, commentaries) that would reveal different understandings and considerations related to possible implementation. Impact assessment is necessary to avoid ineffective legal instruments. Transparency and clarity of regulation is achieved by thorough explanatory notes. Legislation becomes more durable and better understood with the support of clear definitions, principles and mandates.

It is not so important whether a State builds its cybersecurity legislation by way of full codification or employs an approach of patches and adjustments in pre-existing legal instruments. It is essential that regulatory developments are tailored to the unique situation and essential interests of the society in question. While it is useful to track international, regional and other States' regulatory developments and examples, these are best considered as auxiliary sources and guidance. National legislation should adhere to them, but should not always be triggered by them.

Questions as to the balance of law, policy and strategy become irrelevant in action, as these three pillars are intrinsically related to each other. The observation that law is lagging behind technology should not be accepted as a per se justified criticism. A proper balance between policy, strategy and legal moves will allow law to be drafted in a technology neutral and sustainable manner, avoiding unnecessary legal experiments and regulatory burden.

References

1. SO/IEC 27002/2005.
2. Whitman & Mattord, Principles of Information Security (3rd Edition), Thompson, 2009.
3. ISO/IEC 13335-1 (2004).
4. Consider, for instance, the principle, whereby a data controller was required to provide the integrity, confidentiality and availability of that data.
5. Council Directive 91/250/EEC on the legal protection of computer programs, repealed by Directive 2009/24/EC of the European Parliament and of the Council of 23 April 2009 on the legal protection of computer programs.

6. Directive 95/46/EC on the protection of individuals with regard to the processing of personal data and on the free movement of such data, repealed by Regulation (EU) 2016/679 on the protection of natural persons with regard to the processing of personal data and on the free movement of such data. As of 2018, Directive 95/46/EC is repealed by the General Data Protection Regulation.

7. Directive 96/9/EC on the legal protection of databases.

8. Directive 97/7/EC on the protection of consumers in respect of distance contracts, repealed by Directive 2011/83/EU on consumer rights.

9. Directive 98/84/EC on the legal protection of services based on, or consisting of, conditional access.

10. Directive 1999/93/EC on a Community framework for electronic signatures.

11. Directive 2000/31/EC on certain legal aspects of information society services, in particular electronic commerce, in the Internal Market.

12. Directive 2002/19/EC on access to, and interconnection of, electronic communications networks and associated facilities (Access Directive); Directive 2002/20/EC on the authorisation of electronic communications networks and services; Directive 2002/21/EC on a common regulatory framework for electronic communications networks and services; Directive 2002/22/EC on universal service and users' rights relating to electronic communications networks and services; Directive 2002/58/EC concerning the processing of personal data and the protection of privacy in the electronic communications sector; Regulation (EC) No 1211/2009 establishing the Body of European Regulators for Electronic Communications (BEREC) and the Office and Regulation (EU) No 531/2012 on roaming on public mobile communications networks within the Union. See also Directive 2009/140/EC amending Directives 2002/21/EC on a common regulatory framework for electronic communications networks and services, 2002/19/EC on access to, and interconnection of, electronic communications networks and associated facilities, and 2002/20/EC on the authorisation of electronic communications networks and services.

13. Council Framework Decision 2005/222/JHA on attacks against information systems, replaced by Directive 2013/40/EU on attacks against information systems.

14. Directive 2006/24/EC on the retention of data generated or processed in connection with the provision of publicly available electronic communications services or of public communications networks.

15. Council Directive 2008/114/EC on the identification and designation of European critical infrastructures and the assessment of the need to improve their protection.

16. Directive (EU) 2016/1148 concerning measures for a high common level of security of network and information systems across the Union.

17. Federal Law No. 187-FZ "On the Security of the Russian Federation's Critical Data Infrastructure", Federal Law No. 276-FZ "On Amendments to the Federal Law On Data, Information Technologies and Data Security" and Federal Law No. 241-FZ "On Amendments to Articles 10.1 and 15.4 of the Federal Law "On Data, Information Technologies and Data Security".

18. Text available at http://www.npc.gov.cn/npc/xinwen/2016-11/07/content_2001605.htm.

19. See Cybersecurity Information Sharing Act (CISA); Cybersecurity Enhancement Act; Federal Exchange Data Breach Notification Act and National Cybersecurity Protection Advancement Act, all adopted 2014–2015.

20. http://www.dvi.gov.lv/en/legal-acts/law-on-the-security-of-information-technologies/.

21. Act No. 104 of 2014.

22. See the Singaporean draft https://www.csa.gov.sg/~/media/csa/cybersecurity_bill/draft_cybersecurity_bill_2017.ashx?la=en.

23. Foundations of Estonian Information Policy, paras 4–6.

24. Ibid., paras 4–6.

25. Ibid., para 7.
26. Ibid., para 8.
27. Ibid., para 19.
28. Ibid., para 19 (1).
29. As the focus of this article is not on the content, or exact time of adoption, of these instruments, but rather a logical overview, no references have been provided to the laws that have since been often updated, amended, and occasionally repealed.
30. Foundations of Estonian Information Policy 2004–2006, page 3.
31. Ibid., page 3.
32. Ibid., page 4.
33. Ibid., page 7.
34. Ibid., page 9.
35. Contrary to widespread allegations, the CCD COE was not established in the aftermath of the 2007 attacks against Estonian government and private sector information systems. It had been conceptualized in 2003–2004 and the … preparations for establishing the organization begun in 2006 when a core group of scientists were invited to investigate the state of cyber security in Estonia. This group of scientists also formed the initial Estonian personnel component of the CCD COE.
36. OECD Recommendation concerning Guidelines Governing the Protection of Privacy and Transborder Flows of Personal Data (1980), COE Convention for the Protection of Individuals with Regard to Automatic Processing of Personal Data (1981), UN Guidelines for the Regulation of Computerized Personal Data Files (A/RES/44/132) (1989) and A/RES/45/95 (1990), Directive 95/46/EC, Recommendation No. R (99) 5 for the protection of privacy on the Internet (1999), G8 Principles on the Availability of Data Essential to Protecting Public Safety (2002), Directive 2002/58/EC, Supplementary Act on Personal Data Protection within ECOWAS (2010), OECD Recommendation concerning Guidelines Governing the Protection of Privacy and Transborder Flows of Personal Data (2013), UN Resolution on the Right to Privacy in the Digital Age (A/RES/68/167) (2013), European Parliament Resolution on the Electronic Mass Surveillance of EU Citizens (2014, updated in 2015), COE Resolution 2045 (2015) Mass Surveillance (2015), Directive, EU Regulation on the Protection of Natural Persons with regard to the Processing of Personal Data.
37. CoE Declaration on Freedom of Communication on the Internet (2003), Directive on the Re-Use of Public Sector information (2003/98/EC), amended in 2013, Directive 2006/24/EC, CoE Recommendation of the Committee of Ministers to Member States on Measures to Promote the Public Service Value of the Internet (2007), OECD Council Recommendation on Principles for Internet Policy Making (2011), COE Recommendation Rec(2004)11 on Legal, Operational and Technical Standards for E-Voting (2004), OECD Recommendation of the Council on Digital Government Strategies (2014), COE Recommendation CM/Rec(2017)5 of the Committee of Ministers to member States on standards for e-voting (2017).
38. UN Resolution A/RES/36/40 World Communications Year Development of Communications Infrastructures (1982), ITU Resolution 10 World Administrative Telegraph and Telephone Conference (1984), ITU International Telecommunication Regulations (1988, 2012), Constitution and Convention of the International Telecommunication Union (1992), APEC-TEL Mutual Recognition Arrangement for Conformity Assessment of Telecommunications Equipment (1998), Directive 2002/21/EC, Directive 2002/19/EC, Directive 2002/20/EC, Directive 2002/22/EC (the EU package was updated in 2009 and further in 2016).
39. COE Recommendation (No R (89) 9) of the Committee of Ministers to Member States on Computer-Related Crime (1989), UN Manual on the Prevention and Control of Computer Related Crime (1994), CoE Recommendation (No R (95) 13) of the Committee of Ministers

to Member States concerning Problems of Criminal Procedural Law Connected with Information Technology (1995), OAS Final Recommendations of the Second Meeting of Government Experts on Cyber Crime (1999), Combating the Criminal Misuse of Information Technologies (A/RES/55/63) (2000), CIS Agreement on Cooperation among the State Members of the Commonwealth of Independent States in Combating Offences Relating to Computer Information (2001), COE Convention on Cybercrime (2001), G8 Recommendations for Tracing Networked Communications Across National Borders in Terrorist and Criminal Investigations (2002), COE Additional Protocol to the Convention on Cybercrime, concerning the Criminalisation of Acts of a Racist and Xenophobic Nature Committed through Computer Systems (2003), COE Guidelines for the Cooperation between Law Enforcement and Internet Service Providers against Cybercrime (2008), League of Arab States arab Convention on Combating Information Technology Offences (2010), ECOWAS Directive on Fighting Cyber Crime within ECOWAS (2011), COMESA Cyber Crime Model Bill (2011).

40. Decision in the Field of Security of Information Systems (92/242/EEC), OECD Guidelines for the Security of Information Systems (1992), Recommendation on Common Information Technology Security Evaluation Criteria (95/144/EC), OECD Recommendation concerning Guidelines for Cryptography Policy (1997), OECD Guidelines for the Security of Information Systems and Networks Towards a Culture of Security (2002), UN Resolution on Creation of a Global Culture of Cybersecurity (A/RES/57/239), SCO Agreement between the Governments of the Member States of the Shanghai Cooperation Organization on Cooperation in the Field of International Information Security (2009), UN Resolution on Creation of a Global Culture of Cybersecurity and Taking Stock of National Efforts to Protect Critical Information Infrastructures (A/RES/64/211) (2009), Directive 2013-40-EU on Attacks Against Information Systems (2013), OSCE Decision No 1106 Initial Set of OSCE Confidence-Building Measures to Reduce the Risks of Conflict Stemming from the Use of Information and Communication Technologies (2013), African Union Convention on Cyber Security and Personal Data Protection (2014), OSCE Decision No. 1202 OSCE Confidence-building Measures to Reduce the Risks of Conflict Stemming from the Use of Information and Communication Technologies (2016).

41. Recommendation on a European Code of Conduct Relating to Electronic Payment (87/598/EEC), UN Model Law on Electronic Commerce adopted by the United Nations Commission on International Trade Law (A/RES/51/162) (1996), Directive on the Protection of Consumers in Respect of Distance Contracts (97/7/EC), Recommendation on the Development of the Competitiveness of the European Audiovisual and Information Services Industry (98/560/EC), Directive on the Legal Protection of Services Based on, or Consisting of, Conditional Access (98/84/EC), Directive on a Community Framework for Electronic Signatures (1999/93/EC), Directive on Certain Legal Aspects of Information Society Services, in Particular Electronic Commerce, in the Internal Market (2000/31/EC), 2000 e-ASEAN Framework Agreement, Framework Decision Combating Fraud and Counterfeiting of Non-Cash Means of Payment (2001/413/JHA), COE Convention on Information and Legal Co-operation Concerning Information Society Services (2001), COE Improving User Protection and Security in Cyberspace (2014), EU Regulation (EU) No 910/2014 of the European Parliament and of the Council of 23 July 2014 on Electronic Identification and Trust Services for Electronic Transactions in the Internal Market (2014).

42. G8 Principles for Protecting Critical Information Infrastructures (2003), UN Creation of a Global Culture of Cybersecurity and the Protection of Critical Information Infrastructures (A/RES/58/199) (2003), OECD Recommendation of the Council on the Protection of Critical Information Infrastructures (2008).

43. Decision No. 1202 OSCE Confidence-Building Measures to Reduce the Risks of Conflict Stemming from the Use of Information and Communication Technologies, PC.DEC/1202, 10 March 2016.

44. Report of the Group of Governmental Experts on Developments in the Field of Information and Telecommunication in the Context of International Security, 24 June 2013, UN A/68/98), paras 22, 24, 25 and 26); Report of the Group of Governmental Experts on Developments in the Field of Information and Telecommunication in the Context of International Security, 22 July 2015, (UN A/70/174), paras 13, 16 and 17.
45. Human Rights Council and UNGA resolutions.
46. UNGA resolutions.

Sachwortverzeichnis

A

Account 23, 27, 48, 52, 87, 109, 248, 256, 258, 341, 343, 351, 354, 367, 387, 477, 497, 498, 541, 544, 546, 548, 577, 579, 608, 625

Active Cyber Defence 94, 96, 97, 100, 342, 536, 620

Act on the Defence Forces 93

Act on the Protection of Privacy in Electronic Communications 93

Administratoren 275, 280, 281, 283, 329, 470

Advanced Persistent Threat (APT) 350, 502

Agence nationale de la sécurité des systèmes d'information (ANSSI) 48, 56, 519

Air gap 596

Aktionsplan Cyber-Defence 200

Algorithmus 206, 213, 215

Allianz für Cyber-Sicherheit 38

Allied Command 159

Angriffspfad 472

Antimalwareschutz 458, 460

Anti-Viren-Patterns 469

AntiVirus 500

Anwendung 476, 562, 563

API 391, 498, 601, 603, 604

ARAKIS-GOV 51

Artificial Intelligence (AI) 103, 339, 343, 345, 353, 355, 356, 360

Association of Southeast Asian Nations (ASEAN) 218

Attribution 6, 254, 257, 258, 530, 625

Austrian Trust Circle (ATC) 457

Automatisierung 171, 212, 214

Availability 50, 340, 498, 529, 573, 589

Awareness 3, 5, 46, 49, 54, 59, 61, 62, 93–95, 99, 101, 103, 112, 243, 248, 341, 346, 499, 529, 530, 540–544, 547, 574, 580, 596, 619, 623

B

Backdoor 8, 258

BDSAuditG 415

Behörden- und Unternehmens-Cyberstrategie 216

Belfer Centre for Science 113

Belgrade Security Forum 109

Belgrade University 113

Benutzer 425, 476

Big Data 61, 103, 241, 242, 339, 344, 345, 353, 494

Bilanzrechtsmodernisierungsgesetz (BilMoG) 419

BIOS 176

Bitcoin 493, 501

Bitkom Studie Wirtschaftsschutz 74

Blockchain-Technologie 553–554

Body for the Coordination of Information Security 111

Body of European Regulators for Electronic Communications (BEREC) 99

Botmaster-Server 179

Bot-Netz 179

Branche 85, 92, 93, 97

Brickerbot 341

Bring your own device (BYOD) 351, 495, 505

BSI Common Criteria 145–146

BSI-Grundschutz 463, 469

© Springer Fachmedien Wiesbaden GmbH, ein Teil von Springer Nature 2018
M. Bartsch, S. Frey (Hrsg.), *Cybersecurity Best Practices*,
https://doi.org/10.1007/978-3-658-21655-9

Michael Bartsch
Stefanie Frey

Cyberstrategien für Unternehmen und Behörden

Maßnahmen zur Erhöhung
der Cyberresilienz

Springer Vieweg

FSC
www.fsc.org
MIX
Papier | Fördert
gute Waldnutzung
FSC® C083411

Zeitfracht Medien GmbH
Ferdinand-Jühlke-Straße 7
99095 Erfurt, Deutschland
produktsicherheit@kolibri360.de